2 Edition

Introduction to
ABNORMAL CHILD
and ADOLESCENT
PSYCHOLOGY

Introduction to

ABNORMAL CHILD
and ADOLESCENT
PSYCHOLOGY

2 Edition

ROBERT WEIS
DENISON UNIVERSITY

Los Angeles | London | New Delhi
Singapore | Washington DC

Los Angeles | London | New Delhi
Singapore | Washington DC

FOR INFORMATION:

SAGE Publications, Inc.
2455 Teller Road
Thousand Oaks, California 91320
E-mail: order@sagepub.com

SAGE Publications Ltd.
1 Oliver's Yard
55 City Road
London EC1Y 1SP
United Kingdom

SAGE Publications India Pvt. Ltd.
B 1/I 1 Mohan Cooperative Industrial Area
Mathura Road, New Delhi 110 044
India

SAGE Publications Asia-Pacific Pte. Ltd.
3 Church Street
#10-04 Samsung Hub
Singapore 049483

Acquisitions Editor: Reid Hester
Associate Editor: Nathan Davidson
Assistant Editor: Lauren Habib
Editorial Assistant: Lucy Berbeo
Production Editor: Jane Haenel
Copy Editor: Patricia J. Sutton
Typesetter: C&M Digitals (P) Ltd.
Proofreaders: Annie Lubinsky and Susan Schon
Indexer: Terri Corry
Cover Designer: Karine Hovsepian
Marketing Manager: Shari Countryman

Printed in the United States of America

Library of Congress Cataloging-in-Publication Data

Weis, Robert, 1973–

Introduction to abnormal child and adolescent psychology / Robert Weis, Denison University. — 2nd edition.

pages cm
Includes bibliographical references and index.

ISBN 978-1-4522-2525-8
1. Child psychopathology. 2. Adolescent psychopathology. I. Title.

RJ499.W3925 2014
618.92'89—dc23   2013024917

This book is printed on acid-free paper.

SFI Certified Sourcing
www.sfiprogram.org
SFI-00453

14 15 16 17 10 9 8 7 6 5 4 3 2

Brief Contents

Detailed Contents

Preface

Now is an exciting time to study abnormal child psychology. The field of child psychopathology is rapidly changing. The study and practice of abnormal child psychology began when Lightner Witmer established the first psychological clinic for children in 1896. However, some of the most exciting developments in the field have emerged in the past 25 years. For example, the theoretical perspective of developmental psychopathology has shaped the way professionals view children's development (and maldevelopment) across time and from multiple perspectives. Technical advances in clinical neuroscience and neuroimaging have allowed us to better appreciate the genetic and biological underpinnings of childhood disorders. The past two decades have also seen greater importance placed on evidence-based treatments and the dramatically increased use of psychotropic medications for children with behavioral and social-emotional problems. Changes in the demographic and socioeconomic makeup of the United States also require us to view children's development within broader social and cultural contexts. Most recently, the development and publication of the new *Diagnostic and Statistical Manual of Mental Disorders, Fifth Edition (DSM-5),* marks the most significant change to the study of abnormal child psychology in a generation.

Now is a particularly exciting time for students. There is so much new ground to explore! Students can ask relevant, novel questions almost immediately. Important questions such as "Why is Autism Spectrum Disorder more commonly diagnosed today compared to only 10 years ago? Why are adolescent girls more likely than boys to become depressed?" and "What's the best way to help physically abused children?" need answers. The field needs curious, motivated students with a solid understanding of psychological science and research methods to ask, and begin to answer, these (and many other) questions.

There is also much work to be done applying psychological science and evidence-based treatments to help children and families in need. Students often find themselves on the front line of treatment. Some students work in residential treatment facilities with disruptive adolescents. Others serve as behavior therapists for children with developmental disorders. Still other students volunteer: They may tutor children with learning disabilities or spend time as Big Brothers or Big Sisters to neglected youths. There is no shortage of people who want to help children in need; the difficulty is findings individuals who are willing to use scientific principles and evidence-based practices to help them. The field desperately needs bright, empathic students who are willing to devote their professional lives to helping children, using the principles of psychological science.

GOALS OF THIS BOOK

This book is written as an introductory text. I adopted a developmental psychopathology approach to understanding youths with behavioral, developmental, and social-emotional disorders. The developmental psychopathology perspective examines the emergence of child and adolescent disorders over time, pays special attention to risk and protective factors that influence developmental processes and trajectories, and examines child psychopathology in the context of typical child development.

Introduction to Developmental Psychopathology

I have four main goals for this book. First, I want to introduce students to the developmental psychopathology paradigm and show how this perspective can help organize our understanding of various childhood disorders. Examining patterns of development and maldevelopment over time adds a level of complexity that, I hope, will spark their curiosity about child development and the emergence of childhood problems.

In the book, I hope to go beyond merely describing each disorder; I also want to introduce students to the multitude of factors that cause child psychopathology. Potential etiologies are numerous and complex. To help students organize the research literature, I examine each disorder across five broad levels of analysis:

- Genetics (e.g., behavioral and molecular genetics research)
- Biology (e.g., brain structure and functioning, hormones, neuroimaging studies)
- Psychological processes (e.g., the interplay between children's thoughts, feelings, and actions)

- Interpersonal relations (e.g., parent-child attachment, family functioning, peer relationships)
- Social-cultural context (e.g., children's race, ethnicity, socioeconomic status, neighborhood)

The causes of child psychopathology can be analyzed at each of these levels. However, the most complete accounts of child psychopathology usually involve interactions across multiple levels of analysis and across time. In reading this book, I hope students will see that the field of abnormal child psychology is interdisciplinary and complex.

The Integration of Science and Practice

Second, I want to convey the value and interdependence of psychological research and human service. I want to challenge the notion that psychological research and clinical practice are separate professional endeavors. Instead, I hope to illustrate that competent, ethical clinical work draws upon existing psychological research, while the most meaningful psychological research is often inspired by clinical practice.

Perhaps the most salient feature of this text is that it introduces students to the scientist-practitioner approach to abnormal child psychology. The scientist-practitioner perspective assumes that the field of abnormal child psychology is foremost a science. The field needs to be founded in scientific theory and supported by empirical data. Students must appreciate the methods and findings of psychological research in order to accurately understand children's problems. At the same time, the scientist-practitioner perspective assumes that the best psychological research is relevant to the day-to-day lives of children, families, and society. Research allows us to accurately understand children in need, to help alleviate children's problems, and to find ways to promote the welfare of children in society.

Greater Attention to Evidence-Based Treatments

My third goal is to provide students with an understanding of evidence-based treatments. These treatments include psychosocial and pharmacological interventions as well as primary (universal) and secondary (indicated) prevention techniques. To the extent possible, I try to provide a detailed description of each form of therapy so that students can appreciate both the theory behind the intervention and how the treatment plays out in clinics, hospitals, and schools. Then, I briefly review the efficacy and effectiveness of each form of treatment and (more often) limitations in the research literature.

My goal is not to teach students how to conduct therapy. Instead, I have three objectives. First, I hope these accurate and vivid descriptions of treatment will help students draw connections between the causes of each disorder and the methods used to treat them. Such connections will help students integrate material within chapters and (perhaps) across disorders. Second, I hope that my emphasis on evidence-based treatments will help students become better consumers of psychological services. Unfortunately, there are too many interventions available to children and families that lack empirical support and too few evidence-based treatments accessible to families most in need. Perhaps this book will help students discriminate between therapies grounded in science versus well-intentioned treatments that lack empirical support. Third, I hope these descriptions of therapy will motivate students to seek out more information, from their instructors, journals, books, and other reputable sources.

I try to supplement the text with interesting case studies. Although names and other identifying information have been changed, the case studies describe real clients. I hope that these case studies bring to life my descriptions of the various disorders, their causes, and treatments. I also hope these case studies allow students to focus their attention on children and families, rather than on disorders per se.

Relevance to Life

Finally, I want to show students *why* an understanding of child psychopathology and its treatment might be important to them. Most students will not become psychologists or counselors. However, all students have multiple opportunities to influence the lives and developmental outcomes of children and adolescents. Some students will become physicians, nurses, teachers, librarians, day care providers, occupational or recreational therapists, or other professionals who have immediate, frequent contact with children. Other students will volunteer as coaches, tutors, or mentors in schools and in the community. Nearly all students will become parents and have the primary responsibility of raising the next generation of youths. Although few students will become mental health professionals, all can rely on psychological science and critical thinking to make informed decisions about the welfare of our families, schools, neighborhoods, and society.

CHANGES TO THE SECOND EDITION

The second edition of this book offers all of the features instructors and students expected from the first edition, such as (a) a focus on the development of psychopathology over time, (b) the study of childhood disorders from multiple levels of analysis,

(c) detailed descriptions of evidence-based treatments, and (d) a focus on applying information to everyday experience. The second edition offers several new features that I hope readers will find useful and enjoyable.

Changes to Reflect *DSM-5*

The second edition has a new organizational structure to reflect the conceptualization of disorders presented in *DSM-5*. Like *DSM-5*, the second edition adopts a developmental perspective in which disorders that typically emerge in infancy and early childhood are presented fist, followed by disorders most commonly seen in later childhood, adolescence, and emerging adulthood. The second edition includes the new child and adolescents disorders appearing in *DSM-5* (e.g., Disruptive Mood Dysregulation Disorder, Social Communication Disorder), reflects changes in the organization and conceptualization of previously existing disorders (e.g., Autism Spectrum Disorder, Bipolar Disorder), and provides the new *DSM-5* diagnostic criteria for each condition. It also includes several new disorders included in *DSM-5* for future study that are especially relevant to children and adolescents (e.g., Non-suicidal Self-Injury, Attenuated Psychosis Syndrome). The second edition also features text boxes that describe important changes from *DSM-IV* to *DSM-5*. These text boxes should be most beneficial to instructors and students familiar with *DSM-IV* yet will still be interesting to beginning students who want to know how the field has changed over time.

Updated and Expanded Research

The second edition also includes new and exciting developments in the research literature. Not only does the text describe research for new psychological disorders, but it also offers hundreds of new references, published in the last 3 years, on already existing conditions. The second edition is not merely an "updated" version of the previous edition; it expands upon the first edition by discussing new disorders and new research findings.

New Chapters

The second edition offers two new chapters. A new chapter on *Communication Disorders in Children* (Chapter 5) presents a description of language disorders, speech disorders, and Social Communication Disorder as well as information about their causes and treatments. This chapter reflects the Communication Disorder section of *DSM-5* and the research literature on children with speech and language problems. The second edition also includes a new chapter on *Health-Related Disorders and Pediatric Psychology* (Chapter 16). This chapter describes Elimination and Sleep Disorders in children and presents information about the practice of child psychology in hospitals and other medical settings. Because instructors may be less familiar with speech-language disorders and pediatric psychology than other more "traditional" childhood problems (e.g., anxiety, depression, conduct problems), I have tried to write these chapters in a user-friendly, accessible way, emphasizing the application of research to children and families with these problems. I anticipate that instructors will "pick-and-choose" portions of these, and other chapters, based on their knowledge and interests.

The second edition also includes several new subsections of chapters that reflect major changes to *DSM-5*. For example, there are now detailed descriptions of Global Developmental Delay (Chapter 5), Reactive Attachment Disorder and Disinhibited Social Engagement Disorder (Chapter 12), Disruptive Mood Dysregulation Disorder and Non-suicidal Self-Injury (Chapter 13), childhood Schizophrenia (Chapter 14), and Feeding Disorder and Binge Eating Disorder (Chapter 15). These disorders were not covered in the previous edition. I hope that their addition is welcomed by readers.

Greater Focus on Pedagogy

The second edition includes several new features, designed to facilitate teaching and enhance student learning. Each chapter now begins with Learning Objectives to help students identify its most important goals. Chapters also include key terms in bold and detailed summaries for each section, to help students review the text and prepare for exams. The second edition also features text boxes titled "Research to Practice," designed to show students how psychological research can be applied in clinics, schools, and other human-service settings. These boxes include case studies for all of the major disorders, descriptions of assessment and treatment, and therapy transcripts to illustrate important principles or techniques. Chapters end with Critical Thinking Exercises—questions that require students to compare and contrast, integrate, and extend their learning beyond the text. Finally, students are invited to visit the text's website: www.sagepub.com/weis2e for access to videos about the various disorders, their causes, and treatments.

A Final Word to Instructors

To accompany this text, I have created ancillary material for instructors. This material is designed to facilitate lectures, class discussion, and the creation of exams. I hope that this material will allow instructors greater time and flexibility to engage students in the classroom rather than manage the "nuts and bolts" of their courses. The ancillary instructor material includes the following:

- Sample syllabus
- Chapter outlines
- PowerPoint slides for each chapter, including tables and figures from the text
- Supplemental lectures on topics relevant to child/adolescent psychopathology
- Supplemental tables and figures in digital format
- Discussion questions and classroom exercises
- Online videos for each disorder
- Multiple choice, short answer, and essay questions drawn from the book

Instructors can access these resources by visiting www.sagepub.com/weis2e.

I am especially happy to offer instructors a wide variety of exam questions from which to build their tests. The exam questions are organized according to Bloom's (1956) taxonomy of educational objectives. Consequently, questions are grouped according to the level of abstraction, creativity, and critical thinking needed to adequately answer them. I have grouped these questions into five general categories:

1. *Knowledge:* Students must recall facts or define important terms.

2. *Comprehension:* Students must summarize, explain, or give examples of key ideas.

3. *Analysis:* Students must compare and contrast two or more ideas, theories, or therapies.

4. *Application:* Students must use information in the text to solve a problem or apply their understanding to a case study.

5. *Synthesis:* Students must critically examine the strengths and weaknesses of a theory, idea, or therapy and judge its merits.

Multiple-choice questions in the test bank focus on students' (a) knowledge and (b) comprehension of information presented in the text. Short-answer and essay questions in the instructor's material cover all five categories, with emphasis on (c) analysis, (d) application, and (e) synthesis. Although many instructors will write their own exam questions, I hope that these questions will serve as a springboard for exam preparation or class discussion and help instructors develop their students' critical thinking skills.

ACKNOWLEDGMENTS

I am grateful to many people for their support and encouragement. First, I am thankful for the professional training and mentorship of Dr. Chris Lovejoy and the faculty at Northern Illinois University, who embody the spirit of the scientist-practitioner tradition. Second, I want to acknowledge three clinician-scholars who have greatly influenced my view of developmental psychopathology and the delivery of psychological services to children, adolescents, and families: Dr. Thomas Linscheid and Dr. Joseph Hatcher of Nationwide Children's Hospital in Columbus, Ohio, and Dr. Terry Kaddatz of St. Michael Hospital in Stevens Point, Wisconsin. Third, I would like to thank my colleagues at Denison University for their collegiality and support as well as the Denison administration who provided me with an R.C. Good Fellowship to complete this project. Fourth, I must thank the reviewers of this manuscript, who offered many helpful suggestions in its preparation. They are David L. Carlston, Midwestern State University; Robert Devasch, University of South Carolina; Christie Karpiak, University of Scranton; Rich Milich, University of Kentucky; Martin Murphy, University of Akron; Wendy J. Nilsen, University of Rochester; Jill Norvilitis, SUNY College at Buffalo; Elizabeth Soliday, Washington State University, Vancouver; Ric Steele, University of Kansas; and Margaret Wright, Miami University of Ohio.

Finally, I am most indebted to my wife, Jennifer, and three children, Thomas, Marie, and Anne Catherine, who have taught me more about child development that any of my readings or clinical experiences. I hope that this text, in some small way, reflects their love and support for me over the years.

—*Robert Weis*
Denison University
Granville, Ohio

About the Author

Robert Weis is a licensed clinical psychologist and associate professor of psychology at Denison University, a selective liberal arts college near Columbus, Ohio. He earned a BA in psychology from the University of Chicago and a PhD in clinical psychology from Northern Illinois University. He completed his predoctoral and postdoctoral work in clinical child and pediatric psychology at Columbus Children's Hospital (Ohio) and Portage County Mental Health Center (Wisconsin). At Denison, he teaches courses in introductory psychology, research methods and statistics, abnormal psychology, and assessment and psychotherapy. He also supervises an undergraduate internship course in applied psychology. His research interests are in psychometrics, children's mental health program evaluation, and the learning disabilities. His work has been published in *Psychological Science, The Journal of Personality and Social Psychology, The Journal of Abnormal Child and Adolescent Psychology, Psychological Assessment,* and *Psychology in the Schools.* When not working, Robert enjoys spending time with his wife and three children.

PART I

Principles of Science and Practice

CHAPTER 1

The Science and Practice of Abnormal Child Psychology

WELCOME TO THE STUDY OF ABNORMAL CHILD PSYCHOLOGY

Childhood is a time of physical maturation, intellectual development, and social-emotional growth. Ideally, children are provided with ample opportunities for play and exploration within the safety and security of a loving family and supportive social network. However, for a significant number of youths, childhood is marked by biological, behavioral, or social-contextual challenges that can adversely affect their development.

The study of child psychopathology is complex and diverse. The sheer number of psychological disorders that can afflict children and adolescents is daunting, to say nothing of the multitude of causal factors and treatments. However, the last 20 years have witnessed a marked increase in the scientific study of abnormal child and adolescent psychology. Theory and empirical research have helped to advance the field, enabling researchers to more fully understand the causes of childhood disorders. Furthermore, clinicians and researchers have worked together to develop new and exciting methods of treatment. Most recently, the *Diagnostic and Statistical Manual of Mental Disorders, Fifth Edition* (*DSM-5*) has been published, updating the way we define disorders across the life span (American Psychiatric Association, 2013).

There is, perhaps, no more exciting time to be studying abnormal child psychology than now. Students interested in psychological research will discover many areas of child psychopathology that deserve their attention. Each disorder can be explored from multiple perspectives, ranging from its genetic and biological underpinnings to the behavioral and social-cultural factors that cause and maintain it. At the same time, students interested in helping at-risk youths will discover new developments in the application of psychological research to prevent and treat childhood disorders.

The field of abnormal child psychology is broad and constantly changing. There is much work to be done. Geneticists, neuroscientists, physicians, psychologists, counselors, teachers, parents, and all other individuals who interact with youths can play a role in the prevention and alleviation of childhood disorders and the promotion of children's mental health. This text is intended to introduce you to this intellectually exciting and personally rewarding discipline. Welcome!

How Common Are Childhood Disorders?

Epidemiologists are scientists who study the prevalence of medical and psychological disorders in the general population (Maughan & Rutter, 2010). Prevalence refers to the percentage of individuals in a given population who have a medical or psychological condition. To estimate prevalence, epidemiologists collect data from thousands of individuals in the population, recording their current physical or psychological health. To estimate the prevalence of psychological disorders among children and adolescents, epidemiologists usually rely on information gathered from parents, other caregivers, or professionals, and (sometimes) children themselves.

Conducting epidemiological research is difficult for several reasons. First, researchers are challenged by the task of collecting data from thousands of people in the population. Many people do not want to participate in lengthy surveys, others do not understand questions asked of them, and still others provide inaccurate information. Second, the information collected depends greatly on *who* answers the researchers' questions. For example, parents may be able to comment on children's disruptive behavior, but they may be less accurate in estimating children's difficulties with depression or use of alcohol (Loeber, Green, & Lahey, 1990). Third, conducting a large-scale epidemiological survey is costly and time consuming. For these reasons, determining the exact prevalence of childhood disorders has been challenging.

Despite these methodological obstacles, at least seven large epidemiological studies designed to estimate the prevalence of child and adolescent disorders have been conducted in English-speaking countries. Collectively, these studies include data from tens of thousands of youths and their caregivers, using a variety of research strategies. Results indicate that approximately 15% of youths aged 6 to 16 have a diagnosable mental disorder at any given point in time (Breton et al., 1999; British Medical Association, 2006; Costello et al., 1996; Meltzer, Gatward, Goodman, & Ford, 2003; Offord et al., 1987; Shaffer et al., 1996; Simonoff et al., 1997).

A prevalence of 15% indicates that as many as 11,100,000 youths in the United States are experiencing significant psychological distress and impairment (U.S. Census Bureau,

2006). Furthermore, by the time they reach age 16, as many as 30% will have experienced a psychological disorder at some point in their lives (British Medical Association, 2006). The most common category of mental disorders among youths is anxiety disorders (e.g., phobias, fears of separation), followed by Attention-Deficit/Hyperactivity Disorder (ADHD) and conduct problems (e.g., oppositional and aggressive behaviors) (see Table 1.1).

Children's disorders tend to persist over time (Maughan & Rutter, 2010). On average, 40% of children who meet criteria for a psychological disorder tend to also meet criteria for at least one psychological disorder one year later. In some cases, children show **homotypic continuity**, that is, they show the same problem over time. For example, a child diagnosed with ADHD at age seven will likely have the same disorder at age 8 or 9. However, in most instances, children show **heterotypic continuity**, that is, their problems change over time into other, related disorders. For example, a child with separation anxiety in early childhood might develop social anxiety in later childhood and depression in adolescence. Their problems might change, but they do not go away.

Psychological disorders have direct, deleterious consequences on the quality of life of children and their families. The direct cost of child and adolescent mental health care in the United States is approximately $12 million annually (Ringel & Sturm, 2001). Youths who experience mental disorders are at risk for lower academic achievement, which can adversely affect their ability to reach their earning potential as adults. Furthermore, the parents of children

Table 1.1 Prevalence of Psychological Disorders in Children and Adolescents

Problem	Prevalence (%)
Any anxiety disorder	6.5
Attention-Deficit/Hyperactivity Disorder	3.3
Conduct problems	3.3
Any depressive disorder	2.1
Any substance use disorder	0.8
Autism Spectrum Disorder	0.3
Any eating disorder	0.1
Any bipolar disorder	0.1
Schizophrenia	0.1

Source: Based on the Ontario Child Health Study (Offord et al., 1987), the National Institutes of Mental Health Methodology for Epidemiology of Mental Disorders in Children and Adolescents Study (Shaffer et al., 1996), the Great Smoky Mountains Study (Costello et al., 1996), the Virginia Twin Study of Adolescent Behavioral Development (Simonoff et al., 1997), the Quebec Child Mental Health Survey (Breton et al., 1999), the British Child Mental Health Survey (Meltzer et al., 2003), and the British Medical Association Board of Science Survey (British Medical Association, 2006).

and adolescents with mental disorders often show reduced productivity at work because of the demands associated with caring for these youths.

The cost to society of child and adolescent psychological disorders is also enormous. We must not only pay for the direct cost of mental health treatment but also must cover expenses associated with child and adolescent mental illness. These associated costs include incarceration and rehabilitation for youths with conduct problems, drug and alcohol counseling for youths with substance abuse and dependence, and family supervision and reunification services for youths who experience childhood maltreatment. School districts must pay for special educational services for children with cognitive, learning, and behavioral problems that interfere with their ability to benefit from traditional public education. Preventing childhood disorders would spare families considerable suffering and spare society enormous expense. Unfortunately, prevention remains an underutilized approach to dealing with child and adolescent psychopathology in the United States (Tolan & Dodge, 2005).

Although approximately 15% of youths experience full-blown psychological *disorders*, the percentage of youths who encounter significant mental health *problems* is even greater (see Table 1.2). To be classified with a mental disorder, youths must show both significant symptoms and marked distressed or impairment in day-to-day functioning. However, many youths experience serious problems in their family relationships, educational attainment, and social functioning but fall short of meeting diagnostic criteria for a mental disorder. For example, many children experience considerable feelings of sadness and symptoms of social withdrawal, but they do not meet diagnostic criteria for Major Depressive Disorder. Similarly, many adolescent girls show poor body image and unhealthy eating habits, but they do not qualify for a diagnosis of Anorexia or Bulimia Nervosa. Youths with subthreshold emotional or behavioral problems are clearly not reaching their social and emotional potentials and deserve the attention of parents, teachers, and mental health practitioners. Indeed, as

many as 21% of youths in the United States have *either* a diagnosable mental disorder *or* a subthreshold behavioral or emotional problem that significantly interferes with their general functioning and quality of life (Shaffer, Fisher, Lucas, Dulcan, & Schwab-Stone, 2000). Consequently, approximately one in five youths is in need of psychological treatment or support.

Sociodemographics and Children's Mental Health

Mental health problems are not equally distributed across the population (British Medical Association, 2006; Shaffer et al., 1996). First, mental and behavioral disorders are more common among adolescents than among children. Although the prevalence of some disorders, like ADHD, gradually decreases from childhood to adolescence, the prevalence of most disorders, especially substance use problems, depression, and anxiety, increases dramatically during the early teenage years. Although mental health problems can emerge at any age, early adolescence appears to be a time in development that places youths at particular risk.

Second, boys and girls are at different risk for developing psychological disorders across development. Specifically, young boys are more likely than young girls to develop most early childhood disorders, especially developmental disorders (e.g., Autism Spectrum Disorder, Intellectual Disability) and disruptive behavior problems (e.g., ADHD, conduct problems). However, by early adolescence, these differences between genders narrow. By late adolescence, girls show a greater likelihood of emotional disorders, especially depression and anxiety, than do boys.

Third, youths from socially and economically impoverished families and neighborhoods are at increased risk for developing most psychological disorders. Across English-speaking countries, youths from low-income families, single-parent families, parents of low educational attainment, and high-crime neighborhoods show increased prevalence for almost all child and adolescent disorders. In the United States, African American and other ethnic minority children show increased risk for many mental health problems. Researchers are actively searching for the causes of child psychopathology among low-income minority youths, as well as ways to reduce the risks they face.

The Rise of Pharmacotherapy

One of the greatest changes in the field of abnormal child psychology in the last two decades has been the dramatic increase in the use of medication by children and adolescents. The use of psychotropic medication has increased approximately threefold in the past 15 years (Olfson, Marcus, Weissman, & Jensen, 2002). Recent data indicate that approximately 1 in 10 adolescent boys and 1 in 14

Table 1.2	Prevalence of Mental Health Problems Among Youths in the United States

Problem	Prevalence (%)
Anxiety problems	13.0
Disruptive behavior problems	10.3
Mood problems	6.2
Substance use problems	2.0
Any mental health problem	20.9

Source: Based on the Methodology for Epidemiology of Mental Disorders in Children and Adolescents (MECA) Study (Shaffer et al., 1996).

Figure 1.1 Psychotropic Medication Use Over Time

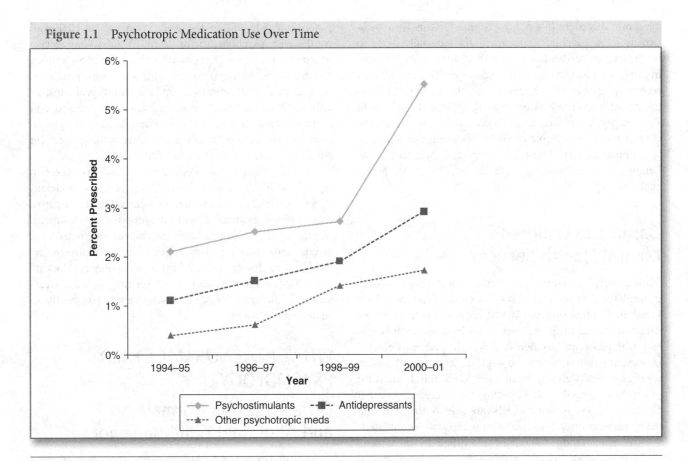

Source: Based on Thomas et al. (2006).

Note: Prescriptions for adolescents have increased 191% since 1994. Approximately 20% of adolescents prescribed psychotropic medications were not diagnosed with a mental disorder.

adolescent girls who visit a physician are prescribed a **psychotropic medication** (Thomas, Conrad, Casler, & Goodman, 2006). Indeed, psychotropic medication prescriptions for adolescents increased 191% from 1994 to

Table 1.3 Psychotropic Medication Use Among Youths in the United States

Medication	Prevalence (%)
Any psychotropic medication	5.2
Psychostimulants (Ritalin, Adderall)	3.4
Antidepressants (Paxil, Prozac)	1.5
Antianxiety medications (BuSpar)	0.4
Antipsychotics (Risperdal)	0.4

Source: Based on Bonati and Clavenna (2005).

Note: Table shows prevalence of medication use among youths with and without psychiatric problems.

2001, compared to an increase of only 6% for nonpsychotropic medications (Thomas et al., 2006; see Figure 1.1).

Estimates of the prevalence of psychotropic medication among youths vary (Bonati & Clavenna, 2005; see Table 1.3). Overall, approximately 5.2% of children and adolescents in the United States are taking at least one psychotropic medication. The most frequently prescribed class of medications for youths are psychostimulants, like methylphenidate (i.e., Ritalin), which are often used to treat ADHD. The second most frequently prescribed medications for youths are antidepressants, especially serotonin reuptake inhibitors like paroxetine (i.e., Paxil) and fluoxetine (i.e., Prozac). In most cases, these medications are prescribed by pediatricians and family practice physicians, rather than psychiatrists.

The use of prescription medications is even higher among youths referred for psychiatric treatment. In one epidemiological study of youths referred to mental health professionals in the United States, approximately 29% were prescribed at least one psychotropic medication (Warner, Pottick, & Mukherjee, 2004). Medication was most frequently used to treat children with ADHD, depression, and psychotic disorders like Schizophrenia. Youths who show two or more psychiatric disorders are especially likely to be prescribed medication. More than 40% of youths with multiple psychiatric disorders receive medication. Youths receiving inpatient psychiatric treatment are most likely to use prescription medication. Indeed, approximately 70% to 75% of psychiatrically hospitalized youths are prescribed at least one psychotropic medication during the course of their inpatient stay (Dean, McDermott, & Marshall, 2006; Lekhwani, Nair, Nikhinson, & Ambrosini, 2004; Najjar et al., 2004).

Barriers to Children's Mental Health Services

Some experts have argued that the child mental health system in the United States is in a state of crisis (President's New Freedom Commission on Mental Health, 2003). Available data indicate that the prevalence of child and adolescent mental health problems has increased over the past two decades. However, families' access to high-quality mental health services remains grossly inadequate. Only about one third of youths who need mental health services receive treatment (Burns et al., 1995). Families who are able to obtain mental health services often find treatment inadequate or outdated.

Tolan and Dodge (2005) have identified several barriers to children's access to high-quality, empirically based mental health services. First, financial hardship often interferes with children's access to comprehensive treatment. In the United States, mental health treatment and medical treatment do not receive equal coverage from insurance companies, despite evidence that mental health problems cost families and society considerable financial expense. Families may find themselves unable to pay for high-quality treatment for their children and adolescents. Families who are uninsured or underinsured face the additional challenge of obtaining treatment from a public social service system that is often overburdened and underfunded.

Second, even if families can pay for high-quality mental health services, they may be unable to find these services. As we will see, evidence-based high-quality mental health treatments are not available in most communities. For example, Multisystemic Therapy (MST) is an empirically supported treatment for older adolescents with serious conduct problems. Many well-designed studies have shown MST to reduce adolescents' disruptive behavior problems, improve their social and academic functioning, reduce their likelihood of arrest and incarceration, and save money (Henggeler & Lee, 2003). However, few clinicians are trained in providing MST, and MST is available in only a small number of communities. Consequently, many clinicians rely on other, less well-supported interventions.

Third, there are simply not enough experts in child and adolescent mental health to satisfy the need for services. Jenkins (1998) estimated that the current mental health care system is able to address the needs of only about 10% of all youths with psychological problems. Youths who receive treatment are typically those who show the most serious distress or impairment. Youths with less severe problems, such as moderate depression, mild learning problems, or unhealthy eating habits, often remain unrecognized and untreated until their condition worsens. Inadequate mental health services are especially pronounced among poor and ethnic minority youths (Ringel & Sturm, 2001).

Finally, stigma can interfere with children's access to mental health treatment. Many caregivers are reluctant to refer their children for therapy because of the negative connotations associated with diagnosis and treatment. Approximately 25% of pediatrician visits involve behavioral or emotional problems that could be better addressed by child and adolescent mental health professionals (Horwitz et al., 2002). Stigma associated with the diagnosis and treatment of childhood disorders causes many at-risk youths to be denied treatment.

WHAT IS *ABNORMAL* CHILD PSYCHOLOGY?
Differentiating Normal and Abnormal Child Behavior

There is no consensus on how to define abnormal behavior in children and adolescents and no agreement on how to best differentiate abnormality from normal functioning. However, mental health practitioners and researchers have proposed several criteria to identify children with behavioral and social-emotional problems.

One approach to defining abnormality is based on **statistical deviancy**. Using this approach, abnormal behaviors are defined by their relative infrequency in the general population. For example, transient thoughts about death are fairly common among adolescents. However, recurrent thoughts about killing oneself are statistically infrequent and could indicate a mood disturbance, such as depression. Advocates of the statistical infrequency approach might administer a rating scale to clients and identify youths who show symptoms well beyond the range of normality, compared to other children and adolescents of the same age and gender.

The chief limitation of the statistical deviancy approach to defining abnormality is that not all infrequent behaviors are indicative of mental disorders. Imagine a child who is tearful, prefers to stay in her room, does not want to play with friends, and is having problems completing schoolwork. From the statistical deviancy perspective, we might diagnose this girl with depression because she shows mood problems that are rare among children her age. However, if we learn that her grandfather died a few days before her assessment, we would likely interpret her behavior as a normal grief reaction, not as an indicator of Major Depressive Disorder. Although statistical infrequency may be an important component of a definition of abnormality, it is insufficient. Statistical deviancy does not take into account the context of children's behavior.

Another approach to defining abnormality is based on **disability or degree of impairment**. From this perspective, abnormal behavior is defined by thoughts, feelings, or actions that interfere with the individual's social, academic, or occupational functioning. For example, an adolescent who feels sad because she broke up with her boyfriend would not be diagnosed with depression, as long as she is able to maintain relationships with friends, get along with parents, and perform adequately in school. However, her behavior might be considered abnormal if her functioning deteriorates in any of these areas.

Defining abnormality by level of impairment has a serious drawback: Many people with mental disorders do not show overt impairment in functioning. For example, an adolescent who carefully plans his suicide may show so few overt problems at home or in school that parents and friends are surprised when he attempts self-harm. By most accounts, Eric Harris and Dylan Klebold, the adolescents who killed 12 classmates and a teacher in Columbine High School in April 1999, showed few symptoms of impairment before they committed their heinous crimes (see Image 1.1).

Yet another definition of abnormality might incorporate the individual's degree of **psychological distress**. People can show psychological distress through depressed mood, irritability, anxiety, worry, panic, confusion, frustration, anger, or any other feeling of dysphoria. Psychological distress is one of the central features of most anxiety and mood disorders.

One limitation of defining abnormality in terms of psychological distress is that distress is often subjective. Some signs of distress can be observed by others, such as sweaty palms and flushed face. However, distress is usually assessed by asking clients to report their feelings. Subjective assessment of distress in children is problematic for at least two reasons. First, not all children are equally aware of their mood states or able to differentiate among various emotions. For example, some children express dysphoria by crying while others develop physical symptoms, like upset stomach. Furthermore, young children often confuse negative emotions, such as "fear" and "anger." Second, children's ratings of distress often cannot be compared against an objective criterion. For example, a child who reports feeling "bad" might be experiencing more distress than another child who reports feeling "terrible."

A second limitation to defining abnormality based on distress is that many youths with serious behavior problems do not experience negative emotions. For example, adolescents with conduct problems often show no signs of anxiety or depression. They may only express remorse when they are caught and punished. Similarly, younger children with oppositional and defiant behavior toward adults rarely express psychological distress. Instead, their disruptive behavior causes distress to their parents and teachers.

Abnormal behavior might also be defined by actions that violate society's standards or rules. Put another way, abnormality may be defined in terms of **cultural deviancy**. For example, Conduct Disorder is characterized by a persistent pattern of behavior that violates the rights of others or the rules of society. Adolescents with Conduct Disorder often have histories of disruptive behavior problems that clearly go against cultural norms and mores: shoplifting, robbery, violence toward others, truancy.

The chief limitation of defining abnormal behavior exclusively by the degree to which it violates social or cultural norms is that these norms can vary considerably from culture to culture. For example, in Western industrialized societies, parents often require young children to sleep in their own beds, usually in separate rooms. Children who refuse to sleep in their own beds may be classified as having a sleep disorder. However, in many non-Western societies, requiring young children to sleep alone is considered cruel and detrimental to their social and emotional development.

Some experts define abnormality in terms of **behavioral rigidity**. From this perspective, abnormal behavior is characterized by the repeated and inflexible display of certain actions, thoughts, or emotional reactions, especially in response to psychosocial stressors. For example, a child who shows fear at the prospect of separating from his mother may be displaying abnormal behavior if he shows this fear in almost all situations. Under some circumstances, clinginess to parents is adaptive, for example, when the child is in an unfamiliar and potentially dangerous setting, such as a crowded airport. Under other circumstances, separation anxiety is clearly maladaptive, such as when a child is unwilling to leave his parents to attend school. Whereas mental health is characterized by flexibility in responding to changes in situational demands, abnormal behavior may be marked by the persistent use of a limited number of behaviors that are clearly not adaptive in all situations. The chief drawback to defining abnormal behavior in terms of rigidity is that terms like *inflexibility* and *maladaptive* are, themselves, vague.

A final way to differentiate abnormality from normal functioning is based on the notion of **harmful dysfunction**. According to Jerome Wakefield (1992), deviation from normality does not necessarily mean a person has a mental disorder. A disorder exists only when two criteria are met. First, the person must show a *dysfunction,* that is, a failure in some internal mechanism to perform a function for which it was naturally selected. Second, the dysfunction *must cause harm,* that is, it must limit or threaten the person in some way. In medicine, heart disease is a disorder because it involves an abnormality in the functioning on the pulmonary system that can greatly interfere with a person's health.

In the field of psychology, whether a person has a disorder based on the "harmful dysfunction" criterion is somewhat less clear. It depends on both scientific objectivity and social-cultural subjectivity (Wakefield, 1997). In determining whether a youth has a mental disorder, clinicians must be mindful of both the child's functioning and his or her development and social-cultural context (Image 1.2). Many behaviors

Image 1.1 Guns in School. A paper submitted by Eric Harris before he and Dylan Klebold shot 12 classmates and one teacher in Columbine High School. His teacher commented on the paper: "Thorough and logical. A few formatting problems, however. Nice job!"

Eric Harris
12/10/97

Guns in School

In the past few weeks there has been news of several shootings in high schools. A student in Texas killed three fellow classmates and injured many more when he fired at a prayer group before school. This student had several other weapons with him when he was apprehended, showing how easy it was to bring so many weapons to school and not be noticed. Students who bring guns to school are hardly ever detected. This is shocking to most parents and even other students since it is just as easy to bring a loaded handgun to school as it is to bring a calculator. *ouch!* The problem of guns in school is a major one faced by many parents, teachers, and citizens these days. Solutions are hard to come by in such a situation because of how widespread the problem is and how different each school in each town can be. Students can get weapons into school too easily and they have to much access to weapons outside of school.

I.

A. Weapons in school are hard to detect and students have ways of getting out of searches or other ways of detection.

  1. One example of students avoiding detection is a 1990 survey conducted by the Centers For Disease Control (CDC) which found that one in 20 high school students carried a gun in school during the past month (CDC).

  2. Students can use their backpacks, purses, or even projects to bring weapons into school.

  3. Metal detectors can be avoided by using other school entrances.

B. Students have access to many weapons and can obtain a gun from many places.

  1. The low price of junk guns (as low as 69 dollars) brings these guns within the economic reach of children (Gun Digest, 288).

JC-001-026352

Source: Released to public domain by the Jefferson County Sheriff's Office, July 6, 2006.

that are objectively dysfunctional may be appropriate or adaptive given the child's context. Consider, Sarah, a girl who lives with her parents on a military base in California. Upon hearing that her mother will soon be deployed to a combat area, she becomes excessively clingy with both parents, has problems eating and sleeping, and refuses to go to school. She may meet diagnostic criteria for Separation Anxiety Disorder, or Major Depressive Disorder. However, her anxiety might be justified given her social context, that is, the imminent deployment of her mother. Wakefield's harmful-dysfunction concept emphasizes that behavior can only be understood in the context of a person's life and surroundings.

Image 1.2 Running away from home, helping a fugitive slave, stealing, and lying might qualify 13-year-old Huck Finn for a diagnosis of Conduct Disorder. According to Wakefield's harmful dysfunction hypothesis, we must consider Huck's social-cultural context, in addition to his behaviors, before assigning a diagnosis.

ON THE RAFT.

Source: Courtesy of Project Gutenberg.

The Psychiatric Definition of Abnormality

Most mental health practitioners and researchers use the *Diagnostic and Statistical Manual of Mental Disorders, Fifth Edition* (*DSM-5*; American Psychiatric Association, 2013) to diagnose mental disorders. *DSM-5* is published by the American Psychiatric Association and reflects the current psychiatric conceptualization of mental illness. The *DSM-5* definition of mental disorder not only reflects Wakefield's notion of harmful dysfunction but also emphasizes the role of impairment and psychological distress in

differentiating normal versus abnormal behavior. According to *DSM-5*,

> a mental disorder is a syndrome characterized by clinically significant disturbance in an individual's cognition, emotion regulation, or behavior that reflects a dysfunction in the psychological, biological, or developmental processes underlying mental functioning. Mental disorders are usually associated with significant distress or disability in social, occupational, or other important activities. An expectable or culturally approved response to a common stressor or loss, such as the death of a loved one, is not a mental disorder. Socially deviant behavior (e.g., political, religious, sexual) and conflicts that are primarily between the individual and society are not mental disorders unless the deviance or conflict results from a dysfunction in the individual, as described above. (American Psychiatric Association, 2013, p. 20)

The *DSM-5* conceptualization of a mental disorder is interesting in several respects. First, it adopts a medical model of mental illness in which disorders reside within individuals, rather than between people (Stein, Phillips et al., 2010). Some people have argued that some disorders are relational in nature and can be understood only in an interpersonal context (Heyman et al., 2009). For example, many young children with Oppositional Defiant Disorder argue with their parents, refuse to comply with parental requests, and tantrum when they do not get their way. Interestingly, their defiant behavior is often directed at some adults (e.g., parents) but not others (e.g., teachers). Therefore, the disorder seems to be dependent on the relationship between people and not merely within the child. Relationships may be especially important to mental disorders in children and adolescents, who are typically more dependent on other people for their well-being.

Second, the *DSM-5* claims that all mental disorders must have an underlying dysfunction that is typically psychobiological in nature. Indeed, some disorders are associated with specific psychobiological causes. For example, children with ADHD often show underactivity in certain areas of the brain responsible for attention, inhibition, and planning. However, requiring an underlying psychobiological cause is problematic in at least three ways:

1. Researchers have not yet identified specific biological causes for most childhood disorders (Frances, 2009). For example, Autism Spectrum Disorder is a highly heritable condition that leads to serious impairment in social communication and behavior. However, researchers have been unable to identify which genes cause this disorder.

2. When specific abnormalities have been identified in research studies, not all children with the disorder show these abnormalities. For example, some children with Autism Spectrum Disorder show reduced synaptic density and abnormalities in their limbic system; however, these differences in brain structure cannot be used to identify children with the disorder. The brains of most children with autism are not different than the brains of typically developing peers.

3. Even when children show specific biological abnormalities, we usually cannot conclude that these abnormalities cause the disorder. For example, some children with autism show underactivity in a brain region responsible for processing human faces (i.e., the right fusiform gyrus). However, we do not know if underactivity in this brain region causes autism or whether their autistic symptoms lead to deterioration in this brain region. Alternatively, a third variable (e.g., exposure to environmental toxins during pregnancy) may cause abnormalities in both brain and behavior.

Consequently, critics have argued that it may be premature to assume that all disorders have an underlying cause that is both psychological and biological. Some disorders may be caused entirely by psychological problems (First & Wakefield, 2010).

Third, it is worth noting that *DSM-5* describes people with mental disorders as "usually" experiencing significant distress *or* disability (i.e., impairment)—they may not always show both characteristics. Some seriously depressed adolescents experience tremendous emotional pain and frequently think about killing themselves, but they do not show marked impairment in their social or academic functioning. Other youths who show serious conduct problems have been arrested and have dropped out of school, but they report no problems with anxiety, depression, or low self-esteem.

Fourth, mental disorders must be assessed in terms of the individual's social and cultural background, a point to which we now turn.

Abnormality, Ethnicity, and Culture

According to *DSM-5*, clinicians must carefully differentiate symptoms of a mental disorder from behaviors and psychological states that are sanctioned in a given culture. Differentiating abnormal symptoms from culturally sanctioned behavior is especially challenging when clinicians are asked to assess youths from other cultures.

Ethnicity and culture can affect the diagnostic process in at least four ways (Alarcon, 2009; Miller & Prosek, 2013):

First, ethnic minority groups living in the United States often have different cultural values that affect their views of children, beliefs about child rearing, and behaviors they consider problematic. For example, white, middle-class parents often place great value on fostering children's social-emotional development and encouraging child autonomy. These parents often provide high levels of warm and responsive behavior during parent-child interactions. In contrast, many African American parents place relatively greater value on children's compliance; consequently, they may adopt less permissive and more authoritarian socialization tactics. Clinicians need to be aware of cultural differences in socialization goals and parents' ideas about appropriate and inappropriate child behavior.

Second, ethnic minorities living in the United States, especially immigrants, encounter psychosocial stressors associated with acculturation. Acculturation stressors can include assimilation into the mainstream culture, separation from extended family and friends, language differences, limited educational and employment opportunities, and prejudice. Many ethnic minorities also face the additional stress of low social and economic status. Many immigrants to the United States, especially those from Latin America, do not share the same legal status as members of the dominant culture. For these reasons, the sheer number of psychosocial stressors encountered by ethnic minority families is greater than those encountered by families who are members of the dominant culture.

Third, language differences can cause problems in the assessment and diagnosis of non-native speakers.

CASE STUDY

CULTURE MATTERS

Julia was a 16-year-old Asian American girl who was referred to our clinic by her oncologist after she was diagnosed with a rare form of cancer. Julia refused to participate in radiation therapy or take medications for her illness. Her physician suspected that Julia was paranoid because she attempted to attack him when he tried to examine her in his office.

With the help of a translator, Julia's therapist learned that she was a second-generation Hmong immigrant from Southeast Asia who lived with her parents and extended family. Julia and her family had limited contact with individuals outside the Hmong community and refused to participate in Western medicine. Instead, Julia and her parents practiced traditional Eastern folk medicine.

Because Julia's therapist doubted that folk medicine alone would help her cancer, she suggested that Julia's community shaman talk with her physician to identify which aspects of medical treatment might be acceptable to Julia and her family. Over time, Julia was able to successfully participate in Western medical treatment by having the shaman attend all of the radiation therapy sessions, bless the medications prescribed by the oncologist, and perform other folk remedies important to Julia and her family.

The assessment and diagnostic process was designed predominantly for English-speaking individuals living in the United States. The words that describe some psychological symptoms are not easily translated into other languages. Furthermore, many symptoms reported by individuals from other cultures do not readily map onto *DSM-5* diagnostic criteria. Psychological tests are almost always developed with English-speaking children and adolescents in mind. For example, white children raised in Columbus, Ohio, will likely find the following question on an intelligence test fairly easy: "Who was Christopher Columbus?" However, Cambodian immigrant children who recently moved to the city might find the question extremely challenging. Psychologists must be aware of differences in language and cultural knowledge when interpreting test results.

Fourth, ethnic minorities are often underrepresented in mental health research. Over the past two decades, researchers have made considerable gains in understanding the causes and treatment for a wide range of child and adolescent disorders. However, researchers know relatively little about how differences in children's ethnicity and cultural backgrounds might place them at greater risk for certain disorders or affect treatment. For example, emerging data suggest that the prevalence of alcohol and drug abuse among adolescents differs, depending on adolescents' ethnicities. Researchers have only recently begun to create treatment programs designed specifically for minority youths. For example, narrative therapies have been developed to help Spanish-speaking children and adolescents overcome mood and anxiety problems, using culturally relevant storytelling (Costantino, Malgady, & Cardalda, 2005). Youths listen to, write, and sometimes enact stories in which the main characters model adaptive responses to stressful life experiences in a manner that is consistent with social-cultural attitudes and values. Clearly, more research needs to be done to investigate the interplay between psychopathology and culture among ethnic minority youths.

WHAT IS ABNORMAL *CHILD* PSYCHOLOGY?

Understanding the Development of Psychopathology

Developmental psychopathology is a broad approach to studying normal and abnormal development across the life span. Developmental psychopathologists believe that development is shaped by the complex interaction of biological, psychological, and social-cultural factors over time. An adequate understanding of development, therefore, depends on the appreciation of each of these domains, how they interact, and how they affect the person from infancy through adulthood (Rutter & Sroufe, 2000).

Developmental psychopathologists study human development across several levels of analysis. These levels include the person's genetics, brain structure and functioning, psychological development (i.e., actions, thoughts, emotions), family interactions and peer relationships, and the broader social-cultural context in which the person lives. Factors on each of these levels can individually affect development. More frequently, however, factors across levels interact over time to shape children's developmental outcomes (Cicchetti & Toth, 1998).

Probabilistic Epigenesis

Developmental psychopathologists use the term **epigenesis** to describe the way biological, psychological, and social-cultural factors interact with each other to influence development over time (see Figure 1.2). Development unfolds as genetic and biological factors guide and direct psychological, familial, and social functioning (Gottlieb & Willoughby, 2006).

Consider Nina, a child with Down Syndrome. Nina's syndrome was caused by a genetic mutation on chromosome 21, probably acquired through an abnormality in her mother's egg cell. This genetic mutation caused Nina's brain and central nervous system to develop in an abnormal fashion. Her neurological development, in turn, shaped her psychological functioning during early childhood. Nina's parents reported delays in her motor development (e.g., sitting up, walking), use of language, and acquisition of daily living skills (e.g., toilet training, dressing). In school, she showed problems in learning to read, write, and count. These psychological characteristics affected the type of care she received from parents and teachers. Nina's mother was understandably very protective, and her teachers often offered Nina extra attention in school. Nina's cognitive functioning also affected her relationships with peers. Nina preferred to play with younger children rather than her classmates. By the time Nina reached junior high school, she was well behind her peers academically. However, Nina was able to spend half the school day in a regular sixth-grade classroom, assisted by an aide. She spent the remainder of the day in a special education class. These extra services offered by her school district (a social-cultural factor) enabled Nina to begin a part-time job during high school.

Nina's story illustrates the unfolding of development over time. Each level of development affects the one beyond it. However, epigenesis is a bidirectional process. Genetic and biological factors certainly affect psychological and social functioning; however, psychological and social factors can also determine the effects of genes and biology on development. Arnold Sameroff (2000) used the term *transactional* to refer to the way factors across levels affect each other over time.

To understand the transactional nature of development, consider Anthony, another child with Down Syndrome. Anthony's mother, Anita, was heartbroken when her obstetrician told her that Anthony had Down Syndrome (Image 1.3). Rather than despair, Anita decided that she was going to

Figure 1.2 Developmental Epigenesis

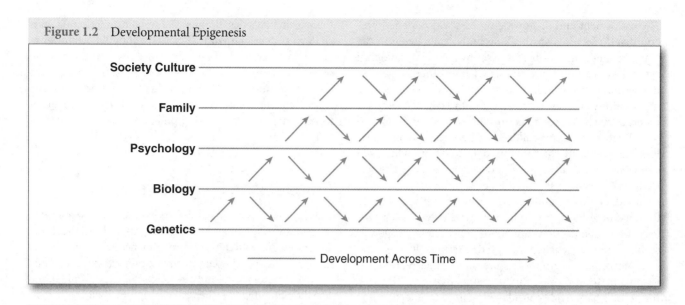

Society Culture

Family

Psychology

Biology

Genetics

⟵————— Development Across Time —————⟶

Source: Based on Gottlieb and Willoughby (2006).

Note: Development unfolds over time. Genetic, biological, psychological, familial, and social-cultural factors interact with each other—across time—to shape children's outcomes. Because of the complex interplay of factors affecting development, children's outcomes are "probabilistic," not predetermined.

Image 1.3 The development of this infant with Down Syndrome will depend on the interaction of biological, psychological, and social-cultural factors over time. Developmental psychopathologists use the term *epigenesis* to refer to this process.

maximize her son's cognitive, social, and behavioral potential by giving him the most enriching early environment that she could provide. Anita spent countless hours talking to Anthony, reading books, listening to music, playing games, and going on outings. Although Anthony acquired language and daily living skills slowly, Anita had high expectations for him. She remained patient and tried to provide structure and help so that Anthony might learn these skills independently. Anita enrolled Anthony in a special needs preschool and was heavily involved throughout his education. Anthony developed fairly good language and daily living skills and was able to graduate with his high school class. Today, Anthony is employed full-time in the mailroom of a large company and lives independently.

Understanding and predicting child development is extremely difficult for two reasons. First, development is influenced by many factors across multiple levels: genes, biology, psychology, family, society. Second, these factors are constantly changing over time, each interacting with the others. Consequently, the unfolding of development is not predetermined by one's genes, biology, or any other factor. Instead, the unfolding of development is **probabilistic**; a person's developmental outcome can vary depending on the interplay of many biological and environmental factors. Developmental psychopathologists use the term *probabilistic epigenesis* to refer to the complex transaction of biogenetic, psychological, familial, and social-cultural factors that shape development over time (Cicchetti & Sroufe, 2000; Gottlieb & Willoughby, 2006).

Developmental Pathways

Developmental psychopathologists often liken child development to a journey along a path. Indeed, they often refer to children as following certain **developmental pathways**, or trajectories, toward either healthy or unhealthy outcomes (Pickles & Hill, 2006).

As children grow, they face certain developmental tasks or challenges along their paths (see Table 1.4). These tasks depend largely on the age and developmental level of

Table 1.4 Developmental Tasks in Childhood and Adolescence

Infants, Toddlers, and Preschool-Aged Children

- Attachment (basic trust) to one or more specific caregivers
- Learning to sit, stand, walk, and jump
- Acquiring functional language
- Obedience to simple commands and instructions of adults
- Toilet training
- Appropriate play with toys and other people
- Achieving a sense of autonomy from parents

School-Aged Children

- Learning reading, writing, mathematics
- Attending and behaving appropriately at school
- Following rules for behavior at home, at school, and in public places
- Getting along with peers at school
- Making friends with peers

Younger Adolescents

- Attending and behaving appropriately at school
- Learning to solve advanced problems with numbers, algebra
- Learning required language, history, and other subjects
- Completing secondary schooling
- Getting along with peers in school

(Continued)

Table 1.4 (Continued)

- Making and maintaining close friendships
- Obeying the laws of society

Older Adolescents

- Working or preparing for future higher education
- If working, behaving appropriately in the workplace
- If in school, meeting academic standards for courses or degrees
- Forming and maintaining romantic relationships
- Obeying the laws of society
- Transitioning from parents, living independently

Source: Based on Masten, Burt, & Coatsworth (2006).

the child. Erik Erikson (1963) outlined some of the most important social and emotional tasks facing individuals as they progress from infancy through old age. For example, the primary developmental task facing infants is to establish a sense of trust in a loving and responsive caregiver. Infants must expect their caregivers to be sensitive and responsive to their physical, social, and emotional needs and to see themselves as worthy of receiving this care and attention from others. A primary developmental task of adolescence is to establish a sense of identity. Adolescents must develop a coherent sense of self that links childhood experiences with goals for adulthood. Adolescents usually accomplish this task by trying out different social roles and behaviors during the teenage years.

Developmental tasks present forks in life's path. The child can either successfully master the developmental task or have problems with its successful resolution. Mastery of developmental tasks leads to social, emotional, and behavioral competence, placing children on course for optimal development. For example, infants who establish a sense of basic trust in caregivers may have greater ability to make and keep friends in later childhood (Image 1.4). Unsuccessful resolution of developmental tasks, however, can lead to problems in later development. For example, failure to establish a sense of trust in caregivers during infancy may interfere with children's abilities to develop close peer relationships later in childhood (Masten et al., 2006).

Progress along developmental pathways, therefore, builds upon itself over time. Early developmental experiences set the groundwork for later developmental experiences. If children show early social, emotional, and behavioral competence, they can use these early skills to master later developmental tasks. However, failure to master early developmental tasks

can interfere with the development of later skills and abilities. For example, a preschool child who learns to control his behavior and emotions during play will likely have an easier time making friends when he enters first grade. However, a preschooler who continues to tantrum or act aggressively when he does not get his way may be ostracized by peers in the first-grade classroom.

To understand the hierarchical nature of development, consider another analogy: Development is like a building. Our genetic endowment might form the foundation of the building, providing us with our physical attributes, raw neurobiological potential, and behavioral predispositions. The ground floor might consist of early environmental experiences, such as our prenatal surroundings or the conditions of our birth and delivery. Subsequent floors might consist of postnatal experiences, such as our nutrition and health care, the relationships we develop with our parents, the quality of our education, and the friends we make in school. The integrity of the upper levels of our "building" is partially determined by the strength of the lower levels. For example, problems with the foundation will place additional challenges on the formation of higher levels. However, especially well-developed higher levels can partially compensate for difficulties in the foundation.

The building does not exist in a vacuum, however. The context in which the structure is created is also important. Just as temperature, wind, and rain can affect the construction of a building, so, too, can the child's social-cultural climate affect his development. Certain social and cultural conditions can promote the child's psychological integrity: high-quality schools, safe neighborhoods, and communities that protect and value children and families. Other social and cultural factors, such as exposure to poverty and crime, can compromise child development.

Image 1.4 At each stage of life, children are confronted with developmental tasks that they must master. This infant must develop a sense of trust in her primary caregivers. Mastery of early tasks can set the stage for competence later in development.

Source: Image courtesy of Flickr Creative Commons (DieselDemon).

Adaptive Versus Maladaptive Behavior

From the perspective of developmental psychopathology, normal and abnormal behavior is determined by the degree to which it promotes children's competence. Behaviors that allow children to develop social, emotional, and behavioral competence over time and meet the changing demands of the environment are regarded as **adaptive**. Examples of adaptive behavior include toddlers learning to understand other people's emotional states, school-age children learning to think before acting, and adolescents using complex moral reasoning to solve interpersonal problems. These behaviors are adaptive because they allow children to understand and interact with their environment in effective and flexible ways (Sroufe, 1997).

Behaviors that interfere with children's social, emotional, and behavioral competence or do not meet the changing demands of the environment are regarded as **maladaptive**. Examples of maladaptive behavior include toddlers who do not understand others' emotional expressions and withdraw from social interactions, school-age children who impulsively

hit others when they are angry, and adolescents who fail to show respect to peers. These behaviors are considered maladaptive because they indicate a failure to develop social competencies and they interfere with children's social-emotional well-being (Sroufe, 1997).

From the perspective of developmental psychopathology, normal behavior is determined by the degree to which the child's actions are adaptive, given his developmental tasks. Consequently, normality and abnormality are dependent on children's *developmental context*. Consider a 2-year-old child who stubbornly refuses to dress in the morning and tantrums when told that he cannot have cookies for breakfast. Although these oppositional behaviors cause parents grief, they are usually not considered abnormal in 2-year-olds. In fact, defiance and stubbornness can reflect toddlers' developmentally appropriate bids for autonomy. However, the same behaviors shown by a 6-year-old child would likely be considered maladaptive and abnormal. In the context of his age and level of development, these behaviors likely reflect problems balancing needs for autonomy with respect for parental authority (Cicchetti & Aber, 1998).

From the perspective of developmental psychopathology, normal and abnormal behaviors are also determined by the degree to which a behavior is adaptive, given the child's environment. Consequently, normality and abnormality are dependent on children's *environmental context*. Consider Xavier, a 13-year-old boy who has a history of running away from home, staying out all night, skipping school, and earning low grades. Clearly, Xavier's behavior is problematic. However, if we discover that Xavier is also experiencing physical abuse at home, we might see how his problematic behavior reflects an attempt to cope with this psychosocial stressor. Specifically, Xavier stays out at night and runs away from home to escape physical maltreatment. Furthermore, he likely has difficulty completing assignments and attending school because of his stressful home environment. Although Xavier's behavior deserves the attention of caring professionals, his actions are best understood in terms of the environmental context.

The Importance of Understanding Normal Development

From the perspective of developmental psychopathology, abnormal development reflects a deviation from normality. Therefore, our ability to recognize, understand, and treat childhood disorders depends on our knowledge of normal child development. Consider George, a 14-year-old boy who begins drinking with friends at parties. Approximately once every month for the past 6 months, George has drunk at least five or more alcoholic beverages while partying with friends. He drinks in order to "have fun" and has never gotten into trouble or put himself in dangerous situations while intoxicated. Consider also a 12-year-old girl, Maria, who is dieting to lose weight. Although Maria's weight is average for a girl her age and height, she is very dissatisfied with her body and feels like she needs to lose at least 15 lbs. Whether we regard George and Maria's actions as abnormal depends partially on whether their behaviors are atypical of adolescents their age or inconsistent with the environmental demands they face. Knowledge of normal development can assist us in identifying and treating children's problems.

Developmental psychopathologists also believe that abnormal behavior can shed light on normal child and adolescent development. Youths who clearly show delays in mastering developmental tasks or failures in meeting environmental demands can teach us about how development typically proceeds. For example, children with autism show unusual deficits in perceiving and interpreting other people's social behavior. By studying these deficits, researchers are beginning to understand how the ability to process social information develops in typically developing infants and children.

Focus on Individual Differences

Developmental psychopathologists are very interested in **individual differences** in child and adolescent development; that is, they want to discover what leads to differences in the way some children develop compared to others. Predicting individual differences in development is extremely difficult because, as we have seen, many factors interact over time to affect children's developmental outcomes. The complex interactions between biogenetic, psychological, familial, and social factors over time produce two phenomena: equifinality and multifinality (Cicchetti, 1990; Sroufe, 1989b).

Equifinality occurs when children with different developmental histories show similar developmental outcomes. For example, imagine that you are a psychologist who conducts psychological evaluations for a juvenile court. As part of your duties, you assess adolescent boys who have been arrested and convicted of illegal activities, such as theft, assault, and drug use, in order to make recommendations to the court regarding probation and treatment. All of the boys that you assess have similar developmental outcomes; that is, they all show conduct problems. However, after interviewing many of the boys, you discover that their developmental histories are quite different. Some boys have long histories of antisocial behavior, beginning in early childhood. Other boys have no histories of conduct problems until their recent arrest. Still other boys' conduct problems are limited to times when they were using drugs and alcohol. Your discovery illustrates the principle of equifinality in child development: There are many different paths to the same developmental outcomes.

The principle of **multifinality** refers to the tendency of children with similar early experiences to show different social, emotional, and behavioral outcomes. For example, imagine that you are a clinical social worker who evaluates children who have been physically abused. During the course of your career, you have assessed a number of children who have been abused by their caregivers. You notice, however, that some of these children show long-term emotional and behavioral problems while others seem to show few adverse effects. Your observation reflects the principle of multifinality: Children with similar early experiences show different outcomes.

The principle of equifinality makes definitive statements about the *causes* of psychopathology extremely difficult. Because of equifinality, we usually cannot infer the causes of children's behavioral problems based on their current symptoms. For example, many people incorrectly believe that all adolescents who sexually abuse younger children were, themselves, sexually abused in the past. In actuality, adolescents engage in sexual abuse for many reasons, not only because they were victimized themselves.

The principle of multifinality limits the statements we can make about children's *prognosis*. For example, many people erroneously believe that if a child has been sexually abused, she is likely to exhibit a host of emotional and behavioral problems later in life, ranging from sexual deviancy and aggression to depression and anxiety. In fact, the developmental outcomes of boys and girls who have been sexually abused vary considerably. Some children show significant maladjustment while others show few long-term effects. Their diversity of outcomes illustrates the difficulty in making predictions regarding development.

Risk and Resilience

What explains equifinality and multifinality? Why is there such great diversity in children's developmental pathways? The answer is that child development is multiply determined by the complex interplay of genetic, biological, psychological, familial, and social-cultural factors. Some of these factors promote healthy, adaptive development, whereas other factors increase the likelihood that children will follow less-than-optimal, more maladaptive, developmental trajectories.

Developmental psychopathologists use the term **risk factors** to describe influences on development that interfere with the acquisition of children's competencies or compromise children's ability to adapt to their environments. In contrast, psychologists use the term **protective factors** to refer to influences on development that buffer the negative effects of risks on children's development and promote adaptive functioning (see Table 1.5). Risk and protective factors occur across levels of functioning: They can be genetic, biological, psychological, familial, or social-cultural (Cicchetti, 2006; Luthar, 2006).

The salience of a risk factor depends on the child's age, gender, level of development, and environmental context. For example, child sexual abuse is a risk factor for later psychosocial problems. However, the effects of sexual abuse depend on the gender of the child and the age at which the abuse occurs. For example, boys often show the greatest adverse effects of sexual victimization when they are abused in early childhood, whereas girls often show the poorest developmental outcomes when abuse occurs during early adolescence (Richters & Cicchetti, 1993).

Similarly, the ability of protective factors to buffer children from the harmful effects of risk depends on context

Table 1.5 Some Risk and Protective Factors Across Childhood and Adolescence

Level	Possible Risk Factors	Possible Protective Factors
Genetic	• Inherited genetic disorders • Genetic mutations	• Genetic screening • Early identification
Biological	• Inadequate prenatal health care • Complications during pregnancy or delivery • Inadequate postnatal health care, immunizations • Malnutrition • Exposure to environmental toxins, teratogens • Childhood illness or injury • Abnormalities in brain development • Speech, language, vision, hearing problems	• Good access to prenatal and postnatal care • High quality nutrition • Early recognition of medical and developmental delays or deficits • Early intensive treatment for medical problems and developmental delays
Psychological	• Cognitive delays or deficits • Hyperactivity, inattention, learning problems • Problems regulating emotions • Problems in social interactions	• Enriched learning, environmental experiences • High-quality special educational services • Help from therapist, school counselor, parents to remedy problems in emotional control or social functioning
Familial	• Parental death, separation, or abandonment • Parental divorce, marital conflict • Cold, distant, intrusive, or harsh parenting • Child abuse or neglect • Placement into foster care, group home • Parental substance abuse or mental illness • Parental antisocial behaviors	• Close relationship with at least one caregiver • Sensitive, responsive parenting behavior • Consistent use of parental discipline • Adequate parental monitoring • Good relationships with peers, extended kin • Adoption by loving parents
Social-Cultural	• Low socioeconomic status (SES) • Dangerous, high-crime neighborhood • Inadequate educational opportunities • Rejected by peers or association with deviant peers • Discrimination	• Peer acceptance, close friends • Involvement in prosocial activities (e.g., sports, clubs) • Relationships with adult mentors (e.g., coaches) • Adequate educational opportunities

(see Image 1.5). For example, many children who experience sexual abuse at the hands of a family member (e.g., stepfather) experience considerable psychological distress and behavioral impairment. However, children who are able to rely on a caring, nonoffending parent are often able to cope with this stressor more effectively than youths without the presence of a supportive parent (Heflin & Deblinger, 2003).

Protective factors are believed to promote resilience in youths at risk for maladaptive development. **Resilience** refers to the tendency of some children to develop social, emotional, and behavioral competence despite the presence of multiple risk factors. Consider the Case Study (Ramon and Rafael) about two brothers growing up in the same impoverished, high-crime neighborhood.

CASE STUDY

RAMON AND RAFAEL: DIVERGING DEVELOPMENTAL PATHS

Ramon, the older brother, begins showing disruptive behavior at a young age. He is disrespectful to his mother, defiant toward his teachers, and disinterested in school. By late elementary school, he has been suspended a number of times for fighting and chronic truancy. In junior high school, Ramon begins associating with peers who introduce him to other antisocial behaviors, such as shoplifting and breaking into cars. By adolescence, Ramon rarely attends school and earns money selling drugs. At 15, Ramon is removed from his mother's custody because of his antisocial behavior and truancy.

Rafael, the younger brother, also shows early problems with defiance and aggression. However, these problems do not persist beyond the early elementary school years. Although Rafael does not enjoy school, he befriends an art teacher who recognizes his talent for drawing. The teacher offers to tutor him in art and help him show his work. Rafael also takes art classes at a local community center to learn new mediums. Through these classes, he meets other adolescents interested in drawing and painting. Rafael's grades in high school are generally low; however, he excels in art, music, and draftsmanship. He graduates with his class and studies interior design at community college.

Image 1.5 Portraits of resilience from both sides of the political spectrum. Barack Obama's parents separated shortly after his birth in 1961. He was estranged from his father and raised by his mother and grandparents. He became the first African American president of the United States. Condoleezza Rice was born in racially segregated Birmingham, Alabama. In 1963, the Sixteenth Street Baptist Church in her neighborhood was firebombed, killing two girls she knew. She later became provost of Stanford University, national security adviser, and secretary of state.

What accounts for Ramon's struggles and Rafael's resilience? Although there is no easy answer, a partial explanation might be the presence of protective factors at just the right time in Rafael's development. Ramon's path to antisocial behavior was probably facilitated by antisocial peers who introduced him to criminal activities. In contrast, Rafael's peer group encouraged prosocial activities and the development of artistic competence. If Rafael's teacher did not encourage the development of his art talents until later in Rafael's development, perhaps after he developed friendships with deviant peers, would he have followed the same developmental pathway as Ramon? Although we do not know for sure, we can speculate that these protective factors played an important role in his ability to achieve despite multiple risks (Cicchetti & Toth, 1991; Sroufe & Rutter, 1984).

Most protective factors occur spontaneously: A teacher nurtures a special talent in an at-risk youth, a coach encourages a boy with depression to join a team, or a girl who has been abused is adopted by loving parents. Sometimes, however, protective factors are planned to prevent the emergence of disorders. For example, communities may offer free infant and toddler screenings to identify children with developmental disabilities at an early age. Identification of developmental delays in infancy or toddlerhood can lead to early intensive intervention and better prognosis. Similarly, schools may offer prevention programs for girls who might develop eating disorders. Volunteers might teach girls about healthy eating, risks of dieting, and stress management. Even psychotherapy can be seen as a protective factor. Therapy helps children and adolescents alter developmental trajectories away from maladaption and toward adaptation (Quinton & Rutter, 1998; Toth & Cicchetti, 1999).

As we have seen, developmental psychopathology is an emerging approach to understanding abnormal child behavior in the context of normal child development, in relation to the environment, and across time. Developmental psychopathology offers a rich and multifaceted perspective on abnormal child psychology across a number of different levels: genetic, biological, psychological, familial, and social-cultural. Throughout this book, the principles of developmental psychopathology will be used to explore the causes and treatment of child and adolescent disorders across these levels and within various developmental contexts.

THE SCIENCE OF ABNORMAL CHILD PSYCHOLOGY
Integrating Science and Practice

The **scientist-practitioner approach** to abnormal psychology assumes that psychological research and clinical practice are interdependent and equally important facets of psychological training. Psychologists trained in the scientist-practitioner tradition are first and foremost scientists. They are committed to understanding human behavior through careful and systematic empirical investigation. Psychological science is concerned primarily with understanding behavior, with the goal of explaining, predicting, and/or influencing aspects of behavior that are relevant to people's lives. Psychological scientists, whether they work in research labs or mental health clinics, rely on scientific principles to inform their work, and they try to base their professional activities on knowledge gained through systematic data collection.

Most scientist-practitioners are clinicians who use scientific knowledge to alleviate distress and promote the welfare of their clients. Clinicians are called to apply information gained through research to help children, adults, and families. Furthermore, they may be asked to consult with other professionals, evaluate the effectiveness of social programs, and teach or supervise new generations of mental health experts. These individuals often work in mental health clinics, hospitals, schools, counseling centers, and other places where psychological services are delivered to individuals or groups.

Other scientist-practitioners are primarily engaged in research. Although they may also see clients on a limited basis, these professionals are devoted to understanding the prevalence, causes, and treatment of mental disorders. Researchers might be employed at a college or university, a medical school, a hospital, or an independent research center.

From the scientist-practitioner perspective, both the science and practice of psychology are important to the discipline. Psychological science informs clinical practice by helping psychologists use the most accurate assessment techniques and effective therapeutic methods possible. At the same time, the practice of assessment and therapy guides research by helping scientists focus their efforts on discovering principles and practices that have real-world applications.

The scientist-practitioner approach has its roots in a 1941 report to the American Association for Applied Psychology written by David Shakow (Baker & Benjamin, 2000). In the report, Shakow outlined the importance of research and clinical training in the education and development of clinical psychologists. He argued that psychologists must be able to integrate scientific principles and knowledge with their expertise as clinicians. Shakow recognized that psychologists could not balance their time equally between research and clinical practice; most would consider themselves either chiefly researchers or primarily practitioners. However, he asserted that an appreciation for science and practice was necessary for all psychologists, regardless of their professional role. As Drabick and Goldfried (2000) explain,

> The scientist practitioner model sought to encourage the development of practitioners who are both consumers of assessment and treatment research findings and evaluators of their own interventions using empirical methods, as well as researchers who are capable of producing and reporting clinically relevant data to the scientific community. Indeed, graduates would be well-trained clinicians who combined practice with an awareness of scientific research; or, conversely, . . . competent researchers with sensitivity to clinical issues. (p. 330)

Shakow's report was used by the American Psychological Association (1947) to formulate the first guidelines for the training of clinical psychologists. Today, most university-based clinical training programs identify themselves in the scientist-practitioner tradition.

Scientifically Informed Practice

The core tenets of the scientist-practitioner approach are outlined by Richard McFall's (1991) "Manifesto for a Science of Clinical Psychology." McFall argued that scientifically based psychology is the only legitimate and acceptable form of understanding and alleviating psychological disorders. Stated another way, psychology is a science that must have its roots in empiricism and objective evaluation. According to McFall, "All forms of legitimate clinical psychology must be grounded in science, . . . all competent clinical psychologists must be scientists first and foremost, and . . . all clinicians must ensure that their practice is scientifically valid" (p. 76).

From McFall's (1991) perspective, the distinction between psychological science and clinical practice is artificial. The only way clinicians can help their clients in a competent and ethical manner is to base their interventions on the research literature and on empirical investigation. Before practicing any form of assessment or treatment, clinicians must ask, "What is the empirical evidence supporting my practice?" Whenever possible, clinicians must rely on assessment strategies and therapy techniques that have empirical support.

Unfortunately, some clinicians do not ground their interventions in the research literature or empirical data (Garb & Boyle, 2004). Instead, they may base their clinical practice on other factors, including theory, clinical experience, and anecdotal information provided by others. Although theories, experience, and anecdotes can be useful when combined with empirical evidence, they are insufficient guides for clinical practice by themselves. Psychological scientists believe that empirical data provide the best evidence either for or against a specific clinical intervention.

Without empirical data, clinicians might intervene in ways that are not effective. Ineffective interventions can harm clients and their families in at least three ways. First, ineffective interventions can cost *significant time and money*—resources that might be better spent participating in treatment with more empirical support. For example, available treatments for childhood disorders include listening to certain types of music, wearing special glasses, taking large doses of vitamins, avoiding certain textured foods, riding on horseback, swimming with dolphins, re-enacting the birth experience, and a host of other therapies with little systematic support. Although most of these interventions do not cause physical or psychological harm to clients, they can cost significant time, energy, and money. Furthermore, when insurance companies compensate individuals for participating in these therapies, resources available for more evidence-based interventions are diminished.

Second, families who participate in ineffective treatment can *lose hope* in the therapeutic process and in psychological treatment more generally. For example, many parents of oppositional and defiant children seek help to manage their children's behavior. Although a number of well-supported interventions exist to treat children's disruptive behavior, many families are given therapy that lacks empirical support. Consequently, they meet with limited success. As a result, many parents come to believe that psychological interventions will not help their children. Some parents simply give up on treatment.

Third, interventions that lack empirical support *can be harmful* to clients, families, and society. The history of psychology is marked by examples of clinicians harming individuals and society by practicing without empirical basis. Perhaps nowhere is this more obvious than in the treatment of autism. In the 1960s, Bruno Bettelheim suggested that autism was caused by parents who were cold and rejecting toward their children. Bettelheim's erroneous theory for the etiology of autism placed unnecessary blame on parents and resulted in a host of interventions that were completely ineffective at alleviating autistic symptoms (Image 1.6).

Later, sociologist Douglas Biklen (1993) recommended that individuals with autism and severe Intellectual Disability might be able to communicate with others if facilitated by a trained therapist. The subsequent practice of "facilitated communication" involved the therapist guiding the client's hand as the client supposedly typed messages on a keyboard. In one case, a client participating in facilitated communication supposedly reported that he had been abused by his family. As a result, the client was removed from his family's custody, despite no corroborating evidence of maltreatment. Later, the technique of facilitated communication was discredited by showing that the messages typed by clients actually reflected knowledge and information provided by therapists, not by the individuals with developmental disabilities.

Even more recently, physician Andrew Wakefield and colleagues (1998) incorrectly suggested that the measles-mumps-rubella (MMR) vaccine caused autism in some children susceptible to the disorder. Consequently, many conscientious parents refused to immunize their infants, resulting in an unnecessary and dangerous increase in these childhood illnesses.

Clinicians also harm clients in more subtle ways when they provide information that lacks empirical support. For example, some clinicians erroneously perpetuate the myth that most sexually abused children victimize other children in the future. This incorrect belief can unnecessarily worry parents and stigmatize young victims. Similarly, other clinicians convey the notion that certain childhood disorders, like ADHD, do not exist; rather, problems with hyperactivity and inattention are caused by inadequate parenting. Such unsupported beliefs can cause parents to feel guilty and ineffective and discourage them from seeking effective treatment.

Scientist-practitioners engaged in full-time clinical practice try to approach their professional activities using the

Image 1.6 A therapist uses Applied Behavior Analysis (ABA) to teach 3-year-old Joey, a boy with Autism Spectrum Disorder, to point to his father's nose. Scientist-practitioners apply evidence-based interventions, like ABA, to help families in need.

Source: Image courtesy of Bruce Cummins.

principles of psychological science. From the scientist-practitioner perspective, clinical work is analogous to a research study in which the practitioner's sample size consists of one individual (i.e., the client). The clinician generates hypotheses about the source of the client's problem and the best form of treatment, based on data gathered from the client and information presented in the research literature. Then, the clinician administers treatment and evaluates the client's outcomes using objective criteria. Finally, the clinician modifies her intervention based on information from the client, in order to improve effectiveness.

Clinically Informed Research

Most professionals have focused on the importance of clinicians applying principles of psychological science to their practice. Somewhat less attention has been directed at the importance of researchers conducting studies that are meaningful to therapists. A scientist-practitioner approach to psychopathology implies that psychological research must be relevant to clinical practice.

A number of researchers have recognized the considerable gap between psychological research and clinical practice (Antony, 2005). Unfortunately, many researchers eschew the lack of scientific rigor that characterizes most clinical interventions, while therapists often find psychological research to be inaccessible and detached from their daily practice.

From the scientist-practitioner perspective, researchers can take at least three steps to bridge this gap between research and practice.

First, psychological research must *address practical problems* that have relevance to clinicians. Although research in basic psychological structure and functioning is extremely important, research that has direct application to clinicians' day-to-day work is most likely to be used by therapists in the community.

Second, researchers must *disseminate their findings* in a manner that clinicians can understand and use. As psychology students know, reading an empirical study from a peer-reviewed journal can be challenging. It is extremely tempting to read the article's abstract, introduction, and discussion and omit the method and results section, in order to avoid the often complex and confusing description of research design and statistics. Furthermore, relatively few research articles are written with clinicians as the primary audience. Often, readers who want to apply findings to their clinical work must determine the implications of research to their practice on their own. Researchers must be more mindful of clinicians when disseminating their research, to maximize the likelihood that clinicians will understand and apply their findings.

Third, the intervention techniques that are developed by researchers must *translate to the real world*. New therapies are usually evaluated in university clinics and research hospitals, and they are evaluated under ideal circumstances. For example, when evaluating a new therapy, researchers carefully select clients with only certain disorders, provide therapists with considerable training in delivering the interventions, and monitor clients' participation in treatment and clinicians' adherence to the treatment program. However, when therapies are used outside research settings, they may not be as feasible to administer or as effective at reducing clients' symptoms. For example, behavioral treatments have been shown to reduce children's disruptive behavior problems in carefully controlled research studies. However, when these programs are administered in real-world clinics, as many as 50% of families drop out of treatment before completion.

From the scientist-practitioner perspective, researchers must be mindful of the needs of clinicians when designing, conducting, and reporting their studies. A closer connection is needed between psychological science and clinical practice if applied psychology is to flourish.

Toward Evidence-Based Treatment

In 1993, the American Psychological Association (APA) organized a task force to identify treatments for psychiatric disorders that have demonstrated effectiveness in research studies. The Task Force on Psychological Intervention Guidelines was convened for two reasons. First, members of the task force hoped that if they identified groups of **evidence-based treatments**, clinicians might have an easier time identifying and using the most efficacious and promising treatments that are available. Second, members of the task force wanted to justify the practice of psychotherapy to insurance companies and show that many forms of psychotherapy are, in fact, supported by empirical data.

The APA task force identified a number of evidence-based psychotherapies for adults. These therapies were divided into three categories. *Well-established/efficacious treatments* showed support from at least two randomized controlled studies demonstrating the therapy's efficacy over a placebo control group or another existing treatment. *Probably efficacious treatments* had empirical support for their efficacy but only from one randomized controlled trial or a small number of single-subject studies. A third category of treatments, *promising treatments*, demonstrated effectiveness in quasi-experimental studies or one single-subject research study and merited further attention.

In 1998, a second task force provided a similar list of evidence-based therapies for child and adolescent disorders (Lonigan, Elbert, & Johnson, 1998). The task force committees identified treatments for ADHD (Pelham, Wheeler, & Chronis, 1998), child and adolescent conduct problems (Brestan & Eyberg, 1998), autism (Rogers, 1998), child and adolescent depression (Kaslow & Thompson, 1998), and child and adolescent anxiety disorders (Ollendick & King, 1998). Treatments for other disorders commonly experienced by youths, such as eating disorders and substance use disorders, were absent from the list because no empirically supported treatments had been identified that met the committee's criteria.

Since the time of the task force's initial identification of evidence-based treatments for child and adolescent disorders, many individuals and professional organizations have suggested modifications to the group's initial criteria for well-established and probably efficacious treatments (Nathan & Gorman, 2002). Many professionals praise the APA's focus on identifying and disseminating evidence-based treatments for specific disorders. Indeed, the focus on evidence-based treatments emphasizes the scientific basis upon which the practice of psychology is founded.

On the other hand, critics have stressed the dangers of overemphasizing the importance of evidence-based treatments in clinical practice (Beutler, Zetzer, & Williams, 1996). Some researchers have challenged the use of randomized, controlled experiments as a means of establishing the efficacy of treatment. These critics argue that randomized, controlled experiments are most sensitive to detecting short-term symptom reduction rather than long-term changes in functioning; consequently, they are more likely to support short-term behavioral interventions rather than long-term therapies. Furthermore, the criteria for well-established treatments favor studies performed in strictly controlled research settings. However, most therapy is practiced under less-than-optimal conditions in community mental health centers and clinics. Critics argue that the results of these studies may not generalize to real-world practice (Westen, Novotny, & Thompson-Brenner, 2004).

Students as Emerging Scientists and Practitioners

Psychology students often find themselves providing services to children and adolescents in distress. Students sometimes act as aides for individuals with Intellectual Disability and developmental delays, behavior therapists for youths with autism, tutors for children with learning disabilities, and psychological technicians in residential treatment facilities, juvenile detention centers, and hospitals. Students can also provide paraprofessional services through volunteer experiences. For example, many students mentor at-risk youths, provide in-services to grade school and high school students, monitor telephone crisis hotlines, and help local community mental health centers.

Because students often provide frontline psychological services, they have enormous potential for improving the functioning of children, adolescents, and families. However, students can also contribute to the propagation of inaccurate information and the dissemination of ineffective and unsupported treatments. Although psychology students are not in a position to direct interventions, they can approach treatment from the perspective of psychological science. Specifically, students can ask the following questions:

1. What is the evidence for the intervention or service that I am providing? Is there a theoretical and empirical basis for my work? Are there alternative services that might provide greater benefits to the people I serve?

2. Am I effective? Am I monitoring the effectiveness of the services I provide to determine whether I am helping my clients? Is there any possibility that I might be harming them?

3. Am I providing ethical, time-effective, and cost-effective services? During my work, do I respect the rights and dignity of others, conduct myself in a responsible and professional manner, and represent the field of psychology with integrity? Are my activities being supervised by someone who practices in an ethical and scientifically mindful manner?

As you read this book, consider how you might use the empirical literature to inform your own understanding of child and adolescent disorders. A scientific approach to child psychopathology is not reserved for licensed psychologists or university professors. Instead, all students, parents, teachers, and individuals who work with youths are called upon to use empirical data to help improve the functioning of others.

ETHICS IN WORKING WITH CHILDREN AND FAMILIES

Mental health professionals are placed in positions of authority and trust. Clients usually come to therapists showing emotional distress and impairment. Clients are often vulnerable, and they seek care that is sensitive and responsive to their needs. The provision of competent and ethically mindful services is especially important when clients are juveniles. Parents place their most valuable assets—their children—in the care of therapists, with expectations that clinicians will help their children overcome problems and achieve the highest levels of competence possible.

Ethics refers to the standard of behavior that is determined to be acceptable for a given profession. Ethics should not be confused with a person's morality, that is, his personal beliefs in the rightness or wrongness of a given behavior. Ethical behavior is determined by group consensus; morality is determined by personal determination and belief.

All mental health professionals adhere to a code of ethics that guides their professional practice. Different professional organizations have different ethics codes. These codes include the APA's (2002) *Ethical Principles of Psychologists and Code of Conduct,* the National Association of School Psychologists' *Professional Conduct Manual and Principles for Professional Ethics,* the American Counseling Association's *Code of Ethics,* and the American School Counselor Association's *Ethical Standards for School Counselors.* Because the APA Ethics Code is the most frequently used system, we will examine it in greater detail.

APA Ethics Code

The primary purpose of the APA Ethics Code is to protect the welfare of individuals with whom psychologists work (e.g., clients, research participants, students). The secondary purpose of the Ethics Code is to educate psychologists, students, and the general public about the ethical practice of psychology. Because the Ethics Code is endorsed by the APA, all APA members and student affiliates are required to be familiar with the code and adhere to its rules. Failure to adhere to the Ethics Code can result in sanctions from the APA, psychology licensing boards, and other professional organizations.

The APA Ethics Code consists of four parts: (a) an Introduction, (b) a Preamble, (c) five General Principles, and (d) specific Ethical Standards. The Introduction and Preamble describe the purpose, organization, and scope of the Ethics Code. The five **General Ethical Principles** are broad ideals for the professional behavior of psychologists. The General Principles are aspirational in nature; they are not enforceable rules. Instead, the General Principles describe the highest ideals of psychological practice toward which all psychologists should strive (APA, 2010, section 4.02):

A. *Beneficence and Nonmaleficence:* Psychologists strive to benefit those with whom they work and they take care to do no harm.

B. *Fidelity and Responsibility:* Psychologists establish relationships of trust, . . . are aware of their professional and scientific responsibilities, . . . uphold professional standards of conduct, clarify their professional roles and obligations, [and] accept appropriate responsibility for their behavior.

C. *Integrity:* Psychologists seek to promote accuracy, honesty, and truthfulness in science, teaching, and the practice of psychology.

D. *Justice:* Psychologists recognize that fairness and justice entitle all persons to access to and benefit from the contributions of psychology.

E. *Respect for People's Rights and Dignity:* Psychologists respect the dignity and worth of all people and the rights of individuals to privacy, confidentiality, and self-determination.

The bulk of the ethics code consists of the **Ethical Standards**: specific rules that guide professional practice. The ethical standards govern all professional activities including assessment, therapy, research, and teaching. Although there are too many Ethical Standards to describe here, we will examine some of the rules that are most relevant to the treatment of children and adolescents.

Competence

The Ethical Standards dictate that psychologists treat, teach, and conduct research only in areas in which they have received appropriate training, supervised experience, or advanced study. Psychologists must be aware of the boundaries of their competence and seek additional training, consultation, or supervision if they want to expand their area of expertise.

Practicing within the boundaries of competence is important because it protects the welfare of children and families. Psychologists who practice outside their areas of training will likely be less effective than therapists who are more knowledgeable and skillful. Therapists who practice outside the boundaries of their competence also risk harming their clients.

Confidentiality

Confidentiality refers to the expectation that information that clients provide during the course of treatment will not be disclosed to others. The expectation of confidentiality serves at least two purposes. First, the expectation of confidentiality increases the likelihood that people in need of mental health services will seek treatment. Second, the expectation of confidentiality allows clients to disclose information more freely and, consequently, it facilitates the therapeutic process.

In most cases, confidentiality is an ethical and legal right of clients. Therapists who violate a client's right to confidentiality may be sanctioned by professional organizations and held legally liable. Most psychologists consider protection of clients' confidentiality to be one of the most important ethical standards.

Although clients have the right to expect confidentiality when discussing information with their therapists, clients should be aware that the information they disclose is not entirely private. There are certain **limitations to confidentiality** that therapists must make known to clients, preferably during the first therapy session. First, if the client is an *imminent danger to self or others,* the therapist is required to break confidentiality to protect the welfare of the client or someone he or she threatens. For example, if an adolescent tells his therapist that he plans on killing himself after he leaves the therapy session, the therapist has a duty to warn the adolescent's parents or the police, in order to protect the adolescent from self-harm. The psychologist's duty to protect the health of the adolescent supersedes the adolescent's right to confidentiality.

Second, if the therapist *suspects child abuse or neglect,* the therapist is usually required to break confidentiality to protect the maltreated child. For example, if during the course of therapy a 12-year-old girl admits to being physically and sexually maltreated by her stepfather, the psychologist would have a duty to inform the girl's mother and the authorities to protect the child from further victimization.

Third, in exceptional circumstances, a judge can issue a *court order* requiring the therapist to disclose information provided in therapy. For example, a judge might order a psychologist to provide information about an adolescent client who has been arrested for serious criminal activity. Sometimes, information about treatment is necessary for the court proceedings. Court orders to disclose information about treatment are rare; however, psychologists are legally obligated to comply with these orders.

Fourth, therapists can disclose limited information about clients in order *to obtain payment* for services. For example, therapists often need to provide information about clients to insurance companies. This information typically includes the client's name, demographic information, diagnosis, and a plan for treatment. Usually, insurance companies are the only parties who have access to this information.

Fifth, therapists can disclose limited information about clients to colleagues *to obtain consultation* or supervision. It is usually acceptable for psychologists to describe clients' problems in general terms in order to gain advice or recommendations from other professionals. However, therapists only provide information to colleagues that is absolutely necessary for them to receive help, and they avoid using names and other identifying information.

In most jurisdictions, the right to confidentiality is held by children's parents, not by children themselves. From a legal standpoint, parents have the right to the information their children or adolescents disclose in therapy.

Samantha was a 14-year-old girl who was referred to Dr. Graham because of disruptive behavior problems. During the course of therapy, Samantha admitted that she frequently drinks alcohol, uses marijuana, and recently began experimenting with prescription pain medications she obtains from friends. Although Dr. Graham was concerned with Samantha's substance use, she decided not to disclose the information to Samantha's parents. Weeks later, Samantha's father called Dr. Graham and demanded to see her therapy notes regarding Samantha. Samantha's father suspected that Samantha was using drugs and wanted information from the therapist about his daughter's substance use.

Dr. Graham needs to balance the father's legal right to receive information about his daughter's treatment with Dr. Graham's ethical obligation to protect Samantha's confidentiality. The APA Ethics Code states that when a psychologist's ethical responsibilities conflict with the law, the psychologist should make known her commitment to the Ethics Code and take steps to resolve the conflict in a responsible manner. In this case, Dr. Graham might consult with a colleague to gain another professional's opinion. Then, she might explain to Samantha's father that disclosing therapy notes would likely violate Samantha's trust and destroy the quality of the therapeutic relationship. If Samantha's father still insists on receiving the information, Dr. Graham might try to reach a compromise between Samantha and her parents. For example, perhaps Samantha could disclose the information to her parents directly, with the therapist facilitating communication between the two parties.

Of course, the best way to deal with a situation like the one described in the Case Study about Samantha is to prevent it. Therapists usually discuss the limitations of confidentiality with youths and their parents, to clarify under what circumstances information will be shared with parents. Ideally, parents and children reach a confidentiality agreement during the first session. Sometimes, therapists create a written contract to avoid ambiguity and prevent future problems.

Multiple Relationships

Psychologists must avoid multiple relationships. A multiple relationship occurs when a psychologist, who is in a professional role with a client, enters into another relationship with the same individual or a person closely associated with that individual. Multiple relationships can impair psychologists' objectivity, competence, and the effectiveness of the services that they provide.

A related ethical issue is therapists' duty to clarify their professional roles. When psychologists provide services to multiple people who have a relationship with one another, they must clarify their relationship with each of these individuals.

Imagine that a mother and her adolescent daughter seek therapy because they frequently argue. At the onset of therapy, the therapist must clarify her relationship with both mother and daughter. One solution is that all parties agree that the clinician will assume the role of primary therapist for the daughter. Although the clinician might occasionally meet with mother and daughter together, the clinician's primary responsibility might be the interests of the daughter. If the mother seeks help with specific problems (e.g., depression), the clinician might refer her to another therapist. An alternative solution is that all parties agree that the parent-adolescent

Dr. Jacoby is a respected psychologist at a child guidance clinic. Her neighbor, and good friend, asks her to provide therapy for her adolescent daughter, Mariah. Mariah has recently been exhibiting problems with anxiety and depression. Dr. Jacoby agrees to treat Mariah and, consequently, enters into a multiple relationship. Mariah is both Dr. Jacoby's client and the daughter of Dr. Jacoby's good friend. During the course of therapy, Mariah tells Dr. Jacoby that she is pregnant and does not want to tell her mother. Dr. Jacoby's objectivity might be compromised because of her dual relationship. Although the needs of her client should be paramount, she might sacrifice Mariah's expectation for confidentiality to maintain her friendship with Mariah's mother.

dyad will be the primary focus of therapy. In this case, the therapist might propose that mother and daughter always meet together for therapy sessions and that the therapist will not meet with either person alone.

Psychologists must carefully identify their relationship with all family members to avoid conflicting roles. When roles are unclear, family members can become estranged from the therapeutic process or feel like their trust has been violated.

Informed Consent

Perhaps the best way to avoid ethical problems is to make sure that children and families know what they are agreeing to before they decide to participate in therapy. The APA Ethics Code requires psychologists to obtain informed consent from individuals before assessment, treatment, or research. Informed consent protects people's right to self-determination. Individuals are entitled to make voluntary and knowledgeable decisions.

Informed consent to therapy includes a number of components. First, individuals are entitled to a description of treatment, its anticipated risks and benefits, and an estimate of its duration and cost. Second, the psychologist must discuss alternative treatments that might be available and review the strengths and weaknesses of the recommended treatment approach. Third, psychologists must remind clients that participation is voluntary and that they are free to refuse treatment or withdraw from therapy at any time. Finally, psychologists should review the limits of confidentiality with their clients.

Children and adolescents, by virtue of their age and legal status as minors, are not capable of providing consent. *Consent* implies that individuals both understand and freely agree to participate. Young children may not fully appreciate the risks and benefits of participation in treatment. Older children and adolescents may not freely agree to participate because they may be pressured by others (e.g., the psychologist, school personnel) to attend treatment. Instead, consent is obtained from parents or legal guardians. Psychologists are required to obtain the *assent* of children and adolescents before providing services. To obtain assent, psychologists typically describe the treatment or research using language that youths can understand. They begin only after receiving permission from children and the consent of their parents or caregivers.

CHAPTER SUMMARY

- Approximately 15% of children meet diagnostic criteria for a psychological disorder at any given point in time. An additional 5 to 6% of youths show subthreshold symptoms. The most common childhood problems are anxiety disorders, conduct problems, and ADHD.
- The prevalence of childhood disorders depends on age, gender, and social-cultural background. Adolescents, girls, and youths from low-income families are at increased risk for developing problems.
- Although disorders are common, children and families often do not receive appropriate treatment. Barriers to treatment include financial hardship, limited availability of high-quality treatment in most communities, and few professionals trained in evidence-based forms of treatment.
- *DSM-5* defines a mental disorder as a behavioral syndrome that exists within the individual, that reflects an underlying psychobiological dysfunction, and that results in clinically significant distress or disability. This definition has been criticized in at least three ways:
  - Some disorders, especially childhood disorders, may be best understood as existing between people (e.g., between parent and child) rather than within an individual.
  - In many instances, people (especially children) with disorders show no biological abnormality that causes their disorder.
  - Socioeconomic background, culture, and ethnicity can greatly influence the way people show psychological symptoms.
- Developmental psychopathology is an interdisciplinary field that seeks to understand childhood disorders from the perspective of normal development. The field assumes that children's problems are best understood across multiple levels (e.g., genetic, neurobiological, family system, social-cultural) and over time. Risk and protective factors affect children's ability to perform tasks at each stage of their behavioral, cognitive, and social-emotional development. Success in early developmental tasks can place children on developmental pathways for success in later tasks and greater competence and adaptive functioning.
- The scientist-practitioner approach to abnormal psychology assumes that psychological research and clinical practice are interdependent and equally important. Clinical practice must be informed by theory and empirical data. Research must address the needs of clinicians in the real world. Students can also act as scientist-practitioners by thinking critically about the services they might provide to children and families in the community.
- The American Psychological Association Ethics Code guides the professional practice of psychology. Both professionals and students should adhere to its ethical principles and standards. Standards relevant to the practice of abnormal child psychology include the following:
  - Practicing only within one's area of competence
  - Protecting the confidentiality of children and families
  - Avoiding multiple relationships and
  - Allowing people to make informed decisions regarding treatment

KEY TERMS

CRITICAL THINKING EXERCISES

1. Some experts believe that the child mental health system is in a state of crisis. Why? What might state governments and/or private social services do to provide high-quality mental health services to children?

2. According to *DSM-5*, a mental disorder is a pattern of behavior characterized by distress or disability (impairment) that resides within the individual. What might be some limitations to this definition of "mental disorder," especially when it is applied to children and adolescents?

3. Sigmund Freud wrote about the difficulty of predicting children's development:

    So long as we trace development from its final outcome backwards, the chain of events appears continuous. . . . But if we proceed the reverse way, if we start from the premises and try to follow these up to the final result, . . . we notice at once that there might have been another result and we might have been just as well able to understand and explain the latter. Hence the chain of causation can always be recognized with certainty if we follow the line of analysis backwards, whereas to predict it is impossible. (quoted in Sroufe & Rutter, 1984, p. 17)

    Apply this passage to the concept of "probabilistic epigenesis."

4. In his "Manifesto for a Science of Clinical Psychology," Richard McFall (1991) argues that the only legitimate form of psychology is *scientific* psychology. How can psychological research guide the practice of psychotherapy? How can the clinical experiences of therapists inform psychological research? In what ways can students think of themselves as scientists and practitioners?

5. Dr. Maeryn, a child psychologist, promises her adolescent client, "It's important for you to be open and honest in therapy. Everything you say will be kept a secret and never shared with anyone else." What is problematic about Dr. Maeryn's statement?

EXTEND YOUR LEARNING

Videos, practice tests, flash cards, study guides, and links to online resources for this chapter are available to students online. Teachers also have access to lecture notes, PowerPoint presentations, suggestions for classroom activities, and possible exam questions. Visit: www .sagepub.com/weis2e.

Exploring the Causes of Childhood Disorders

Research Methods and Theories

LEARNING OBJECTIVES

After reading this chapter, you should be able to answer these questions:

- What is the difference between a correlational study and a true experiment? Why can't we infer causality from a correlational study?
- What is a single-subject research design, and when might it be used in clinical settings?
- What are some of the methods used by behavioral geneticists and molecular geneticists to determine the heritability and causes of childhood disorders?
- What are the major areas of the brain, and what are their functions?
- How might learning theory be used to understand the development of childhood disorders?
- Why is parent-child attachment and parenting behavior important to children's development?
- Explain bioecological systems theory; how does it account for the interaction between proximal and distal influences on child development?

THE SCIENTIFIC STUDY OF BEHAVIOR

Science is the systematic search for order in the natural world. Scientists seek to identify meaningful relationships between observable events, in order to describe, predict, explain, and/or control these events. Physical scientists focus chiefly on the principles of physical matter and movement. Biological scientists concentrate on relationships within and between living systems. Behavioral scientists direct their attention to the structure and functioning of behavior, that is, to people's thoughts, feelings, and actions.

Three Features of Scientific Inquiry

There is no universally accepted method of scientific inquiry. However, science can be differentiated from nonscientific approaches to understanding the world in at least three ways (Newsom & Hovanitz, 2005).

First, to help organize their understanding of nature, scientists *generate hypotheses* about natural phenomena. **Hypotheses** are initial explanations or accounts about the natural world that are based on observation, previous research, and theory.

Hypotheses are stated clearly and unambiguously, using either mathematical formulas or verbal statements. When scientists express hypotheses verbally, they **operationally define** the terms they use; that is, they carefully describe how phenomena can be measured. For example, a behavioral scientist might operationally define the term *aggressive* as "getting into physical fights at least three times per month." Operational definitions translate hypotheses into clear, observable terms and allow scientists to communicate with one another precisely and consistently.

Second, scientists *generate testable hypotheses*. The statements that scientists make about the natural world must be open to evaluation by others. Specifically, hypotheses must be **falsifiable**, that is, capable of being disconfirmed.

Technically speaking, scientists do not seek to prove their hypotheses. Instead, they seek to examine the possibility that their hypotheses might be wrong. Once scientists generate a hypothesis, they re-word the hypothesis as a statement that can be disconfirmed. This falsifiable hypothesis is often called the **null hypothesis**. For example, if a psychologist's hypothesis is "Disruptive adolescents will show higher levels of depression than nondisruptive adolescents," his null hypothesis might be "Disruptive adolescents will show levels of depression *equal* to nondisruptive adolescents." Then, the psychologist examines whether the null hypothesis can be rejected. Rejecting the null hypothesis can provide support for the psychologist's ideas, but it does not *prove* that his ideas are correct.

A third facet of science is that scientists systematically evaluate hypotheses using *empirical data*. One goal of hypothesis testing is to determine causal relationships between two or more events. To establish that variable A causes variable B, three conditions must be met (Alloy, Abramson, Raniere, & Dyller, 1999):

1. *Variable A and variable B must show covariation;* that is, a change in the presence or strength of variable A must be associated with a corresponding change in the presence or strength of variable B. For example, if we say that child physical abuse causes depression, then children who experience abuse should also show greater likelihood of becoming depressed.

2. *Variable A must precede variable B.* For example, if child abuse causes depression, then we would expect children who experience abuse to subsequently show depression. We would not expect depression to exist before the onset of abuse.

3. *Alternative causes for the covariation of variables A and B must be ruled out.* For example, children who have experienced abuse may become depressed, but this covariation does not necessarily imply that abuse *causes* depression. Other variables may account for both abuse and children's depressive symptoms. One alternative explanation is that mothers who are depressed may be more likely to mistreat their children. Furthermore, mothers with depression may pass on genes that predispose their children to problems with depression.

Correlations: Associations Between Variables

What Are Correlational Studies?

Most psychological research examines association between two or more variables (Kazdin, 1999). For example, a researcher might examine whether children who have histories of abuse in early childhood (i.e., variable A) show greater likelihood of depression in later childhood or adolescence (i.e., variable B). Similarly, researchers might examine whether the size or functioning of a certain brain region (i.e., variable A) is associated with the severity of children's autistic symptoms (i.e., variable B). **Correlational studies** allow researchers to determine the relationship between variables (Holmbeck, Zebracki, & McGoron, 2009).

Researchers usually quantify the magnitude of the association between variables, using a correlation coefficient. The **Pearson product-moment correlation coefficient** (r) is the most commonly used statistic (see Figure 2.1). Correlation coefficients range from 1.0 to –1.0. The *strength* of association is determined by the absolute value of the coefficient. Coefficients near 1.0 or –1.0 indicate strong covariation between variables, whereas coefficients near 0 indicate weak or absent covariation. The *direction* of the association is determined by the sign of the coefficient. Positive values indicate a direct association between variables (i.e., as one variable increases, the other increases), whereas negative values indicate an inverse association (i.e., as one variable increases, the other decreases).

Correlations and Causality

Correlational studies allow researchers to notice associations between variables, but they do not allow researchers to infer causal relationships between variables (Holmbeck et al., 2009). Why?

First, a correlation between two variables does not tell us the temporal relationship between the variables. Imagine that researchers notice that the size of a certain brain area is negatively correlated with the severity of children's autistic symptoms: The smaller the brain region, the greater the child's symptoms. We might be tempted to infer a causal relationship between brain and behavior, specifically, that an underdevelopment of this brain region causes autism. However, it is also possible that autistic symptoms, over time, cause this part of the brain to atrophy. Correlations do not allow us to determine temporal relationships between variables. Consequently, they do not allow us to infer causality.

The second reason we cannot infer causal relationships from correlational data is that correlational studies do not rule out alternative explanations for covariation. If we notice a correlation between the size of a brain region and the severity of children's autistic symptoms, we might be tempted to conclude that brain structure influences behavior or behavior affects brain structure. However, an alternative possibility is that a third factor might account for both a reduction in

Figure 2.1 Understanding Correlations

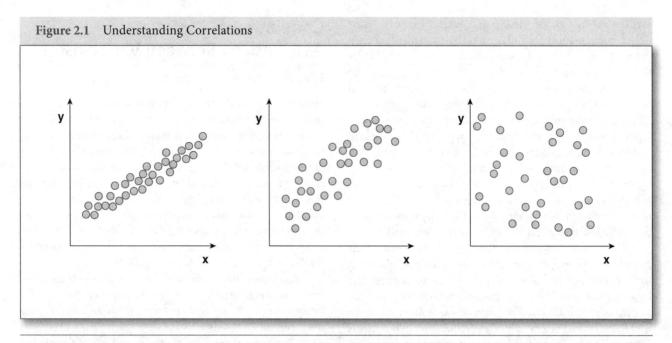

Note: The relationship between two variables are plotted on the X and Y axes respectively. Plots 1 and 2 show positive correlations. The association between variables is stronger for plot 1 ($r = .76$) than plot 2 ($r = .56$). Plot 3 shows no association between the two variables ($r = .00$).

brain size and an increase in autistic symptoms (see Figure 2.2). For example, children exposed to certain toxins during gestation might show both brain abnormalities and features of autism. Correlational studies do not control for these alternative explanations; consequently, they cannot be used to infer causal relationships.

Figure 2.2 Correlation Does Not Imply Causality

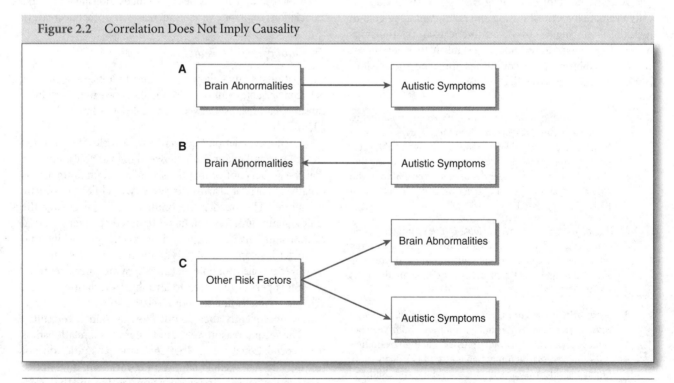

Source: Based on Baron-Cohen (2005) and Lawrence, Lott, and Haier (2005).

Note: Although there is a correlation between brain structure and autistic symptoms, we do not know if (a) brain abnormalities cause autistic behaviors, (b) autistic behaviors lead to abnormal brain development, or (c) other risk factors, like exposure to toxins, cause both brain abnormalities and autism.

Types of Correlational Studies

There are two types of correlational research designs that are especially relevant to scientists who examine the causes of childhood disorders (Alloy et al., 1999). In a **cross-sectional study**, researchers examine the association between variables at the same point in time. For example, researchers might examine the brain structure of children with autism. At the same time, they might ask parents to complete a questionnaire regarding the severity of their children's autistic symptoms. Cross-sectional studies can be conducted relatively quickly. However, because data are collected at the same point in time, researchers cannot determine the temporal relationship between the variables.

In a longitudinal study, researchers specify the temporal relationship between variables by measuring variables at different times. In a **prospective longitudinal study**, researchers measure a hypothesized causal variable at Time 1 and measure its expected outcome at Time 2. For example, researchers might hypothesize that certain brain abnormalities lead to later autistic symptoms. To test this hypothesis, they might assess brain structure during toddlerhood and autistic symptoms one or 2 years later. Prospective longitudinal studies have the advantage over cross-sectional studies of testing temporal relationships between variables.

Prospective longitudinal studies are difficult to conduct because participants often drop out of studies before their completion and researchers must wait a long time to test their hypotheses. Consequently, some researchers use other types of longitudinal designs to test hypotheses about the etiology of disorders. In a **retrospective longitudinal study**, researchers examine individuals with known disorders and ask them (or their parents) to recall events in the past that might have caused the disorder. For example, researchers might ask the parents of children with autism to recall social deficits that their children showed during infancy and that might have preceded the emergence of the disorder. The chief limitation of retrospective longitudinal studies is that they depend on the accuracy of people's memories for events in the past.

In a **follow-back study**, researchers examine the case histories, school records, or medical records of individuals with known disorders to determine whether events in their past may have contributed to the emergence of the disorder. For example, Osterling and Dawson (1994) reviewed videotapes of the first birthday parties of children later diagnosed with autism. Compared to typically developing children, one-year-olds later diagnosed with autism showed deficits during their birthday parties. Although parents usually did not notice these deficits at the time, they were observable on the videotape to researchers. The researchers suggested that early deficits in social and language functioning, often not noticeable by others, may contribute to the development of autism. Follow-back studies, like the one conducted by Osterling and Dawson (1994), do not rely on parents' memories of past events. However, obtaining high-quality records of children's developmental histories is often difficult.

Special Relationships Between Variables

Psychologists have long recognized the complexity of child development. Rarely is there a one-to-one correspondence between a single risk factor and a particular developmental outcome (Alloy et al., 1999).

Instead, researchers are often interested in identifying the conditions under which one variable is associated with another. A **moderator** is a variable that affects the nature of the relationship between two other variables (Baron & Kenny, 1986). For example, harsh physical discipline can contribute to the development of disruptive behavior problems in children. However, the relationship between harsh discipline and child behavior problems seems to be moderated by ethnicity (see Figure 2.3). White preschoolers who experience harsh discipline show increased risk for behavior problems as adolescents. However, African American preschoolers who experience harsh discipline do not show increased risk for later behavior problems; instead, physical discipline predicts fewer behavior problems among African American youths (Deater-Deckard, Dodge, Bates, & Pettit, 1996; Lansford, Deater-Deckard, Dodge, Bates, & Pettit, 2004). Although findings are preliminary, physical discipline may be a risk factor for behavior problems among white children and a possible protective factor among some African American children.

Moderators affect the direction or strength of the association between two variables. In Figure 2.3, ethnicity moderated the relationship between physical discipline and children's disruptive behavior problems. Moderator variables tend to be categorical variables. Some frequently studied moderator variables in child psychopathology research are gender (i.e., boy, girl), age (e.g., child, adolescent, adult), socioeconomic status (e.g., low-income, middle class), and diagnostic status (e.g., diagnosis, no diagnosis).

In other studies, researchers test hypotheses regarding the mechanism by which one variable affects another variable. A **mediator** is a variable that may account for the relationship between two other variables (Baron & Kenny, 1986). Usually, mediators explain how one variable (e.g., a risk factor) might influence another variable (e.g., a disorder).

For example, researchers noticed that children of overly controlling and demanding parents are prone to depression later in development. Until recently, however, researchers did not know exactly how overly controlling parents contributed to children's depressive symptoms. Kenney-Benson and Pomerantz (2005) hypothesized that

Figure 2.3 Understanding Moderation

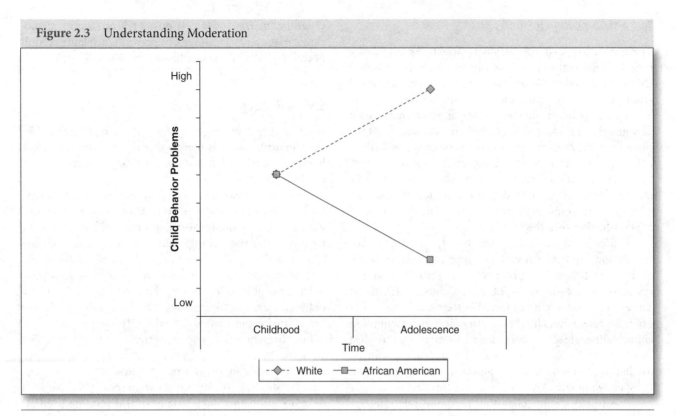

Source: Based on Lansford et al. (2004).

Note: A moderator affects the direction or strength of the association between two variables. In this case, children's ethnicity moderated the effects of physical discipline on children's behavior problems. Harsh discipline is associated with increased behavior problems in white (but not African American) families.

Figure 2.4 Understanding Mediation

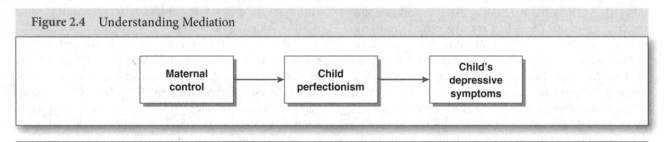

Source: Based on Kenney-Benson and Pomerantz (2005).

Note: A mediator accounts for the mechanism by which one variable affects another variable. In this case, high maternal control is associated with perfectionism in children. Perfectionism, in turn, is associated with childhood depression.

children's perfectionism mediated the relationship between their parents' use of control and their likelihood of developing depression (see Figure 2.4). The children of excessively controlling parents reported high levels of perfectionism. Perfectionism, in turn, predicted children's depressive symptoms (Flett, Hewitt, Oliver, & Macdonald, 2002).

Mediators tend to be continuous variables that explain the mechanism by which a risk factor (e.g., parental overcontrol) leads to a developmental outcome or disorder (e.g., depression). Mediators help researchers explain how risk factors contribute to the development of psychopathology.

DETERMINING CAUSALITY: EXPERIMENTS, QUASI-EXPERIMENTS, AND SINGLE-SUBJECT RESEARCH

What Are Experiments?

Researchers are usually not satisfied with knowing that variables correlate. They also want to determine whether a change in one variable *causes* a corresponding change in another variable. The best way to establish causality between two variables is to conduct an experimental study (Holmbeck et al., 2009). In an experiment, researchers randomly assign participants to two or more groups. Then, they manipulate one variable (i.e., the independent variable) and notice the effects of this manipulation on a second variable (i.e., the dependent variable; Kendall, Flannery-Schroeder, & Ford, 1999). Experiments allow causal inferences because researchers randomly assign participants to treatment and control groups at the onset of the study and treat both groups identically throughout the duration of the study (except for the manipulation of the independent variable; Kazdin, 1999).

In the field of abnormal child psychology, experimental research is most frequently used to examine the effectiveness of treatment. For example, a researcher might be interested in determining the efficacy of a new treatment designed to improve the verbal skills of children with autism. She might randomly assign children with autism to two groups. Children in the treatment group might receive 30 weeks of the new treatment (i.e., the independent variable), while children in the control group might be assigned to a waiting list. After 30 weeks, the researcher examines differences in children's language skills (i.e., the dependent variable) across groups. Differences between groups on the dependent variable might indicate that the new treatment has an effect on children's verbal skills.

A **randomized controlled trial** is a special type of experiment used to test the effectiveness of treatment. Researchers identify a group of individuals with the same disorder. Typically, individuals are recruited from the community, mental health clinics, or hospitals. Then, participants are randomly assigned to at least two groups. One group, the treatment group, receives the intervention. The other group, the control group, is used for comparison. **Random assignment** implies that each participant has an equal chance of being assigned to the treatment or the control group. By randomly assigning participants, the researcher decreases the likelihood that groups differ in meaningful ways before the treatment. Random assignment is essential to experimental research. Without random assignment, differences between groups that emerge at the end of the study might be attributable to differences that existed before the study, rather than to the treatment itself.

Many randomized controlled trials are double-blind. In a **double-blind study**, neither researchers nor participants know to what group participants have been assigned. Double-blind studies reduce biases on the part of researchers and participants. For example, researchers might behave differently toward participants in the treatment versus the control group if they know the group status of participants. Differences in researchers' behaviors toward members of these groups might affect the results of the evaluation.

Participants might also behave differently if they know whether they have been assigned to the treatment or control group. The **placebo effect** refers to the tendency of people to show improvement when they believe they are receiving treatment. Typically, people who believe that they are

receiving treatment pay greater attention to their health and behavior, take better care of themselves, and are more optimistic about their outcomes. Researchers must control for placebo effects; they need to be able to attribute symptom reduction to the treatment itself, not to participants' expectations for improvement (Holmbeck et al., 2009).

A critical decision in randomized controlled studies is what to do with participants in the control group (Kazdin, 2003). Many researchers compare the treatment group to a *no-treatment control group*. In this type of study, participants in the control group receive no treatment whatsoever. The primary shortcoming of using a no-treatment control group is that participants assigned to this group will clearly know that they are not receiving treatment. Consequently, differences between controls and participants in the treatment group can be attributable to placebo effects rather than the treatment per se. A second problem with using a no-treatment control group is that it is often unethical to withhold treatment from people with mental health problems, even for the sake of testing the efficacy of a new therapy. For example, it would be unethical to assign children with learning disorders to a no-treatment control group. By denying children treatment, we would be contributing to their academic delays.

Other researchers compare participants in the treatment group to participants assigned to a *waitlist control group*. In this type of study, participants assigned to the control group are placed on a waiting list to receive treatment. Treatment is delayed but not altogether withheld from participants. Waitlist control groups are usually more ethically justifiable than no-treatment control groups. However, they also have the limitation that participants assigned to the waitlist clearly know that they are not receiving treatment.

A third type of control group used in many randomized controlled studies is the *attention-placebo control group*. In an attention-placebo controlled study, participants assigned to the control group receive a theoretically inert form of treatment that resembles the treatment received by participants in the treatment group. For example, participants in an attention-placebo group might have weekly meetings with a therapist who listens to their concerns and responds in an empathic manner. Participants in the control group would likely believe that they were receiving the active treatment, thereby controlling for placebo effects between groups. However, participants in the attention-placebo group would not receive any specific form of treatment. For example, they would not be taught specific behavioral or cognitive techniques designed to reduce symptoms.

Finally, some researchers compare participants who receive the experimental treatment with participants who receive a treatment that is already available. For example, if a researcher develops a new form of treatment for ADHD, this new treatment might be compared to a treatment that already exists. Use of a *standard treatment control group* is the most stringent test of a new form of therapy. The new treatment must show that it reduces symptoms *and* that its benefits match or exceed those offered by existing therapies. A variant of the use of standard treatment controls is to compare an experimental treatment with "treatment as usual" (TAU). In this case, participants assigned to the treatment group receive the new therapy while participants assigned to the control group are referred to clinicians in the community and receive whatever form of care these clinicians recommend (i.e., treatment as usual).

A recent study conducted by Ronald Rapee and colleagues illustrates a randomized controlled trial. Rapee, Abbott, and Lyneham (2006) recruited 267 children with anxiety disorders and randomly assigned them to one of three conditions. The first group received a cognitive-behavioral treatment program for youths with anxiety problems. The second group received bibliotherapy; that is, their parents were given a book that described ways to treat childhood anxiety problems and parents were encouraged to use the techniques described in the book with their children at home. Children in the third group were placed on a waiting list. Three months after the beginning of the study, researchers examined the percentage of children in each group who no longer met diagnostic criteria for an anxiety disorder (see Figure 2.5). Results showed that significantly more children who participated in bibliotherapy (25.9%) were free of an anxiety disorder than children assigned to the waitlist control condition (6.7%). However, children who received cognitive-behavioral therapy were more likely to be free of their anxiety problems (61.1%) than children assigned to either of the other two groups. Results indicate

that bibliotherapy is effective in reducing childhood anxiety; however, cognitive-behavioral therapy is preferable to bibliotherapy as a primary form of treatment.

Quasi-Experimental Studies

In some cases, random assignment is not possible. For example, researchers might want to examine the effectiveness of a new form of therapy to treat adolescents with severe depression and suicidal thoughts. It would be inappropriate to randomly assign youths to a control group that did not receive the best treatment possible. When random assignment is not possible, the research design is said to be quasi-experimental.

Quasi-experimental research cannot be used to infer causal relationships between variables because improvement in symptoms can be attributable to other factors, not the treatment per se (Maughan & Rutter, 2010). For example, if adolescents with severe depression participate in a new treatment and they show significant symptom alleviation, we might say that the treatment was *associated with* symptom reduction; however, it would be inappropriate to infer that treatment *caused* the adolescents' improvement in functioning.

The **internal validity** of a research study refers to the degree to which we can attribute changes in the dependent variable (e.g., symptom reduction) to manipulation of the independent variable (e.g., treatment). When other factors, besides treatment, can explain symptom reduction, researchers say these factors threaten the internal validity of the study.

Figure 2.5   A Randomized Controlled Trial of Two Treatments for Childhood Anxiety

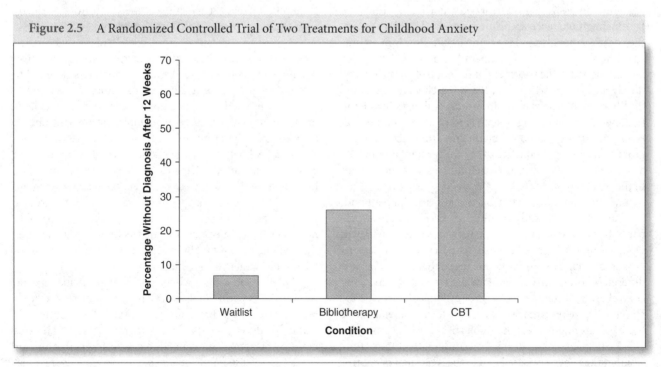

Source: Based on Rapee et al. (2006).

Note: Youths with anxiety disorders were randomly assigned to one of three conditions: (a) waitlist, (b) bibliotherapy, or (c) cognitive-behavioral therapy (CBT). Results showed that youths responded best to CBT; however, bibliotherapy was superior to the waitlist control.

What factors, besides treatment, might cause symptom reduction and threaten the internal validity of a study? Kazdin (2003) identifies at least five threats to internal validity that limit the causal inferences we can make from quasi-experimental research.

First, *maturation* can compromise the internal validity of a treatment study. Maturation refers to changes in the child that occur as a result of the passage of time. For example, in most adolescents, an episode of major depression lasts approximately two to nine months. Over time, depressive symptoms usually decrease even if no treatment is provided. Consequently, a researcher who administers a new therapy to adolescents with severe depression over the course of 6 months might erroneously conclude the treatment is effective if adolescents' symptoms decrease over time. Unless the researcher compares adolescents who received treatment with adolescents in a control group, the effects of treatment cannot be distinguished from maturation.

Second, events in the *surrounding environment* can threaten the internal validity of research. Events might include major news stories (e.g., terrorist attacks), natural disasters (e.g., hurricanes), changes in family environment or schools (e.g., a new teacher), or more subtle changes in temperature, weather, or the quality of the child's life. For example, a researcher might administer a new treatment for adolescent depression beginning in February and ending in May. The researcher might notice that adolescents' depression scores decrease over the course of treatment. She might erroneously attribute symptom reduction to her treatment. However, environmental changes across the duration of treatment might also be responsible for symptom alleviation. For example, adolescents might experience an improvement in mood simply because of more pleasant weather, greater opportunities for outdoor recreational activities, or anticipation of summer vacation.

A third threat to internal validity is *repeated testing*. The act of repeatedly assessing children can cause them to show improvement in their functioning over time. For example, a researcher might administer a 10-week treatment program to youths with math difficulties. To assess his treatment, he might ask the children to complete a math achievement test before the intervention, halfway through the treatment, and again upon completion. Children might show improvement in their math scores over time not because they benefited from the intervention but because they were exposed to the same math problems on three different occasions.

Fourth, in quasi-experimental studies, a *lack of random assignment* can lead to selection biases. Selection biases refer to systematic differences between treatment and control groups that emerge when groups are not randomly assigned at the beginning of the study. Imagine that a researcher investigates the efficacy of a new treatment for depression by recruiting adolescents with depression from hospitals and clinics. She assigns the first 25 adolescents who agree to participate in the study to the treatment group, and she places the remaining 25 adolescents on a waiting list to serve as controls. After 10 weeks of treatment, the researcher notices greater mood improvement among adolescents who received treatment. The researcher cannot attribute these differences to the treatment itself. Instead, selection biases before treatment might account for symptom differences after treatment. For example, the first 25 adolescents who agreed to participate in the study may have been more motivated to participate in treatment than the latter 25 assigned to the control group.

Finally, *attrition* can threaten the validity of all treatment outcome studies, especially studies that involve quasi-experimental designs. Attrition refers to the loss of participants over the course of the study. Attrition most often occurs because participants decide to withdraw from the study or simply stop attending follow-up appointments. When a large percentage of participants who receive treatment withdraw from a study, researchers may not be able to attribute symptom reduction to treatment. For example, a researcher might notice differences between treatment and control groups following a 10-week trial of a new therapy for depression. However, if 50% of participants assigned to the treatment group withdrew from the study before its completion, the researcher cannot be certain whether the 50% who remained in the study were representative of the treatment group as a whole. It is possible that the 50% who withdrew showed an *increase* in depression, prompting them to drop out.

A recent study illustrates how a lack of random assignment to a control group can threaten internal validity. Walker, Roffman, Stephens, Wakana, and Berghuis (2006) randomly assigned 97 high school students who frequently used marijuana to two conditions. The first group received a brief form of cognitive-behavioral treatment called motivational enhancement therapy (MET). The second group was assigned to a waiting list. After 3 months, researchers assessed adolescents' marijuana use (see Figure 2.6). Youths who received MET showed significant reduction in marijuana use. However, youths in the control group, who did not receive treatment, showed a similar reduction in marijuana use. The researchers hypothesized that the act of repeatedly asking adolescents about their marijuana use may have caused a decrease in marijuana smoking across both groups. If the researchers had failed to include a control group in their study, they would have only noticed the decrease in marijuana use among adolescents who received MET and would have mistakenly attributed this decrease to the treatment itself.

Single-Subject Studies

A third way to investigate the efficacy of treatment is to conduct a **single-subject research study**. In a single-subject study, the same individual's behavior is compared before and

Figure 2.6 The Importance of Using Control Groups

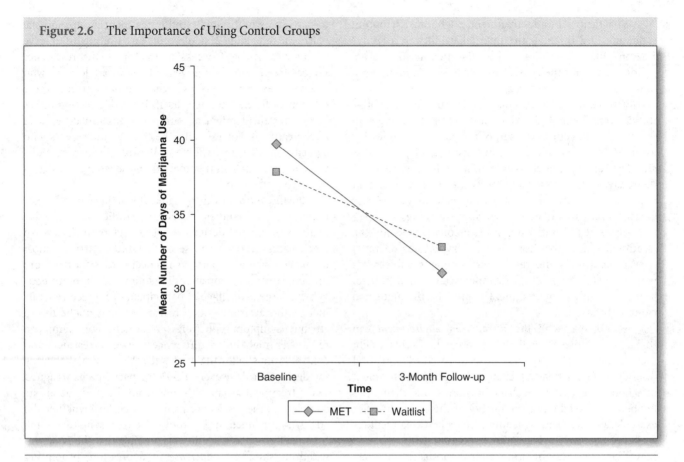

Source: Based on Walker et al. (2006).

Note: Researchers randomly assigned adolescents who frequently used marijuana to one of two conditions: (a) motivational enhancement therapy (MET) or (b) a waiting list. Youths who participated in MET showed a reduction in marijuana use. However, youths assigned to the waiting list also showed a reduction in marijuana use, even though they did not receive treatment.

after treatment. Differences in behavior during or after treatment provide evidence for treatment efficacy. Single-subject studies are sometimes called time-series studies because the same individual's behavior is studied across time (Gaynor, Baird, & Nelson-Gray, 1999).

The simplest way to evaluate treatment effectiveness is to collect data regarding the frequency and/or severity of the child's problematic behavior before and after the intervention. This method is called an **AB design**. The "A" refers to the level of problematic behavior at baseline while the "B" refers to the level of problematic behavior after the intervention. For example, children with autism sometimes engage in high-rate, stereotyped behaviors, such as hand flapping or rocking back and forth, which can be distracting to teachers and classmates. To collect baseline data, a therapist might observe the number of times a child with autism flaps his hands during one hour of class on 3 consecutive days. Then, he instructs the child's classroom aide to reinforce the child with eye contact and a light touch each minute he keeps his hands in his pockets or on his lap. Finally, he observes the child's behavior in the classroom

for another 3 consecutive days after treatment. A decrease in frequency of the child's hand flapping suggests improvement in functioning (see Figure 2.7).

The chief limitation of the AB design is that it suffers from the same threats to internal validity as quasi-experimental research. Without a control group for comparison, clinicians cannot be sure that changes in the child's behavior can be attributed to treatment.

To provide better evidence for a causal relationship between treatment and symptom reduction, many researchers use **ABAB designs**, also called "reversal designs." First, the therapist collects data at baseline and after the intervention, just as in an AB design. Then, she temporarily withdraws treatment and notices any change in the child's behavior (the second A). If the intervention is responsible for improvement in the child's behavior, then withdrawal of the intervention should result in the temporary return of the child's behavior problems. Finally, the therapist would reinstate the intervention (the second B). If the intervention works, the child's behavior problems should subsequently decrease (see Figure 2.8).

Figure 2.7 AB Single-Subject Research Study

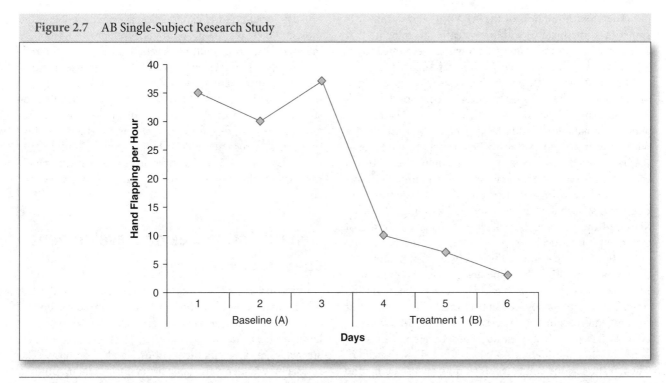

Note: In this study, a child with autism is observed for 3 days to gather baseline data on the frequency of hand flapping (A). Then, the therapist reinforces the child for keeping his hands at his side (B). The reduction in hand flapping suggests that positive reinforcement is effective to treat this problem.

Figure 2.8 ABAB "Reversal" Single-Subject Study

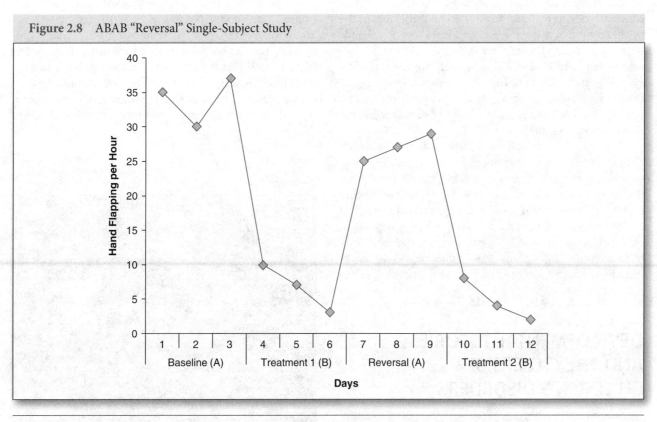

Note: In this study, the therapist collects baseline data on the child's hand flapping (A) and then provides reinforcement contingent on keeping hands at side (B). In the reversal phase (second A), reinforcement is removed, resulting in an increase in hand flapping. Finally, reinforcement is reapplied (second B) to again reduce the behavior.

The chief limitation of the ABAB design is that it is sometimes unethical to withdraw treatment. Imagine that a therapist is treating a young child with severe Intellectual Disability for head banging; the boy repeatedly bangs his head against the wall when he becomes frustrated, angry, or bored. First, the therapist monitors the rate of the child's head banging at baseline (A). Then, the therapist contingently interrupts the child's head banging by misting him with water from a spray bottle when he begins to engage in the behavior (B). To establish a causal connection between the water mist and the decrease in head banging, the clinician would need to withdraw use of the water mist and observe a subsequent increase in head banging. However, because head banging carries serious risks, withdrawal of treatment is unethical.

A third way to examine the effectiveness of treatment is to conduct a **multiple-baseline design**. Here, the therapist identifies two behavior problems and targets them one at a time. For example, a boy with autism might show both hand flapping and rocking in the classroom. First, the therapist collects baseline data regarding the frequency of both behaviors for one hour on 3 consecutive days (baseline). Then, he targets the child's hand flapping by instructing the classroom aide to reinforce the child for keeping his hands in his pockets. He observes the child for another 3 days. If the intervention is effective, he should notice a reduction in the child's hand flapping but not a reduction in the child's rocking. Next, the therapist targets the child's rocking. As the teacher continues to reinforce the child for keeping his hands in his pockets, the therapist instructs the child's classroom aide to reinforce him with a light touch on the shoulders every minute he does not rock. The therapist subsequently observes behavior for an additional 3 days. If the second intervention is effective, the child should show a reduction in both behavior problems.

The chief limitation of all single-subject research designs is that causal inferences are based on data from only one client. Consequently, it is often unclear whether the results of a single-subject study are applicable to other individuals with similar problems. The **external validity** of a study refers to the degree to which results generalize to other people and situations. To establish the external validity of findings generated from single-subject research, results must be replicated, or repeated, with other individuals and in other settings.

DEVELOPMENTAL THEORIES AND THE CAUSES OF CHILDREN'S DISORDERS

Developmental psychopathologists study the potential causes of childhood disorders from multiple levels of analysis. These levels include children's genes, brain structure and functioning, psychological processes, family environment, and broader social-cultural experiences. Researchers obtain the most complete picture of children's development when they integrate data from multiple levels. However, the research methods used at each of these levels are diverse, making communication across levels difficult. Understanding the research methods across levels is especially challenging for students who are new to the field. In this section, we will examine some of the basic principles and methods used by researchers across these levels of analysis. An understanding of these methods is necessary to appreciate research on the various childhood disorders presented in subsequent chapters.

Genetic Influences on Development

Gene Structure and Functioning

Chromosomes are threadlike structures that are found in the nucleus of the cells in our bodies. Each chromosome consists of proteins and *deoxyribonucleic acid (DNA)*. DNA is shaped like a twisted ladder, or double helix. The ropes of the ladder are made up of sugars (deoxyribose) and phosphates. The rungs of the ladder consist of pairs of purine and pyrimidine bases held together by hydrogen bonds (see Image 2.1). Their structures allow them to combine only in certain ways (McClead, Menke, & Coury, 1996).

A **nucleotide** consists of one base pair "rung," a deoxyribose "rope," and a phosphate "rope." Three nucleotides arranged together in the ladder form a trinucleotide, sometimes called a codon. Each trinucleotide instructs the cell to build a specific amino acid. These amino acids are used to build proteins, which form the structure and characteristics of the person. Thousands of trinucleotides form a **gene**. A single human cell contains approximately 30,000 genes (Thapar & Rutter, 2010).

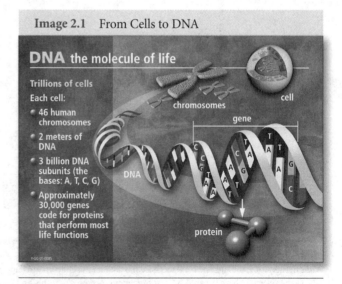

Image 2.1 From Cells to DNA

Source: Courtesy of the U.S. Department of Energy Human Genome Program.

Most of the cells in your body contain 23 pairs of chromosomes. When a cell reproduces, each chromosome splits in two and duplicates itself, resulting in 46 pairs. The cell then divides, forming two daughter cells with 23 pairs each. This process is called *mitosis*. In another process, called *meiosis*, the cell divides before duplicating itself. As a result, the cells that are formed have half the number of chromosomes: 23 total instead of 23 pairs. These cells are sex cells, either sperm or ova. When they unite in fertilization, the resulting zygote has the usual 23 chromosome pairs.

Scientists use the term **genotype** to refer to the collection of genes that we inherit from our parents. Many people erroneously believe that genes determine behavior. For example, newscasters may incorrectly report that researchers have discovered a gene responsible for homosexuality or a gene that makes people behave aggressively. Nothing could be further from the truth. Genes merely form a blueprint for the body's creation of proteins. Some of these proteins partially determine our eye color or skin pigmentation. Others determine whether we have straight or curly hair. No gene directs behavior. However, genes can lead to certain structural and functional changes in our bodies that predispose us to behave in certain ways (Thapar & Rutter, 2010).

Behavioral Genetics

Behavioral geneticists study the relationship between genes and behavior. Behavioral geneticists use three approaches to identifying the relative contributions of genetic and environmental influences on child development. The first, and simplest, approach is by conducting a *family study*. In a family study, researchers determine whether a certain behavior or mental disorder is shared by members of the same family. If the disorder is partially genetically determined, relatives who are closely biologically related will be most likely to be affected.

For example, researchers have examined the heritability of children's intelligence using family studies. If we look at the light gray bars on Figure 2.9, we see that the correlation of children's IQ scores is higher among biological relatives than among nonbiological relatives. The mean correlation between two biological siblings' IQ scores is approximately .45, whereas the mean correlation between two unrelated children's IQ scores is only about .27. These findings suggest that genetic factors play a role in children's intelligence.

The primary limitation of family studies is that they do not adequately control for environmental effects. Although it is true that biological relatives share similar genes, they also

Figure 2.9 The Effects of Genotype and Environment on Children's Intelligence

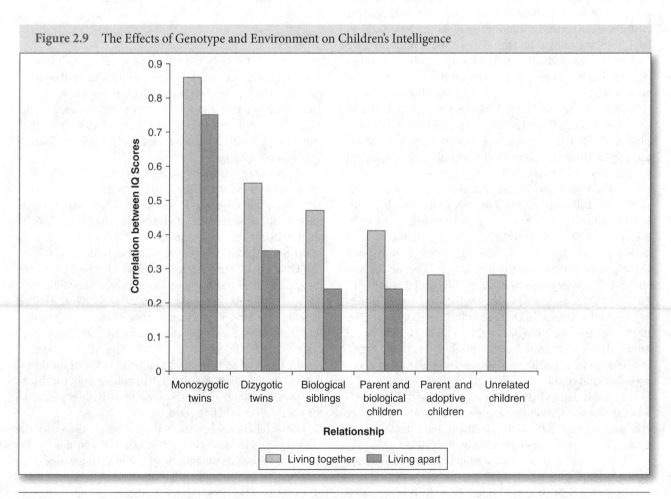

Source: Based on Sattler (2001).

usually live in similar environments. Most family members share the same house, live in the same neighborhoods, enjoy similar pastimes, and come from similar socioeconomic and cultural backgrounds. Therefore, when family studies indicate that closely related relatives are more likely to have a disorder than more distant relatives, we cannot determine whether this similarity is due to common genes or similar environments.

To tease apart the relative effects of genes and environment on behavior, behavioral geneticists conduct *adoption studies*. In an adoption study, researchers examine children who were separated from their biological families shortly after birth. If a behavioral attribute is greatly influenced by genetics, we would expect children to show greater similarity to their biological relatives than to their adoptive relatives.

For example, the mean correlation between parents and their biological children's IQ scores is approximately .40. In contrast, the mean correlation between parents and their adoptive children's IQ scores is only .25. Because children show greater similarity to their biological parents than their adoptive parents, we can conclude that genetic factors play unique roles in the development of children's intelligence.

The primary weakness of adoption studies is that parents who adopt children are often not typical of parents in the general population. Adoption agencies carefully screen prospective adoptive parents before placing a child in their custody. Consequently, adoptive parents are less likely to have mental health problems and are more likely to have higher income and educational backgrounds than other parents. Furthermore, parents who offer their children for adoption often have higher rates of mental illness and lower status social and economic backgrounds than parents in the general population. These systemic differences between biological and adoptive families may partially account for the greater similarity between children and their biological parents compared to their adoptive parents.

A third way that behavioral geneticists identify the relative contributions of genes and environment to behavior is by conducting a *twin study*. In a twin study, researchers compare the behavioral similarity (i.e., concordance) between monozygotic and dizygotic twins. Monozygotic (MZ; identical) twins are the product of the same egg and sperm cell; consequently, they have 100% genetic similarity. Dizygotic (DZ; fraternal) twins are the products of different egg and sperm cells; consequently, they share only 50% of their genes, like biologically related siblings. **Behavioral concordance** is expressed as the correlation between twins, ranging from 1.0 (i.e., perfect behavioral similarity) to 0 (i.e., no behavioral similarity).

The correlation between IQ scores for MZ twins is .85, whereas the correlation for DZ twins is only .55. The higher concordance for MZ twins than DZ twins indicates that intelligence is at least partially genetically determined.

In some cases, twin and adoption studies are combined by examining twins who both live with their biological parents (e.g., the light bars in Figure 2.9) and twins separated at birth (e.g., the dark bars in Figure 2.9). For example, the

mean correlation in IQ for MZ twins reared together is .85, whereas the mean correlation for MZ twins reared apart is .75. The high correlations for twins reared apart and reared together indicate that genetic factors play important roles in the development of intelligence. Even twins separated shortly after birth have remarkably similar IQs.

Behavioral geneticists often divide environmental influences on behavior into two types: shared environmental factors and nonshared environmental factors. **Shared environmental factors** are experiences common to siblings. For example, siblings usually are reared by the same parents, grow up in the same house, attend the same schools, and belong to the same church. Shared environmental experiences make siblings more alike. In contrast, **nonshared environmental factors** are experiences that differ between siblings. For example, siblings may have different friends, play different sports, or enjoy different subjects in school. Siblings may also have different types of relationships with their parents. For example, a girl and boy might have different relationships with their father. These nonshared environmental factors often account for more of the variance in children's behavior than do shared experiences. Nonshared environmental factors help to explain why siblings can be so different even though they grow up in the same home (Caspi & Shiner, 2010).

Molecular Genetics

Another way to study the effects of genes on behavior is to examine children's genes at the molecular (rather than the behavioral) level. Recent advances in our knowledge of the human genome and in gene research technology have allowed scientists to begin to search for specific genes that might be partially responsible for certain disorders (Rende & Waldman, 2006).

In typically developing individuals, genes show a natural amount of variation. For example, some genes code for blue eyes while others code for brown. These variations in the genetic code are called **alleles**. Molecular geneticists can attempt to link the presence of specific alleles (i.e., variations in the genetic code) with certain diseases or disorders.

One way to identify which alleles might be responsible for specific disorders is to conduct a molecular genetic *linkage study*. In a linkage study, researchers search the entire genetic structure of individuals (i.e., perform a "genome scan"), looking for associations between the presence of certain alleles and the existence of a specific disorder. If researchers find certain alleles in individuals with the disorder and do not find these alleles in people without the disorder, they hypothesize that the allele is partially responsible for the disorder (Dick & Todd, 2006).

Researchers tend to use linkage studies when they do not know exactly where to look for genes responsible for the disorder. Given the magnitude of the human genome, it is extremely difficult to identify links between certain alleles and specific disorders. However, researchers have successfully used linkage studies to identify alleles responsible for disorders cause by single genes, such as Huntington's Disease. Linkage approaches have been less successful in identifying the causes of disorders that depend on the presence or absence of multiple alleles.

An alternative technique is to conduct an association study. In an *association study*, researchers select a specific gene that they believe might play a role in the emergence of a disorder. Then, they examine whether there is an association between a particular allele of this "candidate" gene and the disorder (Dick & Todd, 2006).

For example, researchers hypothesized that a specific gene, which affects the neurotransmitter dopamine, might play a role in the development of ADHD. They suspected this particular gene because abnormalities in dopamine have been identified as a specific cause for ADHD. Furthermore, medications that affect dopamine in the brain can reduce ADHD symptoms. The researchers identified a group of children with and without ADHD. Then, they examined whether the two groups of children had different alleles for the candidate gene. The researchers found that a certain allele for this gene was much more common among youths with ADHD compared to youths without the disorder. Consequently, they concluded that the gene may be partially responsible for ADHD (Rende & Waldman, 2006).

Of course, molecular genetics research is much more complicated than has been described here. Nearly all mental disorders are influenced by multiple genes; there is almost never a one-to-one relationship between the presence of a specific allele and the emergence of a given disorder. Furthermore, genes never affect behavior directly; their influence on behavior is always influenced by environmental experience (Rende & Waldman, 2006).

Gene-Environment Interactions

Genes guide our maturation, but they do not determine our development. Our **phenotype**, the observable expression of our genetic endowment, is determined by the interaction between our genes and the environment (Caspi & Shiner, 2010).

We should not think of genes and environment as independently influencing children's development. Rather, there is a correlation between children's genotype and the quality of their environmental experiences. Scarr and McCartney (1983) have identified three ways genotypes and environments are related and how this relationship influences development.

1. *Passive Gene-Environment Correlation.* Although our biological parents determine our genotype, they also determine the quality of our early environmental experiences. Our genes and early experiences are related. For example, parents with high intelligence may pass on this genetic predisposition to their children. At the same time, because of their high intelligence and (perhaps) income, these parents have access to higher quality medical care, more nutritious meals, excellent child care, and better schools. Intelligent parents speak and read to their children frequently, provide stimulating educational toys, and take their children on outings to museums and zoos. In this manner, their children passively receive genotypes and early environmental experiences conducive to high intelligence.

2. *Evocative Gene-Environment Correlation.* As children develop, their phenotype gradually emerges from the interaction between their genotype and early environment. Like their parents, they may begin to show signs of above-average intelligence. They show well-developed verbal skills, learn more quickly than their peers, perform more tasks independently, and are curious about a wide range of topics. These behaviors evoke certain responses in others. School personnel may identify them as "gifted" and provide them with more enriched educational experiences. They may be admitted into accelerated classes in high school and gain academic scholarships to highly selective colleges.

3. *Active Gene-Environment Correlation.* As children continue to develop, they actively select environmental experiences conducive to their genotype. For example, they might develop friendships with other bright children with similar interests and hobbies; seek out clubs that satisfy their curiosity in science, music, or art; and select challenging but rewarding majors in college. Children's tendency to select environmental experiences conducive to their genotypes is sometimes called "niche-picking." As children gain more autonomy, niche-picking plays an increasingly important role in shaping development. In a sense, youths select their own environments based on the cumulative influence of their genes and early environmental experiences.

Biological Influences on Development

Neuroimaging

We have witnessed considerable advances in our understanding of brain development in the past 30 years. Beginning in the 1970s, clinicians and researchers used *computed tomography (CT)* to obtain more detailed images of the brain. In CT scanning, multiple images are taken using a movable X-ray device. These images are then integrated by computer to provide a clearer picture of the brain. Unfortunately, CT scanning, like older X-ray imaging, exposed individuals to radiation. Consequently, it was used sparingly with children.

In the 1980s, a new tool was developed: *magnetic resonance imaging (MRI)*. MRI technology is based on the fact that when body tissues are placed in a strong magnetic field and exposed to a brief pulse of radiofrequency energy, cells from the tissue give off a brief signal, called a "magnetic resonance." Different types of tissue give off slightly different signals. In the brain, neurons (i.e., grey matter), myelin (i.e., white matter), and cerebral spinal fluid give different signals. These signals, associated with a particular type of brain tissue (called a "voxel"), can be detected by a computer and used to generate a digital image (called a "pixel"). MRI machines generate two-dimensional images of brain tissue that can be integrated by the computer (i.e., "stacked" on top of one another) to create a three-dimensional image of the brain (Giedd, Shaw, Wallace, Gogtay, & Lenroot, 2006).

MRI has a number of advantages over CT and most other imaging techniques. First, MRI does not subject individuals to radiation; it is believed to be safe and has even been used to obtain images of the brains of developing fetuses. Second, because it is safe, MRI can be used with healthy children and administered repeatedly over time (see Image 2.2). Consequently, MRI technology allows us to study the same children's brains across development. Third, MRI yields clearer and more precise pictures of the brain than older neuroimaging methods (Giedd et al., 2006).

Besides helping us understand normal brain development, MRI can also allow us to detect structural abnormalities in the brains of youths with mental disorders. In a typical MRI study, researchers scan the brains of youths with and without a specific disorder. For example, Castellanos and colleagues (2002) scanned the brains of children with and without ADHD. The researchers compared the volumes of the frontal cortex of children in the two groups. They found that children with ADHD showed an average 4% reduction in volume of the frontal cortex compared to children without ADHD. These results are important because underactivity in portions of the frontal cortex is believed to account for some ADHD symptoms.

Functional magnetic resonance imaging (fMRI) is a relatively new technique used to measure brain activity (Pine, 2006). The techniques used in fMRI greatly resemble MRI. However, the fMRI device measures changes in oxygenated hemoglobin concentrations in the brain. When the individual engages in mental activity, oxygenated hemoglobin concentrations increase in brain regions that become active. Consequently, fMRI yields a picture of the individual's brain showing regions most active during certain mental activities (Sadock & Sadock, 2003).

To perform fMRI, researchers typically obtain an image of the individual's brain, using traditional MRI. Then, researchers ask the individual to perform a series of mental activities while they collect fMRI data. For example, researchers might ask adolescents with autism to describe the emotional expression on pictures of people's faces, or, ask children with learning disabilities to read or solve math problems. These fMRI images are then superimposed over the traditional MRI to show brain regions that are most active during the mental tasks (Image 2.3).

Tamm, Menon, and Reiss (2006) used fMRI to determine which brain regions might be responsible for the deficits in attention shown by youths with ADHD. They asked 14 adolescents with ADHD and 12 adolescents without ADHD

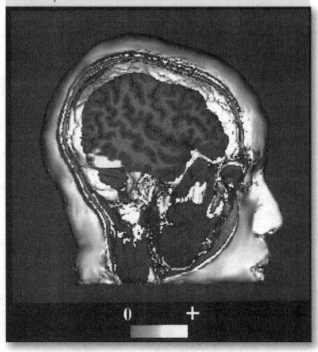

Image 2.3   Functional magnetic resonance imaging (fMRI) can be used to measure brain activity while participants perform cognitive tasks. In this task, an adolescent is asked to look at faces. The right fusiform gyrus (sometimes called the fusiform "face" area) becomes highly active. Adolescents with Autism Spectrum Disorder often do not show activity in this brain area.

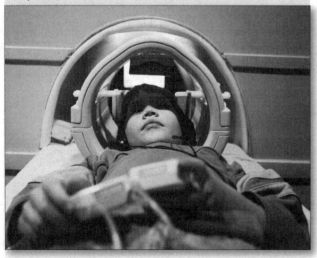

Image 2.2   Nine-year-old Patrick is shown participating in an MRI study of children with dyslexia.

Source: AP Photo/Manuel Balce Ceneta. Used with permission.

Source: Courtesy National Institutes of Health.

to perform a test of attention while they collected fMRI data. In this task, youths were presented with a series of either green circles or green triangles. They were asked to press one button when they saw a circle and a different button when they saw a triangle. As expected, youths with ADHD made significantly more errors in the task than youths without ADHD. Furthermore, youths with ADHD showed significantly less activity in certain brain areas (i.e., their parietal lobes) compared to their healthy peers. The researchers concluded that these brain regions may play a role in people's ability to direct and regulate attention.

Neuroimaging studies involving children and adolescents often yield inconsistent results. The primary reason for the inconsistent results of many neuroimaging studies is that children show enormous variability in their brain volumes and rates of brain development. For example, total brain volumes can differ by as much as 20% based on factors such as children's age, gender, and environment. Researchers wishing to identify structural abnormalities in the brains of children with specific disorders need to carefully control for these factors. A second reason for inconsistent findings is that many studies have been unable to detect structural abnormalities in children because of low image resolution. Even today, with better technology, many children find it uncomfortable to remain in MRI devices for long enough periods of time to obtain the clearest images possible (Giedd et al., 2006).

Perhaps the most important reason for the inconsistent findings is that mental and behavioral disorders in children and adolescents rarely have single causes that can be traced to specific brain regions. For example, ADHD appears to be caused by a complex relationship between biological, psychological, and environmental factors. It would be a mistake to think that a specific brain abnormality would account for all (or even most) cases of ADHD or any other disorder. Instead, it is likely that early differences in brain structure interact with environmental experiences to produce symptoms (Johnson & de Haan, 2006).

Brain Development

The development of the central nervous system begins shortly after conception and continues well into adulthood. During the first month after conception, the *neural tube* is formed. This tissue will later become the basis for the brain and spinal cord. During the second and third months of gestation, the brain gradually begins to take shape at the top of the neural tube, with the foremost part of the brain becoming most prominent. Shortly after the first trimester, there is a rapid proliferation of neurons and an increase in neural density. From month 3 to month 5 of gestation, these neurons gradually make their way from the center of the brain to the outmost areas, a process called migration. These neurons, which migrate to the outermost shell of the brain, will later form the cortex. At the beginning of the second trimester, the brain experiences a period of rapid cell death, called *apoptosis*. Approximately 50% of neurons will die during this process,

presumably to make way for more important neural connections and increased brain organization (Giedd et al., 2006).

During the remainder of gestation, there is a dramatic increase in myelin, the white fatty coating that surrounds neurons and helps with their conductivity. Increased **myelination** is believed to speed up neural activity and make brain processes occur more quickly and efficiently. This increase in myelination continues at a rapid rate until age 2 years. Myelination then slows, but continues through adolescence.

Also during the third trimester of gestation, there is a dramatic increase in the number of connections between neurons. This rapid increase in synaptic connections continues until approximately age two years. Indeed, the average 2-year-old child has approximately 50% more synaptic connections than the average adult. After age 2 years, however, there is a gradual reduction in the number of synaptic connections. Developmental biologists believe that many of the connections that are not needed simply die off, in a process called **synaptic pruning**. Although pruning might seem like a waste of neural connections, it is actually a normal and healthy process. Pruning makes the brain process information more efficiently, by strengthening neural connections that are frequently used and discarding neural connections that are not necessary.

Approximately fifteen years ago, most neuroscientists believed that the brain reached its mature size and structure around age 10 years. However, recent research suggests that the brain continues to change dramatically, at least through late adolescence or early adulthood. Certain brain structures seem to gradually increase in size during childhood and then decrease beginning in adolescence (see Image 2.4).

One brain region, the cortex, follows this pattern of growth and pruning. The **cortex** is divided into four regions or lobes. The occipital lobe, located near the back of the brain, is primarily responsible for visual processing. This brain region appears to undergo the most change during early childhood. In contrast, the volume of the parietal lobe (located on the sides and top of the brain) peaks around age 10 or 11 years and then gradually decreases in size. The parietal lobe is primarily responsible for integrating visual, auditory, and tactile information. Pruning in this region may account for improved sensory and motor functioning that occurs during adolescence. The volume of the frontal lobe peaks shortly thereafter, around age 11 or 12 years. The frontal cortex plays an important role in organizing, planning, and prioritizing behavior. The pruning of the frontal cortex, which begins in early adolescence and continues until early adulthood, is believed to underlie adolescents' increased capacity for attention, inhibition, and overall behavioral control. The temporal lobe (located on the sides and bottom of the brain) shows peak volume around age 16 years. The temporal lobe has multiple functions, including the expression and regulation of emotions. Pruning of the temporal lobe, which usually begins during middle to late adolescence, may underlie adolescents' abilities to understand and regulate emotions (Giedd et al., 2006).

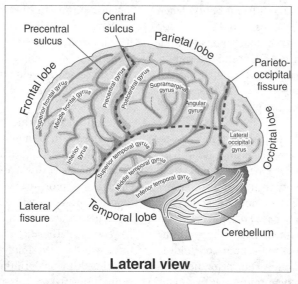

Lateral view

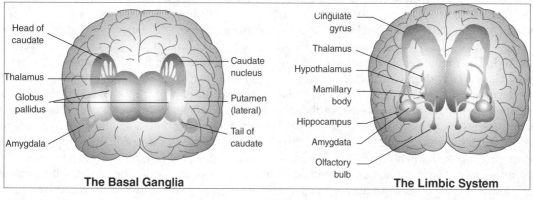

The Basal Ganglia   **The Limbic System**

Source: From Kempler (2005). Used with permission.

Another brain region that seems to change during childhood and adolescence is the basal ganglia. The **basal ganglia** are located under the cortex, between the brain stem and the higher level cortical regions. They consist of a number of structures, including the caudate, putamen, globus pallidus, and substantia nigra. The basal ganglia perform many important functions. One of their primary roles is to help control movement. Another function is to filter incoming information from the senses and relay this information to other brain regions where it can be processed. The basal ganglia have also been implicated in the regulation of attention and emotions. Researchers believe that structural changes in the basal ganglia, especially the pruning that occurs during childhood and adolescence, might account for children's increased motor functioning, attention, and emotional processing across development (Giedd et al., 2006).

A third brain region that appears to change across childhood and adolescence is the **limbic system**. The limbic system is located deep inside the brain, behind the temporal lobes. The primary components of the limbic system are the amygdala and hippocampus. The amygdala aids in our understanding and expression of emotions, especially negative feelings, such as fear and rage. The hippocampus also plays a role in emotional processing, especially the formation of emotion-laden memories. Although neuroimaging studies are just beginning to give us a better understanding of these elusive brain regions, some data indicate that the limbic system may continue to change well into adolescence (Giedd et al., 2006).

A fourth brain structure, the **corpus callosum**, seems to increase in volume from early childhood through adolescence. The corpus callosum is a heavily myelinated structure that connects the left and right hemispheres of the brain. Its primary job is to relay and integrate information across hemispheres. Damage to the corpus callosum is associated with impairments in a wide range of functions, including attention and arousal, memory storage and retrieval, hearing, and language.

A final area of the brain, the **cerebellum**, increases in volume during childhood and undergoes considerable pruning during early adolescence. The cerebellum, or "little brain," is located in the back of the brain, near the brain stem. Neuroscientists originally believed that the cerebellum was chiefly responsible for balance, posture, and coordination. Researchers now believe the cerebellum plays a role in mental gracefulness and efficiency in addition to adroitness in physical movement. Maturation of the cerebellum during adolescence might explain the increased physical gracefulness exhibited by older adolescents as well as a general increase in mental efficiency across development.

Neural Plasticity: How Experience Can Drive Brain Development

So far, we have examined some of the techniques used by neuroscientists to study brain structure and functioning. The notion of gene-environment correlation implies that genes influence brain structure, which, in turn, affects behavior. However, the relationship between brain structure and behavior is bidirectional. Some of the most exciting research in the past 20 years has shown that the brain can change in response to experience.

The structure and functioning of the brain is determined by the interaction of genes and environmental experiences. Specifically, genes and environment interact in three ways to shape the developing brain (Black, Jones, Nelson, & Greenough, 1998). First, certain aspects of brain development are **gene-driven**. These aspects are largely impervious to the effects of experience and almost entirely determined by the person's genetic code. For example, the development of the neural tube and migration of neurons from the center of the brain to the cortex is believed to be genetically preprogrammed and largely insensitive to experience. Developmental psychologists sometimes refer to this importance of genes over experience in embryonic development as *canalization.*

Second, some aspects of brain development are **experience-expectant**; that is, the formation of the brain region is partially dependent on information received from the environment. Infants have an overabundance of neural connections, many of which they do not need. Connections that are used are maintained and strengthened while connections that are not used atrophy and die. Whether a connection is maintained or pruned depends on experience. For example, an infant exposed to the Japanese language during the first few years of life may strengthen neural connections responsible for processing the sounds used in Japanese. However, infants not exposed to Japanese during this early period of development may lose neural connections that might play a role in processing the Japanese language. Consequently, children who are not exposed to Japanese in infancy and early childhood may find it relatively difficult to speak the language without an accent later in life. Developmental psychologists often refer to periods of development in which experience can greatly shape neural structure and functioning as developmentally sensitive periods.

Third, brain development can be **experience-dependent**; that is, environmental experiences in later life can actually lead to the formation of new neural connections or to changes in the brain's organization or structure. The ability of the brain to change after the first few years of life was unimaginable one generation ago. However, recent research points to the ways the brain can change in response to environmental conditions throughout the life span.

Neuroscientists use the term **plasticity** to refer to the brain's malleability, that is, its capacity to change its structure and/or functioning in response to environmental experiences. These environmental experiences can be either internal or external. Internal experiences alter the immediate environment of the brain and nervous system. For example, exposure to too much testosterone or stress hormone can lead to structural changes in various brain regions. In contrast, external experiences come from outside the organism. For example, an infant who ingests environmental toxins can experience brain damage.

Neuroscientists have discovered that the brain is remarkably adaptive to environmental stressors, especially when these stressors occur early in life. Perhaps the most striking example of brain plasticity is seen following a surgical procedure called a functional hemispherectomy. **Functional hemisperectomy** is performed on some children who have medically intractable epilepsy that arises in one hemisphere of the brain. These seizures cause severe impairment, occur very frequently, and are not responsive to medication. To perform a functional hemispherectomy, the surgeon removes the entire parietal lobe of the nonfunctional hemisphere (which is often the origin of the seizures) and severs the corpus callosum (which allows the seizure to travel from one hemisphere to the other; Pulsifer, Brandt, Salorio, Vining, Carson, & Freeman, 2004).

Despite removal or disconnection of several brain regions, children usually show remarkable recovery from the procedure. Children often experience motor deficits on the side of the body opposite the hemisphere that was removed. Furthermore, if the left hemisphere is removed, most children experience temporary disturbance in language. However, children usually recover much of this lost functioning within 6 to 12 months after surgery, as the remaining hemisphere gradually assumes many of these lost functions. Most children are able to return to school 6 to 8 weeks post-surgery (Jonas et al., 2004; van Empelen, Jennekens-Schinkel, Buskens, Helders, & Van Nieuwenhuizen, 2004).

Environmental experiences need not be as dramatic as a hemispherectomy to produce changes in the organization of the brain. Rats reared in isolation show dramatic increases in stress hormone. These chronic elevations in stress hormone seem to alter the rats' stress response. As a result, isolated rats often show long-term propensities toward aggression as adults. Similarly, some children who are repeatedly exposed to physical or sexual abuse show dysregulation of certain brain regions responsible for the body's stress response. This dysregulation, in turn, can cause problems with anxiety and mood later in life.

Environmental experiences also need not be negative to affect brain functioning. Positive environmental experiences can actually increase metabolic activity and lead to the formation of new neural connections. Long ago, the neuropsychologist D. O. Hebb (1949) proposed that the simultaneous activation of neurons can cause the neurons to form new synaptic connections. Hebb suggested that neurons that "fire together, wire together." Recently neuroscientists have been able to show **synaptogenesis**, that is, the formation of new neural connections due to experience. For example, rats reared in enriched living environments (e.g., given extra space and access to toys and mazes) show differences in brain structure and functioning compared to rats reared in typical cages. Humans who receive extensive training in Braille show increases in the size of brain regions responsible for processing the sense of touch. Even skilled musicians show a reorganization of brain regions responsible for controlling the finger positions of their instruments (Cicchetti & Curtis, 2006)!

Gottesman (1963) developed the concept of the **reaction range** to demonstrate the way genes and environment interact to influence development. From Gottesman's perspective, our genotype sets an upper and lower limit, or range, on our intellectual and behavioral potentials. Then, the quality of our environment determines where, within this range, our actual abilities fall. If we are provided with enriched environmental experiences, we may develop toward the higher end of the range. If we encounter impoverished or harmful experiences, our development might be toward the lower end of our potential.

The notion of a reaction range helps to explain why children reared in the same environments can show different developmental trajectories. To take an extreme example, consider two children, one born with Down Syndrome, and the other, a typically developing child. Both children may be raised in the same family and given the same early environmental experiences, but the genotype of the first child places an upper limit on his intellectual development. It is unlikely that he will develop intelligence within the normal range, regardless of the quality of environmental experiences. The second boy, raised in the same environment, would show a different developmental trajectory and much higher intellectual functioning.

Behavioral Influences on Development

Researchers who study the psychological causes of child psychopathology are interested in explaining maladaptation at the behavioral level. The term *behavior* encompasses three important facets of children's functioning: their thoughts, feelings, and actions. Psychologists recognize that thoughts, feelings, and actions are closely connected; each partially influences, and is influenced by, the others.

Psychologists often use learning theory to explain and predict children's behavior. From the perspective of learning theory, children's actions are chiefly determined by environmental factors. Learning occurs in three principal ways: (a) through classical conditioning, (b) through operant conditioning, and (c) through social imitation or modeling.

Classical Conditioning

In classical conditioning, learning occurs when the child associates two stimuli paired together in time. One stimulus is initially called the neutral stimulus (NS) because it does not elicit a response. The other stimulus is initially called an unconditioned stimulus (UCS) because it naturally elicits an unconditioned response (UCR). The organism may come to associate the NS with the UCS if the two stimuli are presented together. For example, Pavlov demonstrated that dogs would associate the sound of a metronome (NS) with the presentation of meat powder (UCS) if the two stimuli were presented contiguously. After repeated presentations, the metronome alone elicited salivation. After conditioning, the previously neutral stimulus (e.g., metronome) is referred to as the conditioned stimulus (CS), whereas the resulting response (e.g., salivation) is referred to as the conditioned response (CR).

Classical conditioning is often used to explain and to treat childhood disorders. For example, a girl who is bitten by a dog might associate the sight of a dog (NS) with the experience of being bitten (UCS). The dog bite, in turn, naturally causes a fear response (UCR). Later, the presence of any dog (CS) may elicit a similar fear response (CR).

One way of decreasing behaviors acquired through classical conditioning is to use **extinction**. Extinction involves repeatedly presenting the CS until it no longer elicits the CR. Extinction is usually accomplished gradually, in a process called graded exposure. For example, a therapist might recommend that a girl with a fear of dogs gradually expose herself to dogs, in order to extinguish this fear. Initially, the girl might simply look at pictures of dogs, then remain in a room with a dog on a leash, and finally pet a dog. After the girl is repeatedly exposed to the dog, the dog's presence no longer elicits a fear response.

Operant Conditioning

Whereas classical conditioning occurs when individuals associate two stimuli, operant conditioning occurs when individuals associate a behavior with a consequence in the environment. Operant conditioning is based on the notion that the consequences of our actions determine the likelihood that the actions will be repeated. If the consequences of our actions increase the likelihood that we will repeat the behavior in the future, these consequences have **reinforced** our behavior. If the consequences of our actions decrease the likelihood that we will repeat our behavior in the future, these consequences have **punished** our behavior. Reinforcement increases the likelihood of future behavior, whereas punishment decreases the likelihood of future behavior (see Figure 2.10).

Figure 2.10 Operant Conditioning

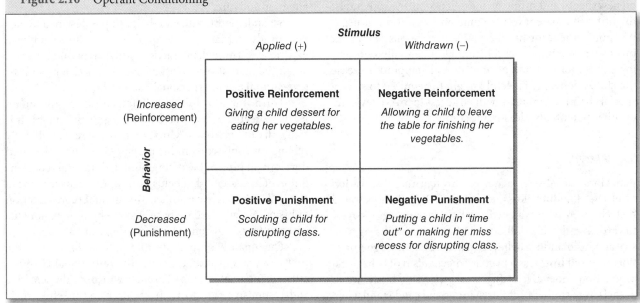

Note: Reinforcement leads to an increase in behavior; punishment leads to a decrease in behavior.

Reinforcement can be positive or negative. **Positive reinforcement** occurs when an individual is presented with a stimulus that increases the likelihood of behavior. For example, a father might give his daughter ice cream after she eats her vegetables at dinner. If the presentation of ice cream following the meal increases the likelihood that the girl eats her vegetables in the future, we say that the ice cream positively reinforced the child's eating.

Many people mistakenly believe that the adjective "positive" in the term *positive reinforcement* refers to the pleasantness of the reinforcer. In fact, the term *positive* simply refers to the fact that the stimulus is *presented* to the individual. Some presumably pleasant stimuli are not positively reinforcing to all children. For example, providing a 2-year-old with one M&M for using the toilet may increase the likelihood that he will use the toilet in the future. However, providing one M&M to a 10-year-old for completing his math homework will likely not increase the likelihood that he will complete his math homework. Additionally, some presumably unpleasant stimuli can be positively reinforcing. For example, a teacher may reprimand her student for disrupting class. If the teacher's reprimand results in an increase in the student's disruptive behavior, the teacher's behavior is positively reinforcing, no matter how aversive it appears.

Negative reinforcement occurs when the withdrawal or avoidance of a stimulus increases the likelihood of behavior. For example, a father might allow his daughter to leave the dinner table only after she finishes her vegetables. If escaping the dinner table by eating vegetables increases the likelihood that the girl eats her vegetables in the future, we say that the father's action negatively reinforced the child's eating.

Negative reinforcement often underlies childhood behavior problems. For example, a mother might ask her son to turn off the television and clean his room. The son might ignore his mother because he prefers to watch his favorite TV program. The mother might withdraw her request and clean her son's room herself. If the mother's behavior (i.e., withdrawal of her request) increases the likelihood that her son will ignore her requests in the future, we say that her actions are negatively reinforcing his disobedience. She is teaching him to disobey.

In contrast to reinforcement, punishment always *decreases* the probability of future behavior. There are two types of punishment: positive and negative. **Positive punishment** involves a stimulus *presentation* that decreases the likelihood of behavior. For example, a mother might spank her son for his disobedience. If spanking results in a decrease in her child's defiance, then the mother's action was a form of positive punishment. **Negative punishment** involves a stimulus *removal* that decreases the likelihood of behavior. For example, a teacher might remove a child from a desirable classroom activity following his disruptive behavior in class. If the teacher's action results in a decrease in the student's disruptive behavior, then the teacher's behavior was a form of negative punishment.

Clinicians prefer to use reinforcement to correct child behavior problems. However, in some cases, punishment can be used therapeutically. For example, a therapist might teach a parent to use positive punishment to correct her son's bed wetting. Specifically, every time the boy wets the bed, the parent might require the boy to perform a series of actions designed to correct the problem behavior. These actions might include stripping the bed, taking the bedding to the washing machine, helping to start the wash, putting on new sheets, and sitting on the toilet. Similarly, a therapist might teach a parent to use "time out" as a form of negative punishment for her disruptive preschooler. Time out involves removing the child from all potentially reinforcing stimuli for a period of time, in an attempt to decrease the child's defiance. The child might be required to sit in a special chair for 3 minutes with no access to toys, television, or other potentially pleasurable stimuli.

Social Learning

Behaviors can also be acquired through the observation of others. Bandura, Ross, and Ross (1961) demonstrated that children who watched adults behaving aggressively toward an inflatable doll often imitated the adults' aggressive actions. Bandura believed that learning through imitation, or **modeling**, was a primary mechanism of behavioral acquisition. Social learning was especially likely when models were similar to children in age and gender and when models were reinforced for their actions.

Modeling is also used to explain and to treat child behavior problems. For example, parents who model anxiety to their children can increase their children's likelihood of developing an anxiety disorder. A mother who is afraid of social situations might model this fear to her daughter. Specifically, she might avoid attending social gatherings and overtly worry about appearing foolish in public. She might also convey to her daughter that other people are often critical and judgmental, thereby, increasing her daughter's fears of social situations. As a result, the daughter might develop anxiety in social situations and a tendency toward social withdrawal.

A therapist might also use modeling as a means to reduce the daughter's social phobia. Specifically, the therapist might ask the child's teacher to pair the girl with a "classroom buddy"—a female classmate who shows well-developed social skills and is willing to model appropriate social behavior. By watching her "buddy," the girl might discover that social situations are often pleasant and are rarely catastrophic. Consequently, her social anxiety may decrease.

Familial Influences on Development

Parent-Infant Attachment

Attachment refers to the affective bond between parent and child that serves to protect and reassure the child in times of danger or uncertainty. According to John Bowlby (1969, 1973, 1980), the parent-child attachment relationship has three basic functions. Most important, the attachment relationship serves to protect the young child from danger. Infants and young children are biologically predisposed to seek contact and proximity to their parents when scared, upset, or unsure of their surroundings. At the same time,

parents are predisposed to respond to their infant's bids for attention and care.

Second, the attachment relationship is designed to provide dyads with an avenue for sharing positive emotional experiences. Through interactions with parents, infants learn about the natural reciprocity of social interactions and the give-and-take of interpersonal relationships.

Third, the attachment relationship helps the infant learn to regulate negative emotions and behaviors. Initially, the infant controls anxiety and distress by directly relying on comfort from his parent. Over time, the child develops an **internal working model**, or mental representation of his parent, that helps him cope with psychosocial stress. The infant learns to use this mental representation of his parent as a "secure base" from which to explore his surroundings and control his emotions and actions.

The quality of parent-child interactions over the first few years of life influences the initial quality of the attachment relationship. Parents who provide sensitive and responsive care to their children, by meeting their children's needs in a consistent and developmentally appropriate fashion, usually develop **secure attachment relationships** with their children. Their children, in turn, come to expect sensitive and responsive care from their parents. At the same time, these children come to view themselves as worthy of receiving sensitive and responsive care from others.

In contrast, parents who do not provide sensitive and responsive care in a consistent fashion are likely to foster **insecure attachment relationships** with their children. When scared or upset, these children do not expect their parents to effectively meet their needs and help them regulate their emotions. They adopt internal working models of their parents as unavailable or inconsistent. At the same time, they may view themselves as unworthy of receiving attention and care from others.

Ainsworth, Belhar, Waters, and Wall (1978) identified three patterns of attachment that develop over the first few months of life. These patterns can be observed in the behavior of 12-month-old infants using the **strange situation**, a laboratory-based test of infant-mother attachment. The strange situation occurs in a laboratory playroom and involves separating infants from their parents for short periods of time (see Table 2.1). Most infants experience distress when separated. However, researchers are primarily interested in how infants respond to their parents when they are reunited. Specifically, researchers observe whether infants are able to use their parents as a means to reduce distress and return to play.

Most children who participate in the strange situation show secure attachment relationships with their parents. These children use their parents as a secure base from which to regulate their emotions, control their behavior, and return to play. Although they usually show considerable distress during separation, they seek comfort and physical contact with their parents when they are reunited. After a little while,

Table 2.1 The Strange Situation

Episode	Persons Present	Duration	Description of Events
1	Mother, infant	30 secs	Parent and infant are introduced to the experimental room.
2	Mother, infant	3 min	Parent and infant are alone. Parent does not participate while infant explores.
3	Mother, infant stranger	3 min	Stranger enters, converses with parent, then approaches infant. Parent leaves.
4	Stranger, infant	3 min	First separation episode. Stranger tries to play with infant.
5	Mother, infant	3 min	First reunion episode. Parent greets and comforts infant then leaves again.
6	Infant alone	3 min	Second separation episode.
7	Stranger, infant	3 min	Stranger enters, tries to play with infant.
8	Mother, infant	3 min	Second reunion episode. Parent enters, greets infant, and picks up infant; stranger leaves inconspicuously.

Source: Based on Ainsworth et al. (1978).

reassurance from caregivers soothes these infants, and they can return to play and exploration.

In contrast, some infants develop **insecure-avoidant attachment** relationships with their parents. When reunited with their mothers, these infants show passivity and disinterest. In fact, many of these infants actively avoid their parents' bids for attention by turning away or ignoring them. Although these infants might be upset by separation, they appear uninterested or resentful of their parents when they return. Instead of using their parents as a secure base from which to regulate their emotions and return to play, these infants attempt to rely on themselves to cope with the stress of separation. Attachment theorists reason that parents who consistently dismiss their children's bids for attention foster insecure-avoidant attachment relationships with their infants.

Other infants develop **insecure-ambivalent attachment** relationships with their parents. When separated, these infants usually respond with considerable distress. However, when reunited with their parents, these infants alternate between seeking and resisting their caregivers' support. For example, an infant might initially motion to be picked up by her mother and then immediately push away. The behavior of these infants conveys the notion that they desperately want comfort from their parents but that they do not expect their parents to adequately provide for their needs. Attachment theorists reason that parents who alternate between providing care and ignoring their children foster this insecure-ambivalent pattern of attachment.

Longitudinal research indicates that the development of secure attachment relationships in infancy and early childhood is associated with later social-emotional competence. For example, infants who display secure patterns of attachment tend to show more flexible and adaptive behavior during childhood and early adolescence. These children show fewer behavior problems at school, are better liked by peers, evidence greater control over their actions and emotions, and have advanced social skills and capacity for empathy. In contrast, infants classified as insecure may be at risk for social-emotional problems later in development. Specifically, these children sometimes have difficulty with self-reliance and flexible problem solving, problems with peer relationships, and difficulty controlling emotions such as anger and anxiety (Main, Kaplan, & Cassidy, 1985; Sroufe, 1989a; Weinfield, Sroufe, & Egeland, 2000).

Parent-Child Interactions

Although parenting practices differ considerably across families and cultures, psychologists have identified at least two dimensions of parenting that are important to most children's cognitive and social-emotional development (Cowan & Cowan, 2006). The first dimension, **parental responsiveness**, refers to the degree to which parents display warmth and acceptance toward their children, orient their behavior to meet their children's needs in a sensitive and responsive fashion, and engage their children through shared activities and positive emotions. The second dimension, **parental demandingness**, refers to the degree to which parents have age-appropriate expectations for their children's behavior, clearly establish and consistently enforce rules governing their behavior, and supervise their children (Maccoby & Martin, 1983).

Diana Baumrind (1991) has classified parents into four parenting types, based on the degree to which they endorse responsiveness and demandingness in their usual interactions with their children (see Figure 2.11).

Figure 2.11 Baumrind's Parenting Typology

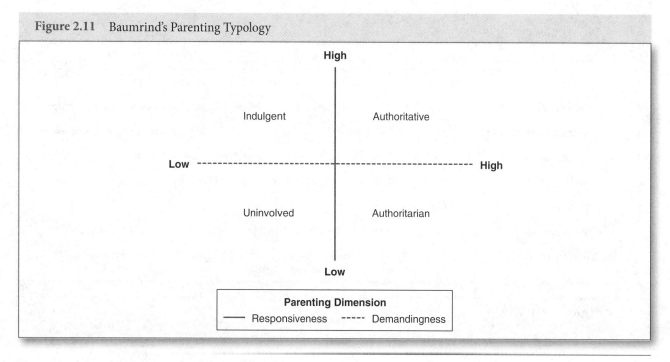

Note: In samples of predominantly white, middle-class families, children of authoritative parents showed the best developmental outcomes.

1. **Authoritative** parents are both responsive and demanding toward their children. These parents set high, but age-appropriate, expectations for their children's behavior and help their children meet these expectations by providing them with nurturance and support. They are assertive in their interactions with their children, but not intrusive. They use discipline to support their children and to teach them how to control their own behavior; they do not use discipline punitively. They value responsibility but also recognize children's needs for sensitive and responsive care.

2. **Authoritarian** parents show high levels of demandingness but low levels of responsiveness. These parents value obedience and achievement in their children. They set high standards for their children and firm limits on their children's behaviors. They establish clear rules and expect them to be obeyed without question. These parents are highly involved in their children's lives, providing them with organized, structured, and supervised educational, extracurricular, and social experiences. They strive to teach self-reliance and responsibility to their children, but they may give their children little support and encouragement to live up to these responsibilities.

3. **Indulgent** parents show high levels of responsiveness but low levels of demandingness. These parents are described as lenient, nondirective, and permissive. They value autonomy and exploration in their children. They place few limits on their children's behaviors and are reticent to discipline.

4. **Uninvolved** parents show low levels of both responsiveness and demandingness. These parents display

infrequent or inconsistent interactions toward their children, often because they are distracted by other psychosocial stressors (e.g., parents working multiple jobs, caring for an elderly relative).

Prospective longitudinal research has shown that children's social-emotional outcomes are related to parenting style (Baumrind, 1991; Weiss & Schwarz, 1996). Overall, children of authoritative parents display the best developmental outcomes. On average, these children show well-developed social skills, emotional competence, and capacity for self-regulation and self-direction. Children of authoritarian parents tend to perform well academically but are at risk for low self-esteem and peer problems, especially in late childhood and early adolescence. Children of indulgent parents often display high levels of self-esteem and well-developed social skills, but they are susceptible to behavior problems during childhood and substance use problems during adolescence. Children of uninvolved parents display the poorest developmental outcomes. These children are at particular risk for low academic achievement, behavior problems, and emotional difficulties across development.

Psychologists have also identified a third dimension of parenting, **parental hostility/coercion**, which is especially relevant to the development of children's behavior problems. Hostile/coercive parenting reflects parenting tactics that express negative affect or indifference toward children or involve the use of threat, harsh physical punishment, or psychological manipulation (Lovejoy, Weis, O'Hare, & Rubin, 1999). Examples of hostile/coercive parenting behavior include threatening to hurt or abandon a child, slapping or handling a child roughly, and using guilt or ridicule to control a child's behavior. Prospective longitudinal research indicates that hostile/coercive parenting behavior may contribute to the development of disruptive behavior problems in childhood and adolescence, especially problems with defiance and aggression (Barber, 2002; Patterson, Reid, & Dishion, 1992).

Social-Cultural Influences on Development

Proximal Versus Distal Risk Factors

Until now, we have focused chiefly on the immediate causes of child psychopathology. These causes include the child's genotype, biological structure and functioning, learning experiences, and familial context. These immediate determinants of children's functioning are often referred to as **proximal risk factors** because they can directly affect children's well-being. For example, a genetic disorder can lead to low intellectual functioning or Intellectual Disability whereas exposure to hostile/coercive parenting can contribute to oppositional and defiant behavior. The overwhelming majority of research addressing the causes of child psychopathology focuses on proximal risk factors because they are typically the easiest to study (Wade & Cairney, 2006).

Researchers have increasingly turned their attention to other, distal risk factors for child behavior problems. **Distal risk factors** are social, cultural, and broader environmental influences on child development that do not directly affect children's functioning but can affect their social, emotional, and behavioral competence.

One important distal risk factor is socioeconomic status (SES), a construct that reflects parents' educational attainment, income, employment status, and living condition. Children from low-SES families are at increased risk for developing behavioral and emotional disorders compared to youths from middle- and high-SES backgrounds. Another frequently studied distal risk factor is ethnicity. For example, some ethnic minority youths show greater likelihood of developing a mental or behavioral disorder than their white counterparts. Other distal risk factors include family structure (e.g., single-parent families), neighborhood quality (e.g., population density, crime), and broader social norms and mores (Wade & Cairney, 2006).

How do distal factors contribute to child psychopathology? According to Wade and Cairney (2006), risk factors like poverty and neighborhood disadvantage can affect child development in at least three ways. First, distal risk factors can *directly influence* child development. For example, infants and toddlers who ingest lead are at risk for developing behavioral and learning problems in early childhood. Typically, youths are exposed to lead from lead-based paint that flakes off the walls of older homes. Children from low-SES families are disproportionately exposed to lead-based paint because they often live in older, more dilapidated homes. Consequently, rates of lead poisoning, and subsequent neurological impairment, are much greater among low-SES ethnic minority youths than among middle-class white children (Dilworth-Bart & Moore, 2006).

Second, proximal factors can *mediate* the effects of distal risks on child development. In this case, distal risk factors undermine parents' abilities to provide optimal care for their children. This less-than-optimal care, in turn, can lead to children's behavioral or emotional problems. For example, Conger, Ge, Elder, Lorenz, and Simons (1994) discovered that the degree to which parents argued over financial concerns predicted the extent to which they showed hostile and coercive behaviors toward their children. Their hostile and coercive parenting behaviors, in turn, predicted the development of their children's behavior problems.

Third, distal risk factors can *moderate* the effects of proximal factors on children's outcomes. For example, the effects of parenting behavior (e.g., a proximal factor) on children's development might differ depending on whether the child is from a low- or high-SES background (e.g., a distal factor). Lundahl, Risser, and Lovejoy (2006) found that psychotherapy that involves teaching parents to reduce hostile/coercive behavior toward their children is often associated with a reduction of children's behavior problems. However, the effects of parental psychotherapy on children's behavior depend on parents' SES. Psychotherapy is more effective among middle-class parents than low-SES parents. Social and economic disadvantage might interfere with parents' abilities to participate in treatment and, consequently, reduce its benefits.

Bioecological Systems Theory

Perhaps the most influential and comprehensive account for the way social and contextual factors affect child development has been offered by the developmental psychologist Urie Bronfenbrenner. According to Bronfenbrenner's (1979, 2000) **bioecological systems theory**, children's environment can be viewed as a hierarchy of four nested social systems, each encompassing the others like Russian dolls.

The **microsystem** reflects children's immediate surroundings and proximal influences on their development. Factors within the microsystem include children's genetic inheritance, biological functioning, psychological processes, and interactions with parents and family. The microsystem also includes children's other significant relationships (e.g., with teachers, coaches, peers) and the various social roles they adopt (e.g., student, athlete, friend). The microsystem is the "primary engine of development," and children's interactions with caregivers and friends are typically the most important proximal determinants of development (Bronfenbrenner & Morris, 1998).

The **mesosystem** refers to the connections between microsystems. For example, children's relationships at home and school are important determinants of their overall functioning. However, the quality of interactions *between* home and school also influences children's well-being. Children whose parents take an active role in their educational and extracurricular activities will likely show different outcomes than children whose parents show disinterest in their activities.

The **exosystem** reflects contextual influences that affect microsystems but do not affect children directly. For example, a father might be required to change work schedules or to work longer hours to keep his job. These work-related changes might influence the amount of time he is able to spend with his child. Similarly, the school board might decide to reduce funding for certain extracurricular activities, causing a child to give up a favorite sport or club. The parent's change in work schedule and the school board's change in funding can alter children's daily experiences and, consequently, their development.

The **macrosystem** refers to broad social, economic, and cultural influences on children's development. Chief among these factors are socioeconomic disadvantage, neighborhood quality, and media exposure.

Bronfenbrenner recognized that the effects of all four systems on development change over time. First, the importance of various systems depends on children's age and developmental level. For example, the relative importance of peers to child development increases across childhood and early adolescence. Second, the nature of proximal and distal risk factors changes across generations. For example, the degree to which children are exposed to violent crime and other social-cultural risk factors has increased dramatically in recent decades (Bronfenbrenner, McClelland, Wethington, Moen, & Ceci, 1996). A full understanding of child development, therefore, depends on an appreciation for children's interactions with these environmental systems and how these interactions vary across time.

CHAPTER SUMMARY

Research Methods

- Psychologists are scientists who seek to understand behavior. Like all scientists, they develop and test hypotheses using empirical data.
- Correlational research allows researchers to examine the relationship between two or more variables. Although correlations can show the direction and strength of these relationships, they cannot be used to infer causality between the two variables. Some commonly used correlational designs are (a) cross-sectional studies, (b) prospective and retrospective longitudinal studies, and (c) follow-back studies.
- Moderators and mediators affect the relationship between two variables.

  - Moderators affect the nature of the relationship between two variables; they are usually categorical variables like age, gender, or ethnicity. For example, the effect of sexual abuse (i.e., variable A) on children's emotional functioning (i.e., variable B) might depend on the child's gender (i.e., the moderator).
  - Mediators help explain the relationship between two variables; they are usually continuous variables measured on a rating scale. For example, child sexual abuse (i.e., variable A) might lead children to have problems trusting caregivers and peers (i.e., the mediator). These problems with trust, in turn, might contribute to social isolation, loneliness, and depression later in childhood (i.e., variable B).

- A randomized controlled study is a type of experimental study in which researchers randomly assign participants to a treatment and control group. Participants in the treatment group receive the primary intervention whereas participants in the control group do not. Different outcomes can be attributed to the intervention. The control group can consist of (a) no-treatment, (b) waitlist, (c) attention-placebo, or (d) standard treatment (i.e., treatment-as-usual).
- Quasi-experimental research is used when random assignment is not possible. Because it lacks random assignment, quasi-experimental research cannot be used to show causality.
- Internal validity refers to the degree to which we can infer causality from a research study. Factors that can affect a study's results and limit its internal validity include the following:

  - Maturation (e.g., depression scores decrease with the passage of time)
  - Environmental factors (i.e., extraneous variables such as the weather influence mood)
  - Repeated testing (e.g., achievement scores improve with repeated practice)
  - Lack of random assignment (e.g., participants in one group are more motivated than participants in another group)
  - Attrition (e.g., people in the treatment group withdraw from the study at a higher rate than people in the control group)

- External validity refers to generalizability of results to a different population or setting.
- Single-subject research is often used by clinicians to evaluate the effectiveness of treatment in their client. Common single-subject research designs include (a) AB designs, (b) ABAB designs, and (c) multiple-baseline designs.

Developmental Theories

- Behavioral geneticists study the association between a person's genotype and his or her likelihood of developing a psychological disorder. Behavioral geneticists use twin, family, and adoption studies to determine heritability.
- Molecular geneticists study the association between specific genes and disorders. They use linkage and association studies to identify genes that place individuals at risk for behavior problems.

- Magnetic resonance imaging (MRI) is frequently used to identify structural abnormalities in the brains of youths with disorders. In contrast, functional magnetic resonance imaging (fMRI) is used to identify functional abnormalities.
- The cortex consists of four lobes: occipital, parietal, frontal, and temporal. Each lobe is associated with specific higher order functions. These lobes develop throughout childhood and adolescence.
- The basal ganglia consists of the caudate, putamen, globus pallidus, and substantia nigra. It is critical to motor control and the regulation of behavior and emotions.
- The limbic system is an evolutionarily older portion of the brain, consisting of the amygdala and hippocampus. These areas are involved in emotional responding, memory, and learning.
- The cerebellum, located at the back of the brain, undergoes considerable pruning in adolescence. It is responsible for balance and coordination as well as mental "gracefulness" and efficient thinking.
- The brain can change and adapt to environmental experiences over the life span. Neural plasticity refers to the brain's malleability in response to experience. Synaptogenesis is the formation of new neural connections associated with learning.
- Three components of learning theory include classical conditioning, operant conditioning, and observational learning (i.e., modeling). Many causes and treatments for childhood disorders can be understood in terms of learning theory.
- Attachment refers to the affective bond between a child and caregiver that emerges over the first few years of the child's life. Attachment relationships provide the child with a sense of safety. These can be secure or insecure, depending on the sensitivity or care the child receives.
- Parenting type depends on the responsiveness and demandingness parents display toward their children. Authoritative parenting (high responsiveness and demandingness) is often associated with the best child outcomes, whereas neglectful parents (low responsiveness and demandingness) is typically associated with the poorest child outcomes.
- Bioecological system's theory asserts that children's development is best understood in terms of nested "systems" each influencing each other:
  - Microsystem: Child's immediate surroundings
  - Mesosystem: Relationships between microsystems
  - Exosystem: Contextual factors that influence the child indirectly
  - Macrosystem: Broad social-cultural factors

KEY TERMS

AB design   36

ABAB designs   36

alleles   40

attachment   48

authoritarian   50

authoritative   50

basal ganglia   44

behavioral concordance   40

behavioral geneticists   39

bioecological systems theory   51

cerebellum   45

chromosomes   38

corpus callosum   44

correlational studies   29

cortex   43

cross-sectional study   31

distal risk factors   51

double-blind study   33

exosystem   52

experience-dependent   45

experience-expectant   45

external validity   38

extinction   46

falsifiable   29

follow-back study   31

functional hemispherectomy   45

gene   38

gene-driven   45

genotype   39

hypotheses   28

indulgent   50

insecure attachment relationships   48

insecure-ambivalent attachment   49

insecure-avoidant attachment   49

internal validity   34

internal working model   48

limbic system   44

macrosystem   52

mediator   31

mesosystem   51

microsystem   51

modeling   48

moderator   31

multiple-baseline design   38

CRITICAL THINKING EXERCISES

1. Why is random assignment essential for experimental research?

2. Imagine that you want to determine the long-term effects of stimulant medication (e.g., Ritalin) on children with Attention-Deficit/ Hyperactivity Disorder. How might you conduct (a) a prospective longitudinal study, (b) a retrospective longitudinal study, or (c) a follow-back study to examine these effects? What are the strengths/weaknesses of each of these research designs?

3. When physicians want to show that a new medication is efficacious for treating a medical disorder, they compare the new medication to a placebo. Why? How might a psychologist use a placebo to investigate the efficacy of a new psychotherapy?

4. As children develop, the relative importance of passive gene-environment effects gradually decreases, while the relative importance of active gene-environment effects gradually increases. Why?

5. The American Academy of Pediatrics has urged parents to monitor young children's access to television and limit infants' exposure to electronic media altogether. Their recommendation is based on the understanding that the infant and toddler brain is developing rapidly. What is the evidence that brain development extends *beyond* early childhood? Should parents also monitor and limit their adolescents' media consumption?

6. Considerable research indicates that children whose parents display high levels of responsiveness and demandingness, but low levels of hostility/coercion, tend to have the best developmental outcomes. However, most of the research supporting this conclusion has been conducted with white, middle-class families. Why might it be important to consider ethnicity and socioeconomic status when making claims about optimal parenting behavior? How might culture affect the relationship between parenting and children's outcomes?

EXTEND YOUR LEARNING

Videos, practice tests, flash cards, study guides, and links to online resources for this chapter are available to students online. Teachers also have access to lecture notes, PowerPoint presentations, suggestions for classroom activities, and possible exam questions. Visit: www .sagepub.com/weis2e.

CHAPTER **3**

Assessing, Diagnosing, and Treating Children's Problems

LEARNING OBJECTIVES

After reading this chapter, you should be able to answer these questions:

- What are the four main ways clinicians can assess children's functioning? Why is multimethod and multi-informant assessment important when assessing children?
- What is a mental status exam and psychosocial history? How are they used as part of the assessment process?
- Explain the major types of norm-referenced child assessment: intelligence, achievement, adaptive functioning, personality, and overt behavior.
- Why is it important to consider the reliability and validity of assessment procedures before using them?
- What is *DSM-5*? How is *DSM-5* different from previous versions of the manual?
- Identify major advantages and disadvantages of psychological diagnosis.
- Compare and contrast the major systems of child and adolescent psychotherapies.
- How does child psychotherapy differ from adult psychotherapy?
- Does child and adolescent psychotherapy work? Under what conditions?

Mental health practitioners spend most of their time engaging in three types of professional activities: assessment, diagnosis, and treatment. **Assessment** refers to the process of gathering information about children and families in order to gain an accurate understanding of their psychosocial functioning. **Diagnosis** refers to the task of describing the client's functioning, usually by matching the client's functioning to descriptions of psychiatric conditions recognized by other practitioners. **Treatment** involves the use of psychosocial and/or medicinal therapies to alleviate distress or impairment and promote children's well-being. In this chapter, we will examine how clinicians perform these three activities.

PSYCHOLOGICAL ASSESSMENT

Purposes of Assessment

Psychological assessment refers to the process of gathering data about children and families in order to reach valid conclusions about their current functioning and future well-being. The assessment of children and adolescents can have many purposes

(Carter, Marakovitz, & Sparrow, 2006; Sattler, 2001). First, assessment can be conducted *to screen* children for possible behavior problems or developmental delays. For example, a pediatrician might ask a psychologist to screen a toddler who is showing delays in language acquisition and social skills despite normal sensory and motor functioning. The psychologist might conduct a brief evaluation in order to determine whether the child has a significant delay that needs greater attention. Early screening can prevent more severe problems later in development.

Second, assessment can be used *to reach a diagnosis*. For example, parents might refer their child to a psychologist because the child is showing a wide range of emotional and disruptive behavior problems. The psychologist would likely conduct a detailed evaluation of the child's strengths and weaknesses in order to identify the nature of the child's problems. The clinician would likely assign one or more diagnostic labels to describe the child's main problem areas. Diagnosis might help parents understand their child's functioning, allow the clinician to estimate the child's prognosis, and help the clinician plan treatment.

Third, some assessments are conducted *to identify and treat a specific behavior problem*. For example, a third-grade teacher might ask a school psychologist to assess a student who repeatedly bullies younger children during recess. In this case, the purpose of the assessment is not to assign a diagnosis. Instead, the purpose of assessment is to identify potential causes of the bullying and to plan an intervention. After careful observation of the bully's behavior, the school psychologist might notice that the boy initiates fights with younger children only in the presence of certain peers. She might recommend that the bully and his peers be separated during recess in order to avoid the problem in the future.

A fourth purpose of assessment is *to monitor progress in treatment*. For example, a pediatrician might prescribe methylphenidate (Ritalin) to a boy with ADHD. She might ask the child's teachers to rate the boy's ADHD symptoms for 3 weeks. During the first week, the boy might not take any medication. During the second week, the boy might take a low dose of the medication. During the third week, the boy might take a slightly higher dose. The pediatrician might use teachers' ratings over the 3 weeks to determine whether the medication reduced the boy's symptoms and which dose was more effective.

The purpose of psychological assessment is to obtain an informed understanding of the child and family. Psychological assessment involves much more than administering a test or assigning a diagnosis. Instead, assessment involves appreciating the strengths and weaknesses of clients within the context of their surroundings and drawing valid conclusions regarding how to help them improve their lives.

Psychological assessment is a *process*. From the scientist-practitioner perspective, each assessment is analogous to a research study with a sample size of one (i.e., $N = 1$, the client). The clinician listens to the family's presenting problem and begins to formulate hypotheses about the child's functioning.

For example, if a mother reports that her child is earning low grades at school, possible hypotheses might be (a) the child has ADHD or a learning disorder that interferes with his academic performance; (b) the child has an emotional problem, such as depression, that distracts him from his work; or (c) the child has high intelligence and is bored with traditional classroom instruction.

The clinician systematically tests each of these hypotheses by gathering data from parents, teachers, and the child. Hypotheses that are supported by data are retained; hypotheses not supported by data are revised or discarded. For example, after careful testing, the clinician might find little evidence of ADHD, a learning problem, or above-average intelligence. However, while interviewing the child, the clinician might find evidence of mood problems, perhaps associated with difficulty making friends in school. The clinician might revise her hypothesis, asserting that the child's academic problems are due to symptoms of depression caused by a lack of peer acceptance.

The clinician's hypothesis can be supported or not supported by the effectiveness of treatment. In this example, the clinician decides to teach the child social skills in order to improve his social standing at school. She reasons that as the child's social functioning improves, so, too, will his mood and academic performance. She provides social skills training to the child and parent for 10 weeks. Each week, she elicits feedback from the child's teacher, regarding his social functioning in the classroom and his academic performance. The clinician notices a modest increase in the child's social functioning over the course of treatment. More important, this increase in social skills is accompanied by improvement in grades and academic motivation.

The process of psychological assessment, therefore, involves generating and systematically evaluating clinical hypotheses using empirical data. This process of assessment begins with the first therapy session and continues until the end of treatment.

The Four Pillars of Assessment

Jerome Sattler (2001) has identified four components of psychological assessment that are optimal for obtaining an accurate understanding of children and families. These four "pillars" of psychological assessment are (a) clinical interviews, (b) observations of children and families, (c) norm-referenced tests, and (d) informal data gathering. From Sattler's perspective, the process of psychological assessment is analogous to the process of erecting a building. The conclusions and treatment recommendations that clinicians make regarding child and family functioning are supported by the four assessment methods. Removal of any of these pillars can compromise the integrity of clinician's inferences, just as removal of one of the support beams of a building can adversely affect its stability.

The most accurate understanding of children's functioning is based on **multimethod assessment**. Multimethod assessment involves gathering data in a number of different ways to obtain a complete picture of children's functioning. Under ideal conditions, multimethod assessment involves all four assessment pillars: interviews, observations, norm-referenced testing, and informal data gathering.

To understand the importance of multimethod assessment, consider the following example. A probation officer refers a 14-year-old boy, Brian, for psychological assessment after the boy is arrested for shoplifting and fleeing from police. The clinician interviews the boy and his mother. Brian's mother tells the clinician that Brian is "a good kid" who has shown an increase in disruptive behavior problems since his father's recent incarceration. Brian expresses remorse for shoplifting and attributes his misbehavior to "family problems" at home. He also begs the clinician for a "second chance" and states that he is willing to "turn over a new leaf." Based on interview data, the clinician erroneously concludes that Brian's behavior reflects problems adjusting to his father's incarceration. However, if the clinician had relied on other assessment methods, his conclusion likely would have differed. For example, informal data gathering from teachers might have revealed that Brian has a history of aggression, callousness, and deceit. Personality test data might have also shown that Brian has disruptive and antisocial behavior tendencies. Relying on a single method of assessment can yield a distorted picture of children's functioning.

Accurate assessment also relies on **multiple informants.** Data should be gathered from many different people knowledgeable about the child's functioning, especially parents, teachers, other caregivers, and the child.

Previous research has shown low correlations between parents, teachers, and children's ratings of child behavior. Correlations between informants tend to range from .30 to .40. In general, parents and teachers tend to report more disruptive behavior problems than do children, whereas children tend to report more anxiety and mood problems than do parents and teachers. Consequently, a clinician who relies only on information provided by one informant will likely obtain an inaccurate picture of children's functioning (Achenbach, McConaughy, & Howell, 1987; Kamphaus & Frick, 2002).

Why do informants disagree so much in their reports of children's functioning? The answer is twofold. First, different informants are privy to different types of information about children's functioning. For example, parents have access to information about children's overt behavior at home, whereas teachers are usually better able to comment on children's academic and behavioral functioning at school. Children, themselves, are often more accurate than parents and teachers in reporting emotional problems, like anxiety and depression.

Second, children's behavior can vary dramatically across settings. For example, children may appear anxious at school but appear relaxed with family members. Similarly, children may be defiant and disrespectful toward parents but be courteous and compliant toward teachers. Disagreement between informants, therefore, often reflects differences in informants' knowledge of the child and variance in the child's behavior across settings.

The art of psychological assessment involves integrating information, using multiple methods from multiple informants to obtain an accurate picture of children's functioning. Often, information is discrepant and clinicians must rely on their experience and knowledge of the child and family to make sense of the data. The science of psychological assessment involves using multimethod, multi-informant data to generate and systematically evaluate hypotheses regarding children's behavior.

Assessment Techniques

Clinical Interviews

Perhaps the most important component of psychological assessment is the **clinical interview.** The interview usually occurs during the first session, and it can sometimes extend across multiple sessions. The interview usually involves the child and his or her parents, and it can sometimes include extended family members, teachers, and other people knowledgeable about the child's functioning. Some clinicians prefer to interview children and parents together, whereas other clinicians separate adults and children.

The assessment interview has three purposes. One purpose of the interview is to identify the family's presenting problem and to begin to establish rapport. The presenting problem is the primary reason(s) the family is seeking treatment. Presenting problems might include a decrease in the child's academic functioning, an increase in disruptive behavior problems, or a referral from a teacher because of a suspected learning disability. The clinician pays special attention to the degree to which all family members, especially the child, want to participate in treatment. The clinician begins to establish rapport with the child and parents by empathically listening to their concerns, accurately reflecting their thoughts and feelings, and offering an initial plan to address their problems.

Another purpose of the interview is to gather data about the child's psychosocial history and current functioning. Typically, clinicians interview the child, parents, and teachers to gain information about the history and current status of the presenting problem; the developmental history of the child; relationships between the child, family, and school; and the child's strengths and weaknesses (see Table 3.1).

During the course of the interview, some clinicians also conduct a **mental status examination** of the child (Groth-Marnat, 2003; Sadock & Sadock, 2003). The mental status examination is a brief assessment of the child's current functioning in three broad areas: (a) overt behavior, (b) emotion, and (c) cognition (see Table 3.2). With respect to behavior, the clinician examines the child's actions and social behavior during the interview session. She is especially interested in the child's general appearance, posture, degree of eye contact, quality of interactions with parents, and attitude toward the therapist.

Table 3.1   Psychosocial History for Children and Adolescents

Dimension	Possible Question(s)
Presenting Problem	
Onset	When did the problem begin?
Course	Has the problem changed, become better, or become worse?
Duration	How long has the problem lasted?
Antecedents	Any psychosocial stressors before problem onset?
Consequences	Any factors that might reinforce or maintain the problem over time?
Attempts to solve	Is there anything that has alleviated the problem?
Family Background	
Parents	Occupations? Educational backgrounds? Marital status?
Siblings	Living in household? Relationship to child?
Socioeconomic status	Family income and financial security? Housing situation?
Family psychiatric history	History of behavioral, emotional, cognitive, or substance use problems in the family?
Culture	Language spoken in home? Religious beliefs? Other relevant cultural or ethnic factors?
Child's Developmental History	
Problems with pregnancy/delivery	Premature birth/low birth weight? Maternal substance use during gestation?
Early development	Attachment to parents? Achievement of developmental milestones (e.g., walking, talking)?
Medical history	Physical health of the child? Injuries/illnesses? Chronic conditions? Medications?
Current physical health	Appetite, energy level, sleep quality?
Child's Academic History	
Academic achievement	Current grade in school? Academic performance? Adjustment to school?
Academic problems	Failed a grade? Received special education services?
Relationship with teachers	Family involvement in child's education? Behavior at school?
Academic/career goal	Will child graduate from high school or college? Are goals realistic?
Child's Social History	
Relationship to parents	Amount of contact with mother, father? Quality of relationships?
Peer status	Friends at school? Rejected by peers?
Social skills	Ability to listen, take turns, develop friendships?
Child's Behavioral History	
Interests, hobbies, activities	Sports, clubs, after-school activities?
Substance use	Cigarette, alcohol, and other drug use? Problems associated with use?
Sexual behavior	Sexually active? Problems with sexual identity?
Child's Psychiatric History	
Previous problems	Previous psychiatric disorders?
History of treatment	Ever participated in therapy? Ever been psychiatrically hospitalized?
Medications	Ever prescribed medication for psychiatric diagnosis?

Table 3.2	Brief Mental Status Examination for Children and Adolescents

1. Overt behavior

- General appearance

- Posture, eye contact, body movements, activity level

- Behavior toward clinician and caregivers

2. Emotion

- Mood

- Affect

- Appropriateness

3. Cognition

- Thought content

- Thought process

- Intelligence

- Attention

- Memory

- Orientation to person, place, and time

- Insight

- Judgment

With respect to emotion, the clinician assesses the child's mood and affect. **Mood** refers to the child's long-term emotional disposition. Mood is usually assessed by asking the child and his parents about the child's overall emotional functioning. Moods can range from shy and inhibited, to touchy and argumentative, to sanguine and carefree. **Affect** refers to the child's short-term emotional expression. Affect is usually inferred by watching the child's facial expressions, posture, and body movements during the session. Affect can include tearfulness, expressions of anger, and social withdrawal. Some children show a range of affective displays whereas others show very little emotional expression. The clinician is especially interested in whether the child's affect is appropriate to the given situation. For example, a child who laughs while talking about a parent's death displays inappropriate affect.

The clinician assesses the child's cognition in several ways. One aspect of cognition is **thought content**, that is, the subject matter of the child's cognition. For example, some children are preoccupied with certain topics or hobbies, whereas other children's thoughts are plagued by persistent worries or fears. In severe instances, children have delusions or bizarre thoughts that do not correspond to reality. Another aspect of cognition is **thought process**, that is, the way in which the child forms associations and solves

problems. Thought process is usually inferred from the child's speech. For example, the clinician observes whether the child's speech is coherent, whether it is rapid and difficult to follow, or whether the child abruptly stops speaking in mid-conversation.

Other aspects of cognition include the child's overall intelligence, attention and memory, and orientation. **Orientation** refers to the child's awareness of himself, his surroundings, and current events. For example, a child involved in a car accident might become disoriented; lack of orientation to person, place, and time usually indicates serious impairment.

Finally, clinicians assess the child's insight and judgment. **Insight** refers to the degree to which the child recognizes that he might have a social, emotional, or behavioral problem. Youths with eating disorders and conduct problems often show poor insight; they often deny having any problems whatsoever. **Judgment** refers to the child's understanding of the seriousness of his behavior problem and its impact on himself and others. Judgment also refers to the child's ability to consider the consequences of his behavior before acting. Disorders such as ADHD are usually characterized by poor judgment.

A third purpose of the interview is to arrive at a psychiatric diagnosis. Many clinicians review diagnostic criteria informally during the course of the interview. Other clinicians conduct structured diagnostic interviews to review criteria with children and parents. In a **structured diagnostic interview**, the clinician systematically reviews all of the major psychiatric diagnoses with children and/or parents to determine whether the child meets criteria for any diagnosis. For example, the Diagnostic Interview Schedule for Children (DISC; Shaffer, Fisher, Lucas et al., 2000) can be administered to children and parents to review the diagnostic criteria for anxiety, mood, behavior, substance use, and thought problems in children and adolescents. The interview takes about 1.5 to 2 hours to complete, but it provides a comprehensive assessment of the child's functioning.

Behavioral Observations

Methods of Observation. Behavioral observations are essential to child assessment. Although parental reports of child behavior are important, there is no substitute for the rich amount of information that can be gathered from watching children. Clinicians observe children in three ways (Groth-Marnat, 2003). First, most clinicians observe children as they participate in the clinical interview. Using this procedure, clinicians note children's activity level, speech and language, emotions, quality of interactions with parents, and other overt actions. The shortcoming of informal clinic observation is that children's behavior in the clinic may not be representative of children's behavior at home and school.

Second, many clinicians observe children performing **analogue tasks** in the clinic. Analogue tasks are designed to mimic activities or situations in which children engage in daily life. For example, a clinician might want to observe the interactions between a mother and her preschool-aged child. The clinician might ask the dyad to play in the clinic playroom for 20 minutes. At the end of the play session, the clinician might ask the mother to tell the child to stop playing and clean up the room. This analogue task allows the clinician to observe firsthand how the mother issues commands to her child, how the child responds to her commands, and how the mother disciplines her child. Information gathered from analogue observation can help the clinician understand how the pattern of interactions between parent and child might contribute to the child's behavior problems. Furthermore, observational data might be used to plan treatment.

A third approach involves **naturalistic observation**. Naturalistic observations are most frequently used by mental health professionals who work in schools. During math class, a school psychologist might monitor the activity level of a child suspected of having ADHD. The frequency of ADHD symptoms shown by the target child might be compared to the frequency of ADHD symptoms shown by another child in the class. The primary strength of naturalistic observation is that it permits clinicians to examine children's behavior in natural settings. The chief weakness of naturalistic observation is that it is time consuming. A second shortcoming of naturalistic observation is **reactivity**; that is, children might react to the fact that they are being observed and act in *un*natural ways.

Functional Analysis of Behavior. During their observations, clinicians often perform a functional analysis of children's behavior. **Functional analysis** is based on the notion that children's behavior is purposeful; that is, their behavior serves a function (Sattler, 2002). In most cases, behavior serves to maximize rewards and minimize punishment. By carefully observing events that occur immediately before and immediately after a behavior, clinicians can determine the behavior's purpose. The clinician can use information about the behavior's purpose to plan treatment (Kamphaus & Frick, 2002; Ramsay, Reynolds, & Kamphaus, 2002).

To perform a functional analysis of behavior, the clinician first defines the child's behavior problem in clear, observable terms. For example, a mother might complain that her preschool-aged child is "defiant." However, terms like *defiant* are vague and not easily observed. Consequently, the clinician might operationally define the term *defiant* as the child's failure to comply with his mother's commands within 10 seconds. By defining the child's behavior in clear, observable terms, the clinician can more easily observe the child's problem behavior and identify its purpose.

Next, the clinician gathers data regarding the antecedents and consequences of the target behavior. **Antecedents** refer to environmental conditions that immediately precede the target behavior, whereas **consequences** refer to conditions that immediately follow the behavior. Clinicians conceptualize the situation in the following terms: A (antecedent), B (behavior), or C (consequence).

For example, the clinician might observe the parent-child dyad during an analogue play session. She might notice that the child refuses to obey his mother's commands when her commands are vague. Specifically, the child obeys his mother when she tells him to perform a single, clear action (e.g., "Pick up *that* toy"), but he often fails to comply when his mother issues a vague or complex command (e.g., "Clean up"). The clinician discovers that vague or complex commands often precede the child's noncompliance. Furthermore, the clinician might notice that the mother often backs down from her commands when her child ignores her or when he refuses to obey. Therefore, the consequence of the child's noncompliance is that the mother stops issuing her request and allows the child to continue playing.

The clinician can use information about the antecedents and consequences of the child's behavior to plan treatment. Because vague and complex commands often precede the child's noncompliance, the clinician might decide to help the mother issue clearer, more concrete commands to her child—commands that the child is more likely to obey. Similarly, because the child's noncompliance is often reinforced by the mother's backing down from her commands, the clinician might teach the mother to be more consistent and insist that her child obey her commands.

Norm-Referenced Testing

Standardization. **Norm-referenced testing** involves the administration of a standardized measure of children's behavior that allows comparisons of that child to other individuals her age. Examples of norm-referenced tests include intelligence tests, personality tests, and behavior rating scales.

All norm-referenced tests are administered, scored, and interpreted in a **standardized format**; that is, each administration of the test involves the same item content, the same administration procedure, and the same method of scoring and interpretation. For example, all 7-year-old children who take the Wechsler Intelligence Scale for Children–Fourth Edition (WISC-IV; Wechsler, 2003) are administered the same test items. Items are presented in the same way to all children according to specific rules described in the test manual. These rules include where participants must sit, how instructions must be presented, how much time is allowed, and what sort of help (if any) examiners can provide. Children's answers are scored in the same way, using specific guidelines presented in the manual.

Standardized test administration and scoring allow clinicians to compare children's test scores. Two children who obtain the same number of correct test items on an intelligence test are believed to have comparable levels of overall intellectual functioning *only* if they were administered the test in a standardized fashion. If one child was given extra time, additional help, or greater encouragement by the test administrator, comparisons would be inappropriate.

Children's scores on norm-referenced tests are always compared to the performance of other children, in order to make these scores more meaningful. For example, imagine that a 9-year-old girl correctly answers 45 questions on the WISC-IV. A clinician would record her "raw score" as 45. However, a raw score of 45 does not allow the clinician to determine whether the girl's performance indicates that she is intellectually gifted, average, or cognitively delayed. To interpret her raw score, the clinician needs to compare her score to a large representative sample of children who have already taken the WISC-IV; that is, he must compare the girl's score to the performance of a **norm group**. If the mean raw score for 9-year-olds in the norm group was 45 and the girl's raw score was 45, the clinician might conclude that the girl's intellectual functioning is within the average range. However, if the mean raw score for 9-year-old children was 30 and the girl's raw score was 45, the clinician might conclude that the girl has above-average intellectual functioning.

The results of norm-referenced testing, therefore, depend greatly on comparison of the individual child with the norm group. At a minimum, comparisons are made based on children's age. For example, on measures of intelligence, 9-year-old children must be compared to other 9-year-old children, not to 6-year-old children or 12-year-old children. On other psychological tests, especially tests of behavior and personality, comparisons are made based on age and gender. For example, boys tend to show more symptoms of hyperactivity than do girls. Consequently, when a clinician obtains parents' ratings of hyperactivity for a 9-year-old boy, he compares these ratings to the ratings for other 9-year-old boys in the norm group.

Standard Scores. Usually, clinicians want to quantify the degree to which children score above or below the mean for the norm group (see text box Research to Practice: Understanding Standard Scores). To quantify children's deviation from the mean, clinicians transform the child's raw test score to a **standard score**. A standard score is simply a raw score that has been changed to a different scale with a designated mean and standard deviation. Examples of standard scores include IQ scores ($M = 100$, $SD = 15$), SAT scores ($M = 1000$, $SD = 200$), T scores ($M = 50$, $SD = 10$), and z scores ($M = 0$, $SD = 1$).

RESEARCH TO PRACTICE

UNDERSTANDING STANDARD SCORES

How do psychologists convert raw scores to standard scores? The answer requires a little bit of statistics. Calculation of raw scores to standard scores is based on the assumption that children's scores fall along a bell-shaped distribution called the **normal distribution**. Most people score very close to the mean of this distribution, while progressively fewer people earn scores at the extremes. Assuming a normal distribution, raw scores can be converted to standardized z scores using the following formula:

$$z = (\text{Person's raw score} - \text{Mean raw score for norm group})/SD$$

For example, if 9-year-old Mary earns a raw score of 45 and the mean raw score for 9-year-old children in the norm group is 45 with a standard deviation of 5, then Mary's z score is

$$z = (\text{Person's raw score} - \text{Mean raw score for norm group})/SD$$

$$z = (45 - 45)/5$$

$$z = 0$$

However, if 9-year-old Julia earns a raw score of 50 and the mean raw score for 9-year-old children in the norm group is 45 with a standard deviation of 5, then Julia's z score is

$$z = (\text{Person's raw score} - \text{Mean raw score for norm group})/SD$$

$$z = (50 - 45)/5$$

$$z = 1$$

(Continued)

The z score tells us the number of standard deviations the person's score is above or below the mean of the norm group. Mary's z score is 0; her score is equivalent to the mean. Julia's z score is 1; her score is 1 standard deviation above the mean.

A z score can be transformed into any other standard score, such as an IQ score or a T score:

$$\text{New standard score} = M_{\text{new distribution}} + z(SD_{\text{new distribution}})$$

If we want to convert Mary's score into an IQ score with $M = 100$ and $SD = 15$, then

$$\text{New standard score} = M_{\text{new distribution}} + z(SD_{\text{new distribution}})$$
$$= 100 + 0(15)$$
$$= 100$$

If we want to convert Julia's score into an IQ score with $M = 100$ and $SD = 15$, then

$$\text{New standard score} = M_{\text{new distribution}} + z(SD_{\text{new distribution}})$$
$$= 100 + 1(15)$$
$$= 115$$

We can also convert Julia's score into any other standard score as long as we know the mean and standard deviation of the scale. For example, if we want to transform her score to a T score with $M = 50$ and $SD = 10$,

$$\text{New standard score} = M_{\text{new distribution}} + z(SD_{\text{new distribution}})$$
$$= 50 + 1(10)$$
$$= 60$$

Julia, therefore, earned a raw score of 45, a z score of 1, an IQ score of 115, and a T score of 60. Transforming raw scores to standard scores to other standard scores is analogous to translating one language into another. A z score of 1, an IQ score of 115, and a T score of 60 all represent the same level of performance, just as the words *house, casa,* and *maison* refer to the same object.

It is important to know that there are different types of standard scores. Nearly all IQ tests yield results in standardized IQ scores; however, most personality tests yield results using standardized T scores.

Standard scores are more meaningful than raw scores (see Figure 3.1). For example, knowing that Anne answered 61 questions correctly on an IQ test and 120 questions on the SAT tells us very little. However, knowing that she earned an IQ score of 130 and an SAT score of 1400 suggests that she is very intelligent.

Intelligence Tests. Over the past 100 years, considerable effort has gone into defining intelligence and developing tests to measure it. Nearly all theorists recognize that intelligence reflects some aspects of the person's mental functioning that has its origins in genetics and biology but is shaped by experience and education. Albert Binet and Theodore Simon (1916), the developers of the first intelligence test, defined intelligence as the ability "to judge well, to comprehend well, and to reason well" (pp. 42–43). Years later, another important figure in the history of intelligence testing, David Wechsler (1958), described intelligence as "the aggregate or global capacity of the individual to act purposefully, to think rationally, and to deal effectively with his environment" (p. 7). Even more recently, John Carroll (1997) claimed that intelligence is "the degree to which, and the rate at which, people are able to learn and retain in long-term memory the knowledge and skills that can be learned from the environment, that is, what is taught in the home and in school, as well as things learned from everyday experience" (p. 44).

Intelligence is a broad construct that is related to people's abilities to adapt to their environments, to solve problems, and to use information accurately and efficiently. According to a survey of experts, the most important components of intelligence include the capacity for reasoning and abstract

Figure 3.1 The Standard Normal Distribution

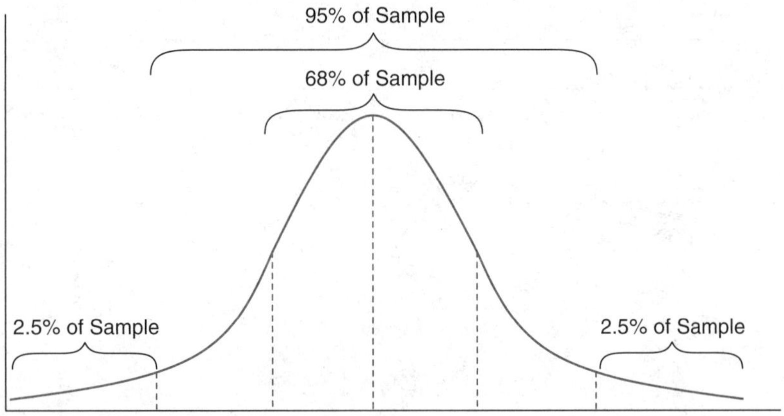

SD	-2σ	-1σ	0	1σ	2σ
z score	−2	−1	0	1	2
T score	30	40	50	60	70
IQ score	70	85	100	115	130
SAT score	600	800	1000	1200	1400

Note: Approximately 68% of people earn scores within one standard deviation from the mean. Approximately 95% of people earn scores within two standard deviations from the mean. Raw scores can be transformed into standard scores to make them easier to understand.

thinking, problem solving, knowledge acquisition, memory, adaptation to one's surroundings, speed of processing information, adroitness with language and mathematics, general knowledge, and creativity (Snyderman & Rothman, 1987).

The WISC-IV (Wechsler, 2003) is the most frequently used measure of intellectual functioning for children and adolescents. Wechsler began developing tests in the 1930s in an attempt to measure facets of adults' intelligence and problem-solving abilities. His first intelligence test, the Wechsler-Bellevue Intelligence Scale, was designed for adults. Later, he created a simplified version of his adult scale to measure children's intellectual functioning (see Table 3.3). The first version of the WISC was created in 1949; subsequent revisions were published in 1974, 1991, and 2003.

Table 3.3 Items Similar to Those on the WISC-IV

Composite/Subtests	Examples
Verbal Comprehension:	
Similarities	In what way are a shoe and a sock alike?
	In what way are a car and a train alike?
Vocabulary	What is a horse?
	What does *jumping* mean?
Comprehension	What should you do if you get lost in a store?
	Why should you look both ways before crossing the street?

(Continued)

Table 3.3 (Continued)

Composite/Subtests	Examples
Perceptual Reasoning:	
Picture Concepts	Select one picture from each row so that the pictures have a characteristic in common:
Matrix Reasoning	Select one of the five choices below to complete the matrix:
Block Design	Reproduce a design using colored blocks:
Working Memory:	
Digit Span	Repeat a string of 2 to 9 numbers from memory. Then, repeat a string of 2 to 8 numbers *backward* from memory.
Letter-Number Sequencing	Listen to a string of 2 to 8 letters and numbers. Then, repeat the string from memory with numbers first (in ascending order), then letters (in alphabetical order). For example, *w 7 b 2* would be repeated *2 7 b w*.
Processing Speed:	
Coding	Copy as many symbols as possible from a key in two minutes. Key:

1	2	3	4	5	6
=	v	/	o	x	L

Composite/Subtests	Examples
Symbol Search	Problems 3 6 1 2 6 4 Decide as fast as possible whether one of two symbols on the left appears in the group of symbols on the right. [Symbol search grid with rows of shapes and YES/NO columns]

The WISC-IV provides five standard scores that psychologists use to form the basis of their evaluations regarding children's intelligence. First, the psychologist examines the child's Full Scale IQ. Full Scale IQ is a broad measure of the child's intellectual ability; it reflects children's performance across all of the components of the test. In most cases, the Full Scale IQ is used to estimate general intellectual functioning.

The WISC-IV also provides four composite scores, each reflecting a slightly different aspect of children's intelligence (Sattler & Dumont, 2004):

- *Verbal Comprehension* reflects knowledge gained through formal and informal educational experiences and reflects the application of verbal skills to new situations. Everyday tasks that require verbal comprehension include providing factual information, defining words, and understanding verbal analogies.
- *Perceptual Reasoning* reflects the ability to organize and interpret visually presented material and to engage in visual-spatial problem solving. Everyday tasks that require perceptual reasoning include solving puzzles and mazes, manipulating geometric shapes, and recognizing and understanding patterns.
- *Working Memory* reflects the ability to attend to information, retain and manipulate information in memory, and apply information when necessary. Everyday tasks that require working memory include remembering someone's telephone number and solving arithmetic problems in one's head.
- *Processing Speed* reflects the capacity to visually scan and process nonverbal information quickly and accurately. Tasks that require processing speed include scanning a supermarket aisle for a specific product or activities that require matching and sorting.

The psychologist examines the child's score on each composite and notes areas of relative strength and weakness. For example, Josh might show a Full Scale IQ within the average range, but his verbal comprehension score might be much lower than his perceptual reasoning score. The psychologist might predict that Josh will have difficulty with traditional verbal instruction in school. He might recommend that teachers use visual demonstrations and hands-on practice to help Josh learn.

Intelligence test scores are normally distributed, with a mean of 100 and a standard deviation of 15. The distribution of test scores in the general population is bell-shaped, with most people earning scores relatively close to 100 and fewer people earning scores at the extremes. Approximately 68% of all people earn IQ scores within one standard deviation about the mean (e.g., IQ = 85–115), which is generally considered the normal range. Furthermore, approximately 95% of people earn IQ scores within two standard deviations about the mean (e.g., IQ = 70–130). The remaining 5% of individuals earn IQ scores at the extremes. Approximately 2.5% have IQ scores less than 70, and they may qualify for the diagnosis of Intellectual Disability. Approximately 2.5% earn IQ scores greater than 130, indicative of superior intellectual functioning (Cohen & Swerdlik, 2005).

Academic Achievement. **Academic achievement** refers to the knowledge and skills that children learn through academic instruction. Some clinicians distinguish between tests of intelligence, which measure a person's intellectual ability or capacity to learn, and tests of achievement, which measure information that the person has already learned and retained.

Tests of academic achievement generally measure three areas of academic functioning: reading, mathematics, and written expression. These three areas reflect the main types of learning disabilities recognized by U.S. public schools. They are also the three dimensions included in the *DSM-5* definition of Learning Disorder. Some tests assess a fourth dimension of academic functioning, oral language, which reflects the child's listening and speaking skills. Problems with oral language are usually diagnosed as communication disorders in *DSM-5*.

The Woodcock-Johnson III Tests of Achievement (WJ-III; Woodcock, McGrew, & Mather, 2001) is a widely used, comprehensive test of academic achievement. The WJ-III assesses academic achievement in four broad areas: reading, mathematics, written language, and oral language (see Table 3.4). The test also allows clinicians to assess children's academic

Table 3.4   Dimensions of the Woodcock-Johnson III Tests of Achievement

Domain/Specific Area	Examples
Reading	
Basic reading	Recognizing letters, reading words, reading fluency, sounding out novel words
Reading comprehension	Understanding the meaning of sentences and paragraphs
Mathematics	
Math calculation skills	Math skills ranging from arithmetic to geometry, math fluency
Math reasoning	Math reasoning, formulating and solving story problems
Written Language	
Basic writing skills	Spelling, editing, grammar, and punctuation
Written expression	Writing sentences and paragraphs, writing fluency
Oral Language	
Listening comprehension	Understanding directions, answering questions about stories
Oral expression	Recalling verbal stories, telling the names of objects

Note: "Fluency" refers to the ability to perform academic tasks quickly and accurately. In a test of academic fluency, the child is asked to correctly solve as many problems as possible in a given period of time (e.g., 3 minutes).

skills and knowledge in specific areas, such as young children's pre-academic skills and older children's ability to sound out new words.

The WJ-III yields standardized scores on each of the four achievement domains with a mean of 100 and standard deviation of 15. Scores more than one standard deviation below the mean (i.e., < 85) can indicate delays in a particular area of achievement, while scores more than 1.5 standard deviations below the mean (i.e., < 78), might indicate a specific learning disability. Usually, clinicians examine children's IQ and achievement test scores together in order to obtain a more complete picture of children's cognitive strengths and weaknesses.

Adaptive Functioning. **Adaptive functioning** refers to how effectively individuals cope with common life demands and how well they meet the standards of personal independence expected of someone in their particular age group, social-cultural background, and community setting. Stated another way, adaptive functioning refers to the child's ability to perform day-to-day activities in an age-appropriate manner and to meet the demands of parents, teachers, and other people with whom they interact. Adaptive functioning is often assessed in children suspected of Intellectual Disability and other developmental delays, to determine their ability to meet the demands of daily life.

To measure adaptive functioning, most psychologists administer a rating scale to caregivers and teachers (see Table 3.5). Like tests of intelligence and academic achievement, adaptive behavior rating scales are norm-referenced measures. That is, the ratings of the parent or teacher can be

Table 3.5   Adaptive Functioning in Young Children

Dimension	Example
Conceptual Skills	
Communication	Follows simple commands, such as "Come here."
	Uses complete sentences.
	Begins and ends conversations appropriately.
Functional academics	Knows colors.
	Counts from 1 to 20.
	Writes first and last name.

Dimension	Example
Self-direction	Follows simple rules, such as "No yelling indoors."
	Controls temper when parent takes a toy away.
	Asks permission before playing with another child's toy.
Social Skills	
Leisure	Asks to be read a favorite book.
	Waits turn during games and activities.
	Plays board games.
Social	Shares toys with others.
	Offers to help others.
	Greets others appropriately with "Hi" and a smile.
Practical Skills	
Community use	Recognizes various public places, like the library and fire station.
	Looks both ways before crossing street.
	Finds restrooms in public places.
Home living	Gets own snacks from pantry.
	Places dirty clothes in laundry basket.
	Wipes dirty feet before entering house.
Health and safety	Avoids hot stove.
	Buckles seatbelt or car seat.
	Carries scissors appropriately.
Self-care	Washes hands with soap.
	Uses bathroom without help.
	Cuts meals into bite-size pieces.

compared to the ratings of parents or teachers in the norm group. The psychologist can convert the parent or teacher ratings into a standard score, just like an IQ score, that tells the child's standing relative to his or her peers.

Personality and Social-Emotional Functioning. Tests of children's personality and social-emotional functioning fall into three categories: (a) self-report personality tests, (b) projective personality tests, and (c) specific measures of social and emotional problems.

Self-Report Measures of Personality. The most frequently used self-report measure of adolescent personality is the **Minnesota Multiphasic Personality Inventory-Adolescent** (MMPI-A; Butcher et al., 1992). Despite its name, the MMPI-A is better viewed as a test of adolescent psychopathology and social-emotional functioning than personality per se. The MMPI-A consists of a series of true/false items

that assess 10 domains of functioning. The names of these 10 clinical domains are somewhat old-fashioned because they are based on the original version of the MMPI, developed in 1943 (see Table 3.6).

Adolescents' responses to test items on each clinical scale are compared to adolescents of the same gender in the norm group. Raw scores are converted to T scores with a mean of 50 and standard deviation of 10. T scores > 65 can indicate clinically significant problems on that dimension of social-emotional functioning. Clinicians usually plot the adolescent's T scores on a personality profile to graphically represent the most salient aspects of the adolescent's functioning (see Figure 3.2).

Projective Measures of Personality. The most well-known projective test is the **Rorschach**, which consists of 10 bilaterally symmetric inkblots. The Rorschach is based on the projective hypothesis, the notion that people who take

Table 3.6 Clinical Scales of the MMPI-A

- **Hypochondriasis (Hs)** reflects excessive concern over physical illness and pain, a tendency to express psychological distress in terms of somatic complaints, and general preoccupation with oneself.

- **Depression (D)** reflects subjective feelings of psychological distress, brooding, apathy, physical slowness, and a general disinterest in other people or activities.

- **Hysteria (Hy)** reflects a tendency to deny psychological distress, to manipulate others, and to seek attention and sympathy from others.

- **Psychopathic Deviate (Pd)** reflects general problems in social functioning, alienation from parents and prosocial peers, resentment of authority, and a tendency toward delinquent behavior.

- **Masculinity-Femininity (Mf)** reflects the degree to which the adolescent endorses traditional masculine or feminine roles or interests.

- **Paranoia (Pa)** reflects suspiciousness, sensitivity to criticism, self-righteousness, and feelings of persecution.

- **Psychasthenia (Pt)** reflects anxiety, obsessive thoughts, compulsive behaviors, unreasonable fears, and excessive doubts.

- **Schizophrenia (Sc)** reflects thought problems, a tendency to withdraw into fantasy, eccentric behavior, and feelings of alienation from self or others.

- **Hypomania (Ma)** reflects feelings of euphoria, increased irritability, inflated mood, and general agitation.

- **Social Introversion (Si)** reflects shyness, lack of social skills, and a tendency to withdraw from social interactions.

Figure 3.2 A Sample MMPI-A Profile

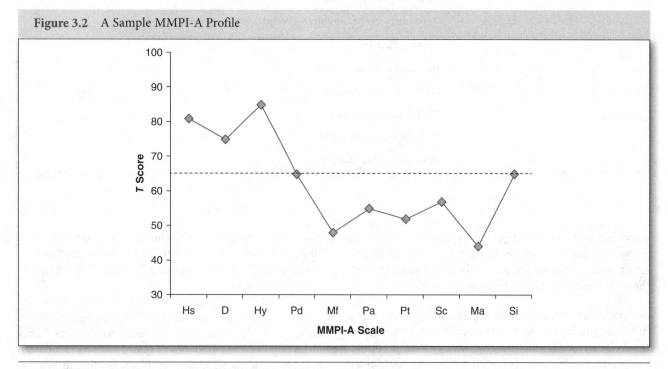

Note: The MMPI-A yields T scores on 10 clinical scales, reflecting the adolescent's social-emotional functioning. Scores > 65 can indicate significant distress or impairment. This girl's scores suggest significant problems with depression, physical complaints, and acting out.

the test "project" or impose structure and organization on the inkblots in order to perceive them in meaningful ways (Beck, 1937). Individuals with social, emotional, or cognitive disturbance will show difficulty in the perceptual-cognitive process required to make sense of the inkblots. Consequently, uncharacteristic ways of responding to the inkblots can reflect distress or impairment (Image 3.1).

John Exner (2003) developed a standardized method for administering, scoring, and interpreting the Rorschach known as the **Comprehensive System**. Clinicians who use

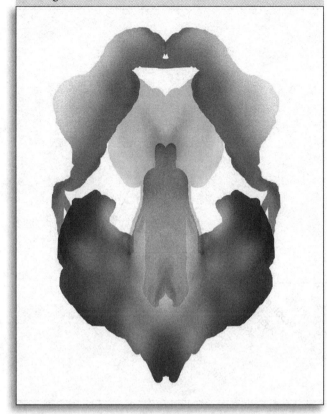

arousal, worry, and social anxiety. The Social Skills Rating System can be completed by parents or teachers to measure children's social skills. Many more measures of specific areas of children's functioning exist—too many to describe here. Selection is based largely on the clinician's hypotheses regarding the nature of children's problems.

Behavioral Functioning. Many clinicians ask parents and teachers to rate children's functioning using behavioral checklists or rating scales. Examples of behavioral rating scales include the Child Behavior Checklist, the Conners Rating Scales-Revised, and the Behavior Assessment System for Children-Second Edition (BASC-2; Reynolds & Kamphaus, 2004). For example, the BASC-2 Parent Rating Scale (PRS) can be completed by parents, whereas the BASC-2 Teacher Rating Scale (TRS) can be completed by teachers or other school personnel (see Figure 3.3). The TRS assesses four broad domains of children's behavior:

- *Externalizing problems* reflect children's disruptive behavior. Externalizing symptoms include hyperactivity, aggression, and conduct problems.
- *Internalizing problems* reflect disturbance in children's emotional functioning. Internalizing symptoms include anxiety, depression, and physical complaints, such as headache or upset stomach.
- *School problems* reflect academic difficulties, including low motivation, inattention, and learning problems.
- *Adaptive skills* reflect behavioral and social-emotional competence, appropriate social and daily living skills, and children's prosocial behavior.

Ratings of children's behavior are compared to the ratings of other parents and teachers, respectively, in the norm group. Raw scores are converted to T scores, just like on the MMPI-A.

Behavior rating scales are a quick and relatively easy way for clinicians to obtain a wide range of data on children's functioning. Furthermore, norm-referenced comparisons allow the clinician to determine whether children's behavior significantly deviates from normality. Behavior rating scales, like the BASC-2, are frequently used in the assessment of disruptive behavior disorders and emotional problems.

Exner's method administer the test in two parts. During the *response phase,* the clinician administers each inkblot, asking the client, "What might this be?" The clinician records responses verbatim for later coding. During the *inquiry phase,* the clinician reviews the client's responses in order to determine which aspects of the inkblots the client used to generate his or her response.

It is commonly assumed that clinicians are interested in what clients see in the inkblots. In Exner's method, however, scoring is based largely on *how* clients perceive the blots rather than *what* they see. For example, clinicians record whether clients use the shape, shading, color, or position of the blot to perceive the image. The clinician calculates the frequency with which clients use each feature of the inkblots in the perceptual process and compares this frequency with other individuals of the same age and gender in the norm group. Deviations can indicate problems in social, emotional, or cognitive functioning.

Specific Tests of Social-Emotional Problems. Clinicians can also administer measures to youths suspected of particular disorders. For example, the Children's Depression Inventory and Reynolds Adolescent Depression Scale are self-report rating scales designed for children and adolescents, respectively, to assess depression and other mood problems. The Revised Children's Manifest Anxiety Scale is another child self-report measure designed to assess physiological

Evaluating Psychological Tests

Although there are many kinds of psychological tests, not all tests are created equal. Before administering a test, clinicians must examine the test's reliability and validity. Reliability refers to the consistency of scores generated by the test; validity refers to the degree to which the test measures aspects of children's functioning that it was designed to measure. Tests must be reliable and valid in order for the clinician to appropriately use test data to understand clients and plan treatment.

Reliability. Reliability refers to the consistency of a psychological test (Anastasi & Urbina, 1997). Reliable tests yield

Figure 3.3 A Sample BASC-2 Profile

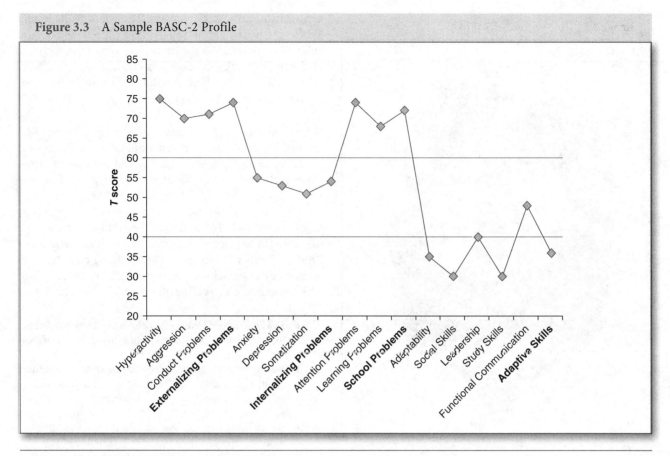

Note: The BASC-2 yields *T* scores on many dimensions of children's behavioral, social, and emotional functioning. A 10-year-old boy's teacher completed this BASC-2. The boy has significantly more externalizing symptoms and school-related problems than his peers. Also, the boy's adaptive skills are significantly lower than those of other boys his age.

consistent scores over time and across administrations. Although there are many types of test reliability, the two most common forms are test-retest reliability and internal consistency.

Test-retest reliability refers to the consistency of test scores over time. Imagine that you go to a shoe store and measure your feet. The foot-measuring device at the store indicates that you wear a size 10. Further imagine that you return to the shoe store one week later and the same device now indicates that you wear a size 8. You would conclude that the foot-measuring instrument has poor test-retest reliability because it yields inconsistent scores across repeated administrations. A psychological test should yield consistent results across repeated test administrations. For example, a child who earns a Full Scale IQ of 110 should earn a similar IQ score if she takes the test 6 months later.

Internal consistency refers to the degree to which test items yield consistent scores. Imagine that the shoe store clerk measured your right foot and the scale indicated that you wear a size 10. Then, imagine that the clerk measured your left foot and the scale indicated that you wear a size 5. You might conclude that the measuring device has poor internal consistency because it yields inconsistent results

when administered to your right and left feet. Psychological tests must also display internal consistency. For example, imagine that we construct a depression test in which children must rate 10 descriptors of mood on a scale of 1 (*low*) to 5 (*high*). These mood descriptors include symptoms of depression, such as feeling "blue," "sad," and "down." We would expect children with depression to rate all of these items highly and children without depression to rate all items low. The consistency with which children rate items reflects the internal consistency of the test.

Test-retest reliability and internal consistency are quantified by the reliability coefficient. Reliability coefficients are analogous to correlation coefficients, but they range from 0 to 1.0. A reliability coefficient of 1.0 indicates perfect consistency. Most tests that measure stable psychological traits have test-retest reliabilities of .80 or higher. Tests that measure more transient psychological states, such as short-term moods, tend to have lower test-retest reliability coefficients.

Validity. Validity refers to the degree to which a test measures what it was designed to measure. More specifically, the validity of a psychological test refers to the degree to which its users can have confidence in the inferences made from the test's results (Anastasi & Urbina, 1997; Sattler, 2001). Tests of intelligence should measure intelligence, tests of math achievement should measure math achievement, and so forth.

Reliability is a necessary, but not sufficient, condition for validity. Imagine that you measure your feet and the scale consistently indicates you wear a size 10. You try on a size 10 shoe, and it fits perfectly. You conclude that the scale is a valid measure of shoe size. Now imagine that you measure your feet and the scale consistently indicates that you wear a size 10. However, when you try on a pair of size 10 shoes, you discover they fit poorly. Your discovery demonstrates that even though a test yields consistent results, the test may not measure what it is supposed to measure (Image 3.2).

Technically speaking, validity is not a property of a test. Rather, validity refers to the ability to use test results for a specific purpose. Imagine that you measure your feet and the scale indicates that you wear a size 10. You subsequently try on a size 10 hat and discover it is much too large. The foot-measuring device is a valid test for shoe size; however, the device is not a valid indicator of hat size. Similarly, results of an IQ test can allow us to infer something about a child's intelligence; these results cannot be used to understand the child's personality.

The validity of psychological tests can be examined in at least three ways. First, psychologists examine the **content validity** of the test. Specifically, the content of test items should be relevant to the test's purpose. For example, a test designed to measure depression should have test items that ask people about various depressive symptoms. Symptoms of other mental disorders, such as anger and anxiety, might not be appropriate for the test. Psychologists often evaluate content validity by asking experts to rate the relevance of test items to the attribute they want to measure.

Psychologists also examine the **construct validity** of the test. Construct validity refers to the degree to which test scores reflect hypothesized behavioral attributes, or constructs. Most psychological variables are constructs: intelligence, depression, anxiety, aggression. Constructs cannot be measured directly; instead, they must be inferred from overt actions or people's self-reports. For example, intelligence might be inferred from superior reading ability, depression might be inferred from frequent crying, and aggression might be inferred from a history of physical fighting.

To investigate the construct validity of a test, psychologists examine the relationship of test scores to other measures of similar and dissimilar constructs. Evidence of *convergent validity* comes from significant relationships between test scores and theoretically similar constructs. Evidence of *discriminant validity* comes from nonsignificant relationships between test scores and theoretically dissimilar constructs. For example, children's scores on a depression test should correlate significantly with other measures of depression; however, their scores should not correlate significantly with measures of intelligence or aggression.

Finally, psychologists examine the test's **criterion-related validity**. Criterion-related validity refers to the degree to which test scores can be used to infer a probable standing on some external variable of interest (i.e., a criterion; Anastasi & Urbina, 1997). One measure of criterion-related

Image 3.2   The ruler consistently shows that this girl wears a size 10 shoe. It is highly reliable. However, when she tries on a size 10 shoe, it doesn't fit. In this case, the ruler is a reliable, but not valid, measure of shoe size.

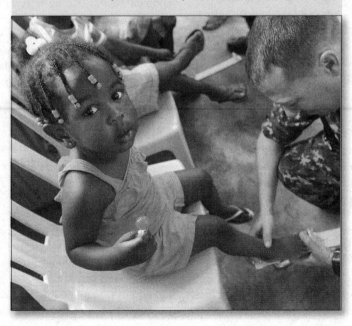

validity is called *concurrent validity*, the degree to which test scores are related to theoretically similar constructs at the same point in time. For example, children's IQ scores should be associated with other external measures of intelligence, such as their grade-point average or the number of honors classes they have taken in high school. Similarly, children's scores on a test of aggression should relate to other indicators of aggression, such as the number of times the child has been disciplined for fighting at school.

Another aspect of criterion-related validity is called *predictive validity*. Predictive validity refers to the ability of test scores to predict theoretically expected outcomes. For example, IQ scores might be expected to predict children's likelihood of attending college or their college grade-point average. Similarly, scores on a childhood aggression test might be expected to predict the likelihood of arrest during adolescence or adulthood.

DIAGNOSIS

DSM-5

The *Diagnostic and Statistical Manual of Mental Disorders-Fifth Edition (DSM-5)* is a compendium of mental disorders published by the American Psychiatric Association (2013) and organized into 20 broad categories based on each disorder's symptom presentation. Each disorder is defined using specific signs and symptoms. To be diagnosed with a given disorder, the individual must show the diagnostic features described in the manual.

DSM-5 uses a categorical approach to diagnostic classification. **Categorical classification** involves dividing mental disorders into types, or categories, based on sets of defining criteria. The categorical approach is also used predominantly in biology and medicine. For example, an animal is classified as a mammal if it (a) has vertebrae, (b) has hair, and (c) feeds its young with mother's milk. An animal that does not possess these features is not a mammal. Similarly, each mental disorder is defined by the presence of specific diagnostic criteria listed in the *DSM-5*. A person without those criteria would not be diagnosed with a given disorder.

The Development of *DSM-5*

The last edition of the diagnostic and statistical manual, *DSM-IV*, was published in 1994 with minor revisions in 2000. Since that time, our understanding of the causes, correlates, and treatment of mental disorders changed because of advances in the research literature. The primary impetus for *DSM-5* was to update the manual to reflect the current research base and the way knowledge was applied in clinical practice.

Psychiatrists, psychologists, and other mental health professionals were invited to serve on work groups to propose changes for *DSM-5*. Each work group focused on a specific class of disorders (e.g., Neurodevelopmental Disorders, Mood Disorders). Each group wanted to use the scientific literature to determine which disorders were most closely associated with one another and how each disorder differed from the others. To accomplish this task, they gathered information in four ways. First, they conducted extensive literature reviews to gain the most up-to-date understanding of each disorder. Second, they reanalyzed data previously collected to determine the effect altering diagnostic criteria might have on the prevalence of each disorder. Third, they asked clinicians to conduct field trials, that is, to use the proposed diagnostic criteria in their practice and report on their reliability, validity, and usefulness in clinical settings. Fourth, they asked for feedback from mental health professionals and members of the public.

Based on this information, the *DSM-5* developers organized disorders using three broad criteria (Robins & Guze, 1970):

1. Do disorders show similar antecedents? For example, disorders caused by similar genetic, sociodemographic, or environmental risks should be grouped together.

2. Do disorders show similar concurrent variables? Disorders that tend to co-occur with each other or are associated with the same underlying biological abnormalities should be grouped together.

3. Do disorders show similar outcomes? Disorders that predict the same outcomes later in life or respond to the same treatments should be grouped together.

The result of their work was a new organization, or "metastructure," for *DSM-5*. Although the number of diagnoses did not change markedly from *DSM-IV* to *DSM-5*, disorders were grouped into broad areas based largely on similar biological and psychological risks, correlates, and outcomes. For example, certain disorders were grouped together into a single diagnostic category because there was little evidence for their differentiation (e.g., Autism Spectrum Disorder, Learning Disorder). Other disorders were separated because they showed different causes, correlates, or outcomes (e.g., Depressive Disorders, Bipolar Disorders). Still other disorders were added to *DSM-5* to reflect recent advances in the research literature (e.g., Disruptive Mood Dysregulation Disorder).

DSM-IV also had several problems that the developers of *DSM-5* wanted to address (Maser et al., 2009). These problems included the following:

• *Co-occurring Disorders:* Many people met diagnostic criteria for multiple disorders at the same time (Krueger & Bezdjian, 2009). Often, the co-occurrence of disorders reflected the actual presence of two distinct disorders in the same person (e.g., a child with both autism and Intellectual Disability). In many cases, however, co-occurrence was the result of the same symptoms acting as criteria for many different disorders. For example, "irritable mood" was a symptom of more than eight disorders in *DSM-IV*; it was not specific to a particular disorder. A person with irritability, therefore, might qualify for several disorders simply because of the way *DSM-IV* was written (Hyman, 2011). To remedy this problem, the developers of *DSM-5* revised the diagnostic criteria for the disorders to make them more specific and thereby reduce artificial comorbidity (Helzer, 2011).

• *Little Developmental Focus:* *DSM-IV* included a category of disorders titled Disorders Usually First Diagnosed in Infancy, Childhood, or Adolescence. These disorders included many conditions often first experienced early in life, such as autism and ADHD. However, it excluded many disorders frequently shown by children and adolescents such as anxiety and depression. By creating a separate childhood disorders category, *DSM-IV* implied that disorders outside this category were reserved for adults. It also implied that disorders such as ADHD were seldom seen in adults (Rutter, 2011).

The developers of *DSM-5* attempted to remedy this problem in three ways (Pine et al., 2011). First, they changed the order of the manual to emphasize the development of psychopathology over the life span. They dropped the "childhood disorders" category and, instead, present disorders in the order in which they typically emerge. For example, disorders such as Intellectual Disability, Autism Spectrum Disorder, and Learning Disorder are presented in the first section of the manual, whereas personality disorders and neurocognitive disorders (e.g., Alzheimer's Disease) occur near the end. Second, the diagnostic criteria vary depending on whether they are applied to children or adults. For example, the symptoms of PTSD are different for preschool-aged children than for older children and adults, because preschoolers often have difficulty describing their thoughts and feelings. Third, *DSM-5* describes how disorders might present differently across the life span. For example, young children with Separation Anxiety Disorder might tantrum to avoid separation from parents whereas older children and adolescents might become "clingy" or avoid peer interactions to avoid separation.

• *Frequent Use of the* "NOS" *Category:* In *DSM-IV*, clinicians were allowed to use the term *Not Otherwise Specified (NOS)* to diagnose people who showed features of a particular disorder but did not meet all of the diagnostic disorder criteria. For example, many children who showed persistent problems with irritable and angry moods were incorrectly diagnosed with Bipolar Disorder, NOS because some of their mood problems resembled Bipolar Disorder. The overuse of the NOS category caused problems because, for some disorders, more children were diagnosed with NOS than the actual disorder itself (e.g., Bipolar Disorder, NOS; Eating Disorder, NOS). To remedy this problem, the developers of *DSM-5* tried to specify when the NOS category should be used for each disorder, to discourage its use as a generic, "catch-all" diagnostic category.

• *International Agreement:* A final limitation of *DSM-IV* was that it did not align with the *International Classification of Diseases (ICD)*, the manual used internationally to classify individuals with medical and psychiatric disorders. Many disorders appearing in the *ICD-10* did not appear in *DSM-IV* and vice versa. Furthermore, disorders with the same title often had different criteria in *DSM-IV* and *ICD-10*. Consequently, the manuals diagnose individuals consistently for some disorders, like depression (87% agreement), but not for others like PTSD (35%) or substance use problems (33%; Andrews, Slade et al., 2009). These differences caused problems when researchers wanted to compare the results of studies conducted in separate countries.

To remedy this problem, the developers of *DSM-5* attempted to align diagnostic criteria with the creation of *ICD-11*. Although there are still points of divergence, the names and criteria for the diagnoses show greater concordance.

Advantages of Diagnosis

Diagnosis has a number of benefits. Perhaps the most obvious benefit to diagnostic classification is parsimony. Imagine that you are a psychologist who has just completed a thorough assessment of a 3-year-old child with suspected developmental delays. You discover that the child shows severe and pervasive problems with social communication and repetitive behavior. Instead of describing each of these symptoms, you can simply use the appropriate diagnostic label: Autism Spectrum Disorder. Diagnostic classification is used for the sake of parsimony in medicine, too. Physicians do not describe children as having mild fever, upset stomach, sweaty palms, flushed face, gastrointestinal upset, vomiting, diarrhea, dizziness, and fatigue; instead, they simply say the child has influenza.

A second advantage to diagnosis is that it can aid in professional communication. Another mental health professional who sees your diagnosis knows that your client exhibits a cluster of symptoms described in *DSM-5*. The second professional does not need to conduct her own assessment of the child to arrive at an independent diagnosis to know something about the child's symptoms.

A third advantage of diagnostic classification is that it can aid in prediction. If you know that your client has Autism Spectrum Disorder, you can use the existing research literature to determine prognosis. For example, most children with autism show chronic impairment in social and communicative functioning; however, prognosis is best among children with higher intelligence and more developed language skills before age 5. The research literature also indicates that children who participate in treatment before age 4 often have the best developmental outcomes. You might use this information to provide parents with realistic expectations regarding their child's future so that they can make more informed decisions regarding treatment.

A fourth and closely related benefit of diagnostic classification is that it can help plan treatment. If you know that your client has Autism Spectrum Disorder, you can also use the existing research literature to plan an intervention. For example, a number of studies have indicated that early, intensive behavioral interventions can be effective in improving the social and communication skills of young children with autism. Other forms of treatment, such as art and music therapy, have far less empirical support. Consequently, you can use knowledge gained from research studies involving other children with autism to help your client.

Fifth, diagnostic classification can help individuals obtain social or educational services. For example, the Individuals with Disabilities Education Act (IDEA; U.S. Department of Education, 2006) is a federal law that entitles children with Autism Spectrum Disorder to special education because of their developmental disability. Special education might involve enrollment in a special needs preschool, early intensive behavioral training paid by the school district, provision of a classroom aide or tutor, academic accommodations, life skills training, and other services. Children may be entitled to receive these services only if they are diagnosed with autism or another developmental disorder. Consequently, diagnostic classification is sometimes a means to obtaining educational or social benefits.

A sixth benefit of diagnostic classification is that diagnosis can sometimes help parents. Although no parent is happy when his or her child has a psychiatric diagnosis, many parents feel relieved when their child's disorder is finally identified. After hearing that her 3-year-old child had autism, one parent said, "Well, I finally know what's wrong. I always suspected it and now I know. I suppose we can finally move forward." Diagnostic labels can also help parents contact the parents of children with similar disorders in order to share information and gain social support.

Finally, diagnostic classification can facilitate scientific discovery. Researchers who conduct studies on the causes and treatment of Autism Spectrum Disorder can compare the results of their investigations with the findings of others. Indeed, many studies are conducted by teams of researchers in multiple locations. As long as researchers use the same diagnostic criteria and procedures to classify children, results can be combined to generate a more thorough understanding of the disorder.

Disadvantages of Diagnosis

The DSM-5 classification system also has some inherent disadvantages and risks (Hyman, 2011; Rutter, 2011). The first main drawback of the DSM-5 classification system is that it often gains parsimony at the expense of detailed information. Although a diagnostic label can convey considerable information to others, it cannot possibly convey the same amount of information as a thorough description of the individual. Of particular concern is the fact that DSM-5 diagnoses do not take into account the individual's environment. Many so-called maladaptive behaviors exhibited by children and adolescents with mental disorders can be seen as attempts to adapt to stressful environments. For example, some physically abused children come to believe that other people have hostile motives and intentions. Although this sense of mistrust is problematic, it may be best understood in terms of the child's attempt to cope with a history of physical abuse.

A second drawback of the DSM-5 lies in its exclusive focus on individuals. DSM-5 conceptualizes psychopathology as something that exists within the person. However, childhood disorders are often relational in nature. For example, Oppositional Defiant Disorder (ODD) is diagnosed in children who show patterns of noncompliant and oppositional behavior toward others, especially adults in positions of authority. Similarly, Separation Anxiety Disorder (SAD) is displayed by children who fear separating from caregivers. Considerable research indicates that the quality of parent-child interactions plays an important role in the development of both ODD and SAD. Furthermore, treatment for both disorders relies heavily on parental involvement. However, in the DSM-5 system, both ODD and SAD are diagnosed in the child. The DSM-5 approach to diagnosis can overlook the role caregivers, family members, and peers play in the development and maintenance of children's problems.

A third drawback in the DSM-5 system is that distinctions between normality and abnormality are sometimes arbitrary. In the categorical approach used by DSM-5, individuals either have a given disorder or they do not. For example, to be diagnosed with ADHD, a child needs to show at least six symptoms of inattention or hyperactivity-impulsivity. If the child displays only five of the required six symptoms, he would not qualify for the ADHD diagnosis. However, as we will see, many youths who show subthreshold symptomatology experience significant distress and impairment and often do not differ appreciably from children who fully meet diagnostic criteria.

An alternative approach to categorical classification is **dimensional (continuous) classification**. Advocates of the dimensional approach to classification recognize that most psychological disorders fall along a continuum ranging from total symptom absence to severe symptom presentation. At any given time, a person can show all, some, or none of the symptoms for a given disorder. Rather than dichotomizing people into either having the disorder or not having the disorder, advocates of the dimensional approach prefer to describe individuals based on the number or severity of their symptoms (Achenbach, 1982; Kamphaus, Reynolds, & Imperato-McCammon, 1999).

For example, a clinician might ask parents to complete the BASC-2 rating scale about their child. Recall that the BASC-2 provides norm-referenced scores on a number of different dimensions, such as attention, aggressive behavior, anxiety, and depression. Instead of diagnosing a child with a single disorder, the psychologist might use BASC-2 ratings to describe the child's functioning on all relevant dimensions.

For example, the clinician might notice that the child has average attention, moderately high levels of aggression, and extremely high levels of anxiety and depression compared to other children his age.

The developers of *DSM-5* (2013) have attempted to incorporate dimensional assessment into their classification system. For example, after determining whether an individual meets diagnostic criteria for a given disorder (a categorical decision), clinicians can specify the severity of the disorder using a semi-continuous rating (e.g., mild, moderate, severe).

A fourth limitation of the *DSM-5* classification system is that there are often unclear boundaries between diagnostic categories. Categorical classification systems, like *DSM-5*, work best when all members of a diagnostic group are homogeneous, when there are clear boundaries between two different diagnoses, and when diagnostic categories are mutually exclusive. Unfortunately, these conditions are not always met.

There are often unclear boundaries between different mental disorders. For example, children with Bipolar Disorder, a serious mood disorder seen in approximately 1% to 2% of youth, often have ADHD. Indeed, some studies indicate that 90% of youths with Bipolar Disorder also meet diagnostic criteria for ADHD. The presence of multiple disorders in the same individual is called **comorbidity**. Comorbidity is actually very common among youths with psychiatric diagnoses; it is more likely that a child referred for treatment will have multiple disorders rather than only one. In some cases, comorbidity is caused by the child actually having two distinct disorders. For example, many children with Bipolar Disorder clearly show symptoms of ADHD, even when they are not having mood problems. Sometimes, however, high rates of comorbidity may be due to unclear boundaries between *DSM-5* diagnostic categories. Both Bipolar Disorder and ADHD are characterized by an increase in behavioral activity, short attention span, distractibility, talkativeness, and impulsive behavior. Some children with Bipolar Disorder may mistakenly be diagnosed with ADHD because of this overlap in symptoms.

A fifth criticism of the *DSM-5* system is that certain diagnostic criteria are subjective and value-laden (Jensen, Hoagwood, & Zitner, 2006). Many terms that are part of the diagnostic criteria are vague and subject to the interpretation of individual clinicians. For example, the *DSM-5* diagnostic criteria include terms like *failure*, *distress*, and *deficit* without clear definitions. Almost every disorder in the *DSM-5* requires the individual to show "clinically significant impairment" in order to be diagnosed; however, the term *clinically significant impairment* is vague and tautological. After all, clinically significant impairment is the type of impairment that a clinician considers severe enough to need treatment (Fulford, 1994; Jensen et al., 2006).

A final weakness of the *DSM-5* approach is that diagnostic classification can lead to stigma. **Stigma** occurs when people judge children, adolescents, or families because of the youth's diagnostic label. Stigmatization of mental illness comes in many forms. During casual conversation, people use terms like *crazy*, *wacked*, *nuts*, and *psycho* without giving much thought to the implications these words have for people with mental illness. Children may use the derogatory term *retard* to describe peers who behave foolishly. Parents of children with psychological and behavioral disorders often report discrimination from school and medical personnel because of their child's illness. Some insurance companies discriminate against individuals with mental disorders by not providing equal coverage for mental and physical illnesses. Movies and television shows depict people with mental illness as violent, unpredictable, deranged, or devious. Even children with mental illness are portrayed in a negative light on film. Broadcasters disproportionately report individuals with mental illness behaving erratically or violently (Hinshaw, 2006).

Stigmatization can negatively affect youths and their families in several ways. First, it can cause a sense of shame or degradation that decreases self-esteem and lowers self-worth. The negative self-image generated by the social judgments of others, in turn, can exacerbate symptoms or hinder progress in therapy. Second, stigmatization can lead to **self-fulfilling prophecies**. Youths may believe that they are deviant, "damaged," or "deranged" because of their diagnostic label. In some cases, children may alter their behavior to fit the diagnostic label or use the diagnosis to excuse disruptive behavior problems. For example, a child might explain the reason for a recent suspension from school: "I can't help it. It's not my fault. It's my ADHD." Third, stigmatization can decrease the likelihood that families will seek psychological services because they want to avoid the shame of the diagnostic label. Indeed, more than three fourths of youths in the United States who show significant behavioral, emotional, and learning problems do not receive treatment, many because parents do not want their children assigned a diagnostic label (Hinshaw, 2005).

PSYCHOTHERAPY

Most mental health professionals spend the majority of their time practicing psychotherapy. However, no one has provided a definition of psychotherapy that satisfies all practitioners. One influential definition of psychotherapy has been offered by Raymond Corsini (2005), an expert in clinical interventions:

> Psychotherapy is a formal process of interaction between two parties . . . for the purpose of amelioration of distress in one of the two parties relative to any or all of the following areas of disability or malfunction: cognitive functions (disorders of thinking), affective functions (suffering or emotional discomforts), or behavioral functions (inadequacy of behavior). . . . The therapist [has] some theory of personality's origins, development, maintenance and change along with some method of treatment logically related to that theory and professional and legal approval to act as a therapist. (p. 1)

According to this definition, psychotherapy is an interpersonal process. Therapy must involve interactions between at least two individuals: a therapist and a client. The therapist can be any professional who has specialized training in the delivery of mental health services. Therapists can include psychologists, psychiatrists, counselors, and social workers; however, therapists can also include teachers and other paraprofessionals who have received training and supervision in the use of psychosocial interventions. The therapist uses a theory about the causes of psychopathology to develop a means of alleviating the client's psychological distress. The client is an individual experiencing some degree of distress or impairment who agrees to participate in the therapeutic interaction to bring about change.

Common Factors in Therapy

The purpose of psychotherapy is to alter the thoughts, feelings, or behaviors of the client. Change occurs primarily through interactions with the therapist. Specifically, the therapist provides certain conditions, consistent with his or her theory of psychopathology, to improve the functioning of the client. Jerome Frank (1973) has suggested that certain factors are common to all forms of psychotherapy. These factors include the presence of a trusting relationship between the client and therapist, a specific setting in which change is supposed to take place, a theory or explanation for the client's suffering, and a therapeutic ritual in which the client and therapist must engage to alleviate the client's suffering. Frank argues these common or "nonspecific" factors of psychotherapy have been primary components of psychological and spiritual healing since ancient times.

In his person-centered approach to counseling, Carl Rogers (1957) identified three **necessary and sufficient factors for therapeutic change.** First, the therapist must provide the client with *unconditional positive regard;* that is, the therapist must be supportive and nonjudgmental of the client's behavior and characteristics in order to establish a relationship built on trust and acceptance. Second, the therapist must respond to the client with *congruence;* that is, the therapist must show his or her genuine feelings toward the client and avoid remaining emotionally detached, distant, or disengaged. Rogers described the ideal therapeutic relationship as "transparent"; that is, the client should easily witness the clinician's genuine feelings during the therapy session. The therapist does not try to hide his or her feelings or put on airs. Third, the therapist must show *empathy* toward the client. Specifically, the therapist must strive to understand the world from the client's perspective and take a profound interest in the client's thoughts, feelings, and actions. Rogers believed that clients whose therapists provided them with these three conditions would experience the greatest benefits from treatment.

Few practitioners dispute the importance of the psychotherapeutic factors identified by Frank (1973) and Rogers (1957). However, most clinicians regard these common factors as necessary but *not* sufficient to bring about change. Most therapists supplement these common factors with specific strategies and techniques consistent with their theories of the origins of psychopathology. The specific therapeutic methods they use depend on the system of psychotherapy they practice and the presenting problem of the client (Frank & Frank, 2004).

Systems of Psychotherapy

There are hundreds of systems or "schools" of psychotherapy. They can be loosely categorized in terms of the level at which they approach clients' presenting problems. Specifically, the various systems of psychotherapy address different levels of the client's behavioral, cognitive, and social-emotional functioning. These levels include (a) the client's overt behaviors and symptoms, (b) the client's patterns of thinking, (c) the client's family relationships, (d) the client's other interpersonal relationships, and (e) the client's knowledge of himself and his intrapersonal functioning (Prochaska & Norcross, 2003).

To understand the various systems of psychotherapy, consider a 16-year-old girl, Anna, who suffers from Bulimia Nervosa, an eating disorder usually characterized by recurrent binge eating and vomiting. The type of treatment that Anna receives will largely depend on the level(s) of functioning to which her therapist attends. Anna may be treated from the approach of behaviorism, cognitive therapy, family system therapy, interpersonal therapy, or psychodynamic psychotherapy.

Behavior Therapy

Behavior therapy focuses primarily on the client's overt actions and maladaptive patterns of behavior. Behavior therapy has its origins in the work of Joseph Wolpe (1958), Hans Eysenck (1959), and B. F. Skinner (1974). Behavior therapists address clients' problems at the symptom level. Behavior therapists do not assume that underlying personality traits or intrapsychic conflicts influence behavior. Instead, behavior is largely determined by **environmental contingencies**, that is, environmental conditions that either reinforce or punish certain behaviors. The goal of behavior therapy is usually to alter these environmental contingencies to increase the likelihood that clients will engage in more adaptive patterns of action.

A behavior therapist would carefully note the frequency of Anna's binge eating. Then, the therapist would likely perform a functional analysis of Anna's maladaptive eating behavior. Specifically, the therapist might find that the antecedents of Anna's bingeing often include being alone and feeling hungry. Furthermore, the consequences of Anna's bingeing might include a temporary reduction in hunger but more lasting feelings of guilt and shame.

Over the course of treatment, the therapist might teach Anna to monitor her binge eating, its antecedents, and its consequences. Then, the therapist might help Anna avoid antecedents that trigger binges. For example, the therapist might help Anna eat more regular, balanced meals to avoid feelings of intense hunger. Similarly, the therapist might help Anna identify ways to avoid the loneliness and boredom that often trigger her binges. The therapist might encourage Anna to become more involved in after-school activities or teach her to develop more satisfying peer relationships. By altering environmental factors that elicit or reinforce her binges, Anna should be able to decrease the frequency of her symptoms.

Cognitive Therapy

Cognitive therapy focuses primarily on the client's patterns of thinking about herself, others, and the future. One cognitive therapist, Aaron Beck (1976), argued that people experience psychological distress and impairment when they engage in systematic errors in thinking called **cognitive distortions.** Specifically, psychological distress occurs when people hold beliefs or perceptions that do not correspond to reality and cast themselves, others, and the world in a bleak, threatening, or dangerous light. For example, people who hold overly negative, pessimistic views of themselves, others, and the future can experience depression. Their beliefs lead them to anticipate failure and doubt their ability to reach their goals. Alternatively, individuals who believe that other people are hostile and critical, who view the world as a dangerous place, and who see themselves as largely unable to control external events may experience anxiety. According to Beck, cognitive therapists help clients identify cognitive distortions and adopt more realistic ways of thinking.

Another cognitive therapist, Albert Ellis, claimed that **irrational beliefs** often contribute to psychological distress and maladaptive ways of acting (Ellis, 2005; Ellis & Harper, 1961). When people engage in absolute, black-or-white thinking, they often place considerable pressure on themselves leading to depression, anxiety, or anger. For example, people who make dogmatic demands on themselves (e.g., "I *must* get into graduate school") often set themselves up for failure and increase their likelihood of low self-worth. Similarly, people who place rigid demands on others (e.g., "My teacher *should* have given me a higher grade on the exam") can experience anger and frustration. According to Ellis, cognitive therapists challenge clients' absolute, dogmatic, and rigid beliefs and teach clients to think more logically.

A cognitive therapist would focus her attention on the thoughts associated with Anna's bingeing and vomiting. A therapist adopting Beck's (1976) approach to cognitive therapy might help Anna identify cognitive distortions that occur before she vomits. Specifically, Anna might think, "I'm afraid of becoming fat. If I become fat, then no one will love me." The therapist might help Anna challenge this belief to determine whether it is true or whether it is a distortion of reality. For example, the therapist might ask Anna, "If you become fat, what's the likelihood that *no one* will love you?" Then the therapist might help Anna think more realistically about her eating behavior. For example, the therapist might encourage Anna to adopt a different thought, like, "I know I feel terrible right now, but if I don't throw up I'll feel OK in a little while."

A therapist adopting Ellis' (2005) perspective of cognitive therapy might help Anna identify irrational beliefs that contribute to her vomiting. For example, Anna might hold the irrational belief, "I need to be thin and beautiful so that people will love me." The therapist would likely challenge this belief, arguing that Anna does not necessarily *need* to be thin or beautiful in order to be loved. Furthermore, the therapist would help Anna identify more logical ways of thinking. For example, the therapist might encourage Anna to think, "I'd *like* to be thin and beautiful, but it wouldn't be terrible if I gained some weight."

Both Beck's (1976) and Ellis' (2005) approaches to cognitive therapy emphasize the connection between thoughts, feelings, and actions. As clients learn to think in more realistic, logical ways, they may experience fewer negative emotions and behave in a more adaptive manner. Often, cognitive therapists incorporate elements of behavior therapy into their treatments. **Cognitive-behavioral therapy** refers to the integrated use of cognitive and behavioral approaches to treatment.

Family Systems Therapy

Family therapists focus on patterns of communication and interaction among family members. There are many different types of family therapy. Most have certain features in common. For example, all family therapists view the family as a **system,** that is, a network of connected individuals who influence and partially direct each other's behavior. Viewing the family as a system has several important implications for therapy. First, family therapists see the entire family as their "client," not just the person who is identified by certain family members as "the one with the problem." Second, a systems approach to treatment assumes that change in one member of the family will necessarily change all members of the family. Consequently, family therapists believe that helping one or two family members improve their functioning can often lead to symptom reduction in the family member with the identified problem.

One form of family therapy, developed by Salvador Minuchin (1974), is **structural family therapy.** Structural family therapists are chiefly concerned with the quality of relationships between family members. In healthy families, parents form strong social-emotional bonds, or alliances, with each other that are based on mutual respect and open lines of communication. Furthermore, in healthy families, parents form boundaries between themselves and their children. Specifically, parents respect children's developing autonomy and provide for their social-emotional needs, but they also remain figures of authority in the family.

In unhealthy families, however, alliances are formed between one parent and the children, leaving the other parent disconnected or estranged from the rest of the family. For example, mother and daughter might form an alliance against father because of father's excessive use of alcohol. Father might feel alienated from his family while mother and daughter might grow to resent father. Furthermore, in unhealthy families, boundaries between parents and children are often overly rigid or excessively diffuse. **Disengaged families** are characterized by overly rigid boundaries, in which open communication between family members is stifled, and members feel disconnected from one another. In contrast, **enmeshed families** are characterized by diffuse boundaries where family members lack autonomy and constantly intrude into one another's lives.

Most family therapists would insist on seeing Anna and her parents together, for at least part of treatment. The therapist would likely pay attention to alliances and boundaries in Anna's family and the way Anna's eating disorder might help to maintain the family system in a maladaptive way. For example, the therapist might discover that Anna's parents frequently argue with one another and are considering a divorce. The therapist might notice that the onset of Anna's symptoms coincided with the onset of her parents' marital problems. The therapist might hypothesize that Anna's eating symptoms serve to maintain the family system by distracting her parents from their marital problems.

A family therapist might also notice that Anna's parents are overprotective and excessively demanding. The therapist might interpret Anna's desire to lose weight as a maladaptive attempt to gain the approval of her parents. The therapist might refer Anna's parents to a marital therapist to help them improve the quality of their relationship. At the same time, the therapist might work with Anna and her parents to help improve communication at home. One goal of therapy might be to help Anna's parents give her more autonomy over her day-to-day behavior.

Interpersonal Therapy

Interpersonal therapy focuses primarily on the quality of clients' relationships with others. Interpersonal therapy is based on the theoretical writings of Harry Stack Sullivan (1953) and John Bowlby (1973). Sullivan believed that interpersonal relationships are essential for mental health. Friendships in childhood help youngsters develop a sense of identity and self-worth and form the basis for more intimate relationships in adulthood. Problems in interpersonal relationships can interfere with social-emotional functioning and self-concept. Bowlby (1969), the founder of attachment theory, believed that people form mental models of interpersonal relationships through their interaction with caregivers and other significant individuals in their lives. Mental models built on trust and expectations for care promote later social-emotional adjustment. However, mental models based on mistrust and inconsistent care can interfere with the development of social-emotional competence.

Interpersonal therapists conceptualize psychopathology as arising from disruptions or problems in interpersonal relationships (Klerman & Weissman, 1993). First, interpersonal relationships can be disrupted when a loved one dies or is separated from the family. Second, relationship problems can arise when a person experiences a major change in social roles (e.g., transitions from junior high to high school). Third, problems can occur when a person's social roles conflict with the expectations of others (e.g., parents and adolescents disagree about dating or the importance of attending college). Finally, interpersonal problems can occur when an individual has interpersonal deficits that interfere with his ability to make and keep friends (e.g., excessive shyness or lack of social skills). An interpersonal therapist attempts to identify and correct relationship problems that might contribute to the client's primary diagnosis (Image 3.3).

An interpersonal therapist might notice that Anna's eating problems occurred shortly after her father changed jobs and the family moved to a new neighborhood and school district. The therapist might interpret Anna's eating disorder as a maladaptive attempt to lose weight, appear attractive to others, and gain acceptance by peers at her new school. Through a combination of support and suggestions, the therapist would help Anna grieve the loss of her old neighborhood and friends, cope with her move to a new school, and find more effective ways to make new friends.

Psychodynamic Therapy

Psychodynamic therapy focuses chiefly on intrapsychic conflict, that is, conflict within the self. Psychodynamic therapy is based on the theoretical and clinical work of Sigmund Freud (1923/1961), Anna Freud (1936), and a host of so-called neo-Freudian theorists. Although there are a vast number of psychodynamic approaches to therapy, almost all believe that unconscious thoughts, feelings, dreams, images, or wishes influence our behavior. According to the **topographic theory of mind**, the mind can be divided into two levels, the conscious and the unconscious. Although unconscious mental activity cannot be directly accessed, unconscious mental processes influence and direct day-to-day actions. The principle of psychic determinism holds that behavior is not random; actions are influenced by both conscious will and unconscious mental activity. From the psychodynamic perspective, psychological symptoms often reflect unconscious mental activity.

The primary goal of psychodynamic therapy is to provide insight, that is, to make the person aware of unconscious mental conflict that contributes to his psychological symptoms. *Insight* is believed to result in symptom alleviation and more adaptive behavior.

The technique that the therapist uses to help the client achieve insight depends on the type of psychodynamic therapy she uses. One way therapists help clients gain insight is by paying attention to the client's **transference**, the attitude and patterns of interaction that the client develops toward

Image 3.3 Interpersonal therapists assume that childhood problems emerge from disruptions in relationships, like separation from loved ones or major life transitions. These children watch a play in which *Sesame Street* characters welcome a girl who just moved to town because her parents were deployed in the military. The children in the audience are also from military families.

Source: Image courtesy of the U.S. Department of Defense.

the therapist. Transference is believed to reflect the client's history of interpersonal relationships and unconscious fantasies projected onto the therapist. For example, an adolescent who has been physically abused or neglected by her parents might express mistrust and hostility toward the therapist in the transference relationship. The client might unconsciously expect the therapist to abandon, reject, or mistreat her in a way similar to her parents. The therapist can use transference to help the client gain awareness of mental conflict. For example, the therapist might interpret the client's transference by suggesting, "I notice that whenever we talk about ending treatment, you get very angry and resentful toward me. I wonder if you're afraid that I'm going to abandon you?" Over the course of therapy, as clients gain greater insight into the causes of their distress, they may experience symptom reduction, develop more effective means of coping with anxiety, and achieve more satisfying relationships with others.

A psychodynamic therapist might focus her attention on Anna's transference. For example, over the course of multiple sessions, the therapist might notice that Anna often acts helpless and childlike during therapy sessions, as if she wants the therapist to tell her what to do. Furthermore, Anna might become frustrated and angry toward the therapist when the therapist remains nondirective and insists that Anna solve problems for herself. The therapist might interpret Anna's transference as an unconscious desire to remain in a childlike state. The therapist might suggest that as long as Anna

remains helpless and childlike, she does not have to assume adult responsibilities that cause her considerable distress: finding a boyfriend, going to college, leaving home. The therapist might suggest that Anna's eating disorder ensures that her parents will coddle her and provide her with attention and sympathy, rather than insist that she develop more autonomous, age-appropriate behavior.

Psychotherapy With Children, Adolescents, and Families

Child Versus Adult Psychotherapy

Child psychotherapy and adult psychotherapy differ in many ways. First, there are often *motivational differences* between child and adolescent clients and their adult counterparts. Most adults refer themselves to therapy; by the time they make the initial appointment, they are at least partially motivated to change their behavior. Indeed, some evidence suggests that the very act of seeking treatment and making an initial appointment is itself therapeutic (Howard, Kopta, Krause, & Orlinsky, 1986; Kopta, 2003). In contrast, children and adolescents are almost always referred by others (e.g., parents and teachers). Youths seldom recognize their behavioral, emotional, and social problems and typically show low motivation to change. Indeed, many youths with psychiatric disorders show very little psychological distress; instead, distress is usually experienced by other people in the children's lives. Most therapists initially try to increase children's willingness to trust the therapist and participate in treatment.

Second, *cognitive and social-emotional differences* between children, adolescents, and adults can influence the therapeutic process. Most forms of child and adolescent therapy are downward extensions of adult therapeutic techniques. However, by virtue of their youth, children and adolescents often lack many of the cognitive, social, and emotional skills necessary to fully benefit from these techniques. For example, cognitive therapy depends greatly on clients' ability to engage in metacognition, that is, to think about their own thinking. However, metacognitive skills develop across childhood and adolescence; some youths may find cognitive therapy too abstract and difficult. Similarly, cognitive and insight-oriented therapies often rely heavily on verbal exchanges between client and therapist. Young children, with underdeveloped verbal abilities, may not benefit from these types of "talk" therapy.

Third, the *goals of therapy* often differ for children compared to adults. In adult psychotherapy, the primary objective of treatment is usually symptom reduction. Most therapists and clients consider treatment to be successful when clients return to a previous state of functioning. In therapy with children and adolescents, return to previous functioning is often inadequate. Instead, the goal of child and adolescent therapy is to alleviate symptoms while simultaneously promoting children's development. For example, a child with ADHD might participate in behavior therapy and take medication to alleviate his hyperactivity and inattention. However, these behavior problems have likely alienated him from classmates. Consequently, the therapist might have an additional goal of helping the child gain acceptance in the classroom and overcome a history of peer rejection.

Fourth, children and adolescents often have less *control over their ability to change* than do adults. Adults usually have greater autonomy over their behavior and environmental circumstances than do children. For example, a woman who is depressed might decide to exercise more, join a social support group, practice meditation, change jobs, or leave her boyfriend. However, a child who is depressed because of his parents' martial conflict has far less ability to alter his environment. Although he might decide to exercise or participate in extracurricular activities, he is unable to leave home or get new parents. Instead, the boy's social-emotional functioning is closely connected to the behavior of his parents. Consequently, the boy's capacity to change is directly associated with his parents' involvement in therapy.

Finally, children and adolescents are more likely to have *multiple psychiatric conditions* compared to adults. In fact, comorbidity is the rule rather than the exception among children and adolescents with psychiatric disorders. Among youths in the community, approximately 50% who have one disorder also have a second disorder. Among youths referred to clinics, rates of comorbidity range from 50% to 90%, depending on the age of the child and the specific problem. Clinicians who treat children and adolescents must address multiple disorders simultaneously, often without the zealous participation of their young clients (Kazdin & Weisz, 2003).

Does Child and Adolescent Psychotherapy Work?

One way to examine the efficacy of child psychotherapy is to use meta-analysis. In a **meta-analysis**, researchers combine the results of several studies into a single analysis. To perform a meta-analysis, researchers locate all of the research examining the efficacy of child and adolescent psychotherapy. Each study typically compares at least one group of children who received treatment with another group of children who served as controls. Then, for each study, researchers calculate a numerical value that indicates the difference between the two groups' scores on some measure of functioning after treatment. Many researchers use the following formula:

$$ES = (M_{\text{treatment group}} - M_{\text{control group}})/SD_{\text{control group}}$$

In this formula, we subtract the mean score for the control group from the mean score for the treatment group to tell us the difference between groups after treatment. Positive scores indicate that the treatment group fared better than the control group after treatment; that is, the therapy worked. Negative scores indicate that the control group fared better than the treatment group; that is, the therapy was harmful.

Next, we take this difference between groups and divide it by the standard deviation of the control group. This tells us how many standard deviations apart the two groups are after treatment. We call this value the **effect size (ES)**.

Since the ES is in standard units, we can combine the effect sizes of many studies, even if they used different measures to evaluate therapy outcomes. Specifically, we might calculate the average effect size across all studies that have investigated the efficacy of some form of psychotherapy. Most researchers consider effect sizes of 0.20 to be small, 0.50 to be medium, and 0.80 to be large (Cohen, 1988).

Four large meta-analyses have investigated the efficacy of child and adolescent psychotherapy (Casey & Berman, 1985; Kazdin, Bass, Ayers, & Rodgers, 1990; Weisz, Weiss, Alicke, & Klotz, 1987; Weisz, Weiss, Han, Granger, & Morton, 1995). Results of these four meta-analyses are quite consistent. Average effect sizes ranged between 0.71 and 0.88 and are considered moderate to large. These average effect sizes are similar to the average effect sizes obtained from studies involving psychotherapy for adults (Shapiro & Shapiro, 1982; Smith & Glass, 1977). These findings suggest that psychotherapy for children and adolescents works, that youngsters who participate in therapy often fare much better than youngsters in control groups, and that the efficacy of child and adolescent therapy is comparable to the efficacy of therapy for adults (see Figure 3.4).

Figure 3.4 Does Psychotherapy Work?

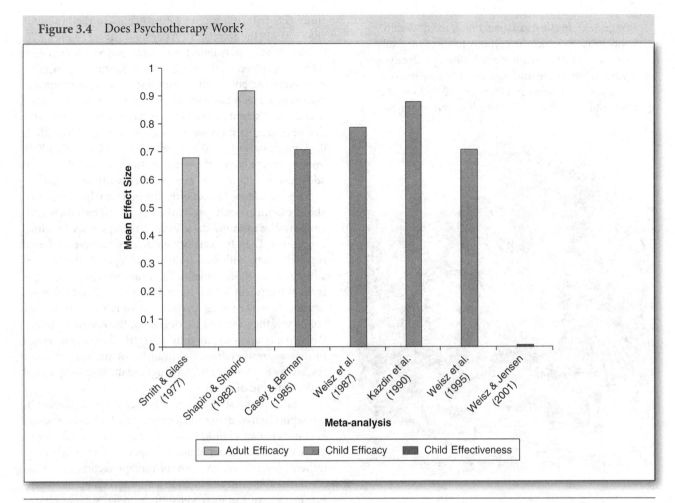

Source: Based on Weisz, Jensen, & McLeod (2005).

Note: Large meta-analyses indicate that adults (light gray) and youths (medium gray) who receive psychotherapy show greater improvement than controls who do not receive therapy. These findings indicate that both adult and child therapy is efficacious. Studies investigating the effectiveness of child therapy (dark gray; final bar only) have yielded more disappointing results in real-life situations.

What Therapies Work Best?

Although it is encouraging to know that therapy for children and adolescents is efficacious, we probably want to know *which* system of therapy works best. Researchers who examine the efficacy of adult psychotherapy have generally concluded that all forms of therapy are approximately equally effective. No single system of psychotherapy works best under all circumstances (Lambert & Ogles, 2004). Some researchers have referred to this phenomenon as the **dodo verdict** (Parloff, 1984; Rosenzweig, 1936). In *Alice in Wonderland,* Alice watches a race in which each contestant starts in a different position, each races in a different direction, and all contestants win. One of the characters in the book, the dodo bird, concludes, "Everybody has won, and all must have prizes." So, too, in adult psychotherapy, there is little evidence that any form of therapy is superior to any other form of therapy, overall (Image 3.4).

Weisz and colleagues (1995) performed a meta-analysis to investigate whether the dodo verdict applied to child and adolescent therapy. Their meta-analysis yielded three important results:

1. Behavioral therapies tended to yield greater effect sizes ($M = 0.76$) than nonbehavioral therapies ($M = 0.35$). Behavioral techniques, such as classical and operant conditioning, modeling, and skills training, yielded more beneficial outcomes than other, nonbehavioral techniques (e.g., psychodynamic treatments).

2. Children's age and gender predicted their response to therapy. Treatment tended to work better for adolescents than for children and was more efficacious for girls than boys. On the other hand, therapy was equally efficacious for both externalizing (e.g., disruptive behavior problems) and internalizing disorders (e.g., depression, anxiety).

3. Children show global and specific improvements in therapy. Previous research with adults showed that therapy often has global effects on clients. Adult clients often experience improvement in a wide range of thoughts, feelings, and

Image 3.4 *In Alice in Wonderland*, the dodo bird holds a race in which "everybody has won, and all must have prizes." In adult psychotherapy, the dodo verdict refers to the finding that all therapies work equally well, on average. However, the dodo verdict may not be true for child and adolescent therapies.

Source: Image courtesy Project Gutenberg.

behaviors, even if these behaviors were not the focus of therapy. Weisz and colleagues (1995) found that children, like adults, experience some global benefits from participating in therapy. However, the greatest improvement in children's functioning occurs in problem areas specifically targeted for treatment. The average effect size for problems specifically addressed in therapy was 0.60, whereas the average effect size for problems not a focus of treatment was 0.30.

Caveats in Efficacy Research

We might conclude from the results of the meta-analyses that psychotherapy usually improves the well-being of children and adolescents who are referred to treatment. However, we must keep in mind the source of the information used in these meta-analyses (Weisz, Doss, & Hawley, 2005). First, the researchers who conducted these meta-analyses tended to calculate the average effect size across all studies. If the effect sizes were 0.50, 0.70, and 0.90 in three studies, respectively, their average effect size would be 0.70. Calculating the average in this way ignores the number of children in each of the three studies. For example, if there were 100 children in the first study (ES = 0.50), 20 children in the second

study (ES = 0.70), and only 10 students in the last study (ES = 0.90), the average effect size for the three studies, 0.70, would not accurately reflect the overall outcome for children who participated in the studies. Consequently, researchers now tend to weight the effect sizes of studies, assigning greater importance to studies with larger samples. If we look at the overall effect size of child and adolescent psychotherapy using the weighting method, we see that the average effect size is 0.54, much lower than 0.70 (Weisz, Weiss, Han et al., 1995). We can conclude that the effects of therapy on children and adolescents are probably "moderate" rather than "strong."

Perhaps more importantly, the meta-analyses reported above examined only psychotherapy efficacy studies. **Efficacy studies** examine the effects of therapy under optimal conditions. They are usually conducted by university-based research teams with well-trained and supervised clinicians administering the treatments. Clinicians tend to use only one form of treatment, which is carefully planned and followed, using a therapy manual. Participants in efficacy studies are voluntary; they agree to participate in the research project. Participants are also carefully selected. They are screened to make sure they have the disorder or problem that the researcher is interested in studying, and they typically do not have comorbid disorders.

However, most child and adolescent psychotherapy is not administered under ideal conditions. Typically, therapy is conducted in clinics, hospitals, and schools. Clinicians are usually not trained in any one specific form of therapy; rather, they rely on an array of therapy techniques. Most often, these techniques include active and empathic listening; expressive and interpretive techniques, such as play or art therapy; addressing children's or parents' weekly concerns; and providing a warm and responsive therapeutic alliance with the family (Weisz, Jensen, et al., 2005). These approaches tend to be based on the clinician's experience as a therapist. Clinicians tend to have large caseloads with little time for careful review and preparation. They may also be limited by insurance companies in the number and kinds of therapies they provide. In most clinical settings, clients are not hand selected; clinicians treat almost anyone who seeks help. Furthermore, children and adolescents are often unwilling to participate in treatment; they are brought to therapy by their parents. Finally, clients tend to have multiple, often poorly defined problems that sometimes do not fit neatly into *DSM-5* diagnostic categories.

Does child and adolescent therapy work in these more ordinary conditions? Little research has been directed to answer this question. A handful of **effectiveness studies** have been conducted, investigating the ability of child and adolescent therapy to improve children's functioning under real-world conditions. The mean effect size for 14 effectiveness studies is –.001 (Weisz, Doss et al., 2005). This suggests that there is little evidence that child and adolescent therapy, as it is typically practiced, benefits children and adolescents as a group. Therapy can and does help individual children; however, there is little research supporting its effectiveness overall. Clearly, more effectiveness studies need to be conducted to examine the usefulness of therapy under real-world conditions.

Summary and Conclusions About Treatment

What can we learn from research on the efficacy and effectiveness of child and adolescent psychotherapy? First, we can say that psychotherapy with children and adolescents is efficacious. Over the past 50 years, researchers have identified a number of therapy techniques that can be used to treat both externalizing and internalizing problems. These interventions produce meaningful improvements in the lives of families who participate in them. Second, for many childhood problems, professionals have limited knowledge of what works. For example, there is yet no consensus on how to treat serious child and adolescent disorders, such as Anorexia Nervosa or Alcohol Use Disorder. Third, although child psychotherapy is efficacious, there is limited evidence for its effectiveness. The few studies examining the effects of child and adolescent therapy in ordinary clinical settings suggest that, on average, therapy yields few benefits. These discouraging findings are probably the result of high therapist workloads, a lack of training in empirically supported interventions, and the complexity and diversity of children's problems encountered in most clinics.

On a more positive note, scientist-practitioners seek to unite the two sometimes disparate factions of clinical child psychology: the researchers who conduct efficacy trials and the clinicians who must meet the mental health needs of families in the community. Some scientist-practitioners, especially those working in university settings, are trying to develop ways to make empirically supported treatments more user-friendly, so that clinicians can access them more easily and make them part of their clinical repertoire. Other scientist-practitioners, especially those working in hospitals, clinics, and schools, are trying to use as many empirically supported interventions as possible in their day-to-day practice, to maximize the effectiveness of their practice. Clearly, much more work needs to be done to bridge the gap between efficacy and effectiveness. However, if clinical psychology is going to remain a viable science in both academic and clinical settings, this bridge must be built.

CHAPTER SUMMARY

Assessment

- Assessment is the process of gathering information about children and families in order to gain an accurate understanding of their psychosocial functioning.
- The purposes of psychological assessment include the following:
  - Screening children for psychological problems
  - Reaching a diagnosis
  - Identifying and treating specific problems
  - Monitoring progress in treatment
- Children and families can be assessed by using four broad methods: (a) clinical interviews, (b) observations, (c) norm-referenced tests, and (d) informal data gathering. Ideally, clinicians rely on information that comes from using multiple methods (e.g., interview *and* observations) and from multiple informants (e.g., parents *and* teachers).
- Clinical interviews usually include assessment of children's mental status and psychosocial history.
  - A mental status exam assesses the child's current functioning across 10 domains, including (a) appearance and overt behavior, (b) affect and mood, (c) thought process and content, (d) attention and memory, and (e) judgment and insight.
  - The psychosocial history assesses the family's presenting problem and current functioning, as well as the child's developmental, medical, academic, behavioral, and social history.
- Clinicians can observe children (a) during the clinical interview, (b) in a naturalistic setting such as school, or (c) while performing a structured analogue task. Often clinicians perform a functional analysis of children's behavior to determine the antecedents and consequences that might cause or maintain children's behavioral problems.
- Norm-referenced tests are administered and scored in a standard way. Children's performance is compared to other youths of the same age and/or gender (i.e., a "norm group" or standardization sample). Tests yield standard scores which quantify the child's performance compared to youths in the standardization sample.
  - Intelligence refers to children's ability to adapt to their environments, to solve problems, and to use information accurately and efficiently. The WISC-IV is a common IQ test administered to children. Most IQ tests have means of 100 and standard deviations of 15.
  - Academic achievement refers to knowledge and skills that children acquire through academic instruction. It usually encompasses reading, mathematics, written language, and oral language. Most achievement tests have means of 100 and standard deviations of 15.
  - Adaptive functioning refers to how effectively children cope with common life demands and how well they met the standard of personal independence expected of someone their age. Adaptive functioning includes (a) conceptual skills, (b) social skills, and (c) practical skills. Most tests of adaptive functioning have means of 100 and standard deviations of 15.

- o Most personality and behavior rating scales assess four domains: (a) internalizing problems, (b) externalizing problems, (c) school problems, and (d) prosocial skills. Most tests have means of 50 and standard deviations of 10.
- Reliability refers to the consistency of test scores.
  - o Test-retest reliability refers to stability over time.
  - o Internal consistency refers to stability of scores within the same administration.
- Validity refers to the degree to which professionals can be confident in inferences drawn from test data; does the test measure what it is designed to measure?
  - o Content validity refers to appropriateness of test items.
  - o Construct validity refers to the test's relationship to tests of other, theoretically similar constructs (e.g., IQ tests should correlate with other measures of intelligence).
  - o Criterion-related validity refers to the test's ability to describe or predict a child's performance on some external variable of interest (e.g., IQ tests should predict children's academic achievement).

Diagnosis

- Diagnosis is the process of describing a child's behavior problems, usually by matching current signs or symptoms to descriptions of disorders recognized by other mental health professionals.
- *DSM-5* is a compendium of mental disorders used by most mental health professionals in the United States. It is based on a medical approach to diagnosis.
- *DSM-5* differs from previous versions of the manual in several ways:
  - o It has a new metastructure (i.e., organization) that reflects advances in the research literature. Disorders are grouped based on underlying genetic and biological correlates, when known.
  - o Definitions are more specific, to avoid artificial co-occurrence of symptoms.
  - o It has greater focus on development and sensitivity to the way youths may manifest disorders differently than adults.
  - o It reduces the use of the generic "NOS" diagnostic category.
  - o It is more similar to international definitions of mental disorders.
- Diagnosis has several advantages.
  - o It is more parsimonious than descriptions of children's functioning.
  - o It facilitates communication between professionals.
  - o It can help professionals make statements about children's prognoses.
  - o It can guide treatment.
  - o It can help children and families access educational or social services.
  - o It can sometimes help parents.
  - o It can facilitate scientific discovery.
- Diagnosis also has limitations:
  - o It often gains parsimony at the expense of detailed information.
  - o It focuses exclusively on individuals.
  - o Differences between normality and abnormality are sometimes arbitrary.
  - o Boundaries between diagnoses are sometime unclear.
  - o Some diagnostic criteria are subjective.
  - o It can lead to stigma.

Psychotherapy

- Psychotherapy is an interpersonal process between a therapist and one or more clients, the goal of which is to alleviate distress and/or improve behavioral, cognitive, and/or social-emotional functioning.
- Jerome Frank and Carl Rogers have described "common" or "necessary" factors in therapy, believed to elicit improvement in clients (e.g., a warm, responsive relationship, a theory to guide treatment). Most professionals regard their factors as necessary, but not sufficient, to help children and families.
  - o Behavior therapy focuses on children's overt actions, especially the way environmental contingencies may reinforce or punish problem behaviors.
  - o Cognitive therapy focuses on the way children's thinking might influence their actions and mood. Cognitive distortions or irrational beliefs often mediate the relationship between specific events and children's behavior problems.
  - o Family systems therapy focuses on patterns of interaction and communication among family members. The entire family is usually viewed as the "client." Change in one family member often elicits change in other family members.
  - o Interpersonal therapy focuses on children's relationships with others in a social context. Children's problems often follow disruptions in interpersonal relationships such as (a) loss or separation from a loved one, (b) a major change in social roles, (c) interpersonal conflicts, or (d) deficits in social functioning.

o Psychodynamic therapy focuses on intrapersonal conflict. The goal of therapy is to provide clients with insight regarding the way unconscious thoughts or feelings might contribute to their current problems. Often, therapists focus on transference, the attitude and patterns of behavior clients develop toward the therapist.

- Child and adolescent psychotherapy differs from adult psychotherapy in several ways:

  o Children often have less motivation to participate in treatment than adults.
  o Child may lack the cognitive or emotional skills to participate in many therapies developed for adults.
  o The goal of adult therapy is to alleviate symptoms whereas the goal of child therapy is also to promote positive development.
  o Children often have less autonomy and control over their environments than adults.
  o Children are more likely to have comorbid problems than adults.

- Meta-analytic studies provide compelling evidence that child and adolescent psychotherapy works when it is administered by well-trained professionals in research settings.
- However, there is much less evidence supporting the effectiveness of child therapy when it is administered by professionals in the community.
- Behavior therapies may be more effective than nonbehavioral therapists for children. On average, older children and girls tend to show the greatest improvement in therapy.

KEY TERMS

academic achievement 65

adaptive functioning 66

affect 59

analogue tasks 59

antecedents 60

assessment 55

categorical classification 72

clinical interview 57

cognitive distortions 77

cognitive-behavioral therapy 77

comorbidity 75

Comprehensive System 68

consequences 60

construct validity 71

content validity 71

criterion-related validity 71

diagnosis 55

dimensional (continuous) classification 74

disengaged families 78

dodo verdict 81

effect size (ES) 80

effectiveness studies 82

efficacy studies 82

enmeshed families 78

environmental contingencies 76

functional analysis 60

insight 59

internal consistency 70

irrational beliefs 77

judgment 59

mental status examination 57

meta-analysis 80

Minnesota Multiphasic Personality Inventory-Adolescent 67

mood 59

multimethod assessment 56

multiple informants 57

naturalistic observation 60

necessary and sufficient factors for therapeutic change 76

norm group 61

normal distribution 61

norm-referenced testing 60

orientation 59

psychological assessment 55

reactivity 60

Rorschach 67

self-fulfilling prophecies 75

standard score 61

standardized format 60

stigma 75

structural family therapy 77

structured diagnostic interview 59

system 77

test-retest reliability 70

thought content 59

thought process 59

topographic theory of mind 78

transference 78

treatment 55

CRITICAL THINKING EXERCISES

1. Why is it important for psychologists to rely on multiple informants when assessing children? Who might be the best person to report (a) a preschool-aged child's disruptive behavior at home, (b) a 7-year-old girl's difficulty with reading, (c) an adolescent suspected of depression?

2. Why is it important for psychologists to rely on multiple methods when assessing children? What assessment techniques might you use to assess (a) Attention-Deficit/Hyperactivity Disorder in a 6-year-old boy, (b) reading disabilities in a 7-year-old girl, (c) depression in a 15-year-old adolescent?

3. Paully is an 11-year-old boy who bullies younger children during recess. How might you conduct a functional analysis of Paully's behavior to determine the antecedents and consequences of his bullying?

4. Can a psychological test be reliable but not valid? Can a test be valid but not reliable?

5. Terry is a 9-year-old boy diagnosed with a learning disability. His guidance counselor explained to his teacher, "Terry has trouble with reading because he has a learning disability." Is the guidance counselor correct? Does Terry's diagnosis actually *explain* his learning problems? What might be the benefit of this diagnostic label?

6. Child and adolescent psychotherapy has been shown to be efficacious; however, data supporting its effectiveness is limited. Why?

7. Maddy is a 14-year-old girl who is experiencing depression following the death of her father. How might her counselor use (a) behavior therapy, (b) cognitive therapy, and (c) interpersonal therapy to help Maddy?

EXTEND YOUR LEARNING

Videos, practice tests, flash cards, study guides, and links to online resources for this chapter are available to students online. Teachers also have access to lecture notes, PowerPoint presentations, suggestions for classroom activities, and possible exam questions. Visit: www .sagepub.com/weis2e.

PART II   Developmental and Learning Disorders

CHAPTER 4

Intellectual Disability and Developmental Disorders in Children

I f you were asked to imagine a child with an Intellectual Disability,[1] what picture would come to your mind? You might imagine a boy with very low intelligence. He might speak using simple sentences, or he might be unable to speak at all. Maybe he looks different from other boys: He has a flatter face, lower set ears, a protruding tongue, and short stature. He might be clumsy, walk in an awkward manner, or need a wheelchair to move about. He might not interact much with other children, and when he does, he might appear unusual or act inappropriately. In school, he might have a classroom aide to help him, but he still might have trouble reading sentences, learning addition and subtraction, and writing. He might be friendly but still seem "different" from most other boys his age.

For most people, our image of children with Intellectual Disability is formed by our personal experiences. We might have attended school with children who had Intellectual Disability, tutored children with developmental delays, volunteered for the Special Olympics or other recreational programs for youths with disabilities, or seen children with Intellectual Disability at the mall, where we work, or elsewhere in the community.

---

[1]Intellectual Disability was called "Mental Retardation" in previous editions of the *DSM*. The term *Mental Retardation* is no longer used because of its negative connotation.

DONTRELL: A FRIENDLY BOY

Dontrell was a 5-year-old African American boy referred to our clinic by his pediatrician. Dontrell showed delays in understanding language, speaking, and performing daily tasks. His mother had used alcohol and other drugs during pregnancy. She did not receive prenatal care because she was afraid that an obstetrician would report her drug use to the police. Dontrell was born with various drugs in his system and had respiratory and cardiovascular problems at birth. Shortly after delivery, Dontrell's mother disappeared, leaving him in his grandmother's care.

Dontrell was slow to reach many developmental milestones. Whereas most children learn to sit up by age 6 months and walk by their first birthday, Dontrell showed delays mastering each of these developmental tasks. Most striking were Dontrell's marked delays in language. Although he could understand and obey simple commands, he was able to speak only 15 to 20 words, and many of these were difficult to understand. He could not identify colors, was unable to recite the alphabet, and could not count. He also had problems performing self-care tasks typical of children his age. For example, he could not dress himself, wash his face, brush his teeth, or eat with utensils.

Dontrell showed significant problems with his behavior. First, he was hyperactive and inattentive. Second, Dontrell showed serious problems with defiance and aggression. When he did not get his way, he would tantrum and throw objects. He would also hit, kick, and bite other children and adults when he became upset. Third, Dontrell's grandmother said that he had "an obsession for food." Dontrell apparently had an insatiable appetite and was even caught hoarding food under his bed and stealing food from relatives.

Dr. Valencia, the psychologist who performed the evaluation, was most struck by Dontrell's appearance. Although only 5 years old, Dontrell weighed almost 85 lbs. He approached Dr. Valencia with a scowl and icy stare. Dr. Valencia extended her hand and said, "Hello." Dontrell grabbed Dr. Valencia's hand and kissed it! His grandmother quickly apologized, responding, "Sorry . . . he does that sometimes. He's showing that he likes you."

Although our image of Intellectual Disability, generated from these experiences, might be accurate, it is probably not complete. Intellectual Disability is a term that describes an extremely diverse group of people. They range from children with severe developmental disabilities who need constant care to youths with only mild delays who are usually indistinguishable from others (Hodapp, Zakemi, Rosner, & Dykens, 2006).

WHAT IS INTELLECTUAL DISABILITY?

The *DSM-5* Definition of Intellectual Disability

According to the *DSM-5*, Intellectual Disability is characterized by significant limitations in general mental abilities and adaptive functioning that emerge during the course of children's development. Limitations must be evident in comparison to other people of the same age, gender, and social-cultural background. (See Table 4.1, Diagnostic Criteria for Intellectual Disability [Intellectual Developmental Disorder].)

All individuals with Intellectual Disability must show significantly low intellectual functioning. These individuals show problems perceiving and processing new information, learning quickly and efficiently, applying knowledge and skills to solve novel problems, thinking creatively and flexibly, and responding rapidly and accurately. In children approximately five years of age and older, intellectual functioning is measured using a standardized, individually administered intelligence test. IQ scores are normally distributed with a mean of 100 and a standard deviation of 15. IQ scores approximately two standard deviations below the

Table 4.1 Diagnostic Criteria for Intellectual Disability (Intellectual Developmental Disorder)

Intellectual disability (intellectual developmental disorder) is a disorder with onset during the developmental period that includes both intellectual and adaptive functioning deficits in conceptual, social, and practical domains. The following three criteria must be met:

A. Deficits in intellectual functions, such as reasoning, problem solving, planning, abstract thinking, judgment, academic learning, and learning from experience, confirmed by both clinical assessment and individualized, standardized intelligence testing.

(Continued)

Table 4.1 (Continued)

B. Deficits in adaptive functioning that result in failure to meet developmental and socio-cultural standards for personal independence and social responsibility. Without ongoing support, the adaptive deficits limit functioning in one or more activities of daily life, such as communication, social participation, and independent living, across multiple environments, such as home, work, and community.

C. Onset of intellectual and adaptive deficits during the developmental period.

Specify current severity: Mild, Moderate, Severe, Profound*

Source: Reprinted with permission from the Diagnostic and Statistical Manual of Mental Disorders, Fifth Edition, (Copyright 2013). American Psychiatric Association.

* Table 4.2 provides a description of each type of severity.

mean (i.e., IQ < 70) can indicate significant deficits in intellectual functioning. The measurement error of most IQ tests is approximately 5 points; consequently, IQ scores between 65 and 75 are recommended as cutoffs in determining intellectual deficits (American Psychiatric Association, 2013). IQ scores below this cutoff are seen in approximately 2.5–3.0% of the population (Durand & Christodulu, 2006).

Second, individuals with Intellectual Disability show significant deficits in adaptive functioning. Adaptive functioning refers to how effectively individuals cope with common life demands and how well they meet the standards of personal independence expected of someone in their particular age group, social-cultural background, and community setting (American Psychiatric Association, 2013). Whereas intellectual functioning refers to people's ability to learn information and solve problems, adaptive functioning refers to their typical level of success in meeting the day-to-day demands of society in an age-appropriate manner.

DSM-IV → DSM-5 CHANGES

A DIAGNOSIS BY ANY OTHER NAME

There has been considerable controversy regarding the name of the disorder "Intellectual Disability." In *DSM-IV*, this disorder was called "Mental Retardation" to reflect the below-average intellectual ability of individuals with this condition. However, the developers of *DSM-5* agreed to abandon this term because of its negative connotation. When revising *DSM-IV*, the American Psychiatric Association's Neurodevelopmental Disorders working group considered renaming the disorder "Intellectual Developmental Disorder." Their proposal drew considerable criticism from the leading professional organization of individuals who work with people with developmental disabilities, the American Association of Intellectual and Developmental Disabilities (AAIDD; Gomez & Nygren, 2012). Instead, The AAIDD argued that the name "Intellectual Disability" (not *Developmental*) be adopted in *DSM-5* for several reasons:

- *Intellectual Disability* is the most commonly used term in the United States and internationally to refer to people with intellectual and adaptive skills deficits.
- The term reflects the World Health Organization's conceptualization of low intelligence and adaptive functioning as a "disability."
- It implies deficits in both intelligence and adaptive functioning, not only low IQ.
- It is less offensive than the often pejorative term *Mental Retardation*.

In 2010, Rosa's Law (PL 111-256) replaced the term *Mental Retardation* with *Intellectual Disability* in federal education, health, and labor laws. The law was named after 9-year-old Rosa Marcellino, a girl with Down Syndrome, whose family worked to have the term *retardation* removed from the educational code in her home state of Maryland.

The APA decided to adopt the term *Intellectual Disability* in *DSM-5* yet retains the term *Intellectual Developmental Disorder* in parentheses.

DSM-5 identifies three domains of adaptive functioning: conceptual, social, and practical. These domains were identified by using a statistical procedure called factor analysis to determine groups of skills that tend to co-occur in individuals with developmental disabilities. To be diagnosed with Intellectual Disability, individuals must show impairment in at least one domain. Usually, children with Intellectual Disability experience problems in multiple areas:

- *Conceptual skills:* understanding language, speaking, reading, writing, counting, telling time, solving math problems, the ability to learn and remember information and skills
- *Social skills:* interpersonal skills (e.g., making eye contact when addressing others), following rules (e.g., turn-taking during games), social problem-solving (e.g., avoiding arguments), understanding others (e.g., empathy), making and keeping friends
- *Practical skills:* activities of daily living including personal care (e.g., getting dressed, grooming), safety (e.g., looking both ways before crossing street), home activities (e.g., using the telephone), school/work skills (e.g., showing up on time), recreational activities (e.g., clubs, hobbies), and using money (e.g., paying for items at a store)

Adaptive functioning can be assessed by interviewing caregivers about children's behavior and comparing their reports to the behavior of typically developing children of the same age and cultural group (Tassé et al., 2012).

Often, psychologists administer a norm-referenced interview or rating scale to caregivers to collect information about children's functioning. For example, the Diagnostic Adaptive Behavior Scale (DABS) is a semi-structured interview that is administered to caregivers of children with developmental disabilities. Based on caregivers' reports, the interviewer rates children's adaptive behavior across the conceptual, social, and practical domains (see text box Research to Practice: Adaptive Functioning Examples). The DABS provides standard scores much like IQ scores, which indicate children's adaptive functioning relative to their peers. Scores more than two standard deviations below the mean (i.e., < 70) on at least one domain could indicate significant impairment in adaptive functioning (Tassé et al., 2011).

It is important to keep in mind that Intellectual Disability is characterized by low intellectual functioning *and* problems in adaptive behavior. Many people believe that Intellectual Disability is determined solely by IQ; however, deficits in adaptive functioning are equally necessary for the diagnosis. A child with an IQ of 65 but with no problems in adaptive functioning would not be diagnosed with Intellectual Disability.

RESEARCH TO PRACTICE

ADAPTIVE FUNCTIONING EXAMPLES

Clinicians assess adaptive functioning by administering semi-structured interviewers to caregivers of children suspected of Intellectual Disability. Adaptive functioning scales allow clinicians to assess children's conceptual, social, and practical skills. Caregivers' reports are converted to standard scores which can be used to determine if children have deficits compared to other children their age in the general population. Below are some areas of adaptive functioning that might be assessed in younger children, older children, and adolescents.

	Younger Children	*Older Children*	*Adolescents*
Conceptual	Can count 10 objects, one by one; Knows day, month, year of birth	States value of penny, nickel, dime; Uses mathematical operations	Sets a watch or clock to correct time; Can complete a job application
Social	Says "hi" and "bye" when coming and going; Asks for help when needed	Reads and obeys common signs (e.g., stop, do not enter); Knows topic of group conversations	Has satisfying friendships; Keeps personal information private
Practical	Uses the restroom; Drinks from a cup without spilling	Answers the telephone; Can safely cross busy streets	Travels to school or work by themselves; Washes clothes, dishes

Finally, all individuals with Intellectual Disability show limitations in intellectual and adaptive functioning early in life. Although some people are not identified as having Intellectual Disability until they are adults, they must have histories of intellectual and daily living problems beginning in childhood. This age-of-onset requirement differentiates Intellectual Disability from other disorders characterized by problems with intellectual and adaptive functioning, such as Alzheimer's Dementia (i.e., cognitive deterioration seen in older adults).

Severity of Impairment

In the past, children with Intellectual Disability were categorized into one of four subtypes based on their IQ. This practice was abandoned in *DSM-5* for three reasons. First, the developers of *DSM-5* wanted to give equal importance to IQ and adaptive functioning in describing children with Intellectual Disability, rather than focus exclusively on IQ alone. Second,

children's IQ scores were less helpful than their level of adaptive behavior in determining their need for support and assistance at home, at school, and in the community. Third, IQ scores tend to be less valid toward the lower end of the IQ range.

Consequently, in *DSM-5*, clinicians specify the severity of Intellectual Disability based on the person's level of adaptive functioning. Adaptive functioning can be assessed using standardized rating scales, clinical interviews, and observations at home and school. Children with mild deficits in adaptive functioning (i.e., standard scores 55–70) in only one domain would presumably need less support from caregivers than children with profound deficits in adaptive functioning (i.e., standard scores <25) across multiple domains. Furthermore, by specifying the domains most in need of support, clinicians can begin to plan interventions to improve children's adaptive functioning or compensate for deficits that might be less responsive to treatment. Table 4.2 provides a general overview of children's adaptive functioning at each level of severity.

Table 4.2 Describing the Severity of Intellectual Disability

Severity	Conceptual Domain	Social Domain	Practical Domain
Mild	Preschoolers may show no obvious conceptual differences. School-aged children show difficulties in acquiring academic skills (e.g., reading, writing, arithmetic, telling time, using money). Abstract thinking and planning may be impaired; thinking tends to be concrete.	Communication, conversation, and language are more concrete or immature than the skills of peers. The child may have difficulty accurately understanding the social cues of others. There may be difficulties regulating emotion and behavior compared to peers.	The child may function in an age-expected manner with regard to personal care. In adolescence, assistance may be needed to perform more complex daily living tasks like shopping, cooking, and managing money.
Moderate	Preschoolers' language and pre-academic skills develop slowly. School-age children show slow progress in academic skills. Academic skill development is usually at the elementary school level.	The child shows marked differences in social and communicative skills compared to peers. Spoken language is simplistic and concrete. Social judgment and decision making are limited. Friendships with peers are often affected by social or communicative deficits.	The child needs more time and practice learning self-care skills, such as eating, dressing, toileting, and hygiene, than peers. Household skills can be acquired by adolescent with ample practice.
Severe	The child generally has little understanding of written language or numbers. Caretakers must provide extensive support for problem solving throughout life.	There are limited spoken language skills with simplistic vocabulary and grammar. Speech may be single words/phrases. The child understands simple speech and gestures. Relationships are with family members and other familiar people.	The child needs ongoing support for all activities of daily living: eating, dressing, bathing, elimination. Caregivers must supervise at all times. Some youths show challenging behaviors, such as self-injury.
Profound	Conceptual skills generally involve the physical world rather than symbols (e.g., letters, numbers). Some visual-spatial skills, such as matching and sorting, may be acquired with practice. Co-occurring physical problems may greatly limit functioning.	The child has limited understanding of symbolic communication. The child may understand some simple instructions and gestures. Communication is usually through nonverbal, non-symbolic means. Relationships are usually with family members and other familiar people. Co-occurring physical problems may greatly limit functioning.	The child is dependent on others for all aspects of physical care, health, and safety, although he or she may participate in some aspects of self-care. Some youths show challenging behaviors, such as self-injury. Co-occurring physical problems may greatly limit functioning.

Source: Based on *DSM-5*, 2013.

Mild Intellectual Disability (Adaptive Functioning Scores 55–70)

As infants and toddlers, children with mild Intellectual Disability usually appear no different than other children (Jacobson & Mulick, 1996). They achieve most developmental milestones at expected ages, learn basic language, and interact with family members and peers. Their intellectual deficits are usually first identified when they begin school. Teachers may notice that they require more time and practice to master academic skills, such as letter and number recognition, reading, and math. As they progress in school and their schoolwork becomes more challenging, these children fall further behind and may repeat a grade. Some children grow frustrated with traditional education and display behavior problems in class. By middle school, these children master basic reading and math but seldom make further academic progress. After school, they typically blend back into society, perform semiskilled jobs, and live independently in the community. They usually require only occasional support from others to overcome their intellectual deficits. For example, they may need help completing a job application, filing a tax return, or managing their finances.

Moderate Intellectual Disability (Adaptive Functioning Scores 40–55)

Children with moderate Intellectual Disability often show signs of their intellectual and adaptive impairments as infants or toddlers (Jacobson & Mulick, 1996). Their motor skills usually develop in a typical fashion, but parents often notice delays in learning to speak and interacting with others. These children often seem less interested in their surroundings compared to their age mates. They are often first identified as having Intellectual Disability as toddlers or preschoolers, when they show little or no language development. Instead, they rely mostly on gestures and single word utterances. By the time they begin school, these children usually speak in short, simple phrases and show self-care skills similar to typically developing toddlers. However, they display problems mastering basic reading, writing, and mathematics. By adolescence, these children are able to communicate effectively with others, have basic self-care skills, and have simple reading and writing abilities. They may continue to have trouble with reading a newspaper, performing arithmetic, or handling money. As adults, some may perform unskilled jobs if they are given training and supervision. They usually live with family members or in residential care facilities.

Severe Intellectual Disability (Adaptive Functioning Scores 25–40)

Children with severe Intellectual Disability are usually first identified in infancy (Jacobson & Mulick, 1996). They almost always show early delays in basic developmental milestones, such as sitting up and walking. They also usually show one or more biological anomalies that are indicative of a genetic or medical disorder. These children often have health problems, are at risk for long-term motor disorders, or have seizures. They require ample supervision from parents and caregivers. By the time they begin school, they may be able to move on their own and perform some basic self-care skills, such as feeding, dressing, and using the toilet. They may communicate using single words and gestures. As adults, their speech continues to be limited and difficult to understand, although their ability to understand others is often better developed. They are usually unable to read or write, but they may be able to perform simple daily living tasks under close supervision. They typically live with family or in residential care.

Profound Intellectual Disability (Adaptive Functioning Scores <25)

Children with profound Intellectual Disability are first identified in infancy (Jacobson & Mulick, 1996). They almost always show multiple biological anomalies and health problems indicative of neurological damage. By the time they reach school age, their skills are similar to those of typically developing one-year-olds. They may be able to sit up, imitate sounds, understand simple commands, and recognize familiar people. About half of the children with profound Intellectual Disability will continue to require help from others throughout their lives. The other half will show slow development of adaptive skills. They may learn to walk, develop some communication skills, and be able to perform some self-care activities. As adults, they usually continue to require constant support and supervision from family and caregivers. They may also show chronic medical problems and sensory impairments.

Remember that the diagnosis of Intellectual Disability is determined by the child's intelligence and adaptive functioning. Two people can show Intellectual Disability but look and act very differently. For example, one person might be a child with Down Syndrome. Another child with the same IQ might have no identifiable cause of their impairments. The label "Intellectual Disability" tells us only about a person's general intellectual and adaptive functioning; the diagnosis says nothing about etiology, symptoms, course, or outcomes (Baumeister & Bacharach, 2000).

The AAIDD Definition of Intellectual Disability

The American Association on Intellectual and Developmental Disabilities (AAIDD) is the oldest professional organization devoted to the study and assistance of individuals with impairments in intellectual and adaptive functioning. The AAIDD consists of professionals and laypersons who research, help, and advocate on behalf of people with intellectual disabilities. Since 1910, they have offered guidelines for the identification of Intellectual Disability and the best methods to help children and adults with this condition. In years past, the *DSM* and AAIDD definitions of Intellectual Disability had differed considerably. Currently, however, the *DSM-5* and AAIDD definitions overlap considerably, which will likely improve communication between members of these two professional organizations (Schalock et al., 2010).

One difference in the AAIDD conceptualization of Intellectual Disability is its emphasis on needed supports (Luck-asson et al., 2002). **Needed supports** refer to a broad array of assistance that helps the individual function effectively in society. Supports can be formal assistance provided by health care providers, mental health professionals, teachers, educational specialists, professional caregivers, or human service agencies. Supports can also refer to informal help from parents, friends, or members of the community. The AAIDD designates four possible levels of supports, based on how much and how long assistance is needed: intermittent (i.e., occasional, in time of crisis), limited (i.e., short-term), extensive (i.e., long-term), and pervasive (i.e., constant).

Rather than categorize clients into mild, moderate, severe, and profound impairment, the AAIDD recommends that professionals describe individuals' need for supports across various areas of functioning. For example, a child with Intellectual Disability might be described as needing "extensive" educational support, such as a full-time classroom aide, for all academic activities, but only "intermittent" support in areas of social functioning, such as one-time training to help him learn to make friends.

The AAIDD has published a semi-structured interview to help clinicians identify the type and intensity of supports needed for adolescents and adults with Intellectual Disability (Schalock et al., 2008). The Supports Intensity Scale measures support needs in the areas of home living, community living, lifelong learning, employment, health and safety, social activities, and protection and advocacy. It ranks each activity according to *frequency* (e.g., none, at least once a month), *amount* (e.g., none, less than 30 minutes), and *type* (e.g., monitoring, verbal gesturing) of support needed.

The AAIDD's approach to classifying individuals with Intellectual Disability in terms of needed supports has two main advantages (Schalock et al., 2008). First, this approach conveys more information about clients than simply classifying them with Intellectual Disability alone. Second, it focuses on clients' abilities rather than on their impairments. The main drawback to the AAIDD approach is that it is complex. Describing clients on so many dimensions of functioning is cumbersome and can hinder communication among professionals. The AAIDD approach can also make research difficult; with so many combinations of needed supports and areas of functioning, it is difficult to identify homogenous groups of individuals for study.

WHAT IS GLOBAL DEVELOPMENTAL DELAY?

Definition and Description

The diagnosis of Intellectual Disability requires significant deficits in intellectual functioning and adaptive skills. Typically, intellectual functioning is assessed using norm-referenced IQ tests. However, it is difficult to obtain an IQ

Image 4.1 The AAIDD conceptualization of Intellectual Disability emphasizes needed supports — assistance from others that helps the person with a disability function effectively in society.

Source: Courtesy of Kiona Miller.

score for very young children. Some tests can be administered to very young children. For example, the Wechsler Preschool and Primary Scales of Intelligence Fourth Edition (WPPSI-IV) can be given to children as young as 2 and a half years, whereas the Bayley Scales of Infant and Toddler Development Third Edition (BSID-III) is appropriate for children aged 1 to 42 months. However, these tests are usually considered measures of children's cognitive, motor, and social development rather than intelligence per se.

The most commonly used intelligence test, the Wechsler Intelligence Scale for Children, Fourth Edition (WISC-IV), can only be administered to children 6 years old or older. Other true IQ tests, like the Stanford-Binet Intelligence Scales Fifth Edition (SB-5), can be administered to 2-year-old children. However, IQ determined prior to age 4 or 5 years is a poor predictor of IQ in childhood or adolescence (Tirosch & Jaffe, 2011). How, then, should infants and toddlers with delays be classified?

Global Developmental Delay (GDD) is a neurodevelopmental disability that is only diagnosed in children less than 5 years of age. GDD is diagnosed when the infant or child fails to meet developmental milestones in several areas. The infant or child's physician or psychologist suspects Intellectual Disability; however, because the child is so young, an individually administered IQ test cannot be administered. Consequently, GDD is assigned as a temporary diagnosis to indicate developmental delays until the child is old enough to participate in standardized IQ testing (American Psychiatric Association, 2013).

GDD is usually diagnosed in infants and toddlers who show significant delays in two or more of the following developmental domains: (a) fine/gross motor skills, (b) speech/language, (c) social/personal skills, and (d) daily living. *Significant delays* are defined by scores two or more standard deviations below the mean (Table 4.3). Typically, children with GDD show delays across most or all domains of functioning (Shevell, 2010).

Children with GDD are usually identified in the first year of life. Some children show physical abnormalities at birth indicative of a developmental disorder. Other children's delays become apparent only when parents notice that their children are not developing in the same way as their peers. For example, a parent might wonder, "Why is my son not sitting up by himself at 9 months or walking at 15 months? Why hasn't my daughter learned to say 'mama' and ask for her cup by 18 months?" (Shevell et al., 2003).

Table 4.3 Developmental Milestones Shown by Infants and Toddlers

Age	Motor	Language	Social	Daily Living
2 mo.	Raises head up in prone position	Differentiated cries	Smiles, follows caregiver w/ eyes	—
3 mo.	Raises head and chest; grasps object	Coos	Laughs	—
4 mo.	Rolls, stretches	—	Social smile in response to others	—
6 mo.	Sits up with support	Babbles, turn to sounds	—	Mouths objects
8 mo.	Sits up without support	Turn to the sound of own name	Stranger anxiety	—
10 mo.	Pincer grasp, crawls	Waves "bye-bye"	Peek-a-boo	Holds bottle with both hands
12 mo.	Walks but falls easily	First words	Separation anxiety	Drinks from a cup
15 mo.	Walks steadily, scribbles	Points to objects, uses single words	—	Uses spoon, helps to dress self
18 mo.	Walks up/down stairs with help; throws ball	Points to body parts when asked, two-word phrases	Plays with others	Builds small tower with blocks
24 mo.	Walks up/down stairs, kicks ball	Uses pronouns, three-word phrases	Says "no" frequently	Tries to feed self without help

Source: Based on Centers for Disease Control (2012).

Note: A pediatrician may consult a table of developmental milestones to determine if an infant is delayed in motor, language, social, or daily living skills. If she suspects delays in a particular domain, she might administer a norm-referenced test to determine the severity of the delay.

SILENT SAM

Sammy was a 34-month-old boy who was referred to our clinic by his pediatrician because of significant language delays. "I'm mostly concerned about his speech," his mother said. "Sammy has never been much of a talker. He only says a handful of words. I'm concerned because most of the kids his age in the neighborhood speak in complete sentences and he doesn't."

Dr. Baer learned that Sammy was born approximately seven weeks premature and continues to be small for his age. His motor skills tended to lag behind his peers throughout his life. When other children were learning to walk, Sammy was just beginning to crawl; when his peers began using a spoon and fork during meals, Sammy used his fingers.

Dr. Baer administered the Bayley Scales of Infant and Toddler Development to Sammy. She observed Sammy complete a series of tasks to assess his functioning and asked questions of Sammy's mother about his development and behavior at home.

Sammy's performance on the Bayley Scales showed delays in language, motor, and social-emotional skills (Figure 4.1). Overall, Sammy's functioning was more than two standard deviations lower than other children his age. Sammy's most prominent delays were in language. He showed problems with receptive vocabulary; for example, he could not correctly point to the parts of his body that Dr. Baer named or demonstrate how to use a cup, shoe, or scissors when asked. Sammy also showed delays in expressive language; he usually spoke in two-word sentences, had difficulty naming pictures of common objects (e.g., apple, bed, car), and did not use pronouns when speaking. Testing also showed similar delays in fine motor skills (e.g., putting coins in a slot), gross motor skills (e.g., climbing stairs, kicking a ball) and social-emotional functioning (e.g., pretend play, interest in peers).

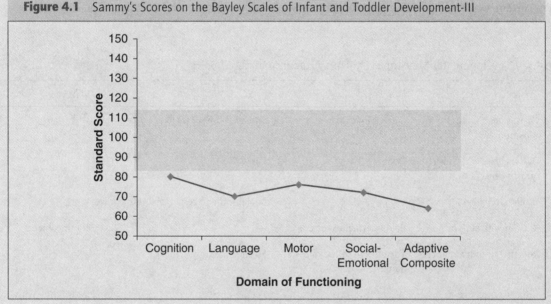

Figure 4.1 Sammy's Scores on the Bayley Scales of Infant and Toddler Development-III

Note: Standard scores have a mean of 100 and standard deviation of 15. Scores between 85 and 115 (shaded area) are within normal limits. Scores approximately two standard deviations below the mean ($\leq$70) indicate significant delays. Sammy would likely qualify for a diagnosis of General Developmental Delay.

"I'm really glad that you brought Sammy to see me," Dr. Baer said to Sammy's mother. "His language and motor skills are lower than what we'd expect from a boy his age. Let's work together to find some ways we can help him develop these skills."

The word "delay" in the name of this diagnosis implies that children with GDD will eventually catch up to their typically developing peers. Unfortunately, longitudinal studies of children with GDD indicate that is not always the case (Shevell, 2008). Many infants and toddlers initially diagnosed with GDD eventually meet criteria for Intellectual Disability by the time they begin preschool. Furthermore, retrospective studies indicate that most older children with Intellectual Disability showed delays in early development that would have merited the diagnosis of GDD. Consequently, some researchers consider GDD to be a "placeholder" diagnosis for children too young to be diagnosed with Intellectual Disability (Shevell, 2010).

Not all children with GDD have concurrent deficits in intellectual functioning, however. In one recent study, researchers examined the WPPSI scores of preschoolers with GDD. Children's scores ranged widely and nearly 20% of children earned scores within the average range (Riou et al., 2009).

Furthermore, some young children with GDD do not develop Intellectual Disability later in life. For example, cerebral palsy is a lifelong, developmental disorder that causes marked delays in fine motor skills, gross motor skills, and (sometimes) eating, speech, and cognition (Hanna et al., 2009). Children with cerebral palsy usually show abnormal muscle tone (e.g., slouching), muscle spasms (e.g., rapid tightening of muscles that control the limbs), involuntary movements (e.g., jerks of the head, facial expressions), unsteady gait, poor balance, and noticeable joint or bone deformities (see Image 4.2). The disorder ranges in severity from mild (i.e., general clumsiness) to severe (i.e., no coordinated motor activity). Although many children with cerebral palsy also show intellectual deficits, approximately one third of children show normal intelligence (Shevell et al., 2003).

Similarly, children exposed to social deprivation or severe economic hardship can show early delays in motor, language, and cognitive development. For example, some infants adopted from developing countries have been raised in orphanages or "baby centers" with very high caregiver-to-child ratios (Van IJzendoorn et al., 2011). Many of these children were provided with inadequate nutrition, cognitive stimulation (e.g., access to books, toys), and interactions with others. Their opportunities to develop motor skills through play and exploration may also be limited. Many of these infants and toddlers show marked delays in development across multiple domains. However, sensitive and responsible care, especially if provided before age 9 months, can remedy these skills deficits. Children who receive care early enough are usually indistinguishable from their typically developing classmates by the time they begin school.

Identifying the Causes of Global Developmental Delay

GDD is not uncommon; between 1% and 3% of infants and toddlers have the disorder (Shevell et al., 2003). In some cases, the cause of GDD can be determined based on physical examination. For example, children with Down Syndrome can be identified by certain physical attributes, such as enlarged and rounded face, wide nasal bridge, and low-set ears. In most cases, however, pediatricians or pediatric neurologists must order blood tests to screen for genetic disorders (Image 4.3). **Chromosomal microarray (CMA)** is a standard test for infants with GDD; this test identifies copy number variants (i.e., unusual duplications or deletions) in major regions of the genome. CMA can be used to create a

Image 4.2 Children with cerebral palsy, like this boy, show significant delays in fine and gross motor development. They may also display problems with speech and language and d0aily living skills. As infants, they often show Global Developmental Delay. However, approximately one third of these children have IQ scores within the normal range.

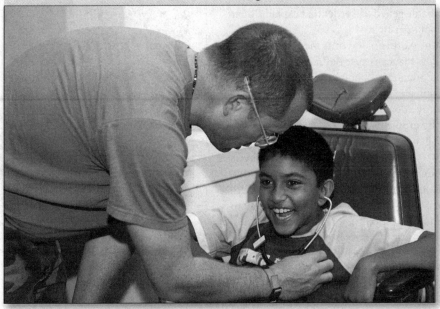

Image 4.3   Two types of genetic testing.

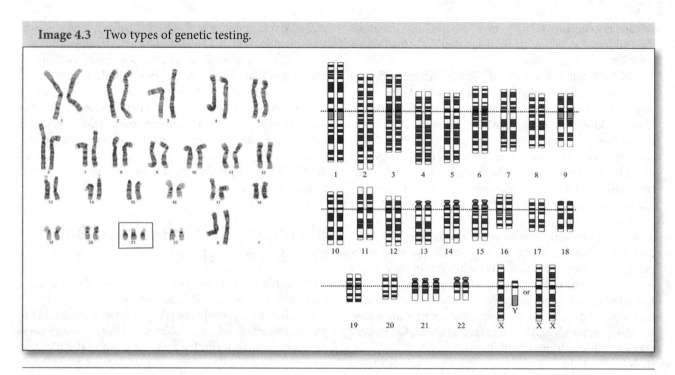

Note: Genetic testing is used to determine the cause of GDD. G-banded karyotyping (*left*) produces a stained image of the child's chromosomes; it is useful for detecting gross genetic abnormalities. In contrast, chromosomal microarray (CMA; *right*) screens the child's genome and generates a high-resolution "virtual karyotype" that can detect small repetitions or deletions of genetic material. These tests above show a child with three (rather than two) 21st chromosomes, the defining feature of Down Syndrome.

"virtual karyotype" of the child's chromosome structure to identify abnormalities. CMA has replaced older forms of genetic testing, such as G-banded karyotyping, which has poorer resolution and may be unable to detect more subtle chromosomal abnormalities (Flore & Milunsky, 2012). The most common genetic disorders that cause GDD are Down Syndrome, Fragile X Syndrome, Rett Syndrome (another X-linked disorder), and subtle translocations or deletions of portions of the genome. Approximately 4% of children with GDD have an identifiable genetic disorder that explains their delays (Stevenson et al., 2012).

Physicians may also order blood or urine tests to screen for metabolic disorders that can cause developmental delays. Some metabolic disorders are phenylketonuria (described later), hypothyroidism, and lead poisoning. These disorders are relatively rare; only about 1% of youths with GDD have identifiable metabolic problems.

If the results of genetic and metabolic testing are negative, physicians may try to determine the source of children's delays using neuroimaging. MRI is usually able to locate structural abnormalities in 30% to 40% of children with GDD. These abnormalities include central nervous system malformation, cerebral atrophy, problems with myelination (i.e., the coating of axons that promotes neural conduction), or cellular damage and lesions (Image 4.4).

Of course, physicians must also rule out the possibility that sensory deficits underlie children's developmental delays. Approximately 13% to 25% of children with GDD also

Image 4.4   MRI abnormality.

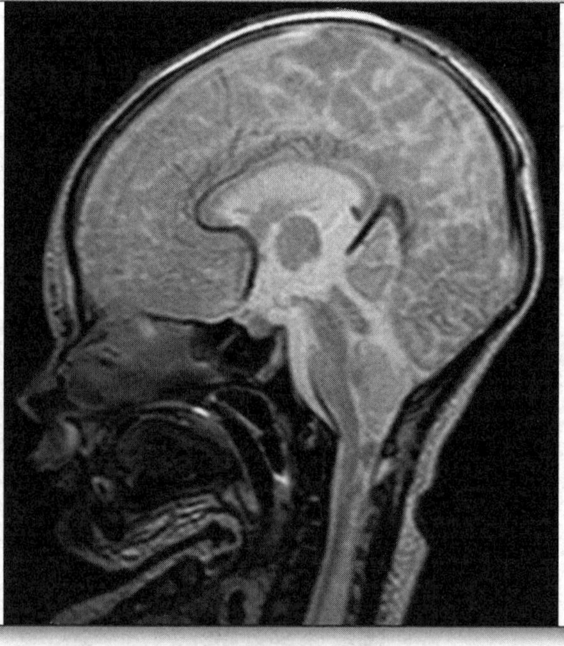

Note: MRI is often used to detect the cause of GDD. This newborn has a malformation of the cerebellum (i.e., Chiari malformation). Notice how the infant lacks a prominent bulge at the base of neck below the occipital lobe where the cerebellum should be. This condition is associated with delays in gross and fine motor development, problems with eating (because of nausea), weight gain, and cognition.

show vision problems, whereas 18% of children with GDD display significant hearing problems (Shevell et al., 2003). Visual and auditory deficits can greatly interfere with the acquisition of children's speech, language, and social skills.

In most cases, the causes of GDD can be determined on the basis of a parental interview, physical exam, genetic and/or metabolic testing, and neuroimaging. In order of prevalence, the most common identifiable causes are (a) genetic disorders or chromosomal abnormalities, (b) perinatal asphyxia (i.e., oxygen deprivation, perhaps during gestation or delivery), (c) brain malformation during gestation, (d) early, severe psychosocial deprivation (e.g., severe neglect), and (e) toxin exposure including maternal alcohol and other drug use (Shevell, 2008).

ASSOCIATED CHARACTERISTICS
Challenging Behavior

Approximately 25% of individuals with Intellectual Disability show challenging behavior. Experts in the field of developmental disabilities use the term *challenging behavior* to describe children's actions which are of such intensity, frequency, or duration that their physical safety (or the safety of others) is placed in jeopardy. Challenging behavior also includes actions that limit the child's access to educational or social opportunities (Didden et al., 2012).

Challenging behavior is problematic because it can affect children's health and development. Specifically, it can adversely affect children and families in several ways:

- It can be physically harmful.
- It can strain relationships with parents and cause children to be rejected by peers.
- It can limit children's access to developmentally appropriate social experiences, such as birthday parties, sleepovers, and participation in sports.
- It can interfere with learning and cognitive development.
- It can place a financial burden on families and the public.

Given their seriousness, challenging behavior is a main target for treatment.

Although children with Intellectual Disability can show many types of challenging behavior, we will focus on the most common: stereotypies, self-injurious behaviors, and aggression.

Stereotypies

Some children with Intellectual Disability show **stereotypies**, behaviors that are performed in a consistent, rigid, and repetitive manner and that have no immediate, practical significance (Carcani-Rathwell, Rabe-Hasketh, & Santosh, 2006). Stereotypies often involve repeated movements of the hands, arms, or upper body. For example, some children flap their hands, repeatedly move their fingers, twirl, fidget with objects,

or rock back and forth. Other common stereotypes are facial grimacing, face and head tapping, self-biting, and licking.

Typically developing infants and toddlers sometimes show stereotyped behaviors, such as arm waving, kicking, or swaying. Some healthy older children and adolescents continue to engage in repetitive behaviors, such as hair twirling, body rocking, and repetitive object manipulation (e.g., twirling a pencil). These behaviors are not problematic unless they come to dominate the youths' behavior, persist over time, and interfere with functioning. *DSM-5* permits clinicians to diagnose children with Stereotyped Movement Disorder when stereotypies become sufficiently impairing.

Stereotypies are fairly common among children with Intellectual Disability. In one large study, 18% of higher functioning and 31% of lower functioning children with developmental disabilities also displayed stereotypies. Moreover, 71% of youths with both Intellectual Disability and Autism Spectrum Disorder showed stereotyped behaviors (Goldman et al., 2009).

Children engage in stereotypies for many reasons (Didden et al., 2012). Certain genetic disorders are characterized by stereotyped movements. More commonly, children engage in stereotypies because these behaviors are self-reinforcing. For example, spinning in place or rocking back and forth can be pleasurable, especially in situations that might otherwise be boring (e.g., sitting at a desk, waiting in line). Still other children engage in stereotypies to regulate anxiety or frustration. For example, a child might suck his fingers or flap his arms to soothe himself or express agitation or excitement.

Self-Injurious Behaviors

Self-injurious behaviors (SIBs) involve repetitive movements of the hands, limbs, or head in a manner that can, or do, cause physical harm or damage to the person. SIBs can be classified in three ways. First, they can be described in terms of their *severity*, from mild (e.g., head rubbing, finger picking, thigh slapping) to severe (e.g., eye gouging, self-scratching, head banging). Second, SIBS can be described in terms of *frequency*, from low-occurrence acts with high potential for harm (e.g., head banging once per day) to high-occurrence acts that may cause harm over time (e.g., hand rubbing). Third, SIBs can be classified in terms of their *purpose*. Some actions seem reinforced by the reactions they elicit in others. For example, a child might gain attention from his teacher by picking his skin. Other actions appear to be reinforcing by themselves. For example, a child might insert objects into his mouth or ears because they produce positive sensations.

Approximately 10% to 12% of children with Intellectual Disability engage in SIBs (Didden et al., 2012). The prevalence of SIBs, like stereotypies, is directly related to the severity of children's intellectual and adaptive impairments. SIBs are most commonly seen in children with severe and profound impairments, children in institutional settings, and children with Autism Spectrum Disorder (Thompson &

Caruso, 2002). Indeed, children with Intellectual Disability and autism may be five times more likely than children with Intellectual Disability alone to show SIBs. Head banging and self-biting/scratching are the two most common SIBs (Kahng, Iwata, & Lewin, 2002).

SIBs usually occur in episodes or "bouts," often occurring many times each day. Children with SIBs usually show the same behaviors in each episode (Kahng et al., 2002). In some children, episodes last only for a few seconds. These episodes are usually triggered by the environment, such as when a child with Intellectual Disability is reprimanded by a caregiver. In other children, episodes last for minutes or hours, more or less continuously. During these episodes, the child may not eat or sleep. Although these episodes may be triggered by environmental events, they are usually maintained over time by neurochemical or other biological factors (Holden & Gitlesen, 2006; Thompson & Caruso, 2002).

There are at least three possible explanations for SIBs in children with Intellectual Disability (Thompson & Caruso, 2002). One explanation is that children show SIBs because these behaviors serve a certain purpose or function. Carr, Levin, McConnachie, Carlson, Kemp, and Smith (1994) have suggested that individuals engage in SIBs when they lack communication or social skills to effectively interact with others. Head banging may be a way of communicating

"I don't like this!" or "I'm bored!" To test this hypothesis, Hanley, Iwata, and McCord (2003) reviewed 536 cases of self-injurious or problematic behavior among people with Intellectual Disability. In 95.9% of cases, the SIBs served some identifiable purpose. These purposes included (a) gaining attention, food, or specific items; (b) escaping a chore, activity, or social interaction that they disliked; (c) providing stimulation or enjoyment; or (d) some combination of these three functions (Figure 4.2).

A second explanation is that SIBs are caused by a hypersensitivity to the neurotransmitter dopamine. Three lines of evidence support this hypothesis. First, destroying dopamine receptors in the brains of neonatal rats causes them to develop a hypersensitivity to dopamine. If these rats are then injected with drugs that activate dopamine in the brain (e.g., dopamine agonists like amphetamine or cocaine), they display severe self-injury. Second, healthy rats given chronic high dosages of dopamine agonists also show self-injury. Third, some antipsychotic drugs, which bind to dopamine receptors, decrease SIBs in humans.

A third possibility is that SIBs are maintained by high levels of endogenous opioids or endorphins (Schroeder et al., 2001). These naturally occurring chemicals bind to certain receptors in the brain and produce analgesia and feelings of pleasure. Children and adults who show SIBs may

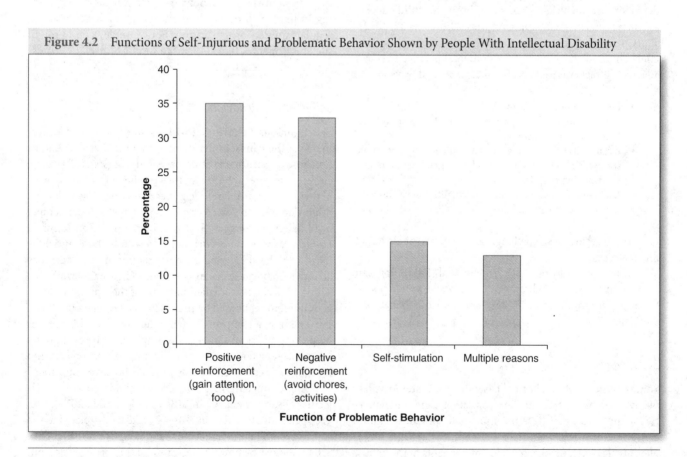

Figure 4.2 Functions of Self-Injurious and Problematic Behavior Shown by People With Intellectual Disability

Source: Based on Hanley et al. (2003).

Note: More than 95% of cases of problematic behavior have some identifiable function, usually maintained by positive or negative reinforcement.

be better able to tolerate the pain because of these analgesic properties. Some individuals who show SIBs may actually derive pleasure from self-injury.

Evidence for the endorphin hypothesis comes from three sources. First, people with Intellectual Disability who show SIBs display a dramatic increase in endorphins immediately after engaging in self-harm; this increase in naturally occurring opioids is much faster than in individuals who do not show SIBs (Sandman, Hetrick, & Taylor, 1997). Second, many people with Intellectual Disability and SIBs have abnormalities in the functioning of opioid receptors and levels in their brains (Sandman, Spence, & Smith, 1999). Third, some studies indicate that SIBs can be reduced by administering drugs that block opioid receptors (i.e., opioid antagonists; Thompson & Caruso, 2002).

Physical Aggression

Youths with Intellectual Disability, like their typically developing peers, sometimes engage in aggression (Farmer & Aman, 2011). **Aggression** refers to behavior that causes (or can cause) property destruction or injury/harm to another person. Aggressive acts include throwing objects, breaking toys, ruining furniture, hitting, kicking, and biting others. Some experts also consider name-calling, screaming, and yelling a form of aggression. By definition, aggressive acts are done deliberately, not by accident. However, it is sometimes very difficult to determine the intentions of children with severe or profound Intellectual Disability (Didden et al., 2012).

Approximately one fifth of children with Intellectual Disability also show recurrent problems with aggression. Most, but not all, studies indicate that children with both Intellectual Disability and Autism Spectrum Disorder are especially likely to display aggression. Furthermore, there is often an inverse relationship between children's IQ scores and the frequency of their aggressive acts (Didden et al., 2012). Interestingly, several studies have shown that deficits in verbal IQ, communication skills, and social skills were especially predictive of aggression. Many children with Intellectual Disability engage in aggression because they lack the language and social skills to convey their thoughts and feelings in more prosocial ways (Kanne & Mazurek, 2011).

Matson and colleagues (2011) reviewed the published literature on the causes of aggression in individuals with Intellectual Disability. Most individuals showed aggression in order to avoid or escape a task, assignment, or chore. For example, a child might push, throw an object, or yell at his teacher because she asked him to put on his coat. Often, the child's aggression is negatively reinforced by the teacher withdrawing her request and allowing the child to avoid the task. Other children engage in aggression for instrumental reasons, that is, to obtain an item or privilege that they want. For example, a child might shove a classmate to access a toy. To a lesser degree, children might engage in aggression, especially property destruction, because it is self-reinforcing.

Some youths find it pleasurable to destroy objects, toys, and furniture.

Comorbid Mental Health Problems

The term *dual diagnosis* refers to the presence of mental disorders among individuals with Intellectual Disability. Until recently, many mental health professionals believed that people with Intellectual Disability could not suffer from other psychiatric disorders. Some experts believed that low intellectual functioning somehow immunized these individuals against depression, anxiety, and psychological distress. Other professionals simply did not differentiate Intellectual Disability from other mental illnesses. Gradually, clinicians became aware that people with Intellectual Disability could suffer from the full range of psychiatric disorders. In fact, the prevalence of psychopathology among individuals with Intellectual Disability may be four to five times greater than the prevalence of mental disorders in the general population (Brereton, Tonge, & Einfeld, 2006; Wallander, Dekker, & Koot, 2006).

The exact prevalence of psychiatric disorders among individuals with Intellectual Disability is unknown because their behavioral and emotional problems are often overlooked. *Diagnostic overshadowing* refers to the tendency of clinicians to attend to the features of Intellectual Disability rather than to the symptoms of coexisting mental disorders. Why might clinicians miss anxiety, depression, and even psychotic symptoms in people with Intellectual Disability? Some mental health professionals simply do not have much experience in assessing and treating people with intellectual disabilities. Others erroneously attribute psychiatric problems to the person's low intelligence or problems in adaptive functioning (Einfeld et al., 2006; Koskentausta, Iivanainen, & Almqvist, 2007).

EPIDEMIOLOGY

Prevalence

Experts disagree about the prevalence of Intellectual Disability. If we assume that IQ scores are normally distributed in the population, we would expect approximately 2.5% of individuals in the general population to earn IQ scores less than 70. Consequently, some people estimate the prevalence of Intellectual Disability to be between 2.5% and 3% of the general population (Hodapp et al., 2006).

Other experts argue that the prevalence of Intellectual Disability is lower (Tirosch & Jaffe, 2011). A meta-analysis suggested that approximately 1.83% of individuals have Intellectual Disability (Yeargin-Allsop, Boyle, & van Naarden, 2008). There are several reasons for this lower estimate. First, Intellectual Disability is not determined by the individual's IQ score alone; the diagnosis also requires impairment in adaptive functioning. Many people with IQ scores in the 55–70 range do not show significant deficits in adaptive functioning. Consequently, they are not diagnosed with Intellectual Disability.

Second, a person's IQ can fluctuate over time. Although IQ scores are quite stable for people with severe and profound impairments, IQs are less stable for individuals scoring on the higher end of the Intellectual Disability continuum (i.e., IQ 55–70). Someone might earn an IQ score below 70 when assessed as a child but earn a score above 75 in adolescence. Consequently, he or she would no longer qualify for the diagnosis (Keogh, Bernheimer, & Guthrie, 1997).

Third, the life expectancy of individuals with severe and profound impairment is less than the life expectancy of typically developing individuals. Because of this reduced longevity, the number of people with Intellectual Disability is likely lower than expected based on the normal curve.

Age and Gender

The prevalence of Intellectual Disability varies by age. Intellectual Disability is more frequently diagnosed among school-age children and adolescents than among adults (Hodapp & Dykens, 2006). If all adults in a town are screened for Intellectual Disability, the prevalence is approximately 1.25% (McLaren & Bryson, 1987); if only school-age children are assessed, the prevalence increases to 2.5% (National Center for Educational Statistics, 2003). Why are more school-age children classified as having Intellectual Disability than people in the general population? The answer

seems to be that the cognitive impairments associated with Intellectual Disability are more noticeable when people are in school. After a person leaves school, these impairments are less noticeable, and people with them are less likely to be identified.

Intellectual Disability is slightly more common in males than in females. The gender ratio is approximately 1.3:1. Experts disagree on why males are more likely to show Intellectual Disability than females. Some people believe the male central nervous system is more susceptible to damage. Others believe that males are more likely to show Intellectual Disability than females because some forms of Intellectual Disability are caused by abnormalities on the X chromosome. Because boys have only one X chromosome, they may be more susceptible to disabilities caused by damage to this chromosome (Hodapp et al., 2006; Stromme & Hagberg, 2000).

ETIOLOGY

Organic Versus Cultural-Familial Intellectual Disability

Edward Zigler (1969) proposed one of the first methods to classify children with Intellectual Disability based on the cause of their impairments. Zigler divided children with Intellectual Disability into two groups (Table 4.4). The first group consisted of children with identifiable causes for their

Table 4.4 Intellectual Disability Classified Into Organic Versus Cultural-Familial Types

	Organic	*Cultural-Familial*
Definition	• Child shows a clear genetic or biological cause for his/her Intellectual Disability	• Child shows no obvious cause for his/her Intellectual Disability • Biological relatives may have low IQ
Diagnosis	• Usually diagnosed at birth or infancy • Frequent comorbid disorders	• Usually diagnosed after beginning school • Few comorbid disorders
Intelligence and Adaptive Functioning	• IQ usually ≤ 50 • Siblings with normal IQ • Greater impairment in adaptive functioning • Often dependent on others	• IQ usually > 50 • Siblings with low IQ • Lesser impairment in adaptive functioning • Can live independently with support
Associated Characteristics	• Similar across ethnicities and SES groups • Associated with health problems and physical disabilities • Higher mortality rate • Unlikely to mate, often infertile • Often have facial abnormalities	• More prevalent in ethnic minorities and low-SES groups • Usually few health problems and no physical disabilities • Normal mortality rate • Likely to marry and have children with low IQ • Normal appearance

Source: Based on Iarocci and Petrill (2012).

Note: Although these names are somewhat misleading, they are useful for broadly differentiating people with intellectual disabilities.

impairments. He classified these children with **organic Intellectual Disability** because most of the known causes of Intellectual Disability at that time involved genetic disorders or biological abnormalities, such as Down Syndrome. As a group, children with organic Intellectual Disability had IQ scores less than 50, physical features indicating neurological problems, and medical complications associated with the disorder. Children with organic Intellectual Disability usually had parents and siblings with normal intellectual functioning and came from families of all socioeconomic backgrounds (Iarocci & Petrill, 2012).

Children in the second group showed no clear cause for their cognitive and adaptive impairments. They tended to earn IQ scores in the 50 to 70 range, had normal physical appearance, and showed no other health or medical problems. They were more likely to have parents, siblings, and other biological relatives with low intellectual functioning. Furthermore, they often came from low-income families. Zigler referred to individuals in this second group as experiencing "familial" Intellectual Disability because children and family members often had low levels of intellectual and adaptive functioning. Today, many experts refer to people in this category as experiencing cultural-familial Intellectual Disability because children in this group are believed to experience Intellectual Disability due to a combination of environmental deprivation (e.g., low levels of cognitive stimulation, poor schools) and genetic diathesis toward low intelligence (Iarocci & Petrill, 2012).

The terms *organic* and *cultural-familial* can be misleading. A child with organic Intellectual Disability does not necessarily have a genetic cause for his impairments. Similarly, the deficits shown by a child with familial Intellectual Disability are not necessarily caused by environmental factors. The organic/familial distinction is based solely on whether we can identify the cause of the child's Intellectual Disability. For example, some cases of organic Intellectual Disability are caused by environmental factors, such as mothers' consumption of alcohol during pregnancy. Similarly, some types of familial Intellectual Disability may be due to genetic anomalies that we have not yet identified. For example, the cause of Fragile X Syndrome, the second-most common genetic cause of Intellectual Disability, was not identified until 1991. Even today, as many as 80% of people with Fragile X do not know they have the disorder (Dykens, Hodapp, & Finucane, 2000). As genetic and medical research progresses, it is likely that more causes of Intellectual Disability will be uncovered (Hodapp et al., 2006).

Similar Sequence and Similar Structure

Typically developing children progress through a series of cognitive stages in a reliable order across their development. Infants learn to represent people in their minds and engage in pretend play, preschoolers show mastery of language,

school-age children develop knowledge of conservation and concrete problem solving, and adolescents show higher level abstract thinking. Zigler (1969) suggested that the sequence of cognitive development among children with Intellectual Disability is similar to the sequence of cognitive development seen in typically developing children. His **similar sequence hypothesis** posits that children with Intellectual Disability progress through the same cognitive stages as typically developing children, albeit at a slower pace.

Zigler (1969) also suggested that the cognitive structures of children with Intellectual Disability are similar to the cognitive structures of typically developing children of the same mental age. His **similar structure hypothesis** indicates that two children of the same mental age (one with Intellectual Disability and the other without Intellectual Disability) will show similar abilities. According to the similar structure hypothesis, a 16-year-old with Intellectual Disability whose intellectual functioning resembles that of a 5-year-old child should show the same pattern of cognitive abilities as a typically developing 5-year-old child.

Subsequent research on children with cultural-familial Intellectual Disability has generally supported the similar sequence and similar structure hypotheses. Children with cultural-familial Intellectual Disability show the expected sequence of cognitive development, although they reach stages at a slower rate than typically developing children (Zigler, Balla, & Hodapp, 1986). Furthermore, children with cultural-familial Intellectual Disability generally show similar cognitive abilities as children without Intellectual Disability of the same developmental age (Weisz, 1990).

Subsequent research involving children with organic Intellectual Disability has yielded mixed results. The cognitive development of children with organic Intellectual Disability does follow an expected sequence, similar to the development of typically developing children. However, children with organic Intellectual Disability often show different cognitive abilities than typically developing children of the same mental age. Specifically, children with organic Intellectual Disability often show characteristic strengths and weaknesses in their cognitive abilities; their cognitive abilities are not uniformly low. Furthermore, these cognitive strengths and weaknesses depend on the cause of the child's Intellectual Disability. For example, children with Down Syndrome often show one pattern of cognitive abilities, whereas children with Fragile X Syndrome show different cognitive profiles.

Behavioral Phenotypes

The finding that children with different types of organic Intellectual Disability show characteristic patterns of cognitive abilities is important. If scientists could identify the cognitive and behavioral characteristics associated with each known cause for Intellectual Disability, this information could be used to plan children's education and improve their adaptive functioning (Hodapp & DesJardin, 2002).

Consequently, researchers have moved away from lumping all children with known causes of Intellectual Disability into one large "organic" category. Instead, researchers study children with Intellectual Disability in separate groups in order to better understand the strengths and weaknesses associated with each disorder. For example, some researchers study the abilities of children with Down Syndrome while others focus on the strengths and weaknesses of children with Fragile X Syndrome (Hodapp et al., 2006).

Stated another way, researchers are interested in determining a **behavioral phenotype** for children with each known cause of Intellectual Disability. According to Dykens (1995), a behavioral phenotype involves "the heightened probability or likelihood that people with a given syndrome will exhibit certain behavioral or developmental sequelae relative to those without the syndrome" (p. 523). Behavioral phenotypes include the appearance, overall intellectual and adaptive functioning, cognitive strengths and weaknesses, co-occurring psychiatric disorders, medical complications, and developmental outcomes of children with specific causes for their Intellectual Disability. Behavioral phenotypes are probabilistic. Although not every child will show all of the features associated with the disorder, a general description might help organize and guide research and assist practitioners in developing empirically based interventions (Dykens, 2001; Hodapp & DesJardin, 2002). In the next section, we examine some of these known causes of organic Intellectual Disability and the characteristic abilities and behaviors shown by children with each disorder.

Causes of Intellectual Disability

More than 750 different causes of Intellectual Disability have been identified. They can be loosely organized into five general categories: (a) chromosomal abnormalities, (b) metabolic disorders, (c) embryonic teratogen exposure, (d) complications during delivery, and (e) childhood illness or injury.

Chromosomal Abnormalities

Down Syndrome. Down Syndrome is a genetic disorder characterized by moderate to severe Intellectual Disability, problems with language and academic functioning, and characteristic physical features. The disorder was first described by John Langdon Down in 1866. It occurs in approximately 1 per 1,000 live births. The likelihood of having a child with Down Syndrome depends on maternal age (Figure 4.3).

Approximately 95% of cases of Down Syndrome are caused by an extra 21st chromosome. This form of the disorder is sometimes called "trisomy 21" because the child shows three chromosome 21s rather than the usual two. Trisomy 21 is not inherited. Instead, it is due to a **nondisjunction**, that is, a failure of the chromosome to separate during meiosis.

Figure 4.3   Risk of Down Syndrome Increases as a Function of Maternal Age

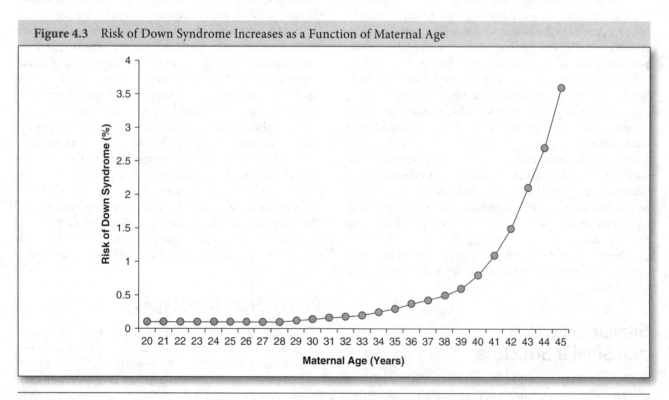

Source: Based on Cuckle, Wald, and Thompson (1987).

Note: After a woman reaches age 35, most physicians recommend prenatal screening due to increased risk.

In most cases, the mother contributes two chromosomes instead of one, but cases of paternal nondisjunction have also been reported.

Down Syndrome can also occur when the child inherits one chromosome 21 from each parent and an abnormally fused chromosome (usually consisting of chromosomes 21 and 15) from one of the parents. This abnormality, called a **translocation**, results in additional genetic material passed on to the child. It occurs in approximately 3% of youths with Down Syndrome. Down Syndrome caused by translocation is inherited. Usually, the parents are unaffected carriers of abnormally fused chromosomes, and they unknowingly pass them on to their children.

Finally, Down Syndrome can occur when some cells fail to separate during mitosis. This causes the child to have some normal cells and some cells with an abnormal amount of genetic information. The mix of normal and abnormal genetic information is called **chromosomal mosaicism**. Just as a mosaic is made up of different colored tiles, people with chromosomal mosaicism have cells of different genetic makeups. Chromosomal mosaicism accounts for approximately 2% of cases of Down Syndrome.

Children with Down Syndrome have characteristic facial features including flattened face, slanting eyes, wide nasal bridge, and low-set ears (Image 4.5). Other physical features include short stature and poor muscle tone (hypotonia). In most typically developing children, the palms show two or more large, horizontal creases. In contrast, children with Down Syndrome often show a single large crease, known as a simian crease, extending from the thumb across the palm. Children with Down Syndrome show small overall brain size and fewer folds and convolutions than in brains of typically developing children. Fewer folds suggest reduced surface area of the cortex and may be partially responsible for low intelligence (Key & Thornton-Wells, 2012).

Children with Down Syndrome are almost always diagnosed with Intellectual Disability; few of these children earn IQ scores greater than 60. Cognitive development progresses in a typical fashion for the first few months of life. After the child's first birthday, however, intellectual development slows and falls further behind typically developing peers. As a result, the delays of children with Down Syndrome become more pronounced with age.

Children with Down Syndrome show significant deficits in language (Dykens & Hodapp, 2001). They often have simplistic grammar, limited vocabulary, impoverished sentence structure, and impaired articulation. In fact, 95% of parents report difficulties understanding the speech of their children with Down Syndrome (Kumin, 1994). These children also show problems with auditory learning and short-term memory. Consequently, they often struggle in traditional educational settings where teachers present most lessons verbally (Chapman & Bird, 2012).

In contrast, children with Down Syndrome show relative strengths in visual-spatial reasoning (Dykens & Hodapp, 2001). For example, these children can repeat a series of

Image 4.5 Michelle is a 7-year-old girl with Down Syndrome, preparing for her first communion. She attended religious education classes with other children her age and received communion with her classmates.

Source: Photo is courtesy of the National Association for Down Syndrome, www.nads.org. Used with permission of her mother.

hand movements presented visually more easily than they can repeat a series of numbers presented verbally (Dykens, Hodapp, & Evans, 2006). Some experts have suggested that teachers should capitalize on these children's visual-spatial abilities in the classroom. For example, Buckley (1999) taught children with Down Syndrome how to read by having children visually match printed words with pictures, play word-matching games with flashcards, and manipulate flashcards with words printed on them into sentences. These techniques, which relied heavily on their propensity toward visual learning, led to increased reading skills. Furthermore, their advances in reading spilled over into other areas, such as speech and language.

Young children with Down Syndrome are usually described as happy, social, and friendly. It is extremely rewarding to volunteer as a tutor for a child with Down Syndrome because these children are often socially outgoing and affectionate. Children with Down Syndrome are less likely to develop psychiatric disorders than other children with Intellectual Disability (Dykens et al., 2006). However, in adolescence they may experience emotional and behavioral problems due to social isolation or increased recognition of their impairments (Reiss, 1990).

Medical complications associated with Down Syndrome include congenital heart disease, thyroid abnormalities, respiratory problems, and leukemia (Chase, Osinowo, & Pary, 2002). After age 35, many adults with Down Syndrome show early symptoms of Alzheimer's Disease (Coppus et al., 2006). Postmortem studies of their brains have shown a high incidence of neurofibrillary tangles and plaques, similar to those shown by older adults with Alzheimer's Disease. The life expectancy for individuals with Down Syndrome is approximately 60 years.

Fragile X Syndrome. Fragile X Syndrome is an inherited genetic disorder that is associated with physical anomalies, moderate to severe intellectual impairment, and social/ behavioral problems. It occurs in 1 per 1,500 live births— about 1 per 1,000 males and 1 per 2,000 females (Sadock & Sadock, 2003).

Fragile X Syndrome is caused by a mutation in a gene on the X chromosome, called the **Fragile X Mental Retardation 1 (FMR1) gene** (Cornish, Bertone, Kogan, & Scerif, 2012). In healthy individuals, this gene contains a three-nucleotide sequence of cytosine-guanine-guanine (CGG) that repeats a small number of times. It produces Fragile X Mental Retardation Protein (FMRP), which assists in normal brain maturation and cognitive development (Comery, Harris, Willems, Oostra, & Greenough, 1997). Children with Fragile X Syndrome show an unusually high number of CGG repeats. Children who inherit 50 to 200 repeated sequences usually show no symptoms. They are typically unaware that they carry the genetic mutation, but they may pass this mutation on to their offspring. Children who inherit more than 200 repeated sequences usually show symptoms. The repeated sequences interfere with the functioning of the FMR1 gene and, consequently, decrease the amount of FMRP produced (Pieretti et al., 1991). The disorder is called "fragile" X because the X chromosome appears broken (Image 4.6). In general, the less FMRP produced, the more severe children's cognitive impairments (Tassone et al., 1999). Brain scans of children with Fragile X show abnormalities of the prefrontal cortex, caudate nucleus, and cerebellum, presumably from less FMRP production (Stevenson et al., 2012).

Boys and girls differ in their presentation of Fragile X Syndrome, with boys showing greater intellectual impairment, more severe behavior problems, and more physical anomalies. Boys show relatively greater impairment because they inherit only one affected X chromosome. Girls, on the other hand, inherit one affected X chromosome and a second X chromosome, which is typically unaffected. The additional unaffected X chromosome produces normal amounts

Image 4.6 Fragile X Syndrome is caused by the FMR 1 gene located at the lower long arm of the X chromosome. This genetic abnormality gives the chromosome a "fragile" or broken appearance.

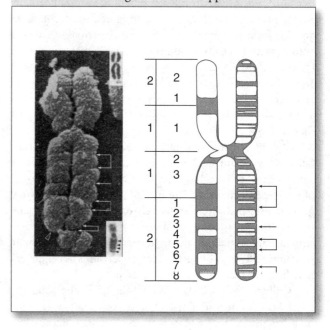

of FMRP and contributes to higher cognitive functioning (Cornish et al., 2012).

Boys with Fragile X tend to have elongated heads, large ears, hyper-flexible joints, and large testicles after puberty (Sadock & Sadock, 2003). They also tend to be shorter than other boys. Medical problems sometimes associated with Fragile X include heart murmur and crossed eyes (Image 4.7).

Image 4.7 Blake is a preschool-age boy with fragile X syndrome. His parents describe him as "a sweet and spunky little guy."

Source: Used with permission from the National Fragile X Foundation, www.fragilex.org.

Boys with Fragile X Syndrome tend to show moderate to severe Intellectual Disability (Abbeduto, McDuffie, Brady, & Kover, 2012). Additionally, they show a curious pattern of strengths and weaknesses in the way they process information and solve problems (Alanay et al., 2007). They perform relatively well on tasks that require **simultaneous processing**, that is, perceiving, organizing, and interpreting information all at once. Solving puzzles or completing mazes demands simultaneous processing. Alternatively, boys with Fragile X Syndrome show relative deficits in **sequential processing**, that is, the capacity to arrange and process information in a certain order. Reading a sentence or following instructions on how to assemble a toy requires sequential processing. These boys also show weakness in planning and organizing activities in an efficient manner (Loesch et al., 2003).

Boys with Fragile X also tend to show characteristic patterns of behavior. Most notably, many show autistic-like behavior, such as a reluctance to make eye contact or be touched by others. However, only about 25% of boys with Fragile X meet diagnostic criteria for autism. The rest appear extremely shy in social situations. Many boys with Fragile X also display hyperactivity and inattention. Perhaps as many as 90% have ADHD (Dykens & Hodapp, 2001; Sullivan, Hooper, & Hatton, 2007).

Girls with Fragile X tend to show higher IQs, less noticeable physical anomalies, and less severe behavior problems than do boys with the disorder. Like boys, girls may have problems with visual-spatial abilities (Cornish, Munir, & Cross, 1998) and inattention (Mazzocco, Pennington, & Hagerman, 1993). They may also show excessive shyness, gaze aversion, and social anxiety (Hodapp & Dykens, 2006).

Prader-Willi Syndrome. Prader-Willi Syndrome (PWS) is a non-inherited genetic disorder characterized by mild Intellectual Disability, overeating and obesity, oppositional behavior toward adults, and obsessive-compulsive behavior (Image 4.8). PWS occurs in 1 per 20,000 live births (Dykens & Shah, 2003).

PWS is usually caused by the deletion of genetic information on portions of chromosome 15. In 70% of cases, the father's information is deleted, so the child inherits only one set of genetic information, from the mother. In most of the remaining cases, the mother contributes both pairs of chromosome 15 (called **maternal uniparental disomy** [UPD]). In both instances, the father does not contribute the significant portion of chromosome 15, resulting in missing paternal genetic information.

Individuals with PWS show either mild Intellectual Disability or borderline intellectual functioning. Average IQs range from 65 to 70 (Dykens & Shah, 2003). These children show characteristic strengths and weaknesses on various cognitive tasks. For example, children with PWS show relative strengths on visual-spatial skills. Indeed, some children with PWS may be able to solve jigsaw puzzles faster than the psychologists who test them (Dykens & Cassidy, 1999). On the other hand, these children show weaknesses in short-term memory. Their adaptive behavior is usually much lower than

Image 4.8 This 15-year-old boy has Prader-Willi Syndrome, a genetic disorder characterized by Intellectual Disability, narrow temples, elongated face, thin upper lip and prominent nose.

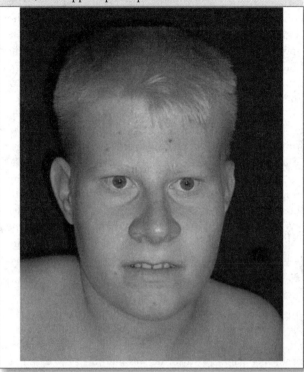

Source: Used with permission.

their IQ because their disruptive behavior often interferes with their acquisition of daily living skills.

The most striking feature of many children with PWS is their intense interest in food (Dykens, 2000; Dykens & Cassidy, 1999). Infants with the disorder show problems with sucking, feeding, and weight gain. However, between 2 and 6 years of age, children with PWS eat enormous amounts of food (i.e., **hyperphagia**). Some evidence suggests that these children have abnormal neural functioning in the paraventricular nucleus of the hypothalamus, the area of the brain that controls hunger and satiety. Since these children never feel full, they eat to excess and are often preoccupied by food. Some children steal food, hoard food, or obtain food from the garbage in an attempt to satisfy themselves. If their diet is not monitored, they will eat to excess and become obese. Medical complications associated with obesity are a leading cause of death among adults with PWS (Dykens & Shah, 2003).

The onset of hyperphagia is also associated with changes in behavior. Many (70%–95%) children with PWS become argumentative, defiant, and throw temper tantrums (Dykens & Cassidy, 1999; Dykens & Kasari, 1997). Approximately 42% of children with PWS destroy property during their disruptive outbursts, while 34% physically attack others (Dykens, Cassidy, & King, 1999).

Most (71%–98%) children with PWS show obsessive thoughts or ritualistic, compulsive behaviors (Dykens & Cassidy, 1999). The most common obsessions concern food (Dykens & Cassidy, 1999). They may eat foods in a certain order or according to color, texture, type, or caloric content (Dykens, 2000). Children with PWS often show nonfood obsessions and compulsive behavior, too. They may hoard paper and pens; order and arrange toys and household objects by color, size, or shape; repeat information or questions; appear overly concerned with symmetry; and redo activities (e.g., untying and tying shoes, rewriting homework) until the behavior is done exactly right (Dimitropoulos, Feurer, Butler, & Thompson, 2001). Most individuals with PWS pick their skin, usually on their head or legs (Dykens & Cassidy, 1999).

In early adulthood, some individuals with PWS show psychotic symptoms, including distorted thinking and hallucinations. In one study, 12.1% of parents of children with PWS reported auditory or visual hallucinations in their children (Stein, Keating, Zar, & Hollander, 1994). Life expectancy among adults with PWS is usually somewhat reduced because of obesity.

Angelman's Syndrome. Angelman's Syndrome is a genetically based developmental disorder characterized by Intellectual Disability, speech impairment, happy demeanor, and unusual motor behavior. The disorder was identified by the English physician Harry Angelman when three children (later diagnosed with the syndrome) were admitted to his hospital at the same time. All three children showed severe Intellectual Disability, an inability to speak, and problems with gait and balance. Their movements were sporadic, jerky, and irregular. They tended to walk with arms uplifted, sometimes on their toes, lurching forward with abrupt starts and stops. Most strikingly, all three children frequently smiled and laughed (Clayton-Smith, 2001; Dykens & Shah, 2003).

Later, while visiting the Castelvecchio Museum in Verona, Angelman saw a painting titled *Boy With a Puppet* that reminded him of the happy disposition of his three young patients (Image 4.9). Angelman subsequently wrote a scientific paper describing his three "Puppet Children," which slowly attracted the attention of clinicians throughout the world (Angelman, 1965). Today, professionals refer to the disorder as Angelman's Syndrome. Approximately 1 per 15,0000 to 20,000 children have the disorder.

Both PWS and Angelman's Syndrome are caused by abnormalities on portions of chromosome 15. Healthy children inherit two chromosome 15s, one from each parent. PWS occurs when children inherit genetic information on chromosome 15 only from the mother. In contrast, Angelman's Syndrome occurs when children inherit genetic information on chromosome 15 only from the father. In 70% of cases of Angelman's Syndrome, genetic information from the mother is deleted. In another 3% to 5% of cases, the father contributes two chromosome 15s and the mother contributes none. In

Image 4.9 *Boy With a Puppet*, Giovanni Francesco Caroto (1520). This oil painting prompted Angelman to write the first scientific account of children with the disorder that now bears his name. The smile of the boy in the painting reminded Angelman of his three patients.

the remaining cases of Angelman's Syndrome, the child shows other genetic mutations in chromosome 15 or the cause is unknown.

The most striking feature of Angelman's Syndrome is the persistent social smile and happy demeanor shown by children with the disorder. Many infants with Angelman's Syndrome begin this persistent smiling between 1 and 3 months of age. Later in development, it is accompanied by laughter, giggling, and happy grimacing. Facial features of children with Angelman's Syndrome often include a wide smiling mouth, thin upper lip, and pointed chin (Williams, 2005).

Despite children's social smiling, Angelman's Syndrome is usually not recognized until toddlerhood. Parents and physicians often suspect the disorder when children continue to show cognitive impairment, lack of spoken language, and movement problems. By childhood, children's intellectual functioning is generally in the range of severe or profound Intellectual Disability. Youths with the disorder show levels of functioning similar to a 2-and-a-half to 3-year-old child.

Most children with Angelman's Syndrome are unable to speak, although some can use a few words meaningfully. They usually can understand other people and are able to obey simple commands.

Nearly all children with Angelman's Syndrome show hyperactivity and inattention. Parents usually describe them as constantly "on the go." Children may flap their arms, fiddle with their hands, and become easily excited. Hyperactivity often interferes with their ability to sleep. Children with Angelman's Syndrome often have difficulty sustaining their attention on one person or task for long periods of time. Problems with hyperactivity and inattention continue throughout childhood but decrease somewhat with age.

Some children with Angelman's Syndrome show skin and eye hypopigmentation; that is, they may appear pale and have light-colored eyes. Hypopigmentation occurs when the gene that codes for skin pigmentation is deleted along with the other information on chromosome 15 that causes Angelman's Syndrome. Other children with Angelman's Syndrome show feeding problems in infancy. They may thrust their tongues outward when fed, have difficulty sucking and swallowing, or drool. In most cases, these problems resolve over time.

More than 90% of children with Angelman's Syndrome have seizures. Sometimes, seizures are difficult to notice because of these children's sporadic motor movements. In most cases, physicians prescribe anticonvulsant medications to reduce the number and severity of seizures. Adults with Angelman's Syndrome have life expectancies approximately 10 to 15 years shorter than typically developing individuals. Life expectancy is dependent on the severity of comorbid medical problems, especially seizures.

Williams Syndrome. Williams Syndrome (WS) is a genetic disorder characterized by low intellectual functioning, unusual strengths in spoken language and sociability, hyperactivity, impulsivity, and inattention (Elsabbagh & Karmiloff-Smith, 2012). Children with WS can be identified by their facial features. They often have broad foreheads; full lips; widely spaced teeth; star-shaped patterns in their irises; and elfin-like noses, eyes, and ears (Image 4.10). Their facial features suggest a mixture of joy and mischievousness. WS is caused by a small deletion in a portion of chromosome 7. The disorder occurs in approximately 1 per 20,000 live births.

Despite their low IQ scores, children with WS show curious strengths in certain areas of language (Mervis, 2012). They have unusually well-developed lexicons (Hodapp & Dykens, 2006). They can tell relatively complex stories with advanced vocabulary and sophisticated grammar (Reilly, Klima, & Bellugi, 1990). They may even use sound effects when telling stories to add emphasis. Some children with WS show relative strengths in auditory memory and music (Hodapp & DesJardin, 2002). Teachers sometimes alter their instructional methods to play to the strengths of children with WS. For example, children with WS might respond best

Image 4.10   Mary is a preschool-age girl with Williams Syndrome. She shows a persistent happy demeanor, characteristic of children with the disorder.

Source: Reprinted with permission of Mary's family.

to verbal instruction rather than to reading and may prefer to work with partners or in groups, rather than independently (Hodapp & DesJardin, 2002).

Children with WS do poorly on visual-spatial tasks. They have great difficulty copying pictures or figures. This relative deficit in visual-spatial abilities is likely due to the genetic deletion that causes WS. Specifically, the portion of chromosome 7 that is deleted contains a gene that codes for an enzyme called LIM kinase. This enzyme is necessary for brain development and functioning, especially in brain regions responsible for visual-spatial processing. Deficits in this enzyme likely underlie the visual-spatial problems shown by children with the disorder (Elsabbagh & Karmiloff-Smith, 2012).

Children with WS are described as friendly and sociable (Rosner, Hodapp, Fidler, Sagun, & Dykens, 2004). They are especially good at remembering faces and inferring a person's mental state and emotions based on his or her affect (Tager-Flusberg, Boshart, & Baron-Cohen, 1998). Sometimes, they are overly trusting of strangers, placing them at risk for exploitation by others.

Children with WS often show problems with high-rate behavior and are easily excitable. They display inattention, hyperactivity, and impulsivity; many are diagnosed with ADHD (Einfeld, 2005). Furthermore, children with WS show hyperacusis, that is, an unusual sensitivity to loud noises. Truck engines, fire alarms, and school bells can cause them considerable distress.

Most children with WS show problems with anxiety. Like typically developing children, young children with WS fear tangible and imposing images and events such as storms, vaccinations, and ghosts. However, unlike typically developing children, older children with WS continue to fear these stimuli and show a marked increase in generalized anxiety. In particular, older children with WS often fear that something bad is about to happen. Many are extremely sensitive to failure and criticism by others (Dykens, 2003). In a sample of 51 individuals with WS, 35% showed full-blown phobias for objects or social situations while 84% showed subthreshold problems with anxiety. In contrast, the prevalence of phobias among children with other types of Intellectual Disability is only about 1% (Landau, 2012)

Dykens and Hodapp (2001) have suggested that the characteristic features of WS may place them at increased risk for developing anxiety problems. For example, their hyperacusis may make them especially sensitive to developing fears of loud noises. Early problems with balance and gait might contribute to fears of falling from high places. Their social sensitivity may place them at increased risk for social anxiety. Consequently, the fears of children with WS may stem from the interaction of genotype, early experiences, and the behavioral characteristics of WS (Dykens & Hodapp, 2001).

Children with WS are at risk for cardiovascular problems. The portion of chromosome 7 that is deleted in WS also contains a gene that codes for elastin. Elastin is used by the cardiovascular system to give connective tissue its elastic, flexible properties. Insufficient elastin can cause hypertension, other cardiovascular diseases, and early death.

Metabolic Disorders

Phenylketonuria (PKU) is a metabolic disorder that is caused by a recessive gene inherited from both parents. In most cases, PKU is characterized by the body's inability to convert **phenylalanine**, an essential amino acid found in certain foods, to paratyrosine. In PKU, the enzyme that breaks down phenylalanine (phenylalanine hydroxylase) is not produced by the liver. As the child eats foods rich in phenylalanine, such as dairy, meats, cheeses, and certain breads, the substance builds up and becomes toxic. Phenylalanine toxicity eventually causes brain damage and Intellectual Disability.

PKU is caused by a recessive gene (Figure 4.4). In order for a child to show PKU, he or she must inherit the gene from

Figure 4.4   PKU Is an Autorecessive Metabolic Disorder

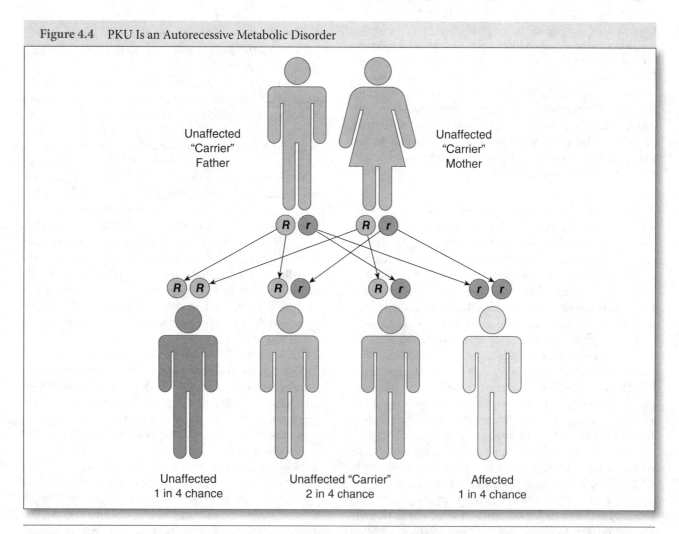

Note: Children must inherit the recessive gene from both parents to develop the disorder. If children inherit only one recessive gene, they will carry the disorder but not show symptoms.

both mother and father. Children who inherit the gene from only one parent are carriers of the disorder but do not display symptoms. If a carrier mates with another carrier, each offspring has a 25% chance of showing PKU. The disorder occurs in approximately 1 per 11,500 children.

Newborns are routinely screened for PKU through a blood test conducted shortly after birth. If the disorder is detected, the child is placed on a diet consisting of foods that are low in phenylalanine. The diet decreases the chances of toxicity; consequently, adherence to the diet results in normal intellectual development. Most physicians suggest the diet should be continued indefinitely. Since phenylalanine is an essential amino acid, children on the diet must be monitored by their pediatricians. They are at risk for low red blood cell count (anemia) and low blood glucose levels (hypoglycemia).

Youths with PKU who do not diet show symptoms several months after birth. By childhood, they often develop severe intellectual impairment. Children with untreated PKU are often hyperactive, show erratic motor movements, and throw tantrums. They also may vomit and have convulsions. They usually cannot communicate with others. These impairments are irreversible, even if a phenyl-free diet is initiated later in childhood.

Embryonic Teratogen Exposure

Intellectual Disability can also occur when children are exposed to certain environmental toxins during gestation. The placenta is a bag-like membrane that partially surrounds the fetus during gestation. It delivers oxygen and nutrients from the mother to the fetus and allows the fetus to excrete waste. The placenta is porous; substances ingested by the mother can pass directly to the fetal system. **Teratogens** are environmental substances that cause maldevelopment in the fetus, often resulting in Intellectual Disability.

Maternal Illness. Viruses acquired by the mother during pregnancy used to be a leading cause of organic Intellectual Disability. Exposure to the **rubella virus**, especially during the first few months of pregnancy, often caused severe Intellectual Disability, cataracts, and deafness. Similarly, **maternal syphilis** was associated with fetal maldevelopment and Intellectual Disability. Other diseases, such as measles, mumps, diphtheria, tetanus, and poliovirus, can also cause Intellectual Disability. Today, these illnesses are largely prevented by childhood immunizations and regular medical care.

Infants can acquire **human immunodeficiency virus** (HIV) from an infected mother either in utero or through breast feeding. HIV causes damage to the child's central nervous and immune systems. The risk of transmission from an infected mother is approximately 30%. However, zidovudine (Retrovir), taken prenatally by mothers, can reduce the likelihood of transmission to less than 5% (Sadock & Sadock, 2003). The progression of HIV in newborns is more rapid than in adults. Most infants born with HIV show progressive brain degeneration, Intellectual Disability, and seizures during their first year of life. Most affected children die before age three.

Maternal Substance Use. Many drugs, if ingested by pregnant women, are associated with low birth weight, small head circumference, and increased risk for behavioral and learning problems in childhood. Interestingly, "hard" drugs, such as heroin and cocaine, are not as consistently associated with children's Intellectual Disability as are more socially accepted drugs like alcohol.

Fetal Alcohol Syndrome (FAS) is caused by maternal alcohol consumption during pregnancy. FAS is characterized by Intellectual Disability, hyperactivity, and slow physical growth as well as characteristic craniofacial anomalies (Figure 4.5). Children with FAS often have cardiac problems. By school age, they tend to show hyperactivity and learning problems.

Figure 4.5 Children With Fetal Alcohol Syndrome

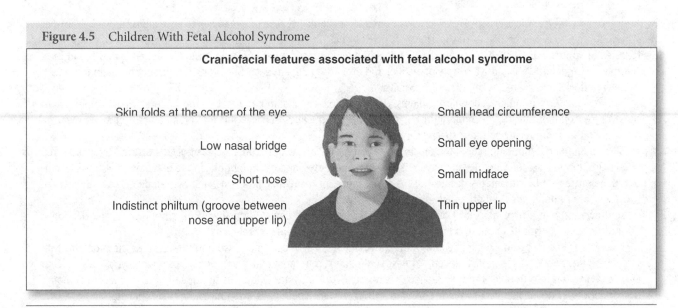

Craniofacial features associated with fetal alcohol syndrome

Skin folds at the corner of the eye

Low nasal bridge

Short nose

Indistinct philtrum (groove between nose and upper lip)

Small head circumference

Small eye opening

Small midface

Thin upper lip

Note: Children with Fetal Alcohol Syndrome often have facial anomalies as well as low intellectual functioning.

The prevalence of FAS is approximately 1 to 3 per 1,000 live births. However, among children of women who have Alcohol Use Disorder, the prevalence is approximately 1 in 3. Experts disagree on how much alcohol must be consumed to produce FAS. Some data indicate that FAS can occur from only 2 to 3 oz. of alcohol per day during gestation. Furthermore, binge drinking during pregnancy greatly increases the chance of FAS. Although occasional consumption of alcohol during pregnancy may not produce FAS, it may lead to subtle cognitive, behavioral, and physical abnormalities, such as mild learning problems, reduced attention span, or short stature. Most physicians recommend abstaining from alcohol entirely during pregnancy.

The intellectual functioning of children with FAS varies considerably. Most children with FAS show mild to moderate Intellectual Disability, although some earn IQ scores within the borderline to low-average range. These children usually have academic problems and may drop out of school. Many have learning disabilities. The most common behavioral problems associated with FAS are hyperactivity, impulsivity, and inattention. Young children with FAS are often diagnosed with ADHD. Older children and adolescents with FAS report feelings of restlessness and difficulty sustaining attention on reading and other homework.

Children with FAS are at risk for mood problems as they enter late childhood and adolescence. They may become depressed because of their academic deficits, behavior problems, or stigmatization associated with the disorder.

Complications During Pregnancy and Delivery

Complications that occur during gestation or delivery can contribute to Intellectual Disability. Maternal hypertension or uncontrolled diabetes during pregnancy are sometimes associated with Intellectual Disability in children. Delivery complications that interfere with the fetus's ability to obtain oxygen for extended periods of time (**anoxia**) can also lead to central nervous system damage and Intellectual Disability. For example, anoxia can occur when the umbilical cord wraps around the fetus's throat, interfering with oxygen intake.

Children born before 36 weeks gestation are also at risk for deficits in intellectual and adaptive functioning in infancy and early childhood. Two meta-analyses have shown an inverse relationship between premature birth and children's subsequent IQ scores (Figure 4.6). Furthermore, a very large, community-based study found that the risk of developmental delays increased exponentially with decreasing gestational age. Approximately 4.2% of full-term infants showed motor, language, social, or daily living delays compared to 37.5% of infants born at 24 to 25 weeks gestation. Controlling for other biological and social factors, such as mother's age and education, did not affect this relationship between prematurity and developmental risk (Kerstjens et al., 2013).

Preterm birth is a risk factor because of the rapid growth of the central nervous system during the third trimester. Between 24 and 40 weeks gestation, the fetus's cortical volume increases fourfold. There is a dramatic increase in the number of neurons,

CASE STUDY

ANDREW: A BOY WITH FAS

Andrew was a 14-year-old boy with FAS who was referred to our clinic because of a marked increase in disruptive behavior at school. Andrew was a large boy, approximately 5 feet, 10 inches and more than 160 lbs. He displayed many of the physical features of youths with Fetal Alcohol Syndrome, including wide-spaced eyes, upturned nose, low-set ears, and broad face. Andrew's mother had an extensive history of alcohol and other drug dependence. She drank throughout her pregnancy with Andrew and was intoxicated at the time of his delivery.

Andrew had long-standing academic problems. His IQ was 67. His reading and mathematics scores were comparable to those of a second- or third-grade child. Andrew received special education services, including remedial tutoring; however, he felt humiliated about receiving these special services.

Since beginning junior high school the previous year, Andrew's behavior became increasingly disruptive. He would often "clown around" in class, play pranks on teachers and other classmates, and get into fights on the playground. Andrew admitted to being teased by classmates because of his appearance, his academic problems, and his family history. "I know I'm slow," he said, "I don't need the other kids to tell me."

Andrew met with a psychologist at our clinic for weekly therapy sessions. Andrew was initially clownish and disruptive during the sessions, but he gradually came to trust his therapist and share his feelings.

During one session, Andrew commented, "You know, if it wasn't for my mom, I wouldn't have all of the problems that I'm having right now." His therapist replied, "I guess you're right. Your mom makes you pretty upset when you visit her. That causes you to get into trouble." Andrew replied, hesitantly, "No. That's not what I mean. I mean, if it wasn't for my mom's drinking—when I was inside her—I wouldn't be so dumb. If only she could have loved me more than drinking."

Figure 4.6 Preterm Birth Places Infants at Greater Risk for Delays

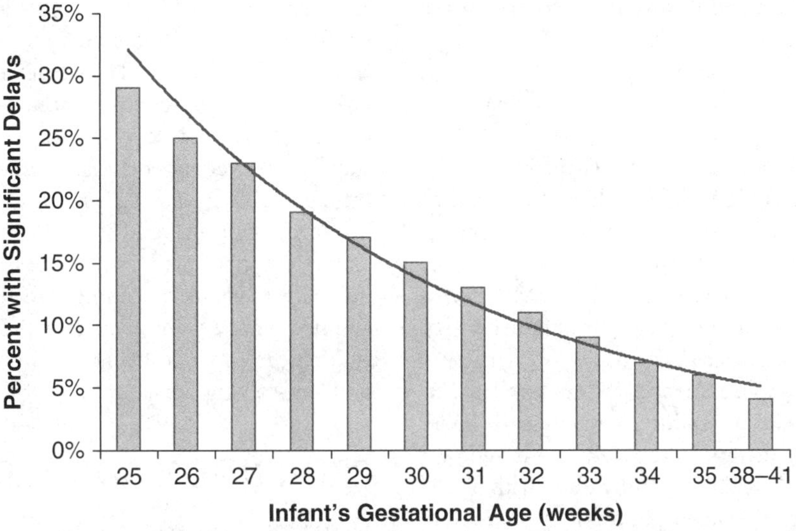

Source: From Kerstjens and colleagues (2013).

Note: Preterm infants are at much greater risk for delays in motor, language, social, and daily living skills than full-term infants. Risk increases exponentially with decreased gestational age.

axons, and synapses; increased myelination; and more complex brain activity. Although maturation can (and does) continue after delivery, the conditions for optimal development occur in utero (Volpe, 2008).

Childhood Illness or Injury

The two childhood illnesses most associated with the development of Intellectual Disability are encephalitis and meningitis. **Encephalitis** refers to the swelling of brain tissue, whereas **meningitis** refers to an inflammation of the meninges, the membrane that surrounds the brain and spinal cord. Both illnesses can be caused by bacteria or viral infections, although viral infections are more serious because they are often resistant to treatment.

All serious head injuries have the potential to cause Intellectual Disability. An obvious source of injuries is car accidents; however, most childhood head injuries occur around the home. Falls from tables, open windows, and stairs account for many injury-related cognitive impairments. Similarly, children who almost drown in swimming pools or bathtubs can experience brain damage and corresponding cognitive problems. Finally, children who are physically abused can experience Intellectual Disability because of environmental neglect or physical trauma (Appleton & Baldwin, 2006).

Lead toxicity is a risk factor for Intellectual Disability. Lead can be found in the paint of older buildings, in lead-soldered water pipes, and in industrial waste. Infants and toddlers may eat paint chips flaking off the walls of older homes. Older children may inhale dust containing lead-based paint from walls, porches, and window panes. Lead enters the child's bloodstream and produces widespread cerebral damage. Exposure can cause Intellectual Disability, movement problems (ataxia), convulsions, and coma. If poisoning is detected early, children can be treated by flushing the lead from the bloodstream. Damage caused by prolonged exposure is irreversible.

The risk of lead poisoning varies by socioeconomic status (SES) and ethnicity. For example, 7% of middle-class white children are exposed to sufficient amounts of lead to cause poisoning. The risk of lead poisoning among low-income white and black children is much higher: 25% and 55%, respectively. Risk is particularly high among poor children living in urban settings (Dilworth-Bart & Moore, 2006; Phelps, 2005).

Causes of Cultural-Familial Intellectual Disability

Cultural-familial Intellectual Disability results from the interaction of the child's genes and environmental experiences over time. Children inherit a genetic propensity toward low intelligence. Furthermore, these children experience environmental deprivation that interferes with their ability to reach their cognitive potentials. Environmental deprivation might include poor access to health care, inadequate nutrition, lack of cognitive stimulation during early childhood (e.g., parents talking, playing, and reading with children), low-quality educational experiences, and lack of cultural experiences (e.g., listening to music, trips to the museum). Over time, the interaction between genes and environment contributes to children's low intellectual functioning.

Socioeconomic Status

Familial Intellectual Disability is more prevalent among children from low-income families than middle-class families. The correlation between SES and children's intelligence is approximately .33. Furthermore, the relationship between SES and children's IQ increases when children experience extreme poverty or socioeconomic disadvantage (Turkheimer, Haley, Waldron, D'Onofrio, & Gottesman, 2003).

Both genetic and environmental factors explain this association between SES and children's intelligence. With respect to genetics, low-income parents tend to have lower IQ scores than middle-class parents. Individuals with higher IQs complete more years of schooling and assume more challenging and higher paying jobs. The children of high-income parents inherit their parents' genotypes that predispose them to a higher range of intellectual and adaptive functioning (Stromme & Magnus, 2000).

Furthermore, children from low-income families are exposed to environments that may restrict their intellectual potential. For example, low-income children are more likely to experience gestational and birth complications, have limited access to high-quality health care and nutrition, have greater exposure to environmental toxins, receive less cognitive stimulation from their home environments, and attend less optimal schools (McLoyd, 1998). These environmental deficits or risk factors limit the child's cognitive and adaptive potential. Young children in poverty earn IQ scores approximately nine points lower than children from middle-class families (Brooks-Gunn & Duncan, 1997; Duncan & Brooks-Gunn, 2000).

Ethnicity

Familial Intellectual Disability is also more frequently seen among ethnic minorities, especially African American children (Raghavan & Small, 2004). This association is partially due to the fact that many African American children live in low-income families and experience the same genetic and environmental risk factors as children from other low-income families. Whereas the average IQ score for middle-class whites is approximately 100, the average IQ score for low-income African Americans is approximately 90. Consequently, African Americans and individuals from low-income families are more frequently diagnosed with mild Intellectual Disability than are white, middle-class children (McLoyd, Hill, & Dodge, 2005).

Home Environment

Many studies suggest a relationship between the quality of the home environment and children's intellectual development.

After reviewing the data, Sattler (2002) identified two broad ways parents can enrich their children's home environment and help them achieve their intellectual potentials. First, families who provide their children with ample verbal stimulation, model and provide feedback regarding language, and give many opportunities for verbal learning appear to foster greater intellectual development in their children. Parents should take every opportunity to interact with their children through talking, playing, and reading. Second, encouraging academic achievement, curiosity, and independence in children is associated with increased intellectual functioning. Parents should encourage creative play, arts and crafts, and homemade games and activities, especially with young children, in order to help them develop novel and flexible problem-solving skills.

PREVENTION AND TREATMENT
Prenatal Screening

Shortly after birth, newborns are routinely administered a series of blood tests in order to determine the presence of genetic and other medical disorders that might cause Intellectual Disability. For example, all infants are administered a genetic test to screen for PKU. If PKU is found, a genetic counselor and nutritionist will meet with parents to discuss feeding options for the child.

If parents are at risk for having children with Intellectual Disability or other developmental delays, a physician may recommend genetic screening during gestation. Parents who may be carriers of specific genetic disorders, parents who have other children with developmental delays, or mothers older than age 35 often participate in screening.

At 15 to 18 weeks' gestation, mothers can undergo **serum screening** (Newberger, 2000). This procedure is usually called the "triple test" or "triple screen" because it involves testing mother's blood for three serum markers: alpha-fetoprotein, unconjugated estriol, and human chorionic gonadotropin. These serums are naturally produced by the fetus's liver and the placenta. If the child has Down Syndrome, alpha-fetoprotein and unconjugated estiol may be unusually low, while human chorionic gonadotropin levels may be unusually high. Significant elevations can be a sign of a genetic disorder, but this test has a high rate of false positives. Consequently, if test results are positive, the physician will usually recommend that the mother participate in additional testing.

Amniocentesis is a more invasive screening technique that is usually conducted during weeks 15 to 20 of gestation. The procedure involves removing a small amount of amniotic fluid with a needle inserted into the abdomen of the mother. The amniotic fluid contains fetal cells, which can be cultured and examined for genetic abnormalities. Amniocentesis is invasive; it carries a 0.5% risk of fetal death. Amniocentesis can also be conducted before 15 weeks' gestation, at the beginning of the second trimester, but the risk of fetal death increases to 1%–2%.

Chorionic villus sampling (CVS) is another genetic screening technique that can be done earlier, usually between 8 and 12 weeks' gestation. In CVS, the physician takes a small amount of chorionic villi, the wisp-like tissue that connects the placenta to the wall of the uterus. This tissue usually has the same genetic and biochemical makeup as the developing fetus. The tissue can be analyzed to detect genetic or biological anomalies. CVS is usually performed only when there is greatly increased risk of the fetus having a developmental or medical disorder. The risk of miscarriage associated with CVS is 0.5% to 1.5%.

Recently, physicians have been using ultrasound to detect structural abnormalities in the fetus that might indicate the presence of a developmental disorder (Rissanen, Niemimaa, Suonpää, Ryynänen, & Heinonen, 2007). Ultrasound is believed to be a relatively safe procedure for both mother and fetus. Between 11 and 14 weeks' gestation, embryos with Down Syndrome often show flatter facial profile and shorter (or absent) nasal bones than typically developing fetuses. The presence of these physical abnormalities, revealed by ultrasound, could indicate the presence of a genetic disorder. Based on the findings, mothers can decide whether they want to pursue more invasive testing.

Infant and Preschool Prevention

A number of state- and locally administered programs have been developed to prevent the emergence of Intellectual Disability in children at risk for low IQ. One of the most recent and, perhaps, the best-designed prevention programs for at-risk children is the **Infant Health and Development Program** (IHDP). Participants in the IHDP were 985 premature infants who showed either low birth weight (weight 2,001 to 2,500 grams) or very low birth weight (weight < 2000 grams). Previous research indicated that these children were at increased risk for developmental delays, including Intellectual Disability and learning problems (Baumeister & Bacharach, 1996). Infants were randomly assigned to either an early intervention group or a control group. The parents of children in the intervention group received regular home visits from program staff. During these visits, staff taught parents games and activities that they could play with their infants to promote cognitive, linguistic, and social development. Staff also served as references to parents, helping parents address problems associated with caring for a preterm, low birth weight infant. When infants turned one year old, parents were invited to place them in a high-quality preschool program. The program was free and transportation to and from the preschool program was provided. The preschool ran year round, 5 days per week, until children were 3 years old. Families assigned to the control group were not given home visits or offered the preschool program.

To evaluate the success of the intervention, children's cognitive development was assessed at the end of the preschool program (age 3 years), at age 5 years, and at age 8 years. Children who participated in the program earned slightly higher IQs than children in the control group at age 3. However, by age 5, these differences in IQ disappeared.

The results of the IHDP indicate that early intervention programs can boost IQ scores among at-risk children, but increases in IQ are not maintained over time. The data are largely consistent with other early intervention programs designed to increase the cognitive functioning of low-income children (Farran, 2000).

Experts have disagreed on how to interpret the findings. Supporters of the IHDP concede that the results of the intervention were "largely negative" (Blair & Wahlsten, 2002, p. 130). However, advocates of the program believe the data speak to the importance of continuing educational enrichment for high-risk children beyond the preschool years. If the program had been extended through elementary school, children in the intervention group might have continued to show higher IQ scores than controls.

Critics of the IHDP argue that early intervention programs do not prevent Intellectual Disability and developmental delays and they should be discontinued (Baumeister & Bacharach, 2000). Instead, the money and time used for early intervention programs could be spent on primary prevention, such as providing at-risk families with better access to health care and nutrition. Critics argue that it is difficult to boost children's IQ because a person's genotype sets an upper limit on his or her intellectual potential (Baumeister & Bacharach, 2000). Furthermore, simply offering intervention services to high-risk families does not mean that they will take advantage of these services. In fact, 20% of children in the intervention group attended the preschool program less than 10 days in 2 years, and 55 children never attended at all (Hill, Brooks-Gunn, & Waldfogel, 2003). Since gains in IQ are directly related to participation in treatment, motivating families to participate in treatment seems to be a critical goal of any effective early intervention program.

Educational Interventions

Mainstreaming and Academic Inclusion

In 1975, Congress passed the Education of All Handicapped Children Act (Public Law 94-142). This act mandated a "free and appropriate public education" for all children with disabilities aged 3 to 18 years. From its implementation in 1977 through the mid-1980s, the practice of mainstreaming became more common in public school systems across the United States. **Mainstreaming** involved placing children with Intellectual Disability in classrooms with typically developing peers, to the maximum extent possible. At first, mainstreamed children with Intellectual Disability were allowed to participate in elective classes, such as physical education, art, and music, with typically developing children. For other subjects, they attended self-contained special education classes for children with developmental delays (Verhoeven & Vermeer, 2006).

In the mid-1980s, many parents argued that children with Intellectual Disability and other disabilities had the right to attend all classes with typically developing peers. This movement, sometimes called the "Regular Education Initiative," gradually led to the practice of inclusion. **Inclusion** involves the education of children with Intellectual Disability alongside typically developing peers for all subjects, usually with the support of a classroom aide.

In 1997, Congress amended PL 94–142 by passing the Individuals with Disabilities Education Act (IDEA; PL 105–17). IDEA codified the practice of inclusion by demanding that children with disabilities be educated in the least restrictive environment possible:

> To the maximum extent appropriate, children with disabilities . . . are educated with children who are not disabled, and special classes, separate schooling, or other removal of children with disabilities from the regular educational environment occurs only when the nature or severity of the disability of a child is such that education in regular classes with the use of supplementary aids and services cannot be achieved satisfactorily. (p. 61)

In addition to providing services for children with disabilities, IDEA also requires local educational systems to identify all infants, toddlers, and children with disabilities living in the community, whether or not they attend school. Once children are identified, a team of educational professionals (e.g., regular education teachers, special education teachers, school psychologists) conducts a comprehensive evaluation of the child's strengths and limitations and designs a written plan for the child's education. Infants and toddlers, aged 0 to 3 years, are provided with an **Individualized Family Services Plan (IFSP)**. For preschoolers and school-aged children, school personnel develop an **Individualized Education Program (IEP)** in consultation with parents. Typically, IEPs provide extra support to children while at school; children may be given special education services or a classroom aide. IEPs also usually specify accommodations for children with disabilities that help them achieve their cognitive, social, emotional, or behavioral potentials. IDEA was revised again in 2004 as the Individuals with Disabilities Education Improvement Act (PL 108–446; Williamson, McLeskey, Hoppey, & Rentz, 2006).

In general, inclusion improves the functioning of children with developmental disabilities, especially children with mild or moderate impairments. Inclusion seems to work best when (a) students with Intellectual Disability can become active in the learning process, and (b) these children frequently interact and cooperate with typically developing classmates. Inclusion may also have benefits for typically developing peers. Specifically, inclusion may teach typically developing children greater tolerance and understanding of individuals with developmental delays and increase students' willingness to welcome children with delays into their peer groups.

The educational rights of children with Intellectual Disability have increased greatly over the past 30 years. The trend toward inclusion has allowed these children to have access to educational experiences that their counterparts, a generation ago, were typically not afforded. Today, the focus of attention has shifted from *where* children are educated (e.g., regular versus special education classes) to *how* they are educated (e.g., the nature and quality of services they receive; Zigler, Hodapp, & Edison, 1990). Simply placing all children with disabilities in regular classrooms is not enough. Now, we must learn to tailor regular educational experiences to the needs of these children in order to allow them to benefit from these experiences. Tailoring might involve smaller class size, more classroom aides, greater access to behavioral or medical consultants, specialized teacher training, and more time for teachers to plan lessons for students with disabilities (Hocutt, 1996).

Universal Design in the Classroom

In recent years, universal design has been a primary method of including children with intellectual and physical disabilities. **Universal design** is an educational practice that involves creating instructional materials and activities that allow learning goals to be achievable by children with different abilities and skills (Schalock et al., 2010). All children (with and without disabilities) use and benefit from these educational materials.

The clearest example of universal design can be seen in accommodations for people with physical disabilities. Many sidewalks now have "curb cuts" or sidewalk ramps that allow people who use wheelchairs to more easily cross the street. Similarly, buses are often built with low floors, rather than steep steps, to allow people with orthopedic problems easier access. These specially designed sidewalks and buses are used by all people; even people without physical disabilities often find them easier to use (Goldsmith, 2012).

Similarly, teachers can design assignments and activities that are accessible to children with a wide range of abilities and skills. These assignments and activities offer alternatives to traditional lecturing, reading, and writing. They can be used to plan (a) the way teachers introduce content to students, (b) the format of instructional material, and (c) the way students demonstrate their learning (Coyne et al., 2012).

First, a teacher might use a wide variety of instructional strategies to match the diversity of students' skills and abilities. For example, a fourth-grade science teacher might find that all children (with and without disabilities) can learn about human anatomy by tracing their bodies on large sheets of paper and then drawing and labeling major organs. Similarly, a fourth-grade English teacher might demonstrate the steps involved in writing a book report using pictures, symbols, and arrows (i.e., graphic organizers) to help all students understand the temporal relationship of elements in a story (Figure 4.7).

Second, a teacher might modify the instructional technology she uses to present material. *Instructional technology* refers to the educational materials instructors use to teach

Figure 4.7 Using Universal Design at School

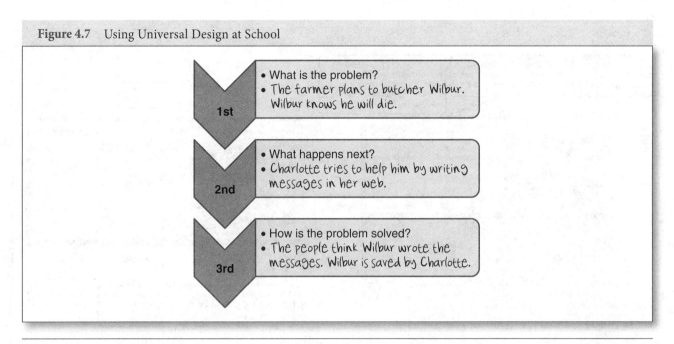

1st
- What is the problem?
- The farmer plans to butcher Wilbur. Wilbur knows he will die.

2nd
- What happens next?
- Charlotte tries to help him by writing messages in her web.

3rd
- How is the problem solved?
- The people think Wilbur wrote the messages. Wilbur is saved by Charlotte.

Note: Teachers might use a graphic organizer, like this flow chart, to help children write a book report.

ideas and concepts. For example, the science teacher might supplement her lessons with a child-friendly website about human anatomy. The website might allow children to enlarge the size of text, to read text aloud, and to access diagrams, pictures, videos. Similarly, the English teacher might use digital media that allows children to simultaneously listen to and read books online.

Third, teachers can measure students' learning in ways that do not penalize them for their disability. One way to accomplish this task is to rely on assistive technology when assessing student learning. *Assistive technology* refers to educational tools students use to compensate for their disabilities. For example, students with mild deficits in writing might be allowed to use text-to-speech software. Children with more profound problems with writing might use a software package, like Widgit Essentials, that allows children to use symbols and pictures to create sentences. Children with impairments in cognitive processing or fluency might be given extra time to complete tests. Indeed, if speed is not an important skill for a given learning domain (e.g., history), all children might be given extra time.

Overall, instructional strategies that adopt principles of universal design are effective. Students with mild to moderate impairments in intellectual and adaptive functioning seem to benefit the most from modifications to instructional methods and materials. For example, Coyne and colleagues (2012) examined the effectiveness of a computer-based reading comprehension program based on principles of universal design (Figure 4.8). The children in the study were in grades K-2; all had a developmental disability (e.g., Down, Fragile X, Prader-Willi Syndromes) and low intellectual functioning. The computer program allowed children to read books along with a narrator, to read with a partner, or to read silently.

Children could also click on words to hear them pronounced and to access definitions, pictures, and videos related to the words. After listening to and reading the books, children could demonstrate their learning by taking a multiple-choice test, typing their responses on a keyboard, or speaking their responses into a microphone. Children in the control group received regular reading instruction. At the end of the school year, students in the universal design reading intervention showed significantly greater improvement in reading and listening comprehension than controls.

Applied Behavior Analysis

Approximately 25% of children with Intellectual Disability show challenging behavior, such as stereotypies, SIBs, or aggression. These behaviors are the primary reason children with Intellectual Disability are referred for treatment (Matson et al., 2011).

Applied behavior analysis (ABA) is a scientific approach to identifying a child's problematic behavior, determining its cause, and changing it (Feeley & Jones, 2006). The principles of ABA are based largely on the work of B. F. Skinner (1974), who believed that the study of behavior should be based on observable, quantifiable data. Skinner asserted that psychologists do not need to rely on latent (unobservable) constructs to explain and predict behavior. Instead, behavior can be understood in terms of overt actions and environmental contingencies. Rather than viewing behavior as originating from within the person, applied behavior analysts understand behavior primarily as a function of environmental antecedents and consequences (Holburn, 2005).

Figure 4.8   Literacy by Design

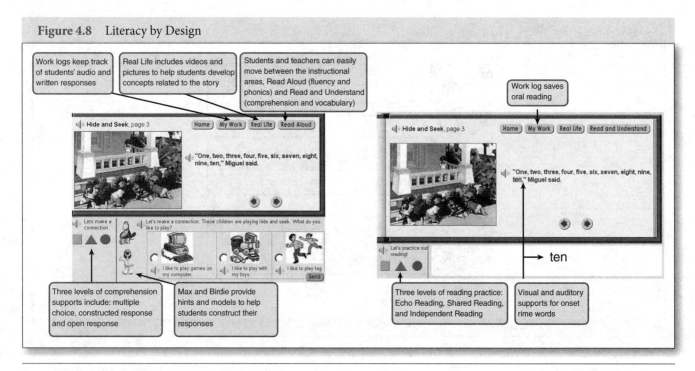

Source: From Coyne and colleagues (2012). Used with permission.

Note: Literacy by Design is a universal design approach to teaching reading comprehension. Children can read along with the narrator (i.e., echo reading), read with a partner, or read to themselves. Children can click on text to hear words or access pictures and videos. Children can demonstrate their comprehension by taking a multiple-choice test, typing their answers, or speaking their answers aloud.

A behavior analysts' first job is to operationally define the child's problem behavior, that is, to describe the behavior in a way that it can be observed and measured. For example, if a child repeatedly behaves "aggressively" in the classroom, the behavior analyst might operationally define the child's behavior in terms of one or two discrete, observation actions, such as "throws objects" or "pushes classmates." Whereas *aggression* is a somewhat vague term that cannot be easily observed or measured, throwing and pushing are more concrete actions that are easily identifiable.

Next, the behavior analyst will carefully observe and record the child's challenging behavior (see text box Research to Practice: Three Ways to Monitor Child Behavior. Several methods of behavioral observation are available (Hurwitz & Minshawi, 2012). One technique is to use *event recording:* The clinician observes the child and records the number of times the problem behavior occurs in an allotted period of time (e.g., 15 minutes). Event recording is suitable for behaviors that occur frequently and have a clear beginning and ending. For example, a school psychologist might record the number of times a child blurts out answers during class. Another technique is *interval recording*. In interval recording, the clinician divides the observation period into brief time segments (i.e., intervals) usually less than 30 seconds in length. Then, the clinician observes the child and notes whether the problem behavior occurred during each interval. Interval recording is useful for frequently occurring behaviors without clear beginnings or endings. For example, a psychologist might use interval recording to determine the percent of class time a child engages in stereotyped rocking or swaying during class. A third technique, *duration recording,* is most appropriate for behaviors that take a long time to resolve. A clinician using this technique would record the duration of a continuously occurring behavior, such as the length of a temper tantrum or the time a child spent out of seat during class.

RESEARCH TO PRACTICE

THREE WAYS TO MONITOR CHILD BEHAVIOR

Event recording is used to assess discrete behaviors that occur frequently. In this case, the clinician records the number of times the child blurts out answers in class.

Child's name: Mark

Target behavior: Blurts out answer without being called on by teacher

Date	Start time	End time	Count
2/20	10:00	10:20	✓✓✓✓✓
2/21	10:05	10:25	✓✓
2/22	9:55	10:15	✓✓✓✓✓✓✓✓

Interval recording is most appropriate for behaviors that occur frequently but do not have clear beginnings or endings. In this case, the clinician records the number of intervals the child showed stereotyped movement during class.

Child's name: Malorie

Interval: 20 seconds

Target behavior 1:   Rocking or swaying in seat

Target behavior 2:   Flapping arms or hands

Behavior	20	40	60	20	40	60	20	40	60
1	✓	✓	✓		✓	✓	✓		
2					✓	✓			

Duration recording is best used to assess discrete behaviors that last a long time. In this case, the clinician records the amount of time the child leaves his seat during class.

Child's name: Miguel

Target behavior: Time child leaves seat until seated again

Start/End time: 9:00 AM–10:00 AM, 60 minutes

Episode	Start time	Stop time	Duration
1	9:05	9:09	4 min
2	9:15	9:24	9 min
3	9:31	9:36	5 min
			Total: 18 min

Observations of children's behavior can help identify the environmental conditions that elicit it or the consequences that maintain it (Lancioni et al., 2012). Is the child's challenging behavior prompted only by certain people or situations? Is it followed by consequences that might be positively or negatively reinforcing? Does the behavior tend to occur at certain times during the day?

Finally, the behavior analyst conducts a functional analysis of the child's behavior in order to identify and alter the causes of the problem behavior (Matson, 2011). **Functional analysis** involves carefully specifying the child's challenging behavior, identifying the environmental contingencies that immediately precede the behavior (i.e., the antecedents), and identifying the environmental events that occur immediately after the behavior (i.e., the consequences) that likely maintain it. A functional analysis of behavior, therefore, involves identifying A (antecedents), B (the behavior), and C (its consequences). To change the child's behavior, the therapist can either alter the antecedents that prompt the undesirable behavior or change the consequences of the behavior so that it is no longer reinforced.

Brian Iwata and colleagues (1994) have developed a method of functional analysis to determine the causes of children's challenging behavior. This method involves observing the child in four conditions and noting the effect of each condition on the child's behavior:

- Attention condition: Whenever the child engages in challenging behavior in this condition, the therapist provides attention by reprimanding him or showing concern. For example, if the child throws an object, the therapist might respond, "Don't do that."
- Demand condition: In this condition, the therapist asks the child to engage in a moderately difficult task (e.g., sorting objects, cleaning a room).
- Alone condition: The child waits in a room with no people or toys present.
- Play condition: The therapist and the child play together.

The frequency and intensity of children's challenging behavior across the four sessions can indicate the behavior's purpose. Relatively high levels of challenging behavior in the attention condition, compared to the other conditions, might suggest that the behavior is maintained by *positive social reinforcement,* that is, to get attention from others.

Relatively high levels of challenging behavior in the demand condition, compared to the other conditions, suggests that the behavior is maintained through *negative reinforcement;* that is, it allows the child to avoid or escape undesired tasks. It is likely that caregivers negatively reinforce the challenging behavior by backing down from requests.

Relatively high rates of challenging behavior in the alone condition compared to the other conditions indicate that the behavior may be *automatically reinforced.* Children may engage in challenging behavior while alone because the behaviors themselves are reinforcing.

Once the purpose of the child's challenging behavior has been identified, the therapist can either alter the antecedents that elicit the behavior or the consequences that follow the behavior. Typically, therapists rely on reinforcement and punishment to accomplish the second objective.

Positive Reinforcement

Whenever possible, therapists use positive reinforcement to strengthen desirable behavior at the same time they reduce undesirable behavior. In a technique called **differential reinforcement**, therapists provide positive reinforcement only for behaviors that are desirable, while they ignore unwanted actions.

The two most common forms of differential reinforcement are (a) differential reinforcement of incompatible behaviors and (b) differential reinforcement of zero behavior. In **differential reinforcement of incompatible behaviors (DRI)**, the therapist provides positive reinforcement when the child engages in a behavior that is incompatible with the problematic behavior. For example, if a child engages in hand flapping or skin picking, the therapist might reinforce

him for keeping his hands in his pockets or holding onto a special toy or blanket. Since the child cannot flap his hands and keep them in his pockets at the same time, the hand flapping should decrease. In **differential reinforcement of zero behavior (DRO)**, the therapist reinforces the child for not engaging in the problematic behavior for a certain period of time. For example, a therapist might give a child an M&M every 30 seconds he does not engage in hand flapping or skin picking.

Positive Punishment

Reinforcement increases behavioral frequency; punishment decreases it (Singh, Osborne, & Huguenin, 1996). Positive punishment involves the presentation of a stimulus that decreases the frequency of a behavior. A common form of positive punishment used by parents is spanking. However, behavior therapists do not use spanking as a means of reducing behavior. Instead, some behavior therapists rely on other forms of positive punishment. For example, some therapists use aversive tastes, water mists, or visual screens to decrease severe behavior problems (Singh et al., 1996).

Since positive punishment techniques are aversive, they are only used under certain conditions such as when children's behaviors are dangerous or life threatening and other methods of treatment have been ineffective at reducing the problematic behavior. Punishment is only used in combination with positive reinforcement, and its use is carefully reviewed and monitored by independent experts. Parents must consent to the use of punishment before it is used to correct their children's behavior problem (APA, 1996).

Salvy, Mulick, Butter, Bartlett, and Linscheid (2004) describe the use of **punishment by contingent stimulation** to reduce self-injurious behavior in a toddler with Intellectual Disability. The girl, Johanna, would bang her head against her crib and other hard surfaces approximately 100 times each day. She had visible bruises on her forehead because of her behavior. Nonaversive interventions were not effective in reducing Johanna's head banging. The therapists and Johanna's mother decided to use punishment to reduce SIBs. The punisher was a brief electric shock that was administered by a device attached to Johanna's leg. The therapists could administer the shock remotely using a handheld activator. The shock was unpleasant (like being snapped by a rubber band), but it did not cause injury.

Treatment involved two phases. In the first (experimental evaluation) phase, Johanna and her mother played in an observation room in the hospital. Observers counted the frequency of her head banging during the first 10 minutes. This provided a baseline of Johanna's behavior to evaluate the effectiveness of the punishment. Then, the shock device was attached to Johanna's leg but shocks were not administered. Observations continued for another 10 minutes to see whether Johanna's behavior would change merely because she wore the device. Next, therapists began administering a brief electrical shock contingent on Johanna's head banging. As before, observations were conducted for an additional 10 minutes. Finally, the shock device was removed and Johanna's behavior was observed for another 10 minutes. Results showed that the frequency of Johanna's head banging decreased from 30 times during baseline observation to 4 times after punishment.

During the second phase of treatment (home implementation), Johanna's mother was taught to punish Johanna's behavior at home. Therapists observed Johanna's behavior in the home for 2 days to obtain baseline data. On the third day, the shock device was attached to Johanna's leg. When Johanna began banging her head, her mother said "No hit, Johanna," retrieved the activator from her purse, and immediately issued a brief shock. The frequency of Johanna's behavior was recorded over the next month, at which time the shock device was removed from the home. Results showed that the frequency of Johanna's head banging at home decreased from 117 times per day at baseline to zero times per day after the contingent administration of shocks. Johanna's mother discovered that the verbal prompt "No hit, Johanna" combined with the action of walking toward her purse was sufficient to stop Johanna's head banging. At one-year follow-up, her mother reported no problems with Johanna's SIBs and no need to use the shock device.

Another form of positive punishment is called **overcorrection**. In overcorrection, the therapist requires the child to correct his problematic behavior by restoring his surroundings to the same (or better) condition than that which existed prior to his disruptive act. Overcorrection is often used when children show chronic problems using the toilet, wetting the bed, or destroying property. In the case of bedwetting, the therapist might require the child to strip his bedding, take his bedding and wet clothes to the laundry, help wash the clothes, and assist in making the new bed. For most children, this procedure is aversive because it is tedious and takes time away from sleep or enjoyable activities.

Overcorrection is often combined with a technique called **positive practice**. In positive practice, the therapist makes the child repeatedly practice an acceptable behavior immediately following his unacceptable act. In the case of bedwetting, the child might be required to sit on the toilet five times to practice the appropriate means of urinating. Positive practice can be aversive to children, but it also teaches children alternative, appropriate behavior.

Negative Punishment

Negative punishment occurs when the therapist withdraws a stimulus from the child, which decreases the recurrence of the child's behavior. Usually, the stimulus that is withdrawn is pleasant to the child. Consequently, the child experiences distress over its removal. Negative punishment is usually less aversive than positive punishment, so it is more often used to reduce problematic behavior.

The most benign form of negative punishment is **extinction**. In extinction, the therapist withdraws reinforcement from the child immediately following an unwanted behavior. Hanley and colleagues (2003) found that some children with developmental delays tantrum in order to obtain attention from caregivers. Caregivers would unknowingly reinforce their children's tantrums by looking at, talking to, and holding them. To extinguish these tantrums, caregivers can withdraw this reinforcement; that is, they can simply ignore their children's bids for attention. This strategy is sometimes called "planned ignoring."

When caregivers begin to extinguish behavior, the rate of children's behavior sometimes temporarily increases. This phenomenon is called an **extinction burst**. Children will usually escalate their problematic behavior in an attempt to gain the reinforcement that was previously provided. Over time, the behavior's frequency and intensity will decrease, as long as reinforcement is withheld. Extinction is a slow, but effective, means of reducing behavior problems. The primary drawback of extinction is that it cannot be used to reduce SIBs because these behaviors cannot be ignored.

A second form of negative punishment is **time out**. In time out, the therapist limits the child's access to reinforcement for a certain period of time. Time out can take a number of forms, but it must involve the complete absence of reinforcement. Children should not be allowed to play, avoid tasks, or gain attention from others while in time out. Time out is usually accomplished by physically removing the child from the reinforcing situation for several minutes.

A final form of negative punishment is **response cost**. In response cost, the therapist withdraws reinforcers from the child immediately following a problematic act. Each problematic behavior "costs" the child a number of tangible reinforcers, such as candy, points, tokens, or other desired objects or privileges. Response cost is similar to time out. In time out, reinforcement is withdrawn *for a specific amount of time*. In response cost, reinforcement is withdrawn *in a specific quantity*. Response cost is often used in combination with token economies. Children may be reinforced with tokens or points for each desirable behavior and required to give up a certain number of tokens or points for each problematic behavior.

Behavioral treatment for people with Intellectual Disability has considerable empirical support. Kahng and colleagues (2002) reviewed 35 years of published research on the effectiveness of behavior therapy to treat SIBs. Data from 706 individuals showed an overall reduction in SIBs of 83.7%. The most effective treatments tended to involve punishment (e.g., overcorrection, shock, time out) with 83.2% effectiveness, followed by extinction (e.g., planned ignoring) with 82.6% effectiveness, and positive reinforcement (e.g., DRI, DRO) with 73.2% effectiveness. Combining behavioral interventions usually resulted in slightly higher effectiveness than the use of any single intervention alone.

Medication

Medication is frequently administered to children and adolescents with Intellectual Disability. Approximately 19% to 29% of people in the community and 30% to 40% of individuals in residential facilities with Intellectual Disability are prescribed at least one psychiatric medication (Singh, Ellis, & Wechsler, 1997). Little research has examined the efficacy of medication in youths with Intellectual Disability, for at least three reasons. First, for a long time, mental health experts did not think that children with Intellectual Disability suffered from psychiatric disorders, or they overlooked their psychiatric symptoms. The problem of dual diagnosis has only recently been recognized. Second, it is difficult to recruit large samples of children with both Intellectual Disability and a psychiatric diagnosis. Consequently, most research has involved very small samples. Third, many research studies have not used adequate experimental designs. Typically, a double-blind, placebo-controlled study is necessary to infer a causal relationship between the use of a medication and symptom reduction, but this type of study has been rare in the research literature (Singh, Matson, Cooper, Dixon, & Sturmey, 2005).

Medications for Disruptive Behaviors

Risperidone (Risperdal) is an atypical antipsychotic medication that blocks certain dopamine and serotonin receptors. It was first released in the United States in 1994 as a medication to treat schizophrenia and other psychotic disorders in adults. Some psychiatrists began using risperidone with developmentally delayed children who showed disruptive behavior problems. Today, risperidone is frequently used to treat oppositional and defiant behavior, destructive behavior, aggression, and SIBs in children and adolescents with Intellectual Disability (Handen & Gilchrist, 2006; Singh et al., 2005).

Evidence supporting the use of risperidone to treat problem behavior comes from a series of double-blind, placebo-controlled studies of children and adolescents who showed behavior problems and low intelligence. For example, Aman, De Smedt, Derivan, Lyons, Findling, and the Risperidone Disruptive Behavior Study Group (2002) examined 118 children aged 5 to 12 years who showed both low intellectual functioning and significant behavior problems. Children were randomly assigned to either an experimental group whose members received a low dose of risperidone or to a control group whose members received a placebo. Six weeks later, 77% of the children in the experimental group showed significant improvement in their behavior, compared to only 33% of children in the control group. Other studies have yielded similar results (Findling, Aman, Eerdekens, Derivan, Lyons, & Risperidone Behavior Study Group, 2004; Snyder et al., 2002).

Medications for Stereotypies and Self-Injurious Behavior

Physicians often prescribe traditional antipsychotic medications to suppress SIBs. Most traditional antipsychotics block dopamine receptors. Interestingly, some individuals who show SIBs also display a hypersensitivity to dopamine. Consequently, there is reason to expect that medications that block certain dopamine receptors would be especially effective at reducing SIBs and stereotypies (Szymanski & Kaplan, 2006).

Research examining the effectiveness of dopamine blockers has been limited, however. Two antipsychotic medications, haloperidol (Haldol) and fluphenazine, appear to be effective in treating adults with SIBs; however, these medications have not been adequately studied with children (Aman, Collier-Crespin, & Lindsay, 2000). Critics argue that these drugs reduce problematic behavior mostly through sedation. Consequently, individuals taking traditional antipsychotics show a general decrease in *all* behaviors, not just SIBs.

Some individuals who engage in self-injurious behavior show high secretions of endogenous opioids. Opioids may reduce pain sensitivity during the SIBs. Consequently, some physicians have used **naltrexone**, a drug that blocks opioid receptors, to curb SIBs. Research investigating the efficacy of naltrexone has been mixed. Unfortunately, some of the largest studies, including those involving children, have not shown naltrexone to be efficacious.

Medication for Anxiety and Mood Disorders

Antidepressants have been used to treat anxiety and mood disorders in adolescents with Intellectual Disability. Unfortunately, research supporting their use has largely involved only case studies and anecdotal reports (Aman et al., 2000). Physicians have also used lithium and valporic acid for children with Intellectual Disability and Bipolar Disorder. However, few large-scale studies have been conducted to investigate their efficacy (Aman et al., 2000).

Support for Parents

Before ending this section on treatment, we should highlight the importance of supporting the parents of children with developmental disabilities. After children are initially diagnosed with GDD or Intellectual Disability, parents are at increased risk for depression. They often report a sense of loss or disappointment associated with their child's diagnosis and apprehension about their child's future or their ability to raise a child with special needs. Over time, however, parents' dysphoria usually decreases (Glidden, 2012). Nevertheless, challenges associated with caring for a child with a developmental disability remain. In one large study of parents of children with GDD, nearly 42% reported significant elevations in stress associated with caring for their children (Tervo, 2012).

Parenting stress can take its toll on the family system (Al-Yagon & Margalit, 2012). Parents of children with developmental disabilities often experience disruptions in the quality of their marriage and family life. However, the effect of having a child with a disability on marital and life satisfaction is complex. Parents who report socioeconomic stress, a high degree of work and interpersonal hassles, and low support from their spouse, often report a marked deterioration in marital and family life after the birth of a child with special needs. In contrast, parents who feel supported by their spouse and who use active, problem-focused coping techniques to deal with family-related stress often report no change in marital satisfaction or quality of life. Indeed, some families report greater cohesion and satisfaction after the birth of a child with a developmental disability (Glidden, 2012).

Some developmental disorders are not strongly associated with increased parental stress. For example, the parents of children with Down Syndrome often report only moderate levels of stress, perhaps because children with this condition typically show mild cognitive impairment and are usually described by others as affectionate and social. There may be less stigma associated with caring for a child with Down Syndrome; most people can easily recognize a child with this condition and generally have some understanding of the disorder. Support groups for families are also available in many communities.

Other developmental disorders are associated with higher levels of parenting stress. Parents can experience considerable stress when the cause of their child's developmental delay cannot be identified. Parents might erroneously blame themselves for their child's limitations or feel uncertain about their child's prognosis. When the cause of children's delays is unknown, or when the disorder is uncommon, parents may also feel misunderstood or alienated. Regardless of etiology, certain child behaviors seem to increase parenting stress: poor motor control, social deficits, and aggression (Tervo, 2012).

Therapists can help children with developmental disabilities by supporting their parents in times of difficulty and uncertainty. Besides providing informational support about their children's development and suggestions for symptom management, therapists can offer emotional support through their willingness to listen to parents' concerns. Parents can also encourage the use of active, problem-focused strategies to deal with parenting stress (Al-Yagon & Margalit, 2012). Parents who are able to cope with their own stress may be better able to care for their children and implement many of the interventions that will promote their children's intellectual and adaptive functioning in the long run.

CHAPTER SUMMARY

What Is Intellectual Disability?

- Intellectual Disability is characterized by significant limitations in cognitive and adaptive functioning that emerge during the course of children's development.

  - IQ scores <70–75 usually indicate limitations in cognitive ability.
  - Adaptive functioning is measured in three broad domains (a) conceptual skills, (b) social skills, and (c) practical skills. Scores <70–75 usually indicate limitations in adaptive functioning.
  - Cognitive and adaptive limitations are equally important to the identification of Intellectual Disability. Children are not diagnosed based on IQ alone.

- The American Association on Intellectual and Developmental Disabilities (AAIDD) offers its own definition on Intellectual Disability. It is largely consistent with the *DSM-5* definition, but it places greater emphasis on contextual factors and the supports children need to succeed academically and socially.
- Global Developmental Delay is characterized by significant deficits in two of the following domains that emerge prior to age 5 years: (a) fine/gross motor skills, (b) speech/language, (c) social/personal skills, and (d) daily living skills.

  - Global Developmental Delay is usually diagnosed in infants and very young children suspected of Intellectual Disability but who are too young to be administered an IQ test.
  - Not all children with Global Developmental Delay will meet criteria for Intellectual Disability when they become older.

Associated Characteristics

- Many youths with Intellectual and Developmental Disabilities show challenging behavior: actions of sufficient intensity, frequency, or duration that children's physical safety (or the safety of others) is jeopardized. Challenging behaviors include the following:

  - Stereotypies are actions performed in a consistent, rigid, and repetitive manner with no immediate practical significance (e.g., hand flapping, rocking back and forth).
  - Self-injurious behaviors are repetitive actions that can, or do, cause physical harm to the person.
  - Physical aggression are actions that cause (or can cause) property destruction or injury to others.

- Children with Intellectual and Developmental Disabilities can experience other psychiatric disorders and are at greater risk than typically developing children their age.

Epidemiology

- Approximately 1.8% of individuals have Intellectual Disability. The disorder is more common among school-age children than adults and is more common among boys than girls.
- According to Edward Zigler, children with Intellectual Disability can be differentiated into two types:
  - Youths with organic Intellectual Disability have known medical causes for their impairments. They tend to have IQ scores <50, physical abnormalities associated with neurological problems, and parents without impairments.
  - Youths with cultural-familial Intellectual Disability have no identified cause for their impairments. They tend to have IQ scores between 50 and 70, have normal physical appearance, have parents with low intelligence, and come from lower income families.
- According to the similar sequence hypothesis, children with Intellectual Disability show cognitive development in the same sequence as typically developing children, albeit at a slower pace. Most research supports this hypothesis.
- According to the similar structure hypothesis, children with and without Intellectual Disabilities who have the same mental age will show the same level of abilities. Although generally supported, some children with organic Intellectual Disability show abilities different than their typically developing peers.
- A behavioral phenotype refers to the curious pattern of strengths and weaknesses shown by children with specific causes for their Intellectual Disability.

Causes of Intellectual Disability

- Chromosomal abnormalities can cause Intellectual Disability.
  - Down Syndrome is usually caused by an extra 21st chromosome (trisomy 21). It is characterized by Intellectual Disability, relative deficits in language, and relative strengths in visual-spatial skills and social functioning in childhood.
  - Fragile X Syndrome is caused by an X-link genetic mutation. The disorder is more severe in boys. It is characterized by Intellectual Disability, relative deficits in sequential processing, relative strengths in simultaneous processing, and problems with social functioning.
  - Prader-Willi Syndrome is caused by a missing paternal chromosome 15. It is characterized by mild Intellectual Impairment, obesity, and obsessive-compulsive behavior.
  - Angelman's Syndrome is caused by a missing maternal chromosome 15. It is characterized by Intellectual Disability, relative deficits in language, and unusually happy demeanor.
  - William's syndrome is caused by deletions on chromosome 7. It is characterized by Intellectual Disability, relative weakness on visual-spatial tasks, well-developed vocabularies and spoken language, and inattention/hyperactivity.
- Metabolic disorders can also cause Intellectual Disability. PKU is caused by a recessive gene which can caused severe disability if children do not abstain from phenylalanine-rich foods (e.g., cheese, meats).
- Teratogen exposure in utero can cause Intellectual Disability. Common teratogens include bacteria, viruses, alcohol, and other drugs.
- Complications during pregnancy or delivery can contribute to Intellectual Disability, especially when they restrict the fetus's access to oxygen.
- Childhood illnesses or injuries can cause Intellectual Disability including encephalitis, meningitis, high fever, and lead toxicity.
- Cultural-familial Intellectual Disability is usually caused by a genetic propensity toward below-average cognitive functioning and environmental deprivation or socioeconomic disadvantage.

Prevention and Treatment

- Women at high risk may participate in prenatal screening to estimate the likelihood of having a child with a genetic disorder. Screening techniques include (a) serum screening, (b) amniocentesis, and (c) chorionic villus sampling.
- Prevention programs for youths at risk for Intellectual Disability, such as the Infant Health and Development Program, are associated with short-term gains in IQ, but, no long-term differences in children's outcomes.
- The Individuals with Disabilities Education Improvement Act requires children with Intellectual Disability to be identified at an early age and provided with services to help them achieve.
  - School-age children receive an Individualized Education Program (IEP) and usually participate in academic inclusion programs alongside typically developing peers.
  - Universal design is an educational practice that involves instructional materials and activities that allow learning goals to be achievable by children with and without disabilities.
- Applied Behavior Analysis (ABA) is typically used to reduce challenging behavior in children with Intellectual Disability.
  - Clinicians can use event recording, interval recording, or duration recording to identify and monitor challenging behavior.
  - Functional analysis can help determine the cause of the behavior:
    - Positive social reinforcement (i.e., to get attention)
    - Negative reinforcement (i.e., to avoid or escape unpleasant tasks)
    - Automatic reinforcement (i.e., self-stimulation)

- ○ Clinicians can use operant conditioning to correct behavior.
  - ○ Positive reinforcement (e.g., differential reinforcement)
  - ○ Positive punishment (e.g., overcorrection, positive practice)
  - ○ Negative punishment (e.g., time out, response cost)
- Medication, such as risperidone (Risperdal) can be used to reduce some challenging behavior.
- Therapists can provide information to families of children with Intellectual and Developmental Disabilities, alleviate parenting stress, and teach problem-focused coping.

KEY TERMS

aggression   101

amniocentesis   114

anoxia   112

applied behavior analysis (ABA)   117

behavioral phenotype   104

chorionic villus sampling   115

chromosomal microarray (CMA)   97

chromosomal mosaicism   105

conceptual skills   91

differential reinforcement   120

differential reinforcement of incompatible behaviors (DRI)   120

differential reinforcement of zero behavior (DRO)   121

encephalitis   113

extinction   121

extinction burst   121

Fetal Alcohol Syndrome   111

Fragile X Mental Retardation 1 (FMR1) gene   106

functional analysis   119

Global Developmental Delay (GDD)   95

human immunodeficiency virus   111

hyperphagia   107

inclusion   116

Individualized Education Program (IEP)   116

Individualized Family Services Plan (IFSP)   116

Infant Health and Development Program   115

lead toxicity   113

mainstreaming   115

maternal syphilis   111

maternal uniparental disomy   107

meningitis   113

naltrexone   122

needed supports   94

nondisjunction   104

organic Intellectual Disability   103

overcorrection   121

phenylalanine   110

positive practice   121

practical skills   91

punishment by contingent stimulation   120

response cost   121

risperidone (Risperdal)   122

rubella virus   111

self-injurious behaviors (SIBs)   99

sequential processing   107

serum screening   114

similar sequence hypothesis   103

similar structure hypothesis   103

simultaneous processing   107

social skills   91

stereotypies   99

teratogens   111

time out   121

translocation   105

universal design   116

CRITICAL THINKING EXERCISES

1. When many people think of Intellectual Disability, they think about a child with Down Syndrome. To what extent is a child with Down Syndrome an accurate portrayal of all children with Intellectual Disability?

2. Until recently, people mistakenly believed that children and adolescents with Intellectual Disability could not experience other psychiatric disorders. Why? Why might it be difficult for a psychologist or physician to assess anxiety and depression in a child with moderate Intellectual Disability?

3. Some professionals classify Intellectual Disability into two broad categories: organic Intellectual Disability and cultural-familial Intellectual Disability. How can these labels be misleading? Why might it be better to describe children with Intellectual Disability based on their behavioral phenotype?

4. How does the treatment for PKU illustrate the interaction of genes and environment in child development?

5. Why are children of lower SES backgrounds at greater risk for certain types of Intellectual Disability? Why might low-SES children with Intellectual Disability have poorer prognoses than middle-class children with Intellectual Disability?

6. Why do clinicians always try to use other forms of behavioral treatments (e.g., positive reinforcement, negative punishment) before using positive punishment? Under what circumstances might it be permissible to use positive punishment to help a child with Intellectual Disability?

EXTEND YOUR LEARNING

Videos, practice tests, flash cards, study guides, and links to online resources for this chapter are available to students online. Teachers also have access to lecture notes, PowerPoint presentations, suggestions for classroom activities, and possible exam questions. Visit: www.sagepub.com/weis2e.

CHAPTER **5**

Communication Disorders in Children

LEARNING OBJECTIVES

After reading this chapter, you should be able to answer these questions:

- What is Language Disorder? What are possible genetic, biological, and environmental causes of Language Disorder in children?

- How can discrete trial training, conversational recast training, and milieu training be used to help children with Language Disorder?

- What is Speech Sound Disorder? How might the disorder be related to problems with either articulation or phonemic awareness?

- How do the causes of Speech Sound Disorder guide treatment?

- What is Childhood Onset Fluency Disorder (stuttering) and why does it occur?

- How can clinicians treat stuttering in children and adolescents?

- What are the characteristics of Social Communication Disorder? How can therapists improve children's pragmatic communication skills?

Communication disorders are among the most common, and most overlooked, problems experienced by children (Bishop & Rutter, 2010). Whereas most people are familiar with Down Syndrome and Autism Spectrum Disorder, relatively few people have heard of Speech Sound Disorder or Language Disorder. Despite their "Cinderella status" among childhood psychiatric disorders, approximately 10% of youths have one or more of these conditions. Indeed, the prevalence of communication disorders is much higher than autism and similar to other—more familiar—conditions, (e.g., learning disabilities). Furthermore, longitudinal studies indicate that communication disorders can lead to short- and long-term problems with children's academic attainment, behavior, and social functioning (Angell, 2009).

The **communication disorders** that appear in *DSM-5* reflect an underlying dysfunction in the verbal and nonverbal exchange of thoughts, ideas, interests, and feelings with others. Effective communication involves three components: (a) language, (b) speech, and (c) social communication. Children can develop disorders in any of these three domains.

WHAT IS LANGUAGE DISORDER?

Language refers to communication in which beliefs, knowledge, and skills can be experienced, expressed, or shared. It involves the complex manipulation and organization of auditory or visual symbols. Language can be spoken, signed, or written. Between 6 and 8 million people in the United States have some form of language impairment that interferes with their ability to communicate with others (Angell, 2009).

Language Disorder is diagnosed when children show marked problems in the acquisition and use of language due to deficits in comprehension or production. Children can manifest Language Disorder in three ways: (a) by showing limited vocabularies, (b) by having problems forming phrases and sentences, or (c) by showing problems explaining or describing their thoughts and feelings. By definition, Language Disorder is not explained by Intellectual Disability or a physical disability, such as hearing loss (Table 5.1, Diagnostic Criteria for Language Disorder).

DSM-5 does not specify exactly how Language Disorder should be assessed. In practice, however, Language Disorder is typically identified in toddlers and preschool age children who earn language scores more than 1.25 standard deviations below the mean on standardized language tests (e.g., <80), have nonverbal IQ scores within with the average range (e.g., >85), and otherwise appear healthy. Children with Language Disorder, therefore, show impairment that is specific to their language skills rather than general intellectual impairments or Global Developmental Delay.

Children with Language Disorder can show problems with receptive language, expressive language, or both aspects of communication. **Receptive language** is the ability to listen to and understand communication. One test of receptive language is the Peabody Picture Vocabulary Test-Fourth Edition. On this test, the psychologist presents four pictures to the child and asks her to point to the picture that shows a specific word or idea. The test assesses receptive vocabulary because the child indicates her understanding by pointing, not by speaking or writing. In contrast, **expressive language** refers to the ability to share beliefs, knowledge, and skills with others. One test of expressive language is the Expressive One-Word Picture Vocabulary Test–Fourth Edition. On this test, the psychologist presents a picture to the child and asks her to name it (Angell, 2009).

The diagnosis of Language Disorder refers to overall delays in language acquisition or skills. It serves as a "red flag" which warns professionals to monitor the child's language development and, if necessary, to intervene early to prevent more serious language deficits. Typically, professionals specify the type of language problem the child displays: (a) late language emergence or (b) specific language impairment.

Late Language Emergence

Late Language Emergence is a type of Language Disorder characterized by significant delays in receptive or expressive language. It is typically diagnosed when children are between 18 and 36 months of age, yet they show marked delays in understanding language or speaking (Figure 5.1). For example, a 24-month-old who cannot follow simple directions

---

Table 5.1 Diagnostic Criteria for Language Disorder

A. Persistent difficulties in the acquisition and use of language across modalities (i.e., spoken, written, sign language) due to deficits in comprehension or production that include the following:

1. Reduced vocabulary (word knowledge and use).

2. Limited sentence structure (ability to put words and word endings together to form sentences based on the rules of grammar and morphology).

3. Impairments in discourse (ability to use vocabulary and connect sentences to explain or describe a topic or series of events or have a conversation).

B. Language abilities are substantially and quantifiably below those expected for age, resulting in functional limitations in effective communication, social participation, academic achievement, or occupational performance, individually or in combination.

C. Onset of symptoms is in the early developmental period.

D. The difficulties are not attributable to hearing or other sensory impairment, motor dysfunction, or another medical or neurological condition and are not better explained by Intellectual Disability or Global Developmental Delay.

Source: Reprinted with permission from the *Diagnostic and Statistical Manual of Mental Disorders, Fifth Edition* (Copyright 2013). American Psychiatric Association.

(e.g., "Pick it up") or a 36-month-old who cannot combine words to form simple sentences (e.g., "Give me the doll") might show Late Language Emergence. Table 5.2 shows other developmental milestones for children's early language skills.

Figure 5.1   Expressive Vocabulary Increases Dramatically in Typically Developing Children

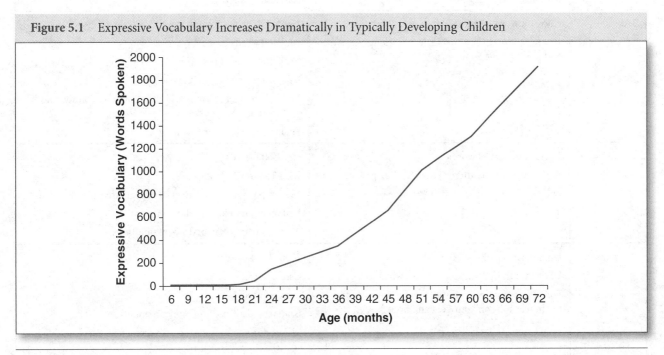

Source: Based on National Institute on Child Health and Human Development (NICHD, 2010), data.

Note: Most children show a marked increase in words between 18 and 36 months of age. Children with Late Language Emergence do not.

Table 5.2   Developmental Milestones for Receptive and Expressive Language

Age	Receptive Language	Expressive Language
2–4 months	Recognizes parent's voice and calms down if crying When feeding, starts or stops sucking in response to sound	Cooing, gooing, laughing Vowel sounds (oooh, eeeh, aaah)
4–8 months	Follows sounds with his or her eyes Has joint attention with parent	Babbles in a speech-like way, using sounds that begin with p, b, and m
8–12 months	Listens when parent speaks Understands words for common items such as "cup," "shoe," and "juice" Responds to requests or questions (e.g., Come here. Want more?)	Babbles using long and short groups of sounds (e.g., tata, upup, bibibi) Communicates using gestures Imitates speech sounds Says one or two words by first birthday (e.g., hi, dog, mama)
1–2 years	Knows some parts of the body and can point to them when asked Follows simple commands (e.g., Roll the ball) Understands simple questions (Where's your shoe?) Points to pictures in books when parent names them	10–15 words at 18 months 40–50 words at 22 months Uses mostly nouns and pronouns

(Continued)

Table 5.2 (Continued)

Age	Receptive Language	Expressive Language
2–3 years	Knows a word for most objects and actions Follows two-step commands (e.g., Pick up the ball, and put it on the table)	150 words at age 2 years 300–400 words at age 3 years Combines 2–3 words (More juice.) Asks simple questions (Go bye-bye?) Makes k, g, f, t, d, n sounds clearly, but other sounds may be problematic Fluency may be poor
3–4 years	Understands 1500 words Recognizes gender differences (he/she), pronouns, plurals, adjectives, shapes, colors	600–1000 words Uses 3–4 word sentences Nouns, pronouns, adjectives used regularly Past tense and plural endings emerge Answers who, what, and where questions
4–5 years	Understands 1500–2000 words Understands if, because, why, and when Follows complex directions (e.g., Before you enter the house, take off your coat and boots)	1000–1600 words Uses 4–6 word sentences Articles used Understandable by nonfamily members Makes most sounds correctly except a few (e.g., l, s, r, v, ch, sh, th) Fluency improving
5–6 years	Understands 2500–2800 words Understands more complex sentences Identifies letters and numbers	1500–2100 words Uses complete 5–6 word sentences Adult grammar Fluent speech

Source: Based on NICHD (2010).

CASE STUDY

CODY'S PROBLEMS WITH LANGUAGE ACQUISITION

Cody was a physically healthy 26-month-old boy referred to our clinic by his pediatrician because of language delays. Cody's mother reported that he was only able to speak a few words clearly, such as "mama," "dada," and "cup." He usually communicated by gesturing and crying. A physical exam indicated that Cody was healthy; his head circumference and weight were within normal limits. He showed no problems with vision or hearing. His motor and social skills were also appropriate for a child his age.

A psychologist at our clinic tested Cody's cognitive functioning and language skills. Although his nonverbal IQ fell within the average range (NVIQ=94), his score on the verbal portion of the IQ test indicated marked delays (VIQ=72). Cody's receptive language skills were approximately one standard deviation below his peers. For example, he was able to follow simple one-word commands, but he had difficulty pointing to pictures of common objects when instructed to do so (e.g., cup, spoon). Cody's expressive language skills were much delayed. His vocabulary consisted of only about 20 to 25 words, most of which served a function (e.g., up, more, mama). He did not combine words to form simple, two-word sentences.

"I'm not sure if Cody really has a language problem or if he's just a late bloomer," said his mother. "I thought I'd just give him a few more months to catch up to the other kids in daycare, but his doctor suggested I have him tested right away."

Late Language Emergence is important because it can be an indicator of later, more serious language problems (e.g., Specific Language Impairment) or an early sign of Autism Spectrum Disorder. Therefore, children diagnosed with Late Language Emergence need to be monitored and, if appropriate, provided with early intervention to improve their language skills (Angell, 2009).

Cody's doctor is probably correct. Prolonged delays in language acquisition can be an indicator of more pervasive neurodevelopmental problems. Buschmann and colleagues (2008) assessed a large sample of 24-month-old children with Late Language Emergence. Approximately 22% showed at least one other developmental delay. For example, 12% showed borderline-significant deficits in nonverbal cognitive functioning, 6% showed significant deficits in nonverbal intelligence, and 4% met diagnostic criteria for Autism Spectrum Disorder. Although most children with Late Language Emergence eventually develop language skills similar to their peers, a sizable minority of these children have potentially serious developmental delays that require early treatment.

Specific Language Impairment

Many young children who show Late Language Emergence eventually catch up to their peers. However, 25 to 50% of these children continue to display problems with language that interfere with their ability to communicate (Kaderavek, 2011). Children with Specific Language Impairment (SLI) show significant deficits in language that are not better explained by Intellectual Disability or another medical or psychiatric condition (Angell, 2009).

Children with SLI are usually diagnosed in preschool or kindergarten, when their language skills significantly lag behind those of their peers (Figure 5.2). Overall, their language is short, simplistic, and filled with errors characteristic of much younger children. Older children with SLI make the same linguistic errors, in roughly the same sequence, as much younger children without language problems. For example, a 7- or 8-year-old child with SLI speaks like a typically developing 3- or 4-year-old preschooler (Cupples, 2011).

Children with SLI show a wide range of language problems. Typically, these children show problems with phonology, morphology, grammar, and semantics (Kamhi, Masterson, & Apel, 2007).

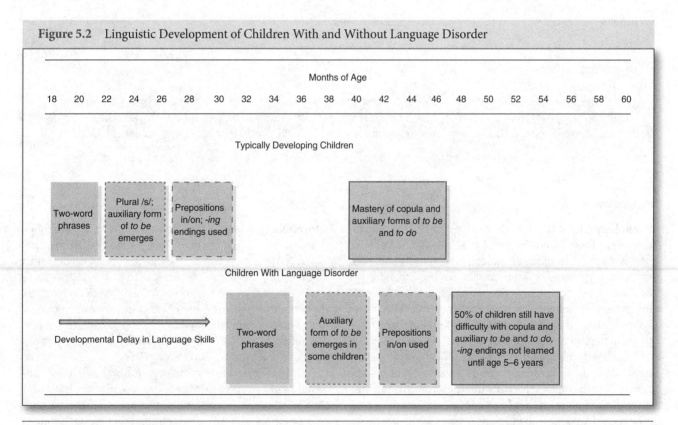

Figure 5.2   Linguistic Development of Children With and Without Language Disorder

Source: Based on Kaderavek (2011).

Note: Children with Language Disorder show delays in language skills. They continue to make the same errors shown by typically developing preschool-age children in kindergarten and early elementary school.

BERNADETTE'S PROBLEMS WITH EXPRESSION

Bernadette was a 5-year-old girl referred to our clinic by her parents because of deficits in expressive language. A cute girl with dark, curly hair, Bernadette had a history of late language emergence. She did not begin talking until 24 months of age and only began speaking in short, two- or three-word sentences the previous year. Her pediatrician initially suspected that Bernadette had Intellectual Disability; however, her cognitive skills and adaptive functioning were within the average range for a girl her age. Indeed, Bernadette was a friendly, outgoing girl whose main limitation was her difficulty expressing herself.

The speech-language pathologist at our clinic showed Bernadette a series of pictures and asked her to tell a story with them. The exchange went as follows:

Therapist: Here's the first picture. Tell me what's going on.

Bernadette: (Pointing to the girl in the picture.) Who her?

Therapist: Her name is Sally.

Bernadette: Sally. Her going shopping. Sally hold . . . (long pause) bag and . . . (pause)—

Therapist: What is she holding?

Bernadette: I don't know.

Therapist: OK. Let's try the next picture. What's going on here?

Bernadette: Her goed into house. Sally. Her eat with mom.

Therapist: What did they eat?

Bernadette: Her eated apple. Her eated . . . (pause) . . . I don't know.

Therapist: It looks like they ate an apple and some grapes.

Bernadette: (Smiles.) Yeah.

"She often can't remember the names of objects," Bernadette's mother reported. "There might be a problem with her memory." The therapist replied, "That is possible. I'll need to assess her more thoroughly to be sure. But I think her main challenge is with expressive language. Luckily, there are some things you and I can do to help Bernadette express herself better."

Phonology

Phonology refers to the sounds of a language and the rules for combining these sounds. English has 42 basic sounds, or phonemes. As children acquire language, they typically make certain errors in phonological processing and articulation. For example, it is common for 3-year-old children to say "ephant" for *elephant* or "sghetti" for *spaghetti*. However, children with Language Disorder often continue to make these characteristic phonological errors into their early school years.

Children with SLI often show a lack of phonemic awareness, that is, the ability to hear, identify, and manipulate these sounds. For example, separating the spoken word "cat" into three distinct phonemes, /k/, /a/, and /t/, requires phonemic awareness. Children with SLI show problems with phonemic awareness in their language when they transpose, substitute, or mispronounce word sounds. For example, they may say "ting" instead of *thing*, "tu" instead of *zoo*, and "dob" instead of *job*.

Morphology

Morphology refers to the study of word structures, quite literally, how words are built from phonemes (Balthazar & Scott, 2007). A morpheme is the smallest unit of language that has meaning. Some morphemes are "free"; that is, they carry meaning on their own as whole words (e.g., tie, walk, dog). Other morphemes are "bound"; that is, they carry meaning only when combined with other morphemes, as in the case of prefixes or suffixes (un– as in "untie"), endings (–ed as in "walked"), or plurals (–s as in "dogs").

Typically developing children follow a relatively consistent pattern in their mastery of morphemes (Bathazar & Scott, 2007). For example, the use of the –ing ending (e.g., swim*ing*) and certain prepositions (e.g., *in* the box) usually develop first. Later, children begin to master the plural –s ending (e.g., hats), the possessive –s ending (e.g., Mommy's hat), and the uncontractible copula "be" (e.g., She *is* my mom. I *am* her son.) Some of the last morphemes that children master include the past tense –ed ending (e.g., walk*ed*), the first-person singular –s ending (e.g., The bird chirp*s*), and the uncontractible auxiliary "be" followed by a verb (e.g., She *is* playing. I *was* running).

Children with SLI show marked deficits in their mastery of morphemes, especially the morphemes which are typically learned later in development (Table 5.3). For example, many youths with SLI omit past-tense endings; they may say, "I walk to school" instead of "I walked to school." Another common error is to omit the third person singular –s ending: "My friend walk with me" instead of "My friend walks with me." A third common error is difficulty with conjugations involving *be*, such as "Mommy bes nice" instead of "Mommy is nice." Although these errors are developmentally normative in 2- and 3-year-old children, children with SLI continue to make these errors in preschool and kindergarten (Bishop, 2006).

Grammar

Linguists use the term *grammar* to describe the rules that govern the use of morphemes and the order of words (syntax) of a sentence. Children with SLI often make serious grammatical errors. For example, they might say "Me go there" instead of "I went there" or "Why he like me?" instead of "Why does he like me?" They may also not appreciate differences in word order. For example, they may have difficulty using puppets to act out the sentence "The dog is chased by the boy" because they are not sure who is chasing whom (Bishop, 2006).

Semantics

Semantics refers to the meaning of language (Gillon, Moran, & Page, 2007). Semantics can refer to the meaning of individual words (lexical semantics) or sentences (sentential semantics). Word meaning is important because it allows children to verbally represent their world, understand others, and convey their thoughts with precision. Children with SLI often show delays in word acquisition and word knowledge. Whereas most 2-year-old children have vocabularies of approximately 200 words, two-year-olds later diagnosed with SLI typically know only 20 (Hegde & Maul, 2006).

Children with SLI typically have semantic skills similar to much younger children (Gillon et al., 2007). For example, preschoolers with SLI often show errors of overextension and underextension similar to 2- and 3-year-olds. **Overextension** is inappropriately generalizing a word

Table 5.3 Morphological and Grammatical Errors Often Shown by Children With Specific Language Impairment

Error	Example
Regular past tense (*–ed*)	He push him. (He pushed him.)
Present possessive verb *–ing*	Cat eat him food. (The cat is eating his food.)
Plural /s/	Me got two toy. (I have two toys.)
Possessive *'s*	That mommy hat. (That is Mommy's hat.)
Simple pronoun errors	He running. (She is running.)
Pronoun case markings	Her do it. (She can do it.)
Omitted copula *be* verb	The bear big. (The bear is big.)
Errors in copula *be* verb	Me happy today. (I am happy today.)
Omitted articles (e.g., a, the)	Give me drink. (Give me a drink.)
Omitted prepositions *in* and *on*	Daddy, put table my paper. (Daddy, put my paper on the table.)
Omitted auxiliary verbs (e.g., is, do, can)	Janie do it. (Janie can do it.)
Overuse of vague demonstratives (e.g., this, that, these, those)	This mine! (This toy is mine.)
Third person singular verbs	Mommy teach me. (Mommy teaches me.)
wh questions	What we can make? (What can we make?)
Embedded clauses with *wh* questions	What do you think what Janie broke? (What do you think that she broke?)

Source: Based on Kaderavek (2011).

(e.g., calling all adult men "daddy") whereas **underextension** is failing to generalize a word (e.g., using the word "cat" to refer only to the family's pet and not to other cats). Children with SLI may also have difficulty with pronouns (e.g., mixing up he/she or him/her). They almost always have underdeveloped vocabularies and experience trouble expressing themselves with precision. Consequently, they may appear to have word retrieval problems, use words incorrectly, invent novel words that have no meaning (e.g., neologisms), or rely on vague, simplistic words (e.g., *thing, this, stuff;* Cupples, 2011).

Finally, children with Language Disorder may be at risk for social and emotional problems across childhood and adolescence. For example, these children often show social withdrawal, tend to play alone, act shy, have poorer quality friendships, are more likely to be bullied, and have more difficulty in peer interactions (Rescorla, Ross, & McClure, 2007; St Clair, Pickles, Durkin, & Conti-Ramsden, 2011).

Although other behavior problems tend to decrease across the school years, the social and emotional difficulties of children with language impairment tend to increase over time. Even at age 16 years, these children show significantly more problems in their social functioning and peer interactions (Snowling, Bishop, Stothard, Chipchase, & Kaplan, 2006). Researchers suggest that their language deficits interfere with their ability to understand others and be understood in return. They learn to adopt social behaviors characterized by avoidance and withdrawal (Redmond & Rice, 1998).

WHAT CAUSES LANGUAGE DISORDER?

Researchers have only begun to determine the causes of Language Disorder in children. Because language is so complex and because it varies considerably in early childhood, there are many possible causes of language problems.

Genetics and Brain Structure

One clear finding is that language impairments are greatly influenced by genetics. Heritability estimates range between .50 and .75 for school-aged children with Language Disorder. Whereas the prevalence of Language Disorder is approximately 7% in the general population, the prevalence increases to 40% for children with at least one family member with the disorder. Furthermore, when the siblings of children with Language Disorder do not meet criteria for the disorder, they often show subtle difficulties with phonemic awareness and grammar. Altogether, these data suggest a common set of genes that predispose youth toward language problems. The greater the genetic risk, the greater the language impairment (Bishop, 2006). Indeed, researchers have started to identify portions of chromosome 16 and 19 that seem to place children at risk for Language Disorder (Newbury, Bishop, & Monaco, 2005).

Some studies have found structural abnormalities in the brain of children with Language Disorder (Hegde & Maul, 2006). These studies have focused on the region surrounding the lateral sulcus. The **lateral sulcus**, also known as the sylvian fissure, is a large gyrus (groove) in the left hemisphere of the brain (Image 5.1). In this area lie several brain regions responsible for language including Broca's area, Wernicke's area, and the primary auditory cortex. Most right-handed children show a normal enlargement of this area; that is, this area of the left hemisphere, which is specialized for language, is larger than the corresponding area in the right hemisphere. However, many children with Language Disorder do not show this typical asymmetry. Instead, both hemispheres may be of equal size, suggesting a lack of linguistic specialization.

Unfortunately, there is not a direct relationship between abnormality of the lateral sulcus and Language Disorder. Many children with Language Disorder do not show this lack of asymmetry, and many children with no language impairments show this abnormality. Therefore, this structural difference cannot explain all cases of Language Disorder.

Cognitive Processing Problems

Many children with Language Disorder have cognitive processing problems that may underlie their language difficulties. Problems in three areas of cognitive processing have been identified so far: (a) auditory perception, (b) rapid temporal processing, and (c) phonological short-term memory (Bishop, 2006).

Auditory Perception Problems

Auditory perception is the ability to identify and differentiate sounds. It can be measured by asking children to detect

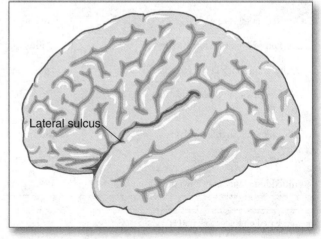

Image 5.1 The lateral sulcus, or sylvian fissure, is a large gyrus (groove) in the left hemisphere of the brain. Abnormalities near this brain region likely play a role in the development of Language Disorder.

Lateral sulcus

differences between two tones with different pitch or two phonemes with slightly different sounds (e.g., the /th/ and /d/ sounds). Auditory perception is important because children must detect subtle differences between phonemes in order to develop phonemic awareness. Typically developing children gradually acquire the ability to differentiate subtle differences in auditory information over the first years of life. However, children with Language Disorder do not. Delays in auditory perception may lead to problems in both speech and language. For example, a child who does not differentiate the /l/ and /r/ sounds may have difficulty accurately producing these sounds (e.g., the word "ring" sounds like "ling."). Furthermore, a child who does not differentiate the word "sing" and "sings" may not produce the plural /-s/ ending when speaking (Weismer, 2008).

Deficits in Rapid Temporal Processing

Children with Language Disorder also show delays in rapid temporal processing (Tallal, 1999). **Rapid temporal processing** is the ability to quickly and accurately process sensory information. Rapid temporal processing is assessed by asking children to discriminate between stimuli presented at increasing speeds. For example, children might be asked to discriminate between two computer-generated sounds (e.g., /ba/ and /pa/) or two multisyllabic words that are presented in rapid succession. When stimuli are presented slowly, all children perform well. However, when stimuli are presented rapidly, children with Language Disorder perform much worse than their peers without language impairments. Interestingly, children with Language Disorder show problems processing a wide range of sensory information in rapid succession, not just linguistic auditory information. For example, children with Language Disorder also show difficulty differentiating tactile stimulation (e.g., touch stimuli presented to fingers, hands, or cheeks) and visual stimuli (e.g., light) compared to their typically developing peers.

Rapid temporal processing is important when auditory information is presented briefly or in rapid succession, such as when a parent speaks quickly to a child. In order for a child to develop phoneme awareness, to learn the names of objects, and to understand sentences, she must be able to encode this auditory information quickly. However, children who have deficits in rapid temporal processing take in and process less fine-grained auditory information. They simply miss out on linguistic input. Problems with rapid temporal processing, therefore, can contribute to delays in children's awareness of phonemes, underdeveloped vocabularies, and difficulty understanding sentences (Weismer, 2008).

Delays in Short-Term Memory

Finally, many children with Language Disorder show problems with phonological short-term memory. **Phonological short-term memory** is the ability to hold auditory material in memory for short periods of time. It is measured by asking children to remember long strings of nonsense syllables, such as "perplisteronk" or "blonterstaping." Phonological short-term memory is important, because the ability to learn and accurately reproduce words depends on this skill.

Problems with phonological short-term memory can cause children to make morphological and grammatical errors. For example, a child who has difficulty remembering auditory information may omit a past-tense or plural ending when completing a sentence (e.g., Yesterday, I walk[ed] to school; Today, John ride[s] his bike.) Similarly, children with phonological short-term memory deficits may have underdeveloped vocabularies or show problems understanding sentences. For example, they may have trouble determining whether "The boy chased the dog" and "The dog was chased by the boy" have the same meaning (Bishop, 2006).

Parent-Child Interactions

A great deal of research has focused on the verbal interactions between children with Language Disorder and their parents. Overall, these studies have shown that the quality of these interactions is impoverished, compared to the verbal exchanges between parents and typically developing children (Hegde & Maul, 2006). On average, the parents of children with Language Disorder

- interact with their children less often,
- ask their children fewer questions,
- use shorter and less complex sentences,
- show less variation in their language toward their children, and
- respond less often to their children's utterances.

It is unknown whether these parenting behaviors are a cause or consequence of Language Disorder. It is possible that impoverished parent-child communication contributes to the language delays shown by children with Language Disorder. Alternatively, the parents of children with Language Disorder may adopt more restricted, less complex language in response to their children's communication problems.

TREATMENT OF LANGUAGE DISORDER

The treatment of Language Disorder is tailored to the needs of the child. Some children, such as those with Late Language Emergence, need help expanding their expressive vocabularies and combining words to form sentences. Other children, such as those with Specific Language Impairment, usually need to correct morphological and grammatical errors in their language, such as problems using the past tense or the omission of articles and prepositions. Treatment, therefore, involves implementing an intervention that capitalizes on children's linguistic strengths to overcome or compensate for their weaknesses (Hoodin, 2011).

Increasing Language Output Through Discrete Trial Training

Teaching Single Words

The expressive vocabularies of many young children with Language Disorder lag far behind their typically developing peers. Whereas most 2-year-old children know approximately 200 words and can speak in two-word sentences, children with Late Language Emergence do not tend to reach these linguistic milestones until age 3 (Kaderavek, 2011). Therefore, a primary goal of therapy is to increase these children's expressive vocabularies, capacity for multi-word utterances, and overall language production.

For children with limited expressive language, discrete trial training may be used. Discrete trial training is an individually administered instructional approach used to teach specific behaviors in a planned, controlled, and systematic manner. Skills are taught, one at a time, using a series of repeated trials. Each trial has three parts: (a) *antecedent*—the presentation of the stimulus, (b) *behavior*—the child's action, and (c) *consequence*—reinforcement for engaging in the desired action.

The **antecedent** is the instruction provided by the therapist. For example, the therapist might want to teach a child to say "cookie." The therapist might present a cookie to the child and ask, "What is this?" If the child does not respond to the therapist's question, the therapist will prompt the child by saying, "This is a cookie. Say 'cookie.'" The goal is for the child to produce the desired verbal response so that the therapist can reinforce the child.

The **behavior** is the child's response to the therapist's instruction. In this case, the child replies "cookie" with or without the therapist's prompt. If the child answers incorrectly, the therapist corrects the child, saying, "No, this is a cookie. Say 'cookie.'" Then, the therapist waits for the correct response.

The **consequence** is the reinforcement provided to the child by the therapist, contingent on the child's production of the correct behavior. For example, the therapist might reinforce the child's reply of "cookie" by smiling, saying "Good. This is a cookie," and giving the child a bite.

Each trial is repeated multiple times until the child correctly produces the desired behavior with minimal prompting. Then, a new behavior is introduced which usually builds upon previously acquired skills.

Teaching Requests and Comments

Discrete trial training can also be used to help children combine words into phrases and simple sentences. One important type of phrase that children learn to use is **mands**, or requests. Mands are important because they allow children to obtain objects, information, or privileges. Mands are also fairly easy to teach because they specify their own reinforcers. For example, a 2-year-old who says "Give drink" can be given a sip of his favorite juice to reinforce his request.

Initially, therapists use discrete trial training to teach simple mands. For example, the therapist might produce a cup of juice and prompt the child's request by saying "You want a drink. Say, 'Give me a drink.'" The therapist would continue to prompt the child until the child produces the request. Then, the therapist would reinforce the mand. Trials would be repeated until the child makes the request with little prompting. Eventually, all prompting would be decreased (or faded) until the child requests on his own.

Another type of phrase that the child learns to use are **tacts**, that is, comments and descriptions. Tacts allow children to combine nouns and verbs to describe their experiences and surroundings. Examples of tacts include

- descriptions of objects (e.g., The dog is black and white);
- descriptions of parts of objects (e.g., The dog has two ears and a nose);
- descriptions of the function of objects (e.g., His nose is for smelling);
- descriptions of actions (e.g., The dog runs fast);
- action sequences (e.g., He runs outside. Then, he gets his ball);
- expression of feelings (e.g., He likes to play).

RESEARCH TO PRACTICE

HOW TO HELP CHILDREN MAKE COMMENTS AND DESCRIBE OBJECTS

A therapist might use discrete trial training to teach tacts. For example, the therapist might show a picture of her dog to the child and say,

Here is a picture of my dog. I want you to tell me about him. You may tell me what he looks like, about the parts of his body, or anything else. For example, say, "He is black and white. He has big ears."

The therapist would praise the child's response and continue with a second trial:

Very good. The dog is black and white. He has big ears. What else does he have? Say, "He has a little nose..."

Over the course of several sessions, the therapist would gradually fade her prompts so that the child can describe objects on his own:

Here is a picture of my house. Tell me three things about my house...

Teaching Questions

Therapists also teach children with limited expressive vocabularies to ask questions. Questions are important because they allow children to gather information about their surroundings and expand their semantic knowledge. The therapist structures a situation that encourages the child to ask a question. Then, the therapist models the question and reinforces the child's attempts to ask the question:

Therapist: [Holds up a magnifying glass.] "Look what I have. You don't know what this is. Ask me, 'What is it?'"

Child: "What is it?"

Therapist: "Great! You asked a good question! It is a magnifying glass. You see with it."

The therapist might introduce other objects, gradually fading her verbal prompt until the child can ask questions on his own. The therapist might use other approaches to teach *who, when, where,* and *why* questions (see Table 5.4). In each case, the therapist initially relies heavily on verbal prompts. Later, the therapist fades the prompts as the child begins to produce questions independently.

Teaching Complex Sentences

Older children with Language Disorder usually have great difficulty forming complex sentences. For example, they often have trouble generating compound sentences (e.g., "Orville climbed aboard the airplane *and* Wilbur started

Table 5.4 Discrete Trial Training to Teach Children to Ask Questions

Question	Example
Who	If you don't know someone, you ask a question that starts with *who*. [Holds up a picture of a boy.] Look at this picture. You don't know this boy. Ask me, "Who is that boy?"
What	If you want to know something, you ask a question that starts with *what*. [Shows a picture of two children playing chess.] Look at this picture. You don't know what the children are doing. Ask me, "What are they doing?"
When	When you want to know when something will happen, you ask a question that starts with the word *when*. Let's pretend that your mother tells you that your grandma is going to visit. You don't know when. Ask, "When is grandma going to visit?"
Where	When you can't find someone or something, you ask a question that starts with *where*. Let's pretend that you want to put on your shoes to go outside, but you can't find them. Ask, "Where are my shoes?"
Why	When you don't understand something, you ask a question that starts with *why*. Let's pretend that your mother gives you a toy car for your birthday, but the car doesn't work. Ask, "Why doesn't the car work?"
How	If you don't know the way to do something, you ask a question that starts with *how*. Here is a new game that you've never played before. Ask, "How do we play the game?"

Source: Based on Hegde and Maul (2006).

HOW TO HELP CHILDREN USE LONGER AND MORE ELABORATE SENTENCES

Using discrete trial training, therapists systematically model, prompt, and reinforce these and other complex sentence structures.

Therapist: Here is a picture of two men. We can tell about these men in one big sentence. Say, "One man is tall *and* the other man is short."

Therapist: Here is a picture of a happy girl. She just won a race. Let's make one sentence, telling why the girl is happy. Say, "The girl is happy *because* she won a race."

Therapist: Here is a picture of two dogs. The dog with the red collar is very dirty. Let's make one sentence, telling which dog is dirty. Say, "The dog, *with the red collar*, is very dirty."

The therapist will gradually fade these prompts until the child can produce these complex sentences independently.

the engine"), dependent clauses (e.g., "*After the engine had started*, Wilbur gave his brother the signal to start"), and embedded clauses (e.g., "The airplane, *which was made of wood and fabric*, went into the air").

Teaching Specific Skills: Conversational Recast Training

Children with Language Disorder typically show specific deficits in morphology and grammar. For example, children may have difficulty using the *to be* form, omit the plural /s/, or leave off the *–ed* ending of the past

tense. Therapists need to target these deficits by modeling, reinforcing, and repeatedly practicing appropriate language skills. A commonly used technique to achieve these goals is conversational recast training (Camarata & Nelson, 2006).

In **conversational recast training**, the therapist structures the child's environment in ways that are likely to elicit the desired verbal behavior. Then, the therapist prompts the child to practice the desired language skill, each time correcting mistakes and reinforcing appropriate language use with eye contact, smiles, attention, and verbal praise.

RECAST TRAINING: PRACTICING SPECIFIC LANGUAGE SKILLS

A therapist wants the child to practice the /s/ ending of the third person singular. The therapist might invite the child to play "zoo" with toy animals (Kaderavek, 2011):

Therapist: The animals are hungry and tired. Let's help the zookeeper feed them and put them to bed. Here is the zookeeper. [Moves human toy figure to giraffe.] He feeds the giraffe every day. What does he do?

Child: He feed giraffe.

Therapist: He feeds the giraffe doesn't he? Let's ask the giraffe what he eats. What do you want to eat, giraffe? You ask the giraffe what he wants to eat?

Child: What you eat?

Therapist: What do you eat, giraffe? Oh, he says he eats hay. He eats hay. Does he eat bananas? No, he eats hay. The monkey eats bananas, doesn't he? Who do you think eats and eats the banana?

Child:	Monkey eats bananas.
Therapist:	Great! The monkey eats and eats the yellow bananas. What does the giraffe eat?
Child:	Giraffe eats hay.
Therapist:	Very good. The monkey eats bananas and the giraffe eats hay. Now let's put the giraffe to bed. Where does the giraffe sleep? Does the giraffe sleep in the pond?
Child:	No, the giraffe sleep under the tree.
Therapist:	Oh, I see. The giraffe sleeps under the tree. He sleeps and sleeps all night. Here is the zookeeper asking the giraffe, "where do you sleep?" Where does the giraffe sleep?
Child:	He sleeps under the tree.
Therapist:	Exactly! He sleeps under the tree.

Ample practice is critical to the success of conversational recast training. Mistakes must be corrected immediately and correct use of the desired language skills must be repeatedly reinforced to maintain its use over time. Most of the deficits shown by children with SLI can be targeted with conversational recast training. The variations of incidental learning are limited only by the goals of treatment and the creativity of the therapist.

Generalizing Language Skills: Milieu Training

Although discrete trial training is very effective at introducing and reinforcing language skills, therapists must rely on other strategies to help generalize these skills to children's homes and schools. **Milieu training** is a treatment approach that uses behavioral principles in contexts that approximate children's real-life environments and experiences. *Milieu* simply means the physical setting in which events typically occur. A young child's milieu might include her home, preschool, day care, and family outings (e.g., shopping, playground). In milieu training, children practice language skills in natural contexts (Hancock & Kaiser, 2006).

Milieu training relies chiefly on contingency management. The therapist observes the child engage in everyday tasks, such as coloring, eating, and playing with toys, and looks for situations in which the child might be able to practice language skills. When such situations arise, the therapist *prompts* the child to practice the language skill, *models* the skill (if necessary), and *reinforces* the child's attempts to use the skill.

There are several specific techniques that may be used in milieu training. The **mand-model technique** is most common. The therapist observes the child approach a desired object, such as a toy car, and immediately prompts (mands) the child to ask for the object (e.g., "Tell me what you want."). If necessary, the therapist provides a verbal prompt to help the child successfully ask for the object (e.g., "Say, 'I want the car.'"), and reinforces the child's request (e.g., "Good question. I'm glad you asked so nicely. Here, take it.").

Another strategy is to use the **delay technique**. This technique is similar to the mand-model approach, but the therapist waits, with an expectant facial expression, for the child to ask for the desired object. The goal of the mand-model technique is for the child to request the object without the therapist asking "What do you want?" or providing a similar verbal prompt. The delay strategy is designed to increase independent verbal output.

A third strategy is **incidental teaching**. In this technique, the therapist simply waits for the child to initiate a topic and then prompts the child to elaborate on that topic using language. After elaboration, the therapist reinforces the child's verbal output.

RESEARCH TO PRACTICE

MILIEU TRAINING: USING THE CHILD'S ENVIRONMENT TO ELICIT LANGUAGE

The therapist uses incidental teaching to prompt the child to ask questions:

Child:	Where daddy.
Therapist:	You want to know where daddy is. Say, "Where *is* daddy?"
Child:	Where is daddy?
Therapist:	Very good. You asked a good question. Let's go find him.

Initially, milieu trainers are professional therapists. Over time, parents can be taught the principles of milieu training so that they can use them with their own children. Parents can effectively implement milieu training after 20 to 30 sessions. Milieu training can also be used for groups of children with language impairment (Kaderavek, 2011).

Augmentative and Alternative Communication

Some children with Language Disorder have considerable difficulty communicating with others. For example, some children with comorbid developmental and neurological disorders, such as Intellectual Disability, Autism Spectrum Disorder, and cerebral palsy, may have great difficulty conveying their needs and ideas using traditional verbal discourse. Many of these children benefit from an augmentative/alternative communication system (Romski, Sevicik, Cheslock, & Barton, 2006).

An **augmentative/alternative communication (AAC) system** compensates for the communication deficits shown by children with severe language impairments and facilitates their communication skills. AAC systems can be used to temporarily augment children's communication as they acquire greater language skills, or they may be used as a permanent means to compensate for language deficits. In either case, AAC devices are meant to complement, not replace, children's verbal language (King, 2011).

There are four components of all AAC systems: symbols, aids, strategies, and techniques (American Speech-Language-Hearing Association [ASHA], 2005). **Symbols** are the representations of objects or actions that the child uses to communicate. For example, a symbol of someone waving might be used to communicate "hello." Symbols can be rudimentary (e.g., a stick figure) or complex (e.g., a photograph).

Aids are the devices that children use to send or receive messages. Some aids use little technology, such as cards containing single drawings (e.g., symbols), which are used to communicate important objects and actions. Other aids are highly sophisticated, such as tablet devices that contain pictures (e.g., symbols) that, when pressed, indicate the desired object or action.

Strategies refer to the method the child uses to communicate more quickly and easily. For example, some low-tech aids rely on a color-coding strategy, in which symbols that represent similar objects or actions are grouped together using the same color (e.g., line drawings for "hungry," "thirsty," and "bathroom" are colored similarly). Other, high-tech aids use prediction strategies to speed communication. For example, electronic devices may try to predict the children's desired word or phrase based on the first few letters he types, much like a search engine.

Finally, **techniques** refers to the methods that the child uses to communicate. Techniques include pointing at a symbol, pressing a button, or scanning through symbols and verbally indicating a choice (Stevens, 2011; Wood & Hart, 2007).

Therapists and families choose from the wide range of the available symbols, aids, strategies, and techniques to build an AAC system for their child. Selection depends mostly on the communication skills and needs of the child and preferences of the family (Ehren & Ehren, 2007). Because there are so many options, we will focus on three of the most popular systems (King, 2011).

Picture Exchange Communication System

Frost and Bondy (2002) developed the **Picture Exchange Communication System (PECS)** as a means to improve the communicative functioning of children with little verbal language. In essence, PECS consists of a series of line drawings or simple pictures printed on cards (Figure 5.3). These symbols represent common objects or actions that children can present to caregivers to communicate their needs. For example, a line drawing of a toilet might be used to communicate "bathroom." Later, children learn to combine cards to ask questions (e.g., "What do you want?") and convey more complex ideas (e.g., "I see . . . ").

Practitioners of PECS use operant conditioning, especially positive reinforcement, to associate picture symbols with objects or activities in the environment. To accomplish this task, therapists teach children to exchange a picture-symbol of an object or activity with a desired item or behavior (Charlop-Christy & Jones, 2006).

Training consists of six phases that can occur over several days to several weeks. In the first phase, the child learns to exchange pictures of commonly used objects in his environment for primary reinforcers, like a favorite food or drink. The child is seated at a table in front of a 2 in. x 2 in. laminated drawing. The drawing represents a common object in the child's environment such as a cup. Two therapists provide the training. One therapist serves as the child's communicative partner. She tells the child to give her "cup." The second therapist sits behind the child and physically guides the child to pick up the card and hand it to the first therapist. The first therapist immediately reinforces the child. The procedure is repeated several times, with the second therapist gradually fading the amount of help she provides. The training session continues until the child is able to independently exchange the picture for the reinforcer 80% of the time.

After the child learns basic exchanges, he develops more complex, expressive language skills. In Phase 2 training, the child is taught to initiate social interactions by getting the attention of adults and handing them a picture card. In Phase 3, the child learns to discriminate among many pictures in an array. For example, if the child is presented with pictures of a tree, a car, and a house, the child learns to successfully give the picture of the house when asked. In phases 4 and 5, children learn to form sentences and answer questions using the pictures. In the final phase, children expand on previously mastered skills to express more complex needs and desires using the picture-symbols.

Figure 5.3   Using PECS to Help Children Communicate

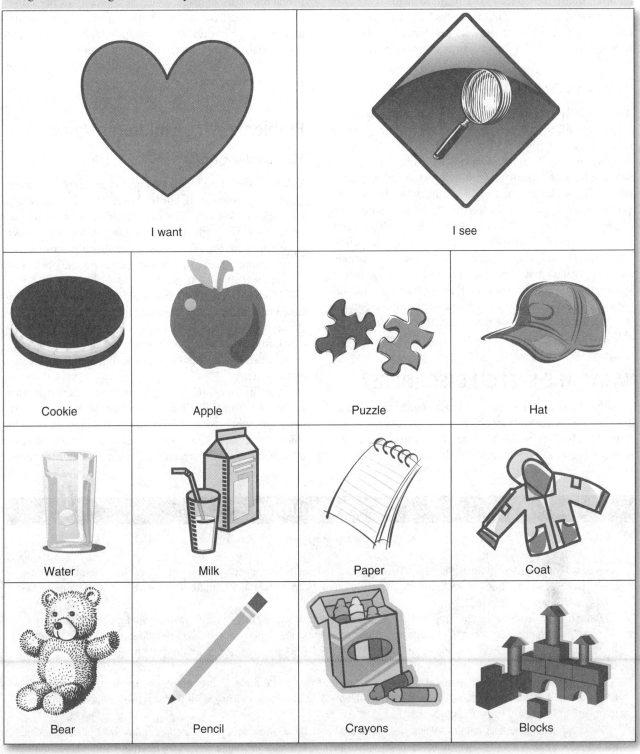

I want	I see

Cookie	Apple	Puzzle	Hat
Water	Milk	Paper	Coat
Bear	Pencil	Crayons	Blocks

Note: Children can use the Picture Exchange Communication System (PECS) to communicate. They might point to "I want" and "water" to request a drink.

System for Augmenting Language

The **System for Augmenting Language (SAL)** is a high-tech AAC system that helps children communicate in their everyday surroundings. Children are given an electronic speech-generating device, like an iPad. Then, children and families select symbols on the device that represent the most commonly needed words and phrases in their child's daily life. Parents, teachers, and other caregivers encourage children to use the device to communicate when necessary. For example, when the child indicates that he is thirsty, the parent might ask him to indicate his desired beverage by pressing the "water" or "juice" symbol on the device.

Visual Scene Displays

An alternative, high-tech AAC system is to use **visual scene displays (VSDs)**. Whereas most systems organize symbols semantically (e.g., by word/phrase meaning), VSDs organize them schematically in the context of a picture. For example, in a VSD, the electronic tablet might include a line picture of the child's classroom. The child might be able to press various "hot spots" on the picture to communicate. For example, pressing the image of the teacher might communicate "I need help" whereas pressing the image of "pencil" on the desk in the picture might indicate "I want my pencil." Different visual scenes can be used in different contexts (e.g., school, mealtime, bedroom). VSDs are especially useful with toddlers who have trouble using more complex pictures or symbols. Indeed, VSDs have been effectively used with children as young as 1 and 2 years of age (Stevens, 2011).

WHAT ARE SPEECH DISORDERS?

Usually, children have no problems acquiring language and developing complex use of morphology, grammar, and semantics. By the time children begin preschool, most children are highly expressive and delightful (albeit sometimes exhausting) conversation partners. Despite having no problems with language, a sizable minority of preschoolers do show deficits in speech, that is, the auditory output of language. Children can show speech problems in three ways: (a) problems with the quality of their voice, (b) problems with speech clarity or articulation, and (c) problems with speech fluency.

Problems With Children's Voice

Pitch, Loudness, and Quality

Voice is the sound children produce using the lungs, diaphragm, and vocal cords. Voice is not synonymous with speech. We can hear an infant's voice when he coos or babbles, although he does not yet show true speech. Approximately 6% of children have disturbances in their voice, characterized by pitch, loudness, or quality that is not typical for their age and gender.

Pitch refers to the highness or lowness of the voice and is determined by the frequency of sound waves generated by the larynx (i.e., voice box).

Loudness refers to the intensity or volume of voice; it is determined by the amplitude of the sound waves generated by the larynx.

Quality refers to the overall tone and clarity of voice. Problems with quality include excessive breathiness, harshness, hoarseness, or vocal fry (i.e., a popping or bubbling sound while speaking). **Dysphonia** (poor voice quality) usually is caused by structural abnormalities of the larynx

---

CASE STUDY

RASPY RAMON

Ramon was an energetic, somewhat husky 8-year-old boy referred to the speech pathologist at our clinic by his school psychologist. "Ray always has a raspy voice. On the playground, I can always differentiate him from the other children based on the hoarseness of its tone."

Ramon bounded into the therapist's office and seemed to talk incessantly. He described his spelling test that morning in school, his friends at lunch, and the upcoming music performance. "I don't like chorus," he added. "Why not?" asked his therapist. "Cause the teacher told me to just "mouth" the words—not to sing them. She said that I have a voice that's better seen than heard."

Indeed, Ramon's voice had a rough, scratchy quality that was moderately aversive to others. He spoke in a loud tone and often quite fast. His mother explained, "Ray's the youngest of four boys. They're all pretty active. He needs to be loud to make himself heard sometimes."

A formal assessment of Ramon's voice was conducted using videostoboscopy. This technique involved placing a small microphone around Ramon's neck to measure his voice quality. At the same time, a very small, fiberoptic camera was placed in the back of his mouth to record the activity of his vocal cords and larynx. The microphone and camera recorded sound and movement in slow motion as Ramon read a passage of text. Results of the test showed moderate to severe hoarseness with frequent breaks in pitch. Furthermore, testing revealed large lesions on the vocal folds, likely caused by vocal straining. The lesions were covered in mucus, adding to the poor quality of Ramon's voice.

His therapist said, "Ray, your vocal cords look like they've been in a boxing match—and lost! First, we need to make sure we let them rest and recover. Then, we're going to train them to get them into shape."

or medical illness. However, dysphonia can also result from anxiety. Sometimes, when children experience stress, their vocal cords remain open during sound production, resulting in "breathy" or airy" speech. In other cases, the vocal cords are held tightly together, producing a harsh or raspy voice. Finally, chronic stress can tire the larynx, causing abnormal pitch.

Other quality problems concern the resonance of children's voices. **Resonance** refers to the modification of sound as it passes through bodily structures. Oral resonance occurs when sound passes through the tongue and jaw. Problems with oral resonance can result in a dull, hollow voice or a voice that sounds infantile (e.g., baby talk). Nasal resonance occurs when sound passes through the nasal cavity when producing the /m/ and /n/ phonemes. The most common problem is hypernasality, which results in a nasally, shrill voice. Hypernasality is usually caused by structural problems with the mouth and nasal cavities (e.g., cleft lip and palate),

Image 5.2 Vocal abuse is the most common cause of voice problems in adolescents. As many as 75% of cheerleaders report voice problems at some point in time.

immaturity of the mouth muscles that restrict flow to the nasal cavity, enlarged adenoids and tonsils, or hearing impairment. However, some children learn to speak in a nasal voice and are candidates for speech therapy. Hyponasality occurs when there is too little nasal resonance. Children with hyponasality sound like they have a cold. The condition is usually caused by enlarged adenoids. Sometimes, hyponasality occurs when those with allergies experience inflammation of the throat and nasal cavity that restricts air flow.

Causes and Treatments

Voice problems are typically caused by structural abnormalities of the larynx, vocal cords, mouth, or nasal cavities. These abnormalities typically result from (a) medical illness, (b) neurological disorders, or (c) vocal abuse.

Several medical disorders are known to cause voice problems. For example, cancer, contact ulcers, gastric (stomach acid) reflux, cysts, endocrine disorders, and papilloma can all adversely affect voice pitch, loudness, or quality. Similarly, many neurological disorders can severely affect control over one's speech centers, leading to marked voice problems. For example, cerebellar lesions, motor neuron damage, and multiple sclerosis (deterioration of the myelin coating of neurons) can greatly impair voice. Fortunately, these disorders are relatively rare in children. More commonly, children develop temporary voice problems because of allergies, asthma, colds, sinus infections, and postnasal drip.

The most common cause of voice problems in children and adolescents is **vocal abuse**. Youths who talk frequently, loudly, or habitually harshly can damage their vocal cords, leading to problems with loudness or quality. As many as 75% of high school cheerleaders report at least moderate voice problems at some time. Excessive cheering at sporting events or yelling to friends at concerts or loud parties can also damage vocal cords. Potential damage includes the development of vocal nodules (i.e., white or pink, callous-like growths), polyps (i.e., soft, fluid-filled sacs), swelling (i.e., laryngitis), or thickening of the vocal cords (Image 5.3). Excessive damage can result in loss of voice or very poor voice quality.

In some cases, voice problems are learned (Fogle, 2008). For example, a child may be positively reinforced with extra help or attention from parents when she uses a high-pitched, sing-songy voice. Alternatively, a child may be negatively reinforced (e.g., excused from giving a class presentation) for speaking in a soft, quiet voice. Still, other children acquire certain voices through imitation. Although the use of these voices may be initially modeled and reinforced, they may eventually hinder the communication and social interactions of children who adopt them.

In most cases, children's voice problems can be treated with rest. In some instances, children must participate in **voice therapy** to learn how to speak with appropriate pitch, loudness, and quality (Colton, Casper, & Leonard, 2011). Speech-language therapists can use a number of techniques,

Image 5.3 This individual has a nodule (i.e., a callous-like growth) on her left vocal fold. This damage may be caused by chronic yelling or cheering and is usually reversible with rest and voice therapy.

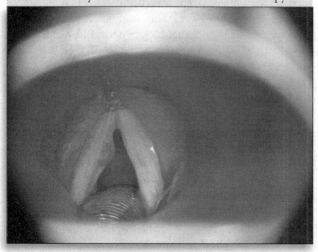

depending on the child's presenting problems. Some examples include (a) vocal abuse prevention, (b) auditory feedback, and (c) voice retraining.

Vocal abuse prevention is a behavioral technique designed for children who yell, scream, or otherwise injure their vocal cords in specific locations (Figure 5.4). For example, an 8-year-old girl who develops polyps on her vocal cords because of frequently yelling on the playground during recess would be a candidate for vocal abuse prevention. First, a teacher or playground supervisor might record the number of times the girl yells during a 25-minute-recess period. Then, the child is asked to monitor her volume on the playground and avoid yelling. Each subsequent recess period, her yelling frequency is recorded on a card, which the girl brings home to her parents. Her parents, in turn, reward her for meeting predetermined goals each day (Colton et al., 2011).

Auditory feedback is a technique that is used to treat a wide range of voice disorders, especially difficulties with pitch and loudness (Stemple & Fry, 2010). Essentially, the therapist records the child's voice and asks him or her to listen to problematic aspects of it. The therapist then teaches the child to modulate his or her voice using a series of exercises. For example, the therapist might ask the child to chant her words to avoid excessive stress on the vocal cords. Alternatively, the therapist might teach the child to alter the focus of her voice by shifting the source of sound from the back of

Figure 5.4 Vocal Abuse Prevention

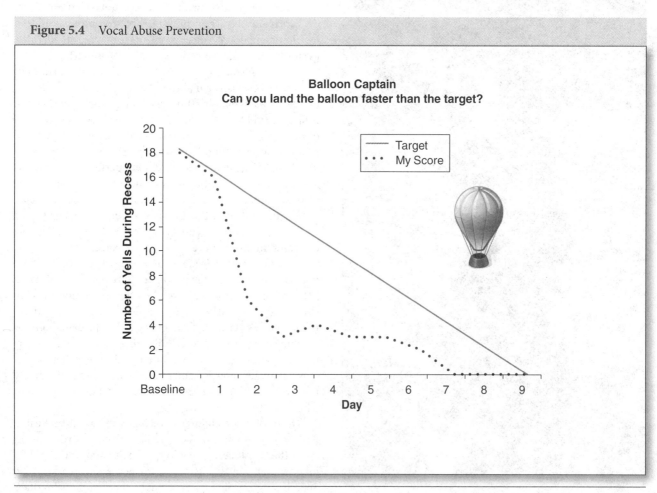

Note. A teacher might monitor the number of times this girl yells during recess. Her goal is to gradually reduce her yelling a little each day.

the throat to the middle of the tongue. As children practice these exercises, they listen to recordings of their voice until their voice improves.

Voice retraining is a third approach to voice therapy often used with older children, adolescents, and adults (Boone, McFarlane, Von Berg, & Zraick, 2010). Voice retraining consists of many different techniques designed to improve voice quality. For example, a therapist might use respiration retraining to reduce the "breathiness" of a child's voice. Another therapist might use nasal/glide training to help youths avoid "nasally" voices that are aversive to others. Yet another therapist might help improve the vocal quality of a child who speaks with tight lips or clenched jaw. The therapist might demonstrate the importance of opening the mouth and lowering the jaw while speaking, using a puppet. The child might then imitate the puppet and watch a video of his successful use of the skill (Behrman & Haskell, 2008).

Speech Sound Disorder

Definition

Speech is produced when young children learn to modulate their voice to produce specific, discernible sounds that have meaning in a particular language. Speech is highly complex; it depends on the maturation of the central nervous system, cognitive development, and coordination of head, neck, mouth, chest, and diaphragm muscles. Over the first 5 years of life, most children transition from unintelligible voice sounds, to idiosyncratic utterances that only their parents understand, to articulate and fluid word production. However, 5% of first-grade students show speech problems that interfere with their ability to communicate (Stemple & Fry, 2010).

Speech Sound Disorder (SSD) is diagnosed when children are unable to produce the expected speech sounds appropriate for their age. Speech production problems interfere with the intelligibility of their speech or prevent communication with others (see Table 5.5, Diagnostic Criteria for Speech Sound Disorder [SSD]). Children with SSD omit, substitute, distort, add, or otherwise incorrectly produce sounds in such a manner that others have difficulty understanding their speech. Usually, children with SSD show problems when producing only one or a few speech sounds. For example, they may have difficulty producing the /l/, /r/, or /s/ sounds, or they may speak with a lisp. Their problem reflects difficulty with articulation (American Psychiatric Association, 2013).

Five sound production problems are common among children with SSD. Omission errors occur when children leave off phonemes, usually at the beginning or end of words. For example, children may say "at" for "cat" or "ba" for "ball." Substitution errors occur when children replace one phoneme with another. For example, they may say "wed" instead of "red" or "thoup" instead of "soup." Sound distortions occur when a phoneme is not produced correctly, usually resulting in a "slushy" sound. Children with SSD most frequently distort the /r/, /l/, /z/, /sh/, and /ch/ sounds. Sylvester the Cat displays distortions when he says "thuffering thuccotash." Addition errors occur when children include an extra phoneme, usually the short /u/ sound, into words. For example, children may say "farog" instead of "frog" or "salow" instead of "slow." Finally, a lisp is a specific and relatively common speech error that usually results in indistinct /s/, /sh/, and /ch/ sounds. Central lisps occur when the tongue is allowed to protrude beyond the front teeth (e.g., "thun" instead of "sun"). Lateral lisps occur when air is allowed to pass between the tongue and the molars, resulting in a slushy /s/ sound.

Some children show more pervasive problems with speech sound production, beyond simple articulation. Furthermore, their speech errors follow a pattern which reflects underlying problems with phonology. For example, these children may consistently add phonemes to words (e.g., "eggi" for "egg"), reverse sounds (e.g., "peek" for "keep"), replace one sound for another (e.g., "hoop" for "soup"), blend or glide sounds (e.g., "yewo" for "yellow"), or delete sounds

---

Table 5.5   Diagnostic Criteria for Speech Sound Disorder (SSD)

A. Persistent difficulty with speech sound production that interferes with speech intelligibility or prevents verbal communication of messages.

B. The disturbance causes limitations in effective communication that interfere with social participation, academic achievement, or occupational performance, individually or in any combination.

C. Onset of symptoms is in the early developmental period.

D. The difficulties are not attributable to congenital or acquired conditions, such as cerebral palsy, cleft palate, deafness or hearing loss, traumatic brain injury, or other medical or neurological conditions.

Source: Reprinted with permission from the *Diagnostic and Statistical Manual of Mental Disorders, Fifth Edition* (Copyright 2013). American Psychiatric Association.

AMIE AND PAUL: SAME DISORDER, DIFFERENT PROBLEMS

Amie and Paul were both young children referred to our clinic because of speech production problems. Both children were diagnosed with Speech Sound Disorder, but they displayed different problems.

Amie was a self-conscious Kindergartener who was teased at school because of her "baby talk." Her speech indicated problems with articulation. She had the most difficulty correctly producing the /l/, /r/, and /s/ phonemes.

Therapist: What did you eat for dinner last night?

Amie: Yast night? I fink we ate fish and wice. I don't wike fish. But I weally wiked dethert.

Therapist: What was for dessert?

Amie: Cake with ithe cream.

Paul was an outgoing preschooler whose speech problems indicated more pervasive problems with language. He showed a pattern of speech production errors during the initial interview that suggested underlying difficulty with phonology. Paul tended to leave off the last phoneme of certain words and substitute phonemes like /th/ and /z/, making his speech very hard to understand.

Therapist: What did you do on Saturday?

Paul: We wen to da do. We saw lot of amals.

Therapist: To the zoo? Which animals did you like?

Paul: The monees, the bi caas. (Pause) And I ga da fee da gos.

Therapist: You got to feed the goats? That sounds like fun.

Amie's prognosis is much better than Paul's. In some cases, articulation problems will resolve themselves over time. When they persist beyond age 4 or 5 years, they are usually responsive to treatment. Paul's problems will likely not resolve on their own and may be more resistant to treatment.

(e.g., "pu" for "pool"). Unlike most children with SSD, their deficits are caused by phonological processing problems rather than difficulties with articulation. Needless to say, these phonological processing problems make these children very difficult to understand.

Very young children frequently make the speech errors shown by children with SSD. For example, many toddlers say *wabbit* for *rabbit*, *dis* for *this*, *pasgehti* for *spaghetti*. Children are diagnosed with SSD only when their speech production errors are developmentally unexpected, that is, when children make significantly more errors (or more severe errors) than might be expected for their age. Approximately 15% of 3-year-olds make significant errors in speech production. By age 6, approximately 75% of these children no longer show speech problems.

Clinicians must be attentive to children's ethnicity and cultural background when diagnosing SSD. SSD is not diagnosed in children who adopt regional dialects. For example,

some African American children use phonemes differently than European American children (e.g., lessening of /l/ phoneme, such as "too" for "tool"; reversals, such as "aks" for "ask"). Similarly, SSD is not diagnosed in bilingual children whose speech sound production reflects their first language. For example, Spanish-speaking children may substitute Spanish language phonemes for English phonemes (e.g., "Yulie" for "Julie") or insert sounds following the rules of Spanish phonology (e.g., "eskate" for "skate"). These cultural differences reflect linguistic variations and not disorders (Hedge, 2008).

SSD is the most common reason young children are referred to speech-language pathologists. Approximately 10% of young children have a communication disorder; as many as 80% of these children have SSD. By first grade, approximately 3.8% of all children meet diagnostic criteria for SSD. Most of these children show articulation problems only; some also show underlying difficulties with phonological processing (Hedge, 2008).

Causes of Speech Sound Disorder

Most children with SSD show problems articulating one or more specific speech sounds. However, some children with SSD display a pattern of speech sound errors that reflect underlying problems with phonological processing. Therefore, SSD is a disorder characterized by problems with articulation and, sometimes, the perceptual and cognitive aspects of speech sounds.

Phoneme acquisition follows an ordered sequence from infancy through age 7-and-a-half years. Typically developing children show a great deal of variability in their speech sound production. For example, children in the same preschool class may vary in their phonemic production by as much as 3 years. Usually, vowel sounds are mastered by age 3, simple consonants sounds (/p/, /m/, /n/, /k/) by age 5, and consonant clusters and blends by age 7 and a half. Because of the wide variability among children, SSD is usually not diagnosed until children's speech skills fall more than one standard deviation behind their peers (Pena-Brooks & Hedge, 2007).

Most explanations for SSD are based on the notion that children's articulation problems reflect a failure to transition from **immature speech production** to more mature speech production. These theories assume that speech is a complex task that takes children several years to master. Very young children discriminate and later imitate speech sounds generated by parents. These children may initially imitate speech sounds using simplistic, yet incorrect, phonemes. For example, a child who initially learns to produce the /s/ sound by thrusting her tongue beyond her front teeth may find this an effective form of communication. Her parents and other family members may understand her and reinforce this habit. Typically, this immature speech fades as children gain greater cognitive and motor control over their speech production. However, in some cases, simplified or immature phoneme production persists beyond an age at which it is developmentally expected. Although a lisp may be acceptable at age 3, it becomes problematic at age 7 when most peers speak clearly (Hedge, 2008).

More pervasive cases of SSD often reflect underlying phonological processing problems. Some experts believe that children who exhibit patterns of speech sound problems have difficulty perceiving and differentiating phonemes, rather than merely articulating them. For example, the **phonological theory of SSD** asserts that children develop underlying mental representations for phonemes as they become exposed to language over their first few years. Children who produce speech sounds normally have formed accurate mental representations of these sounds. However, subtle neurological impairments may interfere with the ability of some children to accurately perceive, differentiate, and mentally represent phonemes, thus leading to impairments in speech production (Bernthal & Bankson, 2004).

A variant of the phonological theory of SSD is **optimality theory of SSD** (Dekkers, van der Leeuw, & van der Weijer, 2000). This psycholinguistic theory of SSD is based on the notion that children learn to speak based on two sets of rules: (a) universal grammar that is common to all human languages and (b) grammatical rules that are specific to the child's language. Over their first years of life, children must learn to use the rules of universal grammar in the context of the specific rules of their language. Most children achieve this process smoothly; however, some children continue to apply principles of universal grammar at the expense of following the rules of their specific language. This can cause a phonological processing problem. For example, innate universal grammar does not place great importance on final consonants (e.g., the /t/ in bat). However, in English, this ending is important to differentiate words (e.g., "bat" and "ball"). English-speaking children who delete these endings (i.e., /ba/ instead of "bat") may be placing excessive emphasis on these universal rules at the expense of rules in the English language (Hedge, 2008).

Genetics also likely plays a role in SSD. Approximately 35 to 40% of children with SSD have a family member with a history of the disorder. It is likely that this familial association is caused by shared genes. However, because parents and other family members usually model speech production to children, this association may also be partially explained by shared environmental experiences. Indeed, parents with poor articulation often have children with similar articulation deficits. SSD is also highly comorbid with Language Disorder. As many as 40 to 80% of children with SSD may also have Language Disorder. It is possible that early deficits in phonological processing underlie children's speech and language problems. In contrast, there is little evidence that ethnicity, bilingualism, socioeconomic status, and intelligence cause SSD (Hedge, 2008).

Treatment of Speech Sound Disorder

The treatment of SSD involves teaching children how to correctly generate speech sounds (Image 5.4). The goals of therapy depend on the specific deficits evidenced by the child. For example, one child might need to improve her articulation of the /r/ sound at the beginning of words, another might need to focus on the /s/ sound at the end of words, and a third might need to correct a lateral lisp. In any case, the therapist uses a combination of modeling and reinforcement to teach children how to produce phonemes in a developmentally appropriate manner. Because most children have never acquired the capacity to produce these word sounds correctly, and may habitually use less complex (and incorrect) sounds, therapy takes considerable effort on the part of therapist and child.

Speech therapy often relies on direct instruction. Therapists break down correct speech into component parts. Then, they model each part and allow ample opportunities for the child to practice its correct use. Over time, basic skills build upon each other until the child is able to correctly produce speech sounds in more complex, flexible ways (Dwight, 2006). Consider the case of Angie:

SPEECH THERAPY FOR SPEECH SOUND DISORDER

Six-year-old Angie incorrectly produced the /l/ sound. First, her therapist must model and reinforce the correct tongue position to produce the /l/ phoneme:

Therapist: (Sitting next to child, facing a mirror.) Look at my tongue. Watch me lift my tongue and put it right behind my front teeth like this. (Demonstrates.) Now you try it. Let's practice lifting our tongues in front of the mirror five times. Each time we do it correctly, we'll color in a happy face circle.

The therapist helps the child attain the correct tongue position and praises correct positioning. In another session, the therapist teaches the child to make the /l/ sound with the tongue in the correct position:

Therapist: Today, I'm going to open my mouth and raise my tongue just behind my front teeth like before. But this time, I'm going to make the /l/ sound. Listen: /l/. (Repeats). Now you try it after me.

Child: wwwlah.

Therapist: That's not exactly it. See how I smile when I make the /l/ sound with my tongue. Raise your tongue just behind your front teeth like me, smile, and make the /l/ sound like this (smiles): /l/.

Child: /l/.

Therapist: Very good /l/ sound. Let's practice it again. Each time we do it right, we'll color a little piece of this picture.

Image 5.4 This picture shows regions of the vocal tract used to produce consonants in American English. The diagram shows /phonetic symbols/ and (examples) if necessary.

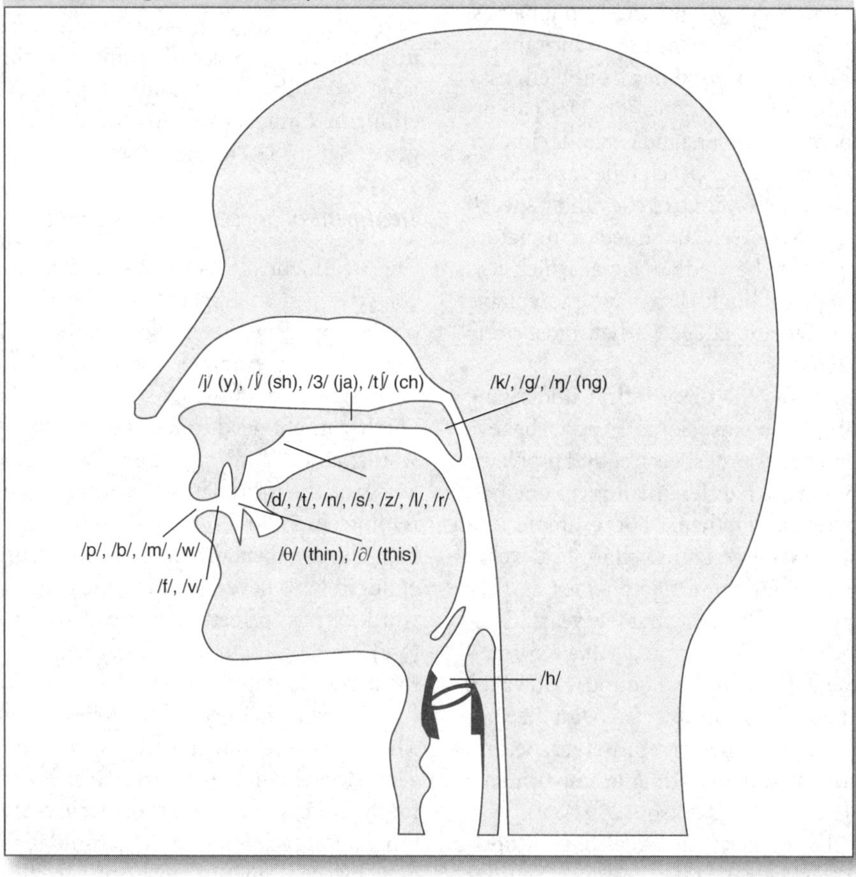

Source: Courtesy of Tavin, Wikimedia Creative Commons.

Subsequent sessions focus on producing *syllables* that either begin (i.e., la, le, li, lo, lu) or end (i.e., al, el, il, ol, ul) with the /l/ phoneme. Then, the therapist and child practice naming *objects* that either begin (e.g., lion), end (e.g., apple), or contain (e.g., balloon) the /l/ phoneme. Still later, sessions focus on blends containing the target phoneme (e.g., clown). Then, words are combined to form phrases, sentences, and stories that the therapist models and the child repeats (e.g., Lucy is a black lab. She is not too little or too large.) Finally, the child and therapist practice correct phoneme production during semi-structured play (see text box Research to Practice: Phonemes in Speech Sound Disorder). The therapist looks for opportunities to model and reinforce correct sound production and immediately corrects any of the child's mistakes (Raz, 1995).

Considerable evidence supports the effectiveness of speech therapy in helping young school-age children overcome SSD. Typically, children can show an 80% reduction

RESEARCH TO PRACTICE

PRACTICING THE /l/ PHONEME TO TREAT SPEECH SOUND DISORDER

A sample story is used to practice the /l/ sound. The therapist reads each part of the story and the child repeats.

Lucy is a black lab.

She is not too little or too large.

Lucy likes to play with her ball.

Lucy plays ball with her pal Lena.

The ball fell into a yellow pail.

The pals laugh and laugh.

in speech-sound errors in 20 sessions, especially if skills are practiced at home by parents. Children who show underlying phonological processing problems or language impairments tend to show fewer gains in therapy, however (Dwight, 2006).

Childhood-Onset Fluency Disorder (Stuttering)

Definition

Fluency refers to the ease and automaticity of speech. Fluency has several components, including *rate* (the speed at which people speak), *duration* (the length of time of individual speech sounds), *rhythm* (the flow and fluidity of sounds), and *sequence* (the order of sounds). Fluency is important to speech because it increases the likelihood that listeners will understand speakers' utterances and respond appropriately (Ratner & Tetnowski, 2006).

Childhood-Onset Fluency Disorder reflects a marked impairment in speech fluency (see Table 5.6, Diagnostic Criteria for Childhood-Onset Fluency Disorder [Stuttering]). It is commonly called stuttering. Stuttering reflects an underlying problem with speech production rather than a language problem. Children who stutter know what they want to say but they have problems saying it. As a result, their speech is disfluent and difficult to comprehend.

Table 5.6   Diagnostic Criteria for Childhood-Onset Fluency Disorder (Stuttering)

A. Disturbances in the normal fluency and time patterning of speech that are inappropriate for the individual's age and language skills, persist over time, and are characterized by frequent and marked occurrences of one (or more) of the following:

1. Sound and syllable repetitions

2. Sound prolongations of consonants as well as vowels

3. Broken words (e.g., pauses within a word)

4. Audible or silent blocking (filled or unfilled pauses in speech)

5. Circumlocutions (word substitutions to avoid problematic words)

6. Words pronounced with an excess of physical tension

7. Monosyllabic whole-word repetitions (e.g., "I-I-I-I see him")

B. The disturbance causes anxiety about speaking or limitations in effective communication, social participation, or academic or occupational performance, individually or in any combination.

C. The onset of symptoms is in the early developmental period.

D. The disturbance is not attributable to a speech-motor or sensory deficit, dysfluency associated with neurological insult (e.g., stroke, tumor) or another medical condition and is not better explained by another mental disorder.

Source: Reprinted with permission from the *Diagnostic and Statistical Manual of Mental Disorders, Fifth Edition* (Copyright 2013). American Psychiatric Association.

CASE STUDY

DAVIS'S STUTTERING

Four-year-old Davis was referred to our clinic by his pediatrician because of problems with stuttering. His father explained, "It started about two months ago. He's always been a good talker. He began saying words at 10 months and could speak in simple sentences by his second birthday. Recently, however, I noticed he's having more trouble getting the words out." His mother added, "At first, Davis just repeated the first syllable of certain words. Then, it occurred more often. Recently, he's been having trouble beginning his sentences." The therapist turned to Davis:

Therapist: Davis, do you like the toys I have in my office?

Davis: (Puts down action figure.) Y-y-y-y-es. (Pauses as if he wants to speak.) B-b-b-b-ut I l-l-l-ike Thomas the Tank Engine b-b-b-etter.

Therapist:	What's your favorite Thomas train?	
Davis:	(Pause.) I l-l-l-l-ike . . .	
Father:	(Interrupts). Davis. Try starting again, this time clearly.	
Davis:	(Frustrated.) I l-l-l-ike . . .	
Mother:	Percy's your favorite, isn't it?	
Davis:	Y-y-y-es.	

His father explained. "That's pretty typical. He just can't get the words out. We make him start over to practice speaking correctly. We don't want him to practice stuttering. Do you think that's a good idea?" The therapist replied, "If you like, I can show you some other strategies that might work better."

Table 5.7 presents some of the most common disfluencies shown by children who stutter. These disfluencies include sound repetitions (e.g., *l-l-l-l . . . listen to me*), broken words (e.g., com—puter), and silent blocking (e.g., problems with word production producing large pauses in speech). Other common problems are sound extensions ("mmmmmy dog") and visible tension while speaking.

Many typically developing children, especially preschoolers, exhibit problems with speech fluency. However, children who stutter exhibit fluency problems more frequently than their typically developing peers (Figure 5.5). Childhood-Onset Fluency Disorder is diagnosed only when it is developmentally inappropriate, that is, when the number of disfluencies exceeds the number expected based on the child's age and gender (Ratner & Tetnowski, 2006).

Many children who stutter show co-occurring behaviors when they exhibit their disfluencies. These behaviors usually involve tension or repetitive movements of the head, face, and neck. Researchers used to believe that children acquired these behaviors over time; they were thought to be coping techniques to help them "get the words out." However, recent research has shown that approximately one half of children show these behaviors soon after the onset of their stuttering symptoms (Yairi & Ambrose, 2005). These behaviors may be part of stuttering itself, rather than secondary to the disorder.

Table 5.7   Common Disfluencies Shown by Children Who Stutter

Disfluency	Description	Examples
Part-word repetitions	Repetition of sounds or syllables	f-five; ba-baby
Single-syllable whole-word repetitions	Repetition of whole words consisting of one syllable	but-but; and-and
Multiple-syllable word repetitions	Repetition of longer words	because-because
Phrase repetitions	Repetition of a phrase (usually two words)	I was I was going . . .
Prolonged sounds	Elongation of vowels or consonants	S>>>>>sometimes . . .
Blocks or broken words	Tongue, lips, or vocal cords held in fixed position	ta—able, c—ake
Tense pause	Unusual breaks between words associated with tension	I like to—go home.
Interjections	Extraneous sounds, often repeated	um, uh, er, hmmm
Revisions	An utterance is modified; content is consistent	I like—I want the ball.
Incomplete utterances	An utterance is abandoned as if there is a change of thought	The baby is—let's do that.

Source: Based on Yairi and Seery (2011).

Figure 5.5 Speech Problems in Children Who Stutter and Their Peers

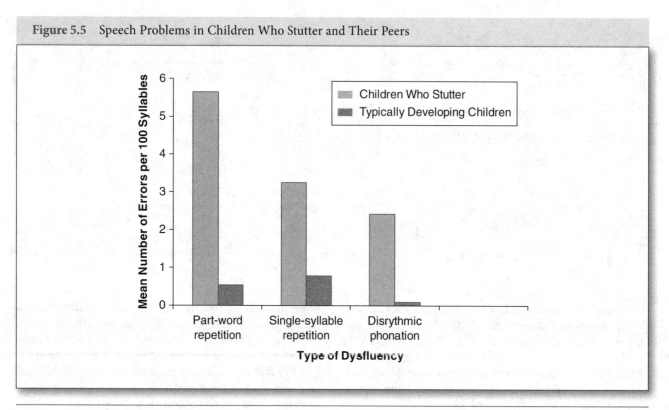

Source: Based on Yairi and Ambrose (2005).

Note: Nearly all young children show occasional problems with speech fluency; however, children who stutter make errors more frequently.

Other communication disorders are fairly common among children who stutter. In one large study, nearly 65% of children who stuttered also showed at least one other problem with communication or learning. The most common comorbid conditions were articulation problems (33.5%), language problems (25.6%), learning disabilities (11.4%), and attention deficits (5.9%; Blood et al., 2003).

Epidemiology and Course

Approximately 5% of youths have problems with stuttering at some point during childhood. Boys are more likely to stutter than girls. Furthermore, the gender ratio for stuttering increases with age. For example, in preschool, boys outnumber girls approximately 2:1. However, by adolescence, the gender ratio increases to 5:1. This gender disparity is probably due to the fact that girls are more likely to naturally recover from stuttering than boys (Bloodstein, 1995; Craig et al., 2002).

Stuttering typically emerges between 24 and 48 months of age and rarely emerges after age 6 years (see Figure 5.6). It usually has an abrupt onset in young children. In one large study, 40% of children who stuttered had their symptoms emerge in less than 2 or 3 days. An additional 33% of children showed intermediate speed of onset, with symptoms emerging over the course of one or

2 weeks. Only 28% of children showed gradual symptom onset (Yairi & Seery, 2011).

Most young children who stutter eventually recover. In several longitudinal studies, 65 to 80% of preschool and young school-age children who stuttered showed either complete or significant symptom reduction within four or five years. Recovery is most common among girls, younger children, and youths with a family member who recovered from stuttering as a child. Unfortunately, approximately 20% of children who stutter experience long-term fluency problems that persist into adolescence or adulthood (Yairi & Seery, 2011).

Often, older children and adolescents who stutter can engage in certain behaviors that reduce the severity of their symptoms. For example, nearly all children report a dramatic reduction in stuttering when they sing, speak to an infant or a pet, talk to themselves or read aloud when no one is else is present, speak in time to the rhythmic swaying of their arm, or read a passage aloud in unison with a large group of students. Other techniques that decrease stuttering for some children include speaking in a sing-song manner, speaking in monotone, whispering, acting a part in a play, repeating sentences after someone else, or simply speaking more slowly. It is unclear why these strategies are helpful in reducing stuttering and why some strategies work for some children but not others (Yairi & Seery, 2011).

Figure 5.6 Onset of Stuttering

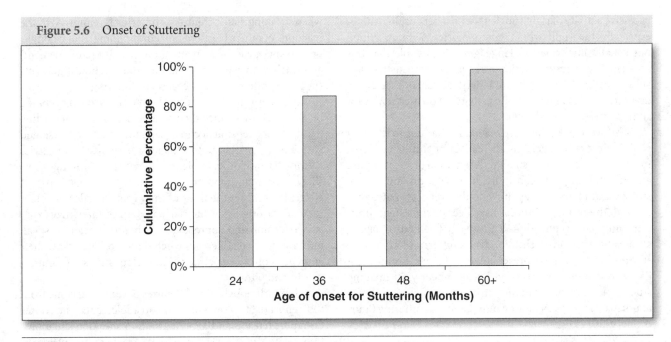

Source: Based on Yairi and Ambrose (2005).

Note: Nearly all children who stutter begin experiencing problems between 24 and 48 months of age.

Etiology

We do not yet have a comprehensive explanation for the causes of stuttering. Models based on neurobiology, learning theory, emotional processing, and cognition likely explain some, but not all, instances of stuttering in children. As is the case with most disorders, stuttering is multidetermined.

Genetics and Neurobiology. Stuttering is heritable. Several studies show that children who stutter often have a relative with a history of stuttering during childhood or adolescence. Overall, 28% of children have a parent who stuttered as a child, 43% have at least one immediate family member with a history of stuttering, and 71% have at least one extended family member with a history of the disorder. Twin studies support the notion that genes can contribute to stuttering in some children. On average, if one identical twin stutters, the likelihood that the other twin will also stutter is approximately 67% (Yairi & Seery, 2011).

On the other hand, some children who stutter have no relative with a history of the disorder. Similarly, one third of identical twins show discordance for stuttering. The genes that play a role in placing children at risk for stuttering remain elusive. Several behavioral genetics studies have shown linkages between stuttering and portions of chromosomes 2 and 9, 7 and 12, and 7 and 18. In addition, the identified chromosomes may differ for males and females who stutter, perhaps explaining the tendency of girls to recover from the disorder more often than boys. Nevertheless, researchers have yet to identify specific genes that underlie stuttering (Yairi & Seery, 2011).

Initially, researchers speculated that stuttering might be explained by abnormal brain structure or functioning. Evidence supporting this notion comes from several sources. First, some individuals begin stuttering after a brain injury. Although these individuals would not be diagnosed with Childhood-Onset Fluency Disorder, their deficits suggest that structural impairments might play a role in stuttering.

Second, some studies suggest minor differences in the size of certain brain regions in individuals who stutter compared to individuals who do not stutter. Most right-handed people show structural asymmetry favoring portions of the left hemisphere of the brain. Brain regions responsible for language processing, especially Wenicke's area in the left hemisphere, tend to be larger than corresponding regions in the right hemisphere. However, some people who stutter show atypical asymmetry favoring the right hemisphere. Neuroimaging shows reductions in the **left planum temporale**, a triangular region inside Wernicke's area, suggesting possible underlying difficulties with language processing.

Other studies have indicated possible functional differences in the brains of people who do and do not stutter. When speaking, most people show greater activation of left-hemisphere brain regions responsible for language, especially **Broca's** and **Wernicke's areas** (Image 5.5). However, PET scans indicate that individuals who stutter often show excessive activity of right (not left) hemisphere brain regions, especially the right frontal motor cortex, a brain region not usually implicated in language. It is possible that this abnormality in brain functioning explains some instances of stuttering (De Nil et al., 2000). Indeed, at least one study has demonstrated changes in brain activity following therapy for stuttering (De Nil et al., 2003).

Unfortunately, there are several limitations to the neurobiological data regarding the causes of stuttering. First, most studies show only small differences in brain structure and functioning between individuals who do and do not stutter, and many studies show no differences whatsoever. Second, the results of studies have been inconsistent; findings often lack replication. Third, very few neuroimaging studies have involved children who stutter, and almost no studies have involved preschoolers—the age group most likely to exhibit the disorder. Because nearly all imaging studies have involved adults, it is unclear whether brain abnormalities are a cause or consequence of stuttering (Yairi & Seery, 2011).

Learning. Several learning theories have been used to explain stuttering. The **two-factor theory of stuttering** posits that both classical and operant conditioning play a role in the onset and maintenance of stuttering (Brutten & Shoemaker, 1967). Specifically, children begin stuttering when normal speech disfluencies are paired with parental disapproval or discipline (e.g., classical conditioning). Children may associate these harsh parenting behaviors with disfluent speech and, consequently, develop tension and apprehensiveness when speaking. Later, children's stuttering is reinforced by the reactions of others (e.g., operant conditioning). For example, parents may give children attention (positive reinforcement) and teachers may excuse children from certain assignments (negative reinforcement) because of stuttering.

Alternatively, the **conflict theory of stuttering** is based on approach-avoidance theory (Sheehan, 1970). According to this theory, tension occurs when individuals are presented with a behavior that both satisfies a basic need and carries risk for harm. For example, in animal studies, hungry rats show tension and apprehension when they must cross an electrified grid on the floor of their cage in order to obtain food on the other side. Similarly, certain children may experience tension and apprehension when they want to speak but experience disfluencies when doing so. They show their apprehension as repetitions and elongations of sounds, words, and phrases.

Support for behavioral theories of stuttering come from self-report data. Older children and adolescents who stutter do report tension and apprehension in speaking situations. Other data also suggest that parents, teachers, and peers can exacerbate children's apprehension by interrupting them, scolding them, ridiculing them, or punishing them when they exhibit disfluencies. On the other hand, there is little evidence that parents cause their children to stutter. Indeed, most parents respond empathically to their children's speech problems.

Emotions. Anxiety can also play a role in stuttering (Karrass et al., 2006). Young children who stutter may

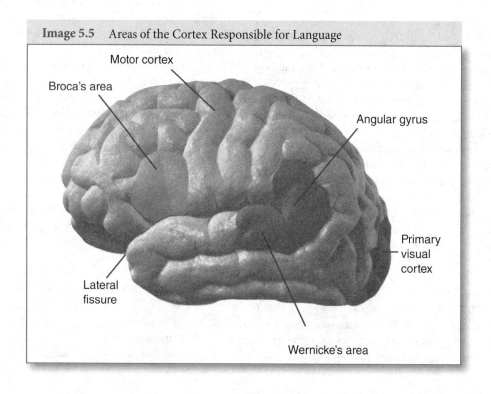

Image 5.5   Areas of the Cortex Responsible for Language

Motor cortex

Broca's area

Angular gyrus

Primary visual cortex

Lateral fissure

Wernicke's area

have difficult temperaments that predispose them to anxiety, such as problems with emotion regulation and self-soothing. Adolescents and adults who stutter report higher levels of state (transient) and trait (dispositional) anxiety than individuals who do not stutter. Finally, nearly all older children and adolescents report intense feelings of anxiety, apprehension, and psychological tension associated with speaking. The negative emotions most commonly reported are fear, dread, feeling trapped, embarrassment, shame, humiliation, resentment, and frustration (Yairdi & Seery, 2011).

The **anticipatory-struggle theory of stuttering** suggests that older children and adolescents with speech disfluencies expect speaking to be anxiety-provoking and difficult (Bloodstein, 1997). Certain situations tend to elicit the most anxiety: public speaking, answering the telephone, and saying one's own name. Children who stutter experience very low self-efficacy in these situations; they severely doubt their ability to speak without mistakes, hesitations, or repetitions. Furthermore, they often report negative thoughts associated with these situations, such as "I won't be able to speak clearly," "I'll make a fool of myself," or "Other people will think I'm stupid." These negative automatic thoughts, and the anxiety they elicit, likely increase the severity of the individual's stuttering.

It is unlikely, however, that anxiety is sufficient to explain all (or even most) instances of stuttering. Recall that stuttering typically emerges between 24 and 48 months of age. Most children in this age range who stutter are largely unaware of their symptoms. Most children who stutter do not report anxiety about public speaking until age 4 or 5 years (Ezrati-Vinacour et al., 2001).

Psycholingustics. A final explanation for the causes of stuttering comes from the field of **psycholinguistics**, the study of the psychological and neurocognitive underpinnings of language. Although there are many psycholinguistic theories of stuttering, they are all based on the premise that fluency depends on three processes: (a) conceptualization, (b) formulation, and (c) articulation. First, children must think about what they want to communicate. Next, they must formulate the appropriate mental representations for their message. Formulation involves encoding the appropriate sounds (phonological representations) and word order (grammatical representations) for the message. Finally, they must articulate these representations through manipulation of the mouth, lips, tongue, and vocal cords. Usually, these three processes occur rapidly and outside children's awareness. Most children simultaneously (and effortlessly) conceptualize, formulate, and articulate their utterances during discourse.

Stuttering occurs when there is a breakdown in one or more of these basic psycholinguistic processes. Most often, breakdowns occur during formulation (i.e., phonological or grammatical encoding). Although children who stutter know what they want to say, they may have difficulty planning out the sound or syllable sequence needed to say it. Consequently, they may be able to utter only the first phoneme or single-syllable word. Alternatively, children may know what they want to say, but, be unable to find the correct word or phrase to communicate their message (i.e., grammatical encoding). Consequently, they may show unusual pauses and repetitions as they struggle to generate the proper mental representations for these words.

According to the **covert-repair hypothesis**, children who stutter show more frequent disruptions in phonological and grammatical formulation than their non-stuttering peers (Postma & Kolk, 1992). They are also highly sensitive to these disruptions and closely monitor their own speech. When they encounter a problem, they attempt to correct it without drawing attention from others. Unfortunately, their covert attempts to repair breakdowns in phonological and grammatical encoding lead to speech disfluencies: They show sound and word repetitions, unusual pauses, and other retrieval problems. Just as traffic stops and starts during road repairs, so too does speech stop and start as children attempt to repair disruptions in speech formulation.

Another psycholinguistic theory is the **auditory processing deficit model**. According to this model, children who stutter do not take in and process sound information, especially linguistic information, the same way as typically developing children. Specifically, children who stutter may have problems with sound localization and lateralization (i.e., identifying the source of sounds), auditory discrimination (i.e., differentiating sounds), auditory pattern recognition (i.e., recognizing groups of sounds, such as phonemes), and temporal aspects of audition (e.g., understanding and processing sounds presented quickly or in a certain order). Problems processing auditory linguistic information are believed to disrupt children's speech because they interfere with the ability to comprehend, formulate, and articulate language.

Evidence supporting the auditory processing deficit model comes from two sources. First, some neuroimaging studies have detected structural and functional deficits in left-hemisphere brain regions in individuals who stutter. These regions, especially portions of Wernicke's area, are believed to be critical to auditory processing and language. Second, many strategies used to reduce stuttering seem to work by compensating for individuals' auditory processing deficits. For example, stuttering often improves when individuals speak more slowly. Speaking at a slower rate can improve auditory processing by slowing the input of auditory information. Stuttering can also be reduced when people are able to listen to their own speech using a hearing device. Listening to oneself speak can improve the auditory feedback that one receives, thus, increasing the likelihood that auditory information will be received and processed correctly (Yairi & Seery, 2011).

Treatment of Childhood Onset Fluency Disorder

Treatment for Younger Children

As many as 75% of preschool-age children who stutter naturally recover from their disfluencies. Not all preschoolers who stutter require therapy. Many clinicians recommend waiting several months after the onset of stuttering before initiating treatment to see if the problem will spontaneously resolve itself. Although some individuals might be concerned about delaying treatment, longitudinal data indicate that a brief delay does not affect the severity of the disorder or the efficacy of treatment once it is initiated (Jones et al., 2000; Kingston et al., 2003).

The decision to formally treat preschoolers who stutter is based on clinical judgment. Many clinicians believe that treatment is needed if stuttering persists for more than 6 to 12 months, if the child shows other speech or language problems, or if the child has a family member who stutters. Treatment may also be warranted if the child's stuttering greatly upsets his or her parents (Yairi & Ambrose, 2005).

The goal of treatment for preschool-age children is **naturally fluent speech**, that is, speech that is indistinguishable from preschoolers who have never stuttered. Most preschoolers who stutter are unaware of their disfluencies; consequently, therapists spend the bulk of their time addressing children's speech problems rather than the social and emotional consequences of stuttering on these children (Yairi & Seery, 2011).

There are many methods to increase fluency in preschoolers who stutter; however, most treatments involve at least one of the following three components: (a) modifying children's speech motor patterns, (b) increasing fluency and decreasing stuttering through operant conditioning, and (c) supporting parents (Ratner & Guitar, 2006).

First, therapists must modify children's speech motor behaviors—behaviors which increase the likelihood that children will pause, repeat, or otherwise linguistically stumble when producing speech sounds. Several **speech modification programs** are available, including the Easy Speaking Voice Program, the Stuttering Intervention Program, and the University of Illinois Stuttering Research Program (Table 5.8). These and other programs involve twice-weekly sessions in which children are systematically trained to (a) use a soft or "easy" voice when speaking, (b) speak at a slower rate, and (c) relax muscles of their mouth and throat and control their breathing.

Initially, children might be taught to whisper when speaking, during therapy sessions. Then, children are asked to utter one-syllable words and to elongate (i.e., draw out) the vowel sounds of these words to increase the likelihood that they will utter them without pauses or repetitions. Later, children might be asked to practice saying two-syllable compound words (e.g., school bus, hot dog) at a very slow rate of speech (60 words/min), elongating vowel sounds and speaking in a soft voice. Still later, children increase the length of utterances (i.e., phrases and sentences) and gradually increase their volume and rate of speech. All the while, therapists model slow speech, controlled breathing, and soft voice in a manner that somewhat resembles Mr. Roger's speech on television.

Most therapists also rely heavily on operant conditioning to improve children's speech motor behaviors. In an early experiment, Martin and colleagues (1972) asked young children who stuttered to carry on a conversation with a puppet. The puppet interacted with the children as long as the child

Table 5.8 University of Illinois Stuttering Research Program for Preschoolers

Week	Description
1	Therapist models a soft voice and slow rate of speech is modeled (i.e., 1 word/sec); children repeat single-syllable words
2	Children practice soft voice and slow rate of speech without modeling; children repeat multiple-syllable words (e.g., school bus, hot dog); parents watch therapy from behind mirror
3	Length of utterances is increased to 2- to 3-word phrases (e.g., ride school bus; eat hot dog); children repeat after therapist; parents watch therapy from behind mirror
4	Length of utterance is increased to 4- to 6 words that form meaningful sentences (e.g., the boy wakes up, he gets dressed, he goes to the grocery store); parents are in therapy room
5	Speaking rate is increased to 1.5 words/sec; parents begin to model 4- to 6-word utterances to the child, using slow and quiet speech
6+	Speaking rate is increased to 2 words/sec; parents take the lead in modeling slow and quiet speech; length of utterances increases to statements and questions

Source: Based on Yairi and Seey (2011).

Note: Sessions are typically held twice weekly.

spoke fluently. However, when the children stuttered, the puppet stopped interacting with the children for 10 seconds. At the end of the study, the children showed significant decreases in stuttering, both in the laboratory and at home.

Several treatment programs capitalize on operant conditioning. For example, the Extended Length of Utterance (ELU) Program requires preschool-age children to name pictures and describe scenes to therapists. The utterances that they must use gradually increase over the course of the program from single-syllable words to multi-word phrases. Fluent speech is liberally reinforced by the therapist saying "Good talking!" or "Excellent speech." In contrast, when children stutter, the therapist immediately says "Stop!" and asks the child to begin the utterance again. Another popular intervention, the Lidcombe Program, also reinforces fluent speech and mildly punishes disfluencies. For example, therapists praise fluent speech by saying "Great job, that was smooth speech." In contrast, they respond to disfluencies with statements such as, "That was bumpy speech. Can you fix that bump?" Both the ELU and Lidcombe Programs are effective for preschool-age children who stutter; as many as 90% of children who participate in these programs show marked symptom reduction within 22 sessions (Yairi & Seery, 2011).

A third component of treatment involves parents. Parental involvement is important in at least two ways. First, parents often have many questions about the causes of stuttering and the prognosis for their children. Therapists can answer parents' questions and provide support and reassurance. Second, therapists can teach parents how to model "easy speech" at home and reinforce their children's fluency.

Treatment for Older Children and Adolescents

If children's stuttering persists into the elementary-school years, it tends to be more resistant to treatment. Therefore, the primary goal for therapy involving older children and adolescents is to reduce the frequency and severity of stuttering and to achieve "deliberately fluent speech." **Deliberately fluent speech** refers to the use of certain strategies and tactics to reduce (not eliminate) disfluencies and cope with speaking situations. Deliberately fluent speech takes considerable effort and practice on the part of children, therapists, and parents. However, it enables children who stutter to speak in a manner that approximates typically developing speakers (Guitar, 2006).

Therapy for older children and adolescents involves three components: identification, modification, and generalization. Identification involves helping the older child recognize instances of stuttering when they occur. Although older children are aware that they stutter, they may not be aware of the frequency of their stuttering, physical behaviors associated with their stuttering (e.g., facial tension, blinking), and speaking situations that are most likely to elicit stuttering. Initially, therapists might use mirrors or video recordings to help children identify and describe instances of stuttering when they occur. Later, the therapist and child might work to identify situations that elicit stuttering, such as answering the telephone or being called upon in class (Montgomery, 2006).

After the child can identify how and when he stutters, the child and therapist can begin modifying the child's speech. The goal of this phase of treatment is similar to the treatment of preschool-age children; the child must learn to switch from "hard speech" to relaxed, slow, "easy speech." Typically, speech modification is taught during the course of conversations between the child and therapist, using a technique called "in-block modification." When the child or therapist notices a disfluency (i.e., a "block"), he or she points it out, and the child must correct it. Table 5.9 shows some of the terms that therapists might use to prompt children to correct disfluent speech.

The actual techniques used to modify children's speech depend on the type of disfluency. However, nearly all therapists

---

Table 5.9 Terms Used by Therapists to Prompt Children's Fluent Speech

Problem	Video Analogy	Football Analogy	For Young Children
Talking too quickly	Fast forward	Rushing	Rabbit talk
Repetition	Rewinds, skips	Fumble	Bumpy talk
Prolongation	Long plays	Holding	Sticky talk
Instruction			
Stop talking	Pause	Time out	Red light
Start talking	Play	In play	Green light
Try again	Erase and replay	Instant replay	Yellow light
Talk more slowly	Try it in slow motion	Stretching	Try it using turtle talk

Source: Based on Yairi and Seery (2011).

model a slow rate of speech (e.g., 1 word/sec), and teach children to begin all speech using gentle onset (e.g., beginning speech with a whisper and gradually increasing volume). Most therapists also teach children to stress and elongate vowel sounds and reduce hard consonants that tense vocal muscles and restrict airflow (e.g., /k/ as in *kite*). Slow, soft speech is initially practiced with single-syllable words and gradually expanded to longer sentences and conversations.

The third component of treatment is generalization. Children must learn to practice their language skills at home and at school. Initially, home and school settings that elicit stuttering might be role-played during sessions. Later, parents and teachers can begin prompting children to use "easy speech" at home and school and reinforcing them for their attempts. Children can also develop communication strategies with their teachers to reduce stuttering in the classroom; for example, if the child raises his hand with an open palm, he signals "I know the answer and want to be called." In contrast, a raised hand with a closed palm might signal, "I know the answer but please don't call on me right now."

Therapists will also address the social and emotional consequences of stuttering on older children and adolescents. Two consequences are particularly salient: teasing from peers and anxiety in speaking situations. With respect to teasing, therapists might work with teachers to identify and rectify situations in which the child is most often teased. Because school personnel cannot monitor all situations, therapists often teach children coping strategies to deal with teasing. For example, some children find that they can effectively deal with teasing using humor: "I guess you noticed that I stutter . . ." or "Don't get too close, or you might catch it too." Other children need to learn problem-solving skills, such as how to deal with embarrassment or avoid fights with peers.

Many children who stutter actively avoid speaking situations because of anxiety. Therapists might use systematic desensitization with older children to help them answer the telephone or answer a question in class (Wolpe, 1958). Systematic desensitization involves pairing an anxiety-provoking stimulus with an incompatible stimulus, relaxation, in an organized manner. Initially, children are taught to use deep breathing, muscle relaxation, and imagery to induce a calm state. Then, they are asked to gradually expose themselves to stimuli that elicit greater anxiety. For example, they may begin by merely listening to a telephone ringing in another room, then by listening to a telephone ringing in their own room, and later by answering the telephone with increasingly longer utterances. Eventually, children learn to confront feared stimuli with reduced anxiety and, presumably, greater fluency (Yairi & Seery, 2011).

Older children and adolescents who stutter may also benefit from cognitive therapies. These therapies identify and combat negative thoughts that may cause anxiety and contribute to disfluent speech. For example, in rational emotive therapy, the client identifies irrational thoughts or images that occur during speaking situations (Table 5.10). With the help of the therapist, the client replaces these irrational thoughts with more rational cognitions or images that lead to reduced anxiety (Ellis, 2011).

Although stuttering is more difficult to treat in older children and adolescents than in preschoolers, therapy can be effective. Overall, interventions that involve the identification, modification, and generalization of children's speech are associated with 85 to 90% reductions in speech disfluencies immediately after treatment. Most children who participate in these interventions stutter only about 1 to 2% of the time. Longitudinal data indicate that stuttering tends to increase slightly after treatment ends, but it still remains below baseline levels. Altogether, these findings provide hope to older youths and their families (Yairi & Seery, 2011).

Table 5.10 Rational Emotive Therapy Applied to Stuttering

Component	Description	Example
Problem		
Activating Event	Distressing situation	Teacher calls on me in class; I freeze and can't get the words out
Irrational Belief	Negative thought or image	I need to speak up; I can't embarrass myself in front of everyone
Consequences	Negative feelings	I feel helpless and ashamed
Treatment		
Dispute Irrational Belief	Replace belief with rational thought	I wish I could say what I want instantly, but I need a little more time; my teacher and friends understand that I stutter
Effective Emotions and Behaviors	New feelings and actions	I feel annoyed that I can't speak like others; I'll try to be patient with myself

Source: Based on Ellis (2011).

WHAT IS SOCIAL (PRAGMATIC) COMMUNICATION DISORDER?

Definition and Description

Some children show no obvious problems with speech production or the basics of language. Specifically, their fluency, phonological processing, morphology, grammar, and semantics are all well developed. However, they still show marked impairments in their ability to communicate with others. **Social Communication Disorder** is characterized by deficits in **pragmatics**, that is, the use of language in specific social contexts (see Table 5.11, Diagnostic Criteria for Social [Pragmatic] Communication Disorder). Children with Social Communication Disorder have an appreciation for the sounds and structure of language, they speak in complete sentences, and their vocabulary may be well developed. However, they lack the ability to use verbal and nonverbal cues to communicate with others effectively in social settings (Redmond & Timler, 2007).

Children with Social Communication Disorder show deficits in four broad areas of social communication. First, they display deficits in using communication for social purposes. For example, they may have problems greeting others, joining a conversation that is in progress, or sharing information. Second, children with Social Communication Disorder have problems switching their communication style to meet the demands of the situation. For example, they may speak the same way with their classmates on the playground as they do with their teacher in the classroom. Third, these youths have marked problems carrying on conversations. For example, they may have problems taking turns in a conversation, identifying when their conversational partner does not understand them, and rephrasing their language when they are not understood. Fourth, older children and adolescents often have great difficulty understanding information that is not explicitly stated but is instead communicated based on context. Puns, jokes, idioms, and double-meanings often go over their heads (American Psychiatric Association, 2013).

Table 5.12 provides examples of some of the most common deficits shown by children with Social Communication Disorder. These deficits lead to problems in effective communication and (often) peer relationships. For example, children with Social Communication Disorder may not know how to begin a conversation with a peer or follow the sometimes subtle rules of taking turns during a conversation. They may also have difficulty maintaining the flow of a conversation without speaking tangentially, or off-topic. These children may not pick up on nonverbal cues from others during conversations—cues that might indicate that others don't want to

---

Table 5.11 Diagnostic Criteria for Social (Pragmatic) Communication Disorder

A. Persistent difficulties in the social use of verbal and nonverbal communication as manifested by all of the following:

  1. Deficits in using communication for social purposes, such as greeting and sharing information, in a manner that is appropriate for the social context.

  2. Impairment of the ability to change communication to match context or the needs of the listener, such as speaking differently in the classroom than on the playground, talking differently to a child than to an adult, and avoiding use of overly formal language.

  3. Difficulties following rules for conversation and storytelling, such as taking turns in conversation, rephrasing when misunderstood, and knowing how to use verbal and nonverbal signals to regulate interaction.

  4. Difficulties understanding what is not explicitly stated (e.g., making inferences) and nonliteral or ambiguous meanings of language (e.g., idioms, humor, metaphors, multiple meanings that depend on the context for interpretation).

B. The deficits result in functional limitations in effective communication, social participation, social relationships, academic achievement, or occupational performance, individually or in combination.

C. The onset of symptoms is in the early developmental period (but deficits may not become fully manifest until social communication demands exceed limited capacities).

D. The symptoms are not attributable to another medical or neurological condition or to low abilities in the domains of word structure and grammar, and are not better explained by Intellectual Disability, Global Developmental Delay, Autism Spectrum Disorder, or another mental disorder.

Source: Reprinted with permission from the *Diagnostic and Statistical Manual of Mental Disorders, Fifth Edition* (Copyright 2013). American Psychiatric Association.

Table 5.12   Pragmatic Deficits Shown By Children With Social Communication Disorder

Problem	Description
Sparse language	Makes fewer comments in general; comments are limited in quality and quantity
Terse responses	Only contributes to conversation when asked a question; gives brief responses without elaboration (e.g., yes/no)
Problems initiating and maintaining conversations	Has difficulty joining peer groups and beginning conversations; has difficulty staying on topic, fluidly switching topics, or elaborating on topic to sustain conversation
Inappropriate turn taking	Interrupts speakers or fails to respond when his or her turn
Irrelevant comments	Makes tangential or off-topic comments that disrupt the flow of conversation
Deficient conversational repair skills	Does not ask for clarification when he/she doesn't understand the speaker; does not alter language when others do not understand him/her
Deficient narrative skills	Has problems telling stories or relating personal experiences; important details are often missing, or events are not in chronological order

Source: Based on Hegde and Maul (2006).

talk about a certain topic or that a particular topic carries a great deal of interest or importance. Consequently, children with Social Communication Disorder may not draw correct inferences from their social interactions and may behave in socially inappropriate ways (Redmond & Timler, 2007).

Children with Social Communication Disorder often show deficits in narrative skills (Boudreau, 2007). **Narrative skills** are used to tell stories or relate personal experiences. Children might rely on narrative skills to describe their favorite movie or their week at summer camp. Narratives are stories; they have a beginning, a middle, and an end. Narratives also include effective vocabulary to convey ideas and events, and they relate events in chronological or logical order. Unfortunately, children with Social Communication Disorder show considerable problems with these elements

RESEARCH TO PRACTICE

DEFICITS IN SOCIAL COMMUNICATION

Consider the following dialogue between Willem, 12-year-old boy with Social Communication Disorder, and his classmate, Mike:

Willem: Hey, Mike, what did you get on the last test?

Mike: I didn't do too well. I studied really hard, but only got a C–.

Willem: Oh. Well, I got an A. I thought it was pretty easy.

Mike: Ah, yeah, good for you. I think my mom and dad are going to be disappointed with me.

Willem: I didn't even study that hard for it.

Mike: Yeah, I'm glad you did well. I'm mostly worried that they may not let me go to the basketball game on Tuesday because they'll want me to study.

Willem: Yeah. I love basketball. Did you see the game yesterday on TV?

Mike: Ah, no. Sorry, I got to go.

of narratives. For example, they may omit important information, use vague or imprecise language because of limited vocabulary, and present information out of order, thus, making their stories difficult to follow.

Children with Social Communication Disorder are also frequently deficient in **conversational repair** skills. Specifically, these children fail to recognize and take action when others do not follow their conversations. Conversational repair skills might include repeating or rephrasing information, providing additional information or examples, or giving background information or context. Children with Social Communication Disorder often have difficulty implementing these skills or are altogether unaware that their communication is not understood by others.

Children with Social Communication Disorder, like children with higher functioning Autism Spectrum Disorder, show problems with social reciprocity and understanding social interactions (see text box *DSM-IV → DSM-5* Changes: Social Communication Disorder). They seem to talk *at* others rather than talk *with* others and show a lack of awareness for others' feelings. However, children with Social Communication Disorder do not show repetitive behaviors and restricted interests like people with Autism Spectrum Disorder. If a child meets diagnostic criteria for Autism Spectrum Disorder, he would not be diagnosed with Social Communication Disorder as well.

Treatment

Children with Social Communication Disorder often require interventions that address the use of language in social settings. The deficits shown by these children tend to fall into the following categories: (a) initiating a social interaction, (b) maintaining a topic of conversation, (c) taking turns during a conversation, (d) speaking in narratives, and (e) using conversational repair strategies (Hegde & Maul, 2006).

Initiating a Conversation

Many children with language impairments avoid conversations because they lack confidence in their language skills. Other children are reluctant to engage in social interactions more generally. Unfortunately, such avoidance deprives them of opportunities to practice their language skills and improve their use of language in social situations. Over time, the language skills of these children decline (Ingersoll & Dvortcsak, 2010).

The therapist's first job is to teach children to initiate conversations. A critical component of beginning a conversation is to maintain eye contact with the conversational partner. The therapist might give instructions on the importance of eye contact, model appropriate eye contact, prompt its use, and reinforce the child's attempts to achieve and maintain it. Next, the therapist must encourage the child to initiate a conversation. To accomplish this goal, the therapist might tempt the child to begin speaking by strategically placing pictures and objects in her office that require the child to ask questions (e.g., What is this toy? How does it work? Will you play it with me?). Alternatively, the therapist might prompt the child to begin a conversation or tell a story by asking him to complete a sentence stem (e.g., Yesterday, I ____. One of my favorite things is ____.) The therapist reinforces all initiations with eye contact and praise, "Oh, I am so happy you told me that. Thanks for sharing it."

Maintaining Conversations and Taking Turns

Next, the therapist encourages children to maintain conversations. Some children provide only brief responses to questions whereas others prematurely end conversations. The therapist teaches children to maintain the conversation with prompts, such as "Tell me more?" "What happened next?" and "What did you like best about it?" Other children include off-topic information or switch topics abruptly. To encourage children to stay on topic, the therapist might gently interrupt and redirect the child, by saying "Stop! I liked how we were talking about your trip to the circus. Tell me more about that trip."

A third component of pragmatics is turn taking. Children must learn the natural reciprocity of language in which both members of the conversational pair exchange verbal information. Children must learn to be attentive to their conversational partners at appropriate times, to avoid interruptions, and to respond to social cues to talk. The therapist can teach turn-taking skills through verbal, symbolic, and physical prompts. Verbal prompts might be specifically telling children when to listen and when to speak (e.g., "It's your turn now"). Symbolic prompts might include gestures (e.g., pointing, motioning) to indicate who is speaking and who is listening. The therapist might even pass a physical prompt, like a microphone, between herself and the child to indicate whose turn it is to speak. The therapist reinforces appropriate turn taking and gradually fades prompts (Ingersoll & Dvortcsak, 2010).

Conversational Repair

Conversation repair skills are the fourth critical component of pragmatic language. Conversational repair skills are techniques that listeners and speakers use when there are breakdowns in communication. For example, when a listener does not understand a word or information presented by a speaker, she might interrupt the speaker and ask for clarification. Similarly, when a speaker detects that a listener does not understand his comment, because the listener has a puzzled look on her face, he may rephrase his statement and ask if she understands.

Children with Social Communication Disorder usually have very poor conversational repair skills. Their deficits in conversational repair are understandable for at least three reasons. First, most people, even people without Social Communication Disorder, are very reluctant to interrupt speakers and ask for more information when they do not understand something. Often, people simply continue the conversation in an attempt to avoid offense or embarrassment. Second, children with Social Communication Disorder often do not understand slang and nonliteral phrases (i.e., figures of speech). Third, children with Social Communication Disorder often have more global deficits in social functioning, making higher order social communication skills (such as conversational repair) challenging.

The first aspect of teaching conversational repair skills is to systematically instruct children how to ask for clarification from speakers. The therapist can teach clarification by deliberately giving ambiguous commands to the child. For example, the therapist might strategically place three toy cars on a table and say "Please give me the car." When the child gives the "wrong" car to the therapist, she might respond, "You don't know which one I want. Ask, 'Which car do you want?'" Later, the therapist will teach appropriate ways to interrupt the speaker, such as by saying "Excuse me . . . " and "I'm sorry, but . . . "

A second aspect of conversational repair skill training is to help children recognize when listeners do not understand them and to take appropriate action. For example, the therapist might show pictures of people who look confused so that children can more easily detect this emotion. Then, the therapist might model appropriate ways to ask for more information from speakers. For example, she might pretend to not understand the child and model appropriate responses: "I don't understand," "Can you say it differently?" "I don't know what (X word) means." Finally, the therapist reinforces conversational repair skills by saying, "Oh, now I get it. Thanks!"

Narratives

Narrative skills are among the most important, and challenging, aspects of social communication. Narratives are children's capacity to tell a story that involves a beginning, middle, and end. Stories can be autobiographical (e.g., what I did after school yesterday) or about others (e.g., the plot of the book I finished reading). Good narratives provide descriptive information, avoid extraneous details, convey a main point, and present elements of the story in an organized, meaningful fashion. Children with Social Communication Disorder have great difficulty speaking in narratives. Their stories often leave out important information, present distracting or irrelevant details, lack a "main point," or present details out of chronological order.

Initially, narrative skills can be introduced, modeled, prompted, and reinforced by using the tell/retell procedure. Specifically, the therapist might tell a familiar story, such as *The Three Little Pigs*, using the aid of picture prompts. Then, with the help of the pictures and verbal prompts, the therapist asks the child to retell the story. Effective narrative skills are reinforced, whereas errors are quickly corrected (e.g., "Hold on! Did the wolf say anything to the pig before he blew down the house?").

Later, the therapist encourages the child to practice narrative skills using autobiographical information. For example, the therapist might first model a simple autobiographical narrative: "Each night, before I go to sleep, I get ready for bed. First, I put on my pajamas . . . " Then, she might encourage the child to recount his own bedtime routine, prompting him if necessary, correcting errors, and reinforcing appropriate narrative skills.

A final technique to teach narrative skills is to use scripts. **Scripts** are descriptions of social interactions in which people routinely engage. Ordering food at a restaurant, shopping at a grocery store, or visiting the doctor for a checkup are examples of scripts. Scripts can either be written down verbatim, represented using pictures, or improvised. In individual therapy, the therapist and child take turns acting out the parts of the main characters in a script (e.g., the child plays the role of waiter and the therapist plays the role of customer). The therapist asks the child to generate the script by explaining the next sequence of events that should occur (e.g., we sit, then we read the menu, and then we order). Then, therapist and child role-play the events and practice other pragmatic language skills (e.g., eye contact, conversational discourse, turn taking, conversational repair). Finally, therapist and child switch roles to reinforce the interactive nature of social communication. Scripts are also useful in group therapy, in which each child takes turns playing various roles and the therapist reinforces appropriate pragmatics.

CHAPTER SUMMARY

Language Disorder

- Communication Disorders fall into three domains: (a) problems with language, (b) problems with speech, and (c) problems with social communication (i.e., pragmatics).
- Language Disorder is characterized by marked problems with receptive and/or expressive language that is not explained by Intellectual Disability or physical impairments.
  - Late Language Emergence is a type of language disorder characterized by significant delays in language acquisition, usually between 18 and 36 months of age.
  - Specific Language Impairment (SLI) is a type of language disorder characterized by problems with phonology, morphology, and/or semantics that persist into childhood.
- Language Disorder is highly heritable and may be associated with a lack of brain symmetry favoring left-hemisphere language areas of the brain, especially the lateral sulcus.
- Children with Language Disorders often show cognitive processing problems than might explain their language deficits. Deficits include (a) auditory perception problems, (b) rapid temporal processing problems, and (c) delays in short-term memory.
- Treatment of Language Disorder depends on children's deficits.
  - Language Disorder is also associated with impoverished communication between parents and children.
  - Discrete trial training can be used to teach single words, simple sentences and questions, and more complex statements.
  - Conversational recast training is effective in teaching specific language skills (e.g., plural endings (/s/), past tense (–ed) for children with SLI).
  - Milieu training is effective at generalizing language skills to new people or situations.
  - Augmentative and Alternative Communication (AAC) can be used with children who have limited expressive language skills.

Speech Disorders

- Speech disorders can arise from difficulty with children's (a) voices, (b) clarity and articulation, or (c) fluency.
- Voice problems usually refer to abnormalities in pitch, loudness, or quality.
  - Pitch refers to the highness or lowness of voice.
  - Loudness refers to the intensity (volume) of voice.
  - Quality refers to breathiness, harshness, hoarseness, or resonance of voice.
- Children's voice problems are usually caused by vocal abuse. Therapists can correct these problems with voice hygiene techniques. Sometimes, auditory feedback or voice retraining is necessary to correct problems with pitch or loudness.
- Speech Sound Disorder (SSD) is characterized by speech production problems unusual for children of the same age.
  - Most children with SSD show specific articulation problems: (a) phoneme omissions, (b) substitutions, (c) distortions, (d) additions, and (e) lisps.
  - Some children with SSD show more pervasive speech production problems indicative of phonological deficits. These children may (a) add phonemes to words, (b) reverse sounds, (c) replace one sound for another, (d) inappropriately blend sounds, or (e) delete sounds when speaking.

Speech Sound Disorder usually occurs when children do not abandon immature speech production strategies developed in early childhood. In some cases, it is caused by underlying problems in the way children mentally represent and understand phonemes. Speech therapy is effective in alleviating both problems.

- Childhood-Onset Fluency Disorder (stuttering) is characterized by abnormalities in the rate, duration, rhythm, or sequence of speech.
  - Stuttering is heritable and is associated with abnormalities in left-hemsiphere speech areas (i.e., Broca's and Wernicke's areas).
  - Learning theory, especially classical and operant conditioning, has been used to explain the causes and maintenance of stuttering.

- The anticipatory-struggle hypothesis suggests that stuttering occurs when children expect speaking to be anxiety-provoking and difficult.
- Psycholinguistic models for stuttering posit that stuttering occurs when children have problems (a) conceptualizing, (b) formulating, or (c) articulating language.
- Several speech modification programs are effective at reducing stuttering in children and adolescents.

Social Communication Disorder

- Social Communication Disorder is characterized by problems with pragmatics, that is, the use of language in specific social contexts. Children with this disorder usually show normal speech and basic language skills, but have difficulty in conversations.
- Children with Social Communication Disorder have social communication deficits like those of children with Autism Spectrum Disorder (ASD), but they do not show stereotyped behavior. If children meet criteria for ASD, they are not also diagnosed with Social Communication Disorder.
- Two areas of deficits include narrative and conversational repair skills.
    - Narrative skills are used to tell stories or relate personal experiences. Children with Social Communication Disorder often tell stories out of order, omit important information, or include unnecessary content.
    - Conversational repair skills are used to recognize and take action when listeners do not understand something a person is saying. Children with Social Communication Disorder often do not know when others are confused by their stories and need clarification.
- Direct instruction and role play can be useful in teaching children how to initiate conversations, ask for more information, and develop narrative and conversational repair skills.

KEY TERMS

CRITICAL THINKING EXERCISES

1. What is the difference between speech and language? Is it possible for a child to have a speech disorder but not a language disorder?

2. Tom and Kelly are parents of a 2-year-old girl with Late Language Emergence. At 24 months, their daughter is able to say only a handful of words and communicates mostly through gestures. Tom and Kelly are wondering if their daughter will eventually catch up to other children her age or if her language delays are a sign of a more serious problem. How might you respond to their concerns? What other information might you need?

3. Children's language problems are sometimes associated with impoverished parent-child interactions. Why can't we conclude that the quality of parent-child interactions causes these language problems?

4. Imagine that your 4-year-old daughter has articulation problems. Specifically, she has difficulty in clearly pronouncing words with the /l/- and /r/- sounds. How would you determine whether her articulation problem merits professional treatment?

5. Some adults try to help children who stutter by encouraging them to "relax" during conversations. Why isn't this strategy usually effective? What might be a more effective intervention for older children and adolescents who stutter?

6. Why aren't children who meet diagnostic criteria for Autism Spectrum Disorder also diagnosed with Social Communication Disorder? How might these two disorders be differentiated?

EXTEND YOUR LEARNING

Videos, practice tests, flash cards, study guides, and links to online resources for this chapter are available to students online. Teachers also have access to lecture notes, PowerPoint presentations, suggestions for classroom activities, and possible exam questions. Visit: www.sagepub.com/weis2e.

CHAPTER 6

Autism Spectrum Disorder

After reading this chapter, you should be able to answer these questions:

- What are the essential features of Autism Spectrum Disorder (ASD)? Why is autism viewed as a "spectrum" in *DSM-5*?
- Describe the intellectual ability and communication skills of children with ASD. What problems do children with ASD often display?
- How common is ASD? How does prevalence vary as a function of gender, ethnicity, and socioeconomic status?
- How might (a) genetic and biological risk factors and (b) early deficits in social cognition play a role in the emergence of ASD?
- What evidence-based treatments are available for preschoolers and older children with ASD?
- What educational interventions are available to children with ASD at school?
- How can therapists improve the social communication skills of infants and of toddlers suspected of ASD and possibly prevent the disorder?

Aristotle called humans "social animals"; he recognized the importance of social interactions and interpersonal relationships in the quality of our lives. Autism Spectrum Disorder (ASD) is one of the most serious, and interesting, childhood disorders because it affects this important dimension of our humanity: the need to effectively interact with others.

Autism Spectrum Disorder (ASD) is characterized by severe impairments in social communication and the presence of restricted, repetitive patterns of behavior, interests, or activities. Most children with ASD begin showing signs and symptoms of the disorder in infancy or very early childhood, although some are not diagnosed until they begin school. Their problems—interacting with others, communicating their thoughts and feelings, and developing relationships—greatly impair their social functioning. Furthermore, their tendency to engage in repetitive behaviors, their adherence to routines, their preoccupation with idiosyncratic topics, or their unusual reactivity to sensory stimulation (e.g., sights, sounds, smells) can appear strange or off-putting to others.

Many, but not all, children with ASD also have Intellectual Disability. Some children and adolescents show severe or profound impairment in intellectual functioning and are unable to communicate verbally. These youths often need constant supervision and care. Other youths with ASD earn IQ scores within normal limits and may even have special talents, skills, or abilities. However, their social communicative and behavioral deficits interfere with their daily functioning.

As its name implies, ASD reflects a "**spectrum**" of signs and symptoms, ranging in severity. Some children show complete disinterest in interactions with others, have few verbal or nonverbal communication skills, and persistently engage in stereotyped, rigid behaviors or rituals. Other children, at the opposite end of the spectrum, are extremely awkward or rigid in their interactions with others, engage in rituals or repetitive behaviors that cause them to be rejected by peers, and need support from others to function in social situations. To say that someone has ASD merely implies that he has marked problems in social communication and behavior. The ASD label does not tell us much about the child's unique strengths and challenges. As we discuss children and adolescents with ASD in this chapter, we need to be mindful of their heterogeneity. There is no such thing as a "typical" child with ASD.

CASE STUDY

I HATE THE WORD "NORMAL"

When I found out I was pregnant, Matt and I were over the moon. Then I had a scan which confirmed that we were having twins. At 37 weeks, I gave birth by C-section to Kylie, who weighed 5 lbs 9 oz, and then Thomas, who was 6 lbs 3 oz. It was hard at first, but then we learned to cope . . . with the lack of sleep at least! By 14 months, Kylie was walking and talking. However, Thomas was a lot slower. Our doctor said he was just the slower twin and not to worry. At 18 months, Thomas finally began to walk, but he never played with his twin sister and wasn't talking. I asked the nurse, who was also beginning to be concerned about him. She got in contact with a local child development center and a lady came to see us.

Image 6.1 Thomas

Source: Used with permission of his mother.

Image 6.2 Kylie

Source: Used with permission of her mother.

Penny came to our house to watch Thomas. I remember he sat on the floor lining his bricks in a row and making unusual sounds. He was disinterested in the rest of us. Penny sat writing in her book. Then she looked at us and said, "I think Thomas may have autism." I actually had an idea that she might say that. I had looked on the Internet and came across a Web site which explained to me what the symptoms were. To be honest, the shock wasn't so bad when we were told. After his assessment, Thomas was diagnosed with severe autism.

The twins are now eight. Thomas is still nonverbal and still in diapers. Kylie is his big sister and always will be. She sits with him and tries so hard to teach him words. I used to be really upset at the stares that Thomas would get from others. But now I just take no notice. I hate the word "normal." Thomas is normal to us.

Source: Reproduced with permission of Kylie and Thomas's mother.

WHAT IS AUTISM SPECTRUM DISORDER (ASD)?

ASD was first described in the research literature by **Leo Kanner** (1943) more than 60 years ago. Kanner used the term *early infantile autism* to describe 11 children who showed difficulty relating to other people and adjusting to new situations. Kanner identified two features that he believed were especially salient in these children. First, the children showed "autistic aloneness" or a tendency toward extreme self-isolation and an apparent lack of interest in social interaction. Second, they displayed an "obsessive insistence on sameness" or a strong desire to avoid novelty or changes to their daily routine.

Kanner also noticed that his patients showed marked delays or deficits in language. All were slow in learning to speak and most showed unusual characteristics in their language use. For example, many of these children repeated words or phrases. Others reversed or misused pronouns in their speech. Still others spoke in an awkward, rigid manner (Witwer & Lecavalier, 2008).

Several years before Kanner's publication, in 1938, the Viennese pediatrician **Hans Asperger** gave a lecture describing children with behavioral characteristics that resembled Kanner's patients. Asperger used the term *autistic psychopathy* to describe their symptoms. Like Kanner's patients, Asperger's patients showed marked problems interacting with others. Asperger noticed that they had considerable problems approaching others and engaging them in conversation, looking others in the eye while speaking, and displaying emotions. The children also tended to be preoccupied with singular topics about which they knew a great deal of information (Feinstein, 2010).

Unlike the children described by Kanner, however, Asperger's patients showed good vocabularies and basic language skills. Indeed, many of these children were very talkative and would carry on lengthy discourses on their favorite, idiosyncratic subjects.

The deficits observed by both Kanner and Asperger remain the essential features of ASD today (Table 6.1. Diagnostic Criteria for ASD). Specifically, ASD is defined by (a) persistent deficits in reciprocal social communication and social interaction and (b) restricted, repetitive patterns of behavior, interests, or activities. These symptoms are present in early childhood and limit or impair everyday functioning (American Psychiatric Association,

---

Table 6.1   Diagnostic Criteria for Autism Spectrum Disorder

A. Persistent deficits in social communication and social interaction across multiple contexts, as manifested by the following, currently or by history:

1. Deficits in social-emotional reciprocity ranging from abnormal social approach and failure of normal back-and-forth conversation; to reduced sharing of interests, emotions, or affect; to failure to initiate or respond to social interactions.

2. Deficits in nonverbal communicative behaviors used for social interaction ranging from poorly integrated verbal and nonverbal communication; to abnormalities in eye contact and body language or deficits in understanding and use of gestures; to a total lack of facial expressions and nonverbal communication.

3. Deficits in developing, maintaining, and understanding relationships ranging from difficulties adjusting behavior to suit various social contexts; to difficulties in sharing imaginative play or in making friends; to absence of interest in peers.

    Specify current severity: Level 1, Level 2, Level 3*

B. Restrictive, repetitive patterns of behavior, interests, or activities as manifested by at least two of the following, currently or by history:

1. Stereotyped or repetitive motor movements, use of objects, or speech (e.g., simple motor stereotypies, lining up toys, echolalia, idiosyncratic phrases).

2. Insistence on sameness, inflexible adherence to routines, or ritualized patterns of verbal or nonverbal behavior (e.g., extreme distress at small changes, difficulties with transitions, rigid thinking patterns, greeting rituals, need to take same route or eat same food every day).

3. Highly restricted, fixated interests that are abnormal in intensity or focus (e.g., strong attachment to or preoccupation with unusual objects, excessively circumscribed or perseverative interests).

4. Hyper- or hyporeactivity to sensory input or unusual interest in sensory aspects of the environment (e.g., apparent indifference to pain/temperature, adverse response to specific sounds or textures, excessive smelling or touching of objects, visual fascination with lights or movement).

Specify current severity: Level 1, Level 2, Level 3*

C. Symptoms must be present in the early developmental period (but may not become fully manifest until social demands exceed limited capacities, or may be masked by learned strategies in later life).

D. Symptoms cause clinically significant impairment in social, occupational, or other important areas of current functioning.

E. These disturbances are not better explained by Intellectual Disability or Global Developmental Delay. Intellectual Disability and Autism Spectrum Disorder frequently co-occur; to make comorbid diagnoses of Intellectual Disability and Autism Spectrum Disorder, social communication should be below that expected for general developmental level.

Specify: With or without accompanying intellectual impairment

With or without accompanying language impairment

Associated with a known medical or genetic condition or environmental factor

Associated with another neurodevelopmental, mental, or behavioral disorder

Source: Reprinted with permission from the *Diagnostic and Statistical Manual of Mental Disorders, Fifth Edition* (Copyright 2013). American Psychiatric Association.

*Severity levels are described in Table 6.2.

2013). Although some children with ASD show dramatic deficits in verbal communication, like Kanner's patients, other children with ASD show only mild problems with expressive and receptive language, like Asperger's patients. Children's language skills, therefore, need not be impaired for the child to be diagnosed with ASD, although most children with the disorder show marked problems with verbal communication.

Essential Features of ASD

Deficits in Social Communication

Perhaps the most salient feature of ASD is the child's persistent deficits in social communication and social interaction. Specifically, children with ASD display deficits in three areas:

- **Social-emotional reciprocity:** the normal back-and-forth of conversation and social interactions through the sharing of interests, affect, or emotions
- **Nonverbal communication:** the effective use of eye contact, gestures, and facial expressions
- **Interpersonal relationships:** showing an interest in others and the capacity to make and keep friends

Each of these deficits can range from moderate to severe, depending on the amount of support children require during social interactions.

Children with ASD are often described as being "in their own world" and largely uninterested in social interactions. They may avoid eye contact with others and seem uninterested in others' activities or reactions to their behavior. They may not respond to the sound of their name, hand clapping and waving, or other bids for their attention. Young children with ASD may not assume an anticipatory posture before being picked up. Indeed, they are often reluctant to let others touch them. They may not respond to hugs and other signs of affection from others, and they may show little emotion. They seldom, if ever, initiate social interactions and usually do not participate in imitative games like "peek-a-boo" or "the itsy-bitsy spider" (Bregman, 2005).

As children with ASD develop, they often begin to show greater tolerance for social interactions with family members. For example, they may allow parents to place them on their laps or let caregivers touch and cuddle with them. Some seem to enjoy being tickled or held in affectionate ways. Nevertheless, children with ASD rarely initiate social interactions or engage in novel activities. They appear relatively uninterested in playing with other children and are generally unable to form friendships. They may interact with others, but their communication and social relationships seem artificial and one-sided.

Older children and adolescents with ASD usually continue to show marked impairments in social functioning. They tend to have few friends and social interests, and they may be ostracized by peers. Some older children with

ASD are able to engage in rigid, scripted play in which they direct activities. For example, high-functioning adolescents with ASD might enjoy playing the role of "banker" in Monopoly. These youths generally avoid unscripted activities, such as "hanging out" with friends. Some of these children and adolescents develop narrow interests or become obsessed with specific hobbies, such as collecting trading cards or certain types of rocks. However, they infrequently join clubs or play spontaneously with peers (Bregman, 2005).

Some older, high-functioning children with ASD like to spend time with family and desire to be accepted by peers. Unfortunately, their social deficits interfere with their abilities to interact with others and make friends. These high-functioning youths with ASD usually appear awkward or insensitive to others during social interactions. For example, they might want to join their classmates in a game of soccer during recess but not know how. Rather than making an appropriate bid to join (e.g., "Hey, can I be on someone's team?"), they might intrude on the activity or insist on directing play around his or her own interests. Over time, the awkward and inappropriate social behavior displayed by these children can cause peer rejection. Sometimes, these youths develop anxiety and depression because they want friends, but they are ostracized by classmates and peers (Tsai, 2004b).

Restricted, Repetitive Behaviors, Interests, or Activities

Children with ASD also show repetitive, ritualistic, or idiosyncratic actions, interests, or activities that interfere with the ability to interact with others. Specifically, they show at least two of the following:

- **Stereotyped or repetitive behaviors** including speech (e.g., repeating words or phrases), motor movements (e.g., gestures), or use of objects (e.g., lining up toys)
- **Excessive adherence to routines or resistance to change** (e.g., need to dress, eat, or bathe at a certain time or in a certain manner)
- **Restricted, fixated interests** that are abnormal in intensity or focus (e.g., constantly talking about idiosyncratic hobbies at inappropriate times)
- **Hyper- or hypo-reactivity to sensory input** (e.g., indifference to pain, unusual sensitivity to certain tastes, textures, or sounds)

Each of these problem areas can be moderate to severe, depending on the amount of support children require to overcome them (Image 6.3).

The most common stereotyped behaviors among lower functioning children with ASD include rocking, hand flapping, whirling, and unusual repetitive mannerisms with hands and fingers (Volkmar, Cohen, & Paul, 1986). Roughly one half of younger children with ASD show at least one of these repetitive behaviors. Stereotypies are most common among younger children with ASD and among individuals with lower intellectual functioning.

Approximately 85% of children with ASD and Intellectual Disability show **echolalia**; that is, they repeat words that they hear others speak or overhear on television and radio. Oftentimes, these words are taken out of context or repeated at inappropriate times, so they seem nonsensical to others.

Complex ritualistic behaviors are more common among older children with ASD and among individuals with higher intellectual functioning. Some children spend hours each day sorting and arranging toys, clothes, or collectables. Other children have food rituals. For example, one child with ASD insisted on eating his foods in a certain order, according to color and texture. Still other children with ASD show compulsive behaviors, such as ritualistic patterns of walking around the room or turning light switches on and off.

A common feature of many children with ASD is their strong desire for daily routines. Many of these children insist on the same day-to-day schedules and become extremely distressed when daily routines are altered or broken. For example, one boy with ASD became argumentative and aggressive because he was unable to watch his favorite television program during a power outage.

Many higher functioning children with ASD develop a fascination with idiosyncratic topics. Some children show intense preoccupation with specific topics such as the batting averages of baseball players, the birth and death dates of U.S. presidents, or the history of certain weather patterns. These highly specialized interests are often appropriate in *content*, but they are always unusual in their *intensity* (Klinger et al., 2003). For example, it is not uncommon to see a 5-year-old fascinated by trains or a 10-year-old interested in baseball statistics. These

Image 6.3   Shaun is a boy with ASD. He is fascinated with the sound of water hitting the pavement outside his house.

Source: Used with permission of his family and photographer Lindsay Weekes.

TYLER'S IDIOSYNCRATIC INTERESTS

Tyler was a handsome, 10-year-old boy who was referred to our clinic by his pediatrician. His doctor said Tyler was having "social problems and issues with self-esteem." Tyler was a healthy child who lived with his father (a software developer), mother (a homemaker), and 3-year-old sister. According to his mother, Tyler had difficulty interacting with children his own age. Tyler desperately wanted friends, but he seemed unable to develop relationships with classmates or other children in the neighborhood.

Tyler had ostracized himself from his peers because of his unusual preoccupation with fantasy role-playing games. Instead of playing sports or talking about movies, Tyler seemed to bring up fantasy and role-playing games whenever he got the chance. Even his classmates, who initially found role-playing games interesting, had been put off by Tyler's persistent discussion of ogres, magic spells, and "hit points."

"Tyler doesn't seem to notice that his preoccupation with role-playing games bores or annoys other kids," reported his mother. "When other kids send him signals that they want to do something else, he doesn't seem to notice. He can get pretty upset when they refuse to play or insist on doing something else."

Because other children will not play with Tyler, he insists that his parents play games with him instead. His mother explained, "He's constantly badgering us to play with him. He even insists on playing before school each morning. I usually humor him, but sometimes we're in a rush and I can't. He gets really upset and refuses to go to school."

"Do you like to do other things, like play sports or watch TV?" asked the psychologist.

Tyler responded, "Of course I do, but they're not as interesting to me." Then, he added, "Do you ever play *Pathfinder* or *Savage Worlds*? If you did you'd understand . . ."

idiosyncratic interests become problematic when they preoccupy the child's time to the extent they interfere with other activities or social relationships. For example, the 5-year-old might spend hours each day playing with and talking about trains, exhausting his parents' patience. He might frequently tantrum if denied access to trains. Similarly, the 10-year-old may be ostracized by classmates and reprimanded by his teachers because of his obsessive interest in earned run averages.

Longitudinal studies indicate that restricted, repetitive behaviors or interests usually emerge *after* deficits in social communication (Klinger et al., 2003). Some experts have suggested that children develop these repetitive behaviors in response to their impairment in their social functioning. For example, children with ASD and severe Intellectual Disability might use stereotyped rocking or hand flapping to escape boredom or alleviate anxiety. Higher functioning youths with ASD might insist on daily rituals in order to gain a sense of control over their otherwise stressful daily lives. Other youths might develop circumscribed interests in response to ostracism by peers.

SPECIFYING SYMPTOMS

DSM-5 allows clinicians to describe the functioning of children with ASD using various "specifiers." Given the heterogeneity of youths with ASD, these specifiers provide other professionals a better picture of the child's strengths, challenges, and need for support (American Psychiatric Association, 2013).

First, the clinician indicates whether the child's symptoms of ASD are associated with a known medical condition or genetic disorder. For example, Rett syndrome is a rare genetic disorder that can cause ASD, Intellectual Disability, loss of purposeful hand movements, and health problems. In most instances, Rett syndrome is caused by mutations on a specific gene that codes for the X-linked methyl-CpG-binding protein 2 (MECP2; Amir et al., 1999). MECP2 plays a role in the development of the brain and central nervous system. Mutations to the gene that codes for MECP2 cause abnormalities in brain development (Tsai, 2004b; Van Acker, Loncola, & Van Acker, 2005). Using the *DSM-5* system, a child with Rett syndrome might be diagnosed with "Autism Spectrum Disorder associated with Rett syndrome."

Second, the clinician describes the severity of the child's symptoms for each of the two broad domains of ASD: (a) social communication and (b) restricted, repetitive behavior or interests. *DSM-5* provides a rating scale to describe severity based on the level of support the child needs in each domain (see Table 6.2, Severity Levels for Autism Spectrum Disorder). The clinician describes each domain separately. For example, a child might be described as "requiring very substantial support for deficits in social communication" and "requiring substantial support for restrictive, repetitive behaviors" (American Psychiatric Association, 2013).

Third, the clinician specifies whether or not the child has language impairment and describes the degree of impairment (if any). For example, a child with language impairment might be diagnosed with "Autism Spectrum Disorder with

Table 6.2 Severity Levels for Autism Spectrum Disorder

Severity Level	Social Communication	Restricted, Repetitive Behavior
Level 3 *Requiring very substantial support*	Severe deficits in verbal and nonverbal social communication skills cause severe impairments in functioning, very limited initiation of social interactions, and minimal response to social overtures from others.	Inflexibility of behavior, extreme difficulty coping with change, or other restricted/repetitive behaviors markedly interfere with functioning in all spheres. Great distress/difficulty changing focus or attention.
Level 2 *Requiring substantial support*	Marked deficits in verbal and nonverbal social communication skills; social impairments apparent even with supports in place; limited initiation of social interactions; and reduced or abnormal responses to social overtures from others.	Inflexibility of behavior, difficulty coping with change, or other restricted/repetitive behaviors appear frequently enough to be obvious to the casual observer and interfere with functioning in a variety of contexts. Distress and/or difficulty changing focus or attention.
Level 1 *Requiring support*	Deficits in social communication cause noticeable impairments without supports in place. Difficulty initiating social interactions, and clear examples of atypical or unsuccessful responses to social overtures of others. May appear to have decreased interest in social interactions.	Inflexibility of behavior causes significant interference with functioning in one or more contexts. Difficulty switching between activities. Problems of organization and planning hamper independence.

Source: Reprinted with permission from the *Diagnostic and Statistical Manual of Mental Disorders, Fifth Edition* (Copyright 2013). American Psychiatric Association.

language impairment-single words only" or "-problems with pragmatic language." Alternatively, a child with adequate language skills might be diagnosed with Autism Spectrum Disorder "without language impairment."

Finally, the clinician specifies any co-occurring neurodevelopmental, mental, or behavioral disorders experienced by the child. For example, some older children with ASD develop problems with depression; they may want friends, but their social communication deficits interfere with the ability to develop peer relationships. By specifying co-existing depression, the clinician can communicate to other professionals this important dimension of the child's social-emotional functioning that might otherwise be overlooked. We will now look at some of these co-occurring conditions.

ASSOCIATED DISORDERS AND CHARACTERISTICS

Intellectual Disability

Intellectual Disability is not part of the diagnostic criteria for ASD. However, a sizable minority of youths with ASD also have very low intelligence. One decade ago, as many as 70% of children and adolescents with ASD earned IQ scores consistent with the diagnosis of Intellectual Disability (Fombonne, 2005). Today, however, large population-based studies indicate that most youths with ASD earn below average, but not deficient, IQ scores (Baron-Cohen et al., 2009).

For example, researchers examined the IQ scores of 8-year-old children with ASD from seven different research centers across the United States (Autism and Developmental Disabilities Monitoring [ADDM] Network, 2012). Overall, 38% of children with ASD earned IQ scores <70. Approximately 24% of children earned intelligence scores in the borderline range (i.e., IQ 71–85) and 38% earned scores in the average or above average range (i.e., IQ >85). Girls with ASD (46%) were more likely than boys with ASD (37%) to have Intellectual Disability.

Experts are not sure why a smaller percentage of children with ASD meet criteria for Intellectual Disability today than in the past. It is possible that as the definition of ASD has been expanded to include high-functioning children with ASD, so a smaller percentage of children with ASD shows Intellectual Disability (Levy et al., 2010).

Children with ASD and Intellectual Disability often develop Tics or Tourette's Disorder. Tics are sudden, rapid, and recurrent motor movements or vocalizations that are beyond the individual's control. Motor tics are most common; they usually involve involuntary movements of the head, face, and neck. Examples include nose twitching, facial grimacing, eye blinks, and head tilting. Vocal tics are less common than motor tics. Examples of vocal tics include brief utterances, such as chirps, grunts, or clicks. Motor and vocal tics usually occur multiple times per day in bouts. They may be triggered or exacerbated by stressful experiences or anxiety. **Tourette's Disorder** is a psychological condition characterized by the presence of multiple motor tics and at least one vocal tic. Some people with Tourette's Disorder show coprolalia; that is, they involuntarily utter obscenities. However, coprolalia is seen in only 10% of people with Tourette's Disorder and is not necessary for the diagnosis (Spessot & Peterson, 2006). Approximately 30% of youths with ASD have tics, while 6.5% meet full diagnostic criteria for Tourette's Disorder (Baron-Cohen, Scahill, Izaguirre, Hornsey, & Robertson, 1999).

Communication Disorders

Communication Disorders are the most common comorbid condition shown by children with ASD. In one large population-based study, 63% of children with ASD also showed deficits in speech and language (Levy et al., 2010). The severity of these communication problems ranges considerably. Some children with ASD are completely mute (Howlin, 2006). Others are able to carry on lengthy conversations with others, using sophisticated vocabularies, but their discourse seems odd, rigid, or peculiar. The severity of these language problems is usually closely associated with children's verbal intelligence; children with higher verbal IQs tend to show superior language skills, although they almost always display some deficits in the use of language during social interactions. Hans Asperger was the first clinician to describe the language deficits of high-functioning children with ASD (Table 6.3). Even today, language problems are often seen among youths with this condition. First, approximately 50% of children with ASD and Intellectual Disability are **mute** (Howlin, 2006). On average, the lower the child's verbal intelligence, the greater the likelihood he or she will be unable to speak.

Second, many children with ASD show **pronoun reversal**. For example, a child with ASD might state, "You are hungry" when he wants to say, "I am hungry." Other children with ASD refer to themselves in the third person, saying, "He wants some water" when they mean to say, "I want some water."

Third, many children with ASD show **abnormal prosody**; that is, their tone or manner of speech is atypical or awkward. For example, some children with ASD speak mechanically. Other children speak with an unusual rhythm or intonation, using a sing-song voice. Still others talk loudly or stress the wrong syllables when speaking.

Fourth, almost all children with ASD who are able to speak show **problems with pragmatics**; that is, they have difficulty using language in a given social context (Tager-Flusberg, Paul, & Lord, 2005). They may speak in grammatically correct sentences, but their sentences do not fit the social situation. For example, many children with ASD do not provide appropriate context for their statements. A boy with ASD might begin a conversation saying, "*We* enjoyed *that* yesterday" without explaining to his friend that he is referring to a movie that he saw with his family earlier in the week. Another example of poor pragmatics is tangential conversation. For example, a schoolmate might ask a girl

with ASD, "How are you today?" The girl might respond in an off-topic, tangential manner, saying, "I ate a hot dog for lunch." Still other children with ASD inappropriately switch topics in the middle of conversations, often confusing and frustrating listeners.

Fifth, the verbal communication of many children with ASD is often **one-sided**. These children communicate primarily to express their needs or to gain information. They seldom talk to others to share their thoughts, past experiences, or feelings. In general, children with ASD do not show the natural reciprocity that characterizes most dialogue. They seem to be talking *to* others rather than talking *with* others (Bregman, 2005). Some high-functioning children with ASD talk constantly. Their discussions are usually described as pedantic ramblings that exhaust their listeners. Often, these children do not seem to care whether anyone is listening to them at all (Klin, McPartland, & Volkmar, 2005).

Some children show language problems, but they do not have deficits in social communication or engage in restricted, repetitive behaviors. These youths would not be diagnosed with ASD. Instead, they would likely be

Table 6.3	Language Characteristics of Children With High-Functioning ASD Seen by Asperger	
Language and Communication	*Percentage*
Not aware of social situation when talking	68
Talks in monologues, comments on own actions, or talks to self	56
Shows deviant modulation (e.g., monotonous) or articulation (e.g., over-exact)	54
Gets off topic or derailed when talking	33
Pedantic or long-winded speech	30
Verbosity or "endless talking"	28
Obsessive questioning, frequently debates with others, argumentative	26
Precocious, "know-it-all"	21
Neologisms (i.e., makes up or uses unusual words or phrases)	21
Common speech problems (e.g., stutters, lisps)	21
Echolalia (i.e., repeating words or phrases)	19

Source: Based on Hippler and Klicpera (2003).

Note: Speech characteristics of 43 children and adolescents initially seen by Hans Asperger and colleagues.

diagnosed with **Social Communication Disorder**, a condition characterized by marked problems with the pragmatic use of language.

Other Behavioral and Medical Conditions

Besides Communication Disorders and Intellectual Disability, the most common co-occurring psychiatric disorder shown by youths with ASD is ADHD. A recent population-based study indicated that 18% of youths with ASD also met criteria for ADHD (Levy et al., 2010).

Rates of anxiety and depression are relatively low among youths with ASD. Population-based data indicate that approximately 3% meet criteria for an anxiety disorder whereas 2% meet criteria for a mood disorder (Levy et al., 2010). Anxiety and mood disorders are most common among older children and adolescents with ASD. It is possible that many high-functioning youths with ASD develop these problems because they are aware of their social deficits or because they are rejected by peers (Kim, Szatmari, Bryson, Streiner, & Wilson, 2000). Youths with ASD and anxiety or depression tend to show increased irritability and agitation, greater social withdrawal, and increased stereotyped behavior.

Approximately 15.5% of individuals with ASD will develop seizures at some time during their childhood or adolescence. Seizures are most common among youths with both ASD and Intellectual Disability and among girls (Levy et al., 2010). The most common seizures shown by youths with ASD are **generalized tonic-clonic (grand mal) seizures**. Generalized seizures are caused by electrical disturbance across both brain hemispheres. They occur abruptly. The first (tonic) phase of the seizure is characterized by a sudden loss of consciousness and posture. The child experiences massive contractions of the entire body and an arching of the back that can last from a few seconds to several minutes. The second (clonic) phase of the seizure is characterized by periodic jerking movements with arms and legs extended. Eventually, the child regains consciousness with no memory of the seizure episode (Tsai, 2005).

Youths with ASD can also experience **absence (petit mal) generalized seizures**. Absence seizures are characterized by momentary lapses of awareness and responsiveness to the environment. Children who experience absence seizures might be playing and then suddenly stop all motor movement and stare momentarily into space. During this brief episode, which usually lasts only a few seconds, the child will not respond to sounds in his environment or to other people calling his name. The child quickly returns to his previous activities after the seizure abates with no memory of the seizure itself. In some cases, children experience dozens or hundreds of absence seizures each day. Because the signs of an absence seizure are so subtle, they are easily overlooked by parents and misinterpreted as "inattention" or "daydreaming" (Tsai, 2005).

A third type of seizure shown by some children with ASD is the **partial seizure**. In contrast to generalized seizures (i.e., tonic-clonic and absence seizures) that affect the entire brain, partial seizures affect only certain brain regions. Children who experience simple partial seizures do not lose consciousness. Instead, they typically experience unusual sensations or motor behaviors that depend on where, in the brain, the seizure occurred. For example, seizures in the part of the brain responsible for sensory perception might cause the child to experience a tingling of the limbs or the perception of flashing lights. Seizure activity in the part of the brain responsible for movement might result in involuntary movements of the limbs, head, or eyes. In most cases, simple partial seizures are not as impairing as generalized seizures (Tsai, 2005).

Changes to ASD in *DSM-5*

Although both Kanner and Asperger published descriptions of children with ASD, they were not aware of each other's writings. Kanner published his description in English, but Asperger's descriptions did not receive attention from the English-speaking world until 1981 when Lorna Wing published *Asperger's Syndrome: A Clinical Account*. Wing's article generated much attention from researchers and clinicians, and studies of children with autistic features but seemingly normal language skills began appearing in the literature. *DSM-IV*, published in 1994, included two separate disorders, Autistic Disorder (defined by problems with social interaction, language, and stereotyped behavior) and Asperger's Disorder (defined by problems with social interaction and stereotyped behavior only). A third diagnostic category, Pervasive Developmental Disorder, Not Otherwise Specified (PDD-NOS), was also included to describe children who met some, but not all, criteria of the other two disorders.

DSM-IV was successful in generating a great deal of research on children with Asperger's Disorder and Pervasive Developmental Disorder, NOS. However, researchers and clinicians began wondering whether these other disorders really differed qualitatively from Autistic Disorder. Wing (2000) and others posited that the autistic disorders should be viewed on a spectrum, rather than categorically. At one end of the autism spectrum are children who show a complete lack of interest in social interactions and engagement, lack interpersonal relationships outside the home, and engage in stereotyped movements and rituals. At the other end of the spectrum are children who show awkwardness during social interactions, difficulty making and keeping friends, and restricted and idiosyncratic interests. Wing and others suggested that these differences in functioning largely reflected children's intelligence, especially their verbal IQs (Georgiades et al., 2007).

Several lines of evidence converged to support Wing's assertion. Researchers used factor analysis to determine the number of core symptoms shown by children with autistic disorders. Specifically, they administered autism rating scales to the caregivers of hundreds of youths with autistic disorders and examined associations among symptoms. They found that children with autistic disorders showed two clusters of symptoms: deficits in social communication and repetitive behaviors or interests. Deficits in language, when they occurred, tended to be related to children's verbal intelligence, rather than the other symptoms of ASD (Frazier et al., 2012; Mandy et al., 2012).

Researchers also examined whether there were any real, qualitative differences between Autistic Disorder, Asperger's Disorder, and PDD-NOS (Witwer & Lecavalier, 2008). Overall, there were few differences in the neuropsychological profiles, comorbid conditions, and prognoses of children with these conditions. When differences in symptom presentation emerged, they tended to be based on degree of impairment, not differences in the symptoms themselves. Furthermore, most differences were associated with children's intelligence. On average, the lower the child's IQ, the greater their language impairment and severity of symptoms.

Consequently, in *DSM-5*, autistic disorders are viewed as a spectrum, ranging in severity (Leventhal, 2012). The diagnoses for Asperger's Disorder and PDD-NOS were removed. The number of core symptoms was reduced from three to two: social communication deficits and repetitive behavior and interests. Deficits in language, which differentiated youths with Autistic Disorder from youths with Asperger's Disorder, was dropped from the diagnostic criteria because these language deficits were largely related to verbal intelligence. Finally, the number of criteria needed in each of the two core symptoms was increased; all three social communication deficits and two out of four restricted behavior symptoms were now required.

We do not yet know the consequences of these changes. The primary criticism of these modifications is that many children who met *DSM-IV* criteria for an autistic disorder might no longer meet *DSM-5* criteria for ASD. ASD classification is important because it is often enables children and families to obtain medical, behavioral, or educational services (Ozonoff, 2012). Indeed, several researchers have applied *DSM-IV* and *DSM-5* diagnostic criteria to children with autistic disorders to determine the number of youths who might fail to meet the newer, more stringent criteria.

For example, Huerta and colleagues (2012) applied *DSM-5* criteria to three large samples of youths previously classified with autistic disorders under *DSM-IV*. They found that 91% of these children continued to meet diagnostic criteria for ASD, using the newer classification system. In contrast, McPartland and colleagues (2012) found that almost 40% of youths formerly diagnosed with an autistic disorder under *DSM-IV* would no longer meet *DSM-5* criteria for ASD. Most of the children who did not meet *DSM-5* criteria were previously classified with Asperger's Disorder (75%) and PDD-NOS (73%). Similarly, Mayes and colleagues (2013) found that most (73%) children previously diagnosed

with PDD-NOS would no longer meet criteria for ASD. These critics argue that the *DSM-5* criteria favor youths with greater symptom severity and impairment. They worry that many higher functioning children with autistic symptoms may be denied access to services they formerly received.

EPIDEMIOLOGY

Prevalence

Overall Prevalence

In 2000, the Centers for Disease Control established the **Autism and Developmental Disabilities Monitoring (ADDM) Network** to collect data regarding the prevalence of ASD at various locations in the United States. The ADDM Network attempts to determine the prevalence of ASD by viewing records in general pediatric health clinics and hospitals, specialized programs for children with developmental disabilities (e.g., early intervention preschools), and special education programs in public schools. Although the ADDM Network cannot identify all youths with ASDs, the data they gather provide one of the best estimates of the disorder's prevalence. The ADDM Network's most recent data indicate that 11.3 per 1,000 children (approximately 1 in 88 children) have ASD (ADDM Network, 2012).

One shortcoming of the ADDM Network's data is that it is not representative of U.S. children because the research team assessed children at 14 specific geographic locations. However, their findings are remarkably consistent with data from the **National Survey of Children's Health** (NSCH) which randomly sampled parents from across the United States (Kogan et al., 2009). The results of this study indicated a prevalence of 11.0 per 1,000 children. The main limitation of this study is that only families with landline telephones could be contacted to participate in the study; families with only cell phones were excluded. However, the consistency between the ADDM Network and NSCH provide some confidence in the data.

Prevalence Over Time

Three large, epidemiological studies allow us to estimate the prevalence of ASD over time. All three studies indicate dramatic increases in prevalence over the last decade (Figure 6.1). The ADDM Network (2012) reported a 78.2% increase in the number of youths with ASD between 2002 (6.4 per 1,000) and 2008 (11.4 per 1,000) and a 22.6% increase between 2006 (9.0 per 1,000) and 2008 (11.4 per 1,000). Data from the National Survey of Children's Health indicated an even greater increase, 289% between 1997 (19 per 1,000) and 2007 (74 per 1,000; Boyle et al., 2011). A third study, which examined only infants and toddlers identified with ASD in Massachusetts, also showed a 66% increase in prevalence from 2001 (56 per 10,000) to 2005 (93 per 10,000; Manning et al., 2011).

Figure 6.1 The Prevalence of ASD Has Increased Dramatically Over the Past 15 Years

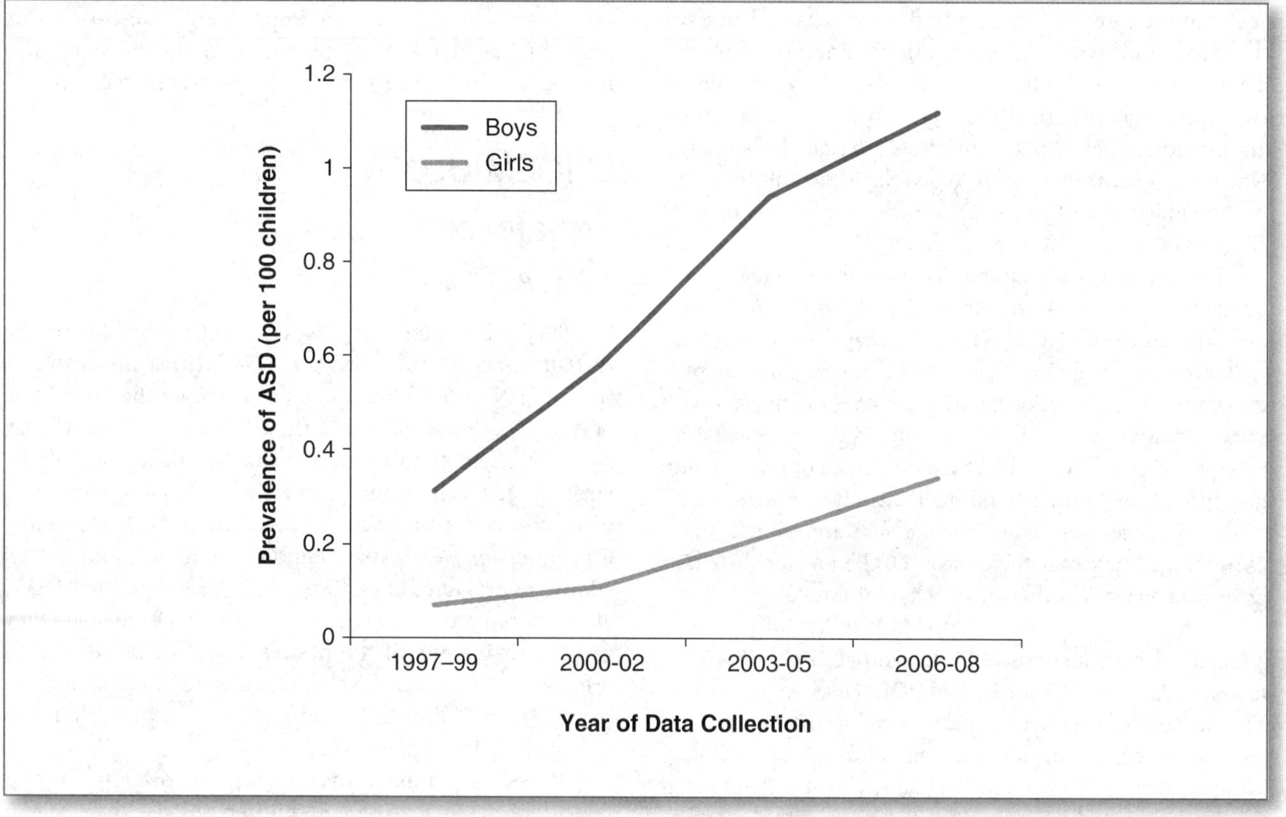

Source: Based on Boyle and colleagues (2011).

Note: Data from the National Health Interview Survey show the increase in ASD is especially noticeable among boys.

Some experts have posited that the United States is experiencing an ASD "epidemic." It is possible that there is a real increase in the disorder among infants and children. Some researchers believe that the recent increase in ASD, food allergies, metabolic disorders, and subtle neurological problems are due to unidentified environmental factors (e.g., foods additives, environmental toxins, or other teratogens) or changes in lifestyle (e.g. delaying pregnancy until later in life).

Alternatively, the increased prevalence of ASD may be explained by a greater number of children being diagnosed with the disorder, rather than an actual increase in the disorder itself (McPartland et al., 2012). First, parents, teachers, and pediatricians have become more aware of the signs and symptoms of ASD over the last 10 years, making them more likely to refer youths to mental health practitioners for diagnosis and treatment. Second, mental health professionals may be more willing to assign the ASD diagnosis now, than in the past, to help families gain access to behavior therapy, special education, or vocational services. Third, in the last decade, there has been a broadening of the conceptualization of ASD to include youths who do not meet full DSM criteria for the disorder but who do show abnormalities in social communication or stereotyped behaviors. Indeed,

in one large epidemiological study, the greatest increase in ASD diagnoses was seen among youths with subthreshold symptoms of ASD diagnosed by school personnel to obtain special educational services (Rosenberg et al., 2009).

Gender, Ethnicity, and Socioeconomic Status

Gender

Nearly every large, epidemiological study indicates that ASD is much more common in boys than in girls. For example, the ADDM Network study demonstrated that ASD is 4.6 times more prevalent in boys (18.4 per 1,000) than girls (4.0 per 1,000). Similarly, the National Survey of Children's Health also revealed a gender ratio of 4:1 favoring boys (17.3 per 1,000) over girls (4.3 per 1,000).

Overall, boys and girls with ASD show only minor differences in their cognition and behavior (Hartley & Sikora, 2009). Studies involving older children with ASD indicate that girls earn lower average IQ scores than boys and are more likely to have severe or profound deficits in intellectual functioning. Studies involving younger children with ASD have found that girls show greater problems with social communication than boys, whereas boys display greater incidence of more restricted, repetitive, and stereotyped behavior than girls. Young girls with ASD are also more likely than boys to experience sleep and mood problems, although the magnitude of this difference is small. In general, boys and girls with ASD show more similarities than differences.

Experts are not sure why boys are more likely than girls to have ASD. One explanation is that girls, in general, have an advantage in social and linguistic functioning compared to boys. Therefore, girls with ASD would need to show greater levels of impairment before they would be diagnosed. Evidence for this explanation comes from studies showing that girls, on average, display superior social and communicative functioning at various times in development. For example, across the life span, girls are better than boys at interpreting other people's facial expressions, emotions, and nonverbal behavior. Similarly, girls show greater tendency to use language to convey emotions and share feelings than do boys. It is possible that these strengths in social and communicative functioning make ASD less noticeable among girls (Koenig & Tsatsanis, 2005).

An alternative explanation is that male hormones lead to the development of ASD disproportionately in boys. Considerable evidence suggests that high levels of male hormones during gestation can affect the developing brain. In particular, prenatal hormones have been shown to affect the limbic system and frontal cortex. This is important because the limbic system and frontal cortex are involved in perceiving, processing, and responding to social information. Furthermore, these brain regions may be underactive in youths with ASD. It is possible that excessive exposure to male sex hormones in utero affects brain development, which, in turn, increases the likelihood of autistic behaviors (Koenig & Tsatsanis, 2005).

Ethnicity and Socioeconomic Status

The prevalence of ASD also varies as a function of ethnicity. The most recent data from the ADDM Network showed greater prevalence among white children (12.0 per 1,000) than among African American (10.2 per 1,000) or Latino (7.9 per 1,000) children. Similarly, data from the National Survey of Children's Health showed greater prevalence among white children (12.5 per 1,000) than African American (6.1 per 1,000), Latino (10.3 per 1,000), and multiracial (7.1 per 1,000) children. Studies have also shown a greater prevalence of ASD among families of higher socioeconomic status (SES). For example, the National Survey of Children's Health indicated that mothers who completed college (8.8 per 1,000) or earned higher incomes (7.8%) were more likely to have a child with ASD than mothers who did not complete high school (3.3 per 1,000) or earned lower incomes (6.9 per 1,000; Boyle et al., 2011). These findings are somewhat counterintuitive, given that lower parental educational attainment and lower family income is typically associated with increased likelihood of childhood disorders.

It is likely that the increased prevalence of ASD among higher SES families may be partially attributable to higher SES families' ability to obtain medical, educational, and behavioral services for their children (Durkin et al., 2010). In one epidemiological study of children in New Jersey, researchers found a higher prevalence of ASD among families earning >$90,000 (17.2 per 1,000) compared to families earning <$30,000 (7.1 per 1,000) annually (Thomas et al., 2012). The researchers also discovered that high-income families participated in a greater number of diagnostic evaluations (e.g., pediatric visits, psychological assessments, school-based evaluations) than lower income families. The children from higher income families were also diagnosed with ASD at an earlier age than the children from lower income families. The data suggest that in higher SES areas, the signs and symptoms of ASD may come to the attention of parents, pediatricians, and mental health professionals sooner than in lower SES areas. Furthermore, high-SES families may be more likely to advocate for the needs of their children than lower SES families, obtaining the ASD diagnosis and access to medical, educational, and community support services. Interestingly, studies conducted in Europe typically show no association between ASD and family income or maternal education, presumably because access to health care and education is independent of SES (Larsson et al., 2005).

Course and Prognosis

Parents of children with ASD often report that their children's symptoms began during the first two years of life. Many parents remember feeling that something was "different" or unusual about their infant's social behavior. Some parents describe their infants as aloof, distant, or avoidant (Lord & Richler, 2006).

Prospective studies of infants later diagnosed with ASD largely confirm parents' reports. Early signs of ASD are sometimes present by age 18 months. For example, 18-month-olds later diagnosed with ASD spend less time looking at others' faces and initiating social interactions with caregivers. They often do not respond when others call their names and do not share interesting toys with caregivers. Young children later diagnosed with ASD seldom direct their attention when other people point to objects or events, and they show delays in make-believe social play (Klinger et al., 2003).

Most parents first seek professional advice shortly after their children's second birthday (Siklos & Kerns, 2007). They usually consult a pediatrician or psychologist because their child shows significant delays in language. Whereas typically developing children are able to speak in simple two-word phrases by their second birthday (e.g., "Give drink" or "Me cookie"), most children later diagnosed with ASD speak few, if any, words by age 2 years.

On the other hand, one third of children with ASD do not show early signs of the disorder. Instead, this sizable minority of children seems to show relatively normal social and linguistic development up to age 2 years. After age 2, however, these children display a lack of social initiative and social skills, a loss of language, and an increase in stereotyped behaviors (Davidovitch, Click, Holtzman, Tirosh, & Safir, 2000).

Experts used to believe that the prognosis of ASD was extremely poor. Recent research, however, indicates that prognosis depends on three factors (Dawson, 2008; Figure 6.2):

1. Children's level of **intellectual ability** predicts their long-term outcomes. In very young children, intellectual ability is assessed by the ability to meet developmental milestones in an age-expected fashion. Infants and toddlers who show interest in a wide range of play materials, who engage others in play, and who begin showing the ability for symbolic play tend to fare well. In contrast, infants and toddlers with restricted interests or repetitive, stereotyped behaviors tend to have worse prognoses.

2. Children's level of **linguistic ability** predicts their social outcomes and later capacity for independent living. Children with ASD who have functional language skills by age 5 years tend to have much better outcomes than their counterparts who lack functional language by the time they begin school.

3. Children's levels of **social engagement** in early childhood greatly predict their long-term social and emotional outcomes. Young children with ASD who show some capacity for joint attention, imitation, and social engagement tend to have better outcomes than children with ASD who show low motivation for social engagement.

Evidence-based treatments for ASD, therefore, tend to target one or more of these three areas: intellectual ability, language, and/or social engagement (Vismara & Rogers, 2010). For example, early intensive behavioral interventions for children with ASD tend to focus chiefly on improving behavioral functioning and language.

ETIOLOGY OF ASD

The earliest hypotheses for the causes of ASD placed considerable blame on families. Kanner (1943) believed that the parents of his patients were emotionally distant from their children. He described these parents as showing little interest in their children's behavior, as socially aloof, and as overly intellectual. Extending these observations, the philosopher and writer Bruno Bettelheim (1967) suggested that cold and rejecting parents *caused* their children to develop autism. His book, *The Empty Fortress: Infantile Autism and the Birth of Self*, blamed cold, emotionally distant "refrigerator mothers" who caused their children to retreat into themselves in response to their dismissive parenting practices. Bettelheim and others suggested that ASD could be treated by helping

Figure 6.2   Predicting the Long-Term Outcomes of Children With ASD

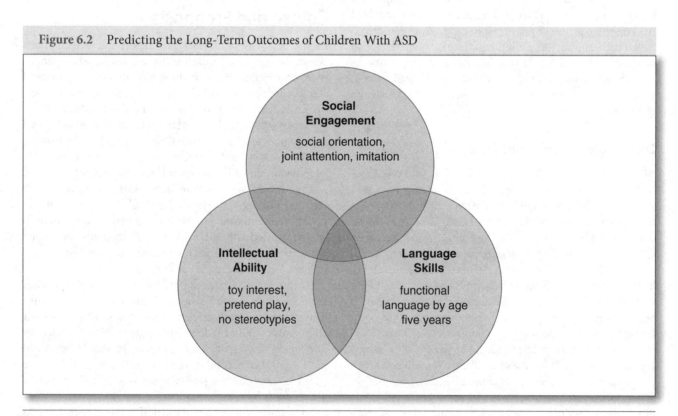

Source: Based on Dawson (2008).

Note: Three factors predict the long-term outcomes of young children with ASD: (a) their intellectual ability, (b) their language skills, and (c) their social engagement.

parents become warmer and more accepting of their children (Feinstein, 2010).

Beginning in the 1960s and 1970s, researchers began challenging the theories of Bettelheim and others regarding the etiology of ASD. Bernard Rimland (1964) first suggested that ASD might have a neurological cause. Empirical data also showed that ASD was not caused by cold or rejecting parenting. In fact, parents of children with ASD were extremely involved in their children's development and care. Unfortunately, many parents assumed that they were somehow responsible for having a child with ASD. New theories, which implicated genetics and neurodevelopment, slowly alleviated some of this guilt.

Today, we still do not know exactly what causes ASD. However, most of the evidence points to a combination of genetic, neurobiological, and early environmental factors. It is clear that there is no single cause for ASD. Instead, ASD is caused by a complex interplay of biological and environmental factors.

Genes and Early Environmental Risk

Genetic Diathesis

ASD has a strong genetic component (Rutter, 2005). Individuals who have a high degree of genetic similarity tend to show high rates of concordance for ASD. If one monozygotic twin has ASD, the other twin has a 31% to 91% chance of also having the disorder. In contrast, concordance rates for dyzygotic twins are generally less than 5%. If the definition of ASD is expanded to include broad social abnormalities, concordance rates for monozygotic twins increase to 92% while concordance rates for dizygotic twins are only about 10% (Tsai, 2005).

ASD also runs in families (Ozonoff et al., 2011). The prevalence of ASD in the general population is approximately 1.5%. However, if one child has ASD, the likelihood of a future sibling also developing ASD is 18.7%. If the later-born sibling is a boy, he has a much greater likelihood of developing ASD (26.2%) than if the sibling is a girl (9.1%). Parents who have two children with ASD are at even greater likelihood of having a third child with the disorder (32.2%).

Despite twin and family data, there is probably not a single gene responsible for ASD. It is more likely that multiple genes predispose individuals to a wide range of autism spectrum behaviors. For example, researchers have studied the behavioral characteristics of twins discordant for ASD; that is, one of the twins has ASD, and the other twin does not. They found that the twin who did not have ASD often displayed mild autism spectrum behaviors, such as social deficits or rigid and obsessive behavior. The severity of these behaviors may depend on the number of affected genes and certain environmental conditions (Freitag, 2007).

Behavioral geneticists have attempted to determine which genes might play a role in ASD. In one of the largest studies so far, the **Autism Genome Project**, researchers in 19 countries studied approximately 1,200 families in which two or more members had ASD. By looking at family members' DNA, the researchers discovered that abnormalities in chromosome 11 were often associated with the presence of the disorder. Furthermore, some people with ASD showed an absence of a particular gene called **neurexin 1**, a gene that produces proteins important to early brain maturation and neural connections. An abnormality or absence of the neurexin 1 gene might underlie some types of ASD (Autism Genome Project Consortium, 2007).

Currently, there is no consensus regarding which chromosomes or genes play the greatest role in ASD. Some experts believe 5 to 10 genes may be responsible for ASD (Klinger et al., 2003; Tsai, 2004a). Other researchers believe that the search for the genes responsible for ASD has been elusive because ASD itself is a heterogeneous disorder. Certain genes may contribute to certain autistic symptoms, but not others (Tager-Flusberg & Joseph, 2003). Despite these challenges, researchers are optimistic that the genes that make children susceptible to ASD will be identified within the next decade (Rutter, 2005).

The Prenatal Environment

Although ASD is a highly heritable disorder, early environmental factors may play a role in the emergence of ASD in some children. Most of these early environmental risks occur in utero. For example, mothers exposed to environmental toxins (e.g., pollutants, pesticides) or viruses (e.g., influenza, rubella) at certain periods during gestation may be at increased risk of having children with ASD. Researchers have also detected an association between maternal allergies and certain autoimmune disorders and the emergence of ASD in their offspring. Furthermore, increased levels of certain sex hormones, a by-product of some types of infertility treatment, may be associated with ASD among offspring.

Brain Structure and Functioning

Synaptic Density and Neural Connections

Neuroscientists have compared the brain structure of children with and without ASD. Youths with ASD tend to show abnormalities in brain size and synaptic density (Tsai, 2005).

Infants and toddlers with ASD often have unusually large head circumference. Longitudinal studies indicate that infants later diagnosed with ASD show an unusual pattern of head growth. At birth, their head circumference is similar to typically developing neonates. However, beginning at age 4 months, children later diagnosed with ASD tend to show a rapid increase in head circumference. By age 12 months, the average head circumference of these children is typically one standard deviation larger than their healthy peers. Then, head growth tends to decelerate, such that the circumferences of children with and without ASD are again similar by late childhood (Dawson, 2008).

This unusual pattern of head growth corresponds to abnormalities in brain density and volume. Several studies have documented an increased density of both white and grey matter beginning in early childhood. For example, in one study, researchers scanned the brains of children with ASD between 6 and 15 years of age (Mak-Fan et al., 2012). Compared to youths without ASD, these children with ASD showed increased brain volume, surface area, and cortical thickness in early childhood but normal structure in later childhood and early adolescence (Figure 6.3).

Together, these findings support the **growth dysregulation hypothesis of ASD**. According to this hypothesis, infants and young children later diagnosed with ASD show unusual maturation of the cortex, characterized by large head circumference, brain volume, and synaptic density. Whereas typically developing infants experience a period of dramatic brain growth followed by synaptic pruning, infants later diagnosed with ASD show only rapid growth. Their brains may form too many neural connections, thus, reducing the efficiency of brain activity (Klinger et al., 2003).

Indeed, recent neuroimaging studies have found that many of the abnormalities shown by children with ASD are in the neural connections *between* brain regions in addition to abnormalities within brain regions. Scientists study connections between brain regions using a technique called **diffusion tensor imaging (DTI)**. DTI is similar to fMRI, but it measures the diffusion of water molecules in brain tissue (Alger, 2012). DTI provides a high-resolution image of the strength or integrity of brain tissue. DTI is especially good at generating images of the brain's white matter, that is, the myelinated axons that form the connections between neurons (Image 6.4). By measuring the structural integrity of white matter, scientists can estimate the strength of connections between brain regions. DTI has shown weakened connections between brain regions responsible for social communication, language, and repetitive, stereotyped movements (Pina-Camacho et al., 2012). Interestingly, these areas correspond to the primary deficits shown by many children with ASD.

Abnormalities of the Limbic System

A second brain area that sometimes differs in individuals with and without ASD is the limbic system (Image 6.5). The **limbic system** is partially responsible for processing social information, such as social behaviors, emotional expressions and reactions, and personally relevant memories.

One component of the limbic system, the **amygdala**, seems particularly important to our social and emotional functioning (Baron-Cohen, 2005; Lawrence et al., 2005). The amygdala is located deep in the temporal lobe of the brain. It becomes highly active when we watch other people's social behaviors and attempt to understand the motives for their actions or their emotional displays. Abnormalities in the structure or functioning of the amygdala might underlie some of the deficits shown by youths with ASD. For example, Baron-Cohen and colleagues (1999) compared the brain activity of individuals with and without ASD as they attempted to infer the mental states of others. Compared to typically developing individuals, people with ASD showed significant reductions in amygdala activity.

A second line of evidence comes from structural studies of the brains of individuals with ASD. Individuals with ASD often show reduced amygdala volume or neural density relative to healthy controls (Schumann & Amaral, 2006).

Figure 6.3   Youths With ASD Show Unusual Cortical Thickness in Early Childhood Compared to Healthy Youths

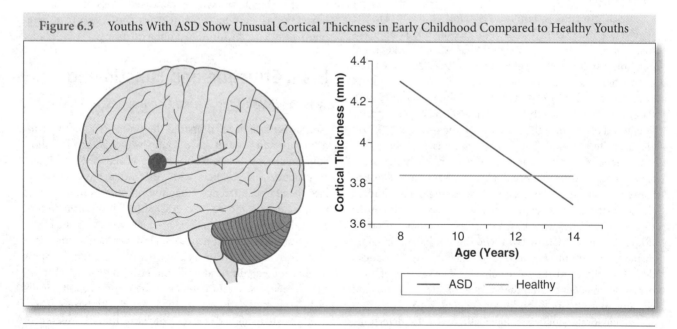

Source: Based on Mak-Fan et al. (2012).

Note: In childhood, cortical thickness is greater in youths with ASD. By adolescence, this difference disappears.

Image 6.4 Diffusion tensor imaging (DTI) can provide detailed pictures of neural connections between brain regions. DTI has shown reduced connectivity between certain regions in children with ASD.

Source: From Wikimedia; Thomas Schultz.

A third line of evidence suggesting the amygdala plays a role in the etiology of ASD comes from studies of animals and humans with damage to this brain region. Humans with damage to the amygdala often show deficits in social understanding that resemble those deficits displayed by high-functioning individuals with ASD. For example, they have problems recognizing and responding to others' facial expressions, detecting social faux pas, and understanding other people's intentions based on their overt behavior. Furthermore, intentional damage to the amygdala in monkeys causes autistic-like behaviors, such as social isolation, lack of eye contact, and stereotyped behaviors (Schultz & Robins, 2005).

Fusiform Gyrus

A third brain region that may be important to the development of ASD is the **right fusiform gyrus** (Image 6.6). This brain region is located on the underside of the temporal lobe, near the occipital lobe. For a long time, this brain area was believed to play a specific role in processing human faces. When healthy adults are asked to view images of human faces, especially faces displaying negative emotions, they show strong activation of their right fusiform gyrus. In contrast, children and adolescents with ASD who are asked to process facial expressions do not show increased activation in this brain region. Instead, people with ASD use a different brain area, the inferior temporal gyri, to process facial information. Interestingly, the inferior temporal gyri are usually used to process information about objects, not people. These findings indicate that people with ASD process facial information using parts of their brains that most people use to process information about objects. This abnormality in information processing may help explain the difficulty that people with ASD have understanding other people's emotions and social behavior (Critchley et al., 2000; Pierce, Muller, Ambrose, Allen, & Courchesne, 2001; Schultz et al., 2003).

The fusiform gyrus does much more than process human faces. It also seems to be important in understanding human

Image 6.5 Structures of the limbic system.

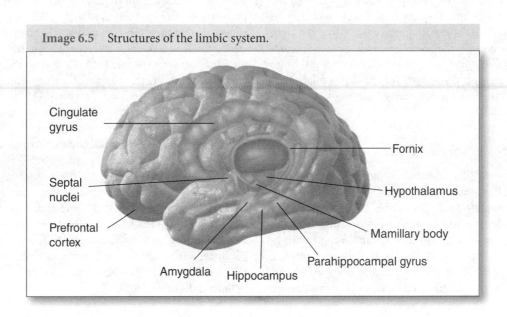

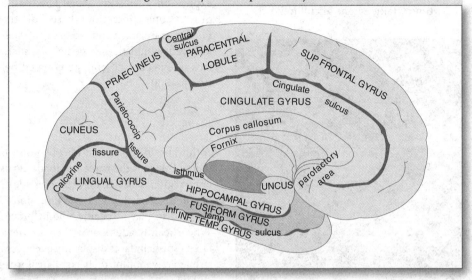

Image 6.6 Most people use the fusiform gyrus (*shaded area*) to process faces. However, children with ASD use the inferior temporal gyrus (just below the shaded area), a brain region usually used to process objects, not faces.

social behavior. In a clever experiment, Castelli, Happe, Frith, and Frith (2000) showed healthy individuals simple cartoons of geometric shapes engaging in humanlike social behavior. For example, one cartoon showed a circle entering a schematic of a house and playing hide-and-seek with a triangle. Another cartoon showed two shapes "fighting" or "chasing" each other. People without ASD almost always described these shapes as having human intentions that motivated their behavior. For example, they reported that the shapes were "playing," "chasing," or "fighting." In contrast, people with ASD usually did not view the shapes as behaving in a social manner. Instead, they sometimes reported that the shapes were simply "bumping into" each other (Klin, 2000).

More important, people with and without ASD showed different levels of activity in their fusiform gyri when watching the shapes. As you might expect, people without ASD showed greater activity of the right fusiform gyrus compared to people with ASD. These findings indicate that the right fusiform gyrus is important to understanding social interactions in general, not just faces. Hypoactivation of this brain region in people with ASD might impair their understanding of social situations and contribute to their social deficits (Schultz et al., 2003).

Functioning of the Prefrontal Cortex

A fourth brain area that may play a role in ASD is the prefrontal cortex. Considerable evidence suggests that this brain region is responsible for higher order cognitive activities, such as regulating attention, extracting information from the environment, organizing information, and using information to solve future problems. The prefrontal cortex acts like the chief executive officer of the brain, directing, organizing, and planning mental activity and behavior. For this reason,

psychologists often say that the prefrontal cortex is responsible for **executive functioning** (Tsatsanis, 2005).

Emerging evidence indicates that children with ASD show marked deficits in attention, organization, and planning—the executive functions. Although their short-term, rote memory is intact (and sometimes exceptional), children with ASD often have difficulty paying attention to important aspects of their environment. For example, when watching a television program, they may pay greater attention to objects in the background than to the activities of the main characters. Their lack of attention to salient social information could interfere with their ability to correctly perceive and respond to social situations (Klin, 2000; Klin, Jones, Schultz, & Volkmar, 2003).

Even high-functioning children with ASD show deficits in organization and planning. Specifically, they tend to have difficulty processing information in flexible ways and solving problems on the spot. Ozonoff and colleagues (2004) have suggested that their rigid cognitive style might explain their strong desire for sameness and repetitive, stereotyped behaviors. Indeed, some people with damage to their prefrontal cortex show a desire for sameness and a propensity for stereotyped behaviors like individuals with ASD (Tsatsanis, 2005).

Regions within the prefrontal cortex are also important in processing social information. Specifically, the **orbital** and **medial prefrontal cortex** become highly active when we engage in tasks that require social cognition, that is, when we watch social interactions and try to understand other people's thoughts, feelings, and intentions. In contrast, people with ASD show underactivity of these brain regions, perhaps explaining their deficits in social understanding. Similarly, damage to these brain regions produces autistic-like symptoms in animals and problems with social cognition in humans (Boddaert et al., 2004; Schultz & Robins, 2005).

Brain imaging and neurological studies indicate that people with ASD often show abnormalities in the structure and functioning of certain brain regions. Of particular interest are three brain areas: the amygdala, the fusiform gyrus, and portions of the prefrontal cortex. These areas play important roles in the perception of, processing of, and responses to social information. Interestingly, researchers have recently discovered neural pathways connecting portions of the prefrontal cortex, the amygdala, and the fusiform gyrus. Furthermore, neuroimaging studies indicate that when healthy individuals process social information, all three areas of this pathway become active. This has led some researchers to suggest that the prefrontal cortex, the amygdala (and other areas of the limbic system), and the fusiform gyrus form a "**social brain**" that is responsible for processing social information (Baron-Cohen, 2005; Frith & Frith, 1999; Schultz et al., 2003). Abnormal functioning of this social brain neural network might underlie many of the psychological and behavioral impairments shown by youths with ASD.

Deficits in Social Cognition

Simon Baron-Cohen (2005) suggested that dysfunction of the social brain leads to early problems in the development of children's **social cognition**. Specifically, social brain dysfunction causes children to perceive, interpret, and respond to social information in a manner qualitatively different from typically developing peers. Problems in social cognition emerge in infancy and may lead to the development of serious deficits in social communication. We will now examine how infants and young children later diagnosed with ASD process social information differently than their typically developing peers.

Lack of Joint Attention

One of the chief ways infants learn about other people and the world around them is through joint attention (Nation & Penny, 2008). **Joint attention** refers to the infant's ability to share attention with his caregiver on a single object or event in the outside world. In typically developing infants, joint attention gradually emerges between 6 and 18 months of age.

To understand joint attention, consider the following example. Imagine that an 8-month-old child is sitting in her high chair. Her mother points to a bowl on the table and says, "Do you want some cereal?" The girl follows her mother's pointing finger, gazes in the direction of the cereal, and squeals. The infant shows **responding joint attention**; she is able to follow the gaze or gesture of her mother (Figure 6.4).

Imagine, also, a 10-month-old girl sitting on the floor inspecting some toys. By chance, the girl swipes at a toy frog and it "ribbits." The girl is surprised by the noise and momentarily shifts her gaze from the toy to her mother. The mother looks at the girl, smiles, and says reassuringly, "That's a frog!" The child smiles at her mother and turns her attention back to the toy. In this case, the child shows a more complex skill, **initiating joint attention**. Specifically, the infant spontaneously initiates a social interaction with her mother through their shared attention on the frog.

Through joint attention, infants learn about the world around them. At the very least, the 10-month-old girl learned the word "frog." Although this seems trivial, consider what might happen if the child did not have the capacity for joint attention. Without joint attention, the child would miss out

---

Figure 6.4   Which Candy Will Charlie Choose?

Note: Young children with ASD may have difficulty answering correctly because of problems with social orientation and joint attention. Typically developing children have no trouble identifying Charlie's favorite candy.

on countless learning opportunities. As her parent tried to teach her about cereal, frogs, and other objects in her environment, she would not be focusing her attention on the same objects or events. As a result, the flow of information to the child would be greatly reduced. The lack of joint attention might cause problems with the acquisition of language, general knowledge, and intelligence (Sullivan et al., 2007).

Indeed, children diagnosed with ASD often show marked problems with joint attention (especially initiating joint attention) during the first 2 years of life. Psychologists have documented these early deficits in three ways. First, researchers have asked parents of children with ASD to recall their children's social functioning when they were infants. Most parents remembered that their children had marked problems with shared attention and eye contact between 12 and 18 months of age. Second, psychologists have reviewed home movies of infants later diagnosed with ASD. Even during their first birthday parties, these children showed deficits in joint attention and social interaction compared to their typically developing peers. Third, several recent studies have shown that deficits in joint attention during infancy are associated with concurrent or later problems with language acquisition and social functioning in early childhood (Charman, 2003; Mundy & Burnette, 2005).

For example, researchers tested the joint attention skills of preschoolers with and without ASD (Falck-Yttr et al., 2012). Specifically, they showed preschoolers silent movies of three toys positioned on the left-hand, center, or right-hand portion of a table. Next, a woman in the movie (1) looked, (2) gestured, or (3) looked and gestured to one of the toys (Image 6.7). The researchers tracked the preschoolers' eye movements to determine if they were able to look at the same toy as the woman in the film. As we might expect, preschoolers with ASD were much less likely than healthy preschoolers to follow the woman's gaze or gesture and look at the correct toy. More importantly, however, the number of errors they made was negatively corrected with their social communication

skills and verbal intelligence. The more errors they showed, the lower their skills. These findings support the idea that joint attention is an important component of children's social functioning and language.

Problems With Social Orientation

Brain abnormalities may also underlie problems with social orientation. Most typically developing infants show well-developed capacities for **social orientation**. For example, if we gave a 12-month-old child a new toy car, he might smile, play with the car briefly, and show the car to his mother. Although the child lacks language, he communicates his enjoyment to his mother by showing her the car and smiling. His mother might acknowledge her son's enjoyment by meeting his gaze, smiling, and enthusiastically saying, "What a great car!"

Early parent-child exchanges teach children about social interactions. Even at 12 months, the infant is learning that social communication occurs between people, that people take turns signaling and responding to one another, that the social exchange is usually centered on a common theme, and that effective communication involves eye contact and emotional expression (Carpenter, 2006; Rogers & Williams, 2006).

Unfortunately, young children who are eventually diagnosed with ASD show problems with social orientation (Image 6.8). Although they might be extremely pleased with a new toy car, they are less likely to share this pleasure with another person. Instead, they would likely appear engrossed in the car and generally uninterested in other people around them. Similarly, these children often do not respond when family members call their names, clap their hands, or otherwise try to attract their attention. Instead, these children often appear distant or aloof (Nadel & Aouka, 2006).

A lack of social responsiveness causes these children to miss out on important social information, especially

Image 6.7 Preschoolers with ASD have problems with joint attention. They make more errors following the woman's gaze (*left*), gesture (*right*), or gaze and gesture (*center*). The number of errors they made was associated with their social communication skills and verbal intelligence.

Source: From Falck-Yttr et al. (2012). Used with permission.

Image 6.8 Researchers tracked the gaze of individuals without ASD (black) and people with ASD (white) as they watched films of social interactions. People without ASD attended to actors' eyes and important objects in the environment. People with ASD attended primarily to inanimate objects in the room and often missed important aspects of the social interaction.

information from people's faces. Researchers asked 2-year-olds with ASD to watch videos of a caregiver and measured the percentage of time the children gazed at the caregiver's eyes, mouth, body, or surrounding objects (Jones et al., 2008). Toddlers with ASD spent the greatest amount of time looking at the caregiver's mouth. In contrast, typically developing toddlers, and toddlers with developmental disorders but not ASD, spent the greatest amount of time looking at the caregiver's eyes (Figure 6.5). The eyes provide a rich source of information, regarding the emotional quality and intent of the other person's communication. In contrast, the mouth is believed to convey less important information about the social interaction. By attending to others' mouths, rather than eyes, children with ASD may miss facial cues important to understanding social situations. Indeed, less time spent gazing at the caregiver's eyes was associated with the degree of social impairment shown by the 2-year-olds with ASD.

Delays in Symbolic Play

Between 18 and 24 months of age, children develop the capacity for symbolic play. *Symbolic play* refers to the child's ability to allow one object to represent (i.e., symbolize) another object. Children show symbolic play in two ways (Image 6.9). First, they can pretend that one object (e.g., a blackboard eraser) represents another object (e.g., a telephone). Thus, a 2-year-old can pretend to talk to her father on the telephone while holding the eraser up to her ear. Second, children can pretend that an inanimate object represents a living thing.

For example, the child might decide to give his teddy bear a drink of water and lay him down for a nap. Symbolic play is often called "pretend play" because children are able to pretend that one object represents another object.

Children who are eventually diagnosed with ASD show delays in symbolic play. When children with ASD begin to show symbolic play, it is usually simplistic and mechanical. For example, typically developing children often show elaborate pretend play involving creative and flexible scripts. My son routinely hosted dinner parties for his toy dinosaurs, complete with appetizers, a main course, and dessert. The pretend play of children with ASD tends to be more repetitive and without flexible, elaborative themes (Wolfberg & Schuler, 2006).

Why is it important that children with ASD show deficits in pretend play? First, a lack of pretend play by 24 months of age can be an early sign of ASD. Although parents and physicians often overlook other signs, such as delays in joint attention or social orientation, the absence of pretend play can be a useful indicator that there might be a problem in the child's development. Since the treatment for ASD is most effective when it is initiated early, recognition and treatment of the disorder during the toddler years can lead to better prognosis (Yoder & McDuffie, 2006).

Second, pretend play is a precursor to language acquisition (Klinger et al., 2003). Jean Piaget believed that children begin to show pretend play when they develop the capacity for complex mental representations. In the case of pretend play, an object (e.g., an eraser) is allowed

Figure 6.5 Toddlers With ASD Show Deficits in Social Orientation

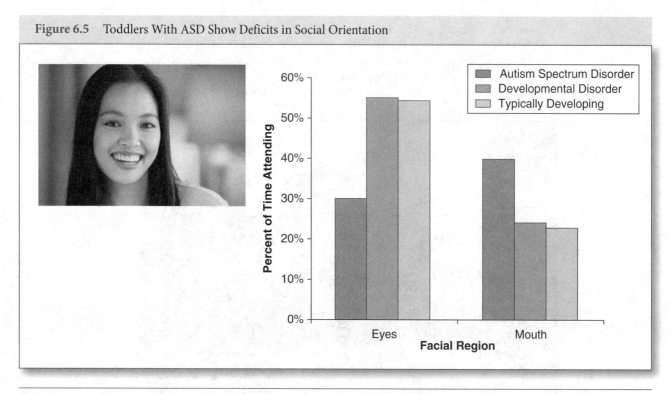

Source: Based on Jones et al. (2008).

Note: When asked to watch a video of a caregiver (left), 2-year-olds with ASD spent less time looking at the caregiver's eyes and more time looking at her mouth than did typically developing toddlers or toddlers with developmental disorders. Furthermore, less time spent gazing at the caregiver's eyes was associated with greater social impairment.

Image 6.9 Three-year-old Nick is playing "restaurant" in his preschool classroom. His hamburger, milk, and juice are not real, and he knows it. Because he has the capacity for symbolic play, he can pretend they are real. Children with ASD show marked delays in symbolic (pretend) play.

to mentally represent another object (e.g., a telephone). A similar process occurs in verbal language. The child learns that a certain utterance (e.g., the sound "cup") represents a particular object (e.g., a cup). Words are, after all, symbols that represent objects and events. Delays in the development of symbolic play, therefore, may be associated with the delays in language shown by people with ASD.

Lack of Empathy

According to Baron-Cohen (2005), children with ASD show deficits in a specific aspect of social cognition: **empathy**. Imagine that you are standing in the hallway of a building on campus and you notice another student suddenly leave a nearby classroom. She quickly exits the classroom, shuts the door behind her, leans her head against the wall, and begins to cry. What just happened? Based on your observations, you might infer that the student received a low grade on an important exam or that her professor chastised her in front of the class. In either case, you would likely feel sorry for her and maybe try to comfort her.

Our ability to react in an empathic manner, therefore, depends on two social abilities. First, we need to understand that the person's mental state (e.g., thoughts, beliefs, feelings) motivated her behavior. By understanding her mental state, we can infer that she either received a low grade on the exam or was humiliated in front of the class. Second, we need to have an appropriate emotional reaction to her crying. We would probably feel troubled by the incident and want to help her in some way. Our ability to empathize allows us to interpret social situations accurately and respond to people in sensitive and appropriate ways.

Sometime during the preschool years, most children begin to understand that people's thoughts, beliefs, intentions, and desires motivate their behaviors. Furthermore, children appreciate that other people's thoughts and intentions can differ from their own. In short, children develop what cognitive psychologists call a **theory of mind**.

Developmental psychologists measure theory of mind using something called a **false belief task**. In one study, the psychologist introduced preschool-age children to a puppet named Sally who hid a toy in a basket and then left the room. While Sally was away, another puppet moved the toy to a different location (a box). The children were asked where Sally would look for her toy when she returned. Young children, without theory of mind, responded that Sally would search for the toy in the box because that is where the toy was moved. These children did not appreciate that Sally's behavior would be motivated by beliefs that differed from their own. Older children, with theory of mind, answered the false belief task correctly: They responded that Sally would search for the toy in the basket because Sally falsely believed the toy was still in its original location (Baron-Cohen, Leslie, & Frith, 1985).

In typically developing children, theory of mind emerges sometime between three and five years of age. However, children with ASD show specific impairment in theory of mind. In one study, 85% of typically developing preschoolers successfully passed a false belief task compared to only 20% of preschoolers with ASD (Figure 6.6). Furthermore, the 20% of children with ASD who passed the false belief task showed great difficulty on other tasks measuring theory of mind.

Why is this deficit in theory of mind important to understanding ASD? The answer is that a well-developed theory of mind is necessary for most complex social interactions. Children with ASD display what Baron-Cohen (1995) calls **mind-blindness**; that is, they are often unable to appreciate that other people have mental states that motivate and direct their actions. If a child with ASD witnessed a student abruptly leaving a classroom and crying, he would likely have difficulty understanding the student's behavior. Specifically, he would have trouble appreciating that some antecedent event and mental state (e.g., failing a test, feeling embarrassed) motivated the student's actions. Because he is unable to infer the student's mental state, he may not respond to the situation in an appropriate way.

Summary of Social Cognitive Deficits

Taken together, the available evidence indicates that ASD is a neurodevelopmental disorder that emerges well before most children receive the ASD diagnosis. Its primary causes are genetic, although the exact genes responsible for ASD remain elusive. Early environmental experiences, such as prenatal exposure to toxins or viruses, may also contribute to the disorder. These genetic and early environmental risk factors, in turn, contribute to abnormalities in brain regions responsible for social and emotional development. Risk factors may lead to abnormalities in the social brain, which, in turn, affect the child's ability to perceive, process, interpret, and respond to social situations. Genetic and early environmental risk factors can also interfere with the connections between brain areas that affect social cognition, language, and overt behavior.

Many experts believe that these neurological abnormalities prompt a cascade of social and emotional deficits that build upon one another and contribute to the signs and symptoms of ASD in early childhood (Dawson, 2008; Figure 6.7). Indeed, recent neuroimaging studies indicate that the abnormal cortical growth seen in many toddlers eventually diagnosed with ASD often precedes or coincides with the emergence of early social cognitive deficits. The early deficits include a lack of interest in others' faces, deficits in joint attention, and delays in social orientation. Instead of interacting with others, these young children miss out on a great deal of social and linguistic information which, in turn, can contribute to deficits in higher order social cognitive skills. As toddlers, these children often show problems with symbolic play, theory of mind, and language.

During the preschool years, deficits in social orientation and language often prompt parents to seek help for

Figure 6.6   Children With ASD Have Deficits in Theory of Mind

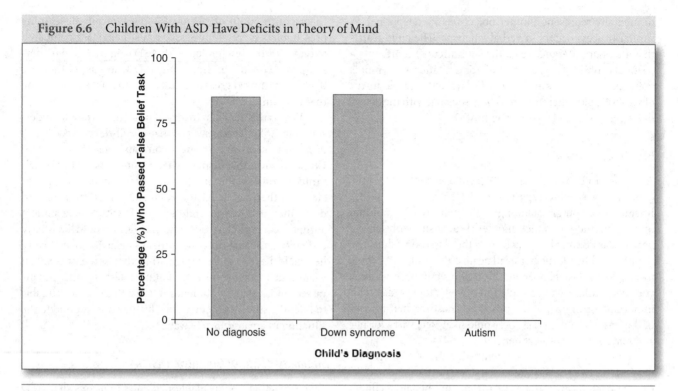

Source: Based on Baron-Cohen et al. (1985).

Note: Children with ASD often fail the false belief task, but healthy children and children with Down Syndrome usually pass this task. These results indicate that children with ASD have problems with theory of mind, that is, understanding the intentions and motives of others.

Figure 6.7   A Developmental Model for ASD

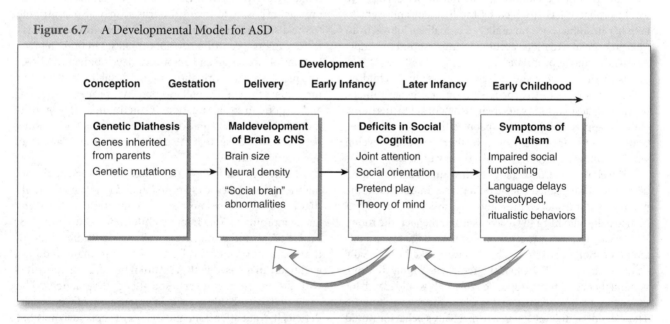

Note: In this general model, individuals show genetic risk for the disorder, which can lead to structural and/or functional differences in the developing brain. Brain abnormalities, in turn, can lead to problems in the development of social cognition during infancy. Social cognitive abnormalities also affect developing brain structure. By early childhood, deficits can be severe enough to merit the diagnosis of autism.

their children. Consequently, most children are not diagnosed with ASD until age 3 years. However, the cascade of events that contributed to this diagnosis likely emerged much earlier.

Repetitive, Stereotyped Behaviors

By definition, children with ASD also show repetitive, stereotyped behaviors, restricted interests, unusual preoccupations, or a desire for sameness. In the past decade, research has implicated the **basal ganglia** in these unusual motor behaviors. Recall that the basal ganglia, located centrally in the brain, are rich in domapinergic neurons. They play a role in motor regulation. The basal ganglia actually consist of several parts: the putamen, caudate, and the globus palidus.

Most neuroimaging studies involving older children and adolescents with ASD have shown enlargement of the basal ganglia, especially the caudate nucleus. Furthermore, the magnitude of the enlargement is correlated with the severity of children's repetitive behaviors and idiosyncratic interests (Pina-Camacho et al., 2012). However, one study involving toddlers and preschoolers with ASD showed *reductions* in the size of the basal ganglia relative to controls, with smaller volumes associated with more repetitive, stereotyped behaviors (Estes et al., 2011). Although the basal ganglia are likely involved in these motor symptoms of ASD, the manner in which they affect these symptoms across development is currently unknown.

Associated Problems With Language

Neuroscientists have identified several abnormalities in children with ASD that might underlie their language problems. In general, language problems can be divided into two types: (a) syntactic-semantic language difficulties and (2) semantic-pragmatic language difficulties.

Syntactic-semantic language problems refer to difficulties with linguistic processing. Children with syntactic-semantic language deficits have trouble understanding the structure and rules of language. Specifically, they may have problems with morphology (i.e., basic linguistic units, such as "root" words, prefixes, and suffixes), syntax (i.e., the rules that govern the way morphemes can be organized, and phonology (i.e., the organization of sounds in spoken language such as the /th/ or /s/ sound). Children with ASD who also show syntactic-semantic language problems would have difficulty understanding and processing language. Their speech would be characterized by frequent grammatical errors, such as dropping the "s" from the end of present-tense verbs, dropping past tense, and asking questions without the usual "be" or "do" verbs. For example, instead of saying, "She rides the horse," a child with syntactic-semantic language problems might say, "She ride the horse." Instead of saying, "He ate the cookie," the child might say, "He eat the cookie." Instead of asking, "Why does he like me?" the child might ask, "Why he like me?" Children with ASD who show syntactic-semantic language deficits may also be diagnosed with Specific Language Impairment, a communication disorder discussed in the previous chapter.

Children with ASD who show syntactic-semantic language problems often display three abnormalities in brain structure and functioning (Pina-Camacho et al., 2012). First, these children often display reversed or reduced left-hemisphere asymmetry when processing language. Whereas most healthy people process language predominantly with the left hemisphere of their brain, these children do not show hemispheric lateralization or may actually show greater activation in their right hemisphere, a region not specialized for language (Image 6.10). Even toddlers later diagnosed with ASD show this reversed or reduced left-hemisphere asymmetry, indicating that this abnormal processing emerges early in development (Eyler et al., 2012). Second, these children often display hyperactivation of Wernicke's area, a brain region responsible for processing linguistic information. Although experts are not certain how to interpret this hyperactivation, it suggests that Wernicke's area is not processing language in the same way as in children without ASD. Third, children with syntactic-semantic deficits often show reduced strength of the arcuate fasciculus, the bundle of neurons that connect Wernicke's area with Broca's area. Consequently, there is

Image 6.10 The brains of 2- and 3-year-olds were scanned while they were listening to a bedtime story. Typically developing toddlers showed greater activation of the left hemisphere than right. (Neuroimages are reversed, such that the right-hand side shows the left hemisphere.) Toddlers later diagnosed with ASD do not show left-hemisphere specialization of language.

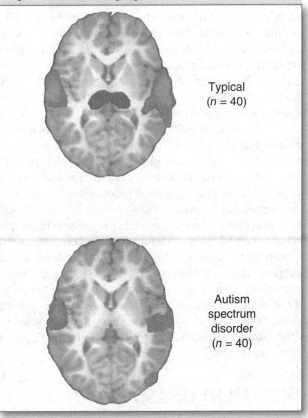

Typical
(*n* = 40)

Autism spectrum disorder
(*n* = 40)

Source: From Eyler et al. (2012). Used with permission.

a lack of connectivity between brain regions that process language (Wernicke's area) and organize spoken language (Broca's area), perhaps contributing to the speech deficits shown by these children.

Semantic-pragmatic language difficulties refer to abnormalities in the use of language in social contexts. Children with semantic-pragmatic language problems show appropriate grammar, but they have difficulty carrying on a conversation and telling stories. They may not understand subtle cues in others' speech, and they may not know how to speak to others in social situations to get their needs met. Put simply, they do not seem to know what to say or when or how to say it. Children with semantic-pragmatic language difficulties may show problems:

- Understanding directions or instructions from others
- Telling a story without going "off topic"
- Picking up on subtle social cues (e.g., irony) in language
- Participating in the natural give-and-take in conversations (i.e., one-sided conversations)
- Understanding jokes, innuendo
- Interpreting body language and nonverbal cues
- Determining socially "appropriate" and "inappropriate" comments
- Showing appropriate prosody (i.e., rhythm, stress, and intonation) and loudness of speech

Most children with ASD who speak show semantic-pragmatic language problems. However, children without ASD can also show semantic-language problems. Like children with ASD, these children show communication deficits; unlike children with ASD, they do not show repetitive behaviors and restrictive interests. Consequently, these children might be diagnosed with Social Communication Disorder, a communication disorder discussed in the previous chapter.

Children with ASD who show semantic-pragmatic language problems tend to show two abnormalities in neural processing (Pina-Camacho et al., 2012). First, they may display hypoactivity in Broca's area, the brain region responsible for fluent language production. Second, they sometimes display reduced connectivity between Broca's area, the prefrontal cortex, and other regions of the temporal and parietal lobes. This functional under-connectivity is important because it interferes with the fluid use of language in social contexts. In several studies, the lower the activity in these neural networks, the greater the severity of children's semantic-pragmatic deficits. Interestingly, these same connections are involved in understanding other people's nonverbal behavior and in the development of theory of mind.

TREATMENT OF ASD

The past decade has seen a marked increase in the number of evidence-based interventions for children with ASD.

Certain treatments, such as early intensive behavioral intervention, have been implemented in research settings for some time and have gradually been expanded to homes and schools to better meet the needs of children and families. Other treatments are new, such as interventions to improve the social communication skills of very young children who first show signs of the disorder. In this section, we will explore these interventions and the evidence that supports their use. We will also examine several other forms of treatment that, while popular, lack empirical support.

Early Identification

Early intervention is critical to children with ASD. Children who begin participating in therapy prior to 36 months tend to show the best outcomes. Consequently, the American Academy of Pediatrics recommends that all 18- and 24-month-old infants be screened for ASD (Johnson et al., 2007).

In practice, however, early detection of ASD is challenging (Charman & Baird, 2002). Several studies indicate that ASD can be reliably and validly diagnosed in children who are at least 36 months of age. The accuracy of ASD diagnosis is greatly improved when clinicians have expertise in assessing ASD and other developmental disabilities in young children and they rely on standardized, norm-referenced developmental measures. Unfortunately, recognizing and diagnosing ASD in one- and 2-year-old children is considerably more difficult.

At least three obstacles hinder clinicians' efforts to diagnose ASD in infants and toddlers (Zwaigenbaum et al., 2009). First, many children with ASD, especially those with average intellectual abilities, show only subtle symptoms at an early age. In many instances, parents do not suspect developmental problems until age 2, when their children continue to show delays in social communication and (often) language acquisition. Second, it is often difficult to differentiate ASD from other developmental problems. For example, many Communication Disorders resemble ASD, especially in young children who are only beginning to develop language. Third, we do not yet know whether ASD is stable over time when it is diagnosed before age 12 months. Very few studies have investigated whether children who show ASD in early infancy continue to meet diagnostic criteria in early childhood.

Despite these challenges, researchers have identified several "red flags" that infants and toddlers might show which may suggest (but do not necessarily indicate) ASD (Wetherby, Watt, Morgan, & Shumway, 2007; Zwaigenbaum et al., 2009). These early warning signs can be organized into three categories.

1. Early social communication deficits: lack of eye contact, limited joint attention, little use of gesturing (e.g., pointing, waving)

2. Limited imaginative play and exploration: absence of pretend play, little imitation of others during play, repetitive actions with toys and objects

3. Language delays; deficits in receptive and expressive language, repetitive use of words, unusual prosody

One recent study investigated early warning signs of ASD in infants aged 8-, 12-, and 24-months (Veness et al., 2012). The researchers compared healthy infants, infants later diagnosed with ASD, and infants with other developmental disorders. At 8 months of age, infants could not be differentiated; however, by 12 months of age, several red flags differentiated infants with ASD from healthy infants, especially the development of joint attention and use of gestures. Unfortunately, few red flags differentiated children with ASD from children with other developmental disorders. These findings speak to the difficulty of early identification.

Home-Based Treatments for Preschoolers and School-Age Children

Early Intensive Behavioral Intervention

Many experts regard **early intensive behavioral intervention (EIBI)** as the gold standard in the treatment of young children with ASD (Maglione et al., 2012). EIBI is a behavioral treatment in which children are taught skills on a one-on-one basis, using principles of operant conditioning and observational learning. Although there are a number of different EIBI programs, they have several features in common (Crockett, Fleming, Doepke, & Stevens, 2007; Lovaas, Cross, & Revlin, 2006).

First, the focus of EIBI is on children's overt behavior. Behavior therapists view ASD as consisting of a pattern of behavioral deficits and excesses. Deficits include problems in communication and social interaction. Excesses include stereotypies and tantrums. Treatment is designed to improve areas of deficit and reduce areas of excess. Behavior therapists do not focus primarily on constructs that are not readily observable, such as the parent-child attachment relationship or the way the child integrates or processes information. Instead, they focus on children's overt actions.

Second, behavior therapists rely on learning theory to guide their interventions. They use modeling, prompting, and positive reinforcement to teach children new skills and to shape appropriate behavior.

Third, behavior therapists structure the child's environment to maximize learning. Typically developing children are constantly learning from their surroundings through their observation and imitation of others, through dialogue, and through exploratory play. However, children with ASD show deficits in all three areas, making it difficult for them to learn like other children. Put another way, there is a mismatch between the abilities of the child with ASD and his or her environment. To compensate for this mismatch, learning experiences are structured so that there is a high probability that children will succeed at learning, rather than fail.

Therapists use **discrete trial training** to simplify the learning experience and increase the probability of skill acquisition. Skills are taught systematically. Behaviors are selected by the therapist and are designed to build upon one another to gradually improve the child's functioning. One of the first behaviors a child may learn is to sit when prompted by the therapist. Another behavior frequently taught in initial training sessions is to maintain eye contact with the therapist. These behaviors are essential for the acquisition of other, more complex behaviors.

Discrete trial training typically occurs in a distraction-free setting. First, the therapist gets the child's attention, usually with a verbal (e.g., calling the child's name) or physical (e.g., gently positioning the child's head) prompt. Then, the therapist issues a clear and succinct verbal command, such as "Sit down." The therapist structures the environment so that it is relatively easy for the child to comply: A chair might be located immediately behind the child. Additionally, the therapist might physically prompt (e.g., nudge) the child backward so that she sits. Immediately after the child complies, she is positively reinforced. The choice of reinforcer depends on the child. Frequently used reinforcers include touching/hugging, verbal praise/smiling, or food/drink. The entire procedure is repeated multiple times and prompting is gradually faded. The learning trial ends when the child successfully displays the behavior 85% to 90% of the time. Parents are then asked to practice the behavior at home.

The most well-known EIBI program is the **UCLA Young Autism Project**, developed by O. Ivar Lovaas. The program accepts children under 4 years of age who have ASD but no other major medical problems. The children participate in intensive behavioral training, approximately 40 hours per week, for about three years. Each child is trained individually; four or five therapists are assigned to each child. Training is typically conducted in the child's home (Image 6.11).

Lovaas's EIBI program consists of six stages. As children progress through the stages, they acquire greater capacity for social interaction, language, and behavioral regulation. The first goal of training (Stage 1) is to establish a teaching relationship between the therapist and child. Discrete trial training is used almost exclusively to teach children basic skills necessary for later learning, such as how to sit down and maintain eye contact. Once children are able to attend to the therapist, training focuses on increasing the child's receptive vocabulary and imitation skills (Stage 2). The child is taught how to obey simple commands (e.g., "Pick up the cup") and discriminate between two commands (e.g., "Pick up the cup" when presented with a cup and a crayon). The child is also taught to imitate the therapist's actions, such as waving or clapping. Imitation is one of the easiest ways for children to acquire new skills or combine behaviors in novel ways. In Stage 3, the therapist tries to increase the child's expressive

Image 6.11 Three-year-old Joey has Autism Spectrum Disorder. He is participating in an early intensive behavior treatment program to help him improve his social communication skills. His therapist provides clear prompts; when he responds correctly, he is reinforced with praise and his favorite snack.

vocabulary. Initially, the child is reinforced for imitating speech sounds (e.g., "aaahhh"), then words, then phrases, and finally simple sentences. The child is also reinforced for correctly labeling objects. Only about half of the children in the program are able to adequately imitate speech (Lovaas & Smith, 2003; Smith, Groen, & Wynn, 2000).

For those who show signs of emerging language, training focuses on expanding communication skills and using language during social interactions (Stage 4). At this stage, the child may begin preschool for typically developing children. The therapist focuses on improving the child's social skills. In Stage 5, the focus of training is on peer interactions. The therapist typically works with the child at home and at school, teaching skills such as initiating play with peers, asking for help in the classroom, and taking turns. Finally (Stage 6), children may be ready to enter a regular kindergarten classroom, and their training is discontinued. These children tend to have the best developmental outcomes. Other children will repeat preschool in order to acquire needed linguistic or social skills. Children who repeat preschool and continue to show marked delays usually need ongoing support services throughout their development (Lovaas, 1987; Lovaas & Smith, 2003).

A number of studies have examined the effectiveness of EIBI at improving the intellectual, linguistic, and behavioral functioning of children with ASD (Anderson, Avery, DiPietro, Edwards, & Christian, 1987; Birnbrauer & Leach, 1993; Fenske, Zalenski, Krantz, & McClannahan, 1985; Harris, Handleman, Gordon, Kristoff, & Fuentes,

1991; Hoyson, Jamieson, & Strain, 1984). Lovaas (1987) evaluated 59 children with ASD who were referred to the UCLA Young Autism Project. Children were assigned to three treatment groups, depending on the availability of therapists: (a) an experimental group that received 40 hours per week of training, (b) a control group that received less than 10 hours per week of training, and (c) a second control group that was referred to other professionals in the community for treatment. Most children referred to professionals in the community participated in special education. Results showed that children in the experimental group earned higher IQ scores than children in the control groups at age 7 years. Furthermore, 47% of children in the experimental group were identified as "best outcome" because they showed IQ scores above 85 and were placed in classrooms with typically developing peers. In contrast, only 3% of children in the control groups were described as "best outcome." Follow-up testing showed that the gains children displayed during preschool were maintained at age 12 years (Lovaas, 1987; McEachin, Smith, & Lovaas, 1993; Table 6.4).

These findings suggest that EIBI can be efficacious in improving the intellectual functioning of children with ASD. However, parents should not routinely expect the remarkable changes in IQ initially reported by Lovaas (1987). Programs that provide fewer hours of training per week are associated with more modest gains in IQ and perhaps no apparent gains in adaptive functioning (Smith, Groen, & Wynn, 2000).

Table 6.4 The Efficacy of Early Intensive Behavioral Intervention

Group	Mean IQ Score			Best Outcome (%)	
	Pretreatment	Age 7	Age 12	Age 7	Age 12
EIBI (40 hrs/wk)	63	83	85	47	42
Minimal treatment (< 10 hrs/wk)	57	52	55	0	0
Special education	60	59	–	5	–

Source: Based on Lovaas and Smith (2003); Lovaas (1987); and McEachin et al. (1993).

Note: EIBI = Early intensive behavioral intervention. Best Outcome = IQ score > 85 and unassisted placement in regular education classroom.

Pivotal Response Training

Although discrete trial training can be effective at improving the intellectual, behavioral, and linguistic functioning of children with ASD, it has some limitations. One limitation is that discrete trial training may not increase children's spontaneous social or linguistic behavior. For example, a child with ASD might be taught to say, "Hello. How are you?" when introduced to a stranger, but she may not spontaneously ask questions or engage others unless prompted by caregivers. Many children with ASD often appear to have a low motivation to engage in spontaneous social or linguistic interactions, even after they have participated in extensive discrete trial training.

A second limitation of discrete trial training is that the skills that children acquire via this method do not automatically generalize to new situations or people. For example, a child with ASD may be able to draw or color when prompted and monitored by her therapist, but she may have difficulty initiating and sustaining the behavior alone. Many children who learn behaviors through discrete trial training may become overly dependent on others to guide and regulate their activities; they often have problems with self-management and self-direction.

Pivotal response training is designed to increase the motivation and self-regulation skills of children with ASD (Schreibman & Koegel, 2005). In pivotal response training, *parents* are taught behavioral techniques to improve children's motivation and self-regulation. Then, parents use these techniques in the home and community. Ideally, parent-guided treatment leads to improvement in children's functioning and the generalization of skills outside the therapy setting (Lovaas, Koegel, Simmons, & Long, 1973).

Pivotal response training differs from discrete trial training in several ways. First, pivotal response training is conducted in naturalistic settings, like the home and community. The diversity of settings fosters generalization of skills. Second, the child, not the therapist, selects the focus of the social interaction. For example, if a child is playing with

a certain toy, the therapist takes the child's lead and begins an interaction addressing aspects of the toy. This technique maximizes the child's interest in learning. Third, the therapist uses reinforcers that are naturally tied to the learning experience or the child's behavior (i.e., **direct reinforcers**). For example, giving the child access to a toy car is a direct reinforcer for saying the word "car." In contrast, giving the child food or drink for saying the word "car" is not directly related to the child's behavior. The use of direct reinforcers strengthens the child's understanding of the behavior-consequence relationship and more closely resembles events in the real world. Finally, the therapist reinforces children for their *attempts* at social or linguistic interaction, rather than for successfully engaging in the behavior. If the therapist reinforces attempts, the child is more likely to initiate novel behaviors in the future.

Pivotal response training can also be used to increase children's *motivation* to verbally engage others (Koegel, Koegel, & Brookman, 2005). For example, parents teach children simple questions, such as "What is that?" "Where is it?" and "Whose is it?" Then, parents model, prompt, and reinforce children's use of the questions in naturalistic settings. As children gradually master the use of these questions, prompts can be faded and reinforcement comes from the child's interactions with the environment, not from the parents. Indeed, simple questions and verbal statements can replace functionally equivalent disruptive behaviors. For example, a child with ASD might tantrum during a meal because his parents do not give him much attention. To correct these tantrums, the child might be taught to use functionally equivalent questions (e.g., "Am I being good?") or statements (e.g., "Talk to me") that attract the parents' attention in more appropriate ways.

Parents use a similar procedure to increase self-management and self-direction. First, they select a target behavior. For example, parents may want their children to be able to play independently for 30 minutes, so that they can perform household chores. Second, parents identify a direct reinforcer for the target behavior. If the child enjoys playing with toy cars, access to the cars can be contingent on independent play. Third, the parent demonstrates appropriate and inappropriate independent play to the child. For example, appropriate play might be sitting in the living room, playing with cars on the floor. Inappropriate play might be leaving the room, playing with the cars on the piano, or engaging in stereotypies or disruptive behavior. Fourth, the parent teaches the child to self-monitor the target behavior. Initially, parents can prompt children every few minutes by asking, "Are you playing quietly?" Appropriate play could be reinforced with access to an additional toy car. Eventually, the prompts are given less often, the schedule of reinforcement is decreased, and children are able to monitor and reinforce their own behavior.

Data supporting the use of pivotal response training comes primarily from studies employing single-subject designs; evidence from randomized clinical trials is limited. However, 85% to 90% of children with ASD show improved communication skills when treated with pivotal response training (Koegel, 1995, 2000). Teaching children to initiate verbal interactions by using simple questions is also associated with increased language skills (Koegel, Carter, & Koegel, 2003; Koegel, Koegel, Shoshan, & McNerney, 1999) and a reduction in problem behavior (Carr & Durand, 1985).

School-Based Interventions for Children

The TEACCH Method

The **Treatment and Education of Autistic and Related Communication-Handicapped Children (TEACCH)** approach was developed by Eric Schopler, a student of Bettelheim. Schopler disagreed with Bettelheim's assertion that cold and rejecting mothers caused autism. Schopler and colleagues developed a comprehensive program for youths with ASD that stressed understanding and compassion for these children and their families (Mesibov, Shea, & Schopler, 2005).

TEACCH relies heavily on principles of operant conditioning and observational learning. It is administered in a specialized classroom environment. The focus of treatment is to help children with ASD fit comfortably and effectively in the classroom. This is accomplished in two ways. First, therapists try to expand children's behavioral repertoire by teaching them new social, communicative, and daily living skills. Second, therapists attempt to structure the child's environment to increase the likelihood that the child can complete activities successfully and as independently as possible (Mesibov et al., 2005; Siegel & Ficcaglia, 2006).

TEACCH practitioners used a method of instruction called **structured teaching**. As its name implies, structured teaching involves a variety of structures and supports to help children understand and master the classroom environment. The technique capitalizes on the developmental principle of **scaffolding**. Just as a physical scaffold supports a building as it is being constructed, a behavioral scaffold guides and supports the developing child as he learns new skills through interactions with his environment (Vygotsky, 1978).

Scaffolding can be seen in the classroom setting. The classroom itself is highly organized and predictable. Activity stations are clearly partitioned, color-coded, and labeled so that children can understand what behavior is to be performed in each location. Stations are also structured to minimize distractions. Within each station, therapists use colors, pictures, shapes, and other prompts so that children can complete activities successfully. For example, in the bathroom area, the soap, water faucet, and towel might be assigned the same color to remind children to use all three objects when washing. In the closet, silhouettes of children's coats might be painted on the wall under pegs, to prompt children to hang up their coats when entering the classroom. Children's desks or work stations might be labeled with their pictures or names (Mesibov et al., 2005).

Scaffolding of daily activities can also be seen in the use of **visual schedules**. Since many young children with ASD have limited language, therapists rely heavily on pictures and symbols to organize and direct children's behavior. A visual schedule might consist of a list of pictures outlining the child's activities for the day. Children can refer to visual schedules throughout the day to help them transition from one activity to the next with minimal instruction from staff. Children can also monitor their progress in daily activities by checking off tasks as they complete them.

Scaffolding is also used to help children perform individual activities. Imagine that the therapist wants to teach the child to brush his teeth. The therapist avoids using verbal instruction (i.e., telling the child what to do). Instead, the therapist teaches the skill by first breaking the activity into small, easy steps and labeling these steps using a visual prompt. The steps required to brush teeth might be presented in picture form on a card placed near the sink. Then, the therapist clearly and slowly demonstrates each step. Next, the therapist helps the child perform each step using **hand-over-hand assistance** (i.e., the therapist guides the child's hands with her own). The therapist gradually replaces her physical prompts with gestures (e.g., pointing to the water faucet) or simple verbal prompts (e.g., "turn off"). The activity is periodically repeated until the child can perform it independently.

Scaffolding is also used to teach communication. First, the therapist teaches the child to associate single objects with specific activities. For example, a spoon might represent "eating lunch," a roll of toilet paper "use of the bathroom," and a small plastic shovel "going outside for recess." Children learn to use these physical objects to communicate a desire to engage in their corresponding activities. A child who wants to use the bathroom might bring the roll of toilet paper to the teacher. Later, physical objects are gradually replaced by more abstract representations for these activities. For example, the child might communicate a desire to use the toilet by presenting the teacher with a photograph or drawing of the toilet.

Techniques used by therapists in the classroom are also taught to parents, so that skills can generalize to the home. Each family is assigned two therapists; one works primarily with the child while the other serves chiefly as a "parent consultant." The consultant helps parents learn about ASD and the basic principles of learning and scaffolding. The therapist then teaches parents the techniques used in the classroom. In most cases, the therapist watches parents use these same techniques with their own children and coaches parents to help them use the techniques most effectively. Consultants may also conduct home visits to help parents structure the home environment in an organized, predictable way (Mesibov et al., 2005).

Most of the data supporting TEACCH come from older studies or research conducted by the developers of the program (Mesibov, 1997; Schopler, Mesibov, & Baker, 1982; Schopler, Mesibov, DeVellis, & Short, 1981). These studies indicate that the program is effective in improving socialization, communication, and daily living skills. More recent research conducted by independent teams supports these findings (Ozonoff & Cathcart, 1998). It appears that children who receive instruction at home, in addition to school, show greater improvement in functioning than do children who participate in school-based programs alone.

Academic Inclusion

Children with ASD are educated in a wide range of settings, depending on their degree of impairment (Mandlawitz, 2004; U.S. Department of Education, 2006). Some children are "mainstreamed" into regular education classrooms. These children spend all or nearly all of their day with typically developing peers. Each mainstreamed child might be provided with a paraprofessional aide who attends classes and helps with activities. Other children are only partially mainstreamed. They may participate in certain regular education classes but be pulled out into special education classes for specific subjects (Handleman, Harris, & Martins, 2005). Children with greater impairments are placed in more restrictive settings. For example, some children with ASD and Intellectual Disability participate in integrated classrooms. These classrooms consist of a mixture of children with and without disabilities, but they are organized with the needs of children with disabilities in mind. Other children with ASD and Intellectual Disability are educated almost exclusively in special education classrooms. These classrooms have a high degree of structure and low student-to-teacher ratios. Young children with ASD may also be educated in special preschools or at home.

Academic inclusion is based on the notion that children with developmental disabilities can benefit from interactions with other typically developing children. Classmates can model appropriate social and linguistic skills and provide academic tutoring and support. Children with ASD also have the opportunity to practice and generalize social and communicative skills more easily when they spend time in regular education settings with typically developing peers. Furthermore, children with ASD who are educated in classrooms with typically developing peers are likely to be held to higher standards than children placed exclusively in special education classrooms.

Unfortunately, research indicates that merely exposing children with ASD to typically developing classmates is of limited benefit. Instead, typically developing classmates need to be systematically taught how to interact with a classmate who has ASD. For example, typically developing peers might be taught to use gestures to get the child's attention, to use physical prompts to guide and direct his behavior, and to issue praise to reinforce appropriate actions. Teachers can also structure group activities that encourage children with ASD and typically developing children to work collaboratively. Some schools have even developed mentoring, tutoring, and "buddy" programs in which children with and without ASD are paired during social activities (Durand, 2005).

The main criticism of academic inclusion is that it is technically not a treatment approach; it simply refers to the setting in which treatment takes place. The effectiveness of academic inclusion depends not so much on *where* the child is taught but *how* and *what* the child is taught. Inclusion might be highly effective for some youths with ASD who are provided high-quality supportive services that enable them to participate in the academic curriculum. On the other hand, inclusion can be ineffective for children who are not provided adequate support services to participate in day-to-day classroom activities (Mesibov & Shea, 1996; Siegel & Ficcaglia, 2006).

Interventions for Infants and Toddlers With ASD

Behavioral interventions that are administered in clinics, homes, and schools are associated with significant improvements in children's verbal abilities and behavior. However, these interventions have been somewhat less effective at improving the social deficits shown by youths with ASD. Many youths who participate in these programs continue to display problems with social communication, repetitive behaviors and restrictive interests, and difficulties with the pragmatics of language. Furthermore, these behavioral interventions are typically designed for preschoolers and school-age children with ASD. Consequently, researchers have started to develop intervention programs that target the social communication skills of younger children with ASD in the hope of preventing or alleviating later social deficits (Ingersoll, 2011).

Social communication prevention and treatment programs typically target older infants and toddlers who first begin to show signs of ASD. These interventions systematically teach early social communication skills that are often delayed in children with the disorder. Skills include children's capacity for joint attention, social imitation, and pretend play. Nonverbal social communication skills are taught in naturalistic settings by clinicians or parents and tailored to the developmental needs of the child. The hope is that improvements in these early social communication skills will lead to corresponding improvements in later social functioning (Ingersoll, 2010b).

For example, Ingersoll (2010b) has developed **reciprocal imitation training (RIT)**, a naturalistic intervention designed to improve imitation skills in toddlers and preschoolers with ASD. RIT is administered by therapists in a clinic playroom. As children play, the therapist imitates the child's action with a duplicate toy in the room. For example, if the child plays with a toy dog, the therapist might imitate the child's action by "walking" the toy dog across the table. As children play, the therapist teaches children to imitate gestures by modeling gestures associated with their play activities. For example, if the child plays with a baby doll, the therapist might put her hands to her lips and gesture "shh" as if the baby is sleeping. Therapists also prompt children to imitate therapists' own actions and gestures and praise children for using imitation during therapy sessions.

Ingersoll (2010a) randomly assigned young children with ASD to receive either 30 sessions of RIT or to participate in treatment as usual in the community. After 10 weeks of treatment, children who received RIT showed a greater increase in elicited and spontaneous imitation of objects and gestures than children in the control group (Figure 6.8). A second randomized controlled trial (Ingersoll, 2012) also showed that children who received RIT showed better social-emotional functioning after treatment than controls. However, increased imitation did not seem to explain the corresponding increase in social-emotional functioning. Nevertheless, these findings provide initial evidence for the usefulness of RIT in improving early social communication skills and behavior.

A second naturalistic intervention for young children is **joint attention symbolic play engagement and regulation (JASPER)**. As its name implies, JASPER was designed to improve the joint attention and symbolic play abilities of 3- and 4-year-olds with ASD (Kasari et al., 2006). In the original version of the therapy, children are taught joint attention and symbolic play in a clinic playroom by therapists. Initially, therapists used principles of applied behavior analysis to prompt, model, and reinforce a desired behavior. Later, however, therapists follow the child's play activities, imitate the

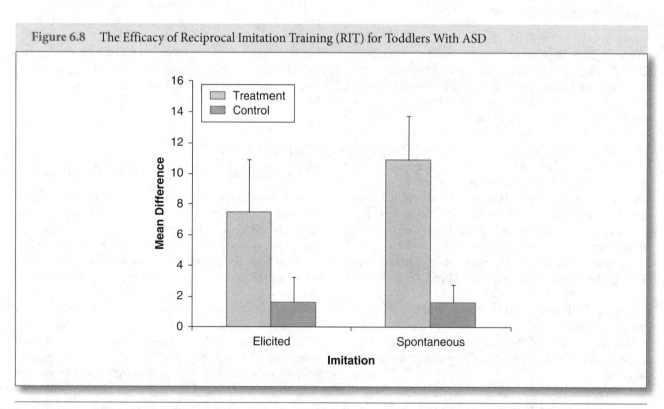

Figure 6.8   The Efficacy of Reciprocal Imitation Training (RIT) for Toddlers With ASD

Source: From Ingersoll (2010a). Used with permission.

Note: RIT increases elicited and spontaneous imitations in toddlers and preschoolers with ASD. Children learn to imitate play with objects and imitate the therapist's gestures.

child's actions, and look for opportunities to model, prompt, and reinforce joint attention and symbolic play.

In one evaluation study, researchers randomly assigned preschoolers with ASD to either a joint attention treatment group, a symbolic play treatment group, or a control group (Kasari et al., 2006). After 5 to 6 weeks of treatment, children in the treatment groups showed significant improvement in their targeted skill compared to children in the control group. Furthermore, children in the treatment groups also exhibited an increase in their targeted behavior while interacting with parents, indicating that they were able to generalize these behaviors to new people. Kasari and colleagues (2012) also examined the long-term outcomes of these children. Five years later, children who participated in the treatment groups showed better language skills than children in the control group. These findings support the efficacy of JASPER in the short term (i.e., improving social communication skills) and long term (i.e., improving language).

Since the initial validation study, JASPER has been developed so that it can be administered by parents (Kasari et al., 2010) and teachers (Lawton & Kasari, 2012) with minimal training. It has also demonstrated efficacy in improving social communication skills in nonverbal preschoolers with ASD (Goods et al., 2013).

Medication

Pharmacotherapy is frequently used to treat many of the co-occurring disorders and behavior problems shown by children and adolescents with ASD. In one study of youths receiving treatment for ASD at a university-based clinic, 55% were taking at least one psychiatric medication, and 29% were taking two or more medications (Martin et al., 1999).

Despite the widespread use of medications for children with ASD, there is very little empirical data regarding their efficacy and safety. One exception has been the **Research Unit on Pediatric Psychopharmacology (RUPP) Autism Network**, which has systematically explored the usefulness of various medications for ASD and other developmental disorders in children (Scahill et al., 2013). Although traditional antipsychotic medications do not seem to be effective in treating children with ASD, newer "atypical" antipsychotics have promise. These medications are called "atypical" antipsychotics because they affect the neurotransmitters dopamine (like traditional antipsychotic medications) and other neurotransmitters like serotonin and norepinephrine.

Two randomized controlled trials have shown that the atypical antipsychotic **risperidone (Risperdal)** is efficacious in reducing behavioral and emotional problems shown by youths with ASD (Image 6.12). For example, risperidone can reduce co-occurring symptoms of hyperactivity and impulsivity as well as decrease irritability, agitation, and crying. Another atypical antipsychotic medication, **aripiprazole (Abilify)** has also been shown to be efficacious in reducing behavior problems in two short-term randomized controlled studies. Atypical antipsychotics do not have the same serious side effects as traditional antipsychotics. However, they frequently cause significant weight gain and sleepiness in children. In rare instances, atypical antipsychotics can also produce motor side effects, such as tremor, rigidity, and dyskinesia (i.e., involuntary movements of the limbs, hands, or face). Finally, these medications can cause a rise in prolactin, a hormone that plays a role in sexual development. Elevated prolactin is a concern because its effect in adulthood is unknown (McPheeters et al., 2011).

Antidepressant medications, especially selective serotonin reuptake inhibitors (SSRIs) are also frequently prescribed to children and adolescents with ASD who experience anxiety and mood problems. Data supporting their efficacy for children with ASD are extremely limited. A randomized controlled study showed fluoxetine (Prozac) to be only slightly superior to placebo in reducing anxiety and repetitive behaviors in children with ASD. Another randomized controlled trial showed that citalopram (Celexa) was not better than placebo at reducing these symptoms. Furthermore, citalopram was associated with increased impulsivity and decreased need for sleep (McPheeters et al., 2011).

In general, medication is not recommended as a first-line treatment for children and adolescents with ASD. Medication is chiefly used to treat comorbid conditions, such as disruptive behavior, repetitive motor movements

Image 6.12 Risperidone is an atypical antipsychotic medication used to treat irritability in children with ASD. Like most antipsychotic medications, it is a dopamine antagonist. However it also affects serotonin and histamine, thereby affecting mood and behavior. Side effects include drowsiness and weight gain.

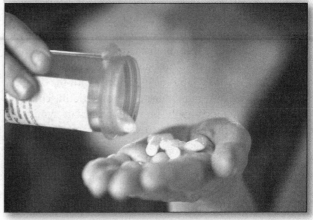

and stereotypies, and anxiety/mood problems. Given the limited number of studies investigating these medications with youths who have ASD, and given their side effects, they are used very cautiously.

Interventions With Little Empirical Support

There are many treatments for ASD that have limited empirical support (Table 6.5). These treatments include interventions designed to increase children's social skills (e.g., "holding therapy" and "pet therapy"), communication skills (e.g., "facilitated communication"), emotional and behavioral functioning (e.g., "art/music therapy"), and sensorimotor functioning (e.g., "auditory integration training"; Simpson et al., 2005). Metz, Mulick, and Butter (2005) conducted a Google search using the terms *autism* and *treatment* and found 65 distinct treatments—most with no empirical basis. These treatments included the use of mental telepathy, the consumption of fish oil and thyme, and the injection of sheep stem cells!

The most frequently used unsupported treatment for ASD is the adoption of special diets or consumption of megavitamins (Senel, 2010). For example, it had been suggested that peptides from gluten (found in wheat products) and casein (found in milk products) might somehow cause ASD or exacerbate symptoms in children with the disorder. Consequently, some individuals believe restricting children's intake of these foods might prevent or alleviate symptoms. Unfortunately, there have been very few randomized controlled studies investigating the efficacy of dietary restriction on ASD. Furthermore, these studies have involved very small samples and have yielded mixed findings. Consequently, more research is necessary before special diets like these can be recommended (Millward et al., 2009). Similarly, some individuals have speculated that large doses vitamin B6 (pyroxidine) might alleviate social communication problems in children with ASD. Unfortunately, there has been a dearth of randomized controlled studies investigating the efficacy of B6 ingestion, with only one study involving eight patients yielding positive results (Nye & Brice, 2009).

A second popular, but unsupported, treatment for ASD is sensory integration training. One form of sensory integration therapy is called auditory integration training. It is designed for children with ASD who show unusual sensitivity to certain sounds. Children who participate in auditory integration training listen to modulated and filtered music during training sessions over the course of several days. Although the training is supposed to reduce the auditory sensitivity of children with ASD, there is little empirical evidence supporting its efficacy (Sinha et al., 2011). Only seven randomized controlled studies, involving very small samples of children with ASD, have been published, and they have yielded mixed results. The American Speech-Language-Hearing Association has concluded that this therapy does not meet scientific standards for safety or efficacy.

Music therapy is sometimes recommended for children with ASD. According to its proponents, music facilitates expression among children with ASD who otherwise show marked deficits in social communication. A recent review of the effects of music therapy on ASD yielded inconclusive findings (Gold et al., 2010). Only three randomized controlled studies have been published involving a very small number of children with ASD. Intensive, short-term music therapy (daily sessions conducted over one week) was associated with gains in verbal behavior and gesturing in two studies, but was not associated with improvements in behavior. The researchers concluded that many more studies are needed before music therapy can be recommended as a treatment for ASD.

Finally, some people have used acupuncture to reduce children's ASD symptoms. Acupuncture involves the insertion of fine needles into certain points in the skin. Several

Table 6.5 Treatments for Autism With Limited Empirical Support

Therapy	Description
Holding therapy	Based on the incorrect notion that children with autism have disturbed attachment to their mothers and that autistic behaviors are the child's way of withdrawing from the mother's rejection; therapist encourages "mother-child holding" to repair the broken attachment bond
Pet therapy	Contact with animals such as cats, dogs, horses, and dolphins is believed to reduce children's anxiety, improve social and communicative skills, and teach decision making and responsibility; some advocates believe dolphins' use of sonar and echolocation causes physiological changes in children's bodies, leading to improvement in functioning
Facilitated communication	Based on the incorrect notion that individuals with autism who are unable to communicate verbally can communicate when assisted by trained professionals; professionals facilitate communication by guiding the patient's hand as he points to symbols/pictures or types messages; evaluations of facilitated communication indicate that "messages" from individuals with autism are likely sent by the professionals who assist them, not by the patients themselves
Auditory integration training	Based on the idea that children with autism have extremely sensitive hearing and that autistic signs are caused by auditory discomfort; children receive auditory training by listening to specialized recordings of music on headphones
Art/music therapy	Art therapy is believed to allow nonverbal expression through drawing, painting, and sculpting; music therapy involves listening to specific musical pieces or playing instruments to reduce anxiety, reinforce positive behavior, and permit self-expression
Megavitamin/diet therapies	Based on the notion that nutritional deficiencies underlie autism; some advocates recommend supplements of B6 and magnesium, other dietary supplements, or avoidance of certain foods
Irlen lenses	Based on the belief that autism is caused by a perceptual disturbance related to difficulties processing light, called scotopic sensitivity; children wear tinted glasses

Source: Based on Simpson et al. (2005).

studies have demonstrated that acupuncture is associated with a reduction of ASD symptoms (Cheuk et al., 2011). However, studies comparing true acupuncture versus sham acupuncture (i.e., needles are inserted in random locations on the skin) found no difference in children's outcomes. Other studies comparing acupuncture plus conventional treatment versus conventional treatment alone also showed no differences in children's ASD symptoms. Several studies have reported adverse effects associated with acupuncture, including bleeding, crying, irritability, sleep disturbance, and hyperactivity.

Why might parents select a treatment with limited empirical support? There are at least three reasons. First, many parents are not aware of the empirical data regarding the treatment for ASD. Most parents do not have access to reputable journals and professional newsletters. Even if they did, published empirical studies are often difficult to read and evaluate. Consequently, most parents might rely on advice from therapists, paraprofessionals, or well-meaning friends—advice that might not be empirically based.

Second, many parents have tried one of the more traditional approaches to treatment and have met with limited

Image 6.13   Equine Therapy

Note: Equine therapy is sometimes recommended for children with ASD and other psychiatric conditions. Proponents argue that children's functioning improves as they interact with horses. No randomized controlled studies support this claim.

success. Understandably, many of these parents turn to other, less supported therapies in the hope that these treatments might help their children.

Third, and perhaps most unfortunately, high-quality, evidence-based treatments for ASD are unavailable to many families. For example, TEACCH programs are generally unavailable outside certain regions of the United States, and behavioral programs in the Lovaas tradition are generally found only in research hospitals and universities. Many local practitioners and well-intentioned volunteer organizations claim to provide "TEACCH" programming or applied behavioral interventions, but they usually do not provide the same high-quality and comprehensive services offered by university-based programs (Metz et al., 2005).

Best Practices

To help parents and practitioners identify interventions that tend to be most effective in the treatment of ASD, the National Research Council commissioned a panel of experts to review the empirical literature. The Committee on Educational Interventions for Children with Autism subsequently identified six components of effective treatment (Lord & McGee, 2001; Scott & Baldwin, 2005).

First, effective treatment involves **early identification and intervention**. The panel recommended that treatment should begin as soon as the child is diagnosed with ASD. The best outcomes occur when treatment begins before age 3 years. Infants, toddlers, and preschool-age children in the community should be periodically screened for ASD to identify the disorder and intervene early (Charman & Baron-Cohen, 2006).

Second, **treatment must be intensive**. Children with the best outcomes participate in full-time educational treatment all year long. Some research suggests a

dose-response effect for treatment. That is, children who received full-time treatment (i.e., 40 hours per week) showed significantly greater improvement than children who received less intensive treatment (e.g., 20 hours per week). The committee recommended a minimum of 25 hours of instruction per week, extended across the entire calendar year.

Third, treatment must involve **repeated, planned, and structured learning opportunities**. Examples of learning opportunities include discrete trial training, pivotal response training, or structured teaching. Regardless of the approach, training should be geared toward the needs of the child and repeated frequently.

Fourth, treatment programs should have **low student-to-teacher ratios**. Ideally, instruction occurs on a 1:1 basis. However, treatment programs for very young children should not have more than two children for each therapist. Ideally, each child should have only a limited number of therapists, to maintain consistency in treatment.

Fifth, **parents must be active in their children's treatment**. Parents' participation in treatment is strongly associated with their children's outcomes. Parents must be not only knowledgeable about the treatment program's strategy and tactics, but also they must implement the program at home. Parental participation in the program increases generalization of children's skills from school to home and provides children with more opportunities to practice skills across contexts.

Finally, programs must constantly **monitor children's progress** in treatment and alter intervention strategies to meet children's needs and developing skills. No two children with ASD are alike. Consequently, not all children with ASD will respond to any single intervention. Intervention strategies need to be tailored to individual children and modified during the course of treatment in order to produce the greatest benefits.

CHAPTER SUMMARY

Definition and Associated Problems

- Autism Spectrum Disorder (ASD) is characterized by impairments in social communication and repetitive behaviors and interests that emerge early in life.

  - Many children with ASD also have Intellectual Disability and/or deficits in expressive language, although these are not required for the diagnosis.
  - ASD exists on a spectrum ranging from mild (e.g., awkward social interactions, ritualistic behaviors) to severe (e.g., complete disinterest in others, persistent stereotypies).
  - ASD was independently identified by Leo Kanner and by Hans Asperger.

- Deficits in social communication are characterized by (a) a lack of social-emotional reciprocity, (b) problems with nonverbal communication, and (c) difficulty forming interpersonal relationships.
- Deficits in restricted, repetitive behaviors and interests include (a) stereotyped or repetitive speech, (b) excessive adherence to routines, (c) restricted interests, and (d) hypersensitivity to sensory input.
- Many children with ASD also have communication disorders. Common communication disorders with verbal communication include (a) muteness, (b) pronoun reversal, (c) abnormal prosody, (d) problems with pragmatics, and (e) one-sided conversations.
- Seizure disorders are also seen in children with ASD. Seizures can be generalized (i.e., tonic-clonic or absence) or partial.

- *DSM-5* has consolidated Autistic Disorder, Asperger's Disorder, and Pervasive Developmental Disorder, NOS into a single spectrum: ASD. It is unclear whether this change will reduce the number of youths who qualify for the ASD diagnosis and receive services.

Epidemiology

- Two large, community-based studies indicate the overall prevalence of ASD is approximately 11 per 1,000 children in the United States.
- All studies indicate that the number of youths diagnosed with ASD is increasing, although some of this increase is likely due to greater awareness of ASD and increased access to services following an ASD diagnosis.
- ASD is approximately four times more common in boys than girls.
- ASD is more common among white, higher SES families than non-white, lower SES families in the United States. This difference is partially attributed to better access to health care (e.g., diagnostic and treatment services) among higher income families.
- The course of ASD is variable. Three factors seem to predict children's outcomes: (a) children's intellectual ability, (b) their linguistic ability, and (c) their degree of social engagement. Early intervention is usually designed to improve one or more of these skills.

Etiology

- Youths with ASD often show abnormalities in the "social brain"—a neural pathway that consists of the prefrontal cortex, limbic system (especially the amygdala), and fusiform gyrus.
  - ASD is highly heritable, although no specific genes have been identified that explain most instances of the disorder.
  - According to the growth dysregulation hypothesis, genes predispose certain infants to show enlarged head circumference and greater synaptic density but decreased neural connectivity.
  - Structural abnormalities in the limbic system, especially the amygdala, may underlie problems in understanding emotions.
  - Youths with autism do not show typical activation of the right fusiform gyrus when processing human faces and interactions. Instead, they typically use a different brain region responsible for processing information about objects.
  - ASD is associated with underactivity of the orbital and medical prefrontal cortex, areas responsible for inferring others' thoughts and feelings.
- ASD is often associated deficits in social cognition that are observable in the first years of life.
  - Joint (shared) attention
  - Social orientation
  - Symbolic (pretend) play
  - Empathy and theory of mind
- Abnormalities of the basal ganglia may underlie some repetitive and stereotyped behaviors shown by children with ASD.
- Language abnormalities include problems with syntactic-semantic language (similar to children with Language Disorder) and problems with semantic-pragmatic language (similar to children with Social Communication Disorder).

Treatment

- Early intensive behavioral intervention (EIBI) is often considered the gold standard home-based treatment for children with ASD. It relies on discrete trial training, a behavioral approach to introducing, modeling, and reinforcing specific skills.
- Pivotal response training is another home-based treatment in which parents use behavioral techniques to improve children's social communication and self-regulation.
- TEACCH is a school-based program for youths with ASD that relies heavily on scaffolding and prompting to improve children's social communication and adaptive skills in the classroom.
- Peer-assisted therapy is often used as a part of academic inclusion for higher functioning children with ASD.
- Social communication prevention and treatment programs are designed to improve the social cognition of infants and very young children suspected of ASD.
  - Reciprocal imitation training fosters imitation and symbolic play in toddlers.
  - JASPER focused on improving children's joint attention and behavioral regulation skills.
- Atypical antipsychotic medication, like risperidone (Risperdal), can reduce behavioral and emotional problems shown by some youths with ASD.
- Many interventions for ASD have limited empirical support. Parents may use these interventions because they seem plausible or because other, evidence-based treatments are not available in their community.
- The National Research Council has established "best practice" guidelines for the treatment of ASD in children. Principles of effective treatment include the following:
  - Early identification and intervention
  - Intensive services
  - Repeated, planned, and structured learning opportunities
  - Low student-to-teacher ratios

- ○ Parental involvement
- ○ Monitoring student progress and modifying treatment when necessary.

KEY TERMS

abnormal prosody   173

absence (petit mal) generalized seizures   174

amygdala   180

aripiprazole (Abilify)   197

Autism and Developmental
   Disabilities Monitoring (ADDM) Network   175

Autism Genome Project   179

Autism Spectrum Disorder (ASD)   166

basal ganglia   189

diffusion tensor imaging (DTI)   180

direct reinforcers   193

discrete trial training   191

early identification and intervention   200

early intensive behavioral intervention (EIBI)   191

echolalia   170

empathy   187

excessive adherence to
   routines or resistance to change   170

executive functioning   182

false belief task   187

generalized tonic-clonic (grand mal) seizures   174

growth dysregulation hypothesis of ASD   180

hand-over-hand assistance   194

Hans Asperger   168

hyper- or hypo-reactivity to sensory input   170

initiating joint attention   183

intellectual ability   178

interpersonal relationships   169

joint attention   183

joint attention symbolic play
   engagement and regulation (JASPER)   196

Leo Kanner   168

limbic system   180

linguistic ability   178

low student-to-teacher ratios   200

medial prefrontal cortex   182

mind-blindness   187

monitor children's progress   200

mute   173

National Survey of Children's Health   175

neurexin 1   179

nonverbal communication   169

one-sided   173

orbital prefrontal cortex   182

parents must be active in their
   children's treatment   200

partial seizure   174

pivotal response training   193

problems with pragmatics   173

pronoun reversal   173

reciprocal imitation training (RIT)   196

repeated, planned, and structured
   learning opportunities   200

Research Unit on Pediatric Psychopharmacology (RUPP)
   Autism Network   197

responding joint attention   183

restricted, fixated interests   170

right fusiform gyrus   181

risperidone (Risperdal)   197

scaffolding   194

semantic-pragmatic language difficulties   190

social brain   183

social cognition   183

Social Communication Disorder   174

social communication prevention and treatment   195

social engagement   178

social orientation   184

social-emotional reciprocity   169

spectrum   167

stereotyped or repetitive behaviors   170

structured teaching   194

syntactic-semantic language problems   189

theory of mind   187

tics   172

Tourette's Disorder   173

Treatment and Education of Autistic and Related
   Communication-Handicapped
   Children (TEACCH)   194

treatment must be intensive   200

UCLA Young Autism Project   191

visual schedules   194

CRITICAL THINKING EXERCISES

1. Significant changes were made to the conceptualization of autism in *DSM-5*. How might these changes affect (a) the prevalence of ASD and (b) children's access to psychiatric and educational services?

2. What is the evidence that genes and abnormal brain development underlie ASD? Why don't all children with ASD show the same brain anomalies?

3. In retrospect, many parents recall that their children with ASD exhibited problems with social communication and behavior in infancy and toddlerhood. However, in most cases, ASD is not diagnosed until the preschool years. Why?

4. Compare and contrast discrete trial training with pivotal response training for ASD. What are the advantages and limitations of each approach to treatment?

5. Why might parents rely on "treatments" for ASD with limited empirical support? What are some of the problems these interventions can cause to children and families?

EXTEND YOUR LEARNING

Videos, practice tests, flash cards, study guides, and links to online resources for this chapter are available to students online. Teachers also have access to lecture notes, PowerPoint presentations, suggestions for classroom activities, and possible exam questions. Visit: www.sagepub.com/weis2e.

CHAPTER 7

Learning Disabilities and Specific Learning Disorder

LEARNING OBJECTIVES

After reading this chapter, you should be able to answer these questions:

- Describe the *DSM-5* and IDEA conceptualization of learning problems in children. How do their conceptualizations differ?
- How are children with learning disabilities usually identified and diagnosed?
- How common are learning disabilities and how does prevalence differ as a function of gender, ethnicity, and socio-economic background?
- What are the causes and treatments for children's problems with (a) basic word reading, (b) reading fluency, and (c) reading comprehension?
- Why do children show problems with written expression? How can deficits in handwriting, spelling, and narrative or expository writing be overcome?
- How do the skills and strategies of children with math disabilities differ from their typically developing peers? What interventions are effective in improving the speed and accuracy of math problem solving?

Learning disabilities are serious conditions that can adversely affect children's academic functioning, career attainment, self-concept, and behavior. Although there is disagreement as to the exact definition of learning disabilities, most experts agree children with learning disabilities have the following characteristics:

1. Children with learning disabilities have marked difficulty learning to read, write, spell, or perform mathematics. These academic skill problems are believed to be due to dysfunction in underlying psychological processes.

2. Genetics plays a role in learning disabilities. Learning problems run in families and monozygotic twins usually show strong concordance for learning disabilities. Genes are believed to cause subtle abnormalities in brain structure, functioning, perception, memory, and information processing, which, in turn, interfere with learning.

3. Children with learning disabilities show marked deficits in academic achievement. If untreated, these deficits usually persist over time; they do not simply reflect delays in the acquisition of academic skills. Children with learning disabilities are not simply "slow learners" or academic "late bloomers."

Daniel was a 9-year-old boy referred to our clinic because of low academic achievement. Daniel began struggling in school as a kindergartener. He had trouble recognizing and writing letters and numbers, answering questions about stories, and following instructions. A medical examination showed that he was healthy. Daniel repeated kindergarten the following year, but his academic problems continued.

In the first grade, Daniel was tested to determine if he had a learning disability. Daniel's IQ score was 103, indicating average intellectual functioning. His standardized scores on tests of reading (75) and writing (81) were significantly below most of his peers. However, Daniel's reading, writing, and math test scores were not low enough for him to receive special education services.

At the time of the evaluation, Daniel was attending a regular third-grade classroom. He showed significant trouble in reading. He often confused letters with similar appearances, like P, B, D, and C, and had trouble differentiating similar-looking words, such as *that, this, those,* and *these.* Daniel could not sound out unknown words; instead, he usually guessed at the pronunciation of words that he did not know. Daniel showed problems with reading comprehension. He would often skip words or whole lines of text while reading and had problems answering questions about what he read.

Daniel hated school. He was especially embarrassed to read out loud in front of the class. He resented the teacher for correcting him when he misread a word. Daniel would often try to avoid schoolwork by averting his eyes in class, volunteering to do chores in the classroom (e.g., clean the blackboards), or charming the teacher. At home, Daniel would whine or tantrum when his mother asked him to do his homework.

Daniel explained, "I'm not dumb or lazy. I just have a hard time with reading. I look at the page, and it's all jumbled up. If I read a sentence or two, I can't tell you about it later." The psychologist at the clinic suggested that Daniel be assessed for a possible learning disability. His mother responded, "OK. But didn't they already test him when he was in the first grade and find out that he wasn't dyslexic? Besides, can't Ritalin work for these sorts of problems?"

4. Although children's intelligence and academic achievement are correlated, learning disabilities are not caused by low intelligence or Intellectual Disability.

5. Learning disabilities are not caused by emotional problems (e.g., test anxiety, depression), socioeconomic deprivation (e.g., malnutrition, poverty), or impoverished educational experiences (e.g., low-quality schools). Although these factors can exacerbate children's learning problems, they do not cause learning disabilities.

There is currently no consensus regarding the best way to identify children with serious learning problems. Indeed, the definition of learning disabilities varies across disciplines. Professionals who work in clinics, hospitals, and other health care facilities (e.g., clinical psychologists, physicians) tend to adopt the medical definition of learning disabilities outlined in *DSM-5.* These professionals diagnose children with Specific Learning Disorder. In contrast, professionals who work in educational settings (e.g., school psychologists, special education teachers) tend to rely on the legal definition of learning disabilities outlined in federal and state laws. These professionals typically classify children with specific learning disabilities. To understand these differences, and some of the controversy that surrounds them, we will examine the *DSM-5* and legal definitions of children's learning problems separately.

WHAT IS SPECIFIC LEARNING DISORDER?
Essential Features

In *DSM-5,* the diagnosis that describes children with persistent difficulties in academic skills is **Specific Learning Disorder** (Table 7.1, Diagnostic Criteria for Specific Learning Disorder). The essential feature of Specific Learning Disorder is a current, normative deficit in reading, writing, and/or mathematics. Specifically, children with Specific Learning Disorder earn reading, writing, and/or math scores well below their peers on standardized measures of academic achievement. "Well below" is usually considered at least 1.5 standard deviations below the mean. Because most achievement tests have a mean of 100 and a standard deviation of 15, a score < 78 might indicate low achievement. These academic skill deficits must be normative, that is, they must be low compared to other children in the general population. Relative deficits in academic skills, such as a lower score in math compared to reading, do not indicate a Specific Learning Disorder (American Psychiatric Association, 2013).

Besides low achievement, children with Specific Learning Disorder must meet three other criteria. First, they must have a history of difficulties acquiring basic academic skills. Specifically, children must experience problems in one or more of the following areas:

Table 7.1 Diagnostic Criteria for Specific Learning Disorder

A. Difficulties learning and using academic skills, as indicated by the presence of at least one of the following symptoms that have persisted for at least 6 months, despite the provision of interventions that target those difficulties:

1. Inaccurate or slow and effortful word reading (e.g., reads single words aloud incorrectly or slowly and hesitantly, frequently guesses words, has difficulty sounding out words).

2. Difficulty understanding the meaning of what is read (e.g., may read text accurately but not understand the sequence, relationships, inferences, or deeper meanings of what is read).

3. Difficulties with spelling (e.g., may add, omit, or substitute vowels or consonants).

4. Difficulties with written expression (e.g., makes multiple grammatical or punctuation errors within sentences; employs poor paragraph organization; written expression of ideas lack clarity).

5. Difficulties mastering number sense, number facts, or calculation (e.g., has poor understanding of numbers, their magnitude, and relationships; counts on fingers to add single-digit numbers instead of recalling the math fact as peers do; gets lost in the midst of arithmetic computation and may switch procedures).

6. Difficulties with mathematical reasoning (e.g., has severe difficulty applying mathematical concepts, facts, or procedures to solve quantitative problems).

B. The affected academic skills are substantially and quantifiably below those expected for the individual's chronological age, and cause significant interference with academic or occupational performance, or with activities of daily living, as confirmed by individually administered standardized achievement measures and comprehensive clinical assessment.

C. The learning difficulties begin during school-age years but may not become fully manifest until the demands for those affected skills exceed the individual's limited capacities (e.g., as in timed tests, reading or writing complex reports for a tight deadline, excessively heavy academic loads).

D. The learning difficulties are not better accounted for by Intellectual Disability, uncorrected visual or auditory acuity, other mental or neurological disorders, psychosocial adversity, lack or proficiency in the language of academic instruction, or inadequate educational instruction.

Note: The four diagnostic criteria are to be met based on a clinical synthesis of the individual's history (developmental, medical, family, educational), school reports, and psycho-educational assessment.

Specify all academic domains and subskills that are impaired. When more than one domain is impaired, each one should be coded individually according to the following specifiers:

Specific Learning Disorder with Impairment in Reading:

Word reading accuracy

Reading rate of fluency

Reading comprehension

Specific Learning Disorder with Impairment in Written Expression:

Spelling accuracy

Grammar and punctuation accuracy

Clarity or organization of written expression

Specific Learning Disorder with Impairment in Mathematics:

Number sense

Memorization of arithmetic facts

Accurate fluency calculation

Accurate math reasoning

Source: Reprinted with permission from the *Diagnostic and Statistical Manual of Mental Disorders, Fifth Edition* (Copyright 2013). American Psychiatric Association.

- *Word reading:* Reading individual words may be inaccurate, slow, or laborious.
- *Reading comprehension:* Children can read the text aloud but are not able to answer questions about it.
- *Spelling:* Children add, omit, or substitute letters.
- *Written expression:* Children make grammatical errors; their writing lacks clarity or organization.
- *Problems mastering number sense, number facts, or math calculations:* Younger children have a poor understanding of numbers. They may have problems conceptualizing the "number line," counting, and adding single digits. Older children use immature strategies (e.g., counting on fingers) to add or subtract.
- *Math reasoning:* Conceptualizing (i.e., "setting up") and solving math problems is ineffective or inaccurate.

Problems in one or more of these areas must exist for at least 6 months and emerge during childhood or adolescence. In most instances, children's academic problems emerge during the early elementary or middle school years and significantly affect school performance. In some cases, however, problems begin in early childhood, but youths are able to compensate for these problems in some way. For example, a child with reading problems who has excellent visual short-term memory might compensate for these problems by memorizing frequently occurring words. His problems may not manifest themselves until later childhood or adolescence, when academic demands (e.g., more complex reading vocabulary) exceed his compensatory strategy.

Second, the deficits shown by children with Specific Learning Disorder must interfere with their academic achievement, work functioning, or everyday life activities. It is not sufficient for children to score low on an achievement test; their academic deficits must also affect their functioning in the real world. For example, children with Specific Learning Disorder might have difficulty meeting educational benchmarks for their grade, adolescents might have trouble maintaining their eligibility to play after school sports, or young adults may experience problems reading instruction manuals, balancing their checkbooks, or writing their resumes.

Third, the academic deficits shown by children with Specific Learning Disorder must not be attributable to Intellectual Disability. The academic deficits shown by children with Learning Disorder must be "specific" to one or more academic

domains—they must not reflect overall low cognitive ability. Children's overall intellectual functioning should be within normal limits with specific deficits in reading, writing, and/or math. Furthermore, Specific Learning Disorder must not be due to other mental or neurological disorders or sensory impairments, such as vision or hearing problems. Psychologists or pediatricians must rule out these other potential causes for low academic achievement, such as anxiety at school, medical problems that might interfere with learning (e.g., seizures), or problems seeing the blackboard or hearing the teacher. Finally, Specific Learning Disorder must not be attributable to sociodemographic factors, such as a lack of proficiency in English or inadequate instruction in school. Learning problems caused by poverty, impoverished educational experiences, or linguistic differences are not Learning Disorders (American Psychological Association, 2013).

Specifiers

When clinicians diagnose Specific Learning Disorder, they specify the area of the child's academic problems (see text box, *DSM-IV* → *DSM-5* Changes: A Broader Approach to Specific Learning Problems). First, clinicians indicate the child's area(s) of impairment: reading, written expression, or mathematics. Then, for each area identified, clinicians indicate the nature of the child's weakness (see Table 7.1, Diagnostic Criteria for Specific Learning Disorder). For example, a child might be diagnosed with "Specific Learning Disorder with Impairment in Reading" and deficits in word reading accuracy, reading fluency (i.e., speed), and/or reading comprehension. Some professionals use the term *dyslexia* to refer to deficits in word reading accuracy and reading fluency. *DSM-5* encourages professionals who use this term to also specify deficits in reading comprehension if they exist. Alternatively, a child might be diagnosed with "Specific Learning Disorder with Impairment in Mathematics" and deficits in number sense, memorization of arithmetic facts, calculation fluency (i.e., speed), and/or math reasoning. Some professionals use the term *dyscalculia* to refer to deficits in number sense, memorization of arithmetic facts, and calculation fluency. *DSM-5* encourages professionals who use this term to also specify deficits in math reasoning if they exist (American Psychological Association, 2013).

Table 7.2   Specific Learning Disorder Severity

Specify the Severity of Specific Learning Disorder:

Mild: Some difficulties learning skills in one or two academic domains, but of mild enough severity that the individual *may be able to compensate or function well* when provided with appropriate accommodations or support services, especially during the school years.

(Continued)

Table 7.2 (Continued)

Moderate: Marked difficulties learning skills in one or more academic domains so that the individual is *unlikely to become proficient without some intervals of intensive and specialized teaching* during the school years. Some accommodations or supportive services at least part of the school day, in the workplace, or at home may be needed to complete activities accurate[ly] and efficiently.

Severe: Severe difficulties learning skills, affecting several academic domains, so that the individual is *unlikely to learn those skills without ongoing intensive individualized and specialized teaching* for most of the school years. Even with an array of appropriate accommodations or services at home, at school, or in the workplace, the individual may not be able to complete all activities efficiently.

Source: Reprinted with permission from the *Diagnostic and Statistical Manual of Mental Disorders, Fifth Edition* (Copyright 2013). American Psychiatric Association.

DSM-IV → DSM-5 Changes

A BROADER APPROACH TO SPECIFIC LEARNING PROBLEMS

DSM-5 includes only one diagnosis for children and adolescents who have learning disabilities: Specific Learning Disorder. In contrast, *DSM-IV* recognized several specific types of learning disorders: Reading Disorder, Mathematics Disorder, Disorder of Written Expression, and Learning Disorder Not Otherwise Specified. The *DSM-5* Neurodevelopmental Work Group consolidated these learning disorders into a single diagnostic category to reflect difficulty differentiating within the different types of learning problems. The new single diagnosis, Specific Learning Disorder, also reflects the high comorbidity of reading, math, and writing problems.

When a child is diagnosed with Specific Learning Disorder, clinicians specify his or her area of academic problems. Specification is important, because different learning disorders are associated with different underlying cognitive processing problems and methods of treatment.

Second, for each diagnosis, clinicians rate the severity of children's academic problems (see Table 7.2, Specific Learning Disorder Severity). Severity ranges from "Mild" (i.e., difficulties that can be compensated by academic accommodations and support services) to "severe" (i.e., difficulties in multiple academic domains that greatly interfere with skill acquisition).

WHAT ARE LEARNING DISABILITIES?

Professionals working in schools tend to use the term *specific learning disabilities*, rather than Specific Learning Disorder, to describe children with serious deficits in specific academic skills (Samms-Vaughn, 2006). The term "learning disability" was coined by Samuel Kirk (1962) to describe children who showed significant delays in the development of reading, writing, math, or oral language. Kirk suggested that these delays interfered with children's ability to learn and were likely caused by structural abnormalities of the brain. Kirk differentiated learning disabilities from other psychological conditions that often interfere with learning, such as low intelligence, blindness, and deafness (Hallahan & Mock, 2003).

In 1975, Congress enacted the Education for All Handicapped Children Act (Public Law 94–142). This law provided free special education services to school-age children with disabilities, including children with learning disabilities (Sotelo-Dynega et al., 2011). The U.S. Department of Education (1977) proposed the following definition of **specific learning disabilities**, which borrows heavily from Kirk's 1962 conceptualization:

The term "specific learning disability" means a disorder in one or more of the psychological processes involved in understanding or in using language . . . which may manifest itself in an inability to listen, speak, read, write, spell, or do mathematical calculations. The term does not include children who have Learning disabilities which are primarily the result of visual, hearing, or motor handicaps, or mental retardation, or emotional disturbance, or of environmental, cultural, or economic disadvantage. (U.S. Department of Education, 1977, *Federal Register, 42*, pp. 65082–65085)

The current definition of learning disabilities is provided in the **Individuals with Disabilities Education Improvement Act** (IDEA, 2004) a federal law (PL 5–17) that provides special education services to children and adolescents with all types of disabilities (Table 7.3). The definition of learning disabilities

Table 7.3	Percent of Children With Disabilities in U.S. Schools
Disability	*Percentage of All Children*
Any Disability	**13.1**
Learning disability	4.9
Speech/language impairment	2.9
Other health impairments	1.4
Intellectual disability	0.9
Emotional disturbance	0.8
Autism	0.8
Developmental delay	0.7
Multiple disabilities	0.3
Hearing impairments	0.2
Visual impairments	0.1
Orthopedic impairments	0.1
Traumatic brain injury	0.1

Source: Based on U.S. Department of Education, National Center for Education Statistics (2012).

Note: Learning disabilities and speech/language impairments (i.e., communication disorders in *DSM-5*) are the most common types of disabling conditions. Other health impairments include chronic or acute health problems, such as a heart condition, asthma, sickle cell anemia, hemophilia, epilepsy, or leukemia.

in IDEA is similar to the one provided by the Education for All Handicapped Children Act. However, IDEA extends this definition by specifying eight areas in which children can be classified with a learning disability:

1. Oral expression
2. Listening comprehension
3. Basic reading skills
4. Reading fluency skills
5. Reading comprehension
6. Mathematics calculation
7. Mathematics problem solving
8. Written expression

For example, a child who shows deficits in reading words might be classified with a learning disability in the area of basic reading; a child who has problems with writing might be classified with a learning disability in the area of written expression (Sotelo-Dynega et al., 2011). Notice how some (but not all) of these academic areas correspond to the domains outlined in *DSM-5* for Specific Learning Disorder. For example, both the *DSM-5* definition of Specific Learning Disorder and the IDEA criteria for learning disabilities permit children to be classified because of problems with basic (word) reading, reading comprehension, mathematics calculation, mathematics (reasoning) problem solving, and written expression. Only *DSM-5* recognizes deficits in spelling as a separate area of academic deficit. Furthermore, according to IDEA, children with oral communication or listening comprehension skills can be classified with a learning disability. In contrast, children with speech and language problems would most likely be diagnosed with a communication disorder in *DSM-5*. Indeed, these communication problems are usually treated by speech and language therapists and not psychologists, counselors, or teachers (Fletcher et al., 2002).

Like *DSM-5*, IDEA lists several exclusionary criteria that must be ruled out before a child can be classified with a learning disability. Specifically, the child's academic problems must not be due to low intelligence, emotional problems, other disabling conditions (e.g., vision, hearing impairment), language differences, or impoverished educational experiences (U.S. Department of Education, 2006).

IDENTIFYING LEARNING DISABILITIES IN SCHOOL-AGE CHILDREN

IDEA does not specify how professionals must identify youths with learning disabilities. Instead, IDEA gives state governments freedom to determine the specific classification criteria they will use. Different states use different criteria. Currently, there are three general approaches used by most clinicians: (a) the IQ-achievement discrepancy method, (b) responsiveness to intervention, and (c) comprehensive assessment.

IQ-Achievement Discrepancy

The **IQ-achievement discrepancy method** was once the most widely used procedure for identifying learning disabilities in school-age children. Prior to IDEA (2004 Amendment), federal law defined learning disabilities in terms of a significant discrepancy between a child's IQ and at least one domain of academic achievement. Similarly, *DSM-IV* also conceptualized Specific Learning Disorder in terms of a significant discrepancy between cognitive ability (i.e., intelligence) and academic achievement (American Psychiatric Association, 2000).

Professionals who use the discrepancy approach compare children's IQ and academic achievement using standardized tests. Significantly low achievement, relative to IQ, can indicate the presence of "unexpected underachievement," an indicator of a learning disability. Previous federal regulations did not specify the magnitude of the discrepancy needed to classify children with a learning disability. Instead, state governments adopted different criteria. Typically, discrepancies between 1 and 2 standard deviations (i.e., IQ 15–30 points higher than academic achievement) were required for a child to be classified with a learning disability and gain access to special educational services.

Today, there is general consensus that the IQ-achievement discrepancy approach is *not* a valid method of identifying youths with learning disabilities when used alone (Johnson et al., 2010; Scanlon, 2013). The IQ-achievement discrepancy method has at least four weaknesses.

First, the IQ-achievement discrepancy approach is often not useful in differentiating youths with and without learning problems. Many young children who show marked delays in reading fall short of the discrepancy needed to be classified with a learning disability. Although these children (like Daniel; see text box Case Study: Waiting to Fail) display serious delays in reading, they are often denied special education because they do not meet the discrepancy cutoff specified by their state. Over time, these children often fall further behind their peers. Consequently, the IQ-achievement discrepancy approach to classification has been called the "wait to fail" approach, because children do not receive help for their learning problems until *after* they show serious delays in academic skills (Reynolds & Shaywitz, 2009).

Second, neuroimaging studies have not shown differences between children who show significant IQ-achievement discrepancies and children with academic problems who do not show significant discrepancies. For example, poor readers show underactivation of left-hemisphere brain regions responsible for reading (Tanaka et al., 2011). There are no differences in brain activity between children who do and do not show significant discrepancies between IQ and achievement. Similarly, the heritability of learning problems is similar in children who do and do not show IQ-achievement discrepancies (Skiba Landi, N., Wagner, R., & Grigorenko, 2011). There is little evidence that youths with discrepancies are biologically or genetically different than other low-achieving children.

Third, children identified with learning disabilities using the IQ-achievement method do not show different patterns of cognitive abilities than youths with learning problems who fall short of the IQ-achievement cutoff. For example, youths with reading problems who do and do not show significant discrepancies display similar problems with sounding out words, recognizing letters and words, knowledge of vocabulary, short-term memory, speech and language, and classroom behavior. There is little evidence that youths who meet the IQ-achievement discrepancy process information differently than youths who fall short of this discrepancy (Maehler & Schuchardt, 2009; Stuebing et al., 2002).

Fourth, youths with reading problems who do and do not show significant IQ-achievement discrepancies display similar outcomes. Children in both groups display long-term problems with reading. Youths with reading problems who do and do not have significant IQ-achievement discrepancies

respond similarly to treatment. There is little evidence that youths with IQ-achievement discrepancies need to be taught using different methods than other youths with reading problems (Hoskyn & Swanson, 2000; Shaywitz et al., 2002; Stuebing et al., 2002; Vellutino, Scanlon, & Lyon, 2000).

Despite problems with reliability and validity, the discrepancy approach is still used in many school districts to classify children with learning disabilities. Although the discrepancy approach should not be used as the only means to identify learning disabilities, it can be an important part of the assessment process (Zirkel & Thomas, 2010).

Response to Intervention (RTI)

A second way to identify learning disabilities in school-age children is **response to intervention (RTI)**. Instead of relying on standardized IQ and achievement testing, RTI identifies learning disabilities based on children's educational progress and outcomes (Reschly, 2006). Specifically, children with learning disabilities can be identified based on their inability to respond to "scientific, research-based" teaching methods (U.S. Department of Education, 2006). Children who are provided with high-quality, empirically based instruction but who fail to show academic progress may be classified with learning disabilities (Tannock, 2013).

School systems that use RTI usually rely on a three-tier system to identify children with learning disabilities (Reschly & Bergstrom, 2009; Figure 7.1). Tier I is characterized by "universal" or "primary preventative" screening; all children in a class are evaluated to assess their acquisition of basic academic skills (Berkeley, Bender, Peaster, & Saunders, 2009). Typically, screenings are brief and administered periodically over the course of the academic year. Furthermore, screening often relies on curriculum-based assessment. **Curriculum-based assessment** involves measuring children's acquisition of academic skills in the classroom. Rather than comparing children's scores to a norm group (like standardized achievement testing), children's scores are evaluated in terms of the school's learning goals. Alternatively, an individual child's performance is compared to other children in the same grade at that school.

For example, many school districts use the Dynamic Indicators of Basic Early Literacy Skills (DIBELS) to identify children with delays in word reading (Kaminski & Cummings, 2008). The DIBELS consists of a series of very brief tests that require students in early elementary school to read words or short passages of text. Testing takes only a few minutes and is repeated across the school year to monitor students' progress with reading acquisition. Children's performance on the DIBELS is compared to other students in their class and evaluated based on the school district's learning objectives.

Approximately 85% of all children show adequate progress in reading, writing, and math. However, the remaining 15% who lag behind their peers or fall short of the district's

Figure 7.1 Response to Intervention (RTI)

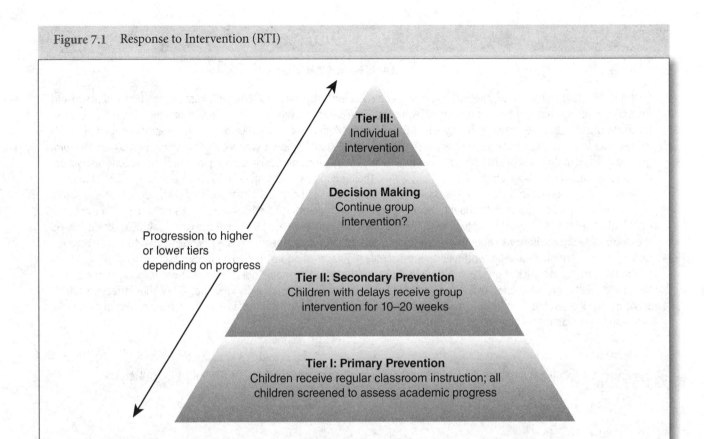

Progression to higher
or lower tiers
depending on progress

Tier III:
Individual
intervention

Decision Making
Continue group
intervention?

Tier II: Secondary Prevention
Children with delays receive group
intervention for 10–20 weeks

Tier I: Primary Prevention
Children receive regular classroom instruction; all
children screened to assess academic progress

Source: Based on Reschly and Bergstrom (2009).

Note: RTI usually consists of three tiers of increasingly more individualized and intensive instruction. Children who fail to respond progress up the tiers and may eventually receive special education services and be classified with a learning disability.

standards are considered "nonresponsive" to treatment and progress to Tier II. This tier is called "secondary prevention" because interventions in this tier are administered to children who show academic delays but have not yet been identified with learning disabilities. Children in Tier II typically receive supplemental, small-group instruction in the academic domain in which they show delays. For example, children who lag behind their peers in reading might receive regular reading instruction in the classroom and additional, small-group instruction several times per week. Reschly and Bergstrom (2009) recommend that Tier II interventions last 10 to 20 weeks. In practice, the frequency and duration of group interventions range considerably, from weekly sessions lasting a few months to daily sessions lasting most of the academic year (McKenzie, 2009). After small-group instruction, schools reevaluate children's need for continued services in Tier II. Children who meet learning benchmarks may return to Tier I; students who show some improvement may remain in Tier II; and children who do not respond to group intervention may progress to Tier III (Reschly & Bergstrom, 2009).

Between 5 and 10% of school-age children continue to show academic deficits even when provided with supplemental group instruction (Image 7.1). These youths may progress to Tier III of RTI (Berkeley et al., 2009). The services

delivered to children in Tier III vary from school to school. In most instances, Tier III involves individualized instruction or one-on-one tutoring, targeting children's academic deficit.

Image 7.1 In RTI, children who fail to respond to instruction will likely be referred for special education.

RAFE, RICKY, AND RTI

Rafe and Ricky are 7-year-old boys in the same first-grade class. Both boys had problems with letter recognition and basic word reading in kindergarten and have continued to lag behind their peers this year as well. Periodic screenings conducted by their teacher indicated that they could read only about 8 to 10 words/minute, compared with their classmates who read 20 to 25 words/minute on average. Because the boys were not making adequate progress with regular classroom instruction, they progressed to Tier II of their school's RTI program. Tier II consisted of regular reading class and supplemental small-group instruction, designed to improve the boys' ability to sound out words. Their group met approximately 20 minutes each day for 20 weeks.

Figure 7.2(a) shows Rafe's progress. The dark line shows the school's benchmark criterion for first graders; that is, it shows how many words a first-grade child should be able to read at each point in the school year. Rafe's reading specialist set the goal (light line) that he should be able to read three more words/minute each week over the course of the intervention. As the dotted line shows, Rafe was able to meet his goals and catch up to his peers. Because he responded to Tier II intervention, it was discontinued, and he continued to receive only regular reading instruction with his class.

Figure 7.2(b) shows Ricky's progress. Although Ricky and Rafe had the same goals, Ricky did not respond to the group-based intervention (dotted line). Ricky's parents, teacher, and reading specialist decided that Ricky should receive Tier III services, which consisted of individual reading instruction for the remainder of the academic year. Their goal is to help Ricky catch up to his classmates before transitioning to the second grade.

Figure 7.2 Rafe (a) Responded to Group-Based Reading Intervention in Tier II of RTI but Ricky (b) Did Not

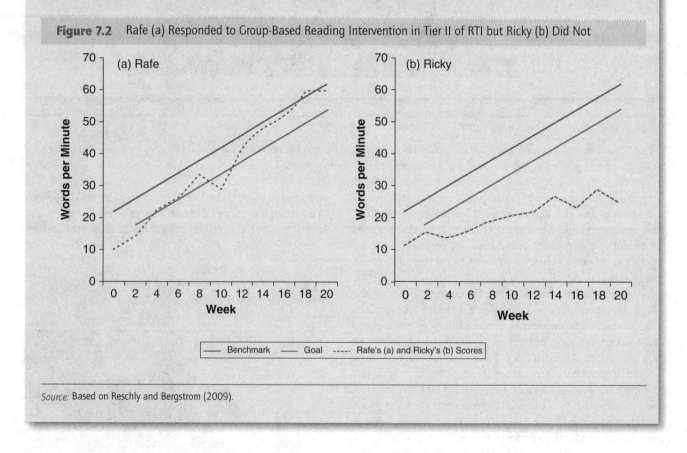

Source: Based on Reschly and Bergstrom (2009).

Some experts regard Tier III as "special education" whereas others believe that children should only be placed in special education if they fail to show progress in Tier III (Kavale et al., 2008; Reschly and Bergstrom, 2009).

RTI is an increasingly popular method of learning disability identification. Its popularity can be attributed to at least two factors. First, most research indicated low validity of the IQ-achievement discrepancy method. RTI offered an alternative method of assessment. Second, federal law (IDEA, 2004 Amendment) specifically stated that school districts could not require a significant IQ-achievement discrepancy for learning disability classification. Instead, IDEA permitted RTI, claiming, "a local educational agency may use a process that determines if the child responds to scientific, research-based intervention as part of the evaluation process" (IDEA, 2004 Amendment). Currently, approximately one third of states either require RTI for the assessment of learning disabilities or permit RTI to be used as part of the evaluation process. Several more states are planning to implement RTI in the near future.

Supporters of RTI point out its benefits. The chief benefit is that RTI allows school personnel to identify and help children with learning disabilities at an earlier age (Yssledyke et al., 2010). Recent research indicates that RTI can be useful in identifying children whose academic skills lag behind their peers as early as kindergarten. Because RTI is based on observations of children's performance in class, RTI allows teachers to identify youths' academic delays much earlier than more traditional discrepancy approaches. Presumably, early identification and intervention would improve the academic outcomes of these youths (Reschly, Tilly, & Grimes, 1999).

Early identification and remediation of learning problems might also decrease the number of children referred to special education. Because RTI uses a "tiered" approach to identification and treatment, only children who fail to respond to lower level interventions are referred for more intensive (and costly) special education services. Fewer children referred to special education not only saves money but also reduces stigma for the children associated with being classified with a learning disability and (in some cases) being removed from the regular education classroom.

RTI also has several limitations (Hale et al., 2010). Although IDEA recommends RTI as a method to assess learning disabilities, federal law does not provide guidelines regarding how it should be implemented (Cavendish, 2013). Consequently, states (and even school districts within the same state) that use RTI may implement it in different ways. Thus, there is variability in the way children are identified with learning disabilities from state to state or school district to school district. A child might be classified with a learning disability in one state but not another (McKenzie, 2009).

Second, RTI is based on the premise that children with learning disabilities fail to respond to "scientific, research-based" teaching methods. However, there is disagreement as to what constitutes evidence-based methods of teaching, especially in certain academic domains such as math. Similarly, RTI assumes that teachers are well trained in administering and evaluating these evidence-based methods of instruction. However, we simply do not know whether teachers are familiar with many of these relatively new techniques. Although reading specialists and special education teachers with advanced training may be skilled at implementing these interventions, regular education teachers, who perform most interventions in the RTI model, may not be (Tannock, 2013).

Third, it is unclear whether RTI reduces the number of children diagnosed with learning disabilities and referred to special education. Several early studies investigating referrals in specific states or school districts indicated modest reductions (i.e., 3–5%) in the number of children identified with learning disabilities (Torgeson, 2009). However, more recent studies have found only negligible reductions in the number of referred children using RTI Fuchs et al., 2012).

Fourth, it is unclear whether RTI actually identifies children with learning disabilities earlier than alternative approaches to classification. Children must progress through several tiers of RTI before being classified with a disability and receiving special education services. Consequently, critics have claimed that RTI is a "watch them fail" model that replaced the older "wait and fail" discrepancy approach (Reynolds & Shaywitz, 2009). Tran and colleagues (2011) conducted a meta-analysis examining the academic and cognitive processing scores of children with reading problems who participated in RTI. They discovered that children's baseline test scores, especially scores on measures of basic word reading and the ability to sound out novel words predicted their response to RTI. Although one of the assumptions of RTI is that it more quickly and accurately identifies children who fail to respond to instruction, Tran and colleagues' (2011) findings indicate that many children could be identified even before RTI was implemented by using their baseline test scores. Their results are consistent with other studies that indicate that cognitive processing problems predict children's ability to respond to regular classroom instruction (Al Otaiba & Fuchs, 2002; Nelson et al., 2003). Consequently, many experts argue that children's cognitive processing abilities are a critical component in the assessment of learning disabilities (Compton et al., 2012).

Comprehensive Assessment

The psychometric problems of the discrepancy method and questions about RTI have led many clinicians to adopt a third approach to learning disability classification (Hale et al., 2010). **Comprehensive assessment** refers to the identification of learning disabilities by integrating classroom observations of academic performance with norm-referenced testing that includes measures of academic achievement, intellectual ability, and cognitive processing. Advocates of comprehensive assessment point out that children can fail to respond to evidence-based academic instruction for many reasons, only one of which is learning disabilities (Hale et al., 2010). Alternative reasons might include low intellectual functioning, attention problems, anxiety or mood disorders, low motivation, poor parental involvement or support, linguistic or cultural differences, health or nutritional problems, or other difficulties stemming from social-cultural disadvantage (Tannock, 2013). Although all children with learning disabilities have academic delays, all children with academic delays do not necessarily have learning disabilities. Comprehensive assessment permits clinicians to differentiate learning disabilities caused by underlying cognitive processing problems from low achievement caused by these other factors.

Imagine a second grader who struggled with reading since beginning school. Because he persistently lagged behind his classmates in basic reading, he progressed through tiers II and III of RTI and received more intensive reading instruction. Nevertheless, he continues to earn reading achievement scores in the bottom 15 to 20% of his class. Professionals using RTI might conclude that the child has a learning disability and refer him for special education services. In contrast, advocates of comprehensive assessment would be interested in measuring his cognitive functioning to determine whether below average cognitive ability or cognitive processing problems might partially explain his reading deficits. If the child's verbal IQ score was similar to his reading achievement (e.g., both scores in the 80–85 range), we might conclude that he does not have a learning disability but, rather, that his reading is consistent with his intellectual abilities (McKenzie, 2009).

Advocates of comprehensive assessment argue that the assessment of cognitive ability and cognitive processing problems is essential to learning disability identification. Indeed, both the *DSM-5* and IDEA define Learning Disorder/learning disabilities as academic deficits caused by cognitive or psychological processing problems. Furthermore, research over the past two decades has shown that children with learning disabilities have underlying cognitive processing problems that their healthy classmates do not have (Compton et al., 2012; Fiorello et al., 2009). In many cases, specific types of learning disabilities are associated with particular cognitive processing problems. Cognitive processing problems also predict children's response to treatment (Al Otaiba & Fuchs, 2002; Frijters et al., 2011; Fuchs et al., 2012). For example, children with reading problems who display underlying problems with phonemic awareness and phonics skills tend to show improvement when provided with reading instruction designed to remedy these cognitive processing deficits.

Dawn Flanagan and colleagues (2010, 2011) have developed a **comprehensive model for learning disability identification** that integrates RTI with norm-referenced cognitive and academic achievement testing. Like RTI, children progress through a series of tiers, each characterized by more insensitive and individualized services provided to the child. Unlike RTI, clinicians assess the cognitive abilities and processing skills of children who fail to respond to intensive, individualized instruction. Results of cognitive testing can either rule out the presence of a learning disability or confirm the diagnosis and aid in treatment planning (Figure 7.3).

The first part of the comprehensive model capitalizes on the strengths of RTI. Children who show delays in academic skills compared to their peers (Tier I) are provided with additional group-based instruction (Tier II). If children continue to lag behind their classmates, they may receive individualized instruction and practice (Tier III). Ideally, this higher level intervention should target specific areas of weakness. For example, children who show deficits in retrieving math facts (e.g., $7 \times 7 = ?$) would receive a different intervention than children who can recall math facts quickly and accurately but are unable to understand math story problems.

If children continue to show deficits despite individual instruction, they might have a learning disability. Determination is based on the following criteria:

1. The child shows a normative deficit in academic skills. Typically, the child earns a standard score <85 (lowest 16th percentile) in one or more academic domains, such as basic reading or reading comprehension.

2. The child shows a cognitive processing problem that is related to his or her academic skill deficit. For example, cognitive testing might show that a child with poor reading fluency displays underlying problems with processing speed. Alternatively, a child with poor math calculation skills might have underlying deficits in working memory. Although clinicians cannot conclusively say that these cognitive processing problems cause the child's learning problems, they are consistent with the conceptualization of learning disabilities as cognitive processing disorders.

3. Although the child shows specific cognitive processing problems, his or her intellectual functioning in other domains is intact. For example, a child with reading disability might have underlying problems with sounding out words and processing speed. However, his verbal IQ should be within normal limits and most of his other cognitive processing scores should fall into the average range. The existence of specific academic and cognitive processing problems in an otherwise normal cognitive profile is consistent with the notion of learning disabilities as "unexpected underachievement." An otherwise normal cognitive profile allows the clinician to differentiate children with learning disabilities from children who experience learning problems because of low intelligence.

4. Alternative explanations for the child's academic deficit are explored and ruled out. For example, the clinician must determine that the child's achievement deficit is not due to language differences or problems with acculturation, socioeconomic disadvantage, anxiety or mood disorders, or other psychiatric problems (e.g., ADHD).

Children who meet criteria for learning disabilities according to the comprehensive model may be referred for high-intensity, individualized instruction to help them overcome their academic deficits. More importantly, the results of comprehensive assessment provide information to school personnel that might help them tailor intervention to suit the cognitive strengths and weaknesses of the child.

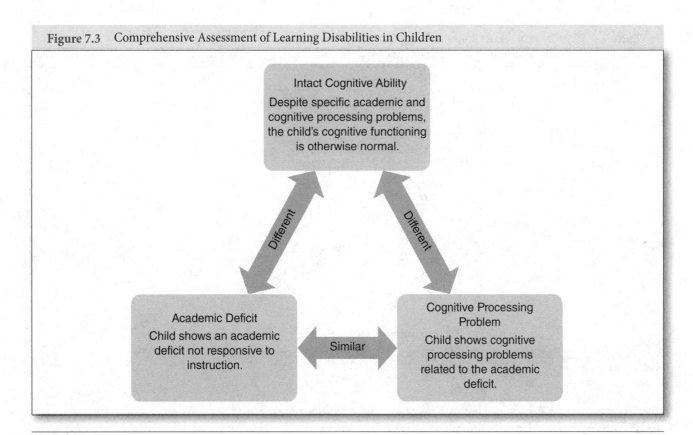

Source: Based on Flanagan and colleagues (2010).

Note: Children with learning disabilities show (a) an academic skill deficit, (b) underlying cognitive processing problems associated with that academic deficit, and (c) otherwise normal cognitive functioning (IQ). Furthermore, alternative explanations for the child's academic problem (e.g., cultural or economic disadvantage) must be ruled out.

EPIDEMIOLOGY

Prevalence

Approximately 4.9% of children have been classified with learning disabilities and are receiving special education services in U.S. schools (U.S. Department of Education, 2012). This percentage has remained relatively stable for the past decade (Figure 7.4). This percentage likely underestimates the actual number of children with learning disabilities because not all youths receive a formal disability classification and receive services.

An alternative way to estimate prevalence is to ask parents if their child has even been diagnosed with a learning disability, either by school officials or private practitioners (e.g., pediatricians, psychologists). Results of the National Health Interview Surveys, a very large epidemiological study, revealed that 7.2% of parents report that their child has a learning disability (Boyle et al., 2011). This finding is consistent with the results of a second population-based study that investigated the prevalence of learning disabilities in the areas of reading and mathematics separately (Landerl & Moll, 2010). In this study, 7% of parents reported having a child with reading disabilities whereas 6.1% reported a child with a disability in mathematics.

Reading disability is the most common learning disability; as many as 80% of children with diagnosed learning disabilities have reading problems. The prevalence of writing disabilities (8%–15%) and mathematics disabilities (5%–8%) is much lower. Many children with learning disabilities experience problems in two or more academic domains. For example, roughly half of all youths with math-related problems also show difficulty reading. Furthermore, children with both mathematics and reading problems show greater impairment in each of these areas than do children with mathematics or reading problems alone (Augustyniak, Murphy, & Phillips, 2006; Loomis, 2006).

Gender

Studies examining gender differences in the prevalence of learning disabilities have yielded mixed results. Most community-based studies have shown equal rates of learning disabilities for boys and girls (Dirks, Spyer, van Lieshout, & de Sonneville, 2008). However, some studies have found a higher percentage of boys (8.9%) than girls (5.0%) with the disorder (Boyle et al., 2011). Landerl and

Figure 7.4 The Percentage of Children Classified With Disabilities (including learning disabilities) in U.S. Schools Remained Relatively Stable in the Past Decade

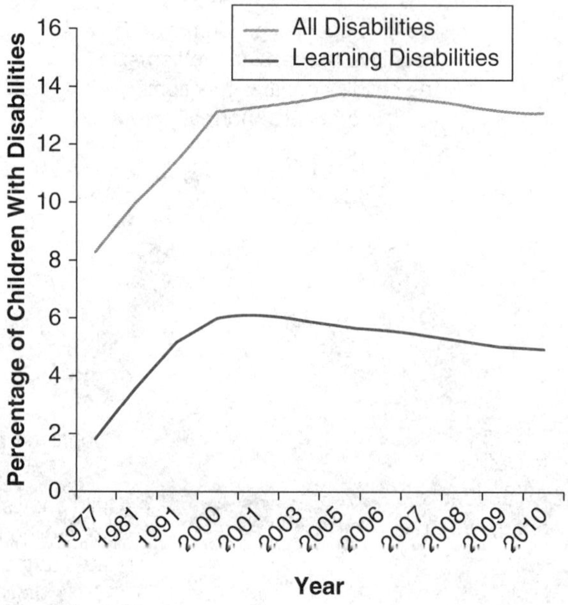

Source: Based on U.S. Department of Education (2012).

Moll (2010) concluded that although there was no *overall* difference in the prevalence of learning disabilities across gender, girls were twice as likely as boys to be diagnosed with mathematics disability.

In contrast to community-based research, studies involving youths referred to special education have consistently shown a greater percentage of boys than girls. Shifrer and colleagues (2011) found that boys were twice as likely as girls to be classified with a learning disability and receive special education. Their findings are consistent with previous studies showing that boys are 1.7 to 2.7 times more likely to receive special education services for learning disabilities than girls. Boys may be more likely to receive learning disability classification because they also tend to show more disruptive behavior than girls. Their disruptive behavior may increase the likelihood that they will be referred for testing and, consequently, receive special education.

Race and Ethnicity

Several large, population-based studies also indicate that racial and ethnic minorities in the United States are more likely to be classified with learning disabilities than nonminority children. For example, Shifrer and colleagues (2011) found that African American, Hispanic, and American Indian children were 1.43 to 1.56 times more likely than white children to be diagnosed with learning disabilities. Although some experts have attributed this increased likelihood of classification to racism or biased assessment strategies (Skiba et al., 2008), the researchers found a more likely culprit: low socioeconomic status. Low family income consistently predicted a child's likelihood of disability classification; furthermore, when the researchers controlled for SES, differences in the prevalence of learning disabilities across these ethnic and racial groups disappeared. The researchers hypothesized that low family income, low parental education, and barriers to high-quality schools, nutrition, and health care place children at risk for learning disabilities, not race or ethnicity per se (Figure 7.5).

What about children whose native language is not English? Overall, children whose primary language is not English are *not* more likely than native English speakers to be diagnosed with learning disabilities (Shifrer et al., 2011). However, children who do not gain proficiency in English by the time they begin school or children who are placed in an English as a Second Language (ESL) class in school are at increased likelihood of learning disability classification. This increased risk is not explained by race, ethnicity, or SES. The researchers suggest that school personnel may misinterpret these children's difficulty with English as evidence of a learning disability. These findings speak to the importance of linguistically sensitive assessment of children's academic skills.

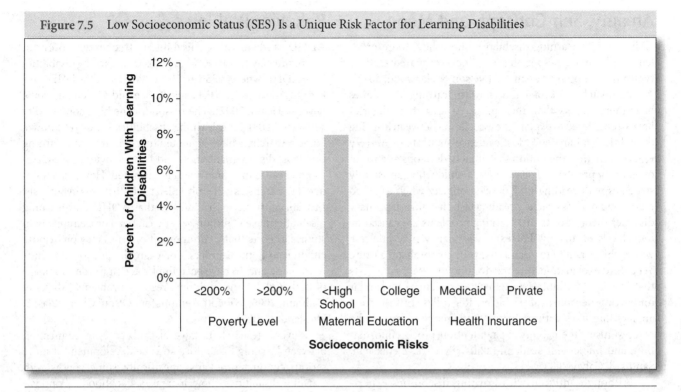

Source: Based on Boyle and colleagues (2011).

Note: Children who live in poverty, whose mothers did not complete high school, or who receive Medicaid are at increased risk for developing learning disabilities.

COURSE

Children with learning disabilities are at risk for long-term academic difficulties. Many youths begin to show learning problems in kindergarten but are not identified until their academic problems worsen. Approximately 70% of children with reading disabilities who are not identified until the third grade continue to show reading problems in adolescence and early adulthood. Children with learning disabilities are more likely than typical learners to earn low grades, to repeat a grade in school, and to drop out of school before graduation. The high school dropout rate for youths with learning disabilities is approximately 37%, compared to an average of 12% nationally (National Center for Educational Statistics, 2003).

The long-term outcomes for children with learning disabilities depend on at least three factors: (a) early intervention, (b) familial support, and (c) the child's personal resiliency. First, youths who receive high-quality, empirically based interventions, especially before the third grade, tend to show marked improvement in their academic skills. Consequently, they are less likely to experience long-term achievement problems. Second, youths who receive support from their families are often better able to cope with their learning problems. Parents can emotionally support their children and advocate for their children's educational needs. Third, youths can rely on other, nonacademic skills to compensate for their academic problems. For example, some children develop competence in sports, art, music, or community service and derive self-esteem, motivation, and career interests from these other accomplishments (Loomis, 2006).

COMORBIDITY

Overlap in Academic Problems

Children with learning disabilities in one academic area often have problems in other academic areas as well. In a recent population-based study of elementary school children, researchers examined the presence of learning disabilities in the areas of reading, mathematics, and spelling (Landerl & Moll, 2010). As we might imagine, disabilities in the areas of reading and spelling tended to co-occur most often: 49% of children with reading disability also had problems with spelling whereas 39% of youths with spelling disability also experienced difficulty with reading. Comorbid mathematics disabilities were also relatively common: 23% of children with reading disability and 25% of children with spelling disability also showed problems with mathematics. Although children with a learning disability in one domain may have a disability in another domain, learning problems are also somewhat specific. Many children showed problems with reading, mathematics, or writing/spelling alone.

Anxiety, Self-Concept, and Mood

Children with learning disabilities often show more problems with anxiety, especially in school, compared to their typically developing classmates (Nelson & Harwood, 2011). Approximately 70% of children with learning disabilities have more anxiety than their peers. At least three theories have been offered to explain the association between learning disabilities and anxiety. Most evidence supports **secondary reaction theory**, the notion that anxiety develops as a result of learning problems. For example, a child who consistently struggles with reading may develop anxiety when asked to read aloud in class or take a reading test. In contrast, primary disorder theory posits that learning problems are caused by high levels of anxiety. For example, anxiety may interfere with a child's ability to attend to text or comprehend stories. Yet a third explanation, cerebral dysfunction theory, suggests that learning disabilities and anxiety are caused by similar underlying neurological problems. Regardless of the cause, anxiety interferes with children's academic performance by compromising their ability to pay attention, process information, and implement academic skills (Eysenck, Derakshan, Santos, & Calvo, 2007).

Although children with learning disabilities experience elevated levels of anxiety, on average, these children are not more likely than their non-disabled peers to have anxiety disorders. Although youths with learning disabilities may experience elevated anxiety in educational settings, they do not seem to be at increased risk for pervasive problems with agitation, nervousness, or worry. Furthermore, parents and teachers have a tendency to overreport anxiety in children with learning disabilities whereas students themselves have a tendency to minimize their anxiety. Therefore, it is important to ask parents, teachers, and children themselves about anxiety in order to determine if anxiety is interfering with the child's academic functioning (Nelson & Harwood, 2011).

The impact of learning disabilities on children's self-esteem is mixed. Some data indicate that youths with learning disabilities are at risk for developing negative self-concepts because of their academic struggles. However, most recent research indicates that children with learning disabilities show specific deficits in academic self-concept, but they do not show problems with low self-concept overall. Consequently, they may have a dim view of their academic skills but not a negative impression of themselves in general (Lackaye, Margalit, Ziv, & Ziman, 2006; Lipka & Siegel, 2006).

Research regarding the association between learning disabilities and mood is also mixed. Some research indicates that youths with learning problems are at risk for a host of negative emotions. These feelings range from self-blame and anger to helplessness and despair (Loomis, 2006). However, other research indicates that depression is equally common among children with and without learning problems (Lipka & Siegel, 2006).

Behavior Problems

ADHD and learning disabilities frequently co-occur. Approximately 15% to 40% of youths with learning disabilities have ADHD whereas 25% to 50% of youths with ADHD have learning disabilities (Palacios & Semrud-Clikeman, 2005; Silver & Hagin, 2002). The reason for the high comorbidity between ADHD and learning disabilities is not yet known. Some researchers have suggested that children with learning problems display inattention and hyperactivity in the classroom because they are frustrated or bored. However, subsequent research has generally failed to confirm this hypothesis. Instead, most research indicates that ADHD and learning disabilities have common genetic causes. For example, twin studies indicate that a common set of genes may predispose children to both disorders. For example, portions of chromosomes 6 and 16 have been implicated in the development of both ADHD and children's reading problems (Mayes & Calhoun, 2006; Willcutt, Pennington, Olson, Chhabildas, & Hulslander, 2005).

Several researchers have also observed a connection between learning disabilities and the development of more serious conduct problems. Specifically, some youths with learning disabilities show increased likelihood of oppositional-defiant behavior toward adults, aggression, theft, vandalism, robbery, and chronic truancy. Conduct problems are especially likely among children with significant learning problems and below average intelligence (Palacios & Semrud-Clikeman, 2005).

Two hypotheses have been offered to explain the relationship between learning disabilities and conduct problems. The *school failure hypothesis* suggests that academic failure mediates the relationship between children's learning problems and the development of conduct problems. Specifically, children and adolescents with learning problems struggle academically and show less involvement in school-related activities. Consequently, they may associate with deviant peers who model and reinforce delinquent behaviors. Alternatively, the *susceptibility hypothesis* posits that children with learning disabilities often have other personality and behavioral attributes that place them at risk for conduct problems. For example, youths with learning disabilities often display ADHD symptoms that compromise their decision making and judgment. Consequently, these youths may be prone to disruptive behaviors, such as losing their temper, taking risks, and responding aggressively (Lipka & Siegel, 2006).

Peer Interactions

Children with learning disabilities are at risk for peer rejection for at least three reasons. First, children's academic skill deficits and low grades can make them less attractive to classmates. Peers might view them as unintelligent or lazy. Indeed, children with learning disabilities show the same likelihood of peer rejection as children who earn low grades but do not have learning disabilities (Nowicki, 2003). Second, children with learning disabilities often show disruptive behavior problems, such as hyperactivity and impulsivity. Classmates might find these disruptive behaviors aversive and avoid children with learning disabilities who display them (Samms-Vaughn, 2006). Third, children with learning disabilities often show deficits in social skills. They may prefer younger playmates and display less stable friendships. Some youths with learning disabilities have difficulty understanding other people's emotional expressions and acting appropriately in social situations. They may have low social self-efficacy; that is, they lack confidence in their ability to get along with others. These social deficits and doubts can compromise their peer interactions and friendships (Lackaye et al., 2006; Lipka & Siegel, 2006).

ETIOLOGY

The Genetic Basis for Learning Disabilities

Learning disabilities are heritable conditions. Family studies indicate that 35% to 40% of children with reading or writing disabilities, compared to only about 5% of the general population, have an immediate family member with at least one learning disability. Familial concordance seems to be stronger for boys than for girls. Approximately 40% of boys and 18% of girls who have a parent with a learning disability show serious learning problems themselves. Twin studies provide further evidence that learning disabilities have a genetic component. Concordance rates for monozygotic and dizygotic twins are .85 and .35, respectively (Grigorenko, 2001; Hawke, Wadsworth, & Defries, 2006).

Learning disabilities in the area of mathematics have similar heritability (Geary, 2011). Mathematics disabilities run in families; roughly 50% of children with mathematics disabilities have a sibling with the disorder. Concordance rates for monozygotic and dizygotic twins are .73 and .56, respectively (Butterworth, 2005). Children with certain X-linked genetic disorders, such as Turner Syndrome or Fragile X Syndrome, often show marked impairment in their mathematical abilities. Turner Syndrome is caused by the absence or inactivity of a portion of the X chromosome. Fragile X Syndrome usually results from a genetic mutation of the X chromosome. Girls with these disorders display underlying deficits in behavioral inhibition, reasoning, short-term memory, and visual-spatial skills that seem to impair their math performance. The fact that girls with these X-linked disorders show specific deficits in mathematical abilities supports the notion that mathematics disabilities is partially influenced by one's genotype (Mazzocco & McCloskey, 2005).

Approximately 50 to 67% of the variance of children's math achievement is attributable to genetics. The remainder of the variance can be explained by shared environmental experiences (i.e., experiences common to all siblings, such as nutrition, SES) and unshared experiences (i.e., experiences unique to the child, such as having a particularly good math teacher in third grade). We can look at the percentage of variance explained by genetics and examine it more closely. Approximately one third of this variance in math achievement that is explained by genetics overlaps with the percentage of variance explained by children's intelligence. Intelligence is highly heritable; furthermore, children with high intelligence tend to have high math achievement. An additional one third of the variance explained by genetics overlaps with children's reading skills. Reading ability is also highly heritable; furthermore, children's math achievement often depends on their reading abilities (e.g., the ability to read math story problems). Only about one third of the variance explained by genetics is specific to mathematics. Contrary to popular opinion, there is no "math gene" that allows people to be either very good or very bad at math.

The familial transmission of learning disabilities tends to be somewhat specific (Figure 7.6). Researchers investigated the prevalence of learning disabilities in the areas of reading and mathematics in a large sample of elementary-school children and their parents (Landerl & Moll, 2010). They found that children with disabilities in the area of reading tended to have a parent with a history of reading disability. Similarly, children with disabilities in the area of mathematics tended to have a parent with a history of mathematics disability. Although some children with learning disabilities had parents without a history of learning problems or learning problems in a different academic area, most children had a family history of learning problems in the same academic area.

Although learning disabilities are believed to have underlying genetic and neuropsychological causes, experience also plays a role in the development and maintenance of learning problems. Recall that the principle of passive gene-environment correlation asserts that parents provide not only their genotypes to their children but also their early environmental experiences. Parents who have difficulty with reading, writing, and math may be less likely to model and reinforce these academic skills to their children. Indeed, Byrne and colleagues (2006) noticed that parents with reading problems had fewer books and magazines in their home, read to their children less often, and placed less emphasis on literacy than parents with average reading skills. Genetic risk, combined with impoverished early learning experiences, likely underlie many children's academic problems.

BASIC READING

Word Reading

Approximately 80% of children with learning disabilities have difficulty with reading. *DSM-5* recognizes two reading problems: (a) inaccurate or slow and effortful word reading, and (b) difficulty with reading comprehension. In contrast, IDEA recognizes an additional disability in reading fluency,

Figure 7.6 Parent-Child Transmission of Learning Disabilities Is Somewhat Specific

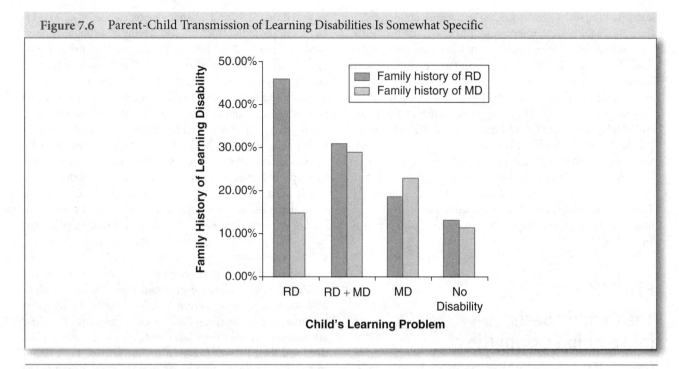

Source: Based on Landerl & Moll (2010).

Note: Children with reading disabilities (RD) tend to have a first-degree family member with RD whereas children with mathematics disabilities (MD) tend to have a first-degree family member with MD.

that is, the speed of reading. Because word reading, fluency, and comprehension involve different processes, we will discuss them separately.

Word Reading Skills

Reading is a complex task that children do not acquire naturally. As children learn to read, they progress along a continuum of reading skills. First, children learn basic reading skills. These skills include (a) the ability to recognize letters, (b) the awareness of phonemes or the basic sounds of language, (c) an understanding of the connection between letters and the sounds they make, and (d) the capacity to sound out novel words (Linan-Thompson & Miciak, 2012). Problems in any one of these early skills can lead to difficulty with word reading. Consider Alex, a girl with basic reading skill deficits:

CASE STUDY

ALEX: JUST GETTING BY IN SCHOOL

Alex was a 9-year-old girl with a history of low academic achievement, especially in the areas of reading. Alex displayed problems mastering basic phonics skills. Because she could not sound out words, she guessed at their meaning based on their initial letters, length, or context. She often confused words with similar appearance. For example, Alex sometimes read "what" instead of "that" and often mistook "thought" for "though" and "through." Alex was unable to sound out novel words or read stories at her grade level that did not contain pictures or other contextual cues.

Alex had difficulty understanding directions and completing tasks in a timely manner. In school, she frequently made mistakes because she did not understand written directions. Alex performed best when her teacher presented instructions orally, demonstrated tasks, and monitored her progress as she completed her work. Alex admitted that she was frequently confused by assignments at school. "Sometimes, I just guess at what I'm supposed to do because I don't understand the directions. I also look at the other kids in the class to find out what to do. I have a lot of friends who are willing to help me, so I get by."

Children learn to recognize individual letters by their names and sounds. For example, preschool-age children learn to recognize the letter *s* from a list of printed letters, to name the letter *s*, and to tell a parent that the *s* makes the /s/ sound. Letter recognition is essential to the development of all other reading skills.

After letter recognition, children must develop phoneme awareness. **Phonemes** are the smallest units of spoken language; they are the sounds that individual letters or combinations of letters make. Examples of phonemes include the /s/ sound, as in *sip*, or the /sh/ sound, as in *ship*. There are 41 phonemes in the English language. These phonemes can be combined in many ways to form the English spoken language. **Phoneme awareness** refers to children's recognition that spoken language can be broken down into phonemes and that phonemes can be combined to create spoken language (Samms-Vaughn, 2006).

Phoneme awareness does not come naturally to children. Spoken language is seamless. When we speak, we usually blend sounds together. We usually do not clearly articulate each sound of each word. For example, when we ask a friend, "What do you want to do today?" our question might sound like, "Waddayawanna do today?" Children must learn that these strings of spoken language can be segmented into discrete sounds or phonemes.

Typically, children need systematic instruction to develop phoneme awareness. Indeed, a considerable percentage of time that children spend in early elementary school is devoted to learning phoneme awareness. Table 7.4 shows several ways parents and teachers can teach phoneme awareness to young children.

Phoneme awareness is essential for the acquisition of the next basic reading skill: understanding the connection between printed letter combinations and the sounds they make. Specifically, children must learn to translate graphemes into phonemes. **Graphemes** are the units of written language that represent phonemes. For example, the grapheme *ship* represents the three phonemes /sh/ /i/ /p/. Children with adequate phoneme awareness are able to use their understanding of phonemes to decode written words into spoken language.

The ability to decode written words into phonemes depends on children's phonics skills. **Phonics** instruction emphasizes the correspondence between letters and sounds. Although there are many ways to teach phonics, all phonics-based teaching methods help children see the basic relationship between letter combinations and the sounds letters make (Image 7.2).

One of the most widely studied methods for teaching phonics is direct instruction. **Direct instruction** involves the systematic presentation and practice of basic skills in highly structured settings. Skills are broken down into simple steps. Then, each step is introduced, modeled, and practiced. In direct phonics instruction, children are initially taught to convert letters into sounds. Later, they are taught to combine or blend sounds into recognizable words.

Almost any skill can be taught by breaking it down into component steps, providing clear instructions and ample practice, immediately correcting mistakes, and liberally reinforcing its appropriate use (Table 7.5).

Table 7.4   Methods to Teach Phoneme Awareness

1. Phoneme isolation: Recognizing individual sounds in words

    Tell me the first sound in "paste." Answer: /p/

2. Phoneme identity: Recognizing a common sound in different words

    Tell me the sound that is the same in "bike," "boy," and "bell." Answer: /b/

3. Phoneme categorization: Recognizing the phoneme that does not belong

    Which word does not belong: bus, bun, rug? Answer: rug

4. Phoneme blending: Listening to separately spoken phonemes and combining them to form a spoken word

    What word is /s/ /k/ /ü/ /l/? Answer: school

5. Phoneme segmentation: Breaking words into sounds by counting phonemes

    How many sounds are in "ship"? Answer: three (/sh/ /i/ /p/)

6. Phoneme deletion: Recognizing the word that remains when a phoneme is deleted

    What is "smile" without the /s/? Answer: mile

Source: From National Reading Panel (2000). Used with permission.

Image 7.2 A Phonics-Based Reading Program. Texts emphasize the repetition of words with the same phonemes.

The cat sat on Sam's lap.
The cat had a nap.
Sam will pat the cat.

Typically, children are first taught very basic tasks that have a high probability of success. Then, teachers help children build upon early skills until they demonstrate mastery in more advanced tasks. Advocates of direct instruction believe that children who continue to show learning problems despite average cognitive ability lack adequate instruction; they do not have some underlying disorder that renders them unable to learn (Adams & Carnine, 2003).

Decoding Unfamiliar Words

The final basic reading skill is the ability to read unfamiliar words. New readers can approach novel words in at least two ways. The first method is called **phonemic mediation**. Readers with adequate phoneme awareness and phonics skills can sound out unfamiliar words, translating them into spoken language. Then, they examine whether the word they decode is familiar and makes sense in the sentence.

Consider the following sentence: Cat has a snack. A beginning reader might know the first three words in the sentence but be unfamiliar with the word *snack*. He might use phonics skills to sound out the word by translating each letter into its corresponding phoneme: /s/ - /n/ - /a?/ - /k/. Then, he examines whether the resulting combination of phonemes corresponds to his existing spoken vocabulary. For example, he might think to himself, "The word sounds like *snack*. I know what a *snack* is. The word *snack* makes sense in the sentence, so the word must be *snack*."

A second method to decode unfamiliar words relies on children's memories and the use of contextual cues. If children lack phoneme awareness or phonics skills, they may try to infer words based on their appearance, other words in the sentence, or contextual cues (e.g., pictures).

In the sentence "Cat has a snack," a beginning reader might attempt to guess at the meaning of the word *snack* based on its length or beginning letter. Then, he might use pictures to test whether his inference is correct. In many cases, use of appearance and contextual cues result in successful reading. However, in some cases, these strategies lead to reading errors. For example, a child might incorrectly read the sentence as "Cat has a sack" because he sees a picture of the cat holding a bag of candy.

Table 7.5 Using Direct Instruction to Teach Reading

Step 1: The teacher explicitly states the goals for the lesson.

Today, we are going to learn how to read words that contain the letters "st" and make the sound /st/. By the end of the lesson, you will be able to read words that have /st/ in them.

Step 2: The teacher breaks down material into small steps, giving students the chance to practice each step.

Here are the letters "st." What are the letters? (Child answers "st.")

They make the /st/ sound. What sound do they make? (Child answers /st/.)

Step 3: Teacher provides clear and detailed instructions.

Let's practice some words that start with /st/. All of these words begin with the /st/ sound. Ready? (Teacher gives examples.)

Step 4: Teacher provides guidance during initial practice.

Start with this word. (Teacher points to each part of the word as child reads it.)

Step 5: Teacher provides systematic feedback and corrects child's mistakes immediately.

Now read this word. (Child correctly reads the word "stop.")

Good. Now this one. (Child incorrectly reads the word "stem.")

No. The word is "stem." Read it again with me.

Step 6: Teacher gives additional practice, either during seatwork, homework, or during the next lesson.

During the last lesson, we learned about words that begin with /st/. Today, we're going to review and practice more /st/ words.

Brain Areas Involved in Word Reading

Three areas of the brain are important to reading (Image 7.3). The first area is the left occipito-temporal cortex, a brain region located near the boundary of the occipital and temporal lobes. In this region, a small area known as the left fusiform gyrus seems to be critical to our ability to detect words. Functional MRI studies indicate that the **left fusiform gyrus** helps us recognize familiar printed words. It is likely that this brain region is especially involved in our ability to read rapidly and accurately. Damage to the left fusiform gyrus renders people unable to recognize familiar words. Instead, people with damage to this brain region must sound out even simple, frequently occurring words. Their reading is slow and laborious (L. Cohen et al., 2002; McCandliss, Cohen, & Dehaene, 2003).

Two other brain regions are responsible for converting graphemes into phonemes (Kovelman et al., 2012). The first is the left inferior frontal cortex, located in a portion of the frontal lobe known as **Broca's area**. The second is the left temporo-parietal cortex. This brain region is located between the temporal and parietal lobes and roughly corresponds to **Wernicke's area**. These brain regions seem to be responsible for our ability to sound out novel words (Frackowiak et al., 2004; Shaywitz & Shaywitz, 2005).

Evidence implicating the left inferior frontal cortex and left temporo-parietal cortex in reading comes from two sources. First, damage to these regions renders people unable to sound out novel words. However, people with damage to these regions are often able to recognize and read familiar words based on their appearance. Second, electrical stimulation of these brain areas disrupts the ability to sound out novel words in healthy individuals. However, electrical stimulation to these regions does not interfere with the ability to recognize familiar words (Cao, Bitan, Chou, Burman, & Booth, 2006).

By measuring activity in the brain, researchers have identified a neurological pathway that underlies our ability to read. Approximately 200 milliseconds after a word is presented, it is processed by the left occipito-temporal regions. These regions are involved in detecting and processing familiar words. Words that require phonological decoding (i.e., unfamiliar words) are further processed by the left temporo-parietal area approximately 150 milliseconds later. This area allows us to sound out novel words. Complex words may also be processed by the left inferior frontal region approximately 100 milliseconds later. The left inferior frontal region helps us understand the word's meaning and its association with other words in the sentence (Rayner et al., 2001; Simos et al., 2005).

Image 7.3 Brain Areas Involved in Word Reading

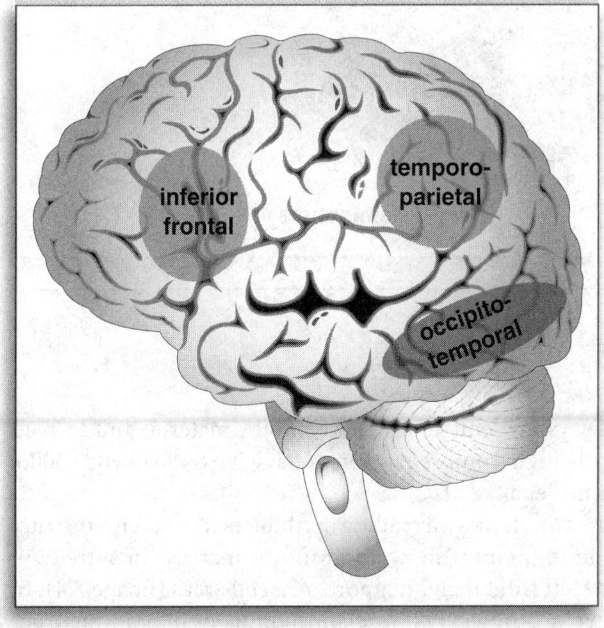

Source: From Rayner, Foorman, Perfetti, Pesetsky, and Seidenberg (2001).

Note: Printed words are first processed by the left occipito-temporal region, which allows us to recognize and read common words. Uncommon words are processed by the left temporo-parietal cortex, which allows us to sound out novel words. The left inferior frontal regions help us interpret the word's meaning and context within the sentence.

Causes of Word Reading Problems

Brain Abnormalities

Abnormal functioning of the left inferior frontal cortex and left temporo-parietal cortex probably underlies many instances of reading disabilities. Children with reading disabilities show less activity in these brain regions when processing novel words compared to youths without reading problems. Decreased activity of these left hemisphere brain regions might explain deficits in phonological awareness among youths with reading disabilities (Shaywitz & Shaywitz, 2005; Simos et al., 2002).

Instead of relying on the left frontal and temporo-parietal areas to process language, children with reading disabilities often use other brain areas in the right hemisphere. Specifically, many children with reading disabilities rely on the right frontal cortex, a brain area believed to be responsible

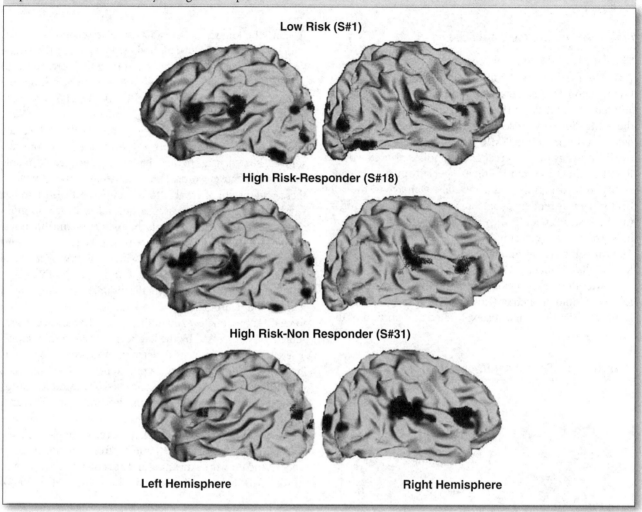

Image 7.4 Effects of Phonics Instruction on Brain Activity. Researchers classified kindergarteners into three groups: children who showed normal reading (top row), children who showed initial reading problems but improved following phonics instruction (middle row), and children who showed initial reading problems but did not improve following phonics instruction (bottom row). Normal readers and children who improved their reading learned to rely on left hemisphere brain regions responsible for language processing. Children who continued to have reading problems continued to rely on right hemisphere areas.

Source: From Simos et al. (2005). Used with permission.

for processing visual information. Interestingly, older children with reading disabilities show greater reliance on right hemisphere brain regions than younger children with the disorder (Kovelman et al., 2012).

These findings indicate that older children with reading disabilities may learn to compensate for their poor phonics skills in three ways. First, they may rely on the appearance of the word to guess its meaning. Second, they may use the context of the sentence or the story to infer the word's meaning. Third, they may simply memorize words based on their appearance. Although these strategies can be effective for early readers, they are almost always inadequate to read complex material and to read with high comprehension (Shaywitz & Shaywitz, 2005; Simos et al., 2002).

Children with reading disabilities who receive instruction in phonics show a significant increase in activity in the left frontal and temporo-parietal areas (Image 7.4). In several studies, two to eight months of phonics instruction caused significant increases in left hemisphere activity. After instruction, the brain activity of children with and without reading disabilities was indistinguishable. Phonics instruction may normalize brain activity among children with reading disabilities, helping these children process words like normal readers (Aylward et al., 2003; Shaywitz et al., 2004).

Cognitive Processing Problems

Most children with reading disabilities have underlying deficits in basic reading skills. These children often display marked deficits in phonological awareness, that is, the ability to perceive, understand, and process individual sounds in a stream of speech. A recent meta-analysis, investigating the relationship between underlying cognitive processing skills and children's academic functioning, showed the strongest association between phonological processing and children's ability to decode words. Overall, children with reading disabilities show phonological processing scores that are one and one-third standard deviations lower than their typically developing classmates (Johnson et al., 2010).

Phonological processing skills are important because they form the basis of later phonics skills. For example, children initially learn to isolate phonemes (i.e., the first sound in "car" is /c/), segment phonemes (e.g., there are three sounds in "shop": /sh/ /o/ /p/), blend phonemes (e.g., the sounds /s/ /t/ /r/ /ee/ /t/ make "street"), and manipulate phonemes (e.g., "car" with a /f/ instead of a /c/ is "far"). Later, they are able to use these phonemic skills to phonetically sound out words (e.g., the letters C-A-T spell /c/ /a/ /t/ or "cat"). Children who have deficits in phonological awareness will likely have difficulty with phonetic mediation. Instead of using phonics principles to decode words, these children often rely on memory, word appearance, and contextual cues to infer word meaning. When reading frequently occurring words, they show few problems, because they have memorized each word's appearance. When reading novel words, however, they are prone to mistakes because they are unable to decode the word.

Children's lack of phoneme awareness and phonics skills are especially noticeable when they are asked to read pseudowords, that is, words that follow basic principles of the English language but have no meaning. Examples of pseudowords include *throught*, *plesh*, and *britter*. Children with adequate phoneme awareness and phonics skills are able to sound out these words. Children without adequate phoneme awareness are usually unable to correctly decode pseudowords. Instead, they may mistakenly "read" these words according to their appearance: *thought*, *flesh*, and *bitter*.

Treatment of Word Reading Problems

Explicit Instruction in Phoneme Awareness and Phonics

The National Institute for Child Health and Human Development commissioned a group of experts to determine the most effective methods of reading instruction.

The group, called the **National Reading Panel** (NRP), gathered data from numerous studies, comparing different methods to teach reading. The panel concluded that methods that provided explicit instruction in letter recognition and phoneme awareness were most effective in helping children learn to read (National Reading Panel, 2000).

More recent research has confirmed the importance of systematic instruction in phoneme awareness and phonics. Children who receive direct instruction, in particular, show large gains in phoneme awareness, word recognition, and reading comprehension relative to children who do not receive direct instruction. Furthermore, direct instruction is effective in improving the reading skills of children with reading disabilities. The best outcomes are generally attained by children who begin receiving direct instruction in kindergarten and continue to participate in direct instruction through the second or third grade (Adams & Carnine, 2003; Carlson & Francis, 2002).

Figure 7.7 summarizes the NRP findings with respect to phoneme awareness. Explicitly teaching children to recognize and manipulate phonemes had a large and direct effect on their phoneme awareness skills. Explicit training in phoneme awareness was also associated with significant gains in reading and spelling.

Figure 7.8 summarizes the NRP's (2000) findings regarding the effects of explicit phonics instruction on children's reading. Overall, children who receive systematic instruction in phonics show significantly greater gains in reading than children who do not receive phonics instruction. Phonics programs that encourage children to convert letters (graphemes) into sounds (phonemes) and combine or blend sounds into recognizable words were associated with the greatest improvement in reading. Systematic phonics instruction is most effective when it is administered individually or in small groups and when it is initiated before second grade. Phonics-based reading instruction is also associated with gains in children's reading comprehension (Kerins, 2006).

Whole Language Instruction

Whole language instruction is based on the belief that learning to read is a natural process that occurs through continued exposure to spoken and written language. Advocates of whole language instruction criticize systematic phonics instruction in which teachers carefully introduce, model, and reinforce the relationship between words and sounds. Instead, proponents of whole language argue that children will naturally discover the rules of reading on their own, as long as they are given opportunities to read and they are allowed to direct their own learning (Y. M. Goodman, 1989; K. S. Goodman, 1992).

Whole language approaches to reading instruction are "learner-centered" and designed to increase children's interest in reading. Although instructional approaches vary, teachers who adopt the principles of whole language allow

Figure 7.7   Effects of Phoneme Awareness Training on Children's Reading and Spelling

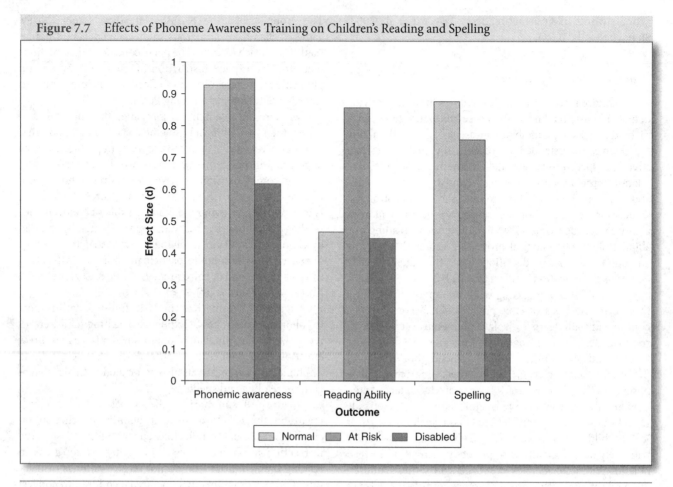

Source: Based on NRP (2000).

Note: Children who receive systematic instruction in phoneme awareness show greater gains in phoneme skills, reading, and spelling compared to children who do not receive training in phoneme awareness. Training can improve phoneme awareness and reading skills in normal children, at-risk children, and youths with reading disabilities.

children to select their own reading materials in order to capitalize on their motivation to learn. In some cases, children might dictate stories to the teacher. After the teacher transcribes the stories, children are encouraged to read them. Teachers also encourage students to use contextual cues and pictures to interpret the meaning of the stories they read.

Little research supports the efficacy of whole language instruction. Stahl, McKenna, and Pagnucco (1994) found only 14 studies that included quantitative data for investigating the efficacy of whole language approaches to teaching reading. These studies provided some evidence that whole language reading instruction increased children's reading comprehension. However, Stahl and colleagues concluded that there were too few studies to support the adoption of whole language techniques in the classroom.

Whole Word Instruction

Whole word instruction is an extension of the whole language approach. Both whole word and whole language

approaches emphasize the meaning behind printed material rather than the ability to sound out words. In whole word instruction, teachers encourage children to process words as wholes, rather than break them down into phonemes. Initially, children learn to recognize a limited number of common words on sight. Then, their reading vocabulary is gradually expanded as teachers introduce new words during the course of reading practice.

In traditional whole word instruction, teachers usually do not provide explicit instruction in phonics. Advocates of the whole word approach believe that breaking words down into phonemes is artificial and not meaningful to students. Instead, teachers might present whole words on flashcards and encourage students to recognize words based on their appearance. This approach is believed to have two chief advantages over phonics-based instruction. First, by learning words as wholes, children may be less likely to be confused by irregular phonemes in the English language. For example, *pint* and *hint* have different pronunciations despite the fact they both end in *int* (Rayner et al., 2001). Second, practitioners of

Figure 7.8 Effects of Systematic Phonics Instruction on Reading and Spelling

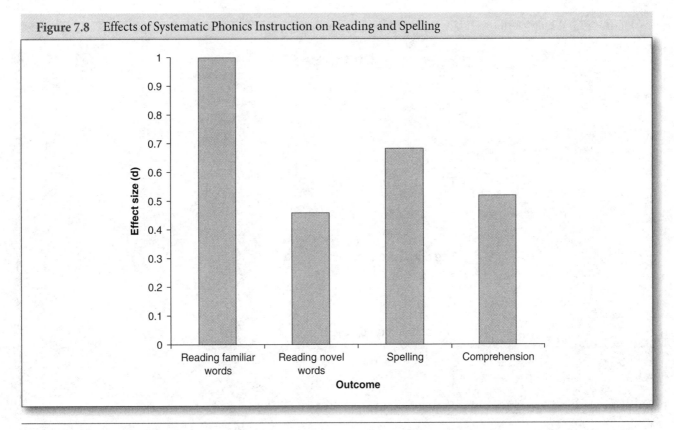

Source: Based on NRP (2000).

Note: Children who receive systematic phonics training, especially training conducted before the second grade, show improvements in basic reading, spelling, and reading comprehension compared to children who do not receive systematic phonics instruction.

the whole word approach argue that this approach is more meaningful to children than phonics instruction and, consequently, improves children's motivation to read.

Whole word instruction often relies on leveled texts to increase children's reading vocabulary. **Leveled texts** are short books that are ordered according to the difficulty of vocabulary, repetition of words, inclusion of novel words, use of picture cues, and complexity of sentence structure (Figure 7.9). Children are initially assigned to low-leveled texts, based on the number of sight words they know. Then, teachers gradually present more difficult texts to expand the child's reading vocabulary.

Reading Recovery is one of the most frequently used whole word approaches to reading instruction. Some data indicate that Reading Recovery is effective at reducing reading problems among children with reading delays. Several studies indicate that as many as 81% of children with reading problems show marked improvement in their reading ability following participation in Reading Recovery (Zane, 2005).

On the other hand, much of the research supporting Reading Recovery is flawed (D'Agostino & Murphy, 2004; Zane, 2005). First, in several studies, attrition was very high among children who received Reading Recovery compared to children who received other forms of reading instruction.

For example, in one study, more than one third of youths who participated in Reading Recovery dropped out of the program before completion. Only those children who successfully completed the Reading Recovery program (and who presumably had the best outcomes) were used to evaluate the program's effectiveness.

Second, teachers who administered Reading Recovery were often better trained than teachers in the comparison groups. In one study, Reading Recovery teachers received two years of training in the program, whereas teachers who administered the comparison treatment received only 2 weeks of training. The efficacy of Reading Recovery, therefore, may be due to the expertise of teachers rather than the efficacy of treatment.

Finally, Reading Recovery is less efficacious when administered to children with reading disabilities compared to youths without serious reading problems (Elbaum, Vaughn, Hughes, & Moody, 2000). Chapman, Tunmer, and Prochnow (2001) showed that Reading Recovery improved the decoding skills of youths *without* Reading Disorder but was largely ineffective for youths *with* serious reading problems. Reading Recovery, therefore, may be most efficacious for youths *least* in need of reading remediation.

Figure 7.9 Whole Word Instruction

On the Bed

The mouse sat on the bed.

The cat sat on the bed.

The dog sat on the bed.

The cow sat on the bed.

The elephant sat on the bed.

Note: Children read leveled texts, like this one. Each text introduces new words, such as "elephant." Children are encouraged to use pictures and other contextual cues to derive the meaning of words.

READING FLUENCY AND COMPREHENSION

Fluency and Comprehension Skills

Fluency

Reading fluency refers to the ability to read rapidly, accurately, and with proper expression. Fluent readers recognize words quickly, attend to important words in sentences more than unimportant words, and emphasize critical words so that sentences make sense.

Reading fluency is important. Fluent readers spend less mental energy processing text. Instead, their cognitive resources can be directed at other tasks, like extracting meaning from what they read. Fluent readers also spend less time reading individual words and sentences. Therefore, they encounter more words and gain relatively greater practice with reading than do disfluent readers. Finally, fluent readers are able to determine where to place emphasis or where to pause so that sentences makes sense. Reading fluency, therefore, allows readers to better interpret and understand text.

Children become fluent readers through extensive practice with reading. Initially, children must sound out almost all words in order to gain familiarity with the irregularities of the English language. Over time, children begin to recognize frequently occurring words on sight. Consequently, their speed and accuracy increases. As children's reading experience accumulates, they encounter more novel words, which gradually become familiar "sight" words. Practice allows children to make reading automatic; that is, practice lets children "turn low-frequency words into high-frequency words" (Rayner et al., 2001, p. 40).

Comprehension

Reading comprehension refers to children's ability to read text for meaning, to remember information from the text, and to use information to solve problems or share with others. Reading comprehension is an active process in which children construct meaning from what they read. Reading comprehension, therefore, depends on the interaction between the reader and the text. The reader's understanding of the text will depend on her basic reading skills, reading fluency, and prior knowledge.

Reading comprehension depends principally on children's basic reading skills and reading fluency. In order to understand text, children must be able to recognize words. If children are unable to recognize familiar words or incorrectly decode novel words, their reading comprehension will suffer. Children's reading comprehension also depends on their ability to read quickly. To understand text, children must be able to combine information from the beginning and end of the passage. Consider the following sentence:

Matt has a fat cat that likes to wear a hat.

A child who must sound out individual words in the sentence might have difficulty remembering information presented early in the sentence by the time he reaches the end of the sentence. For example, a disfluent reader might be able to answer the question, "What does the cat like to wear?" but not "Whose cat likes to wear a hat?"

Reading comprehension also depends on children's general language skills. Indeed, the correlation between people's spoken language comprehension and reading comprehension is .90 (Rayner et al., 2001). Many of the same abilities important to reading comprehension are also important to the comprehension of spoken language. First, children must possess adequate information processing skills to comprehend passages. For example, when listening to or reading a passage, children must be able to attend to the most important information, ignore irrelevant information, notice the sequence of events, and pay attention to causal relationships in the story. Second, listening and reading comprehension depends greatly on children's working memory. Children must be able to remember information from passages long enough to answer questions. Third, children must also have adequate contextual knowledge about the story in order to make sense of the information that is presented. For example, children who read a story about Vikings will have difficulty comprehending the story if they have never been taught about Vikings before.

Reading comprehension is influenced by practice. Children with greater exposure to stories gain experience understanding passages. Reading experience also increases children's reading vocabulary, fluency, and general knowledge, which further promote reading comprehension. Ironically, children with adequate basic reading skills are more likely to practice reading and, therefore, develop high levels of reading fluency and comprehension. In contrast, children with basic reading skill deficits are less likely to practice and, consequently, are more likely to show problems with fluency and comprehension (Rayner et al., 2001; Shaywitz, Holford, Holahan, & Fletcher, 1995).

Fluency and Comprehension Problems

Phoneme Awareness and Phonics Skill Deficits

Children with reading fluency and comprehension problems often have histories of poor phoneme awareness and word-decoding skills. Many of these children never developed the basic reading skills necessary to sound out novel words. Consequently, their exposure to novel words and practice with reading was limited. Problems reading novel words often lead to an overall reduction in the rate of reading (i.e., fluency) and accuracy with which children can answer questions about the passages they read (i.e., comprehension; Lyon, Fletcher, & Barnes, 2003).

Cognitive Processing Problems

Reading fluency and comprehension problems are also associated with specific cognitive processing problems. Several studies have shown three deficits to be associated with reading fluency and comprehension problems: (a) slow processing speed, (b) poor verbal working memory, and (c) deficits in rapid automatized naming (Johnson et al., 2010).

Processing speed refers to a child's cognitive efficiency, that is, her ability to quickly and accurately perform relatively simple tasks without expending a high degree of effort. Processing speed is usually measured by asking children to scan a visual array and identify a specific object (e.g., if given a page of shapes, find as many triangles as possible), to match objects (e.g., match the correct symbol with its number), or to make simple decisions (e.g., which of the three pictures doesn't belong?) in a short period of time. Children with above average processing speed can perform simple cognitive tasks automatically and, therefore, can devote cognitive resources to high-level thinking and reasoning. Because these children can read quickly and accurately, they can spend more energy thinking about the meaning of the text. Children with below average processing speed find lower level cognitive tasks slow and effortful; consequently, they have fewer resources available for higher order mental activity. Often, these children read slowly and spend a great deal of energy sounding out words; as a result, they have less energy to spend on comprehension.

Working memory is the ability to simultaneously hold and manipulate multiple pieces of information in short-term memory to solve problems. Verbal working memory is a specific kind of working memory for verbal information (e.g., words, sentences). In everyday life, verbal working memory allows you to remember the names of new friends you meet at a party. In clinical settings, verbal working memory is measured by asking children to recall and manipulate a series of numbers, words, or sentences:

I am going to read a list of numbers and letters to you in mixed-up order. When I am finished, tell me the numbers first in numerical order, followed by the letters in alphabetical order.

Children with above average verbal working memories can keep verbal information in short-term memory long enough so that it can be used to solve immediate problems. When reading, these children can keep details about the early part of a sentence or paragraph in mind while simultaneously reading the later part of a sentence. Their verbal working memory permits greater reading comprehension. Children with below average verbal working memories have difficulty maintaining and manipulating information in short-term memory. When reading, these children may forget important information presented earlier in the text and, consequently, show poor comprehension (Swanson & Stomel, 2012).

A third cognitive processing problem related to reading fluency and comprehension is **rapid automatized naming** (RAN; Denckla & Rudel, 1976). RAN refers to the ability to recall the names of a series of familiar items as quickly as possible. In everyday life, RAN might be measured by counting the number of songs on your iPOD that you can name in one minute. In clinical settings, RAN is measured by counting the number of items in a certain category that children can name while working against a time limit (e.g., "Name as many foods as possible in one minute"). It can also be assessed by presenting an array of pictures, colors, letters, or numbers in random order and asking children to name each stimulus in the array while working against a time limit.

Experts are not certain why RAN is important to reading. It is possible that RAN depends on both verbal working memory (e.g., the recall of words) and processing speed (e.g., the automaticity of processing), which are, themselves, important to language. Whatever the reason, considerable research has shown that children's capacity for RAN predicts their reading achievement. Furthermore, deficits in RAN are associated with the emergence of reading disability (Norton & Wolf, 2012).

Double Deficits

Children with reading disability can be differentiated into three groups based on the nature of their reading problems and underlying cognitive processing deficits (O'Brien et al., 2012). Wolf and Bowers (1999) developed the **double-deficit model** to explain this differentiation. Some children show problems with word reading. These children often have deficits in phonological processing, phonics skills, and pseudoword reading. In early elementary school, they may rely on sight words and orthographic recognition to read. However, by middle school, these children experience problems with word reading and reading comprehension because of the greater frequency of novel words (e.g., *chlorophyll, diffusion, photosynthesis*). Their deficits in phonetic mediation catch up to them.

A second group of children shows few problems with word reading or phonemic awareness but does display poor reading fluency. These children often have underlying deficits in processing speed, verbal working memory, and/or RAN. They can read words accurately, but their reading is slow and laborious. These children may also have poor reading comprehension because of their slow reading speed and working memory deficits. They often have difficulty remembering information from the beginning of the passage by the time they reach the end of the passage.

A third, small group of children shows impairments in both basic reading skills and reading fluency. These children with double-deficits show the greatest level of reading problems overall (Frijters et al., 2011).

It is rare for children to show problems with reading comprehension but no deficits in phoneme awareness, decoding, or fluency. Only about 6% of youths with reading problems show difficulty in comprehension alone. Youths with comprehension problems, but not basic reading or fluency problems, tend to have underlying difficulties with oral language and reasoning (Leach, Scarborough, & Rescorla, 2003; Ransby & Swanson, 2003).

Treatment of Fluency and Comprehension Problems

Improving Fluency

Reading fluency depends on practice. Keith Stanovich (1986) noticed how children who had success with reading in the first few years of school, tended to become fluent readers in later childhood and adolescence. In contrast, children who struggle initially with reading, especially beyond the third grade, often have lifelong fluency problems. Stanovich described this divergence in reading skills as the **Matthew Effect**, based on Matthew 25:29, "To everyone who has, more will be given; but from the one who has not, even what he has will be taken away." To develop reading fluency, children must practice. However, children with initial reading problems often avoid reading and fall further behind their classmates.

Most teachers rely on one of two approaches to provide children with reading practice. One tactic is called **guided oral reading**. In guided oral reading, the child reads and rereads a text aloud until she becomes proficient. Teachers or peers listen to the child, provide assistance sounding out words, and correct reading errors. Sometimes, children read along with audiotapes, videos, or computer programs.

A second strategy to improve fluency is **independent silent reading**. For example, teachers who use the Sustained Silent Reading (SSR) or Drop Everything and Read (DEAR) programs devote 15 to 30 minutes of class time each day to independent silent reading. Students are allowed to select their own reading material, and they do not receive systematic help and correction from teachers or peers.

The NRP (2000) reviewed the effect of guided oral reading and independent silent reading on children's reading fluency and comprehension. Children who participated in guided oral reading showed increased reading accuracy, reading speed, and reading comprehension compared to children who did not receive opportunities for guided oral reading (Figure 7.10). Guided oral reading is effective for normal readers and children with reading disabilities (Chard, Vaughn, & Tyler, 2003; Kuhn & Stahl, 2003). The NRP (2000) was unable to draw firm conclusions regarding the merits of independent silent reading. Too few studies were conducted

Figure 7.10 Effects of Guided Oral Reading on Accuracy, Speed, and Comprehension

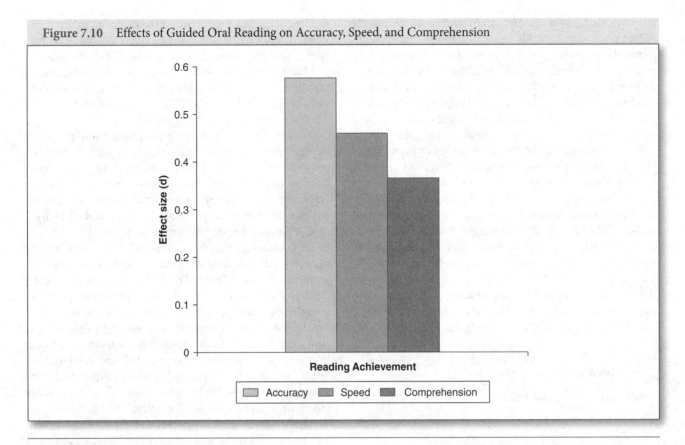

Source: Based on National Reading Panel (2000).

Note: Guided oral reading is associated with increases in children's fluency and comprehension.

to adequately evaluate this approach. However, most of the research that had been conducted indicated that silent reading is not associated with increases in reading fluency.

What about children who continue to struggle with reading fluency despite ample practice? Interventions for these children should target underlying deficits in cognitive processing. For example, many children read slowly because of deficits in phonemic awareness and phonetic decoding skills. These children would likely benefit from a phonics-based intervention that systematically teaches them the relationships between orthography and phonology.

Some children, however, exhibit adequate word reading skills but still read slowly. Often, these children show deficits in verbal working memory, processing speed, and RAN. Until recently, effective treatment for these children had remained elusive. However, Maryanne Wolf and colleagues (2000) have developed a comprehensive intervention program to improve the reading fluency of children with underlying memory and automatized naming deficits. Their intervention is called retrieval, automaticity, vocabulary, elaboration, and orthography (**RAVE-O**), an intensive program designed to improve children's ability to automatically decode, identify, and understand words. RAVE-O has three components: (a) automaticity, (b) semantic facilitation, and (c) lexical retrieval (Wolf, Gottwald, & Orkin, 2009).

A primary goal of RAVE-O is to improve the **automaticity** of children's reading (Wolf, Barzillai, et al., 2009). To help children read words more quickly, and with less effort, teachers emphasize certain "core words" that form the basis of their reading vocabulary. These words are organized in groups based on similar rhymes. For example, "hat," "mat," and "cat" share the /at/ rhyme. Children learn to recognize related core words each week as well as common rhyme patterns. They also begin to recognize words quickly based on orthographic patterns (e.g., –at). Teachers play various games to emphasize these patterns so that children can identify them quickly. For example, "sound sliders" is a game in which children combine initial phonemes with base rhymes to make new words (e.g., /f/ + at = fat, /m/ + at = mat, /r/ + at = rat). Children also practice recognizing orthographic patterns, discriminating patterns (e.g., –at versus –an), and matching patterns to word sounds while playing computer games. With practice, children are able to process common words with greater automaticity.

A second objective of RAVE-O is **semantic facilitation**. This component of treatment is based on the notion that word recognition can be increased by greater semantic knowledge. That is, if children had larger reading vocabularies, they would read more quickly. As we have seen, one method to increase children's semantic knowledge is to teach "core words" each week. Another strategy is to use image cards to help children learn and recall frequently encountered words quickly and easily. Image cards contain pictorial representations of common words designed to help children with memory deficits recall them. Multiple meanings for each word might be displayed on the card, to help children appreciate the flexibility of language. For example, the word "jam" might be shown as "a topping for toast" and as "a child in trouble." Teachers can also use very short stories, called "minute stories," which contain only words previously introduced in the program, to give students repeated practice reading and recalling the meaning of these words.

A final component of treatment involves improving children's **lexical retrieval** strategies. Often children with RAN deficits have difficulty retrieving words. Image cards can help with lexical retrieval. Another technique to improve word recall is the Sam Spade technique. In the movie *The Maltese Falcon*, Sam Spade is a private detective who uses clues to solve a case. Children are taught to be word detectives to correctly retrieve words that might be "on the tip of their tongues." Specifically, they are taught to use the following cues:

1. What does the word start with?

2. What does it sound like?

3. What is it similar to?

4. Is it a short word (or a long word)?

These four questions (each remembered by an s) can prompt children to recall words more quickly.

The efficacy of RAVE-O was investigated in a randomized, controlled study of 279 children with reading disabilities (Morris et al., 2012). Youths were randomly assigned to one of four conditions: (a) traditional phonemic awareness and word identification skills training, (b) RAVE-O, (c) phonemic awareness training plus study skills training, or (d) math instruction and study skills training (a control condition). All interventions were conducted 5 days per week for 70 sessions. As we might expect, at the end of treatment, children in the three active treatment groups showed significantly more improvement in word reading than children in the control group. More importantly, children who participated in RAVE-O showed the greatest improvement in reading fluency. RAVE-O was also effective at improving reading comprehension. These findings indicate that intensive instruction in automaticity, semantic knowledge, and lexical retrieval can help children with deficits in reading fluency (and comprehension).

Improving Comprehension

Children with reading disability will not develop adequate reading comprehension on their own. Reading comprehension skills must be systematically introduced and modeled in the classroom. Children who are provided with systematic training in reading comprehension show significant improvements compared to youths who do not receive explicit instruction. Systematic instruction is associated with increases in children's memory for information, speed of reading, understanding, and ability to apply information to answer questions or solve problems (NRP, 2000; Rosenshine et al., 1996; Therrien, Wickstrom, & Jones, 2006).

Interventions for reading comprehension programs depend on the nature of the text. Children with reading disability often have difficulty with narrative texts (e.g., stories) because they show deficits in story grammar (Mason & Hagaman, 2012). *Story grammar* refers to knowledge of the components and structure of stories, such as their characters, setting, action or problem to be resolved, conclusion or resolution, and tone or emotion. Children with reading disability are often unaware of many of these aspects of story grammar and recall fewer of them than typically developing children. Furthermore, they exhibit deficits in story grammar regardless of whether they are listening to or reading stories.

Interventions to improve **narrative text comprehension** systematically teach children to recognize and retain information about story grammar (Mason & Hagaman, 2012). For example, story mapping is a technique suitable for younger readers. As children read stories aloud, the teacher emphasizes aspects of story grammar when they occur. Then, she organizes each aspect as a visual representation in a picture or schematic to aid children's recall (e.g., images of straw, sticks, and brick to represent events in *The Three Little Pigs*). With practice, children learn to recognize aspects of story grammar independently and complete their own story maps. Another technique, appropriate for older children, is self-questioning. Although good readers naturally ask questions about story grammar while reading a narrative, poor readers need to be taught this skill. In self-questioning, children are initially prompted by teachers to ask questions about purpose, characters, plot, and resolution before, during, and after reading. With practice, children begin to ask (and answer) these questions independently.

Understanding **expository writing** is especially challenging to children with reading disability. Expository text, which conveys facts and information, tends to use relatively unfamiliar text structure (e.g., lists, compare-and-contrasts), adopts complex vocabulary, and assumes prior knowledge that children might lack (Saenz & Fuchs, 2002). To understand expository writing, children need to be taught to break down and reorganize the text, using text enhancements. **Text enhancements** are visual aids or routines that assist students in identifying, organizing, understanding, and recalling important information (Image 7.5). Text enhancements can be simple (e.g., highlighting key terms in a textbook) or elaborate (e.g., drawing Venn diagrams to represent similarities and differences between groups). The most commonly used text enhancements (Mason & Hagaman, 2012) are the following:

- *Graphic organizers:* Diagrams, figures, or charts that display information simply and make abstract concepts concrete

- *Cognitive maps:* Lines, arrows, or flowcharts that show relationships between concepts, to reflect cause-and-effect or similarities and differences
- *Semantic mapping:* Hierarchies that show how subordinate constructs (e.g., lizards, snakes, turtles) relate to a superordinate construct (e.g., reptiles)
- *Visual displays:* Graphic organizers that represent temporal information (e.g., the life cycle of the frog, a timeline of events leading up to the American Revolution)
- *Mnemonics:* Memory aids to increase recall (e.g., HOMES can help you recall the names of the Great Lakes)
- *Computer-assisted instruction:* Enhancements embedded in digital text (e.g., hypermedia that displays definitions, pictures, or video of key terms)

A recent meta-analysis provides support for the efficacy of interventions designed to increase reading comprehension in children with reading disabilities (Berkeley et al., 2010). Overall, interventions designed to improve reading comprehension yielded a moderate effect size ($d = .65$). Approximately 40% of children with reading disabilities who participate in these interventions earn higher reading comprehension scores than youths with learning disabilities in the comparison groups. Furthermore, these interventions produced both immediate gains in reading comprehension and sustained improvement in reading comprehension over time. There was also some evidence that the interventions produced improvement in other areas such as word reading and fluency.

Interestingly, Berkeley and colleagues (2010) found that certain factors moderated the relationship between reading comprehension interventions and children's learning outcomes. First, interventions administered in universities and research facilities tended to yield stronger effects than interventions administered by teachers, other adult tutors, or computers. Second, interventions administered to small groups of children tended to be more efficacious than interventions administered to whole classrooms. Third, focused interventions of medium duration (1–4 weeks) tended to

more useful than very brief or very long interventions. Together, these findings indicate that the best interventions provide systematic, high-quality, and focused reading comprehension strategies to small groups of children.

Unsupported Therapies

There is a long history of attempting to treat reading disabilities using vision therapy. Beginning in the 1920s, one of the pioneers of learning disability research, Samuel Orton, suggested that reading disabilities are caused by problems with the visual system. His assertion led to a proliferation of training programs designed to correct visual-perceptual or visual-motor problems that presumably underlie children's reading problems. These therapies were later discredited and their use waned during the 1960s and 1970s. Today, however, some individuals continue to assert that learning disabilities are caused by subtle vision problems including abnormal focusing, jerky eye movements, misaligned or crossed eyes, visual-motor dysfunction, impairments in binocular vision, or perceptual or sensory-integration disturbances. These individuals claim that special vision therapies such as visual "training," muscle exercises, ocular "pursuit-and-tracking" exercises, or the use of special glasses, lens, or colored filters can correct these problems and improve academic performance.

After reviewing the scientific literature, the American Academy of Pediatrics concluded that children with learning disabilities have the same visual functioning as their classmates without disabilities (Handler et al., 2011). Furthermore, there is no consistent relationship between subtle visual abnormalities and academic performance. There is also no evidence that vision therapies improve children's academic skills. They conclude, "These ineffective, controversial methods of treatment may give parents and teachers a false sense of security that the child's reading difficulties are being addressed, may waste family and/or

Image 7.5 A timeline is one example of a text enhancement that can help children with reading comprehension. This fifth-grader's timeline shows events leading up to the American Revolution.

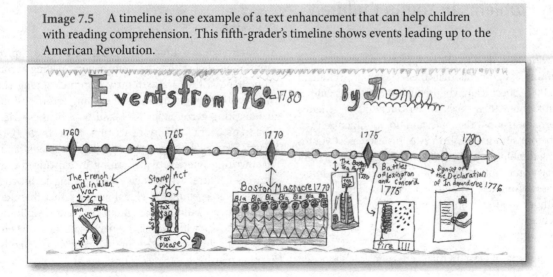

school time and resources, and may delay proper instruction or remediation" (p. 848).

WRITTEN EXPRESSION
Basic Writing Skills

Writing is a complex task that takes years to master. For most children, the writing process involves three steps: planning, translating, and reviewing (Hayes & Flower, 1980). First, children *plan* the writing task. Planning involves determining the purpose of the writing, generating a main topic and supporting ideas, and organizing these ideas so that they make sense.

Imagine that a teacher asks students to write a report on sharks. Most children would begin the writing process by identifying the purpose of the writing assignment and an appropriate format for the paper. An essay on shark behavior would be written differently than a creative story about a fictional shark. Then, children might gather information about sharks, identify the most important information that they want to include in their essays, and discard irrelevant information. Finally, children would likely spend time organizing their thoughts—generated from the information they gathered. Some children might outline their essays, whereas others might use diagrams or flow charts.

Second, children *translate* their ideas into written text. Translation depends on children's phoneme awareness, their knowledge of vocabulary and spelling, and the mechanics of writing (e.g., how they hold a pencil).

Third, children *review* their writing. Reviewing involves rereading their stories, identifying mistakes, and making changes. Mistakes can be at the level of individual words (e.g., illegible handwriting, misspellings), sentences (e.g., missing subject, predicate), or paragraphs (e.g., no topic sentence). Editing can also involve analyzing the composition's grammar and punctuation (e.g., are singular and plural verbs used correctly?) or theme (e.g., does the sentence make sense?).

Writing Problems in Young Children

Planning

Children with writing disabilities spend far less time and effort planning assignments than their classmates (Graham & Harris, 2000). Specifically, children with writing disabilities do not think about their goals for writing, do not generate much information about the topic, and do not organize their thoughts before sitting down to write. Instead, most youths with writing disabilities begin writing about the first relevant concept that comes into their minds. Then, they add information that is prompted by their first sentence. For example, a child without writing problems might write the following topic sentence:

> Sharks are some of the most dangerous animals in the ocean.

Then, she might follow up with additional sentences supporting her topic:

> Sharks have hundreds of teeth that are as sharp as knives.
>
> An adult shark can eat 100 pounds of fish each day.
>
> Sharks have been known to eat fish, seals, and even other sharks!

In contrast, a child with writing difficulties might begin his essay in the same way:

> Sharks are some of the most dangerous animals in the ocean.
>
> Sharks have hundreds of teeth that are as sharp as knives.

Then, he might follow up with a series of sentences that are prompted by the sentence that immediately precedes it. The result is a list of ideas that strays from the topic:

> If one cuts you, you will be in a lot of trouble.
>
> You will need to swim to shore and see a doctor.
>
> The doctor will tell you not to go out into the ocean again.
>
> You might swim in swimming pools.

This lack of planning, often shown by children with writing problems, has two adverse consequences. First, the stories of children with writing disabilities tend to be disjointed and difficult to follow. In the above example, the reader expects that the paragraph will be about shark's teeth or the fact that they are dangerous, but the actual text conveys a story about a swimmer. Second, the stories of children with disabilities tend to be brief. Indeed, children with writing disabilities tend to generate stories approximately one third shorter than those of their classmates. Because children with disabilities do not plan and organize their writing before they begin, they run out of ideas earlier than their peers (Graham, Harris, MacArthur, & Schwartz, 1991).

Translation

Children with writing disabilities often show problems translating their thoughts onto paper. Spelling errors and poor handwriting are extremely common among children with writing problems. Indeed, spelling errors and illegible handwriting account for 41% and 66% of the variance in children's overall quality of writing, respectively (Graham, Harris, & MacArthur, 2004). Spelling problems and poor handwriting interfere with writing by slowing the writing process. Children who struggle with spelling devote cognitive resources to spelling individual words, rather than focusing on sentence quality or paragraph coherence. Children who have difficulty with mechanics may write too slowly to keep up with the thoughts they want to convey. Consequently, their writing may be disorganized or illogical.

Reviewing

Children with writing disabilities review and edit their work differently than their classmates. When most children review their writing, they attend to all aspects of the text, including whether individual sentences make sense and whether paragraphs are organized into a coherent story.

In contrast, children with writing disabilities focus primarily on low-level writing mistakes when editing. Low-level mistakes include errors in capitalization, mistakes in punctuation, and illegible handwriting. A child with writing disabilities might write, "The boy and the girl *is* going to the party." However, he might edit the sentence by changing the order of the boy and the girl in the sentence, altering the punctuation, or rewriting the sentence so that it is more legible. In one study, approximately 70% of the revisions made by youths with writing problems involved surface-level changes that did not correct substantive errors (De La Paz, Swanson, & Graham, 1998; MacArthur, Graham, & Schwartz, 1991).

Writing Problems in Older Children

Older children with and without writing disability differ greatly in the quality of their composition. Specifically, they differ in six areas:

- *Productivity:* Children with writing disability simply write fewer words than their typically developing classmates. On average, their compositions are one-third shorter than those of children with average writing skills. Their lack of productivity is seen in both narrative and expository writing.
- *Lexical diversity:* Lexical diversity is typically assessed by counting the number of different root words in a composition. Children with writing disability write fewer words and use language that is less varied and more redundant.
- *Grammar:* Grammatical errors are the most noticeable and common problem shown by children with writing disability. They often omit essential parts of a sentence, have difficulty with subject-verb agreement, or mistakenly use pronouns and contractions (e.g., *their* vs. *they're*).
- *Sentence complexity:* Children with writing disability use less descriptive sentences than their peers. Sentence complexity is typically assessed by determining the average length of main clauses and dependent clauses in the child's writing. Consider the following narratives:

  I followed the rabbit all day until it ran into its hole.

  I followed the rabbit all day. It ran into its hole.

  Although both narratives have the same meaning, the first is more complex.

- *Spelling accuracy:* Children with writing disability often make spelling errors. Children with underlying phonological processing problems and reading disability often make dysphonetic spelling errors; that is, their errors indicate that they do not have an understanding of the relationship between phonetics and orthography. For example, a young child with adequate phonemic processing might spell

"telephone" as "telafone." However, a child without adequate phonemic processing might spell the word "talnofe," which does not correspond to the sound of the word. Dysphonetic spelling errors make children's compositions extremely difficult to read.
- *Story content:* Children with writing disability also receive lower ratings for overall story content than do their typically developing classmates. Specifically, they have difficulty (a) relating experiences or presenting information in a clear and focused manner, (b) structuring their writing in such a way that their main idea is clear and supported, (c) using an appropriate tone of voice and degree of formality for the purpose of the writing and the audience, and (d) adopting the writing conventions (e.g., punctuation, capitalization, paragraph breaks).

Treatment of Writing Problems

General Principles

Children with writing disability need systematic instruction, ample practice, and frequent feedback to help them overcome deficits in their spelling or writing skills (Mather & Wendling, 2011). MacArthur and colleagues (2012) offer the following general principles for treating children with writing disability:

- Children should be given systematic instruction in writing for different audiences and purposes.
- Instruction should involve the basic skills required for fluent text production, such as spelling, grammar, and punctuation.
- Instruction should teach the writing process: planning, translating, and reviewing. Children should also be taught writing strategies to help them engage this process with increasing independence.
- Writing instruction should be integrated with learning in content areas (e.g., history, literature). Children learn as they write.
- Children need ample time and practice to write and a supportive social environment in which to write and evaluate their writing.

Cognitive Strategy Instruction

One of the most effective methods of teaching writing skills to children with writing problems is Cognitive Strategy Instruction. Cognitive Strategy Instruction is based on the notion that poor writers lack effective strategies for planning, implementing, and evaluating their writing. Teachers provide students with various strategies for writing, appropriate for a wide range of writing tasks, give specific feedback regarding the quality of their writing, and offer ample opportunities to practice and improve their writing over time.

Cognitive Strategy Instruction relies on a model called **self-regulated strategy development (SRSD)**. The SRSD model consists of a series of stages that children learn to implement, practice, and evaluate (Graham, 2006; Reid et al., 2012). The SRSD stages include:

1. Develop and activate background knowledge: The teacher explains or models any skills or information needed to complete the writing assignment. For example, if the

assignment involves autobiographical writing, the teacher might explain the term *autobiography* and provide a short example of an autobiographical narrative.

2. Discuss the strategy: The teacher suggests a specific strategy for completing the writing task.

3. Model the strategy: The teacher presents each step in the strategy, emphasizing why each step is important. The teacher "thinks aloud," explaining her thought process behind each step. Modeling is extremely important because it makes normally covert processes overt and accessible to students.

4. Memorize the strategy: Students memorize each step in the strategy through repetition and variation. The more practice they receive, the easier they will recall the strategy when necessary.

5. Support the strategy: Teachers use scaffolding to make sure students are successful implementing the strategy. Initially, teachers offer a great deal of assistance; as students become more familiar with the strategy, they gradually reduce their level of support until students can implement it independently.

6. Independent performance: The teacher continues to monitor the students' use of the strategy and help them modify it, when necessary, to suit different situations.

The specific strategies used in the SRSD model vary depending on the writing task (Common Core State Standards, 2013). Tasks include argumentative writing (i.e., persuasion), explanatory writing (i.e., providing information), and narrative writing (i.e., conveying real or imagined experiences).

For example, teachers might use the planning, organizing, writing, editing, revising (POWER) strategy to help students recall the steps involved in writing a narrative. First, the student *p*lans her story. What is the purpose of the story? What background information or knowledge do I need to write it? Second, the student *o*rganizes her thoughts before writing. She completes a worksheet that prompts her to identify the main characters, the setting, the problem or action, and the resolution or ending. Third, the teacher models the *w*riting process using the think-aloud technique. The teacher might explicitly show how he uses the students' ideas to create sentences and why the order of events is important to a story's coherence. Fourth, the student *e*dits her own writing. She reads her story, stars portions that she likes, and marks sections that need improvement. She also receives feedback from classmates. Fifth, the teacher models ways to *r*evise the story to make it better. The student ultimately decides which changes she will make based on feedback from the teacher and peers (Figure 7.11).

Another strategy, titled DEFENDS, or decide, examine, form, expose, note, drive, search—is useful in expository writing, when children must defend a thesis statement. Using the SRSD approach, the teacher introduces, models, and supports each step in the strategy. First, the child *d*ecides on an exact position (e.g., *Geckos make the best pets for fourth-grade boys.*) Second, he *e*xamines possible reasons for his position, perhaps by generating them on his own or consulting other people or books (e.g., *They are interesting to feed*). Third, the student *f*orms a list of points that explains each reason (e.g., *They eat live crickets and mealworms. They shake their tails before attacking their prey. Their food crunches in their mouths*). Fourth, the child is ready to begin writing. He *e*xposes his position in the first sentence of the essay. Then, he *n*otes each reason for his position and supporting points.

Figure 7.11   Improving Children's Writing Using SRSD

Albert the Fish

On a warm, sunny day two years ago **(When)**, there was a big gray fish named Albert **(Who)**. He lived in a big icy pond near the edge of town **(Where)**. Albert was swimming around the pond when he spotted a big juicy worm on top of the water. Albert knew how good worms tasted and wanted to eat this one for dinner **(What He Wanted To Do)**. So he swam very close to the worm and bit into him. Suddenly, Albert was pulled through the water into a boat **(What Happened)**. He had been caught by a fisherman **(Ending)**. Albert felt sad **(Feelings)** and wished he had been more careful.

Source: Based on the National Center on Accelerated Student Learning (http://kc.vanderbilt.edu).

Note: Students are taught to identify the parts of their story to determine whether it makes sense. Children focus chiefly on errors in grammar, sentence structure, and logical organization rather than on low-level mistakes.

Sixth, the student *drives* home his main idea in the final sentence. Finally, he *searches* for mistakes and makes necessary corrections.

There are many other strategies that can be taught using the SRSD model (Mather & Wendling, 2011). Empirical studies have investigated the efficacy of SRSD for children with and without writing problems. Four aspects of children's writing have been evaluated: (a) writing quality, the overall value of the composition; (b) writing elements, such as identification of main characters, location, time frame, and conclusion; (c) grammar; and (d) length.

Overall, children who participate in SRSD show increased writing skills in all four areas compared to youths who receive other forms of writing instruction. SRSD is associated with improvements in the writing skills of youths with writing disabilities and typically developing children (Figure 7.12). Furthermore, the benefits of SRSD are maintained over time and generalize to other types of writing assignments. For example, children who are initially taught to write essays also show improvement in writing book reports and short stories. The benefits of SRSD are attributed to the fact that teachers systematically introduce and model planning and reviewing strategies and encourage students to actively participate in the writing process (Graham & Harris, 2003). Similar results have been obtained by other writing instruction techniques that explicitly teach planning, translating, and reviewing (Graham, 2006; Wong, 1997).

Improving Translation: Handwriting and Spelling

Some children show writing problems because they have difficulty with mechanics (Monroe & Troia, 2006). Techniques that improve handwriting and spelling often lead to improvements in the overall quality and length of children's writing (Graham, Harris, & Fink, 2002).

The goal of **handwriting instruction** is to help students write legibly and quickly. Students must be able to write automatically, so that they can direct their attention to the

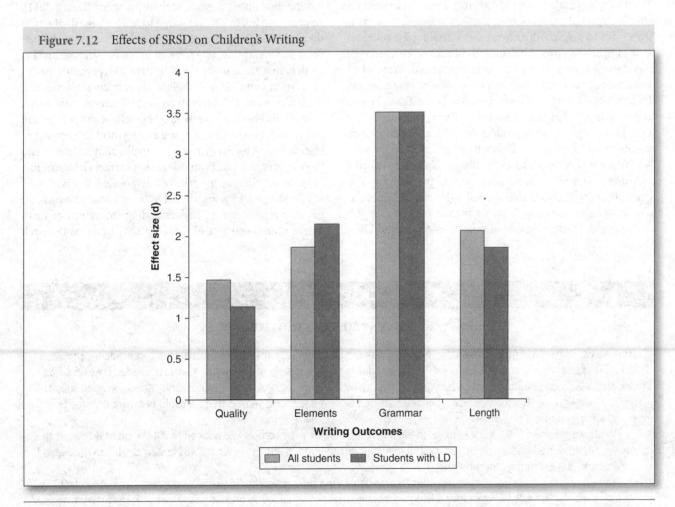

Figure 7.12 Effects of SRSD on Children's Writing

Source: Based on Graham and Harris (2003).

Note: Children who participate in SRSD show improvements in four areas of writing compared to youths who receive traditional writing instruction. SRSD is associated with improvements in both typical readers and children with learning disabilities.

quality of their composition rather than to the mechanics of writing. One method of handwriting instruction consists of four steps:

1. *Alphabet warm-up:* Students learn to name and identify letters.

2. *Alphabet practice:* Three lowercase letters with similar shapes are presented (e.g., l, i, t). First, the teacher models how to write each letter. Students practice writing the letters with guidance from the teacher. Students practice writing words containing the letters.

3. *Alphabet rockets:* Children rapidly copy sentences with words that contain the previously introduced letters.

4. *Alphabet fun:* Children are taught to write the letters in a creative way (e.g., making the *t* into a tomahawk; Graham, Harris, & Fink, 2000).

Spelling instruction involves three components (Graham et al., 2004). First, teachers help students learn to spell frequently occurring words. Teachers might use "word banks" or flashcards to familiarize children with the correct spelling of common words. Repeated exposure to commonly misspelled words is important to help children learn about spelling irregularities in the English language. Graham and colleagues (2002) recommend using a word sorting activity in which children are asked to sort common words based on similar phonemes (e.g., *made*, *laid*, and *say* belong in the same group). Students might also engage in games designed to reward spelling improvement. For example, in a game called Spelling Road Race, students move tokens around a game board when they correctly spell words.

A second component of spelling instruction involves teaching children to spell novel words by analogy. For example, a child who is able to spell *ought* might be able to use this knowledge to spell words such as *bought*, *brought*, and *thought*. Students might also be taught word-building

activities. For example, teachers might encourage students to generate as many words as they can that end with "oy."

A final component of spelling instruction involves proofreading. Children are taught to review their own writing and identify and correct spelling mistakes. In some cases, students review each other's compositions and correct misspellings.

Handwriting and spelling instruction is associated with improvements in the quality of children's overall writing. Effective instruction seems to have two components. First, effective instruction is explicit; teachers introduce, model, and reinforce children as they engage in each activity. Second, effective instruction is repeated. Children are given opportunities to practice new skills until they demonstrate proficiency.

MATHEMATICS
Math: A Critical Skill

Although learning disabilities in the area of mathematics do not receive the same amount of attention as reading and writing disabilities, they are serious problems (Geary, 2011). Approximately 6 to 7% of children have a learning disability in the area of mathematics. An additional 10 to 15% of children show persistently low achievement in mathematics, defined as math performance in the lowest 10th to 25th percentile multiple years in a row. Math disability and persistent problems with math achievement contribute to lower academic attainment, reduced likelihood of completing high school and college, and difficulty gaining and sustaining employment in high-status, high-income jobs. Furthermore, math disability interferes with tasks in everyday life, from calculating correct change from a $5 bill to determining the price of a new sweater that is 15% off.

In the past 15 years, there has been a dramatic increase in research directed at understanding the causes of math disabilities (Geary et al., 2011). This body of research

---

CASE STUDY

LUKE'S PROBLEMS WITH MATH

Luke was a 10-year-old African American boy who was referred to our clinic because of behavior and academic problems. Luke earned below average grades in most subjects, but he performed poorest in math. As a fifth grader, Luke could add and subtract simple numbers, but he had great difficulty with multiplication, division, and computations involving "borrowing" or "remainders." His teacher recommended that he be "held back" next year so that he could get extra practice before progressing to junior high school.

Dr. Ideran observed Luke as he completed some math problems in her office. She noticed that Luke often arrived at the correct answer for addition, subtraction, and simple multiplication problems. However, he was largely unable to divide, and his progress was extremely slow and effortful.

"You got a lot of them right," she said, "but it takes you a long time, doesn't it?" Luke replied, "Yeah. I'm not too fast." Dr. Ideran asked, "So, how do you go about solving a problem like 4 × 7?" Luke was reluctant to answer. After a long pause and sigh, tears rolled down his cheeks. Embarrassed, Luke said, "I just start with four... and keep counting up by fours... until I get to the answer." Dr. Ideran said, "Yes. That takes a lot of work and energy doesn't it? Maybe I can teach you a better way?"

---

suggests that children with math disabilities show problems in the development of three cognitive processes important to higher order mathematics calculation and problem solving: (a) number sense, (b) counting, and (c) arithmetic.

Number Sense

Typical Development

Some experts have argued that children are biologically predisposed to understand and process mathematics information. Infants may have inherent number sense or **numerosity**, that is, they may have an understanding that a group of stimuli can be understood in terms of their number (Geary, 2010).

Karen Wynn (1992) examined whether 5-month-olds could discriminate between a correct numerical expression $(1 + 1 = 2)$ and an incorrect expression $(1 + 1 = 1)$. She showed infants a case containing a doll. Then, the case was obscured by a screen. Next, infants saw a hand apparently place a second doll behind the screen. Finally, the screen was removed and infants were shown either a correct display (i.e., two dolls) or an incorrect display (i.e., one doll). Infants looked at the incorrect display significantly longer than the correct display, suggesting that they had an appreciation for simple numerosities.

Similarly, Starkey and Cooper (1980) examined whether 4- through 7-month-old infants could differentiate groups of dots presented in different numbers. First, infants were presented with a group of three dots. When infants became habituated, or no longer responded to the dots, the researchers changed the number of dots in the display. Infants who habituated to three dots showed renewed interest when presented with only two dots. Starkey and Cooper's findings indicate that young infants appreciate simple numerosities. More recent research has shown that young infants can also discriminate between sounds of different numbers (Lipton & Spelke, 2003) and older infants can order sets of items from largest in number to smallest (e.g., A > B > C; Xu & Spelke, 2000). By the time most children begin school, their ability to discriminate small quantities is greatly refined. Six-year-olds can easily tell that a basket containing 25 M&Ms contains more candy than another basket containing only 20 M&Ms. By late childhood, this capacity for numerosity is similar to that of adults (Halberda & Feigenson, 2008).

Numerosity permits the development of all other math abilities (Geary, 2010). It allows very young children to subitize, that is, to judge the number of objects in a small group, rapidly and accurately, without counting them. For example, young children can easily report that there are three cookies on a plate without actually counting the cookies. Furthermore, they can quickly differentiate between a plate with three cookies and a plate with five cookies (a useful skill for a hungry preschooler).

As children get older, numerosity allows them to mentally represent quantities. For example, young children learn the correspondence between Arabic numerals and discrete quantities (e.g., 3 = ■■■). At about the same time, children also begin to mentally represent quantities along a number line. Young children easily understand that numbers are positioned in ordinal fashion, that is, first, second, third, and so on. Over time, children also learn that the intervals between numbers are equal (i.e., the difference between 1 and 2 equals the difference between 8 and 9). The capacity to mentally represent quantities permits basic math calculation in early elementary school (e.g., addition, subtraction).

Delays in Number Sense

Unfortunately, children with mathematics disabilities tend to show delays in the development of number sense. Geary and colleagues (2007) developed a brief test of numerosity called the **Number Sets Test** (Figure 7.13). It consists of a series of numerals (e.g., 1, 3) or groups of objects (e.g., ■, ◆◆◆) that children must group to match a target number presented at the top of the page. Children can use subitizing, counting, or a combination of both strategies to group the stimuli as fast and as accurately as possible. Typically developing children show improvement on this test from first through fourth grade. However, children with mathematics disabilities perform more slowly and make more errors than their healthy classmates at each grade level. Specifically, children with mathematics disorder lag approximately three years behind their peers (Geary et al., 2009). Furthermore, children's performance on the Number Sets Test at the beginning of first grade (before most children even know how to add and subtract) predicts their reading achievement and likelihood of developing mathematics disability by the time they reach third grade. First-graders' scores on the Number Skills Test predict later math skills better than their intelligence, memory, and baseline knowledge of math! This finding indicates that numerosity is critically important to later math skills.

Children with mathematics disorder also have difficulty mentally representing numbers (Geary et al., 2011). The **Number Line Test** requires children to locate the position of numbers on a physical number line. For example, if given a line labeled *1* on the far left-hand side and *10* on the far right-hand side, most children would correctly locate the number 5 in the middle of the line. Interestingly, however, young school-age children produce a number line that looks like the natural logarithm with the distance between 1 and 2 being much farther apart than the distance between 8 and 9. Although young children understand the difference between numbers representing small quantities, numbers representing increasingly larger quantities seem more and more alike (Figure 7.14). With maturation and experience, children acquire the ability to correctly represent numbers on the line. However, children with mathematics disorder continue to struggle with this task and usually lag one year behind their typically developing classmates. Their problems mentally representing numbers hinder their ability to perform higher order math calculations.

Figure 7.13   The Number Sets Test

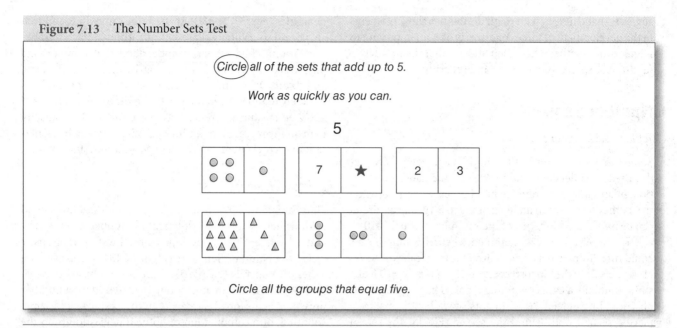

Figure 7.14   Number Line Tests for Children With and Without Math Disabilities

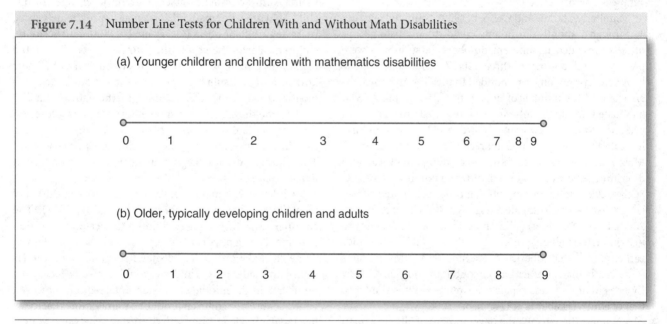

Source: Based on Geary and colleagues (2011).

Note: This test can be used to predict mathematics disorder in young children. Children with mathematics disorder are 3 years behind their typically developing classmates in their capacity for numerosity.

Note: Very young children and youths with mathematics disability have difficulty mentally representing numbers: (a) On a physical number line, the difference between 1 and 2 seems larger than the difference between 4 and 5. As numbers become larger, they seem more and more alike. In contrast, typically developing older children (b) know that the intervals between numbers are equal.

What explains these delays in numerosity? Brian Butterworth (2005) has developed the **defective number module hypothesis** to explain the cause of certain math disabilities. According to this hypothesis, the neurological system that is believed to underlie infants' appreciation for numerosity does not develop properly. This neurological system involves many brain areas, especially portions of the parietal lobes known as the right intraparietal sulci (IPS). The right IPS seems to play an important role in estimating numerosity for small sets of stimuli, a capacity displayed by infants and young children. The left IPS seems to be important for more complex numerical processing and arithmetic calculations shown by older children. Problems in the development of either right or left IPS would affect mathematical ability.

Indeed, neuroimaging studies indicate that some youths with mathematics disability show abnormalities in these brain regions (Dehaene, Piazza, Pinel, & Cohen, 2003; Piazza, Giacomini, Le Bihan, & Dehaene, 2003).

Counting

Typical Development

Children's ability to count develops between the ages of 2 through 5 years. Young children obey certain rules of counting that follow a fixed sequence (Gelman & Gallistel, 1978):

- *One-to-one correspondence:* One number is assigned to each object.
- *Stable order:* Numbers are counted in a specific order.
- *Cardinality:* The last number stated reflects the quantity of the items counted.
- *Abstraction:* Objects of any kind can be grouped and counted.
- *Order irrelevance:* Objects can be counted in any order.

Children's counting skills increase with experience. However, typically developing children universally progress through similar stages of counting, suggesting that counting is mediated by brain maturation.

Counting Errors

Children with mathematics disability also progress through the same sequence of counting skills. However, in early elementary school, they make counting errors not often shown by their classmates (Geary et al., 2011). To study these errors, researchers ask children to help a puppet learn to count objects. On some counts, the puppet deliberately makes mistakes. The researchers record whether the child detects the mistake and corrects the puppet. Children with mathematics disabilities sometimes show two types of errors. First, they may become confused when counting occurs from right to left, rather than in the typical left-to-right order. They do not seem to understand the principle of order irrelevance. Second, they often fail to detect errors when the puppet double-counts the first object in the row (e.g., the puppet points to the first object and counts "one, two" and then points to the second object and counts "three"). In contrast, they are able to detect double-counting when it occurs on the last object. It seems that these children have difficulty remembering the double-counting error.

Arithmetic Computation

Typical Development

Beginning in elementary school, children's math skills become more complex, as children transition from simple counting to arithmetic. Addition depends greatly on children's counting abilities. For example, young children use fairly immature strategies to add numbers. Initially, they might count on their fingers to solve addition problems. Later, addition is performed verbally or mentally.

Young children also use less efficient strategies to add. For example, very young children use the **counting-all strategy**; when asked to add $7 + 4$, they first count from 1 to 7 and then count four more numbers until they arrive at the correct answer. In contrast, older children use the **counting-on strategy**; they begin with the larger number (i.e., 7) and then count four more digits until they arrive at the answer. Similar shortcuts are used for subtraction and other mathematical operations (Augustyniak et al., 2006).

With experience, children learn to store math facts in long-term memory. For example, children begin to use **direct retrieval** to recall that $7 + 6 = 13$; they no longer need to count to arrive at the correct answer. Alternatively, they may use a process called **decomposition** to solve the same problem; they might break up the problem into smaller components that are more easily remembered. For example, children might directly recall that $6 + 6 = 12$ and then add one to this partial sum to obtain the correct answer. Direct retrieval and decomposition permit more rapid and automatic math computation. Children can direct their attention to conceptualizing arithmetic problems rather than to counting. Direct retrieval and decomposition also free short-term memory, allowing children to perform more complex calculations in their heads (Geary & Hoard, 2005).

Calculation Problems

Children with math disabilities often show marked delays in math calculation skills. They calculate more slowly and make more errors than their typically developing classmates (Figure 7.15). Several studies indicate that deficits in semantic memory underlie many of their difficulties with math calculations (Geary et al., 2011). Semantic memory refers to the ability to retrieve ideas, concepts, and facts from long-term memory to solve immediate problems. Children with math disability have difficulty remembering math facts (Geary et al., 2012). Whereas most fourth graders can effortlessly recall $4 + 5 = 9$, children with mathematics disability often need to count to recall the correct answer. Consequently, children with mathematics disabilities spend greater cognitive resources performing basic calculations and fewer resources conceptualizing the problem itself (Andersson, 2010).

Youths with mathematics disabilities also frequently show problems remembering math procedures. For example, when presented with a problem such as $41 - 29 = ?$, children with disabilities may forget how to "borrow" and, consequently, they provide an incorrect answer (Temple & Sherwood, 2002).

Because of their difficulty retrieving math facts and procedures from long-term memory, children with mathematics disabilities often rely on immature strategies to solve math problems. For example, many first graders count on

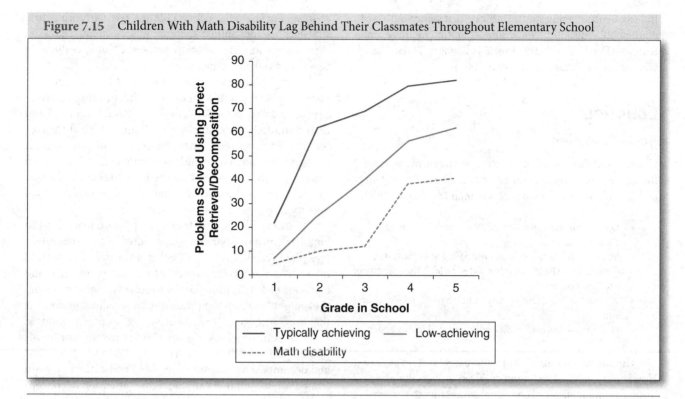

Figure 7.15   Children With Math Disability Lag Behind Their Classmates Throughout Elementary School

Source: Based on Geary and colleagues (2012).

Note: In this longitudinal study, children with math disabilities used direct retrieval or decomposition less frequently than did typically achieving children and low-achieving children. Instead, youths with math disability relied heavily on immature (i.e., counting) strategies.

their fingers to solve addition problems. However, children with mathematics disabilities often continue to rely on this immature tactic into the third and fourth grades. Furthermore, when young children with disabilities count, they often count all digits rather than rely on more advanced "add-on" strategies. These immature strategies result in slow, error-prone calculations (Butterworth, 1999; Geary & Hoard, 2005; Jordan, Hanich, & Kaplan, 2003).

Math Reasoning and Problem Solving

Deficits in Working Memory

By late childhood, children begin to develop more complex math problem-solving skills. These skills include the ability to solve story problems, to interpret charts and graphs, and to perform mathematical operations with complex sets of numbers (i.e., borrowing, long division, fractions). These higher order math skills depend on several underlying cognitive abilities.

Children's ability to solve higher order math problems depends on their capacity for working memory (Toll et al., 2011). Working memory refers to the ability to keep multiple units of information in short-term memory simultaneously,

ignore extraneous information, manipulate this information, and use this information to solve an immediate problem. Working memory consists of two components: a "phonological loop" that allows children to understand and process auditory-verbal information and a "visual-spatial sketchpad" that allows children to understand and process visual-spatial information (Baddeley & Hitch, 1974). For example, the ability to remember (and not confuse) two people's telephone numbers depends on the phonological loop, whereas the ability to mentally recall the map to a job interview likely depends on the visual-spatial sketchpad.

Children with mathematics disabilities often experience problems with *verbal and phonological* working memory. Some children have reading disabilities that interfere with their ability to comprehend math story problems. Other children have difficulty with auditory working memory, attention, and concentration; they are unable to hold mathematical information in short-term memory long enough to process it and arrive at the correct answer. For example, they may forget important bits of information at the beginning of story problems, become distracted by extraneous information, or transpose digits when converting a story problem to a math calculation (Toll et al., 2011).

Other children with mathematics disorder seem to have problems with *visual-spatial* working memory. Children's abilities to use charts and graphs depend on their visual-spatial reasoning skills and attention-concentration. They must appreciate the relationship between visually presented information in a chart or graph and the quantities these illustrations represent. Furthermore, they must identify important elements of the chart or graph and ignore extraneous details. Problems with visual-spatial working memory can lead to errors in both processes. Children's abilities to perform complex mathematical calculations, like adding three-digit numbers or performing long division, also depend on their visual-spatial skills. Deficits in visual-spatial working memory can cause children to misalign numbers, leading them to use the wrong digits for their calculations (Geary & Hoard, 2005).

David Geary and Mary Hoard (2005) have proposed a **developmental model for mathematics disability** to explain these children's higher order math deficits (Figure 7.16). According to this model, children's math skills depend on underlying cognitive processing skills including their (a) language abilities and (b) executive functioning. Children's language skills enable them to understand the correspondence between spoken numbers (e.g., "twenty-two") and Arabic numerals (e.g., 22). Language skills also help children listen to and understand orally presented math problems and to read math story problems. Some youths with mathematics disabilities may have underlying verbal deficits that interfere with their math skills.

Children's executive functioning allows them to attend to important information in mathematics problems, ignore unimportant details, retrieve math facts from long-term memory, and perform mathematic operations, using working memory. Youths with mathematics disabilities have difficulty with all four tasks. They often have difficulty recognizing important elements of story problems and are easily distracted by extraneous information. They may also be unable to inhibit irrelevant mathematical operations when presented with math problems. For example, when they see the problem $6 \times 4 = ?$, children with mathematics disabilities might answer "10" because of their failure to inhibit the use of addition. These children also have difficulty retrieving math facts and, consequently, rely on immature strategies (e.g., counting) to solve math problems. As a result, their working memories are often overly taxed, and they are unable to devote sufficient resources to understanding and effectively framing math problems (Barrouillet, Fayol, & Lathuliere, 1997; Geary & Hoard, 2005). A recent meta-analysis on examining cognitive processing in children with learning problems showed that impairments in executive functioning ($d = 1.05$) and working memory ($d = 0.59$) differentiated children with and without mathematics disability (Johnson et al., 2010).

Deficits in Rapid Automatized Naming (RAN)

Recent research has also shown that children with mathematics disability, like children with reading disability, often show deficits in RAN (Heikkila et al., 2009). Below average RAN is associated with more errors in math calculation, slow calculation fluency, and problems retrieving math facts (e.g., $6 \times 6 = 12$). Interestingly, the RAN deficits shown by children

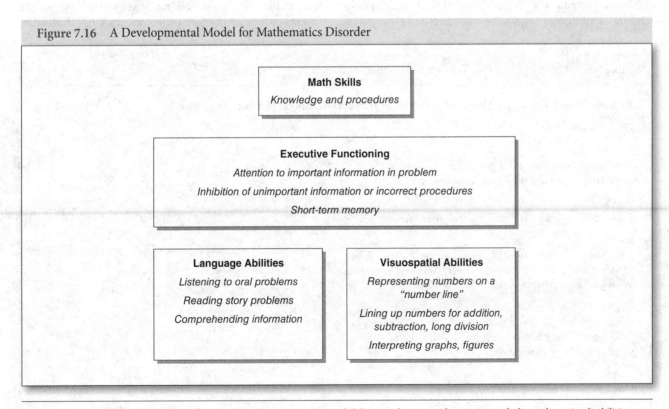

Figure 7.16   A Developmental Model for Mathematics Disorder

Note: According to Geary and Hoard (2005), problems in language, visuospatial abilities, and executive functioning underlie mathematics disabilities.

with reading disabilities and math disabilities are somewhat domain specific (Pauly et al., 2011). Whereas children with reading disability have difficulty retrieving the names of letters and objects, children with math disability have trouble retrieving the names of Arabic numerals and the number of dots on dice. It is likely that problems with number-specific RAN leads to poor retrieval of math facts and procedures as well as slower, laborious, and more error-prone math problem solving.

Treatment of Mathematics Disabilities

Targets of Instruction

To treat Mathematics Disorder, therapists can target three areas: (a) preparatory arithmetic skills, (b) basic math computation skills, and (c) math problem solving (Kroesbergen & VanLuit, 2003). Interventions designed to teach preparatory arithmetic skills are usually directed toward very young children and youths with developmental delays. These interventions help children develop an appreciation for numerosity, the ability to recognize numerals, and basic counting skills.

Interventions designed to teach basic computational skills are directed at elementary school-age children with mathematics disabilities. These interventions focus primarily on addition, subtraction, multiplication, and division. Often, interventions address more complex mathematic operations, such as operations involving three-digit numbers, long division, fractions, and decimals. These interventions help children acquire and automatize math facts and procedures.

Interventions that focus on math problem solving are usually reserved for older children who show adequate computational skills. These interventions provide children with training in understanding story problems and applying math facts and procedures.

Methods of Instruction

Clinicians generally rely on one of three methods for math instruction: (a) direct instruction, (b) self-instruction, or (c) mediated/assisted instruction (Goldman, 1989; Table 7.6). **Direct mathematics instruction** involves the systematic presentation of math knowledge and skills. In direct instruction, the teacher introduces and demonstrates the skill following a carefully designed script. Then, the skill is broken down into specific steps, which children perform. Teachers provide help and feedback regarding children's performance, correcting children's mistakes. Gradually, teacher assistance is faded as children gain mastery of the skill. Children are given repeated opportunities to practice the skill and extend it to new problems. Direct instruction tends to be most effective in improving basic math computation skills in younger children (Kroesbergen & VanLuit, 2003).

Self-instruction is a second method to improve children's math skills. In self-instruction, teachers systematically present a series of verbal steps or "prompts" that children can use to solve math problems. Teachers model the use of these prompts as they complete problems on the blackboard in front of the class. Then, children are encouraged to use the prompts when solving their own problems, while the teacher

Table 7.6   Three Methods for Teaching Mathematics Skills

Problem: Anne had 9 apples. She gave 4 apples to her friend. How many apples does Anne have left?

Direct Instruction[a]

Step A
Read the problem with me. *Teacher reads the problem.*
What kind of problem is it? *Answer: Subtraction*

Step B
Good. It's subtraction. Is the big number given? *Answer: yes*

Step C
Let's read the problem again. *Teacher reads the problem again.*
Is 9 the big number or the small number? *Answer: The big number.*
What kind of number is 4? *Answer: the small number.*

Step D
Good. Now let's take 9 and subtract 4. Watch me. Nine minus four is five.
Now you say "Nine minus four is five." *Child repeats.*
Good. What is the answer? *Answer: Five*

Step E
Good. Now let's read the next problem.

Self-Instruction[b]

Teacher introduces and demonstrates the following steps to solve story problems. Teacher encourages children to use the steps (first aloud, then silently) as she monitors.

What are you asked?	*How many apples does Anne have left?*
What numbers do you have?	*9 and 4*
What number(s) do you need to know?	*How many left?*
What must you do?	*Subtract, 9 – 4*
What is the answer?	*5*
Check your answer.	*4 + 5 = 9, so it checks out!*

Mediated/Assisted Instruction[c]

Teacher provides a structured sequence of hints to help the child complete the problem. Hints become gradually more specific and content-related until the child is able to arrive at the correct answer.

Hint Strategy	*Example*
Simple negative feedback: Teacher asks child to check answer.	Your answer is not quite right. Try again.
Working memory refresher: Teacher reminds child of important parts of the problem.	Remember, she has 9 and gives away 4.
Numerals as memory aids: Teacher asks child to write down important parts of problem.	Let's write it down in numbers: 9 – 4.
Enumeration: Teacher uses a series of verbal instructions and numbers to guide child.	Nine apples [points to nine] minus four apples [points to four] is what?
Complete demonstration: Teacher completes problems for child, giving rationale.	See. Nine minus four is five.

a. Based on DISTAR Arithmetic (Engelmann & Carnine, 1975).

b. Based on Fleischner and Manheimer (1997).

c. Based on Goldman (1989).

monitors their use. Initially, teachers provide careful assistance to children in using the prompts. Eventually, teacher assistance is faded until children can use the prompts to solve problems on their own. Self-instruction tends to be most effective in teaching higher order math problem-solving skills to older children.

Teachers who use **mediated/assisted instruction** begin with the student's understanding of the mathematical problem. Then, they offer assistance and guidance to the child to help him solve the problem correctly. Mediated/assisted instruction does not involve the use of a script (as direct instruction) or a series of steps (as self-instruction). Instead, the teacher offers increasingly detailed hints at solving the math problem until the child is able to complete the problem successfully. In this way, children are encouraged to derive their own way of solving math problems, rather than rely on a formal set of rules provided by the teacher. Overall, mediated/assisted instruction is the least efficacious method of math instruction (Kroesbergen & VanLuit, 2003; Figure 7.17).

Efficacy of Specific Methods

Gersten and colleagues (2009) conducted a meta-analysis investigating the efficacy of instructional strategies to improve the achievement scores of children with mathematics disability (Table 7.7). The two strategies that yielded the largest effect sizes (e.g., showed the greatest superiority of the treatment group compared to the control group) were direct mathematics instruction and the use of heuristics. Both strategies were uniquely associated with positive learning outcomes, even when they were combined with other instructional methods.

As indicated above, direct instruction involves (a) the teacher explicitly demonstrating a step-by-step method or strategy to solve a specific problem, (b) multiple opportunities for the student to practice the step-by-step method with reinforcement and, if necessary, corrective feedback, and (c) additional practice generalizing the step-by-step method to similar problems.

Heuristics are "rules of thumb" or general approaches to problem solving. The use of heuristics to teach math is similar to the use of direct instruction except the student learns

Figure 7.17   Effects of Mathematics Instruction

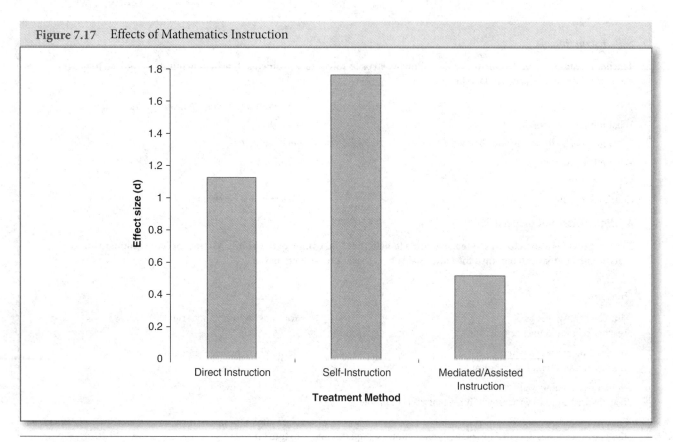

Source: Based on Kroesbergen and VanLuit (2003).

Note: Youths who receive self-instruction show the greatest improvement in math skills. However, direct instruction was particularly effective in improving children's computational skills.

Table 7.7   Math Instruction: What Works and What Doesn't?

	Effect Size (d)
Largest Effects	
Use of heuristics*	1.56
Direct (explicit) instruction*	1.22
Student verbalizations	1.04
Sequence and/or range of problems	0.82
Use of visuals or manipulatives	0.47
Smallest Effects	
Student feedback and goal setting	0.17 (ns)
Peer-assisted learning or tutoring	0.14 (ns)

Source: Based on Gersten and colleagues (2009).

Note: Direct instruction and the use of heuristics yielded the largest effect sizes and (*) were independently related to outcomes even when combined with other instructional methods. Providing feedback to students and encouraging classmates to tutor each other yielded nonsignificant (ns) effect sizes.

a general problem-solving strategy rather than a specific step-by-step method to solve a particular problem. For example, to teach math story-problem solving, the teacher might coach a student in the following ways:

1. Read the problems
2. Underline the key facts
3. Cross out the unimportant information
4. Solve the problem
5. Check his work

Self-Regulated Strategy Instruction (SRSD), used to teach writing strategies, can also be applied to teach math problem-solving strategies. Heuristics may be especially useful for children who have problems generalizing strategies learned through direct instruction.

The use of visual representations yields moderate effects on children's math achievement. Visual representations might include a picture, diagram, chart, or physical object that helps the child understand the relationship between a math quantity, concept, or process and the physical world. For example, a teacher might use a number line to help students learn about ordinal position, arithmetic, or negative numbers. Similarly, he might use slices of a pizza to demonstrate fractions.

Another technique that is effective in improving math skills is verbalization. Clinicians want to encourage students to verbalize their steps when solving math problems. According to Lev Vygotsky's (1962) influential theory of cognitive development, children acquire the ability to engage in higher level cognitive processes through a gradual process of verbalization and internalization. First, a teacher presents the process aloud, then children repeat the process while verbalizing the steps, and still later the child is able to internalize the steps without verbalizing them (as thoughts). By encouraging children to verbalize math problem-solving steps, teachers may facilitate this process of internalization.

Finally, both learning theory and educational research highlight the importance of providing students with a range and sequence of examples. *Range* refers to the variability of math problems. Initially, problems should be similar to one another, to allow children practice in mastering basic concepts or skills. Over time, problems should vary to maintain children's interest and permit children to generalize skills to new problems. *Sequence* refers to the order of problems. Vygotsky (1978) posited that optimal learning occurs when instruction is directed within a child's **zone of proximal development**. This "zone" reflects the difficulty of problems that a child can perform with and without help. If problems are too easy, the child will not learn new skills. If problems are too difficult and cannot be solved even with help from others, the child will not learn. Optimal instruction depends on presenting problems that fall within this zone, that is, problems that children can solve correctly with effort and/or assistance. Ideally, problems should increase in complexity, based on the child's acquisition of knowledge and skills. To teach in this zone of proximal development, teachers use a process called "scaffolding." Like the scaffolding that supports a building when it is first being constructed, teachers provide cognitive scaffolding to support students as they begin to build new concepts or skills. As children begin to master basic tasks, the teacher's help is gradually reduced, the scaffolding is gradually removed, to permit children to solve problems more independently.

CHAPTER SUMMARY

Definitions

- There is no consensus for the best way to characterize children with specific deficits in reading, writing, and math. *DSM-5* used the diagnosis Specific Learning Disorder to describe these problems whereas the Individuals with Disabilities Education Improvement Act (IDEA) classifies these conditions as "learning disabilities."

  o Specific Learning Disorder is defined by low academic achievement that interferes with a person's school performance, work, or everyday life. The academic problems must emerge in childhood and cannot be attributable to Intellectual Disability, sensory impairments, or social-cultural factors.

  o The IDEA definition of *learning disabilities* is similar to that provided by *DSM-5*. However, the IDEA permits children to be classified with learning disabilities in areas not described in *DSM-5*, such as reading fluency and oral language.

- Three broad approaches to learning disability classification are used by clinicians.

  o The IQ-achievement discrepancy method is based on academic achievement significantly lower than intellectual ability. Although this method is still used by some clinicians, it is not considered a valid approach to classification.

  o Response to Intervention (RTI) is used by many schools to identify children with learning disabilities based on their failure to respond to evidence-based academic instruction. It relies chiefly on observations and curriculum-based assessment.

  o Comprehensive assessment involves integrating classroom observations and RTI approaches with the results of standardized IQ and achievement tests to identify children with learning disabilities. The clinician tries to identify a cognitive processing problem that underlies the child's disability.

Epidemiology

- Approximately 5% of school-age children are receiving educational services because of a learning disability. Approximately 7% of parents report that their child has been diagnosed with a learning disability at some point in childhood.
- Reading disabilities are the most common learning problems. They are seen in 80% of youths with learning disabilities.
- Approximately equal numbers of boys and girls have learning disabilities. However, boys are approximately twice as likely as girls to be diagnosed with a learning disability and receive treatment.
- The prevalence of learning disabilities is higher among African American, Latino, and American Indian children than white children. Their increased prevalence is largely attributable to low-SES, which places youths at risk for learning problems.
- The course of learning disabilities is usually chronic. Youths are at risk for lower academic attainment and dropout. Outcomes are improved with early intervention and family support.
- Associated problems include (a) academic anxiety and low self-concept, (b) ADHD and behavior problems, and (c) risk for peer rejection.

Reading Disabilities: Causes and Treatments

- Learning disabilities are heritable conditions; 35 to 40% of children with learning disabilities have a family member with a disability. Genetic transmission tends to be somewhat specific; children and parent often show the same types of academic deficits.
- Deficits in word reading are often caused by poor phonemic awareness, that is, children's recognition that spoken language can be broken down and analyzed by phonemes.
  - Poor phonemic awareness interferes with phonetic mediation, that is, the ability to sound out novel words.
  - Children with reading disabilities often do not use the same brain areas to phonetically decode novel words as do typically developing children. Instead of using left-hemisphere language centers, they process using right-hemisphere visual areas.
  - Direct, phonics-based instruction can improve children's ability to decode novel words and increase left-hemisphere processing.
- Deficits in reading fluency are often caused by underlying problems with (a) processing speed, (b) verbal working memory, and (c) rapid automatized naming.
  - Children with double-deficits (i.e., poor word reading and fluency) tend to be most impaired.
  - Some children show improvements in fluency in response to additional guided reading practice.
  - Other children need systematic instruction to improve their reading automaticity, word facilitation, and retrieval skills, such as the RAVE-O program.
- Reading comprehension problems are usually the result of (a) low overall verbal ability or (b) previous problems with word reading or fluency problems. Text enhancements are especially useful in fostering reading comprehension in children.

Writing Disabilities: Causes and Treatments

- Most writing disabilities are caused by problems with (a) planning, (b) translating, or (c) reviewing written expression.
- Self-regulated strategy development (SRSD) is an effective approach to systematically introducing, modeling, and reinforcing writing skills to children. Different strategies can be used to teach narrative writing, expository writing, and other types of writing.
- Handwriting instruction can use helpful for children with poor penmanship.
- Spelling instruction is effective in improving the accuracy of children's spelling.

Mathematics Disabilities: Causes and Treatments

- Very young children who are later diagnosed with math disabilities often show deficits in number sense (i.e., numerosity). They are slow to recognize the correspondence between Arabic numerals and sets of objects and to understand the "number line."
- Very young children who are later diagnosed with math disabilities sometimes make counting errors not shown by typically developing children.
- Children with math disabilities often use immature calculation strategies that make problem solving slow and error prone. They sometimes have problems recalling math fact and procedures.
- Children with math disabilities often show underlying problems with verbal working memory that interferes with their ability to solve story problems and visual-spatial working memory that interferes with their ability to solve lengthy calculations and interpret charts and graphs.
- Direct instruction in mathematics and the use of heuristics are effective in helping children with math disabilities. Self-Directed Strategy Instruction is particularly useful in teaching children approaches to problem-solving.
- Children with math disabilities also benefit from systematic practice that involves varying the range and sequence of problems so that children are challenged but not overwhelmed by problems.

KEY TERMS

automaticity   231

Broca's area   223

comprehensive assessment   213

comprehensive model for learning disability identification   214

counting-all strategy   241

counting-on strategy   241

curriculum-based assessment   210

decomposition   241

defective number module hypothesis   240

developmental model for mathematics disability   243

direct instruction   221

direct mathematics instruction   244

direct retrieval   241

double-deficit model   230

dyscalculia   207

dyslexia   207

expository writing   232

graphemes   221

CRITICAL THINKING EXERCISES

1. The *DSM-5* definition of Specific Learning Disorder does not require children with learning deficits to show underlying cognitive processing problems. Why might a clinician want to assess children's cognitive processing when diagnosing Specific Learning Disorder?

2. Response to Intervention (RTI) is widely used in schools to identify children with learning disabilities. Identify and explain two limitations to the RTI method.

3. Children from low-SES families are at disproportionate risk for being classified with a learning disability. Why? How might school psychologists and other professionals avoid misdiagnosing these children?

4. Compare and contrast phonics-based direct instruction with whole word approaches to treating reading disabilities. Which treatment strategy seems to have greater empirical support for young children with reading problems?

5. Develop an intervention program for the following students:

   o An 8-year-old boy who reads accurately but very slowly
   o A 12-year-old boy with difficulty in writing research papers for history class
   o A 10-year-old girl who has difficulty with math story problems

   How would you know if treatment was effective?

EXTEND YOUR LEARNING

Videos, practice tests, flash cards, study guides, and links to online resources for this chapter are available to students online. Teachers also have access to lecture notes, PowerPoint presentations, suggestions for classroom activities, and possible exam questions. Visit:www .sagepub.com/weis2e.

PART III

Disruptive Disorders and Substance Use Problems

CHAPTER 8

Attention-Deficit/Hyperactivity Disorder

LEARNING OBJECTIVES

After reading this chapter, you should be able to answer these questions:

- What are the characteristics of ADHD in preschoolers, school-age children, and adolescents? How does the disorder differ from developmentally expected inattention and hyperactivity/impulsivity?

- What other mental disorders and psychosocial problems are often experienced by children with ADHD? What might explain these co-occurring problems?

- How common is ADHD? How and why has its prevalence changed over the past 30 years? How does its prevalence vary as a function on age, gender, and social-cultural background?

- What are the most common causes of ADHD? Why is ADHD best viewed as a "neurodevelopmental" disorder that is influenced by genetic, neurological, and cognitive-behavioral factors?

- What medications and psychosocial treatments are effective for ADHD? What percentage of youths responds to treatment? What treatment options are available for families who do not want to use medication to manage their children's symptoms?

WHAT IS ATTENTION-DEFICIT/HYPERACTIVITY DISORDER (ADHD)?

When most people think of Attention-Deficit/Hyperactivity Disorder (ADHD), they usually envision children who have difficulty paying attention in class, are easily distractible, have trouble remaining seated, and are restless, talkative, and impulsive. In other words, most people view "typical" children with ADHD as having two general behavior problems: (a) inattention and (b) hyperactivity and impulsivity.

In fact, most people's impressions of ADHD are accurate. Many children and adolescents with ADHD show problems with both inattention and hyperactivity/impulsivity (Taylor & Sonuga-Barke, 2010). *DSM-5* lists behavioral symptoms that define problems in each of these domains (Table 8.1 Diagnostic Criteria for Attention-Deficit/Hyperactivity Disorder). Children with significant **attention problems** show persistent and developmentally unexpected difficulties with attention to detail, sustaining attention over time, listening to others and following through with assignments, organizing tasks, staying focused, and remembering information and where they placed objects. Children who have significant problems with **hyperactivity** fidget and squirm, have difficulty remaining seated and staying still when expected, show problems playing quietly, are talkative, and "on the go." They often exhaust others' patience with their high-rate behavior or annoy others with their restlessness. Children

252

Table 8.1 Diagnostic Criteria for Attention-Deficit/Hyperactivity Disorder

A. A persistent pattern of inattention and/or hyperactivity-impulsivity that interferes with functioning or development, as characterized by (1) and/or (2):

   1. **Inattention:** Six (or more) of the following symptoms have persisted for at least 6 months to a degree that is inconsistent with developmental level and that negatively impacts directly on social and academic/occupational activities[1]:

      a. Often fails to give close attention to details or makes careless mistakes in schoolwork, at work, or during other activities (e.g., overlooks or misses details, work is inaccurate).

      b. Often has difficulty sustaining attention in tasks or play activities (e.g., has difficulty remaining focused during lectures, conversations, or lengthy readings).

      c. Often does not seem to listen when spoken to directly (e.g., mind seems elsewhere, even in the absence of any obvious distraction).

      d. Often does not follow through on instructions and fails to finish schoolwork, chores, or duties in the workplace (e.g., starts tasks but quickly loses focus and is easily sidetracked).

      e. Often has difficulty organizing tasks and activities (e.g., difficulty managing sequential tasks; difficulty keeping materials and belongings in order; messy, disorganized work; has poor time management; fails to meet deadlines).

      f. Often avoids, dislikes, or is reluctant to engage in tasks that require sustained mental effort (e.g., schoolwork or homework; for older adolescents and adults, preparing reports, completing forms, reviewing lengthy papers).

      g. Often loses things necessary for tasks or activities (e.g., school materials, pencils, books, tools, wallets, keys, paperwork, eyeglasses, mobile telephones).

      h. Is easily distracted by extraneous stimuli (for older adolescents and adults, may include unrelated thoughts).

      i. Is often forgetful in daily activities (e.g., doing chores, running errands; for older adolescents and adults, returning calls, paying bills, keeping appointments).

   2. **Hyperactivity and impulsivity:** Six (or more) of the following symptoms have persisted for at least 6 months to a degree that is inconsistent with developmental level and that negatively impacts directly on social and academic/occupational activities:[1]

      a. Often fidgets with or taps hands or feet or squirms in seat.

      b. Often leaves seat in situations when remaining seated is expected (e.g., leaves his or her place in the classroom, in the office or other workplace).

      c. Often runs about or climbs in situations where it is inappropriate. (Note: In adolescents or adults, may be limited to feeling restless.)

      d. Often unable to play or engage in leisure activities quietly.

      e. Is often "on the go," acting as if "driven by a motor" (e.g., is unable to be or is uncomfortable being still for extended time, as in restaurants, meetings; may be experienced by others as being restless or difficulty [sic] to keep up with).

      f. Often talks excessively.

      g. Often blurts out an answer before a question has been completed (e.g., completes people's sentences; cannot wait for turn in conversation).

      h. Often has difficulty waiting his or her turn (e.g., while waiting in line).

      i. Often interrupts or intrudes on others (e.g., butts into conversations, games, or activities; may start using other people's things without asking or receiving permission; for adolescents and adults, may intrude into or take over what others are doing).

B. Several inattentive or hyperactive-impulsive symptoms were present prior to age 12 years.

C. Several inattentive or hyperactive-impulsive symptoms are present in two or more settings (e.g., at home, school, or work; with friends or relatives; in other activities).

D. There is clear evidence that the symptoms interfere with, or reduce the quality of, social, academic, or occupational functioning.

(Continued)

Table 8.1 (Continued)

E. The symptoms do not occur exclusively during the course of Schizophrenia or another psychotic disorder and are not better explained by another mental disorder.

Specify whether:

Combined presentation: If both Criterion A1 (inattention) and Criterion A2 (hyperactivity-impulsivity) are met for the past 6 months.

Predominantly inattentive presentation: If Criterion A1 (inattention) is met but Criterion A2 (hyperactivity-impulsivity) is not met for the past 6 months.

Predominantly hyperactive/impulsive presentation: If Criterion A2 (hyperactivity-impulsivity) is met but Criterion A1 (inattention) is not met for the past 6 months.

Source: Reprinted with permission from the *Diagnostic and Statistical Manual of Mental Disorders, Fifth Edition* (Copyright 2013). American Psychiatric Association.

[1]The symptoms of inattention and/or hyperactivity-impulsivity are not solely a manifestation of oppositional behavior, defiance, hostility, or failure to understand tasks of instructions. For older adolescents and adults (age 17 and older), at least *five* symptoms are required.

who have significant problems with impulsivity act without forethought; they may blurt out answers in class, have trouble waiting their turn in line, and intrude into others' conversations or activities. They often have problems delaying gratification in order to achieve long-term goals. Older children and adolescents may also make decisions or begin tasks without first considering the long-term consequences of their actions (American Psychiatric Association, 2013).

Children can be diagnosed with ADHD if they show significant symptoms of inattention *or* hyperactivity/impulsivity. By definition, children must show at least six out of a possible nine symptoms of *either* inattention *or* hyperactivity/impulsivity to be diagnosed with the disorder.

The fact that children can be diagnosed with ADHD if they show *either* significant hyperactivity/impulsivity *or* significant inattention means that two children diagnosed with ADHD can have qualitatively different symptoms. A fourth grader with predominantly hyperactive/impulsive symptoms might wander about the classroom, talk excessively with peers, interrupt the teacher, and disrupt learning. In contrast, his classmate with predominantly inattentive symptoms might sit quietly at her desk, look out the classroom window, think about events occurring in the hallway, and daydream (Bauermeister, Alegria, Bird, Rubio-Stipec, & Canino, 1992; Hudziak et al., 1998; Lahey, Carlson, & Frick, 1997; McBurnett, 1997). The diagnostic label *ADHD* reflects a heterogeneous mix of children.

After reading the diagnostic criteria for ADHD, presented in Table 8.1, many students begin to think, "Maybe I have ADHD?" Don't all students sometimes have difficulty attending to lectures, show poor time management, forget appointments or assignments, and dislike or avoid long and complex tasks like term papers? In fact, nearly all of the symptoms of ADHD are also seen in typically developing individuals from time to time. However, people with ADHD can be differentiated from their peers without ADHD in three ways. First, people with ADHD show a *persistent pattern* of inattention and/or hyperactivity-impulsivity that lasts for at least 6 months.

Second, people with ADHD show symptoms *in multiple settings.* Typically, individuals with ADHD have problems with inattentions and/or hyperactivity-impulsivity at home, at school, and in other settings (e.g., work, with friends). Symptoms may be less noticeable or impairing during some activities (e.g., playing sports) than others (e.g., attending class), but they are present. By definition, a child cannot be diagnosed with ADHD if he shows symptoms only with parents but never with teachers or adults outside the home.

Third, people with ADHD show inattention and/or hyperactivity-impulsivity that *is inconsistent with their developmental level.* All children show problems with inattention and hyperactivity/impulsivity from time to time. Younger children generally have more frequent problems than older children. To qualify for a diagnosis of ADHD, individuals must show symptoms that greatly exceed symptoms of inattention and/or hyperactivity and impulsivity shown by people of the same age (see Research to Practice: ADHD Across Development). Psychologists can compare a person suspected of having ADHD with other individuals of the same age by using norm-referenced rating scales. For example, the psychologist might administer an ADHD rating scale to a child's parents and teachers to assess the child's behavior at home and school, respectively. The rating scale would ask informants to evaluate the severity of the child's *DSM-5* ADHD symptoms. If the parents' and teacher's ratings indicate that the child's symptoms exceed 95% or 97% of children his age in the norm group, the child might qualify for a diagnosis of ADHD (Taylor & Sonuga-Barke, 2010).

ADHD ACROSS DEVELOPMENT

All children, especially preschoolers and young school-age children, show attentive, hyperactive, and impulsive behavior. These symptoms indicate ADHD only if they are inconsistent with the person's developmental level and persistent over time and across settings. Clinicians might use a chart like this one to identify non-normative patterns of behavior.

	Preschool	School-Age	Adolescence	College
Inattention	Child plays for short periods of time (<3 min)	Activities are brief (<10 min); forgetful, disorganized, easily distracted	Less persistent in tasks than peers (<20-30 min); doesn't focus on details; forgets assignments	Forgets appointments or assignments; doesn't plan ahead for long-term projects
Hyperactivity	Overactive; can't be settled, acts like a "whirlwind"	Restless, excessive movement, leaving seat in school	Fidgets with object; squirms in seat; movement of legs and limbs	Subjective sense of restlessness
Impulsiveness	Doesn't listen to adults' warnings; no sense of danger	Blurts out answers in class; interrupts others; gets into many accidents	Speaks or acts before thinking; doesn't plan ahead; risk taking	Quick and unwise decision making; impatient; reckless driving

Source: Based on Taylor and Sonuga-Barke (2010).

Children's symptoms must also interfere with their everyday functioning. To be diagnosed with ADHD, children must show clear impairment in academic, social, or occupational activities. For example, inattentive symptoms might interfere with their ability to pay attention in class and do well in school. Alternatively, hyperactive/impulsive symptoms might lead to peer rejection. Adolescents might get into trouble at work because of careless mistakes, rushing through activities, or forgetting important tasks.

Finally, *DSM-5* conceptualizes ADHD as a disorder that emerges in childhood. In order to be diagnosed with ADHD, individuals must have at least some symptoms of inattention *or* hyperactivity/impulsivity before age twelve (see text box *DSM-IV* → *DSM-5* Changes: A New Age of Onset Criterion for ADHD).

DSM-IV → *DSM-5* CHANGES

A NEW AGE OF ONSET CRITERION FOR ADHD

The criteria for ADHD in *DSM-IV* required children to show symptoms of inattention or hyperactivity-impulsivity prior to age 7 years. The rationale for this age-of-onset criterion was to differentiate children with ADHD from children who showed inattention or hyperactivity-impulsivity as a reaction to school-related stress. Unfortunately, there was no empirical justification for this criterion; it was selected rather arbitrarily by the developers of *DSM-IV*. Furthermore, research conducted after the publication of *DSM-IV* showed that nearly 50% of children with ADHD (especially those with predominantly inattentive symptoms) do not show symptoms until *after* age 7. Furthermore, individuals who show symptoms before age 7 do not differ from individuals who first show symptoms after age 7. Consequently, in *DSM-5*, the age of onset criterion was pushed back to age 12. Polanczyk and colleagues (2010) showed that extending the age of onset criterion resulted in a negligible increase (.1%) in children with ADHD, yet they correctly identified many older children and adolescents who showed serious symptoms that first emerged in middle to late childhood. By changing the age of onset criterion from 7 to 12, the developers of *DSM-5* hope that children with later symptom onset may be better identified and treated.

COREY: THE ENERGIZER BUNNY

Corey was an 8-year-old boy who was referred to our clinic by his mother. His mother reported that Corey showed significant problems with hyperactivity and impulsiveness at home. "Most second-grade boys are active, but Corey is always on the go," she reported. "Watching him tires me out." According to his mother, Corey had difficulty remaining seated during meals, constantly fidgeted with objects around the house, talked incessantly, and engaged in high-rate, restless behavior. "He's very impulsive," she added. "As soon as I let him out of the car, I know he'll run right out into the parking lot. He's constantly doing dangerous stunts with his bike. He just doesn't think things through."

Corey also showed problems with inattention at home. Corey had difficulty sustaining his attention on any activity that required concentration or effort. "He can't focus on his homework for more than a few minutes at a time," his mother said. "I tried to reward him for completing his work, but then he rushes through it sloppily." Corey was also extremely forgetful. He often neglected his chores, forgot to complete school assignments, and lost belongings for school. His mother said, "This is the third schoolbag he's had this year. He'd forget to put on his underwear if I didn't remind him."

Corey showed similar problems with hyperactivity, impulsivity, and inattention at school. Corey completed assignments quickly, making careless mistakes. His work was often difficult to read. His grades were slightly below average because he often forgot to turn in assignments, lost his work, or rushed through tests without reading directions. "When I remind him to obey the class rules, he's always apologetic," his teacher said. "He wants to be good, but he just can't follow through."

A psychologist in our clinic interviewed Corey in her office. "You have a hard time doing what you're supposed to do at home and in school?" she asked. "Yeah," admitted Corey, "I'm always getting into trouble because I'm so hyper. My mom calls me her 'Energizer Bunny.'"

Specifying Current Symptoms

When clinicians diagnose ADHD, they specify children's current symptom presentation in one of three ways: (a) combined presentation, (b) predominantly hyperactive/impulsive presentation, or (c) predominantly inattentive presentation (Coghill & Seth, 2011; Tannock, 2013) (see *DSM-IV → DSM-5* Changes: Subtypes to Specifiers).

Combined Presentation

Children with combined presentation show significant inattentive and significant hyperactive/impulsive symptoms for the past 6 months. When most people think of ADHD, they are probably envisioning a child with combined symptom presentation. Parents and teachers describe these children as careless, forgetful, sloppy, distractible, rushed, irresponsible, or restless (Lahey et al., 1997). Children with combined presentation have underlying problems with behavioral inhibition, that is, the ability to control or regulate immediate impulses to achieve more long-term goals. Disinhibition causes them to have difficulty with sustained attention and to show over-activity and impulsiveness at school and home. Most children diagnosed with ADHD in clinics and hospitals display combined symptoms.

DSM-IV → DSM-5 CHANGES

SUBTYPES TO SPECIFIERS

In *DSM-IV*, children were diagnosed with various "subtypes" of ADHD based on their predominant symptom presentation: (a) ADHD, Inattentive Type, (b) ADHD, Hyperactive-Impulsive Type, or (c) ADHD, Combined Type. However, research conducted after the publication of *DSM-IV* showed that these subtypes were unstable over time; children diagnosed with one subtype of ADHD would often meet criteria for a different subtype of ADHD a few years later. On average, only 35% of children continued to have the same subtype of ADHD over a 5-year period (Willcutt et al., 2012).

Because of their poor reliability, the ADHD subtypes were abandoned in *DSM-5*. However, both researchers and clinicians recognized the value of describing children in terms of predominantly inattentive, hyperactive/impulsive, or combined symptoms. Research studies indicated that children's predominant symptom presentation was often associated with specific comorbid problems (e.g., inattentive symptoms are often associated with academic problems whereas hyperactive/impulsive symptoms place children at risk for conduct problems). Similarly, clinicians often used the inattentive, hyperactive/impulsive, and combined labels as convenient ways to describe their clients.

Consequently, in *DSM-5*, various "specifiers" are used to indicate the child's current symptom presentation. By calling these labels *specifiers* rather than subtypes, *DSM-5* acknowledges their somewhat lower reliability while retaining their use by researchers and clinicians.

Predominantly Hyperactive/Impulsive Presentation

Children with predominantly hyperactive/impulsive presentation show significant hyperactive and impulsive symptoms but only subthreshold problems with inattention. They are usually described as "driven by a motor" or "constantly running and on the go." These children may have problems with attention and concentration, but their inattention is not severe enough to merit combined type specification (Frick et al., 1994; Owens & Hoza, 2003).

Children with predominantly hyperactive/impulsive presentation tend to be younger than children with combined presentation. Indeed, roughly three fours of children who show predominantly hyperactive/impulsive symptoms are 7 years old or younger. Several longitudinal studies suggest that predominantly hyperactive/impulsive symptoms are an early manifestation of ADHD. Young children with these symptoms often show increasingly more inattentive symptoms over time. By middle childhood, many will display significant hyperactive/impulsive *and* inattentive symptoms and be classified with combined symptom presentation (Faraone, Biederman, Weber, & Russell, 1998; Lahey et al., 1998; Marsh & Williams, 2004).

Predominantly Inattentive Presentation

Children with predominantly inattentive presentation show significant problems with inattention but subthreshold symptoms of hyperactivity and impulsivity. These children are typically described as "distractible, forgetful, and disorganized." They often do not pay attention to teachers at school or parents at home and may get into trouble because of their distractibility and lack of focus (Owens & Hoza, 2003).

Although predominantly inattentive presentation is the second most common presentation in clinical settings, it is the most common presentation in community studies. Children with predominantly hyperactive/impulsive symptoms are more likely than children with predominantly inattentive symptoms to be referred for treatment because of their high-rate, over-active behavior. In contrast, children with predominantly inattentive symptoms are often overlooked by parents and teachers, despite their higher frequency in the general population (Carlson, Shin, & Booth, 1999).

Predominantly inattentive presentation is usually seen in older children and adolescents. Typically, children who show predominantly inattentive symptoms are not diagnosed with ADHD until after they enter school. It is likely that inattentive symptoms exist at an earlier age, but they may not be recognized until children are required to sustain attention for longer periods of time.

Most children with predominantly inattentive presentation show at least six inattentive symptoms and a moderate (but still subthreshold) number of hyperactive-impulsive symptoms. However, a subset of children with predominantly inattentive presentation show few or no symptoms of hyperactivity and impulsivity (Langberg et al., 2013). These children are sometimes described as having a "restrictive inattentive presentation" or a **sluggish cognitive tempo** (Table 8.2). They often daydream, appear drowsy, and act confused. Interpersonally, they are described as lethargic, hypoactive, or passive. In school, they often appear spacey and disoriented, as if their minds were constantly wandering from topic to topic. They may not be aware of events around them (e.g., a teacher giving instructions) and take a long time to respond when asked a question. These children often do not get into trouble at school, but they may have problems making friends and getting along with classmates (Carlson & Mann, 2002; McBurnett, Pfiffner, & Frick, 2001). Consider Brandy, a girl with sluggish cognitive tempo.

Table 8.2 Behaviors of Children With Sluggish Cognitive Tempo

Forgetful	Drowsy/sleepy	Stares into space
Daydreams	Easily confused	Acts overtired
Sluggish/slow to respond	Seems to be "in a fog"	Underactive/lacks energy

Source: Based on McBurnett et al. (2001).

WELL-BEHAVED BRANDY

Brandy was a 10-year-old African American girl with a history of low academic achievement. She was referred to our clinic for psychological testing by her pediatrician, who suggested that she might have a learning disability.

Brandy's academic problems emerged 2 years earlier, when she was in the third grade. She began making careless mistakes on homework and often asked teachers to repeat instructions on assignments. In class, Brandy had difficulty listening and often daydreamed. "Brandy always seems to be off in her own little world," her teacher reported. "She seems more interested in doodling or staring out the window than in listening to me. I called her mother to make sure that Brandy was getting enough sleep, but she assured me that wasn't the problem."

Brandy's mother reported similar trouble with inattention at home: "She never seems to listen to me. It's not that she's being disrespectful; it's just that I have to remind her a thousand times to do something." Brandy's mother also remarked about her daughter's forgetfulness: "She's always asking, 'Where's my shoes, where's my homework?'" Brandy was generally compliant, except during homework time. Her mother explained, "I'll tell her to go upstairs and to do her homework, but when I check on her, she's listening to music or drawing. She says she'll get to work, but she never does."

A psychologist at our clinic administered an IQ and academic achievement test. Brandy's scores indicated average intelligence and academic skills. The psychologist shared his findings with Brandy's mother: "I don't think your daughter has a learning disability. I need a little more information, but I think that she might have ADHD." Her mother replied, "ADHD? That can't be. She's such a quiet, well-behaved girl."

We do not know whether children who show sluggish cognitive tempo are simply less hyperactive and impulsive than other children with ADHD or if children with sluggish cognitive tempo have a qualitatively different disorder altogether. Because the features of sluggish cognitive tempo are so different from the other symptoms of ADHD, some experts consider it a separate condition (Garner et al., 2012). Indeed, children with sluggish cognitive tempo often show different cognitive processing problems, such as slow processing speed and working memory deficits, than other children with ADHD. Children with sluggish cognitive tempo are also more likely to show problems with internalizing disorders (e.g., anxiety, depression, social withdrawal), whereas other children with ADHD are more likely to develop externalizing disorders (e.g., conduct problems, substance abuse). Finally, medications used to treat ADHD are often less effective for youths with sluggish cognitive tempo than youths with other ADHD symptoms. Consequently, researchers are continuing to study children with sluggish cognitive tempo to determine if there is a need for a separate disorder in future versions of the *DSM* (Harrington & Waldman, 2010).

Specifying Symptom Severity

DSM-5 also instructs clinicians to specify the severity of ADHD symptoms. Individuals with "Mild" ADHD have few, if any, symptoms in excess of the required number for the ADHD diagnosis and only minor impairment in social, academic, or occupational functioning. In contrast, people with "Severe" ADHD have many more symptoms beyond the number required for the ADHD diagnosis and marked impairment in functioning. Clinicians can also rate severity

as "Moderate," that is, severity between "Mild" and "Severe" (American Psychiatric Association, 2013).

Adult ADHD

ADHD used to be considered a childhood disorder. It is now well established that adolescents and adults can also have ADHD. However, older adolescents and adults usually manifest symptoms differently than children. *DSM-5* provides several examples of ADHD symptoms that might be especially relevant to college students and other adults. For example, whereas children might display hyperactive/impulsive symptoms by leaving their seat in class or blurting out answers, college students are more likely to experience subjective feelings of restlessness during lectures or have difficulty waiting their turn while in line at the registrar's office. Similarly, whereas children might display inattention by not listening to parents or being easily distractible in school, college students might show inattention by daydreaming during lectures, forgetting to keep appointments, or submitting late assignments with many careless mistakes (Tannock, 2013).

DSM-5 also requires older adolescents and adults (>17 years of age) to show only five, rather than six, symptoms of either inattention or hyperactivity/impulsivity to be diagnosed with the disorder. The reduced symptom count is allowed because, on average, adults with significant impairments due to ADHD often endorse fewer symptoms than children with the disorder. Indeed, as many as 50% of adults with persistent problems with inattention and hyperactivity/impulsivity fall short of the six-symptom criterion established for children. Adults who exhibit only five symptoms tend to have equal levels of impairment in tasks requiring attention or behavioral control as adults who meet six or more symptoms (Solanto, Wasserstein, Marks, & Mitchell, 2013).

ASSOCIATED DISORDERS AND FEATURES
Comorbid Disorders

Comorbid psychiatric disorders are common among children with ADHD. In one large epidemiological study, 44% of children with ADHD had at least one other psychiatric disorder, 32% had at least two other disorders, and 11% had at least three other disorders (Szatmari, Offord, & Boyle, 1989).

Conduct Problems

Many youths with ADHD develop significant conduct problems at some point in their lives. Approximately 54% to 67% of children with ADHD show Oppositional Defiant Disorder (ODD), a psychiatric disorder characterized by persistent stubbornness and noncompliance toward adults. Children with ODD refuse to obey, talk back, throw tantrums, and are otherwise spiteful and argumentative toward caregivers.

Approximately 30% to 56% of adolescents with ADHD show Conduct Disorder (CD), a more serious behavioral disturbance characterized by a persistent disregard for the rules of society. Youths with CD show a wide range of disruptive and destructive behaviors, including physical fighting, theft, vandalism, and truancy (Whittinger, Langley, Fowler, Thomas, & Thapar, 2007).

Approximately 18% to 24% of youths with ADHD develop Antisocial Personality Disorder (APD) as adults. APD is a serious personality disturbance defined by a persistent disregard for the rights of others. Adults with APD often have histories of aggression and illegal behavior. Overall, the presence of ADHD in childhood increases the likelihood of developing ODD, CD, and/or APD 10-fold. Many experts believe ADHD acts like a "motor" that drives certain children toward oppositional, defiant, and sometimes aggressive/destructive behavior (Angold, Costello, & Erkanli, 1999; Barkley, 1998; Fischer, Barkley, Smallish, & Fletcher, 2002).

Although ADHD and conduct problems frequently co-occur, they are considered separate disorders. Indeed, *DSM-5* specifically warns clinicians that ADHD symptoms are not solely a manifestation of oppositional, defiant, or antisocial behaviors (see Table 8.1; American Psychiatric Association, 2013), Many children with ADHD are hyperactive, impulsive, and/or inattentive but do not talk back to parents, fight with classmates, or skip school. Other children and adolescents show serious patterns of defiant and aggressive behavior toward family and peers but show no problems with hyperactivity or inattention (S. King et al., 2005).

Furthermore, ADHD and conduct problems in childhood and adolescence seem to have different underlying causes. ADHD is viewed predominantly as a neurodevelopmental disorder, characterized by problems with impulse control and information processing. ADHD shows high heritability and appears to be strongly influenced by genetics (Barkley, 1998). In contrast, conduct problems are viewed primarily as learned disorders, associated with problematic parent-child interactions, inadequate parental monitoring, association with deviant peers, and socioeconomic disadvantage. CD also has a somewhat lower heritability than ADHD (Loeber & Stouthamer-Loeber, 1986).

On the other hand, both ADHD and conduct problems are characterized by difficulties in "executive" functioning, that is, the ability to plan, prioritize, and regulate behavior. Indeed, some experts believe that the strong co-occurrence of ADHD and conduct problems in childhood and adolescence is due to abnormalities in the development of executive functioning (Coolidge, Thede, & Young, 2000).

Substance Use Problems

ADHD places children at greater risk for substance use problems during adolescence (Bukstein, 2011). On average, children with ADHD are 6 times more likely than typically developing peers to abuse nicotine, alcohol, or other drugs during adolescence. Approximately 22% of adolescents with ADHD have at least one substance use disorder; rates are slightly higher for girls with ADHD than boys (Biederman & Faraone, 2004; Biederman, Mick et al., 2002). The drug most frequently used by adolescents with ADHD is nicotine, although the abuse of alcohol, marijuana, inhalants, and stimulants is also common (Charach et al., 2011; Lee et al., 2011).

Why are adolescents with ADHD at increased risk for substance use problems? The answer depends on the type of substance that adolescents use. Most studies indicate that the association between ADHD and alcohol and other drug abuse is mediated by comorbid CD (Bukstein, 2011). ADHD places some children at risk for CD; CD, in turn, is associated with substance abuse. Longitudinal studies indicate that children with hyperactive/impulsive symptoms are often rejected by their typically developing classmates. They may associate with older, deviant peers who model and reinforce antisocial behavior and substance use. Children with ADHD may succumb to peer pressure in order to gain acceptance and to avoid further social rejection (Marshal et al., 2003).

In contrast, ADHD is a specific, unique predictor of smoking. Even after controlling for comorbid conduct problems, adolescents with ADHD are approximately twice as likely to smoke as their typically developing peers. Youths with ADHD begin smoking at an earlier age, have more difficulty quitting the habit, and have higher relapse rates after they quit. In one large, population-based study, there was a linear relationship between the number of ADHD symptoms reported by youths and their risk of smoking: the more symptoms, the greater the risk. Adolescents and young adults with ADHD often report that nicotine improves their concentration and behavioral inhibition. It is likely that many youths use nicotine to regulate their attention and behavior (Bukstein, 2011).

Anxiety and Mood Disorders

Internalizing disorders are also fairly common among youths with ADHD (Bagwell, Molina, Kashdan, Pelham, & Hoza, 2006). Approximately 25% of children and adolescents with ADHD have at least one anxiety disorder while 20% to 30% experience depression (Fischer et al., 2002; Tannock, 2000). Most data indicate that anxiety and mood problems are more common among girls with ADHD than boys with ADHD. Girls who show sluggish cognitive tempo are particularly prone to anxiety and mood problems (Carlson & Mann, 2002; Power, Costigan, Eiraldi, & Leff, 2004). These girls show a curious mixture of depressive, drowsy, passive, and withdrawn behavior that is usually not seen in other youths with ADHD.

The relationship between ADHD and Bipolar Disorder is unclear. Bipolar Disorder is a serious emotional disorder characterized by at least one episode of elevated, expansive, or irritable mood. Many children and adolescents with Bipolar Disorder show recurrent episodes of irritability and depressed mood. Early research indicated that children with ADHD were at increased risk for Bipolar Disorder, but later research did not replicate these findings (Barkley, 2004). The best data available suggest that the presence of Bipolar Disorder greatly increases a child's likelihood of developing ADHD; however, the presence of ADHD does not greatly increase a child's likelihood of developing Bipolar Disorder (Singh, DelBello, Kowatch, & Strakowski, 2006).

Associated Problems

Problems in Parent-Child Interactions

Children with ADHD often have problematic interactions with their parents. One way psychologists study parent-child interactions in young children is to observe dyads playing or performing a structured task (e.g., reading a book, cleaning up after play). During these interactions, mothers of children with ADHD are more negative and hostile and less sensitive and responsive to their children than are mothers of children without ADHD. Their children, in turn, engage in more aversive and noncompliant behavior (Barkley, 1988). Researchers believe that these parent-child behaviors are reciprocal: Parents engage in more hostile-intrusive parenting tactics because they are frustrated by their children's high-rate behavior; children engage in more disruptive behavior because of their parents' punitive discipline (Chronis, Lahey, Pelham, Kipp, Baumann, & Lee, 2003).

Mothers of children with both ADHD and conduct problems are at particular risk for mood disorders and substance use problems (Chronis et al., 2003). These mothers often blame themselves for their children's disruptive behavior and doubt their competency as parents (Mash & Johnston, 1990). Their feelings of low parenting efficacy may contribute to the development of depression.

The relationship between children's disruptive behavior and parents' substance use is more complex. One possibility is that parental alcohol and drug abuse causes children to show high-rate, aversive behaviors. Another possibility is that similar genes (shared by both parents and children) account for both children's disruptive behavior problems and their parents' substance use disorder. A third possibility is that children's disruptive behavior may increase parents' use of alcohol and other drugs. Pelham and colleagues (1998) asked the parents of disruptive children to interact with another child (i.e., not their own child) for a short period of time. The child, who was actually a confederate, engaged in either normal or disruptive behavior during the session. After the session, adult participants were offered alcoholic beverages while completing follow-up questionnaires. As expected, parents who interacted with children behaving disruptively reported greater feelings of inadequacy and more negative emotions than parents who interacted with children behaving normally. Furthermore, parents with family histories of substance use disorders consumed more alcohol after interacting with children behaving disruptively than with children acting compliantly. Pelham and colleagues (1998) suggested that some parents, particularly those with a genetic diathesis toward alcohol abuse, may cope with their children's disruptive behavior by drinking.

Problems With Peers

It is extremely important for school-age children to be accepted by peers and to develop friendships with children in their age group (Sullivan, 1953). These peer relationships are believed to contribute to children's self-esteem, to serve as models for adult interpersonal relationships, and to promote the development of children's identity and their capacity for intimacy in adolescence and adulthood. Indeed, the degree to which we are liked and accepted by peers in early elementary school is one of the best predictors of our social and emotional well-being in adolescence (Rubin, Bukowski, & Parker, 1998).

Unfortunately, children with ADHD are frequently disliked by peers. Their hyperactive and impulsive behavior often interferes with their ability to behave appropriately during peer interactions. Children's ADHD symptoms often cause peers to reject them quickly. In one study, unfamiliar children rated children with ADHD as less desirable play partners after only two brief play sessions (Pelham & Bender, 1982). In another study, children at a summer camp rejected children with ADHD after only 3 days (Erhardt & Hinshaw, 1994). After children are rejected by some of their peers, they often develop negative reputations among the rest of the peer group. As many as 70% of children with ADHD may not have a single friend in their class.

Hoza and colleagues (2005) used **sociometric ratings** to determine the peer status of school-age children with and without ADHD. All children in a class were asked to privately identify the children with whom they most and least enjoyed playing. Then, researchers tallied children's nominations to determine the peer status of each child. Children were categorized into one of five groups based on their peer nominations. *Popular* children received the greatest number of positive nominations. *Rejected* children received the greatest number of negative nominations. *Controversial* children received a large number of both positive and negative nominations. *Neglected* children received few nominations altogether. *Average* children received an average number of nominations, both positive and negative.

Hoza and colleagues (2005) discovered that children with ADHD were not only unpopular, they were also actively rejected by their classmates (Figure 8.1). Indeed, 52% of children with ADHD were rejected. Although children with ADHD sought friendships with their classmates, especially popular children, these high-status popular children were *most* likely to reject and avoid them. The tendency for children with ADHD to be rejected was not merely due to comorbid problems, such as oppositional or defiant behavior. Children were rejected based on their ADHD symptoms alone. Even children as young as 7 years old were rejected because of their ADHD symptoms.

Peer rejection can contribute to the development of conduct problems. Once children develop negative reputations, these reputations are difficult to change (Hoza, Mrug, Pelham, Greiner, & Gnagy, 2003; Price & Dodge, 1989a). Even if children's ADHD symptoms can be decreased (e.g., with medication), children may still be rejected by peers because of their history of hyperactivity and impulsivity. If

children are unable to develop meaningful, prosocial peer relationships before middle childhood, they may seek friendships with other peer-rejected children. These peer-rejected friends may introduce them to more serious antisocial and disruptive acts (Dishion, Andrews, & Crosby, 1995; Dishion, Eddy, Haas, Li, & Spracklen, 1997).

Academic Problems

Children with ADHD often show difficulties across academic domains, with particular problems in reading and math (DeShazo Barry, Lyman, & Grofer Klinger, 2002; Rapport, Scanlan, & Denney, 1999). Approximately 56% of children with ADHD require tutoring, 30% to 49% receive special education services, 30% repeat a grade, and 10% to 35% do not complete high school (Barnard et al., 2010). Longitudinal studies show that symptoms of ADHD in early childhood predict academic problems into adolescence, with more severe early symptoms associated with greater academic impairment later in development (DeShazo Barry et al., 2002; Fergusson & Horwood, 1995; Fergusson, Lynskey, & Horwood, 1997).

It is unclear exactly how ADHD interferes with children's academic performance. One hypothesis is that conduct problems mediate the relationship between ADHD in early childhood and academic underachievement in middle to later childhood. It is possible that ADHD contributes to

Figure 8.1 Peer Status of Children With ADHD

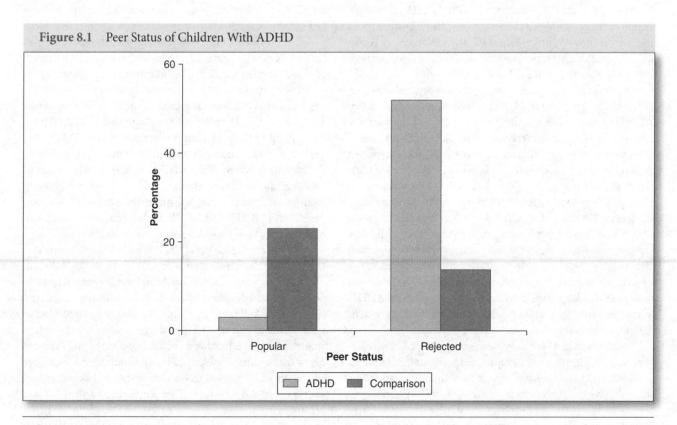

Source: Based on Hoza et al. (2005).

Note: Compared to healthy children, youths with ADHD are less popular and more frequently rejected by classmates. Peer rejection can lead to association with deviant peers and more severe behavior problems later in childhood.

conduct problems in some children and these conduct problems, rather than ADHD per se, lead to academic deficits. Support for this hypothesis is weak, however. Several studies indicate that the association between ADHD and academic deficits remains even after controlling for conduct problems (Rapport et al., 1999).

A more likely explanation is that children with ADHD have cognitive processing problems that interfere with their ability to learn in traditional academic settings (Rapport et al., 1999). For example, children with ADHD may miss information presented by teachers and opportunities to practice newly learned academic skills. Missed learning experiences may contribute to a generally lower fund of information (Buckley et al., 2006). Similarly, children with ADHD often have deficits in working memory that interfere with their ability to perform multistep academic tasks (Renz, Lorch, Milich, Lemberger, Bodner, & Welsh, 2003). They may have problems holding information in working memory long enough to use this information effectively to solve academic problems. They may also show difficulty organizing information and relaying information to others. These deficits interfere with their ability to learn new information and to perform adequately on academic tasks.

Sleep Problems

Between 25% and 50% of children with ADHD experience persistent sleep problems (Cassoff et al., 2012). Disturbances include problems falling asleep, difficulty staying asleep (early morning waking), excessive movement during sleep, restless leg syndrome, and enuresis (i.e. bed-wetting).

It is currently unclear whether these sleep disturbances place children at risk for ADHD, whether they are caused by ADHD symptoms, or whether they are a comorbid condition affected by similar underlying neurobiological problems. Evidence supporting the notion that sleep problems cause ADHD symptoms comes from two sources. First, when children's sleep is restricted by only one or two hours per night, their problems with attention and hyperactivity/impulsiveness often increase. Increased ADHD symptoms are even observable by teachers who are unaware that children's sleep is restricted. Second, longitudinal studies have shown that children's sleep problems at age 2 to 4 years predict the emergence of ADHD symptoms at age 5. However, children whose early sleep problems subsided show fewer ADHD symptoms in later childhood than children with persistent sleep problems (Gruber, Michaelson, et al., 2012).

Alternatively, there is evidence that ADHD may interfere with children's sleep. Several studies report that children with ADHD exhibit more restless, low-quality sleep. Their sleep behavior is also characterized by greater physical movements of the torso and limbs. Children with hyperactive/impulsive symptoms often experience problems settling into bed at night; consequently, they may have delayed sleep onset or refuse to go to bed altogether.

Finally, both ADHD and sleep problems are associated with similar underlying mechanisms. Like children with ADHD, children deprived of sleep often exhibit problems with attention and behavior regulation. The prefrontal cortex, a brain region largely responsible for these functions, has been implicated in both ADHD and several sleep disorders. Furthermore, the neurotransmitter dopamine is also implicated in both ADHD and sleep disorders. Dopaminergic underactivity has been suggested as a cause of ADHD whereas low levels of dopamine have been implicated in problems with arousal and wakefulness.

Taken together, these findings indicate an association between sleep and ADHD. Most experts regard this association as bidirectional; sleep disturbance likely exacerbates ADHD symptoms and these symptoms worsen the quality of children's sleep (Alfano & Gamble, 2009).

EPIDEMIOLOGY
Prevalence

Approximately 3% to 7% of children in the general population currently meet diagnostic criteria for ADHD. Prevalence is higher among school-age children compared to preschoolers, adolescents, and adults. For example, approximately 5% to 9% of school-age children have ADHD while only about 4% to 5% of adolescents and adults have the disorder (Akinbami et al., 2011).

The prevalence of ADHD has increased dramatically over the last 30 years (Figure 8.2). Data from the U.S. Department of Health and Human Services indicate that approximately 1% of children aged 3 to 18 years were diagnosed with ADHD in the late 1980s (Olfson, Gameroff, Marcus, & Jensen, 2003). Today, 9% of children have been diagnosed with ADHD at some point in time. The largest increase in ADHD has been seen in African American and low-income children. Today, the lifetime prevalence of ADHD is similar for white (10.6%) and African American children (9.5%). However, children from low-income families are more likely to have been diagnosed with ADHD (10.3%) than children from middle- or high-income families (7.2%; Akinbami et al., 2011).

Olfson and colleagues (2003) offer four explanations for the increase in the prevalence of ADHD. First, the Individuals with Disabilities Education Act (IDEA), a federal law that addresses the education of children with disabilities, began recognizing ADHD as a potential disability in 1990. Consequently, many parents sought diagnoses for their children in order to gain educational accommodations and services. Second, the number of school-based health clinics increased during this time period, giving low-income children greater access to mental health services. Third, the 1990s witnessed advances in the assessment of ADHD, leading to better identification of children with the disorder. Fourth, there was a general increase in public awareness of the disorder and, perhaps, a decrease in stigma. Organizations such as

Figure 8.2 Approximately 9% of Children 5 to 17 Years of Age Have Been Diagnosed With ADHD

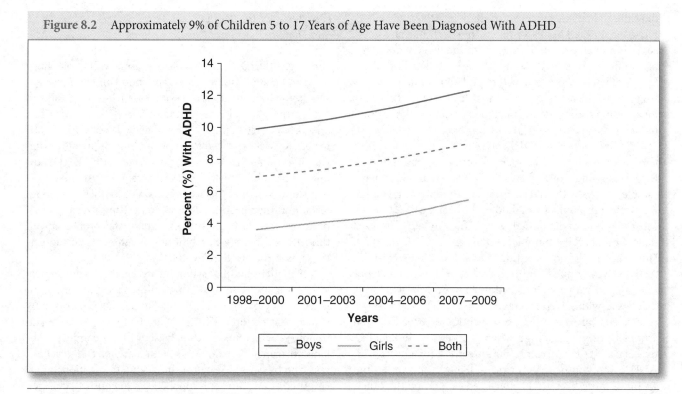

Source: From Akinbami and colleagues (2011). Used with permission.

Note: The prevalence is much higher for boys than girls and has increased over the past 15 years.

Children and Adults with Attention-Deficit/Hyperactivity Disorder (CHADD) and the Attention Deficit Disorder Association (ADDA) advocated for the rights of individuals with ADHD and their families.

Gender Differences

ADHD is more common in boys than in girls. Among clinic-referred children, the gender ratio is approximately 10:1 in favor of boys. In community samples, the gender ratio favors boys 3:1 (Arnold, 1996; Gaub & Carlson, 1997). The large gender ratio among clinic-referred children may be partially due to referral bias, not actual differences in boys' and girls' behavior. Boys with ADHD are more likely to be referred to clinics because of their coexisting disruptive behavior problems. Girls with ADHD, who are less likely to show oppositional and defiant symptoms than boys with the disorder, may not be referred for treatment.

Overall, girls with ADHD usually show better functioning than boys (Arnold, 1996; Gaub & Carlson, 1997). Girls display fewer and less severe ADHD symptoms than boys (Abikoff et al., 2002; Biederman, Mick et al., 2002; Newcorn et al., 2001). They are less likely than boys to have other disruptive behavior problems and substance use disorders (Biederman, Mick et al., 2002; Levy, Hay, Bennett, & McStephen, 2005; Wilens, Spencer, & Biederman, 1996). They are also less likely to have learning difficulties (Biederman, Mick et al., 2002; Doyle, Faraone, DuPre, & Biederman, 2001).

Girls with ADHD also show slightly different symptoms than boys. Girls are 2 times more likely to display predominantly inattentive symptoms than boys (Biederman & Faraone, 2004; Biederman, Mick et al., 2002). Furthermore, girls with ADHD have slightly lower average IQ scores than boys with the disorder, although the magnitude of the difference is very small.

Course

Persistence of ADHD

Many parents of children with ADHD ask, "Will my child grow out of it?" Unfortunately, longitudinal studies indicate that ADHD is fairly stable across childhood and adolescence (Sibley, Waxmonsky, Robb, & Pelham, 2013). Preschoolers with ADHD almost always continue to show symptoms into early childhood (Lahey et al., 2004). Furthermore, children with ADHD in early elementary school usually continue to show symptoms in high school (Larsson, Larsson, & Lichtenstein, 2004). Longitudinal studies have followed children with ADHD for 8 to 11 years (Lahey & Willcutt, 2010). These studies generally find that children with ADHD continue to show impairment one decade after their initial diagnosis.

On the other hand, approximately 25% to 35% of children diagnosed with ADHD no longer meet diagnostic criteria by the time they reach adolescence (Barkley, 1997a; Claude & Firestone, 1995). This discontinuity in ADHD during adolescence is probably due to changes in the adolescent brain that occur during puberty (Larsson et al., 2004; Willoughby, 2003). Developments in brain structure and functioning that are triggered by the onset of puberty may lead to greater capacity for attention and behavioral inhibition in some children, thus, reducing the severity of ADHD symptoms.

Adolescents with ADHD often continue to have problems with academic and social functioning in adulthood. Biederman and colleagues (2010, 2011) studied a large sample of boys with ADHD from late childhood (mean age = 11 years) through early adulthood (mean age = 22 years). Most (65%) boys diagnosed with ADHD in late childhood no longer met full criteria for ADHD as adults (Figure 8.3). However, 78% of boys continued to show either significant ADHD symptoms, subthreshold ADHD symptoms, or problems in daily living related to ADHD. Boys previously diagnosed with ADHD were more likely to repeat a grade, receive special education, be suspended or expelled from school, or drop out of high school than boys without a history of ADHD. Furthermore, boys previously diagnosed with ADHD were approximately twice as likely to be arrested and 14 times more likely to be convicted of a crime than their typically developing peers.

Persistence of Inattentive and Hyperactive/Impulsive Symptoms

Although ADHD is fairly stable over time, children's symptom presentation is not. Across childhood and adolescence, symptoms of inattention often increase while symptoms of hyperactivity/impulsivity tend to decrease (Barkley, Fischer, Smallish, & Fletcher, 2002; Hart, Lahey, Loeber, Applegate, Green, & Frick, 1995). Instead of climbing on furniture and running around the classroom, adolescents with ADHD show low motivation to engage in tasks that require sustained effort (e.g., homework), difficulty organizing activities (e.g., long-term, multistep projects, such as completing a term paper), poor self-control (e.g., reckless stunts), and problems with time management (e.g., submitting assignments late, forgetting appointments; Barkley, 2004).

Although children's symptom presentation is not entirely stable, it is useful in predicting children's concurrent problems (Lahey & Willcutt, 2010). Studies have consistently shown that children with predominantly hyperactive and impulsive symptoms are at increased risk for conduct problems, disrupted relationships with parents and teachers, rejection by peers, substance abuse, and unintentional injuries (Elkins, McGue, & Iacono, 2007). In contrast, children with predominantly inattentive symptoms are at increased

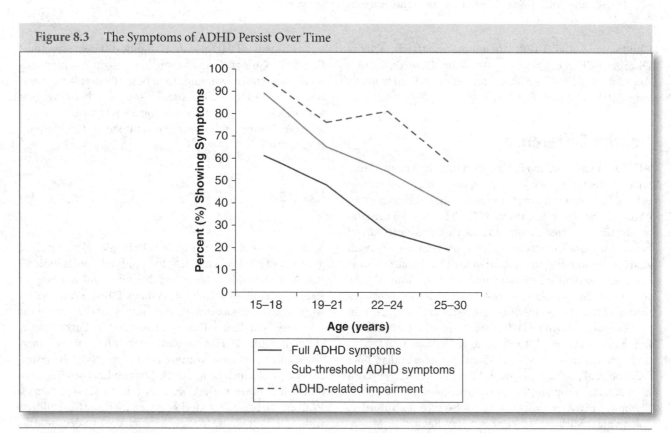

Figure 8.3 The Symptoms of ADHD Persist Over Time

Source: Based on Biederman and colleagues (2010, 2011).

Note: Most boys previously diagnosed with ADHD in childhood do not meet criteria for ADHD in young adulthood. However, most *do* show subthreshold symptoms or functional impairments related to ADHD.

risk for academic problems (especially in mathematics), social withdrawal, and internalizing disorders (Breslau, Lane, Sampson, & Kessler, 2008).

ETIOLOGY

Genetics and Early Environmental Risks

Behavioral Genetics

ADHD is a neurodevelopmental disorder with a strong genetic basis. Although the exact genes that underlie ADHD have not been identified, genetic factors may explain as much as 80% of the variance in ADHD symptoms among children with the disorder (Brookes et al., 2006).

Twin studies suggest that ADHD is heritable. Concordance between monozygotic twins is 50% to 80%, whereas concordance between dizygotic twins is only 33% (Bradley & Golden, 2001; Larsson et al., 2004). Concordance rates are higher for hyperactivity/impulsivity symptoms than for symptoms of inattention (Sherman, Iacono, & McGue, 1997).

ADHD also runs in families. Children with ADHD are more likely to have a biological parent with the disorder (18%) than children without ADHD (3%). Adults with ADHD have a 57% chance of having at least one child with the disorder. Furthermore, the siblings of children with ADHD are 3 to 5 times more likely to have the disorder compared to controls. Adoption studies consistently show that children show a much greater similarity in ADHD symptoms with their biological parents than their adoptive parents (Asherson & Gurling, 2011).

The *symptoms* of ADHD are also highly heritable (Nikolas & Burt, 2010). Genetic factors account for 71% and 73% of a child's inattentive and hyperactive/impulsive symptoms, respectively. Interestingly, however, these symptom clusters are distinct in their type of genetic inheritance. **Additive genetic effects** largely explain the heritability of hyperactive and impulsive symptoms. Additive effects represent the sum of all genetic influences from both parents on multiple parts of the genome. For example, height is an additive genetic effect because it is determined by the sum of multiple genes provided by both parents. Because hyperactive and impulsive symptoms are largely explained by additive genetic effects, there is correspondence between the hyperactive/impulsive symptoms of children and their parents.

In contrast, inattentive symptoms are largely explained by **dominant (i.e., non-additive) genetic effects**. Dominant genetic effects represent the interaction of genes from both parents on specific points in the genome. For example, eye color is a dominant genetic effect because it depends on the interaction of genes provided by each parent. Traits influenced by dominant genetic effects, like eye color, sometimes show little correspondence between a parent and child (e.g.,

a girl can have brown eyes and her mother might have green). Consequently, children and parents may show less similarity in inattentive symptoms.

Molecular Genetics

Genes associated with the dopamine neurotransmitter system probably play a primary role in the development of ADHD. Evidence for their involvement comes from four sources. First, dopamine receptors are especially prevalent in brain regions responsible for regulating attention and inhibiting behavior, especially the prefrontal cortex and striatum (Jackson & Westlind-Danielsson, 1994; Missale, Nash, Robinson, Jaber, & Caron, 1998). Second, people with lesions to these areas (and presumably damage to the dopamine neurotransmitter system) often show ADHD symptoms (Misener et al., 2004). Third, medications used to treat ADHD stimulate the dopamine system (Seeman & Madras, 1998; Stein et al., 2005). Fourth, mice lacking genes that code dopamine receptors show hyperactivity and impulse-control problems (Clifford, Tighe, Croke, Sibley, Drago, & Waddington, 1998).

Several genes involved in the synaptic transmission of dopamine are implicated in ADHD (Asherson & Gurling, 2011). One gene is the **dopamine transporter gene (DAT1)** located on chromosome 5. This gene codes for proteins that pump dopamine out of the synaptic cleft back into the presynaptic neuron. Some children with ADHD show mutations of this gene, such as an unusual repetition of gene sequences (i.e., the "10-repeat allele"). Mutations like these may cause disruption in the dopamine reuptake process. Medications such as methamphetamine, used to treat ADHD, inhibit the reuptake of dopamine, allowing dopamine to remain in the synaptic cleft longer and be detected by the postsynaptic neuron. The result is better synaptic activity and behavioral control.

The **dopamine D4 and D5 receptor genes** are also likely involved in ADHD. These genes code for proteins that act as receptors for dopamine in postsynaptic neurons. Some children with ADHD show mutations in these genes. For example, the "D4 long variant mutation" occurs when portions of the D4 gene incorrectly repeat seven times. Certain stimulant medications, such as Ritalin, bind to D4 receptors in frontal brain regions, stimulating these regions, and producing greater attention and behavioral control. Other genes that have been implicated in ADHD are the dopamine beta-hydroxylase gene (DBH), the serotonin transporter gene (5HTT), and the serotonin 1B receptor gene (HTR1B; Asherson & Gurling, 2011).

Early Environment

Although genetics accounts for the lion's share of the variance of ADHD symptoms, environmental factors also play important roles. **Nonshared environmental factors**—experiences unique to individual children—seem especially important in predicting the development of ADHD (Larsson et al., 2004). Prenatal environmental risk factors include maternal alcohol and drug use, exposure to toxins, and infections during gestation (Root & Resnick, 2003). Maternal cigarette and alcohol use during pregnancy is a particular risk (Linnet et al., 2003; Mick, Biederman, Faraone, Sayer, & Kleinman, 2002). Perinatal risks include premature birth, low birth weight, and complications with delivery involving hypoxia (i.e., restricted oxygen). Medical conditions that deprive the fetus or neonate of oxygen for extended periods of time present the greatest risk. Areas of the brain responsible for behavioral inhibition and executive functioning (i.e., frontal-striatal regions) seem to be highly susceptible to damage caused by hypoxia. Indeed, animals deliberately deprived of oxygen during their neonatal period show increased hyperactivity later in life (Brake, Sullivan, & Gratton, 2000). Several postnatal factors have also been identified, such as poor nutrition, limited access to neonatal care, and teratogen exposure, such as lead poisoning (Millichap, 2010).

Brain Structure and Functioning

Prefrontal Cortex

MRI studies have compared the brains of youths with and without ADHD. Relative to controls, children with ADHD show an average 5% reduction in cerebral volume. This reduction includes both gray and white matter and tends to be more pronounced in the right hemisphere (Almeida et al., 2010).

Other studies have investigated differences in specific brain regions. Several studies have found an overall reduction in the volume and thickness of the prefrontal cortex among children with ADHD (Castellanos et al., 1994, 1996, 2001, 2002; Filipek, Semrud-Clikeman, Steingrad, Kennedy, & Biederman, 1997; D. E. Hill, Yeo, Campbell, Hart, Vigil, & Brooks, 2003; Kates et al., 2002; Mostofsky, Cooper, Kates, Denckla, & Kaufmann, 2002; Seidman, Valera, & Makris, 2005). For example, Almeida and colleagues (2010)

measured the cortical thickness of the brains of children, adolescents, and adults with ADHD. They found that all three groups of participants showed significant reductions in the thickness of the right prefrontal cortex compared to healthy controls.

The prefrontal cortex is largely responsible for **executive functioning**, a person's capacity to effectively perceive, process, and use information in order to solve problems and attain long-term goals (Riccio, Homack, Jarratt, & Wolfe, 2006). Just as an executive of a company is responsible for organizing and implementing the company's resources in order to meet its objectives, the executive functioning areas of the brain are responsible for organizing and utilizing one's cognitive resources in order to effectively meet the demands of the environment (Figure 8.4). The executive functions include the ability to attend to relevant information, to ignore distractions, to quickly shift from one task to another, to organize information, to plan and prioritize future actions, and to follow through with one's plans in a logical and efficient manner (Biederman, Monuteaux et al., 2004). The prefrontal cortex also has connections to other areas of the brain responsible for the regulation of motor behavior, such as the basal ganglia and thalamus (Almeida et al., 2010).

Children with ADHD show deficits in executive functioning (Pennington & Ozonoff, 1996). Indeed, children with ADHD show more severe problems with executive functioning than do healthy controls (Seidman, Biederman, Faraone, Weber, & Ouellette, 1997) and clinic-referred children without ADHD (Seidman, Biederman, Monuteaux, Weber, & Faraone, 2000). Executive functioning deficits tend to be relatively stable over time. Children with ADHD who also have deficits in executive functioning usually continue to show executive functioning deficits throughout childhood and adolescence (Seidman et al., 1997) and into adulthood (Seidman, Biederman, Weber, Hatch, & Faraone, 1998).

Figure 8.4 Continuous Performance Tests to Measure Executive Functioning

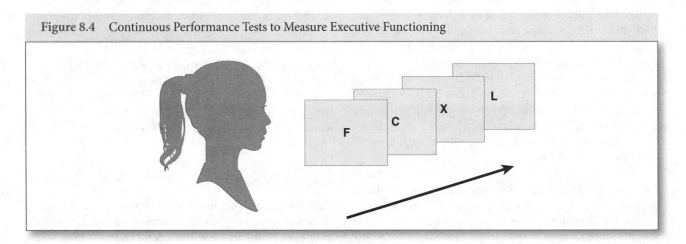

Note: Continuous performance tests are often used to measure executive functioning, especially children's ability to sustain attention and inhibit an immediate impulse. In the Conners' Continuous Performance Test 3. a computer monitor presents individual letters. Children must press a key when they see any letter but *X*, and must refrain from pressing when *X* is presented.

Two subdivisions of the prefrontal cortex seem to underlie these deficits in executive functioning: the orbitofrontal region and the dorsolateral prefrontal region (Image 8.1). The **orbitofrontal cortex** is responsible for inhibition and impulse control. The **dorsolateral prefrontal cortex** plays a role in organization, planning, and attending. Both regions tend to be smaller in children with ADHD than in controls. Furthermore, children with ADHD show underactivity in both of these brain regions, during tasks requiring behavioral inhibition and memory (Langleben, Austin, Krikorian, Ridlehuber, Goris, & Strauss, 2001; Lee et al., 2004; Seidman et al., 2005; Sowell, Thompson, Welcome, Henkenius, Toga, & Peterson, 2003).

Striatum

The striatum is another brain region that has been implicated in ADHD (Shafritz, Marchione, Gore, Shaywitz, & Shaywitz, 2004). The **striatum** is the major input station of the basal ganglia and consists of the caudate, putamen, and globus pallidus; however, the caudate seems to be especially important in the development and maintenance of ADHD (Image 8.2). The caudate is responsible for higher order motor control, learning, and memory. It is especially important in regulating behavior in response to feedback from the environment (e.g., reinforcement, punishment).

Structural and functional neuroimaging studies indicate that the development of the striatum (and the caudate in particular) is delayed in children with ADHD (Vaidya, 2011). Typically developing children show dramatic growth in this brain region, peaking between 7 and 8 years of age. Then, between late childhood and adolescence, neural connections important to behavioral control and learning are

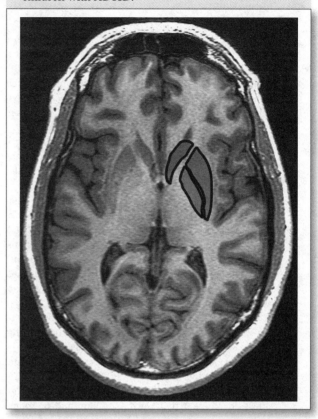

Image 8.2 The striatum receives input from the frontal cortex and is responsible for the regulation of behavior. It consists of the caudate (top), putamen (lower right), and globus pallidus (lower left). Development of the striatum is often delayed in children with ADHD.

Source: Courtesy L. Hanford and G. Hall. Used with permission.

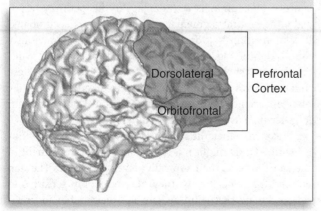

Image 8.1 The prefrontal cortex is responsible for higher order executive functions. The orbitofrontal region is responsible for inhibition and impulse control. The dorsolateral region plays a role in organization, planning, and attending. Both are smaller and underactive in children with ADHD.

Source: From Zahr and Sullivan (2008). Used with permission.

strengthened, while nonessential connections atrophy. This developmentally normal process of neural "pruning" allows the child's brain to function more efficiently. However, children with ADHD show delays in brain growth and pruning. First, growth of the striatum peaks much later than in typically developing children, usually between the ages of 10 and 11 years. Second, there is less pruning in late childhood and adolescence. Together, these findings indicate that ADHD may reflect a delay in brain development.

The Frontal-Striatal Neural Circuit and Executive Functions

The striatum is functionally connected to the prefrontal cortex through a series of neural pathways. The prefrontal cortex, striatum, and the pathways that connect them collectively form the frontal-striatal neural circuit. The **frontal-striatal neural circuit** is essential to the executive functions because it relays information between the prefrontal cortex, which is responsible for attention and inhibition, and the striatum, which plays a role in learning, memory, and behavior (Taylor & Sonuga-Barke, 2010).

Many symptoms of ADHD are produced by dysfunction in the frontal-striatal neural circuit (Faraone & Biederman, 1998; Giedd, Blumenthal, Molloy, & Castellanos, 2001). Evidence for this claim comes from four sources:

- Damage to the frontal-striatal circuit in humans (because of injury) or animals (in experimental studies) produces ADHD symptoms. In particular, humans or animals with damage to this pathway exhibit problems inhibiting their behavior, ignoring distractions, and remembering previously learned information or actions (Pliszka, Lancaster, Liotti, & Semrud-Clikeman, 2006).
- Children with ADHD often show structural and functional abnormalities in the right prefrontal cortex and caudate, two essential components of this pathway. Specifically, children with ADHD often show reduced thickness and underactivity of the frontal cortex compared to controls as well as delayed maturation and underactivity of the caudate compared to controls (Pliszka et al., 2006). Developmental delays and underactivity in these regions, which are responsible for regulating attention and behavior, might underlie many ADHD symptoms (Castellanos, 2003; Pliszka et al., 2006; Wellington, Semrud-Clikeman, Gregory, Murphy, & Lancaster, 2006).
- Children with ADHD typically perform poorly on neuropsychological tests that measure executive functioning. Adequate performance on these tests depends on the frontal-striatal circuit. Their low performance indicates deficiencies in this neural pathway (Vaidya, 2011).
- Stimulant medications, such as methylphenidate (Ritalin), affect dopamine activity in the striatum and prefrontal cortex and cause an increase in activity. This activity is associated with improvements in children's behavioral control and attention (Carrey et al., 2002; Lee et al., 2004; Seidman et al., 2005; Vaidya, 2011).

The Mesolimbic Neural Circuit and Reward Sensitivity

Years ago, Jeffrey Gray (1982, 1987) hypothesized the existence of two neuropsychological systems that govern overt behavior. The first system, the **behavioral inhibition system (BIS),** is responsible for slowing or stopping behavior in response to punishment or a lack of reinforcement. Imagine a child who engages in high-rate behavior on the playground. At recess, boisterous behavior is appropriate; however, when recess ends, the child must reduce the frequency and intensity of his behavior to meet the expectations of the classroom. The BIS is responsible for inhibiting his behavior and making it conform to environmental expectations.

Clearly, children with ADHD show underactivity of the BIS. These children are unable to adjust their behavior to meet the demands of new situations, such as the transition from recess to the classroom. They may show difficulties inhibiting their boisterous play even when classmates no longer reciprocate (i.e., a lack of reinforcement) or the teacher becomes angry (i.e., punishment). Although children with ADHD know how they should behave in class, their underactive BIS interferes with their ability to follow classroom rules.

Children with ADHD also show problems with the second behavioral system, the **behavioral activation system (BAS)**. The BAS is responsible for adjusting behavior to achieve reinforcement. Imagine that a boy is playing on his school's basketball team. In order to be successful, the boy must follow the rules of the game, pass the ball to other players, and play defense. To win the game, the boy must delay immediate gratification in order to work with the team. If the boy is able to engage in these behaviors, he is likely to enjoy playing the game, to be praised by his teammates, and to be encouraged by his coach.

Youths with ADHD often show over-activity of the BAS. Their behavior is governed primarily by a strong need for immediate reinforcement. Indeed, some theorists have argued that these children have a greater sensitivity to immediate rewards than other children (Nigg, 2001). Consequently, a boy with ADHD might behave impulsively on the basketball court in order to achieve immediate gratification, rather than work with his teammates. For example, he might ignore the referee, refuse to share the ball with other players, and avoid parts of the game that are less exciting (e.g., defense).

Structural and functional neuroimaging studies have largely confirmed Gray's theory regarding dysregulation of the BIS and BAS (Taylor & Sonuga-Barke, 2010). Our response to reinforcement and punishment is mediated by a brain pathway called the **mesolimbic neural circuit**. This pathway consists of the ventral tegmental area and nucleus accumbens (located in the middle of the brain), the amygdala and hippocampus (located in the limbic area), and the ventromedial prefrontal cortex. The mesolimbic pathway is rich in dopamine receptors and involves areas of the brain responsible for learning, memory, and emotion. It has long been considered the brain's "pleasure pathway" and is important to understanding most addictive behaviors.

However, the mesolimbic pathway is also responsible for motivating us to engage in tasks for which we anticipate rewards. Evidence supporting this claim comes from two sources. First, animals with damage to this pathway (especially the ventral tegmental area and nucleus accumbens) lack motivation to work for food rewards they previously found reinforcing. Second, adolescents and adults with ADHD often show underactivity of this brain pathway. These individuals respond to immediate reinforcement, but they often experience problems in delaying gratification to attain long-term goals or objectives (Vaidya, 2011).

Taken together, the available data indicate that individuals with ADHD might not be sensitive to reinforcement in the same way as their typically developing peers (Luman et al., 2012). Specifically, they may be highly sensitive to reinforcement that is immediate and pleasurable and relatively insensitive to reinforcement that is less salient, due to underactivity of the mesolimbic circuit. Dysregulation of the mesolimbic pathway might explain why many children with ADHD can play video games for hours (i.e., a task with immediate, salient reinforcement) but cannot sustain their attention on math homework for more than a few minutes (i.e., a task with delayed, less salient reinforcement). This difference in reinforcement sensitivity has implications for treatment: To influence the behavior of children with ADHD, parents and teachers must administer reinforcement frequently and immediately following appropriate behavior.

Barkley's Neurodevelopmental Model for ADHD

So far, we have seen that genetic and biological factors are associated with the development of ADHD. Now, we will examine the mechanism by which these risk factors lead to the disorder. One of the most influential explanations for the development of ADHD in children has been offered by Russell Barkley. According to **Barkley's neurodevelopmental model** (1997a, 1998), problems in neural development, caused primarily by genetic and early biological risks, lead to problems with behavior later in life. His model offers one explanation for how early neural development can contribute to the emergence of later ADHD.

At the heart of Barkley's model is the concept of behavioral inhibition. According to Barkley (1997a, 1998), the chief problem with ADHD is not inattention; instead, the

fundamental deficit in ADHD is a lack of behavioral inhibition. **Behavioral inhibition** refers to the ability to inhibit immediate responses, especially responses that usually provide immediate gratification. Children show behavioral inhibition when they resist the impulse to act, when they stop responding in the middle of an action, or when they ignore a distracting stimulus in order to complete another behavior. Behavioral inhibition allows children time to consider other, more adaptive ways of responding.

For example, children show behavioral inhibition when they resist the urge to blurt out answers in class. Although blurting out answers might provide them with immediate reinforcement (e.g., teacher gives them attention, classmates laugh), it may not be the most beneficial way of responding. By inhibiting this behavior, children can consider alternative ways of responding (e.g., raising their hands) that could be more reinforcing in the long term (e.g., teacher provides praise for correct answer).

According to Barkley (1997a, 1998), children with ADHD show fundamental deficits in their capacity for behavioral inhibition (Figure 8.5). These deficits arise primarily from genetics but also from early environmental experiences (e.g., prenatal distress, birth complications). In typically developing children, behavioral inhibition gives children time to develop more sophisticated cognitive processes that allow them to regulate behavior and solve complex problems.

Barkley (1997a, 1998) asserts that the capacity for behavioral inhibition permits the development of four

Figure 8.5   Barkley's Neurodevelopmental Model for ADHD

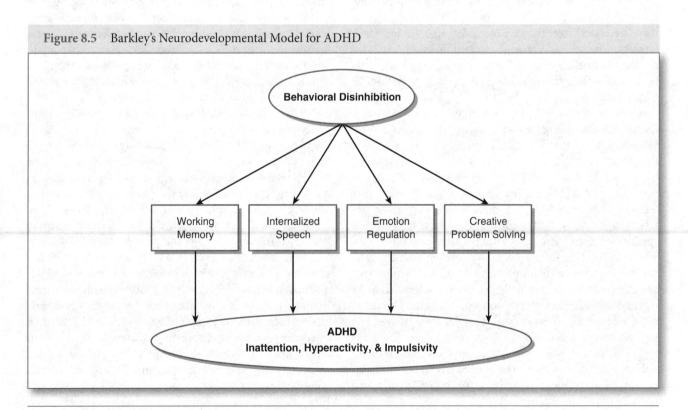

Note: Early problems with behavioral inhibition can adversely affect the development of the four executive functions. Executive functioning deficits underlie symptoms of ADHD.

basic executive functions. Each of these executive functions begins as an overt, observable behavior. Gradually, each function is internalized into mental representations or thoughts.

The executive functions serve three primary purposes. First, they allow children to determine their own behavior, rather than to be controlled by environmental stimuli. For example, the executive functions allow schoolchildren to ignore noises in the hallway and, instead, to focus on their teacher. Second, the executive functions allow children to be influenced by delayed reinforcers rather than by immediate gratification. For example, the executive functions allow children to resist the temptation to play video games (i.e., an immediate reinforcer) and, instead, complete their homework to earn a high grade (i.e., a delayed reinforcer). Third, executive functions allow children to set long-term goals. For example, executive functions allow children to plan and organize their behaviors (e.g., setting sequential short-term tasks) to accomplish long-term goals (e.g., completing a class presentation).

The first executive function to emerge is **working memory**. Working memory involves holding information in short-term memory; analyzing this information to detect useful patterns, principles, or rules; and applying this information to solve future problems. Stated another way, working memory allows us to remember past experiences and use these experiences to plan for the future. Children with ADHD often have difficulty with working memory. They appear forgetful, do not seem to listen to others or learn from past experiences, and do not consider the consequences of their behaviors before they act. Instead, their behavior is tied largely to the here and now. They are influenced primarily by stimuli in their immediate environments rather than by past events or future consequences (Wu, Anderson, & Castiello, 2006).

The second executive function to emerge is **internalized speech**. Children's inner speech guides and directs their overt behavior, giving them increased control over their actions (Vygotsky, 1978). As toddlers, children use speech primarily to communicate with others. As preschoolers, children begin to speak to themselves while performing tasks. This "self-directed" speech helps organize their actions and regulate their behavior. By the early school years, self-directed speech becomes even less overt, perhaps noticeable only when the child learns new behaviors or when he is trying to solve particularly difficult problems. By middle childhood, self-directed speech is usually completely internalized. In essence, self-directed speech becomes thought. Thoughts, or private speech, allow children to guide their behavior in logical and organized ways.

A lack of behavioral inhibition interferes with the internalization of speech. Children with ADHD have difficulty organizing and directing their behavior, following rules, and obeying others' instructions. Instead of being motivated by internalized speech and thoughts, they rely on other people and their environment for direction.

The third executive function to develop is **emotion regulation**. As children become better at inhibiting immediate behaviors, they also gain greater capacity to control the emotions that would normally follow those behaviors. Consequently, they are less influenced by immediate, transitory emotions and more influenced by expectations for long-term rewards. For example, children become increasingly better at suffering through the short-term boredom of studying for a test in order to achieve future rewards associated with the studying (e.g., good grades, praise from parents). In short, children's motivation becomes less extrinsic and more intrinsic.

Children with ADHD, however, continue to show problems with emotion regulation. They have difficulty regulating their moods, show reduced ability to maintain their motivation on tasks that require sustained effort, and appear heavily dependent on immediate reinforcement from the environment to direct their behavior. Consequently, children with ADHD can spend hours engaged in tasks that provide immediate reinforcement, but they quickly lose interest in other activities that depend on intrinsic motivation (e.g., reading, drawing, collecting).

The fourth and most complicated executive function to develop is the capacity for **creative problem solving**. Initially, children learn about their surroundings by physically manipulating objects in their environment. During play, children discover the properties of objects by disassembling them, performing simple experiments, and combining objects in new and creative ways (e.g., a child playing with bristle blocks or Legos). Later in development, objects can be mentally manipulated, analyzed, and combined in novel ways in order to solve problems. Whereas younger children might build a "fort" in their living room out of pillows and blankets through trial and error, older children can mentally plan the "fort" before beginning actual construction.

By late childhood, children can also combine words, images, information, and ideas in novel ways. This allows them to organize information, plan strategies, and solve increasingly more complex problems before acting. For example, middle-school students arranging a Halloween party can plan the guest list, refreshments, entertainment, and each person's responsibilities for the party well in advance. Children with ADHD, however, show difficulty with organization, planning, and problem solving.

In summary, Barkley's (1997a, 1998) neurodevelopmental model posits that the underlying problem with ADHD is a deficit in behavioral inhibition. Problems with behavioral inhibition are primarily determined by genetics and early environmental risks. Difficulty with behavioral inhibition interferes with the development of the executive functions during infancy and early childhood. Children show impairments in working memory, internalized speech (thinking), emotional regulation, and creative problem solving. Over time, these impairments in executive functioning can interfere with subsequent brain development and lead to the emergence of ADHD.

TREATMENT

Evidence-Based Treatment

If we view ADHD as a neurodevelopmental disorder, we notice some important implications for its treatment. First, because we have little control over children's genes and early neurological development, we should not expect to cure ADHD (Barkley, 2004). Instead, ADHD should be viewed as a developmental disorder, analogous to Intellectual Disability or Specific Learning Disorder. Treatment primarily involves symptom alleviation. Clinicians focus mostly on reducing children's disruptive behavior problems and increasing their social functioning, rather than in eliminating the disorder, per se. Because the disorder often continues into adolescence and early adulthood, treatment requires long-term intervention.

Second, because ADHD is primarily a neurodevelopmental disorder, traditional psychosocial interventions will likely have limited effects (Barkley, 2004). Early treatments for ADHD involved social skills training, that is, teaching children skills to help them learn rules and obey others. Unfortunately, these interventions were largely ineffective. Children with ADHD know how they should behave at home and school; they simply have difficulty obeying rules and adjusting their behavior to meet the expectations of the situation. According to Barkley (2004), "ADHD can be viewed as a disorder of performance—of *doing* what one knows rather than *knowing* what to do" (p. 43). The most effective treatments for ADHD help children engage in appropriate behavior at the proper point in time.

Finally, because children with ADHD often show poor executive functioning and problems with reward sensitivity, interventions must not rely on children's internal motivation to change (Barkley, 2004). The very nature of ADHD makes it difficult for children to organize and direct their behavior over sustained periods of time. Instead, children with ADHD are primarily motivated by immediate reinforcement from the environment. Consequently, interventions that provide children with immediate, tangible rewards will be most effective.

For example, if we want a child with ADHD to complete her math homework, we might offer her access to her favorite TV program contingent on the homework's completion. One tactic might be to break the assignment into small steps (e.g., five math problems) and immediately reward completion of each step with a token that can be exchanged for 5 minutes of TV. A child without ADHD would use her executive functions to sustain her attention long enough to complete the entire homework assignment. However, a child with ADHD would need more frequent reinforcement to sustain her attention over time.

Medication

Psychostimulants and Other Medications

Pharmacotherapy is currently the first-line treatment for children with ADHD. Bradley (1937) is credited with accidentally discovering the effectiveness of stimulant medications more than 75 years ago. He prescribed DL-amphetamine to a boy complaining of headaches and academic problems. He noticed significant improvement in the boy's attention, concentration, and capacity for behavioral control. Bradley (1950) began trying other stimulants like D-amphetamine (a precursor to today's Adderall) on other children with over-activity and noticed similar benefits.

Today, **psychostimulants** are the most commonly prescribed medications for ADHD. These medications affect the neurotransmitters dopamine and norepinephrine (Figure 8.6). They cause increased attention and behavioral inhibition (Greenhill, Pliszka, & Dulcan, 2002). There are two broad classes of psychostimulants: amphetamines and methylphenidates. The most frequently prescribed **amphetamines** are Adderall, Dexedrine, and Vyvanse. The most commonly prescribed **methylphenidates** are Concerta, Daytrana, Focalin, and Ritalin. Approximately 3% of all school-age children and 1.2% of all preschoolers take one of these medications, totaling more than 2.5 million children in the United States (Olfson et al., 2003; Stevens, Harman, & Kelleher, 2005; Thomas, Conrad, Casler, & Goodman, 2006).

Amphetamine and methylphenidate have slightly different chemical structures and mechanisms of action (Heal et al., 2011). Both medications stimulate the central nervous system by increasing dopamine and norepinephrine levels in the synaptic cleft. Amphetamine works primarily by increasing the release of dopamine from presynaptic storage vesicles, resulting in more dopamine output to the cleft. Methylphenidate slows the dopamine transporter system that removes dopamine from the cleft, thereby, allowing dopamine to remain in the cleft for longer periods of time. The overall effect of both of these medications is a net increase in dopamine activity in brain regions that are typically underactive in children and adolescents with ADHD, particularly the frontal-striatal circuit. This increase in dopamine activates the regions that are responsible for executive control, behavioral inhibition, and working memory (Greenhill, 2005). Youths taking these medications experience increased ability to attend, ignore distractions, inhibit behavior, and engage in organization, planning, and problem solving.

The various medications for ADHD also target different brain regions (Heal et al., 2011; Spencer et al., 2010). For example, Adderall and Ritalin are older stimulants that bind to D2 and D4 receptors in frontal brain regions, implicated in executive functioning. In contrast, Focalin is a second-generation stimulant that specifically binds to dopamine receptors in the striatum. Medications also differ in their method of delivery. For example, Adderall begins binding to dopamine receptors within minutes of ingestion; children usually show peak effects in 30 to 40 minutes, lasting approximately 4 to 5 hours. In contrast, Adderall XR (extended release) consists of a 50:50 ratio of immediate-release and delayed release capsules, resulting in effects that last 6 to 8 hours in most children. Children who refuse to swallow pills can use a methylphenidate transdermal

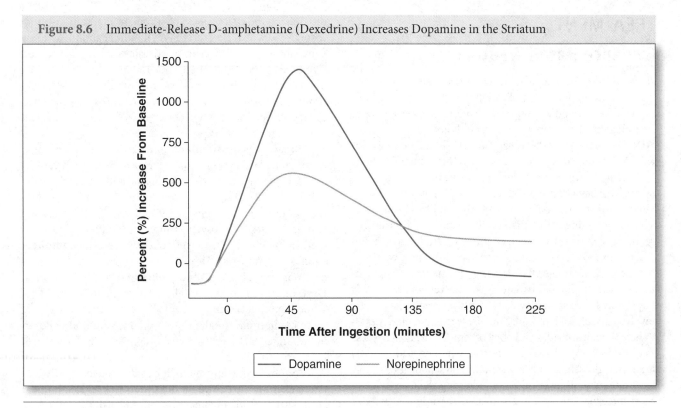

Source: Based on Heal at al. (2011).

Note: Immediate-release D-amphetamine (Dexedrine) increases dopamine in the striatum by 1500% and norepinephrine in the prefrontal cortex by 500% approximately 45 minutes after ingestion.

patch, Daytrana, which is applied to the skin once daily and produces sustained effects that last 6 to 10 hours.

What would happen if youths without ADHD took stimulant medication? Neuroimaging studies suggest that the same brain circuitry is used to regulate attention and achieve behavioral inhibition, regardless of a person's diagnostic status. Specifically, the frontal-striatal neural circuit seems to be largely responsible for attention and inhibition, with other brain regions (e.g., corpus callosum, cerebellum) playing important supportive roles. Stimulant medication seems to activate frontal-striatal brain regions, especially by increasing dopamine in the striatum (Vaidya et al., 1998; Volkow et al., 2001). Consequently, low doses of stimulant medication reduce impulsivity and increase attention in individuals with and without ADHD (Shafritz et al., 2004; Solanto, 1998).

Because stimulant medication affects individuals with and without ADHD, it has high potential for misuse (Image 8.3). In the United States, the psychostimulants are Schedule II Drugs that are restricted by the Controlled Substances Act. (Other drugs on this list include cocaine, morphine, and pentobarbital.) They are typically misused by adolescents in two ways. First, adolescents without ADHD may use these medications as "study enhancers" by orally ingesting other people's medications. These medications improve students' attention and concentration while studying. Approximately 15% of adolescents with ADHD report giving away their medication to friends, 7% admit to selling their medication, and 4% indicate

that their medication was stolen in the previous 12 months. Second, immediate-release medications can be crushed and inhaled, producing a short-lasting euphoric effect. Approximately 2.7% of eighth graders and 5% of 12th graders admit to abusing stimulant medication in this manner (Bukstein, 2011).

Not all ADHD medications are stimulants, however (Spencer et al., 2010). Atomoxetine (Strattera) is a **selective norepinephrine reuptake inhibitor (SNRI)**. Like the stimulants, Strattera seems to affect the norepinephrine system; unlike the stimulants, it appears to have little effect on dopamine activity. Effects tend to occur 2 to 3 weeks after first administration. Several randomized clinical trials have shown Strattera to be superior to placebo and comparable to methylphenidate in reducing ADHD symptoms. For example, Spencer et al. (2002) found that 69% of children responded to atomoxetine, compared to 73% taking methylphenidate and 31% taking placebo. Because atomoxetine is not a stimulant, it has lower risk of misuse.

Atomoxetine is often prescribed to the 20 to 30% of children who do not respond to stimulants (Millichap, 2010). It can also be given to children with other behavioral or medical conditions that might be exacerbated if administered stimulant medication. For example, some children with tics or heart conditions may experience increased symptoms when taking stimulants. Finally, atomoxetine may be appropriate for adolescents with a history of conduct problems or substance abuse who might misuse stimulants if they were prescribed.

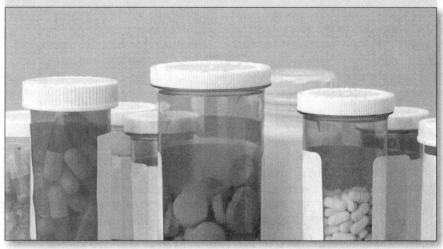

Image 8.3 Methylphenidate (Ritalin) is a Schedule II Drug that is restricted by the Controlled Substances Act in the United States. It has a high potential for misuse.

Source: Upadhyaya et al. (2013).

Efficacy

More than 200 placebo-controlled studies have demonstrated the effectiveness of stimulant medication in reducing ADHD symptoms in children older than 5 years of age (Joshi, 2004; Wilens & Spencer, 2000). For example, Biederman, Lopez, Boellner, and Chandler (2002) investigated the long-term effects of Adderall on 509 children (aged 6–12 years) with ADHD (Figure 8.7). Children were randomly assigned to either a placebo group or to a treatment group that received 10 mg, 20 mg, or 30 mg of Adderall for three weeks. Clinicians and parents, who were "blind" to children's group status, rated children's ADHD symptoms at the end of the 3-week intervention. Results showed that all doses of medication were superior to the placebo. Furthermore, there was a dose-response relationship between children's improvement and dosage; children receiving more medication were more likely to improve (McGough et al., 2005).

Across studies, approximately 70% of children with ADHD respond to medication compared to only 13% taking a placebo (Greenhill & Ford, 2002). The response rate increases to 75 to 80% if children try a second type of stimulant medication if they do not respond to the first type (Pliszka, 2003). Medication seems to affect ADHD symptoms and reduce other disruptive behavior problems, such as oppositional behavior, defiance, and some conduct problems (Joshi, 2004). A recent meta-analysis suggests that amphetamine (effect size = 1.03) is slightly more effective than methylphenidate (effect size = .77) in alleviating ADHD symptoms; however, both medications are clearly superior to placebo (Faraone & Buitelaar, 2010).

Stimulant medication is associated with improvements in children's academic, cognitive, and social functioning in addition to ADHD symptoms (Spencer et al., 2010). Several studies have demonstrated better academic performance and productivity as well as improvements in working memory and executive functioning. For example, Barnard and colleagues (2010) used data from the Special Education Elementary Longitudinal Study to examine the effects of stimulants on the academic achievement of 2,844 children with ADHD. Their analyses showed that medication was associated with higher achievement test scores across the duration of the study (i.e., 4 years). Furthermore, the association between medication and improved educational outcomes was similar for children who showed predominantly inattentive symptoms, predominantly hyperactive/impulsive symptoms, and combined symptoms.

Recent research also indicates that stimulants can be effective for preschoolers (Spencer et al., 2010). In the **Preschool ADHD Treatment Study (PATS)**, 3-and-a-half to 5-year-old children with ADHD were randomly assigned to receive various doses of immediate-release methylphenidate or placebo for 8 weeks. Results showed significant improvement in ADHD for children in the medication conditions, except those taking the lowest dose. In contrast, there was no improvement in children prescribed placebo. Only 21% of preschoolers who took medication achieved complete symptom remission, however. Furthermore, 30% of parents reported that their children experienced significant side effects (e.g., sleep or behavior problems). These findings indicate that medication is often helpful for preschoolers with ADHD, but most young children will remain symptomatic.

The most common side effects of stimulants are insomnia (59%), decreased appetite (56%), stomachache (34%), headache (30%), and dizziness (13%; Ahmann, Waltonen,

Figure 8.7 Stimulant Medication Is Efficacious in Reducing ADHD Symptoms

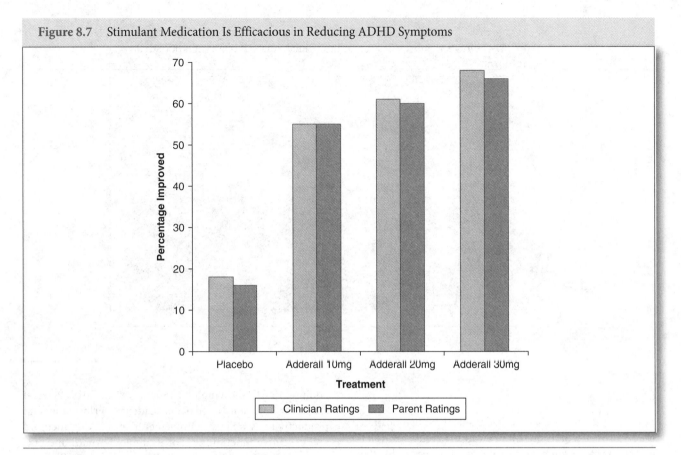

Source: Based on Biederman, Lopez et al. (2002).

Note: In this randomized, controlled study, both clinicians and parents noticed an improvement in children's ADHD symptoms.

Olson, Theye, Van Erem, & LaPlant, 1993). These side effects are usually minor and go away when dosage is reduced. Early research indicated that children who take stimulant medication may experience a slowdown in their physical development. However, more recent research suggests that children with ADHD who do not take stimulant medication also show slower growth rates, so the exact effects of stimulants on children's growth is still debated (Spencer, Biederman, Harding, Faraone, & Wilens, 1996).

There had been concern that stimulants might be associated with cardiovascular problems in children. The Canadian Department of Health temporarily prohibited certain extended-release amphetamines for children with ADHD, following anecdotal reports of sudden death, heart attack, and stroke. In the United States, several regulatory agencies recommended black-box warning for stimulants frequently prescribed to children. Indeed, the American Heart Association suggested that children taking stimulants participate in periodic electrocardiograms to monitor their safety. Recently, however, a large epidemiological study indicated that these concerns are likely unwarranted. Researchers analyzed health records of 1,200,438 children and young adults, including 373,667 individuals prescribed stimulant medication. They found that the risk of a cardiovascular event was very low overall (i.e., 81 people in the sample),

and there was no association between stimulant use and cardiovascular problems.

The non-stimulant medication atomoxetine is associated with fewer side effects (Spencer et al., 2010). For example, insomnia and appetite suppression are less common with atomoxetine than methylphenidate. Furthermore, atomoxetine is not associated with weight reduction and slowed growth. However, because axomoxetine affects norepinephrine, like many antidepressant medications, it carries a black-box warning which indicates that children who take this medication may be at increased risk for suicidal ideation. In one large study, 0.4% of children taking atomoxetine showed suicidal ideation compared to 0% of children taking placebo. Risk of suicidal ideation is very rare. However, clinicians and parents must weigh the risks of suicidal ideation versus the benefits of atomoxetine when deciding to use this medication.

Limitations of Pharmacotherapy

Medication for ADHD has several limitations. First, not all children respond to medication. Even in carefully controlled research studies, as many as 15% to 30% of children with ADHD do not show improvement. In the community, nonresponse rates may exceed 50% (MTA Cooperative Group, 1999). Clearly, medication is not a panacea for ADHD.

Second, discontinuation of medication almost always results in the return of ADHD symptoms. Consequently, most physicians view stimulant medication as a long-term treatment for ADHD. Longitudinal studies indicate that stimulant medications remain safe and effective for at least 2 years (Joshi, 2004), but their effects after that duration are largely unknown.

Third, stimulant medications should be used cautiously in children with tics or Tourette's syndrome. Overall, there is little evidence that stimulant medications elicit tics. However, very high doses of stimulants may exacerbate tics in certain children who already have them. These children may be prescribed atomoxetine instead of stimulants, which is not associated with motor control problems (Pringsheim & Steeves, 2012).

Finally, many families are reluctant to use medications to manage their children's ADHD symptoms. For these families, psychosocial interventions offer an alternative avenue of treatment.

Psychosocial Treatments

Clinical Behavior Therapy

Clinical behavior therapy is the most frequently used evidence-based, non-pharmacological treatment for ADHD (Young & Amarasinghe, 2010). This form of treatment is called "clinical" behavior therapy because clinicians typically administer treatment from hospitals and clinics, rather than in people's homes. The focus of therapy is on children's overt behavior. Clinical behavior therapy has three main components: (a) parent consultation, (b) school consultation, and (c) a combined home-school reward system.

Parent consultation, sometimes called "**parent training**," involves helping the caregivers of children with ADHD learn more effective ways to manage their children's behavior. Typically, the therapist meets with parents on a weekly basis, over the course of 2 to 3 months. Each week, the therapist introduces a new parenting principle or tactic designed to improve the quality of parents' interactions with their children or help parents manage their children's high-rate behaviors. Early sessions focus on teaching parents how to attend to children's positive behavior and reinforce children for obeying rules. These sessions help parents acknowledge and strengthen desirable aspects of their children's behavior—behaviors that are often overshadowed by children's ADHD symptoms.

Later sessions focus on setting clear expectations for children and administering consistent discipline for children's misbehavior. Clinicians usually teach parents of young children to use time out to address disruptive behavior problems. Parents of older children may be taught how to use tokens or points to reinforce appropriate behavior and penalize inappropriate actions. The purpose of these sessions is to help parents address their children's misbehavior without yelling, threatening, or resorting to hostile and coercive interactions.

In addition to meeting with parents, clinicians consult with teachers and other school personnel and implement a home-school reward system. Clinicians usually help teachers identify times or situations when the child is most often off task. Then, clinicians help teachers change the environment to reduce disruptive behavior and encourage on-task activities. Clinicians also encourage teachers to keep a **daily report card** of children's appropriate behavior at school, which can be monitored and rewarded by parents at home. Finally, clinicians may help teachers develop a classroom-wide token economy or point system to encourage students' attention and compliance. Tokens can be exchanged for privileges enjoyed by all students in the class.

Recently, researchers have developed a parent training program specifically for the fathers of children with ADHD (Fabiano et al., 2012). The intervention is called **COACHES (coaching our acting-out children, heightening essential skills)**. It consists of 8 weekly sessions, each 2 hours in duration. During the first hour, fathers learn the basic components of operant conditioning, including the importance of giving clear commands, attending to and reinforcing appropriate behavior, and ignoring or punishing high-rate behavior. During the second hour, fathers and children play soccer. During the game, fathers practice parenting skills and therapists offer assistance. In a randomized controlled study, fathers who participated in the COACHES program praised their children more often and were critical of their children less often than fathers assigned to a waitlist control group. Furthermore, their children showed significant reductions in the intensity of behavior problems. These findings suggest that a program like COACHES, which combines parent training with sports, can be an effective way to engage fathers who might otherwise be reluctant to participate in therapy.

Clinical behavior therapy is effective in improving the functioning of children with ADHD and their families (Lundahl et al., 2006). A meta-analysis of 68 studies showed that parent training was associated with moderate improvements in children's behavior (effect size = .42), parents' behavior (effect size = .47), and parents' perceptions of their children (effect size = .53). Up to one year after treatment, gains made in therapy were attenuated but remained significant. Children who showed the most severe behavior problems tended to benefit the most from parent training. Interestingly, parent training was much more effective when it was administered to individual families rather than to groups of parents. However, parent training was least effective for families from disadvantaged backgrounds. It is possible that socioeconomic hardships interfere with parents' abilities to attend therapy sessions, to learn strategies taught during sessions, and to practice these strategies at home. The researchers suggest that disadvantaged families might benefit from individual parent-training sessions, during which the therapist might tailor interventions to each family's needs.

Clinical behavior therapy for ADHD also has several limitations. First, the efficacy of parent training is strongly related to parents' involvement in the program. For example, in one study of kindergarten children with ADHD, clinical behavior therapy led to improvements in children's behavior at school, but not at home (Barkley et al., 2000). The failure of treatment to improve home behavior was probably due to the fact that most parents did not consistently attend the parent training program. When parents consistently attended training sessions, treatment was associated with improvements across home and school contexts (Anastopoulos, Shelton, & Barkley, 2005).

Second, parent training is typically effective only as long as parents actively implement strategies and tactics learned in therapy. Although most children show symptom reduction immediately after their parents' completion of the training program, the effects of therapy tend to be reduced 6 to 12 months later (Hinshaw et al., 2002).

Third, parent training does not always normalize child behavior (Hinshaw et al., 2002). *Normalization* refers to whether, at the end of treatment, children cannot be distinguished from children without significant behavior problems. Even after parent training, children tend to show symptoms of ADHD and continue to merit the ADHD diagnosis. In fact, only about 25% of children whose parents participate in treatment no longer meet diagnostic criteria for ADHD (Anastopoulos et al., 2005; Hinshaw et al., 2002; Klein et al., 1997).

Fourth, parent training programs are less effective with adolescents than with children (Barkley, 2004). Parent training works best when parents have a high degree of control over their children's environmental contingencies. However, parents have much less control over adolescents than over school-age children. Consequently, some clinicians supplement traditional parent consultation with parent-adolescent problem-solving and communication training (Barkley, DuPaul, & Connor, 1999). Specifically, clinicians teach parent-adolescent dyads how to solve problems and handle disputes constructively—rather than by resorting to yelling, sarcasm, criticism, or "shutting down." Unfortunately, supplementing traditional parent training with communication training does not seem to be more effective than traditional parent training alone (Barkley, Edwards, Laneri, Fletcher, & Metevia, 2001). Only about 23% of adolescents show reliable improvement in their behavior, and 17% of dyads actually showed a worsening of family disputes, perhaps because they were encouraged to discuss conflicts openly rather than to avoid them.

Direct Contingency Management (Summer Treatment Program)

A second form of behavioral treatment for ADHD is direct contingency management (Pfiffner & O'Leary, 1993). **Direct contingency management** is used in schools and specialized classroom settings, in which therapists have a great deal of control over children's surroundings. In direct contingency management, therapists alter children's environments to maximize the frequency of desired actions. They rely heavily on systematic rewards and punishments to shape behavior. Usually, environmental contingencies are used to increase attention, reduce disruptive behavior in the classroom, and improve the quality of children's interactions with peers.

One of the best known examples of a direct contingency management program for children with ADHD is the **Summer Treatment Program (STP)** developed by William Pelham (Pelham, Fabiano, Gnagy, Greiner, & Hoza, 2005). The STP provides comprehensive treatment for children with ADHD over the summer months, a time during which most children do not receive treatment for their ADHD symptoms. The STP is an 8-week program for children aged 5 through 15 years with ADHD and other disruptive behavior problems.

Children are divided into age-matched teams led by staff members, usually college students who are trained as behavior therapists. Teams stay together throughout the summer in order to foster friendships and improve the social functioning of members. Each group spends 3 hours per day in a modified classroom setting, led by special education teachers. Children participate in one hour of academic instruction, one hour of computer assisted instruction, and one hour of art class. Children spend the rest of the day in recreational group activities that are highly structured, such as soccer, softball, and swimming. These activities are designed to improve children's social and motor skills.

STP differs from traditional summer camps; staff members use direct contingency management to modify children's behavior. The tactics used by staff members resemble the strategies taught to parents during clinical behavior therapy. The low staff-to-child ratio allows staff to closely monitor children's behavior throughout the day and provide immediate reinforcement contingent on children's appropriate behavior. The intervention is intensive and comprehensive.

First, staff members issue brief, clear, and specific commands to children and only when certain children are attending. Clear directions reduce the chance that children will not comply with the command because of inattention, ambiguity, or distraction. Second, staff members provide immediate and liberal reinforcement contingent on desirable behavior. Social reinforcers include eye contact and smiles, touch (e.g., a high five), or recognition (e.g., buttons, stickers). Third, staff members use tokens with younger children and a point system with older children to foster desirable behavior. Staff award tokens or points for appropriate behavior in the classroom (e.g., attending to the teacher, working quietly) and during recreation (e.g., listening to coaches, following pool safety rules). Tokens or points can be exchanged for privileges. Response cost is used to reduce inappropriate behavior. Staff take away tokens or deduct points contingent on unwanted behaviors (e.g., excessive talking in class, teasing peers on the soccer field). For more serious rule violations, staff use time out. For example, children who deliberately hurt others or destroy property are removed from positive reinforcement (e.g., no swim or computer time).

The behavioral interventions used by STP staff are supplemented by social skills training, parent training, and medication assessment and management. First, all children participate in 10 minutes of formal social skills training each day. Staff members initially introduce a social skill (such as raising your hand before speaking in class) by talking about it, demonstrating it, and breaking it down into steps. Then, children are encouraged to practice the skill during a role play. Staff members remind children to use the new skill throughout the day and reward them liberally for its use. Second, caregivers participate in weekly group parent training sessions designed to teach them how to use behavioral principles in the home. Staff members give parents a daily report card and encourage them to reward their children for appropriate behavior at camp. Finally, children in the STP are assessed to determine the appropriateness of medication to treat their ADHD symptoms. If medication is warranted, the effectiveness of the medication is monitored during camp.

Direct contingency management appears to greatly improve children's behavior (DuPaul & Eckert, 1997; DuPaul & Stoner, 2003). Treatment programs using direct contingency management have been shown to increase attention and appropriate social behavior, reduce disruptive behavior and aggression, and improve children's self-esteem (Barkley et al., 2000; Pelham, Carlson, Sams, Dixon, & Hoza, 1993). Furthermore, parents report a high degree of satisfaction with intensive classroom or summer camp interventions (Pelham, Fabiano et al. 2005; Wells et al., 2000).

For example, Chronis and colleagues (2004) performed one of the first controlled studies of the effectiveness of STP for children with ADHD (Figure 8.8). In their study, 44 children (90% Caucasian, 90% boys) aged 6 to 13 years participated in an 8-week STP modeled after the one developed by Pelham and Hoza (1996). All children had ADHD and 85% also showed either Oppositional Defiant Disorder or Conduct Disorder.

The researchers used a BAB within subjects design to evaluate the effectiveness of the STP. For the first 5 weeks of camp (Phase B), staff used direct contingency management to modify children's behavior. For 2 days during Week 6 (Phase A), staff refrained from using direct contingency management. For the final 2 weeks of the STP, direct contingency management procedures were reinitiated (Phase B). Independent observers rated children's behavior during all three phases of the evaluation. Children showed a significant increase in disruptive behavior when treatment was removed compared to when direct contingency management was used.

Direct contingency management has some important limitations (Hinshaw et al., 2002). First, treatment gains acquired in the special classrooms or summer camps do not generalize to children's homes and are not well-maintained after the program ends (Pelham & Hinshaw, 1992). Second, direct contingency management procedures are not typically associated with better academic functioning (Pelham et al., 1993). Although children who participate in these special programs show improvements in behavior, their academic skills usually remain unimproved. Third, almost no studies have investigated the efficacy of direct contingency management

with adolescents who have ADHD. Finally, summer treatment programs are not available in most communities. Parents who want their children to attend a summer camp program may be unable to find one near their home (Barkley, 2004).

Multimodal Psychosocial Therapy

Multimodal psychosocial therapy (MPT) is a broad-based treatment for children with ADHD that integrates psychosocial, educational, and behavioral treatment (Hechtman, Abikoff, & Jensen, 2005; Klein, Abikoff, Hechtman, & Weiss, 2004). MPT is designed to improve children's (a) home behavior, (b) academic skills, and (c) social functioning with peers and adults. MPT consists of a number of treatment components, each targeting one or more of these domains of functioning.

To improve behavior at home, parents participate in small-group parent training sessions (Hechtman et al., 2004a). This component of treatment is similar to the parent training provided in clinical behavior therapy. Parents are taught principles of operant conditioning and how these principles can be used to manage the behavior of children with ADHD. Key components of treatment involve learning how to give effective commands, to attend and reinforce appropriate child behavior, and to selectively ignore and punish inappropriate child behavior. Teachers provide feedback regarding children's behavior at school, using a daily report card. Parents can reinforce appropriate behavior at school by rewarding children at home, based on these reports.

To improve academic functioning, children receive **educational skills training**, support, and tutoring (Hechtman et al., 2004a). For example, in one MPT program, children participated in a 16-week study skills program designed to teach time management, listening comprehension, organization of written work, and various study skills. They also received individualized academic plans and remedial tutoring in spelling, writing, and arithmetic.

To improve social functioning, children participate in **social skills training** (Abikoff et al., 2004a). In small groups, children are taught basic interaction skills, how to get along with peers, how to interact with adults, how to carry on a conversation, and how to deal with conflict situations. In each training session, the therapist introduces a specific skill, breaks it down into small steps, models it, and encourages children to practice the skill in a role play. Sometimes, children are videotaped while practicing the skill, and group members provide feedback after watching the tape. Outside the class, parents and teachers remind children to practice the skill in real-life situations and reinforce its appropriate use.

MPT is effective in reducing ADHD symptoms in school-age children (Abikoff et al., 2004a, 2004b; Hechtman et al., 2004a, 2004b, 2005). Specifically, treatment is associated with fewer disruptive behavior problems, better academic performance, improved social functioning, and more satisfying parent-child interactions. The effectiveness of MPT may be attributed to the fact that it is an intensive, comprehensive form of treatment.

Figure 8.8 Summer Treatment Program for Youths With ADHD

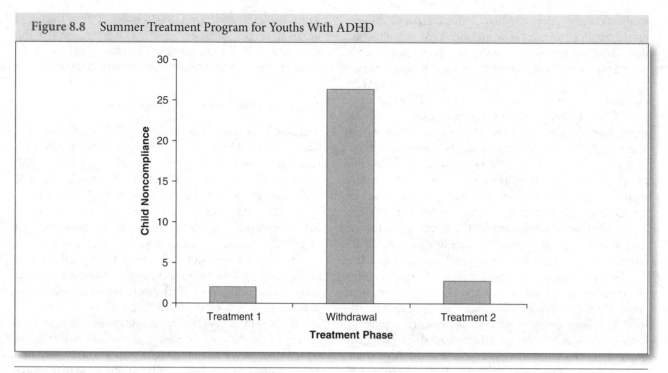

Source: Based on Chronis et al. (2004).

Note: Chronis and colleagues (2004) used direct contingency management during treatment phases 1 and 2, but withdrew contingencies between treatment phases. Children's noncompliance increased during treatment withdrawal, indicating that treatment was effective.

MPT has two primary limitations. First, most communities do not offer MPT. The limited access to MPT is probably because there are few professionals trained in MPT and fewer clinics able to devote the time and resources to develop MPT programs. The second drawback to MPT is that it may be less effective for younger children compared to older children (McGoey, DuPaul, Eckert, Volpe, & van Brakle, 2005). Its efficacy with adolescents has not been adequately examined.

Working Memory Training

Working memory refers to the ability to temporarily hold information in short-term memory, manipulate it, and use it to solve problems (Castellanos & Tannock, 2002). Working memory is important to many cognitive tasks including remembering instructions, planning work, and completing assignments. Working memory is one of several executive functions believed to be underdeveloped in children with ADHD (Barkley, 1998). Furthermore, children and adolescents with ADHD often show deficits in working memory compared to their typically developing peers (Martinussen et al., 2005; Engelhardt et al., 2008). For example, children with ADHD often forget to complete a chore at home because they are distracted by a telephone call, or they forget an important step in a math problem because they were eavesdropping on a conversation between two classmates. Deficits in working memory likely contribute to children's symptoms of inattention and associated academic problems.

Indeed, working memory deficits often underlie learning disabilities (Geary et al., 2012).

Although stimulant medication is effective at improving the behavior of children with ADHD, its effects on working memory are less robust. Consequently, Beck and colleagues (2010) have developed an intervention program designed to improve the working memory skills of youths with ADHD (Figure 8.9). The computer-based program is administered at home and is supervised by parents. It consists of 25 sessions, each lasting 30 to 40 minutes, administered over the course of 6 weeks. Each session consists of activities designed to strengthen children's working memory skills. Some activities involve verbal working memory (e.g., remembering names or objects) whereas other activities are designed to strengthen visual-spatial working memory (e.g., remembering patterns, shapes, or puzzles). The computer adjusts the difficulty of items based on children's performance, so they are neither bored nor overwhelmed by the activities.

A randomized controlled study of the working memory intervention yielded promising results. The parents of children who participated in the program reported significant reductions in their children's inattentive symptoms over time. Furthermore, these gains were maintained 4 months later. Teachers reported borderline-significant improvement in children's inattentive symptoms as well. No such improvement was seen among youths in the comparison group. These findings are noteworthy because this program was relatively brief, easy to administer, and did not involve the use of medication.

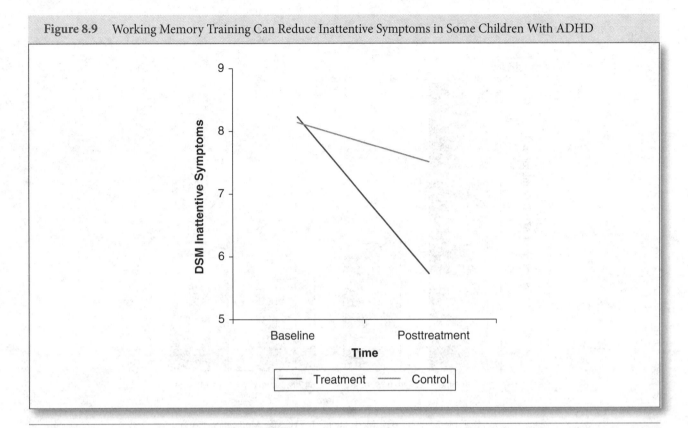

Source: Based on Beck and colleagues (2010).

Note: This brief and easy-to-use program led to a significant reduction in parent-reported symptoms.

Medication Versus Psychosocial Treatment

Both stimulant medication and certain psychosocial treatments can effectively reduce ADHD symptoms in children. Is one treatment better than the other? Should we combine treatments to produce the greatest effects?

Fortunately, several studies have compared the efficacy of pharmacological and psychosocial treatments. In one recent study, researchers examined 103 children with ADHD (93% boys; Abikoff et al., 2004a, 2004b; Hechtman et al., 2004a, 2004b). Children were randomly assigned to one of three treatment groups. The first group received only methylphenidate. The second group received methylphenidate plus MPT. The third group received methylphenidate plus an attention placebo. The children in this third condition worked on projects with staff members, received help with homework, and participated in nondirective therapy with a counselor about day-to-day problems. Their parents also attended a parent support group but did not receive parent training. Parents, teachers, psychiatrists, and independent observers rated children's behavior every 6 months for 2 years. The researchers were interested in whether children who received both medication and MPT would fare better than children in the other two groups.

Results were consistent across all outcome variables. First, all three groups of children showed improved functioning from the beginning of the study to the time the study ended. For example, children in all three treatment groups showed fewer disruptive behavior problems, improved academic functioning, better social functioning, and better quality parent-child interactions over the course of treatment. Most of the improvement in children's behavior occurred during the first 6 months of treatment. The second important finding of the study was that all three groups of children showed generally equivalent outcomes at 1- and 2-year follow-up. Contrary to the researchers' expectations, children who received methylphenidate plus MPT fared no better than children who received methylphenidate alone or methylphenidate plus placebo (Figure 8.10).

A larger study comparing the pharmacological and psychosocial treatments for ADHD yielded similar results. In the **Multimodal Treatment Study of Children with ADHD (MTA Study),** 579 children with ADHD were randomly assigned to one of four treatment groups (MTA Cooperative Group, 1999; Swanson et al., 2001). The first group received medication for 14 months. Most of the children in this group were prescribed stimulant medication, usually methylphenidate. The second group participated in approximately 8 months of behavioral treatment. Treatment included both clinical behavior therapy and a summer camp treatment

Figure 8.10   Should We Combine Medication and Behavior Therapy?

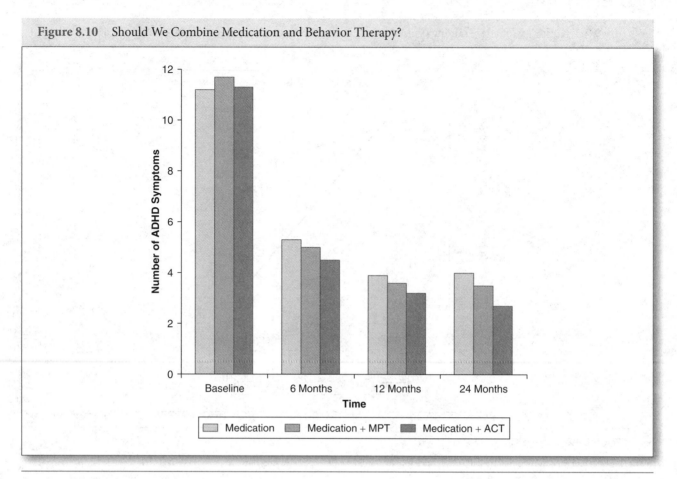

Source: Based on Abikoff et al. (2004b).

Note: Results of one large study indicated that combining medication with Multimodal Psychosocial Treatment (MPT) or Attention Control Treatment (ACT) did not lead to better improvement than using medication alone.

program. Children in this group did not receive medication. The third group received a combination of medication and the behavioral treatments. The fourth group received community care; that is, they were not treated by the research team. Instead, they were referred to mental health professionals in their communities. Most (67%) children who received community care were eventually prescribed medication. Researchers assessed the functioning of children after 14 months of treatment to examine outcomes.

Results indicated that all four treatments were reasonably effective at reducing ADHD symptoms and other disruptive behaviors (Swanson et al., 2001). However, children who participated in either medication management or combined treatment were two times more likely to improve compared to children who received only behavioral treatment or community care (Figure 8.11). The addition of behavioral treatment to medication alone produced a statistically significant but small improvement in children's behavior.

Taken together, the MTA study suggests that medication alone is superior to behavioral treatment alone for children's ADHD symptoms. Adding behavioral treatment

to medication can lead to a slight improvement in children's functioning over medication alone. However, other data indicate that psychosocial treatment may be as efficacious as medication. Pelham and colleagues (2000) reanalyzed data from the MTA study. The researchers compared children's functioning while they were participating in the summer treatment program with the functioning of children who were receiving medication alone. They found that children actively participating in STP showed levels of functioning comparable to children receiving medication. By analyzing children's outcomes after the STP had ended, the MTA evaluation may have missed the program's benefits for children's functioning.

Moreover, recent research conducted after the MTA study provides additional support for the efficacy of psychosocial treatments alone. Fabiano and colleagues (2009) reviewed 175 studies, involving more than 2,000 participants, investigating the usefulness of psychosocial interventions. Overall, the effects of these interventions on children's ADHD symptoms were large. For example, across all between-group studies, participants who received psychosocial treatment

Figure 8.11   Results of the MTA Study

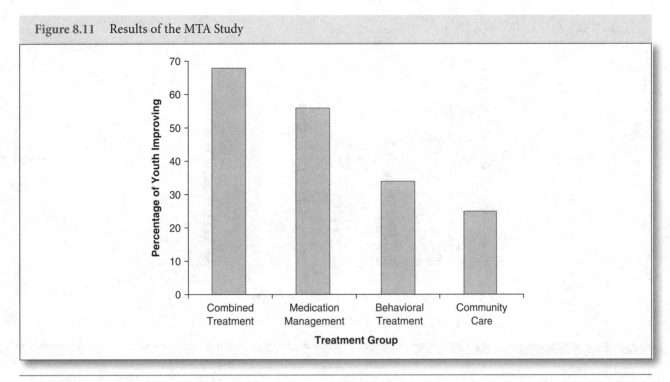

Source: Based on Swanson et al. (2001).

Note: Combining medication with behavior therapy, or using medication alone, is superior to behavior therapy alone to treat ADHD.

showed greater symptom reduction than approximately 80% of controls. Similarly, in within-group studies, children who received psychosocial interventions showed an average of 2.64 standard deviations improvement from pretest to posttest.

There are at least three additional reasons for using psychosocial treatments (Pelham, Fabiano et al., 2005). First, parents strongly prefer behavioral treatments over pharmacological ones. Parents are understandably wary of administering stimulant medication to their children, especially those for which we have limited data regarding their long-term impacts on health and behavior. Second, not all children respond to pharmacological treatments for ADHD. Psychosocial interventions offer an alternative form of treatment to non-responders. Third, there is some evidence that combining psychosocial interventions with medication leads to better outcomes than using medication alone (Pelham & Waschbusch, 1999). The evidence for this claim is mixed, but most practitioners argue that combined treatment is preferable to medication alone.

Special Diets

Many parents believe that certain foods or food additives can exacerbate hyperactive and impulsive symptoms in children with ADHD. The notion that diet might be related to ADHD began in 1973 when Benjamin Feingold, Chief of the Department of Allergy at the Kaiser Permanente Foundation Hospital, suggested that certain foods might increase symptoms. He suggested restricting foods containing salicylic acid, such as apples, berries, green peppers, oranges, and tomatoes, as well as artificial preservatives. He claimed that 60 to 70% of children with ADHD improved on the Kaiser-Permanente Diet. Similar diets recommend avoiding artificial colors and flavors and restricting foods containing dairy or wheat (e.g., chocolate, eggs, milk, breads).

Do special diets help children with ADHD? On average, the difference between children with ADHD who adopt special diets versus those that eat all foods is small (effect size = .28; Schab & Trinh, 2004). Furthermore, the benefits of special diets tend to be reported by parents but not observed by clinicians or teachers. However, the effects of special diets seem to be much larger for children whose parents previously reported a sensitivity to certain food or additives (effect size = .54) compared to children in general (effect size = .09). Furthermore, special diets do not seem to significantly affect the behavior of children without ADHD (effect size = .12).

Altogether, these findings indicate that a subgroup of children with ADHD may have sensitivities to certain foods or artificial colors, flavors, or preservatives (Figure 8.12). Restricting these substances may result in modest improvement in these children. Dietary restriction will likely have little to no effect on many children with ADHD and most children without the disorder (Stevens et al., 2011).

Figure 8.12   Can Artificial Colors in Foods Increase ADHD Symptoms?

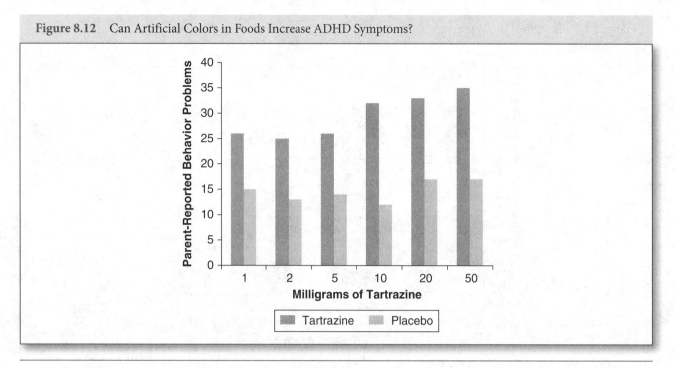

Source: Based on Stevens and colleagues (2011).

Note: Researchers administered either tartrazine (yellow and green food coloring) or placebo in varying doses to children with ADHD who showed sensitivity to food additives. Results indicated that this subgroup of children showed an increase in irritability, sleep problems, restlessness, aggression, and inattention after ingesting tartrazine.

Sleep and Exercise

Before ending our discussion of the treatment of ADHD, we should keep in mind that most families do not have access to well-designed medication management programs, intensive summer treatment programs, or multimodal interventions. Instead, most (92%) children with ADHD receive only medication prescribed by physicians in the community. Only 26% of children with ADHD participate in some form of psychosocial intervention. Sadly, as the MTA study shows, community care often yields only modest benefits. We must remember that the efficacy of medication and behavioral treatment depends greatly on the skill and scientific judgment of the scientist-practitioners who administer them (Olfson et al., 2003).

Thankfully, new research indicates that parents can adopt two simple strategies to help their children cope with symptoms of inattention or hyperactivity/impulsivity. The first strategy is to make sure their children get enough sleep. Recall that children with ADHD often experience sleep disturbance; they may be reluctant to go to bed at night, have difficulty falling or staying asleep, and show more restless sleep than their typically developing classmates (Alfano & Gamble, 2009). Furthermore, most children (with or without ADHD) show an increase in inattentive and hyperactive/impulsive symptoms when deprived of sleep. Consequently, researchers speculated that sleep might be a mechanism by which ADHD symptoms might be alleviated in certain children.

Gruber and colleagues (Gruber, Cassoff, Frenette, Wiebe, & Carrier, 2012) randomly assigned children to two conditions. Parents in the first condition were asked to put their children to bed one hour earlier than usual; parents in the second condition were asked to put their children to bed one hour later. On average, children in the sleep enhancement condition gained an extra 27 minutes of sleep per night, whereas children in the sleep restriction condition lost 54 minutes per night. Teachers, who were blind to the children's condition, reported improvements in the behavior of children in the sleep enhancement condition; they noted less daytime sleepiness, better emotional stability, and fewer restless and hyperactive behaviors at school. In contrast, teachers reported deterioration in children whose sleep was restricted. Altogether, these results indicate that sleep enhancement might be a free, no-risk strategy that parents can implement to improve their children's behavior.

A second strategy to improve children's attention is physical exercise. Pontifex and colleagues (2012) asked children to perform two simple tasks (a) read a book while seated for 20 minutes and (b) run on a treadmill for 20 minutes. All children performed both tasks in counterbalanced order (i.e., some children read first whereas others exercised first). After each task, children completed a continuous performance test of attention and concentration and paper-and-pencil tests of reading and mathematics. Regardless of the order of the tasks, children showed faster reaction times and better response accuracy on the computerized test of attention after exercising than after sitting (Image 8.4). Furthermore,

Image 8.4 Children with ADHD showed more brain activity *(lighter gray)* indicative of attention and concentration after 20 minutes of cardiovascular exercise than after 20 minutes of reading. After exercising, children also showed better performance on standardized tests of reading and math. Exercise might be a no-cost, no-risk means of improving attention and academic performance in children with ADHD.

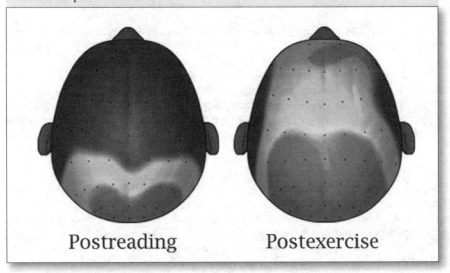

Postreading   Postexercise

Source: Based on Pontifex and colleagues (2012). Used with permission.

children's reading and math scores were significantly higher after exercising than after sitting. Interestingly, electroencephalograms (EEGs), performed during the study, indicated that exercise was associated with greater allocation of resources to areas of the brain responsible for attention and concentration—areas typically underactive in children with ADHD. Exercise might stimulate those brain areas and improve attention and concentration.

CHAPTER SUMMARY

Definitions

- ADHD is characterized by persistent problems with inattention and/or hyperactivity/impulsivity not shown by other individuals of the same age and gender. These problems must emerge in childhood, be present in multiple locations, and interfere with daily functioning.
- Children are diagnosed based on their symptom presentation:

  - Combined presentation
  - Predominantly hyperactive/impulsive presentation
  - Predominantly inattentive presentation
  - Restrictive inattentive presentation (i.e., few symptoms of hyperactivity)

- Some children with restrictive inattentive symptoms show "sluggish cognitive tempo," characterized by lethargy, passivity, forgetfulness, and a tendency to daydream.
- Adults can be diagnosed with ADHD. *DSM-5* provides examples of how adults may manifest the disorder differently than children. Adults require fewer symptoms than children to meet diagnostic criteria.

Comorbidity and Epidemiology

- Associated Problems

  - Children (especially boys) with ADHD often show conduct problems. The hyperactive/impulsive symptoms of ADHD may predispose some youths to develop Oppositional Defiant Disorder in childhood and (less commonly) Conduct Disorder in adolescence.
  - Older children and adolescents with ADHD are at increased risk for substance use problems. ADHD is a unique predictor for nicotine use. In contrast, children with ADHD who misuse alcohol and other drugs tend to have comorbid conduct problems.

- ADHD often co-occurs with anxiety and depression. Children with inattentive symptoms are most likely to develop these internalizing disorders.
- Many children with Bipolar Disorder also meet diagnostic criteria for ADHD; however, most children with ADHD do not have Bipolar Disorder.
- ADHD can disrupt parent-child and peer relationships, leading to hostile parenting behavior and peer rejection and ostracism.
- Youths with ADHD are at increased risk for academic problems, Specific Learning Disorder, and school dropout.
- Sleep problems, especially insomnia and poor sleep quality, are common among children with ADHD.

- Prevalence

  - Approximately 3% to 7% of youths currently meet diagnostic criteria for ADHD. The disorder is more common among school-age children than preschoolers, adolescents, and adults.
  - The prevalence of ADHD has increased dramatically in the past 30 years.
  - Among clinic-referred children, boys are 10 times more likely than girls to be diagnosed with ADHD. Among children in the community, boys are 3 times more likely than girls to be diagnosed with the disorder.
  - Girls are more likely than boys to show inattentive symptoms and to manifest the disorder later in childhood.
  - ADHD tends to be stable across childhood. Approximately 35% of children with ADHD no longer meet criteria in adolescence. However, ADHD-related impairments usually persist into adolescents and early adulthood.

Causes

- ADHD is highly heritable. Monozygotic twin concordance is 50% to 80% whereas dizygotic twin concordance is only 33%. Molecular genetic studies suggest that genes that regulate dopamine predispose some youths to ADHD.
- Early nonshared environmental factors can increase the likelihood of ADHD, especially among children at genetic risk for the disorder. These environmental risks often occur during gestation or delivery.
- ADHD is often associated with deficits in executive functioning, that is, the ability to perceive, process, and use information efficiently in order to ignore distractions, solve problems, and reach long-term goals. Underactivity of the prefrontal cortex may cause these deficits.

  - The orbitofrontal cortex is responsible for inhibition and impulse control.
  - The dorsolateral cortex is responsible for organizing, planning, and attending.

- The striatum helps regulate high-order motor behavior and plays a role in learning and memory. Children with ADHD often show underactivity in the frontal-striatal neural circuit that connects the striatum with the prefrontal cortex.
- Youths with ADHD also show abnormalities in the mesolimbic neural circuit, a brain region that plays a role in learning and response to reinforcement. These youths are highly sensitive to immediate reinforcement and have difficulty delaying impulses to attain long-term objectives.
- Barkley's neurodevelopmental model suggests that ADHD is caused by problems with behavioral inhibition. Problems with behavioral inhibition, in turn, are caused by deficiencies in four executive functions:

  - Working memory: Children with ADHD have problems keeping future rewards in mind and, instead, seek immediate gratification.
  - Internalized speech: Children with ADHD cannot direct their own actions; instead, they are highly influenced by their situation.
  - Emotion regulation: Children with ADHD have problems inhibiting immediate emotional displays and regulating their emotions in different contexts.
  - Creative problem solving: Children with ADHD have difficulty "thinking ahead" before beginning multistep activities.

Treatment

- Medication is typically regarded as a first-line treatment for ADHD. Approximately 60% to 70% of youths respond to medication, although most will continue to experience symptoms.

  - Psychostimulants include amphetamines (e.g., Adderall) and methylphenidates (e.g., Ritalin). They primarily affect dopamine receptors and stimulate brain regions responsible for behavior inhibition.
  - Atomoxetine (Strattera) is a non-stimulant that inhibits the reuptake of norepinephrine and is associated with improvements in behavior and attention.

- Common side effects include insomnia, appetite problems, and other gastrointestinal problems. Serious side effects are rare. Many stimulant medications have high potential for misuse, especially among adolescents.
- Clinical behavior therapy is a behavioral approach to managing the hyperactive and impulsive behavior of children with ADHD. It consists of parent training, school consultation, and a home-school reward system. It is effective at improving children's behavior as long as it is actively administered.
- Direct contingency management is a behavioral approach to managing the hyperactive and impulsive behavior of children with ADHD in schools and structured activities outside the home.

  - Youths are systematically reinforced for appropriate behavior and negatively punished (e.g., using response cost or time out) for inappropriate behavior.
  - The Summer Treatment Program for ADHD relies on direct contingency management as children participate in classroom and athletic activities.
  - Direct contingency management is highly effective in improving youth's behavior as long as it is actively administered.

- Multimodal Psychosocial Therapy (MPT) is an intensive approach to treatment that involves improving children's home behavior, academic skills, and social functioning with peers.
  - MPT consists of parent training, educational skills training, and social skills training.
  - It is highly effective for older children with ADHD but is not available in many communities.
- Some data indicate that youths with ADHD may be able to improve their working memory through systematic, computer-based training.
- Most research indicates that the combination of medication and psychosocial treatment is only moderately more effective than medication alone. However, psychosocial treatments are usually recommended as part of treatment because (a) they are as effective as medication as long as they are actively used and (b) many youths do not respond to medication.
- Special diets are associated with modest improvements in ADHD among some children with sensitivities to certain foods or additives. Special diets have no effect on most children with ADHD and nearly all children without ADHD.
- Research studies indicate that improving children's sleep and encouraging children to engage in physical exercise can lead to improvements in ADHD symptoms.

KEY TERMS

additive genetic effects   265

amphetamines   271

attention problems   252

Barkley's neurodevelopmental model   269

behavioral activation system (BAS)   268

behavioral inhibition   269

behavioral inhibition system (BIS)   268

COACHES (coaching our acting-out children, heightening essential skills)   275

creative problem solving   270

daily report card   275

direct contingency management   276

dominant (i.e., non-additive) genetic effects   265

dopamine D4 and D5 receptor genes   265

dopamine transporter gene (DAT1)   265

dorsolateral prefrontal cortex   267

educational skills training   277

emotion regulation   270

executive functioning   266

frontal-striatal neural circuit   267

hyperactivity   252

internalized speech   270

mesolimbic neural circuit   268

methylphenidates   271

multimodal psychosocial therapy (MPT)   277

Multimodal Treatment Study of Children with ADHD (MTA Study)   279

nonshared environmental factors   265

orbitofrontal cortex   267

parent training   275

Preschool ADHD Treatment Study (PATS)   273

psychostimulants   271

selective norepinephrine reuptake inhibitor (SNRI)   272

sluggish cognitive tempo   257

social skills training   277

sociometric ratings   260

striatum   267

Summer Treatment Program (STP)   276

working memory   270

CRITICAL THINKING EXERCISES

1. Nearly all young children show occasional problems with inattention and hyperactivity/impulsivity. How might a psychologist or physician differentiate developmentally expected hyperactivity or inattention from ADHD?

2. Why are children with ADHD at risk for problematic parent-child interactions? Why are children with ADHD at risk for peer rejection? If you were a clinician, how might you prevent these social problems among young children with ADHD?

3. Barkley claims that ADHD is not primarily a disorder of inattention; rather, it is a disorder caused by a lack of behavioral inhibition. How does behavioral inhibition play a critical role in Barkley's model for ADHD?

4. Under what circumstances might a physician decide to prescribe a non-stimulant medication, such as Strattera, to a child or adolescent with ADHD?

5. Philip is an 8-year-old boy who was recently diagnosed with ADHD with combined presentation. His mother is reluctant to use medication to manage his symptoms; instead, she wants Philip to participate in "talk therapy" with a counselor to help him "learn how to behave." What might you say to Philip's mother regarding (a) the merits and limitations of medication for ADHD and (b) the benefits and drawbacks of psychosocial treatments?

EXTEND YOUR LEARNING

Videos, practice tests, flash cards, study guides, and links to online resources for this chapter are available to students online. Teachers also have access to lecture notes, PowerPoint presentations, suggestions for classroom activities, and possible exam questions. Visit: www.sagepub.com/weis2e.

CHAPTER 9

Conduct Problems in Children and Adolescents

LEARNING OBJECTIVES

After reading this chapter, you should be able to answer these questions:

- What are the essential features of Oppositional Defiant Disorder (ODD) and Conduct Disorder (CD)? How do these disorders differ?
- How do children's conduct problems depend on (a) gender, (b) age of symptom onset, and (c) the presence or absence of prosocial emotions?
- What other externalizing and internalizing disorders often occur with ODD and CD?
- How might the causes of children's conduct problems be partially explained by (a) genetics and difficult temperament, (b) parenting behavior and early social learning, (c) parents' and children's information processing, (d) peer relationships, and (e) social-cultural factors?
- What evidence-based treatments are available for (a) young children with oppositional behavior and (b) older children and adolescents who engage in disruptive and aggressive acts?

I f you were asked to generate a mental picture of a child with "conduct problems," what image would come to mind? Perhaps you might think about the 5-year-old boy you saw at the checkout isle of the grocery store who was screaming at his mother because she wouldn't buy him his favorite candy bar. Alternatively, you might recall a middle school classmate, who deliberately bullied other kids and picked fights after school. A third image might be of an adolescent gang member who was arrested for the third time for physical assault by the age of 15. These mental images, although somewhat disparate, all depict different facets of conduct problems in youths.

DSM-5 recognizes two conduct problems that typically emerge in childhood or adolescence: Oppositional Defiant Disorder and Conduct Disorder. Both disorders bring children into significant conflict with caregivers and other authority figures, place great strain on relationships with parents, teachers, and (sometimes) peers, and, can lead to acts that violate the standards of society and the rights and dignity of others (American Psychiatric Association, 2013). Equally important, these disorders can adversely affect children's behavioral and social-emotional development and place them at risk for interpersonal and occupational problems later in life.

Fortunately, over the past 30 years, researchers have identified several factors that contribute to the development of children's conduct problems and have found effective ways to treat these disorders. Indeed, we now know many ways that parents and other caregivers can promote behavioral and emotional self-regulation in their children and prevent the emergence of conduct problems. We also know practical steps that adults can take to alleviate conduct problems in children once they emerge. If you are a parent or grandparent, if you are a teacher or tutor, if you are a coach or mentor, if you are in the position to influence the development of a child, read on.

WHAT ARE CHILD AND ADOLESCENT CONDUCT PROBLEMS?

Oppositional Defiant Disorder

DSM-5 identifies two disorders that describe children and adolescents with conduct problems: Oppositional Defiant Disorder (ODD) and Conduct Disorder. ODD is characterized by a persistent pattern of angry and irritable mood with defiant and vindictive behavior (see Table 9.1, Diagnostic Criteria for Oppositional Defiant Disorder). Children with ODD show at least four symptoms of noncompliant and defiant behavior toward adults that fall into three groups:

1. **Angry or irritable mood** (i.e., losing temper, being touchy or easily annoyed by others, acting angry and resentful)

2. **Argumentative or defiant behavior** (i.e., arguing with adults, defying adults' requests, deliberately annoying others, blaming others for his or her own behavior)

3. **Vindictiveness** (i.e., acting spiteful or seeking revenge against others)

Notice that the three groups of symptoms are somewhat heterogeneous. The first group of symptoms refers chiefly to problems regulating emotions (i.e., angry or irritable behavior),

---

Table 9.1   Diagnostic Criteria for Oppositional Defiant Disorder

A. A pattern of angry/irritable mood, argumentative/defiant behavior, or vindictiveness lasting at least 6 months as evidenced by at least four symptoms from any of the following categories, and exhibited during interaction with at least one individual who is not a sibling.

Angry/Irritable Mood

1. Often loses temper.

2. Is often touchy or easily annoyed.

3. Is often angry and resentful.

Argumentative/Defiant Behavior

1. Often argues with authority figures or, for children and adolescents, with adults.

2. Often actively defies or refuses to comply with requests from authority figures or with rules.

3. Often deliberately annoys others.

4. Often blames others for his or her mistakes or misbehavior.

Vindictiveness

1. Has been spiteful or vindictive at least twice within the past 6 months.

Note: The persistence and frequency of these behaviors should be used to distinguish a behavior that is within normal limits from a behavior that is symptomatic. For children younger than 5 years, the behavior should occur on most days for a period of at least 6 months unless otherwise noted. For individuals 5 years and older, the behavior should occur at least once per week for at least 6 months unless otherwise noted. While these frequency criteria provide guidance on a minimal level of frequency to define symptoms, other factors should also be considered, such as whether the frequency and intensity of the behaviors are outside a range that is normative for the individual's developmental level, gender, and culture.

B. The disturbance in behavior is associated with distress in the individual or in others in his or her immediate social context (e.g., family, peer group), or it impacts negatively on social, educational, occupational, or other important areas of functioning.

C. The behaviors do not occur exclusively during the course of a psychotic, substance use, depressive, or bipolar disorder. Also, the criteria are not met for Disruptive Mood Dysregulation Disorder.[1]

Specify current severity:

Mild: Symptoms are confined to only one setting (e.g., at home, at school, with peers).

Moderate: Symptoms are present in at least two settings.

Severe: Symptoms are present in three or more settings.

Source: Reprinted with permission from the *Diagnostic and Statistical Manual of Mental Disorders, Fifth Edition* (Copyright 2013). American Psychiatric Association.

[1]Disruptive Mood Dysregulation Disorder is a depressive disorder described in Chapter 13.

the second group refers principally to difficulties regulating overt actions (i.e., argumentative and defiant behavior), and the third group seems to reflect problems controlling both emotions and overt actions (i.e., vindictiveness). As we will see later in this chapter, most children with ODD show symptoms in two or all three groups. However, some children with ODD only show problems regulating overt behavior; they do not show persistent problems with angry or irritable mood. These differences in children's symptoms are important because they predict different developmental outcomes and may be important to selecting the best method of treatment for these youths (American Psychiatric Association, 2013).

Most children show oppositional or defiant behaviors from time to time. After all, nearly all parents routinely describe children entering "the terrible twos" or "the horrible threes."

Usually, children show a developmentally normative increase in oppositional and defiant behavior during the toddler and early preschool years. Two-year-olds may insist on selecting their own clothes in the morning, even though they prefer to wear shorts and a T-shirt in the middle of winter. Three-year-olds may tantrum when told to go to bed. Four-year-olds may stubbornly refuse to eat their vegetables and sit at the table for an hour to see whether their parents will acquiesce to their demands to be excused. In one study, 97% of toddlers initially ignored or refused to obey adults' requests to clean up after play (Klimes-Dougan & Kopp, 1999).

How can we distinguish normative child behavior from childhood behavior problems? Although there is no easy answer to this question, *DSM-5* suggests that differentiating normal from abnormal behavior must be determined based

DSM-IV → DSM-5 CHANGES

ODD SYMPTOM CLUSTERS

Although the core symptoms of ODD remain the same from *DSM-IV* to *DSM-5,* they are now grouped into three clusters: (a) irritable/angry mood symptoms, (b) defiant/headstrong behavior, and (c) vindictiveness. This change is based on several factor-analytic studies which showed that certain ODD symptoms tended to occur together and that different symptom clusters predicted different outcomes.

For example, Stringaris and Goodman (2009) showed that young children's irritable or angry mood symptoms predicted later internalizing problems, especially depression and anxiety. In contrast, young children's headstrong symptoms predicted externalizing symptoms, such as ADHD and the nonaggressive symptoms of Conduct Disorder. Finally, children's vindictive symptoms often coincided with the presence of limited prosocial emotions and predicted physical aggression.

A second study, involving clinic-referred boys, yielded similar findings (Burke, 2012). In this study, boys' disruptive behavior problems were assessed for the first time between the ages of 7 and 12 years. Then, boys' psychosocial outcomes were measured at age 18 years. Most boys showed classic ODD symptoms: arguing, defying, and annoying others. However, a subset of boys showed ODD symptoms more characteristic of emotional problems: anger, touchiness, and irritability. These early emotional symptoms predicted anxiety through adolescence and early adulthood.

A third study replicated these findings with girls from the community (Burke, Hipwell, & Loeber, 2010). Researchers examined a large sample of 5- to 8-year-old girls annually over a 5-year period. They discovered that girls who showed irritable or angry mood symptoms were at specific risk for developing depression later in childhood or adolescence.

Based on these findings, clinicians can use the ODD symptom clusters to better predict children's outcomes and, perhaps, tailor treatment accordingly.

on (a) symptom number and frequency, and (b) children's overall development context (American Psychiatric Association, 2013). First, children with ODD show a greater number of problematic behaviors, and they show these behaviors more frequently than their typically developing peers. Whereas many children occasionally defy their parents' requests or complain when they do not get their way, children with ODD repeatedly tantrum, defy parents, argue with adults, and act in mean and spiteful ways.

Indeed, empirical research has consistently shown that children with ODD show more frequent and severe behavior problems than other children their age. For example, Keenan and Wakschlag (2004) compared the frequency of disruptive behaviors of young children referred for psychiatric treatment with the behavior of children in the community (Figure 9.1). Among clinic-referred children, disruptive behavior was common. Approximately 70% of referred children repeatedly denied an adult's requests or threw tantrums. In contrast, such oppositional behavior was relatively rare among nonreferred children; only about 4% to 8% showed these disruptive behaviors. Although strong-willed behavior is common among preschoolers, symptoms of ODD are not (Eyberg, 2006).

Second, children with ODD engage in disruptive behaviors that are developmentally unexpected. Their behaviors are problematic because they persist beyond an age at which they are developmentally normative. For example, when a 2-year-old tantrums because his father asks him to clean up his toys, we might consider the child's behavior as developmentally normative. However, when a 5- or 6-year-old child tantrums when asked to put away his toys, we would likely consider the behavior as atypically oppositional (Lahey & Waldman, 2003).

How do clinicians determine if a child's behavior is uncharacteristic for his or her age? Clinicians typically administer norm-referenced behavior rating scales to children's parents and teachers in order to compare the severity of their conduct problems with other children. Elevated ratings, beyond the 93rd or 95th percentile, would likely indicate significant oppositional or defiant symptoms. Furthermore, *DSM-5* provides guidelines to clinicians to differentiate developmentally expected oppositional and defiant behavior from behavior that merits professional attention. Specifically, children under 5 years of age should show symptoms most days for at least 6 months to be diagnosed with ODD. Children 6 years and older may show

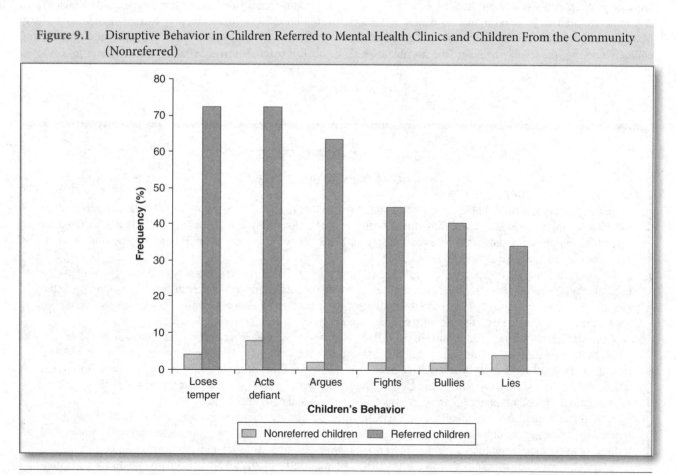

Figure 9.1 Disruptive Behavior in Children Referred to Mental Health Clinics and Children From the Community (Nonreferred)

Source: Based on Keenan and Wakschlag (2004).

Note: Most young children in the community do not show serious conduct problems like physical fighting, bullying, and lying.

symptoms less often (i.e., at least once per week) for at least 6 months and be diagnosed with ODD. In all cases, symptoms must cause impairment in children's social or educational functioning. Typically, ODD strains children's relationships with parents, teachers, and peers (American Psychiatric Association, 2013).

Children can be diagnosed with ODD if they show symptoms in only one setting. For example, some children with ODD are defiant toward parents but appear compliant and respectful toward teachers, coaches, and other adults. In fact, some children with ODD only show symptoms toward one parent but not the other. The fact that children with ODD can show symptoms in certain situations or with specific people suggests that environmental factors greatly influence the development and maintenance of the disorder. ODD differs from ADHD, in which symptoms are present across multiple settings (Eyberg, 2006).

Clinicians are able to classify children's ODD symptoms based on their severity. Mild symptoms occur in only one setting (e.g., at home, at school, or with peers), moderate symptoms occur in two settings, and severe symptoms occur in three or more settings. ODD symptoms are almost always directed at parents (96%) or teachers (85%). Less commonly, they are directed toward peers (67%). Most children with ODD (62%) show symptoms at home, school, and with peers (Youngstrom, van Meter, & Algorta, 2010).

Conduct Disorder

Conduct Disorder (CD) is a more serious and persistent condition that usually manifests in late childhood or adolescence. CD is characterized by a repetitive and persistent pattern of behavior in which the basic rights of others or major age-appropriate societal norms or rules are violated (Table 9.2 Diagnostic Criteria for Conduct Disorder).

The symptoms of CD can be grouped into four broad categories: (a) aggression to people and animals, (b) destruction of property, (c) deceitfulness or theft, and (d) serious violations of rules. Aggression to people and animals involves initiating physical fights, physical cruelty to or assault of others, and robbery. Destruction of property involves intentionally damaging others' belongings through vandalism, arson, or other reckless acts. Deceitful behaviors include breaking and entering, stealing, or lying to earn a reward or to avoid a responsibility. Other serious rule violations include staying out all night, running away from home, or truancy.

Conduct problems exist along a continuum, ranging from mild difficulties with oppositional and defiant behavior (e.g., tantrums, refusing to obey) to serious violations of the rights of others (e.g., assault, rape). Children with ODD and CD show the same pattern of oppositional, defiant, and disrespectful attitudes toward adults in authority. However, children with ODD typically do not show physical aggression to people or animals, deliberately destroy property, or

CASE STUDY

DAVIDSON'S ESCAPE

"If you don't sit down and behave this minute your dad will hear about it when we get home!" Upon hearing those words, Dr. Anders knew that 6-year-old Davidson and his mother, Mrs. Lepper, had arrived for their 9:30 appointment and were waiting in the reception area of our clinic. Dr. Anders invited her two clients into her office and asked how she might help.

"Davidson's a handful and I don't know what to do. He won't listen to anything I say and he seems to enjoy giving me grief." As Mrs. Lepper explained Davidson's frequent tantrums and defiance at home, Davidson interrupted, saying, "Hey mom, this is boring, can I have some gum?" Mrs. Lepper replied, "Not now sweetie." Dr. Anders added, "I have some coloring books and crayons for you on this table here. Let's see if we can find one you like."

Davidson remained interested in coloring for only a few minutes, then, he returned to nagging his mother and interrupting her conversation. His mother explained, "It's like this all the time at home. I can't talk on the telephone without him bothering me. I can't shower in the morning; he'll scream outside the bathroom door or walk in on me if I don't lock it. I can't go shopping with him because he won't stop grabbing things from the shelves or crawling on the floor."

By this time, Davidson grew impatient and walked to Dr. Ander's office door. After checking to make sure that the adults were watching, Davidson slowly turned the door handle and opened the door slightly. His mother replied, "If you leave this room, you're going to get it when we get home." With an ever-widening smile, Davidson opened the door a bit more and placed one foot in the hallway. His mother stood up and began to count, "1 . . . 2 . . . Davidson." Her son responded by ducking into the hallway, closing the office door behind him.

Mrs. Lepper bolted toward the door with an angry expression. Dr. Anders interjected, "Mrs. Lepper, please have a seat." Exasperated, Mrs. Lepper replied, "I need to go get him." Dr. Anders said, "Why? This end of the hallway is empty and he can't enter the rest of the clinic without a keycard. He's safe and can't get into any trouble. Davidson decided he doesn't want to color and that's fine. Now he can sit in the hallway for a while." For the first time, a smile flickered across Mrs. Lepper's face.

Table 9.2   Diagnostic Criteria for Conduct Disorder

A. A repetitive and persistent pattern of behavior in which the basic rights of others or major age-appropriate societal norms or rules are violated, as manifested by the presence of at least three of the following 15 criteria in the past 12 months from any of the categories below, with at least one criterion present in the past 6 months:

Aggression to People and Animals

1. Often bullies, threatens, or intimidates others.

2. Often initiates physical fights.

3. Has used a weapon that can cause serious physical harm to others (e.g., a bat, brick, broken bottle, knife, gun).

4. Has been physically cruel to people.

5. Has been physically cruel to animals.

6. Has stolen while confronting a victim (e.g., mugging, purse snatching, extortion, armed robbery).

7. Has forced someone into sexual activity.

Destruction of Property

1. Has deliberately engaged in fire setting with the intention of causing serious damage.

2. Has deliberately destroyed others' property (other than by fire setting).

Deceitfulness or Theft

1. Has broken into someone else's house, building, or car.

2. Often lies to obtain goods or favors or to avoid obligations (e.g., "cons" others).

3. Has stolen items of nontrivial value without confronting a victim (e.g., shoplifting, but without breaking and entering; forgery).

Serious Violations of Rules

1. Often stays out at night despite parental prohibitions, beginning before age 13 years.

2. Has run away from home overnight at least twice while living in the parental or parental surrogate home, or once without returning for a lengthy period.

3. Is often truant from school, beginning before age 13 years.

B. The disturbance in behavior causes clinically significant impairment in social, academic, or occupational functioning.

C. If the individual is age 18 years or older, criteria are not met for Antisocial Personality Disorder.

Specify whether:

Childhood-onset type: Individuals show at least one symptom characteristic of Conduct Disorder prior to age 10 years.

Adolescent-onset type: Individuals show no symptom characteristic of Conduct Disorder prior to age 10 years.

Unspecified onset: Criteria for a diagnosis of Conduct Disorder are met, but there is not enough available to determine whether the onset of the first symptom was before or after age 10 years.

Specify current severity:

Mild: Few if any conduct problems in excess of those required to make the diagnosis are present, and conduct problems cause relative minor harm to others (e.g., lying, truancy, staying out after dark without permission, other rule breaking).

Moderate: The number of conduct problems and the effect on others are intermediate between those specified in "mild" and those in "severe" (e.g., stealing without confronting a victim, vandalism).

Severe: Many conduct problems in excess of those required to make the diagnosis are present, or conduct problems cause considerable harm to others (e.g., forced sex, physical cruelty, use of a weapon, stealing while confronting a victim, breaking and entering).

Source: Reprinted with permission from the *Diagnostic and Statistical Manual of Mental Disorders, Fifth Edition* (Copyright 2013). American Psychiatric Association.

frequently engage in theft and deceitfulness (Frick et al., 1992; see text box *DSM-IV → DSM-5* Changes: Changes in the Relationship between ODD and CD).

The symptoms of CD include 15 indicators of serious conduct problems. To be diagnosed with CD, youths must show at least three symptoms in the past 12 months. Because the criteria reflect such diverse behaviors, two children with CD can show dramatically different behavioral profiles. Consider the following 15-year-old boys, each of whom might be diagnosed with CD (Tremblay, 2003):

- Anthony has run away from home, is frequently truant from school, and stays out all night without his parents' permission.

- Brett initiates physical fights with peers, uses a knife to rob others, and forces girls into sexual activity.
- Charles deliberately vandalizes school property, sets fires, and tortures animals.
- Dean breaks into others' homes, shoplifts, and steals credit cards.

Although all of these boys might be diagnosed with CD, each shows a different pattern of symptoms. The diagnostic label *CD* reflects a large and heterogeneous group of children and adolescents.

Because of the diverse symptoms of CD, researchers have been interested in differentiating children and adolescents into groups based on the pattern of symptoms they

CASE STUDY

MAKING MOM MISERABLE

Brandyn was a 9-year-old boy who was referred to our clinic by his third-grade teacher because of defiant and aggressive behavior at school. According to his teacher, Mrs. Miller, Brandyn became angry and resentful whenever she placed limits on him. For example, he would often tantrum, throw objects, and hit her when she asked him to pick up his belongings. Brandyn also bullied and intimidated other children in the class in order to obtain toys and to get his way. His teacher explained, "Brandyn seeks out the younger kids and torments them until he gets what he wants. If they stand up to him, he pushes or pinches them. He even choked a classmate because he wouldn't give him a scented pencil that he wanted."

Brandyn engaged in other acts of aggression designed to get attention from others. For example, he cut a girl's ponytail off during class and repeatedly destroyed other students' belongings. On two occasions, he was caught stealing items from lockers and desks. Classmates often avoided playing with Brandyn because of his aggressive acts. Mrs. Miller commented, "I don't know what to do with him. He doesn't seem bothered when we reprimand him and we can't keep him in the time-out chair."

Brandyn's mother reported similar problems with aggression and defiance at home. "He doesn't listen to me at all," she explained. "He seems to enjoy making my life miserable." She explained, "It's hard enough being a single mother and working a crummy job. Then, I have to come home and deal with him. I love him, but I don't know what to do. It scares me sometimes because I see him heading down the same road as his father. I guess the apple doesn't fall too far from the tree."

show. Researchers have attempted to classify youths with CD in four ways:

1. The nature of their conduct problems: covert or overt

2. Their type of aggression: reactive or proactive

3. Their age of symptom onset: childhood or adolescence

4. Their capacity for prosocial emotions

We will now examine each of these four dimensions.

Overt Versus Covert Conduct Problems

The diagnostic criteria for CD can be loosely divided into two broad clusters: overt symptoms and covert symptoms (see Table 9.3). **Overt symptoms** refer to observable and confrontational antisocial acts, especially acts of physical aggression. Examples of overt symptoms include physical assault, robbery, and bullying. In contrast, **covert symptoms** refer to secretive antisocial behaviors that usually do not involve physical aggression. Examples of covert symptoms include breaking into someone's home, burglary, lying, skipping school, and running away from home. Although most youths with CD show both overt and covert symptoms, these two symptom clusters can be differentiated. Some children, especially boys, tend to show mostly overt symptoms of CD, whereas other children, especially girls, are more likely to show covert symptoms (Achenbach, Howell, Quay, & Conners, 1991; Biederman, Mick et al., 2002; Frick et al., 1993; Loeber & Hay, 1997; Tackett, Krueger, Iacono, & McGue, 2005; Tackett, Krueger, Sawyer, & Graetz, 2003).

Frick and colleagues (1993) reviewed 60 published studies on youths with CD. The researchers discovered that children's conduct problems could be described in terms of two independent dimensions: (a) overt versus covert and (b) destructive versus nondestructive. Children's behavior could be overt-nondestructive (e.g., defiance, talking back), overt-destructive (e.g., fighting, bullying), covert-nondestructive (e.g., truancy, running away), or covert-destructive (e.g., vandalism, theft). Overt-nondestructive behaviors reflect ODD. The other types of behaviors reflect CD (Monuteaux, Fitzmaurice, Blacker, Buka, & Biederman, 2004; Tackett et al., 2005).

Reactive Versus Proactive Aggression

Overt conduct problems can further be differentiated into two types of aggression: reactive and proactive. Children show **reactive aggression** when they engage in physical violence in response to a threat, a frustrating event, or a provocation. For example, a child might shove a classmate because the classmate stole his pencil (Connor, Steingard, Cunningham, Anderson, & Melloni, 2004).

Reactive aggression usually occurs because children act impulsively and automatically (out of anger), without considering alternative, prosocial ways of responding (e.g.,

Table 9.3 Children's Conduct Problems

Overt Symptoms	Covert Symptoms
Bullies, threatens, or intimidates others	Steals without confrontation
Initiates physical fights	Runs away from home
Physically cruel to people	Breaks into a house, building, or car
Physically cruel to animals	Often truant from school
Uses a weapon	

Source: Based on Tackett et al. (2003).

asking a teacher for help, finding another activity). Reactive aggression is most often seen in younger children and children with ADHD—children who have difficulty controlling their emotions or inhibiting their behavior. Children with a history of physical abuse and/or bullying by peers are also likely to show reactive aggression (Coie, Dodge, Terry, & Wright, 1991; Connor et al., 2004; Dodge & Coie, 1987; Dodge, Pettit, Bates, & Valente, 1995; Waschbusch, Willoughby, & Pelham, 1998).

Children show **proactive aggression** when they deliberately engage in an aggressive act in order to obtain a desired goal (Connor et al., 2004; Dodge, Pettit, & Bates, 1997). For example, a child might shove a classmate and steal his pencil because he wants it.

Most experts believe that children *learn* to use proactive aggression. Learning occurs through modeling and reinforcement. First, parents model proactive aggression when they use hostile behaviors in the home, such as yelling and harsh physical discipline, to force children to comply with their commands. By observing their parents, children learn that proactive aggression is a legitimate and effective way of achieving one's short-term objectives. Second, children's use of proactive aggression is strengthened through positive reinforcement. Children learn that they can acquire objects, money, and social status through fighting or bullying (Bandura, 1973).

Although occasional aggressive outbursts are common during childhood, repeated displays of reactive and proactive aggression are infrequent. Approximately 7% of children show recurrent problems with reactive aggression, 3% show patterns of proactive aggression, and 10% show a mixture of reactive and proactive aggression (Dodge et al., 1997; Waschbusch et al., 1998).

Childhood-Onset Versus Adolescent-Onset Conduct Problems

Most mental health practitioners and researchers distinguish between two types of childhood conduct problems, based on the age at which children begin showing symptoms and the persistence of symptoms across development (Frick & Munoz, 2006; Moffitt, 2003). Indeed, *DSM-5* requires clinicians to specify the age of onset of children's CD symptoms (American Psychiatric Association, 2013).

The differentiation between childhood-onset and adolescent-onset conduct problems is based on a 30-year longitudinal study of 1,000 New Zealand youths called the Dunedin Multidisciplinary Health and Development Study (Moffitt, Caspi, Rutter, & Silva, 2001). In the Dunedin study, researchers identified two developmental pathways for childhood conduct problems: the life-course persistent path and the adolescence-limited path.

Individuals with life-course persistent conduct problems first show symptoms in preschool or early elementary school. Some children with life-course persistent symptoms can be identified as early as age 4-and-a-half years (Kim-Cohen, Arseneault, Caspi, Tomas, Taylor, & Moffitt, 2005). These youths display difficulties in emotional control in infancy and early childhood, neurological abnormalities and delayed motor development in preschool, lower IQ and reading problems in school, and later neuropsychological deficits, especially in the areas of decision making, judgment, and memory (Moffitt, 2003). More important, children with life-course persistent conduct problems show an increase in conduct problems throughout childhood and adolescence (Lahey & Loeber, 1994; Moffitt, 1993, 2003). As adults, they are at risk for antisocial behaviors, mental health and substance use problems, work and financial difficulties, domestic abuse and relationship problems, and incarceration (Frick, 2004; Moffitt & Caspi, 2001; Moffitt, Caspi, Harrington, & Milne, 2002).

Youths with adolescence-limited conduct problems show their first symptoms after puberty (Moffitt, 1993). They usually do not show psychosocial risk factors for the disorder (e.g., emotional control problems, cognitive/academic deficits). They tend to engage in covert, nonconfrontational antisocial acts (e.g., stealing, truancy, running away) rather than overt acts of aggression. Their behavior problems tend to persist into middle adolescence and then gradually taper off. Most individuals who show adolescence-limited conduct problems do not show serious symptoms in adulthood. However, a small percentage of these adolescents engage in petty crimes and experience financial problems into their middle 20s (Moffitt et al., 2002).

DSM-5 requires clinicians to identify the onset of children's Conduct Disorder symptoms. Youths with Conduct Disorder, Childhood-Onset Type have at least one Conduct Disorder symptom prior to age 10 years. In contrast, youths with Conduct Disorder, Adolescent-Onset Type do not have a Conduct Disorder symptom prior to age 10 years. If clinicians cannot determine the age of symptom onset, they can diagnose youths with Conduct Disorder, Unspecified Onset (American Psychiatric Association, 2013).

Limited Prosocial Emotions

Some children with CD also show a lack of prosocial emotions in their interactions with others. In addition to persistent violations of the rights of others, these youths also show two or more of the following features:

- A lack of remorse of guilt: When these children and adolescents do something wrong, they do not experience guilt or feel "sorry" for their behavior. They might regret "getting caught," but they do not show remorse for the act itself.
- Callousness or a lack of empathy: These children and adolescents are unconcerned about the feelings of others. They experience little discomfort when witnessing others' misfortune and disregard others' suffering.
- Lack of concern about performance: These children and adolescents do not care about their performance in school, work, or sports. They are not bothered even when failing a class or fired from a part-time job.
- Shallow or deficient affect: These children and adolescents often show only superficial emotions and do not confide in others or express their feelings in emotionally vulnerable ways. They may only express emotions to manipulate or "con" others and frequently show emotions that are incongruent with their actions (e.g., smiling or laughing while hurting others).

Children and adolescents who show two or more of these traits are said to display "limited prosocial emotions" (American Psychiatric Association, 2013, p. 470). Note that these characteristics reflect the youth's typical pattern of interpersonal and emotional functioning, not an occasional behavior toward specific people or in specific situations. By definition, the characteristics of "limited prosocial emotions" must exist for at least 12 months and must be displayed in multiple relationships and settings. Consequently, it is necessary for clinicians to gather data from multiple people (e.g., parents, teachers, other adults involved in the child's life) to assess these features. It is especially important for clinicians to supplement youths' self-reports with data from other informants, because children and adolescents with limited prosocial emotions often deny or minimize the number and severity of their problems (American Psychiatric Association, 2013).

Children with limited prosocial emotions have many characteristics of adults with psychopathy. **Psychopathy** is a behavioral syndrome characterized by antisocial behavior, impulsivity, shallow affect, narcissism, and disregard for the suffering of others. They often show callousness and a lack of emotional responsiveness. Indeed, researchers used to describe children with these features as having "**callous-unemotional traits.**" Adults with psychopathy often have histories of physical aggression and blatant violations for the rights and dignity of others (e.g., physical assault, rape). Similarly, research has shown that children with CD who also show limited prosocial emotions are at considerable risk for serious violations of others' rights and dignity beyond what might be expected by CD alone (Frick & Moffitt, 2010).

For example, Kahn and colleagues (2012) assessed conduct problems in 1,700 children from the community and children referred to mental health clinics. Among children in the community, 32% of children who met criteria for

CD also showed limited prosocial emotions. Among clinic-referred youths, 50% of children with CD also showed limited prosocial emotions. Perhaps more importantly, youths who showed limited prosocial emotions (independent of whether they were from the community or clinic) showed more serious antisocial and aggressive behavior than youths without CD or youths with CD but without limited prosocial emotions (Figure 9.2).

A second, very large community-based study examined conduct problems in boys for 2 years (Pardini & Fite, 2010). Approximately 5.9% of boys met criteria for CD, almost all of whom showed symptom onset in childhood. Interestingly, youths with CD and limited prosocial emotions were significantly more likely to engage in serious criminal activity than youths with CD alone. Interestingly, limited prosocial emotions predicted only serious, violent crime rather than less serious criminal activity (e.g., shoplifting, truancy).

Still other studies have shown that a lack of prosocial emotions is associated with poorer response to treatment (Frick & Moffitt, 2010). Although CD is difficult to treat in general, children and adolescents who show both CD and limited prosocial emotions are especially resistant to treatment. Treatment seems to be less effective for two reasons.

First, children with limited prosocial emotions may be less willing to establish a relationship with a therapist based on trust and may be reluctant to disclose thoughts or feelings that make themselves emotionally vulnerable. Second, youths with limited prosocial emotions seem to be less sensitive to punishment than other children; consequently, behavioral interventions may be less effective for them. For example, Hawes and Dadds (2005) found children with CD and limited prosocial emotions tended to respond to interventions based on positive reinforcement (e.g., rewarding children for compliant behavior) but not punishment (e.g., response cost).

A lack of prosocial emotions in children predicts physical aggression, serious criminal behavior, and resistance to treatment above and beyond CD alone (see text box *DSM-IV → DSM-5* Changes: Everything Old Is New Again). Consequently, *DSM-5* allows clinicians to use the specifier "with limited prosocial emotions" at the end of their diagnosis (i.e., Conduct Disorder with Limited Prosocial Emotions). The specifier can also be used by researchers who want to study differential outcomes and treatments for youths with and without this attribute (American Psychiatric Association, 2013).

Figure 9.2 Children With CD and Limited Prosocial Emotions Show More Aggression and Cruelty

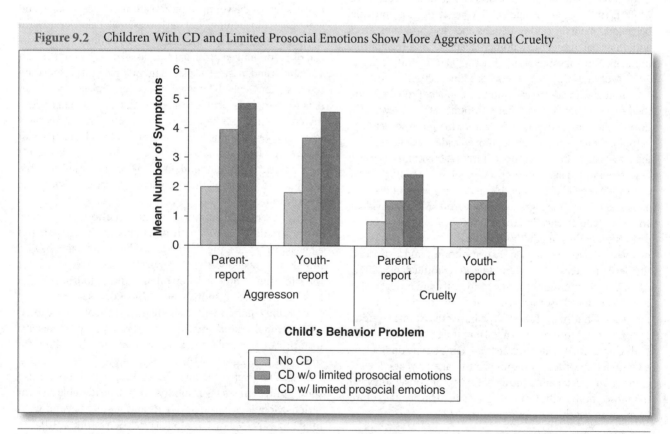

Source: Based on Kahn and colleagues (2012).

Note: Children with CD and limited prosocial emotions are more likely to show physical aggression and cruelty toward people and animals than clinic-referred children without CD or clinic-referred children with CD but without limited prosocial emotions. Limited prosocial emotions predict aggression and cruelty as reported by both parents and children themselves.

DSM-IV → DSM-5 CHANGES

EVERYTHING OLD IS NEW AGAIN

DSM-5 permits clinicians to use the specifier "with limited prosocial emotions" to describe youths who act callously and unemotionally toward other people. These youths show limited empathy and little concern for the feelings, wishes, and well-being of others.

Although the addition of the limited prosocial emotions specifier is new to *DSM-5*, a similar specifier appeared in *DSM-III* more than 30 years ago. *DSM-III* included two subtypes of Conduct Disorder: "socialized" and "undersocialized" (American Psychiatric Association, 1980). Children with the socialized type of CD engaged in repeated antisocial acts, but they were able to form attachments to parents, other adults, and friends. For example, these youths often associated with deviant peers (e.g., gangs) to whom they were very attached. In contrast, children with the undersocialized type of CD were "characterized by a failure to establish a normal degree of affection, empathy, or bond with others" (p. 45). They generally lacked close friends and had only superficial relationships. They tended to interact with others only when it suited their needs. Their relationships tended to be exploitative and they were largely unconcerned with the feelings of others.

The socialized and undersocialized subtypes of CD were dropped in *DSM-IV* for two reasons. First, many people misunderstood the label "undersocialized." They believed that it referred to CD caused by parental neglect. Second, the term was considered pejorative and potentially stigmatizing.

In the last 20 years, however, research has demonstrated the predictive value of differentiating children with and without "limited prosocial emotions." Furthermore, the label is likely less stigmatizing than other terms used by researchers such as *undersocialized*, *callous-unemotional*, or *narcissistic*. Consequently, the developers of *DSM-5* hoped the addition of this specifier might be useful to clinicians and stimulate research into the causes and treatment of youths with these traits (Frick & Moffitt, 2010).

CASE STUDY

CALLOUS CADE

Cade was a 14-year-old boy who was referred to our clinic by his caseworker from the department of juvenile justice. Cade had a history of disruptive behavior. His mother remembered, "As a toddler, he was a handful. He was always getting into mischief, disobeying me, and throwing tantrums. When he was five, he cut all of the whiskers off our cat and set our living room rug on fire."

By the time Cade was in second grade, he had been suspended twice for physical aggression. Once, he stuck a nail from the inside of his shoe through the toe and kicked classmates on the playground. On another occasion, he shoved a classmate down the stairs. Cade got in trouble for playing pranks, such as "mooning" other children in gym class, spraying classmates with a bottle of urine, and pulling the fire alarm on several different occasions.

By the time Cade reached the sixth grade, he had few friends his own age. He preferred to spend time with older boys at the nearby junior high school who introduced him to more serious antisocial behaviors. Cade began using alcohol and marijuana and skipping school. He was arrested for the first time in seventh grade for vandalizing 17 school buses, causing several thousand dollars of damage.

At the time of the referral, Cade was attending an eighth-grade classroom for youths with behavior problems. He had gotten into trouble earlier in the year for making sexually suggestive and racially offensive comments to two girls at the school. Most recently, he injured a classmate during a fight with a box cutter. One teacher said, "Cade deliberately tries to provoke others—calling people names, swearing, making offensive remarks. He seems to take delight in hurting others, and he doesn't care about being punished."

Dr. Witek, the psychologist who interviewed Cade, was most concerned about Cade's fascination with fire and explosives. Cade said proudly, "About two years ago, I began building bombs in my house. I use cigarette lighters, aerosols, gasoline, fireworks, batteries, Styrofoam containers . . . whatever I can get my hands on. My friends and me build them and set them off in the field."

Cade's mother said to Dr. Witek, "I know Cade has made a lot of trouble, but he's really not a bad kid. I think if his father played a larger role in his life, he'd be OK."

ASSOCIATED DISORDERS

Most youths with conduct problems show other cognitive, behavioral, or emotional disorders (Essau, 2003). In fact, it is more common to see a child with conduct problems and some other disorder than conduct problems alone (McMahon & Frick, 2005).

ADHD

Many children and adolescents with conduct problems have ADHD. Overall, approximately 36% of boys and 57% of girls with conduct problems also meet diagnostic criteria for ADHD (Waschbusch, 2002). Comorbid ADHD is more common among youths with CD (75%) than youths with ODD (27%; Whittinger et al., 2007).

Although there is little disagreement that ADHD and conduct problems co-occur, there is considerable debate regarding the nature of their association. Many experts believe the hyperactive-impulsive symptoms of ADHD act as the "motor" that drives youths to engage in aggression and other antisocial acts. Children's high-rate and impulsive behaviors in early childhood elicit negative reactions from caregivers and lead to problems in caregiver-child interactions. These problems, in turn, often contribute to the development of oppositional and defiant behaviors. Early problems with ODD, in turn, can lead to CD in adolescence (Lahey, McBurnett, & Loeber, 2000).

Other research suggests that the strong association between conduct problems and ADHD is due to shared genetic factors. In a large twin study, Nadder, Rutter, Silberg, Maes, and Eaves (2002) concluded that a common set of genes underlies both ADHD and ODD. The mechanism by which genes influence behavior is unknown. One possibility is that genes directly predispose children to both ADHD and ODD. Another possibility is that genes predispose children to show symptoms of ADHD, which, in turn, evoke hostile behavior by parents, teachers, and peers. These hostile behaviors can lead to the emergence of ODD.

Although they frequently co-occur, ADHD and conduct problems are probably caused by different underlying neural impairments (van Goozen et al., 2004). According to Gray's (1994) neuropsychological theory, behavior is regulated by two neuropsychological systems: the behavioral activation system (BAS) and the behavioral inhibition system (BIS). The BAS is controlled by a neural pathway that connects the brain's pleasure center (in the hypothalamus) to other brain regions. The primary job of the BAS is to motivate behavior. The BAS is responsible for our desire for pleasure, excitement, satiety, and well-being. In contrast, the BIS is regulated primarily by the prefrontal cortex and neural pathways that connect the frontal lobe to other brain regions. The chief job of the BIS is to inhibit a person's activity when behavior might not be reinforced or when it might be punished. The BAS and BIS are competing neuropsychological systems that regulate behavior. The BAS might motivate us to drive fast because we derive pleasure from the exhilaration of going 90 mph; the BIS would cause us to slow down in order to avoid getting a speeding ticket.

Children with ADHD show deficits in BIS activity. These children display problems inhibiting behaviors, even when they know those behaviors will be punished. For example, children with ADHD are talkative and blurt out answers in class even when they know those behaviors will result in a detention.

In contrast, children with conduct problems (but not ADHD) do not consistently show problems with behavioral inhibition (van Goozen et al., 2004). Instead, they show a more general dysregulation of both BAS and BIS (Nigg, Hinshaw, & Huang-Pollock, 2006). First, children with conduct problems become highly aroused by potential reinforcement. They tend to focus primarily on the pleasurable aspects of their misbehavior (e.g., stealing a candy bar), while they minimize or ignore the potentially negative aspects (e.g., getting caught). This high saliency of reward reflects an overactive BAS. Furthermore, once their BAS becomes active, these children show a general insensitivity to punishment. Despite threats of negative consequences, these children continue to misbehave. This perseveration, despite punishment, reflects an underactive BIS.

Anxiety Disorders

Children with conduct problems are more likely to have anxiety disorders than children without conduct problems. Furthermore, girls with conduct problems are more likely than boys with conduct problems to have anxiety disorders. Approximately 14% of boys and 22% of girls with ODD show significant anxiety, while 9% of boys and 16% of girls with CD have comorbid anxiety disorders (Maughan, Rowe, Messer, Goodman, & Meltzer, 2004).

The relationship between conduct problems and anxiety is unclear (McMahon & Frick, 2005). Some studies have shown that children with comorbid conduct and anxiety disorders are less impaired than children with conduct problems alone (Fergusson, Horwood, & Nagin, 2000). Other studies have shown the opposite effect, specifically, that children with both conduct and anxiety problems display more severe symptoms of both disorders (McMahon & Frick, 2005).

It is likely that the relationship between conduct problems and anxiety depends on the personality characteristics of the child. Moderate levels of anxiety allow children to benefit from parental discipline. Some children may display lower levels of conduct problems because they fear parental disapproval or punishment. For these children, comorbid anxiety problems decrease the severity of their conduct symptoms. However, certain children and adolescents have personality traits that make them slow to respond to punishment. These children may have underactive BIS, making them persist in misbehavior despite threats of discipline. For these children and adolescents, comorbid anxiety might be associated with an increase in conduct problems, especially hostile and aggressive behaviors (Frick & Loney, 2002).

Depression

Some children who show conduct problems also experience depression. Approximately 2% to 4% of children with ODD and 11% to 13% of youths with CD experience depression (Maughan et al., 2004).

Years ago, researchers thought that depression and feelings of low self-worth caused children's conduct problems. Some people believed that depressive symptoms were masked by children's disruptive and aggressive behavior. Subsequent research has not supported this theory of **masked depression** (Toolan, 1962).

Instead, longitudinal studies indicate that children's conduct problems usually precede their symptoms of depression. Today, most researchers believe that conduct problems can contribute to children's mood symptoms. Patterson and Capaldi (1991) have offered the **dual failure model** to explain the association between conduct problems and depression. According to this model, conduct problems cause children to experience failure in two important areas of functioning: peer relationships and academics. Peer rejection and academic problems, in turn, can cause depression and feelings of low self-worth (Ezpeleta, Domenech, & Angold, 2006).

The relationship between conduct problems and depression is especially strong for girls (Ehrensaft, 2005). Disruption of family and peer social networks may be particularly stressful for girls, causing depressed mood and increased disruptive behaviors. These disrupted interpersonal relationships can lead to despair and feelings of hopelessness.

Adolescents with conduct problems often show problems with impulsivity and poor problem solving, putting them at increased risk for suicide (Ruchkin, Schwab-Stone, Koposov, Vermeiren, & King, 2003). In one study, two thirds of adolescents who completed suicide had histories of antisocial behavior; about 50% were retrospectively diagnosed with CD (Ezpeleta et al., 2006).

Substance Use Problems

Youths with conduct problems are at increased risk for substance use disorders (Clark, Parker, & Lynch, 1999). Children and adolescents with conduct problems often begin using nicotine, alcohol, and other drugs at earlier ages than children without conduct problems (McGue, Iacono, Legrand, & Elkins, 2001; McGue, Iacono, Legrand, Malone, & Elkins, 2001). In one study, 41.9% of youths with conduct problems tried alcohol and 23.1% tried marijuana by their 14th birthday (see Figure 9.3). In contrast, only 26.9% and 6.9% of 14-year-olds without conduct problems had tried alcohol and marijuana, respectively (S. M. King, Iacono, & McGue,

2004). Conduct problems also place children and adolescents at increased risk for using alcohol and marijuana on a regular basis and using multiple substances simultaneously (Button, Hewitt, Rhee, Young, Corley, & Stalling, 2006; K. M. King & Chassin, 2004).

What causes adolescents with conduct problems to use alcohol and other drugs? First, there seems to be a common set of genes that predisposes individuals to both conduct problems and substance use disorders (McGue, Iacono, Legrand, & Elkins 2001; McGue, Iacono, Legrand, Malone et al., 2001). Studies of twins and adopted children reared apart indicate a significant association between children's genes and the emergence of both conduct problems and substance use disorders (Clark, Vanyukov, & Cornelius, 2002). Some researchers have suggested that children inherit genes that cause over-activity in the BAS neurotransmitter system, making them highly sensitive to rewards and pleasure (Vanyukov & Tarter, 2000). This sensitivity might predispose them to both conduct problems (e.g., to obtain excitement) and substance use (e.g., to obtain pleasure from the drug).

Second, disruptive children are typically first introduced to alcohol and other drugs by older, deviant peers (Van Kammen, Loeber, & Stouthamer-Loeber, 1991). Deviant peers provide access to these substances, model their use, and reward adolescents with acceptance into the peer group. Substance use problems, therefore, are typically part of a larger spectrum of Conduct Disorder symptoms fostered by deviant peers.

Learning Problems

Young children with conduct problems usually show considerable difficulties in school (Dishion, Capaldi, Spracklen, & Li, 1995). They are more likely to earn low grades, to repeat a grade, and to drop out of school before graduation than youths without conduct problems (Kazdin, 2005b). Disruptive youths usually show problems in critical areas of academic achievement, especially reading and mathematics. Approximately 25% of children with conduct problems show academic underachievement; that is, their academic performance is significantly lower than what might be predicted by their age and intelligence. Academic underachievement is especially likely when children have both ADHD and conduct problems (Finch, Nelson, & Hart, 2006).

By middle childhood, children's academic difficulties often lead to negative attitudes toward school and teachers (Sameroff, Peck, & Eccles, 2004). Youths with conduct problems often devalue education, put less effort and time into their school work, and show reduced confidence in their ability to perform. These negative attitudes can cause youths with conduct problems to distance themselves from school, teachers, and prosocial peers.

Schools, too, sometimes play a role in the development of conduct problems. Schools that place little emphasis on academic work, hold low expectations for students' academic

Figure 9.3 Substance Use Among Adolescents With and Without Conduct Problems

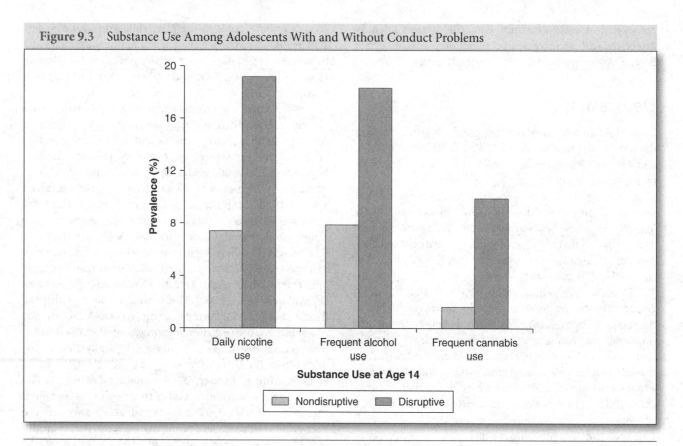

Source: Based on S. M. King et al. (2004).

Note: Fourteen-year-olds with behavior problems are more likely to use cigarettes, alcohol, and marijuana on a regular basis than are youths without behavior problems.

achievement and classroom behavior, and provide students with poor working conditions can contribute to children's disruptive behavior problems. Unfortunately, these characteristics are often seen among schools in low-income, high-crime neighborhoods (Sameroff et al., 2004).

EPIDEMIOLOGY

Prevalence

The prevalence of conduct problems depends on gender (Maughan et al., 2004). With respect to ODD, prevalence for boys ranges from 1.9% to 13.3%, with most estimates being within the 3% to 5% range. For girls, the prevalence of ODD ranges from 1.1% to 9.4%, with most estimates being approximately 3%. With respect to CD, prevalence estimates for boys range from 1.7% to 14%, with most estimates being within the 5% to 10% range. For girls, prevalence ranges from approximately 1% to 8%, with most estimates being within the 2% to 4% range.

The prevalence of conduct problems also varies by age. Across development, rates of ODD decrease and rates of CD increase. Approximately 3% of preschoolers have ODD compared to less than 1% of adolescents; conversely, less than

1% of preschoolers meet diagnostic criteria for CD, whereas approximately 5% of adolescents may have the disorder (Lahey et al., 2000; Maughan et al., 2004).

The apparent decrease in ODD with age is largely due to the fact that an older version of the *DSM*, the *DSM-IV*, did not permit ODD to be diagnosed when CD is present. Older children who met diagnostic criteria for both ODD and CD were given only the CD diagnosis. If we simply look at the percentage of children who meet diagnostic criteria for ODD (regardless of whether they have CD), we see that the prevalence remains fairly stable across childhood and adolescence. These data suggest that ODD symptoms do not disappear; instead, they are usually overshadowed by more serious CD symptoms (Maughan et al., 2004).

Gender Differences

Research investigating gender differences in children's conduct problems has yielded complex results. Overall, boys are more likely than girls to show conduct problems. For example, in one large community sample of twins, boys (13.9%) were about three times more likely than girls (4.9%) to meet diagnostic criteria for CD (Gelhorn et al., 2005).

However, the exact prevalence of conduct problems by gender depends on the age of the child. For example, conduct problems in boys typically emerge in preschool and are characterized by hyperactivity, destructive behavior, and physical aggression (Loeber & Stouthamer-Loeber, 1998). In contrast, conduct problems in girls usually do not emerge until adolescence and often involve more covert symptoms. Consequently, in early childhood, boys are approximately three times more likely than girls to show serious conduct problems (Biederman, Mick et al., 2002). However, by adolescence, the gender ratio for CD may be 2:1 (Finch et al., 2006).

Until recently, most experts believed that girls simply showed less aggression than boys. However, emerging data suggest that girls aggress in different ways than boys—ways that can be easily overlooked. Specifically, girls often use **relational aggression**; that is, they harm other people's mood, self-concept, or social status by damaging or manipulating interpersonal relationships (Crick & Grotpeter, 1995). Relational aggression can occur in a number of ways. Girls can spread rumors, ostracize another girl from a social network, share another girl's secrets without her consent, steal another girl's on-line identity, or make fun of another girl's weight, clothes, or general appearance. These tactics can be used either reactively (e.g., because the girl is angry at something another girl did) or proactively (e.g., because the girl wants to gain popularity or social status by harming a peer).

Girls may show relational aggression more than boys for at least three reasons (Ehrensaft, 2005). First, parents socialize girls differently than boys. From an early age, girls are discouraged to show anger through physical aggression. They may learn to use relational aggression to express anger, frustration, and discontent. Whereas physical aggression by girls is usually punished, relational aggression is often overlooked. Second, relational aggression may be more effective than physical aggression at harming other girls. Because girls' moods and identities are so connected with their social relationships, damage to these relationships might be more hurtful than physical assault. In fact, girls view relational aggression as extremely distressing and comparable to physical bullying (Crick, 1995, 1997; Crick & Grotpeter, 1995). Third, girls' relatively more advanced language skills make relational aggression possible. Relational aggression does not typically emerge until late childhood and adolescence, when children's verbal skills are developed enough to engage in these complex, socially aggressive acts (Tiet, Wasserman, Loeber, McReynolds, & Miller, 2001). Since young girls' verbal skills are often better developed than those of boys, girls may be able to show relational aggression at younger ages than boys.

Course

Most children show an increase in disruptive behavior from late infancy through the preschool years. Beginning in early childhood, however, disruptive behavior problems typically decline. Some young children continue to show an increase in oppositional and defiant behavior during early childhood and merit the diagnosis of ODD (Gelhorn et al., 2005).

In samples of clinic-referred children, there is a strong relationship between ODD and CD. In one study, 80% of clinic-referred children with ODD eventually developed CD (Lahey, Waldman, & McBurnett, 1999). In samples of children from the community, only about 25% to 33% of children with ODD develop CD (Keenan, Loeber, & Green, 1999; Rowe, Maughan, Pickles, Costello, & Angold, 2002). These differences are likely due to the fact that children with more severe and persistent problems are more likely to be referred to treatment.

Most experts view ODD and CD as distinct, but related, disorders. For example, Lahey, Loeber, Quay, Frick, and Grimm (1992) suggest that ODD is a precursor to CD in some children. Although most children with ODD do not develop CD, a certain percentage of children will show more severe conduct problems.

The developmental outcomes of children with conduct problems depend greatly on the age at which they first showed symptoms. Children with childhood-onset conduct problems have poorer prognoses. These youths are at risk for antisocial and criminal behavior (Caspi, 2000; Farrington, 1998), educational and employment problems (Caspi, Wright, Moffitt, & Silva, 1998), mental health problems (Darke, Ross, & Lynskey, 2003; Fergusson & Lynskey, 1998), and teenage pregnancy (Bardone, Moffitt, Caspi, Dickson, Stanton, & Silva, 1998; Woodward & Fergusson, 1999). In a 25-year longitudinal study of almost 1,000 children with early-onset conduct problems, Fergusson, Horwood, and Ridder (2005) found that children who showed the most serious conduct problems at age 7 also showed the worst developmental outcomes in adulthood. A second longitudinal study followed preschoolers with CD for 5 years (Kim-Cohen et al., 2009). Although many children no longer met full criteria for CD at age 10, most continued to show problems with aggression, delinquency, and academics (Figure 9.4).

Boys with CD are at particular risk for developing Antisocial Personality Disorder (APD) as adults. Approximately 40% to 70% of adolescent boys with CD will develop APD by early adulthood (Fombonne, Wostear, Cooper, Harrington, & Rutter, 2001; Lahey, Loeber, Burke, & Applegate, 2005). A boy's likelihood of developing APD depends on two factors. First, the sheer number of covert (but not overt) symptoms that the boy shows in adolescence predicts his likelihood of showing future antisocial behavior. Deceitfulness, property destruction, and theft are some of the best predictors of the development of APD. Second, adolescents with CD who come from low-income families are at particular risk for developing APD in adulthood. In one study, adolescents from low-SES backgrounds (65%) were much more likely to develop APD than adolescents from middle-class families (20%; Lahey et al., 2005).

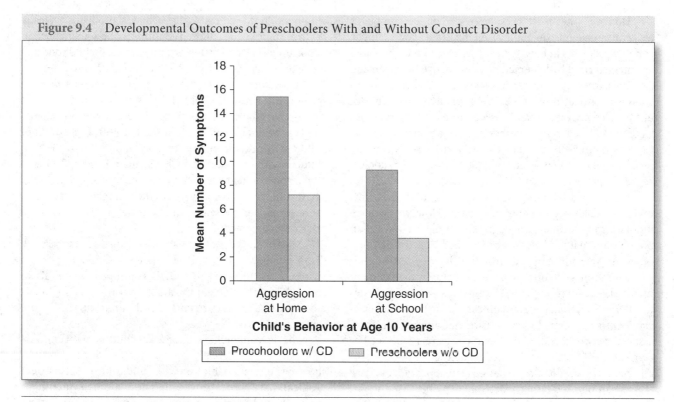

Source: Based on Kim-Cohen and colleagues (2009).

Note: Preschoolers with CD were followed from age 5 to age 10. They showed more aggression at home and school in later childhood than did their peers without CD.

Girls with CD are at risk for internalizing disorders in adolescence and adulthood. As young adults, 75% of girls previously diagnosed with CD show some type of internalizing disorder, including depression and anxiety. Some girls previously diagnosed with CD develop Borderline Personality Disorder (BPD) in adulthood. BPD is a serious personality disorder characterized by tumultuous interpersonal relationships, mood dysregulation, impulsive and reckless behavior, and self-harm. The symptoms of CD in adolescence may interfere with girls' development of identity and healthy relationships, thus, leading to the emergence of BPD in later life (Bardone, Moffitt, Caspi, Dickson, & Silva, 1996; Ehrensaft, 2005; Moffitt et al., 2001; Woodward & Fergusson, 1999).

Youths with adolescence-limited CD have better developmental outcomes than children whose symptoms begin in childhood. Nevertheless, youths with adolescence-limited symptoms show considerable impairment during their teenage years. These youths are at risk for academic failure, suspension, expulsion, legal problems, and conflicts with parents and peers. Some of their antisocial behaviors during adolescence can have long-term consequences. For example, youths who drop out of high school or are arrested may have limited employment opportunities in adulthood. Longitudinal studies indicate that youths with adolescence-limited conduct problems often show residual effects of their disruptive behavior in early adulthood (Moffitt et al.,

2002). Consequently, youths who begin to show disruptive behavior in adolescence merit the attention of parents, teachers, and mental health professionals as much as youths with childhood-onset conduct problems.

ETIOLOGY

Genetics

Conduct problems run in families. Youths with ODD or CD often have first-degree relatives with histories of conduct problems or antisocial behavior (Meyer et al., 2000).

However, family studies do not tell us whether the transmission of conduct problems from parent to child is due to shared genes or common environmental experiences.

The results of twin studies have yielded inconsistent findings. Heritability estimates range from 6% to 71%. Across all studies, genetic factors account for approximately 40% to 50% of the variance in children's conduct problems, broadly defined (Dick, Viken, Kaprio, Pulkkinen, & Rose, 2005; Gelhorn et al., 2005; Rhee & Waldman, 2002). Recent molecular genetics studies indicate that portions of chromosomes 2 and 19 may be partially responsible for this heritability (Dick et al., 2004).

If we assume that approximately 50% of the variance in children's conduct problems is attributable to genetics, then the remaining variance must be attributable to environmental causes (see Figure 9.5). Nonshared environmental factors account for the lion's share of the remaining variance in children's conduct problems, with estimates ranging from 31% to 86%. In contrast, shared environmental experiences typically account for very little of the variance in conduct problems, with estimates ranging from 0% to 37% (Tackett et al., 2005).

Temperament and Early Neurological Development

Youths with childhood-onset conduct problems often have certain temperamental characteristics that contribute to their disruptive behavior (Dodge & Pettit, 2003; Loeber & Farrington, 2000). **Temperament** refers to the physiological, emotional, and behavioral responses a child typically displays in response to environmental stimuli (Nigg, 2006). A child's temperament is chiefly determined by genetic factors; temperament can be observed at birth or shortly thereafter. Some newborns show "easy" temperaments: They display moderate levels of emotional activity, do not react negatively or fearfully to novel situations, readily engage their environment, and are able to cope with changes in their routine. Other infants show "difficult" temperaments: They display either extremely high or extremely low levels of emotional activity, are quick to cry and fuss at novel stimuli, are easily frustrated, and have difficulty adjusting to change. Children with early-onset conduct problems often show difficult temperaments in infancy and early childhood (Frick, Cornell, Barry, Bodin, & Dane, 2003; Frick, Cornell, Bodin, et al. 2003; Loney, Frick, Clements, Ellis, & Kerlin, 2003).

Recently, researchers have begun examining *how* difficult temperament can contribute to the development of conduct problems (Frick, 2004; Frick & Morris, 2004). So far, two developmental pathways have been identified: (a) problems with emotion regulation and (b) problems with low emotional arousal.

Figure 9.5 The Effect of Genetic and Environmental Factors on Children's Conduct Problems

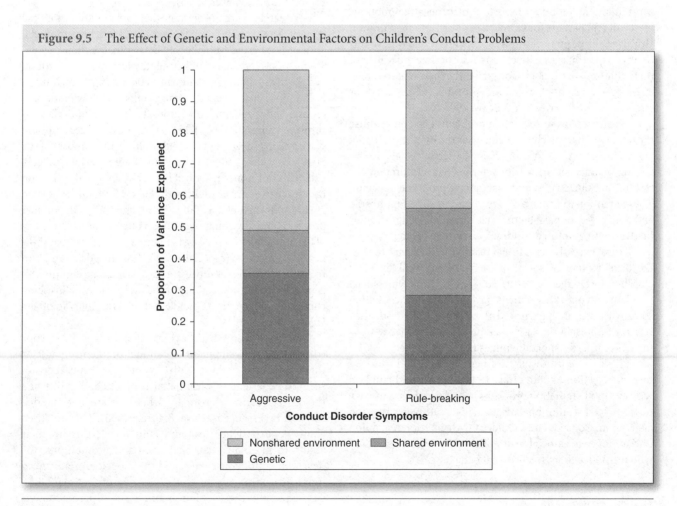

Source: Based on Tackett et al. (2005).

Note: The type of disruptive behavior that children show determines how important genetic and environmental factors are in children's conduct problems. Genetic and nonshared environmental factors account for most of the variance in children's aggressive symptoms. However, nonaggressive conduct symptoms (e.g., stealing, lying, truancy) are explained by genetic, nonshared, *and* shared factors.

Problems With Emotion Regulation

Some children with difficult temperament show problems with **excessive emotional reactivity** (Eisenberg et al., 2001; Eisenberg, Fabes, Guthrie, & Reiser, 2000; Frick, Cornell, Barry et al., 2003). When confronted with an environmental stressor, these children display intense, negative emotional reactions and take an unusually long time to soothe (Keenan, Gunthorpe, & Young, 2002). Keenan and Shaw (2003) believe this tendency is caused by an underlying problem with emotion regulation. These children have difficulty controlling negative emotions and responding to stressors in adaptive, flexible, and age-appropriate ways. When frustrated, these children often react with extreme emotional outbursts including anger and aggression. Problems with emotion regulation emerge between 6 and 24 months of life.

Difficulty with emotion regulation can lead to the development of conduct problems in several ways (Frick, 2004; Frick & Morris, 2004; Keenan & Shaw, 2003). First, young children's early emotional displays can interfere with the development of more effective emotion regulation skills. Most infants and toddlers learn to control negative emotions by relying on parents for comfort, support, and reassurance. However, the parents of these at-risk children may have difficulty responding sensitively and appropriately because of their children's outbursts. Consequently, their children may enter their preschool years with diminished capacity for emotional control (Keenan & Shaw, 2003).

Second, emotion regulation problems can compromise the quality of parent-child interactions during the preschool years (Kochanska & Aksan, 2006; Patterson et al., 1992). Crying, yelling, and aggression interfere with children's abilities to internalize rules and maintain appropriate behavior. These emotional displays also lead parents to adopt hostile and angry disciplinary tactics that can model aggression or inadvertently reinforce children's disruptive behaviors.

Third, excessive emotional reactivity can interfere with the development of social problem-solving skills in early childhood (Dodge & Pettit, 2003). Children with social problem-solving skills deficits have difficulties negotiating social disputes in logical and flexible ways. Instead, they rely on impulsive decision making and aggressive actions to resolve interpersonal dilemmas (Crick & Dodge, 1996).

Finally, intense displays of negative emotion can lead to peer rejection (Rubin et al., 1998). Peers avoid children with emotion regulation problems because of their tendency toward aversive emotional displays, high-rate behaviors, and aggression. Consequently, children with emotion regulation difficulties may associate with other peer-rejected children who introduce them to antisocial behaviors.

Low Emotional Arousal

Other children with difficult temperament show extremely low levels of emotional arousal (Frick & Morris, 2004). These youths have a reduction in overall autonomic activity: low resting heart rate, reduced brain activity, low galvanic skin response (Frick & Morris, 2004; Raine, 2002). Because of their low level of arousal, these children need more intense stimulation to experience the same feelings as typically developing children. Consequently, they tend to engage in high-rate, high-risk activities and be less responsive to punishment.

Toddlers with low levels of emotional arousal are slow to react to pleasurable stimuli, appear less afraid of frightening or dangerous situations, and do not seem to adjust their behavior when punished (Shaw, Gilliom, Ingoldsby, & Nagin, 2003). By middle childhood, these children often show an inability to feel empathy for others' suffering or distress, a lack of remorse for misbehavior, a desire to use others for personal gain, and a lack of response to discipline or punishment (Frick, Bodin, & Barry, 2000; Pardini, Lochman, & Frick, 2003; Silverthorn, Frick, & Reynolds, 2001; van Goozen, Fairchild, Snoek, & Harold, 2007). Adolescents who show limited prosocial emotions often display a fascination with impulsive, dangerous, or delinquent behaviors (Dadds, Fraser, Frost, & Hawes, 2005).

Researchers are not certain what explains low emotional arousal. Most data point to three causes. First, low emotional arousal is believed to be largely determined by one's genes. Twin studies indicate high heritability for emotional arousal and reactivity (Lahey & Waldman, 2003; Viding, Blair, Moffitt, & Plomin, 2004). Second, some youths with low emotional arousal show general underarousal of the **hypothalamus-pituitary-adrenal (HPA) axis**, the body's stress-response system (van Goozen & Fairchild, 2006). Underarousal of the HPA axis causes reduced secretion of epinephrine and cortisol, two hormones responsible for physiological activation in response to threat (McBurnett, Lahey, Rathouz, & Loeber, 2000; McBurnett et al., 2005). Third, children with conduct problems and low emotional arousal often show hypoactivity of the **amygdala** when asked to look at human faces that show negative emotions (especially fear). The amygdala is a brain region responsible for processing and expressing emotions. It is possible that underactivity of the amygdala explains these children's lack of empathy and emotional reactivity to others (Blair et al., 2005).

Early problems with low emotional arousal can contribute to the development of conduct problems in at least three ways. First, children with low emotional arousal do not seem to experience typical patterns of fear and guilt when they engage in misbehavior and when they are reprimanded by parents (Essau, Sasagawa, & Frick, 2006). This impaired ability to experience fear and guilt interferes with their ability to internalize parental rules and prohibitions, the development of conscience, and the capacity for advanced moral reasoning (Essau et al., 2006; Pardini et al., 2003). Consequently, these children often show premeditative, aggressive behaviors without regard for the rights of others (Frick, Cornell, Bodin et al., 2003).

Second, children with low emotional arousal show an overall reduction in autonomic reactivity that renders them less sensitive to punishment (Frick, Cornell, Barry et al., 2003; Frick & Morris, 2004). Consequently, they do not correct their misbehavior when disciplined by adults. Indeed, discipline appears to have little effect on these children, making the process of socialization challenging (Dadds & Salmon, 2003).

Third, children's low autonomic arousal may render them less able to experience pleasure, excitement, and exhilaration (Frick, Cornell, Barry et al., 2003; Frick, Cornell, Bodin et al., 2003). Whereas typically developing children and adolescents derive pleasure from moderate levels of stimulation (e.g., playing sports, going to the movies), children with low autonomic activity need to engage in high-rate, novel, and sometimes dangerous activities to obtain the same pleasurable experience (e.g., reckless skateboarding, driving). Many people describe these youths as "unusually daring," prone to "sensation seeking," or "risk takers" (Essau et al., 2006).

Children who show limited prosocial emotions are at increased risk for serious aggressive behaviors in late childhood and adolescence (Frick, Cornell, Bodin et al., 2003; Frick, Stickle, Dandreaux, Farrell, & Kimonis, 2005). For example, low emotional activity predicts future antisocial behavior, delinquency, and violent criminal offenses (Kruh, Frick, &

Clements, 2005; van Goozen, Fairchild, Snoek, & Harold, 2007). The presence of low emotional reactivity may be a better predictor of future antisocial behavior than the presence of CD alone (Caputo, Frick, & Brodsky, 1999; Essau et al., 2006). Frick, Cornell, Barry et al. (2003) studied 98 school-age children, separated into four groups based on the presence or absence of (a) conduct problems (CP) and (b) low emotional arousal. As we might expect, children with CP at the beginning of the study were more likely than children without CP to show disruptive behaviors 4 years later. However, children who showed limited emotional arousal at the beginning of the study, regardless of whether they also showed CP, displayed the greatest likelihood of aggressive and delinquent behavior at follow-up (see Figure 9.6).

Taken together, research indicates that the presence of difficult temperament in infancy can predispose children toward conduct problems in later childhood and adolescence (Moran et al., 2009). Problems with emotional reactivity or unusually low emotional arousal can independently contribute to later behavior problems. Although difficult temperament is largely determined by genetic factors, the emergence of later conduct problems is caused by a complex interplay of temperamental and environmental factors that are just beginning to be understood.

Figure 9.6 Effects of Low Emotional Arousal on Children's Likelihood of Aggression

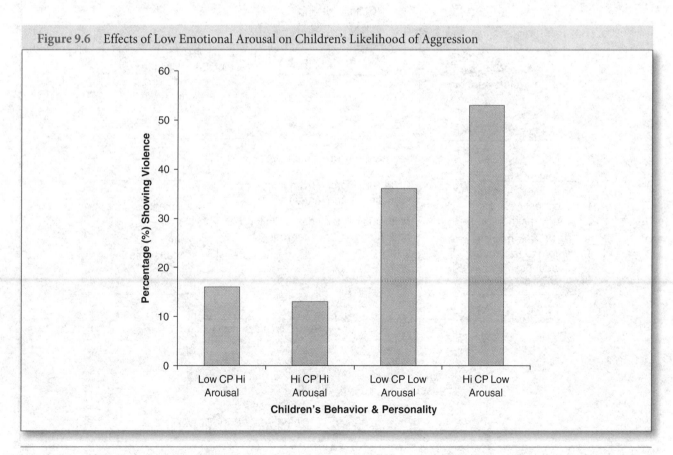

Note: Frick, Cornell, Barry, and colleagues (2003) divided children into four groups based on the presence or absence of conduct problems (CP) and low emotional arousal. Four years later, they assessed children's aggressive behavior. Children with low emotional arousal showed more aggressive behavior, regardless of whether they also had histories of conduct problems.

Parent-Child Interactions

Parenting Behavior

Although genetic and temperamental factors can predispose children to conduct problems, the development of ODD and CD depends greatly on early learning experiences. Chief among these experiences is the quality of early parent-child interactions (Constantino et al., 2006; Guttmann-Steinmetz & Crowell, 2006).

Hostile-coercive parenting behavior is associated with the development of children's conduct problems. **Hostile-coercive parenting behavior** includes harsh disciplinary tactics, such as yelling, arguing, spanking, hitting, or criticizing children in response to their misbehavior. Hostile parenting can also involve using guilt and shame to correct children's misbehavior or relying on parental power to make children comply with requests or commands. Usually, hostile parenting is administered in an inconsistent fashion. Parents are often unwilling to hit or yell at their children for every misbehavior. Instead, parents tend to rely on hostile practices only when other tactics have proved ineffective or when they have become increasingly frustrated. Consequently, hostile parenting is almost always associated with parental anger and resentment (Baumrind, 1991).

Gerald Patterson and colleagues (1992) have identified a particularly problematic pattern of parent-child interactions known as the **coercive parent-child cycle** (Figure 9.7). In coercive parent-child interactions, parents and children teach each other to behave in ways that predispose children to act in oppositional and defiant ways. The cycle is based on learning theory, especially principles of operant conditioning.

Coercive parent-child interactions often begin with the parent issuing a command to a child. For example, a boy might be playing in the living room and his mother might ask him to set the table for dinner. The boy might

Figure 9.7   The Coercive Parent-Child Cycle

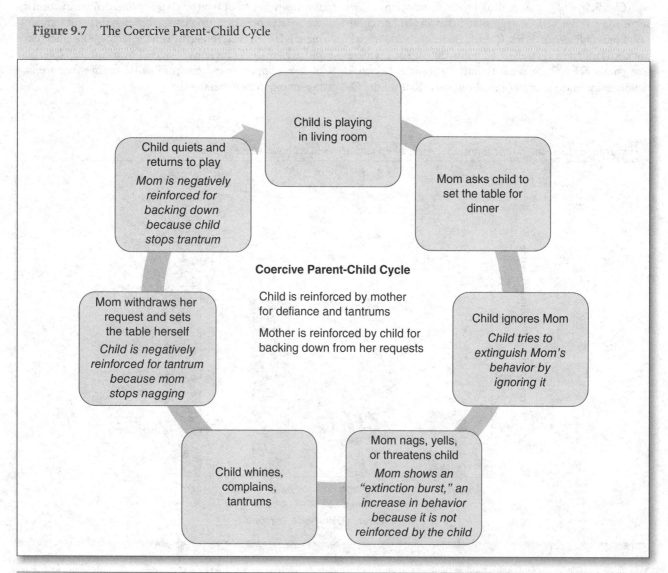

Note: Patterson and colleagues (1992) showed that oppositional-defiant behavior was often maintained through negative reinforcement. Parents reinforced children for throwing a tantrum while children reinforced parents for backing down from their requests.

initially ignore his mother's request. In behavioral terms, he is attempting to **extinguish** her behavior by not reinforcing it with his compliance. His mother will probably repeat her request, this time more forcefully. She might nag, yell, or threaten the boy with punishment. In behavioral terms, the mother is showing an **extinction burst**, that is, a marked increase in the frequency or intensity of a behavior that occurs when the behavior is not reinforced. In response, the boy may issue a more forceful refusal; he might whine, yell, or throw a tantrum to avoid setting the table. Consequently, his mother decides that it is too much trouble to argue with her son and decides to set the table herself. She withdraws her request and stops nagging her son. In behavioral terms, the mother negatively reinforces her son for throwing tantrums; she withdraws an aversive stimulus (e.g., nags) in response to his tantrums, making it more likely that he will tantrum in the future. At the same time, her son negatively reinforces his mother's acquiescence; he stops whining and complaining in response to her decision to "give in" and allow him to play. Consequently, she will be more likely to give in in the future.

The coercive cycle can also begin with the child, rather than the parent. For example, a girl and her father might be in the check-out aisle of the grocery store when the girl asks her father for some candy. Her father denies her request, saying that the candy will spoil her dinner. The girl may exhibit an extinction burst, in this case, a dramatic increase in whining, crying, or throwing tantrums in response to her father's refusal to purchase the candy. Embarrassed and frustrated, the father might acquiesce and give her daughter the candy. The daughter is positively reinforced for her tantrums; she learns that throwing tantrums allows her to obtain candy. Her father, in turn, is negatively reinforced for giving in to his daughter's tantrums; he learns that he can avoid embarrassment and frustration in a crowded store by giving her what she wants. Each member of the dyad teaches the other to act in a way that elicits the child's opposition-defiant behavior.

In most coercive exchanges, parents inadvertently reinforce children for ignoring or defying their commands. In some instances, however, parents become angry and insist on compliance (Snyder, 2001). In these cases, parents may engage in hostile behaviors, such as yelling, threatening, or physically disciplining children, while in a state of anger. In these instances, parents model hostile-aggressive behaviors for their children. They show their children that verbal and physical aggression are effective ways of dealing with problematic social situations (see Research to Practice, Problems with Positive Punishment).

Parents of disruptive children frequently alternate between overly permissive and hostile-coercive parenting behaviors (Cunningham & Boyle, 2002). Typically, parents are lax on discipline, perhaps because they want to avoid stress associated with correcting their children's misbehavior (McKee, Harvey, Danforth, Ulaszek, & Friedman, 2004). However, when parents become frustrated or threatened by children's misbehavior, they may respond in a hostile or aggressive fashion: yelling, threatening, grabbing, or hitting. Parents' reliance on overly permissive and hostile-coercive parenting behaviors is one of the best predictors of conduct problems in young children (Chamberlain, Reid, Ray, Capaldi, & Fisher, 1997; Patterson et al., 1992; Sameroff et al., 2004). Frequent use of these tactics also predicts conduct problems in elementary school and middle school (Ackerman, Brown, & Izard, 2003). Furthermore, harsh discipline is one of the best predictors in determining whether a child with ODD will develop CD as an adolescent (Rowe et al., 2002).

RESEARCH TO PRACTICE

PROBLEMS WITH POSITIVE PUNISHMENT

Many parents rely on positive punishment (e.g., yelling, spanking) to stop children from engaging in aversive behavior. Although positive punishment can be effective in the short term, it has several long-term disadvantages:

- Positive punishment models hostile and aggressive behaviors to children. Children learn that yelling and spanking are appropriate and effective ways to deal with interpersonal conflict.
- Positive punishment does not teach children new, prosocial behaviors. Punishment teaches children what not to do (e.g., cry, complain) rather than what to do (e.g., obey adults, make appropriate requests).
- To be effective, positive punishment must be used consistently; however, parents usually use it only intermittently (especially when they are angry).
- If punished often, children learn to avoid or escape these punishments through negative reinforcement. For example, they may avoid interacting with parents.
- Positive punishment, when administered when parents are angry or frustrated, can lead to verbal and physical abuse.

Because of these limitations, treatment for oppositional behavior relies chiefly on positive reinforcement, extinction, and negative punishment (e.g., time out).

Parenting Cognition

Parents' thoughts about their children's misbehavior can affect both their parenting behavior and their children's developmental outcomes (Dix, 1993). Suppose that a mother notices that her preschool-age child often tantrums in the late afternoon. She could make two different **attributions** for her child's misbehavior. First, she might attribute her misbehavior to *external* and *unstable* causes, saying, "Oh, she just gets tired during that time of the day. She needs a longer nap." Alternatively, she might attribute the child's tantrum to *internal* and *stable* causes, saying, "Oh, she's such a bad girl. She seems to enjoy making me upset."

Parents of children with conduct problems are more likely to attribute behavior problems to internal and stable factors (Dix & Lochman, 1990; Johnston & Freeman, 1997). Internal and stable attributions increase the likelihood that parents will respond to misbehavior in hostile or coercive ways (Bugental, Johnston, New, & Silvester, 1998). If a parent believes that her child misbehaves because she is "a bad girl" or "deliberately being naughty," the parent is prone to anger and resentment. However, if a parent attributes her child's misbehavior to transient, situational factors (e.g., fatigue, hunger, boredom), the parent is more likely to respond in a more sympathetic way (Snyder, Cramer, Afrank, & Patterson, 2005).

The way parents think about their own parenting skills can also affect their disciplinary tactics (Johnston, 2005; Johnston & Freeman, 1997). The parents of disruptive children frequently feel powerless over their children, and they often report little confidence in their caregiving abilities (see Figure 9.8). Parents who feel powerless over their children's behavior may give up trying to discipline their children. In one study, the parents of disruptive preschoolers disciplined their children *less* often than the parents of nondisruptive preschoolers, despite the fact that children in the former group showed more behavior problems. These feelings of powerlessness can also cause parents to resent their children's misbehavior and increase the likelihood that parents will discipline in a hostile or coercive manner (Cunningham & Boyle, 2002).

We need to remember that the relationship between parenting behavior and child misbehavior is transactional; parents and children influence each other's behaviors over time. For example, a child who has difficulty regulating his emotions might engage in more crying, tantrums, and disruptive behavior than most children his age. His aversive emotional displays might cause his mother to adopt hostile-coercive strategies to manage his behavior. These less-than-optimal parenting behaviors might, in turn, contribute to more severe oppositional-defiant behaviors and future conduct problems. In fact, children with difficult temperaments and affect regulation problems seem to elicit hostile-coercive behaviors from their parents (Moffitt et al., 2001; Stoolmiller, 2001). These parenting behaviors, in turn, contribute to the development of conduct problems throughout childhood (Dodge, 2006; Patterson, DeGarmo, & Knutson, 2000; Shaw, Lacourse, & Nagin, 2005).

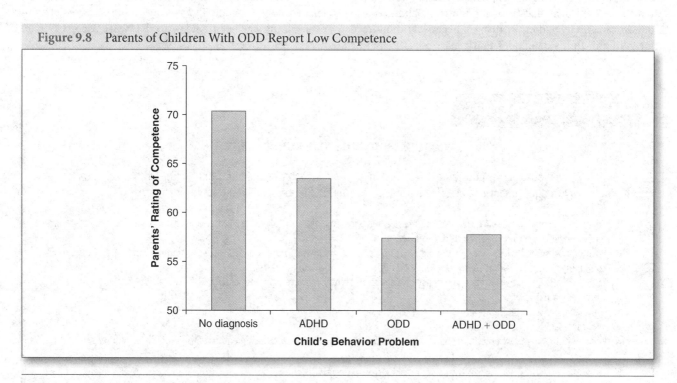

Figure 9.8   Parents of Children With ODD Report Low Competence

Source: Based on Cunningham and Boyle (2002).

Note: Parents' doubts and frustrations can cause them to respond in hostile ways, exacerbating their children's conduct problems.

Parents' Mental Health

Parental psychopathology also predicts children's conduct problems (Crnic & Low, 2002). Maternal depression, paternal antisocial behavior, and parental substance abuse are all associated with children's disruptive behavior problems. Marital conflict, too, is associated with children's conduct problems (Chronis et al., 2007). Parents' emotional and behavioral problems can contribute to children's disruptive behavior by interfering with the quality of parent-child interactions. For example, mothers with depression are often less supportive and more coercive toward their children than mothers without depression; their emotional distress and low energy interferes with the care and discipline they give their children (Lovejoy, Graczyk, O'Hare, & Neuman, 2000). Additionally, parents with disruptive behavior problems often model hostile and aggressive behaviors in the home (Calzada, Eyberg, Rich, & Querido, 2004; Frick & Loney, 2002; Querido, Eyberg, & Boggs, 2001).

Low Parental Monitoring

By late childhood and early adolescence, children assume greater autonomy over their behavior. They are given greater freedom to plan their day, and they are able to participate in more activities without parental supervision. However, the increased autonomy that children enjoy also provides them with more opportunities to engage in disruptive and antisocial acts.

Low parental monitoring is strongly associated with the development of conduct problems in late childhood and adolescence (Loeber & Farrington, 2000; Rowe et al., 2002; Wasserman & Seracini, 2001; see Figure 9.9). **Parental monitoring** has three components. First, parents must know children's whereabouts, activities, and peers. Second, parents must set developmentally appropriate limits on children's activities. Third, parents must consistently discipline children when they fail to adhere to rules (Snyder, Reid, & Patterson, 2003). Children whose parents fail to monitor or supervise their activities show increased likelihood of conduct problems; however, children whose parents set firm limits on after-school activities show decreased rates of delinquency (Chronis et al., 2007; Galambos, Barker, & Almeida, 2003; Laird, Pettit, Dodge, & Bates, 2003).

Patterson and Yoerger (2002) have argued that low parental monitoring is one of the chief mechanisms by which children's disruptive behavior continues into adolescence. They encourage parents to set clear expectations on their children's behavior, to supervise their children's activities, and to administer consequences for their children's rule violations. Although these are wise suggestions, some data suggest that these tactics are more easily said than done. Adolescents are adroit at keeping parents in the dark about potentially delinquent activities. Furthermore, excessive

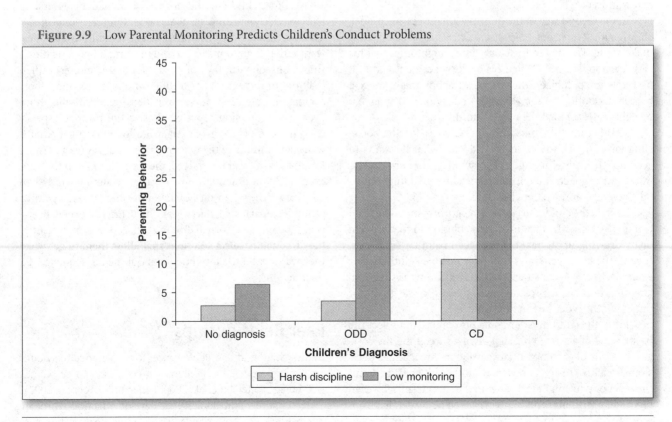

Figure 9.9 Low Parental Monitoring Predicts Children's Conduct Problems

Source: Based on Rowe et al. (2002).

Note: The parents of youths with ODD and CD engage in more harsh discipline and less parental monitoring than do the parents of youths without conduct problems.

parental supervision can actually lead to an *increase* in adolescent behavior problems if teens feel overcontrolled by parents (Kerr & Stattin, 2000).

Social Information Processing

Children with conduct problems often show characteristic biases in their social information processing, that is, the way they perceive, interpret, and solve social dilemmas and interpersonal disputes (Dodge, 2003; Reinecke, 2006). Crick and Dodge (1994) developed **social information processing theory** to explain how children solve interpersonal problems. According to this theory, the way people think and feel about social situations influences their actions.

In social information processing theory, a child must perform five mental processes in order to solve an interpersonal problem. First, the child must *encode cues* about the social situation; that is, he or she must take in information about the situation in order to understand it. Cues can include external information about the situation itself or internal information about the child. Imagine that a 10-year-old boy is waiting in line in the school lunchroom. He is suddenly struck from behind and notices milk running down his back. He further notices that a larger, older boy is standing behind him, looking sheepish, while other children in the lunchroom are beginning to snicker. The younger boy feels embarrassed and confused.

In the second step of the information processing model, children must *interpret internal and external cues* so that they make sense. The boy in the story above might infer that his classmate spilled milk down his back by accident and that he wants to apologize. Alternatively, the boy might make a hostile attribution for the older boy's behavior, believing that he deliberately spilled the milk to humiliate him.

Third, the child must *clarify his goals* for the social situation. That is, the child must decide what he wants to accomplish. One goal might be to avoid further embarrassment and to get cleaned up. An alternative goal might be to take revenge on the older classmate.

Fourth, the child must *develop a plan of action*. The child can do this either by creating a new solution to the problem or by drawing upon past experiences in similar situations. Ideally, the child generates multiple possible solutions. For example, he might consider walking away from the situation, laughing over his misfortune with the rest of his peers, or punching the older boy in retaliation.

Fifth, the child must *evaluate his options* and select the best course of action. This step involves weighing the costs and benefits of each potential solution and reaching a decision about how to act. For example, if the child decides to hit the older boy, he might feel better in the short term. However, he will likely get in trouble and may even be suspended from school.

Finally, the child *enacts the solution* to the problem that he believes is the best. Then, the cycle begins anew, as the child begins to process others' reactions to his solution. According to Crick and Dodge (1994), the information-processing steps occur extremely rapidly, usually without children knowing that they are engaging in them.

Considerable research has shown that aggressive children tend to show biases in their social information processing. Furthermore, these deficits differ depending on whether children show reactive or proactive aggression (Kempes, Matthys, de Vries, & van Engeland, 2005). Children who show reactive aggression tend to have problems with the first two steps: encoding and interpreting cues (Crick & Dodge, 1996; Schwartz et al., 1998). Specifically, they take in less information about the situation. For example, they might attend to one or two salient features of the situation (e.g., the milk, the other children laughing) and ignore other potentially important cues (e.g., the boy behind saying, "I'm sorry"). These children also have difficulty understanding their own emotional reactions to the situation. For example, they might mistake feelings of embarrassment for feelings of anger. Consequently, children who engage in reactive aggression usually show a **hostile attribution bias** for others' behavior; they are likely to interpret others' benign behavior as hostile or threatening (Dodge, 1993; Dodge et al., 1995).

Children who show proactive aggression tend to have difficulty with the last three steps: clarifying goals and developing and evaluating possible solutions (Crick & Dodge, 1996). First, children who engage in proactive aggression tend to select instrumental goals rather than relational goals. That is, their objective is often to get something that they want rather than to make a friend or to maintain a relationship. Consequently, they often act out of self-interest rather than out of respect for the feelings of others. Second, when evaluating potential courses of action, children who show proactive aggression often emphasize the positive aspects of aggressive behavior (e.g., it will allow me to get what I want) and minimize the negative aspects of aggression (e.g., I might get in trouble). Indeed, these children seem to focus excessively on potential rewards (e.g., stealing a candy bar or a car) rather than on possible punishment (e.g., getting grounded or arrested; Barry et al., 2000; Frick, Cornell, Barry et al., 2003; Frick, Cornell, Bodin et al., 2003). Consequently, they frequently select solutions that allow them to get what they want with little forethought about the consequences of their actions.

Peer Relationships

Across childhood and adolescence, friends gradually assume greater importance to children's self-concepts and emotional well-being (Patterson et al., 2000; Patterson & Yoerger, 2002). Older children and adolescents develop identities through interactions with their friends; friends influence their thoughts, feelings, and actions. Prosocial peers can protect youths from stressors by providing them with a social support system independent of their families (Brendgen, Wanner, Morin, & Vitaro, 2005). Deviant peers, however, can contribute to children's behavior problems (Moffitt et al., 2001).

Boys who show academic and conduct problems in school are often rejected by prosocial peers (Dishion, Andrews et al., 1995; Dodge et al., 2003; Snyder et al., 2003). Children with low academic achievement are seldom selected for group projects and may be teased by classmates. Even in kindergarten, children avoid classmates who are hyperactive or highly disruptive (Lacourse, Nagin, Vitaro, Cote, Arseneault, & Tremblay, 2006). Youths who show problems with affect regulation, anger, or aggression are actively avoided because of their impulsive and aversive displays (Price & Dodge, 1989b; Schwartz et al., 1998). Interestingly, children who show angry reactive aggression are more likely to be rejected by peers than children who show proactive aggression (Dodge & Coie, 1987; Price & Dodge, 1989b). Some bullies are popular, especially among younger children (Price & Dodge, 1989b).

Socially ostracized boys may seek out other boys who are socially rejected, a tendency known as **selective affiliation** (Snyder et al., 2003). These deviant peers introduce boys to more serious antisocial behaviors, such as physical aggression, vandalism, truancy, theft, and alcohol use (Haselager, Cillessen, Van Lieshout, Riksen-Walraven, & Hartup, 2002; Petras et al., 2004).

Boys learn to engage in antisocial behavior from peers through a process called **deviancy training** (Dishion, McCord, & Poulin, 1999). In deviancy training, peers positively reinforce boys for talking about antisocial activities. In one study, researchers compared the conversations of disruptive and nondisruptive peer groups (Dishion, Spracklen, Andrews, & Patterson, 1996). Nondisruptive boys tended to reinforce each other for telling jokes and interesting stories. In contrast, disruptive boys reinforced each other for discussions about antisocial behavior, such as getting into trouble at school, shoplifting, or bullying.

Over time, boys engage in increasingly more severe antisocial behaviors in order to obtain further reinforcement from the deviant peer group. Deviant conversations among peer group members in late childhood predict delinquency, aggression, and substance use problems by early adolescence (Lacourse et al., 2006; Patterson et al., 2000). Deviant peers, therefore, amplify boys' emerging behavior problems, leading them to engage in more severe and problematic antisocial acts. The process of deviancy training seems to begin early. In fact, deviant discussions with peers predict future behavior in children as young as 6 years old (Snyder et al., 2003).

For girls, the emergence of conduct problems tends to coincide with puberty. Early menarche places girls at risk for later conduct problems (Burt, McGue, DeMarte, Krueger, & Iacono, 2006). Among girls who already show conduct problems before puberty, the stressors of puberty seem to exacerbate disruptive behavior symptoms, leading to a general increase in the severity and frequency of behavior problems (see Figure 9.10). However, even girls without prepubertal behavior problems are at risk for conduct problems, following early menarche. The physical changes of puberty can attract older, deviant boys who introduce early maturing girls to antisocial and sexually precocious behavior.

Neighborhoods

Children's neighborhoods may also affect their likelihood of conduct problems (Boyle & Lipman, 2002; Leventhal & Brooks-Gunn, 2000). Youths from disadvantaged, high-crime neighborhoods are more likely to develop ODD and CD than children from middle-class communities (Brooks-Gunn, Duncan, Klebanov, & Sealand, 1993; Chase-Lansdale & Gordon, 1996; Greenberg, Lengua, Coie, & Pinderhughes, 1999; Ingoldsby & Shaw, 2002).

Neighborhoods can influence child development in several ways (Kroneman, Loeber, & Hipwell, 2004). First, neighborhoods may lack institutional resources to meet the needs of children in the community. For example, poor neighborhoods often have lower quality day care centers and public schools. Children who attend these schools may not receive optimal educational services, especially if they show a developmental or learning disability. As a result, they may experience academic difficulties, come to devalue learning, and begin to show problematic behavior in and out of school.

Second, neighborhoods may provide inadequate supervision and monitoring of children's activities, especially after school. For example, children living in low-income neighborhoods often have limited access to prosocial activities. High-quality recreation centers, after-school programs, and organized athletics tend to be disproportionately available in middle- and upper-class neighborhoods. In the absence of prosocial programming, youths from disadvantaged neighborhoods may engage in unsupervised, antisocial activities (Brody et al., 2001; Kim, Hetherington, & Reiss, 1999; Kupersmidt, Griesler, DeRosier, Patterson, & Davis, 1995).

Third, low-income, high-crime neighborhoods often have weak social control networks; that is, these neighborhoods often lack organizations and community members that encourage prosocial behavior and limit antisocial activity (Kroneman et al., 2004). For example, in upper- and middle-class neighborhoods, children's disruptive behavior is kept in check by police, neighborhood watch groups, and concerned community members. Adolescents who wander the neighborhood at night or vandalize property are quickly brought to the attention of authorities. In contrast, community members living in poorer neighborhoods often tolerate higher levels of antisocial behavior among youths. After all, in high-crime neighborhoods, adolescents wandering the streets at night or engaging in petty acts of vandalism do not merit as much attention as people who engage in other, more serious criminal activities.

Of course, not all children who grow up in disadvantaged neighborhoods develop conduct problems. Certain factors can protect children from environmental risks posed by their surroundings. Chief among these protective factors is family cohesion and parental monitoring. Children whose parents set high expectations for their behavior, support their

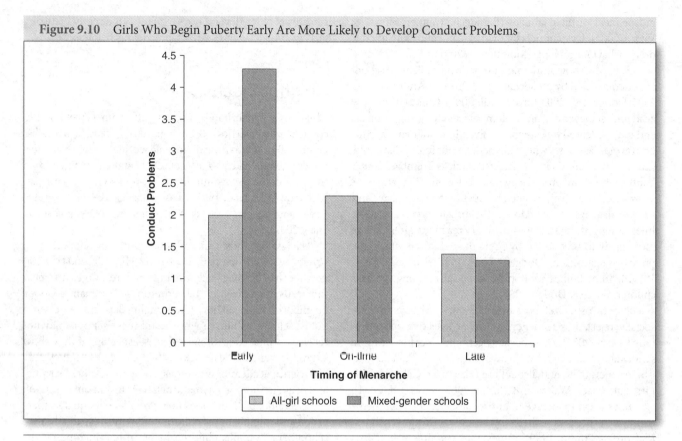

Figure 9.10 Girls Who Begin Puberty Early Are More Likely to Develop Conduct Problems

Source: From Caspi, Lynam, Moffitt, and Silva (1993). Used with permission.

Note: Early-maturing girls may associate with older, deviant boys who introduce them to antisocial behaviors. However, early-maturing girls who attend all-girl schools do *not* show increased risk of conduct problems.

prosocial activities, and monitor their whereabouts are more likely to have positive developmental outcomes, regardless of neighborhood risks (Gorman-Smith, Tolan, & Henry, 2000; Plybon & Kliewer, 2001; Shaw, Ramirez, Trost, Randall, & Stice, 2004).

What About Adolescence-Limited Conduct Problems?

Up until now, we have examined the causes of conduct problems that emerge in early childhood and often persist into adolescence. However, we should remember that many youths display adolescence-limited conduct problems (Moffitt, 2003). These adolescents begin showing symptoms shortly after puberty and then display a pattern of antisocial behavior during early adolescence. Their delinquent acts are almost always rebellious but not aggressive (Piquero & Brezina, 2001). Behaviors include destruction of property (e.g., vandalism, joyriding), deceitfulness (e.g., lying, shoplifting), and other rule violations (e.g., staying out all night, running away from home, truancy). These children typically engage in delinquent behavior only when encouraged by deviant peers (Moffitt & Caspi, 2001). In middle or late adolescence, the frequency and severity of these behaviors begin to decrease.

Youths with adolescence-limited conduct problems usually do not show the same genetic, temperamental, and psychosocial risk factors as individuals with childhood-onset conduct problems. Adolescence-limited conduct problems are often viewed as an extreme, maladaptive form of adolescent rebellion (Frick, 2004). Moffitt (2003) asserts that adolescents often find themselves in a "maturity gap"; that is, they possess many of the cognitive and physical attributes of adults, yet they do not have access to the privileges and responsibilities of adulthood. Encouraged by antisocial peers, these adolescents engage in disruptive acts in order to develop a sense of autonomy and identity independent of parents and family (Moffitt, 1993). As these adolescents gradually assume more positive adult responsibilities, their disruptive behaviors usually decrease.

TREATMENT

Treatment for Younger Children

Parent Management Training

Parent management training (PMT) is the most widely used and best supported treatment for conduct problems in children. PMT is based on the notion that children's disruptive behaviors often develop in the context of hostile-coercive parent-child interactions (Patterson et al., 1992). The clinician assesses the quality of parent-child interactions and notes how parents might inadvertently reinforce or model oppositional, defiant, or aggressive behavior. During the course of therapy, the clinician teaches parents how to interact with their children in more adaptive ways and how to avoid coercive parent-child exchanges (Schultz, 2006; Steiner & Remsing, 2007).

There are a number of different PMT programs designed for children of various ages (Harwood & Eyberg, 2006; Markie-Dadds & Sanders, 2006). In most cases, parents participate in weekly PMT sessions without their children. Parents learn new child management skills each week and practice these skills at home. Barkley's (1997b) Defiant Children parent training program is often used with disruptive preschool- or school-aged children. There are 10 steps in the program; each step consists of a principle or skill that parents learn in the session and apply in their home during the course of the week (see Table 9.4). Some parents can complete one step each week, but most parents require multiple weeks to master some steps. The steps can be loosely categorized into four phases of treatment (Image 9.1).

In the first phase (Step 1), parents learn about the causes of children's disruptive behavior problems. Although parents frequently blame themselves for their children's misbehavior, therapists show how children's misbehavior is influenced by parent, child, and environmental factors.

In phase two (Steps 2–4), parents are taught basic learning principles, with an emphasis on positive reinforcement. Parents who seek treatment for their disruptive children usually attend predominantly to their children's misbehavior. Consequently, therapists teach parents how to attend to and praise appropriate behavior. First, parents learn to attend to children's desirable behavior. Then, parents learn to use positive reinforcement to increase the frequency of children's compliance. Parents are taught that in order for reinforcement to be effective, it must be contingent on appropriate behavior; that is, it must occur *immediately* following the appropriate behavior, and it must be *consistently* provided. Later, parents learn to extinguish many of their children's inappropriate behaviors through selective ignoring. That is, parents systematically ignore unwanted behaviors that are aversive but not dangerous (e.g., tantrums, interruptions while parents are on the phone). Finally, parents learn to establish either a token economy (for younger children) or a point system (for older children) in the home. Children earn tokens or points contingent on specific appropriate behaviors, such as compliance with parental requests or homework completion.

In phase three (Steps 5–7), parents learn how to reduce children's disruptive behavior, using discipline and environmental structuring. First, parents learn how to use time out for serious rule violations. Time out is first practiced at home, with a single behavior problem. Later, time out is used for other behavior problems at home. Finally, parents extend time out to public settings (e.g., restaurants, shopping trips). Parents also learn how to avoid behavior problems by structuring the environment to help their children behave. For example, before going grocery shopping, a parent might decide to bring snacks and a few small toys for the child so that she does not fuss or tantrum during the trip.

Image 9.1 In Parent Management Training (PMT), caregivers learn how to attend to their children's appropriate behaviors, ignore inappropriate behaviors, and discipline in noncoercive ways. Parents often meet together, with a therapist, to develop skills and share strategies for dealing with difficult child behavior.

Table 9.4   Parent Management Training

Step	Topic/Description
1	**Why do children misbehave?** The therapist teaches parents the causes of child misbehavior, how these causes interact, and what parents can do to identify these causes in their own families.
2	**Pay attention!** Many parents of disruptive children focus primarily on their children's misbehavior. In this session, the therapist teaches parents to attend to and appreciate their children's appropriate actions.
3	**Increasing children's compliance** After parents learn to attend to their children's appropriate behavior, the therapist teaches them to contingently reinforce their children's appropriate actions, using praise and attention. The therapist especially encourages parents to attend to and reward their children when they are not interrupting or bothering them, such as when they are playing quietly.
4	**Using token economies** Parents are taught how to implement a token economy in the home to increase child compliance with commands, rules, and chores.
5	**Using time out at home** The therapist teaches parents how to use the token system as a form of punishment using response cost; tokens are withdrawn for inappropriate actions. Parents also learn how to use time out in the home. Initially, time out is used for only one or two problem behaviors.
6	**Practicing time out** Parents gradually expand their use of time out to other behavior problems. During the session, the therapist and parents address problems using the time out procedure.
7	**Managing children in public places** Parents are taught how to use modified versions of time out to discipline children outside the home in stores, restaurants, church. Parents are also taught how to "think ahead" and plan for children's misbehavior in public.
8	**Using the daily school behavior report card** Teachers are asked to complete a daily report card regarding the child's behavior at school. Parents use the home token economy to reinforce appropriate behavior at school, based on teachers' reports on the card.
9	**Handling future behavior problems** The therapist and parents discuss how to deal with future behavior problems and challenging situations. Parents are shown how to use the skills they acquired in the parent training course to address future behavior problems.
10	**Booster session and follow-up meetings** The therapist asks parents to attend a follow-up "booster" session one month after the training ends to check on the family's progress. Parents can use this session to troubleshoot new problems or discuss ways to fade the token system. Follow-up visits may be scheduled every 3 months as needed.

Source: Based on Barkley (1997b).

The fourth phase (Steps 8–10) involves generalizing children's appropriate behavior to the school setting and maintaining behavioral gains in the future. Teachers are asked to complete a daily report card on children's behavior at school. Parents monitor children's school behavior, using the daily report card, and reward children for their compliance when they are at home. Later, parents and therapists work together to plan for other potential behavior problems. Many therapists encourage parents to attend a follow-up or "booster" session sometime after training has ended, in order for therapists to check in on the progress of families.

PMT has received considerable empirical support (Kazdin, 2005b). Children whose parents participate in PMT show decreased oppositional, defiant, and aggressive behavior at home and at school. They show more prosocial behavior at home, get into fewer disciplinary problems at school, and are less likely to show serious disruptive behavior problems in the future. After treatment, their functioning is similar to peers without conduct problems. Most longitudinal studies have shown that the effects of treatment last at least one to 3 years; however, some studies have shown that treatment gains are maintained 10 to 14 years after the end of treatment (Kazdin & Whitley, 2006).

PMT also has some limitations. First, PMT is less effective for parents under high stress. Single parents, low-income parents, parents experiencing marital conflict, and parents who have substance use or mental health problems tend to drop out of PMT or progress slowly (Dadds & McHugh, 1992; Kazdin, 2005b). Psychosocial stressors can interfere with parents' abilities to attend sessions, practice parenting skills, and persevere in the face of environmental challenges. Second, PMT has received less empirical support when used with adolescents (Kazdin, 2005b). Adolescents typically show more severe conduct problems than children, perhaps making them more resistant to treatment. Furthermore, parents tend to have less control over their adolescents' environments and, consequently, have less ability to change environmental contingencies to alter their adolescents' behavior.

Third, most clinicians in the community have not received formal training in PMT (Kazdin, 2005b). Parents who want to participate in PMT may be unable to find skilled therapists in their communities.

Parent-Child Interaction Therapy

Parent-child interaction therapy (PCIT) is a variant of PMT designed for families with disruptive preschoolers and young school-age children (Nixon, 2002; Querido & Eyberg, 2005). As with PMT, the focus of PCIT is on the way parents interact with their children and address child misbehavior. Unlike PMT, parents and children attend therapy sessions together. Clinicians observe parent-child interactions and teach parents techniques for managing their children's behavior, during the sessions.

PCIT is divided into two phases. In the first phase, **child-directed interaction**, the goal of treatment is to increase parents' sensitivity and responsiveness toward their children and to improve the quality of the parent-child relationship (Image 9.2). These sessions resemble play; children select a play activity and parents follow their lead. One component of this phase of treatment is to help parents develop a set of skills—praising, reflecting, imitating, describing, and enthusiasm—that spell the acronym PRIDE. While playing with their children, parents practice praising, reflecting, imitating, and describing their children's appropriate behavior in an enthusiastic way (see Table 9.5). Furthermore, parents are discouraged from assuming too

Image 9.2   In Parent-Child Interaction Therapy (PCIT), caregivers are initially taught to pay attention to their child's appropriate behavior and follow their child's lead in activities. Therapists coach parents as they practice these skills.

Source: Image courtesy of Kaitlyn M. Scarboro-Vinklarek.

Table 9.5 Parent-Child Interaction Therapy: PRIDE Skills

Skill	Reason	Examples
PRAISE appropriate behavior	Causes your child's good behavior to increase	Parent: Good job putting the toys away!
REFLECT appropriate talk	Shows your child that you are listening	Child: I drew a tree.
IMITATE appropriate play	Lets your child lead; shows your child that you approve of his or her game	Child: I put a nose on the potato head.
DESCRIBE appropriate behavior	Shows your child that you are interested in what he or she does	Parent: You're making a tower with Legos.
ENTHUSIASM show it	Lets your child know that you are enjoying the time you are spending together	Parent: You are a REALLY hard worker!

Source: Based on T. Patterson and Kaslow (2002).

much control over the play situation, from asking questions or making demands to being critical of their child's behavior. In this way, parents strengthen children's appropriate actions and convey acceptance and warmth (Eyberg, 2006).

In the second phase of PCIT, **parent-directed interaction**, the goal of treatment is to help parents create more realistic expectations for their children's behavior, to reduce hostile and coercive parent-child exchanges, and to promote fair and consistent use of discipline. An important component of this phase of therapy is learning how to give effective commands to children. Commands must be given when children are paying attention; these must be stated clearly and concretely, and, must be followed up immediately by consequences, either praise (for compliance) or discipline (for noncompliance). Another component of this phase is teaching parents how to use time out effectively (Eyberg, 2006).

In PCIT, the therapist meets with the parent and child together. The therapist acts as the parent's teacher and coach. The therapist demonstrates all of the skills to the parent in the therapy session. Then, the therapist coaches the parent, during the session, until the parent has performed the skill adequately with her child. The therapist also troubleshoots specific behavior problems as they arise in the session and helps the parent tailor treatment to meet her child's specific needs. In general, PCIT is a hands-on approach to PMT.

Several studies have shown PCIT to be effective at reducing disruptive behavior in very young children, both at home and in the classroom (Herschell & McNeil, 2005; Nixon, Sweeney, Erickson, & Touyz, 2003; Schuhmann, Foote, Eyberg, Boggs, & Algina, 1998). Furthermore, PCIT seems to improve the sensitivity and care parents show to their children, decrease parental hostility and criticism toward their children, and reduce parenting stress (Eisenstadt, Eyberg, McNeil, Newcomb, & Funderburk, 1993; Werba,

Eyberg, Boggs, & Algina, 2006). Improvements in children's behavior are maintained for at least one to 2 years after treatment (Boggs et al., 2004; Eisenstadt et al., 1993; Eyberg, Funderburk, Hembree-Kigin, McNeil, Querido, & Hood, 2001; Funderburk, Eyberg, Newcomb, McNeil, Hembree-Kigin, & Capage, 1998; Nixon, Sweeney, Erickson, & Touyz, 2004) and possibly up to 6 years after treatment (Hood & Eyberg, 2003). An abbreviated version of the PCIT has also been developed that seems to be equally efficacious (Nixon et al., 2003, 2004).

Videotaped Modeling and the Incredible Years Program

Carolyn Webster-Stratton (2005) has developed a comprehensive program for young children with emerging conduct problems. The Incredible Years program consists of separate modules for parents, teachers, and children. The program was designed especially for low-income, high-stress families—families most likely to drop out of traditional PMT (Webster-Stratton & Reid, 2007).

The **Incredible Years BASIC** parent training program resembles Barkley's Defiant Children program, with certain modifications made for children aged 2 to 10 years. The program consists of 14 parent training sessions, each approximately two hours long. Parents learn to attend to children's behavior, to reinforce appropriate actions, and to punish inappropriate actions using noncoercive methods. In the program, parents watch videotaped vignettes of parent-child interactions. These vignettes are designed to illustrate the problematic parent-child interactions that underlie children's conduct problems and to teach alternative, effective parenting behaviors. Parents watch the vignettes with other parents and then discuss the child management principles and parenting skills with each other and the therapist. The therapist acts as a collaborator and supporter rather than as a teacher.

The therapist encourages parents to decide for themselves how to implement the parenting principles introduced by the program into their daily lives and to tailor the program to meet their individual needs.

The **Incredible Years ADVANCE** parent training program is offered to parents as a supplement to the BASIC program. Webster-Stratton (1990) realized that parents with high levels of stress and conflict in the home have difficulty implementing the BASIC program and avoiding hostile-coercive exchanges with their children (Webster-Stratton & Hammond, 1999). The ADVANCE program consists of 14 additional sessions that teach parents self-control and anger management strategies, communication skills, interpersonal problem-solving skills, and techniques to strengthen their social support network. These skills are designed to improve parents' mood states, to decrease family discord and tension, and to provide parents with the support they need to effectively implement the BASIC program.

The **Incredible Years Academic Skills Training (SCHOOL)** and **Teacher Training (TEACHER)** programs were developed as adjuncts to the BASIC and ADVANCE parent training programs. These programs were designed to improve the academic, behavioral, and social competence of children at school. The SCHOOL program consists of four to six sessions attended by groups of parents. It focuses on improving parents' involvement in their children's education, fostering parental collaboration with teachers, and increasing parents' monitoring of children's activities with peers. The TEACHER program is a workshop for teachers. Topics in this program include classroom management strategies, strengthening children's social skills and avoiding peer rejection, improving communication with parents, monitoring children's activities, and reducing physical aggression and bullying.

The **Incredible Years Child Training Program** was developed for 4- to 8-year-old children with emerging conduct problems. This 22-week program is administered to small groups of children and uses a series of videotaped vignettes, puppets, and role play activities to improve children's social functioning, especially at school. The program consists of empathy training, problem-solving skills training, anger control, friendship skills, and communication skills training. The overall goal is to teach children how to behave in class, how to make and keep friends, and how to play appropriately with peers (Webster-Stratton, 2005).

The efficacy of the Incredible Years BASIC and ADVANCE parent training programs have been investigated in a series of randomized, controlled studies (Webster-Stratton, 2005). Results show that the BASIC program is efficacious in improving parents' attitudes toward childrearing, their quality of parent-child interactions, and their children's behavior. Parents who participate in the program display fewer hostile-coercive behaviors toward their children; their children display fewer conduct problems over time. Parents who also participate in the ADVANCE program report improved interactions with their spouses, better communication and problem-solving skills, and greater satisfaction with

treatment than do parents who participate only in the BASIC program. These improvements in marital quality, communication, and problem solving are associated with improved parent-child interactions, especially for fathers.

The efficacy of the entire program has been evaluated on children with emerging conduct problems and low-income children at risk for developing conduct problems (Beauchaine, Webster-Stratton, & Reid, 2005; Webster-Stratton, Reid, & Hammond, 2001, 2004). Overall, children whose families participate in either parent-based, school-based, or child-based interventions show greater improvement in behavior than children whose families do not participate in treatment. Furthermore, children whose families participate in more of the treatment components (e.g., parent, teacher, *and* child training) fare better than families that participate in only one component. Across studies, the BASIC program tends to be the most effective component of the Incredible Years program. However, the ADVANCE program is especially efficacious for mothers with depression, fathers with histories of substance abuse, and families experiencing psychosocial stress (e.g., single-parent or low-income families).

Despite the success of the Incredible Years program, 25% to 46% of parents report significant child behavior problems 3 years after completing treatment (Webster-Stratton, 1990; Webster-Stratton & Hammond, 1990). The best predictors of continued child behavior problems are high marital distress or spousal abuse, single-parent status, maternal depression, low socioeconomic status, high life stress, and a family history of substance abuse. These findings speak to the importance of programs like ADVANCE, which are designed to improve the social-emotional functioning of parents. Improvements in parents' mood and social functioning might help them respond to their children's needs and discipline in a consistent and noncoercive fashion.

Treatment for Older Children and Adolescents

Problem-Solving Skills Training

Problem-Solving Skills Training (PSST) is based on the notion that youths with disruptive behavior problems show characteristic biases in the way they perceive, interpret, and respond to interpersonal problems. These social information-processing biases interfere with their ability to respond to social dilemmas in prosocial ways and increase the likelihood that they will show hostile and aggressive behaviors (Reinecke, 2006).

Recall that social information processing consists of five steps: (a) encoding cues about the social situation, (b) interpreting these cues, (c) clarifying goals, (d) developing possible plans for action, and (e) evaluating and implementing the best plan to solve the problem. Children who show high levels of aggression often display biases in the ways they solve social problems. PSST attempts to correct the biased information-processing styles of aggressive children by teaching them how to systematically progress through these social problem-solving steps. In PSST, the child and therapist meet together for 12 to 20 sessions, each approximately 30 to 50 minutes in length.

The therapist initially teaches the child a simplified social problem-solving strategy (see Table 9.6). Each step prompts the child to attend to certain aspects of the interpersonal problem and helps the child solve the problem in prosocial ways. First, the child asks himself, "What am I supposed to do?" This requires the child to identify the problem and determine how he should act in the situation. Second, the child asks, "What are all my possibilities?" This step reminds the child to generate as many courses of action as possible. Third, the child says, "I'd better concentrate and focus in." This step encourages the child to evaluate the possible courses of action. Fourth, the child says, "I need to make a choice." This step requires the child to select the best response. Fifth, the child evaluates his actions and concludes either "I did a good job" or "I made a mistake." The steps slow the problem-solving process and help the child consider more information before acting.

In each session, the therapist usually begins by describing an interpersonal problem that the child might encounter in everyday life, for example, arguments during recess, on the bus, or in the hallways at school. The therapist then shows the child how to use the steps to solve the problem. Next, the therapist and child might role-play the situation. In the first few sessions, the child says each step aloud as he works through the problem. After the child becomes more familiar with the steps, he can solve the problem silently. Throughout each session, the therapist coaches the child in the use of the steps and provides praise and encouragement. Some

therapists will also use a token economy during sessions. They reinforce the child's attention and participation in the session and withdraw tokens for inattentive, disruptive, or inappropriate behavior. If possible, parents are also taught the problem-solving steps. Parents are encouraged to prompt and reward the child for using the steps at home.

PSST has been shown to be effective in reducing aggressive and disruptive behavior in school-aged children (Kazdin, 2005a). In several studies, children who participated in PSST showed greater symptom reduction than children who participated in an attention control group. Both inpatient and outpatient children showed improved functioning, relative to controls, and treatment gains were maintained one year later. Furthermore, children who participated in both PSST and PMT showed better outcomes than children who received either treatment alone (Kazdin, 2005a).

Multisystemic Therapy

Multisystemic therapy (MST) is an intensive form of family- and community-based treatment that has been shown to be effective in treating serious conduct problems in adolescents (Henggeler & Lee, 2003). Whereas PMT is frequently used for children and adolescents who show oppositional and defiant behaviors, MST is used most often used with adolescents who show more serious antisocial and violent behavior. In fact, MST has been used successfully with adolescents exhibiting chronic juvenile delinquency, violent crime, substance abuse, psychiatric crisis, and sexual offenses (Henggeler & Lee, 2003). In short, MST is one of the most successful interventions for adolescents with long-standing and serious behavior problems.

MST therapists target three systems essential to the adolescents' welfare: (a) family, (b) school, and (c) peers

Table 9.6 Problem-Solving Steps and Self-Statements

Step	Self-Statement	Purpose
1.	What am I supposed to do?	This step requires the child to identify and define the problem.
2.	I have to look at all my possibilities.	This step asks the child to generate alternative solutions to the problem.
3.	I'd better concentrate and focus in.	This step instructs the child to concentrate and evaluate the solutions he has generated.
4.	I need to make a choice.	In this step, the child chooses the best action.
5.	I did a good job. [or] I made a mistake.	In the final step, the child verifies whether the solution was the best among those available, whether the problem-solving process was correctly followed, or whether a less-than-desirable solution was selected.

Source: Based on Kazdin and Weisz (2003).

Note: Problem-solving steps are taught and practiced during role play. The child and therapist alternate turns practicing the steps. The therapist prompts and shapes the child's use of the steps using reinforcement. As the child learns the steps, prompts are gradually faded. The child also progresses from saying the steps aloud (overt), to saying them silently (covert).

(Saldana & Henggeler, 2006). In the family, therapists might help parents develop more effective skills for interacting with their adolescents. For example, MST therapists might administer a parent training program, teach parents how to monitor their adolescents' whereabouts after school, or help parents learn to avoid conflict situations with their adolescents. MST therapists also try to remove obstacles that interfere with parents' abilities to provide supportive and consistent care. For example, therapists might address parents' marital discord, assist a parent in overcoming alcohol dependence, or increase the social support network of a single parent. In any case, MST therapists see themselves as resources and allies for parents. Therapists hope that by improving the skills and well-being of parents, these parents will more effectively manage their adolescents' behavior.

A second realm of intervention is the adolescent's school. Most MST therapists seek to increase parental involvement in their adolescents' education. Therapists might serve as liaisons between parents and teachers or help parents advocate for their children's educational needs. Therapists might teach parents to monitor their adolescents' attendance at school and behavior in the classroom. Again, therapists try to remove obstacles to the adolescents' academic achievement. For example, MST therapists might help to resolve any conflicts between parents and teachers or deal with practical problems, like helping parents find time to attend parent-teacher conferences.

A third avenue of intervention involves the adolescents' peers. Association with deviant peers is one of the best predictors of adolescent behavior problems. Consequently, MST therapists attempt to limit adolescents' opportunities for interactions with deviant peers and increase opportunities for interactions with prosocial youths. At the very least, MST therapists encourage parents and other people involved in the adolescent's life (e.g., family members, teachers, police) to closely monitor his whereabouts, especially after school. At the same time, therapists might help the adolescent develop new peer networks. For example, a MST therapist might encourage an adolescent to try out for a sports team, join a club at school, or volunteer in the community. The therapist might also help the adolescent improve his social skills, in order to increase the likelihood that he will be accepted by prosocial peers (Saldana & Henggeler, 2006).

MST is an intense, flexible, and family friendly intervention. MST therapists usually work in teams of three to five, and they are available 24 hours a day, 7 days a week. Therapists usually meet with family members in their home or in the community, rather than in an office, in order to increase the family's attendance and involvement. MST usually lasts three to five months.

There is considerable evidence supporting the efficacy of MST for adolescents with conduct problems (Hart, Nelson, & Finch, 2006; Saldana & Henggeler, 2006). Across a number of randomized controlled trials, adolescents whose families participate in MST are 25% to 70% less likely to be rearrested and 47% to 64% less likely to be removed from their homes 1 to 4 years after treatment than are adolescents of families who do not participate in MST. Treatment appears to improve family functioning and parenting skills, which, in turn, decrease adolescents' association with deviant peers and their disruptive behavior (Huey, Henggeler, Brondino, & Pickrel, 2000; Saldana & Henggeler, 2006).

Recently, researchers examined the long-term outcomes of adolescents who participated in MST. In this study, 176 adolescents previously arrested for serious crimes were randomly assigned to receive either MST or traditional individual psychotherapy (Schaeffer & Borduin, 2005). The adolescents in the study averaged 3.9 arrests for felonies and 47.8% had at least one arrest for violent crime (e.g., sexual assault, assault and battery with intent to kill). Researchers examined arrest records approximately 13 years after treatment. Results showed that adolescents who participated in MST were less likely than adolescents who participated in individual therapy to be arrested for a future serious offense (see Figure 9.11). Furthermore, adolescents who participated in MST committed half as many offenses overall as adolescents who participated in individual therapy. These results suggest that MST is not only effective in reducing adolescent antisocial behavior, but also it may have long-term effects on adolescents' developmental outcomes.

Unfortunately, MST programs are available to only about 1% of adolescents with serious conduct problems. Most therapists do not have formal training in MST. Although MST is intensive, it is less costly than out-of-home placement or incarceration. One study concluded a cost savings of approximately $60,000 per adolescent who participated in MST compared to adolescents who did not. Hopefully, continued research supporting MST will prompt individuals and agencies to develop programs in their communities (Henggeler & Lee, 2003).

Aggression Replacement Training

Aggression Replacement Training (ART) is a multimodal treatment designed for adolescents with histories of disruptive, aggressive, and antisocial behavior (Glick & Gibbs, 2011; Reddy & Goldstein, 2001). ART is founded on the premise that adolescents who engage in antisocial acts lack the behavioral, affective, and cognitive skills that underlie prosocial actions. Instead, these adolescents show delays in social skills, social problem-solving, emotion regulation, and moral reasoning that interfere with their ability to engage in compliant, constructive behaviors. Furthermore, disruptive and aggressive behavior is sometimes modeled and reinforced by other people in these adolescents' lives, especially family members and peers (Goldstein, 2002).

In ART, adolescents engage in structured group activities designed to teach behavioral, emotional, and cognitive skills (Glick, 2006; Goldstein & Martens, 2000; Hollin, 2004). These skills are systematically taught using a system of modeling, behavioral rehearsal, and social reinforcement. Specifically,

Figure 9.11   The Efficacy of Multisystemic Therapy (MST)

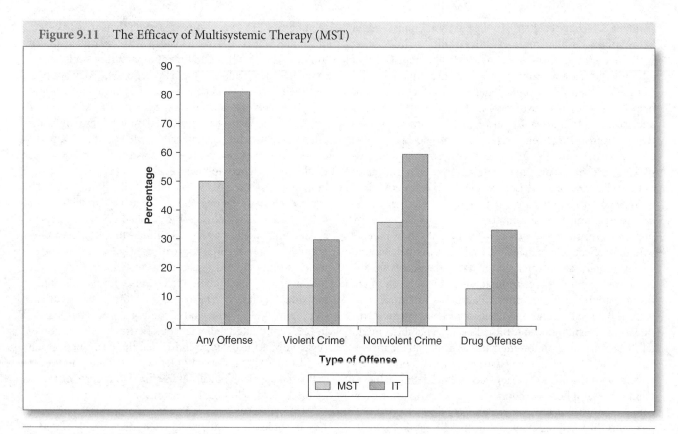

Source: Based on Schaeffer and Borduin (2005).

Note: Researchers compared the behavioral outcomes of adolescents with conduct problems who participated in MST versus interpersonal therapy (IT), a nonbehavioral form of treatment. Adolescents who participated in MST were less likely to show future antisocial behavior.

ART consists of three components: (a) skillstreaming, (b) anger control training, and (c) moral reasoning training.

The goal of skillstreaming, the behavioral component of ART, is to enhance prosocial skills that help adolescents avoid arguments and aggressive displays and promote social competence (Goldstein, 1997). These skills are taught in small groups through a combination of modeling, role play, reinforcement and feedback, and they transfer to other settings. Skills fall into six categories: beginning social skills (e.g., listening), advanced social skills (e.g., apologizing), skills for dealing with feelings (e.g., understanding the feelings of others), skill alternatives to aggression (e.g., keeping out of fights), skills for dealing with stress (e.g., dealing with group pressure), and skills related to planning (e.g., setting a goal).

Skillstreaming is a structured, psychoeducational activity. First, a skill is introduced by the facilitator and defined by the group. It is important for the group members to collectively synthesize a definition of the skill and outline the behavioral steps needed to practice it. Second, the skill is modeled by the facilitator in a fashion that clearly follows each step. The facilitator then prompts each group member to identify how they might utilize the skill in their everyday life.

Next, a volunteer is selected from the group to role-play the skill. The volunteer describes a real-life situation in which he or she might practice the skill and gives details about the setting, preceding events, and feelings of everyone involved. The volunteer assumes the role of the main actor and chooses another group member to play the part of the individual with whom he or she might use the skill. The pair rehearses their role play outside the group setting, reviewing each step of the skill with the facilitator. While the pair rehearses, a second facilitator asks other members to carefully observe the role play and evaluate each step of the skill, so that they might later provide feedback to the actors. When ready, the actors return to the group and role-play. The observers, the actors, and the facilitator, in turn, provide feedback on the main actor's ability to use the skill. The role play and feedback process is repeated until all group members have the opportunity to practice the skill. Then, the facilitator asks each group member to practice the skill outside the group and reflect on the outcome of this practice.

Anger control training comprises the emotion regulation component of ART (Feindler & Engel, 2011; Hollin & Bloxsom, 2007; Novaco, 1975). A primary goal of anger control training is to help adolescents understand the angry behavior cycle—a model for the external triggers and internal cues that prompt adolescents' anger. The group first discusses and role-plays situations that trigger anger. Once group members have identified their triggers, the facilitator encourages them to recognize what physiological markers serve as cues that they are angry. Next, anger-reducing techniques, such as deep breathing, are presented and practiced. Members are also taught to use "reminders"—self-statements designed to decrease arousal, such as "Take it easy, he didn't mean to bump into me on purpose." Group members are also encouraged to identify and use skillstreaming techniques to solve social problems and avoid angry or aggressive displays. In later sessions, facilitators teach "self-evaluation," in which adolescents review their handling of a conflict, reward themselves for successfully avoiding anger, or find ways to deal with social problems more effectively in the future. Throughout anger control training, skills are practiced step-by-step via role play and feedback.

The final element of ART is moral reasoning training (Arbuthnot & Gordon, 1986; Gibbs, 2010; Palmer, 2007). The goal of moral reasoning training is to move group members from immature moral reasoning to more advanced stages of moral development. Facilitators provide the group with a relatable story in which an adolescent encounters a moral dilemma (e.g., cheating, stealing, fighting).

Group members discuss questions posed by facilitators, which highlight cognitive distortions, moral values, and the rights and feelings of others. During the course of discussion, facilitators challenge group members to adopt more mature, less egocentric moral decision making.

The first evaluations of ART, conducted by its developers, were encouraging (Weis & Pucke, 2013). Overall, youths who participated in ART showed moderate acquisition and application of social skills compared to comparison youths who did not receive ART. Furthermore, in half of the studies, youths also showed increased anger control, improved moral reasoning, and decreased recidivism. The results of independent, peer-reviewed evaluations were more mixed. On one hand, these studies also showed increased social skill acquisition associated with ART. On the other hand, the effects of ART on observed behavior were inconsistent. Furthermore, none of the studies showed increased moral reasoning associated with ART. Currently, ART is classified as a *Model Program* by the United States Office of Juvenile Justice and Delinquency Prevention and is classified as a *Promising Program* by the United States Department of Education (Glick & Gibbs, 2011).

CHAPTER SUMMARY

Definitions

- Oppositional Defiant Disorder (ODD) is characterized by a persistent pattern of angry and irritable mood and defiant or vindictive behavior. Symptoms can be shown toward parent, teachers, and/or peers.

  - Most symptoms must be shown for at least 6 months, indicating long-standing oppositional behavior.
  - Symptoms must be developmentally unexpected and interfere with children's social or academic functioning.

- Conduct Disorder (CD) is a more serious condition characterized by repetitive behaviors in which the basic rights of others and age-appropriate social norms are violated. Symptoms fall into four groups:

  - Aggression to people and animals
  - Destruction of property
  - Deceitfulness or theft
  - Age-inappropriate rule violations (e.g., truancy, staying out all night)

- Children can be diagnosed with both ODD and CD if they meet diagnostic criteria for each disorder.
- Behavior problems can be categorized based on several dimensions:

  - Overt conduct problems are observable and confrontational (e.g., assault), whereas covert conduct problems are secretive (e.g., burglary).
  - Reactive aggression is shown in response to a frustrating event or provocation, whereas proactive aggression is a deliberate act to achieve a desired goal.
  - Life-course persistent conduct problems emerge before puberty and typically last into late adolescence or adulthood, whereas adolescence-limited conduct problems emerge in adolescence and typically do not persist more than a few years.

- Some children with CD show limited prosocial emotions. These youths show increased likelihood of violent criminal behavior and resistance to treatment. Characteristics include the following:

  - Lack of remorse or guilt
  - Callousness, lack of empathy
  - Little concern about performance
  - Shallow or deficient affect

Associated Features and Epidemiology

- ADHD is highly comorbid with both ODD and CD. ADHD may be viewed as the "motor" which drives some children's oppositional and disruptive behavior.
- Children with ODD and CD can develop anxiety and depression. According to the dual failure model, internalizing symptoms occur in youths with conduct problems due to failure in (a) relationships and (b) academics.
- Youths with CD are at increased risk for substance use problems. A common set of genes may underlie problems with both behavior and substance use. Furthermore, deviant peers often model and reinforce substance use to youths with CD.
- Between 3% and 5% of youths have ODD, whereas 2% to 4% of youths have CD.
- The prevalence of ODD and CD is higher for boys than girls. Girls often show relational aggression, rather than physical aggression. Consequently, they may be less likely to meet diagnostic criteria for CD which include few symptoms of relational aggression.
- Nearly 80% of clinic-referred children with ODD will develop CD in adolescence; however, conversion to CD is much lower among children with ODD in the community.
- Between 40% and 70% of boys with CD in adolescents will develop Antisocial Personality Disorder in adulthood. As many as 75% of girls with CD in adolescence develop mood and anxiety disorders in adulthood.
- Youths with adolescent-limited CD usually do not meet criteria in adulthood; however, they often experience problems with relationships, academics, and employment.

Causes

- Heritability estimates for ODD and CD tend to be modest, typically below 50%. It is likely that some children inherit a genetic risk for difficult temperaments and hyperactivity/impulsivity that predisposes them toward conduct problems.
- Some children with conduct problems show excessive emotional reactivity; they are easily upset by novel stimuli and have difficulty regulating their emotions.
- Other children with conduct problems show low emotional arousal.

  o These children do not become aroused and excited by typical sensory stimuli and are slow to respond to punishment.
  o Underactivity of the HPA axis and amygdala may underlie these symptoms.

- Many children with limited prosocial emotions display underarousal.
- Many children with conduct problems engage in coercive parent-child interactions with their caregivers. Their parents unknowingly reinforce their defiant behavior while they reinforce their parents' tendency to back down from requests.
- The parents of children with conduct problems often attribute their children's misbehavior to internal, stable causes. These attributions (a) can lead them to react in hostile ways and (b) make them feel helpless and powerless.
- The caregivers of youths with CD often show low parental monitoring. Their children are often allowed to engage in activities without their parents' knowledge and approval.
- Crick and Dodge's social information processing theory posits that youths with conduct problems show biases in the ways they solve interpersonal problems. These biases lead them to react to problems impulsively and aggressively.
- Youths with conduct problems are often rejected by prosocial peers. They may associate with deviant peer groups who model and reinforce disruptive behavior, antisocial acts, and substance abuse.
- Neighborhoods characterized by (1) socioeconomic disadvantage, (2) low child monitoring, and (3) high crime may contribute to CD among adolescents.

Treatment

- Parent management training (PMT) is the most widely used treatment for childhood conduct problems. PMT is based on learning theory. Parents learn principles of operant conditioning to reinforce appropriate behavior and extinguish or punish negative behavior in a noncoercive manner.
- Parent-Child Interaction Therapy (PCIT) is a variation of parent management training designed for caregivers and their preschool-age children. Therapists coach parents as they practice principles with their children.
- The Incredible Years program is another parent management training program for groups of parents and/or teachers. Adults learn principles of behavior management by watching videotapes of parent-child interactions and discussing effective practices. A separate module is available for children.
- Problem-Solving Skills Training (PSST) is designed for older children with conduct problems. Youths overcome biases in social information processing by learning steps to effective social problem solving. Therapy is usually administered to groups of children.
- Multisystemic Therapy is an intensive form of family- and community-based treatment designed for adolescents with serious conduct problems. Therapists coordinate services provided to parents, adolescents, and teachers to provide comprehensive treatment.
- Aggression Replacement Training (ART) is also designed for adolescents with serious conduct problems and aggression. Treatment consists of training in (a) social skills, (b) anger control, and (c) moral reasoning.

KEY TERMS

CRITICAL THINKING EXERCISES

1. Although ODD and CD often co-occur, they are separate disorders. What is the evidence for and against viewing ODD as a developmental precursor for CD?

2. Why is CD much more commonly diagnosed among adolescent boys than adolescent girls? Are the diagnostic criteria for CD gender biased? Should they be changed?

3. Why might a clinician ask a parent *at what age* his child's conduct problems emerged? Will a young child with conduct problems "grow out of it"?

4. How might a child's temperament and early neurological development influence his likelihood of developing conduct problems later in life? Why don't all children with difficult temperaments develop CD?

5. David is a 10-year-old boy. During recess, David is hit in the head by a kickball, leaving mud and grass stains on his face and shirt. He notices that the ball was kicked by Goliath, an older and larger boy who was playing kickball with his friends nearby. According to Crick and Dodge's (1994) social information-processing theory, what steps will David go through to solve this social problem? If David showed a hostile attributional bias in his problem solving, how might he interpret and respond to the situation?

6. Monica participated in 20 sessions of parent-child interaction therapy with her 5-year-old son, Augustine. After treatment, Augustine showed a marked decrease in behavior problems at home but not at school. Why?

EXTEND YOUR LEARNING

Videos, practice tests, flash cards, study guides, and links to online resources for this chapter are available to students online. Teachers also have access to lecture notes, PowerPoint presentations, suggestions for classroom activities, and possible exam questions. Visit: www.sagepub.com/weis2e.

CHAPTER **10**

Substance Use Disorders in Adolescents

LEARNING OBJECTIVES

After reading this chapter, you should be able to answer these questions:

- What are Substance Use Disorders? How do clinicians differentiate substance *use* from Substance Use Disorders?

- How do older children and adolescents show Substance Use Disorders differently than adults?

- How common is alcohol and other drug use among older children and adolescents? How does prevalence differ as a function of age, gender, and ethnicity?

- What causes Substance Use Disorders? How do the causes differ in adolescents compared to adults?

- What programs (if any) are effective for preventing alcohol and other drug use in children and adolescents?

- What evidence-based treatments are available for older children and adolescents with Substance Use Disorders? How is treatment for adolescents different than treatment for adults?

Adolescents' involvement with alcohol and other drugs falls on a continuum which ranges from complete abstinence to chronic use and dependence. Of course, the vast majority of adolescents fall between these extremes. Most youths experiment with cigarettes, alcohol, and (perhaps) marijuana; relatively few develop problematic patterns of use that lead to distress or impairment (Johnston, O'Malley, Bachman, & Schulenberg, 2006).

When they do occur, substance use problems carry immediate and delayed risks to adolescents' health and well-being. In the short-term, problematic use of alcohol and other drugs can lead to motor vehicle accidents, sexual risk taking, sexual victimization, and unintentional injuries. More prolonged use can contribute to relationship problems with parents and peers; withdrawal from sports, clubs, and other extracurricular activities; and poor school performance. Long-term risks include chronic health problems, low educational attainment and employment, and anxiety and mood disorders (Heath, Lynskey, & Waldron, 2010).

Adolescence is an important developmental period for the emergence of Substance Use Disorders. Youths who develop moderate to severe Substance Use Disorders by age 18 show higher lifetime consumption of alcohol and other drugs, more risky patterns of substance use, and poor social-emotional and occupational outcomes (Bukstein & Deas, 2010). In contrast, some studies suggest, if a person does not develop a Substance Use Disorder by early adulthood, it is unlikely they ever will (Chen & Kandel, 1995).

In this chapter, we will focus on the *DSM-5* conceptualization of Substance Use Disorders and how the research literature on addictions has changed over the past three decades. We will then focus on two substances in particular, alcohol and marijuana, and use them as a model for the other Substance Use Disorders. We will examine the effects of these substances on adolescents' development and learn about ways to prevent and treat Alcohol and Cannabis Use Disorders in youths.

WHAT ARE SUBSTANCE USE DISORDERS?

Overview

People are diagnosed with Substance Use Disorders when they show a problematic pattern of alcohol or other drug use that interferes with their daily functioning or causes significant psychological distress. Each substance is associated with a particular cluster of behavioral, cognitive, and physiological symptoms. People with Substance Use Disorders show these symptoms yet persist in using the substance(s) that cause them (American Psychiatric Association, 2013). *DSM-5* uses the term *substance* to refer to alcohol, drugs, and medications that can be abused. People can develop a Substance Use Disorder for eight different classes of substances:

- *Alcohol*: Alcohol is a depressant that enhances GABA, the brain's primary inhibitory neurotransmitter. Alcohol also blocks glutamate, a major excitatory neurotransmitter. It produces a biphasic effect on the nervous system, resulting in euphoria and sociability in low doses and slurred speech, coordination problems, and cognitive impairment in higher doses.
- *Cannabis*: Cannabis is a naturally occurring drug that contains delta-9-tetrahydrocannabinol (THC). When ingested, it affects a wide range of neurotransmitters and brain areas. Its effects including euphoria, anxiety reduction, unusual perceptions and thoughts, slowed reaction time, increased appetite, and low motivation for goal-directed activity.
- *Hallucinogens*: Hallucinogens include substances, such as lysergic acid diethylamide (LSD), psilocybin ("mushrooms"), and 3, 4-methylenedioxymethamphetamine (MDMA, "ecstasy"). These medications typically bind to serotonin receptors and stimulate the locus coeruleus, an area of the brain that regulates many other brain regions. These substances typically cause unusual perceptions and thoughts, distortions in sense of time, disorientation, and anxiety reduction. They can also elicit anxiety, depression, paranoia, and impaired judgment and decision making.
- *Inhalants*: Inhalants include substances, such as gasoline, glue, paint thinners, spray paints, and household cleansers. When ingested, ingredients in these substances produce a wide range of effects on the brain and central nervous system. Effects include euphoria, anxiety reduction, and passivity. However, they can also produce disorientation, slurred speech, slow reaction time, poor judgment, and death.
- *Opioids*: Opioids include natural opioids (e.g., morphine), semisynthetics (e.g., heroin), and synthetic drugs that act like these substances (e.g., codeine, oxycodone, fentanyl). Synthetic opioids are often prescribed for pain reduction. Besides alleviating pain, they may produce euphoria, anxiety reduction, and disorientation. Tolerance can develop quickly. Withdrawal symptoms can be severe and include dysphoria, nausea and vomiting, insomnia, muscle aches, and fever.

- *Sedatives, Hypnotics, and Anxiolytics*: Substances in this class include nearly all medications used to treat anxiety and insomnia (e.g., benzodiazepines, barbiturates). They tend to augment GABA, the brain's primary inhibitory neurotransmitter. Their immediate effect is drowsiness and anxiety reduction. Tolerance can develop quickly. Withdrawal symptoms include autonomic hyperactivity (e.g., sweating, rapid pulse), hand tremor, insomnia, agitation, and anxiety.
- *Stimulants*: Stimulants include medications and drugs that typically enhance dopaminergic activity in the central nervous system. They include medications used to treat ADHD, such as amphetamine and methylphenidate, as well as illegal drugs, such as cocaine. Stimulants have immediate effects on the central nervous system, producing extreme euphoria, energy, and sociability. However, they can also produce anxiety, agitation, and anger; racing heart; shallow breathing; and cognitive problems.
- *Tobacco*: The chemical nicotine, found in tobacco, has both stimulating and anxiety-reducing effects. Short-term use can result in pleasure, enhanced concentration, reduced tension and anxiety, and decreased restlessness and agitation. Prolonged use is associated with health problems and dependence.

Although each class of substances is unique, all classes have abuse potential. People can develop a Substance Use Disorder for any of these substances because they all affect the brain's reward pathway. Their physiological affects are different, but they all typically alter the individual's mood state, resulting in increased pleasure and/or decreased negative affect. The physiological effects of these substances can be so marked that individuals neglect normal activities and adopt behaviors that interfere with their academic, emotional, social, and/or occupational functioning (American Psychiatric Association, 2013).

People are diagnosed with a Substance Use Disorder for each drug that they abuse (Heath et al., 2010). For example, an adolescent who abuses alcohol might be diagnosed with Alcohol Use Disorder whereas another adolescent who abuses marijuana might be diagnosed with Cannabis Use Disorder. Individuals can be diagnosed with multiple Substance Use Disorders. The diagnostic criteria for Substance Use Disorders are the same for alcohol, cannabis, and other substances (Table 10.1. Diagnostic Criteria for Substance Use Disorder). Consequently, in this chapter, we will focus our attention on alcohol and marijuana use in adolescents as a model for understanding and treating Substance Use Disorders more generally.

DSM-5 Conceptualization

According to *DSM-5*, a **Substance Use Disorder** is a maladaptive pattern of substance use leading to clinically significant impairment or distress. Individuals with Substance Use Disorders, including children and adolescents, show at least two of 11 possible symptoms within a 12-month period. The symptoms can be organized into four clusters: (a) impaired

Table 10.1   Diagnostic Criteria for Substance Use Disorder

A. A problematic pattern of substance use leading to clinically significant impairment or distress, as manifested by at least two of the following, occurring within a 12-month period:

1. The substance is taken in larger amounts or over a longer period than was intended.

2. There is a persistent desire or unsuccessful efforts to cut down or control substance use.

3. A great deal of time is spent in activities necessary to obtain the substance, use the substance, or recover from its effects.

4. Craving, or a strong desire to use the substance.

5. Recurrent substance use resulting in a failure to fulfill major role obligations at work, school, or home.

6. Continued substance use despite having persistent or recurrent social or interpersonal problems caused by or exacerbated by the effects of the substance.

7. Important social, occupational, or recreational activities are given up or reduced because of substance use.

8. Recurrent substance use in situations in which it is physically hazardous.

9. Substance use is continued despite knowledge of having a persistent or recurrent physical or psychological problem that is likely to have been caused or exacerbated by the substance.

10. Tolerance, as defined by either of the following:

   a. A need for markedly increased amounts of the substance to achieve intoxication or desired effect.

   b. A markedly diminished effect with continued use of the same amount of the substance.

11. Withdrawal, as manifested by either of the following:

   a. The characteristic withdrawal syndrome for the substance.

   b. The substance (or a closely related substance) is taken to relieve or avoid withdrawal symptoms.

Specify if:

In early remission: After full criteria for a substance use disorder were previously met, none of the criteria for a substance use disorder have been met for at least 3 months but for less than 12 months (with the exception that criterion A4 , "craving, or a strong desire to use the substance," may be met).

In sustained remission: After full criteria for a substance use disorder were previously met, none of the criteria for a substance use disorder have been met at any time during a period of 12 months or longer (with the exception that criterion A4 , "craving, or a strong desire to use the substance," may be met).

Specify current severity:

Mild: Presence of 2-3 symptoms.

Moderate: Presence of 4-5 symptoms.

Severe: Presence of 6 or more symptoms.

Source: Reprinted with permission from the *Diagnostic and Statistical Manual of Mental Disorders, Fifth Edition* (Copyright 2013). American Psychiatric Association.

control, (b) social impairment, (c) risky use, and (d) pharmacological criteria (American Psychiatric Association, 2013).

Impaired Control

- *Use in large amounts.* Adolescents might initially try alcohol or marijuana at a party or with friends. Over time, they might use more frequently and consume greater amounts of these substances than originally intended.

- *Problems cutting down.* Adolescents experience problems stopping or reducing their substance use despite a desire to do so. They may find themselves drinking on days they did not want to (e.g., before an important test) or be unable to refuse drinks at parties.

- *Time spent obtaining the substance or recovering from its effects.* Adolescents spend a great deal of time acquiring alcohol or recovering from its effects. Time spent in alcohol-related activities begins to interfere with their day-to-day school, peer, and extracurricular activities.

- *Craving.* Adolescents might experience a strong desire or intense urge to drink or use other drugs. Certain people (e.g., friends who drink), places (e.g., a party where alcohol is available), or situations (e.g., a stressful day) can prompt these cravings.

Social Impairment

- *Recurrent failure to fulfill major role obligations.* Adolescents who abuse alcohol or other drugs may miss school or work because of their substance use. They may forget to complete assignments or neglect to study for tests, resulting in low grades. They may be suspended from school for alcohol or other drug use or possession.
- *Continued use despite recurrent interpersonal problems.* Adolescents who abuse alcohol and other drugs may argue with parents about their substance use or problems in school. Adolescents may experience deterioration in their peer relationships. They may physically fight with others while intoxicated.
- *Important activities are given up.* Adolescents might feel like they have no time for sports, clubs, or hobbies they formerly enjoyed. They may also experience decreased energy or motivation for these activities. They may abandon friendships with peers who do not drink or use other drugs.

Risky Use

- *Recurrent use in physically hazardous situations.* Adolescents might drink and drive or repeatedly place themselves in risky social situations while under the influence of alcohol or other drugs.
- *Continued use despite physical or psychological problems.* In some cases, adolescents recognize the negative effects that their drinking and other drug use has on their health, mood, relationships, and academic functioning. Nevertheless, they may continue to drink or use other drugs despite these problems.

Pharmacological Criteria

- *Tolerance.* **Tolerance** occurs when the person (a) needs more of the substance to achieve intoxication or (b) the same amount of the substance produces diminished effects over repeated use. Adolescents might discover that they need to drink more beer to achieve a "buzz" at parties or smoke more marijuana to experience a reduction in anxiety.
- *Withdrawal.* **Withdrawal** occurs when the person (a) experiences negative physiological symptoms when they

stop or reduce substance use or (b) takes a different substance to avoid these negative symptoms. Adolescents who frequently use marijuana for many years may develop withdrawal symptoms if they discontinue use. Symptoms might include increased anxiety, agitation, irritability, and concentration problems.

The pharmacological criteria for Substance Use Disorders can vary considerably, depending on (a) the class of substance and (b) the person using the drug. For example, depressants, like alcohol, often produce withdrawal symptoms of anxiety, agitation, and insomnia. In contrast, stimulants, like methamphetamine, often produce withdrawal symptoms of daytime drowsiness and fatigue. Furthermore, people show great variability in their sensitivity to various classes of substances and their likelihood of developing tolerance and withdrawal symptoms. For example, some people use alcohol and other drugs for years without developing tolerance whereas others develop tolerance almost immediately (American Psychiatric Association, 2013).

If someone meets diagnostic criteria for a Substance Use Disorder, clinicians specify the severity of the problem. Severity is determined by the number of criteria met: two to three criteria (mild), four to five criteria (moderate), or >6 criteria (severe). Clinicians can also indicate if the person's symptoms are in **remission**; that is, symptoms that used to be present no longer exist. A person in "early remission" has remained symptom free (except for cravings) for 3 to 11 months. A person in "sustained remission" has remained symptom free (except for cravings) for 12 months or more.

Substance use disorders are diagnosed only when adolescents repeatedly use alcohol and other drugs in a manner that causes significant distress or impairment. Substance use disorders, therefore, can be differentiated from substance use by their (a) recurrence and (b) effects on adolescents' functioning. A single episode of "drinking and driving," although very serious, is not sufficient to diagnose an adolescent with Alcohol Use Disorder. The behavior must be *recurrent* and at least one other symptom must be present to merit the diagnosis. Similarly, repeated marijuana use with friends, although concerning, is probably not sufficient to diagnose an adolescent with Cannabis Use Disorder. The behavior must *impair* the adolescent's health or social-emotional functioning to merit a diagnosis (Heath et al., 2010).

CASE STUDY

ERICA'S EMERGING ALCOHOL USE PROBLEM

Erica is a 16-year-old girl who was referred to our clinic by the juvenile court after she was arrested for driving a car while intoxicated. Two weeks earlier, Erica had attended a party at her friend's house. She consumed approximately

(Continued)

(Continued)

six or seven alcoholic beverages and drove home. A police officer noticed Erica driving erratically, pulled her over, and determined that her blood alcohol content was .09. Erica was arrested. Her father made her spend the night in jail "to teach her a lesson."

Erica resented having to meet with her substance abuse counselor, Randy Moore. She explained, "I don't know why I'm here. I'm not an addict, I don't use hard drugs, and I didn't do anything that a million other kids my age haven't done." Nevertheless, the judge ordered Erica to participate in a substance abuse evaluation, 12 sessions of counseling, and community service.

Erica began drinking alcohol, at parties and on weekends with friends, when she was 14 years old. She said that she hated beer but liked sweet drinks. "I mostly drink to relax and have fun with my friends," Erica said. "They call me 'Captain Cook' because that's the kind of champagne I like to drink. Drinking helps me unwind and have a good time." Erica admitted to also using marijuana at parties and other social gatherings, but denied using other drugs.

"Has your drinking ever gotten in the way of your daily life?" asked Randy. Erica replied, "Not really, although I have been hung over a few times this year." Randy asked, "What about school?" Erica responded, "I guess my grades are lower now than when I started high school. But I think that's because I hang around with different kids than I used to. I don't think it's the drinking."

"What's your relationship with your mom and dad like?" asked Randy. Erica replied, "It's fine. My mom's a doctor and my dad's an investment advisor, so they're pretty busy. As long as I bring home good grades and stay out of trouble, they leave me alone. Now they're on my case because of the arrest."

After the initial session, Erica stated, "I know I have to be here, and I'm really sorry for what I did, but I obviously don't have a drinking problem. Besides, I'm sure you have people worse off than me who really need your help." Randy responded, "Let's schedule an appointment for next week and talk some more."

Changes From DSM-IV to DSM-5

People familiar with *DSM-IV* will notice a major change to the conceptualization of Substance Use Disorders in *DSM-5*. In *DSM-IV*, Substance Use Disorders were split into two categories: *Substance Abuse* and *Substance Dependence*. Substance Abuse Disorder was considered less severe. It was defined by the first three symptoms of the current diagnostic criteria for Substance Use Disorders and a fourth criterion: substance-related legal problems. To be diagnosed with Substance Abuse Disorder, a person needed to show only one symptom. Substance Dependence Disorder was considered more severe. If a person met criteria for dependence, he or she would not also be diagnosed with abuse. Dependence was defined by the remaining criteria in the current conceptualization of Substance Use Disorders except the presence of cravings. Three symptoms were required for dependence.

The decision to differentiate "abuse" and "dependence" was based on an old conceptualization of addiction called Alcohol Dependence Syndrome (Edwards & Gross, 1976). According to this conceptualization, substance use problems existed on two dimensions. On one hand were people who abused alcohol and other drugs; they experienced immediate problems associated with recurrent substance use. On the other hand were individuals who were physiologically and psychologically dependent on substances; they experienced tolerance, withdrawal, and disruptions in daily life because of their prolonged use. Over time, individuals were believed to transition from abuse to dependence.

In the past 30 years, researchers have identified four problems with the distinction between abuse and dependence:

1. Symptoms fall along one dimension rather than two. Researchers have used factor analysis, a statistical technique to examine the way symptoms correlate with each other. They have discovered that symptoms often co-occur and are not easily split into "abuse" and "dependence" symptoms as suggested by *DSM-IV*. Adolescents' symptoms, in particular, seem to fall into one general cluster rather than two independent clusters (Gelhorn et al., 2008; Hartmen et al., 2008).

2. Most people who abuse substances never become dependent. Prospective longitudinal studies show that abuse is usually not a precursor to dependence. Adolescents and young adults are especially likely to show abuse but not dependence (Grant et al., 2009; Verges, Steinley, Trull, & Sher, 2010).

3. Using *DSM-IV* criteria, many people were diagnosed with alcohol abuse after showing only one symptom: drinking while driving. Although this behavior is risky, it might not merit a psychiatric diagnosis. Furthermore, labeling someone with alcohol abuse might be stigmatizing (Hasin & Paykin, 1999).

4. Using *DSM-IV* criteria, some individuals with serious alcohol and other drug problems did not meet criteria for either abuse or dependence. These "diagnostic orphans" showed only two (not the required three) symptoms of dependence. Approximately 20% of adolescents with substance use problems failed to meet *DSM-IV* criteria. Because they were never diagnosed, many were denied treatment (Harford, Yi, Faden, & Chen, 2009).

To remedy these problems, *DSM-5* collapsed Substance Abuse and Substance Dependence into one disorder: Substance Use Disorder (O'Brien, 2011). The criteria for Substance Use Disorder consist of the criteria for abuse and dependence, except that the criterion "substance-related legal problems" was removed because of difficulty applying this criterion across regions where drug laws might vary. One symptom, the presence of "cravings," was added to make the criteria more consistent with the International Classification of Disease.

It is also noteworthy that the number of symptoms required for Substance Use Disorder was increased from one (required by Substance Abuse) to two. The increased symptom threshold was designed to exclude people who might have been erroneously diagnosed with Substance Abuse, following a single potentially harmful act like drinking and driving. Furthermore, in *DSM-5*, people can meet criteria by showing *any* two symptoms; therefore, the new threshold should eliminate diagnostic orphans who formerly went undiagnosed (Dawson, Goldstein, & Grant, 2013).

Some experts worried that increasing the number of required symptoms from one to two would decrease the number of people who would qualify for a Substance Use Disorder diagnosis. They worried that people formerly diagnosed with Substance Abuse would no longer be diagnosed and receive treatment. However, recent epidemiological studies indicate that the number of people who meet criteria will likely not change appreciably from *DSM-IV* to *DSM-5* (Agrawal, Heath, & Lynskey, 2011; Dawson et al., 2013).

Problems Diagnosing Substance Use Disorders in Adolescents

DSM-5 includes many improvements to the conceptualization of Substance Use Disorders. However, some experts have pointed out several limitations of the current diagnostic criteria, especially when they are applied to children and adolescents (Chung, Martin, Armstrong, & Labouvie, 2002; Deas, Roberts, & Grindlinger, 2005; Martin, Chung, Kirisci, & Langenbucher, 2006).

One criticism is that the *DSM-5* criteria are developmentally insensitive (Winters, Martin, & Chung, 2011). The symptoms most commonly seen among adolescents who misuse or abuse alcohol and other drugs are absent from the *DSM-5* criteria. For example, two of the most frequently occurring signs of alcohol use problems among adolescents are low grades and truancy. However, neither sign is included in the current diagnostic criteria. Consequently, some researchers have developed more developmentally appropriate criteria for adolescent substance use problems. These criteria include (a) breaking curfew, (b) lying to parents, (c) showing a reduction in grades, and (d) engaging in truancy (E. F. Wagner & Austin, 2006).

A second concern is the possibility that some criteria are overidentified in adolescents, compared to adults. Two

---

RESEARCH TO PRACTICE

ADDICTS IN *DSM-5*?

Careful readers will notice that the term "addiction" is not used in *DSM-5* or in this textbook to describe problematic alcohol or other drug use. The term *addiction* is sometimes used by people to describe severe problems related to compulsive and habitual use of alcohol and other drugs. *DSM-5* adopts the more general term *Substance Use Disorder* to describe the range of problems people can experience as a result of using substances. These problems range from problematic but relatively mild use (e.g., drinking while driving, school/work problems because of drinking) to severe use (e.g., excessive daily consumption, tolerance and withdrawal symptoms). An addiction would probably reflect the more severe end of this spectrum. However, *DSM-5* and many mental health professionals avoid using this term because of its uncertain definition and potentially negative connotation, especially when applied to children and adolescents (American Psychiatric Association, 2013).

Interestingly, however, *DSM-5* describes Gambling Disorder as an "addictive disorder" that shares many features of compulsive and habitual substance use. It is defined by persistent and recurrent maladaptive gambling that disrupts a person's family, interpersonal, and/or vocational activities. People with Gambling Disorder and people with Substance Use Disorders often experience problems stopping or "cutting back" on their behavior. Furthermore, both disorders are believed to be maintained by the brain's reward pathway—making them particularly resistant to treatment. Other addictive disorders have not yet been included in *DSM-5*. These disorders include "sex addiction," "exercise addiction," and even "shopping addiction." On the other hand, Internet Gaming Disorder, characterized by compulsive video game playing, is considered a "Disorder for Future Study." Additional research might support its inclusion in [a future] *DSM-6* (American Psychiatric Association, 2013).

---

studies (Harford, Grant, Yi, & Chen, 2005; Harford et al., 2009) have compared the prevalence of specific symptoms in adolescents (12–17 years) versus adults (>25 years). Three symptoms are more likely to be reported by adolescents and their families compared to adults: (a) tolerance, (b) time spent obtaining substances, and (c) substance use in hazardous situations (Figure 10.1).

In adults, tolerance tends to occur after years of frequent drinking. The amount of alcohol adults need to consume to achieve the same level of intoxication gradually increases. However, because adolescents are typically new to drinking, tolerance may develop more rapidly. For example, a 14-year-old who drinks at a party might become intoxicated after only one or two beers. If his drinking persists for several weeks or months, he might need three or four beers to achieve the same euphoric mood state. "Tolerance" in adolescence, therefore, may be more easily achieved than tolerance in adulthood, thus, leading to over-endorsement of this symptom by youths.

Similarly, adults who spend a great deal of time on substance-related activities tend to have chronic alcohol and other drug problems. For example, an adult who is dependent on prescription pain medication may spend considerable time convincing physicians to prescribe the medicine to him, stealing and selling items to raise money to buy the drug, or buying the medicine illegally. In contrast, adolescents who endorse this symptom tend to have less severe problems with alcohol and other drugs. Typically, adolescents endorse this criterion because they spend considerable time trying to access alcohol. For example, they may make fake IDs, try to find older friends who will buy alcohol for them, or acquire alcohol from parents. These youths are much less likely to have serious substance use problems than adults who endorse this symptom.

Youths are also more likely than adults to report substance use in situations that might be hazardous. It is likely that youths are more likely to use substances in hazardous situations because of their increased probability of engaging in impulsive, high-rate behaviors in general. Youths may be more likely than adults to drive or engage in other high-risk behaviors while intoxicated because of their underdeveloped capacities for forethought, planning, and considering the long-term consequences of their actions.

A third criticism of *DSM-5* criteria is that adolescents often show different patterns of alcohol and other drug use than adults (E. F. Wagner & Austin, 2006; Ray & Dhawan,

Figure 10.1   Alcohol Use Disorder Symptoms Reported by Adolescents (12–17 Years) Versus Adults (>25 Years).

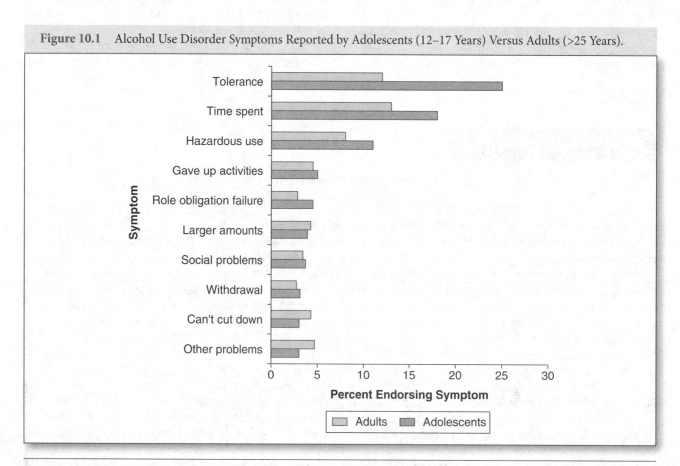

Source: Based on Harford and colleagues (2009).

Note: Adolescents are more likely than adults to report problems with tolerance, time spent acquiring alcohol, and hazardous alcohol use. Consequently, some experts worry that *DSM-5* criteria may overdiagnose adolescents.

2011). Adolescent substance use differs from adult substance use in several ways:

- Adolescent substance use, especially alcohol use, is more episodic than alcohol use by adults. Most adolescents tend to drink in binges, especially at parties. They usually do not drink every day.
- Adolescents often use a greater number of substances simultaneously than do adults. Indeed, it is more common for adolescents to misuse alcohol and marijuana together than to misuse either substance alone. In contrast, most adults who show substance use problems have a single substance of choice.
- Adolescents with Substance Use Disorders are more likely to show comorbid behavior problems than are adults with Substance Use Disorders. Furthermore, adolescents are more likely to show disruptive and antisocial behaviors, whereas adults are more likely to develop mood and anxiety disorders associated with their substance use.

Finally, adolescents are more likely than adults to "outgrow" their substance use problems. Because of the great number of physiological and psychosocial changes that occur during adolescence, many adolescents show a gradual reduction in substance use by the time they reach early adulthood. For example, many older adolescents use alcohol fairly regularly, especially during their late teens and early twenties. However, most young adults dramatically reduce their alcohol consumption after they assume more adult-like responsibilities (e.g., gain full-time employment, have children). Although all serious substance use problems merit treatment regardless of the person's age, adolescents usually show a different course of substance use than do adults.

Assessing Adolescent Substance Use Disorders

To obtain the most reliable and valid information, clinicians often rely on questionnaires or semi-structured interviews to assess child and adolescent substance use. One simple screening measure, often used with adults suspected of alcohol use problems is the CAGE questionnaire (Ewing, 1984, pp. 1905–1907). The acronym CAGE reminds clinicians of the four domains of alcohol use problems: (1) Have you ever tried to Cut down on your drinking? (2) Have people Annoyed you by criticizing your drinking? (3) Have you ever felt Guilty about your drinking? and (4) Have you ever felt you needed a drink first thing in the morning (as an Eye-opener) to steady your nerves or get rid of a hangover? Adults who respond affirmatively to two or more CAGE questions should be further assessed for an Alcohol Use Disorder.

Although the CAGE questionnaire is an effective screening measure for substance use problems in adults, it is less applicable for children and adolescents suspected of substance use problems. Indeed, the CAGE does not assess many features of child and adolescent substance use, such as binge drinking, drinking in hazardous situations (e.g., while driving), or experiencing academic or peer problems because

of continued alcohol use (Rumpf, Wohlert, Freyer-Adam, Grothues, & Bischof, 2012). Consequently, clinicians might use a different screening tool to assess adolescent substance use. One option is the CRAFFT (Knight et al., 1999). The CRAFFT questionnaire assesses substance use problems most likely to be exhibited by adolescents and includes questions about alcohol, marijuana, and other drugs.

First, the questionnaire asks if the adolescent has consumed alcohol, smoked marijuana, or used any other drugs to get "high" in the past 12 months. Then, the adolescent answers a series of questions reflecting the acronym CRAFFT:

C Have you ever ridden in a **CAR** driven by someone (including yourself) who was "high" or had been using alcohol or drugs?

R Do you ever use alcohol or drugs to **RELAX**, feel better about yourself, or fit in?

A Do you ever use alcohol or drugs while you are **ALONE**?

F Do you ever **FORGET** things you did while using alcohol or drugs?

F Do your family or **FRIENDS** ever tell you that you should cut down on your drinking or drug use?

T Have you ever gotten into **TROUBLE** while you were using alcohol or drugs?

Adolescents who answer "yes" to any of the six CRAFFT items should be more carefully assessed for a Substance Use Disorder. Overall, the CRAFFT has adequate reliability and validity as a brief screening measure (Dhalla, Zumbo, & Poole, 2011, pp. 57–64).

Another questionnaire that is useful in assessing a wide range of child and adolescent Substance Use Disorders is the Alcohol, Smoking, and Substance Involvement Screening Test (ASSIST; National Institute on Drug Abuse, 2013). One advantage of the ASSIST is that it screens for a wide range of substance use problems. A second strength of the ASSIST is that it can be administered to both youths and their parents. Gathering data from both parents and adolescents is important because youths sometimes deny or minimize the frequency and severity of their alcohol and other drug use. Furthermore, parents are sometimes not knowledgeable about the extensiveness of their child's substance use. Indeed, the overall agreement between parent-reported and adolescent-reported alcohol use is approximately 22%. Therefore, data from both parents and adolescents are necessary to obtain the most complete picture of the youths' use of substances (Delaney-Black et al., 2010).

The ASSIST asks parents and adolescents to independently report the frequency of adolescents' alcohol and other drug use over the previous 2 weeks (see Table 10.2). Elevated ratings could indicate a Substance Use Disorder (Humeniuk, Henry-Edwards, Ali, Poznyak, & Monteiro, 2010).

Table 10.2 Dimensions of the Alcohol, Smoking, and Substance Involvement Screening Test (ASSIST)

During the past 2 weeks, how often did you/your child . . .

Have an alcoholic beverage?

Have four or more drinks in a single day?

Smoke a cigarette or use chewing tobacco?

During the past 2 weeks, how often did you/your child use any of the following medicines without a doctor's prescription or in greater amounts or longer than prescribed?

Painkillers (like Vicodin)?

Stimulants (like Ritalin, Adderall)?

Sedatives or tranquilizers (like sleeping pills)?

During the past 2 weeks, how often did you/your child use any of the following drugs . . .

Steroids?

Marijuana?

Cocaine or crack?

Club drugs (like ecstasy)?

Hallucinogens (like LSD)?

Heroin?

Inhalants (like glue)?

Methamphetamine (like speed)?

Source: Based on National Institute on Drug Abuse (2013).

Substance-Induced Disorders

Up until now, we have examined Substance Use Disorders, the persistent use of alcohol and other drugs despite behavioral, cognitive, and physiological symptoms that cause distress or impairment. By definition, Substance Use Disorders describe symptoms that emerge only after continued substance use. In contrast, Substance-Induced Disorders describe substance-specific syndromes caused by either the ingestion of alcohol or other drugs or their withdrawal. *DSM-5* recognizes three Substance-Induced Disorders: (a) Substance Intoxication, (b) Substance Withdrawal, and (c) Substance-Induced Mental Disorder.

Intoxication is defined as "a disturbance of perception, wakefulness, attention, thinking, judgment, psychomotor and/or interpersonal behavior" caused by the ingestion of a substance (American Psychiatric Association, 2013, p. 485). Usually, intoxication does not cause distress or impairment, such as when a person experiences a sense of relaxation and gregariousness after a few drinks at a party. However, if intoxication causes distress or impairment, the person can be diagnosed with Substance Intoxication. The specific symptoms of Substance Intoxication differ based on the drug consumed. For example, Table 10.3 presents the symptoms of alcohol and cannabis intoxication.

Withdrawal is defined as a "substance-specific problematic behavioral change . . . that is due to the cessation of, or reduction in, heavy and prolonged substance use" (American Psychiatric Association, 2013, p. 486). Withdrawal symptoms can include changes in overt actions (e.g., pacing), emotions (e.g., anxiety), cognitions (e.g., unpleasant dreams), and physiological functioning (e.g., rapid heart rate, nausea). By definition, withdrawal symptoms are always problematic, causing distress or impairment in academic, occupational, or social functioning. The specific symptoms of Substance Withdrawal depend on the drug used. Table 10.3 also presents the symptoms of alcohol and cannabis withdrawal.

Finally, individuals can be diagnosed with a Substance-Induced Mental Disorder. A Substance-Induced Mental Disorder occurs when someone develops a mental disorder that is caused by the use or withdrawal of a substance. Any of the classes of substances can induce a mental disorder.

Table 10.3   Symptoms of Alcohol and Cannabis Intoxication and Withdrawal

	Alcohol	*Cannabis*
Intoxication	Psychological changes: labile mood, impaired judgment, inappropriate sexual/aggressive behavior Slurred speech Incoordination Unsteady gait Nystagmus[1] Impaired attention/memory Stupor or coma	Psychological changes: euphoria, anxiety, sensation of slowed time, impaired coordination, impaired judgment, social withdrawal Conjunctival injection[2] Increased appetite Dry mouth Tachycardia (i.e., increased heart rate)
Withdrawal	Autonomic hyperactivity Increased hand tremor Insomnia Nausea or vomiting Hallucinations Psychomotor agitation Anxiety Generalized tonic-clonic seizures	Irritability, anger, or aggression Nervousness or anxiety Sleep difficulty Decreased appetite or weight loss Restlessness Depressed mood Physical symptoms: abdominal pain, shakiness, sweating, fever, headaches

Source: American Psychiatric Association (2013).

[1]Involuntary movement of the eyes resulting in jerky or saccadic movements while tracking an object.

[2]Reddening of the eyes due to increased prominence of the conjunctival blood vessels.

However, two classes of disorders are most common. First, depressants, such as alcohol, sedatives, and hypnotics (e.g., sleep medications), sometimes elicit depressive disorders after prolonged use, and, anxiety disorders and insomnia upon withdrawal. Second, stimulants, such as amphetamine and cocaine, sometimes elicit psychotic disorders after their use and depressive disorders upon withdrawal. Indeed, certain adolescents are at risk for developing psychotic disorders, such as Schizophrenia, after using stimulant medication (American Psychiatric Association, 2013).

ALCOHOL AND MARIJUANA USE AND MISUSE

Alcohol

Alcohol is the drug most widely used by adolescents. Alcohol is often overlooked as a possible drug of abuse because of its widespread availability in the United States. Alcohol is legal in nearly all parts of the country, and it is heavily advertised on television and in magazines. Furthermore, many adolescents and parents regard alcohol consumption as part of adolescent culture. After all, most adolescents drink alcohol at least occasionally at some point during their high school years.

For these reasons, adolescents and adults tend to minimize the risks associated with alcohol use (Johnston, O'Malley, Bachman, & Schulenberg, 2005).

Psychological Effects of Alcohol

Alcohol is technically a **sedative**. It falls into the same class of drugs as benzodiazepines, barbiturates, and most sleeping pills. The effects of alcohol depend on the amount consumed. Experts usually describe its effects as **biphasic**. Mild to moderate alcohol use produces one set of (largely desirable) effects: increased arousal, sociability, euphoria, and reduced anxiety. Extended alcohol consumption produces a different cluster of (largely aversive) effects: sedation, cognitive and motor impairments, heart and respiratory problems, and other health risks (Perham, Moore, Shepherd, & Cusens, 2007).

Moderate alcohol consumption usually produces pleasurable effects. Consequently, many adolescents will continue to drink in order to maintain or enhance these subjective feelings of well-being. Unfortunately, excessive alcohol consumption produces less-than-desirable effects in most people. Excessive alcohol use can result in **binge drinking**, that is, consuming five or more alcoholic beverages in a single episode. Binge drinking can cause fatigue, dizziness, nausea, and blackout. Bingeing may also produce severe impairment in judgment and problem solving. Physiologically, binge drinking is associated with disturbances in balance and coordination, slurred speech, restlessness and irritability, and problems with heart rate and respiration. In rare cases, excessive alcohol consumption can cause coma and death.

Physiological Effects of Alcohol

Alcohol is rapidly absorbed by the gastrointestinal tract and quickly diffuses throughout the bloodstream. It is metabolized primarily by the liver. The enzymes **alcohol dehydrogenase** and **acetaldehyde dehydrogenase** are chiefly responsible for its metabolism. The exact mechanisms by which alcohol affects mood, cognition, and behavior are unknown. However, alcohol seems to affect the functioning of at least five major neurotransmitters: norepinephrine, glutamate, dopamine, opioids, and GABA (g-aminobutyric acid; Kosten, George, & Kleber, 2005; Meyer & Quenzer, 2005; Nace, 2005).

First, low doses of alcohol stimulate the norepinephrine system, causing increased feelings of arousal and behavioral excitation. Alcohol seems to target a brain region known as the reticular formation, located near the base of the brain. The **reticular formation** is responsible for alerting us to important information in the environment and initiating attention and arousal. Increased norepinephrine activity in this brain area is probably responsible for the increase in alertness, sociability, and

talkativeness shown by most people after one or two alcoholic beverages.

At the same time, alcohol affects glutamate functioning. Glutamate is a major excitatory neurotransmitter in the central nervous system. Alcohol acts to inhibit the neurotransmission of glutamate, thereby, slowing neuronal activity. Specifically, alcohol interferes with certain glutamate receptor sites, especially the N-methyl-D-aspartate (NMDA) receptor. Consumption of one or two alcoholic beverages can begin to decrease glutamate activity, producing feelings of relaxation and stress reduction. Reduced glutamate activity might partially explain the negatively reinforcing properties of alcohol; alcohol can alleviate anxiety. Glutamate is also partially responsible for associative learning and memory. Excessive alcohol use, therefore, can lead to memory problems including difficulty forming new memories and periods of memory loss (i.e., blackouts).

Moderate alcohol consumption affects dopamine activity. Researchers have identified a neural pathway that they believe is responsible for the pleasurable effects of most addictive drugs, including alcohol. This "reward pathway" extends from the ventral tegmental area (VTA) of the midbrain to the nucleus accumbens, amygdala, and hippocampus, located in the limbic system (Image 10.1). This neural pathway responds primarily to dopamine, a neurotransmitter responsible for feelings of pleasure, positive affect (i.e., energy, sociability), and increased motor activity. Because this dopamine-rich pathway extends from the midbrain

Image 10.1   In the brain, dopamine plays an important role in the experience of pleasure. As part of the reward pathway, dopamine is manufactured in nerve cell bodies located within the ventral tegmental area (VTA) and is released in the nucleus accumbens and the prefrontal cortex.

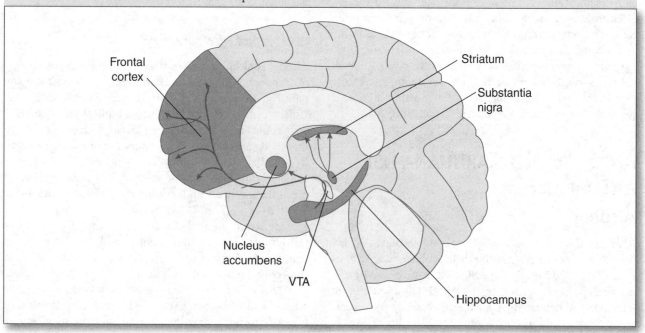

Source: Image courtesy of the National Institutes of Health.

(VTA) to the limbic system, it is called the **dopaminergic mesolimbic pathway**.

How does the dopaminergic mesolimbic pathway operate? Alcohol stimulates dopaminergic neurons in the VTA. The VTA, in turn, increases dopamine levels in a nearby brain area, the nucleus accumbens, producing subjective feelings of euphoria, pleasure, and emotional well-being (Image 10.2). These pleasant effects constitute the first phase of the "biphasic" response to alcohol, and they are the primary reason most people, especially adolescents, drink. Furthermore, these pleasurable feelings also positively reinforce alcohol use, making the person consume more of the drug. Alcohol also increases neuronal activity in the amygdala and hippocampus, brain areas responsible for processing emotions and forming new memories. The increased activity of these brain regions may account for the highly emotional memories associated with alcohol consumption and the "cravings" for alcohol experienced by chronic drinkers.

Alcohol produces other pleasurable effects through its activity on the body's production of natural opioids. Researchers have discovered opioid receptors throughout the brain. These receptors are primarily responsible for subjective feelings of satisfaction and alleviation of pain. Typically, the body makes natural opioids (i.e., endorphin, enkephalin) to cope with stressful or painful situations. These opioids are produced by the pituitary gland and released into the bloodstream to circulate throughout the body. Alcohol consumption increases the release of endogenous opioids, producing these pleasurable effects.

Finally, moderate alcohol consumption affects GABA, a major inhibitory neurotransmitter. GABA binds to receptor sites throughout the central nervous system, causing cells to rapidly take in negatively charged chloride ions (Figure 10.2). This increase in negatively charged particles makes cells less likely to fire. Alcohol enhances the effects of GABA, producing a rapid influx of chloride into cells and a general decrease in neuronal activity. This decrease in neuronal activity is partially responsible for many of the sedating effects of alcohol: relaxation, cognitive sluggishness, and slowed reaction time.

Most adolescents who use alcohol experience tolerance; that is, they report needing more alcohol to achieve previous levels of euphoria (Chung et al., 2002). Researchers distinguish between two types of tolerance (Meyer & Quenzer, 2005). First, adolescents can experience **acute tolerance** during a single drinking episode. Specifically, people experience the greatest effects of alcohol after only a few drinks, with diminishing effects after each successive drink. Many adolescents often try to "chase the high" by continuing their alcohol use after reaching this period of diminishing returns. Unfortunately, continued use results in increased sedation rather than increased pleasure.

Second, chronic alcohol use is associated with **pharmacodynamic tolerance** (Koob & LeMoal, 2006). Over sustained periods of time, the sensitivity of the neuroreceptors

Image 10.2   This rat can stimulate his nucleus accumbens by pressing a lever in his cage. The nucleus accumbens is part of the dopamine-rich mesolimbic pathway, the brain's pleasure center. Most addictive drugs stimulate the nucleus accumbens. The rat will press the lever to exhaustion. He will also transverse an electric grid, enduring painful shocks, to access the lever and stimulate his brain.

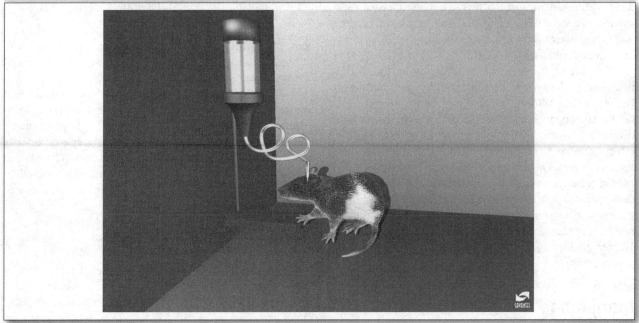

Source: Image courtesy of the National Institute of Mental Health.

Figure 10.2 A GABA Receptor in the Brain

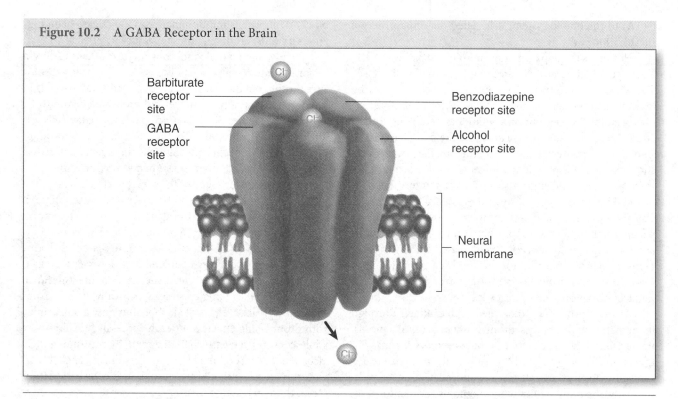

Barbiturate receptor site

GABA receptor site

Benzodiazepine receptor site

Alcohol receptor site

Neural membrane

Note: Alcohol enhances the effects of the inhibitory neurotransmitter GABA. Chloride (Cl-) ions enter through the channel, making the neuron less likely to fire.

that respond to alcohol gradually decreases. For example, long-term alcohol use is associated with decreased sensitivity of GABA and dopamine receptors. Individuals who drink frequently may not exhibit the same sedating effects of alcohol due to this decrease in sensitivity to GABA. Frequent drinkers may also require more alcohol to achieve a state of euphoria due to decreased dopamine activity. Decreased receptor sensitivity is believed to be a homeostatic mechanism, that is, a way for the body to compensate for the individual's history of excessive alcohol use (Image 10.3).

Because of this decrease in sensitivity, abrupt discontinuation of alcohol can produce withdrawal symptoms in chronic users. Without alcohol, the body's sensitivity to GABA and dopamine is diminished. Consequently, chronic drinkers who stop using alcohol may experience negative effects due to the relative underactivity of these neurotransmitters. Decreased GABA sensitivity can produce feelings of anxiety, excitability, irritability, restlessness, and excessive motor activity. Some adults experience delirium tremens, a cluster of symptoms that include tremors, seizures, confusion, and visual and tactile hallucinations. Decreased dopamine activity can cause low energy, fatigue, and depression.

Marijuana

Marijuana is the most commonly used illegal drug. Marijuana contains dozens of compounds known to affect brain chemistry. These compounds fall into a certain class called cannabinoids. The most powerful cannabinoid is **delta-9-tetrahydrocannabinol** (THC; O'Brien et al., 2005).

Psychological Effects of Marijuana

When someone smokes a marijuana cigarette, approximately half of the THC enters the lungs and is rapidly absorbed. Within seconds of the first puff, THC enters the brain and affects mood, cognition, and behavior.

Moderate doses of marijuana usually produce mild intoxication. Within seconds of use, people often feel lightheaded and dizzy. Some people report tingling sensations in their limbs. After a few minutes, most people experience feelings of euphoria, disinhibition, and increased energy and sociability. Continued use (10–30 minutes) produces reductions in anxiety, a general sense of relaxation, and a state of emotional well-being or contentment. Cognitive and motor processes are usually slowed. For example, marijuana users may show slowed movements, speech, or problem-solving ability. Slowed cognitive and motor responses can interfere with people's abilities to perform complex mental activities (e.g., complete homework) and motor activities (e.g., drive a car). Effects typically last a few hours. Larger doses of marijuana can cause paradoxical effects: increased anxiety and agitation, perceptual distortions or visual hallucinations, and paranoia.

Image 10.3 Repeated exposure to drugs decreases sensitivity of dopamine receptors in the brain (*light areas*). Decreased sensitivity can produce tolerance and withdrawal.

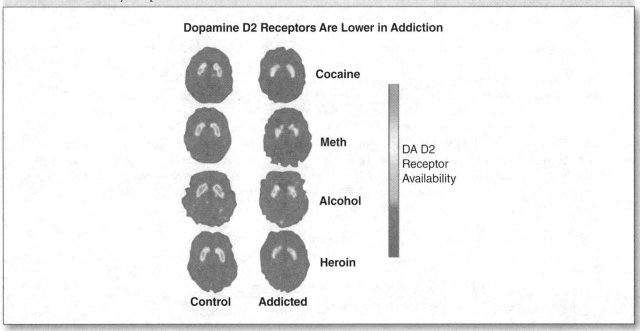

Source: Image courtesy of the National Institute on Drug Abuse.

Physiological Effects of Marijuana

THC is detected by cannabinoid receptors located throughout the brain. The largest concentrations of these receptors are in the basal ganglia, cerebellum, hippocampus, and cortex. When THC is detected by these receptors, it causes a reduction in the cell's metabolic activity and the activity of neurotransmitters. The specific effects of THC depend on *where* it is detected. For example, THC detected by the basal ganglia affects movement and coordination, whereas THC detected by receptors in the cortex affects thinking, judgment, and problem solving.

THC is known to affect a wide range of neurotransmitters, including norepinephrine, dopamine, glutamate, GABA, and serotonin. The multiple brain areas and neurotransmitters affected by THC likely account for the diverse effects of the substance on people's behavior.

Experts disagree about the long-term physiological risks of repeated marijuana use (O'Brien et al., 2005). People who frequently use marijuana often show impairments in attention, memory, and problem-solving ability relative to individuals who do not use the drug. Some researchers, but not all, have found that these cognitive impairments persist for weeks or months after discontinuing marijuana use (Pope & Yurgelun-Todd, 2004). Many chronic users show decreased motivation and goal-directed behavior, a phenomenon called **amotivational syndrome** (Meyer & Quenzer, 2005). However, experts are unsure whether this lack of motivation is caused by the physiological effects of the drug or by environmental factors associated with drug use. For example, people who frequently use marijuana may drop out of mainstream culture and adopt an unconventional lifestyle characterized by low achievement motivation.

Perhaps the most serious effect of chronic marijuana use is health impairment. Smoking marijuana is associated with the same health risks as smoking cigarettes: respiratory problems, circulatory problems, and cancer. Marijuana can also suppress immune functioning. Finally, the effects of marijuana can impair people's sensory and motor functioning, increasing their likelihood of injury.

Most people show acute tolerance to marijuana. During the course of a single marijuana episode, most people need to use more of the drug to achieve the initial state of intoxication. Animal studies demonstrate pharmacodynamic tolerance to marijuana. Long-term use causes reductions in the number and sensitivity of cannabinoid receptors in animals. There is less evidence for pharmacodynamic tolerance in humans; however, many people who frequently use marijuana report needing more of the drug after months or years of use.

Frequent marijuana use can cause dependence. Individuals who are dependent on marijuana report cravings for the drug and show a characteristic pattern of withdrawal symptoms associated with abstinence. Frequent users who are denied the drug can experience sleep and appetite disturbance, anxiety, agitation, restlessness, and general irritability. Sometimes, marijuana withdrawal is also associated with physical symptoms, such as sweating, chills, and nausea. Chronic marijuana users show more severe withdrawal symptoms including intense cravings for the drug, depression, anger, bizarre dreams, and headaches. Withdrawal symptoms typically last only a few days.

VIDEO GAME ADDICTION?

Do you know someone who plays video games for several hours every day? Do they become agitated, moody, or restless when they are unable to play? Does their gaming negatively affect their relationships, schoolwork, or health? For now, their behavior does not reflect a mental disorder—but it could in the future.

Internet Gaming Disorder is a "condition for further study" in *DSM-5* (American Psychiatric Association, 2013). The developers of *DSM-5* reviewed more than 240 peer-reviewed research studies examining individuals who experienced clinically significant distress and impairment because of persistent Internet gaming. Many of the people described in the studies showed several features displayed by people with Substance Use Disorders, such as repeated unsuccessful attempts to stop their behavior, tolerance, and withdrawal. However, these studies lacked a standard definition of the disorder, making comparison across studies difficult. Consequently, *DSM-5* includes diagnostic criteria for Internet Gaming Disorder, so that researchers can assess the disorder more reliably and share their findings more easily with others. The criteria include five (or more) of the following symptoms in a 12-month time period:

1. Preoccupation with Internet games (i.e., gaming is a dominant activity in daily life).

2. Withdrawal symptoms when games are taken away (i.e., anxiety, irritability, sadness).

3. Tolerance (i.e., increased amount of time playing Internet games).

4. Unsuccessful attempt to cut down or control Internet gaming.

5. Loss of interest in other hobbies or activities.

6. Continued gaming despite awareness that it causes psychological problems.

7. Deceived other people (e.g. parents) regarding the amount of Internet gaming.

8. Uses Internet gaming to escape or relieve negative mood (e.g., anxiety, depression).

9. Problems in relationships, school, or work because of gaming.

What is the evidence that individuals can develop problems with online gaming? In one important study, Douglas Gentile (2009) assessed the presence of problematic gaming using a random sample of youths, aged 8 to 18 years. Approximately 8% of youths showed significant symptoms. Boys (12%) were significantly more likely to show problematic use than girls (3%). Youths who showed problematic video game use also reported more problems with peers, lower grades in school, and greater difficulty with inattention and impulsivity. Similar results were obtained from a large sample of Asian youths (Gentile et al., 2011).

Source: DSM-5, 2013; Gentile, D. (2009); Gentile et al. (2011).

ASSOCIATED DISORDERS

Approximately 50% of adolescents in the community with Substance Use Disorders show at least one other mental disorder. Among adolescents referred to treatment, comorbidity ranges from 50% to 90% (Rowe, Liddle, Greenbaum, & Henderson, 2004).

Adolescents who have both a Substance Use Disorder and a psychiatric diagnosis show greater impairment than adolescents with either substance use or psychiatric problems alone. Specifically, adolescents with dual diagnoses show more school-related difficulties, greater family conflict, more emotional distress, and more legal problems than adolescents

with either Substance Use Disorders or psychiatric disturbances alone (Grella, Hser, Joshi, & Rounds-Bryant, 2001). Adolescents with dual diagnoses also show poorer prognoses. They are more likely to have substance use problems during adulthood, experience long-term psychiatric illness, and develop personality disorders.

Adolescents with both substance use and mental health disorders may be less responsive to treatment than adolescents with substance use or mental disorders alone. Adolescents with dual diagnoses are more likely to drop out of treatment or relapse within one year of treatment completion (Rowe et al., 2004; Wise, Cuffe, & Fischer, 2001).

Behavior Problems

ADHD is the most frequently occurring psychiatric disorder shown by adolescents with Substance Use Disorders (Dennis et al., 2002, 2004). Approximately 15% to 30% of adolescents with ADHD eventually develop a Substance Use Disorder. Conversely, most (50%–75%) adolescents with Substance Use Disorders have ADHD. Adolescents with ADHD and substance use problems show more severe symptoms of both disorders and greater impairment in overall functioning. Their substance use tends to be longer and more resistant to treatment than that of individuals without ADHD. After treatment for substance use problems, youths with ADHD are more than twice as likely to relapse compared to adolescents without ADHD (Latimer, Ernst, Hennessey, Stinchfield, & Winters, 2004).

The relationship between ADHD and Substance Use Disorders is unclear (J. J. Wilson & Levin, 2005). At least three hypotheses have been offered to explain their high comorbidity. First, ADHD and substance use problems can have a common genetic or biological cause. For example, adolescents with both disorders display problems with executive functioning and behavioral inhibition that could stem from their genetic makeup. Second, both ADHD and substance use problems are correlated with other disruptive behavior disorders. For example, children with ADHD show increased likelihood of developing ODD and CD later in their development. ODD and CD, in turn, are associated with adolescent substance use problems. It is possible that ADHD, ODD and CD, and substance use problems are part of a spectrum of externalizing behavior that unfolds across development. Third, symptoms of ADHD could increase the probability of substance use problems. For example, individuals with ADHD often show problems with decision making, social problem solving, and peer relations. These problems can cause peer rejection, social isolation, and depression. Rejected children with ADHD might use substances to gain acceptance from peers or to cope with feelings of loneliness.

Approximately 35% to 40% of adolescents with substance abuse also meet diagnostic criteria for CD (Henggeler, Pickrel, Brondino, & Crouch, 1996; Kaminer, Burleson, & Goldberger, 2002). Furthermore, nearly 90% of youths with Substance Use Disorders show at least some problems with oppositional, defiant, or disruptive behavior (Waldron, Slesnick, Brody, Charles, & Thomas, 2001). Among adolescents with CD, alcohol and other drug abuse is usually part of a much larger problem with impulsive, disruptive, and destructive behavior.

Depression and Anxiety

Approximately 25% to 50% of adolescents with substance use problems are depressed. Longitudinal data indicate that most adolescents do not use alcohol and other drugs primarily to cope with depression. Instead, mood disorders often develop after the onset of adolescents' substance use problems. Comorbid depression and substance use problems can sometimes be explained by shared genetic and psychosocial risk factors, as well (Goodwin, Fergusson, & Horwood, 2004).

Adolescents with substance use problems show greater likelihood of suicidal thoughts, suicide attempts, and suicide completion than their counterparts without Substance Use Disorders (Kaminer & Bukstein, 2005). Mood problems, especially depression, associated with substance use partially account for the relationship between substance use and suicidal ideation. However, at least one study showed that the likelihood of suicide attempts remained elevated even after controlling for co-occurring depression (Wu et al., 2005). It is possible that alcohol and other drugs increase the likelihood of adolescent suicide by producing feelings of dysphoria, by lowering adolescents' inhibitions against self-harm, and by increasing impulsive and risky decision making.

Approximately 10% to 40% of adolescents with substance use problems show comorbid anxiety (Kaminer & Bukstein, 2005; Waldron et al., 2001). The relationship between substance use and anxiety is complex. Some anxiety disorders usually precede the development of adolescents' substance use problems. For example, some adolescents use alcohol and other drugs to cope with social anxiety or unwanted memories of traumatic experiences. Alternatively, other anxiety disorders usually develop after the onset of substance use problems. For example, chronic use of alcohol can produce a gradual increase in worry and generalized anxiety.

Psychotic Disorders

Three large community-based studies have demonstrated an association between adolescent marijuana use and the development of psychotic symptoms later in life (Crome & Bloor, 2005). Adolescents who regularly used marijuana were more likely to report psychotic symptoms (e.g., hallucinations, delusions) or develop Schizophrenia in late adolescence or early adulthood compared to adolescents who did not use marijuana. The association between marijuana use and psychotic symptoms could not be explained by adolescents' levels of psychological distress. Therefore, it is unlikely that adolescents who eventually showed psychotic symptoms used marijuana to treat early symptoms of psychosis. Instead, the data suggest that repeated marijuana use may increase the likelihood of psychotic symptoms, especially among those adolescents who have a genetic predisposition toward Schizophrenia.

EPIDEMIOLOGY

Prevalence

Prevalence of Adolescent Substance Use

To estimate prevalence, scientists at the University of Michigan Institute for Social Research have annually assessed adolescent substance use in a project called Monitoring the Future (MTF; Johnston et al., 2006). These researchers collect data regarding adolescents' attitudes and overt behavior regarding substance use. In recent years, approximately 50,000 youths in eighth, tenth, and twelfth grades have completed anonymous surveys. Their data allow us to determine normative substance use throughout adolescence and see trends in adolescents' substance use over the past 30 years.

Recent data indicate that adolescent alcohol use is common (Johnston et al., 2006). By their senior year in high school, nearly 75% of adolescents have used alcohol at some point in their lives, approximately 65% have used alcohol in the past year, and almost 50% have used alcohol in the past 30 days. A sizable minority of younger adolescents also report alcohol use. Approximately 40% of students in eighth grade report trying alcohol at some point in their lives, while 15% report alcohol use in the previous month (see Figure 10.3).

Marijuana use is also fairly widespread, especially among older adolescents. Approximately 45% of high school seniors have tried marijuana; almost 18% have used it within the past month. Marijuana use is less common among younger adolescents. Only about 15% of eighth-grade students report having tried the drug.

Although many adolescents report having tried alcohol and marijuana, most adolescents do not try other illicit drugs. Only about 25% of high school seniors have tried another illicit substance in their lifetime. Excluding alcohol and marijuana,

the most commonly used drugs among twelfth-grade students were prescription medications, including Vicodin (10%), other medicinal narcotics (9%), medicinal amphetamines (9%), barbiturates (7%), tranquilizers (7%), and OxyContin (6%). Less than 6% of high school seniors reported trying other so-called street drugs, like hallucinogens, crack cocaine, heroin, and methamphetamines (Feinberg, 2006).

In general, substance use has decreased over the past decade (Kuehn, 2006). The greatest reductions in substance use have been for drugs like marijuana, LSD, methamphetamine, and ecstasy. Although these drugs reached peak levels in the middle to late 1990s, their use has been decreasing ever since. In contrast, occasional alcohol use among adolescents has remained fairly steady over the years. Use of other drugs, especially prescription medications, seems to be on the rise among adolescents.

Data from MTF indicate that alcohol use during adolescence is developmentally normative. Furthermore, marijuana use by older adolescents is fairly common, with almost half of twelfth-grade students admitting to trying marijuana. Besides alcohol and marijuana, the illicit drugs most frequently used by adolescents appear to be prescription medications. Adolescent substance use is largely opportunistic. Most adolescents obtain alcohol, marijuana, and prescription drugs from friends, classmates, and family (e.g., stealing from parents). In contrast, use of street drugs like cocaine and methamphetamine is relatively uncommon.

Figure 10.3 Percentage of Youths Who Have Used Various Substances in the Past Year

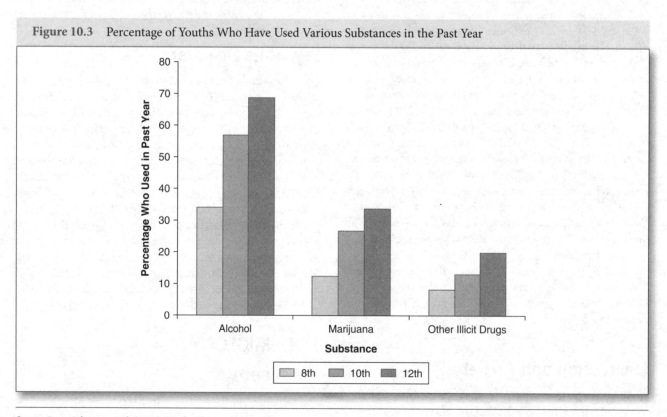

Source: From Johnston et al. (2006). Used with permission.

Note: Most tenth through twelfth graders have tried alcohol; approximately 25% have tried marijuana.

Prevalence of Adolescent Substance Use Disorders

What about Substance Use Disorders? Studies assessing prevalence have yielded inconsistent findings. Results vary depending on the sample of adolescents studied, the method of questioning, and the researcher's definition of "problematic" use.

One method of defining substance use problems is to use *DSM* criteria. When researchers use *DSM* diagnostic criteria, the prevalence of mild Substance Use Disorder among adolescents in the community ranges from 1% to 9%, while the prevalence of moderate or severe Substance Use Disorder among adolescents in the community ranges from 1% to 5%.

A second method of classifying substance use problems is to base classification on the frequency of use. For example, many researchers believe that daily use of alcohol or marijuana for one month or longer indicates a significant Substance Use Disorder. Using this criterion, almost 3% of high school seniors abuse alcohol while almost 5% abuse marijuana (Johnston et al., 2006; see Figure 10.4).

Yet a third technique involves classifying alcohol abuse in terms of binge drinking. Binge drinking is often associated with increased intoxication, risk-taking behavior, and many of the harmful effects of alcohol use. Unfortunately, binge drinking is fairly common among adolescents. Approximately 25% of high school seniors admit to binge drinking in the past 2 weeks, while less than 10% of eighth-grade students admit to bingeing (see Figure 10.5). Interestingly, there is a moderate, inverse relationship between binge drinking and perceived risk associated with bingeing. Adolescents who show the greatest rate of binge drinking are least likely to view their consumption as dangerous.

Gender Differences

Patterns of substance use differ slightly for boys and girls. Boys usually begin using cigarettes, alcohol, and marijuana at earlier ages than girls (Andrews, 2005). At any given age, the percentage of boys who have tried any of these substances is slightly higher than the percentage of girls (Johnston et al., 2005; see Figure 10.6). Boys are also more likely than girls to binge drink, to engage in dangerous activities as a result of their substance use, and to get into trouble at school because of alcohol or other drugs.

Figure 10.4 Percentage of Youths Who Use Alcohol or Marijuana Daily

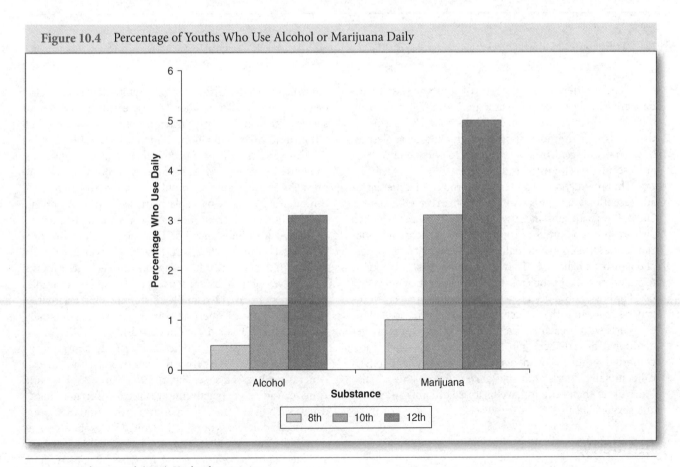

Source: From Johnston et al. (2006). Used with permission.

Note: Most people regard daily use of alcohol and marijuana by adolescents as problematic. Using this criterion, approximately 3% to 5% of youths have substance use problems.

Figure 10.5   Binge Drinking Among Adolescents

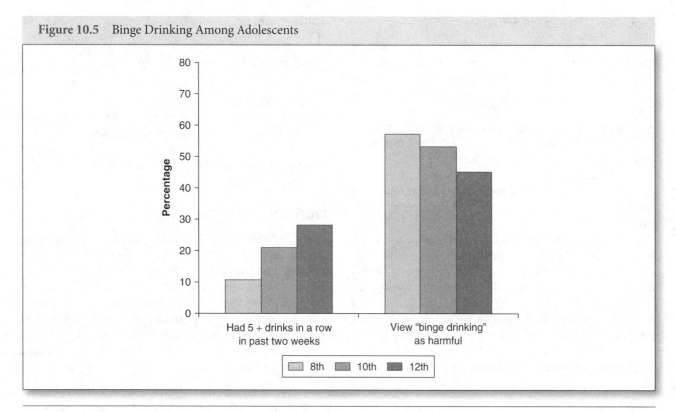

Source: From Johnston et al. (2006). Used with permission.

Note: Approximately 25% of twelfth graders binge drink. Although binge drinking carries serious risk, most older adolescents do not regard it as harmful.

Gender differences in the rates of Substance Use Disorders are less clear. Some research indicates that adolescent boys show greater prevalence of Substance Use Disorders than girls. For example, approximately 30% of adolescent boys report binge drinking compared to only about 22% of adolescent girls (Johnston et al., 2005).

The presentation of substance use problems is different for adolescent boys and girls (Andrews, 2005; Hsieh & Hollister, 2004). Boys with substance use problems are more likely than girls to show comorbid disruptive behavior. Boys with Substance Use Disorders show high rates of impulsivity, aggression, and antisocial behaviors. They are also more likely than girls to experience legal problems associated with their substance use. For boys, Substance Use Disorders usually reflect a more general problem with conduct and antisocial behavior.

Girls with substance use problems often report greater emotional disturbance than boys. These girls often show comorbid problems with depression, anxiety, and physical complaints. Girls with substance use problems are also more likely than boys to have histories of family problems and sexual abuse.

Ethnicity

Substance use differs by ethnicity (Wagner & Austin, 2006). Native American youths show the highest rates of substance use disorders overall, followed by white and Hispanic

adolescents. Native American and white adolescents also begin using alcohol and other drugs at earlier ages and may show greater comorbid psychiatric problems than most other ethnic minorities living in the United States (Abbott, 2007).

African American and Asian American adolescents show the lowest rates of substance use problems. The low prevalence of substance use problems among African American adolescents is remarkable because African American adolescents are disproportionately exposed to risk factors associated with Substance Use Disorders, such as low SES (Gil, Vega, & Turner, 2002). It is possible that certain aspects of African American culture somehow protect these youths from developing substance use problems. For example, involvement in extended family kinships or church activities may buffer African American youths against the potentially harmful effects of socioeconomic hardship.

Hispanic American adolescents usually show prevalence rates somewhere between those of white and African American adolescents (see Figure 10.7). However, Hispanic American adolescents show the greatest use of certain "hard" drugs, such as cocaine and heroin. Furthermore, Hispanic American adolescents born in the United States show greater rates of drug abuse and dependence than Hispanic American adolescents born in other countries (Vega, Gil, & Wagner, 1998). Among foreign-born adolescents, acculturation and ethnic identity seem to influence their likelihood of using alcohol and other drugs.

Figure 10.6   Gender Differences in Substance Use

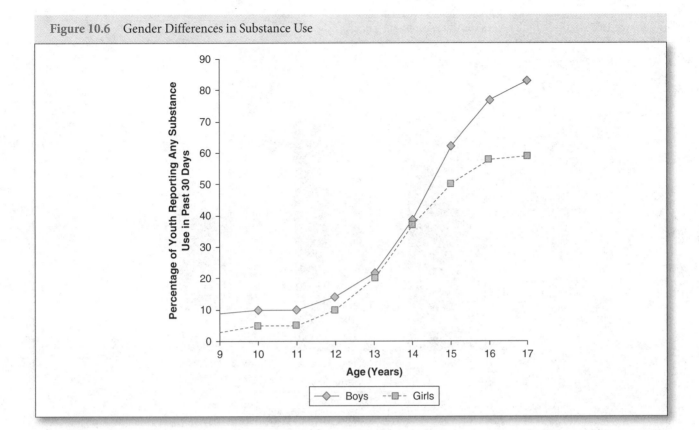

Source: Based on Sambrano, Springer, Sale, Kasim, and Hermann (2005).

Note: Boys tend to use alcohol and other drugs at slightly earlier ages than girls.

Course

Adolescents tend to use substances in an orderly, predictable fashion (Kandel, Yamaguchi, & Chen, 1992). Among adolescents who use alcohol and other drugs, a typical pattern of use begins in late childhood with cigarettes. Then, sometime during adolescence, youths may begin to use alcohol and try marijuana. Some individuals subsequently try other illicit drugs, such as stimulants or prescription medications. This progression from "soft" to hard drugs has led some people to suggest that marijuana is a "gateway drug" that introduces youths to other illicit substances.

Evidence supporting the **gateway hypothesis** is limited. On the one hand, longitudinal data indicate that the vast majority of adolescents who abuse stimulants and prescription medications have also used cigarettes, alcohol, and marijuana. On the other hand, most adolescents who use cigarettes, alcohol, and marijuana *do not* use other illicit substances. We might conclude, therefore, that the abuse of hard drugs is almost always dependent on the use of cigarettes, alcohol, and marijuana; however, use of these softer drugs does not imply an escalation to other illicit substances (Tucker, Ellickson, Orlando, Martino, & Klein, 2005).

Why do most youths stop at alcohol and marijuana while some youths progress to using other illicit substances?

Recent longitudinal studies have shed some light on this question (Stice, Kirz, & Borbely, 2002; Wagner & Austin, 2006). At least three factors seem to predict escalation in substance use. First, adolescents with histories of impulsive and disruptive behavior are more likely to escalate their use of alcohol and other drugs and develop Substance Use Disorders. Their substance use may be part of a larger problem with disruptive and antisocial activity. Second, adolescents whose parents model excessive substance use in the home are at increased risk of developing substance use problems. Parents who drink or use other drugs to excess may provide adolescents with access to these substances and model their use. Third, and most important, friends' use of alcohol and other drugs strongly predicts the adolescents' likelihood of escalated substance use. Peers introduce adolescents to illicit substances then model and reinforce their use (Kessler, Berglund, Dernier, Jin, & Walters, 2005; O'Brien et al., 2005).

Adolescents who develop Substance Use Disorders are at risk for a host of deleterious outcomes. First, substances carry direct risks to adolescents' health. For example, excessive use of alcohol can cause transient illness, impairment in cognitive functioning, and, in rare cases, coma and death. Substance use can also place adolescents in hazardous situations. For example, adolescents who binge drink may drive while intoxicated,

Figure 10.7   Ethnic Differences in Adolescent Substance Use

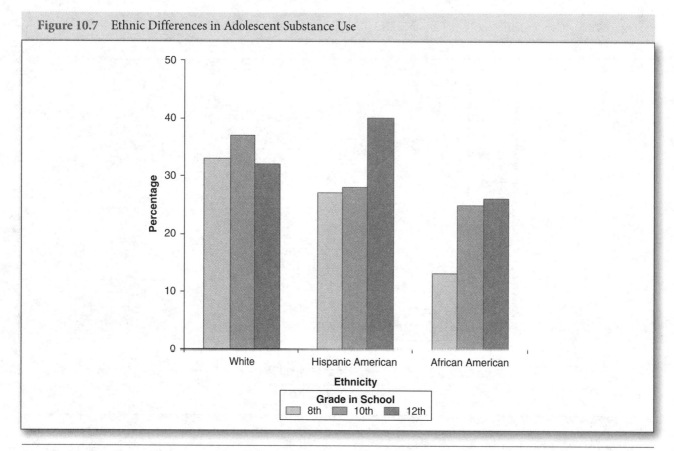

Source: From Johnston et al. (2006). Used with permission.

Note: White adolescents show the highest rates of problematic drinking and marijuana use, while African American adolescents show the lowest prevalence. Hispanic adolescents tend to show slightly higher use of so-called hard drugs.

practice risky sexual behavior, or engage in aggressive or anti-social activity. Substance use also carries psychosocial risks. Adolescents with substance use problems show increased conflict and decreased communication with parents, greater likelihood of school-related problems and academic difficulties, and poorer peer relationships. Certainly, problems with family, school, and peers are partly responsible for adolescents' substance use. However, adolescents who use alcohol and other drugs likely exacerbate these social difficulties and compound their substance use problems (Tucker et al., 2005).

What happens to adolescents who use alcohol and other drugs after they finish high school? Recent data indicate that the risk for developing chronic substance use problems increases dramatically after adolescents leave high school, regardless of whether they drop out of high school, graduate and enter the workforce, or graduate and attend college (White, Labouvie, & Papadaratsakis, 2005). Risk for problematic substance use peaks between the ages of 18 and 22 years. By age 25 years, there is usually a dramatic decline in substance use and misuse, especially among people who attended college. This decrease in substance use with age is probably caused by young adults entering the workforce, assuming more adult-like responsibilities, marrying, and

having children (Rohrbach, Sussman, Dent, & Sun, 2005; White et al., 2006).

Substance use problems during adolescence can have negative effects on psychosocial functioning in adulthood. Most adolescents who use alcohol and other drugs during adolescence *do not* continue to show substance use problems as adults, especially if the onset of their substance use was in later adolescence. However, some adolescents, especially those who begin using substances before age 14 years, show long-term substance use problems. These adolescents are also likely to display lower levels of social competence, decreased employment, and increased likelihood of depression and criminal behavior (Caspi, Harrington, Moffitt, & Milne, 2002; Chassin, Pitts, & DeLucia, 1999).

ETIOLOGY

The development of Substance Use Disorders is complex. A model that explains the emergence of substance use problems must take into account a wide range of genetic, biological, psychological, and social-cultural factors. One biopsychosocial model has been offered by Sher (1991) to explain the development of alcohol use problems. Sher's model suggests that alcohol use disorders can emerge along three possible developmental pathways. First, alcohol problems can develop when people inherit a genetic or biological sensitivity to the effects of alcohol and derive a great deal of pleasure from its use (the enhanced reinforcement pathway). Second, alcohol abuse can arise when people rely on alcohol to cope with depression or anxiety. In this case, alcohol use is negatively reinforced by the alleviation of psychological distress (the negative affect pathway). Third, alcohol abuse can emerge as part of a larger pattern of antisocial behavior. In this pathway, alcohol use problems emerge in the context of CD (the deviance-prone pathway).

These three pathways to substance use problems are not mutually exclusive; many people abuse alcohol and other drugs for multiple reasons. However, these pathways are useful for organizing our understanding of the etiology of Substance Use Disorders (Chassin, Ritter, Trim, & King, 2003).

Enhanced Reinforcement Pathway

Genetic Diathesis

At the beginning of all three pathways lies a biological diathesis toward developing Substance Use Disorders (see Figure 10.8). Considerable research has shown an association between problematic substance use in parents and the development of Substance Use Disorders in their offspring. Approximately two thirds of adolescents who show substance use problems have at least one biological parent with a history of Substance Use Disorders (Winters, Stinchfield, Opland, Weller, & Latimer, 2000). Substance Use Disorders are especially common among biological fathers (Henggeler et al., 1996).

Having a parent with a history of Substance Use Disorders increases one's likelihood of developing a Substance Use Disorder two- to ninefold (Chassin et al., 2003). Twin and family studies indicate that this association between parent and child substance use is at least partially heritable, with 60% of the variance of alcohol use and 33% of other drug use attributable to genetics (Han, McGue, & Iacono, 1999). Genetic factors predict the likelihood of using alcohol and other drugs, the age at which people first begin using substances, and the overall probability of a Substance Use Disorder (McGue, Pickens, & Svikis, 1992).

Positive Expectations and Pleasurable Effects

Although having a parent with a Substance Use Disorder places the child at risk for future substance use problems, the mechanism by which biological diathesis leads to Substance Use Disorders is not known. The enhanced reinforcement pathway assumes that biological diathesis makes offspring unusually sensitive to the pharmacological effects of the substance. For example, individuals who have this biological diathesis may respond more intensely to the effects of alcohol, may experience more pleasure from drinking, or may

have fewer negative side effects from drinking excessively (Zuckerman, 2007).

At the same time, as adolescents experiment with alcohol and other drugs, they learn about the effects of these substances on their behavioral, social, and emotional functioning. Eventually, they come to expect substances to be beneficial. As use increases, the substances assume reinforcing properties by either bringing about pleasure (i.e., positive reinforcement) or alleviating distress or boredom (i.e., negative reinforcement).

A biological sensitivity to the effects of the substance and an expectation that the substance will have positive effects can lead to problematic use. For example, adolescents at risk for Substance Use Disorders often have unusually positive expectations for substance use; that is, they expect substances to produce a great number of benefits with few drawbacks (van Voorst & Quirk, 2003). Indeed, distorted beliefs in the positive effects of alcohol can increase the frequency or amount of drinking (Barnow et al., 2004; Kirisci, Tarter, Vanyukov, Reynolds, & Habeych, 2004). In contrast, adolescents who have negative experiences with alcohol and other drugs or adolescents who are anxious about substance use, are less likely to develop substance use problems.

Negative Affect Pathway

Individuals can also develop substance use problems in response to stress and negative affect (see Figure 10.8). Stress can arise from negative early childhood experiences, such as growing up in an abusive or neglectful home. Stress can also be caused by later environmental factors, such as witnessing marital conflict, experiencing disruptions in family and interpersonal relationships, or encountering school-related difficulties (Bond, Toumbourou, Thomas, Catalano, & Patton, 2005; A. M. Libby et al., 2004; A. M. Libby, Orton, Stover, & Riggs, 2005). These stressors, in turn, can cause anxiety, depression, and low self-worth. Adolescents who are unable to cope with these negative emotions may use alcohol and other drugs to alleviate psychological distress. Substance use, therefore, is negatively reinforced by the reduction of anxiety and depression. Over time, substance use can increase and lead to abuse (K. G. Anderson, Ramo, & Brown, 2006).

The stress and negative affect pathway has not enjoyed widespread empirical support as an explanation for substance use problems among adolescents. Most cross-sectional studies show only moderate associations between adolescents' ratings of negative affect and their alcohol use. Furthermore, most longitudinal studies have shown that adolescents' symptoms of depression and anxiety usually *do not* precede the emergence of their substance use problems. Instead, some data indicate the opposite effect: Adolescent substance use often leads to social and academic problems that elicit depression and anxiety. When mood and anxiety problems predict later substance use, the relationship between mood and substance use is usually weak (S. M. King et al., 2004)

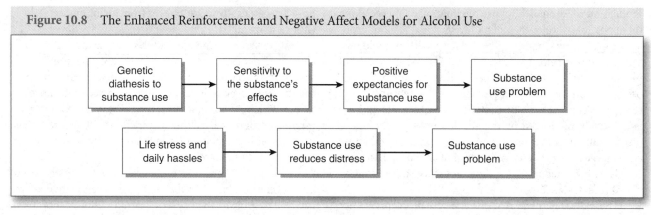

Source: From Sher (1991). Used with permission.

or attributable to other factors such as disruptive behavior problems (Bardone et al., 1998; Goodman & Capitman, 2000; Goodwin, Lieb et al., 2004; Patton et al., 2002; Rao, Daley, & Hammen, 2000).

On the other hand, recent data indicate that the stress and negative affect model might apply to a subset of adolescents who experienced child maltreatment (Libby et al., 2005; B. A. Miller & Mancuso, 2004). Physically abused boys and sexually abused girls show increased likelihood of developing mood problems associated with their victimization. They may rely on alcohol and other drugs to cope with these mood problems.

Furthermore, specific mood and anxiety disorders may place children at risk for substance use problems. For example, adolescents who experience extreme anxiety in social situations often use alcohol to cope with anticipatory anxiety. These adolescents might drink *before* going to a party, in order to relax. Their repeated alcohol use can lead to abuse (Merikangas, 2005). Adolescents with Bipolar Spectrum Disorder also show greater likelihood of developing substance use problems (Wilens et al., 2004).

Finally, the stress and negative affect pathway might apply to youths from affluent families. Suburban children living in affluent households may use alcohol and other drugs to cope with depression and anxiety. Furthermore, affluent adolescent boys use alcohol to gain social standing with peers. Luthar and Latendresse (2005) suggest that affluent adolescents lead overly scheduled lives and experience considerable pressure to excel academically, athletically, and socially. At the same time, their parents are often less involved in their lives because of career and social demands. This combination of high stress and low parental supervision places affluent youths at risk.

Deviance-Prone Pathway

The deviance-prone pathway offers a third explanation for the development of adolescent substance use problems (Chassin et al., 2003). According to this model, adolescent substance use is part of a much larger problem with general antisocial behavior (see Figure 10.9).

Consequently, the causes of adolescent substance use problems are similar to the causes of other disruptive behavior problems. These causes include early problems with neurobehavioral inhibition, cognitive and academic delays, peer rejection, and low parental monitoring.

Neurobehavioral Disinhibition

Young children who show neurobehavioral disinhibition are at increased risk for developing substance use problems later in life (Tarter et al., 2003; Zuckerman, 2007). **Neurobehavioral disinhibition** is characterized by three features: (a) behavioral undercontrol, (b) emotional reactivity, and (c) deficits in executive functioning.

First, children with behavioral undercontrol show high-rate, risky, and impulsive behaviors (Elkins, King, McGue, & Iacono, 2006). These children have a strong need for excitement and are often described as "sensation-seekers" or "daredevils." The tendency toward behavioral undercontrol is likely inherited; twin and family studies show strong heritability for risk-taking and sensation-seeking behavior (Iacono, Carlson, Taylor, Elkins, & McGue, 1999; Young, Stallings, Corley, Krauter, & Hewitt, 2000). Adults with Substance Use Disorders often display behavioral undercontrol, and they may genetically predispose their children to similar behaviors (King & Chassin, 2004). Indeed, behavioral undercontrol is a strong predictor of later disruptive behavior problems and substance use.

Second, children with neurobehavioral disinhibition display a high degree of emotional reactivity (Chassin et al., 1999). As young children, they display difficult temperaments. Their caregivers describe them as irritable and fussy. Later in childhood, these children often overreact to stress and display a tendency toward irritability, anger, and aggressive outbursts.

Third, children with neurobehavioral disinhibition show deficits in executive functioning (Kirisci, Vanyukov, & Tarter, 2005; Tarter, Kirisci, Habeych, Reynolds, & Vanyukov, 2004). Executive functioning refers to the cognitive processes

Figure 10.9 The Deviance-Prone Model for Alcohol Use

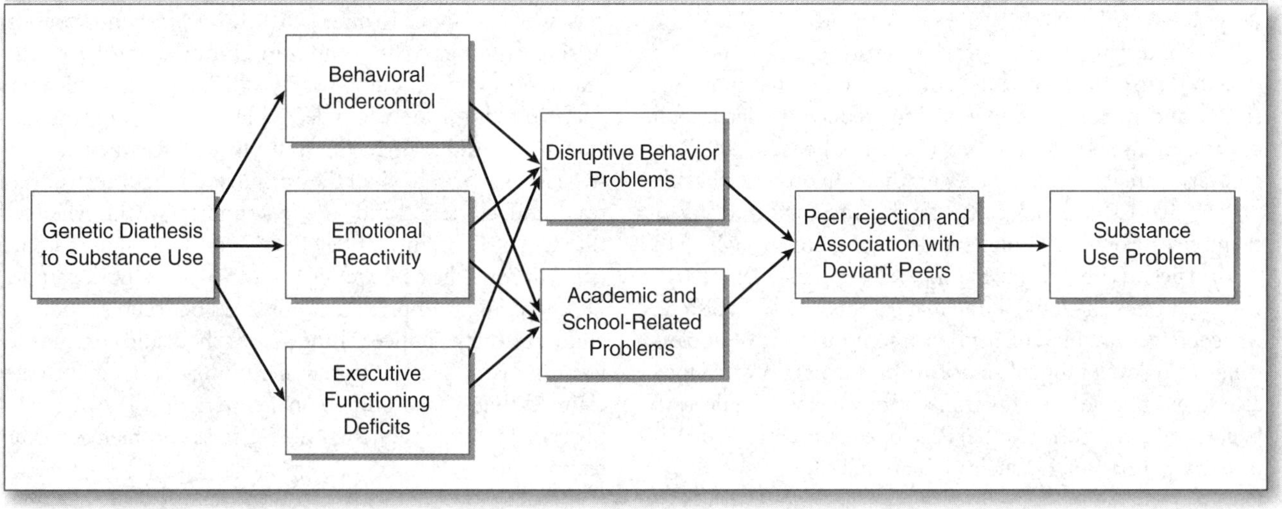

Source: From Sher (1991). Used with permission.

that allow children to inhibit immediate impulses, plan and prioritize behavior, and achieve long-term goals. Children with deficits in executive functioning display problems with inattention, hyperactivity, and impulsivity.

Academic and Peer Problems

According to the deviance-prone model, problems with neurobehavioral disinhibition can interfere with children's academic performance. Specifically, children who show problems with behavioral undercontrol may have difficulty attending to teachers and adhering to classroom rules. They may also have trouble staying on task in class and completing exams. Deficits in executive functioning can also interfere with children's abilities to complete assignments in a timely fashion, to plan and organize academic activities, and to accomplish long-term projects. Children with neurobehavioral disinhibition often have negative views of school, earn low grades, and struggle academically (Gau et al., 2007).

Problems with disinhibition can also affect children's interactions with peers. Peers often find these children's high-rate, disruptive behavior aversive. They may avoid interacting with them in the classroom and during recess. Furthermore, children who display emotional reactivity, especially aggression, are often rejected by peers.

Association With Deviant Peers

Academic problems and peer rejection can cause children to distance themselves from classmates and mainstream peer groups. Instead of associating with prosocial peers, these disruptive children associate with other rejected youths. Typically, rejected peers display similar histories of academic and disruptive behavior problems (Pearson et al., 2006).

Early substance use often occurs when deviant peers introduce children to alcohol and other drugs. Peers model substance use, encourage experimentation, and reinforce continued use over time. Rejected children might initially engage in substance use to gain acceptance into the deviant peer group. Over time, repeated use can lead to an exacerbation of social and academic problems and the development of Substance Use Disorders (Barnes, Hoffman, Welte, Farrell, & Dintcheff, 2006).

The relationship between deviant peers and substance use may be different for boys and girls. Some girls associate with deviant peers for the same reasons as boys: They are ostracized by prosocial peers because of their behavioral and academic problems. However, early pubertal maturation also increases the likelihood that girls will associate with deviant peers. Older boys, in particular, may introduce early-maturing girls to alcohol and other drugs, encourage antisocial behavior, and pressure them to engage in sexual activity. Despite their appearance, these early-developing girls may lack the maturity to resist social pressures. Indeed, early-developing girls show greater consumption of alcohol and other drugs than typically developing girls. Furthermore, they are more likely to develop substance use problems than their typically developing peers (Andrews, 2005).

Protective Factors

The association between academic and/or peer problems and children's substance use is moderated by parenting. Parents can affect their children's likelihood of developing substance use problems in two ways. First, children whose parents monitor their daily activities are less likely to develop substance use problems, regardless of their academic and peer status (Barnes et al., 2006). Parents who monitor their children provide fewer opportunities for their children to associate with deviant peers and experiment with alcohol and other drugs (Gau et al., 2007).

Second, parents who provide sensitive and responsive care to their children and discipline their children in a consistent and noncoercive manner can reduce the likelihood of their children's substance use (Parker & Benson, 2005). In contrast, parents who interact with their children in a hostile or coercive fashion can cause children to further distance themselves from the family and affiliate more strongly with deviant peers (Urberg, Luo, Pilgrim, & Degirmencioglu, 2003). King and Chassin (2004) found that parents' use of consistent, noncoercive discipline can protect some disruptive adolescents from developing substance use problems. However, they also found that adolescents with a strong genetic diathesis to behavioral undercontrol often developed Substance Use Disorders regardless of the quality of parental care.

TREATMENT
Primary Prevention Programs

Primary prevention programs target all youths, regardless of their risk status for developing a psychological disorder. Primary prevention programs generally fall into two categories: school-based programs and community-based programs.

D.A.R.E.

Drug Abuse Resistance Education, or D.A.R.E., is the best known school-based program designed to prevent substance use problems (Image 10.4). D.A.R.E. originated in Los Angeles in 1983. It was originally intended to increase contact between police and school-age children. The program consisted of weekly visits by uniformed police officers to fifth- and sixth-grade classrooms. Officers discussed the dangers of substance use, ways to avoid peer pressure to use alcohol and other drugs, and techniques to promote abstinence. It has since been expanded to elementary and junior high school classrooms across the United States.

Despite its popularity, D.A.R.E. does not appear to be effective in reducing alcohol and other drug use. The first meta-analysis of D.A.R.E., funded by the National Institute of Justice, revealed that children who did and did not participate in D.A.R.E. had equal rates of substance use by early adolescence (Ennett, Tobler, Ringwalt, & Flewelling, 1994). Other randomized controlled studies showed that D.A.R.E. produced increases in children's knowledge of substance use problems but did not cause changes in children's substance use (Clayton, Cattarello, & Johnstone, 1996; Dukes, Stein, & Ullman, 1997; Rosenbaum, Gordon, & Hanson, 1998).

Although D.A.R.E. is not effective in preventing alcohol use, nearly 80% of public schools in the United States continue to offer the program. Birkeland, Murphy-Graham, and Weis (2005) interviewed school and community officials who continued to offer D.A.R.E. despite being aware of its shortcomings. School and community leaders gave three reasons for continuing to use D.A.R.E. First, many leaders claimed that they never expected D.A.R.E. to prevent substance use problems in the first place; consequently, they were not surprised when they discovered that the program was ineffective. Second, many supporters acknowledged that D.A.R.E. might not be effective in reducing substance use, but it might be beneficial in other ways. For example, D.A.R.E. might improve relationships between school-age children and the police. Third, some school and community leaders dismissed the research findings altogether. They claimed that, based on personal experience, D.A.R.E. was highly effective at reducing substance use problems in their community.

Media Campaigns

Two national media campaigns have also targeted alcohol and other drug use among children and adolescents (O'Brien et al., 2005). Beginning in 1987, the Partnership for a Drug Free America (PDFA) produced television ads designed to provide substance abuse education to youths and their parents. Evaluation of the campaign indicated that it was successful in reaching a large number of families across the United States. Furthermore, the media campaign coincided with an overall decrease in substance use among American youths. Proponents of the program concluded that it was effective in preventing substance use problems. However, critics argued that the general decrease in substance use actually *preceded* the onset of the media campaign; therefore, it may be inappropriate to attribute this reduction in substance use to the campaign.

In the late 1990s, a second media campaign was conducted by the White House Office of National Drug Control Policy. This campaign resembled the PDFA campaign and consisted largely of television ads directed toward parents and children. The ads were designed to (a) increase parent-child communication about alcohol and other drugs, (b) increase parental monitoring of children's peer groups and after-school activities, (c) decrease children's positive beliefs and expectations about substance use, and (d) decrease youths' actual use of alcohol and other drugs.

An evaluation of the campaign demonstrated that the program reached a large number of families. It also increased parent-child communication about substance use. However, the campaign was largely unable to increase parental monitoring or decrease children's subsequent substance use. In fact, exposure to the media campaign was actually associated with an *increase* in children's intentions to use marijuana! It is possible that youths who were told to abstain from certain drugs, like marijuana, strongly resented these prohibitions. To exert their autonomy, they may have decided to use the drug.

Image 10.4 Fifth-grade students sit during a Drug Abuse Resistance Education (D.A.R.E.) graduation ceremony. Daren the Lion presents each student with a certificate, a T-shirt, and water bottle.

Source: Image courtesy of the U.S. government.

Overall, evaluations of school- and media-based prevention campaigns have not been encouraging. Nevertheless, policy makers will likely continue to implement these programs, despite limited evidence regarding their effectiveness. All too often, people form opinions and shape public policy based on anecdotal evidence rather than on carefully collected data (Birkeland et al., 2005). In the case of D.A.R.E., policy informed by anecdotal impressions and ideology alone seems to have resulted in a considerable loss of time and money. In the case of certain media campaigns, failure to evaluate outcomes may have caused an increase in the behavior the program was designed to prevent.

Secondary Prevention Programs

Secondary prevention programs are designed for youths at risk for developing substance use problems. Most secondary prevention programs are **ecologically based**; that is, they target at-risk youths in certain areas or neighborhoods (Pumariega, Rodriguez, & Kilgus, 2004). Programs are usually designed for middle-school students who are about to transition from childhood to early adolescence. Program developers reason that a successful transition from preadolescence to adolescence can protect youths from developing substance use problems.

Ecologically based prevention programs target multiple risk factors simultaneously. First, information is provided to adolescents about substance use and misuse. Adolescents are also taught techniques to avoid substance use with peers. Second, parents are taught about adolescent substance use problems and steps that they can take to decrease the likelihood that their adolescents will use alcohol and other drugs. Many programs emphasize the importance of improving parent-child communication, monitoring children's friends and activities, and setting clear but developmentally appropriate limits on children's behavior. Third, ecologically based programs address the child's larger social system: school, peers, and the community. Some programs offer after-school activities to promote abstinence to entire peer groups. Other programs work with community officials and police to limit adolescents' access to alcohol and other drugs.

Researchers evaluated the effectiveness of 48 secondary prevention programs using a sample of approximately 10,000 adolescents (Sambrano et al., 2005). Roughly half of the sample participated in a prevention program, while the remaining adolescents served as controls. Results of the evaluation were disappointing. Overall, adolescents who participated in the prevention programs did not differ in their alcohol and marijuana use compared to controls. However, when researchers looked at the data more carefully, they noticed that the programs that provided high-intensity, comprehensive services reduced substance use more among participants than controls. These findings indicate that all prevention programs are not equal. To be effective, prevention programs must target multiple risk factors in the adolescent's life and teach skills to avoid substances and develop positive relationships with peers.

Medication

Medication is often used in the treatment of Substance Use Disorders in adults (Bukstein & Deas, 2010). Furthermore, approximately 55% of adolescents who receive treatment for Substance Use Disorders are prescribed at least one medication (Clark, Wood, & Cornelius, 2003). Medication can be used in at least five ways.

First, **substitution therapy** involves administering a medication that is designed to eliminate cravings for alcohol or other drugs. For example, adults who are addicted to opioids, like heroin, might be prescribed methadone, a synthetic opioid that binds to receptors and produces mild analgesia and anxiety reduction. Adults can gradually wean off heroin with methadone as they participate in treatment. Similarly, adolescents might use nicotine replacement therapy to reduce their use of cigarettes.

Second, medication can be used during **detoxification** to help patients cope with withdrawal symptoms. For example, adults who are addicted to opioids might be prescribed clonidine, a medication that reduces heart rate, blood pressure, and physiological arousal. Clonidine can reduce some of the arousal symptoms associated with opioid withdrawal. Similarly, adolescents and adults who are addicted to alcohol might be prescribed benzodiazepines, medications that reduce anxiety and agitation. Benzodiazepines are often useful in reducing withdrawal symptoms.

Third, some clinicians use medications that **block the effects** of alcohol and other drugs, reducing their pleasurable consequences. For example, naltrexone is an opioid receptor antagonist which significantly reduces the euphoric effects of alcohol after it is consumed. Similarly, bupropion is an atypical antidepressant that affects dopamine and norepinephrine and blocks the pleasurable effects of nicotine.

Fourth, some physicians use medication as part of **aversion therapy**. For example, disulfiram (Antabuse) is a medication that prohibits alcohol from being metabolized. Several minutes after alcohol is consumed, the person experiences accelerated heart rate, shortness of breath, vomiting, nausea, and headache (i.e., symptoms of a hangover). This aversive reaction may help individuals decrease their alcohol consumption.

Fifth, and most commonly, medication is used to treat **comorbid disorders.** Double-blind, controlled studies have demonstrated that medication can be useful in alleviating depression (Riggs, Mikulich-Gilbertson, & Davies, 2007), Bipolar Disorder (Geller, Cooper, and Sun, 1998), and ADHD (Riggs, Hall, & Mikulich-Gilbertson, 2004) in adolescents with comorbid Alcohol Use Disorder. Unfortunately, medications used to treat these disorders seem to have little effect on alcohol consumption. It is also noteworthy that many psychotropic medications have potential for abuse themselves. For example, some adolescents with ADHD will sell stimulant medication used to treat their disorder, a practice known as "diversion." Alternatively, some psychostimulants can be crushed and ingested to produce euphoria and a rush of energy. Benzodiazepines have high potential for dependence given their antianxiety properties. Consequently, physicians, therapists, and parents must carefully monitor youths with Substance Use Disorders who are prescribed these medications.

Psychosocial Treatments

Psychotherapy is typically regarded as the treatment of choice for adolescents who show substance use problems. Overall, youths with Substance Use Disorders who participate in therapy experience better outcomes than youths who do not participate in therapy (Deas & Thomas, 2001). Psychosocial interventions are associated with reductions in substance use, criminal activities, and improvements in emotional and social functioning. In some studies, therapy is also associated with improvements in academic performance (Hser, Grella, & Hubbard, 2001; Williams, Chang, & Addiction Center Adolescent Research Group, 2000). Youths with more extensive substance use, youths with history of conduct problems, and youths with comorbid anxiety and depression are less responsive to treatment (Grella et al., 2001; Tomlinson, Brown, & Abrantes, 2004).

Despite its effectiveness, most youths with Substance Use Disorders never participate in psychotherapy. In one population-based study, 4.9% of adolescents in the United States (12–17 years) exhibited a significant alcohol or drug use problem that merited treatment. However, only 11.3% of these youths were referred to an inpatient or outpatient treatment program for their substance use problem (Substance Abuse and Mental Health Services Administration, 2007). Clearly, there is much work to be done in the identification and provision of services to youths with alcohol and other drug problems.

Inpatient Treatment and Twelve-Step Programs

Some adolescents with serious Substance Use Disorders participate in **28-day inpatient treatment** programs. Although inpatient treatment programs vary, most have three goals: (a) to attend to the adolescent's immediate medical needs and to detoxify her body, (b) to help the adolescent recognize the harmful effects of the substance on her health and functioning, and (c) to improve the quality of the adolescent's relationships with others.

To accomplish these goals, nearly all inpatient programs require adolescents to abstain from alcohol and other drug use during treatment. Staff members educate adolescents about the process of substance dependence and the physiological, psychological, and social effects of substance use. Inpatient programs typically provide individual and group therapy to adolescents. Staff members also offer family therapy sessions designed to improve parent-adolescent communication and problem solving. Before the end of treatment, staff members help the adolescent and family members prepare for a return to school and home.

Most inpatient programs incorporate twelve-step philosophies into their treatment package. **Twelve-step programs** include Alcoholics Anonymous (AA) and Narcotics Anonymous (NA). Proponents of these programs conceptualize alcohol and other drug use as a disease. From this perspective, Substance Use Disorders are medical conditions that develop because of genetics, are maintained because of biology and "brain chemistry," and deleteriously affect the person's social, emotional, and spiritual life. Proponents of twelve-step programs argue that individuals must first acknowledge that they have the disease and that they are powerless to overcome its effects.

Participants progress through a series of 12 steps designed to help them cope with their substance use and remain abstinent. At some point in their participation, they must recognize their inability to overcome their substance use problem, and they must surrender themselves to a "higher power." Indeed, they are taught to rely on spirituality and support from others to cope with urges to drink or use other drugs. Participants attend group meetings to gain the support of other people struggling with Substance Use Disorders. Each participant also selects a mentor who provides individual support and advice to help her maintain sobriety.

Twelve-step programs are the most frequently used means of treating Substance Use Disorders in the United States. Typically, twelve-step programs are initiated during inpatient treatment. After the individual completes inpatient treatment, he or she is encouraged to continue participating in twelve-step programs in the community. Very often, individuals participate in twelve-step group meetings while simultaneously meeting with an individual therapist.

Twelve-step programs have demonstrated efficacy among adults with substance use problems. However, less information is available regarding the efficacy of twelve-step treatment for adolescents (Elliott, Orr, Watson, & Jackson, 2005). Twelve-step programs that are administered as part of inpatient treatment tend to be highly effective, probably because adolescents are living in controlled environments with limited opportunities for substance use. Some participants are able to maintain treatment gains 6 to 12 months after program completion (Winters et al., 2000). However, adolescents released from these inpatient programs have high rates of relapse. Approximately 60% relapse within 3 months of discharge and as many as 80% relapse within one year (Kaminer & Bukstein, 2005).

Cognitive-Behavioral Therapies

Cognitive-behavioral therapy (CBT) for Substance Use Disorders has gained considerable popularity in recent years (Waldron & Kaminer, 2004). Practitioners of CBT view problematic substance use as a learned behavior that is acquired and maintained in four ways.

First, people often learn to use alcohol and other drugs through *operant conditioning*. For example, alcohol can be positively reinforcing to the extent that it gives people a subjective sense of satisfaction and well-being or enhances enjoyment during social interactions. Alcohol can also be negatively reinforcing to the extent that it reduces tension or alleviates pain. Over time, the reinforcing properties of alcohol lead to increased use.

Second, through *classical conditioning*, people learn to associate substance use with certain situations or mood states. For example, an adolescent might use marijuana with a certain group of friends. He discovers that smoking with these friends allows him to relax and have a good time. Through classical conditioning, he associates this group of friends with marijuana use. In the future, these friends might serve as a trigger or "stimulus cue" for him to use again.

Third, substance use is often maintained through *social learning*. Specifically, family members sometimes model substance use. Adolescents might view substance use as an acceptable means to cope with stress or facilitate social interactions. Similarly, peers often model and reinforce drug and alcohol use, communicating that to gain social approval, drug and alcohol use is not only acceptable but also expected.

Fourth, adolescents' *beliefs* mediate the relationship between events that trigger substance use and consumption of alcohol and other drugs (J. S. Beck, Liese, & Najavits, 2005). Strictly speaking, events do not cause people to use substances; rather, people's interpretations and thoughts about events lead to either substance use or abstinence. Adolescents often hold distorted beliefs about situations that prompt their substance use (see Figure 10.10). These distorted beliefs elicit drinking or other drug use.

Figure 10.10 Cognitive Model for Adolescent Alcohol Use

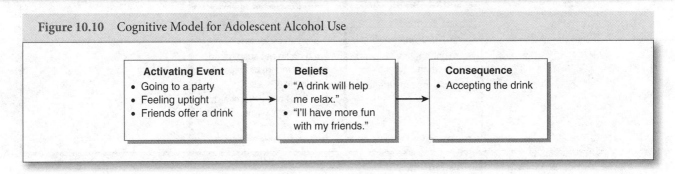

Note: Cognitions mediate the relationship between events and people's overt behavior. Adolescents who believe that alcohol will facilitate social interactions or help them have more fun are more likely to drink than adolescents who believe that alcohol will not produce pleasurable effects.

To understand the way beliefs mediate the relationship between events and behavior, consider the following example. Sam is a shy tenth grader who has been invited to a party. When his friends pick him up to go to the party, they offer him some beer to help him relax. Sam's decision to drink or abstain will depend largely on his thoughts about the situation. Beliefs, such as "Having a couple of drinks will help me relax and get into a good mood," will increase his likelihood of accepting the drink. Alternatively, beliefs, such as "I'll be OK without the drink; Jim isn't having any," may lead him to decline the drink.

The techniques used in CBT target each of the four ways substance use problems develop and are maintained: (a) operant conditioning, (b) classical conditioning, (c) social learning, and (d) ways of thinking. First, the therapist asks the adolescent to monitor her substance use and note environmental factors or mood states that precede substance use. For example, an adolescent might discover that she only drinks when she is nervous before or during a party. With this information, the therapist and adolescent try to find ways for her to avoid feelings that trigger alcohol use. The adolescent might decide to ask a friend to go to parties with her so that she does not experience as much anticipatory anxiety.

Second, the therapist encourages the adolescent to consider the consequences of her substance use. Specifically, the therapist and adolescent might conduct a **cost-benefit analysis** of using alcohol or other drugs (see Figure 10.11). For example, the adolescent might list certain benefits of drinking before attending a party: It helps her relax; it allows her to have a good time. However, these benefits might be overshadowed by potential drawbacks: She drinks too much and gets sick; she feels guilty afterward; her parents become angry.

Third, to help adolescents avoid substance use, therapists teach their clients specific skills to reduce the reinforcing effects of alcohol. The skills that they teach depend largely on the adolescents' reasons for using. Adolescents who consume alcohol to reduce anxiety before a party might benefit from relaxation or social skills training. If they felt more relaxed or confident before the party, they might experience less desire to drink. Adolescents who drink in order to gain peer acceptance might be taught alcohol refusal skills. During the session, the therapist and adolescent might generate and practice ways to refuse alcohol when peers offer it.

Fourth, most cognitive-behavioral therapists examine the beliefs that adolescents have about substances and challenge distorted cognitions that lead to problematic use. Many adolescents overestimate the benefits of alcohol and dismiss its potentially harmful effects. An adolescent might reason, "It's fun to get wasted with my friends; we always have a great time." The therapist might encourage the adolescent to look at his alcohol use more objectively, by considering the negative consequences of use.

Similarly, an adolescent might overestimate the frequency with which peers use alcohol and other drugs, claiming, "I drink about as much as everybody else." In response, the therapist might share data regarding typical alcohol use among adolescents of the same age and gender. Consider the following transcript of a therapy session:

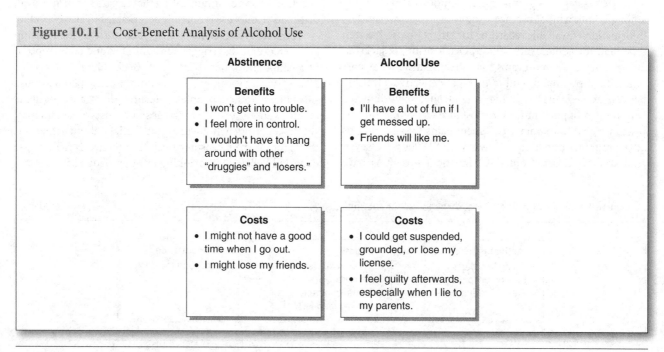

Figure 10.11   Cost-Benefit Analysis of Alcohol Use

Abstinence

Benefits
- I won't get into trouble.
- I feel more in control.
- I wouldn't have to hang around with other "druggies" and "losers."

Costs
- I might not have a good time when I go out.
- I might lose my friends.

Alcohol Use

Benefits
- I'll have a lot of fun if I get messed up.
- Friends will like me.

Costs
- I could get suspended, grounded, or lose my license.
- I feel guilty afterwards, especially when I lie to my parents.

Source: Based on J. S. Beck et al. (2005).

Note: Cognitive-behavioral therapists often ask adolescents to consider the pros and cons of (a) abstinence and (b) continued drinking.

CHALLENGING DISTORTED THOUGHTS ABOUT DRINKING

Therapist: We've been talking for quite a while, and I've noticed that you put a lot of pressure on yourself to drink when you're hanging out.

Adam: Well, sort of. It's more like the other guys put a lot of pressure on me. I'm fine when I'm with them most of the time. It just gets a little hard when I go to parties or things like that.

Therapist: So, when you go to one of these parties, what's it like?

Adam: Well, I usually see a lot of my friends and the other kids from school. They look like they're drinking and having a good time. It's like they expect me to drink too. And I want to have a good time, too—to have fun. I also don't want to let them down and ruin their fun.

Therapist: You mean if you don't drink, you might be ruining their good time?

Adam: Yeah, I guess. I just think that they'd think, "What's the matter with him. Doesn't he want to have fun? Does he think he's better than the rest of us?" It makes me nervous.

Therapist: And *how do you know* that's what's going through their minds? What's the evidence?

Adam: I don't know. I can just tell, you know. I get real nervous about the situation, and I can just tell that's what they're thinking.

Therapist: It sounds to me like you're reasoning with your emotions, not with your head. This can sometimes get us into a lot of trouble and cause us to feel nervous. Let's see if we can look at the situation a little more objectively. Was everyone else at the party drinking?

Adam: Yeah, most people.

Therapist: But not everyone?

Adam: No, there were a few guys who weren't drinking.

Therapist: Did the other kids make fun of these other guys?

Adam: No. Everyone was OK with it.

Therapist: And did you think these kids (who didn't drink) were somehow weird or strange or better than you?

Adam: No. I guess I didn't think anything of it. Everyone just wanted to have a good time.

Therapist: So no one at the party was really interested in who drank and who didn't. They were more interested in having fun themselves.

Adam: Yeah. I guess so, now that I think about it.

Within the past 10 years, a number of randomized controlled studies involving adolescents with substance use problems have shown CBT to be efficacious (Patterson & O'Connell, 2003). Adolescents who participate in CBT show greater reductions in substance use than adolescents who receive individual supportive therapy, group therapy, or information about substance use problems alone (Kaminer, Blitz, Burleson, Sussman, & Rounsaville, 1998; Kaminer et al., 2002; Waldron et al., 2001).

Motivational Enhancement Therapy

Another method of treatment involves **motivational enhancement therapy**, sometimes referred to as "motivational interviewing" (Tevyaw & Monti, 2004). The primary goal of motivational enhancement therapy is to increase the adolescent's desire to reduce his alcohol consumption. Practitioners of motivational enhancement therapy recognize that most adolescents are referred to therapy by parents, teachers, or other adults; rarely do adolescents seek treatment themselves. Consequently, adolescents usually have low motivation to participate in treatment and less motivation to change their drinking habits.

Practitioners of motivational enhancement therapy help adolescents increase their willingness to change (Figure 10.12). Adolescents progress through a series of steps, or **stages of change,** as they move from a state of low motivation to change to a state of high readiness to change (Prochaska, DiClemente, & Norcross, 1992). The stages are

Figure 10.12 Practitioners of Motivational Enhancement Therapy Help Adolescents Increase Their Willingness to Change

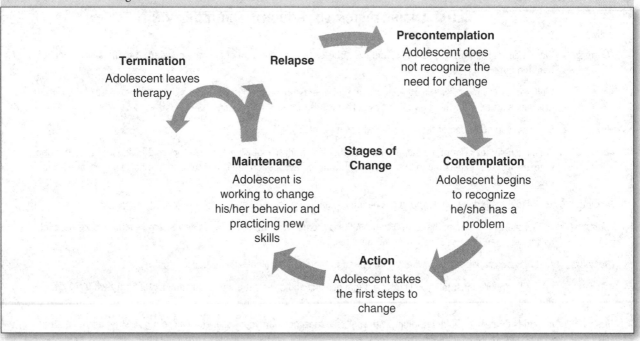

Source: Based on Prochaska, DiClemente, and Norcross (1992).

Note: Adolescents progress through a series of steps, or stages of change, as they move from a state of low motivation to change to a state of high motivation to change.

precontemplation (not recognizing that their alcohol use is a problem), contemplation (considering the possibility that their alcohol use is problematic), action (making initial steps to change, such as making an appointment with a therapist), and maintenance (avoiding relapse).

To increase the adolescent's motivation to change, the therapist uses five principles of motivational interviewing (Miller & Rollnick, 2002). First, she approaches the adolescent in an accepting and nonjudgmental way. The therapist *expresses empathy, warmth, and genuine concern* for the adolescent and avoids signs that she disapproves of the adolescent's alcohol use or disagrees with his attitudes about drinking. She actively listens to the adolescent's point of view in order to accurately understand his perspective. The therapist's initial goal is to understand and accept the adolescent, not to persuade him to adopt others' beliefs about drinking. Second, the therapist *develops discrepancies* between the adolescent's short- and long-term goals and his current alcohol use. For instance, the therapist might surmise that athletic achievement is important to the adolescent. She might ask him whether drinking, which jeopardizes his eligibility to compete, is consistent with his goal to be a star athlete. Third, the therapist *rolls with resistance and avoids argumentation.* If the adolescent becomes defensive, angry, or avoidant, the therapist assumes it is because she is not adequately understanding and appreciating the adolescent's perspective. Fourth, the therapist *supports any commitment*

to change, no matter how small. The therapist sees herself as being "in the adolescent's corner," that is, supporting and encouraging his decisions regardless of whether they agree with her own. For example, the therapist might support the adolescent's decision to cut back on his drinking, even if this falls short of complete abstinence. Fifth, the therapist promotes the adolescent's *self-efficacy*, by pointing out successful change no matter how small (Figure 10.13).

Practitioners of motivational enhancement therapy usually do not see abstinence as the primary goal of therapy. Instead, these practitioners often adopt a **harm reduction** approach to treatment (Miller, Turner, & Marlatt, 2001). According to the harm reduction perspective, the primary goal of therapy is to help adolescents identify and avoid alcohol use that has great potential for harm. For example, the therapist might support the adolescent's decision to drink fewer than four beers at a party, even if this decision might not make the adolescent's parents very happy. Any reduction in alcohol use that decreases risk or harm to the adolescent is viewed as successful.

Some people question the ethics of using a harm reduction approach with adolescents under 18 years of age (Bukstein & Deas, 2010). After all, is it appropriate for therapists to support an adolescent's decision to engage in an illegal behavior? Although ethical questions like these cannot easily be answered, we should consider three points. First, therapists who adopt a harm reduction perspective must obtain

Figure 10.13   Principles of Motivational Interviewing

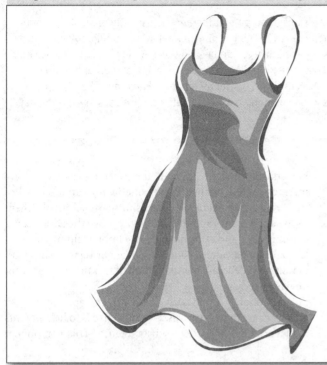

Develop a discrepancy between goals and current behavior.

Roll with resistance; don't argue.

Express empathy, warmth, and concern through active listening.

Support the client's efforts to change, no matter how small.

Success should be acknowledged to build the client's self-efficacy.

parental consent prior to treatment. Although adolescents have basic rights to autonomy and self-determination, parents have the ultimate responsibility for their children's welfare and development. The therapist cannot ethically proceed with a harm reduction approach to therapy without parental consent. Second, most therapists who adopt a harm reduction perspective would probably argue that abstinence is the *ideal* goal of therapy. To the extent that abstinence has low probability, any reduction in alcohol use can be seen as beneficial. Finally, practitioners need to consider empirical data, in addition to personal beliefs, when they judge the merits of a harm reduction approach to treatment. If harm reduction works and clinicians do not use it, can they defend their practice?

Emerging data indicate that motivational enhancement therapy can be effective for high school students at risk for substance use problems. In two studies, adolescents who presented to a hospital emergency department because of an alcohol-related event were randomly assigned to either one session of motivational enhancement therapy or usual care. At 6-month follow-up, adolescents who participated in motivational enhancement therapy showed lower rates of alcohol-related problems and injuries than controls. Furthermore, adolescents with the lowest motivation to change before treatment showed the greatest benefits from their participation in treatment (Monti et al., 1999; Monti, Barnett, O'Leary, & Colby, 2001).

Two additional studies examined the efficacy of motivational enhancement among high school students who frequently used alcohol and marijuana (Grenard, Ames, Wiers, Thush, Stacy, & Sussman, 2007; McCambridge & Strang, 2004). Adolescents received either one session of motivational enhancement therapy or no intervention. Three months later, adolescents who participated in motivational enhancement therapy showed significant reductions in alcohol and marijuana use. Furthermore, reductions were greatest among adolescents who showed the most frequent use before treatment (see Figure 10.14).

CASE STUDY

ERICA'S TREATMENT

Erica met diagnostic criteria for Alcohol Use Disorder of mild severity. Erica was at particular risk for more severe and long-standing substance use problems because her friends often encouraged her to drink at parties and her parents did not monitor her behavior.

(Continued)

Her therapist, Randy, continued to meet with Erica for 12 sessions of outpatient therapy. He used the principles of motivational enhancement therapy to help Erica increase her readiness to change her drinking behavior. Both Randy and Erica agreed that it was probably unrealistic for her to avoid drinking at parties altogether. However, Randy helped Erica weigh the benefits of drinking (e.g., having fun) with the potential costs of earning lower grades in school and getting arrested.

Erica completed mandated therapy and community service. Several months after termination, Erica called Randy to thank him for being her counselor. Apparently, one of Erica's friends was injured in an alcohol-related car accident. "I suppose that could have just as easily been me," said Erica.

Family Therapies

The most extensively studied treatment for adolescent substance use problems is **family therapy** (Hogue, Dauber, Samuolis, & Liddle, 2006; Liddle, 2004). Practitioners of family therapy view adolescent substance use as a family problem. The causes of adolescent substance abuse must be understood in light of the adolescent's family and her surrounding social system. Consequently, family therapists are interested in how the adolescent's relationships with parents, home environment, and school influence her substance use. Since all three ecological factors are interconnected, change in any one factor can affect all of the others. For example, increasing parents' involvement in the adolescent's activities could improve the adolescent's commitment and attitude toward school. Helping the adolescent manage anger could enhance her relationship with parents and decrease her likelihood of seeking support from deviant peers.

Although the tactics used by family therapists vary, they usually share two objectives. One objective is to help parents manage their adolescent's substance use. This component

Figure 10.14 Efficacy of Motivational Enhancement Therapy for Adolescents With Alcohol or Marijuana Use Problems

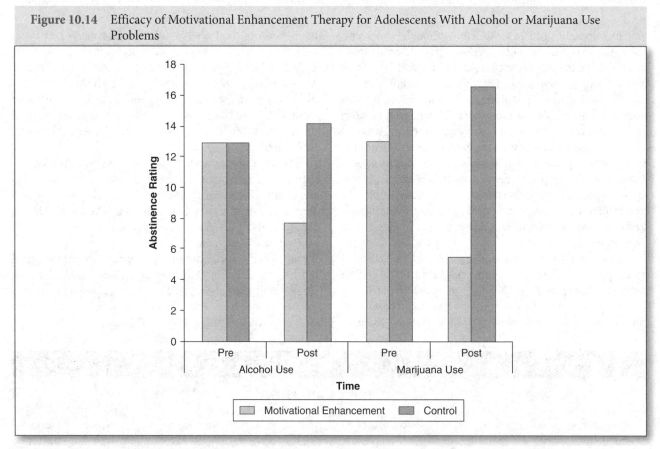

Source: Based on McCambridge and Strang (2004).

Note: Individuals in the treatment group received only one session of motivational enhancement. Three months later, they were less likely to use drugs than adolescents who served as controls.

of treatment typically involves education about normal and atypical adolescent development, the causes and consequences of adolescent substance abuse, and the role parents play in their adolescent's alcohol use. Therapists usually stress the importance of placing developmentally appropriate limits on adolescents' behavior, disciplining adolescents in a manner that is fair and consistent, and monitoring adolescents' activities.

The second objective of family therapy is to improve the quality of family functioning. Typically, therapists meet with adolescents and parents together and observe the quality of family interactions. Most therapists are chiefly interested in patterns of communication among family members. For example, some families avoid direct confrontation with each other and rarely talk about topics that make them angry, worried, or upset. Other families show frequent emotional outbursts and criticism toward each other, behaviors that often leave family members feeling isolated or rejected. Therapists often point out these communication patterns and teach family members to use different, more effective strategies (Hogue et al., 2006).

Family therapists are usually interested in the way parents and adolescents solve problems. They want to know how parents balance the adolescent's needs for autonomy with their desire to direct their adolescent's activities. Some parents adopt authoritarian practices that deny adolescents appropriate self-determination. Excessive parental control can cause adolescents to defy parental commands. Other parents are overly permissive. These parents place too few constraints on their adolescents' activities. Permissive parenting increases adolescents' opportunities to associate with deviant peers (Hogue et al., 2006).

One type of family therapy that has been used for adolescents with substance use problems is **multidimensional family therapy** (MDFT; Liddle, Dakof et al., 2001). MDFT targets four dimensions of family functioning that are relevant to the adolescent's well-being: (a) the adolescent's substance use, (b) the caregiving practices of the adolescent's parents, (c) the quality of the parent-adolescent relationship, and (d) other social factors that can influence the adolescent's substance use, such as his peer relationships or involvement in school.

MDFT involves a series of individual sessions with the adolescent, individual sessions with the parents, and combined family sessions over the course of several months. Individual sessions with the adolescent focus on increasing the adolescent's social skills and involvement with prosocial peers, helping the adolescent recognize and manage negative emotions, and reducing the adolescent's contact with deviant peer groups.

Individual sessions with parents include teaching parents about the causes of adolescent Substance Use Disorders, outlining ways parenting behaviors can contribute to these disorders, and helping parents monitor adolescent behavior. The therapist also tries to stress the importance of parental involvement in their adolescents' activities.

Family sessions are dedicated primarily to improving dyadic communication and problem-solving skills. Near the end of treatment, family sessions are meant to help maintain treatment gains and develop a plan in case of relapse. Throughout the course of treatment, therapists can help families manage specific problems, involving systems outside the family. For example, the therapist might facilitate the adolescent's participation in court-ordered substance counseling or his return to school after suspension.

Family therapy for adolescent substance use problems has been supported by a number of randomized controlled trials. For example, Liddle, Rowe, Dakof, Ungaro, and Henderson (2004) randomly assigned 80 children and adolescents (11–15 years) with marijuana use problems to two treatment conditions: (a) MDFT or (b) traditional group therapy. Outcomes were assessed 6 weeks into treatment and at termination. Results showed that adolescents in both groups displayed reductions in marijuana use. However, MDFT produced more rapid results and was more effective than group therapy in improving adolescents' social, emotional, behavioral, and academic functioning.

Results of other studies indicate that family therapies are efficacious in reducing the use of alcohol, marijuana, and other drugs relative to controls (Ozechowski & Liddle, 2000). Furthermore, family therapies have been shown to be more efficacious than individual supportive therapy, group supportive therapy, and family-based education about substance use (Liddle, 2004).

Comparison of Treatments

Until recently, little was known about the relative effectiveness of treatments for adolescent substance use problems. The most promising treatments, CBT, motivational enhancement therapy, and family systems therapy, had been studied independently. Recently, the Center for Substance Use Treatment conducted the first large-scale comparison study to determine which treatment reduced adolescent substance use in the most time- and cost-effective manner (Dennis et al., 2002). This comparison study, the **Cannabis Youth Treatment Study**, has provided researchers and clinicians with new information about the treatment of adolescent substance use problems.

Dennis and colleagues (2004) conducted two studies administered at four treatment centers across the country. Participants were 600 adolescents with marijuana use problems and their parents. Most adolescents reported daily or weekly marijuana use; almost 20% also reported daily or weekly alcohol use.

In the first study, adolescents were randomly assigned to one of three treatment conditions (Diamond et al., 2002). The first group received five sessions of motivational enhancement therapy and CBT (MET/CBT 5). The second group received 12 sessions of the same treatment (MET/CBT 12). The third group received 12 sessions of motivational enhancement therapy and CBT and an additional 6 sessions of family supportive therapy (MET/

CBT 12 + family support). The parent-family sessions were designed to improve parents' behavior management skills, improve parent-adolescent communication, and increase parents' involvement in their adolescents' treatment. Researchers assessed adolescent outcomes 12 months after treatment. Results of the first study showed that all three forms of treatment were equally efficacious in reducing adolescent substance use. Five sessions of MET/CBT was the most time- and cost-efficient treatment.

In the second study, adolescents were randomly assigned to one of three treatment conditions (Diamond et al., 2002). The first group received five sessions of MET/CBT. The second group participated in a behaviorally based family therapy program. The third group participated in 15 sessions of MDFT. Results of the second study yielded similar findings. Adolescents in all three treatments showed similar reductions in substance use. In this study, however, MET/CBT 5 and the behaviorally based family therapy program were the most cost-effective interventions.

Results of the Cannabis Youth Treatment Study seem to suggest that five sessions of MET/CBT can be sufficient to treat adolescent Substance Use Disorders (see Figure 10.15). However, other research indicates that family therapy may be an important supplement to motivational enhancement and cognitive-behavioral interventions. Liddle and colleagues

(Liddle & Hogue, 2001; Liddle & Rowe, 2006; Waldron et al., 2001) compared CBT with family therapy for adolescents with alcohol use problems. Overall, they found that both CBT and family therapy were efficacious in reducing substance use; however, family therapy sometimes produced more rapid reductions in alcohol use and more lasting abstinence than CBT. The superiority of family therapy over CBT is attributable to its greater emphasis on decreasing family conflict, improving parent-adolescent communication, and strengthening parenting skills (Hogue, Liddle, Dauber, & Samuolis, 2004). Indeed, many professional organizations recommend including families in the treatment of adolescent Substance Use Disorders, even when practicing motivation enhancement therapy and CBT (American Academy of Child and Adolescent Psychiatry, 2001).

Relapse Prevention

Results of the Cannabis Youth Treatment Study highlighted a glaring problem in the treatment of adolescent Substance Use Disorders: Most adolescents who respond to treatment will eventually relapse. In the cannabis study, 66% to 83% of adolescents who participated in treatment had either not responded to therapy or had relapsed within 12 months of completing therapy (Diamond et al., 2002). Across other

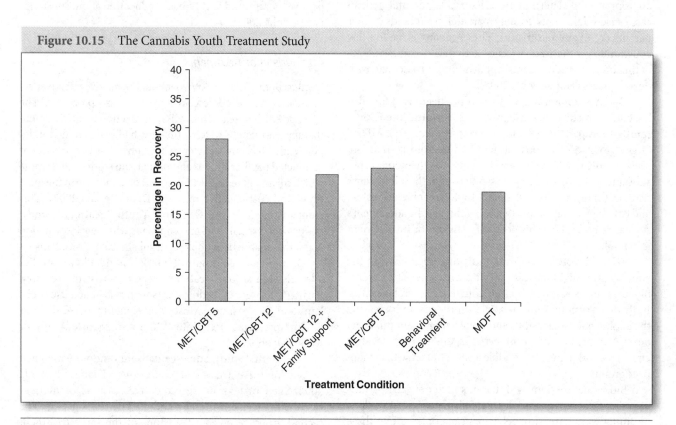

Figure 10.15   The Cannabis Youth Treatment Study

Source: From Dennis et al. (2004). Used with permission.

Note: All groups of adolescents who participated in treatment showed similar rates of recovery. Five sessions of MET/CBT or behavioral treatment were most time- and cost-effective. Notice, however, that only 20% to 30% of youths remained abstinent after treatment. Most relapsed.

studies of adolescents with alcohol use problems, approximately 50% of youths relapse within 3 months after treatment, 66% relapse after 6 months, and as many as 75% to 80% relapse after one year (Wagner & Austin, 2006).

Therapists have begun to systematically address the possibility of relapse during the course of therapy. Indeed, Marlatt and Gordon (1985) developed a relapse prevention component to therapy for adults with substance use problems. This approach has subsequently been adapted for use with adolescents (Patterson & O'Connell, 2003).

Relapse prevention is most often used with motivational enhancement and cognitive-behavioral therapy. After the adolescent has shown a decrease in substance use, the therapist begins to discuss the possibility of relapse. The therapist might mention that relapse is likely when the adolescent encounters any high-risk situations. High-risk situations usually involve **stimulus cues** that trigger substance use. Cues might include certain people (e.g., friends who expect the adolescent to drink), situations (e.g., parties or being alone), and negative mood states (e.g., feeling depressed or bored). The strongest stimulus cues seem to be exposure to family members and friends who use substances (Latimer, Newcomb, Winters, & Stinchfield, 2000).

Stimulus cues can trigger relapse even if adolescents have been abstinent for long periods of time. Often, adolescents feel shame and guilt after breaking a period of abstinence, an experience referred to as the **abstinence violation effect** (Marlatt & Gordon, 1985). Adolescents may attribute their relapse to internal, stable, and global causes; that is, they blame their relapse on their weak morals, their lack of will power, or their general inability to control their lives. Consequently, many adolescents continue to drink, believing that abstinence is impossible.

Adolescents' thoughts about the relapse greatly affect their ability to maintain sobriety. After having one drink, many adolescents show a number of cognitive distortions that make them more likely to continue their alcohol use. For example, many adolescents engage in **catastrophic thinking**; that is, they expect the worst possible consequences from "falling off the wagon." They might reason, "Well, now that I've had one drink, everything is ruined. I'm going to hit rock bottom again, my parents are going to kill me, I'm going to get kicked out of school, and I'm probably not going to graduate." As a result of catastrophic thinking, adolescents conclude, "I guess there's no use; I might as well get drunk."

Therapists who incorporate relapse prevention into their treatment not only help clients develop a plan for responding to a possible relapse, but they also teach youths to learn from the relapse experience. First, the therapist encourages the client to identify stimulus cues that might lead to relapse and generate ways to avoid these cues. Second, the therapist and client might create a concrete strategy for dealing with a relapse. For example, if the adolescent uses alcohol, she might agree to contact the therapist or a support group member immediately, before she has another drink. The therapist or friend might then encourage her to avoid the situation that triggered the relapse and take steps to maintain sobriety. The therapist might help the client to attribute the relapse to external, transient causes (e.g., a stressful day, a lot of pressure from friends) rather than to personal weakness.

Similarly, the therapist might challenge the adolescent's catastrophic thoughts or other cognitive distortions that could increase his likelihood of drinking even more. Consider the following transcript from a therapy session.

RESEARCH TO PRACTICE

LEARNING FROM RELAPSE

Mike:	Before I knew it, I had had five or six beers at the party and I was doing a lot of stupid stuff. At first, I felt really good. But then I just thought, "What a loser." I'd been so good not drinking for those months and now I just threw that all away.
Therapist:	You felt as if all your work had been for nothing?
Mike:	Exactly. Like, no matter what I do, I'm going to end up a drunk like my dad. I figure, what's the use?
Therapist:	It sounds like you're being a little too hard on yourself. Just because you had a few drinks at the party that night, does that really mean you're going to be a drunk? After all, wasn't there a lot of encouragement from friends to drink that night?
Mike:	Well, yeah. I really wanted to have a good time with everybody else.
Therapist:	And you didn't get into any serious trouble like last time [when you drove off the road and hit a tree]?
Mike:	No, I made it home fine.
Therapist:	Then maybe we can look at the situation a little more closely and learn from it. Maybe we can see what triggered your decision to drink and figure out how to avoid these triggers in the future.

As the above narrative suggests, the therapist encourages the adolescent to view the lapse as a possible learning experience rather than a sign of failure. If the adolescent views the lapse as an indicator that she is "back at rock bottom," then she might drink even more heavily. Alternatively, the therapist and client might analyze the antecedents and consequences of the lapse and develop ways to avoid another lapse in the future.

Researchers are only beginning to study factors that affect the likelihood of relapse among junior and senior high school students. Our current knowledge of relapse among adolescents can be summarized as follows. First, adolescents seem to relapse for different reasons than adults. Adolescents are more likely than adults to relapse because of exposure to substance-using peers, pressure or encouragement from friends, and a desire to enhance mood or enjoy the pleasurable effects of the drug. In contrast, adults often relapse when depressed, anxious, or otherwise distressed (Curry et al., 2012; Ramo, Anderson, Tate, & Brown, 2005). Second, adolescents' self-efficacy regarding their ability to abstain is inversely related to their likelihood of relapse. Adolescents who are confident that they can resist the pleasurable effects of substances and avoid social pressures to use are more likely to maintain abstinence (Burleson & Kaminer, 2005). Third, adolescents who do not regard their substance use as problematic are far more likely to relapse than adolescents committed to long-term behavior change (Callaghan, Hathaway, Cunningham, Vettese, Wyatt, & Taylor, 2005; Ramo et al., 2005). Since both situational (e.g., peers) and cognitive (e.g., beliefs, readiness to change) factors affect likelihood of relapse, both are targets of relapse prevention.

CHAPTER SUMMARY

Definitions

- People are diagnosed with Substance Use Disorders when they show a problematic pattern of alcohol or other drug use that interferes with their daily functioning or causes significant psychological distress.

  - *DSM-5* uses the term *substance* to refer to alcohol, drugs, and medications that can be abused. It identifies eight classes of substances: (a) Alcohol, (b) Cannabis, (c) Hallucinogens, (d) Inhalants, (e) Opioids, (f) Sedatives, Hypnotics, and Anxiolytics, (g) Stimulants, and (h) Tobacco.

- Youths must show at least two of 11 possible symptoms to be diagnosed with a Substance Use Disorder. The same symptoms are used for all substances. However, each disorder is labeled separately (e.g., Alcohol Use Disorders, Cannabis Use Disorder).

  - Tolerance occurs when the person (a) needs more of the substance to achieve intoxication or (b) the same amount of the substance produces diminished effects over repeated use.
  - Withdrawal occurs when the person (a) experiences negative physiological symptoms when they stop or reduce substance use or (b) takes a different substance to avoid these negative symptoms.

- Clinicians specify the severity of the problem. Severity is determined by the number of criteria met: two to three criteria (mild), four to five criteria (moderate), or >6 criteria (severe). Clinicians can also indicate if the person's symptoms are in remission; that is, symptoms that used to be present no longer exist.
- Substance Use Disorders can be differentiated from substance use by their (a) recurrence, and (b) effects on adolescents' functioning.
- There are several changes from *DSM-IV* to *DSM-5* in the conceptualization of Substance Use Disorders.

  - *DSM-5* no longer distinguishes substance abuse and substance dependence. All symptoms are now included in a single diagnosis: Substance Use Disorder.
  - At least two (rather than one) symptom is now required for a diagnosis. This change was made to eliminate the possibility that someone might be diagnosed without clinically significant problems.
  - Youths can be diagnosed with a Substance Use Disorder by showing only two symptoms. (In the past, three symptoms were required for Substance Dependence.) This changed eliminated "diagnostic orphans who had substance use problems but fell short of the three symptoms needed for Substance Dependence.

- *DSM-5* criteria for Substance Use Disorders have several limitations when applied to adolescents. The diagnostic criteria are developmentally insensitive and may overidentify adolescents with substance use problems.
- Alcohol is a depressant. It is similar to benzodiazepines, barbiturates, and most sleeping pills.

  - Low doses of alcohol stimulate the norepinephrine system, causing increased feelings of arousal and behavioral excitation.
  - Consumption of one or two alcoholic beverages can begin to decrease glutamate activity, producing feelings of relaxation and stress reduction.
  - Moderate alcohol consumption affects dopamine activity; researchers have identified a neural pathway, the dopaminergic mesolimbic pathway, that they believe is responsible for the pleasurable effects of most addictive drugs, including alcohol.
  - Moderate alcohol consumption affects GABA, causing relaxation, cognitive sluggishness, and slowed reaction time.
  - Pharmacodynamic tolerance over prolonged periods of time is rare among adolescents.

- Marijuana contains dozens of compounds, cannabinoids, known to affect brain chemistry; the most powerful cannabinoid is delta-9-tetrahydrocannabinol (THC). Using it, most people experience feelings of euphoria, disinhibition, and increased energy and sociability. Continued use (10–30 minutes) produces reductions in anxiety, a general sense of relaxation, and a state of emotional well-being or contentment.
  - THC is detected by cannabinoid receptors located throughout the brain, especially the basal ganglia, cerebellum, hippocampus, and cortex.
  - THC is known to affect a wide range of neurotransmitters: norepinephrine, dopamine, glutamate, GABA, and serotonin.
  - Some chronic users show decreased motivation and goal-directed behavior. Discontinuation after habitual use can cause withdrawal symptoms, such as cravings, sleep and appetite disturbance, agitation, anxiety, and irritability.

- The University of Michigan Institute for Social Research has annually assessed adolescent substance use in a project called Monitoring the Future.
  - Nearly 75% of adolescents have used alcohol at some point in their lives; approximately 65% have used alcohol in the past year and almost 50% have used alcohol in the past 30 days.
  - Approximately 45% of high school seniors have tried marijuana; almost 18% have used it within the past month.
  - Only about 25% of high school seniors have tried another illicit substance in their lifetime.

- The prevalence of Substance Use Disorder depends on the sample of adolescents studied, the method of questioning, and the researcher's definition of these disorders.
  - Using DSM criteria, the prevalence of mild Substance Use Disorders among adolescents in the community ranges from 1% to 9%, while the prevalence of moderate to severe Substance Use Disorders ranges from 1% to 5%.
  - Almost 3% of high school seniors use alcohol daily while almost 5% use marijuana daily.
  - Approximately 25% of high school seniors and 10% of eighth graders admit to binge drinking in the past 2 weeks.
  - Prevalence is greater for older adolescents, boys, and white youths.

- Sher's biopsychosocial model offers three pathways toward the development of Substance Use Disorders.
  - The enhanced reinforcement pathway model posits that a combination of genetic risk and positive expectations for the effects of the substance predispose individuals to substance use problems.
  - The stress and negative affect pathway model posits that individuals use alcohol and other drugs to cope with dysphoria and other negative feelings. Negative reinforcement maintains the disorder.
  - The deviance-prone pathway posits that some youths are rejected by prosocial peers. They associate with deviant peers who introduce them to alcohol and other drugs.

- Primary prevention programs, such as D.A.R.E. and the Partnership for a Drug Free America (PDFA) campaign have increased awareness of alcohol and other drugs, but may not reduce substance use or Substance Use Disorders.
- Results from ecologically-based secondary prevention programs have been mixed; the most effective programs target multiple risk factors in the adolescent's life and teach them skills to avoid substances and develop positive relations with peers.
- Inpatient treatment is frequently used to treat adolescents with Substance Use Disorders who require hospitalization.
- Twelve-step programs include Alcoholics Anonymous (AA) and Narcotics Anonymous (NA); proponents of these programs conceptualize alcohol and other drug use as a disease; treatment is usually based on abstinence.
- According to the cognitive-behavioral approach, substance use problems are acquired and maintained in three ways: (a) operant conditioning, (b) classical conditioning, and (c) social learning. Beliefs mediate the relationship between events that trigger substance use and consumption of alcohol and other drugs.
- Practitioners of motivational enhancement therapy help adolescents increase their willingness to change their substance use behavior.
- The most extensively studied treatment for adolescent substance use problems is family therapy. One objective in family therapy is to help parents manage their adolescent's substance use. A second objective of family therapy is to improve the quality of family functioning.
- Many therapists include a relapse prevention component in treatment; relapse prevention helps adolescents plan for relapse before it occurs.

KEY TERMS

28-day inpatient treatment   350

abstinence violation effect   359

acetaldehyde dehydrogenase   334

acute tolerance   335

alcohol dehydrogenase   334

amotivational syndrome   337

aversion therapy   350

binge drinking   333

biphasic   333

block the effects   350

Cannabis Youth Treatment Study   357

catastrophic thinking   359

CRITICAL THINKING EXERCISES

1. What physiological changes explain the biphasic effects of alcohol? How can the biphasic effects lead adolescents to binge drink?

2. Many adults use alcohol and marijuana to alleviate anxiety and depression. To what extent does the negative affect model explain adolescent alcohol and drug use?

3. In the 1980s, First Lady Nancy Reagan initiated an anti-drug campaign toward school-age children called "Just Say No!" The campaign consisted of speeches and rallies, television commercials, and school-based programs. During the 1980s and early 1990s when this campaign was in effect, the use of alcohol and marijuana among older children and adolescents decreased. Why *can't* we conclude that the "Just Say No" campaign caused this reduction in substance use?

4. Compare and contrast the twelve-step approach to treating adolescent alcohol abuse with cognitive-behavioral therapy. According to these models, (a) What causes Alcohol Use Disorder? (b) What is the best way to treat substance use problems?

5. Some clinicians who treat adult Substance Use Disorders adopt a "harm reduction" approach. Why is harm reduction controversial when it is used with adolescents? What is the evidence (for or against) using a motivational enhancement or harm reduction approaches to treat adolescents with substance use problems?

OTHER RESOURCES

Videos, practice tests, flash cards, study guides, and links to online resources for this chapter are available to students online. Teachers also have access to lecture notes, PowerPoint presentations, suggestions for classroom activities, and possible exam questions. Visit: www.sagepub.com/weis2e.

PART IV

Emotion and Thought Disorders

CHAPTER 11

Anxiety Disorders and Obsessive-Compulsive Disorder

LEARNING OBJECTIVES

After reading this chapter, you should be able to answer these questions:

- How do psychologists differentiate developmentally expected anxiety from anxiety disorders?
- How common are anxiety disorders in children and adolescents? How do age, gender, and social-cultural background affect their prevalence?
- What are some likely causes for each of the anxiety disorders shown by children and adolescents? To what extent is each disorder caused by (a) genetic and biological risk factors, (b) early social-emotional experiences that make children vulnerable to anxiety, and (c) specific social-emotional experiences that contribute to fears or worries?
- What is Obsessive-Compulsive Disorder (OCD)? How do biological and psychosocial factors help explain the emergence and maintenance of OCD in children?
- What is Tourette's Disorder, Trichotillomania, and Excoriation Disorder? How are these disorders similar to OCD?
- What evidence-based psychosocial treatments are available for childhood anxiety disorders and OCD? Is medication also effective for these conditions?

WHAT IS CHILD AND ADOLESCENT ANXIETY?

Anxiety: Adaptive and Maladaptive

We all know what it is like to be anxious. Think about how you felt before your last important exam or job interview. You probably experienced physiological symptoms like butterflies in your stomach, a rapid heartbeat, or sweaty palms. You might have also shown anxiety through your behavior, by fidgeting with your clothes, pacing about the room, or acting restless and agitated. You probably also had certain thoughts that accompanied your physiological and behavioral symptoms. These thoughts might have included self-statements like, "I really *need* to do well on the test" or "I *have* to get the job" or "*What if* I fail?" **Anxiety** is a complex state of psychological distress that reflects emotional, behavioral, physiological, and cognitive reactions to threatening stimuli (Barlow, 2002).

Psychologists often differentiate between two types of anxiety: fear and worry (Weems & Watts, 2005). **Fear** is primarily a behavioral and physiological reaction to immediate threat, in which the person responds to imminent danger. People respond to fearful stimuli by confrontation (e.g., fighting) or escape (e.g., fleeing). We might experience fear when we discover that we are poorly prepared for an important exam. As we stare at the test, our pulse quickens, our breathing becomes shallow, and we may become dizzy or light-headed. Subjectively, we might experience a sense of panic or terror and a strong desire to run out of the classroom.

In contrast, **worry** is primarily a cognitive response to threat, in which the person considers and prepares for future danger or misfortune. We might worry about next week's exam, an upcoming job interview, or tomorrow's big game. The subjective experience of worry is a chronic state of psychological distress that can cause uneasiness, apprehension, and tension. Worry is typically accompanied by thoughts and self-statements about the future, such as "What is going to be on the exam?" "What should I wear to the interview?" or "What if I make a mistake and lose the game?" (Ramirez, Feeney-Kettler, Flores-Torres, Kratochwill, & Morris, 2006).

In most cases, anxiety is a beneficial emotional state that helps us deal with immediate threats to our integrity or prepare for future danger. For example, a moderate amount of anxiety can help us stay alert and cautious while driving our car during a thunderstorm. Similarly, a moderate degree of apprehension before an important exam can motivate us to study.

Maladaptive anxiety can be differentiated from adaptive, healthy anxiety in at least three ways: (a) by its intensity, (b) by its chronicity, and (c) by its degree of impairment. First, maladaptive anxiety tends to be *intense and out-of-proportion* to the threat that triggered the anxiety response. For example, many students experience apprehension about giving an oral presentation in front of the class. In most cases, moderate anxiety is appropriate and adaptive; it can motivate students to prepare for the presentation. However, apprehension becomes maladaptive when it causes intense feelings of distress or psychological discomfort. For example, a student's mind may "go blank" during the presentation, or she may become physically ill shortly before the presentation because of her anticipatory anxiety (Ramirez et al., 2006).

Second, maladaptive anxiety tends to be *chronic*. Worry about an upcoming exam is appropriate and adaptive when it motivates individuals to prepare for the exam and terminates after the exam's completion. Chronic worry, however, is maladaptive. Chronic worriers, who always anticipate disasters on the horizon, tend to experience long-standing agitation as well as physical and emotional discomfort.

Third, maladaptive anxiety *interferes* with people's ability to perform daily tasks. For example, most people experience moderate anxiety before a job interview. Anticipatory anxiety becomes maladaptive when people decide to keep their current, low-paying job in order to avoid the anxiety-provoking interview. Similarly, many people experience moderate apprehension before riding in an airplane. This apprehension becomes problematic, however, if the person is unable to attend his best friend's wedding because of his fear of flying.

Anxiety in the Context of Development

Children's anxiety also exists on a continuum from developmentally expected and adaptive to developmentally divergent and maladaptive (Table 11.1). At any given point in time, children's fears and worries reflect their present stage of cognitive, social, and emotional development (Pine & Klein, 2010). For example, a critical developmental task in infancy is to establish a sense of basic trust in a primary caregiver—someone who will provide safety and security in times of danger or distress. The natural emergence of object permanence (4–10 months), stranger anxiety (6–12 months), and separation anxiety (12–18 months) promotes the mastery of this social-emotional task. It is developmentally normative, and expected that younger infants will display a wariness of strangers and anxiety upon being separated from their mothers. However, some children display separation anxiety of unusual intensity, chronicity, or impairment. Their fears might be out-of-proportion to the actual threat that might confront them (e.g., screaming or clinging to avoid separation at day care). Furthermore, their anxiety may extend beyond the typical developmental period (e.g., beyond toddlerhood). Finally, their anxiety may interfere with their ability to master other developmental tasks at later points in time. For example, a child who fears separation may refuse to play at a friend's home or attend sleepovers. These developmentally unexpected signs of anxiety might indicate an anxiety disorder.

Similarly, a critical task in older childhood and early adolescence is to develop a sense of competence in life domains: school, friendships, and extracurricular activities like sports and music. Children's increasingly more sophisticated abstract thinking, capacity for empathy, and growing ability to engage in metacognition (e.g., thinking about their own thinking) aids them in their academic achievement and social interactions. However, with these increased abilities come the capacity for self-doubts and insecurities. For example, it is developmentally normative for older children to show increased self-consciousness and a preoccupation with what others are thinking about them (Elkind & Bowen, 1979). However, some children's fears and doubts become unusually intense, extend beyond the typical developmental period, and interfere with their overall functioning. Their anxiety about school or interactions with teachers and peers can cause sleep problems, depressed mood and irritability, or avoidance of social situations. At that point, they might be classified with an anxiety disorder.

It should now be obvious that children's fears, anxieties, and worries exist along a continuum (Goldberg, Krueger, Andrews, & Hobbs, 2009). On one end of this continuum is developmentally expected and adaptive anxiety that can help children achieve developmental tasks and interact

Table 11.1   A Continuum of Fears and Worries Across Childhood

Age	Developmentally expected fears/ worries	Symptoms that might indicate a disorder	Corresponding DSM-5 Anxiety Disorder
Toddlerhood (2–3 years)	Shyness, anxiety with strangers; Fears of separation from caregivers	Extreme panic when separated after age 2 years, sleep disturbance, nighttime panic attacks, oppositional behavior toward adults	Separation Anxiety Disorder
Preschool (4–5 years)	Fear of separating from parents to go to preschool or day care; Fear of thunderstorms, darkness, nightmares; Fear of specific animals	Clinging to parents, crying, tantrums, freezing, sneaking into parents' bed at night, avoiding, avoiding feared stimuli, sleep refusal, bed-wetting	Separation Anxiety Disorder Specific Phobia (natural environment) Specific Phobia (animals)
Elementary School (6–8 years)	Fear of specific objects (animals, monsters, ghosts); Fear of germs or illnesses; Fear of natural disasters or injuries; Anxiety about school	Avoidance of feared stimuli, refusal to attend school, extreme anxiety/panic during tests, academic problems	Specific Phobia (animals, situations)
Middle School (9–12 years)	Anxiety about school or tests, worry about completing assignments; Worries about making and keeping friends, concerns about pleasing others	School refusal, academic problems, procrastination, insomnia, tension or restlessness, social withdrawal, timidity, extreme shyness in social situations, persistent worry	Social Anxiety Disorder Generalized Anxiety Disorder
High School (13–18 years)	Concerns about acceptance and rejection by peers, teachers; Worries about grades, sports, relationships	Academic problems, persistent worry, sleep/appetite disturbance, depressed mood or irritability, substance abuse, recurrent panic attacks, social withdrawal	Social Anxiety Disorder Generalized Anxiety Disorder Panic Disorder, Agoraphobia

Source: Based on Beesdo and colleagues (2009.

effectively with the world. Anxiety helps children study for tests, prepare for important presentations, and seek safety in times of danger. At the other extreme is intense anxiety, fear, or worry that extends beyond the usual development period and interferes with children's capacities to meet the expected challenges at their stage of development (e.g., trust in a primary caregiver, autonomy and independence at school, confidence in social situations). Many children fall somewhere in between these extremes. It takes both scientific knowledge and clinical skills to determine where normal anxiety ends and anxiety disorders begin (Beesdo et al., 2009; Connolly & Suarez, 2010).

CASE STUDY

TAMMIE'S SLEEPLESS NIGHTS

Tammie Velazquez was a 12-year-old girl who was referred to the hospital by her parents because she was having difficulty going to sleep at night. "A few months ago," Mrs. Velazquez explained, "Tammie started complaining about having problems falling asleep. We'd put her to bed, but she'd lie awake for several hours. Then, she'd wander out of her room and ask for a drink of water. Sometimes, she's not asleep until 11:30 or midnight and then she's exhausted the next day."

Dr. Baldwin reviewed Tammie's developmental and medical history, her diet, and her habits before bed. However, he couldn't find any explanation for her sleep problems. Tammie's father said, "Tammie's never been a problem. She's very smart and does extremely well in school—a real perfectionist. She's popular with the other kids and has a lot of friends. She's very mature for her age and almost always listens to her mother and me."

Dr. Baldwin interviewed Tammie: "When you're in bed at night, how do you feel?" Tammie replied, "At first I feel good, because I'm so tired. Then, I sort of tense up and feel nervous. I get tingly in my stomach." Dr. Baldwin asked, "Do you think about anything?" Tammie responded, "I start to think about all the things I need to do the next day for school. I worry about my homework, tests, volleyball . . . stuff like that. Then, I get more and more nervous and tingly. I just can't stop. I start to bite my lip or pick at my fingernails until they bleed. When I've had enough, I get out of bed."

Dr. Baldwin continued, "And is there anything you can do to make yourself relax and go to sleep?" Tammie responded, "If my mom or dad give me a hug or talk to me, I can usually stop worrying and think about other things and calm down. Sometimes, though, the worrying starts up again and I know it's going to be a long night."

ANXIETY DISORDERS
Overall Prevalence and Associated Features

Anxiety disorders are among the most frequently diagnosed psychiatric conditions in children and adolescents (Curry, March, & Hervey, 2004). Approximately 15% to 20% of children and adolescents will develop an anxiety disorder before reaching adulthood (Figure 11.1). At any given time, approximately 5% of youths have an anxiety disorder (Costello, Egger, & Angold, 2004). The prevalence of anxiety disorders is higher for adolescents than for children. The prevalence is also higher for girls than boys. The gender ratio of anxiety disorders tends to increase with age, reaching 1:2 or 1:3 by adolescence (Beesdo et al., 2009).

Anxiety disorders tend to be persistent across childhood and adolescence (Beesdo et al., 2009). Specifically, anxiety disorders show modest **homotypic continuity** (i.e., stability for the same specific disorder) and strong **heterotypic continuity** (i.e., stability for the same general class of disorders). The Early Developmental States of Psychopathology (EDSP) study followed a large group of children with anxiety disorders over time. On average 25% to 30% of children diagnosed with a specific anxiety disorder at baseline met diagnostic criteria for the same disorder 10

Figure 11.1 Prevalence of Anxiety Disorders in Children and Adolescents

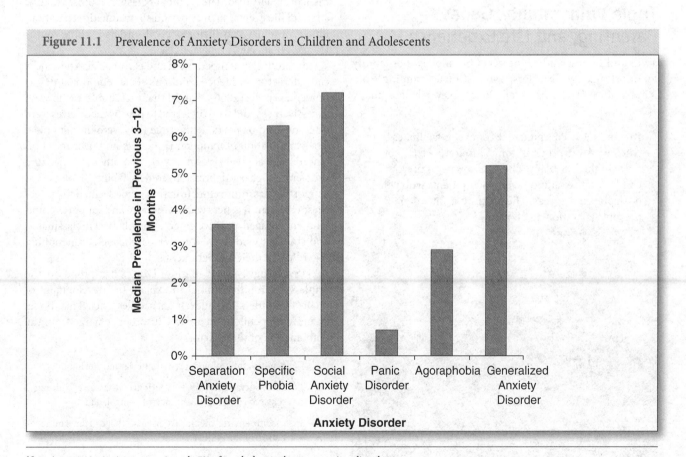

Note: At any point in time, approximately 5% of youths have at least one anxiety disorder.

Source: Based on Pine and Klein (2010).

years later (homotypic continuity). Furthermore, more than 70% of children who met criteria for an anxiety disorder at baseline also met criteria for an anxiety or mood disorder a decade later (heterotypical continuity). Although the stability of individual anxiety disorders is modest, the stability of anxiety problems in general is high.

Several longitudinal studies have also demonstrated an association between childhood anxiety disorders and the development of depressive disorders in adolescence and young adulthood (Beesdo et al., 2007; Bittner et al., 2004; Colman et al., 2007; Wittchen et al., 2000). For example, one prospective longitudinal study followed a large sample of children from New Zealand for 21 years (Woodward & Fergusson, 2001). Childhood anxiety disorders predicted a litany of negative developmental outcomes including Major Depressive Disorder, Substance Use Disorder, and suicide attempts. In another study, depression tended to emerge, on average, 5 years after the onset of anxiety (Goldberg et al., 2009). Certain childhood anxiety disorders, especially those characterized by chronic worry or extreme panic, are particularly predictive of later depression (Moffitt et al., 2007). These findings have led many researchers to conclude that early problems with anxiety can adversely affect the developmental trajectories of children and adolescents who experience them (Pine & Klein, 2010).

Triple Vulnerability: Genes, Parenting, and Life Experience

Twin and family studies indicate only modest heritability for most anxiety disorders, with estimates ranging from 30% to 40% (Hettema et al., 2001). Nevertheless, many anxiety disorders are associated with abnormalities in the structure or functioning of various regions of the central nervous or endocrine systems. The most consistent findings suggest dysregulation of the **amygdo-cortical neural circuit** (Stein, Fineberg, et al., 2010). This neural pathway consists of two important brain regions: the amygdala and the ventromedial prefrontal cortex.

The **amygdala**, part of the limbic system, is a brain area responsible for learned fear responses; it regulates the fight or flight response when a person is confronted with threat. The **ventromedial prefrontal cortex**, part of the frontal lobe, is a brain area that modulates fear and controls behavior. People with anxiety disorders often display hypersensitivity of the amygdala and underactivity of the ventromedial prefrontal cortex. This combination of hypersensitivity and underactivity results in excessive anxiety and difficulty regulating fear and panic.

Early social and emotional experiences also play a role in the development of pediatric anxiety. Children with "difficult" temperaments are at risk for anxiety problems. Youths high in neuroticism (e.g., proneness to negative affect) or behavioral inhibition (e.g., extreme shyness) seem to be particularly at risk. Furthermore, parents who model anxiety, who show low warmth toward their children, or who act in an overprotective manner may contribute to the development of anxiety disorders (Gunnar & Fisher, 2006). Similarly, stressful life events, such as periods of traumatic separation, illness, or injury, can elicit anxiety disorders in some youths (Moffitt et al., 2007; Image 11.1).

Interestingly, temperament and early social experiences can interact to influence children's social-emotional development. Gazelle (2006) showed that preschoolers who were excessively shy and who preferred to play by themselves were often rejected by peers by the time they were in first grade. The combination of temperamental risk and peer rejection placed them at great risk for anxiety and other internalizing problems, such as depression and irritability. However, a supportive classroom climate in first grade seemed to protect these children. Teachers who were warm and supportive, and who encouraged positive interactions between classmates, had students who showed better psychosocial functioning regardless of their temperament.

Psychologist David Barlow (2002) has proposed the **triple vulnerability model** to explain the development of anxiety disorders in children and adolescents. This model assumes that childhood anxiety disorders emerge from the combination of three factors:

1. genetic and biological risk that is largely heritable,

2. early social-emotional experiences that give children a sense of vulnerability or lack of control, and

3. specific environmental experiences that can determine the nature of the children's fears.

First, genetic and biological factors can predispose youths to experience greater levels of negative affect or to

Image 11.1 This guidance counselor facilitates the Anchors Away program for children whose parents serve in the U.S. Navy. The program helps prepare children for separation from their parents who will be deployed overseas. The program is intended to prevent separation anxiety.

Source: Photo by John K. Hamilton.

develop excessive inhibition and shyness. Second, shared environmental experiences can shape the development of these predispositions in early life. For example, parents who are overprotective may communicate to children that the world is a dangerous place, thereby, reinforcing their children's propensities toward clinginess and inhibition. Third, specific environmental experiences may determine the nature of the anxiety disorder that children are likely to develop. For example, a child at risk for anxiety, who almost drowns while learning to swim, might develop a fear of water. Another child, at risk for anxiety, who is embarrassed while giving a class presentation, might develop a fear of public speaking (Suarez et al., 2008).

DSM-5 Anxiety Disorders Across Childhood

DSM-5 identifies six anxiety disorders that can be diagnosed in children, adolescents, and adults. They are (a) Separation Anxiety Disorder, (b) Specific Phobia, (c) Social Anxiety Disorder, (d) Panic Disorder, (e) Agoraphobia, and (f) Generalized Anxiety Disorder.

Longitudinal and retrospective studies indicate that these anxiety disorders tend to emerge at different periods in children's development (Figure 11.2). Three disorders typically emerge in early or middle childhood: **Separation Anxiety Disorder**, **Specific Phobia**, and **Social Anxiety Disorder**. These disorders are characterized by recurrent, unwanted fears of specific objects or situations. A child with

Separation Anxiety Disorder might fear leaving her parents during the day to attend school, a child with Specific Phobia might fear snakes or spiders, and a child with Social Anxiety Disorder might fear attending parties or other social gatherings. These disorders are usually considered "fear" disorders because they are characterized by persistent, unwanted fears that greatly interfere with children's social-emotional functioning and overall quality of life.

The next two anxiety disorders, Panic Disorder and Agoraphobia, are rare in children. These disorders tend to emerge in adolescence or early adulthood. They are characterized by feelings of intense apprehension, dread, or panic. Panic Disorder and Agoraphobia often, but not always, co-occur. Adolescents and adults with **Panic Disorder** experience recurrent intense panic attacks, characterized by discrete episodes of severe, unpleasant autonomic arousal (e.g., rapid breathing, heart rate, and negative thoughts, feelings, and actions). Adolescents and adults with **Agoraphobia** fear situations in which escape might be difficult or embarrassing (e.g., movie theaters, shopping malls). Often, adolescents fear having a panic attack in these situations and, consequently, avoid them.

The final anxiety disorder, **Generalized Anxiety Disorder (GAD)**, is unlike the other anxiety disorders because it is characterized by persistent worry, rather than fear or panic. Youths with GAD do not fear specific situations, objects, or events; instead, they chronically worry about future misfortune. GAD usually does not develop until late childhood or adolescence because only older children have the cognitive capacity to contemplate (and worry about) events in the future.

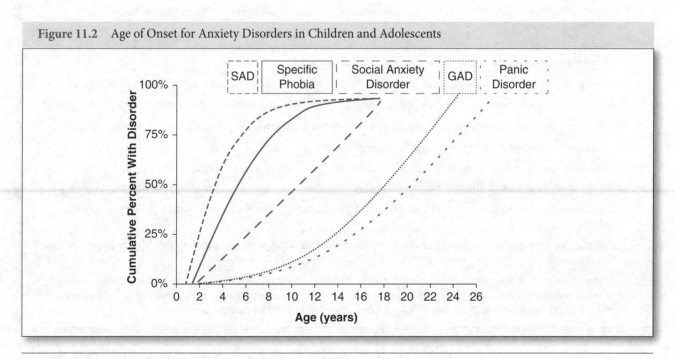

Figure 11.2 Age of Onset for Anxiety Disorders in Children and Adolescents

Source: Based on Beesdo and colleagues (2009).

Note: Separation Anxiety Disorder (SAD), Specific Phobia, and Social Anxiety Disorder (Social Phobia) usually emerge in childhood. Generalized Anxiety Disorder (GAD) and Panic Disorder tend to emerge in adolescence.

In this chapter, we will also consider Obsessive-Compulsive Disorder (OCD). OCD is characterized by (a) persistent thoughts, urges, or images (i.e., obsessions) that cause anxiety or distress and (b) repetitive behaviors or mental acts (i.e., compulsions) that the person performs to reduce these negative emotions. Although OCD is not classified as an anxiety disorder in *DSM-5*, youths with this disorder often experience anxiety. Furthermore, children and adolescents with OCD often have histories of other anxiety disorders or co-occurring anxiety problems.

SEPARATION ANXIETY DISORDER, SPECIFIC PHOBIA, AND SOCIAL ANXIETY DISORDER

Separation Anxiety Disorder, Specific Phobia, and Social Anxiety Disorder (Social Phobia) are sometimes referred to as conditioned fear disorders. Children with these anxiety disorders display fear or apprehension when confronted with specific objects or situations. Although their etiology cannot always be determined, these disorders are often caused by a combination of genetic-biological risk and specific learning experiences. Often, they are acquired through classical conditioning or social learning and maintained through negative reinforcement (Pine & Grun, 1999).

What Is Separation Anxiety Disorder?

Definition

Children with Separation Anxiety Disorder (SAD) show excessive anxiety about leaving caregivers and other individuals to whom they are emotionally attached (Table 11.2, Diagnostic Criteria for Separation Anxiety Disorder). Typically, these youths are preoccupied by fears that misfortune or harm will befall themselves or their caregivers during the separation period. For example, young children with SAD may believe that monsters might kidnap them while their parents are away. Older children might fear that their parents will become injured at work. Children with SAD usually insist that caregivers remain in close proximity, and they may become angry, distressed, or physically ill upon separation. Many refuse to attend school, summer camps, and activities with friends to avoid separation.

Table 11.2 Diagnostic Criteria for Separation Anxiety Disorder

A. Developmentally inappropriate and excessive fear or anxiety concerning separation from those to whom the individual is attached, as evidenced by at least three of the following:

  1. Recurrent excessive distress when anticipating or experiencing separation from home or from major attachment figures.

  2. Persistent and excessive worry about losing major attachment figures or about possible harm to them, such as illness, injuries, disasters, or death.

  3. Persistent and excessive worry about experiencing an untoward event (e.g., getting lost, being kidnapped, having an accident, becoming ill) that causes separation from a major attachment figure.

  4. Persistent reluctance or refusal to go out, away from home, to school, to work, or elsewhere because of fear of separation.

  5. Persistent and excessive fear of or reluctance about being alone or without major attachment figures at home or in other settings.

  6. Persistent reluctance or refusal to sleep away from home or to go to sleep without being near a major attachment figure.

  7. Repeated nightmares involving the theme of separation.

  8. Repeated complaints of physical symptoms (e.g., headaches, stomachaches, nausea, vomiting) when separation from major attachment figures occurs or is anticipated.

B. The fear, anxiety, or avoidance is persistent, lasting at least 4 weeks in children and adolescents and typically 6 months or more in adults.

C. The disturbance causes clinically significant distress or impairment in social, academic, occupational, or other important areas of functioning.

D. The disturbance is not better explained by another mental disorder, such as refusing to leave home because of excessive resistance to change in Autism Spectrum Disorder; refusal to go outside without a trusted companion in Agoraphobia; or worries about ill health or other harm befalling significant others in Generalized Anxiety Disorder.[1]

Source: Reprinted with permission from the *Diagnostic and Statistical Manual of Mental Disorders, Fifth Edition* (Copyright 2013). American Psychiatric Association.

[1] Agoraphobia and Generalized Anxiety Disorder are presented later in this chapter.

VALERIE: CONCERNED ABOUT HER DAD

Valerie was a 14-year-old girl referred to our clinic because she persistently refused to go to school. According to her father, Valerie would feign sickness, lie, tantrum, and do "just about anything" to stay home. Her father explained, "Last week, she promised me that she would go. I watched her get on the bus, but she never made it to school. She was back home 25 minutes later saying that her stomach hurt."

Valerie's mother added, "It's really getting to be a problem. All she wants to do is stay home. I ask her, 'Don't you want to go to Julie's or shopping with your friends?' but she always prefers to be with us."

A psychologist at our clinic, Dr. Saunders, asked Valerie about her reluctance to go to school. "Did something bad happen at school? Are you having trouble there?" Valerie responded, "No. I get along fine with the other kids and I'm getting good grades. I just like being at home better, near my dad." Dr. Saunders learned that Valerie's school refusal began last autumn, shortly after her father had heart surgery. Valerie was asked to take care of her father, while her mother was at work, as he recovered from the surgery. Since that time, Valerie's father had worked from his home, and Valerie showed especially strong attachment to him.

After several sessions, Dr. Saunders asked, "Are you worried that something bad might happen to your father, like maybe he'll have another heart problem?" Valerie responded, "Of course not! The doctors say he's fine." After a long pause, she added, "I just want to make sure."

SAD in Children and Adolescents

Among infants and young children, a certain degree of separation anxiety is adaptive (Bernstein & Victor, 2010). Fear of separation tends to emerge in infants at 6 months of age and peaks between 13 and 18 months. Older infants and toddlers show separation anxiety as they develop a sense of trust in the availability of their caregivers. Separation anxiety keeps infants in close proximity to caregivers and helps protect them from harm. Separation anxiety typically declines between the ages of 3 and 5 years. However, preschoolers and young school-aged children continue to require reassurance from caregivers when scared, upset, or unsure. The tendency to seek out caregivers when scared or upset indicates that the young child expects her parents to provide comfort and care.

Periodic concerns about separation are also common among school-aged children. Indeed, approximately 70% of school-aged children admit to occasional anxiety when separating from parents, and 15% report occasional nightmares about being kidnapped or harm befalling loved ones (Muris, Merckelbach, Mayer, & Meesters, 1998; Muris, Merckelbach, Gadet, & Moulaert, 2000). However, only about 15% of school-aged children report persistent fears about separation, and 3% to 4% meet diagnostic criteria for SAD (Muris, Merckelbach et al., 2000; Perwien & Bernstein, 2004). SAD is differentiated from developmentally expected fears of separation by the intensity of the fear, its persistence, and the degree to which the fear interferes with the child's overall functioning.

The presentation of SAD varies by age (Fischer, Himle, & Thyer, 1999). Young children with SAD worry about physical harm befalling themselves or their parents, usually through unlikely means. For example, a 7-year-old boy with SAD might worry about being kidnapped on the way to school or

his parents being abducted by robbers while at work. Young children with SAD may refuse to attend school and throw tantrums if forced to go. When their parents are home, young children may "shadow" them from room to room or engage in other clinging behavior. Parents often regard these children as excessively needy. They may become frustrated with their children's strong desire for reassurance. Young children with SAD often experience nightmares about harm befalling themselves or family members. They may have difficulty going to sleep, insist on a parent staying in their room, or ask to sleep in their parents' bed. If denied, some youths with SAD will sleep outside their parents' bedroom door in order to gain closer proximity.

Older children with SAD often worry about more realistic events that might separate them from parents. For example, a 12-year-old with SAD might worry about her parents contracting a terrible disease or getting into an auto accident. Adolescents with SAD often have diffuse fears of separation. They might report only a vague sense that "something bad will happen" if they are separated from their parents or loved ones.

Older children and adolescents with SAD usually tolerate separation better than younger children; however, older children still experience considerable anxiety and sadness when separated. Some become physically ill if forced to separate from parents. Others show severe social withdrawal, concentration problems, and symptoms of depression. Many older children and adolescents sacrifice time with peers to be near their families. Often, these fears of separation interfere with academic and social functioning (Silverman & Dick-Niederhauser, 2004).

SAD is associated with a wide range of psychiatric conditions (Bernstein & Victor, 2010). In younger children, the most common comorbid problems are Specific Phobia

(13%–58%), ADHD (17%–22%), and Oppositional Defiant Disorder (12%–17%). In older children, SAD often occurs with Generalized Anxiety Disorder (33%–74%) and Social Anxiety Disorder (8%–20%). Approximately 8% of youths with SAD show sleep problems, especially enuresis (i.e., bed-wetting) and sleep terrors (i.e., panic-like symptoms during deep sleep). The prevalence of mood disorders and OCD is lower than the prevalence of other anxiety disorders.

The onset of SAD is usually between 7 and 9 years of age. Some children first show symptoms following a stressful event. Events that threaten the availability of parents or the child's security may be most likely to elicit SAD: illness of a family member, parental divorce, a change in home or school. However, many families cannot identify a specific stressor associated with onset (Bernstein & Victor, 2010).

Experts disagree about the course of SAD. Most children experience a marked decrease in separation fears over time (Bernstein & Victor, 2010). For example, longitudinal research indicates that only about 20% to 25% of youths initially diagnosed with SAD continue to meet full diagnostic criteria 18 months later. However, most children continue to show subthreshold symptoms that cause them (or their families) distress. In some instances, SAD can persist into adolescence and adulthood. Data from a large epidemiological study showed that 36% of adults who reported a history of SAD in childhood continued to report fears of separating from loved ones and "being alone."

SAD in childhood may also predispose youths to a wide range of anxiety disorders in adolescence and young adulthood. In one study, children with SAD were more likely to develop other anxiety disorders 7 years later than children with other psychiatric conditions (Aschenbrand, Kendall, Webb, Safford, & Flannery-Schroeder, 2003). SAD in childhood is closely associated with Panic Disorder in adulthood. Retrospective studies show that many adults with Panic Disorder experienced SAD in their youths (Perwien & Bernstein, 2004).

Etiology

Compared to other anxiety disorders, genetic factors play a relatively small role in the development of SAD. Genetic factors likely predispose children to SAD by increasing their level of autonomic arousal and general anxiety in novel situations. Consequently, these children often demand considerable reassurance and comfort from parents to help them regulate their physiological arousal and feel safe (Barlow, 2002).

The quality of parent-child interactions, especially early attachment relationships, likely plays an important role in the development of anxiety problems, including SAD, among inhibited youths (Manassis, 2001). According to John Bowlby (1973), the purpose of **parent-child attachment** is to provide safety and security to the child. Attachment behaviors, such as approaching the parent when scared, are evolutionarily adaptive; they keep children in close proximity to their caregivers.

Insecure attachment relationships in early life predispose individuals to anxiety problems in childhood (Manassis, Bradley, Goldberg, Hood, & Swinson, 1994). Several prospective, longitudinal studies suggest that insecure attachment in infancy predicts anxiety problems during childhood. Furthermore, risk for anxiety is greatest among youths with both high levels of behavioral inhibition and a history of insecure attachment (Manassis, 2001; Warren, Emde, & Sroufe, 2000). Children who show behavioral inhibition in infancy and early childhood are extremely sensitive to psychosocial stressors, and they often demand considerable reassurance and comfort from parents. However, if parents are unable to meet their needs for comfort and security, these infants may experience prolonged and considerable feelings of insecurity and distress.

Insecure attachment in infancy may also predispose youths to anxiety problems in adolescence. Warren, Huston, Egeland, and Sroufe (1997) examined the relationship between the quality of the attachment relationship in infancy and the prevalence of anxiety disorders, including SAD, during adolescence. Infants who initially displayed insecure attachment relationships with their mothers at age 12 months were more likely to develop anxiety disorders by late adolescence. Furthermore, a particular pattern of insecure attachment predicted later anxiety. This pattern, called **insecure-ambivalent attachment**, is associated with inconsistent parental care. It is possible that children who receive inconsistent care from parents experience considerable anxiety in times of stress because they do not know when (or if) parents will come to their aid. They seem to lack a secure base from which they can derive comfort and protection.

On the other hand, parents who provide their infants and young children with sensitive and responsive care may prevent the emergence of SAD and other anxiety problems later in childhood. Warren and Simmens (2005) examined the quality of parent-child interactions in families with infants who had difficult temperaments or high levels of behavioral inhibition. The researchers found that infants whose parents provided sensitive and responsive care were less likely to have anxiety problems during toddlerhood.

Parents' own levels of anxiety and insecurity can contribute to the development of SAD in their children (Silverman & Dick-Niederhauser, 2004). The parents of children with SAD often appear overly involved, controlling, and protective of their children's behavior. Rather than encouraging independent play and exploration, these parents may model anxiety and fearfulness to their children and encourage their children to be excessively cautious (Dadds et al., 1996; Hudson & Rapee, 2002). The tendency to parent in a highly controlling, overprotective manner is strongest among mothers with histories of insecure attachment relationships with their own parents (Rapee, 1997).

It is important to remember that insecure parent-child attachment relationships are not indicative of early child abuse or neglect. Children who develop insecure attachment relationships with their parents *are* attached to them—they love them, care about them, and experience distress when unexpectedly separated from them. These children simply feel less secure in their parents' ability to provide comfort and protection. In contrast, some children who are deprived of parental care during infancy and early childhood can fail to develop an attachment relationship to any caregiver. Infants raised in orphanages, toddlers who move from foster family to foster family, and severely neglected children may develop no attachment to any caregiver whatsoever (van IJzendoorn et al., 2011).

What Is Specific Phobia?

Definition

Specific Phobia is one of the most common, and most untreated, anxiety disorders in children and adolescents. Specific Phobia is defined as a marked fear of clearly discernible, circumscribed objects or situations (Table 11.3, Diagnostic Criteria for Specific Phobia). Although people can fear a wide range of stimuli, most phobias fall into five broad categories:

- Animals—fear of snakes, spiders, dogs, birds
- Natural environment—fear of thunderstorms, heights, water
- Blood, injections, and injuries—fear of receiving an injection, seeing blood
- Specific situations—fear of airplanes, elevators, enclosed places
- Other stimuli—fear of choking, contracting an illness, costumed characters

Individuals with Specific Phobia immediately experience anxiety symptoms when they encounter a feared situation or object. Sometimes, they may show extreme panic, characterized by racing heart, rapid and shallow breathing, sweaty palms, dizziness, and other somatic symptoms. Younger children might cry, tantrum, freeze, or cling to their parents. Often, individuals with Specific Phobia avoid situations in which they might encounter feared stimuli. For example, a child who is afraid of dogs might plan her walk to school in order to avoid encountering a neighbor's dog. Although some people with Specific Phobia recognize that their fears are excessive and unreasonable, many children do not have this degree of insight.

The fears displayed by people with Specific Phobia must be out-of-proportion to the actual danger posed by the specific object or situation. Usually, it is fairly easy for a parent or clinician to determine whether a fear is disproportionate to the threat of danger. A child who panics at the sight of a clown at her friend's birthday party is clearly showing a disproportional degree of anxiety. In some instances, however, determining the appropriateness of the child's reaction is less straightforward. For example, a child's fear of storms might be appropriate if she lives in an area plagued by hurricanes or tornadoes.

Table 11.3 Diagnostic Criteria for Specific Phobia

A. Marked fear or anxiety about a specific object or situation (e.g., flying, heights, animals, receiving an injection, seeing blood).

   Note: In children, the fear or anxiety may be expressed by crying, tantrums, freezing, or clinging.

B. The phobic object or situation almost always provokes immediate fear or anxiety.

C. The phobic object or situation is actively avoided or endured with intense fear or anxiety.

D. The fear or anxiety is out of proportion to the actual danger posed by the specific object or situation and to the sociocultural context.

E. The fear, anxiety, or avoidance is persistent, typically lasting for 6 months or more.

F. The fear, anxiety, or avoidance causes clinically significant distress or impairment in social, occupational, or other important areas of functioning.

G. The disturbance is not better explained by the symptoms of another mental disorder, including fear, anxiety, and avoidance of situations associated with panic-like symptoms or other incapacitating symptoms (as in Agoraphobia); objects or situations related to obsessions (as in Obsessive-Compulsive Disorder); reminders of traumatic events (as in Posttraumatic Stress Disorder); separation from home or attachment figures (as in Separation Anxiety Disorder); or social situations (as in Social Anxiety Disorder).[1]

Source: Reprinted with permission from the *Diagnostic and Statistical Manual of Mental Disorders, Fifth Edition* (Copyright 2013). American Psychiatric Association.

[1]Agoraphobia, Social Anxiety Disorder, and Obsessive-Compulsive Disorder are presented later in this chapter. Posttraumatic Stress Disorder is presented in Chapter 12.

Children are only diagnosed with Specific Phobia if (a) their anticipatory anxiety or fear significantly interferes with their day-to-day functioning or (b) their symptoms cause significant distress. An adolescent who fears the sight of blood and avoids watching gory movies might not be diagnosed with Specific Phobia because her fears do not seriously affect her daily activities. However, if she wants to become a doctor, but pursues another career path because of her fear of blood, then the diagnosis of Specific Phobia might be appropriate.

Specific Phobia in Childhood and Adolescence

Specific phobias are seen in approximately 2% to 9% of children and adolescents (LeBeau et al., 2010). Animal phobia is the most common type; between 3.3% and 7% of youths show intense fear for at least one specific animal. Natural environment phobias are also common. Approximately 9% to 11% of youths fear natural stimuli, if we lump them all together into a single category (e.g., storms, water, heights). Fear of blood, injection, and injuries occurs in 3% to 4.5% of youths. Situational phobias are somewhat less common; they include fear of flying (2.7%) and fear of enclosed spaces (3.2%). Fear of the dark is especially common among younger children (3%–4%).

The fears shown by children and adolescents usually reflect their level of cognitive development (Warren & Sroufe, 2004). Young children tend to fear concrete objects such as animals and monsters. Indeed, animal phobias tend to emerge between 8 and 9 years old on average. Older children tend to fear situations that might result in injury to themselves or others. The mean age of onset for blood-injection-injury phobia is age 9 to 10 years whereas onset for natural disaster phobias is typically in early adolescence (13–14 years old). Adolescents' fears also reflect their interest in social interactions and achievement. Common phobias among adolescents include fear of being alone and fear of exams (LeBeau et al., 2010).

Girls are more likely than boys to develop most types of phobias. Fear of specific animals (91% female), situations (87% female), and natural disasters (70% female) is much more common in girls. Situational phobias, such as fear of heights, are more equally distributed (60% female). Blood-injection-injury phobia is equally common among boys and girls (LeBeau et al., 2010).

When children with specific phobias confront feared stimuli, they show changes in cognition, physiology, and behavior (N. J. King, Muris, & Ollendick, 2004). With respect to cognition, children make negative self-statements that maximize the danger of the situation (e.g., "That dog is going to bite me") and minimize their ability to cope (e.g., "There's nothing I can do to stop it"). With respect to physiological responses, children show changes in autonomic functioning, such as increased heart rate, rapid breathing, sweatiness, dizziness, or upset stomach. Finally, with respect to behavior, children may attempt to flee the situation. If they cannot flee, they may become clingy, panicky, or irritable.

Specific phobias rarely occur in isolation. Approximately 75% of youths who have one specific phobia report another phobia as well. Specific Phobia also co-occurs with other anxiety disorders. The most common comorbid anxiety problems are fears of social situations (Social Anxiety Disorder) and fears of separation from parents (SAD; Costello et al., 2004; Ginsburg & Walkup, 2004). Youths with Specific Phobia may also show other mental health problems. Approximately 36% have depression, while 33% show comorbid physical illnesses caused by stress (Essau, Conradt, & Petermann, 2000).

Phobias typically last one to 2 years and cause considerable distress and impairment if left untreated. Most childhood phobias do not persist into adulthood. However, children's phobias can develop into other anxiety, mood, and somatic problems later in adolescence and adulthood. Consequently, childhood phobias merit clinical attention if they cause significant impairment or distress (Ginsburg & Walkup, 2004; N. J. King et al., 2004).

Etiology

Genes play a relatively small role in the development of most phobias (N. J. King et al., 2004). Fears of specific stimuli (e.g., dogs, clowns) usually do not run in families. Instead, people may inherit a general tendency toward anxiety, which can later develop into a specific fear.

However, genetics seems to play a relatively greater role in the development of blood-injection-injury phobias than in other phobias. Individuals with blood-injection-injury phobias become dizzy or faint when confronted with blood, needles, or open wounds. Their reaction may be due to an unusual sensitivity of the **vasovagal response**, a physiological response that involves a rapid increase and sudden decrease in blood pressure. People typically feel dizzy and light-headed. There is a strong relationship between parents' and children's fear of blood and needles, indicating that shared genetic factors could be partially responsible for blood-injection-injury phobias (Dejong & Merckelbach, 1998).

Interestingly, people with blood-injection-injury phobia seem to process feared stimuli differently than people with other types of phobias (Caseras et al., 2010). For example, when people with spider or snake phobia are shown pictures of these animals, they may display unusual activation of cingulate cortex and insula. These areas of the brain play critical roles in emotional responses, memory, and learning. It would be adaptive to have these brain regions active when confronting potentially threatening stimuli, such as dangerous animals. In contrast, people with blood-injection-injury phobia do not show activation in this brain region. Instead, people with blood-injection-injury phobia display increased activity in the occipito-parietal cortex and thalamus. These areas are responsible for focusing visual attention and regulating basic automatic activity (e.g., breathing, blood pressure). Activation of these regions might underlie the tendency of individuals with blood-injection-injury phobia to become light-headed.

Most phobias are acquired chiefly through experience. One method of acquisition is **classical conditioning**. Watson and Rayner (1920) demonstrated that fear could be acquired through classical conditioning. In the famous "Little Albert" study, Watson and Rayner conditioned a fear response in an 11-month-old boy by pairing a white rat with a loud sound. Initially, the child was not afraid of the rat (NS), but the loud noise (UCS) produced an intense fear response (UCR). After repeated pairing of the rat and noise, the rat alone (CS) produced a fear response (CR). Classical conditioning might explain some common childhood fears. For example, a child who is bitten by a dog or frightened by a mysterious noise at night might develop phobias of dogs or the dark, respectively.

One brain region, the **median raphe nucleus,** seems to be particularly important in classically conditioned fears (Sweeney & Pine, 2004). The median raphe nucleus is located in the pons, a portion of the brain stem just in front of the cerebellum (Image 11.2). Melik, Babar-Melik, Ozgunen, and Binokay (2000) classically conditioned a fear response in rats and then produced lesions in the median raphe nuclei of some of the rats. Although all of the rats initially showed the conditioned fear response, rats with lesions showed a decrease in fear 48 hours after the surgery. Results indicate that conditioned fear responses are partially dependent on the raphe nucleus. Indeed, the raphe nucleus is connected to the hippocampus, another brain structure partially responsible for remembering emotion-laden events.

Image 11.2 The median raphe nucleus (#18) is located in the pons, a portion of the brain stem. It seems to play a role in conditioned fears and specific phobias.

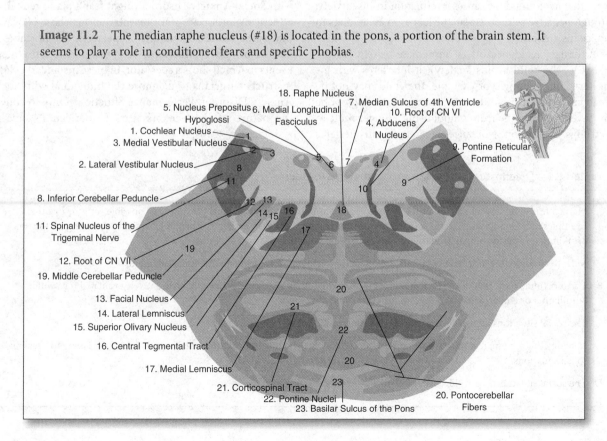

An alternative means of fear acquisition is through **observational learning**. Children can acquire fears by watching other people respond with fear or avoidance to certain objects, events, or situations. For example, parents who avoid visiting the dentist or show fear while getting a flu shot can convey this anxiety to their children. Mary seemed to develop her fear of dogs after witnessing someone being bitten by a dog.

A third way of acquiring fears is through **informational transmission**. Children can learn to fear objects or situations by talking with others or overhearing others' conversations. For example, hearing about a friend's dog bite or reading a story about a child lost in the dark can contribute to the development of phobias.

Children who are genetically susceptible to anxiety can develop specific fears through classical conditioning or social learning. However, classical conditioning and social learning do not explain why children's fears persist over time. Imagine that a child is bitten by a dog and subsequently develops dog phobia. As he encounters more and more friendly dogs, we would expect his fear to decrease over time. However, most children with dog phobia continue to fear dogs for months or years.

Why do phobias persist? According to the **two-factor theory of anxiety**, phobias *develop* though classical conditioning and other forms of social learning, but they are *maintained* through operant conditioning, namely, negative reinforcement (Mowrer, 1960). A child who is bitten by a dog subsequently develops dog phobia. Whenever he encounters a dog, he experiences extreme fear. However, the child discovers that avoiding dogs causes a reduction in his anxiety. Through negative reinforcement, he learns to avoid dogs to manage his anxiety.

Although avoidance offers immediate benefits to the child (e.g., the child avoids anxiety), it interferes with his long-term functioning. For example, the child may not be able to visit friends or family members who have dogs, or he may have to walk home from school using a longer route to avoid dogs. In addition, avoidance of feared stimuli interferes with the child's development of coping strategies to deal with anxiety. If the child never confronts his fear of dogs, he may never be able to learn how to cope with other, similar anxiety-provoking situations.

What Is Social Anxiety Disorder?

Definition

Social Anxiety Disorder is characterized by a marked and persistent fear of social or performance situations in which scrutiny or embarrassment might occur (Table 11.4, Diagnostic Criteria for Social Anxiety Disorder). Like individuals with Specific Phobia, people with Social Anxiety Disorder show immediate anxiety or panic symptoms when they encounter feared situations. For people with Social Anxiety Disorder, feared situations involve social settings in which they might be judged, criticized, or negatively evaluated by others. These settings include public speaking, attending a party or social gathering, or performing in front of others. People with Social Anxiety Disorder worry that they will be embarrassed in front of others, that others will think they are "crazy" or "stupid," or that others will notice their anxiety symptoms (e.g., shaking hands, sweaty palms). People with Social Anxiety Disorder often avoid social or performance situations. If forced to attend social gatherings, they endure them with extreme distress.

Some people with Social Anxiety Disorder only experience apprehension in performance situations; they do not fear other social settings. For example, an adolescent with Social Anxiety Disorder might fear a piano recital, an athletic event, or an oral presentation for class. However, that same adolescent might be perfectly comfortable in nonperformance situations, such as parties or athletic events in which she is a spectator. In these instances, *DSM-5* instructs clinicians to diagnose the individual with Social Anxiety Disorder, Performance Situations Only to convey the nature of the person's fears (American Psychiatric Association, 2013).

Table 11.4 Diagnostic Criteria for Social Anxiety Disorder

A. Marked fear or anxiety about one or more social situations in which the individual is exposed to possible scrutiny by others. Examples include social interactions (e.g., having a conversation, meeting unfamiliar people), being observed (e.g., eating or drinking), and performing in front of others (e.g., giving a speech).

   Note: In children, the anxiety must occur in peer settings and not just during interactions with adults.

B. The individual fears that he or she will act in a way or show anxiety symptoms that will be negatively evaluated (i.e., will be humiliating or embarrassing; will lead to rejection or offend others).

C. The social situations almost always provoke fear or anxiety.

   Note: In children, the fear or anxiety may be expressed by crying, tantrums, freezing, clinging, shrinking, or failing to speak in social situations.

D. The social situations are avoided or endured with intense fear or anxiety.

E. The fear or anxiety is out of proportion to the actual threat posed by the social situation and to the sociocultural context.

F. The fear, anxiety, or avoidance is persistent, typically lasting 6 months or more.

G. The fear, anxiety, or avoidance causes clinically significant distress or impairment in social, occupational, or other important areas of functioning.

H. The fear, anxiety, or avoidance is not attributable to the physiological effects of a substance (e.g., a drug of abuse, a medication) or another medical condition.

I. The fear, anxiety, or avoidance is not better explained by the symptoms of another mental disorder, such as Panic Disorder[1] or Autism Spectrum Disorder.

J. If another medical condition (e.g., obesity, disfigurement from burns or injury) is present, the fear, anxiety, or avoidance is clearly unrelated or is excessive.

Specify if:

Performance only: If the fear is restricted to speaking or performing in public.

Source: Reprinted with permission from the *Diagnostic and Statistical Manual of Mental Disorders, Fifth Edition* (Copyright 2013). American Psychiatric Association.

[1]Panic Disorder is presented later in this chapter.

Social Anxiety Disorder in Children and Adolescents

Social Anxiety Disorder usually emerges in late childhood or early adolescence. Indeed, it is usually not diagnosed before age 10 (Albano, Chorpita, & Barlow, 1996). The two most common situations that are feared by youths with Social Anxiety Disorder are formal presentations and unstructured social interactions (Beidel, Morris, & Turner, 2004). Most youths with Social Anxiety Disorder report intense anxiety associated with reading aloud in class, giving a class presentation, performing for others on stage, or competing in an athletic event. Youths with Social Anxiety Disorder often experience anxiety when initiating conversations with strangers, asking questions, or attending parties (Table 11.5).

Any situation in which the person might be judged or evaluated negatively by others can potentially be a source of anxiety for a person with Social Anxiety Disorder. Many children with Social Anxiety Disorder experience distress while taking tests because they fear criticism by teachers. Some children experience anxiety eating in public because they believe others may be watching them and criticizing their diet or etiquette.

Youths with Social Anxiety Disorder experience considerable impairment in their social and emotional functioning (Beidel, Turner, & Morris, 1999). Usually, youths with Social Anxiety Disorder avoid situations that elicit anxiety. Social avoidance is negatively reinforced by anxiety reduction. For example, by avoiding the school cafeteria, a child with Social Anxiety Disorder will not experience anxiety associated

---

CASE STUDY

ERIN'S SOCIAL ANXIETY

"I've been dealing with Social Anxiety Disorder since I was 10 or 11. I struggled all through middle school, crying every day, feeling like I had no friends, wondering why I couldn't just be normal! Meeting new people without other friends around to make me feel 'normal' was extremely difficult. I hated parties, dances, interviews, class presentations, and get-to-know-you type of games. I dreaded any type of social setting.

I didn't ever want to share my writing in my composition class, even though I was friends with just about everyone in the class. I found that I had trouble being creative. . . . I edited all my ideas as being too 'weird' or 'stupid.' I worried all the time about how I looked. I also worried about calling my friends or asking them to do things with me. I thought that I might be bothering them.

I kept a lot of things to myself and never told anyone what I felt. When they asked me what was wrong, I was sure that they would think that I was ridiculous."

Source: Used with permission of the author.

Table 11.5 Situations Feared by Children With Social Phobia

Situation	% Endorsing
Reading aloud in front of the class	71
Musical or athletic performances	61
Joining in on a conversation	59
Speaking to adults	59
Starting a conversation	58
Writing on the blackboard	51
Ordering food in a restaurant	50
Attending dances or activity nights	50
Taking tests	48
Parties	47
Answering a question in class	46
Working or playing with other children	45
Asking a teacher for help	44
Physical education class	37
Group or team meetings	36
Having picture taken	32
Using school or public bathrooms	24
Eating in the school cafeteria	23
Walking in the school hallway	16
Answering or talking on the telephone	13
Eating in front of others	10

Source: From Beidel et al. (2004). Used with permission.

with interacting with classmates. However, social avoidance also reduces children's contact with peers. Over time, peer avoidance can cause social impairments. Approximately 60% of youths with Social Anxiety Disorder show school problems, 53% display serious social withdrawal and lack of friends, and 27% report difficulty engaging in sports, clubs, and other leisure activities (Essau, Conradt, & Petermann, 1999). Children with Social Anxiety Disorder are at particular risk for depression, social isolation, and loneliness. Adolescents with Social Anxiety Disorder are at additional risk for substance use problems (Beidel et al., 2004; Chavira, Stein, Bailey, & Stein, 2004).

Most children with Social Anxiety Disorder do not have the disorder long term. In one study, nearly half of children with Social Anxiety Disorder did not show the disorder 3 years after initial diagnosis (Last, Perrin, Hersen, & Kazdin, 1996). In another study, most adolescents with Social Anxiety Disorder did not continue to meet diagnostic

criteria in adulthood (Pine, Cohen, Gurley, Brook, & Ma, 1998). However, most adolescents with histories of Social Anxiety Disorder develop other mental health problems, especially other anxiety and depressive disorders (Albano & Hayward, 2004).

Etiology

Genetic factors seem to underlie children's risk for developing Social Anxiety Disorder. Twin studies indicate that 50% of the variance in children's symptoms of Social Anxiety Disorder is attributable to genetics. Family studies indicate that the tendency to experience anxiety in social situations, and the diagnosis of Social Anxiety Disorder in particular, runs in families (Albano & Hayward, 2004; Hirshfeld-Becker, Biederman, & Rosenbaum, 2004).

Emerging evidence suggests that children inherit a temperamental predisposition toward social anxiety that can develop into Social Anxiety Disorder later in life (Figure 11.3). Infants and young children at risk for later anxiety disorders, especially Social Anxiety Disorder, tend to show temperaments characterized by a high degree of **behavioral inhibition**. Behavioral inhibition was first described by Jerome Kagan and colleagues (Kagan, Reznick, & Snidman, 1988) to describe children's tendency to withdraw when confronted with unfamiliar situations. Children who show high levels of behavioral inhibition are reluctant to explore new settings, are reticent to engage new playmates or enter new peer groups, and are avoidant of novel situations and strangers. Approximately 10% to 15% of children show high levels of behavioral inhibition.

Social Anxiety Disorder also depends on environmental factors, especially classical conditioning and negative reinforcement (Beidel et al., 2004). For example, a child who makes many mistakes when asked to read aloud in front of the class may associate public speaking with humiliation. Consequently, she may experience anxiety when asked to perform in other social settings. Over time, she may learn to avoid social and performance situations in order to avoid these negative feelings. Indeed, approximately 50% of youths with Social Anxiety Disorder are able to report a specific humiliating or embarrassing social experience that was associated with the onset of their Social Anxiety Disorder.

Parent-child interactions can also contribute to the development of Social Anxiety Disorder. The parents of children with Social Anxiety Disorder are more likely to have problems with social anxiety themselves (Morris, 2004). Although this suggests a genetic transmission of anxiety from parent to child, it also indicates that anxious parents might teach anxiety responses to their children during parent-child interactions (Biederman et al., 2006).

First, the parents of children with Social Anxiety Disorder are often described as more *controlling* than the parents of nonanxious children (Ginsburg, Siqueland, Masia-Warner,

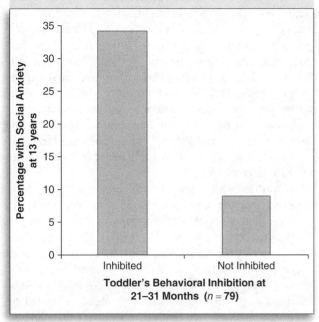

Figure 11.3 Behavioral Inhibition in Toddlerhood Predicts Social Anxiety Symptoms in Adolescence

Source: Based on Schwartz and colleagues (1998).

& Hedtke, 2004; Morris, 2004). For example, the parents of children with anxiety problems often intrude on their children's behavior and do not allow their children to make decisions for themselves. This highly controlling behavior may stifle the development of children's autonomy. Overcontrolling parents may communicate to children that they are not capable of coping with challenges in life (Hudson & Rapee, 2004). As a consequence, children of overcontrolling parents may require frequent reassurance from parents when completing tasks or solving problems.

Second, the parents of children with Social Anxiety Disorder are often described as *overprotective*; that is, they excessively restrict children's exploration and play because they fear harm befalling their children (Ginsburg, Siqueland et al., 2004). For example, it is reasonable for a mother to prohibit her 14-year-old daughter from attending a party that might involve older boys, a lack of adult supervision, and alcohol consumption. However, it is probably not reasonable for a mother to prohibit her 14-year-old daughter from attending a similar party with same-age peers, responsible adult supervision, and nonalcoholic beverages. Although the world can be a dangerous place, overprotective parents can convey to their children an excessive degree of risk and worry. Children can learn to overestimate the degree of threat in their surroundings and become excessively inhibited (Bogels & van Melick, 2004).

Third, the parents of children with Social Anxiety Disorder often show high levels of *hostile and critical* behavior toward their children (Ginsburg, Siqueland et al., 2004). Not

only are these parents highly controlling, but they are also prone to criticizing and rejecting their children when they do not live up to their high expectations. Such critical behavior may communicate to children that the world is a hostile and dangerous place and that they should not expect sympathy from caregivers if they take risks and fail (Moore, Whaley, & Sigman, 2004).

Fourth, parents of children with Social Anxiety Disorder may inadvertently *teach their children to be anxious* in social situations. Specifically, these parents may model anxiety and reinforce their children's anxiety reactions (Barrett, Rapee, Dadds, & Ryan, 1996). Dadds, Barrett, Rapee, and Ryan (1996) observed anxious children and their parents discussing hypothetical, ambiguous social situations. Some of the situations described people experiencing physical ailments, like an upset stomach. Other situations involved ambiguous social situations, like a group of peers laughing and joking. Youths with anxiety problems interpreted these ambiguous situations negatively. For example, they often interpreted the upset stomach as a sign of serious illness or the laughing peers as a sign of teasing or bullying. The parents of these anxious children also interpreted a great deal of hostility and danger in these ambiguous situations. Perhaps more important, the parents often supported children's decisions to overreact or withdraw from these social situations (Creswell, Schniering, & Rapee, 2005).

Fifth, parents can contribute to their children's social anxiety by *avoiding emotionally charged discussions*. Children's emotional well-being depends greatly on their ability to discuss and think about their feelings. One way children learn to recognize, understand, and discuss their feelings is through interactions with their parents. Parents model emotional expression, teach children how to label emotions, and communicate socially acceptable ways to discuss emotions with others (Eisenberg, Cumberland, & Spinrad, 1998). However, the parents of anxious children often avoid discussions about their children's feelings (Suveg, Zeman, Flannery-Schroeder, & Cassano, 2005). This lack of emotional expressiveness in the family can deprive children of skills and opportunities to label, talk about, and process emotions and, consequently, it can contribute to their social anxiety.

Keep in mind that parent-child interactions are bidirectional (Ginsburg & Schlossberg, 2002). Although parents can contribute to children's anxiety, children's behavior can also cause their parents to be excessively controlling, protective, or critical. For example, young children with high levels of behavioral inhibition often demand considerable reassurance and protection from their parents (Bogels & van Melick, 2004; Moore et al., 2004). Children's behavioral inhibition also seems to elicit harsh, critical, and demanding parenting practices (Chen, Hastings, Rubin, Chen, Cen, & Stewart, 1998; Hirshfeld, Biederman, Brody, Faraone, & Rosenbaum, 1997; Smoller et al., 2005). It is likely that parent and child behaviors mutually influence each other across development and, together, contribute to children's emerging anxiety.

Test Anxiety and School Refusal

Test anxiety and school refusal are not official *DSM-5* diagnoses. However, they are problems frequently experienced by children and families. In most cases, youths who show these problems meet criteria for an anxiety disorder.

Test Anxiety

Test anxiety is characterized by extreme fear of poor performance on tests and other examinations (LeBeau et al., 2010). Test anxiety can be very problematic for children and adolescents, who frequently confront test situations in school and other activities (e.g., driving test, piano recitals). Children with test anxiety, like children with other phobias, tend to worry about exams before they occur; endure tests with apprehension; and experience problems with concentration and memory during exams. In some cases, children will try to escape or avoid exams altogether (e.g., feigning physical illness). Test anxiety can lead to academic underachievement, low self-esteem, and depressed mood.

Test anxiety is relatively common among school-age children. As many as 38% of white and 52% of African American children report anxiety in test situations (Beidel, Turner, & Trager, 1994). However, the percentage of youths with clinically significant anxiety, that would require treatment, is much lower. In a large, epidemiological study involving more than 3,000 adolescents, 11% reported clinically significant elevations in anxiety in response to tests (Knappe et al., 2011).

Girls are more likely to be classified with test anxiety than boys. However, the greater prevalence of test anxiety in girls is almost certainly due to girls' willingness to admit to symptoms more than boys (Putwain, 2007). Test anxiety can be seen in children as young as 9 or 10 years of age. Mean age of onset is 14.7 years (Knappe et al., 2011).

DSM-5 does not have a diagnostic category for test anxiety. In most cases, children with extreme anxiety in test situations would be diagnosed with Social Anxiety Disorder. Indeed, approximately 75% of adolescents with Social Anxiety Disorder report test anxiety, and 14% of these youths fear only test situations (Knappe et al., 2011). Most children who experience test anxiety specifically fear negative appraisal by others if they perform poorly on the exam. Before exams, these children report high levels of worry about criticism from teachers and parents, or (to a lesser extent) teasing from peers. During exams, children with test anxiety often report negative automatic thoughts about criticism from others. For example, during exams, children with high test anxiety might say to themselves, "What am I going to do if I fail?" or "What will dad say?" Ironically, these cognitions usually exacerbate their anxiety and hinder their performance.

School Refusal

School refusal is defined as difficulty attending school as the result of emotional distress, such as anxiety and depression (King & Bernstein, 2001). Children may tantrum, play sick, or plead with their parents to avoid going to school in the morning. Alternatively, they may go to school but leave class early without permission. Still other children go to school reluctantly but then engage in disruptive behavior that prompts teachers to send them home. In all cases, school refusal is associated with emotional distress. The term *school refusal* is usually not used to describe youths who skip class because of truancy, conduct problems, or defiance of parents and other adults (Bernstein & Victor, 2010).

Children with school refusal may meet diagnostic criteria for several anxiety or mood disorders. The exact disorder depends on the child's symptom presentation and reasons for school refusal. SAD is often diagnosed when children avoid school because of fears of separation from parents. In contrast, Social Anxiety Disorder is probably a more appropriate diagnosis when children skip school to avoid a situation in which they might be judged or evaluated by others (e.g., eating in the cafeteria, giving an oral presentation). A mood disorder, such as depression, might also be considered if children are being teased or ostracized at school. Approximately 25% of youths with school refusal meet diagnostic criteria for at least one disorder, compared to 6.8% of children without school refusal (Egger et al., 2003).

Approximately 1% of school-aged children in the community and 5% of clinic-referred children exhibit school refusal. In the largest study to date, the Great Smokey Mountains Study (Egger et al., 2003), 1.3% of all children refused to go to school because of anxiety or mood problems. (An additional 5.8% of children showed chronic truancy associated with oppositional and antisocial behavior.) An equal percentage of boys and girls exhibited school refusal with a mean age of onset at 11 years. Another study showed a bimodal age of onset, corresponding to the beginning of kindergarten (5–6 years) and middle school (10–11 years). Beginning school or transitioning to a new school may be particularly distressing to a subset of children.

Learning theory is usually used to explain school refusal (Kearney & Albano, 2000). In most instances, negative reinforcement maintains children's reluctance to attend school. For example, a child might want to avoid an unpleasant situation (e.g., encountering bullies) or a social-evaluative situation (e.g., giving a class presentation) at school. In some instances, however, positive reinforcement maintains the problem. For example, a child might enjoy playing videogames at home or spending the day with his mother.

Parenting and the quality of children's home environment may also play a role in the development or maintenance of school refusal. Approximately 81% of children with school refusal have at least one parent with a psychiatric disorder; 41% have both parents with a psychiatric condition. Approximately 78% of mothers and 54% of fathers have an anxiety disorder whereas 51% of mothers and 22% of fathers have depression. Several studies have indicated that the parents of these children are either overprotective and highly controlling or emotionally distant and disengaged. Family conflicts and tension are also common (Bernstein & Victor, 2010).

PANIC DISORDER AND AGORAPHOBIA

Panic Disorder and Agoraphobia are rare in children. These disorders tend to emerge in adolescence or early adulthood. They are characterized by feelings of intense apprehension, dread, or panic. Although they are separate disorders, Panic Disorder and Agoraphobia often co-occur. Indeed, many people develop Agoraphobia because they fear panic attacks in specific places or situations. Both disorders are due to a combination of biogenetic and environmental factors that lead to (a) higher levels of general physiological arousal, (b) unusual sensitivity to threats or danger, and (c) a tendency to engage in catastrophic thinking (Pine & Grun, 1999).

What Is Panic Disorder?

Panic Disorder is a serious condition characterized by the presence of recurrent, unexpected panic attacks that cause the person significant distress or impairment (Table 11.6, Diagnostic Criteria for Panic Disorder). A **panic attack** is an acute and intense episode of psychological distress and autonomic arousal. During the attack, people experience physiological symptoms that fall into three broad clusters: cognitive symptoms (e.g., thoughts of losing control or going crazy), emotional symptoms (e.g., feelings of unreality or detachment), and somatic symptoms (e.g., heart palpitations, chest pain, dizziness). People who experience panic attacks feel as if they are having a heart attack, believe that they are dying or going crazy, or experience a strong desire to flee the situation. Indeed, panic attacks can be extremely scary because they are so severe and because people seem to have little control over their onset.

Table 11.6   Diagnostic Criteria for Panic Disorder

A. Recurrent unexpected panic attacks. A panic attack is an abrupt surge of intense fear or intense discomfort that reaches a peak within ten minutes, and during which time four (or more) of the following symptoms occur:

  1. Palpitations, pounding heart, or accelerated heart rate.

  2. Sweating.

  3. Trembling or shaking.

  4. Sensations of shortness of breath or smothering.

  5. Feelings of choking.

  6. Chest pain or discomfort.

  7. Nausea or abdominal distress.

  8. Feeling dizzy, unsteady, light-headed, or faint.

  9. Chills or heat sensations.

  10. Paresthesias (numbness or tingling sensations).

  11. Derealization (feelings of unreality) or depersonalization (being detached from oneself).

  12. Fear of losing control or "going crazy."

  13. Fear of dying.

B. At least one of the attacks has been followed by one month (or more) of one or both of the following:

(Continued)

Table 11.6 (Continued)

1. Persistent concern or worry about additional panic attacks or their consequences (e.g., losing control, having a heart attack, "going crazy").

2. A significant maladaptive change in behavior related to the attacks (e.g., behaviors designed to avoid panic attacks, such as avoidance of exercise or unfamiliar situations).

C. The disturbance is not attributable to the physiological effects of a substance (e.g., a drug of abuse, a medication) or another medical condition (e.g., hyperthyroidism, cardiopulmonary disorders).

D. The disturbance is not better explained by another mental disorder (e.g., panic disorders do not only occur in response to separation from attachment figures as in Separation Anxiety Disorder; in response to circumscribed phobic objects or situations as in Specific Phobia; in response to feared social situations as in Social Anxiety Disorder; or in response to reminders of traumatic events as in Posttraumatic Stress Disorder[1]).

Source: Reprinted with permission from the *Diagnostic and Statistical Manual of Mental Disorders, Fifth Edition* (Copyright 2013). American Psychiatric Association.

[1]Posttraumatic Stress Disorder is presented in Chapter 12.

Panic attacks may reach their peak intensity in about 10 minutes. However, many research studies indicate that adolescents and young adults often show very rapid symptom onset. Several studies indicate that maximum heart rate is reached within 3 or 4 minutes after the onset of a panic attack. In one large study of adolescents, only 35% reported onset greater than 10 minutes (Essau, Conradt, & Petermann, 1999).

Typically, adolescents and young adults who experience panic attacks report four or more symptoms (Craske et al., 2010). The most commonly reported symptoms are palpitations or "pounding heart" (78%–97%) and dizziness (73%–96%). The least common symptoms are numbness or tingling sensations (26%–29%) and choking (24%). The greater the number of symptoms experienced, the greater the likelihood an individual will seek treatment. In one study, an adolescent's risk of being taken to the emergency room increased 20% for every symptom he or she experienced beyond the four required by *DSM-5* (Craske et al., 2010).

The duration of panic attacks is variable. The median duration is approximately 12.6 minutes. However, average durations have ranged from 23.6 minutes to 45 minutes, depending on the study (Craske et al., 2010).

Typically, panic attacks are "unexpected"; that is, they come "out of the blue." For example, an adolescent might be working on her physics lab assignment when she suddenly begins to feel her heart race, her breathing to become shallow, and her palms to sweat (Figure 11.4). She might feel dizzy and hot and experience an urge to run out of the classroom. She might leave class, enter the bathroom, and splash water on her face to cool down. Adolescents who experience unexpected attacks often report feeling as though they were having a heart attack or that they were overcome with terror.

To get a sense of what an unexpected panic attack feels like, try to remember a time when you were driving and you suddenly saw the flashing lights of a police car in your rearview mirror. For an instant, you may have experienced many physiological symptoms of panic: pounding heart, rapid breathing, and dizziness. Perhaps you also had fleeting thoughts such as, "What did I do wrong?" or "Oh no, now I'm in trouble." Now, imagine that these sensations came out of the blue, that is, that they emerged suddenly while you were driving, without ever seeing the police lights. You might ask yourself, "What's wrong with me? Am I going crazy or dying?" Finally, imagine that these feelings increased over the next 5 minutes and lasted for the next half hour. This experience is similar to a panic attack.

To be diagnosed with Panic Disorder, an individual must have recurrent, unexpected panic attacks followed by (a) one month of persistent concern about having another panic attack, (b) worry about the implications of the attacks, or (c) a significant change in daily routines because of the attack. For example, many people who have had a panic attack fear having another one. They might believe that the attacks are a sign of psychosis or serious physical illness. They may also avoid situations where they experienced attacks in the past to prevent their recurrence. Some people experience unexpected panic attacks but do not worry about them or change their day-to-day behavior because of them. If panic attacks do not cause the person distress or impairment, they do not meet the criteria for Panic Disorder (American Psychiatric Association, 2013).

Children, adolescents, and adults with other anxiety disorders can also experience panic attacks. For example, children with Separation Anxiety Disorder might experience panic separating from their mothers. Alternatively, a boy with Specific Phobia for water might panic when his swimming teacher asks him to dive into the deep end of the pool. Children with other disorders can also show panic

Figure 11.4 Three Types of Panic Attacks

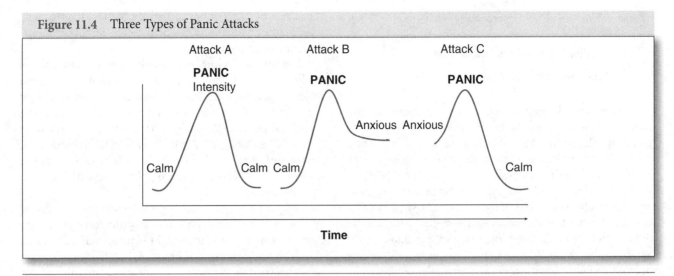

Source: Based on Craske and colleagues (2010).

Note: Attack A shows an attack that occurs out of the blue, when the adolescent is in a relaxed state. After the attack, the adolescent returns to a relaxed state. Attack B also shows an attack that occurs during a relaxed state, but after the attack, the adolescent returns to a state of anxiety. Attack C shows an attack that occurs during an anxious state, such as during a test or stressful social situation. After the attack, the adolescent returns to a relaxed state.

attacks. For example, some people develop Posttraumatic Stress Disorder from exposure to life-threatening negative events, such as serious car accidents or violent crimes. These people sometimes have panic attacks when they are reminded of these traumatic events. In all of these cases, panic attacks are "expected"; that is, specific events, situations, or memories triggered their onset. When other medical or mental disorders explain the causes of recurrent panic attacks, individuals are diagnosed with these other disorders rather than Panic Disorder, per se. *DSM-5* instructs clinicians to include the specifier "with Panic Attacks" at the end of the diagnosis to more accurately describe the person's symptoms. For example, the individual might be diagnosed with "Specific Phobia with Panic Attacks" or "Posttraumatic Stress Disorder with Panic Attacks" (American Psychiatric Association, 2013).

What Is Agoraphobia?

Agoraphobia is characterized by marked anxiety about places or situations from which escape or help is not possible without considerable effort or embarrassment (Table 11.7, Diagnostic Criteria for Agoraphobia). Common fears for people with Agoraphobia include:

1. Using public transportation (e.g., airplanes, buses, trains)
2. Being in open spaces (e.g., parking lots, shopping malls)

CASE STUDY

PAUL: HEART ATTACK AT AGE 16

Paul was a 16-year-old boy who was sent to the emergency department of the hospital after two episodes of "heart problems" in one week. Paul's mother told the emergency room physician that Paul had experienced symptoms of a heart attack after dinner at home. Specifically, Paul's heart raced, his breathing became shallow, he experienced dizziness, and his skin became clammy to the touch. "It came out [of] nowhere. I felt like my heart was going to explode in my chest. Then, I got a terrible urge to run way, but I couldn't. I just froze. I was scared and shaking all over."

The physician at the hospital determined that Paul was medically healthy and showed no signs of heart problems. Dr. Dresser, a pediatric psychologist at the hospital, suggested that Paul may have had a panic attack. She asked Paul and his parents, "Do anxiety problems run in your family?" Paul's father admitted to taking medication for both anxiety and depression. Paul worried, "Do you mean that I'm going to have more of these attacks?" Dr. Dresser replied, "That is a possibility. The important thing is that you learn to cope with them if they recur. Do you want to learn some techniques that can help?"

3. Being in enclosed places (e.g., stores, movie theaters, or stadiums)

4. Standing in line or being in a large crowd

5. Being outside the home alone

People with Agoraphobia fear these situations because they believe escape might be difficult in the event of a panic attack, panic-like symptoms, or an embarrassing event. For example, a woman might avoid traveling on an airplane because she knows she cannot easily exit the plane in the event of a panic attack. The woman does not have Specific Phobia (i.e., a fear of flying); instead, she has a fear of places or situations in which escape might be impossible or extremely difficult. Similarly, a man with Irritable Bowel Syndrome might avoid sporting events in large stadiums because he fears incontinence. The man might love watching his favorite football team, but he avoids games because he worries that he might embarrass himself in the crowded stadium. The man does not have Social Anxiety Disorder (i.e., a fear of social or performance situations); instead, he fears places or situations in which escape might be impossible or extremely difficult.

Not all people with Agoraphobia fear the same places or situation. For example, one adolescent with Agoraphobia might be afraid of leaving her house to attend school or her after-school job. Another adolescent with Agoraphobia might fear going to the mall, movie theater, or gymnasium to watch her school's basketball team play. By definition, people with Agoraphobia must fear at least two situations; however, most people with Agoraphobia report anxiety in multiple settings.

People with Agoraphobia try intensely to avoid feared situations. For example, an adolescent who fears leaving her home and attending school might tantrum, feign illness, or skip school in order to stay home. An adolescent who fears large, crowded public places might decline invitations from friends to go shopping or attend a concert. Agoraphobic avoidance can restrict adolescents' educational and social functioning. Agoraphobia limits adolescents' abilities to

---

Table 11.7 Diagnostic Criteria for Agoraphobia

A. Marked fear or anxiety about two (or more) of the following five situations:

  1. Using public transportation (e.g., buses, trains, ships, planes).

  2. Being in open spaces (e.g., parking lots, marketplaces, bridges).

  3. Being in enclosed places (e.g., shops, theaters, cinemas).

  4. Standing in line or being in a crowd.

  5. Being outside of the home alone.

B. The individual fears or avoids these situations because of thoughts that escape might be difficult or help might not be available in the event of developing panic-like symptoms or other incapacitating or embarrassing symptoms.

C. The agoraphobic situations almost always provoke fear or anxiety.

D. The agoraphobic situations are actively avoided, require the presence of a companion, or are endured with intense fear or anxiety.

E. The fear or anxiety is out of proportion to the actual danger posed by the agoraphobic situations and to the sociocultural context.

F. The fear, anxiety, or avoidance is persistent, typically lasting 6 months or more.

G. The fear, anxiety, or avoidance causes clinically significant distress or impairment in social, occupational, or other important areas of functioning.

H. If another medical condition is present, the fear, anxiety, or avoidance is clearly excessive.

I. The fear, anxiety, or avoidance is not better explained by the symptoms of another mental disorder—for example, the symptoms are not confined to fear of separation (as in Separation Anxiety Disorder); fear of specific objects or situations (as in Specific Phobia); fear of social situations (as in Social Anxiety Disorder); or reminders of traumatic events (as in Posttraumatic Stress Disorder[1]).

Source: Reprinted with permission from the *Diagnostic and Statistical Manual of Mental Disorders, Fifth Edition* (Copyright 2013). American Psychiatric Association.

Note: Agoraphobia is diagnosed irrespective of the presence of Panic Disorder. If an individual's presentation meets criteria for Panic Disorder and Agoraphobia, both diagnoses should be assigned.

[1]Posttraumatic Stress Disorder is presented in Chapter 12.

attend school, participate in after-school activities, and spend time with friends.

Sometimes, adolescents with Agoraphobia are forced into feared situations. For example, an adolescent who is afraid of leaving her home will eventually need to go to school; an adolescent afraid of certain modes of public transportation may eventually find herself on an airplane during a family vacation. In many cases, adolescents are able to endure these situations with intense, emotional discomfort. In some cases, they rely on another person (e.g., parent, older sibling, close friend) to accompany them and provide them with reassurance and a sense of safety.

Panic Disorder and Agoraphobia in Children and Adolescents

Panic attacks are relatively common among youths. As many as 18% of adolescents have had at least one full-blown panic attack (Essau et al., 1999; Hayward, Killen, Kraemer, & Barr Taylor, 2000). Furthermore, 60% of adolescents may have had subthreshold panic symptoms (Ollendick, Birmaher, & Mattis, 2004). Panic attacks are equally common in boys and girls, but they may be more severe in girls (Ollendick et al., 2004).

Although panic attacks occur relatively frequently, Panic Disorder is relatively uncommon among adolescents and rare in children. The onset of Panic Disorder is usually between the ages of 15 and 19 (Curry et al., 2004). However, there are isolated instances of its onset occurring before puberty (Ollendick, Mattis, & King, 1994). Most cases of Panic Disorder in children and adolescents go undetected. Parents and physicians usually interpret panic symptoms as medical problems. Consequently, youngsters who are eventually diagnosed with Panic Disorder wait, on average, 12.7 years until their disorder is properly identified and treated (Essau, Conradt et al., 1999, 2000).

Researchers are not sure why Panic Disorder is seldom seen in prepubescent children. Clearly, young children can experience panic attacks. For example, a young child separated from her parents in a crowded department store might experience extreme panic. However, few children develop Panic Disorder. Some data indicate that young children do not develop Panic Disorder because they lack the cognitive capacity for **metacognition**, that is, the ability to think about their own thoughts and feelings. Indeed, younger adolescents who have had at least one panic attack worry less about having additional attacks and think less about the implications of these attacks than older adolescents and young adults. It is likely that younger children's cognitive immaturity protects them from thinking about (and worrying about) recurrent problems with panic (Wittchen et al., 1998).

DSM-IV → DSM-5 CHANGES

AGORAPHOBIA AS A SEPARATE DISORDER

In *DSM-III* and *DSM-IV*, Agoraphobia was not a separate disorder. It could only be diagnosed in relation to Panic Disorder. Researchers believed that most people with Agoraphobia also had Panic Disorder or, at least, a history of recurrent panic attacks. Through classical conditioning, individuals might associate a specific place or situation (e.g., a shopping mall) with a panic attack. Then, because of negative reinforcement, individuals would avoid that place or situation in order to reduce fears of having another attack. Individuals with both panic and agoraphobic avoidance would have been diagnosed with *Panic Disorder with Agoraphobia*. In rare instances, when individuals did not meet criteria for Panic Disorder, they would be diagnosed with *Agoraphobia without History of Panic Disorder*.

In *DSM-5*, Agoraphobia is classified as a separate disorder that can co-occur with a wide range of other psychiatric conditions (Wittchen et al., 2010). The Anxiety Disorders Work Group made this change for three reasons:

1. Although many people referred to hospitals and clinics for Agoraphobia also had Panic Disorder, 25% to 50% of people in the community with Agoraphobia have no history of panic attacks. Among people in the general population, Agoraphobia frequently develops in the absence of panic.

2. When people do show both Panic Disorder and Agoraphobia, their panic attacks do not always precede their agoraphobic avoidance. In some cases, people have panic attacks after the emergence of Agoraphobia.

3. No other disorders are organized hierarchically (e.g., one disorder is viewed as a subset of another disorder). Panic Disorder and Agoraphobia should be separated to maintain consistency across the *DSM-5*.

(Continued)

People with Panic Disorder often have co-occurring Agoraphobia. Across all studies, between 50% and 75% of individuals with Panic Disorder also have Agoraphobia. Experts used to believe that Agoraphobia existed almost exclusively in people with Panic Disorder (see text box *DSM-IV* → *DSM-5* Changes: Agoraphobia as a Separate Disorder). We now know that approximately 25% of people referred to mental health clinics and 50% of people in the community with Agoraphobia have no history of Panic Disorder. The two disorders can occur independently (Wittchen et al., 2010).

Youths with Panic Disorder almost always have other anxiety problems. The most commonly occurring anxiety disorder is Generalized Anxiety Disorder, a condition characterized by persistent psychological tension and worry about the future (Last, Perrin, Hersen, & Kazdin, 1992). Generalized anxiety during childhood might predispose adolescents to experience Panic Disorder in late adolescence (N. J. King, Gullone, Tonge, & Ollendick, 1993).

Panic Disorder in adolescence or adulthood is also associated with childhood-onset Separation Anxiety Disorder (Craske et al., 2010). Family studies indicate that adults with Panic Disorder are at elevated risk of having children who develop SAD. Furthermore, several retrospective and longitudinal studies indicate that children with SAD may be 2 to 4 times more likely to develop Panic Disorder in late adolescence or early adulthood. Indeed, both children with SAD and adults with Panic Disorder show subtle abnormalities in respiration that may make them susceptible to panic symptoms (i.e., rapid, shallow breathing). Some experts have argued that these two disorders are different developmental manifestations of the same underlying condition.

Panic Disorder can also lead to mood problems. Adolescents and young adults with Panic Disorder show increased risk for depression and suicide (Birmaher & Ollendick, 2004). Risk is approximately three times higher in youths with Panic Disorder compared to youths without anxiety. Panic Disorder typically precedes mood and substance use problems by 3 years, indicating that panic symptoms may cause later emotional impairment (Craske et al., 2010). Panic Disorder also frequently precedes substance use problems in adolescents. Adolescents with Panic Disorder are most likely to use alcohol and other depressant drugs to reduce anxiety and cope with panic symptoms. In one large, longitudinal study, the onset of Panic Disorder in adolescence and early adulthood predicted the emergence of Substance Use Disorders 5 years later (Goodwin, Lieb et al., 2004).

Etiology of Panic Disorder

The causes of Panic Disorder are complex; no single theory can adequately explain all of the features of this disorder. However, cognitive and behavioral models of Panic Disorder have received the most empirical support from studies involving adolescents (Barlow, 2002; Beck & Emery, 1985; Clark, Salkovskis, & Chalkley, 1985). According to these models, biological, cognitive, and behavioral factors interact to produce recurrent panic attacks and (sometimes) Agoraphobia.

Individuals prone to Panic Disorder may inherit a biological disposition toward anxiety sensitivity (Dehon, Weems, Stickle, Costa, & Berman, 2005; Ollendick et al., 2004; Silverman & Dick-Niederhauser, 2004). **Anxiety sensitivity** refers to the tendency to perceive the symptoms of anxiety as extremely upsetting and aversive. For example, most people experience moderate anxiety before an important exam. A person with low anxiety sensitivity might be able to acknowledge her anxiety, cope with its symptoms (e.g., take deep breaths), and proceed with the exam. In contrast, a person with high anxiety sensitivity might experience pre-exam anxiety as extremely distressing and respond with fear. This unusual sensitivity to the physiological symptoms of anxiety (e.g., shakiness, rapid heartbeat, unusual body sensations) can lead to panic (Hale & Calamari, 2007).

According to the **expectancy theory of panic**, people with high anxiety sensitivity are unusually sensitive to the physiological symptoms of anxious arousal. Specifically, individuals with high anxiety sensitivity pay special attention to the increase in heart rate and shallowness of breathing that characterizes the early signs of anxiety. Additionally, these individuals show characteristic ways of thinking that exacerbate their anxiety symptoms (Weems, Berman, Silverman, & Saavedra, 2001).

First, these individuals tend to *personalize* negative events; that is, they blame themselves for negative outcomes.

For example, an adolescent with high anxiety sensitivity who experiences anxiety during an exam might blame herself for her anxiety: "I didn't study enough—it's my own fault that I'm not prepared." Personalization exacerbates the adolescent's anxiety and interferes with coping.

Second, adolescents with high anxiety sensitivity often engage in *catastrophic thinking*. When distressed, they anticipate the worst possible outcomes. For example, when an adolescent with high anxiety sensitivity experiences mild anxiety before an exam, she might expect her anxiety to escalate and become uncontrollable. She might think, "Oh no, I'm having one of those attacks again. I'm going to blank out and forget everything I studied! What am I going to do?" Catastrophic thinking is often self-fulfilling; it leads to an escalation of psychological distress.

Anxiety sensitivity, and the tendency to personalize and catastrophize negative events, can trigger a panic attack (Ginsburg, Lambert, & Drake, 2004). Unfortunately, one panic attack can cause adolescents to pay excessive attention to early warning signs of future attacks. Consequently, these adolescents become highly aware of even the mildest symptoms of anxious arousal. Even mild anxiety symptoms can cause them to think, "Oh no! Am I going to have one of those attacks again?"

Etiology of Agoraphobia

Approximately 30% of adolescents with Panic Disorder eventually develop Agoraphobia (Essau et al., 1999; Hayward et al., 2000). Usually, Agoraphobia develops when adolescents associate certain places or situations with a panic attack, through classical conditioning. For example, an adolescent who experiences a panic attack while shopping might avoid the mall. Similarly, a girl who experiences a panic attack at school might refuse to attend school. Agoraphobic avoidance is maintained through negative reinforcement. By avoiding the mall or school, these youths experience anxiety reduction. Consequently, they are more likely to avoid these places in the future.

Agoraphobia also seems to be related to the interaction of genetic risk and environmental factors (Wittchen et al., 2010). The heritability of Agoraphobia is particularly high; as much as 61% of an individual's risk for agoraphobic avoidance can be attributed to genetic factors. Furthermore, youths who develop Agoraphobia often come from families characterized by low warmth, high demandingness, and overprotection. Authoritarian parents place high expectations on their children yet often do not provide enough support or guidance to help them reach these expectations. Furthermore, they may communicate to their children that the world is a threatening, dangerous place. The combination of genetic risk, authoritarian parents, and panic symptoms greatly increases the likelihood of Agoraphobia.

In some cases, Agoraphobia can develop in the absence of Panic Disorder (Figure 11.5). Agoraphobia without Panic Disorder can develop in at least three ways (Headley & Hoffart, 2001). First, some individuals experience panic-like symptoms, but not true panic attacks. Panic-like symptoms include headaches, migraines, and gastrointestinal problems that cause distress or embarrassment. Through classical conditioning, individuals learn to associate these symptoms with specific situations. Through negative reinforcement, they learn to avoid these situations. For example, a child who develops migraines at school might develop agoraphobic avoidance of school because he fears their return. He would not be diagnosed with Panic Disorder because he has recurrent migraines, rather than panic attacks.

Second, some people develop agoraphobic avoidance of certain places or situations because they experience a negative external, rather than physiological, incident in that place. For example, a child who is bullied at school or an adolescent who is teased at the swimming pool by peers might develop Agoraphobia to avoid future victimization.

Third, some people who develop Agoraphobia also earn high scores on general anxiety and dependency. These individuals seem to worry a great deal about future misfortunes and doubt their ability to cope with psychosocial stress. They often report low self-efficacy and need frequent reassurance from others. These individuals may develop agoraphobic avoidance of certain places or situations if they are not accompanied by a family member or close friend who can provide this reassurance. For example, an adolescent might insist that her older sister go with her to the grocery store or the shopping mall, because she doubts her ability to visit these places alone.

CHRONIC WORRY: GENERALIZED ANXIETY DISORDER

Generalized Anxiety Disorder (GAD) is unlike the other anxiety disorders in two respects. First, GAD is characterized by worry rather than fear or panic. People with GAD do not fear specific objects, situations, or sensations; instead, they worry about future misfortune (Andrews et al., 2010). Second, GAD is more closely associated with depression than the other anxiety disorders. Children with GAD are especially likely to develop depression later in life. Adolescents with GAD often have co-occurring problems with depressed mood and dysphoria (Goldberg et al., 2009).

What Is Generalized Anxiety Disorder?

The hallmark of GAD is **apprehensive expectation**, that is, excessive anxiety and worry about the future (Table 11.8, Diagnostic Criteria for Generalized Anxiety Disorder). Adults with GAD worry about aspects of everyday life, such as completing tasks at work, managing finances, meeting appointments, and performing household chores. Children

Figure 11.5 Panic Disorder and Agoraphobia Can Occur Together or Separately

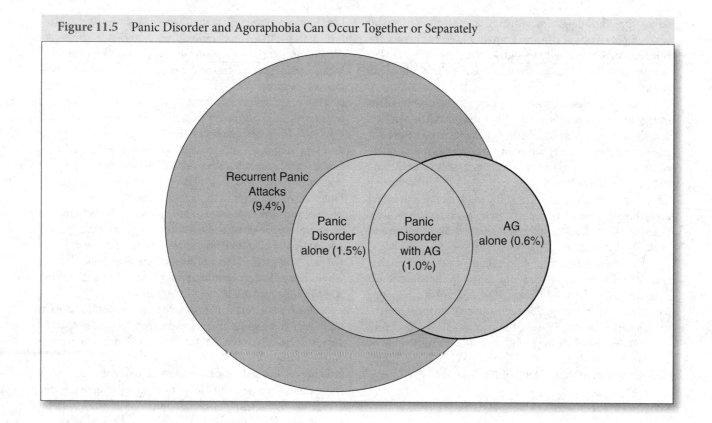

Source: Based on Wittchen and colleagues (2010).

Note: Usually, Agoraphobia (AG) develops after recurrent panic attacks or Panic Disorder. In some cases, however, Agoraphobia can develop without a history of panic symptoms.

and adolescents with GAD also worry about activities and events in their day-to-day lives, especially performing well on exams, school assignments, athletics, and extracurricular activities. By definition, youths with GAD must worry about at least two activities or events. On average, however, most people with GAD report many domains of worry (Niles et al., 2012).

Table 11.8 Diagnostic Criteria for Generalized Anxiety Disorder

A. Excessive anxiety and worry (apprehensive expectation), occurring more days than not for at least 6 months, about a number of events and activities (such as work or school performance).

B. The individual finds it difficult to control the worry.

C. The anxiety and worry are associated with three (more) of the following six symptoms (with at least some symptoms having been present for more days than not for the past 6 months):

Note: Only one item is required in children.

1. Restlessness or feeling keyed up or on edge.

2. Being easily fatigued.

3. Difficulty concentrating or mind going blank.

4. Irritability.

5. Muscle tension.

6. Sleep disturbance (difficulty falling asleep or staying asleep, or restless unsatisfying sleep).

D. The anxiety, worry, or physical symptoms cause clinically significant distress or impairment in social, occupational, or other important areas of functioning.

E. The disturbance is not attributable to the physiological effects of a substance (e.g., a drug of abuse, a medication) or another medical condition (e.g., hyperthyroidism).

F. The disturbance is not better explained by another mental disorder (e.g., worry about separation from attachment figures as in Separation Anxiety Disorder; worry about negative evaluation as in Social Anxiety Disorder; or worry about having panic attacks as in Panic Disorder).

Source: Reprinted with permission from the *Diagnostic and Statistical Manual of Mental Disorders, Fifth Edition* (Copyright 2013). American Psychiatric Association.

Children and adolescents with GAD worry about the same topics as people without GAD, such as work, school, relationships, and achieving goals for the future (Layne et al., 2009). The difference between the worries of people with and without GAD lies in their (a) number, (b) intensity, and (c) duration (Figure 11.6). First, people with GAD report a greater *number* of worries than people without GAD.

Second, people with GAD rate their worries as *more intense* or distressing than people without GAD. Furthermore, they often report greater impairment associated with worrying: daytime restlessness, sleep problems, fatigue, muscle tension, irritability, and difficulty concentrating. Third, people with GAD spend a greater *percentage of their day* worrying than most other individuals (Niles et al., 2012).

Figure 11.6   Children With and Without GAD Worry About Similar Topics

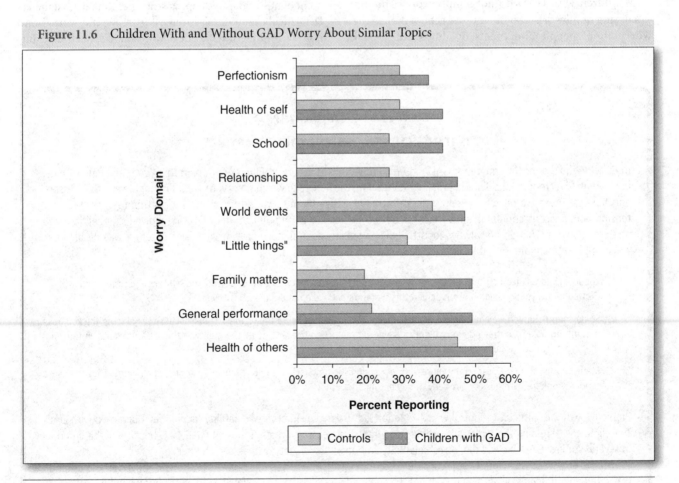

Source: Based on Layne and colleagues (2009).

Note: Children with GAD, however, report a greater number of worries and associated symptoms (e.g., restlessness, trouble concentrating, trouble sleeping) than their peers without GAD.

Generalized Anxiety Disorder (GAD) in Children and Adolescents

Worry is a cognitive activity characterized by repeated and increasingly elaborated thoughts about future negative events and their consequences (Borkovec & Inz, 1990). Children might worry about an upcoming exam, the possibility of not studying adequately for the exam, and the repercussions of earning a low grade or gaining the disapproval of teachers and parents. Children begin to show the ability to worry around age four or five years (Muris, Merckelbach et al., 2000). However, the ability to think about and dwell upon negative events in the distant future does not seem to emerge until after age 8 (Vasey, Crnic, & Carter, 1994). The onset of GAD is usually after this cognitive capacity for worry develops, that is, between 8 and 10 years of age (Keller, Lavori, Wunder, Beardslee, Schwartz, & Roth, 1992; Last et al., 1992). As children's capacity for worry increases with age, so does the frequency and severity of GAD (Kendall, Pimentel, Rynn, Angelosante, & Webb, 2004).

Children with GAD do not simply worry about an upcoming homework assignment or a school dance; they worry about people and events in almost all areas of their lives (see text box *DSM-IV* → *DSM-5* Changes: Is It Difficult to Control Your Worrying?). The most common worries among children with GAD include health problems (e.g., getting sick and dying), school problems (e.g., failing, being ridiculed by teachers, not getting admitted to college), disasters (e.g., harm in a thunderstorm, terrorist attacks), and personal harm befalling others (e.g., a loved one hit by a car, a parent losing a job). Children with GAD also have many adultlike worries, such as whether a parent might lose her job or whether the family has enough money (Weems, Silverman, & La Greca, 2000).

The worries shown by children with GAD interfere with their daily functioning (Flannery-Schroeder, 2004; Masi, Millepiedi, Mucci, Poli, Bertini, & Milantoni, 2004; see Figure 11.7). First, worry causes significant distress and consumes significant time and energy. Second, worry interferes with children's abilities to concentrate on important activities such as listening to parents or completing homework assignments. Third, worry can cause mood problems, frustration, and irritability. Fourth, worry can cause somatic problems, such as headaches, sleep problems, or fatigue. Finally, worry can interfere with the development of more adaptive coping strategies (Shoal, Castaneda, & Giancola, 2005). Children who frequently worry may not learn other ways to deal with anxiety, such as using

---

DSM-IV → *DSM-5* CHANGES

IS IT DIFFICULT TO CONTROL YOUR WORRYING?

In *DSM-IV*, the diagnostic criteria for GAD required individuals to report problems controlling their worrying. Indeed, most adults with GAD report considerable problems controlling the degree to which they worry about minor life events, stressors, and hassles. These worries often keep them up at night, make them tired and irritable, and contribute to restlessness, tension, and concentration problems. However, data collected since the publication of *DSM-IV* showed that children and adolescents with GAD do not always report similar problems controlling their worrying. This criterion was problematic when applied to children for at least three reasons:

1. Younger children did not often understand what clinicians meant when they asked, "Do you find it difficult to control your worry?" Consequently, young children often denied this symptom and were not diagnosed with GAD.

2. Some young children were not able to control their worrying, not because they had GAD but because they lacked the cognitive maturity to do so. Controlling worry requires advanced metacognitive skills (e.g., the ability to think about your own thinking) that typically does not emerge until late childhood or adolescence.

3. Many youths with GAD, especially those with perfectionistic tendencies, do not even try to control their worry. They may have serious problems with anxiety but deny this symptom altogether.

Problems with the "difficult-to-control worry" criterion led to very low inter-rater reliability for children diagnosed with GAD. Two clinicians, assessing the same child, would frequently disagree as to whether the child had GAD because of this criterion. In several studies, GAD showed the lowest reliability among all the anxiety disorders in children.

The Anxiety Disorder Work Group considered dropping this criterion from *DSM-5*. In the end, however, the criterion was retained. Clinicians need to be mindful of the challenges of diagnosing anxiety disorders in young children, especially when information must come from children's self-reports (Andrews et al., 2010).

---

relaxation or play, expressing negative emotions to parents or peers, or engaging in a sport or hobby. *DSM-5* requires children with GAD to experience at least one symptom as the result of their worrying. In contrast, adults with GAD must show at least three symptoms (American Psychiatric Association, 2013).

DSM-5 warns clinicians that GAD may be overdiagnosed in children and adolescents (American Psychiatric Association, 2013). Overdiagnosis likely occurs for two reasons. First, many older children and adolescents report considerable stress or anxiety in their daily lives. It is sometimes difficult for clinicians to differentiate normal concerns from the symptoms of GAD. Second, many other childhood anxiety disorders can by mistaken for GAD. For example, children with Separation Anxiety Disorder often worry about separation from loved ones or the health and welfare of their parents. Similarly, youths with Social Anxiety Disorder often worry persistently about social or performance situations. When worry is better explained by these other disorders, youths should be diagnosed with these other disorders rather than GAD.

Children with GAD are often described by parents and teachers as "little adults" (Kendall, Krain, & Treadwell, 1999). These youths are often perfectionist, punctual, and eager to please. They are usually quite self-conscious around others, especially adults and people in authority. They also tend to be highly conforming to rules and social norms. For these reasons, Kendall and colleagues (1999) suggest that children with GAD create an "illusion of maturity" that makes them appear more emotionally competent than they really are.

Beneath this illusion of maturity, children with GAD harbor feelings of self-doubt, self-criticism, and uncertainty. They may strive for perfection when completing a homework assignment, preparing for a piano recital, or practicing for an athletic competition. However, they often require excessive reassurance from teachers, tutors, and coaches to make sure that they gain the approval of others. Children with GAD may also refuse to submit homework, play, or compete unless they know their performance will be perfect. They often interpret signs of imperfection (e.g., homework mistakes, misplayed notes, coming in second) as indicators of failure and worthlessness.

Children with GAD are at risk for other anxiety disorders. In one large study, 75% of youths with GAD showed one comorbid anxiety disorder and 38% showed two or more coexisting anxiety disorders (Masi et al., 2004). The most common comorbid anxiety disorders are SAD, Specific Phobia, and Social Anxiety Disorder (Kashani & Orvaschel, 1990; Masi et al., 2004). It is possible that persistent worry sensitizes children to developing specific fear of objects or social situations.

Figure 11.7   Anxiety Symptoms in Youths With GAD

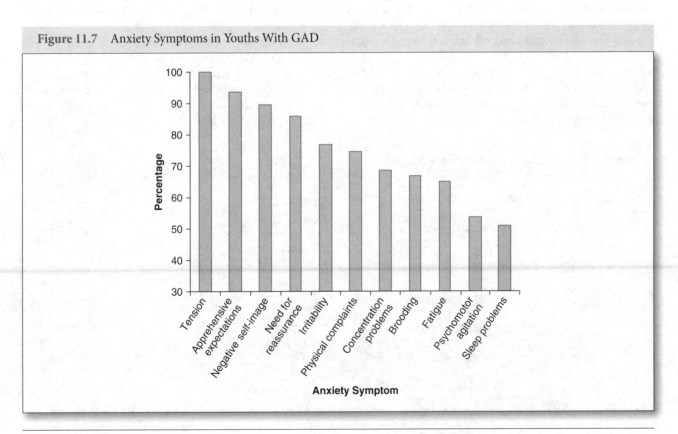

Source: Based on Masi et al. (2004).

Note: Children and adolescents with GAD show a wide range of impairments, including tension, apprehension about the future, and negative self-image.

GAD also shows closer associations with depression than any of the other anxiety disorders (Goldberg et al., 2009). Three lines of evidence indicate its close relationship to depression. First, GAD and Major Depressive Disorder show high comorbidity in older children and adolescents. Approximately 50% of youths with GAD also have depression (Masi, Favilla, Mucci, & Millepiedi, 2000; Masi et al., 2004).

Second, longitudinal research indicates that children with GAD are at particular risk for developing depression later in life. For example, Moffitt and colleagues (2007) examined a large sample of individuals with GAD and depression from adolescence through young adulthood. In most cases (68%), participants' anxiety problems preceded or appeared simultaneously with their depressive symptoms. Only about one third of participants experienced anxiety problems after depression. Another longitudinal study showed that adolescents developed depressive symptoms 5 years after the emergence of their anxiety, on average (Cole, Peeke, Martin, Truglio, & Seroczynski, 1998).

Third, factor analysis has shown that GAD and depressive symptoms tend to naturally co-occur in the general population (Krueger, 1999; Slade & Watson, 2006; Vollebergh et al., 2001). Factor analysis is a statistical technique that identifies underlying constructs, or "factors," that explain relationships between observable traits or symptoms. In this case, factor analysis is performed by examining associations between children's symptoms and identifying clusters of symptoms that tend to occur together. Several factor analytic studies have shown that children's internalizing symptoms can be explained by two factors (Figure 11.8). A "fear" factor explains the relationship between most anxiety disorders characterized by anxiety, fear, and panic: Specific Phobia, Social Anxiety Disorder, Agoraphobia, and Panic Disorder.

However, a second "anxious-misery" factor explains the relationship between GAD, Major Depressive Disorder, and Dysthymic Disorder (i.e., persistent dysphoria). Children with GAD are more likely to show problems with depression than symptoms of fear or panic.

Etiology

Little is known about the causes of GAD in children (Kendall, Pimentel et al., 2004). Most research has examined the causes of childhood anxiety more generally. Many of the risk factors of anxiety disorders in general apply to GAD. For example, children with difficult temperaments, behavioral inhibition, and less-than-optimal parent-child interactions are probably at risk for GAD, in addition to the other anxiety disorders (Flannery-Schroeder, 2004; Hale, Engels, & Meeus, 2006).

From a behavioral perspective, worrying seems to make little sense. Most people consider worrying to be an aversive activity. Consequently, worrying appears to have no reinforcing properties. However, cognitive-behavioral theorists suggest that worrying serves a special purpose for children and adolescents with GAD. According to Thomas Borkovec's **cognitive avoidance theory**, worrying helps people avoid emotionally and physically arousing mental images (Borkovec & Inz, 1990; Roemer & Borkovec, 1993). Worry allows people to replace these emotion-laden images of imminent danger with more abstract, analytical thoughts about future misfortune. Worry, therefore, is a form of avoidance and is negatively reinforcing.

To understand how worry can be negatively reinforcing, consider Elsa, a perfectionistic 12-year-old with GAD. Elsa's teacher has assigned her to work with three classmates on an important science project. As a group, the students must

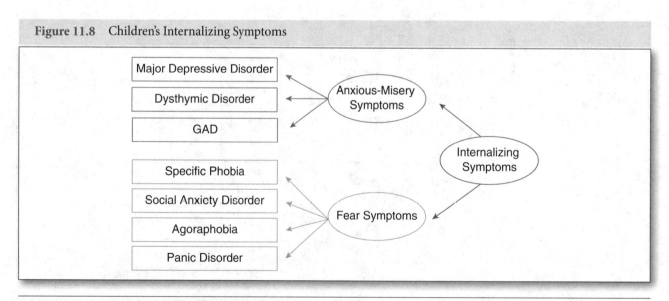

Figure 11.8 Children's Internalizing Symptoms

Source: Based on Goldberg and colleagues (2009).

Note: Children's internalizing symptoms can be divided into two groups based on how they typically co-occur: fear symptoms and anxious-misery symptoms. GAD tends to be more like depression than the other anxiety disorders.

PART IV EMOTION AND THOUGHT DISORDERS

complete the project, write a poster, and present their findings at the school science fair. Most children would experience some apprehension when faced with this assignment; however, Elsa shows great distress. She imagines the group failing miserably in their experiment, making countless mistakes on their poster, and humiliating themselves during the presentation. Furthermore, she foresees chastisement and disapproval from her teacher and parents. To cope with these mental images, Elsa thinks about the situation in more abstract, verbal terms—she worries. She thinks to herself, "What if my classmates don't follow through with their part of the project?" or "I had better double-check our spelling on the poster" or "Maybe I'm not prepared enough for the oral presentation—I should rehearse one more time." These worries occupy Elsa's time and energy. They serve an important function: They allow Elsa to avoid imagining the terrible consequences of failing the project. To the extent that worry allows children like Elsa to avoid or escape distressing images, worry can be negatively reinforcing (Borkovec, Ray, & Stober, 1998).

Most data supporting the cognitive avoidance theory of worry come from adults with GAD. However, one recent study showed that children and adolescents who experience excessive worrying engage in more cognitive avoidance strategies than youths who experience only moderate worry (Gosselin et al., 2007). For example, chronic worriers often used strategies like distraction (e.g., playing video games) or thought suppression (e.g., telling oneself not to think about a given topic) to avoid dealing with future problems. In contrast, low level worriers tended to use more active problem-solving strategies that helped them address problems directly (e.g., studying for an upcoming test). Furthermore, the researchers found that the number of avoidance strategies used by children predicted the severity of their worrying.

In fact, children with GAD worry to *avoid* thinking about problems, not to solve them. Most children use worrying to anticipate future problems and generate possible solutions ahead of time. For example, a child worrying about an upcoming exam might reason, "The test is going to be very hard, so I'm going to have to start studying right away—a little bit each night—in order to do well." In this case, worrying serves a positive, problem-solving function. In contrast, children with GAD show very little problem solving while worrying (see Figure 11.9). Instead, these children simply ruminate about the negative event (Szabo & Lovibond, 2004). For example, a child with GAD who is worrying about a future exam might think, "The exam is going to be really difficult. What if I fail? What will my mom say?" Because children with GAD are less likely to generate solutions for their worries, their worries persist uncontrollably.

Youths with GAD may show **cognitive distortions** that cause them to worry. Weems and Watts (2005) identified three cognitive distortions seen in children's worries: catastrophizing, overgeneralizing, and personalizing. *Catastrophizing* occurs when children expect disastrous outcomes from mildly aversive events. For example, a girl with GAD who has an upcoming dance recital might anticipate disaster: She

Figure 11.9   How Do You Worry?

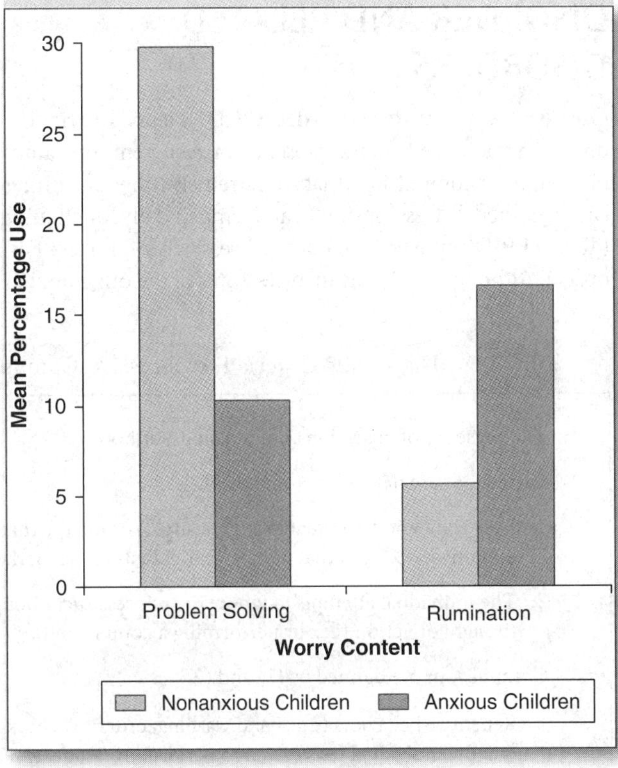

Source: Based on Szabo and Lovibond (2004).

Note: Children without anxiety disorders tend to generate solutions to future problems when they worry. In contrast, children with anxiety disorders, like GAD, tend to ruminate about potential trouble in the future.

might forget her dance shoes, trip on stage, and humiliate her family. *Overgeneralizing* occurs when children assume that a single adverse event is an indicator of future misfortune. For example, a child who makes a mistake in her first recital might anticipate mistakes in all subsequent performances. Finally, *personalizing* occurs when children assume personal responsibility for misfortune. For example, a child who trips during a dance recital might attribute her mistake to her own clumsiness, rather than to a slippery floor (Weems et al., 2001).

Youths with GAD also underestimate their ability to cope with threatening events (Weems & Watts, 2005). Children with anxiety disorders in general, and GAD in particular, often display an **external locus of control**; that is, they believe events and situations are largely determined by external causes (e.g., luck, fate) rather than internal causes (e.g., hard work). Youths with GAD, in particular, often show low self-efficacy (Weems & Watts, 2005). **Self-efficacy** is a concept created by Albert Bandura (1973) to describe a person's appraisal of her ability to accomplish tasks and control her surroundings. When faced with threatening situations, children with GAD are often doubtful of their abilities to confront and overcome their problems. Low self-efficacy, therefore, breeds rumination and worry. In contrast, high self-efficacy fosters confidence about the future.

OBSESSIVE-COMPULSIVE DISORDER AND RELATED DISORDERS

Obsessive-Compulsive Disorder (OCD) is a psychiatric condition characterized by the presence of recurrent, unwanted obsessions or compulsions that are extremely time consuming, cause marked distress, or significantly impair daily functioning (Table 11.9, Diagnostic Criteria for Obsessive-Compulsive Disorder). Although OCD has many features of the other anxiety disorders, it is placed in a separate diagnostic group in *DSM-5* (see text box *DSM-IV* → *DSM-5* Changes: OCD: Not an Anxiety Disorder). Recent research indicates that OCD likely has different causes than the anxiety disorders. Furthermore, OCD tends to respond to different forms of treatment. In this section, we will also consider three other related conditions: (a) Tic Disorders, (b) Trichotillomania (i.e., hair-pulling), and (c) Excoriation Disorder (i.e., skin-picking). OCD, tics, Trichotillomania, and Excoriation often co-occur and are all characterized by obsessive preoccupation, unwanted urges, and/or repetitive actions (Stein, Fineberg et al., 2010).

Table 11.9 Diagnostic Criteria for Obsessive-Compulsive Disorder

A. The presence of obsessions, compulsions, or both:

Obsessions are defined by (1) and (2):

1. Recurrent and persistent thoughts, urges, or images that are experienced, at some time during the disturbance, as intrusive and unwanted, and that in most individuals cause marked anxiety or distress.

2. The individual attempts to ignore or suppress such thoughts, urges, or images, or to neutralize them with some other thought or action (i.e., by performing a compulsion).

Compulsions are defined by (1) and (2):

1. Repetitive behaviors (e.g., hand washing, ordering, checking) or mental acts (e.g., praying , counting, repeating words silently) that the individual feels driven to perform in response to an obsession or according to rules that must be applied rigidly.

2. The behaviors or mental acts are aimed at preventing or reducing anxiety or distress, or preventing some dreaded event or situation; however, these behaviors or mental acts are not connected in a realistic way with what they are designed to neutralize or prevent, or are clearly excessive.

Note: Young children may not be able to articulate the aims of these behaviors or mental acts.

B. The obsessions or compulsions are time-consuming (e.g., take more than 1 hour per day) or cause clinically significant distress or impairment in social, occupational, or other important areas of functioning.

C. The obsessive-compulsive symptoms are not attributable to the physiological effects of a substance (e.g., a drug of abuse, a medication) or another medical condition.

D. The disturbance is not better explained by the symptoms of another mental disorder (e.g., repetitive patterns of behavior as in Autism Spectrum Disorder; impulses as in Conduct Disorder; preoccupation with substances as in Substance Use Disorders; excessive worries as in Generalized Anxiety Disorder; hair pulling as in Trichotillomania[1]; skin picking as in Excoriation Disorder[1]; or guilty ruminations as in Major Depressive Disorder.[2]

Specify if:

With good or fair insight: The individual recognizes that obsessive-compulsive disorder beliefs are definitely or probably not true or that they may or may not be true.

With poor insight: The individual thinks that obsessive-compulsive disorder beliefs are probably true.

With absent insight: The individual is completely convinced that obsessive-compulsive disorder beliefs are true.

Specify if:

Tic-related: The individual has a current or past history of a Tic Disorder.

Source: Reprinted with permission from the *Diagnostic and Statistical Manual of Mental Disorders, Fifth Edition* (Copyright 2013). American Psychiatric Association.

[1]Trichotillomania and Excoriation Disorder are presented later in this chapter.

[2]Major Depressive Disorder is presented in Chapter 13.

What Is Obsessive-Compulsive Disorder?

Obsessions are "recurrent and persistent thoughts, urges, or images that are experienced as intrusive and unwanted" (American Psychiatric Association, 2013, p. 235). Obsessions include thoughts about contamination (e.g., touching "dirty" objects like door handles), repeated doubts (e.g., wondering whether someone left the door unlocked), need for order or symmetry (e.g., towels arranged a certain way), aggressive or horrific impulses (e.g., thoughts about swearing in church), and sexual imagery.

Most people with OCD attempt to ignore or suppress obsessions. However, ignoring obsessions usually causes an increase in anxiety and subjective distress. To reduce feelings of distress, most people engage in compulsions. **Compulsions** are "repetitive behaviors or mental acts that an individual feels driven to perform in response to an obsession or according to rules that must be applied rigidly"

(American Psychiatric Association, 2013, p. 235). Common compulsions include washing, cleaning, counting, checking, repeating, arranging, and ordering. Compulsions are usually performed in a highly rigid and stereotyped manner, often according to certain idiosyncratic rules. For example, an adolescent with recurrent obsessions involving sexual imagery may feel compelled to pray to alleviate anxiety or guilt. If she makes mistakes in her prayers, she may require herself to repeat them until they are flawlessly recited.

Obsessions and compulsions tend to be time consuming, distressing, and impairing. It is not uncommon for obsessions and compulsions to occupy hours of the individual's time each day (Lin et al., 2007).

Many adults and adolescents with OCD recognize that their unwanted thoughts, urges, or images are a product of their own mind; they will likely not occur or "come true." Consider the following transcript between 12-year-old Richard and his therapist:

RICK'S RECURRENT THOUGHTS

Therapist: So, tell me about these thoughts you have before going to bed.

Rick: I feel the need to check my backpack many times. I have these thoughts like, "I've forgotten to pack something important." They fill up my head until I've had enough.

Therapist: Then what do you do?

Rick: I get out of bed and check. Sometimes, I check five or 10 times. I know it's funny, but if I don't check, I can't relax and get to sleep.

Therapist: What do you mean when you say "it's funny?"

Rick: I mean, checking once is fine—just to make sure. I don't *need* to check five or 10 times. But I still do.

Therapist: So, what's the likelihood that after you've checked once, you'll still forget something important.

Rick: Pretty low. But that doesn't make a difference. I still can't get to sleep until I check many times and feel good about it.

Many adults and adolescents, like Rick, realize that their obsessive thoughts and/or compulsive behaviors are not true. However, many individuals with OCD, especially children, may be convinced that their obsessions and/or compulsions will materialize. *DSM-5* requires clinicians to specify the person's insight into his or her obsessive-compulsive symptoms (see Table 11.9, Diagnostic Criteria for Obsessive-Compulsive Disorder). Specification is important because people with good insight may be more motivated to participate in treatment than people with poor or absent insight (Geller, 2010).

Obsessive-Compulsive Disorder (OCD) in Children and Adolescents

Approximately 1% to 2% of children and adolescents have OCD. Epidemiological studies suggest that at any given point in time, 90% of these children are not receiving treatment for the disorder. In childhood, OCD is more common among boys than girls, with a gender ratio of 2:1. By late adolescence, many girls begin to manifest the disorder and the gender distribution becomes roughly equal (Geller, 2010).

CASE STUDY

TONY: A BOY WHO NEEDS THINGS DONE "JUST RIGHT"

Tony was a 12-year-old boy who was referred to our clinic by his mother after she noticed him repeatedly engaging in "bizarre rituals" around the house. Mrs. Jeffries first became aware of Tony's ritualistic behavior when she noticed his persistent habit of turning lights on and off multiple times before entering or leaving a room. When she asked about this habit, Tony seemed embarrassed and dismissed it as "nothing." Mrs. Jeffries subsequently noticed other rituals. Tony avoided cracks in sidewalks, always entered rooms with his right foot, and always opened doors with his right hand. Mrs. Jeffries confronted Tony about these behaviors. In tears, Tony eventually admitted to being bothered by a persistent need to engage in these compulsive acts.

Dr. Saunders interviewed Tony. "Do you have any thoughts that pop into your mind before you perform these acts?" Tony replied hesitatingly, "Yeah, but they're hard to describe. I sort of feel nervous. I feel like something bad is going to happen to me or to my mom . . . like maybe I'll get an F in school or my mom will lose her job. Then, I just feel like I need to do something in a certain way, like turn the lights on and off three times, or open and close the refrigerator three times, or enter and exit a room three times." Dr. Saunders asked, "Always in threes?" Tony explained, "Yeah, it has to be in threes and just right so that I don't feel nervous anymore."

The most common obsessions among children and adolescents are fear of germs (e.g., contamination), fear of harm befalling self or others, and an overwhelming need for order or symmetry (Figure 11.10). The most common compulsions are washing and cleaning, checking, counting, repeating, touching, and straightening (March et al., 2004).

Children's obsessions and compulsions differ somewhat from those of adults. First, it is not unusual for children to change obsessions and/or compulsions over time. Second, children's obsessions and compulsions are often more vague, magical, or superstitious than those of adults (Franklin, Rynn, Foa, & March, 2004). Third, many children have difficulty describing their obsessions. For example, they might report fearing "bad things" rather than contamination or asymmetry. Fourth, some children who are able to articulate their obsessions are unwilling to do so because they fear that stating them aloud will make their feared consequences come true.

Technically, individuals can be diagnosed with OCD if they show *either* obsessions *or* compulsions. In reality, most children show both symptoms (March et al., 2004). Sometimes, children appear to display only obsessions because their compulsions involve mental rituals. For example, obsessions regarding harm befalling a loved one might be accompanied by ritualistic counting or praying. These mental acts might be easily overlooked by parents and clinicians who mistakenly conclude that no compulsions exist. Indeed, the treatment of mental compulsions is more difficult than the treatment of behavioral compulsions because they are difficult to detect and monitor.

As many as 80% of children and adolescents with OCD have at least one other psychiatric disorder (Geller, 2010). The most commonly co-occurring problems are other anxiety disorders, depression, and tics. Among clinic-referred children, as many as 70% of children with OCD have another anxiety disorder, while approximately 70% of adolescents with OCD have depression (Curry et al., 2004). OCD and tics may have a common genetic etiology. For example, individuals with OCD often have first-degree

Figure 11.10 Common Obsessions and Compulsions Shown by Children and Adolescents With OCD

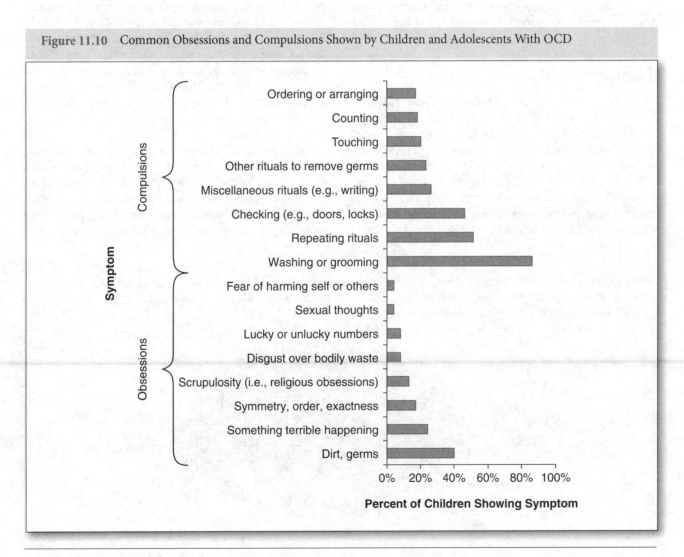

Source: Based on Rapoport and Shaw (2010).

relatives with tics, while individuals with tics often have first-degree relatives with OCD. Children and adolescents with both OCD and tics tend to show the greatest degree of anxiety and impairment (March et al., 2004). On average, 25% of youths with OCD also meet criteria for ADHD. Boys whose OCD symptoms emerge in childhood are especially likely to show comorbid inattentive and hyperactive/impulsive symptoms (Geller, 2010).

Childhood OCD is a serious disorder that is persistent over time. On average, 41% of youths with OCD continue to meet diagnostic criteria for the disorder 5 years later. An additional 20% of youths continue to show subthreshold OCD symptoms. Youths with early symptom onset, longer duration of symptoms, and symptoms requiring hospitalization are most likely to show persistent symptoms. On the other hand, approximately 40% of youths with OCD show a marked reduction in symptoms in late adolescence and early adulthood. Many adolescents will experience complete symptom remission. Nevertheless, youths with OCD are at significantly greater risk for relationship, employment, and emotional problems in young adulthood compared to their typically developing peers (S. E. Stewart, Geller et al., 2004).

Etiology

OCD is moderately heritable. The disorder appears to run in families; individuals with first-degree relatives with OCD are at increased risk for developing OCD. Approximately 10% to 25% of youths with OCD have at least one parent with the disorder (Hanna, 2000). Twin studies indicate that genetic (45%–58%) and nonshared environmental (42%–55%) factors explain about the same amount of variance in OCD symptoms. Shared environmental experiences (e.g., parenting, SES) account for very little variance (Hudziak et al., 2004).

The heritability of obsessions is slightly higher than the heritability of compulsions (Geller, 2010).

OCD is best viewed as a neuropsychiatric disorder that is caused by abnormalities in brain structure and functioning (Rapoport & Shaw, 2010). A neural pathway, known as the **cortico-striatal-thalamic circuit**, seems to be particularly important in the disorder (Image 11.3). This circuit forms a feedback loop, involving three brain regions: (a) the orbital-frontal cortex; (b) the caudate, which is part of the striatum; and (c) the thalamus.

The orbital-frontal cortex is responsible for detecting abnormalities or irregularities in the environment and initiating a behavioral response to correct these irregularities. For example, the orbital-frontal cortex might be activated when a person notices dirt on his hands. Signals from the orbital-frontal cortex pass through the caudate to the thalamus, which becomes highly active. The thalamus routes the information to various brain regions to initiate a behavioral response (e.g., wash hands) and sends a feedback signal back to the orbital-frontal cortex. In healthy people, the caudate inhibits information from the cortex to the thalamus, thereby, regulating the amount of arousal experienced by the thalamus. However, individuals with OCD often show irregularities in the structure and functioning of the caudate. Consequently, the cortico-striatal-thalamic circuit is not inhibited. Instead, the orbital-frontal cortex continues to send signals to the thalamus, increasing the person's desire to perform the behavior or ritual (March et al., 2004; Rosenberg & Keshavan, 1998).

Interestingly, abnormalities in the cortio-striatal-thalamic pathway tend to be specific to the types of obsessions shown by individuals with OCD (Leckman et al., 2010). For example, researchers examined the brain activity of people with obsessions about germs using fMRI. When these people were shown pictures related to washing, they

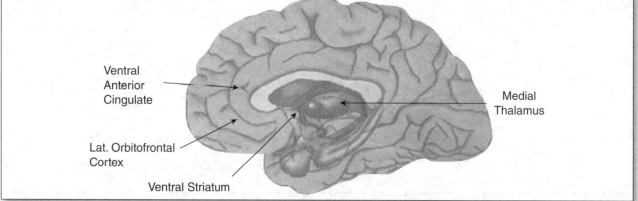

Image 11.3 The cortico-striatal-thalamic circuit likely underlies OCD. This circuit forms a feedback loop, involving (a) the orbital-frontal cortex, (b) the striatum, and (c) the thalamus. Dysregulation of this circuit may produce obsessive thoughts and compulsive behaviors.

Source: From National Institutes of Mental Health.

showed increased activation in the insular cortex, a brain region in this pathway involved in the emotion of "disgust." In contrast, patients with checking and counting obsessions showed activation in a different portion of this pathway, the cingulate, a brain area responsible for noticing irregularities in environmental stimuli (e.g., items "out of order" or "not quite right").

Serotonin also likely plays a role in OCD. Medications like fluoxetine (Prozac) that inhibit the reuptake of serotonin reduce OCD symptoms in adolescents with the disorder (Franklin, March, & Gracia, 2007). Furthermore, drugs that artificially increase serotonergic activity often exacerbate symptoms. Consequently, many researchers believe that OCD symptoms are partially caused by excessively high levels of serotonin. Medications may reduce OCD symptoms by decreasing the number or sensitivity of serotonin receptors (March et al., 2004).

Genetic and biological factors might underlie OCD symptoms, but the disorder is probably maintained through learning. Obsessions develop when people associate specific environmental stimuli with anxiety-provoking thoughts or beliefs. For example, a door handle might be paired with anxiety-provoking thoughts of contamination. Later, the individual learns that washing reduces anxiety; consequently, he is more likely to wash his hands in the future. Compulsions, therefore, are negatively reinforced by anxiety reduction.

Cognitive theorists have argued that the way adolescents think can also contribute to the development of OCD (Salkovskis, Forrester, & Richards, 1998). Adolescents with OCD show two ways of thinking that contribute to their symptoms (S. Libby, Reynolds, Derisley, & Clark, 2004). First, adolescents with OCD experience inflated responsibility for misfortune. For example, if the adolescent's mother is fired from her job or the adolescent's father experiences car trouble on the way home, the adolescent might blame herself for their misfortune. She might think, "My mother lost her job because I'm too much of a burden for her. She can't handle me and her job at once" or "My father had car trouble because I was late in getting the oil changed last week. It must be my fault." These appraisals of misfortune contribute to feelings of guilt and self-doubt.

Second, adolescents with OCD often display **thought-action fusion**, the erroneous belief that merely thinking about an event will increase its probability. For example, an adolescent might believe that simply because he thought of his grandfather becoming sick and dying, his grandfather's likelihood of dying actually increased. Because the adolescent believes her thoughts can influence the external world, she attempts to control negative thoughts to prevent future disaster. Thought-action fusion causes adolescents to feel great distress when they experience transient negative thoughts. Whereas most people dismiss such thoughts as "irrational" or "unlikely," an adolescent with OCD might take them seriously because she believes she has the ability to mentally influence outside events.

Certain personality styles are also associated with OCD. Compared to their typically developing peers, adolescents with OCD are more likely to show a tendency toward anxiety and psychological distress (e.g., neuroticism) as well as a trend toward overestimating threats to their personal security and well-being. Like many youths with anxiety disorders, these adolescents may simply perceive the world as more threatening and themselves as more vulnerable to these threats. Furthermore, adolescents with OCD tend to score higher than their typically developing peers on measures of perfectionism, cognitive rigidity, and intolerance of uncertainty. Youths with OCD may have trouble seeing themselves, others, and the world around them in flexible ways and have problems adapting their thoughts and actions to meet the changing demands of their surroundings. These personality attributes probably do not cause OCD, but it is likely that they do exacerbate OCD symptoms once they develop (Reuther et al., 2013; C. Wilson et al., 2012).

Some cases of pediatric OCD may be caused by a beta-hemolytic streptococcus infection (Singer et al., 2011). The most common infection of this type is strep throat. According to the **Pediatric Autoimmune Neuropsychiatric Disorder Associated with Streptococcus (PANDAS) theory**, a subset of children who show these infections develops rapid-onset OCD symptoms and tics (i.e., involuntary movements or vocalizations). These children may have other symptoms such as irritability, enuresis, anxiety, and deterioration in fine motor skills (e.g., handwriting). These symptoms are caused by an autoimmune reaction that produces white blood cells which interfere with the functioning of the striatum. Antibiotic medication is not effective in preventing the onset of these symptoms. In most cases, children are later diagnosed with OCD and must receive treatment for the disorder (Murphy et al., 2010).

Associated Disorders

OCD bears resemblance to several other psychiatric conditions. Like OCD, these conditions are not anxiety disorders. However, they are associated with anxiety, tension, and negative affect. These conditions have in common obsessive preoccupations, unwanted urges, and/or repetitive actions that cause great distress or impair day-to-day functioning (Stein et al., 2011; Stein, Grant, et al., 2010). We will examine the three conditions most commonly seen in children and adolescents: (a) Tic Disorder and Tourette's Disorder, (b) Trichotillomania (i.e., hair-pulling disorder), and (c) Excoriation Disorder (i.e., skin picking).

Tic Disorders

Tics are sudden, rapid, non-rhythmic, and stereotyped behaviors. They can be either motoric (e.g., a facial grimace, neck twitch, or limb movement) or vocal (e.g., a grunt, chirp, or clearing of the throat). Tics can also be either simple or complex. Simple tics last a short duration (i.e., milliseconds) and consist of one type of motor behavior (e.g., eye blink, shrug) or vocalization (e.g., grunt, clearing one's throat). Complex tics last several seconds and usually consist of a combination of several simple tics (e.g., simultaneous head turning and shrugging). Complex tics sometimes appear to have a purpose or are volitional. For example, some people with tics make sexual or obscene gestures (i.e., copropraxia), utter obscenities or racial or religious slurs (i.e., coprolalia), imitate other people's movements (i.e., echopraxia), or repeat their own sounds or words (i.e., echolalia). In all cases, however, tics do not have a purpose and are done involuntarily.

Tics are similar to OCD; both disorders involve a sequence of events in which a stimulus is followed by a largely habitual response. In the case of OCD, the stimulus is an obsession, and the response is a compulsion. In the case of tics, the stimulus is a sudden, unwanted urge, and the response is the motor or vocal behavior. Furthermore, both tics and obsessions can be suppressed for brief periods of time but cause increasingly greater discomfort the longer they are suppressed (Leckman & Bloch, 2010).

OCD and tics also differ from one another. People with OCD almost always perform compulsions in response to certain obsessive thoughts or mental images (e.g., thoughts about contamination). In contrast, not all people with tics report obsessive thoughts that prompt their motor or vocal behaviors (Phillips et al., 2010). Only about one half of people with tic disorders report specific obsessions that occur prior to a tic. These obsessions often include thoughts

Image 11.4 Tourette's Disorder gets its name from Georges Gilles de la Tourette, who described nine patients with multiple motor and vocal tics in 1884. Tourette was a student of the famous neurologist Jean-Martin Charcot at the Salpêtrière Hospital in Paris. Charcot's other famous students include Alfred Binet, William James, and Sigmund Freud.

about symmetry, counting, ordering, or repeating actions until everything seems "just right." However, 57% to 80% of people with tic disorder report only premonitory urges prior to their tics. These urges are often described as having a "physical quality," much like an itch or muscle tension localized to a specific area of the body (Towbin, 2010).

Tics can range in severity from mild to severe. Many youths describe them as unwanted urges, similar to the feeling that you might get when you want to scratch your nose or sneeze. Usually, you can ignore or stifle this urge for a short period of time. However, suppressing the urge usually causes an increase in its intensity and feelings of discomfort. For this reason, tics are usually considered "largely involuntary"—youths are able to control tics, but only for short periods of time (Towbin, 2010).

There are several different tic disorders. *DSM-5* arranges them in a hierarchical fashion from least to more severe. First, Provisional Tic Disorder is characterized by single or multiple motor or vocal tics (or both) lasting less than one year. Second, Persistent Motor or Vocal Tic Disorder is defined by multiple motor or vocal tics (but *not* both) lasting for more than one year. Finally, **Tourette's Disorder** is defined by multiple motor *and* vocal tics lasting for more than one year (Image 11.4). Many people believe that Tourette's Disorder is defined by coprolalia, the involuntary utterance of obscene words. In fact, less than 10% of individuals with Tourette's Disorder show these types of vocal tics (Leckman & Bloch, 2010).

The lifetime prevalence of Tourette's Disorder ranges from 0.4% to 1.8%. Chronic Tic Disorder is more common, appearing in 2% to 4% of children and adolescence. Between 5% and 18% of youths experience transient tics, often at stressful times in their lives. Tics are 2 to 10 times more common in boys than in girls (Towbin, 2010).

Tic disorders and OCD often emerge in childhood or adolescence. The median age of onset for tics is 5.5 years; in contrast, OCD usually does not emerge until late childhood (in boys) or adolescence (in girls). Both disorders tend to wax and wane over time and are usually exacerbated by psychosocial stress. For example, before final exams or an important athletic competition, youths with these disorders often experience greater frequency and intensity of unwanted urges. Usually, symptoms peak in early to middle adolescence and decline by early adulthood (Bloch et al., 2009).

Tics usually appear first in the face (e.g., eye blinks, grimaces) and then progress to other areas of the body, such as the neck, shoulders, arms, and legs. Tics usually affect the same body region over a period of hours or days and then spread to new body regions over months or years. Specific tics appear, disappear, and reappear over time (Towbin, 2010).

Tic disorders are highly comorbid with OCD. Between 25% to 50% of youths with Chronic Tic or Tourette's Disorder will develop OCD at some point in adolescence or early adulthood. Conversely, approximately 30% of youths with OCD also show Tic or Tourette's Disorder. Because tics are rare in the general population, their high comorbidity with OCD suggests a common underlying cause (Richter et al., 2003).

Indeed, both tic disorders and OCD are heritable conditions. The concordance of tic disorders among monozygotic twins ranges from 77% to 94%, whereas the concordance for dizygotic twins is only 23%. Furthermore, both conditions run in families. Children with tic disorders have a 15% to 53% likelihood of having a relative with a history of tics. Children with tic disorders are also 10 to 20 times more likely than unaffected children to have a family member with OCD (Towbin, 2010).

Finally, both tics and OCD are associated with dysfunction of the cortico-striatal-thalamic circuit. Structural and functional abnormalities of the caudate nucleus, part of the striatum, have been specifically implicated in both disorders. This region is rich in dopamine receptors, perhaps explaining why atypical antipsychotic medications, which block dopamine, are often useful for treating tic disorders (R. A. Anderson & Rees, 2007).

Trichotillomania

Individuals with **Trichotillomania** repeatedly pull out their own hair, resulting in hair loss. For example, a girl might pull hair from the top of her head or bite and chew long hair dangling into her face. Alternatively, an adolescent boy might ritualistically pluck whiskers from his sideburns or face. Although the person's hair loss may not be noticeable to others, the practice of hair pulling causes the person distress or interferes with his or her functioning. In the context of hair-pulling, "distress" includes negative emotions, such as feeling a loss of control, embarrassment, or shame. For example, a child might become very upset because she feels like she cannot stop her hair pulling. Alternatively, an adolescent might be consistently late for school because she spends excessive time plucking hair in the morning. Many individuals remove unwanted hair when they groom or occasionally pluck or pull hair to escape boredom (e.g., during a boring lecture or while reading this book). Trichotillomania is only diagnosed when the person's hair pulling is recurrent and results in distress or impairment (American Psychiatric Association, 2013).

Clinical observations and recent research studies have identified two subtypes of Trichotillomania. "Focused" hair pulling involves conscious, deliberate pulling, usually in response to unpleasant thoughts or feelings. Adolescents who engage in focused hair pulling tend to report distress immediately prior to pulling and relief immediately after the act. Focused hair pulling resembles many features of OCD. In contrast, "automatic" hair pulling involves habitual pulling, usually outside the person's awareness. Automatic pulling usually occurs while the adolescent is engaged in other tasks (e.g., completing homework, talking on the telephone) and is usually not elicited by distress or negative affect (Stein, Grant, et al., 2010).

Like OCD, Trichotillomania involves repetitive behaviors that can cause distress. Furthermore, many adolescents with Trichotillomania engage in ritualistic behaviors associated with hair pulling. For example, some youths will remove hair from only certain parts of the body whereas other youths will "mouth" hair before biting it off.

Trichotillomania differs from OCD in several respects. First, people with Trichotillomania usually do not report obsessive thoughts or mental images. In contrast, nearly all patients with OCD report obsessions. Second, people with Trichotillomania sometimes report pleasure or satisfaction from hair pulling. In contrast, people with OCD usually report relief (but not pleasure) after their compulsions. Third, people with Trichotillomania usually recognize that their behavior is unusual, whereas individuals with OCD (especially children) may not (Stein, Grant, et al., 2010).

Trichotillomania and OCD have a similar onset and course. Both disorders typically emerge in early adolescence. The mean age of onset for Trichotillomania is 11.8 years, although it has been observed in toddlers and preschoolers. Onset is usually insidious (i.e., slow and increasingly more severe) and symptoms tend to worsen with psychosocial stress. Although symptoms of OCD tend to peak in late adolescence, symptoms of Trichotillomania tend to peak slightly later, in young adulthood. Symptoms of Trichotillomania and OCD are also comorbid. Although Trichotillomania occurs in less than 1% of the general population, 9% of individuals with OCD have Trichotillomania.

Trichotillomania and OCD also have similar underlying causes. The two disorders tend to run in families. In one study, 5% of patients with Trichotillomania had a relative with OCD; in contrast, 0% of healthy controls had a family member with OCD. Both disorders are also associated with dysfunction of the striatum. Interestingly, however, medications that are often effective for OCD (e.g., serotonin reuptake inhibitors) are less effective for Trichotillomania, suggesting a possible difference between these two disorders (Phillips et al., 2010).

Excoriation Disorder

Excoriation Disorder is new to *DSM-5*. It is characterized by recurrent skin picking that results in lesions. Individuals with Excoriation Disorder have made repeated attempts to decrease or stop their recurrent skin picking, but have been unable to do so. Their habitual picking, or inability to stop, causes them distress or impairment in school, work, or social functioning (American Psychiatric Association, 2013).

Skin picking is usually considered a minor problem or bad habit. In most cases, people pick at their skin in order to remove a blemish, tag, or other minor imperfection. Youths with Excoriation Disorder, however, repeatedly pick at their skin and find it difficult to stop. Between 2% and 5.4% of adolescents and young adults have Excoriation Disorder. Usually, individuals with this condition pick at skin on their face, head, and neck. Usually, picking is done with the fingernails, although some people use tweezers, scissors, nail files, or other objects. Needless to say, repeated picking can cause lesions, abrasions, and scarring. Typically, youths with Excoriation Disorder are first referred to a pediatrician or dermatologist because of tissue damage. Sometimes, medication is necessary because of infection and, in rare cases, cosmetic surgery is needed to repair damage (Grant et al., 2012).

Excoriation Disorder is similar to OCD because it is usually elicited by feelings of negative affect or distress. Many, but not all, individuals with Excoriation Disorder experience an urge to pick immediately following psychosocial stress and report alleviation of negative affect immediately after picking. Like people with OCD, individuals with Excoriation Disorder can spend hours each day engaged in their compulsive behavior. Their skin picking can greatly interfere with school, work, and friendships. Furthermore, adolescents with OCD and Excoriation Disorder are often embarrassed by their symptoms. Most will go to great lengths to avoid detection and are very reluctant to seek treatment.

Excoriation Disorder often co-occurs with OCD, Trichotillomania, depression, and other anxiety disorders (Stein, Grant, et al., 2010). The comorbidity between Excoriation Disorder and these other conditions may be due to common genetic risks and neural pathway dysfunction (Snorrason et al., 2012). Excoriation Disorder is also seen in young adults with impulse-control problems, such as compulsive gambling, buying, stealing (i.e., kleptomania), and sexual behavior (Odlaug et al., 2013).

TREATMENT FOR CHILDHOOD ANXIETY

Anxiety disorders in children often go undetected and untreated. As many as 86% of youths with anxiety disorders never see mental health professionals (Costello, 2005). Even among children attending outpatient clinics, almost 70% never receive treatment for their anxiety disorder (Chavira & Stein, 2005). Anxiety disorders are easily overlooked by parents and teachers, the people most likely to refer children for treatment. After all, internalizing symptoms, like anxiety, demand less immediate attention than externalizing symptoms, like physical aggression or hyperactivity. Furthermore, many children recognize their anxiety symptoms are unusual, and they attempt to hide their symptoms from adults. Ethnic minority children and children from lower-SES backgrounds are especially likely to be overlooked (Chavira & Stein, 2005; Costello et al., 2004).

Almost all efficacious psychosocial treatments for childhood anxiety disorders involve exposure therapy (Bouchard, Mendlowitz, Coles, & Franklin, 2004). **Exposure therapy** occurs when the client confronts a feared stimulus for a discrete period of time. Over time, and across multiple confrontations, the client's anxiety gradually decreases. Exposure

therapy can occur in many ways. Exposure can occur gradually (i.e., graded exposure) or rapidly (i.e., flooding). The client can confront real objects, people, or situations (i.e., in vivo exposure) or the client can imagine the feared stimulus (i.e., imaginal exposure). Exposure can occur multiple times over a number of weeks (i.e., spaced exposure) or over the course of hours or days (e.g., massed exposure). Although all forms of exposure can be used with children, exposure therapy is usually most effective when it is graded, in vivo, and massed.

Behavior Therapy for Phobias

Behavioral treatments for children's phobias have existed for nearly 80 years. Mary Cover Jones (1924), a student of John Watson, used behavioral techniques to reduce a fear response in a 34-month-old child named Peter, who was afraid of rabbits. Jones used three techniques to reduce Peter's fear. First, she gradually exposed Peter to a rabbit for progressively longer periods of time. Initially, the rabbit remained on the other side of the room and in a cage. In subsequent sessions, assistants brought the rabbit closer to Peter, released it from the cage, and encouraged Peter to touch it. Second, Peter was provided with candy whenever he tolerated the rabbit's presence; that is, he was positively reinforced for coming into contact with the rabbit and not running away. Third, other children Peter's age, who were not afraid of rabbits, were asked to play with Peter while the rabbit was present. Peter observed these children approach and pet the rabbit without fear. Over the course of several weeks, Peter's fear of the rabbit decreased.

Contingency Management

Behavioral techniques, like the ones used to treat Peter's phobia, are still used today (Ginsburg & Walkup, 2004). Jones's (1924) primary technique is now called **contingency management**. Contingency management is based on the principles of operant conditioning; it involves exposing the child to the feared stimulus and positively reinforcing the child contingent on the exposure. At the same time, the child is *not* allowed to avoid or withdraw from the feared stimulus. Jones progressively exposed Peter to the rabbit and reinforced him with candy. Furthermore, she prohibited him from running away.

Today, a therapist who wants to use contingency management would first meet with parents and the child to establish a **behavioral contract**. The contract specifies exactly what behaviors the child is expected to perform and what reinforcement will be provided when the child follows through with the behavior. Usually, parents and the child rank order the child's behavior in a hierarchical fashion. Behaviors that elicit mild anxiety are introduced first, while behaviors that cause high anxiety are presented last.

The child is required to come into closer and closer contact with the feared stimulus for longer and longer periods of time. When the child successfully completes the required behavior, he is positively reinforced (e.g., given praise, access to toys and games). At the same time, he is not permitted to run away, tantrum, or otherwise avoid the feared stimulus. The child is encouraged to confront the feared stimulus until his anxiety dissipates.

Modeling

A second technique to treat phobias, also used by Jones (1924), involves observational learning or modeling. In modeling, the child watches an adult or another child confront the feared stimulus. For example, a child with dog phobia might watch his therapist approach, pet, and play with a dog during the therapy session. He might also see another child his age perform the same behaviors. The child sees that confronting the feared stimulus does not result in punishment (e.g., the model is not bitten by the dog) and often results in positive reinforcement (e.g., the model enjoys playing with the dog). Jones used modeling to extinguish Peter's fear; Peter watched other toddlers approach and play with the rabbit.

Modeling can occur in real life (i.e., in vivo modeling) or by watching video tapes (i.e., videotaped modeling). Some therapists use a third strategy called participant modeling. In **participant modeling**, the therapist first models the behavior for the child and then helps the child perform the behavior himself.

Systematic Desensitization

A third behavioral technique to treat phobias is **systematic desensitization**, a technique based on the principle of classical conditioning. In systematic desensitization, children learn to associate a feared stimulus with a response that is incompatible with fear. Usually, this incompatible response involves relaxation.

First, parents and the child create a hierarchy of feared stimuli, just like in contingency management. The goal is to gradually progress up the fear hierarchy by exposing the child to the feared stimulus for longer periods of time. However, before exposure begins, the child is taught an incompatible response to use when confronting the feared stimulus. Some therapists teach children deep breathing techniques to help them relax. Other therapists teach children how to relax their muscles.

Then, children gradually progress up the fear hierarchy. When they experience anxiety, children use their relaxation skills to produce an incompatible (relaxation) response. Through classical conditioning, children come to associate the previously feared stimulus with the relaxation response.

Efficacy of Behavioral Techniques

Research supports the efficacy of behavior therapy for phobias in children and adolescents (Barrios & O'Dell, 1998; Ollendick & King, 1998). Behavioral techniques have been successfully used to reduce fears that range from the commonplace (e.g., animals, the dark, heights) to the atypical (e.g., menstruation, bowel movements).

Ollendick and King (1998) performed an extensive review and analysis of behavioral treatments of childhood anxiety. Contingency management, modeling, and systematic desensitization all enjoyed at least some support in the treatment literature. The greatest support was found for contingency management and participant modeling. These techniques seem to be superior to no treatment and other, nonbehavioral interventions. Systematic desensitization was also found to be efficacious, especially when it involves in vivo confrontation of the feared stimulus. These results suggest that behavioral techniques that involve direct exposure to the feared stimulus and positive reinforcement contingent on that exposure seem to produce the greatest benefits.

Cognitive-Behavioral Therapy for Separation Anxiety Disorder (SAD), Social Anxiety Disorder, and Generalized Anxiety Disorder (GAD)

Description of CBT

Cognitive-behavioral therapy (CBT) is an effective treatment for many childhood anxiety disorders, especially SAD, Social Anxiety Disorder, and GAD. The underlying premise of CBT is that there is an interrelationship between a person's thoughts, feelings, and actions. Changes in thinking can affect the way people feel and act. Similarly, changes in overt behavior can influence thought patterns and mood. In CBT, children with anxiety disorders are taught to recognize anxiety (feelings) and use cognitive and behavioral coping strategies to reduce the anxiety until it is more manageable (Beidel & Turner, 2007).

Philip Kendall and colleagues (Kendall, Hudson, Choudhury, Webb, & Pimentel, 2005) have examined the efficacy of a 16-week cognitive-behavioral treatment for children. The program is divided into two phases: education and practice. In the first phase, children learn about the relationship between thoughts, feelings, and actions, and they are taught new ways to cope with anxiety and worry. Therapy is structured around a personalized **FEAR plan**. The steps in the plan are represented by the acronym FEAR: feelings, expectations, attitudes, and results (see Table 11.10). When the child confronts an anxiety-provoking situation, she uses the FEAR steps to manage her anxiety.

First, children learn to identify feelings and somatic sensations associated with anxiety. Children learn to ask themselves, "Am I feeling frightened?" Children are taught to use muscle relaxation when frightened as a way to reduce distress.

Next, children learn to recognize and modify negative thoughts (i.e., self-talk) that contribute to their anxiety. They ask themselves, "Am I expecting bad things to happen?" The

Table 11.10 Sample FEAR Plan for a Socially Anxious Child Giving a Class Presentation

Step	*Example*
F: Feeling frightened	"Well, I have butterflies in my stomach and my palms are kind of sweaty."
E: Expecting bad things to happen	"I will mess up." "The other kids will make fun of me." "I'm going to look stupid and they'll laugh at me."
A: Attitudes and actions that will help	"I can practice beforehand and make sure I know what I'm going to say." "I didn't mess up the last time and the teacher said I did a good job." "Even if I mess up, it's not a big deal anyway because everybody messes up sometimes."
R: Results and rewards	"I was nervous in the beginning, but I felt OK by the end." "Nobody laughed at me." "I think I did a pretty good job and I tried really hard." "My reward is to go to the movies with Mom and Dad this weekend."

Source: Based on Kendall et al. (2005).

therapist uses a workbook, games, and role-playing exercises to show how changes in thoughts can influence changes in feelings and actions. For example, the *Coping Cat Workbook* (Kendall, 1992) consists of a series of exercises designed to teach children to recognize and alter negative self-talk (see Figure 11.11).

Therapists help children reduce the frequency of negative self-statements (Kendall et al., 2005). Children with anxiety disorders engage in many more negative self-statements, but the same number of positive self-statements, as nonanxious children (Treadwell & Kendall, 1996). The therapist's goal is not to increase the child's positive cognitions, that is, to help the child see the world through "rose-colored glasses." Rather, the therapist focuses on helping the child see the world more realistically, rather than negatively or catastrophically. According to Kendall (1992), the goal of therapy is to teach children the power of "non-negative" thinking. Reductions in negative self-talk predict success in therapy (Treadwell & Kendall, 1996; Wilson & Rapee, 2005).

In subsequent sessions, children learn cognitive problem-solving skills designed to cope with anxiety-provoking situations. They try to develop attitudes that can help. Problem solving training is designed to help children view social situations or problems realistically, generate as many solutions to these problems as possible, consider the benefits and costs of each solution, and select the best course of action.

Finally, in the results and rewards component of treatment, children are encouraged to realistically judge the effectiveness of their problem solving and to reward themselves for addressing the feared situations. Since

Figure 11.11 The Coping Cat

Some type of thoughts can help people deal with the situation, while other thoughts might make people feel more nervous or scared. Take a look at this cartoon scene. Circle the cat that would be most frightened. Why do you think he would feel more scared?

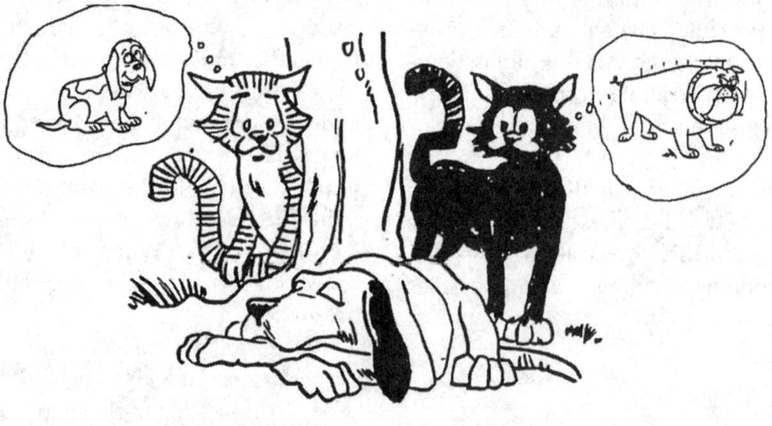

Source: From Kendall (1992). Used with permission.

Note: Children complete the *Coping Cat Workbook* to help them make connections between their thoughts and feelings.

anxious children often place unrealistic expectations on themselves or exaggerate negative events, it is important for them to view outcomes in a realistic light and to take pride in *attempting* to cope with anxiety-provoking situations (Kendall et al., 2005).

After children have mastered the FEAR plan, they begin using it in the community. Use of the FEAR steps in the community involves graded exposure. The type of exposure largely depends on the child's disorder. Children with Social Anxiety Disorder might be asked to approach a group of children playing a game; adolescents with SAD might be encouraged to separate from their parents for 15 minutes during a shopping trip. Initially, children report intense anxiety following exposure. However, as children habituate to the anxiety-provoking situation, anxiety levels drop. Children learn that exposure does not result in catastrophe.

Several randomized, controlled studies indicate that CBT is efficacious (Barrett, Dadds, & Rapee, 1996; Cobham, Dadds, & Spence, 1998; Kendall, 1994; Kendall, Flannery-Schroeder, Panichelli-Mindel, Southam-Gerow, Henin, & Warman, 1997; Silverman, Kurtines, Ginsburg, Weems, Lumpkin, & Carmichael, 1999; Spence, Donovan, & Brechman-Toussaint, 2000). Research has typically involved children aged 7 to 13 years diagnosed with Social Anxiety Disorder, SAD, and GAD. CBT is associated with improvements in self-report, parent-report, and behavioral observations of children's anxiety symptoms, compared to control groups. Furthermore, reductions in anxiety tend to be clinically significant; most children who participate in CBT no longer meet diagnostic criteria for anxiety disorders after treatment (Kendall et al., 1997; Kendall, Marrs-Garcia, Nath, & Sheldrick, 1999). Gains are maintained from one to 7 years after treatment (Barrett, Duffy, Dadds, & Rapee, 2001; Cobham et al., 1998; Kendall, 1994; Kendall & Southam-Gerow, 1996; Kendall, Safford, Flannery-Schroeder, & Webb, 2004; see Figure 11.12). CBT can also be administered to groups of children at the same time (Flannery-Schroeder & Kendall, 2000; Flannery-Schroeder, Choudhury, & Kendall, 2005).

Most recently, CBT treatment packages have been modified so that children and adolescents can participate via the computer. A computer-based CBT program called *Cool Teens* has been developed for youths with Social Anxiety Disorder, SAD, and GAD (Cunningham, Rapee, & Lyneham, 2007). Similarly, a computer-administered version of the *Coping Cat Workbook* has been developed for youths with

Figure 11.12   Efficacy of CBT for Children With Social Phobia, SAD, and GAD

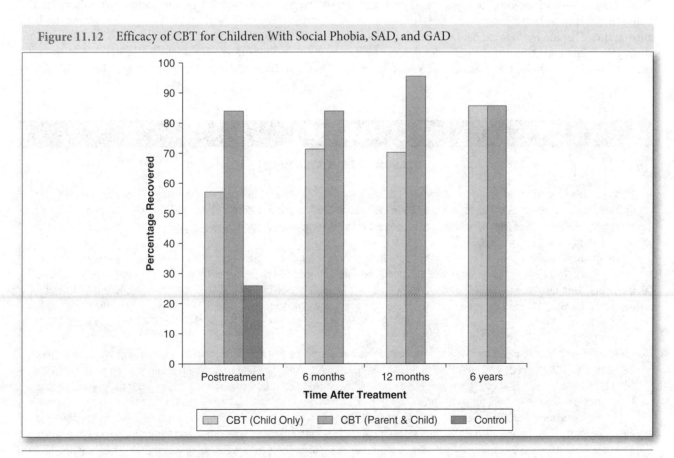

Source: Based on Barrett, Dadds et al. (1996) and Barrett et al. (2001).

Note: CBT is more effective than placebo. Furthermore, providing therapy to parents and children may produce faster results than providing treatment only to children. Consequently, involving parents in therapy is usually recommended.

a wide range of anxiety problems (Khanna, Aschenbrand, & Kendall, 2007). Both programs teach youths the relationship between thoughts, feelings, and actions and encourage them to change their patterns of thinking and behaving to improve their mood. Youths who have tried these computer-based programs report that they are convenient, easy to use, and fun. Computer-based programs might be used to supplement traditional therapy or as an alternative to traditional therapy.

Cognitive-Behavioral Therapy for Panic Disorder

There is currently no evidence-based treatment specifically designed for children or adolescents with Panic Disorder or Agoraphobia (Craske et al., 2010). No randomized, controlled trials of any form of psychotherapy or medication have been published that have included more than 30 participants. Thankfully, however, several studies have investigated the efficacy of psychotherapy and medication for adults with these disorders. Among the psychotherapies with the greatest empirical support is cognitive-behavioral therapy.

Cognitive-behavioral therapy for adolescents with Panic Disorder involves four components: (a) relaxation training, (b) interoceptive exposure, (c) cognitive restructuring, and (d) graded in vivo exposure (Birmaher & Ollendick, 2004). In **relaxation training**, the adolescent learns ways to reduce physiological arousal when he begins to experience panic. Relaxation training is designed to combat the adolescent's anxiety sensitivity and tendency to overreact to stress. Most therapists teach breathing exercises, muscle relaxation, or calming self-statements to help clients learn to relax.

Interoceptive exposure is a technique unique to the treatment of panic disorder. In interoceptive exposure, the adolescent learns to produce some of the physiological symptoms of panic and then use relaxation techniques to cope with these symptoms. Panic-like symptoms can be intentionally produced by spinning in a chair, hyperventilating into a paper bag, or running in place for 1 to 2 minutes. Mimicking panic symptoms has at least three benefits. First, adolescents recognize that panic symptoms can be intentionally produced and, therefore, are not always beyond their control. Second, adolescents learn that they will not die or pass out from panic. Although distressing, panic symptoms decrease over time. Third, adolescents learn that relaxation techniques can be used to effectively cope with panic symptoms.

Cognitive restructuring is also used to treat Panic Disorder. Cognitive restructuring techniques generally involve challenging cognitive biases and distortions that lead to panic attacks. The main target of cognitive restructuring is catastrophic thinking. Some therapists play the "detective game" with their adolescent clients to help them critically evaluate the likelihood of catastrophic events occurring as a result of a panic attack. For example, a therapist might challenge her client's distorted beliefs

---

CASE STUDY

TAMMIE'S PROGRESS IN CBT

Tammie, the 12-year-old girl who experienced problems falling asleep at night, displayed many symptoms of GAD. Her problems falling asleep seemed connected to her persistent worries about school, sports, and friends. Furthermore, these worries caused her to feel restless and "edgy," interfered with her sleep and caused fatigue, and produced feelings of agitation and tension.

Dr. Baldwin suggested that Tammie participate in cognitive-behavioral group therapy for older children and adolescents with anxiety problems. In the group sessions, Tammie learned to recognize the connection between her patterns of thinking (i.e., worry) and her feelings (i.e., tension, anxiety). Then, she learned how to look at her worries more critically and realistically. For example, when she worried about failing an upcoming test, she learned to ask herself, "What's the chance that I'll actually fail? Isn't it more likely that I'll do OK since I studied hard and have always done fine in the class?" Challenging unrealistic worries helped Tammie gain some control over them.

Tammie also found that she could manage her nighttime worries by writing them down during the day. With the help of her therapist, Tammie kept a list of all the things she worried about. When she began worrying at night, she told herself, "It's OK. I don't need to worry about this now. I have it on my list so that I can think about it tomorrow." Her list seemed to give her permission to worry at appropriate times during the day.

Dr. Baldwin met with Tammie's parents on several occasions to give them information about GAD in children. He encouraged them to be sensitive to Tammie's anxiety and to be ready to listen when she wanted to talk about her worries. After approximately 20 weeks of group and individual-family therapy, Tammie was better able to manage her worrying and her sleep improved greatly. "I'm still a worry-wart," Tammie said, "but now I can control myself better than before." As a reward, Tammie and her mother had their nails professionally manicured.

by asking for evidence for and against those beliefs (see Research to Practice: Challenging Catastrophic Thoughts That Lead to Panic).

The final component of CBT for Panic Disorder is graded exposure. Graded exposure is primarily used to correct agoraphobic avoidance. The therapist and adolescent create a hierarchy of situations or events that range from moderately distressing to extremely feared. The adolescent is encouraged to face each feared situation until she experiences a reduction in anxiety.

RESEARCH TO PRACTICE

CHALLENGING CATASTROPHIC THOUGHTS THAT LEAD TO PANIC

Marie:	When I start to get those feelings, you know, with my heart beating fast and hyperventilating, I feel like I'm having a heart attack, like I'm going to die!
Therapist:	What's the likelihood that you're *actually* going to die when you feel that way?
Marie:	Pretty high; at least, it feels that way.
Therapist:	Yes, but you've had a number of these attacks before.
Marie:	Uh-huh.
Therapist:	And you obviously haven't died from them.
Marie:	No.
Therapist:	And you've never even fainted or lost consciousness before, right?
Marie:	No. I never have.
Therapist:	So what's the likelihood that you will die, faint, or lose consciousness from an attack in the future?
Marie:	I guess pretty low since it's never happened before.
Therapist:	You're probably right. You can even tell yourself, when you feel an attack coming on, that you'll be OK, that you're not going to die or faint or pass out.
Marie:	Yes. But it sure feels like I will.
Therapist:	Yes, it does. But *feeling* like it will happen and *actually* fainting are two different things. Besides, what is the worst possible thing that could happen?
Marie:	Well, I could sweat all over and hyperventilate and get all pale and clammy. I'd have to run out of class and go to the bathroom to feel better. The teacher and the other kids in class would think I was crazy.
Therapist:	OK. So we agree that you'll probably not die or pass out, right?
Marie:	Yeah, but I would probably make a fool out of myself.
Therapist:	Well, if you saw another kid in your class suddenly look sweaty and clammy and then run out of class for the bathroom, what would you think?
Marie:	I'd think she was sick.
Therapist:	Would you think she was crazy?
Marie:	No. I'd think she had the flu.
Therapist:	Would you tease her after class or talk about her with your friends?
Marie:	Of course not. I'd probably ask her if she was feeling OK.
Therapist:	Don't you think your teacher and classmates would react the same way if they saw you do the same thing?
Marie:	Yes. I suppose they would.

Cognitive-Behavioral Therapy for Obsessive-Compulsive Disorder (OCD)

CBT is currently the treatment of choice for youths with OCD. Usually, CBT is administered as a treatment package consisting of three basic components: (a) information gathering, (b) exposure and response prevention, and (c) generalization (Grabill, Storch, & Geffken, 2007).

First, the clinician interviews the parents and child to obtain information regarding the family's psychosocial history, the child's symptoms, and the onset and course of the disorder. It is important for the clinician to determine exactly what kinds of obsessions and compulsions the child shows. For example, treating a child's ritualistic actions (e.g., hand washing, checking) would require different methods than addressing a child's mental rituals (e.g., counting, praying silently; Franklin et al., 2007).

The next step is **exposure and response prevention (EX/RP)**. Using information gathered during the interview, the child and clinician develop a hierarchy of feared stimuli. Over several weeks, the child exposes himself to each of the feared stimuli, gradually progressing up the hierarchy. At the same time, the child must not engage in the rituals he feels compelled to do after confronting the feared stimuli.

To illustrate EX/RP, imagine a 10-year-old boy who obsesses about contamination. After he touches certain objects that he considers "dirty," he feels compelled to wash his hands. His obsession is contamination by "dirty" objects; his compulsion is ritualistic washing. The boy and his therapist develop a fear hierarchy, ranging from behaviors that elicit only mild anxiety (e.g., sitting in the therapist's chair) to strong anxiety (e.g., touching a public toilet). During each session, the boy and his therapist confront a different feared stimulus, gradually moving up the hierarchy. The therapist might teach the boy relaxation techniques, like controlled breathing, to help him cope with anxiety during the exposure. The therapist might also use modeling, positive reinforcement, and the strength of their therapeutic relationship to help the boy to successfully confront the stimuli. At the same time, the therapist prohibits the boy from washing.

EX/RP works through the principle of extinction. Initially, exposure produces a rapid surge of anxiety. Over time, however, the child's anxiety gradually decreases and becomes more manageable.

Older children and adolescents with OCD might benefit from cognitive therapy in addition to EX/RP. Cognitive techniques do not reduce OCD behaviors directly; rather, they help some children engage in the EX/RP exercises. Many therapists use cognitive restructuring to help children view feared situations more realistically, rather than in an excessively negative light. For example, a child might initially think, "That chair is disgusting. It has germs all over it, and I'll get sick if I touch it." The therapist might challenge the child's thinking by asking, "Lots of other people have sat in that chair; have they all gotten sick?" Some therapists help children replace self-defeating, negativistic self-statements with more realistic statements. For example, after confronting a feared stimulus, a child might initially say, "I just can't stand it. I have to wash." The therapist might encourage him to say, "It's tough, but I can do it. I just need to hang in there" (Franklin et al., 2007).

The final component of CBT involves **generalization training and relapse prevention**. Parents play an important role in this part of treatment. The therapist teaches parents how to coach their children through the EX/RP tasks and asks parents and children to continue confronting feared stimuli outside the therapy setting. In the final sessions, the therapist, child, and parents discuss what to do in case symptoms return. Most therapists suggest viewing relapses as learning experiences, rather than as signs of failure. If relapses occur, the family can try using EX/RP techniques or they can call the therapist for additional training and support.

The efficacy of CBT for children and adolescents is supported by a number of uncontrolled studies (de Haan, Hoogduin, Buitelaar, & Keijsers, 1998; Franklin et al., 2007; March, 1998; March, Franklin, & Foa, 2005) and some randomized controlled trials (Pediatric OCD Treatment Study Team, 2004). These studies showed reductions in OCD symptoms ranging from 50% to 67% among children who participated in CBT. Furthermore, a few small-scale studies show that treatment gains are maintained at least 9 months after therapy (Franklin, Kozak, Cashman, Coles, Rheingold, & Foa, 1998; March, Mulle, & Herbel, 1994). EX/RP seems to be the most important component of treatment (March et al., 2005). Relaxation training and cognitive interventions that are often part of OCD treatment packages may be useful, but they do not seem to be critical to treatment (March et al., 2005; van Oppen, de Haan, van Balkom, Spinhoven, Hoogduin, & van Dyck, 1995).

Treatment of Tic Disorders

Tic and Tourette's Disorders can also be treated with a combination of behavior therapy and medication (Towbin, 2010). The first method of treatment is typically **self-monitoring**. Children, with the help of parents, are asked to monitor and record the frequency of tics during the course of the day. Families can use a small notebook or handheld clicker. Sometimes, children are not aware of the frequency of their tics. In these cases, self-monitoring raises awareness of their tics and decreases their frequency. In rare cases, however, self-monitoring can make children uncomfortable and actually exacerbate the problem. Even if self-monitoring does not alter the child's behavior, it can provide baseline data regarding the frequency, time, and location of children's tics (Azrin & Peterson, 1988).

A second behavioral strategy is **habit reversal training** (Peterson & Azrin, 1992). Habit reversal training involves teaching the child to engage in a behavior that, when carried out, makes it impossible to produce the tic. For example, a boy with a neck or arm tic might be instructed to tense his muscles in such a way that it is physically impossible for him to engage in the tic. Alternatively, a girl with a vocal tic might be taught to breathe in a certain way that is incompatible with the tic. Habit reversal training can be highly effective in reducing the frequency of tics. Furthermore, habit reversal techniques are usually not noticeable by others. However, they take motivation to learn and practice to implement.

Pharmacotherapy

Exposure-based, psychosocial interventions are the first-line treatment for most pediatric anxiety disorders (Connolly & Bernstein, 2007). However, many children do not respond to exposure-based therapy, or symptom reduction may not occur fast enough to satisfy families. For these children, medication can sometimes be helpful (Stein & Seedat, 2004).

SAD, Social Anxiety Disorder, and GAD

In several studies, researchers have investigated the efficacy of selective serotonin reuptake inhibitors (SSRIs) in the treatment of pediatric Social Anxiety Disorder, SAD, and GAD (Beidel et al., 2004). Trials of fluoxetine (Prozac), sertraline (Zoloft), fluvoxamine (Luvox), and paroxetine (Paxil) indicate that these medications are superior to placebo in treating anxiety problems, especially symptoms of

Social Anxiety Disorder. For example, in the **Research Unit on Pediatric Psychopharmacology Anxiety Study** (2001), researchers randomly assigned 128 children and adolescents with SAD, Social Phobia, or GAD to receive either fluvoxamine (Luvox) or placebo. After 8 weeks, youths taking the medication showed greater symptom reduction than controls. In another study, researchers randomly assigned 74 children with SAD to receive either fluoxetine (Prozac) or placebo. Approximately twice as many youths taking the medication (61%) improved compared to youths in the placebo condition (35%; Birmaher et al., 2003). Across studies, approximately 45% to 65% of youths prescribed these medications show at least moderate improvement (Bernstein & Victor, 2010).

Combining cognitive-behavior therapy with medication will likely improve children's outcomes. The **Child-Adolescent Anxiety Multimodal Study (CAMS)** compared various treatments for 488 youths with SAD, Social Phobia, and Generalized Anxiety Disorder (Walkup et al., 2008). Specifically, youths were randomly assigned to one of four conditions: (a) sertraline alone, (b) CBT alone, (c) sertraline plus CBT, or (d) placebo. All three treatments were more effective than placebo (Figure 11.13). Furthermore, youths who received medication alone showed similar outcomes as youths who received CBT alone. However, youths who received the combined treatment were more likely to improve than youths in any of the other treatment groups (Compton et al., 2010).

It is noteworthy that medication is associated with a significant reduction in symptoms but not symptom remission.

Figure 11.13   The Child-Adolescent Anxiety Multimodal Study (CAMS)

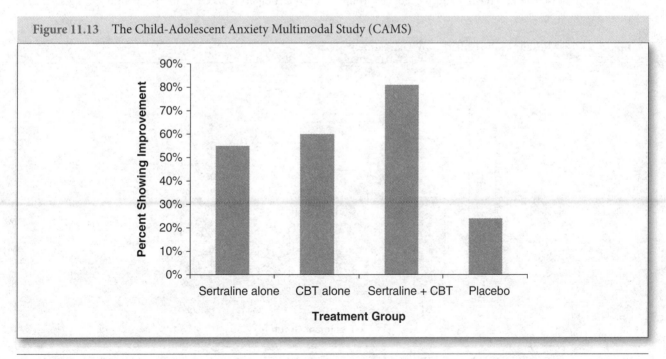

Source: Based on Compton and colleagues (2010).

Note: CAMS showed that youths who received both sertraline (Zoloft) and CBT were more likely to experience a reduction in anxiety symptoms than youths receiving either treatment alone.

For example, in the CAMS study, "improvement" was defined as a 30% reduction in symptom severity. Most youths who "improved" after taking medication continued to experience symptoms of anxiety (Bernstein & Victor, 2010).

Obsessive-Compulsive Disorder

Both tricyclic antidepressants and SSRIs have demonstrated efficacy in treating children and adolescents with OCD (Franklin et al., 2004). Randomized controlled studies indicate that both classes of medications are more effective than placebo in reducing OCD symptoms in youths. The mean effective size across all studies is moderate (ES = .42), suggesting that approximately one third of youths taking medication show better outcomes than youths taking placebo. Two meta-analyses suggest that the tricyclic antidepressant clomipramine (Anafranil) yields the largest effects ranging from .69 to .85 (Watson & Rees, 2008). Some physicians will prescribe both clomipramine and an SSRI, like sertraline (Zoloft), to treat children who do not respond to a single medication alone. However, studies supporting the use of combining these medications involve adults with OCD, not children (Geller, 2010).

In an important study, the **Pediatric OCD Treatment Study** (POTS, 2004) team examined the relative efficacy of medication and CBT for pediatric OCD (see Figure 11.14). Researchers studied 112 children and adolescents (aged 7–12 years) with OCD. Children and adolescents were assigned to one of four groups. The first group received CBT alone. The second group received sertraline, an SSRI. The third group received both CBT and medication. The fourth group received a placebo. Children participated in their respective treatments for 12 weeks.

Results showed that the children who received combined CBT and medication showed greater symptom reduction than children who received either CBT or medication alone. Children who received either of the treatments alone showed approximately equal symptom reduction. Furthermore, youths who received either treatment alone showed greater symptom reduction than children who received a placebo. The researchers also examined the percentage of children who no longer showed significant OCD symptoms after treatment in each group. Results showed that 53.6% of children in the combined group, 38.3% in the CBT-only group, 21.4% in the medication-only group, and 3.6% in the placebo group showed significant symptom reduction. These results suggest that both CBT and medication are efficacious at reducing OCD symptoms in children and adolescents.

The POTS study showed that combining CBT with medication was more effective than using medication alone. However, CBT can take many sessions to implement. Furthermore, there are not enough clinicians trained in using CBT for youths with OCD. The researchers wanted to know if providing children and parents with information about CBT and instructions on how to implement exposure with response prevention might be as effective as actual CBT in alleviating OCD symptoms. To answer this question, the **Pediatric OCD Treatment Study II** (Franklin et al., 2011) team examined 124 children and adolescents with OCD, randomly assigned to one of three conditions: (a) youths taking sertraline alone, (b) youths taking sertraline and participating in CBT, and (c) youths taking sertraline

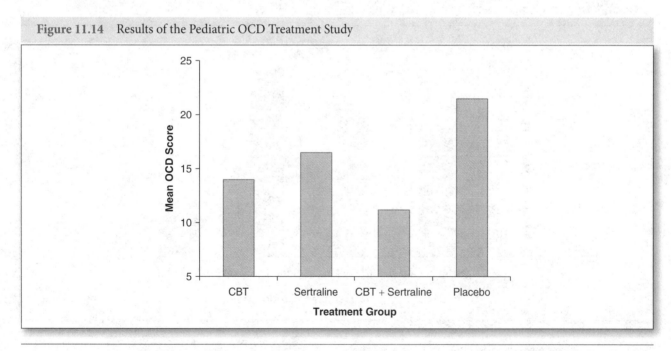

Figure 11.14 Results of the Pediatric OCD Treatment Study

Source: Based on Pediatric OCD Treatment Study Team (2004).

Note: After treatment, youths with OCD who participated in either CBT or pharmacotherapy showed greater improvement than youths who received a placebo. However, combining CBT with medication was associated with greater symptom reduction than either therapy or medication alone.

who received information about OCD and instructions on exposure therapy. Results (Figure 11.15) showed that youths who received medication plus actual CBT were significantly more likely to improve (68.6%) than youths who received medication alone (30%) or medication plus instructions about using CBT (34%). A trained cognitive-behavior therapist seemed to be critically important to the effectiveness of treatment.

Tic Disorders

The goal of pharmacotherapy is to reduce, not eliminate, tics. Physicians try to find a medication that reduces children's tics to a level that allows them to function at home, school, and with peers yet does not elicit too many side effects. **Dopamine antagonists**, which block dopaminergic activity in portions of the frontal-striatal neural circuit, are often recommended. Overall, older medications like haloperidol (Haldol) and pimozide (Orap), and newer medications like risperidone (Risperdal) and ziprasidone (Geodon), result in a 22% to 56% reduction in tics, compared to a 16% reduction using placebo. These medications are associated with sedation, weight gain, and metabolic problems. As many as 40% of youths discontinue them because of these side effects (Towbin, 2010).

A second class of medications used to treat tics include the **alpha-2 adrenergic agonists**. These medications affect serotonin and norepinephrine in a brain area called the median raphe nucleus which, in turn, reduces dopamine activity in the striatum. The effect is usually a reduction in tics without the risk of metabolic problems associated with dopamine antagonists. Studies investigating the efficacy of alpha-2 adrenergic agonists have yielded mixed results. Some studies have shown a 20% to 31% reduction in tics when using clonidine (Catapres) or guanfacine (Tenex), whereas others have shown no improvement associated with the medication. The chief side effects of alpha-2 adrenergic agonists are sedation and low blood pressure (Towbin, 2010).

Other Anxiety Disorders

Few randomized, controlled studies have investigated the efficacy of medication for other pediatric anxiety disorders. SSRIs have been effectively used to treat Specific Phobias and Panic Disorder in children and adolescents. However, studies have tended to rely on small sample sizes and have lacked control groups for comparison. Most experts do not consider medication to be a first-line treatment for these disorders, although they might be helpful as an adjunct to cognitive and behavioral treatments (Birmaher & Ollendick, 2004; N. J. King et al., 2004; J. A. Cohen & Mannarino, 2004; Silverman & Carmichael, 1999).

Figure 11.15   The Pediatric OCD Treatment Study II

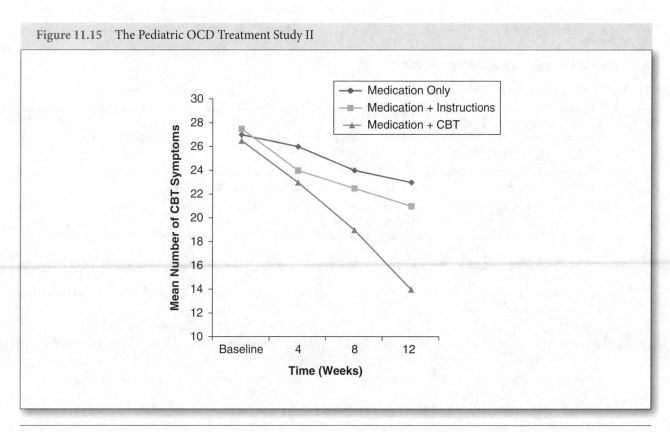

Source: Based on Franklin and colleagues (2011).

Note: This study compared youths in three conditions: (a) sertraline alone, (b) sertraline plus instructions on using CBT to treat OCD, and (c) sertraline plus actual CBT. Youths in the third group showed superior outcomes. These results indicate that a skilled cognitive-behavior therapist is important for treatment.

Child and Adolescent Anxiety

- Anxiety is a complex state of psychological distress that reflects emotional, behavioral, physiological, and cognitive reactions to threatening stimuli.

  - Fear is primarily a behavioral and physiological reaction to an immediate threat.
  - Worry is primarily a cognitive response to a future threat or possible negative event.

- Anxiety is usually adaptive; it helps protect us from immediate danger or motivates us to prepare for negative events in the future. Maladaptive anxiety can be differentiated from adaptive anxiety in three ways:

  - Intensity: Maladaptive anxiety is out-of-proportion to the threat.
  - Chronicity: Maladaptive anxiety begins before the threat and continues after the threat has passed.
  - Impairment: Maladaptive anxiety interferes with functioning.

- Psychologists also differentiate maladaptive anxiety from adaptive anxiety in children in terms of the degree to which children's anxiety responses are developmentally expected.
- Approximately 15% to 20% of youths will develop an anxiety disorder at some point in childhood. Girls and older children are especially likely to develop anxiety disorders.
- Anxiety disorders tend to persist over time and can greatly affect children's functioning. Children with anxiety disorders are at particular risk for long-term problems with anxiety and depression.
- Barlow's triple vulnerability theory offers a general model for the development of anxiety disorders in children. According to this model, anxiety disorders result from the interaction of (a) genetic and biological risk, (b) early social-emotional experiences that give children a sense of vulnerability, and (c) specific social-emotional experiences that cause specific fears or worries.
- *DSM-5* anxiety disorders tend to emerge in childhood and adolescence in predictable ways.

  - SA, Specific Phobia, and Social Anxiety Disorder usually first emerge in childhood.
  - Generalized Anxiety Disorder typically emerges in later childhood or early adolescence.
  - Panic Disorder and Agoraphobia tends to emerge in late adolescence or adulthood.

- Although OCD is not an anxiety disorder, it often co-occurs with anxiety disorders. Furthermore, youths with OCD often report anxiety and psychological distress.

SAD, Specific Phobia, and Social Anxiety Disorder

- Children with SAD show excessive anxiety about leaving caregivers and other people to whom they are emotionally attached.

  - Young children's separation fears are usually less realistic than older children's fears. Adolescents often have vague fears of harm befalling loved ones.
  - Insecure parent-child attachment may contribute to separation anxiety. Children who do not expect sensitive and responsive care from parents may seek frequent reassurance regarding their safety.

- Children with Specific Phobia fear discernible, circumscribed objects or situations. Common phobias include (a) animals, (b) natural environment, (c) blood-injection-injuries, (d) specific situations, and (e) other stimuli such as clowns.

  - Children's fears are typically associated with their social-emotional and cognitive development. Young children often fear monsters whereas older children often fear more realistic negative events (e.g., storms).
  - Learning theory is used to explain most phobias. Phobias can develop from classical conditioning, observation, or information transfer.
  - According to two-factor theory, phobias are often acquired through classical conditioning and are marinated through negative reinforcement (e.g., avoidance).
  - Blood-injection-injury phobias seem to have a different cause than other phobias. They are associated with an unusual sensitivity of the vasovagal response.

- Children with Social Anxiety Disorder fear social or performance situations in which they might be scrutinized by others or embarrassed. Although many older children and adolescents are self-conscious in social situations, youths with this disorder experience significant distress and impairment.

  - Social Anxiety Disorder is more heritable than SAD and Specific Phobia. Young children often inherit temperaments characterized by high behavioral inhibition.
  - Parents may contribute to Social Anxiety Disorder in several ways:

    - They are often overcontrolling, denying autonomy to their children.
    - They are often overprotective, restricting children's play and activities.
    - They often make hostile and critical comments to their children, increasing their children's sense of vulnerability.

- o They often model anxiety to their children.
- o They often avoid emotionally charged discussion, providing their children with less insight into effective emotion-regulation strategies.
- Test Anxiety and School Refusal are not official *DSM-5* diagnoses; however, they are frequently shown by children and adolescents.
  - o Youths with test anxiety often fear scrutiny by others (e.g., parents, teachers) and may meet criteria for Social Anxiety Disorder.
  - o School refusal can be the result of fears of separation (SAD), social anxiety (Social Anxiety Disorder), or specific negative events at school (e.g., bullying).
  - o Both problems are usually characterized by anxiety, impairment, and avoidance of the feared stimuli (i.e., tests, school). Treatments for anxiety disorders are often effective in helping children with test anxiety and school refusal.

Panic Disorder and Agoraphobia

- Adolescents with Panic Disorder worry about recurrent panic attacks that cause distress or impairment. A panic attack is a brief, intense episode of distress and autonomic arousal.
- Adolescents with Agoraphobia avoid places or situations in which escape or help is not possible without considerable effort or embarrassment. Common agoraphobic situations are (a) outside the home alone, (b) on public transportation, (c) shopping malls and open spaces, (d) theaters and stadiums, and (e) large crowds.
- Panic Disorder and Agoraphobia usually do not emerge until later adolescence, perhaps because children usually do not worry persistently about recurrent panic attacks.
- Often, adolescents develop agoraphobic avoidance of places in which they have experienced a panic attack. However, some youths develop agoraphobia without a history of panic.
- Youths with Panic Disorder often show high anxiety sensitivity in childhood. They are more easily upset by negative emotions than their peers.
- According to the expectancy theory of panic, people with high anxiety sensitivity may be predisposed to recurrent panic attacks when they also show certain cognitive distortions:
  - o They personalize the attacks, blaming themselves for their occurrence.
  - o They engage in catastrophic thinking, anticipating the worst possible outcomes.
- Many adolescents and adults with Panic Disorder and Agoraphobia have histories of SAD in childhood. Some experts believe the two conditions are different manifestations of the same underlying problem.

Generalized Anxiety Disorder

- Youths with GAD experience chronic worry, rather than fear. The essential feature of GAD is apprehensive expectation, excessive worry about future negative events.
- Children with and without GAD report similar worries. However, the worries of children with GAD differ in their (a) number, (b) intensity, and (c) duration.
- The persistent worries shown by children with GAD adversely affect their daily functioning. Often, they cause distress, interfere with social relationships, and cause sleep problems.
- Youths with GAD often present as highly responsible and conscientious. However, most harbor insecurities and self-doubts.
- GAD is more closely associated with depression than the other anxiety disorders. In most cases, youths develop GAD before the onset of Major Depressive Disorder.
- According to Borkovec's cognitive avoidance theory, youths with GAD worry about minor hassles to avoid emotionally and physiologically arousing mental images associated with major negative events.
- Youths with GAD also show cognitive distortions, such as (a) catastrophic thinking, (b) overgeneralizing, and (c) personalizing. They often have an external locus of control, believing that outcomes are largely due to luck rather than hard work and preparation.

Obsessive Compulsive Disorder and Related Conditions

- OCD is characterized by recurrent, unwanted obsessions and compulsions that are time consuming, cause distress, and/or impair daily functioning.
  - o Obsessions are persistent thoughts, impulses, or images experienced as intrusive and inappropriate, which cause anxiety or distress.
  - o Compulsions are repetitive behaviors or mental acts designed to reduce anxiety or prevent an imaginary dreaded event from occurring.
- Approximately 1% to 2% of youths have OCD. Prevalence is more common in boys during childhood. However, the gender distribution becomes equal by late adolescence.
- OCD is associated with dysregulation of the cortico-striatal-thalamic circuit. This circuit responds to irregularities in the environment (e.g., contamination, objects "not quite right").

- Cognitive factors also contribute to OCD. Some youths show thought-action fusion, the incorrect belief that thinking about a negative event makes it more likely to occur. Thought-action fusion may elicit anxiety and the need for compulsions.
- PANDAS theory posits that some youths develop OCD symptoms following certain streptococcus infections.
- Several disorders resemble OCD and often co-occur with the disorder:

  o Tics are sudden, rapid, non-rhythmic and stereotyped movements. They can be motoric or vocal. Tourette's Disorder is characterized by multiple motor and vocal tics.
  o Trichotillomania is characterized by repeated hair pulling resulting in hair loss and distress.
  o Excoriation Disorder is characterized by recurrent skin picking that results in lesions. It causes distress and tissue damage.

Treatment

- An important component of psychosocial treatment for anxiety disorders is exposure therapy. People with anxiety disorders must confront their feared stimulus without escape or avoidance.
- Treatment for phobias is typically behavioral in nature.

  o Using contingency management, children are reinforced for behaviors that bring them closer to their feared stimulus.
  o Often therapists will model behavior and invite children to imitate.
  o In systematic desensitization, children use relaxation techniques to cope with anxiety as they progress up a fear hierarchy.

- Treatment for SAD, Social Anxiety Disorder, and GAD often relies on cognitive-behavior therapy (CBT).

  o CBT is based on the notion that thoughts, feelings, and actions are interrelated. To change problematic feelings (e.g., anxiety) children can be taught to think and act in different ways.
  o Kendall's CBT for anxiety disorders teaches children to identify and label their feelings and challenge automatic thoughts that might predispose them toward anxiety. Children learn to use the FEAR approach to coping with anxiety.

- Cognitive-behavioral therapy can also be used to treat Panic Disorder in adolescents.

  o Relaxation training helps adolescents recognize the first signs of panic and avoid a full-blown attack.
  o Using interoceptive exposure, adolescents deliberately produce panic symptoms and practice using coping skills.
  o Cognitive restructuring is necessary to change cognitive distortions (e.g., catastrophic thinking) that elicits panic.

- Exposure with response prevention is the treatment of choice for pediatric OCD. Youths gradually expose themselves to stimuli that elicit obsessions and avoid engaging in compulsions.

  o Usually, exposure progresses up a hierarchy of feared stimuli.
  o Clients and therapists try to generalize skills to new situations and plan for relapse.

- Tics and other OCD-like behaviors can be managed by using self-monitoring and habit-reversal training.
- Medication is often frequently used to manage pediatric anxiety disorders. Medication is typically effective only while it is administered. Relapse is high after it is discontinued if psychosocial treatments are not also used.

  o SSRIs have shown effectiveness for treating SAD, Social Anxiety Disorder, and GAD. Combining medication with therapy results in better outcomes than medication alone.
  o Similarly, in the Pediatric OCD Treatment Study (POTS), youths who received SSRI and therapy showed greater improvement than youths who received medication alone.
  o Tic disorders often respond to dopamine antagonists rather than SSRIs.

KEY TERMS

Agoraphobia   369

alpha-2 adrenergic agonists   411

amygdala   368

amygdo-cortical neural circuit   368

anxiety   364

anxiety sensitivity   386

apprehensive expectation   387

behavioral contract   402

behavioral inhibition   378

Child-Adolescent Anxiety Multimodal Study (CAMS)   409

classical conditioning   375

cognitive avoidance theory   392

cognitive distortions   393

cognitive restructuring   406

cognitive-behavioral therapy (CBT)   403

compulsions   395

contingency management   402

cortico-striatal-thalamic circuit   398

dopamine antagonists   411

Excoriation Disorder   401

CRITICAL THINKING EXERCISES

1. Many children fear snakes, although relatively few children have ever been bitten by snakes. If a child has *never* been attacked by a snake, how can he or she develop snake phobia?

2. Some people believe that children with Social Anxiety Disorder are simply "extremely shy." How is Social Anxiety Disorder different from shyness?

3. Mallorie is a 16-year-old girl who experienced two panic attacks while at school. Since that time, she has been reluctant to go to school. How might learning theory be used to explain Mallorie's school refusal?

4. How might an adolescent develop Agoraphobia *without* having Panic Disorder or ever experiencing a panic attack?

5. Christian is a 14-year-old boy with GAD. During an important basketball game, Christian mistakenly passed the ball to an opponent, and his team lost the game. After the game, Christian thought, "How could I have been so incredibly stupid? The coach is never going to let me play again! I single-handedly ruined the game." Explain how Christian's thoughts about the event contribute to his negative feelings.

6. How might exposure be used to treat most child and adolescent anxiety disorders and OCD?

EXTEND YOUR LEARNING

Videos, practice tests, flash cards, study guides, and links to online resources for this chapter are available to students online. Teachers also have access to lecture notes, PowerPoint presentations, suggestions for classroom activities, and possible exam questions. Visit: www.sagepub.com/weis2e..

CHAPTER 12

Trauma-Related Disorders and Child Maltreatment

After reading this chapter, you should be able to answer these questions:

- What are the essential features of Posttraumatic Stress Disorder (PTSD)? How do preschoolers, older children, and adults show PTSD differently?

- How common is PTSD? How do characteristics of the traumatic event, the child, and the family influence a child's likelihood of developing the disorder?

- What evidence-based treatments are available to children exposed to trauma (a) immediately following a traumatic event and (b) months or years later?

- What is Reactive Attachment Disorder (RAD) and Disinhibited Social Engagement Disorder (DSED)? How do they differ?

- What causes RAD and DSED? Given their causes, what treatments are available?

- Explain the four types of child maltreatment? What are their potential effects on children's development?

- What evidence-based treatments can be used for children exposed to abuse and neglect?

O n December 14, 2012, Adam Lanza fatally shot 20 children and six adult staff members at Sandy Hook Elementary School in Newtown, Connecticut. The incident was the deadliest shooting in an American elementary school.

Lanza forced his way through a locked glass door at the school entrance. Armed with a rifle and carrying several hundred rounds of ammunition, he killed the school principal, school psychologist, and other teachers who were meeting in a conference room that morning. The school intercom was on at the time of the shooting; several children reported that they could hear gunshots and screaming through the intercom system.

Lanza then entered a first-grade classroom, killing a teacher and almost all of her students. One 6-year-old girl survived by playing dead and fleeing after Lanza left the room. When she was reunited with her mother, she reported, "Mommy, I'm okay but all of my friends are dead."

Many other teachers attempted to hide students or barricade themselves in their classrooms. One first-grade teacher hid 19 students in a bathroom, blocked the door, and told them to "be completely quiet to stay safe." Another teacher barricaded her fourth-grade students in a tiny supply closet. Lanza reportedly tried to open the closet several times before leaving. A third teacher discovered two students in the hallway, chosen classroom helpers who were delivering morning attendance. The teacher hid the children only moments before Lanza arrived in that area of the school.

The Sandy Hook Elementary shooting was a traumatic event for children, parents, school personnel, and the community (Image 12.1). Unfortunately, the shooting was not an isolated incident. Fifteen people died at Columbine High School in 1999, eight perished at Red Lake Senior High School in 2005, and dozens were killed in shootings at Virginia Tech (2007), Northern Illinois University (2008), and the University of Alabama (2010).

Although terrible, massacres like these can direct our attention away from other traumatic (and, unfortunately, more common) experiences that can adversely affect children's behavioral, social, and emotional well-being. Children are much more likely to be involved in a serious car accident or an at-home injury than a school shooting or terrorist attack. Sadly, children are also at surprisingly high risk for physical maltreatment, sexual victimization, and physical or emotional neglect. All of these experiences have the potential to negatively affect their development (Norris, 2007).

In this chapter, we will examine psychological problems that can arise from three types of psychosocial stressors: (a) traumatic experiences, (b) early social and emotional deprivation, and (c) child maltreatment. First, we will examine Posttraumatic Stress Disorder (PTSD), an adverse reaction to a catastrophic event, such as a car accident, home fire, or natural disaster. Then, we will discuss a rare, but equally traumatic experience for infants—deprivation—and

its effects on their social, emotional, and behavioral development. Finally, we will study one of the most common sources of psychosocial stress that face children and adolescents throughout the world: child abuse and neglect.

Although these topics are not pleasant to study, they are extremely important. As many as 30% of youths are exposed to a serious, traumatic event at some point in their childhood and roughly one third of these children will develop symptoms of PTSD (Yule & Smith, 2010). Furthermore, between 1% and 2% of children in the United States are confirmed victims of child maltreatment, to say nothing about the many children who are victimized but never brought to the attention of officials. We sorely need dedicated researchers to discover the best ways to identify and treat these youths and caring practitioners to help children and families cope with these painful experiences.

POSTTRAUMATIC STRESS DISORDER

What Is Posttraumatic Stress Disorder (PTSD)?

PTSD in Older Children and Adolescents

Posttraumatic Stress Disorder (PTSD) is defined by a characteristic set of behavioral, cognitive, emotional, and physiological symptoms that emerge following exposure to a traumatic or catastrophic event (Table 12.1,

Image 12.1   A memorial to the victims of the Sandy Hook Elementary School shootings.

Diagnostic Criteria for Posttraumatic Stress Disorder). By definition, a traumatic event is a psychosocial stressor that involves actual or threatened death, serious physical injury, or sexual violation. To be diagnosed with PTSD, a person must be exposed to the event in at least one of four ways:

- by directly experiencing the event,
- by witnessing the event in person,
- by learning that the event occurred to a close family member or close friend, or
- by firsthand exposure to aversive details about the event (e.g., first responders observing the effects of a trauma).

Table 12.1 Diagnostic Criteria for Posttraumatic Stress Disorder

A. *Exposure* to actual or threatened death, serious injury, or sexual violence in one (or more) of the following ways:

1. Directly experiencing the traumatic event(s).

2. Witnessing, in person, the event(s) as it occurred to others.

3. Learning that the traumatic event(s) occurred to a close family member o[r] close friend. In cases of actual or threatened death of a family member or friend, the event(s) must have been violent or accidental.

4. Experiencing repeated or extreme exposure to aversive details of the traumatic event (e.g., first responders collecting human remains; police officers repeatedly exposed to details of child abuse).

Note: Criterion A4 does not apply to exposure through electronic media, television, movies, or pictures, unless this exposure is work related.

B. Presence of one (or more) of the following *intrusion symptoms* associated with the traumatic event(s), beginning after the traumatic event(s) occurred:

1. Recurrent, involuntary, and intrusive distressing memories of the traumatic event(s). Note: In children older than 6 years, repetitive play may occur in which themes or aspects of the traumatic event(s) and [*sic*] expressed.

2. Recurrent or distressing dreams in which the content and/or affect of the dream are related to the traumatic event(s). Note: In children, there may be frightening dreams without recognizable content.

3. Dissociative reactions (e.g., flashbacks) in which the individual feels or acts as if the traumatic event(s) were recurring. Note: In children, trauma-specific reenactment may occur in play.

4. Intense or prolonged psychological distress at exposure to internal or external cues that symbolize or resemble an aspect of the traumatic event(s).

5. Marked physiological reactions to internal or external cues that symbolize or resemble an aspect of the traumatic event(s).

C. *Persistent avoidance* of stimuli associated with the traumatic event(s), beginning after the traumatic event(s) occurred, as evidenced by one or both of the following:

1. Avoidance of or efforts to avoid distressing memories, thoughts, or feelings about or closely associated with the traumatic event(s).

2. Avoidance of or efforts to avoid external reminders (people, places, conversations, activities, objects, situations) that arouse distressing memories, thoughts, or feelings about or closely associated with the traumatic event(s).

D. *Negative alterations in cognitions and mood* associated with the traumatic event(s), beginning or worsening after the traumatic event(s) occurred, as evidenced by two (or more) of the following:

1. Inability to remember an important aspect of the traumatic event(s).

2. Persistent and exaggerated negative beliefs or expectations about oneself, others, or the world (e.g., "I am bad," "No one can be trusted," "The world is completely dangerous," "My whole nervous system is permanently ruined").

3. Persistent, distorted cognitions about the cause or consequences of the traumatic event(s) that lead the individual to blame himself/herself or others.

4. Persistent negative emotional state (e.g., fear, horror, anger, guilt, or shame).

5. Markedly diminished interest or participation in significant activities.

6. Feelings of detachment or estrangement from others.

7. Persistent inability to experience positive emotions (e.g., inability to experience happiness, satisfaction, or loving feelings).

E. Marked *alterations in arousal and reactivity* associated with the traumatic event(s), beginning or worsening after the traumatic event(s) occurred, as evidenced by two (or more) of the following:

1. Irritable behavior and angry outbursts (with little or no provocation) typically expressed as verbal or physical aggression toward people or objects.

2. Reckless or self-destructive behavior.

3. Hypervigilance.

4. Exaggerated startle response.

5. Problems with concentration.

6. Sleep disturbance (e.g., difficulty falling or staying asleep or restless sleep).

F. Duration of the disturbance is more than 1 month.

G. The disturbance causes clinically significant distress or impairment in social, occupational, or other important areas of functioning.

H. The disturbance is not attributable to the physiological effects of a substance (e.g., medication, alcohol) or another medical condition.

Specify whether:

With dissociative symptoms: The individual's symptoms meet criteria for Posttraumatic Stress Disorder, and in addition, the individual experiences persistent or recurrent symptoms of either of the following:

1. Depersonalization: Persistent or recurrent experiences of feeling detached from, and as if one were an outside observer of, one's mental processes or body (e.g., feeling as though one were in a dream; feeling a sense of unreality of self or body or of time moving slowly).

2. Derealization: Persistent or recurrent experiences of unreality of surroundings (e.g., the world around the individual is experienced as unreal, dreamlike, distant, or distorted).

Specify if:

With delayed expression: If the full diagnostic criteria are not met until at least 6 months after the event (although the onset and expression of some symptoms may be immediate).

Source: Reprinted with permission from the Diagnostic and Statistical Manual of Mental Disorders, Fifth Edition (Copyright 2013). American Psychiatric Association.

Note: These criteria apply to adults, adolescents, and children older than 6 years. For children 6 years and younger, see corresponding criteria in Table X.

By definition, events must be serious and are often life threatening. Events can be either intentional (e.g., a physical assault), accidental (e.g., a car crash), or natural (e.g., a fire). People need not show anxiety or distress during or immediately after the event, but they must show PTSD symptoms at some point after the trauma.

Note also that the traumatic event must occur either to the individual directly or to a close family member or friend. Hearing about a traumatic event occurring to a distant friend or stranger (e.g., in the newspaper) does not satisfy this criterion. Similarly, watching a real or fictitious traumatic event on television or in a movie is insufficient for the diagnosis of PTSD (see text box *DSM-IV → DSM-5* Changes: A New View of PTSD).

After exposure to the traumatic event, people with PTSD show characteristic symptoms that fall into four

DSM-IV → *DSM-5* CHANGES

A NEW VIEW OF PTSD

In *DSM-5*, individuals with PTSD must be exposed to actual or threatened death, serious injury, or sexual violation. "Exposure" can occur by having the event happen to you, witnessing the event, or learning that the event occurred to a loved one. *DSM-IV* merely required that people were "confronted with" a traumatic event and that they reacted to the event with "fear, helplessness, or horror" (Resick & Miller, 2009).

(Continued)

(Continued)

The wording of the old diagnostic criteria was problematic in at least two ways. First, the criteria were too broad (McNally, 2003). Although PTSD was initially meant to describe negative reactions to events that were injurious or life-threatening (e.g., combat, physical or sexual assault), the disorder was gradually expanded to include events that some people considered "traumatic" but were probably not life-threatening (e.g., delivery of a baby, hearing sexual jokes, wisdom tooth extraction; McNally, 2009). Diagnosticians wondered whether a child who is upset after the death of his pet hamster or Bambi's mother might also meet criteria (Elhaie et al., 2005).

Second, many people reacted to life-threatening events with dysphoria and lack of feeling rather than with anxiety. For example, military personnel and first-responders often report that they did not show the typical fear-based response following a traumatic incident because of their training. Consequently, the criterion requiring an anxiety response has been eliminated in *DSM-5* (Moran, 2013).

Individuals familiar with the *DSM-IV* criteria will notice several other changes to the conceptualization of PTSD:

- Exposure to traumatic events through the media is not sufficient for a PTSD diagnosis. Although watching violence on television can be distressing, it cannot be the only event that elicits symptoms.
- There are now four symptom "clusters" rather than three. The "avoidance" and "numbing" symptoms have been split into two separate clusters because of their importance.
- The number of symptoms required for PTSD is lower for children than adults. Furthermore, *DSM-5* now specifies signs of PTSD typically shown by preschool-age children exposed to trauma. These signs are largely behavioral, given that young children have difficulty reporting cognitive and emotional symptoms.

The creators of *DSM-5* hope that these changes will make the diagnostic criteria more sensitive to children (Scheeringa et al., 2011).

---

clusters. First, they experience *intrusive symptoms* associated with the trauma; they persistently reexperience the event, often in the form of recurrent dreams, transient images, or unwanted thoughts. In some cases, people with PTSD experience dissociative reactions or "flashbacks"; that is, they temporarily feel as if the traumatic event is recurring to them in the present moment. An adolescent involved in an auto accident might have nightmares about the incident or have recurrent images of the accident pop into his mind while attending school. In contrast, a 7-year-old girl who witnessed a violent storm destroy her house might have persistent thoughts about the disaster. Her parents might observe her reenacting the event during play (e.g., with Legos or a doll house) or overhear her dolls "talking" to each other about the storm and their relocation to a new house.

Second, people with PTSD persistently *avoid stimuli associated with the trauma*. Avoidance might come in the form of an unwillingness to discuss the traumatic experience or visit people or places associated with the trauma. For example, a child who was sexually assaulted by a relative will likely avoiding thinking about or discussing the incident. He might also try to avoid that relative by refusing to visit him on a family outing or by feigning illness.

Third, PTSD causes *a negative alteration in the person's feelings or thoughts*. These alterations are sometimes referred to as emotional or cognitive "numbing." Emotional numbing might include the inability to experience joy or positive emotions, a lack of interest in activities that used to be pleasurable, or feelings of detachment or estrangement from others (Forbes et al., 2011). Individuals might also experience persistent negative emotions, such as anger, guilt, or shame, regarding the traumatic event. For example, an adolescent who witnesses his friend drown might feel guilty for not having rescued him.

Cognitive numbing might manifest as problems in remembering details about the traumatic event, a tendency to blame oneself or others for the trauma, or a dramatic and negative change in the person's view of self, others, or the world. For example, a girl who is sexually assaulted might blame herself for being raped or view herself as "damaged goods" following the incident.

Fourth, individuals with PTSD show alteration in *physiological arousal* or reactivity. These symptoms include overactivity of the "fight" or "flight" response. Symptoms might include difficulty sleeping, irritability or aggression, concentration problems, and excessive vigilance. Many individuals personally involved in traumatic events show exaggerated startle response. For example, if an adolescent involved in an auto accident hears a loud noise similar to the sound of a crash, he might jump or panic (McKnight, Compton, & March, 2004).

PTSD symptoms must cause significant distress or interfere with the person's social interactions, capacity to work or attend school, and other activities (e.g., sports, clubs, hobbies). Usually, PTSD greatly interferes with all aspects of an individual's life.

It is not necessary for children (or adults) to react to traumatic experiences with fear, helplessness, or horror (Brewin et al., 2009). Indeed, children react to catastrophic events in many ways (see text box *DSM-IV* → *DSM-5* Changes: PTSD: Not an Anxiety Disorder Anymore).

A recent survey of parents indicated that some children respond to traumatic events with anxiety (39.6%), sadness (39.6%), or fear (32.1%). However, children also show other emotions such as excitement (22.6%), enjoyment (3.8%), or no emotion whatsoever (11.3%; Sheeringa et al., 2011).

No matter how individuals manifest the disorder, symptoms must be present for at least one month to qualify for the diagnosis of PTSD. In some instances, individuals do not meet all diagnostic criteria for PTSD until several months after the trauma. For example, an adolescent girl who is sexually victimized might avoid thinking and talking about the incident (i.e., avoidance symptoms), experience increased irritability and sadness (i.e., alterations in mood symptoms), and problems with sleep and concentration (i.e., arousal symptoms), but she might not develop intrusive thoughts or dreams about the event until several months later. When people do not meet full PTSD criteria until 6 months (or more) after the trauma, *DSM-5* instructs clinicians to add the specifier "with delayed expression" to the PTSD diagnosis (American Psychiatric Association, 2013).

Although not required for the diagnosis of PTSD, some people exposed to traumatic events also experience dissociative symptoms. **Dissociative symptoms** involve persistent or recurrent feelings of detachment from oneself or one's surroundings (American Psychiatric Association, 2013).

Often, individuals use dissociative symptoms to cope with extremely traumatic events by cognitively or emotionally distancing themselves from memories of the event. Two types of dissociative symptoms are especially relevant to PTSD: (1) depersonalization, and (2) derealization.

Depersonalization describes persistent or recurrent experiences of feeling detached from one's own body or mental processes. People who experience episodes of depersonalization often feel like they are watching themselves in a movie, like they are in a dream, or like they are somehow disconnected from their own thoughts and actions. Some people report, "I felt as if I was floating away," "I felt disembodied, disconnected, or far away from myself," or "I could see and hear everything around me but couldn't respond." **Derealization** involves persistent or recurrent thoughts and feelings that one's surroundings are not real. People who experience episodes of derealization see the world around them in an unusual or distorted manner. Some individuals report, "My surroundings seemed unreal and far away," "I felt like I was looking at everything through a strange lens or a glass," or "Objects seemed smaller than usual, drab, or artificial."

When individuals with PTSD also show dissociative symptoms, *DSM-5* instructs clinicians to add the specifier "with dissociative symptoms" to the PTSD diagnosis. This specifier provides additional information to other professionals regarding the person's symptoms (American Psychiatric Association, 2013).

Exposure to trauma is not uncommon among youths in the United States. Approximately 40% of adolescents in the general population have experienced at least one serious trauma (Giaconia et al., 1995). The most common traumatic events involving youths include exposure to violent crime, auto accidents, home fires and injuries, natural disasters, domestic violence, physical and sexual abuse, and serious physical illnesses. Exposure to violence is especially

PRESTON: A STORY OF SURVIVAL

Preston was a 17-year-old boy referred to our clinic by his parents because of severe depression and self-injury. "He's been 'different' since the accident," reported his mother. "That night, three other mothers lost their sons, but I also lost my boy (pointing to her heart) inside."

Preston was a tall, good-looking high school senior who excelled at cross country and had many friends. Preston had no history of emotional or behavioral problems before his car accident 3 months earlier.

Preston and three friends were driving home from a party on a rural highway. Although Preston had not been drinking, his friends had consumed several beers and were acting in a loud and boisterous manner. Preston, who was driving, became distracted. His car verged off the side of the road, entered a ditch, and rolled over. It finally stopped after hitting a utility pole. Preston broke his arm and clavicle in the accident. Two friends died instantly, and the third died in the hospital the next day.

"I don't really want to do anything anymore. Sometimes, I don't know why I didn't die that night like the others," Preston explained to Dr. Foster. "I know I'm to blame for the accident and that it should have been me (to die) and not them."

Dr. Foster asked, "Do you think about the accident a lot?" Preston replied, "Actually, I try not to think about it. I try to keep myself distracted with school or work, but that doesn't work. I'm on Ambien because I can't sleep at night and I have terrible dreams. During the day, I snap at my parents and sister all the time. I can't concentrate at school either. I keep thinking 'why me?' and thinking about their families. There's no way I can go to graduation."

"You were sent to me partially because you were cutting on your arm," added Dr. Foster. After a long pause and heavy sigh, Preston replied, "It's really the only way I can feel anything at all."

common in urban settings. In one study of predominantly African American low-income children, 39% had witnessed a shooting, 35% had seen a stabbing or physical assault, and 24% had observed an attempted killing. Nearly one half of the sample reported being a victim of violent crime (Jenkins & Bell, 1994).

Older children typically display a closer correspondence between their PTSD symptoms and the trauma that they experienced. For example, a child involved in a fire at school may subsequently exhibit school refusal. Older children are also more likely to report intrusive thoughts and nightmares associated with the trauma. They sometimes show omen formation. **Omen formation** refers to the belief that warning signs immediately preceded the traumatic event; consequently, the child constantly scans the environment, looking for similar signs of impending misfortune. For example, if a certain song was playing on the radio shortly before a serious auto accident, the child may believe that hearing the song again indicates another upcoming disaster. Omen formation is likely formed through classical conditioning. It occurs when the child incorrectly assumes a causal relationship between two stimuli that occur together in time (e.g., the "omen" and the trauma).

Adolescents tend to show PTSD similar to adults. However, unlike adults, adolescents usually do not experience flashbacks. Instead, adolescents are more likely to have intrusive and recurrent thoughts, images, and dreams. Nightmares associated with the trauma are particularly common among older children and adolescents (McKnight et al., 2004).

PTSD in Preschoolers and Young Children

Very young children exposed to traumatic events may not show PTSD in the same way as older children, adolescents, and adults. Young children often have difficulty articulating their thoughts and fears. Consequently, it can be difficult for clinicians to use the same diagnostic criteria for PTSD with preschool-age children as they might with older children, adolescents, and adults. For example, when very young children experience an increase in sleep problems and frightening dreams following a traumatic event, it may be difficult or impossible to determine if the content of these dreams is connected to trauma. Similarly, it is very unlikely that children will be able to describe symptoms of avoidance or negative changes in their thoughts and feelings—characteristics essential to PTSD in older children, adolescents, and adults. Instead, it is more likely that their parents will notice behaviors that suggest intrusive thoughts or dreams, avoidance of people or places associated with trauma, and negative changes in overt behavior and mood.

Because very young children manifest PTSD differently than adults, *DSM-5* includes specific criteria for PTSD in preschool children. These criteria (Table 12.2, Diagnostic Criteria for PTSD for Children 6 Years and Younger) are similar to PTSD in adults; they require symptoms to follow a serious, traumatic event. Furthermore, they require the presence of at least one intrusive symptom, such as recurrent memories or thoughts about the event, distressing dreams, dissociative symptoms, or distress when confronted with people or places associated with the trauma. The criteria for PTSD in preschoolers differ from the criteria for older children, adolescents, and adults in several respects:

Table 12.2 Diagnostic Criteria for PTSD for Children 6 Years and Younger

A. In children 6 years and younger, *exposure* to actual or threatened death, serious injury, or sexual violence in one (or more) of the following ways:

   1. Directly experiencing the traumatic event(s).

   2. Witnessing, in person, the event(s) as it occurred to others, especially primary caregivers.

   Note: Witnessing does not include events that are witnessed only in electronic media, television, movies, or pictures.

   3. Learning that the traumatic event(s) occurred to a parent or caregiving figure.

B. Presence of one (or more) of the following *intrusion symptoms* associated with the traumatic event(s), beginning after the traumatic event(s) occurred:

   1. Recurrent, involuntary, and intrusive distressing memories of the traumatic event(s). Note: Spontaneous and intrusive memories may not necessarily appear distressing and may be expressed as play reenactment.

   2. Recurrent or distressing dreams in which the content and/or affect of the dream are related to the traumatic event(s). Note: It may not be possible to ascertain that the frightening content is related to the traumatic event.

   3. Dissociative reactions (e.g., flashbacks) in which the child feels or acts as if the traumatic event(s) were recurring. Trauma-specific reenactment may occur in play.

   4. Intense or prolonged psychological distress at exposure to internal or external cues that symbolize or resemble an aspect of the traumatic event(s).

   5. Marked physiological reactions to reminders of the traumatic event(s).

C. One (or more) of the following symptoms, representing either *persistent avoidance* of stimuli associated with the traumatic event(s), or *negative alterations in cognitions and mood* associated with the traumatic event(s), must be present, beginning after the traumatic event(s) occurred or worsening after the event(s):

   Persistent Avoidance of Stimuli

   1. Avoidance of or efforts to avoid distressing activities, places, or physical reminders that arouse recollections of the traumatic event(s).

   2. Avoidance of or efforts to avoid people, conversations, or interpersonal situations that arouse recollections of the traumatic event(s).

   Negative Alterations in Cognitions or Mood

   1. Substantially increased frequency of negative emotional states (e.g., fear, guilt, sadness, shame, confusion).

   2. Markedly diminished interest or participation in significant activities, including constriction of play.

   3. Socially withdrawn behavior.

   4. Persistent reduction in expression of positive emotions.

D. *Alterations in arousal and reactivity* associated with the traumatic event(s), beginning or worsening after the traumatic event(s) occurred, as evidenced by two (or more) of the following:

   1. Irritable behavior and angry outbursts (with little or no provocation) typically expressed as verbal or physical aggression toward people or objects (including extreme temper tantrums).

   2. Hypervigilance.

   3. Exaggerated startle response.

   4. Problems with concentration.

   5. Sleep disturbance (e.g., difficulty falling or staying asleep or restless sleep).

(Continued)

Table 12.2 (Continued)

E. Duration of the disturbance is more than 1 month.

F. The disturbance causes clinically significant distress or impairment in relationships with parents, siblings, peers, or other caregivers or with school behavior.

G. The disturbance is not attributable to the physiological effects of a substance (e.g., medication, alcohol) or another medical condition.

Source: Reprinted with permission from the *Diagnostic and Statistical Manual of Mental Disorders, Fifth Edition* (Copyright 2013). American Psychiatric Association.

Note: These criteria apply to children 6 years and younger.

1. Preschooler's symptoms are expressed in terms of actions or observable behaviors, because it is often difficult for preschoolers to express thoughts and feelings. For example, adults might report feeling detached or estranged from others and experience a lack of interest in activities they previously found enjoyable. In contrast, preschoolers might show social withdrawal and restricted play.

2. Preschoolers need to show only one persistent avoidance symptom *or* one negative alteration in cognition and mood symptom to meet criteria for PTSD. In contrast, adults must show one persistent avoidance symptom and two symptoms of negative alteration in cognition and mood to meet criteria. The lower symptom threshold for preschoolers reflects their difficulty in articulating their thoughts and feelings.

3. Preschoolers' symptoms must cause them distress, interfere with their behavior at school, or impair their relationships with parents, siblings, or caregivers. In contrast, PTSD symptoms in adults must cause distress or impairment to the individual themselves (not necessarily others).

DSM-5 also shows sensitivity to the ways children might express PTSD symptoms differently than adults. For example, young children with significant PTSD symptoms may not appear distressed immediately following a traumatic event. Similarly, they might engage in repetitive play instead of experiencing intrusive memories of events. For example, a child who underwent a painful or frightening medical procedure might reenact the event with her dolls (e.g., reassuring a doll that everything will be fine on a pretend trip to the hospital). Similarly, children with PTSD may experience nightmares after the traumatic experience, but they may not be able to connect their bad dreams to the experience itself. Other young children with PTSD show regressive behaviors. They might suck their thumb, refuse to go to bed at night, or tantrum. Still other children might experience other anxiety problems, such as separation anxiety, fear of the dark, or monsters under the bed.

Acute Stress Disorder

By definition, PTSD symptoms must occur after a traumatic event and must last for at least one month. The diagnosis Acute Stress Disorder is assigned when people show PTSD symptoms for at least 3 days but less than one month. The symptoms of Acute Stress Disorder fall into five clusters. These clusters overlap with the four essential symptoms of PTSD and a fifth cluster which includes dissociative symptoms (American Psychiatric Association, 2013). The five symptom clusters are the following:

Intrusive Symptoms: Recurrent, involuntary, and intrusive memories, distressing dreams, or flashbacks associated with the traumatic event.

Avoidance Symptoms: Efforts to avoid distressing memories, thoughts, feelings or reminders (e.g., people, places, activities) associated with the traumatic event.

Dissociative Symptoms: An altered or distorted sense of the reality of one's self or one's surroundings or the inability to remember important aspects of the traumatic event.

Negative Mood: Persistent inability to experience positive emotions following the traumatic event.

Arousal Symptoms: Hypervigilence, exaggerated startle response, irritable behavior and angry outbursts, or problems with sleep and concentration following the traumatic event.

DSM-5 lists a total of 14 possible symptoms of Acute Stress Disorder, falling into these five clusters. People can meet criteria for Acute Stress Disorder by showing nine symptoms from any of these clusters. Consequently, individuals with Acute Stress Disorder need not show all five symptom clusters; they can exhibit symptoms from two or three clusters only. This flexibility reflects the diverse ways people may respond to traumatic events. It also increases the likelihood that someone with Acute Stress Disorder will be identified and receive treatment before the development of PTSD.

Epidemiology of PTSD

Prevalence

As many as 30% of youths are exposed to a serious, traumatic event at some point in their childhood and roughly one third of these children will develop symptoms of PTSD. The number of children who meet full criteria for PTSD is likely much smaller. The only published epidemiological study involving children in the United States showed a 3-month prevalence of .03% and a lifetime prevalence of .1% (Copeland et al., 2007). Low prevalence has also been seen among children in other countries such as the United Kingdom and Germany. In contrast, the prevalence among adults is approximately 8%. It is noteworthy that these prevalence estimates are based on older (*DSM-IV*) diagnostic criteria that were not designed for children. Recent studies indicate that the current criteria are more sensitive to PTSD symptoms in children and, therefore, will detect a larger percentage of youths who experience clinically significant symptoms (Sheeringa et al., 2011).

Recall that the number of symptoms required for a PTSD diagnosis is lower in children than in adults. Several studies indicate that this lower symptom threshold makes the diagnostic criteria more sensitive to children with posttraumatic stress. For example, researchers examined the number of young children who met PTSD, using the *DSM-5* adult and child symptom thresholds (Figure 12.1).

All children had experienced a household accident resulting in a burn (e.g., scalding water in the bath, touching a hot stove). Approximately 25% of children met the reduced (i.e., child) threshold criteria for PTSD one month after the accident. Although these children were highly symptomatic and showed impairment, only one fifth of these children met the adult PTSD criteria.

The prevalence of pediatric PTSD depends largely on the trauma to which children have been exposed. Children exposed to chronic or repeated traumatic events show the highest likelihood of developing PTSD. Between 40% to 60% of refugees from war-torn countries, chronic victims of physical or sexual abuse, and children who are repeatedly exposed to domestic violence meet diagnostic criteria for PTSD. The prevalence of PTSD among youths exposed to single-incident traumatic events is somewhat lower. For example, between 25% and 30% of children caught in building fires or involved in serious auto accidents develop PTSD. Rates of PTSD associated with single-incident household accidents are lower still. For example, between 14% and 26% of young children burned or otherwise injured at home later meet criteria for the disorder (Yule & Smith, 2010).

Course and Comorbidity

The course of PTSD is variable. Most adults with PTSD recover from the disorder without treatment. Furthermore,

Figure 12.1 The Most Common PTSD Symptoms Shown by Children One Month After a Household Injury

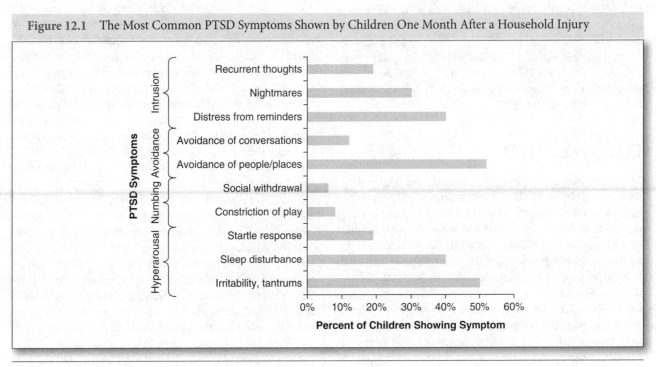

Source: Based on DeYoung and colleagues (2011).

retrospective studies indicate that two thirds of adults who had PTSD as adolescents no longer experience the disorder in adulthood (Yule & Smith, 2010).

Prospective, longitudinal studies involving children reveal a different picture, however. These studies suggest that childhood PTSD often persists over time. For example, Meiser-Stedman and colleagues (2005) conducted a prospective, longitudinal study of children involved in assaults or traffic accidents. Two to 4 weeks after the trauma, 20% of children met criteria for Acute Stress Disorder. Six months after the incident, 12% still met criteria for PTSD. Another study assessed children who developed PTSD after surviving Hurricane Andrew in Florida (Shaw et al., 1996). Although their symptoms decreased over time, 70% of children still met criteria for PTSD 21 months after the storm. Children who were victims of fires, car accidents, and other injuries showed similar persistence in PTSD (Scheeringa et al., 2011).

PTSD merits treatment for several reasons. First, many youths who "recover" from PTSD continue to show subthreshold PTSD symptoms and problems with depression and anxiety. Irritability and sleep disturbance are the most common lingering symptoms in children. Second, early treatment might prevent Acute Stress Disorder from developing into PTSD or facilitate the recovery of PTSD once it emerges. Third, PTSD interferes with children's emotional well-being. Youths with PTSD often have other anxiety disorders, especially phobias. In most cases, phobias exist before the development of PTSD (LaGreca, Silverman, & Wasserstein, 1998).

Depression and suicidal ideation are also comorbid with PTSD. In one study of adolescents with PTSD, 41% met criteria for depression (Giaconia et al., 1995). As many as 46% of adolescents with PTSD develop alcohol use problems, while 25% abuse other drugs (Giaconia et al., 1995). Adolescents with PTSD seem to use substances to cope with anxiety and depression associated with the trauma (Chilcoat & Breslau, 1998).

Etiology of PTSD

Many children are exposed to traumatic events, but relatively few develop PTSD. Although catastrophic events are necessary for the development of PTSD, they are not sufficient. In order to understand why some children exposed to trauma develop PTSD symptoms and others do not, researchers have developed a risk and resilience approach to understanding the disorder. Recall that **risk factors** increase the likelihood that children will develop a particular disorder, whereas **resilience factors** buffer children from the potential harmful effects of risk. Although our understanding of PTSD is not complete (especially in children), the emergence of the disorder depends largely on the complex interaction of risk and resilience.

Functioning Before the Trauma

One fairly consistent finding has been that children's social-emotional functioning *before* a traumatic event predicts the severity of their posttraumatic symptoms. Several studies have found that children with elevated anxiety and/or depression levels before the September 11th terrorist attacks in New York were more likely to develop distress and impairment after the attacks (Gil-Rivas, Holman, & Silver, 2004; Hock, Hart, Kang, & Lutz, 2004; Lengua et al., 2005; Whalen et al., 2004). In one study of New York schoolchildren, the relationship between exposure to the trauma and PTSD symptoms disappeared after researchers controlled for children's pretraumatic psychological functioning (Aber, Gershoff, Ware, & Kotler, 2004). Similarly, children's emotional functioning *before* hurricane Katrina predicted their likelihood of PTSD, general anxiety, and depression after the hurricane (Weems et al., 2007). Collectively, these findings indicate that children already showing mood or anxiety disorders are most susceptible for developing PTSD following a traumatic event.

Proximity to the Trauma

The likelihood of developing PTSD depends on the child's proximity to the traumatic event (McKnight et al., 2004). In 2001, a 15-year-old Santana High School student opened fire during the school day, killing two classmates and wounding 10 other people. Several months after the incident, researchers assessed PTSD symptoms among students at the high school (Wendling, 2009). In total, 247 students witnessed a student being shot or receiving medical treatment, 590 had heard or seen a shot fired in the distance, and 323 were not directly exposed to the trauma. The researchers found a dose-response relationship between proximity to the trauma and PTSD (Figure 12.2). Overall, 4.9% of students met criteria for PTSD. Rates were highest for students directly exposed to the trauma (9.7%) and lowest for students only indirectly exposed (3.4%). These findings indicate that the more youths are exposed to traumatic events, the greater their likelihood of PTSD. However, even youths more distally exposed to trauma can develop PTSD symptoms.

Children can also be traumatized by hearing about a catastrophic event occurring to their parents, relatives, or loved ones. Many children attending school near the World Trade Center on September 11, 2001, were directly exposed to the terrorist attack. Overall, 76% of children witnessed the attack themselves, were evacuated from their schools, or were otherwise involved in the events of that day. Furthermore, 8% of children had a family member who worked at the World Trade Center or who was in one of the buildings at the time of the attack. More than 3,250 children lost their parents in the disaster (Hoven, Mandell, & Duarte, 2003).

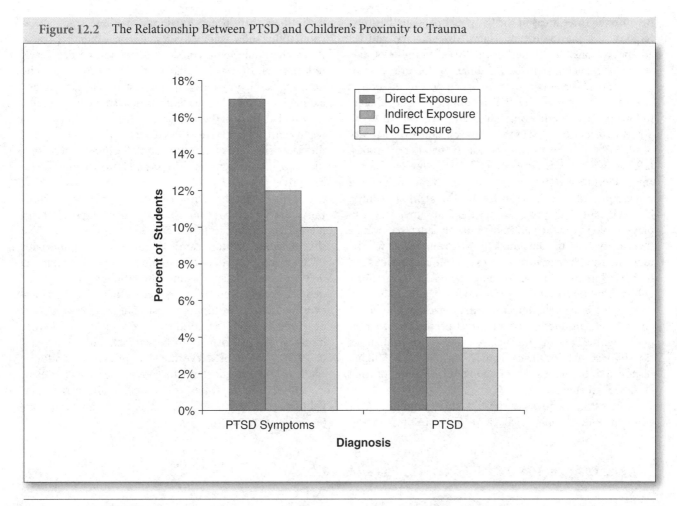

Figure 12.2 The Relationship Between PTSD and Children's Proximity to Trauma

Source: Based on Wendling (2009).

Note: Children who saw a classmate shot or receiving medical treatment (direct exposure) were more likely to develop PTSD symptoms or to meet full criteria for PTSD than children who heard or saw shots only from a distance (indirect exposure) or who attended the school but did not witness the shooting.

Data collected after 9/11 demonstrated that children who were directly exposed to the trauma, or whose family members were directly exposed to the attack, were more likely to develop psychiatric problems than children who were only exposed to the attacks through television. For example, 87% of children who were exposed to the trauma (directly or through parents) displayed at least one PTSD symptom after the attacks. Almost 25% of these children showed intrusive thoughts, concentration problems, *and* sleep disturbance (Aber et al., 2004; Schlenger et al., 2002). After the attacks, approximately 27% of youths met diagnostic criteria for at least one anxiety or mood disorder. The most common psychiatric disorders were Separation Anxiety Disorder (12.3%), PTSD (10.6%), Generalized Anxiety Disorder (12.3%), Panic Disorder (8.7%) and depression (8.1%; Aber et al., 2004; Hoven et al., 2003; Stuber et al., 2005).

Brain and Endocrine Functioning

The **amygdala** plays a role in the development of PTSD. In healthy people, the amygdala is the starting point for the body's physiological stress response (Figure 12.3). When a person encounters a stressful event, the amygdala causes the periventricular nucleus of the hypothalamus to release a hormone called corticotropin releasing factor (CRF). CRF is detected by a second brain area, the pituitary, which releases the hormone corticotropin. Finally, corticotropin triggers the release of cortisol by the adrenal gland. Cortisol, the body's primary stress hormone, activates the sympathetic nervous system and prepares the body for confronting or fleeing potential dangers. After the body has produced sufficient levels of cortisol to effectively deal with the stressful situation, the amygdala inhibits further activity by the hypothalamus.

Because the three areas of the body that regulate the stress response are the (a) hypothalamus, (b) pituitary, and (c) adrenal regions, this system is usually called the **HPA axis** (J. A. Cohen, Perel, DeBellis, Friedman, & Putnam, 2002).

Traumatic events can cause disruption in the body's stress response system (DeBellis et al., 1994). Immediately following a traumatic event, children who develop Acute Stress Disorder or PTSD often show chronic over-activity of the HPA axis, even while at rest (Carrion et al., 2002). HPA over-activity results in high baseline levels of cortisol, blood pressure, and heart rate, which can make these individuals unusually sensitive to threatening stimuli, hypervigilant, and prone to startle. The amygdala also plays a role in the formation of emotion-laden memories. Over-activity of the amygdala may be responsible for the unwanted and intrusive memories of traumatic events seen in PTSD. Furthermore, some youths with PTSD show difficulty inhibiting cortisol secretion once it begins. In healthy people, the amygdala detects cortisol levels in the blood and inhibits production after a threat passes. However, in people with PTSD, this normal feedback loop is sometimes slow or dysfunctional, causing the body's "fight" or "flight" response to be mobilized for an extended period of time (J. A. Cohen et al., 2002).

Interestingly, however, several studies indicate that children with chronic PTSD have *lower* resting cortisol levels than their peers. Furthermore, these traumatized youths often show a blunted corticotropin response to stress. Researchers believe that these unusually low cortisol levels reflect the body's way of compensating for chronic stress by downregulating its stress-response system. This downregulation helps the body cope with chronic stress, but it seems to be maladaptive in the long term. When children with low resting cortisol levels are exposed to another major stressor, they may show an exaggerated stress response, increasing their likelihood of greater distress and impairment (DeBellis, 2001).

High levels of cortisol can damage the **hippocampus**, a brain region responsible for converting short-term memories to long-term memories. Several studies have shown decreased hippocampal volume among adults with PTSD symptoms. Reduced volume of the hippocampus may underlie some of the unwanted thoughts or memory deficits experienced by many people with PTSD. However, reductions in hippocampal volume have not been observed in children with the disorder. It is possible that hippocampal malformation is observable only after years of PTSD symptoms. Nevertheless, children and adolescents with PTSD do tend to show other, more global, structural abnormalities including small intracranial volume and reduction in the size of the corpus callosum (Yule & Smith, 2010).

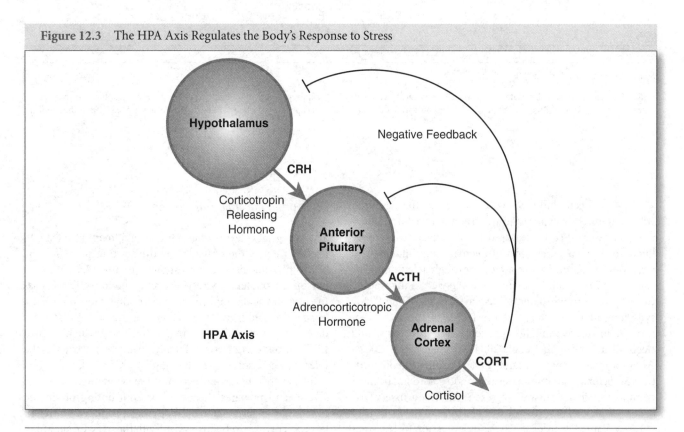

Figure 12.3   The HPA Axis Regulates the Body's Response to Stress

Source: From Brian M. Sweis.

Note: Children with PTSD often show dysregulation of this axis and abnormally high or low levels of cortisol, the body's main stress hormone.

Cognitive Appraisal and Coping

Children's cognitive appraisal of traumatic events can greatly influence their response to these events (Yule & Smith, 2010). **Cognitive appraisal theory** asserts that the way people feel about situations depends on their evaluations (i.e., appraisals) of those situations. Children who experience trauma as personally relevant typically show more distress than children who cognitively distance themselves from catastrophic events (Meiser-Stedman et al., 2005). For example, children who knew someone involved in the 9/11 terrorist attacks or who believed that they or their families could be victims of a similar event in the future were likely to develop PTSD symptoms. In contrast, children who believed that it was unlikely that their families would be harmed in subsequent attacks showed relatively few anxiety and mood problems (see text box Research to Practice: Children's Appraisals of the September 11 Terrorist Attacks).

Children's coping strategies immediately following a traumatic event can also greatly influence their behavioral and social-emotional functioning. **Coping** refers to thoughts and actions that protect oneself from psychological damage following a stressful event. Coping mediates the relationship between stress and a person's emotional response. Most theories of coping assert that a person's coping strategy largely determines his or her response to a psychosocial stressor, rather than aspects of the stressor itself. Consequently, the same stressor can have different effects on different people.

Psychologists differentiate between two types of coping: problem-focused and escape-avoidance. **Problem-focused coping** is often considered more adaptive. It involves modifying or eliminating the conditions that gave rise to the psychosocial stressor or changing the perception of an experience in a way that reduces or neutralizes the problem. In many cases, children and adolescents cannot "fix" traumatic events once they occur; however, they can change the way they think about the stressor in order to make them feel more in control of the situation. For example, an adolescent who is sexually assaulted may not be able to "take back" her virginity. However, she may reduce feelings of guilt or loss by talking to a loved one about the incident and realizing that she was not to blame.

In contrast, **escape or avoidance coping** involves disengaging from a stressful situation and its behavioral, cognitive, emotional consequences. After a traumatic event, most people want to avoid people, places, thoughts, and feelings associated with the event. They might become increasingly isolated or try to distract themselves with other activities. Some people will use medication, alcohol, and other drugs to cope with negative

---

RESEARCH TO PRACTICE

CHILDREN'S APPRAISALS OF TO THE SEPTEMBER 11 TERRORIST ATTACKS

Below are verbatim statements given by school-aged children living in New York to open-ended questions about the 9/11 attacks. Children's cognitive appraisals of the trauma influenced their emotional reactions. Children who personalized the attacks were more likely to develop PTSD symptoms than children who distanced themselves from the attacks.

Personalization

- It was scary. If they could do it to the World Trade Center, they could do it to our house. It bothered me because so many people died.
- Yes, I was worried because not far from where I live there are tall buildings.
- I don't like to go into tall buildings.
- I didn't like it. It was sad and scary. It made me worry about going on planes and living next to a stadium that they might bomb.
- I'm afraid that Dad might get drafted if they lose too many soldiers. My mom is a nurse so I kind of worry about her.
- The week after it happened my dad had to fly to [city name]. That made me scared.
- I was worried something would happen when they [Mom and Dad] would go someplace alone. I wanted to go, but I couldn't go.

Distancing

- There are a billion people in the world; it would be like a one in a billion chance that something like that would happen to me.
- The school is the safest place I can be—they just have to push buttons to get the cops here.
- I was a little bit scared after the attack, but now I know I'm safe. Here in [city name], what are the odds of someone crashing? There are no big monuments.
- No, I don't think something bad might happen to my parents. My dad doesn't work in a big building, only 20 stories, and my mom only works in a one-story building.
- It made me mad and I wished the U.S.A. could get revenge. It did not really cause me to worry. I've never been on an airplane before.

Source: Adapted from Hock et al. (2004).

emotions, whereas others will cognitively and emotionally "shut down" in order to avoid any feeling whatsoever.

Escape and avoidance coping is negatively reinforcing because it temporarily removes psychological distress and discomfort. In the short term, escape-avoidance coping can also be adaptive; it can allow people to meet school, work, or family obligations immediately following a major stressor. In the long term, however, escape-avoidance coping predisposes people to social-emotional problems, especially anxiety disorders and PTSD. Because individuals do not confront people, situations, thoughts, and feelings associated with the stressor, negative emotions associated with the stressor tend to linger, leading to long-term impairment. For example, adolescents who responded to the 9/11 terrorist attacks with emotional numbness displayed the poorest social and emotional outcomes: depression, hopelessness, suicidal ideation, and PTSD. In contrast, youths with fewer "numbing" symptoms were less likely to develop these emotional problems (Lengua et al., 2005).

Family Functioning

Parental support can protect youths from anxiety and mood disorders following a major trauma. Anna Freud first observed that children whose mothers held and reassured them during the air raids over London during World War II were less likely to develop adverse emotional reactions to the bombings (Freud & Burlingham, 1943). More recently, researchers have noticed that parents' emotional reactions to trauma influence their children's adjustment (Fremont, 2004). Specifically, parents who are able to provide stable and consistent care, to model constructive coping, and to reassure their children of their availability and safety often buffer their children from the adverse effects of the trauma.

What else can parents and teachers do to protect children from the potentially deleterious effects of traumatic events, like terrorist attacks (LaGreca & Silverman, 2006)? First, caregivers must appreciate the sensitivity of children to these traumatic events and take them seriously. Even children living thousands of miles away from events can experience distress. After the 9/11 attacks, many children personalized the incident, expecting future attacks in their own communities. Parents should not underestimate the influence of indirect exposure on children's social-emotional health (LaGreca, Silverman, Vernberg, & Roberts, 2002).

RESEARCH TO PRACTICE

TALKING TO KIDS AFTER A DISASTER

Children vary in their capacity to make connections between events and emotions. Many children will benefit from a basic explanation of how disaster-related experiences produce upsetting emotions and physical sensations. Suggestions for working with children include the following:

- Don't ask children directly to describe their emotions (like telling you that they feel sad, scared, confused, or angry), as they often have a hard time finding the words. Instead, ask them to tell you about physical sensations, for example, "How do you feel inside? Do you feel something like butterflies in your stomach or tight all over?"
- If they are able to talk about emotions, it is helpful to suggest different feelings and ask them to pick one ("Do you feel sad right now, or scared, or do you feel okay?") rather than asking open-ended questions ("How are you feeling?").
- You can draw (or ask the child to draw) an outline of a person and use this to help the child talk about his or her physical sensations.

The following gives a basic explanation that helps children to talk about common emotional and physical reactions to disaster.

When something really bad happens, kids often feel funny, strange, or uncomfortable, like their heart is beating really fast, their hands feel sweaty, their stomach hurts, or their legs or arms feel weak or shaky. Other times, kids just feel funny inside their heads, almost like they are not really there, like they are watching bad things happening to someone else.

Sometimes, your body keeps having these feelings for a while even after the bad thing is over and you are safe. These feelings are your body's way of telling you again how bad the disaster was.

Do you have any of these feelings, or other ones that I didn't talk about? Can you tell me where you feel them and what they feel like?

Sometimes, these strange or uncomfortable feelings come up when kids see, hear, or smell things that remind them of what happened, like strong winds, glass breaking, the smell of smoke, and so on. It can be very scary for kids to have these feelings in their bodies, especially if they don't know why they are happening or what to do about them. If you like, I can tell you some ways to help yourself feel better. Does that sound like a good idea?

Source: From the National Child Traumatic Stress Network and the National Center for PTSD (Brymer et al., 2006).

Second, parents can limit children's exposure to traumatic events by regulating access to media images and conversations about traumatic events. For example, researchers have found moderate correlations between children's access to television stories about traumas and children's anxiety (Lengua et al., 2005; Schuster et al., 2001). It is particularly important to shield children from extremely distressing images of destruction that could cause them to personalize the attack to their own lives.

Third, it is important for parents to provide consistent, sensitive care to children following trauma and avoid displays of hostility or anxiety. For example, hostile parent-child interactions or displays of parental anxiety predicted children's negative emotional reactions to the 9/11 attacks (Gil-Rivas et al., 2004; Phillips, Prince, & Schiebelhut, 2004). In contrast, children whose parents helped them cope with the trauma in a sensitive and supportive fashion displayed better outcomes. Parents must give children the opportunity to discuss their impressions of the traumatic event in a safe, supportive environment. The nature of these parent-child conversations will depend on the child's age and development but should always involve reassurance that the parents will provide physical security and emotional support.

Treatment of PTSD

Psychological Debriefing and Psychological First Aid

One of the most popular forms of treatment for victims of traumatic events has been psychological debriefing. Technically, **psychological debriefing** is not a "treatment" as much as a method of helping victims cope with distressing mental images, thoughts, and feelings associated with a catastrophic evident. It is usually administered by first-responders or mental health professionals who arrive at the scene of traumatic events within minutes or hours of the event's occurrence. Psychological debriefing consists of a single session, usually conducted on location, in which the practitioner helps the victim describe memories of the event as well as corresponding cognitions and emotions. Most proponents believe that psychological debriefing provides victims with a cathartic experience that facilitates coping.

Although psychological debriefing might seem appropriate, nearly all research has failed to show that it is effective in reducing psychological distress or preventing anxiety disorders, mood disorders, or PTSD (Rose et al., 2002). Furthermore, at least two randomized controlled studies have shown that people who participated in psychological debriefing immediately following an injury (e.g., burns, traffic accidents) actually showed an increase in PTSD symptoms compared to individuals who did not receive this intervention. It is possible that by encouraging victims to talk about traumatic experience before they are ready, practitioners of psychological debriefing may hinder, rather than help, the recovery process. Indeed, psychological debriefing

is currently not recommended by either the National Center for PTSD or the World Health Organization.

Instead, PTSD experts have developed an alternative intervention for children, adults, and families exposed to trauma: **psychological first aid** (PFA; Watson et al., 2011). Like psychological debriefing, PFA is typically administered by first-responders or mental health professionals at the site of a catastrophic event (Image 12.2). Unlike psychological debriefing, PFA provides victims with a sense of safety and security and meets their immediate physical, social, and emotional needs. PFA is based on several core principles including (a) fostering a sense of safety, (b) promoting calming, (c) increasing self-efficacy, (d) achieving connectedness and social support, and (e) instilling hope for the future. Although providers of PFA are certainly willing to listen to victims' thoughts and feelings about the traumatic event, their focus is chiefly on meeting victims' immediate needs (Ruzek et al., 2007).

For example, a primary goal in working with traumatized children is to make sure that they feel safe, that they know their parents and loved ones are also safe, and that they will soon be reunited with their family (Koocher & LaGreca, 2010). The practitioner introduces herself to the child and tries to offer comfort and reassurance:

> Hi. I'm Lisa, and I'm here to try to help you and your family. Is there anything you need right now? There is some water and juice over there, and we have a few blankets in those boxes. Your mom and dad are here, and many people are all working hard so that you and your family will be safe. Do you have any questions about what we're doing to keep you safe? (Brymer et al., 2006, p. 24).

Next, the individual providing PFA tries to determine other needs, besides safety, that the child might have and begins to develop a plan with the child and family to meet those needs:

> It sounds like you are really worried about several different things, like what happened to your house, when your dad is coming, and what will happen next. Those are all important things. Let's think about what's most important right now, and then make a plan. (Brymer et al., 2006, p. 66)

The practitioner will encourage the child to engage in active coping strategies, by talking with parents and other adults that are available to help. The goal is not to get the child to discuss the trauma but, rather, to know that adults are willing to listen and connect with her if she does need tangible or emotional support:

> You are doing a great job letting grown-ups know what you need. It is important to keep letting people know how they can help you. The more help you get, the more you can make things better. Even grown-ups need help at a time like this. (Brymer et al., 2006, p. 72)

Sometimes, PFA might involve teaching children simple relaxation strategies, such as focused breathing, to help them

Image 12.2 Psychological first aid can be used by paraprofessionals to help families feel safe and make sure their immediate physical and psychological needs are met. This photograph shows counselors and volunteers helping victims of Hurricane Katrina.

Source: FEMA photo/Andrea Booher.

regulate their emotions. Relaxation is also useful in helping children sleep:

> Let's practice a way of breathing that can help calm our bodies down. Put one hand on your stomach, like this [demonstrate]. Okay, we are going to breathe in through our noses. When we breathe in, we are going to fill up with a lot of air and our stomachs are going to stick out like this [demonstrate]. Then, we will breathe out through our mouths. When we breathe out, our stomachs are going to suck in and up like this [demonstrate]. We can pretend that we are a balloon, filling up with air and then letting the air out, nice and slow. We are going to breathe in really slowly while I count to three. I'm also going to count to three while we breathe out really slowly. Let's try it together. (Brymer et al., 2006, p. 83)

Finally, practitioners of PFA will attempt to normalize the child and family's stress response by explicitly stating that their emotional reactions are expected given the severity of the situation. Practitioners will usually provide families with the names and contact information of mental health professionals in case families need treatment.

The essential elements of the intervention are supported by research. For example, techniques such as active listening, supporting individuals through normalization, and providing informational, tangible, and emotional support to foster a sense of self-efficacy and control are all associated with

enhanced coping (Bisson & Lewis, 2009). Future research needs to include randomized controlled studies of the entire treatment package to determine its effectiveness with children and families.

Trauma-Focused CBT

Trauma-Focused CBT (TF-CBT) involves exposing children to memories or stimuli associated with traumatic events and then encouraging them to think about and cope with the trauma in more adaptive ways. TF-CBT has several important features (Cohen & Mannarino, 2004; McKnight et al., 2004). First, early treatment sessions are used to teach families about PTSD. It is usually helpful for parents and children to know that PTSD symptoms are relatively common among individuals who experience trauma and that treatment can be effective in reducing children's distress.

Second, the therapist teaches the child coping skills to deal with the anxiety associated with the trauma. Most therapists teach relaxation skills, such as deep breathing or muscle relaxation. Some therapists also teach children to engage in positive self-talk that is designed to give them greater confidence and security when they encounter memories of the trauma. For example, a child might practice saying to herself, "It's going to be OK" when she experiences distress or, "I can do it" when she attempts to use relaxation techniques to combat anxiety.

Third, TF-CBT involves gradually exposing children to stimuli or memories associated with the traumatic event. At a minimum, exposure usually involves the therapist encouraging the child to imagine the traumatic event in the safety and security of the therapy session. The therapist might ask the child to give a play-by-play account of the event and pay attention to sights, sounds, images, and feelings associated with the trauma. The goal is to expose the child to the anxiety-provoking stimuli for progressively longer intervals. Many therapists also ask the child to provide increasingly more detailed narratives of the traumatic event, either orally or in writing. Ideally, the child will eventually feel comfortable enough to share his narrative with others. If possible, some therapists use in vivo exposure to correct avoidance of situations associated with the trauma. For example, a child might avoid recess at school because he witnessed a classmate being severely injured in a car accident in the school parking lot. The therapist, with the help of parents and teachers, might encourage the child to gradually expose himself to the parking lot to overcome his anxiety (J. A. Cohen, 2005).

Fourth, TF-CBT involves identifying and changing children's maladaptive cognitions about the traumatic event (Stallard & Smith, 2007). Many children believe they somehow caused the traumatic event or are to blame for the misery and hardship the event placed on others. For example, an adolescent who is sexually abused might assume blame for her maltreatment because she acquiesced to the demands of her abuser. Another child, whose mother died in an auto accident, might believe that he is to blame because he was arguing with his sister in the car when the accident occurred. The clinician identifies and challenges these maladaptive beliefs. The therapist might ask children to provide evidence for their beliefs. A clinician might say to a sexually abused child, "It is true that you never told anyone about the abuse. However, didn't he threaten to kill you and your mother if you didn't give in to his demands? Were you really free to say 'no'?"

At least four randomized controlled studies have investigated the efficacy of TF-CBT for children with PTSD that was caused by sexual abuse (Nemeroff et al., 2004). In general, children who participate in trauma-focused CBT show reductions in PTSD symptoms and increases in social competence greater than youths who receive no treatment or nondirective counseling. For example, Smith and colleagues (2007) randomly assigned youths with PTSD following assault to either TF-CBT or a waitlist control condition. After treatment, 92% of youths who participated in TF-CBT no longer met criteria for PTSD compared to 42% of children on the waitlist. Children who received TF-CBT also showed significant reductions in anxiety and depression. These benefits remained 6 months after treatment. Other studies have demonstrated the efficacy of CBT in reducing PTSD symptoms in children exposed to natural disasters and abuse (Chemtob,

Nakashima, & Carlson, 2002; Cohen & Mannarino, 2004; Goenjian et al., 1997).

Eye Movement Desensitization and Reprocessing

Eye movement desensitization and reprocessing (EMDR) is a technique developed by Francine Shapiro (2001) to treat PTSD in adults. The technique involves asking an adult patient to generate a mental image related to the traumatic experience during the therapy session. With this image in mind, the patient is instructed to follow the therapist's moving finger as the therapist rapidly moves it across the patient's visual field, back and forth, for approximately 30 seconds. Then, the therapist asks the patient to report his or her current thoughts and feelings. The procedure is typically repeated several times during a single therapy session.

EMDR is as effective as cognitive-behavior therapy at alleviating PTSD in adults (National Institute for Health and Clinical Excellence [NICE], 2005). However, relatively few studies have investigated its efficacy with children. One team of researchers compared EMDR to CBT for 523 children involved in a fireworks disaster in the Netherlands (de Roos et al., 2011). Although children improved in response to both treatments, EMDR yielded benefits in fewer sessions. Another group of researchers used EMDR to treat 32 children who did not respond to other forms of psychosocial interventions (Chemtob et al., 2002). In this study, three sessions of EMDR were associated with reductions in PTSD, anxiety, and depression.

The main drawback to EMDR is that the mechanism by which it reduces PTSD is unknown. Proponents claim that saccadic eye movements somehow integrate memories of traumatic events into individual's long-term memory, thereby, reducing intrusive thoughts, images, and dreams. However, several studies indicate that the effects of EMDR are attributable to exposing patients to images related to the trauma and allowing them to cognitively and emotionally process these events (Bisson et al., 2007; Seidler & Wagner, 2006). Although the mechanism by which EMDR "works" has yet to be determined, it has been shown to be promising treatment for children with the disorder (Yule & Smith, 2010).

Medication

Medication is not considered a first-line treatment for pediatric PTSD. Only two randomized controlled studies have investigated the efficacy of medication with children. The first study showed that the tricyclic antidepressant imipramine (Tofranil) was superior to the sedative chloral hydrate in alleviating PTSD symptoms in children hospitalized for serious burns (Robert et al., 1999). However, tricyclic antidepressants can cause cardiac problems in children. Consequently, imipramine is typically not prescribed to youths.

The second study compared TF-CBT plus sertraline (Zoloft) and TF-CBT plus placebo in adolescents with PTSD (Cohen et al., 2007). Both groups of adolescents experienced significant reductions in PTSD and depression, with no differences between groups. Other studies have demonstrated the usefulness of other SSRIs, propranolol, and clonidine in alleviating PTSD symptoms. However, these studies did not involve control groups; it is possible that children may have experienced symptom reduction without medication or that the benefit of medications are attributable to placebo. Furthermore, these medications have side effects which often contraindicate their use (Cohen & Mannarino, 2010).

SOCIAL AND EMOTIONAL DEPRIVATION IN INFANCY

In the last section, we examined PTSD, a disorder caused by exposure to a traumatic experience. Clearly, life-threatening events, such as car accidents, home fires, and natural disasters, are catastrophic to people of all ages. However, the nature of "trauma" might be different for children than adults. Because children are dependent on caregivers for their physical and social-emotional needs, they may be just as traumatized by disruptions in their relationships as by threats to their physical integrity. For example, when maltreated children are asked to report their "worst" or most frightening experience, they usually do not recount an incident of abuse; rather, they describe their placement in foster care, separation from their family, or seeing their parents cry during the process. These disruptions in children's relationships would not constitute a "life threatening event" as required for the diagnosis of PTSD, but they can certainly adversely affect children's development (Scheeringa et al., 2011).

There are few things more traumatic to young children than to be lost or separated from their parents. Parents and other caregivers are a source of comfort, support, and reassurance to children. Children rely on parents for protection, nurturance, and direction. Moreover, humans are biologically predisposed to form attachment relationships with their caregivers and to rely on caregivers for support in time of need. When caregivers are absent, infants and young children lack their primary sources of behavioral, social, and emotional support to help them cope effectively with their surroundings (Sroufe & Waters, 1977).

Approximately 8 million infants and children worldwide have no parent or primary caregiver (United Nations Children's Fund [UNICEF], 2012). Most of these youths are raised in orphanages, "baby centers," or other institutions (Image 12.3). Many of these orphanages are located in countries ruled, or formerly ruled, by totalitarian regimes (e.g., Romania, Korea), plagued by war or disease (e.g., Mali, Sudan), or troubled by financial instability (e.g., portions of Latin America, Eastern Europe). Some institutions

Image 12.3   Some Romanian orphans who were raised in institutions, like this boy, showed stereotypies, low cognitive functioning, inattention, and inappropriate social behavior. These problems often persisted even when children were adopted into loving homes in the United States, the United Kingdom, and other countries.

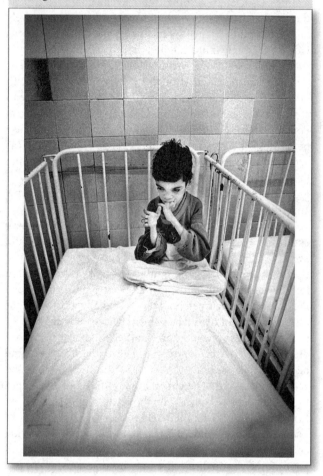

Source: Photo by Anglea Catlin.

provide adequate physical care and cognitive stimulation to children whereas the conditions of other orphanages have been described as "abusive" and "deplorable" (Van IJzendoorn, 2011).

Despite their heterogeneity, most institutions have the following characteristics in common:

- High child-to-caregiver ratios ranging from 1:8 to 1:31.
- High caregiver turnover which often leaves children exposed to 50 to 100 caregivers during their first 18 months of life.
- High regimentation and periods of isolation; in one Greek orphanage children spent 3.5 hrs per day at play and 17.5 hrs per day in their cribs or beds.

- Caregivers focusing chiefly on children's physical health (e.g., feeding, cleaning) rather than children's social-emotional well-being.
- Caregivers providing little warmth, sensitivity, and responsiveness.

Even if institutionalized children are given adequate physical care and cognitive stimulation, these children lack attention and nurturance from a primary caregiver. Orphanages are no substitute for home-based care from loving families (Van IJzendoorn, 2011).

DSM-5 identifies two disorders that can develop in infants and young children when they lack developmentally appropriate care from parents or other primary caregivers early in life: Reactive Attachment Disorder (RAD) and Disinhibited Social Engagement Disorder. Typically, these disorders are seen in infants and young children raised in orphanages, group homes, or multiple foster care settings. More rarely, abused and neglected children can also develop these disorders.

What Is Reactive Attachment Disorder (RAD)?

Definition

Reactive Attachment Disorder (RAD) is a rare disorder seen almost exclusively in infants and young children who experience extreme deprivation (Table 12.3, Diagnostic Criteria for Reactive Attachment Disorder). According to *DSM-5*, infants and young children with RAD show disturbed or developmentally inappropriate attachment behaviors. Most children display attachment behaviors when they are scared, upset, or unsure of their surroundings. Attachment behaviors, such as crying, clinging, and gesturing to be picked up, bring the child closer to his or her caregiver and help the child attain safety (Ainsworth et al., 1978; Bowlby, 1969). Children with RAD do not seek comfort from caregivers when distressed, and they do not respond to comfort when it is provided. Instead, these children are inhibited and emotionally withdrawn from their caregivers. Caregivers sometimes describe these children as "emotionally absent" and lacking the usual social reciprocity that characterizes most parent-infant interactions. Furthermore, children with RAD often show very little positive affect (e.g., smiles, hugs, and kisses) but, instead, present as sad, anxious, or irritable (American Psychiatric Association, 2013).

By definition, RAD is caused by pathogenic care, such as severe physical or emotional neglect, frequent and repeated changes in primary caregivers, such as frequent relocations to different foster homes or institutions with little emotional contact between children and caregivers. In the United States, RAD is most often seen among international adoptees who spent their first 12 to 24 months of life in orphanages characterized by an absence of close caregiver-child interactions (Glowinski, 2011).

Table 12.3   Diagnostic Criteria for Reactive Attachment Disorder

A. A consistent pattern of inhibited, emotionally withdrawn behavior toward adult caregivers, manifested by both of the following:

  1. The child rarely or minimally seeks comfort when distressed.

  2. The child rarely or minimally responds to comfort when distressed.

B. A persistent social and emotional disturbance characterized by at least two of the following:

  1. Minimal social and emotional responsiveness to others.

  2. Limited positive affect.

  3. Episodes of unexplained irritability, sadness, or fearfulness that are evident even during nonthreatening interactions with adult caregivers.

C. The child has experienced a pattern of extremes in insufficient care as evidenced by at least one of the following:

  1. Social neglect or deprivation in the form of persistent lack of having basic emotional needs for comfort, stimulation, and affection met by caregiving adults.

  2. Repeated changes of primary caregivers that limit opportunities to form stable attachments (e.g., frequent changes in foster care).

  3. Rearing in unusual settings that severely limit opportunities to form selective attachments (e.g., institutions with high child-to-caregiver ratios).

(Continued)

Table 12.3   (Continued)

D. The care in criterion C is presumed to be responsible for the disturbed behavior in criterion A.

E. The criteria are not met for Autism Spectrum Disorder.

F. The disturbance is evident before age 5 years.

G. The child has a developmental age of at least 9 months.

Specify current severity:

Reactive Attachment Disorder is specified as severe when a child exhibits all symptoms of the disorder, with each symptom manifesting at relatively high levels.

Source: Reprinted with permission from the *Diagnostic and Statistical Manual of Mental Disorders, Fifth Edition* (Copyright 2013). American Psychiatric Association.

RAD should not be diagnosed in children less than 9 months of age, because attachment relationships are not believed to develop until after this period in development. Similarly, RAD should not be first diagnosed after age 5 years, because attachment relationships are typically formed during the first few years of life.

Early Studies on Infant Deprivation

During World War II, psychologists became interested in the development of infants and young children separated from their caregivers for prolonged periods of time (Spitz, 1965). Pioneering work was conducted by Anna Freud, who opened the Hampstead (England) War Nursery for children separated from their parents because of the war (Image 12.4). Some children were sent to the nursery to escape bombing raids over London (like the children in the book *The Lion, the Witch, and the Wardrobe*); others were separated from parents who were serving in the war effort (Burlingham & Freud, 1962). Later, Freud and her colleagues established a second residential facility for children who survived concentration camps. Freud (1956)

published some of the first papers describing the harmful effects of maternal deprivation on these children's physical and emotional health.

At about the same time, Rene Spitz and Katherine Wolf (1946) described the behavior of infants and toddlers abandoned by their parents and raised in orphanages. Although their physical care was adequate, these infants were given very little physical and social stimulation from caregivers at these institutions. Spitz and Wolf described these infants as listless, withdrawn, and emotionally unresponsive. They did not show interest in seeking closeness with caregivers, even when they were scared or upset. Many infants failed to make normal gains in weight and some engaged in stereotypies, such as unusual and repetitive hand or body movements. Spitz and Wolf believed these infants experienced "anaclitic depression," a sadness and withdrawal caused by the loss of their parents and the absence of an alternative caregiver with whom to bond.

Shortly after World War II, John Bowlby (1951) was asked by the World Health Organization to review research on the developmental outcomes of children who experienced parental deprivation in postwar Europe. Bowlby

CASE STUDY

AN EARLY DESCRIPTION OF RAD

This is a moderately intelligent, unusually beautiful child with enormously big blue eyes and golden curls. At the end of the 11th month, the child, who never has been very active, began to lose even more interest in playing with the experimenter. In the following 2 weeks, the behavior was more marked. The child was not only passive, but she also refused to touch any toys offered to her. She sat in a sort of daze, by the hour, staring silently into space. She did not even show the apprehensiveness in the presence of an approaching observer that was shown by other children. If a toy was put into contact with her, she would withdraw into the farthest corner of her bed and sit there wide-eyed, absent, and without contact, with an immobile, rigid expression on her beautiful face.

Source: From Spitz and Wolf (1946).

met with researchers and clinicians in the United States and Europe who worked with youths raised in orphanages, group homes, and other institutions. Bowlby also noticed a form of "depression" shown by infants and young children deprived of a primary caregiver during their first year of life. He described these children as "listless, quiet, unhappy, and unresponsive." They showed

> an emotional tone of apprehension and sadness. The child withdraws himself from all that is around him; there is no attempt to contact a stranger and no brightening if this stranger contacts him. The child often sits or lies inert in a dazed stupor. Lack of sleep is common and lack of appetite is universal. Weight is lost and there is a sharp drop in general development. (Bowlby, 1954, pp. 23–24)

Bowlby concluded that a "warm, intimate, and continuous relationship" between young children and a primary caregiver was essential to children's physical, cognitive, and social-emotional development (see text box Research to Practice: Differentiating RAD and Autism Spectrum Disorder).

RAD and Parent-Child Attachment

Bowlby's observations of deprived children led to the development of **attachment theory**. Bowlby (1969, 1973) posited that infants are biologically disposed to form attachment relationships with one or a few primary caregivers over the first few years of life. Attachment is adaptive; it brings the infant in close proximity to the caregiver in times of danger

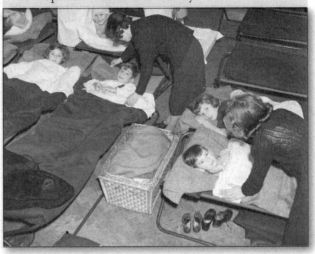

Image 12.4 Homeless and orphaned children settle down to sleep on beds in a British air raid shelter during World War II. The basket in the center of the photograph probably contains a small baby. Observations of children like these led to the development of attachment theory.

or uncertainty. Infants and toddlers show proximity-seeking behavior when they cry, approach, or motion to be picked up. Caregivers, in turn, are biologically disposed to respond to proximity bids with sensitivity and care.

Between 12 and 36 months, children form **internal working models** (schemas or mental representations) of themselves and their caregivers (Bowlby, 1988; Main et al.,

---

RESEARCH TO PRACTICE

DIFFERENTIATING RAD AND AUTISM SPECTRUM DISORDER

It is often very difficult for clinicians to determine whether a child has RAD or Autism Spectrum Disorder. Children with both disorders typically show dampened expression of positive emotions, cognitive and language delays, and impairments in social functioning. However, the disorders can be differentiated in at least three ways:

1. Children with RAD always have early histories of extreme social-emotional neglect. In contrast, children with Autism Spectrum Disorder usually do not have histories of extreme deprivation.

2. Children with RAD show few, if any, attachment behaviors (e.g., showing distress when separated from primary caregiver, seeking proximity when reunited). In contrast, children with Autism Spectrum Disorder usually show attachment behaviors consistent with their level of development.

3. Children with both disorders can show stereotypies, such as rocking and flapping. However, children with RAD usually do not show restricted interests or ritualized behaviors. In contrast, children with Autism Spectrum Disorder often do show restricted interests and behaviors.

DSM-5 indicates that a child who meets criteria for Autism Spectrum Disorder should not also be diagnosed with RAD (American Psychiatric Association, 2013).

Source: McCall, R., McCall, R. B., & Grotevant, H. D. (2011). *Children without permanent parents: Research, practice, and policy.* Wiley.

1985). These models are based on the history of interactions between each child and his or her caregiver. Some infants develop models based on attachment security; they expect that their caregivers will provide care, comfort, and support in a sensitive and appropriate fashion when they are scared, upset, or unsure (Ainsworth et al., 1978). Other infants develop models based on attachment insecurity; they expect that their caregivers will be dismissive, inappropriate, and/or inconsistent in the care they provide. They may believe that in times of trouble they cannot rely on anyone, other than themselves, for help. Finally, some infants develop disorganized attachment models. These children do not have a coherent set of expectations for their caregivers when they are in distress. Sometimes, their caregivers might be helpful, but at other times, their caregivers might be unresponsive or even frightening.

Several points follow from Bowlby's conceptualization of attachment (Bretherton, 1992). First, parent-child attachment is an **experience-expectant** process. Because humans are biologically predisposed to form attachments, and because attachments are evolutionarily adaptive, all infants who are exposed to a primary caregiver early in life will develop an attachment relationship with that caregiver. Even infants who are mistreated by their primary caregivers will form attachment relationships with these caregivers because the human nervous system is so disposed to form attachments early in life. The time period between 6 and 12 months of age appears to be a particularly sensitive period in attachment formation, that is, a time period in which the human nervous system is especially prepared to organize itself in response to care from one or more attachment figures. Before 6 months, children show little preference for their primary caregiver, whereas after 6 months, children begin showing stranger anxiety and attachment behaviors.

Second, Bowlby's theory asserts that attachment relationships vary in their quality; some relationships are secure, others are insecure, and others are disorganized. Whereas forming an attachment is experience-expectant and common to the entire human species, the quality of the attachment that is formed (secure, insecure, disorganized) is **experience-dependent**; it is unique to each caregiver-infant dyad and is based on the quality of their interactions over time (C. A. Nelson, Bos, Gunnar, & Sonuga-Barke, 2011).

Caregivers who meet their children's needs in sensitive and responsive ways are likely to develop secure relationships with their children. Attachment security, in turn, places these children on developmental pathways toward satisfying future relationships.

How does RAD fit into Bowlby's conceptualization of attachment? RAD occurs when infants are deprived of even minimal care from a primary caregiver during this sensitive period of attachment formation (i.e., after age 6 months). Such deprivation results in the absence of a clear attachment relationship and corresponding attachment behaviors (e.g., making eye contact, smiling, cuddling, using the caregiver as a means of comfort). Consequently, infants with RAD appear listless, withdrawn, and sad. RAD should not be confused with insecure or disorganized attachments. Whereas insecure or disorganized children have developed attachment relationships with a primary caregiver, children with RAD have absent or minimal attachments to any caregivers whatsoever (C. A. Nelson et al., 2011).

What Is Disinhibited Social Engagement Disorder (DSED)?

Definition

DSM-5 also recognizes another disorder caused by early deprivation. Children with **Disinhibited Social Engagement Disorder (DSED)** show a pattern of behavior that involves culturally and developmentally inappropriate, overly familiar behavior with strangers (Table 12.4, Diagnostic Criteria for Disinhibited Social Engagement Disorder). Beginning at age 6 or 7 months, typically developing children begin showing wariness of strangers. In contrast, children with DSED do not. Instead, children with DSED readily approach and interact with unfamiliar adults. Unlike their same-age peers, children with DSED do not "check back" with their caregivers to make sure that they are safe and that their caregiver knows their whereabouts. Perhaps most concerning, children with DSED will often talk to strangers, make inappropriate physical contact with strangers (e.g., sit on their laps, hold hands), and wander off with strangers without their caregivers' permission (American Psychiatric Association, 2013).

By definition, DSED is diagnosed only if children have a history of severe neglect or social-emotional deprivation. Many children with DSED have experienced deprivation in institutions. However, signs of DSED can also be seen among children who experienced frequent disruptions in their caregiving over the first year of life. For example, DSED is observed in some children who have been relocated to multiple foster homes and in some children exposed to inconsistent care because of parental abuse or neglect.

Early Studies on "Indiscriminately Friendly" Children

In his research for the World Health Organization, Bowlby (1954) described a small group of children who showed "undiscriminating and shallow friendliness" (p. 29). These children sought social and emotional contact with almost all adults, including strangers. Although they appeared charming to adults in their orphanages, and often became "favorites" among nursing staff, their relationships tended to be superficial and one-sided. Bowlby (1951, 1954) noted that many of these indiscriminately friendly children experienced frequent disruptions in their caregiving relationships over their first years of life. He also observed that these children experienced

Table 12.4 Diagnostic Criteria for Disinhibited Social Engagement Disorder

A. A pattern of behavior in which a child actively approaches and interacts with unfamiliar adults and exhibits at least two of the following:

  1. Reduced or absent reticence in approaching and interacting with unfamiliar adults.

  2. Overly familiar verbal or physical behavior (that is not consistent with culturally sanctioned and age-appropriate social boundaries).

  3. Diminished or absent checking back with adult caregiver after venturing away, even in unfamiliar settings.

  4. Willingness to go off with an unfamiliar adult with minimal or no hesitation.

B. The behaviors in criterion A are not limited to impulsivity (as in ADHD) but include socially disinhibited behavior.

C. The child has experienced a pattern of extremes in insufficient care as evidenced by at least one of the following:

  1. Social neglect or deprivation in the form of persistent lack of having basic emotional needs for comfort, stimulation, and affection met by caregiving adults.

  2. Repeated changes of primary caregivers that limit opportunities to form stable attachments (e.g., frequent changes in foster care).

  3. Rearing in unusual settings that severely limit opportunities to form selective attachments (e.g., institutions with high child-to-caregiver ratios).

D. The care in criterion C is presumed to be responsible for the disturbed behavior in criterion A.

E. The child has a developmental age of at least 9 months.

Specify current severity:

Disinhibited Social Engagement Disorder is specified as severe when the child exhibits all symptoms of the disorder, with each symptom manifesting at relatively high levels.

Source: Reprinted with permission from the *Diagnostic and Statistical Manual of Mental Disorders, Fifth Edition* (Copyright 2013). American Psychiatric Association.

problems bonding with their biological or adoptive parents after leaving their institutions.

The first systematic, longitudinal study of infants raised in institutions corroborated Bowlby's findings. Barbara Tizard and colleagues (1974, 1976, 1978) studied 65 children who spent their first years in a London residential nursery. These children were provided with adequate nutrition, physical care, toys, and books. However, caregivers were explicitly told to avoid bonding with these children. Furthermore, caregiver turnover in the nursery was very high; infants had few opportunities to form attachment relationships. Tizard found that 18 out of 26 children reared in the institution until aged 4-and-a-half years showed social-emotional problems. Eight "emotionally withdrawn and unresponsive" children did not seem to form attachment relationships with any caregiver, nor did they show distress or make bids for closeness and social engagement. Today, these children would likely be diagnosed with RAD. Tizard also described 10 other children as "indiscriminate, attention seeking, and socially superficial." These children were "exceptionally affectionate" toward most caregivers, would beg for attention and physical proximity from anyone who entered the room, and showed no wariness of strangers. This "overly friendly and attention seeking" behavior persisted across development; even at the age of 16, these children continued to display superficial relationships with others (Hodges & Tizard, 1989). Tizard's description of these children formed the basis for the *DSM-5* conceptualization of DSED (Zeanah & Gleason, 2010).

Causes of RAD and DSED

RAD: An Absence of Attachment

Although RAD and DSED are both caused by early deprivation, they differ in several important ways (Table 12.5; Zeanah & Smyke, 2008). To study these differences, researchers examined 136 children who spent their early years in impoverished Romanian orphanages (Fox et al., 2011; Gleason et al., 2011). Conditions in these orphanages were terrible. Many children were undernourished, staff-to-child ratios were extremely high, children were left unattended in cribs for long periods of time, and there was little to no social interaction between children and staff. Worse yet, Romania at that time, had no effective foster care system.

Consequently, the researchers began the **Bucharest Early Intervention Project (BEIP)**; they found foster homes for children in the orphanages and provided education and support to foster parents. Because there were not enough foster parents for all infants, the researchers randomly assigned infants to either foster placement or care as usual (i.e., staying in the orphanage). Then, the researchers examined the children's development until age 54 months to determine their outcomes. Because the BEIP is a prospective, randomized controlled study, it allows us to examine the outcomes of institutionalized children over time and to see whether foster care improves the outcomes of these infants (McLaughlin et al., 2012; Zeanah et al., 2012).

The results of the BEIP provide strong evidence that the signs and symptoms of RAD are associated with a lack of attachment in infancy and early childhood (Figure 12.4). The BEIP team compared three groups of children: (a) children raised in Romanian orphanages, (b) children initially raised in Romanian orphanages but placed in foster homes before age 24 months, and (c) Romanian children living with their families. At age 24 months, all of the non-institutionalized children showed a clear attachment to their primary caregiver. In contrast, only 3.2% of institutionalized children showed a clear attachment pattern. Indeed, 9.5% of institutionalized children showed no attachment behavior toward caregivers and no differentiation between familiar and unfamiliar adults whatsoever. An additional 25.3% of institutionalized infants showed only slight preference for their primary caregiver over a stranger but no positive affect when interacting with their caregiver (Zeanah, Smyke, Koga, & Carlson et al., 2005). The researchers also found that the severity of RAD was inversely associated

with the quality of care infants received: The more sensitive and responsive the care, the fewer signs of RAD children displayed (Gleason et al., 2011).

On a more positive note, the BEIP team discovered that foster placement was helpful in reducing RAD over time. Whereas children who remained in the orphanage showed relatively stable RAD signs and symptoms into early childhood, children placed in foster care showed decreased RAD signs and symptoms over time. Altogether, the results of the BEIP, and a similar study conducted in a Ukrainian institution (Bakermans-Kranenburg, Dobrova-Krol, & van IJzendoorn, 2012), suggest that most institutionalized children develop attachment relationships, even under conditions of extreme deprivation. However, a small percentage of children seem to lack attachment relationships altogether, appear emotionally flat, and act behaviorally passive. These children likely meet criteria for RAD. The good news is that if children are removed from the institution before age 24 months, they can form attachment relationships with foster parents. Furthermore, the quality of care largely predicts children's ability to overcome previous deprivation (Bos et al., 2011).

DSED: A Lack of Inhibition (not attachment)

In contrast to RAD, many more (31.8%) infants in the BEIP showed symptoms of DSED. Curiously, DSED signs and symptoms were not consistently associated with the quality of care infants received in the institution or in foster homes. Furthermore, there was little relationship between infants' attachment security and DSED; even security-attached infants sometimes showed signs and symptoms of DSED.

Table 12.5 Major Differences Between RAD and DSED

	RAD	*DSED*
Children's characteristics	Little interest in social interactions, passive, do not show preference for primary caregivers	Interested in social interactions, willingly approach and seek contact with strangers
Cause	Social deprivation in infancy	Social deprivation in infancy
Frequency	Rare in institutionalized children; almost never seen in children adopted out of institutions	Sometimes seen in institutionalized children, children adopted out of institutions, and maltreated children
Relationship to attachment	Child lacks clear attachment relationship to a caregiver	Child typically shows attachments to caregivers, attachment may be secure
Relationship to caregiving	Associated with a lack of sensitive and responsive care	Not associated with the quality of care
Associated disorders	Many children also show depressed mood, irritability	Some children show hyperactivity-impulsiveness
Course-Prognosis	Often persistent if child remains in institution; remits after child forms attachment to adoptive parents	Usually persists into childhood even if child is adopted

Source: Adapted from Zeenah & Gleason (2010).

Figure 12.4   Attachment Among Infants Raised in Romanian Orphanages

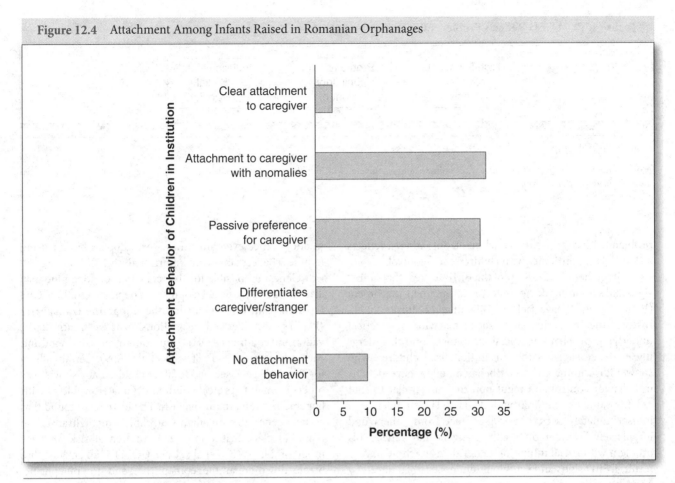

Source: Based on Zeanah and colleagues (2005).

Later in childhood, infants with signs of DSED did not show problems with depression; rather, they often displayed difficulty with attention and social inhibition, that is, controlling impulses in social situations.

Late infancy and early childhood may be a sensitive period for the development of social inhibition. Parents play a central role in helping infants and young children regulate and control their behavior (Hofer, 2006). For example, parents direct young children's attention to social situations and cues, model and reinforce appropriate social interactions, and teach impulse control, especially in potentially dangerous situations. How many times did your parents warn, "Look both ways before crossing the street" or "Don't talk with strangers?" Young children deprived of parents may miss out on many of these social learning experiences. Consequently, they may show delays or deficits in social inhibition. Indiscriminately social behavior, such as touching or wandering off with strangers, may reflect these underlying deficits in social inhibition (Bakermans-Kranenburg et al., 2011).

To test this hypothesis, Bruce, Tarullo, and Gunnar (2009) measured the behavioral and social-emotional functioning of children adopted from orphanages and foster care settings in China, Eastern Europe, and South Korea. As expected, adoptees showed more problems with social inhibition than nonadopted children; furthermore, children who spent more time in institutions or foster care showed more "indiscriminately friendly" behavior at 7 years of age. Interestingly, "indiscriminately friendly" behavior was not correlated with children's attachment to parents; it was associated only with underlying problems with inhibitory control.

Additional support for the inhibitory control hypothesis came from a second study, comparing 93 maltreated preschool-aged children in foster care to 60 children living with their parents in the community (Pears, Bruce, Fisher, & Kim, 2010). Again, as expected, foster care children showed more symptoms of indiscriminately social behavior than controls. More importantly, children who had more changes in their foster care placements showed more indiscriminately social behavior. The most important finding was that children's inhibitory control mediated the relationship between the number of foster caregivers and their indiscriminately social behavior: A high number of different foster caregivers predicted problems with inhibitory control; problems with inhibitory control, in turn, predicted indiscriminately social behavior (Figure 12.5). These studies provide evidence that indiscriminately social behavior does not reflect a

Figure 12.5 DSED Reflects Problems With Inhibitory Control

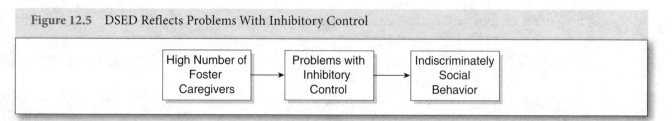

Source: Pears et al., 2010.

Note: Children placed in multiple foster care settings showed problems with inhibitory control. Problems with inhibitory control, in turn, predicted indiscriminately social behavior.

problem with parent-child attachment, but rather, it reflects an underlying difficulty with children's self-control.

Altogether, the findings of the BEIP suggest that DSED signs and symptoms do not reflect a disruption in attachment (Potter, Chevy, Amaya-Jackson, O'Donnell, & Murphy 2009). Instead, the indiscriminately social behavior may reflect underlying problems in social inhibitory control. Emerging evidence suggests that institutionalized children who show indiscriminately social behavior often have deficits in behavior control and regulation that are similar to (but not the same as) children with ADHD. Their tendency to indiscriminately seek physical contact from others and impulsively "wander off" with strangers may reflect this problem with social inhibition rather than attachment. As a result, DSED signs and symptoms are not easily reduced by providing youths with sensitive and responsive foster parents (Schechter, 2012).

Gene-Environment Interactions

Although many children experience social deprivation, relatively few develop DSED and fewer still show RAD (Bakermans-Kranenburg et al., 2011). Consequently, environmental experience is not sufficient to explain the emergence of these disorders. Recently, independent research teams have found intriguing evidence that early experiences of deprivation and children's genotypes interact to influence the likelihood that children will develop these disorders.

Two independent research teams have suggested that the **serotonin transporter gene** may play a role in the developmental outcomes of children exposed to early deprivation. In one study of Ukrainian orphans, deprived children who inherited two short alleles for this gene were at greatly increased risk for developing attachment problems with their caregivers compared to children who inherited one long and one short allele from their parents. Interestingly, the presence of two long alleles seemed to protect children from attachment problems, even when they experienced severe deprivation in early childhood (Bakermans-Kranenburg et al., 2012). In another study of Romanian orphans, the serotonin transporter gene predicted children's emotional problems

in adolescence even after they were adopted by nurturing families (Bakermans-Kranenburg et al., 2011).

Genes responsible for the regulation of dopamine may also play a role in the development of deprived children. One research team discovered that the **dopamine transporter (DAT) gene** moderated the relationship between early deprivation and children's ADHD symptoms in late childhood and early adolescence (S. E. Stevens et al., 2009). Certain alleles for the DAT gene seemed to place children at risk whereas others seemed to protect children from later problems with hyperactivity and impulsiveness. The BEIP team found that certain genes that regulate Catechol-O-methyltransferase (COMT) place institutionalized children at risk for later mood problems (Bos et al., 2011). COMT is an enzyme that breaks down dopamine, epinephrine, and norepinephrine. Children who inherit certain alleles for genes that regulate COMT show a 108% increased risk in developing mood problems in adolescence compared to their peers who do not inherit these genetic risks.

Studies supporting gene-environment interactions are preliminary. However, these studies help explain multifinality in child psychopathology: Why do children exposed to the same risks show such different outcomes? One answer may be that we carry inside of us certain risk and protective factors—just as important as our environments—that can greatly influence our outcomes in life.

Associated Features of Deprived Children

Brain and Endocrine Functioning

Many institutionalized children show below average height, weight, and head circumference compared to children living with their families (van IJzendoorn et al., 2011). On average, the head circumference of deprived children is 1 to 2 standard deviations smaller than their non-deprived peers. Small head circumference is important because it is correlated with brain maturation. Children typically show "catch-up" growth immediately following placement into nurturing foster homes. By age 6 years, height and weight is usually similar to never-institutionalized peers (D. E. Johnson & Gunnar, 2011). Unfortunately, the head circumference of institutionalized children often remains below average through early adolescence. Reduced head circumference, and corresponding brain size, may underlie some of the behavior problems shown by these children that persist over time (Rutter, Sonuga-Barke, & Castle, 2011).

Many institutionalized children and maltreated children in foster care show dysregulation of the HPA axis (Bruce et al., 2009; Schuengel, Oosterman, & Sterkenburg, 2009). Recall that the HPA axis is the body's primary mechanism for responding to stress. It controls the secretion of cortisol, the stress hormone which releases energy (for the fight or flight response) and stimulates the body's immune system. Typically developing children show a "diurnal" pattern of cortisol secretion: high secretion in the morning and lower secretion in the afternoon. However, studies involving Chinese, Romanian, and Russian orphans show abnormalities in this diurnal pattern (van IJzendoorn et al., 2011). Some children show unusually high morning cortisol levels; others display a flattened pattern of cortisol secretion. In either case, these abnormalities suggest HPA dysregulation in response to chronic stress. HPA dysregulation is important because it is implicated in many anxiety and mood disorders later in life. HPA dysregulation may be correctable if children are provided sensitive and responsive care. Two independent studies have attempted to improve parent-child interactions by providing support to foster parents of at-risk children (Dozier, Dozier, & Manni, 2002; Fisher & Stoolmiller, 2008). Both studies improved not only the quality of parent-child interactions but also helped prevent or correct atypical cortisol secretion in these children over time.

Cognition and Stereotypies

Infants and young children raised in institutions are at particular risk for lower cognitive functioning. Overall, institutionalized children earn IQ scores approximately one standard deviation (15 points) below average (van IJzendoorn et al., 2011). Furthermore, delays in cognitive functioning seem to persist across childhood. The BEIP team examined the cognitive functioning of three groups of children: (a) children raised in institutions through age 54 months, (b) institutionalized children placed in foster homes before age 24 months, and (c) never-institutionalized children (Figure 12.6). As expected, children raised in institutions for their first 54 months of life showed low cognitive functioning which persisted into middle childhood. Children placed in foster homes before age 24 months showed better cognitive functioning than their peers who remained in the institutions. However, foster children's cognitive functioning still remained below average. Interestingly, malnutrition did not predict the development of children's cognitive abilities. Instead, it appears that a lack of cognitive and social

stimulation between 0 and 24 months of age was responsible for these cognitive deficits. Deprivation during this period in children's development appears to affect cognition, leading to later deficits in verbal and problem-solving skills. Unfortunately, these deficits are only partially ameliorated by foster care (Fox et al., 2011; Nelson et al., 2007).

Approximately 60% of children living in impoverished institutions show **stereotypies**, that is, repetitive body movements, such as hand gesturing, rocking, or swaying (Bos, Zeanah, Smyke, Fox, & Nelson, 2010). Some children engage in stereotypies to escape boredom. Others use stereotypies to soothe themselves or cope with stress. Still others show stereotypies to express anxiety or frustration. The severity of stereotypies tends to decrease over time, even among children who remain in institutions. Furthermore, stereotypies are greatly reduced after children are placed in nurturing foster homes. Nevertheless, approximately 25% of formerly institutionalized children show stereotypies after foster placement. Persistent stereotypies are most often seen among children with cognitive and language problems (van IJzendoorn et al., 2011).

Behavior and Emotional Problems

Infants exposed to early deprivation are also at increased risk for psychiatric disorders in childhood (Table 12.6). Data from the BEIP indicate that children who spend their first several years of life in institutions are much more likely than home-raised children to be diagnosed with an externalizing or internalizing disorder in childhood. However, infants adopted out of institutions before age 24 months showed reduced likelihood of future psychiatric problems (Figure 12.7). These findings provide more evidence that early home placement is critical to infant's behavioral and social-emotional development.

Institutionalized children are especially likely to show symptoms of ADHD in later childhood. Studies of both Spanish and Romanian children raised in institutions indicate increased risk for hyperactivity and impulsivity by middle childhood (Juffer et al., 2011; Zeanah, Egger et al., 2009). For example, in one sample of institutionalized Romanian orphans adopted into Canadian homes, 34% developed ADHD by age 10 years (Juffer et al., 2011). Furthermore, this increased risk for ADHD is only moderately reduced by placement into foster care. For example, in the BEIP study, children raised in institutions (23.1%) and children placed in foster care before age 2 years (18.6%) were much more likely to be diagnosed with ADHD at 54 months than their never-institutionalized counterparts (3.4%).

Why are institutionalized children at particular risk for ADHD? It appears that cognitive and social-emotional deprivation, especially after age 6 months, leads to delays in brain regions associated with behavioral inhibition. These deficits may lead to both problems with social inhibition (seen in DSED) and ADHD (Bakermans-Kranenburg,

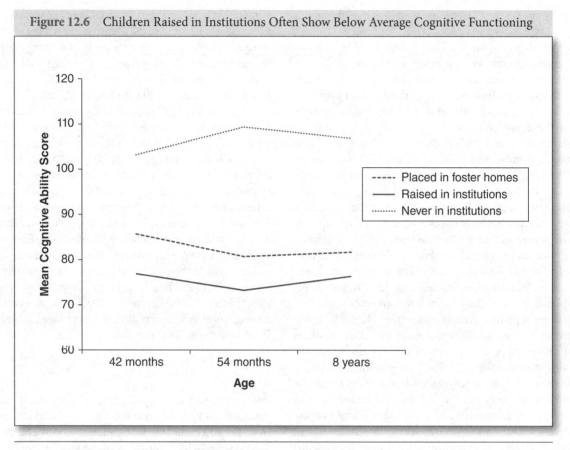

Figure 12.6 Children Raised in Institutions Often Show Below Average Cognitive Functioning

Source: Based on Nelson, Furtado, Fox, & Zeanah (2009), and Fox et al. (2011).

Note: Even children who leave institutions and are placed in foster homes continue to show cognitive delays.

2011). In one large sample of international adoptees from Russia, East Asia, and Latin America, children who spent longer periods of time in institutions showed greater deficits in attention, behavioral inhibition, impulse control, and academic problems at age 9 years. Interestingly, children adopted out of institutions before age 8 months showed no attention or behavioral problems (Pollack et al., 2010).

Table 12.6 Psychiatric Disorders Among Institutionalized Children (Age 54 Months)

Disorder	Stayed in Institution	Adopted before Age 24 Months	Never in Institution
Any Disorder	61.5%	45.8%	22.0%
Any Externalizing Disorder	28.8%	25.4%	6.8%
Any Internalizing Disorder	44.2%	22.0%	13.6%

Source: Adapted from Zeanah et al. (2009).

In another longitudinal study, institutionalized toddlers showed abnormal EEG activities, characterized by reduced high-frequency brain activity (alpha relative power) and increased low-frequency brain activity (theta relative power). This pattern of EEG activity is typical of younger infants and older children with ADHD. Furthermore, this pattern of EEG activity predicted which children would develop ADHD in later childhood (Bos et al., 2011; McLaughlin, Fox et al., 2011). Together, these findings indicate the importance of early care on the development of children's capacity for behavioral inhibition.

Deprivation Specific Psychological Patterns

Michael Rutter and colleagues (Rutter, Sonuga-Barke, & Castle, 2011) have suggested that some children exposed to severe deprivation show a syndrome of behaviors that are socially impairing and relatively persistent over time. Rutter led a team of researchers who studied large groups of institutionalized Romanian children who were adopted by families in the United Kingdom: the **English and Romanian Adoptees (ERA) Study**. The researchers (Kumsta et al., 2011) noticed that approximately one fourth of these children showed a distinct syndrome characterized by four core symptoms:

Figure 12.7 Persistence of RAD and DSED Over Time

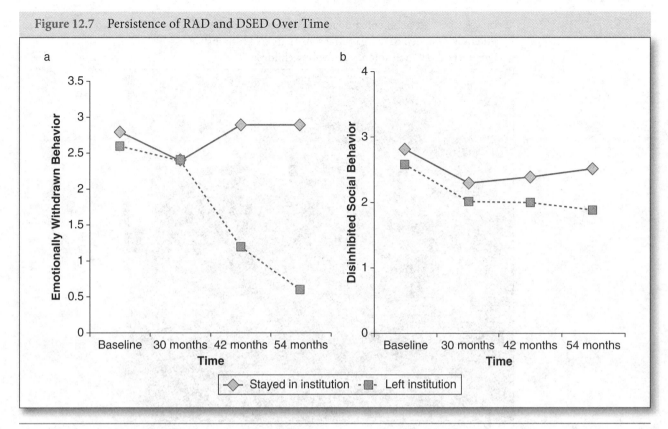

Source: Adapted from the BEIP.

Note: The emotionally withdrawn behavior of children raised in institutions tends to decrease after children are placed in foster homes. However, disinhibited social behavior tends to persist over time.

- Quasi-autism: Children had difficulty reading social cues and understanding social situations. Many developed circumscribed interests or preoccupations (e.g., fascination with watches, shiny objects) in later childhood.
- Disinhibited attachment: Children inappropriately approached and often made physical contact with strangers (i.e., DSED).
- Cognitive impairment: Children often earned IQ scores one standard deviation below average.
- Inattention and over-activity: Children were at increased likelihood for ADHD by middle childhood.

Rutter believed this cluster of symptoms was "deprivation-specific" because it was seen only among formerly institutionalized children. The ERA Study group discovered that children's head circumference mediated the relationship between early deprivation and this deprivation specific pattern (DSP). Early deprivation was associated with reduced head circumference (a proxy for brain maturation) and reduced head circumference in turn predicted the severity of DSP symptoms. This pattern was likely the result of atypical brain development, and it was persistent over time. Rutter and his colleagues followed children with DSPs through age 15 years. Although symptoms tended to decrease in severity, they were still present in many of the adolescents.

Treatment for RAD

Evidence-Based Attachment Programs

Prognosis for children with RAD is good if these children are provided sensitive and responsive care by foster or adoptive parents. Outcomes seem to be especially positive if home placement occurs early in development. For example, Mary Dozier and colleagues (2002) asked foster mothers to keep diaries about their interactions with their babies for 60 days after placement into their homes. Parents were asked to pay special attention to situations in which children felt scared, hurt, or otherwise distressed. The researchers coded parents' diaries in terms of the quality of parent-child interactions. Three findings emerged. First, parents and infants began forming attachments within days of children being placed in foster homes. Second, the security of attachment relationships was greatest when children were placed in foster homes before age 10 months. Third, mothers and babies showed reciprocity in their interactions; both mothers and babies influenced each other's behaviors. For example, mothers of overly passive babies often had difficulty reading their babies' signals and meeting their needs. Similarly, mothers of irritable babies often had trouble providing sensitive and patient care.

Image 12.5 Attachment and biobehavioral catch-up (ABC) is a therapy designed to increase the sensitivity and responsiveness caregivers show their infants and young children.

Source: Photo by Robert Whitehead

Based on the results of the diary study, Dozier developed an intervention to promote attachment security between infants and foster parents at risk for attachment problems (Image 12.5). The intervention, **attachment and biobehavioral catch-up (ABC),** consists of 10, one-hour sessions for parent-child dyads.

ABC has three components. First, parents are taught to meet their infants' needs even when these needs are not clearly communicated. Recall that many children with RAD symptoms are passive and show little interest in receiving care. Foster parents are taught the importance of providing warmth and nurturance to their children even when they fail to ask for contact or actively spurn their efforts. For example, therapists ask parents to keep a record of instances in which their children avoided or resisted their attempts at nurturance. Therapists review this record with parents and help parents find ways to persist in offering sensitive and responsive care to their children despite their children's passivity or irritable behavior.

Second, parents are encouraged to give their infants greater autonomy in parent-child interactions and to be sensitive and responsive to their needs and signals during play. Recall that many children with RAD symptoms have little experience being in control over their surroundings. Instead, they may view the world as unpredictable and caregivers as uncaring or intrusive. Foster parents are

taught to interact with their children in ways that respect their emerging autonomy and self-direction. For example, parents and infants are asked to engage in structured activities designed to give children greater latitude in directing parent-child interactions. Activities include eating, looking at a picture book, and playing with blocks. Therapists provide real-time coaching to parents, encouraging them to let their children take the lead during play. Activities are also videotaped so that therapists and parents can later review parents' attempts at sensitive and responsive care and monitor their progress.

Third, therapists help parents overcome barriers to meeting their children's needs in sensitive and responsive ways. Because foster children do not come with instruction manuals, parents often rely on their own caregiving experiences to decide how to interact with their infants. However, parents who have experienced neglectful or abusive parenting themselves may have difficulty meeting their infants' needs. Parents are taught to recognize when their caregiving histories interfere with their ability to provide sensitive care to their infants and find ways to overcome these negative experiences for the benefit of their children. Often, this involves helping parents identify negative automatic thoughts that distort their perceptions of their children. Consider the following exchange between a foster mother and therapist:

EXPLORING MOTHERS' THOUGHTS ABOUT THEIR OWN PARENTS

Therapist: When your baby cries, what goes through your mind?

Mother: I feel terrible. You know, completely helpless. I try to do everything I can think of to get her to settle down, but I can't.

Therapist: That's how you *feel*. Now, tell me what you *think*. Is there a thought or a picture that pops into your mind when she cries and cries?

Mother: It's funny, but I think about my own mom when I was a little girl. She was never really there for me very much. She was always working and never had time for me and my sister. I used to think, "When I become a mom, I don't want to be like her. I want to be warm, and loving, and caring to my children."

Therapist: And now you are a mom.

Mother: Yes. And no matter what I do, she doesn't seem to respond to me. She doesn't like to be cuddled or soothed. She doesn't seem to need me at all. I might as well not even be there.

Therapist: Like your mom.

Mother: Something like that.

Therapists might teach mothers to recognize the ways their caregiving histories can negatively impact their current parent-child interactions, using the "shark music" analogy. In the movie *Jaws*, ominous music precedes each shark attack. When you hear the music, you instantly feel anxiety. Memories of negative caregiving experiences are like shark music; they compromise parents' abilities to attend to their children's needs and signals by producing anxiety, anger, or other negative emotions. Therapists help parents recognize situations that likely lead to shark music and cope with these situations with more objective (less distorted) thoughts.

Efficacy

A recent randomized, controlled trial of ABC indicates that it can be efficacious in promoting secure parent-child attachment. Bernard and colleagues (2012) randomly assigned 120 foster parents of children between 11 and 31 months of age to either ABC or an educational control group. All dyads were at risk for attachment problems because of domestic violence, parental substance abuse, neglect, or similar stressors. After treatment, more parent-child dyads who received ABC intervention (52%) were securely attached than were dyads in the control group (33%). Furthermore, fewer dyads who participated in ABC showed disorganized attachment (32%) than did dyads in the control condition (57%).

Several other interventions are also available to help improve the quality of parent-child interactions in foster and adoptive families. For example, video-based intervention to promote positive parenting is designed to improve maternal sensitivity toward very young infants through the use of videotaped feedback. Alternatively, the Circle of Security

program offers both group and individual interventions for parents to encourage greater caregiver sensitivity and child autonomy during play. Both interventions have demonstrated effectiveness in improving parent-child interactions in at-risk families (Zeanah, Berlin, & Borris, 2011). Unfortunately, none of the interventions have been investigated with children diagnosed with RAD. Given the low prevalence of RAD, it is likely that clinicians will need to continue using attachment-based interventions, like ABC, for some time.

Treatment for DSED

Treatment for Children Living in Institutions

Providing children with sensitive and responsive foster parents may not be sufficient to reduce indiscriminately social behavior. Several longitudinal research studies suggest that once indiscriminately social behaviors emerge in late infancy or early childhood, they often persist into late childhood or early adolescence (Gunnar, 2010).

Nearly all studies indicate that institutionalized infants who are adopted into nurturing homes prior to age 6 months do *not* develop significant symptoms of DSED. Therefore, prevention of DSED is best accomplished by home placement before age 6 months. Infants who remain socially deprived after age six months are at increased risk for indiscriminately social behavior. The number of different caregivers and disruptions to the caregiving environment between 6 and 24 months of age is associated with later social disinhibition (Zeanah et al., 2011). Consequently, researchers have tried to provide more stable and consistent care to institutionalized infants in the hope of reducing DSED symptoms.

Smyke, Dumitrescu, and Zeanah (2002) compared two groups of children living in Romanian orphanages: (a) children assigned to usual care and (b) children assigned to a pilot program designed to reduce the number of caregivers to whom each child was exposed. Children in both groups had the same child-to-caregiver ratio (1:12). However, children in the usual care group were exposed to a wide range of different caregivers whereas children in the pilot program saw the same caregivers each day. Over time, children in the pilot program displayed fewer symptoms of both RAD and social disinhibition than children receiving usual care (Smyke, Zeanah et al., 2010).

A second study involved young infants living in Russian orphanages (McCall and St. Petersburg-USA Orphanage Research Team, 2008). Researchers compared three groups of children. The caretakers of children in the first group were specifically trained to provide sensitive and responsive care to their children; furthermore, the caregiver-to-child ratio for infants in their group was reduced. The caretakers of children in the second group received training only; these children had the same high caregiver-to-child ratio. Children in the third group received usual care in the orphanage. As expected, infants in the first group showed the best outcomes: more positive emotions, greater exploration and play, more attempts to gain proximity to caregivers, and less indiscriminately social behavior.

Treatment for Children in Foster Care

What can be done for children who already show a lack of social disinhibition? Three large longitudinal studies, the BEIP, the ERA study, and the St. Petersburg-USA Orphanages Research Project, suggest that socially disinhibited behavior often persists, even after children are adopted into nurturing homes (Zeanah et al., 2011). Although social disinhibition tends to decrease over time, it can continue to interfere with children's interactions with parents and peers in late childhood and early adolescence. Early deprivation likely takes its toll of the development of children's abilities for behavioral control. These underlying neurological deficits, once they appear, are resistant to change and may manifest themselves in hyperactivity, impulsiveness, and social disinhibition (Ghera et al., 2009).

Some researchers have suggested that indiscriminately social behaviors can be corrected by targeting the neurological deficits that likely underlie these behaviors, namely, problems with behavioral inhibition (Pears et al., 2010). For example, researchers have developed a computer program which fosters the development of attentional control in typically developing young children (Rueda et al., 2005). Children who completed the program showed increased capacity for inhibition and greater activation of the brain areas believed responsible for inhibition, especially the prefrontal cortex. However, this program has not yet been used to teach indiscriminately social behavior specifically. Clearly, more research must be directed at finding effective treatments for children with DSED.

MALTREATMENT IN CHILDHOOD AND ADOLESCENCE

Although early deprivation is relatively rare in the United States, other forms of child maltreatment are, unfortunately, too common. Each year, approximately 2.6 million youths in the United States are referred to child protective services for suspected maltreatment. After review and investigation, almost 900,000 of these reported cases are substantiated. These statistics indicate that approximately 1.3% of children and adolescents are abused or neglected every year. However, this estimate does not include the vast number of maltreated youths who are never reported.

Child maltreatment places considerable financial demands on society. Most obvious are the direct financial costs associated with child maltreatment: the cost of providing medical, mental health, and home placement services to victims; the cost of providing training and rehabilitative services to offending parents; and (in some cases) the cost of prosecuting and incarcerating adult offenders. Less noticeable are the indirect financial costs associated with maltreatment: lower academic and job attainment by victims, lost wages and productivity by parents, and the negative impact on the community caused by antisocial behavior shown by many maltreated youths who do not receive treatment. The estimated annual financial cost of child maltreatment in the United States is approximately $50 billion to $100 billion (Cicchetti, 2004).

Child maltreatment has less tangible, but no less important, emotional costs. Child victims typically experience considerable emotional pain and psychological distress, family members often report increased conflict and reduced quality of life, and perpetrators must face the consequences of their acts, ranging from humiliation to social ostracism to imprisonment. Child maltreatment seriously affects victims, families, and society.

What Is Child Maltreatment?

Public policy and research have been limited by a lack of consensus regarding the definition of child maltreatment. Put simply, experts cannot agree what behaviors constitute abuse and neglect. Indeed, definitions of child maltreatment vary from state to state and from professional to professional.

The first general definition of child maltreatment was presented in the Child Abuse Prevention and Treatment Act of 1974 (PL 93–247). This act defined maltreatment as the physical or mental injury, sexual abuse, exploitation, negligent treatment, or maltreatment of a child under the age of 18 . . . by a person who is responsible for the child's welfare under circumstances which indicate that the child's health or welfare is harmed or threatened.

Although somewhat vague, this definition is noteworthy because it identifies four types of child maltreatment: (a) physical abuse, (b) sexual abuse, (c) psychological abuse (i.e., "mental injury"), and (d) neglect. *DSM-5* also recognizes these same four domains of child maltreatment (See Table 12.7, *DSM-5* Definitions of Child Maltreatment). However, abuse and neglect are not considered mental disorders in *DSM-5*. Indeed, children who are victims of maltreatment vary considerably in their behavioral, cognitive, social-emotional, and physiological outcomes: Some children develop disorders whereas others do not. Clinicians can describe a child as the victim of abuse or neglect and assign diagnoses if the child meets diagnostic criteria. For example, a child who experiences abuse might be diagnosed with Posttraumatic Stress Disorder, an anxiety disorder, or a sleep disorder depending on his or her symptoms (American Psychiatric Association, 2013).

Physical Abuse

Physical abuse includes deliberate behaviors that result in injury, or the serious risk of injury, to a child. Examples of physically abusive behavior include hitting, kicking, shaking, throwing, burning, stabbing, or choking an infant or child. States have different definitions of physical maltreatment. Some states use the harm standard to identify cases of physical abuse; that is, the abusive act must result in physical harm to the child. Other states apply the endangerment standard, in which the *potential* for harm is sufficient to merit the classification of physical abuse. For example, dangling a small child over a balcony in order to punish him would be considered physical abuse according to the endangerment standard, even if the child did not experience physical injury.

Table 12.7   *DSM-5* Definitions of Child Maltreatment

Child Physical Abuse is nonaccidental physical injury to a child, ranging from minor bruises to severe fractures or death, occurring as a result of punching, beating, kicking, biting, shaking, throwing, stabbing, choking, hitting (with a hand, stick, strap, or other object), burning, or any other method that is inflicted by a parent, caregiver, or other individual who has responsibility for the child. Such injury is considered abuse regardless of whether the caregiver intended to hurt the child. Physical discipline, such as spanking or paddling, is not considered abuse as long as it is reasonable and causes no bodily injury to the child (American Psychiatric Association, 2013, p. 717).

Child Sexual Abuse encompasses any sexual act involving a child that is intended to provide sexual gratification to a parent, caregiver, or other individual who has responsibility for a child. Sexual abuse includes activities such as fondling a child's genitals, penetration, incest, rape, sodomy, and indecent exposure. Sexual abuse also includes noncontact exploitation, for example, forcing, tricking, enticing, threatening, or pressuring a child to participate in acts for the sexual gratification of others, without direct physical contact between child and abuser (American Psychiatric Association, 2013, p. 718).

Child Psychological Abuse is nonaccidental verbal or symbolic acts by a child's parent or caregiver that result, or have reasonable potential to result, in significant psychological harm to the child. Examples include berating, disparaging, or humiliating the child; threatening the child; harming/abandoning people or things that the child cares about; confining the child (as by tying the child's arms and legs together or binding a child to furniture, or confining a child to a small enclosed area [e.g., a closet]); egregious scapegoating of the child; coercing the child to inflict pain on himself or herself; and disciplining the child excessively (i.e., at an extremely high frequency or duration) through physical or nonphysical means (American Psychiatric Association, 2013, p. 719).

Child Neglect is defined as any confirmed or suspected egregious act or omission by a child's parent or other caregiver that deprives the child of basic age-appropriate needs and thereby results, or has reasonable potential to result, in physical or psychological harm to the child. Child neglect encompasses abandonment; lack of appropriate supervision; failure to attend to necessary emotional or psychological needs; and failure to provide necessary education, medical care, nourishment, shelter, and/or clothing (American Psychiatric Association, 2013, p. 718).

Source: *DSM-5*, American Psychiatric Association, 2013, pp. 717–719.

Note: Child maltreatment is not considered a mental disorder in *DSM-5*. Clinicians can describe a child as a victim of abuse or neglect (based on the definitions above) and then diagnose the child with one or more mental disorders, depending on his or her symptoms.

Sexual Abuse

There is no consensus regarding the definition of child sexual abuse (Bergevin, Bukowski, & Karavasilis, 2003). In fact, experts disagree about the precise meaning of each component of the term: *child*, *sexual*, and *abuse*.

Experts disagree regarding the age of "child" victims. Some professionals limit their definition of child sexual abuse to sexual acts committed against individuals 14 years of age and younger. Other experts, adopting a more liberal definition, classify all individuals under the age of 18 as "children." Still others consider the age difference between the victim and the perpetrator of the abuse.

Experts also disagree about the types of sexual acts that constitute sexual abuse. Some individuals only consider penetration as sexually abusive. Others believe all sexual activity that involves physical contact merits the definition of sexual abuse (e.g., fondling, open-mouth kissing). Still other experts include sexual acts that do not involve physical touching in their definition of abuse, so long as these acts are directed toward children and intended to sexually gratify the adult. From this perspective, voyeurism, exhibitionism, and the use of children for sexually explicit pictures or videos constitute sexual abuse.

Finally, experts disagree about the exact definition of abuse. Some individuals claim that physical force or coercion is necessary for a sexual act to be considered abusive. Other experts believe that *all* sexual activity toward children and adolescents is abusive, even those acts that are seemingly performed willingly by adolescents.

According to Lucy Berliner (2000), child sexual abuse involves any sexual activity with a child in which consent is not or cannot be given. Berliner's definition includes all sexual behavior regardless of whether the interactions are physical or nonphysical. Consequently, both physical contact (e.g., touching, penetration) and nonphysical sexual interactions (e.g., voyeurism, exhibitionism) with children can be considered sexual abuse (Bonner, Logue, & Kees, 2003).

Berliner's definition of sexual abuse also includes all sexual interactions between adults and nonadults (i.e., children and adolescents). Even sexual contact between adults and adolescents can be considered abusive, despite the fact that some adolescents may want to engage in the sexual activity. Adult sexual contact with children and adolescents is *always* abusive because nonadults are incapable of consenting to sexual activity. In order to consent, people must (a) understand all of the implications associated with their sexual behavior and (b) freely decide to engage in the sexual activity without any outside pressure. Of course, most youths are unable to appreciate the full implications of engaging in sexual behavior with an adult. Furthermore, by virtue of their age and developmental status, children and adolescents are always at a power disadvantage in their interactions with adults. Consequently, they can *never* consent to sexual activity without adults influencing their decision.

Of course, there are gray areas in determining what constitutes child sexual abuse. For example, experts disagree how to classify sexual contact between two children or two adolescents. Furthermore, experts disagree whether sexual contact between a minor adolescent (e.g., 16 years) and a young adult (e.g., 19 years) constitutes abuse. In these cases, professionals usually consider the age and developmental status of the two youths, their relationship to each other, and any power differentials that might have led to coercion.

up in a tumultuous home. Angela's biological father had a history of aggressive and antisocial behavior. He was incarcerated for domestic violence at the time of the evaluation. Angela's mother had a history of alcohol abuse and had been arrested for selling narcotics on two occasions. Mrs. Alosio used alcohol, cocaine, and other drugs during her pregnancy with Angela. Angela was born prematurely and showed cognitive delays.

Angela's mother married Jason Valenta when Angela was 6 years old. Mr. Valenta appeared to provide a stable home and family life for Angela and her sisters. However, several weeks before Angela's referral, Mrs. Alosio discovered Mr. Valenta engaging in sexual intercourse with Angela. Shocked and repulsed, Mrs. Alosio yelled at both Mr. Valenta and Angela and ordered them to leave the house.

Angela had been repeatedly sexually abused for at least 5 years. Mr. Valenta eventually admitted to seeking out Mrs. Alosio, whom he described as "emotionally and financially vulnerable," to gain access to her daughters. Mr. Valenta instructed Angela never to tell anyone about the abuse because disclosure would cause his imprisonment, family disunification, and Mrs. Alosio's return to poverty and drug abuse.

In foster care, Angela showed problems with anxiety and depression. She displayed sleep difficulties, fear of the dark, and frequent nightmares associated with the abuse. Angela also had unwanted memories of abuse (e.g., a flashback) while in church. During the sermon, Angela showed extreme panic, ran from the congregation, and repeatedly cried, "I'm so bad!"

Angela preferred to play with the 6- and 7-year-old children in her foster home, rather than with girls her own age. She had few friends at school. Angela was reprimanded for kissing several boys during recess because "they asked her to." In foster care and at school, Angela tended to act helpless or to use "baby talk" to get special favors. Most of all, Angela seemed to need constant approval and reassurance from adults. Her foster mother described her as "needy" and "crushed by the slightest reprimand or criticism."

Psychological Abuse

Psychological maltreatment is more difficult to identify and substantiate than physical or sexual abuse. The American Professional Society on the Abuse of Children (APSAC) defines psychological maltreatment as a pattern of caregiver behavior that "conveys to children that they are worthless, flawed, unloved, unwanted, endangered, or only of value in meeting another's needs" (Briere, Berliner, Bulkley, Jenny, & Reid, 1996, p. 2). According to the APSAC definition, psychological maltreatment includes six types of behaviors: (a) spurning, (b) terrorizing, (c) isolating, (d) exploiting and corrupting, (e) denying emotional responsiveness, and (f) neglecting children's health and educational needs (Table 12.8).

Psychological maltreatment denies children the respect and dignity that is the inherent right of all human beings. At one extreme, psychological maltreatment involves the repeated and outright rejection of children through seriously hostile, aggressive, or coercive displays. These behaviors are included under the APSAC domains of spurning, terrorizing, isolating, and exploiting children. At the other extreme, psychological maltreatment communicates to children that their needs, interests, emotions, and bids for autonomy lack value. These sentiments are conveyed when parents deny emotional responsiveness or neglect children's health and emotional needs.

One particularly troubling form of psychological maltreatment is exposing children to domestic violence

Table 12.8   Six Types of Psychological Abuse

Type of Abuse	Description
Spurning	Verbal and nonverbal acts that reject or degrade a child: • Ridiculing a child for showing normal emotions (i.e., crying). • Consistently singling out a specific child for punishment or chores. • Showing extreme favoritism to one child and neglecting another. • Humiliating a child in public.
Terrorizing	Threatening to hurt or abandon a child or injure/kill a child's loved one: • Threatening to hurt or kill a child if he/she does not obey. • Allowing the child to witness domestic violence. • Threatening to kill the child's pet if the child does not obey. • Threatening to leave the child.

(Continued)

Table 12.8 (Continued)

Isolating	Denying a child opportunities to interact with peers or adults outside the home: <ul><li>Refusing the child's reasonable requests to interact with peers.</li><li>Denying the child telephone contact or legal visitation with parent.</li></ul>
Exploiting	Encouraging a child to adopt inappropriate, maladaptive behaviors: <ul><li>Modeling, permitting, or encouraging antisocial acts.</li><li>Using the child to sell or transport drugs.</li><li>Asking the child to engage in prostitution or pornography.</li></ul>
Denying emotional responsiveness	Ignoring the child's bids for attention and emotional interactions: <ul><li>Remaining emotionally detached, cold, distant from the child.</li><li>Rarely showing care, affection, or love toward the child.</li><li>Failing to comfort the child when he/she is scared, upset, or unsure.</li></ul>
Health and educational neglect	Failing to meet a child's medical, mental health, and educational needs: <ul><li>Failing to provide medical care to the child when necessary.</li><li>Ignoring or refusing to participate in the child's psychological treatment when necessary.</li><li>Ignoring or refusing to participate in the treatment of the child's learning problems.</li></ul>

Source: Based on Hart, Brassard, Binggeli, and Davidson (2002).

(Graham-Bermann, 2002). In the United States, domestic violence occurs in approximately one fourth of all marriages, with rates possibly much higher among cohabitating nonmarried couples. No one knows how many children witness acts of domestic violence each year. However, the effects of domestic violence on children are striking. Children exposed to violence in the home show a wide range of internalizing and externalizing behavior problems, especially depression, anxiety, conduct problems, and PTSD. Many adults who physically abuse their spouses also engage in child maltreatment (Appel & Holden, 1998).

Neglect

Neglect occurs when caregivers do not meet children's essential needs and when their negligence harms or threatens children's welfare. There are at least four ways caregivers can neglect children: physically, emotionally, medically, and educationally (Erickson & Egeland, 2002).

Physical neglect occurs when caregivers fail to protect children from danger and provide for their physical needs. Failing to provide food, shelter, and clothing is usually considered neglectful. Physical neglect is, perhaps, the most common form of neglect and the easiest to identify. However, it

---

CASE STUDY

DEE'S STORY: WORDS CAN HURT TOO

One Saturday night, I went with my friend to a restaurant. My mother found out, and she came to the restaurant and yelled at me in front of my friends. She pulled me home, where she threw me to the floor and started kicking me and slapping me.

The next day, she called me to her bed and gave me a 2-hour lecture on how it was my fault that I had forced her to hit me because I wouldn't listen to her. I then had to write a sorry letter to her for forcing her to hit me. It was like that every time after we got hit. She would always make us tell her that we were sorry for forcing her to hit us, and we were forced to thank her for doing it because it was for our own good.

Every night we fell asleep, knowing sooner or later we would be awakened for a lecture about something we had done. It would go on for 2 to 3 hours. And just wanting it to end, we had to agree she was right. She forced us to repeat after her:

"I am a lazy, clumsy girl."

"I am stupid."

"I don't respect my parents enough."

Michael was a 5-year-11-month-old boy who was referred to our hospital by the department of child protective services. Michael and his half siblings were removed from their grandmother's care because of neglect. The children were discovered living in a dirty apartment with little food and almost nonexistent daytime supervision. They had an inconsistent history of medical care (e.g., immunizations, well-child checks), were malnourished, and were generally unkempt. All of the children were physically sick, and Michael's 2-year-old sister had extensive diaper rash that needed medical attention.

Michael displayed below average social and self-care skills. Upon arriving in foster care, he was unable to wash his face, brush his teeth, bathe, dry, and dress. Michael hoarded food, displayed poor table manners, and did not know how to use utensils. He also showed excessive preoccupation with food. His teeth were decayed.

Michael displayed poor social skills. He refused to share toys, wait his turn, pick up his clothes, or obey other rules of the home. He usually settled interpersonal disputes through physical violence. Ironically, Michael was expelled from Sunday School for punching a classmate. Michael's foster mother said that he intimidated and bullied the other children in the home. "Michael is a needy kid," his foster mother explained. "He demands constant reassurance. He's always acting up and then asking us, 'Am I a good boy?'"

is sometimes difficult to differentiate parents who physically neglect their children from parents who, because of economic hardship, are unable to provide for their children's needs.

Emotional neglect occurs when caregivers fail to provide for children's social and emotional needs. Erickson and Egeland (2002) describe emotionally neglectful caregivers as "psychologically unavailable" to their children. These caregivers do not provide sensitive and responsive care to their children, ignore their children's bids for comfort and attention, and remain physically and emotionally distant or disconnected.

Medical neglect occurs when children's basic health care needs are unmet (Dubowitz & Black, 2002). Basic health care refers to medical procedures or treatments that, if not administered, would seriously jeopardize the health of the child. Medical neglect might include failing to provide children with necessary immunizations, not taking children for a medical examination when they display serious illness, or refusing to follow doctors' recommendations regarding the treatment or management of a severe illness (e.g., parents not helping a young child with diabetes management).

Educational neglect usually occurs when parents do not enroll their children in school or otherwise provide for their education. Educational neglect might also occur when parents repeatedly allow their children to skip school.

Prevalence of Child Maltreatment

For several reasons, it is difficult to estimate the prevalence of child maltreatment. First, many instances of child abuse are never identified. For example, many abused children never disclose their victimization because they feel shame, others are intimidated by the adults who victimize them, and still

others are simply too young to tell others about their experiences. Similarly, many psychologically abused and neglected children never come to the attention of teachers or neighbors because their maltreatment does not result in a deterioration in their appearance or behavior (Dubowitz et al., 2005).

Second, even when child maltreatment is identified, it is not always reported to authorities. Many parents decide not to report instances of child maltreatment to authorities, believing that they can help their children cope with the experience themselves. Other adults avoid reporting maltreatment in order to avoid the stigma associated with an investigation.

Third, no government agency collects data on all reported cases of child maltreatment. Instead, different government agencies and independently funded researchers collect data from local areas that may or may not be representative of all children across the country.

How common is child maltreatment? In a recent survey of a large, nationally representative sample of youths, Finkelhor, Cross, and Cantor (2005) estimated that 13.8% of children and adolescents have experienced at least one form of maltreatment (Figure 12.8). This estimate is based on a definition of maltreatment that involves the *potential* for the child to experience serious harm. When researchers limit their definition of maltreatment to include only instances that resulted in *actual* injury, then the estimated prevalence of maltreatment decreases to 12.4%. This percentage reflects approximately 8,000,000 youths in the United States.

If we use the harm standard to identify maltreated youths, the most common form of child maltreatment in the United States is neglect, accounting for 60% of reported cases (Runyon, Kenny, Berry, Deblinger, & Brown, 2006). Approximately 19% of maltreated children experience physical abuse, 10% experience sexual abuse, and 8% experience psychological abuse. The remaining children experience acts of maltreatment that are undifferentiated or difficult to

Figure 12.8   Prevalence of Child Maltreatment in the United States

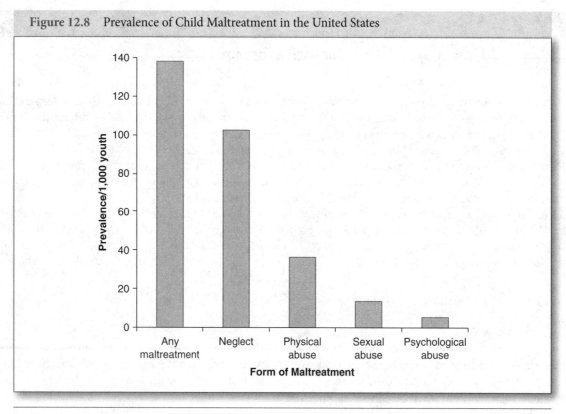

Source: Based on Finkelhor et al. (2005).

classify. It is important to remember that most children who experience maltreatment are victimized in multiple ways. The statistics provided above reflect children's most frequent or severe experience of maltreatment.

Overall, boys and girls show approximately equal likelihood of experiencing physical abuse, psychological abuse, and neglect. Girls, especially adolescent girls, are more likely than boys to be sexually abused.

Research is mixed regarding the prevalence of child maltreatment as a function of age. Most data indicate that infants, toddlers, and preschoolers are at greater risk for physical abuse and neglect than older children and adolescents (Stevens, Ruggiero, Kilpatrick, Resnick, & Saunders, 2005). Young children may be more susceptible to maltreatment because they depend heavily on the nurturance and protection of adults. However, some research shows that older children and adolescents show greater prevalence of maltreatment than younger children. Older children may be at particular risk for psychological and sexual abuse (Finkelhor et al., 2005).

Most acts of sexual abuse are committed by people the child knows (Figure 12.9). Approximately 85% of sexually maltreated children are victimized by their parents or stepparents. The vast majority of other cases of abuse are committed by other family members, babysitters, teachers, and coaches. Strangers are responsible for only about 2% of cases of sexual abuse.

EFFECTS OF PHYSICAL ABUSE AND NEGLECT
Physical Health Problems

Child physical abuse and neglect can take its toll on children's physical health. Severely neglected infants can exhibit non-organic failure to thrive, which can cause long-term health and behavior problems or death. Children who experience physical abuse often suffer bruises, broken bones, burns, and scars. These injuries are sometimes accompanied by neurological damage due to head trauma or abnormally elevated levels of stress hormone. As many as 35% of physically abused children suffer serious injury that requires medical or psychiatric treatment to prevent long-term impairment (Sedlak & Broadhurst, 1996).

The most serious and potentially lethal form of child physical abuse is shaken baby syndrome (Johnson, 2002). Shaken baby syndrome occurs when a caregiver vigorously shakes an infant back and forth, causing a rapid acceleration and deceleration of the brain within the skull. This shaking can cause severe damage to brain tissue. The syndrome is characterized by initial drowsiness or sleepiness, failure to respond to outside stimulation, breathing problems, vomiting, seizures, coma, and death. Usually, symptoms are not apparent until hours or days after the damage has been inflicted.

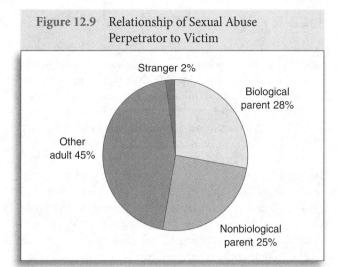

Figure 12.9 Relationship of Sexual Abuse Perpetrator to Victim

Stranger 2%

Biological parent 28%

Other adult 45%

Nonbiological parent 25%

Source: Based on Fagan, Wise, Schmidt, and Berlin (2002) and U.S. Department of Health and Human Services (2002).

Note: Strangers perpetrate only about 2% of sexual abuse cases.

Behavior Problems

Children who experience physical abuse or neglect are at risk for developing disruptive behavior problems. Children with histories of maltreatment are frequently diagnosed with Oppositional Defiant Disorder. At home, they are often spiteful and argumentative toward caregivers. At school, they are frequently disruptive and defiant. Most research indicates that this tendency toward negativistic, disruptive behavior continues throughout childhood and early adolescence. Children exposed to physical abuse or neglect also show increased risk for aggression, especially toward other children. When these children experience interpersonal problems, they are prone to angry outbursts or fits of rage. Physically abused and neglected children tend to use aggression both proactively (i.e., to get what they want) and reactively (i.e., in response to being frustrated by others; Koenig, Cicchetti, & Rogosch, 2004).

Older children and adolescents with histories of physical abuse and neglect are at risk for Conduct Disorder. Abused youths have greater likelihoods of engaging in serious antisocial behavior, especially stealing, cheating, physical assault, and chronic truancy. Underlying deficits in moral reasoning may partially account for these antisocial tendencies. As adolescents, they are twice as likely as nonabused youths to be suspended from school, arrested, or involved in a violent crime. Boys who experience maltreatment show increased likelihood of developing Antisocial Personality Disorder as adults. Girls who experience physical abuse or neglect show increased risk for underemployment and prostitution later in life (A. L. Koenig et al., 2004; Luntz & Widom, 1994; Maxfield & Widom, 1996; Widom & Kuhns, 1996).

Why do maltreated children show increased likelihood of disruptive behavior later in life? One explanation is based on **learning theory**. Physically abused children may model the hostile and aggressive behavior of caregivers (Dodge et al., 1997). Indeed, children exposed to child maltreatment often witness other aggressive acts, such as domestic violence, parental antisocial behavior, and violent crime. Children may learn, through their observations, that disruptive and aggressive behavior is an effective way to solve interpersonal problems.

Another explanation for the relationship between early maltreatment and later disruptive behavior problems is based on **social information-processing theory** (Dodge & Pettit, 1990; Rieder & Cicchetti, 1989; Rogosch, Cicchetti, & Abre, 1995). According to this theory, children solve social problems by engaging in a series of cognitive steps: (a) taking in and interpreting information about the social situation, (b) generating and evaluating a number of possible ways of responding, and (c) selecting and implementing the best plan. Physically abused children show difficulty with all three steps, making them more likely to use hostile and aggressive means to solve interpersonal problems.

First, physically abused children show hostile attributional biases when solving social problems. That is, they expect others to behave in a hostile and aggressive manner toward them. Consequently, they often misinterpret the benign behaviors of others as hostile and aggressive. Second, abused children usually have difficulty generating solutions to social problems; furthermore, the solutions that they are able to generate are usually hostile or aggressive in nature. Third, abused children impulsively select a plan of action; that is, they often do not consider the consequences of their behavior before they act. These social problem-solving deficits increase the likelihood that children will act aggressively in ambiguous social situations (Price & Glad, 2003).

What about neglected youths; how might they develop disruptive and antisocial behaviors? Children who experience neglect often have peer problems and low social functioning. Indeed, many neglected youths have few friends and are actively rejected by classmates. Because neglected children are often ostracized by prosocial peers, they may seek friendships with other rejected children. These rejected peers can introduce them to disruptive and antisocial behaviors, such as aggression, delinquency, and substance use. Furthermore, parents who neglect their children usually do not sufficiently monitor their children's activities (Knutson, DeGarmo, Koeppl, & Reid, 2005). Consequently, neglected children are free to engage in antisocial activities with little adult supervision. Association with deviant peer groups and low parental monitoring are primary predictors of conduct problems.

Mood and Anxiety Problems

Many physically abused and neglected children develop mood disorders (Clark, De Bellis, Lynch, Cornelius, & Martin, 2003; Kilpatrick et al., 2003). Comorbid mood problems include Major Depressive Disorder (MDD), Dysthymic Disorder, and general feelings of hopelessness (Kolko, 2002). Child maltreatment, especially psychological maltreatment, can also lead to more diffuse emotional problems. For example, many psychologically maltreated children report low self-esteem and self-efficacy. These mood problems are especially common in youths who experience multiple types of maltreatment and among girls (Danielson, de Arellano, Kilpatrick, Saunders, & Resnick, 2005).

Maltreated youths are also at risk for developing anxiety disorders. The most common anxiety disorder associated with physical abuse is PTSD. Approximately 16% to 36% of youths exposed to physical abuse develop PTSD (Danielson et al., 2005; Famularo, Fenton, Kinscherff, Ayoub, & Barnum, 1994). Furthermore, approximately one third of children who develop abuse-related PTSD continue to show symptoms 2 years after the end of their physical maltreatment (Famularo, Fenton, Augustyn, & Zuckerman, 1996).

How does child abuse place children at risk for mood and anxiety disorders? Hart, Brassard, Binggeli, and Davidson (2002) have used **Maslow's hierarchical theory of human needs** to explain the negative effects of child maltreatment on children's social and emotional development. According to Maslow's theory, optimal social-emotional development depends on children's abilities to satisfy certain fundamental needs. These needs are arranged in hierarchical fashion and fall into two general categories. The first category, basic needs, includes the child's physiological needs (e.g., food, shelter, clothing) and psychological needs (e.g., a sense of safety, belongingness, self-esteem). The second category, growth needs, includes the need for knowledge and beauty as well as the tendency toward self-actualization. According to Maslow, **self-actualization** refers to the innate tendency to become fully functioning in all areas of life and is characterized by a sense of high self-efficacy and intrinsic motivation.

From the perspective of human needs theory, child maltreatment interferes with children's attainment of their basic needs. Physical and emotional neglect denies children's physiological needs. Physical and psychological abuse interfere with children's pursuit of psychological needs, especially safety and emotional connectedness with others. Since these basic needs are unsatisfied, high-order needs that promote social and emotional well-being are often left unfulfilled.

Physical abuse, psychological abuse, and neglect also can cause children to adopt negative views of themselves, others, and the future (Runyon & Kenny, 2002; Toth, Cicchetti, Macfie, Maughan, & Vanmeenen, 2000). Compared to nonabused children, maltreated children are more likely to believe that they are inherently unworthy, bad, or flawed (Harter, 1997, 1999). The attributions children make about their maltreatment predict the severity of their internalizing symptoms. Children who blame themselves for their victimization show much greater mood disturbance than children who do not assume responsibility for their maltreatment (Brown & Kolko, 1999).

Quality of Attachment

Abused and neglected children show greater likelihood of developing insecure attachment relationships with parents and other adults responsible for their care. Approximately two thirds of maltreated children develop insecure attachment relationships with their caregivers, compared to approximately one third of nonmaltreated children (Cicchetti & Barnett, 1991; Cicchetti, Toth, & Maughan, 2000; Crittenden, 1992).

Insecure attachment might mediate the relationship between child maltreatment and behavioral-emotional problems later in development. That is, child maltreatment can lead children to adopt internal working models of themselves and others that are based on interpersonal mistrust and self-doubt. Although rarely articulated, these working models might include the following beliefs: "The world is dangerous. I cannot trust others. I must rely on myself. I am not worthy of receiving help from others, anyway." These models subsequently color all of the child's future relationships and his self-view. The result could be disruptive behavior, social isolation, and a host of mood and anxiety problems (Erickson & Egeland, 2002).

Some maltreated children display **disorganized patterns of attachment** toward their caregivers (Main, Kaplan, & Cassidy, 1985). Children who form disorganized attachments behave in bizarre, erratic, or unpredictable ways during the Ainsworth strange situation procedure. Some children who are classified as having disorganized attachment show considerable distress when separated from their mothers during the strange situation procedure, but they attempt to flee from their mothers when their mothers reenter the room. Other children classified as having disorganized attachment also show distress during separation, but when their mothers return, they seek comfort from inanimate objects (e.g., the leg of a table) instead of their mothers. Still other children appear hesitant or fearful of their mothers. Disorganized attachment is most common among children who have experienced physical abuse or neglect. Maltreatment may cause children to expect that their parents will behave in unpredictable or threatening ways (Barnett, Ganiban, & Cicchetti, 1999).

Cognitive Delays

Physically abused and neglected children are more likely to show cognitive delays than their nonabused peers (Kolko, 2002). Cognitive problems include difficulty with executive functioning, working memory, and language (Eigsti & Cicchetti, 2004). Abused and neglected children often lack impulse control and have difficulty on a wide range of mental tasks. These cognitive problems tend to be long lasting; they may persist well after the termination of abuse (Claussen & Crittenden, 1991; Crittenden, Claussen, & Sugarman, 1994).

The academic achievement of maltreated youths tends to be less well-developed than the achievement of nonabused children. Academic problems seem to be pervasive; they exist across all major areas of academic functioning (Kolko, 2002). Maltreated children are more likely to repeat a grade, receive special education services for learning problems, and miss school. They are also more likely to show behavior problems at school, to be suspended, and to drop out before graduation. Neglected children tend to show the lowest academic achievement of any group of maltreated youths (Dubowitz et al., 2005).

EFFECTS OF SEXUAL ABUSE

Finkelhor and Browne (1985) suggest that childhood sexual abuse traumatizes children in four ways. Specifically, sexual abuse contributes to (a) traumatic sexualization, (b) feelings of betrayal, (c) powerlessness, and (d) stigmatization. Abuse places children on deviant developmental pathways that can lead to impairment.

Traumatic Sexualization

Sexually abused children sometimes show increased levels of sexualized behavior compared to nonabused peers (Kendall-Tackett, Williams, & Finkelhor, 1993). **Sexualized behaviors** are actions that are either not typical for the child's age and development or inappropriate to the social situation. Sexualized behaviors include excessive or public masturbation, preoccupation with sex, sexualized play with dolls, forced sexual activity with playmates, and seductive language and behavior (Heiman & Heard-Davison, 2004).

It is sometimes difficult to differentiate normative and non-normative sexualized behavior during childhood because little research has been conducted on typical sexual activity in children (Friedrich, 1997; Friedrich et al., 2001). Some sexualized behaviors are normative at certain ages. For example, many toddlers engage in self-stimulation, preschoolers try to look at adults while naked or undressing, and school-age children ask parents sex-related questions. However, other sexual behavior is usually never developmentally appropriate, such as sexualized play with dolls, forced sexual behavior, or the insertion of objects into sexual body parts.

Age-inappropriate sexual behavior is *not* a reliable indicator of child sexual abuse (Friedrich, 1997; Johnson & Friend, 1995). Although many sexually abused children show sexualized behavior, most (66%) do not. Even the most problematic sexualized behaviors (e.g., a child forcing sexual activity on a playmate, insertions) differentiate sexually abused and nonabused children with only 75% accuracy. Instead of behavior, emerging data indicate that the presence of **precocious sexual knowledge** might better differentiate sexually abused and nonabused youths (Brilleslijper-Kater, Friedrich, & Corwin, 2004). Young, sexually abused children often have greater knowledge of sexual behavior than their nonabused peers.

Emerging data indicate that child sexual abuse can speed up sexual maturation, especially in girls (Bergevin et al., 2003). In one study, sexually abused girls who experienced vaginal penetration showed menarche approximately one year earlier than their nonabused peers. The mechanism by which child sexual abuse leads to early menarche is unknown, but researchers have suggested that the abuse experience could stimulate hormonal or biochemical (e.g., pheromone) secretions.

Sexually abused girls are at risk for being sexually victimized as adults. A meta-analysis of studies investigating the association between sexual abuse in children and sexual victimization in adults revealed an overall effect size of .59 for women (Roodman & Clum, 2001). Overall, women who were sexually abused as children were 2 to 3 times more likely to be sexually assaulted during adulthood than their nonabused peers (Rich, Combs-Lane, Resnick, & Kilpatrick, 2004).

Retrospective studies also indicate that girls who are sexually abused show increased risk for sexual disorders and risky sexual behavior as adults (Koenig & Clark, 2004; Rich et al., 2004). For example, some sexually abused girls show higher rates of sexual arousal problems as adults than their nonabused peers (Laumann, Paik, & Rosen, 1999). Other women with histories of child sexual abuse display hypersexual behavior. Specifically, they are more likely to show sexual promiscuity, engage in unsafe sexual practices, such as one-time-only sexual encounters, become involved in prostitution, and contract human immunodeficiency virus (HIV) than their nonabused peers.

The relationship between childhood sexual abuse and sexual revictimization is less clear for boys. Most research indicates that boys who are sexually abused are not more likely to be sexually assaulted as adults (Purcel, Malow, Dolezal, & Carballo-Dieguez, 2004). However, some data indicate that homosexual men with histories of childhood sexual abuse do show increased risk for adult sexual victimization by other men.

Men with histories of sexual abuse are also more likely to show sexual adjustment problems than their nonabused peers (Heiman & Heard-Davison, 2004; Purcel et al., 2004). Although data are somewhat inconsistent, men with histories of sexual abuse show increased likelihood of sexual dysfunction (e.g., premature ejaculation, erectile dysfunction, low sexual desire), sexually coercive and aggressive behaviors toward their partners, sexual promiscuity, risky sexual behavior, and HIV infection.

Feelings of Betrayal

Sexual abuse traumatizes children through betrayal. Sexual abuse breeds mistrust, especially when the abuser is a family member or caregiver. Abuse during childhood can also cause mistrust toward adults and authority figures in general. Loss of trust can contribute to feelings of anger, rage, and anxiety in interpersonal relationships (Gold, Sinclair, & Balge, 1999).

Attachment theorists argued that the experience of child sexual abuse contributes to the development of insecure attachment (Howes, Cicchetti, Toth, & Rogosch, 2000). Abused children fail to develop internal working models of caregivers based on trust, security, sensitivity, and support. Instead, the worldview of sexually abused youths is often characterized by insecurity, doubt, and the anticipation of harm. In times of crisis, individuals with histories of abuse may not feel confident in their partner's sensitivity and responsiveness to their needs. Consequently, these individuals may avoid close attachments with others or excessively cling to others because they fear abandonment.

Indeed, many sexually abused children display problems in their adult interpersonal relationships (Finkelhor, Hotaling, Lewis, & Smith, 1989; Gold et al., 1999; Mullen, Martin, Anderson, Romans, & Herbison, 1994). Some women with histories of sexual abuse sacrifice their freedom and autonomy in order to please their partners. Although they describe their partners as overly controlling and unsympathetic to their needs, they remain in these relationships to avoid rejection and abandonment. Other women with abuse histories report a general dissatisfaction in their romantic relationships, pervasive feelings of mistrust and insecurity toward their partners, and an overall lack of emotional intimacy. Both groups of women are more likely to divorce than their nonabused counterparts.

Powerlessness

Sexual abuse victimizes children by making them feel powerless. Children who are abused often feel helpless and unable to cope with the abuse experience or its social-emotional effects. Children who adopt internal, stable, and global attributions for their abuse are especially at risk for feelings of powerlessness and helplessness (Gold et al., 1999; Sinclair & Gold, 1997). Some maltreated children assume responsibility for their abuse, believe that abuse-related problems will persist, and believe that the effects of abuse will affect many aspects of their lives and day-to-day functioning. Over time, feelings of powerlessness can lead to anxiety and depression, emotional numbing, and hopelessness.

The most common psychological disorder associated with sexual abuse is PTSD (Berliner & Elliott, 2002). Among children referred to psychiatric clinics for sexual abuse, as many as 50% meet diagnostic criteria for PTSD, while another 30% show at least some PTSD symptoms (Ackerman, Newton, McPherson, Jones, & Dykman, 1998; McLeer, Deblinger, Henry, & Orvaschel, 1992). The likelihood of developing PTSD symptoms following sexual abuse is related to the severity of the abuse, especially the degree to which the perpetrator used violence or physical coercion, intimidated the victim, or instilled fear and terror (Chaffin, Silovsky, & Vaughn, 2005; Hanson et al., 2001).

Children can show a host of other internalizing disorders ranging from anxiety, depression, somatic complaints, eating problems, sleep disturbance, and loss of bowel and bladder control. For example, sexually abused children are 4 times more likely than nonabused youths to develop anxiety disorders. Abused children are at risk for anxiety even if they do not immediately perceive the sexual abuse incident as traumatic (Chaffin et al., 2005).

Stigmatization

Finally, sexual abuse can lead to stigmatization (Browne & Finkelhor, 1986; Feiring & Taska, 2005). Many abused children believe that they are "damaged goods" because of their maltreatment. As a result, abused children may engage in self-destructive behaviors to express their feelings of low self-worth or replace emotional discomfort with physical pain. Self-injury, suicidal behavior, and Substance Use Disorders can be seen as the outward manifestations of stigmatization.

Although the concept of stigmatization is difficult to measure, adult survivors of child sexual abuse are more likely to display these hypothesized effects of stigmatization than their nonabused peers (Heiman & Heard-Davison, 2004). For example, self-harming behaviors, such as burning and cutting, are 2 to 5 times more common among sexually abused adolescent girls and women than among nonabused females (Figure 12.10). In one study of adolescent girls who recently disclosed their sexual abuse, 62% admitted to some form of self-harm (Cyr, McDuff, Wright, Theriault, & Cinq-Mars, 2005). Child sexual abuse is often seen in the histories of women with Borderline Personality Disorder, a serious disorder characterized by an unstable sense of identity, emotional dysregulation, tumultuous interpersonal relationships, and self-harm.

Sexual abuse also predicts suicidal thoughts and suicide attempts in adolescence and adulthood (Martin, Bergen, Richardson, Roeger, & Allison, 2004; Ystgaard, Hestetun, Loeb, & Mehlum, 2004). Interestingly, the relationship between child sexual abuse and suicidality differs by gender. For girls, child sexual abuse is associated with depression and feelings of hopelessness. These negative emotions, in turn, predict suicidal ideas and plans. For boys, there is a direct relationship between history of sexual abuse and later suicidal thoughts and behavior. This direct relationship between abuse and suicide indicates that sexually abused boys may be at risk for suicide even if they do not show depression. Indeed, even after controlling for current levels of depression, adolescent boys with histories of sexual abuse are 15 times more likely than nonabused boys to attempt suicide.

TREATMENT FOR PHYSICAL ABUSE AND NEGLECT
Supportive Therapy for Children

Most maltreated children do not receive mental health services. Indeed, only about 13% of abused and neglected youths

Figure 12.10 Self-Harm Among Youths With Histories of Sexual Abuse

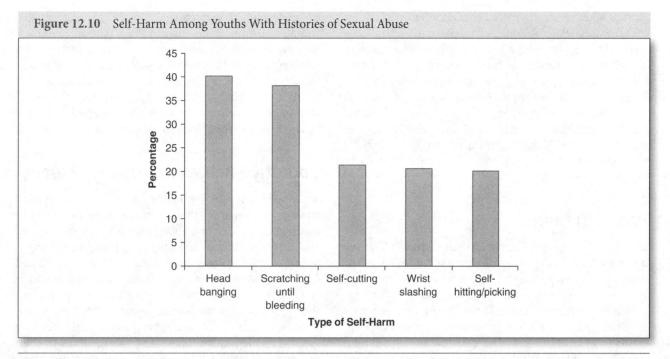

Source: Based on Cyr et al. (2005).

receive any type of treatment after their abuse is discovered (Kolko, Selelyo, & Brown, 1999).

The most common form of treatment given to abused and neglected children is supportive therapy. The primary goal of **supportive therapy** is to help children cope with feelings and memories associated with their maltreatment and to improve their sense of self and relationships with others. William Friedrich (2002) has developed an integrated approach to the treatment of abused and neglected children. In his approach, treatment addresses three core areas of children's functioning: (a) attachment to caregivers, (b) behavioral regulation, and (c) self-perceptions.

Abuse and neglect seriously jeopardize the security of the parent-child attachment relationship (Cassidy & Shaver, 1999). Under optimal conditions, children expect sensitive and responsive care from parents when they are scared, upset, or unsure. However, acts of maltreatment rob children of that security. Physical and emotional neglect communicate to children that parents are not able or willing to provide for their basic material and psychological needs. Furthermore, parents who physically abuse children are, simultaneously, the source of danger and support. The result of maltreatment is an attachment relationship built on mistrust and doubt. In the worst cases, attachment is disorganized, as children learn to fear their caregivers.

Early in therapy, the clinician uses the therapeutic relationship as a source of support, care, and nurturance. The clinician's primary goal is to establish a sense of trust between himself and the maltreated child. Fostering trust is initially a difficult task because maltreated children often expect rejection and abandonment by others. Indeed, children may engage in disruptive behaviors and aversive emotional displays to elicit anger and resentment from the therapist and thereby confirm their expectations that others will reject them.

To establish a sense of trust, clinicians strive to provide a safe, consistent, and accepting therapeutic environment. Therapy sessions are typically used to help children process feelings associated with maltreatment. Some children harbor anger toward parents for their neglectful and abusive behavior. Other children resent the police, child protective services, and foster families for keeping them away from their parents. Still other children blame themselves for their mistreatment, believing they were somehow responsible for their caregivers' actions. Finally, a large number of children deny having problems altogether. The therapist tries to validate children's feelings by listening to them in a supportive, nonjudgmental way.

Later in therapy, the clinician might help children recognize their feelings and understand how these feelings affect their thoughts and actions. For example, feelings of anger and resentment could lead to aggressive outbursts at school and problems with teachers or peers. Peer problems, in turn, could contribute to additional feelings of loneliness, resentment, and hostility. The therapist might teach children more effective ways to cope with negative feelings, in order to avoid long-term emotional and social problems. Some therapists teach children relaxation techniques, others encourage participation in art or sports, while others ask children to keep journals about their memories and experiences.

The clinician hopes that the therapeutic relationship can become a corrective emotional experience for the child, perhaps the first relationship that the child has ever had in which her needs are placed above the needs of others (Friedrich, 2002). Establishing such a corrective relationship is usually quite difficult because many maltreated children are reluctant to trust or confide in another adult who they believe (based on previous experience) will reject, abandon, or mistreat them. By supporting the child, the clinician shows that the child is worthy of receiving care and attention from others. The experience of unconditional positive regard from the therapist can correct self-perceptions of worthlessness or guilt that interfere with the child's self-esteem and self-efficacy.

Parent Training

Most caregivers who physically abuse or neglect children are offered therapy that involves behavioral parent training. The primary goal of parenting training is to teach parents more effective ways to socialize children. Specifically, parents are shown how to (a) attend to children's activities and positively reinforce appropriate behavior, (b) give clear and developmentally appropriate commands to maximize children's compliance, (c) ignore inappropriate behaviors and avoid hostile-aggressive displays, and (d) use noncoercive forms of discipline, such as time out (with young children) and response cost (with older children and adolescents).

Parent training can be administered either individually or in group format. Each week, the therapist introduces a new parenting skill and encourages parents to practice the skill at home with their children. The following week, parents provide feedback to the therapist and the therapist offers suggestions on how to tailor the treatment to meet parents' needs. When administered in group format, the therapist might use video demonstrations to elucidate parenting principles and tactics. The therapist might also allow time for parents to discuss their experiences with each other.

Parent training is efficacious in improving the quality of parent-child interactions. Specifically, parent training is associated with improvements in the quality of care parents provide their children, reductions in hostile and coercive parenting behaviors, and a decrease in children's behavior problems. The efficacy of parent training is based primarily on research involving children with disruptive behavior disorders, not abused and neglected children per se (Chaffin & Schmidt, 2006).

A specific parent training program, Parent-Child Interaction Therapy (PCIT), has been effectively used with caregivers who abused their children. Chaffin and colleagues (2004) randomly assigned parents to one of three treatment conditions: (a) PCIT, (b) PCIT plus individual counseling for parents, and (c) a traditional group-based parenting training program. Results showed that PCIT alone (Group 1) was superior to a traditional parenting program (Group 3) in decreasing re-referral to child protective services. These results indicate that the hands-on "coaching" approach used in PCIT may be especially

useful to high-risk parents (Figure 12.11). Interestingly, adding individual counseling to PCIT (Group 2) did not increase the efficacy of treatment; in fact, parents who participated in PCIT plus individual therapy showed *greater* likelihood of re-abusing than parents who participated in PCIT alone. The researchers suggest that the addition of individual counseling may have diluted the efficacy of PCIT by decreasing parents' interest in treatment.

Cognitive-Behavioral Family Therapy

Many clinicians use a combination of behavioral parent training and cognitive therapy to help families who have experienced child maltreatment (Azar & Wolfe, 1998; Kolko, 2002). Melissa Runyon and colleagues (Runyon, Deblinger, Ryan, & Thakkar-Kolar, 2004) have developed a combined CBT program for abusive and neglectful parents and their children. Parent-child dyads participate in 16 weekly group therapy sessions, each lasting approximately two hours. Initially, parents and children are separated. Parents receive specific training in the causes and consequences of child maltreatment, child behavior management, stress reduction, and social problem solving.

One important aspect of cognitive therapy is to help parents form more realistic expectations for their children's behavior. Physically abusive parents often set extremely high and developmentally inappropriate expectations for their children. When their children fail to live up to these expectations, parents can become angry and respond with verbal or physical aggression.

Additionally, cognitive interventions for parents often involve challenging caregivers' cognitive distortions that lead up to child maltreatment. For example, a parent might think, "My child is always disrespectful; he never listens to me." The therapist might challenge this distorted belief by asking the parent to provide evidence for and against this claim. In fact, there are probably many instances each day in which the child obeys the parent, but these situations are often overshadowed by acts of noncompliance.

Another cognitive technique is to improve parents' problem-solving skills. Specifically, parents are taught to avoid blaming themselves or their children for children's misbehavior. Instead, parents are encouraged to look for alternative (and more benign) reasons for their children's acting out. For example, if the child becomes disruptive during a shopping trip, the parent might initially blame herself (e.g., "I'm a terrible parent") or the child (e.g., "He's a naughty kid"). Alternatively, the parent might attribute the child's misbehavior to situational factors (e.g., "He missed his nap today" or "He's bored and needs something to do"). Alternative attributions that do not place blame on the parent or child can reduce feelings of guilt, helplessness, or anger and, consequently, the likelihood of maltreatment.

Still another cognitive intervention involves improving parents' coping skills. Since distress, resentment, and anger

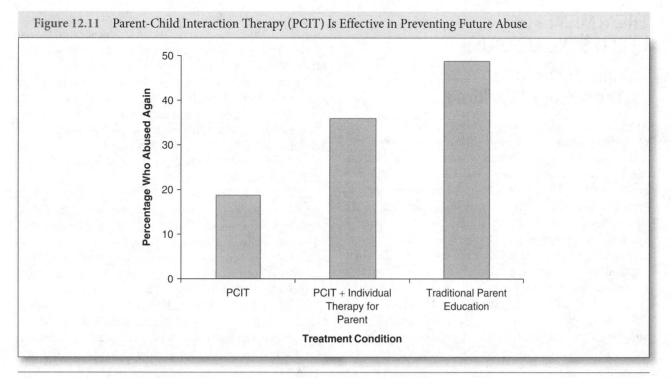

Source: Based on Chaffin and colleagues (2004).

Note: Interestingly, PCIT alone yielded better outcomes than more extensive forms of treatment.

usually precede child abuse, it is important for parents to learn ways to reduce these emotional states. The techniques that therapists use depend largely on the needs and preferences of parents. Some parents prefer breathing exercises, others respond to muscle relaxation, and still others like journaling. Most therapists also try to increase parents' social support as a way to buffer them against the harmful effects of parenting stress.

While parents participate in cognitive group therapy, their children simultaneously participate in group treatment. During the initial sessions, children learn about child abuse and neglect and the possible consequences that child maltreatment can have on children and families. In the early phase of treatment, therapists attempt to normalize children's feelings of anger, sadness, or anxiety. Therapists also help children identify and label their feelings and examine how feelings, thoughts, and actions are connected. This can be accomplished through games, role play, and discussion.

Later, children and therapists develop a **safety plan**. The safety plan is a specific strategy for dealing with future episodes of maltreatment. The safety plan involves (a) learning how to identify signs that abuse might occur (e.g., "Mom gets very angry and starts to threaten me; Dad starts drinking again"), (b) engaging in an immediate behavior to keep the child safe (e.g., leave the house), and (c) going to a trusted person for help (e.g., grandmother, neighbor). Other child therapy sessions are designed to increase children's anger management, social skills, and problem-solving strategies.

After separate parent and child sessions, dyads participate in joint sessions that focus on the quality of parent-child interactions. For most of these combined sessions, parents practice behavior management skills with their children in the room, while they receive coaching from therapists. During some of these combined sessions, therapists encourage parents and children to openly discuss the abuse incident and to talk about ways to prevent it from happening in the future.

CBT for abused and neglected children is promising. Two randomized controlled studies indicate that CBT is efficacious in reducing punitive parenting practices (Whiteman, Fanshel, & Grundy, 1987). An additional study shows that CBT is associated with reductions in maltreated children's PTSD symptoms, anxiety, and anger (Swenson & Brown, 1999).

To date, only one study has examined the efficacy of combined parent-child CBT. Kolko and colleagues (Kolko, 1996; Kolko & Swenson, 2002) randomly assigned families to one of three treatment conditions: (a) family therapy, (b) parent-child CBT, and (c) treatment in the community. Results showed that parents who participated in either family therapy or CBT reported greater reductions in psychological distress, family conflict, and children's behavior problems than parents who received treatment in the community. Additionally, parents who participated in CBT reported lower levels of anger and physical punishment than parents who participated in family therapy (Chaffin & Valle, 2003).

TREATMENT FOR CHILD SEXUAL ABUSE

Trauma-Focused CBT for Abused Children

Trauma-focused cognitive-behavioral therapy (TF-CBT) incorporates elements of exposure therapy, cognitive restructuring, parent training, and family support into a single treatment package for sexually abused children. The initial goal of TF-CBT is to help children identify and manage negative emotions associated with the traumatic experience. In the first session, children are encouraged to identify positive and negative feelings associated with various social situations and to recognize that negative feelings are acceptable. Then, children are encouraged to describe their own traumatic experience and the feelings associated with it. In the second session, children learn stress management techniques, such as focused breathing, muscle relaxation, and **thought stopping**. When unwanted and intrusive memories come into the child's mind, the child might mentally say, "Stop! Stop! Stop!" and focus her attention away from the thoughts. The therapist also helps the child identify other stress reduction techniques, such as listening to music, drawing, or playing with friends.

Next, treatment involves exposing the child to memories of the traumatic event and altering the child's thoughts regarding the event. In session three, the therapist teaches the relationship between thoughts, feelings, and actions. Then, children explore how different ways of thinking and feeling change the way they act. In sessions four through six, children gradually disclose more of their traumatic experiences in writing. Children read books written by other youths who were abused. Then, children are encouraged to write their own stories, detailing the events, thoughts, and feelings associated with their abuse. Very young children are encouraged to draw picture books about their abuse experiences (Knell & Ruma, 2003). By session seven, the therapist begins to challenge and reframe children's maladaptive thoughts about the abuse experience. For example, a child might initially think, "It's my fault that I was abused. I let my stepfather do it, and I didn't tell anyone." The therapist might reframe this statement as, "It's not my fault; I was scared and couldn't tell anyone."

While children participate in therapy activities, nonoffending parents also meet with the clinician for individual sessions. For the most part, parent sessions mirror the child sessions. For example, both children and parents learn to identify and accept feelings regarding the traumatic experience and to develop coping strategies to deal with negative affect and stress. In addition, parents participate in training designed to improve the support and consistency they give to their children and to teach effective ways of addressing children's problem behavior that might arise after the abuse.

In the final phase of therapy, children and nonoffending parents meet together. Children are encouraged to read their abuse stories to their parents and to discuss their thoughts and feelings about the trauma. Parents are asked to listen with acceptance and understanding and to answer children's questions regarding their abuse. Finally, parents and children develop new strategies to keep children safe. For example, parents might be encouraged to monitor their children more frequently, whereas children might pledge to come to parents immediately if they feel uncomfortable about a person or situation.

The efficacy of TF-CBT has been investigated in a number of randomized controlled studies. For example, J. A. Cohen, Mannarino, and Knudsen (2005) examined 82 children and adolescents (ages 8–15 years) with histories of sexual abuse. Youths were randomly assigned to either TF-CBT or supportive therapy, which involved art, play, and therapists listening to children's feelings. Children's PTSD symptoms, behavior problems, and sexual behavior were assessed before treatment, after treatment, and at 6- and 12-month follow-ups. Results showed that both forms of treatment were efficacious in reducing children's mood and anxiety symptoms. However, children were more likely to complete TF-CBT (73%) than nondirective therapy (46%). Furthermore, at 12-month follow-up, children who participated in TF-CBT showed fewer problems with depression, anxiety, inappropriate sexual behaviors, and PTSD symptoms compared to children who received supportive therapy (Figure 12.12).

Several other randomized controlled trials have yielded similar results (J. A. Cohen, Deblinger, Mannarino, & Steer, 2004; J. A. Cohen et al., 2005; J. A. Cohen & Mannarino, 1996, 1997, 2004; Deblinger, Lippmann, & Steer, 1996; Deblinger, Steer, & Lippmann, 1999a, 1999b). These trials support the use of TF-CBT as a first-line treatment for sexually abused children who display PTSD, other mood and anxiety disorders, and aberrant sexual behaviors (Berliner, 2005).

Cognitive Restructuring for Abused Adolescents

Older children and adolescents who have been sexually abused often report negative thoughts about themselves, others, and the world that contribute to their anxiety and mood problems (J. B. Cohen, Deblinger, Maedel, & Stauffer, 1999; Deblinger & Heflin, 1996). First, sexually abused children often hold negative appraisals of themselves. They may view themselves as worthless, as "damaged goods," or as unlovable by others. They may also blame themselves for the abuse, especially if they feel that they were somehow complicit in the sexual act.

Second, sexually abused children often hold negative views of others. They may view other people as untrustworthy, self-centered, and coercive. Consequently, they may be suspicious of others' motives and avoid asking other people for help or support.

Figure 12.12 Effectiveness of TF-CBT for Sexually Abused Youths

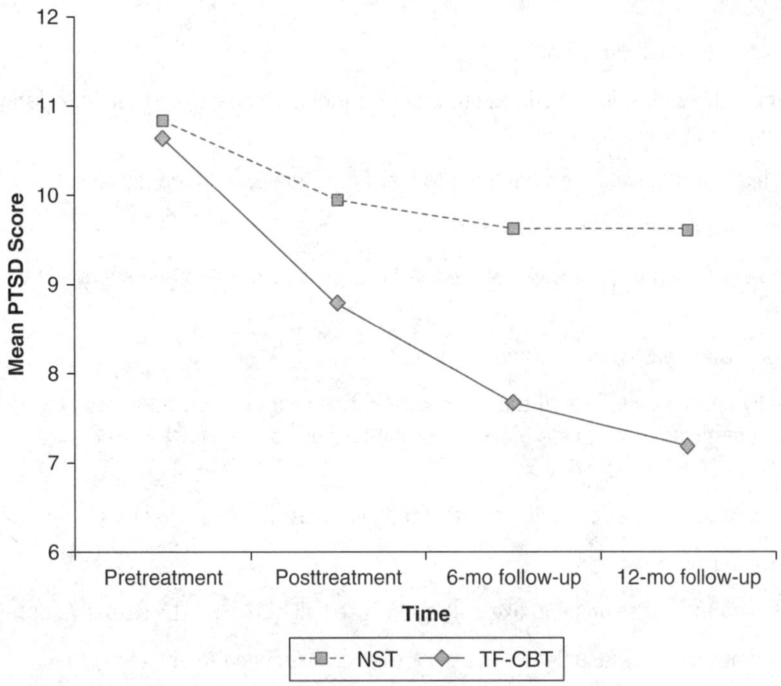

Source: Based on J. A. Cohen et al. (2005).

Note: Both TF-CBT and nondirective supportive therapy (NST) led to reductions in children's symptoms. However, one year after treatment, youths who participated in TF-CBT showed fewer problems with depression, anxiety, inappropriate sexual behaviors, and PTSD.

Finally, sexually abused children may adopt negative views of the world and the future. Abused children often view the world as a dangerous place. Some children report a pessimistic attitude toward the future and an inability to think about long-term plans.

The way children think about themselves, others, and the world can color their experiences and influence their feelings and actions. A child who believes "No one can be trusted" will likely have difficulty forming attachments with caregivers and friends. An adolescent who believes "I am worthless—even my own father mistreated me" may have problems with low self-esteem and self-efficacy. These negative beliefs, in turn, can cause individuals to distort interpersonal experiences to confirm their pessimistic and mistrustful schemas.

Therapists try to challenge cognitive distortions and help youths find ways to think about their abuse experiences (Heflin & Deblinger, 2003). Consider Michelle, a 14-year-old adolescent who was sexually abused by her father. In the transcript below, the therapist identifies a cognitive distortion that may be contributing to Michelle's guilt. Then, the therapist asks Michelle to critically examine the validity of her distorted belief.

RESEARCH TO PRACTICE

CHALLENGING COGNITIVE DISTORTIONS

Therapist: When something reminds you of the abuse now, what feelings do you have?

Michelle: I guess I mostly feel bad.

Therapist: I'm not sure what you mean by "bad." Can you tell me a little more about which kind of bad feelings you have?

(Continued)

Michelle:	Well, I just feel guilty about all of it.
Therapist:	OK, remember how we said sometimes our thoughts influence how we are feeling? Can you tell me what you are thinking about when you feel guilty?
Michelle:	I just feel like I must have done something to make my dad decide to do it to me.
Therapist:	What do you think you might have done?
Michelle:	I don't know. He used to always yell at me for the clothes I wore, so I guess maybe I wore the wrong kind of stuff.
Therapist:	What do you think was wrong with your clothes?
Michelle:	I don't really know. I dress like all the other kids, but he said I was trying to look too grown up, too sexy. He even said sometimes that I made him do it to me because of the way I walked around in really short shorts and miniskirts.
Therapist:	Well, let's think about that carefully. You said that you dress like the other kids?
Michelle:	Yeah, pretty much.
Therapist:	And so, do you think that dressing like that also caused all of *them* to be sexually abused?
Michelle:	Well, not all of them, no. Actually, I don't think this has happened to any of my friends.
Therapist:	So, if dressing like that hasn't caused them to be sexually abused, it doesn't make sense that it caused you to be abused, does it?
Michelle:	No, I guess not.

Source: From Heflin and Deblinger (2003). Used with permission.

The negative cognitions evidenced by abused children contribute to their psychological and somatic symptoms (Heflin & Deblinger, 2003; Mannarino & Cohen, 1996). Cognitive therapy is designed to challenge these negative cognitions and help children view themselves, others, and the world more realistically.

CHAPTER SUMMARY

Posttraumatic Stress Disorder

- PTSD is characterized by cognitive, behavioral, emotional, and physiological symptoms that emerge following a traumatic or catastrophic event. The person must (a) directly experience the event, (b) witness the event, or (c) learn about the event that is occurring to a family member or close friend. Furthermore,
  - they persistently reexperience the event,
  - they avoid stimuli associated with the event,
  - they experience a negative alteration of thoughts and feelings (i.e., numbing),
  - they experience physiological arousal.
- *DSM-5* shows sensitivity to the way children may manifest PTSD differently than adults. The number of symptoms required for PTSD is lower for children and adolescents compared to adults. Furthermore, there are different criteria for preschoolers compared to children and adolescents.
- Acute Stress Disorder is diagnosed in children who show PTSD symptoms for more than 3 days but less than one month. Symptoms need not fall into all four symptom areas.
- The development of PTSD depends on risk and protective factors:
  - Youths with poorer social-emotional functioning before the trauma are more likely to develop PTSD after the trauma.
  - Children directly exposed to the trauma are more likely to develop PTSD than children indirectly exposed to the trauma.

- Dysregulation of HPA axis likely underlies many physiological symptoms of PTSD.
- Cognitive appraisal theory asserts that children who personalize trauma are more likely to develop PTSD. Furthermore, escape-avoidance coping increases the likelihood of PTSD.
- Parents' reactions to traumatic events and the care they afford their children influences their children's ability to cope with these events.

- Several evidence-based treatments are available for PTSD in children.

  - Psychological debriefing has not been shown to be effective in reducing PTSD. Two studies also suggest that it may exacerbate PTSD symptoms; consequently, it is not recommended as a first-line treatment.
  - Psychological first aid can provide informational and tangible support to victims of trauma immediately after the event. It can be used effectively with children and families.
  - Trauma-focused CBT involves exposing children to memories or traumatic events in the safety of a trusting therapeutic relationship and teaching children to use problem-solving coping strategies. Four randomized controlled studies support its effectiveness.
  - EMDR may be effective in reducing PTSD symptoms in children. However, the mechanism by which it alleviates symptoms is not known.
  - Medication is generally not regarded as a first-line treatment for pediatric PTSD.

Social-Emotional Deprivation

- Reactive Attachment Disorder (RAD) is a rare disorder shown by children who experienced extreme social-emotional deprivation in infancy. They are "emotionally absent" and do not show preference for a primary caregiver.

  - RAD was first observed among orphans during World War II. Infants provided adequate physical care, but inadequate social-emotional contact, showed inadequate weight gain, depressed and irritable mood, and passivity.
  - Bowlby asserted that deprived children failed to develop attachment relationships with their primary caregivers during a sensitive stage in their social-emotional development.

- Disinhibited Social Engagement Disorder (DSED) is characterized by inhibiting social behavior caused by disruptions in caregiving that occur in infancy and early childhood.

  - Youths with DSED show "indiscriminately friendly" behavior. They are prone to show affection and wander off with strangers.
  - Tizard's longitudinal research showed that children's indiscriminately social behavior can persist throughout childhood and into adolescence.

- The Bucharest Early Intervention Project followed social-emotionally deprived infants into early childhood. Some infants were raised in institutions while other were adopted.

  - Results showed that RAD developed when infants did not form attachment relationships with a primary caregiver. Children adopted in infancy generally recovered from RAD as they became attached to their adoptive parents.
  - Results showed that DSED was not associated with attachment. Instead, DSED was associated with deficits in social inhibition. These deficits often persisted, even if children were adopted by supportive families.
  - Certain alleles for the serotonin and dopamine transporter genes may place children at greater risk for these disorders of they are faced with early deprivation. Other alleles may protect children.

- Deprived infants are at risk for small head circumference and brain size, disruption of the HPA axis, cognitive deficits, and stereotypies. Youths raised in institutions often display emotional and behavioral problems (especially ADHD) in childhood and adolescence.
- Rutter has observed "deprivation specific patterns" in some children reared in institutions. Features include the following:

  - Quasi-autism
  - Indiscriminately social behavior
  - Cognitive impairment
  - Inattention and hyperactivity

- Evidence-based treatment for RAD involves teaching parents to provide sensitive and responsive care to their infants.

  - Attachment and biobehavioral catch-up is effective in helping dyads develop secure attachment relationships and improving children's functioning.
  - Treatment involves helping parents come to terms with their own caregiving histories that might interfere with their caregiving.

- Several studies have shown that DSED can be prevented by improving the sensitivity and care provided to children in institutions. However, effective treatment for DSED in older children and adolescents is limited.

Child Maltreatment

- Child maltreatment is a significant problem in the United States. Each year, approximately 2.6 million youths are referred to child protective services for suspected maltreatment.
- Maltreatment has four components:

- Physical abuse includes deliberate behaviors that result in injury, or the serious risk of injury, to a child.
- There is no consensus regarding the definition of child sexual abuse. Berliner argues that child sexual abuse involves any sexual activity with a child in which consent is not or cannot be given.
- Psychological abuse is a pattern of caregiver behavior that conveys to children that they are worthless, flawed, unloved, unwanted, endangered, or only of value in meeting another's needs.
- Neglect occurs when caregivers do not meet children's essential needs and when their negligence harms or threatens children's welfare.

- Child maltreatment can adversely affect children's health and development.

  - Child physical abuse and neglect can take its toll on children's physical health.
  - Children who experience physical abuse or neglect are at risk for developing disruptive behavior problems, mood disorders, and anxiety.
  - The theory of "traumatic sexualization" posits that sexual abuse can contribute to maladaptive sexual development and feelings of (a) betrayal, (b) powerlessness, and (c) stigmatization.

- Evidence-based treatments are available for maltreated children and adolescents.

  - The most common form of treatment given to abused and neglected children is supportive therapy; the goal is to help children cope with feelings and memories associated with their maltreatment and to improve their sense of self and relationships with others.

    - Early in therapy, the clinician uses the therapeutic relationship as a source of support, care, and nurturance; the clinician's primary goal is to establish a sense of trust.
    - Later in therapy, the clinician might help children recognize their feelings and understand how these feelings affect their thoughts and actions.
    - The clinician hopes that the therapeutic relationship can become a corrective emotional experience for the child.

  - Most caregivers who physically abuse or neglect children are offered therapy that involves behavioral parent training. The primary goal of parenting training is to teach parents more effective ways to socialize children.

    - Parent training is efficacious in improving the quality of parent-child interactions.
    - PCIT has been effectively used with caregivers who abused younger children.
    - Runyon and colleagues (2004) have developed a combined CBT program for abusive and neglectful parents and their children.

  - Trauma-focused cognitive-behavioral therapy (TF-CBT) incorporates elements of exposure therapy, cognitive restructuring, parent training, and family support into a single treatment package for sexually abused children.
  - With older children and adolescents who have been sexually abused, therapists often use cognitive restructuring; therapists try to challenge cognitive distortions and help youths find ways to think about their abuse experiences in more objective and realistic ways.

KEY TERMS

amygdala   427

attachment and biobehavioral catch-up (ABC)   446

attachment theory   437

Bucharest Early Intervention Project (BEIP)   440

cognitive appraisal theory   429

coping   429

depersonalization   421

derealization   421

Disinhibited Social Engagement Disorder (DSED)   438

disorganized patterns of attachment   456

dissociative symptoms   421

dopamine transporter (DAT) gene   442

English and Romanian Adoptees (ERA) Study   444

escape or avoidance coping   429

experience-dependent   438

experience-expectant   438

eye movement desensitization
   and reprocessing (EMDR)   433

hippocampus   428

HPA axis   428

internal working models   437

learning theory   455

Maslow's hierarchical theory of human needs   456

omen formation   422

Posttraumatic Stress Disorder (PTSD)   417

precocious sexual knowledge   457

problem-focused coping   429

psychological debriefing   431

psychological first aid   431

Reactive Attachment Disorder (RAD)   435

resilience factors   426

risk factors   426

safety plan   461

self-actualization 456

serotonin transporter gene   442

sexualized behaviors   457

CRITICAL THINKING EXERCISES

1. Image that your friend's teenage son was involved in a serious car accident in which one of his friends died. Although the accident occurred 3 months ago, her son refuses to talk about the accident, despite the fact that it continues to cause him distress and interfere with his daily functioning. Your friend thinks it might be best to let him "put it in the past and move on with his life." How might you respond to her suggestion?

2. What role can parents play in helping their children cope with a major traumatic event?

3. In *DSM-IV*, both RAD and DSED were considered "attachment disorders." Why is this label misleading in the case of DSED?

4. Your sister and her husband recently adopted a 12-month-old boy from South America who was abandoned by his mother shortly after birth. Prior to your adoption, he lived in an orphanage which met his physical needs but had a very high caregiver-to-child ratio and turnover among workers. Although they love him very much, he seems emotionally "detached" and is often very difficult to soothe. What might you say to your sister?

5. Maslow's hierarchy of human needs has been used to explain why abused and neglected children often show emotional and behavioral problems. Are there any weaknesses in Maslow's theory? Why might children show resilience *despite* histories of abuse and neglect?

6. Mark was sexually abused by his stepfather during infancy and early childhood. Now a college student, Mark is worried that he will someday sexually abuse children himself. He visits the counseling center at his university and shares his concerns with the therapist. If you were his therapist, what might you say to Mark?

7. What is the effectiveness of (a) behavioral parent training and (b) cognitive-behavioral family therapy for the treatment of physical abuse and neglect? If you were a therapist, which approach would you use?

EXTEND YOUR LEARNING

Videos, practice tests, flash cards, study guides, and links to online resources for this chapter are available to students online. Teachers also have access to lecture notes, PowerPoint presentations, suggestions for classroom activities, and possible exam questions. Visit: www .sagepub.com/weis2e.

CHAPTER 13

Depressive Disorders and Self-Injury

After reading this chapter, you should be able to answer these questions:

- What is Disruptive Mood Dysregulation Disorder (DMDD)? Why is it considered a depressive disorder?
- What are the causes of DMDD, and what evidence-based treatments are available to children with this disorder and their families?
- What is Major Depressive Disorder (MDD) and Persistent Depressive Disorder? How might children and adolescents show these disorders differently than adults?
- How common is MDD? How does its prevalence, onset, and course depend on age, gender, and children's social-cultural background?
- How do (a) biological, (b) psychological, and (c) interpersonal factors contribute to the development of MDD in children and adolescents?
- What medications and psychosocial treatments are available for youths with MDD? How effective are they?
- What is Non-Suicidal Self-Injury (NSSI), and how common is it among children and adolescents?
- What are the causes of NSSI and what evidence-based treatments are available for youths who show this behavior?

Everyone has felt "sad," "down," or "blue" from time to time. Occasionally, we even experience prolonged episodes of dysphoria, perhaps after losing someone we love or experiencing a major life change. During these times, we may be less motivated to go to school or work, to spend time with friends and family, or to participate in sports or hobbies we typically enjoy. We may even feel tired and sluggish, be irritable or "crabby," and have difficulty eating, sleeping, or concentrating. Mood problems like these are common; however, they are also characteristics of depressive disorders. Determining when simple dysphoria ends and clinically significant depression begins is a major task facing mental health practitioners and the family and friends who refer individuals to their care.

Mood refers to people's pervasive and sustained emotions. Common moods include happiness, depression, irritability, anxiety, or anger. These feelings color people's perceptions of themselves, others, and the world around them and, consequently, influence their thoughts and actions. Because mood is subjective, it is usually assessed by asking people how they feel. In contrast, **affect** refers to a person's immediate emotional responsiveness, inferred by their facial expression and other observable behaviors. In most cases, affect is congruent with mood: Happy people smile and laugh, sad people engage others with downcast eyes, angry people scowl or stare. Sometimes, however, affect is incongruent with mood, such as when a student laughs when discussing worries about an upcoming test or smiles while describing the hurt of her parent's divorce (Sadock & Sadok, 2003).

Mood disorders occur when people experience mood problems that are prolonged and cause distress or impairment in functioning (Image 13.1). There are two broad classes of mood disorders: Depressive Disorders and Bipolar Disorders. **Depressive Disorders** are characterized by predominantly depressed or irritable mood, a lack of interest in people and activities, and problems meeting the demands of everyday life. Sometimes, depressive disorders are called "unipolar" mood disorders, because people predominantly experience moods at the negative (i.e., depressed) end of the mood spectrum. In contrast, **Bipolar Disorders** are characterized by discrete periods of mania or hypomania, that is, feelings of euphoria, energy, and grandiosity. Often (but not always), people with Bipolar Disorders also experience periods of depression; consequently, these disorders are called "bipolar" to reflect mood episodes at both ends of the spectrum.

Depressive disorders in children and adolescents have received serious attention from researchers and clinicians only in the past few decades. A generation ago, many mental

Image 13.1 Depression can be differentiated from sadness by its severity, its duration, and the way it interferes with people's daily activities.

health professionals believed that children were incapable of developing depression. We now know that mood disorders not only exist in children and adolescents, but also they are actually fairly common. Advances in research and clinical practice are leading to new and exciting developments in how we diagnose and treat childhood mood disorders.

In this chapter, we will examine three of the most common depressive disorders experienced by children and adolescents. First, we will learn about Disruptive Mood Dysregulation Disorder (DMDD), a condition new to *DSM-5*. Children with DMDD show persistently irritable mood and frequent tantrums. Usually, DMDD is seen in young school-age children. It is significant because many young children with DMDD eventually develop depression and anxiety. Second, we will discuss Major Depressive Disorder, the most common mood disorder seen in older children and adolescents. Finally, we will examine Persistent Depressive Disorder, a condition characterized by long-standing symptoms of depression.

This chapter will also present information about two phenomena closely associated with depressed mood: suicide and Non-Suicidal Self-Injury. Approximately 2% of older children and adolescents report thoughts of killing themselves, usually prompted by intense dysphoria and feelings of hopelessness (Vander Stoep et al., 2009). Approximately 1500 adolescents in the United States commit suicide each year, making it the third leading cause of death among youths (Shain, 2007). In contrast to suicide, Non-Suicidal Self-Injury refers to repeated and deliberate self-harm without suicidal intent. As many as one fourth of adolescents have engaged in some form of deliberate self-injury making it a common, but often unspoken, problem among youths (Muehlenkamp et al., 2012).

MOOD PROBLEMS IN EARLY CHILDHOOD

What Is Disruptive Mood Dysregulation Disorder (DMDD)?

Disruptive Mood Dysregulation Disorder (DMDD) is a mood disorder characterized by severe and recurrent temper outbursts (Table 13.1, Diagnostic Criteria for Disruptive Mood Disregulation Disorder). Although many children, particularly preschoolers and young school-age children, display temper tantrums, children with DMDD have outbursts that are out of proportion to the situation in terms of their intensity or duration. These outbursts can be verbal or behavioral. For example, many children with DMDD display sudden, intense verbal outbursts that observers describe as "rages" or "fits." They may scream, yell, and cry for excessively long periods of time, sometimes for no apparent reason. Other children with DMDD show intense physical aggression toward people or property. During an outburst, children may destroy toys or household objects (e.g., furniture, television); throw things; hit, slap, or bite others; or otherwise act in a harmful manner. Often, children's outbursts are both verbal and physical. In all cases, these outbursts are inconsistent with the child's developmental level. To be diagnosed with DMDD, temper outbursts must occur, on average, three or more times per week (American Psychiatric Association, 2013).

In addition to temper outbursts, children with DMDD display a persistently irritable or angry mood that is observable by others. Irritability is a feature of many childhood psychological disorders. For example, children with behavior problems (e.g., Oppositional Defiant Disorder), anxiety disorders (e.g., Generalized Anxiety Disorder), and other mood disorders (e.g., Major Depressive Disorder) can show irritability. However, the irritability or anger displayed by children with DMDD is "persistent," that is, it is shown nearly every day, most of the day. Their irritability or anger is not episodic; they have displayed these mood problems for months or years. Parents, teachers, or classmates describe these children as habitually angry, touchy, grouchy, or easily "set off."

Children with DMDD, therefore, show persistently irritable or angry mood overlain with recurrent, severe temper outbursts. *DSM-5* includes several additional diagnostic criteria which specify the duration, setting, and onset of the disorder:

- The outbursts and mood problems must be present for at least 12 months. This criterion highlights the *chronicity* of the problem and differentiates DMDD from mood disorders that are characterized by discrete episodes of dysphoric mood, irritability, or excitement, such as Major Depressive Disorder or Bipolar Disorder.
- The outbursts and mood problems must occur in at least two settings (e.g., home, school, with peers) and must be severe in at least one setting. This criterion highlights the *severity* of the problem and differentiates DMDD from disruptive behavior that might occur only in one setting (e.g., a child tantrums only at home to avoid chores, a child shows anger only at school because of learning difficulties or peer problems).
- The disorder should be first diagnosed only between the ages of 6 and 18 years. Furthermore, symptom *onset* must

Table 13.1   Diagnostic Criteria for Disruptive Mood Disregulation Disorder (DMDD)

A. Severe recurrent temper outbursts manifested verbally (e.g., verbal rages) and/or behaviorally (e.g., physical aggression toward people or property) that are grossly out of proportion in intensity or duration to the situation or provocation.

B. The temper outbursts are inconsistent with developmental level.

C. The temper outbursts occur, on average, three or more times per week.

D. The mood between temper outbursts is persistently irritable or angry most of the day, nearly every day, and is observable by others (e.g., parents, teachers, peers).

E. Criteria A–D have been present for 12 months or more. Throughout that time, the individual has not had a period lasting 3 or more consecutive months without all of the symptoms in criteria A–D.

F. Criteria A and D are present in at least two settings (i.e., at home, at school, with peers) and are severe in at least one of these.

G. The diagnosis should not be made for the first time before age 6 years or after age 18 years.

H. By history or observation, the age of onset of criteria A–E is before age 10 years.

I. There has never been a distinct period lasting more than 1 day during which the full symptom criteria, except duration, for a manic or hypomanic episode have been met.

Note: Developmentally appropriate mood elevation, such as occurs in the context of a highly positive event or its anticipation, should not be considered as a symptom of mania or hypomania.

J. The behaviors do not occur exclusively during an episode of Major Depressive Disorder and are not better explained by another mental disorder.

Note: This diagnosis cannot coexist with Oppositional Defiant Disorder (ODD) or Bipolar Disorder. Individuals who meet criteria for both DMDD and ODD should only be given the diagnosis of DMDD. If the individual has ever experienced a manic or hypomanic episode, the diagnosis of DMDD should not be assigned.

K. The symptoms are not attributable to the physiological effects of a substance or to another medical or neurological condition.

Source: Reprinted with permission from the *Diagnostic and Statistical Manual of Mental Disorders, Fifth Edition* (Copyright 2013). American Psychiatric Association.

occur prior to age 10 years. These criteria highlight the fact that DMDD is a childhood disorder that should not be diagnosed in toddlers or preschoolers. Very young children might show developmentally expected temper outbursts (e.g., tantrums to obtain dessert or a toy) which are not symptoms of DMDD. Furthermore, mood problems or temper outbursts that first emerge in adolescence likely reflect other problems besides DMDD, such as other mood disorders or difficulties adjusting to psychosocial stressors.

It is also important to differentiate developmentally expected temper tantrums from persistent irritability and anger (Figure 13.1). Among preschool-age children, tantrums are fairly common. In one recent survey, 83.7% of young children had a tantrum at home or school at least once in the previous month. However, frequent displays of temper were not normative; only 8.6% of preschoolers had a tantrum every day (Wakschlag et al., 2012). Furthermore, temper displays seem to exist along a continuum, with most young children showing only mild displays of temper. Angry, aggressive, or destructive outbursts are rare, even among preschoolers. For example, many youths lose their temper when angry or frustrated, some have a "short fuse" and yell at

others when upset, but less than 5% have severe tantrums or "meltdowns" that last until they are exhausted, tantrum with nonfamily members (e.g., teachers, babysitters), or hit, kick, or bite others during tantrums. These severe and aggressive-destructive symptoms are not normative and likely merit clinical attention.

Differential Diagnoses

The core features of DMDD, irritability and temper outbursts, are seen in children and adolescents with several other psychiatric disorders. Therefore, differentiating DMDD from these other disorders can be difficult. Three disorders most closely resemble DMDD: Attention-Deficit/Hyperactivity Disorder (ADHD), Oppositional Defiant Disorder (ODD), and Bipolar Disorder.

ADHD

ADHD is a neurodevelopmental disorder characterized by problems with inattention and/or hyperactivity-impulsivity. Children with DMDD often show several features of

Figure 13.1 Temper Loss Falls on a Continuum in Young Children

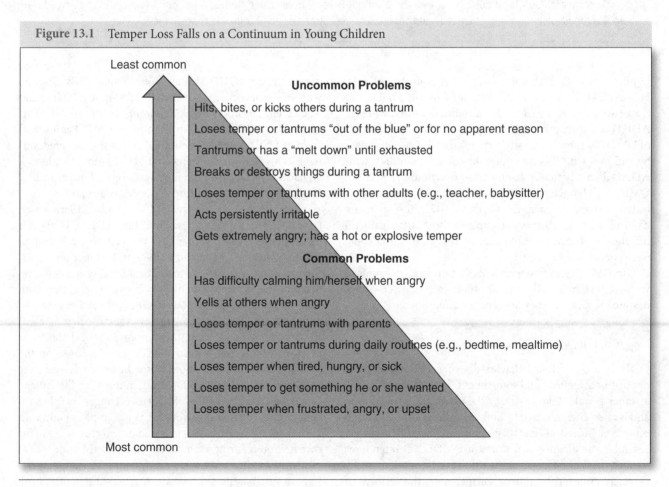

Note: Most young children tantrum occasionally with parents; less than 5% of young children show frequent and severe tantrums marked by aggression or destructiveness.

Source: Based on Wakschlag et al., 2012.

REESE: MOOD PROBLEMS IN EARLY CHILDHOOD

Reese was a 9-year-old African American girl who was referred to our clinic by her pediatrician. Her pediatrician had attempted to treat Reese's hyperactive and disruptive behavior for several years with various medications, to little effect. Reese's mother also participated in a parenting program to help her manage Reese's temper tantrums, but they seemed to be worsening rather than getting better.

Reese had a long-standing history of behavior problems. Her mother said Reese was a "colicky" infant who never seemed to be able to settle down. As a toddler, Reese would frequently throw tantrums, "sass," and disobey. About the same time, Reese began to show high-rate, disruptive behavior that interfered with her ability to pay attention and follow the rules at home and preschool. In kindergarten, she was diagnosed with ADHD and Oppositional Defiant Disorder. The pediatrician began prescribing stimulant medications to help Reese manage her hyperactivity; however, these medications had little effect on her behavior.

By the time Reese was in first grade, she had been expelled from two schools for throwing violent temper tantrums. During one tantrum, she threw a chair at her teacher; during another tantrum, she bit several classmates and stabbed a girl with a pencil. At the time of the interview, Reese was receiving special education for children with "emotional disturbance." Reese continued to throw tantrums multiple times each week, at home and at school. These tantrums usually lasted 30 minutes to two hours. During her "meltdowns," Reese would scream, cry, throw objects, destroy toys and clothing, and finally collapse from exhaustion.

Reese also had a history of mood problems. According to her mother, Reese was "always" irritable, spiteful, and "touchy." In the past 3 years, Reese began to have crying spells in her room, which usually followed her tantrums. On two occasions, her mother overheard Reese crying, "I want to die. Just let me die. Nobody loves me."

Her mother stated, "I just don't know what to do about Reese. I'm so scared for her, and I don't know who to turn to for help. Everybody keeps saying, 'she just needs more discipline,' but I just don't think it's that simple."

hyperactivity and impulsiveness common to ADHD. However, DMDD can be differentiated from ADHD in at least two ways. First, DMDD is a mood disorder, whereas ADHD is a disruptive behavior disorder. A salient feature of DMDD is the persistently angry or irritable mood shown by children with this condition. In contrast, children with ADHD do not typically display anger or irritability. Second, DMDD is characterized by severe, recurrent temper outbursts that are not characteristic of ADHD. Although many children with ADHD behave impulsively, they typically do not show verbal rages or physical aggression toward people or property.

In *DSM-5*, children with DMDD can also be diagnosed with ADHD. In fact, the two disorders frequently co-occur, despite the fact that they are separate conditions.

Oppositional Defiant Disorder

ODD is a disruptive behavior disorder characterized by oppositional, defiant, and sometimes hostile actions directed at other people. Like DMDD, ODD emerges in childhood and is often characterized by both irritable mood and temper outbursts. Indeed, several diagnostic criteria of ODD closely resemble the diagnostic features of DMDD: (a) often loses temper, (b) is often angry or resentful, and (c) is often touchy or easily annoyed by others. Furthermore, the features of ODD and DMDD are persistent; children with these disorders show problems for months or years. ODD and DMDD are highly comorbid. Nearly all children with DMDD also

meet criteria for ODD. However, only about 15% of children with ODD meet criteria for DMDD (*DSM-5* Childhood and Adolescent Disorders Working Group, 2010a, 2010b). This finding has led many experts to think of DMDD as a severe form of ODD in which emotional symptoms are predominant. With *DSM-5*, children cannot be diagnosed with both ODD and DMDD. If a child meets criteria for both disorders, only DMDD, the more serious disorder, is diagnosed.

Despite their similarity, DMDD can be differentiated from ODD in several ways. First, like ADHD, ODD is a disruptive behavior disorder not a mood disorder. Although children with ODD can show anger and temper outbursts, their most salient problems are oppositionality and defiance. Second, the disruptive behavior shown by children with ODD is typically directed toward other people. For example, children with ODD may tantrum or otherwise defy a parent in order to avoid cleaning their rooms. These defiant acts are usually directed toward specific people, based on the child's history of interactions with those people (e.g., the child tantrums only with his mother, not with his father). In contrast, children with DMDD direct anger and physical aggression to people *and* property. For example, a child with DMDD may break his own toys and destroy furniture in his own bedroom during a temper outburst. Furthermore, these tantrums are directed toward many people in many settings (e.g., toward parents at home and teachers at school). Third, DMDD differs from ODD in the duration and severity of children's temper outbursts. Whereas a child with ODD may ignore parents' requests or stubbornly refuse to comply with their commands, a child with DMDD might yell, scream, hit, kick, and destroy objects to express anger. These outbursts may appear for no apparent reason and usually last much longer than expected.

A final, critical difference between ODD and DMDD come from longitudinal studies showing different developmental trajectories for youths with these disorders (Stringaris & Goodman, 2009). For example, researchers have found a relationship between chronically irritable mood in early childhood and internalizing symptoms in later childhood and adolescence. In one study (Drabick & Gadow, 2012), researchers compared children and adolescents who showed anger and/or irritability symptoms and youths with behavior problems without anger or irritability. Compared to youths with behavior problems alone, youths with anger and irritability were at significantly greater risk for developing problems with anxiety and depression later in childhood.

Pediatric Bipolar Disorder

Bipolar Disorder is a serious mood disorder characterized by the presence of discrete manic or hypomanic episodes. These episodes are usually characterized by feelings of euphoria, energy, and grandiosity. However, many children and adolescents with Bipolar Disorder also show periods of irritability and moodiness.

Beginning in the 1990s, clinicians began observing children and adolescents who showed hyperactivity, irritability, and severe temper outbursts that greatly impaired their lives at home, at school, and with friends (Leibenluft, 2011). Because other diagnoses, such as ADHD and ODD, did not seem to capture the severity of their irritability, anger, and disruptive behavior, many of these children were diagnosed with Bipolar Disorder. Some experts asserted that children and young adolescents manifested Bipolar Disorder differently than adults. Whereas adults with Bipolar Disorder typically display discrete episodes of mania and discrete episodes of depression lasting several weeks or months, children with Bipolar Disorder may not show discrete manic and depressive episodes. Instead, these experts argued, children with "pediatric bipolar disorder" may show relatively persistent dysphoria with frequent, severe temper outbursts or "rages." Furthermore, children's mood episodes may last only several hours or days. This "ultra-rapid" cycling of moods, the persistent irritability or anger, and the recurrent temper outbursts were unique features of the disorder in children (Biederman, Faraone, et al., 2004; Biederman, Kwon et al., 2004; Mick et al., 2005).

Because of this expanded definition of pediatric bipolar disorder, the number of children and adolescents diagnosed with the disorder increased dramatically (Leibenluft et al., 2012). In the previous 15 years, the number of outpatient psychiatry visits for children with this diagnosis increased 40-fold (Moreno et al., 2007). Similarly, the number of youths discharged from hospitals with the primary diagnosis of Bipolar Disorder increased from 1.3 to 7.3 per 10,000 patients (Blader & Carlson, 2007).

In fact, recent research indicates that children with chronic irritability and angry outbursts showed the same symptom severity and degree of impairment as children with classic Bipolar Disorder. For example, clinicians' ratings of impairment, number of medications prescribed, and number of previous hospitalizations are similar among children with chronic, non-episodic irritability and classic Bipolar Disorder. In one study, nearly 35% of youths with chronic irritability were previously hospitalized because of their angry outbursts. Like children with classic Bipolar Disorder, children with chronic irritability experience real-world problems that need to be identified and treated (*DSM-5* Childhood and Adolescent Disorders Working Group, 2010a).

However, recent research indicates that children with persistent irritability and angry outbursts do NOT have Bipolar Disorder (Leibenluft, 2011). Researchers at the National Institutes for Mental Health (NIMH) conducted a series of longitudinal studies, examining children with chronic, non-episodic irritability and angry outbursts over time (Leibenluft et al., 2003). These, and other, studies indicated that chronic irritability in early childhood is more closely associated with depression and anxiety than Bipolar Disorder. At least four lines of evidence support this claim:

1. Children and adolescents can show "classic" symptoms of Bipolar Disorder. Youth with classic bipolar symptoms show discrete episodes of mania or hypomania, lasting several days to weeks. These episodes are characterized by many of the same symptoms shown by adults, such as excessive energy, decreased need for sleep, and a lack of goal-directed (i.e., purposeful) behavior. Furthermore, these children often show discrete episodes of depression either before or after the manic or hypomanic episode. Their depressive episodes also resemble those of adult depression: sadness, a lack of interest in activities they used to find enjoyable, and disturbances in eating and sleeping (*DSM-5* Child and Adolescent Disorders Working Group, 2010a).

2. The biological relatives of children with chronic irritability often have problems with anxiety and depression, not Bipolar Disorder. Brotman and colleagues (2007) examined the parents of children with chronic irritability or classic Bipolar Disorder. Whereas the parents of children with classic bipolar symptoms often showed Bipolar Disorder themselves (33%), the parents of children with chronic irritability did not (2.7%).

3. The gender distributions of youths with chronic irritability and classic Bipolar Disorder are different. Roughly equal numbers of males and females develop classic Bipolar Disorder. However, children with chronic irritability in the community (Brotman et al., 2006) and in psychiatric clinics (Stringaris, 2011) are twice as likely to be boys than girls.

4. Children with chronic irritability show different developmental outcomes than youths with classic Bipolar Disorder. Brotman and colleagues (2006) analyzed data from a very large, community-based sample of older children and adolescents, called the Great Smokey Mountains Study. The researchers identified children who showed chronic irritability and angry outbursts at age 10 years and examined their outcomes in early adulthood. Contrary to expectations, these children were 7 times more likely to develop major depression in adulthood than healthy children. In contrast, very few children in the sample developed Bipolar Disorder (0.1%).

A second study, called the Children in the Community Study, also examined a large sample of youths in the general population (Stringaris et al., 2009). However, in this study, youths were studied from the age of 13 years to 33 years. In this study, youths who showed chronic irritability at age 13 years, were at increased risk for developing Generalized Anxiety Disorder, Major Depressive Disorder, and Persistent Depressive Disorder at age 33 years. Chronic irritability did not predict later Bipolar Disorder (Figure 13.2).

A third study, conducted at the NIMH, involved youths referred for psychiatric treatment because of either chronic irritability and angry outbursts or classic Bipolar Disorder (Stringaris et al., 2010). Both groups of youths were studied for 28 months. As expected, most (62%) youths with classic Bipolar Disorder symptoms showed recurrent problems with mania or hypomania during the course of the study. However, only one out of 84 children (1.2%) with chronic irritability later experienced a hypomanic episode.

Because of its close association with depression and anxiety, DMDD is classified as a Depressive Disorder in *DSM-5* (Leibenluft et al., 2012; see text box *DSM-IV → DSM-5* Changes: DMDD: A Diagnostic "Home"). The chronic irritability and angry outbursts of children with DMDD seem qualitatively different than the manic episodes shown by youths with classic Bipolar Disorder (Stringaris, 2011). Clinicians are urged to diagnose children with persistent irritability and angry outbursts with DMDD and to reserve the diagnosis of Bipolar Disorder for only those youths who show classic symptoms of mania (American Psychiatric Association, 2013).

Figure 13.2 Youths With Chronic Irritability and Angry Outbursts Are At-Risk for Anxiety and Depression

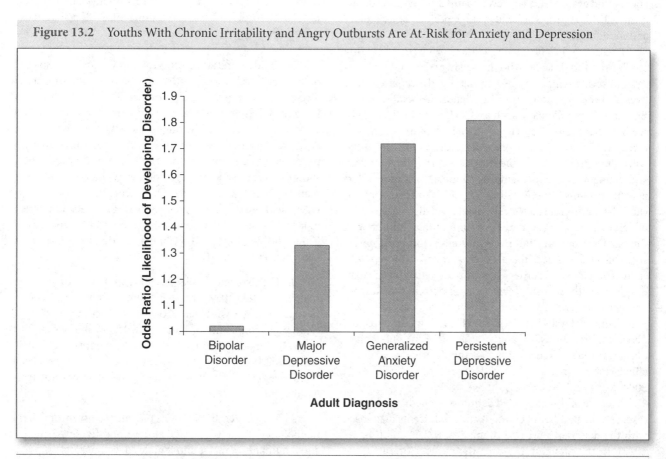

Source: Based on Stringaris and colleagues (2009).

Note: These youths often developed depressive and anxiety disorders in adulthood, but rarely developed Bipolar Disorder.

Epidemiology and Course

Because DMDD is a new diagnosis, we do not yet have a good understanding of its prevalence. However, some data indicate it is fairly common among youths in the general population. For example, Brotman and colleagues (2006) found that 3.2% of youths in the Great Smokey Mountains Study showed chronic irritability and angry outbursts, the essential features of DMDD.

Additional data suggest that irritability and angry outbursts are very common among clinic-referred youths. In one study conducted at Maudsley Hospital in the United Kingdom, approximately one third of all youths admitted for psychiatric treatment showed chronic irritability. In another study conducted in the United States, 47% of children referred to an outpatient clinic had a history of temper outbursts at home or school; 14% displayed "rages" in both locations (Stringaris, 2011). Margulies and colleagues (2012) found that 30.5% of children hospitalized for psychiatric problems met diagnostic criteria for DMDD, based on parental report, and 15.9% met criteria based on observations made by hospital staff.

As indicated above, several other disorders often co-occur with DMDD. The most frequently comorbid conditions are ADHD (86.3%), ODD (84.9%), Generalized Anxiety Disorder (58.4%), and depression (16.4%; Leibenluft et al., 2012).

Very little is known about the course of DMDD. In one study of children hospitalized because of DMDD, parents reported that the onset of their irritable mood and angry outbursts began in infancy or preschool. Nearly all met diagnostic criteria for DMDD before the age of 10 years (Margulies et al., 2012). These problems with irritability and temper appear to be frequent and long-standing. They tend to persist at least through childhood and early adolescence if untreated.

Etiology

Several recent studies indicate that many youths with DMDD have difficulty with attending, processing, and responding to negative emotional stimuli and social experiences. This difficulty may predispose them to instances of anger and aggression in social settings (Leibenluft, 2011).

Youths with DMDD have problems interpreting social cues and the emotional expressions of others. Guyer and colleagues (2007) asked youths to label the emotional expressions shown in photographs of faces. Youths with DMDD made significantly more errors than youths with anxiety and depression or youths without emotional problems. Youths with DMDD were particularly bad at judging negative emotions such as "sad," "fearful," and "angry." In a similar study using fMRI, youths with DMDD showed underactivity of the amygdala during a facial perception task, compared to youths with ADHD, Bipolar Disorder, and healthy controls (Brotman, Rich et al., 2010). This finding is important because the amygdala is believed to play a role in the interpretation and expression of emotions. The capacity to correctly interpret emotions is partially controlled by the amygdala and medial frontal gyrus (MFG). Deficits in processing emotional stimuli can cause youths to misinterpret social cues (e.g., misinterpret a "smile" as a "smirk") and respond inappropriately or aggressively in social situations.

Children with DMDD may also have difficulty regulating negative emotions once they are elicited. Rich and colleagues (2011) asked older children and adolescents with DMDD to perform a simple, computerized task while their brain activity was monitored. Youths were asked to look at two boxes in a visual field and indicate whether a target stimuli appeared in the left-hand or right-hand box. Because the researchers were interested in how these youths processed negative emotions, they rigged the task so that youths often received false negative feedback, even when they gave the correct answer. The researchers were interested in what areas of the brain might be activated during this frustrating task. They also compared the brain activity of youths with DMDD with the brain activity of youths with Bipolar Disorder and healthy controls.

Two important findings emerged (Figure 13.3). First, youths with DMDD reported significantly less happiness and more agitation and negative arousal than comparison youths in the rigged task. Furthermore, youths with DMDD showed significantly greater activation of the right **medial frontal gyrus (MFG)** and slightly greater activation in the left **anterior cingulate cortex (ACC)** than comparison youths in the rigged task. These brain regions are important because they are involved in evaluating and processing negative situations, monitoring one's own emotional state, and selecting an appropriate, effective behavioral response when upset, angry, or frustrated. The ACC, in particular, seems to be important in formulating a course of action in response to negative emotional stimuli. Altogether, these findings indicate that youths with DMDD are more strongly influenced by negative events than other youths. They may become more upset and select less effective and acceptable ways to deal with negative emotions (e.g., screaming, throwing objects, aggression) than their peers.

Deficits in inhibition, face perception, and emotional processing may lead to the development of DMDD in at least three ways. First, youths with DMDD may selectively attend to negative social cues that predispose them to anger, destructiveness, and aggression. For example, in social situations, these youths may attend to the most salient environmental (e.g., others scowling, teasing) or internal (e.g., feeling cheated, embarrassed) cues and minimize or ignore all other aspects of the event. Consequently, they may respond impulsively, selecting an emotional and behavioral response characterized by anger or aggression.

Second, youths with DMDD often show deficits in recognizing and interpreting others' emotions. Furthermore, they may be especially likely to misinterpret negative emotional expressions. Consequently, these youths may misperceive benign social stimuli as hostile or threatening. Consequently, they may respond with anger and aggression.

Third, youths with DMDD show marked problems monitoring their own emotions and behaviors, especially when they are angry, frustrated, or upset. Leibenluft (2011) uses the term "decreased context-sensitive regulation" to describe these deficits. That is, youths with DMDD do not modify or regulate their feelings and actions based on the situation. When their goals or objectives are blocked (e.g., a parent denies a request to stay up late; a coach asks the child to share the ball), these youths are unable to regulate their feelings and adjust their behavior. Instead, youths

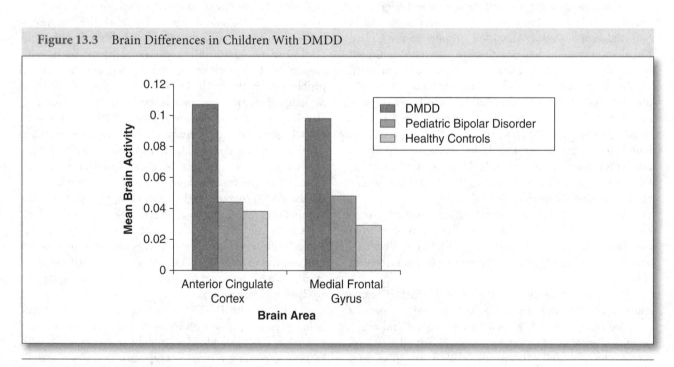

Figure 13.3   Brain Differences in Children With DMDD

Source: Based on Rich and colleagues (2011).

Note: Youths with DMDD show over-activation of the anterior cingulate and medial frontal cortex when performing a frustrating task. These brain regions are important when evaluating and processing negative situations, monitoring one's own emotional state, and selecting an appropriate, effective behavioral response when upset, angry, or frustrated.

with DMDD experience these events as more distressing than most other children.

Treatment

Medication

Very little is known about the effectiveness of medication for DMDD. Because the mood stabilizing medication lithium is effective in adults with Bipolar Disorder, psychiatrists have speculated that it might be useful for children with DMDD. However, when researchers randomly assigned youths with DMDD to receive either lithium or placebo, youths in both conditions failed to show improvement (Dickstein et al., 2009). In contrast, the antipsychotic medication risperidone (Risperdal) has been shown to be effective in reducing irritability and depressed mood in older children and young adolescents with chronic irritability and anger (Krieger et al., 2011). However, the study demonstrating its effectiveness did not include a placebo control group for comparison (Figure 13.4). Furthermore, side effects such as anxiety and excessive sleepiness, affected approximately one third of children in the study.

Currently, most physicians recommend treating DMDD by using a combination of medications depending on the youth's symptom presentation (Jairam et al., 2012). For youths with DMDD alone, many physicians recommend antidepressant medications to alleviate irritability and dysphoria. For youths with both DMDD and ADHD, stimulant medication may also be used to reduce hyperactivity and impulsivity.

Behavioral Interventions

Because DMDD is a new disorder, our knowledge of effective treatments is limited. However, several cognitive-behavioral interventions have been developed for youths with chronic irritability and temper outbursts that may be useful in treating DMDD. These treatments have typically involved one or more of the following three components: (a) parent training, to help parents manage their children's disruptive behavior; (b) cognitive-behavioral interventions for youths, to help them manage negative emotions and avoid angry outbursts; and (c) family therapy, to improve the quality of parent-child interactions.

Because many youths with DMDD tend to show problems with both ADHD and oppositional-defiant behavior, researchers initially attempted to treat these children with traditional parent training. Recall that parent training involves teaching caregivers to use contingency management (e.g., positive reinforcement for desired behavior, punishment for problem behavior) to increase compliance and decrease defiance at home. Researchers soon discovered that traditional parent training was not particularly effective for youths with DMDD, because it did not address these children's most salient problems: irritability and anger.

Researchers also attempted to treat youths with chronic irritability using therapeutic summer treatment programs, like the kind developed for children with ADHD. Recall that these summer treatment programs consisted of psychoeducation, social skills training, and extracurricular activities (e.g., sports) in which children

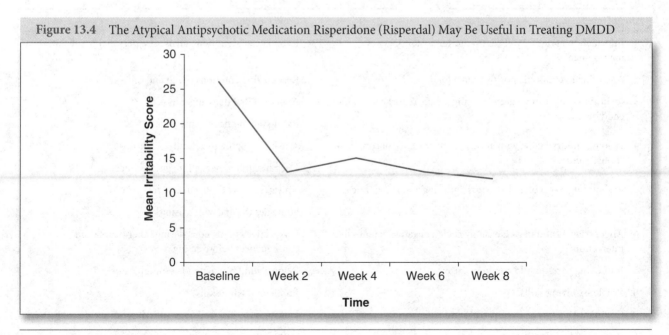

Figure 13.4 The Atypical Antipsychotic Medication Risperidone (Risperdal) May Be Useful in Treating DMDD

Source: Based on Krieger and colleagues (2011).

Note: However, the study showing its effectiveness did not include a control group. We do not know if children might have improved even without the medication over time.

received positive reinforcement for appropriate behavior and received negative punishment (e.g., response cost) for inappropriate behavior. Although these therapeutic camps are effective for youths with ADHD, most youths with DMDD continued to show symptoms during this intervention (Waxmonsky, Pelham et al., 2008).

Comprehensive Family Treatment

To address the irritability and angry outbursts of children with DMDD, some clinicians have used cognitive-behavioral interventions designed to improve anger management, social skills, and social problem solving. Recall that youths with DMDD often show problems with impulsivity, interpreting others' emotions, and regulating their own emotions when their goals are blocked. These youths may selectively attend to negative events (e.g., focus on others laughing at them or teasing), interpret benign events as hostile or threatening (e.g., perceive a joke as a mean comment), and select responses to these events based on their immediate, negative emotional reactions rather than their long-term interests (e.g., hit someone rather than walk away). Cognitive-behavioral interventions target these deficits in attention, emotion-recognition and regulation, and social problem solving by teaching youths anger management and social skills.

Waxmonsky, Wymbs, and colleagues (2012) have developed a comprehensive treatment package for youths with DMDD and their parents. Their treatment includes education about DMDD, traditional behavior parent training and cognitive-behavioral interventions for youths. However, all sessions are run concurrently with groups of parents and children. While groups of children learn and practice anger management and social skills in one room, groups of parents learn similar child management techniques in an adjacent room. Concurrent sessions ensure that parents learn the same skills as their children, so that they can encourage and reinforce these skills at home. Previous research has also shown that parent sessions are helpful in increasing caregivers' knowledge of their children's mood problems and improving their beliefs and attitudes toward treatment. Parents also appreciate support and encouragement from each other during the parent sessions (Mendenhall et al., 2009).

The treatment package consists of nine parent and child sessions, each lasting 105 minutes (Table 13.2). Parent sessions initially introduce caregivers to principles of contingency management. They stress the importance of attending to and praising appropriate behaviors, ignoring inappropriate behaviors, giving effective instructions, and using time out or response cost to decrease inappropriate actions. Later, parents learn strategies to respond to children's outbursts. For example, parents learn how to recognize when their child is in a dysphoric mood, how to avoid triggers that might elicit an angry outburst, and how to cope with their own negative emotions that might exacerbate their children's tantrums. Still other sessions emphasize the need for consistency in caregiving. Parents discuss the value of regulating

Table 13.2   Psychosocial Treatment for DMDD

Parent Group	Child Group
1. Information about DMDD; introduction to contingency management	Icebreakers; identifying goals for a personal "fix it" kit
2. Attending to children's positive behavior	Recognizing emotions in self and others
3. Identifying anger in your child; using a daily report card to monitor child behavior	Anger I: What does anger look like?
	Rating the intensity of my anger
4. Helping children cope with anger; the importance of consistent "house rules"	Anger II: Coping to get calm
	Deep breathing, relaxation, guided imagery
5. Responding to problem behaviors; ignoring and using time out	Anger III: How to stay in control
	Strategies to cope with teasing
6. Anger triggers and negative family cycles; negative parent-child interactions	Perspective taking, considering other people and consequences before acting
7. Improving parent-child communication	Being a good listener and communicator
8. Problem-solving skills	Problem-solving skills
9. Coping with depression in parents and kids	How to recognize and cope with depression
10. Review and graduation ceremony	Putting it together and awards ceremony

Source: Based on Waxmonsky et al. (2012).

their children's sleep-wake cycles and daily activities. Skills are taught using a combination of videotaped vignettes of parent-child interactions and discussion.

Child sessions mirror the parent sessions. During sessions, children's behavior is monitored by therapists and appropriate behavior is recognized and reinforced using a point system. Initial sessions focus on helping children accurately identify emotions in themselves and others. Subsequent sessions focus chiefly on anger: what it feels like, how to calm oneself when angry, and how to find nonaggressive solutions to social problems when one is angry. Children learn to recognize situations, thoughts, and feelings that might elicit an angry outburst and cope with these potential "triggers" in effective ways. They build a "tool kit" to cope with problem situations. Skills are taught using a combination of semi-structured physical activities, videotaped vignettes, and discussion.

An initial evaluation of the comprehensive treatment program indicated that families found it helpful in reducing children's disruptive behavior, alleviating depression, and improving the quality of parent-child interactions (Waxmonsky et al., 2012). Most children showed a marked reduction in disruptive behavior and angry outbursts and approximately one half of youths also showed improvements in depressive symptoms.

Sleep Enhancement

Children with DMDD often experience difficulty sleeping. In one large, epidemiological study, the Cologne Sleep Study, researchers identified youths who showed both severe mood problems and temper outbursts (Legenbauer et al., 2012). These youths reported significant problems getting to sleep, staying asleep, and sleeping in a restful manner. We do not yet know if sleep problems cause irritability and anger, whether irritability has a deleterious effect on sleep, or whether a third variable, such as ADHD, might predispose youths to both angry outbursts and sleep problems.

Despite the limited data, several experts have argued that youths with DMDD should be assessed for sleep problems. If sleep difficulties are reported by parents, these youths may benefit from behavioral interventions to improve their **sleep hygiene**. Some basic interventions include establishing a consistent sleep-wake cycle; creating a relaxing routine prior to bedtime (e.g., washing face, brushing teeth, putting on pajamas, reading a book); and avoiding excessive stimulation that might delay sleep onset (e.g., drinking caffeinated beverages, watching television prior to bed). Clinicians hope that improving sleep hygiene and restfulness will lead to subsequent improvements in youths' ability to regulate their mood and behavior during the day.

Other experts have observed that youths with DMDD often have disrupted sleep-wake cycles (Heiler et al., 2011). Specifically, these youths often go to bed late, experience poor sleep quality, and have difficulty rising in the morning. To regulate these cycles and improve mood, these experts recommend chronotherapy. **Chronotherapy** is the deliberate, controlled presentation of light in order to regulate the sleep-wake cycle, establish better sleep quality, and improve mood (Image 13.2).

Image 13.2 Special high-intensity lamps can be used to help regulate the sleep-wake cycles of children with DMDD.

Chronotherapy takes advantage of the fact that the human body responds physiologically to changes in the light-dark cycle. Specifically, changes in lightness and darkness are detected by the suprachiasmatic nucleus (SCN), which then regulates two hormones important to restfulness: melatonin and cortisol. Controlled studies have shown that when individuals are exposed to light immediately after waking, the light suppresses melatonin production and decreases cortisol levels, thereby, advancing the sleep-wake cycle and producing greater arousal and alertness over time. Chronotherapy, combined with improved sleep hygiene, is an effective component of treatment for depression, Bipolar Disorder, and some types of anxiety. Experts hope it might be useful for youths with DMDD as well (Heiler et al., 2011).

DEPRESSION AND SUICIDE IN CHILDREN AND ADOLESCENTS
What Is Major Depressive Disorder?

To be diagnosed with **Major Depressive Disorder (MDD)**, a person must experience a "major depressive episode," that is, a discrete period of dysphoria that lasts for at least 2 weeks. Specifically, people experiencing a major depressive episode must show five out of a possible nine symptoms (Table 13.3, Diagnostic Criteria for Major Depressive Disorder). At least one of these symptoms must be either (a) depressed mood or (b) a diminished interest or pleasure in most activities.

1. *Depressed mood.* People with depression often feel sad, blue, or "down." Most people report these feelings directly. Other people show signs of sadness and emotional pain in their facial expressions and nonverbal behavior. Still others, especially children, express dysphoria through somatic complaints, such as headaches and upset stomach. Children and adolescents may show a predominantly irritable mood rather than a more traditional "depressed" mood. For example, children with depression may appear angry, "touchy," easily upset, or annoyed. Parents and other adults may describe these children as crabby or cranky.

2. *Diminished interest or pleasure in most activities.* Most people with depression, regardless of age, also show a marked loss of interest or pleasure in activities they used to enjoy. Children with depression might drop out of sports or clubs. Adolescents with depression might avoid parties and other social gatherings. This loss of interest is often referred to as *anhedonia*—literally, a loss of pleasure.

3. *Significant change in appetite or weight.* Many people with depression show a marked decrease in appetite. These individuals often report that they "don't feel hungry," and they may need to be reminded and encouraged to eat. Their decreased appetite often leads to weight loss. In adults, a loss of more than 5% body weight in one month indicates significant weight reduction. In children and adolescents, failure to make age-expected weight gains meets this criterion. Some people with depression show increased appetite and weight gain. Increased appetite and weight gain are atypical and are more often seen in adults than in youths.

4. *Significant change in sleep.* The most common sleep problem among people with depression is **insomnia**. Typically, individuals with depression will wake in the middle of the night or during the early morning hours and be unable to return to sleep. Insomnia is one of the best predictors of mood problems in late childhood and early adolescence. In contrast, **hypersomnia** (i.e., sleeping too much) is more common among adults than among youths (van Lang, Ferdinand, & Verhulst, 2007).

5. *Psychomotor agitation or retardation.* **Psychomotor agitation** refers to a noticeable increase in motor activity. Children and adolescents with psychomotor agitation may appear restless, have problems sitting still, pace or wander about the room, or fidget with their hands or clothing. These behaviors seem to have no purpose, and they reflect an increase in children's usual activity level. Agitation must be severe enough to be observable by others. In some cases, individuals with depression show **psychomotor retardation**, that is, a general slowness or sluggishness in movement. Psychomotor retardation is more common in adults than in children and adolescents.

6. *Loss of energy or fatigue.* Most people with depression experience a loss of energy, tiredness, or fatigue. Adults and adolescents may report that even trivial daily tasks seem to require an enormous amount of energy. An adolescent with depression might have great difficulty getting ready for school or completing a short homework assignment. Children are less likely to report a loss of energy or fatigue than are adolescents and adults. Instead, they may appear unusually resistant or oppositional when asked to perform household chores and participate in activities with family members.

7. *Feelings of worthlessness or guilt.* Many people with depression are preoccupied by feelings of worthlessness or excessive feelings of guilt. Typically, these individuals ruminate on personal shortcomings or failures and overlook their strengths and successes. For example, a child with depression might get into frequent arguments with parents because of her irritable mood. Then, she might feel terribly guilty for having these arguments, believing that she is not worthy of her parents' love and attention. Similarly, an adolescent with depression might fail to complete homework assignments because he believes that he is unintelligent, or he might avoid sports because he believes that he is not athletic.

8. *Thought and concentration problems.* People with depression often report problems with attention and concentration. They may be easily distracted, have problems thinking, or report difficulty making decisions. People with depression often show clouded judgment or lapses in memory.

Table 13.3 Diagnostic Criteria for Major Depressive Disorder

A. Five (or more) of the following symptoms have been present during the same 2-week period and represent a change from previous functioning: at least one of the symptoms is either (1) depressed mood or (2) loss of interest or pleasure.

1. Depressed mood most of the day, nearly every day, as indicated by either subjective report (e.g., feels sad, empty, hopeless) or observation made by others (e.g., appears tearful). *Note:* In children and adolescents, can be irritable mood.

2. Marked diminished interest or pleasure in all, or almost all, activities most of the day, nearly every day (as indicated by either subjective account or observation).

3. Significant weight loss when not dieting or weight gain (e.g., a change of more than 5% of body weight in a month), or decrease or increase in appetite nearly every day. *Note:* In children, consider failure to make expected weight gain.

4. Insomnia or hypersomnia nearly every day.

5. Psychomotor agitation or retardation nearly every day (observable by others, not merely subjective feelings of restlessness or being slowed down).

6. Fatigue or loss of energy nearly every day.

7. Feelings of worthlessness or excessive or inappropriate guilt nearly every day (not merely self-reproach or guilt about being sick).

8. Diminished ability to think or concentrate, or indecisiveness, nearly every day (either by subjective account or as observed by others).

9. Recurrent thoughts of death (not just fear of dying), recurrent suicidal ideation without a specific plan, or a suicide attempt or a specific plan for committing suicide.

B. The symptoms cause clinically significant distress or impairment in social, occupational, or other important areas of functioning.

C. The episode is not attributable to the physiological effects of a substance or to another medical condition.

   Note: Criteria A–C represent a major depressive episode.

D. The disturbance is not better explained by Schizophrenia or a psychotic disorder.[1]

E. There has never been a manic episode or hypomanic episode.

Specify course:

Single Episode: Only one major depressive episode.

Recurrent: Two or more major depressive episodes, with at least two months between episodes in which the individual does not meet criteria.

Specify current severity:

Mild: Few, if any, symptoms in excess of those required to make the diagnosis are present, the intensity of the symptoms is manageable, and the symptoms result in minor impairment.

Moderate: The number of symptoms, intensity of symptoms, and/or functional impairment are between those specified for "mild" and "severe."

Severe: The number of symptoms is substantially in excess of that required to make the diagnosis, the intensity of the symptoms is seriously distressing and unmanageable, and the symptoms markedly interfere with functioning.

Source: Reprinted with permission from the *Diagnostic and Statistical Manual of Mental Disorders, Fifth Edition* (Copyright 2013). American Psychiatric Association.

[1]Schizophrenia is presented in Chapter 14.

For example, adolescents with depression may have problems performing complex mental activities at school, such as writing a science report or performing a difficult musical arrangement. Children and adolescents with depression show increased difficulty in completing homework assignments and may experience a sudden drop in grades.

HANNAH MISUNDERSTOOD

Hannah was a 10-year-old girl who was sent to the emergency department of our hospital following a suicide attempt. The previous evening, Hannah had a fight with her mother, who had asked Hannah to clean her room. After 15 minutes of shouting, Hannah locked herself in the bathroom and swallowed an entire bottle of Tylenol capsules.

The pediatric psychologist at the hospital, Dr. Loebach, interviewed Hannah and her mother. According to her mother, Hannah had shown a gradual deterioration in her mood over the past several months. She had been increasingly irritable and moody. Her mother said, "Hannah just flies off the handle for no apparent reason. I'll ask her to set the table or to turn off the TV and she'll scream, swear, or throw a tantrum. Then she'll run into her room and cry." Her mother was most concerned that Hannah might hurt herself. "Twice, I've had to stop her from banging her head against the wall. She kept crying, 'I want to die. I wish I was dead.'"

Hannah also showed problems with her behavior. In recent months, her appetite greatly decreased, and she had problems going to sleep. Hannah used to have many friends at school, but in recent months she stopped playing with peers. She dropped out of the Girl Scouts and the 4-H club, two activities that she formerly enjoyed. "She used to be the perfect child—getting good grades, asking to help around the house, trying to do everything to please us. Now, she deliberately tries to upset us."

Hannah's family life was stressful. Her mother had a history of depression and had attempted suicide on two occasions. Although she took antidepressant medication, she still admitted to periods of intense sadness and loneliness. Hannah's father, a photographer, had long-standing problems with alcohol dependence. According to her mother, "Hannah thinks the world of her dad, and why shouldn't she? He's really fun when he's drunk. Hannah hates me because I'm the one who makes her do her homework, pick up her room, and eat her vegetables."

Dr. Loebach attempted to interview Hannah. "I feel terrible," said Hannah, her mouth covered with charcoal residue. Dr. Loebach explained, "They needed to put that stuff in your stomach to get all the Tylenol out of your system." Hannah said, "I didn't want to kill myself; I just wanted to show my mom that I'm serious. When I say 'no' I mean 'no.' She just doesn't understand how much my life sucks. No one understands."

9. *Recurrent thoughts of death or suicide.* Thoughts of death and suicide are common among people with depression, including children and adolescents. We commonly think of adolescents and adults as committing suicide, but prepubescent children also attempt and complete suicide.

Once a clinician determines whether a child or adolescent meets criteria for a major depressive episode, he or she assesses whether the child has ever experienced a depressive episode in the past. If the child's current depressive episode is the only period of time in which she experienced depression, she would be diagnosed with **Major Depressive Disorder, Single Episode.** However, if the child had had a history of depression in the past, she would be diagnosed with **Major Depressive Disorder, Recurrent.** It is important to differentiate between single and recurrent depression because the latter is associated with poorer prognosis and is often more resistant to treatment.

Finally, the clinician determines the severity of the individual's most recent symptoms. Severity can be described as mild, moderate, or severe. Severity is based on the number of depressive symptoms the person experiences, the intensity of symptoms and distress they cause, and the degree to which symptoms impair functioning (American Psychiatric Association, 2013).

What Is Persistent Depressive Disorder?

In adults, **Persistent Depressive Disorder** is defined by the presence of chronically depressed mood, occurring most days for at least 2 years. In children and adolescents, Persistent Depressive Disorder is characterized by chronically depressed or irritable mood that lasts at least one year (Table 13.4, Diagnostic Criteria for Persistent Depressive Disorder).

Children with Persistent Depressive Disorder are often described as moody, sluggish, down, or cranky. Adolescents with Persistent Depressive Disorder often regard themselves as uninteresting, unlikable, and ineffective. For example, an adolescent with Persistent Depressive Disorder might not believe that classmates want to spend time with her or select her to be part of a group activity. Another adolescent with the disorder might doubt his ability to make a sports team or to gain admission to college. Youths with Persistent Depressive Disorder are also prone to self-criticism. They might dwell upon their shortcomings, belittle themselves in front of others, and constantly doubt themselves and their abilities. They usually show very poor self-esteem and express pessimism and hopelessness about the future.

Table 13.4 Diagnostic Criteria for Persistent Depressive Disorder

A. Depressed mood for most of the day, for more days than not, as indicated by either subjective account or observation by others, for at least 2 years. *Note:* In children and adolescents, mood can be irritable and duration must be at least one year.

B. Presence, while depressed, of two (or more) of the following:

　　1. Poor appetite or overeating.

　　2. Insomnia or hypersomnia.

　　3. Low energy or fatigue.

　　4. Low self-esteem.

　　5. Poor concentration or difficulty making decisions.

　　6. Feelings of hopelessness.

C. During the 2-year period (1 year in children and adolescents) of the disturbance, the individual has never been without the symptoms in criterion A and B for more than 2 months at a time.

D. Criteria for Major Depressive Disorder may be continuously present for 2 years.

E. There has never been a manic episode or a hypomanic episode, and criteria have never been met for Cyclothymic Disorder.[1]

F. The disturbance is not better explained by Schizophrenia or a psychotic disorder.[1]

G. The symptoms are not attributable to the physiological effects of a substance or another medical condition.

H. The symptoms cause clinically significant distress or impairment in social, occupational, or other important areas of functioning.

Specify if:

With pure dysthymic syndrome: Full criteria for a major depressive episode have not been met in the preceding two years.

With persistent major depressive episode: Full criteria for a major depressive episode have been met through the preceding 2-year period.

With intermittent major depressive episodes, with current episode: Full criteria for a major depressive episode are currently met, but there have been periods in the preceding 2 years with symptoms below threshold for a full major depressive episode.

With intermittent major depressive episodes, without current episode: Full criteria for a major depressive episode are not currently met, but there has been one or more major depressive episodes in the preceding 2 years.

Source: Reprinted with permission from the *Diagnostic and Statistical Manual of Mental Disorders, Fifth Edition* (Copyright 2013). American Psychiatric Association.

[1]Bipolar Disorders (including Cyclothymic Disorder) and Schizophrenia are presented in Chapter 14.

Persistent Depressive Disorder is a long-lasting condition. If we think of MDD as a severe bout of the flu, we might liken most cases of Persistent Depressive Disorder to chronic problems with allergies. These symptoms are not as severe, but they last a long time, and they affect nearly all aspects of the person's life. The symptoms of Persistent Depressive Disorder occur for so long that many people with the disorder do not even realize that they have mood problems. Some adults and adolescents with Persistent Depressive Disorder see these symptoms as part of their personality, claiming, "I've always been this way" or "That's just how I am."

Persistent Depressive Disorder can be differentiated from MDD by its onset, duration, severity, and (to some extent) its symptoms. Persistent Depressive Disorder usually begins gradually. In contrast, the onset of MDD is usually rapid. By definition, Persistent Depressive Disorder is a long-term condition, whereas MDD usually lasts for only a few months. Although MDD and Persistent Depressive Disorder share some of the same symptoms, symptoms of MDD are more severe. Furthermore, certain symptoms like anhedonia and suicidal ideation are characteristic of MDD but not Persistent Depressive Disorder.

To diagnose a child or adolescent with Persistent Depressive Disorder, the clinician first determines whether the youth has experienced depressed mood for at least one year and has at least two of the other required symptoms, such as sleep and appetite disturbance. Then, the clinician specifies the type of Persistent Depressive Disorder the child shows. Specification is based on whether the child has ever had a major depressive episode in the previous 2 years (American Psychiatric Association, 2013).

Some youths meet criteria for Persistent Depressive Disorder but have never experienced a major depressive episode. Youths with this condition would be diagnosed with Persistent Depressive Disorder with Pure Dysthymic Syndrome. Clinicians often refer to the presence of long-term dysphoria without major depression as **dysthymia**, which comes from the Greek words meaning "bad-mind." People with pure dysthymia feel chronically dysphoric and often cannot conceptualize an existence in which they feel happy or satisfied with life.

Other youths meet criteria for both Persistent Depressive Disorder and have experienced a major depressive episode. If the duration of the major depressive episode lasts for one year or more, the child or adolescent is diagnosed with Persistent Depressive Disorder with Persistent Major Depressive Episode. Clinicians often refer to this condition as **chronic depression**. It can be extremely distressing and debilitating to children and families.

Finally, some youths meet criteria for Persistent Depressive Disorder and have experienced a major depressive episode during the course of the disorder. For example, an adolescent might be chronically dysphoric for several months, experience a severe depressive episode for 4 months, and return to his previous state of persistent dysphoria. Youths with these symptoms would be diagnosed with Persistent Depressive Disorder with Intermittent Major Depressive Episode. Clinicians sometimes refer to the presence of a depressive episode on top of persistent dysphoria as "double depression"—a condition that can be especially resistant to treatment.

Associated Problems

Anxiety

Anxiety disorders are highly comorbid with depression. Approximately 40% to 50% of adolescents with depression have an anxiety disorder (Kovacs & Devlin, 1998; Lewinsohn, Hops, Roberts, Seeley, & Andrews, 1993). The most common anxiety disorder among children with depression is Social Anxiety Disorder (Treatment for Adolescents With Depression Study Team [TADS], 2005). Both depression and Social Anxiety Disorder can lead to social withdrawal and avoidance. Youths with both disorders show greater impairment in interpersonal functioning than youths with either disorder alone.

Disruptive Behavior

Childhood depression and conduct problems frequently co-occur; furthermore, the presence of both mood problems and conduct disturbance is associated with high levels

---

CASE STUDY

A CASE OF BAD GENES

Elizabeth (Eppy) Andersen was a 15-year-old girl who was referred to our clinic by her mother. According to Mrs. Andersen, Eppy had been experiencing long-term problems with depressed mood and irritability. "For a while now," her mother explained, "Eppy's been withdrawn and moody. Sometimes, she just shuts herself in her room as soon as she gets home from school, and we don't see her again until the next morning. At other times, she just mopes around the house, never wanting to do anything with anyone. When we ask her what's wrong, she just snaps at us, 'Nothing! Can't you just leave me alone?'"

Eppy had to deal with many stressors in her childhood. Mrs. Andersen had a history of MDD. Eppy's father abandoned Eppy and her mother when Eppy was in the second grade. Eppy had long-term academic problems. She earned mostly Cs and Ds, even though she studied very hard.

During the course of the interview, Eppy admitted to persistently feeling "not quite right." She admitted to "snapping" at family members and reported that her moodiness, tendency toward social isolation, and low self-esteem had caused her to lose friends. Eppy added, "My friends will invite me over to cheer me up. But I always just blow them off or say something stupid to make them mad at me. Afterward I feel terrible. I wonder, 'Why was I so mean to them?' But, you know, I'd just rather be by myself." Eppy admitted to feeling depressed and tired most of the time. She napped each afternoon, despite sleeping nine or ten hours every evening. She often felt tired and "run down," as if she never had enough energy to get things done.

Eppy denied suicidal thoughts, but she showed extreme pessimism about the future. "Nothing I do is ever good enough," she explained. "At home, my mom's always nagging me. At school, I work hard and never get anywhere. My friends don't care. I'll probably just end up like my mom—a basket case . . . or worse, like my dad." Her therapist asked, "How do you know that?" Eppy responded, "I just know. It's in the genes."

---

of impairment (Angold et al., 1999). The comorbidity of depression and ADHD ranges from 12% to 45% (Biederman et al., 1999; Kennard, Ginsburg, Feeny, Sweeney, & Zagurski, 2005; TADS, 2005). Youths with both disorders show problems with attention and concentration and are easily distractible. They may also have difficulty performing homework assignments and earning high grades in school.

Approximately 23% of depressed youths show ODD or CD (TADS, 2005). When conduct problems and depression co-occur, conduct problems usually precede depression (Biederman, Milberger, & Faraone, 1995; Rohde, Lewinsohn, & Seeley, 1991). Capaldi (1992) examined conduct problems and depression in boys from sixth through eighth grades. Approximately 31.5% of boys with conduct problems alone in sixth grade showed comorbid depression by eighth grade. In contrast, only 12.9% of boys with depression alone in sixth grade showed conduct problems by eighth grade. Most experts believe conduct problems lead to conflict with family members and peers. These interpersonal problems, in turn, place children at risk for social isolation, low self-worth, and depression.

Little and Garber (2005) provided support for the notion that peer rejection explains the relationship between conduct problems and depression. In a study of sixth graders, the researchers found that conduct problems predicted interpersonal problems. These interpersonal problems, in turn, predicted depression one year later. However, interpersonal stressors predicted depression only for children who showed high levels of interpersonal orientation (i.e., a strong need for connectedness with others). The authors concluded that children who place great value on interpersonal relationships, yet experience social problems because of their disruptive behavior, may be particularly prone to depression.

Substance Use

Some studies have shown a relationship between adolescent depression and substance use problems (Henry, Feehan, McGee, Stanton, Moffitt, & Silva, 1993). The strength of this relationship seems to depend on the age and gender of the adolescent. Older adolescents with depression are more likely to show substance use problems than younger adolescents and children. Furthermore, boys with depression are somewhat more likely than girls to show substance use problems (Maag & Irvin, 2005). In one study, approximately 33% of boys with depression and 16% of girls with depression also showed signs of problematic alcohol use (Windle & Davies, 1999).

Why are youths with depression at increased risk for substance use problems? In some cases, particularly among older adolescents, depression precedes alcohol use (Costello, Erkanli, Federman, & Angold, 1999). These adolescents may use alcohol and other drugs to cope with psychological distress, a practice sometimes called **self-medication**. Alcohol consumption is negatively reinforced by a reduction in depressed mood (Khantzian, 1995).

However, most research suggests that a third variable, peer rejection, predicts both adolescents' likelihood of depression and their likelihood of using alcohol and other drugs. Some children, especially those with disruptive behavior problems, experience conflict with family members, rejection by classmates, and low academic achievement. Peer rejection, in particular, can cause these adolescents to become depressed. At the same time, peer rejection can prompt many of these youths to associate with deviant peers who encourage them to use alcohol and other drugs. These youths, therefore, develop both mood problems and substance use problems as a consequence of peer rejection (S. M. King et al., 2004).

Suicide

Children and adolescents with depression are at increased risk for suicide. Suicide is the third leading cause of death among adolescents (Shain, 2007). Suicide kills more children and adolescents than cancer, heart disease, AIDS, birth defects, stroke, and chronic lung disease combined. Approximately 4,000 youths die by suicide annually (World Health Organization, 2001).

Suicidal thoughts and behaviors are alarmingly common among adolescents. In one very large epidemiological study, 28.6% of adolescents reported feeling sad or hopeless almost every day for at least 2 weeks, 16.5% had planned a suicide attempt, 8.5% had attempted suicide, and 2.9% had made an attempt that required hospitalization (Centers for Disease Control and Prevention, 2004). Suicide attempts are twice as common in girls than boys; however, boys are much more likely to complete suicide than girls. The greater lethality of suicide attempts among boys is partially due to their methods of injury. Boys are more likely than girls to use firearms; in contrast, girls are more likely than boys to ingest pills (American Academy of Child and Adolescent Psychiatry, 2001). Approximately 1 in every 100 suicide attempts results in death (Pomerantz, 2005).

Mental health professionals should always assess a youth's suicide risk. The best way to assess a child or adolescents' suicidal thoughts is to ask him or her directly. The American Academy of Pediatrics (Shain, 2007) recommends that professionals ask direct questions such as the following:

- Have you ever thought about killing yourself or wished you were dead?
- Have you ever done anything on purpose to hurt or kill yourself?
- If you were to kill yourself now, how would you do it?

Youths' responses to these (and other follow-up) questions can help determine their risk for suicide. Contrary to popular belief, asking an adolescent about suicide does not increase his suicidal ideations (Gould et al., 2005).

Although predicting suicide is impossible, three important risk factors have been identified: (a) does the adolescent express a desire to die, (b) does the adolescent have a plan to kill himself, and (c) is the plan feasible? Transient thoughts of one's own death are fairly common among children and adolescents; they usually indicate low risk by themselves. For example, it is fairly common for a child to ask, "I wonder if Mom and Dad would miss me if I caught a terrible disease and died?" Recurrent thoughts of suicide, with no specific suicide plan, merit greater concern. For example, a child might admit, "I've thought about killing myself, to make everyone feel bad about being mean to me, but I don't know how I'd do it."

Even more risky are youngsters who report recurrent thoughts of suicide with specific suicide plans. For example, an adolescent with depression might state, "I've thought about killing myself a few times, by shooting myself or taking pills, but I'm not sure whether I could go through with it." Of greatest concern are children and adolescents who show high motivation to kill themselves and have a well-thought-out suicide plan. For example, an adolescent might want to die, know that a combination of certain medications and alcohol can be lethal, and have access to these substances.

Researchers have identified several other risk factors for suicide among adolescents (Shain, 2007). These risks include abuse or neglect, high family conflict, social or environmental stressors (e.g., peer rejection, romantic problems), and mental health problems. More than 90% of adolescents who complete suicide have at least one psychiatric disorder at the time of their death. Disorders that cause severe emotional suffering and pain, such as MDD and PTSD, place adolescents at particular risk for suicide (Figure 13.5). Although depression is the best predictor of suicide, it is not a reliable predictor. Most youths who are depressed never attempt suicide, and some youths who attempt suicide do not experience depression (Wild et al., 2004).

Epidemiology

Prevalence

The prevalence of depression varies by age (Brent & Weersing, 2010). Most young children show few problems with mood; only 1% to 2% experience MDD (P. Cohen et al., 1993; Fleming & Offord, 1990; Keenan, Hipwell, Duax, Stouthamer-Loeber, & Loeber, 2004). In childhood, boys and girls are approximately equally likely to show depression (Costello, Pine, Hammen, John, Plotsky, & Weissman, 2002; Hankin et al., 1998). In adolescence, the prevalence of depression increases dramatically. At any given time, 3% to 7% of adolescents are depressed (Costello et al., 2002; Hankin et al., 1998). Furthermore, as many as 20% of youths may experience MDD at some time during adolescence (Cole et al., 2002; Garber, Keiley, & Martin, 2002; Lewinsohn, Rohde, & Seeley, 1998).

The dramatic increase in the prevalence of depression from late childhood to early adolescence is largely due to a corresponding increase in the number of adolescent girls with depression. Indeed, adolescent girls are twice as likely

Figure 13.5 Risk Factors for Adolescent Suicide

Family Risks	Parental mental health problems
	History of child abuse or neglect
	Parent-child conflict
Social & Environmental Risks	Peer rejection, social isolation
	Romantic problems
	Difficulty in school
	Immediate psychosocial stressor
Mental Health Risks	Major Depressive Disorder
	Posttraumatic Stress Disorder
	Bipolar Disorder
	Substance Use Disorder

Source: Based on Shain and the American Academy of Pediatrics (Shain, 2007).

Note: It is impossible to predict suicide; however, a greater number of risk factors should prompt parents and professionals to ask adolescents about suicidal thoughts and plans.

as adolescent boys to experience a depressive disorder. By age 18, as many as 28% of girls and 14% of boys have experienced either MDD or Dysthymic Disorder. The prevalence of child and adolescent depression *has not* increased over the past several years (Costello, Erkanli, & Angold, 2006).

Gender Differences

Depression is not only more common among adolescent girls, it may also be more impairing. Compared to adolescent boys with depression, girls with depression show a greater number of symptoms, more severe symptoms, and greater likelihood of self-harm. Initial depressive episodes last longer for adolescent girls than boys and are more likely to lead to long-term mood problems (Kovacs, 1997; McCauley, Myers, Mitchell, Calderon, Schloredt, & Treder, 1993).

Keenan and Hipwell (2005) developed a theoretical model to explain gender differences in adolescent depression. According to their model, girls who are at risk for depression have three personality characteristics that predispose them to mood problems.

First, some girls display *excessive empathy*; that is, they are unusually sensitive to the emotional well-being of others and may assume unwarranted responsibility for others' negative emotions. Consequently, girls may try to solve other people's problems and experience excessive guilt and helplessness when they are unable to alleviate others' distress.

Second, some girls show *excessive compliance*; that is, they have a strong need to meet others' needs and to gain others' approval. Often, they sacrifice their own well-being and autonomy in order to please others. Excessive compliance can be problematic in two ways. First, depression can occur when girls comply with others' requests in situations when noncompliance might be more appropriate (e.g., a girl giving in to a boy's demands for sex). Second, depression can occur when girls repeatedly remain passive in interpersonal situations to meet the social expectations of others (e.g., a girl reluctant to speak up in class). Excessive compliance can stifle the development of autonomy and individuality and contribute to low self-esteem and depression.

Third, some girls show *problems with emotion regulation*; that is, they have difficulty modifying and altering negative moods. Keenan and Hipwell (2005) argue that some girls have a limited number of coping strategies to deal with negative emotions. When these strategies are ineffective, they can become either excessively distressed or overcontrolled. Rather than displaying negative emotions in open and adaptive ways, these girls hide their feelings and develop mood problems.

A combination of biological and environmental factors can lead to excessive empathy, overcompliance, and emotional overcontrol in girls. Indeed, young girls are more likely than boys to display higher levels of all three risk factors (Keenan & Hipwell, 2005). These three characteristics limit girls' social and emotional competencies, especially their self-confidence, assertiveness, and emotional expressiveness. When they enter adolescence, they may be unprepared to cope with the biological and psychosocial stressors of puberty (Zahn-Waxler, 2000; Zahn-Waxler, Cole, & Barrett, 1991). Consequently, they may show rates of depression much higher than do boys.

Age Differences

Depression in Childhood. Depression is fairly rare in prepubescent childhood; most young children show few symptoms. Depressive symptoms increase considerably after puberty, with the increase occurring earlier and more dramatically in girls than boys (Birmaher et al., 1996; Lewinsohn et al., 1998). Symptoms tend to be at their greatest during late adolescence, after which they usually decline in a linear fashion into early adulthood (Wight, Sepulveda, & Aneshensel, 2004).

Depressive symptoms also show moderate to high stability over time. If left untreated, the duration of depressive episodes ranges from 8 to 13 months in children and 3 to 9 months in adolescents. Approximately 90% of children and 50% to 90% of adolescents recover from these episodes. Relapse is fairly common (Birmaher, Arbelaez, & Brent, 2002; Birmaher, Williamson et al., 2004). Approximately 60% of depressed youths have another depressive episode within 2 years after recovery, whereas 72% have another depressive episode within 5 years of recovery (Simons, Rohde, Kennard, & Robins, 2005).

Post, Weiss, Leverich, George, Frye, and Ketter (1996) developed the **kindling hypothesis** to explain the tendency of depressed individuals to have recurrent depressive episodes. According to this hypothesis, early depressive episodes sensitize individuals to stressful life events and depression. After multiple depressive episodes, less severe stressors can trigger major depressive symptoms. Support for the kindling hypothesis has been found in adults, but it remains untested in children.

Depression in Adolescence. In order to investigate the course of depression, researchers have conducted longitudinal studies assessing children's mood symptoms from childhood through adolescence. Based on this longitudinal research, researchers have identified four distinct patterns of mood functioning among youths (Brendgen et al., 2005; Figure 13.6).

First, 50% of children and adolescents show very low levels of depression across childhood and adolescence. These youngsters are at low risk for developing mood problems. Boys are the overwhelming majority of children in this group.

Second, 30% of youths show consistent but moderate levels of depressive symptoms throughout childhood and adolescence. These youths experience mild dysphoria, but their mood problems usually do not interfere with day-to-day activities. Boys outnumber girls in this group as well.

Third, 10% of youths show chronically high levels of depression, beginning in late childhood and continuing through adolescence. These youngsters are disproportionately girls with histories of early parent-child conflict and difficulties with emotion regulation. These girls often show difficult temperaments that interfere with their social and emotional functioning. They are at risk for long-term problems with mood and behavior.

The remaining 10% of youths show low levels of depressive symptoms in childhood but dramatically higher levels of depression in adolescence. These youngsters also tend to be girls with difficult temperaments and histories of parent-child conflict. However, they frequently experience peer rejection and social alienation during late childhood or early adolescence. It is likely that peer rejection and other psychosocial stressors of puberty exacerbate social and emotional problems in this group of children.

Taken together, these findings indicate that approximately 20% of youths will have mood problems during childhood or adolescence. This is consistent with other longitudinal research that suggests that 20% to 25% of youths show moderate to long-term mood problems (Fombonne et al., 2001). Indeed, youths with depression are 4 times more likely to experience mood disorders in adulthood compared to their nondepressed peers (Harrington, Fudge, Rutter, Pickles, & Hill, 1990).

Etiology

Genetics

MDD in children and adolescents is partially determined by genetics. Research involving adults with MDD has shown

Figure 13.6   Developmental Pathways for Child and Adolescent Mood Disorders

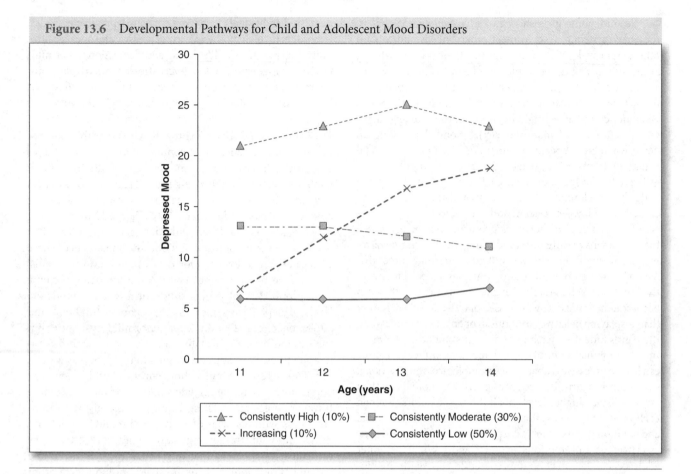

Source: Based on Brendgen et al. (2005).

Note: Most children show either chronically low (50%) or chronically moderate (30%) levels of depressive symptoms and are not at risk for mood disorders. Approximately 10% of youths show chronically high levels of depression through childhood and adolescence. An additional 10% show low levels of depression in childhood but high levels in adolescence.

a strong genetic component to the disorder. For example, some studies involving adult monozygotic (MZ) twins reared together have yielded concordance rates as high as 70% to 85%. Furthermore, adult MZ twins reared apart show approximately 67% concordance for depression. In contrast, dizygotic twins reared together show only about 19% concordance for the disorder. Taken together, these findings indicate that genetic factors place individuals at considerable risk for depression. Having a parent with depression increases one's risk of developing the disorder threefold (Reinecke & Simons, 2005).

Unfortunately, genetic studies of children and adolescents with depression have been plagued by methodological problems. Most studies have relied on extremely small sample sizes. Also, studies have often used different methods to identify depression in youths, making these studies difficult to compare to each other. Furthermore, researchers have often failed to separate the effects of genes from the effects of the environment in their studies of depressed youths. For example, the fact that depression runs in families provides evidence for both genetic and shared environmental causes. Future research that more carefully teases apart the relative

effects of genes and environment on children's depression is sorely needed (Reinecke & Simons, 2005).

Neurotransmitters

It is likely that genetic factors contribute to depression by affecting children's neurotransmitter functioning. The **monoamine hypothesis** for depression asserts that two neurotransmitters, in particular, play roles in depressive disorders: serotonin and norepinephrine. These neurotransmitters are monoamines, hence the name of the hypothesis. According to the theory, depression is associated with dysregulation in one or both of these neurotransmitters.

Evidence for the monoamine hypothesis comes primarily from research with adults. The hypothesis is supported by the fact that antidepressant medications, which regulate serotonin and/or norepinephrine, can alleviate depression in adults. Adolescents treated with certain antidepressant medications can also show changes in serotonin functioning; furthermore, the magnitude of these changes is directly associated with the degree of adolescents' symptom reduction (Axelson et al., 2005).

Other evidence for the monoamine hypothesis comes from molecular genetics research. Eley and colleagues (2004) examined genes responsible for serotonergic functioning. They discovered a number of genes that predicted depression in adolescent girls. Furthermore, some of the genes predicted depression only when girls also experienced adverse life events. The authors argued that genes responsible for serotonergic activity play roles in the emergence of depression in youths. However, these genes may require certain adverse environmental conditions to produce their harmful effects.

Temperament

A second mechanism by which genes might contribute to the development of mood problems is through temperament. Recall that temperament refers to the physiological, emotional, and behavioral responses a child typically displays when she encounters environmental stimuli (Rothbart & Bates, 1998). Temperament is largely genetically determined; however, it can be modified by children's early experiences.

Temperament can contribute to the development of mood disorders in at least three ways (Compas, Connor-Smith, & Jaser, 2004). First, difficult temperament can directly contribute to children's depressive symptoms by increasing children's negative emotions. Children with difficult temperament (e.g., excessive irritability, moodiness, difficulty soothing) often overreact to negative life events and have difficulty regulating their emotions. They may simply experience more frequent and intense levels of negative affect than other children their age.

Second, difficult temperament in childhood may elicit negative reactions from caregivers and peers. For example, irritability in early childhood might lead caregivers to adopt more angry, hostile, and coercive parenting tactics. These adverse parenting behaviors can cause parent-child conflict, behavior problems, low self-worth, and depression.

Third, children with difficult temperaments may show greater problems coping with early childhood stressors. These coping problems, in turn, can contribute to mood problems. For example, children with difficult temperaments may become overwhelmed when they encounter stressful life events. When faced with a psychosocial stressor, these children might show high levels of anger, irritability, or moodiness. Alternatively, other children with difficult temperaments may avoid coping with the stressor altogether by emotionally shutting down, withdrawing, or developing anxiety and depression.

HPA Dysregulation

Early childhood stressors can contribute to later mood problems by affecting the body's stress response system. The body's response to stress is regulated by the **hypothalamus-pituitary-adrenal (HPA) axis**. When the child encounters a psychosocial stressor, brain regions that process and regulate emotions (especially the amygdala and hippocampus) activate the HPA axis. When activated, components of the HPA axis release a series of hormones. First, the hypothalamus releases corticotropin-releasing hormone (CRH). CRH is detected by the pituitary gland, which, in turn, secretes a second hormone, adrenocorticotropin-releasing hormone (ACTH). ACTH, in turn, triggers the release of cortisol from the adrenal cortex. **Cortisol** is the body's main stress hormone; it activates the sympathetic nervous system. Cortisol initiates fight-or-flight behavior and increases feelings of alertness and apprehension.

In typically developing individuals, cortisol flows through the bloodstream and is detected by the hypothalamus, pituitary, and hippocampus. These brain regions shut off production of cortisol, returning the body to a more relaxed state. However, adults with depression often show chronically high levels of cortisol. Furthermore, they often have difficulties stopping cortisol production once it starts. For example, if researchers give adults with depression a synthetic form of cortisol (i.e., dexamethasone), many adults do not show the normal "shutting off" of cortisol production. In fact, as many as 60% of depressed adults do not pass this **dexamethasone suppression test (DST)** and show chronically high levels of cortisol, even when not experiencing an immediate stressor. This dysregulation of the HPA axis is believed to partially explain their depressed mood (Shea, Walsh, MacMillan, & Steiner, 2005).

Depressed youths may also show dysregulation of the HPA axis. First, many depressed youths show elevated cortisol activity, even while at rest (Goodyer, Herbert, Tamplin, & Altham, 2000; Goodyer, Park, & Herbert, 2001). Second, some depressed adolescents show structural abnormalities in parts of the HPA axis. Compared to healthy adolescents, depressed adolescents show smaller amygdalae and hippocampi (MacMaster & Kusumakar, 2004; Rosso et al., 2005) and enlarged pituitary (MacMaster & Kusumakar, 2004).

Stress and Coping

Stressful Life Events. Stressful life events are associated with child and adolescent depression. Several studies have shown that major life stressors predict the onset of MDD (Burton, Stice, & Seeley, 2004; Goodyer, Herbert, & Tamplin, 2000; Lewinsohn, Allen, Gotlib, & Seeley, 1999; Luby, Belden, & Spitznagel, 2006). Furthermore, depressed children and adolescents report more frequent and serious stressful life events than their nondepressed peers (Sandberg, McGuinness, Hillary, & Rutter, 1998; Williamson, Birmaher et al., 1998). In fact, children's risk of depression is directly associated with the number of stressful life events that they encounter (Monroe, Rhode, Seeley, & Lewinsohn, 1999; Steinhausen & Metzke, 2000).

The timing of stressful life events may also be important. Events that occur during adolescence seem to be especially problematic. Perhaps stressful life events that occur during adolescence magnify the stress adolescents experience during this developmental period. Stressful events that occur during or shortly after puberty may have especially adverse effects for girls (Ge, Coger, & Elder, 2001). Again, the combination of puberty and the stressful event might be too taxing on girls' coping skills.

Although stressful life events are associated with depression in youths, they are not robust predictors of depression (see text box *DSM-IV → DSM-5 Changes: When Does Bereavement End and Depression Begin?*). On average, stressful life events explain only 2% of the variance in adolescents' depressive symptoms (Garber et al., 2002; Lewinsohn, Roberts et al., 1994). Furthermore, the importance of stressful life events in triggering depressive episodes may diminish over time. Lewinsohn and colleagues (1999) found that adolescents' first depressive episodes were strongly associated with a negative life event. However, later depressive episodes were less closely connected to psychosocial stressors.

Although stressful life events and depression are correlated, stressful life events may not necessarily *cause* adolescents to become depressed. Waaktaar, Borge, Fundingsrud, Christie, and Torgersen (2004) assessed adolescents' depressive symptoms and stressful life events at two times, approximately one year apart. Consistent with previous research, they found a moderate correlation between depressive symptoms and life stressors. Contrary to expectations, however, the researchers discovered that early symptoms of depression predicted *later* stressful life events.

The researchers suggested that the traditional view—that stressful events cause depression—is too simplistic. Instead, the relationship between stressful events and depression may be bidirectional. Of course, stressful events can contribute to depression. However, depressed youths may also elicit stressful events from the environment (Hammen, 1991). For example, children who are rejected by peers may experience depression. Depression, in turn, can lead to social avoidance and increased problems in social interactions.

DSM-IV → DSM-5 CHANGES

WHEN DOES BEREAVEMENT END AND DEPRESSION BEGIN?

A major psychosocial stressor for children is the loss of a parent or other close family member. Approximately 30% of children and adolescents who experience the death of a loved one meet diagnostic criteria for MDD within one year (Brent & Weersing, 2010).

In *DSM-IV*, clinicians were instructed to avoid diagnosing MDD until 2 months after the loved one's death. The developers of *DSM-IV* considered the first 2 months to be a period of "bereavement." However, the "bereavement exclusion" rule in *DSM-IV* implied that normal grief lasts only 2 months. In fact, most individuals grieve for 1 to 2 years, especially when the loved one was a parent, close family member, or friend. Furthermore, the bereavement exclusion may have caused some clinicians to overlook people who had MDD following the death of a loved one. When MDD occurs during the grief process, it is often characterized by greater emotional pain and somatic complaints, greater impairment in daily functioning, and greater likelihood of suicidal thoughts than MDD alone.

Consequently, *DSM-5* no longer contains the bereavement exclusion; individuals can be diagnosed with MDD after the death of a loved one. *DSM-5* also offers five ways to differentiate developmentally expected bereavement from MDD (American Psychiatric Association, 2013):

- In grief, the predominant feelings are typically emptiness and loss; in MDD, people feel depressed mood and the inability to experience happiness or pleasure.
- In grief, painful feelings come in waves (i.e., the pangs of grief). Usually, negative feelings lessen over time. In MDD, thoughts and feelings are almost constantly negative.
- The grieving individual is often preoccupied by thoughts and memories of the deceased. In contrast, people with MDD are usually preoccupied by self-critical or pessimistic thoughts about themselves or their future.
- In grief, the person still maintains self-esteem; in MDD, the individual typically feels worthless and experiences self-loathing.
- When grieving individuals think about death, they often think about the deceased loved one and the possibility of "joining" him or her. In contrast, people with MDD often think about death because of feelings of worthlessness or an inability to cope with emotional pain.

Bereavement also varies as a function of a person's age, relationship to the deceased, and socio-cultural background. The death of a loved one can precipitate MDD, as can other major life events. Differentiating grief from MDD requires both clinical sensitivity and scientific knowledge.

Coping

Although many youths experience stressful life events, most do not show depression. Stressful events, alone, are often insufficient to explain the emergence of depression. Hammen (1992) has suggested that the effects of stress on children's emotional functioning depend partly on the way children attempt to cope with stress. Stressful life events are not harmful per se; rather, it is the child's ability to cope with these events that determines whether or not he will become depressed (Murberg & Bru, 2005).

Children can cope with stress in two ways (Li, DiGiuseppe, & Froh, 2006). First, children can use **active coping**. Active coping involves taking steps to address the source of psychosocial stress or, at least, to reduce its harmful effects. For example, a child who is bullied at school might actively cope with this stressor by confronting the perpetrator or asking a teacher for help. Most studies have shown that active coping strategies protect children from depression (Vickers et al., 2003).

Alternatively, children can use **avoidance coping** to deal with stress. Children use avoidance coping when they physically or emotionally distance themselves from the stressor. One way to cope with stress, but avoid the stressor, is to act out or show other disruptive behavior problems. For example, a child who is bullied at school might act out in class. Unfortunately, disruptive coping is associated with peer rejection and decreased self-worth (Coie, Dodge, & Kupersmidt, 1990). A second form of avoidance coping is to withdraw from the stress-evoking situation. For example, a child who is bullied might refuse to attend school. Social withdrawal, too, is associated with depression (Li et al., 2006).

A final form of avoidance coping is to mentally disengage from the stressful situation. Children can distract themselves from stressful events by thinking other, more pleasant thoughts or engaging in pleasurable activities. Rather than ruminate about being bullied at school, a child might take his mind off the situation by playing video games or reading a book. In general, mental disengagement has benefits and drawbacks. On the one hand, distraction stops children from dwelling on negative events. On the other hand, excessive use of distraction can interfere with children's use of active coping (Nolen-Hoeksema, 2000).

Cognition

Contemporary models of child and adolescent depression emphasize the role of cognition in the emergence and maintenance of depressive symptoms (Reinecke & Simons, 2005). According to cognitive models, early stressful experiences adversely affect the way children think about themselves and their surroundings. These experiences also color the attributions they make about other people's behavior and the way they interpret events. Cognitions, in turn, can affect children's moods (Mezulis, Hyde, & Abramson, 2006; Spence & Reinecke, 2003).

Beck's Cognitive Theory of Depression

Aaron Beck (1967, 1976) developed a model of depression that focuses primarily on people's cognitions. According to Beck, thoughts, feelings, and actions are intricately connected. The way people think influences the way they feel and act. Beck posited that individuals who are depressed show two characteristic ways of thinking that predispose them to negative emotions and maladaptive behaviors: cognitive biases and cognitive distortions.

First, people with depression often show **cognitive biases**. A bias is a cognitive shift toward looking at the world in a certain way. People with depression show a negative cognitive bias in their view of themselves, the world, and the future. Although these people encounter pleasant and unpleasant experiences every day, they tend to selectively attend to negative experiences while ignoring or dismissing positive aspects about themselves and their surroundings. For example, an adolescent with depression might dwell upon a low grade that she receives on a particular math exam rather than on her otherwise good performance in math class.

Second, people with depression show **cognitive distortions**. A cognitive distortion involves adjusting one's perceptions or interpretations of the world in a manner that is inconsistent with reality (Table 13.5). Individuals with depression interpret events in an excessively negative light, causing them to feel helpless and hopeless (Brozina & Abela, 2006). For example, after receiving a low grade on a math exam, an adolescent with depression might believe that she is "stupid" and that she will "never get into college." These distortions are untrue; one low math grade is not sufficient evidence that someone is "stupid." Furthermore, one low grade will probably not affect one's chances of gaining college admission. These beliefs reflect distortions of reality that confirm the adolescent's view that she is worthless, that the world is cruel, and that the future is bleak.

According to Beck (1967, 1976), cognitive distortions are especially salient in people's **negative automatic thoughts** about themselves, the world, and the future. Automatic thoughts are transient self-statements or mental images that pop into people's minds immediately after they experience a psychosocial stressor. For example, after missing a game-winning free throw, a child might think to himself, "I'm such a loser" or "Nothing I do ever goes right." Alternatively, he might have a mental image of his friends or family members teasing or ostracizing him for missing the basket. These transient negative thoughts color people's interpretation of events and can contribute to feelings of depression.

Depressed children and adolescents show both cognitive biases and distortions. Furthermore, the number of cognitive biases and distortions shown by youths is associated with the severity of their depressive symptoms (Tems, Stewart, Skinner, Hughes, & Emslie, 1993). Depressed youths typically report more negative automatic thoughts than their emotionally healthy peers (Figure 13.7). Furthermore, depressed youths tend to dwell upon their negative

Table 13.5   Examples of Cognitive Distortions That May Contribute to Depression

Distortion	Explanation/Examples
Catastrophizing	Overestimating the chances of disaster; expecting something terrible to happen
	• *What if I go to the party and no one asks me to dance?*
	• *What if I mess up on the presentation and everyone thinks I'm stupid?*
Overgeneralization	Abstracting a general rule (or coming to a general conclusion) based on a single isolated incident
	• *After breaking up with a boyfriend: I'll never find anyone as good as him again.*
	• *After failing a test: I'm just not very smart*
Dichotomous thinking	Categorizing experiences at the extremes (either all good or all bad)
	• *Unless I make the honor roll, I'm a dummy.*
	• *If I can't get an A in the class, I just won't even try.*
Mind reading	Making assumptions about other's thoughts, feelings, or behaviors without evidence
	• *I can tell they hate my clothes.*
	• *They're probably thinking, "Look how dumb he is."*
Personalization	Taking personal responsibility for something that is not one's fault
	• *Bill walked by me in the hallway and didn't say hello. I must have said something to make him mad.*
	• *He didn't ask me out; it must have been my weight.*
Absolute thinking	Beliefs that involve "must," "should," or "have to"
	• *I must get into college, otherwise I'm a complete failure.*
	• *My parents have to let me go camping this weekend, otherwise I'll just die.*

Source: Based on J. S. Beck et al. (2005) and A. T. Beck and Weishaar (2005).

thoughts and personal failures (Burwell & Shirk, 2007; Wilkinson & Goodyer, 2006). The negative automatic thoughts reported by depressed youths differ from the negative automatic thoughts reported by youths with other disorders. For example, depressed youths frequently report beliefs characterized by personal loss and failure, whereas anxious youths are more likely to report automatic cognitions about threat and personal vulnerability (Schniering & Rapee, 2004a, 2004b).

Reciprocal Vulnerability

Cognitive theorists argue that ways of thinking, especially negative cognitive biases and distortions, place individuals at risk for depression. However, critics of the traditional cognitive approach argue that depressive symptoms themselves can lead to an increase in negative beliefs and automatic thoughts (Coyne & Whiffen, 1995). Negative beliefs can be a consequence, in addition to a cause, of depression.

Using a large sample of sixth- and seventh-grade girls, Shahar, Blatt, Zuroff, Kuperminc, and Leadbeater (2004) tested the idea that negative self-statements and depressed mood are reciprocally related. By observing adolescents over a one-year period, the research team found that negative automatic thoughts led to increased feelings of depression. This finding supported Beck's (1967, 1976) cognitive theory. However, the researchers also found that feelings of depression led to an increase in self-criticism and other negative automatic thoughts. This finding supported the notion that depression can also affect cognition. In another study involving a large sample of adolescents, depressive symptoms predicted the emergence of cognitive distortions *better* than cognitive distortions predicted later depressive symptoms (Stewart, Kennard et al., 2004).

Taken together, these results suggest that negative beliefs and depressive symptoms reciprocally affect the emergence of depression in adolescents. Shahar and colleagues (2004) suggest that negative automatic thoughts (especially self-critical statements) and depressive symptoms contribute to a vicious cycle, especially in girls. Girls who set unrealistically high standards and criticize themselves when these standards are not met set themselves up for depression. Their depressed mood, in turn, may interfere with their social and academic functioning, causing them to experience more failure and, consequently, more self-criticism. The reciprocal effects of self-criticism and depression may account for the chronic nature of depression in some adolescent girls (Rice, Leever, Noggle, & Lapsley, 2007).

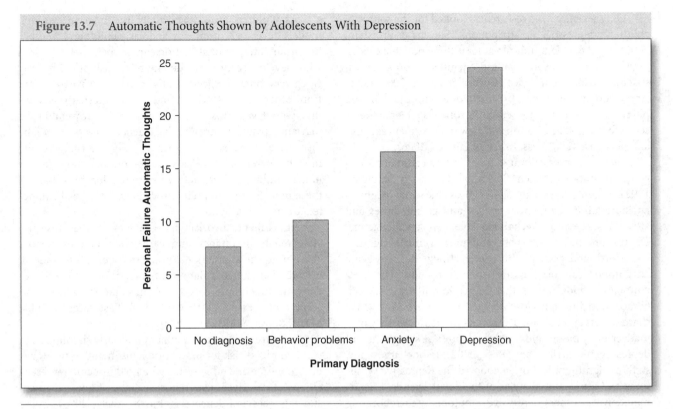

Figure 13.7 Automatic Thoughts Shown by Adolescents With Depression

Source: From Schniering and Rapee (2004b). Used with permission.

Note: Automatic thoughts dealing with personal failure (e.g., "I'm a loser. Nothing I do ever goes as planned") are associated with childhood depression.

Learned Helplessness

Martin Seligman (1975) hypothesized that feelings of hopelessness and despair contribute to the emergence of depression. In a now-famous study, Seligman and colleagues attempted to condition fear in dogs by restraining them and administering a mild electrical shock. The researchers expected that when the restraints were removed, the dogs would actively avoid the shock by jumping away. However, to their surprise, the previously restrained dogs passively succumbed to shocks even when they were given the opportunity to escape or avoid them. Seligman believed the dogs learned to helplessly succumb to the shocks. Since the dogs had no control over the shocks, they were unmotivated to avoid the shocks later when given the opportunity.

Seligman proposed that learned helplessness might explain depression in humans (Hiroto & Seligman, 1975). He suggested that people who are exposed to stressful but apparently uncontrollable life events would become passive and depressed. They would not actively cope with stressors but, instead, succumb to feelings of pain and despair.

Reformulated Learned Helplessness Model

Later, Abramson, Seligman, and Teasdale (1978) adjusted the learned helplessness theory of depression to explain *how* negative life events can contribute to depressed mood.

They suggested that the **attributions** we make about success and failure in our lives affect our mood. Specifically, depressed individuals attribute *negative* events to internal, stable, and global factors. For example, if an adolescent boy asks a girl for a date and she turns him down, he might attribute his rejection to internal, stable, and global factors. He might reason that he was rejected because he is ugly (internal), he will always be ugly (stable), and no one, no matter how desperate, will ever want to go out with someone as ugly as him (global). This **depressogenic attributional style** can lead to feelings of helplessness, hopelessness, and depression.

Depressed people also tend to attribute *positive* life events to external, unstable, and specific causes. For example, if a child with depression gets an A on an exam, she might attribute her success to the fact that the teacher is an easy grader (external), that she was lucky (unstable), or that she just happened to study the information that was on the exam (specific). These attributions can contribute to her negative mood and low self-regard.

Most research has shown a relationship between depressogenic attributional styles and depressed mood in adults (Sweeney, Anderson, & Bailey, 1986). Similarly, depressed children and adolescents show pessimistic attributions for negative events (Gladstone & Kaslow, 1995; Joiner & Wagner, 1995).

Only recently have researchers looked for the source of children's depressogenic attributions (Stevens & Prinstein, 2005). Available data indicate at least three possible causes. First, negative life events can cause youths to adopt depressogenic attributional styles (Garber & Flynn, 2001; Gibb, Abramson, & Alloy, 2004). For example, children who are physically or sexually abused can erroneously blame themselves for their victimization and view maltreatment as stable and pervasive (Harkness, Bruce, & Lumley, 2006).

Second, depressed mood, itself, might cause depressogenic attributions (Nolen-Hoeksema, Girgus, & Seligman, 1992). When adolescents feel helpless, they may begin to attribute failure to internal, stable, and global causes and attribute success to external, unstable, and specific factors. Depression, therefore, may beget depressogenic thoughts.

Third, and perhaps most interestingly, depressogenic attributions can be acquired though friends. The **peer contagion model** posits that depression, like a cold, can be acquired through close contact with peers. As friends share secrets and talk about stressors in their lives, they may inadvertently model and reinforce depressive symptoms and depressogenic attributions (Rose, 2002). In one large study, sixth to eighth graders often adopted the depressive symptoms and attributional styles of their best friends. Friends maintain each others' depressive symptoms by corroborating depressogenic attributions or avoiding other positive social experiences (Stevens & Prinstein, 2005).

Interactions With Parents

Children's relationship with parents can also affect their likelihood of developing depression. Although a number of parenting variables can place youths at risk for depression or buffer them from the deleterious effects of psychosocial stressors, three of the most important variables are (a) the quality of parent-child attachment, (b) parents' social-emotional health, and (c) conflict in the home (MacPhee & Andrews, 2006).

Parent-Child Attachment

According to the principles of attachment theory, children construct mental representations or **internal working models** of caregivers during the first few years of life (Bowlby, 1969, 1980). These mental representations are based on the quality of parent-child interactions during infancy and childhood. Children whose parents provide sensitive and responsive care during their first few years of life come to expect accessibility and responsiveness from others. Parent-child dyads that develop relationships based on the expectancy of care and sensitivity are said to have developed *secure* attachment relationships. In contrast, children whose parents provide intrusive or unresponsive care come to expect that others will be inaccessible or unavailable in times of stress or crisis. These children are said to have developed *insecure* attachment relationships with their parents.

As children grow, they apply the internal working models developed in infancy and early childhood to other important interpersonal relationships in their lives. Children who develop secure attachment relationships with early caregivers come to expect sensitive and responsive treatment from other adults, teachers, and peers. Alternatively, children who develop insecure relationships in early childhood may anticipate that other adults, teachers, and peers will be dismissive, unavailable, or uncaring. The internal working models, therefore, serve as social-emotional templates for understanding and predicting future relationships. Indeed, these models seem to predict social and emotional competence across childhood.

Attachment theorists have suggested that insecure attachments in infancy and early childhood predispose children to social-emotional problems later in life. Indeed, research has shown a significant correlation between insecure attachment and mood problems among children and adolescents (Essau, 2004; Graham & Easterbrooks, 2000; Muris, Mayer, & Meesters, 2000).

Insecure attachment in infancy and early childhood can place youths at risk for mood problems in one of two ways. First, children and adolescents who hold insecure representations of caregivers also report feelings of low self-worth and low self-confidence (Hankin & Abela, 2005). These youngsters derive self-esteem from their accomplishments and approval of others, rather than from an intrinsic sense of self-worth (Shirk, Gudmundsen, & Burwell, 2005). They need attention and reassurance from caregivers to maintain a sense of worthiness and self-confidence (Joiner, Metalsky, Katz, & Beach, 1999). Youths with insecure attachment histories and feelings of low self-worth are at increased risk for depressive symptoms (Abela, Hankin et al., 2005; Shirk et al., 2005).

Second, adolescents who hold insecure representations of caregivers do not rely on others for support in times of crisis (Shirk et al., 2005). Although these individuals appear self-reliant under usual circumstances, they may be alone and easily overwhelmed by stress when negative events occur. Children with histories of insecure attachment may be reluctant to seek help from parents or teachers to solve personal problems. Adolescents with insecure attachment histories often underutilize social support networks in times of crisis (Connor-Smith, Compas, Wadsworth, Thomsen, & Saltzman, 2000). Excessive self-reliance predisposes youths to isolation, failure, and depression.

Maternal Depression

The children of depressed mothers are at risk for depression themselves (Beardslee, Versage, & Gladstone, 1998). As many as 60% of the children of depressed parents show depression by young adulthood. The risk for depression is 6 times greater for the children of depressed mothers compared to the offspring of nondepressed women (Essau & Merikangas,

1999). The relationship between mother and child depression is complex and not fully understood. However, there are three general approaches to explaining the transmission of depression across generations (Goodman & Gotlib, 1999).

First, some research suggests there might be a genetic component to the relationship between parent and child depression (Goodman & Gotlib, 1999; Gotlib & Sommerfeld, 1999). It is possible that depressed mothers and their offspring share similar genes that predispose them both to mood disorders.

Second, maternal stress during pregnancy might compromise the development of children's neurological and endocrine systems. These developmental problems, in turn, can lead to childhood depression. For example, women's anxiety levels during gestation predict their offspring's ability to regulate cortisol during late childhood (O'Connor, 2003). Maternal stress hormones during pregnancy might adversely affect the development of their children's HPA axis. Furthermore, women's levels of depression shortly after delivery predicted their children's cortisol levels and regulation during childhood and adolescence (Essex, Klein, Cho, & Kalin, 2002; Halligan, Herbert, Goodyer, & Murray, 2004). Being cared for by a depressed parent early in life places considerable stress on infants. This increased stress might lead to dysregulation of the HPA axis and later mood problems.

The **intergenerational interpersonal stress model** of depression offers a third explanation for the relationship between parent and child depression (Hammen, 1991, 2002). According to this model, children of depressed mothers experience two problems. First, they must face many of the same family stressors that their mothers experience (e.g., conflict between parents, economic hardship). Second, the children of depressed mothers are not taught effective problem-solving and social skills to cope with these stressors. Instead, depressed parents often model ineffective problem-solving skills and discipline their children in less-than-optimal ways. Consequently, the children of depressed mothers often display behavior problems and show difficulty in interpersonal relationships themselves. These difficulties, in turn, lead to their own problems with depression and low self-worth (Goodman & Gotlib, 1999).

Several studies have supported the intergenerational interpersonal stress model. For example, longitudinal research shows that maternal depression is associated with more hostile and less responsive parenting behavior. This negative parenting behavior subsequently predicts childhood depression (Bifulco et al., 2002; Burt et al., 2005; Johnson, Cohen, Kasen, Smailes, & Brook, 2001). Furthermore, Hammen, Shih, and Brennan (2004) found the relationship between maternal depression and children's mood problems was explained by mothers' tendencies to use parenting techniques characterized by low warmth and high hostility. Family stress and problematic parenting predicted adolescents' mood problems.

Family Conflict

Parent-child conflict is strongly associated with childhood depression (Marmorstein & Iacono, 2004). Depressed youths often come from families characterized by less cohesion, communication, and responsiveness. Furthermore, parents of depressed youths are often described as antagonistic, punitive, and critical (Kaslow, Deering, & Racusin, 1994; Lewinsohn, Roberts et al., 1994).

Harsh, critical family interactions can lead to the emergence and exacerbation of children's depressive symptoms (Hooley & Gotlib, 2000; MacPhee & Andrews, 2006). Researchers sometimes use the term **expressed emotion (EE)** to refer to caregivers' hostile behavior and criticism directed at family members. Examples of high expressed emotion include belittling children for inappropriate behavior or criticizing adolescents for low grades. High expressed emotion can lower children's self-esteem and deprive them of parental support. High expressed emotion also increases the likelihood of depression and relapse of mood episodes after recovery. Asarnow, Goldstein, Tompson, and Guthrie (1993) showed that 53% of depressed children from low EE families recovered within one year, compared to 0% of depressed children from high EE families.

Interactions With Peers

Friendships. Other researchers have examined the role that peers play in child and adolescent depression. Harry Stack Sullivan (1953) described the importance of peer relationships to the emotional well-being of children. He claimed that children develop the capacity for empathy and emotional autonomy through their friendships in late childhood and adolescence. Through interactions with peers, children learn the emotional give-and-take that characterizes healthy, intimate adult relationships. Through friendships, children also learn about themselves and develop a sense of identity. For example, children compare themselves to peers to determine their strengths and weaknesses. They also derive self-esteem from friends' acceptance of their personality and behavior (Parker, Rubin, Erath, Wojslawosicz, & Buskirk, 2006).

Research has shown that acceptance by peer networks (i.e., "crowds" or "cliques") is important to children's self-concepts and emotional well-being (Klomeck, Marrocco, Kleinman, Schonfeld, & Gould, 2007). Children who are rejected or victimized by peers are more likely to show depressive symptoms. Both physical victimization (e.g., bullying) and relational aggression (e.g., teasing, spreading rumors) are associated with depression in boys and girls (Crick & Bigbee, 1998; Prinstein, Boergers, & Vernberg, 2001). In one study, relational aggression predicted adolescent depression better than physical aggression (LaGreca & Harrison, 2005). This finding contradicts the old saying about "sticks and stones." It also suggests that school-based interventions designed to reduce the harmful effects of bullying must also target relational aggression in order to prevent children's mood problems (LaGreca & Harrison, 2005).

Prinstein and Aikins (2004) showed how the relationship between peer rejection and depressive symptoms is moderated by adolescent cognitions. As expected, peer rejection predicted later depressive symptoms in a sample of tenth graders. However, the relationship was strongest for adolescents who (a) also showed depressogenic attributional styles and (b) placed a great deal of importance on peer acceptance. The researchers suggested that adolescents who attribute peer rejection to internal, stable, and global causes (e.g., "I'm no good") are more likely to become depressed than adolescents who hold less pessimistic attributions for their rejection (e.g., "The other kids are jerks"). Furthermore, adolescents who are rejected, but who desperately want to be accepted by peers, may be especially prone to depression. Prinstein and Aikins's (2004) study is significant because it shows how cognitive factors can moderate the effects of psychosocial stressors on adolescent depression.

Friendships and romantic relationships can also be stressful to adolescents. Friendships characterized by conflict or coercion can negatively affect the emotional well-being of adolescents and contribute to depression (LaGreca & Harrison, 2005). Stressful romantic relationships during adolescence also predict depressive symptoms (Davila, Steinberg, Kachadourian, Cobb, & Fincham, 2004; LaGreca & Harrison, 2005).

What about the possible positive effects of peer relationships? Can peers buffer adolescents from other psychosocial stressors by offering them a source of support? The answer appears to be "no." In their review of the adolescent depression literature, Burton and colleagues (2004) found very little evidence supporting the idea that positive peer relationships protect children from the effects of other psychosocial stress. However, problematic peer relationships did independently predict depression. Although the buffering effect of peer relationships seems intuitive, it may not have much empirical support (LaGreca & Harrison, 2005).

Social Information Processing

In previous chapters, we examined how biases in children's information processing can lead to externalizing behavior problems. Crick and Dodge (1996) found that aggressive boys tend to show hostile attributional biases when solving interpersonal problems. These boys interpret others' benign behavior as malevolent, and they rely on hostile strategies to resolve interpersonal disputes.

Recently, some authors have applied similar information-processing models to explain childhood depression (Prinstein, Cheah, & Guyer, 2005). According to the **social information-processing theory of depression**, children with depression display two types of biases when solving interpersonal problems (Figure 13.8). First, like aggressive

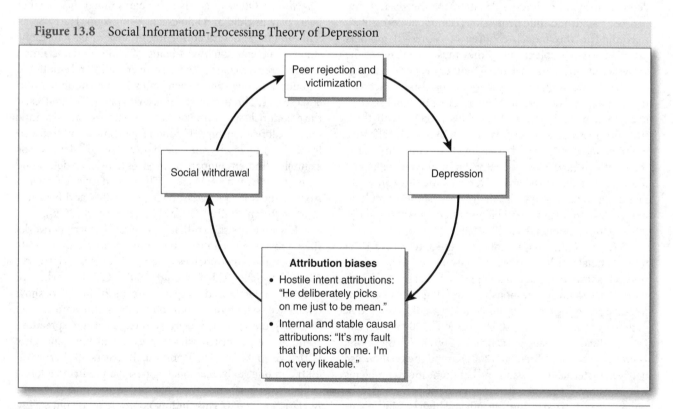

Figure 13.8 Social Information-Processing Theory of Depression

Source: Based on Prinstein et al. (2005).

Note: Children at risk for depression believe that (a) other people have hostile intentions and (b) other people's hostility is their fault. Consequently, these children withdraw from social situations, causing them to experience peer rejection, teasing, and depression.

children, depressed children attribute hostile intentions to other people's ambiguous behavior. For example, imagine that a child is playing outside during recess. While playing, a peer kicks a soccer ball, and it hits the child in the head. The child might show a hostile attributional bias by attributing hostile intentions to the peer's behavior (e.g., "That kid is picking on me").

Second, children with depression often show internal and stable causal attributions; that is, they attribute social problems or failures to internal and stable causes. For example, the child who is hit by the soccer ball might blame himself for his perceived victimization (e.g., "He hit me in the head because he doesn't like me. I'm no fun to be with").

The social information-processing model of depression suggests that depressed children interpret others' behavior as hostile and attribute others' hostile actions to internal and stable factors (e.g., their own fault). These cognitions can influence children's long-term self-perceptions and social behaviors. Children who adopt these information-processing biases are likely to view themselves negatively and avoid social situations. They are at risk for peer rejection and victimization, which, in turn, can lead to more hostile and depressogenic problem solving (Rubin & Rose-Krasnor, 1992).

The social information-processing model of depression is relatively new. A few studies have shown that the combination of hostile and depressogenic attributions leads to decreased self-esteem, loneliness, and depressive symptoms in children and adolescents (Graham & Juvonen, 2001; Prinstein et al., 2005; Suarez & Bell-Dolan, 2001). Perhaps more important, these attributional biases lead children to withdraw from social situations (Prinstein et al., 2005; Quiggle, Garber, Panak, & Dodge, 1992). Social withdrawal, in turn, is associated with peer victimization, which confirms children's belief that they are partially to blame for their own peer problems.

Treatment

Antidepressants

Does Medication Work? Until the early 1990s, the pharmaceutical treatment of depression in children and adolescents was limited. Most physicians prescribed **tricyclic antidepressants**. These medications, which affect levels of serotonin and norepinephrine, included amitriptyline (Elavil), desipramine (Norpramin), and imipramine (Tofranil). Tricyclic antidepressants were effective in treating depression in adults. However, two meta-analyses revealed that tricyclic antidepressants were largely ineffective in reducing depressive symptoms in youths, especially prepubescent children (Hazell, O'Connell, Heathcote, & Henry, 2002; Figure 13.9). This is probably because the serotonin and norepinephrine neurotransmitter systems upon which these medications work are not fully developed until late adolescence or early adulthood (D. Cohen, Gerardin,

Mazet, Purper-Ouakil, & Flament, 2004). Researchers also discovered that tricyclic antidepressants caused severe side effects in some children, including cardiac arrhythmia, suicidal behavior, and death (D. Cohen et al., 2004). In one study, 14% of youths taking imipramine reported cardiovascular side effects that caused them to discontinue the medication (Findling, 2005).

In the early 1990s, physicians began prescribing **selective serotonin reuptake inhibitors** (**SSRIs**) to youths with depression. These medications slow the reuptake of serotonin, allowing the neurotransmitter to remain in the synaptic cleft for longer periods of time. The percentage of children taking antidepressant medication, mostly SSRIs, increased markedly from 1.6% in 1998 to 2.4% in 2002 (Delate, Gelenberg, Simmons, & Motheral, 2004).

A recent meta-analysis indicates that SSRIs are superior to placebo in alleviating depression in children and adolescents. On average, 60% of youths respond to SSRIs, whereas 49% improve with placebo. The overall effect size of SSRIs is small, mostly because approximately one half of depressed children and adolescents improve when taking placebo rather than actual medication (Bridge et al., 2007).

Currently, the only SSRI that has received FDA approval for the treatment of depression in children is fluoxetine (Prozac). Three published studies of youths with depression have compared fluoxetine to placebo. All three studies have shown fluoxetine to be superior in reducing depressive symptoms with minimal side effects (Figure 13.10). Despite these results, the efficacy of fluoxetine in children and adolescents has been questioned. First, the magnitude of the difference between youths taking fluoxetine versus placebo is somewhat small. For example, in one study, approximately 65% of youths improved with fluoxetine compared to approximately 52% with placebo. Although fluoxetine decreases children's depressive symptoms, some of its benefits can be attributed to placebo. Second, the superiority of fluoxetine over placebo depends partially on *who* is reporting children's symptoms. In another study, medication was associated with symptom reduction when reported by clinicians, but *not* when reported by parents or children (Emslie et al., 2002). Third, the superiority of fluoxetine over placebo may be largely due to its efficacy in reducing symptoms of comorbid anxiety, not depression per se (Garland, 2004).

Two other SSRIs have also been shown to be superior to placebo in treating pediatric depression. Wagner and colleagues (2003) showed that 69% of depressed children improved after using sertraline (Zoloft) compared to 59% of children receiving placebo. Again, the magnitude of the difference between children receiving the medication versus placebo was small. Wagner, Robb, and colleagues (2004) also showed that citalopram (Celexa) was more effective than placebo in reducing depression among children and adolescents. However, only 36% of the sample responded to citalopram. A second study of citalopram did not demonstrate its superiority over placebo (Wagner, 2005).

Figure 13.9 Results of Major Randomized Controlled Trials Investigating the Efficacy of Tricyclic Antidepressants on Child and Adolescent Depression

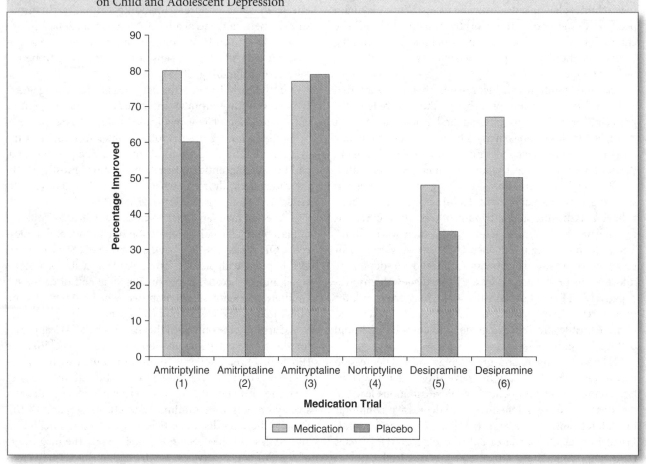

Source: Based on D. Cohen et al. (2004).

Note: In general, tricyclics do not show superiority over placebo. In addition, they can cause dangerous side effects, including death, in some children.

Other antidepressant medications have *not* been shown to be superior to placebo in treating child or adolescent depression. Five large, randomized controlled studies of the SSRIs paroxetine (Paxil) and escitalopram (Lexapro) have shown these medications to be no better than placebo in reducing core depressive symptoms. Venlafaxine ER (Effexor), a medication that inhibits the reuptake of both serotonin and norepinephrine, has also been shown in two independent trials to be equivalent to placebo in treating childhood depression (Wagner, 2005).

Are Antidepressant Medications Safe? In 2003, regulatory agencies in the United States, Great Britain, and Canada issued warnings against prescribing SSRIs to children and adolescents. The warnings followed a series of unpublished studies of two SSRIs frequently used with children: paroxetine (Paxil) and venlafaxine (Effexor). These studies showed that the SSRIs were not effective in reducing depression in children and that they doubled children's likelihood of suicide and aggression (Garland, 2004).

The U.S. Food and Drug Administration (Wagner, 2005) subsequently conducted its own study of nine antidepressant medications for depressed youths and found that the risk of suicidal ideation and behavior was roughly twice for patients on medication (4%) compared to patients receiving placebo (2%). However, a more recent study indicated that only 2.5% of youths taking medication showed suicidal thoughts or actions compared to 1.7% of children taking placebo—only a 0.8% increase (Bridge et al., 2007). Nearly all of these children showed increased suicidal thoughts; suicidal actions were extremely rare, and no child actually completed suicide in any study. Furthermore, researchers have not identified a mechanism by which SSRIs might lead to suicidal thoughts and behaviors in children (Brent & Weersing, 2010).

Nevertheless, most physicians are extremely cautious when prescribing antidepressant medication to youths. Their caution arises primarily because (a) some of these medications have shown limited effectiveness beyond placebo and (b) they are associated with adverse side effects including

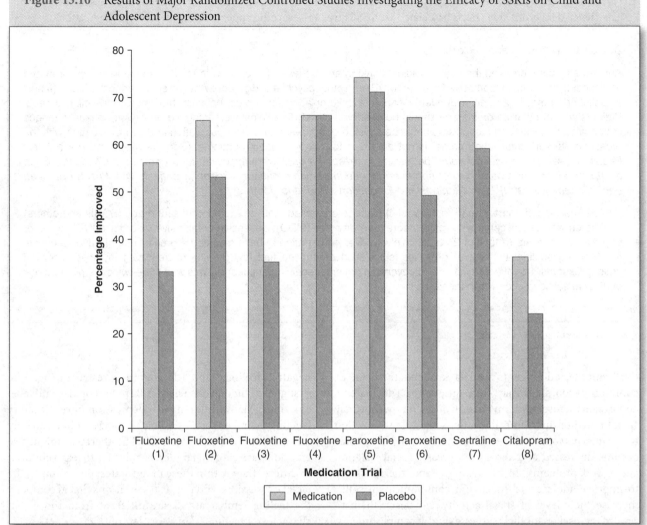

Source: Based on (1) Emslie et al. (1997); (2) Emslie et al. (2002); (3) TADS (2004); (4) Simeon, Dinicola, Ferguson, and Copping (1990); (5) Milin, Walker, and Chow (2003); (6) Keller et al. (2001); (7) Wagner et al. (2003); (8) Wagner, Berard et al. (2004).

Note: In general, only fluoxetine (Prozac) is associated with consistent improvement in depressive symptoms with minimal side effects. However, most SSRIs (including fluoxetine) perform only slightly better than placebo.

slightly elevated risk of suicidal thoughts and actions. The FDA directed pharmaceutical manufacturers to post "black box" warnings on all antidepressant medications, informing caregivers of the apparent increased risk of suicidal ideation and behavior associated with SSRI treatment (Wagner, 2005; Image 13.3). Professional organizations, such as the American Psychiatric Association and the American Academy of Child and Adolescent Psychiatry, have criticized the FDA's action, claiming that such warnings limit patients' access to pharmaceutical treatment (Whittington et al., 2004; Wohlfarth, Lekkerkerker, & van Zwieten, 2004). Physicians and parents must weigh the potential benefits of SSRI against their possible costs when deciding whether to use these medications (Birmaher & Brent, 2010).

Cognitive-Behavioral Therapy

Although cognitive-behavioral therapy (CBT) for depression is typically offered as a single treatment "package," it actually consists of two separate treatment components (Kazdin & Marciano, 1998). First, cognitive therapy for depression is based on the notion that maladaptive patterns in thinking contribute to people's depressed mood. In cognitive therapy, clients learn more accurate and realistic ways to perceive themselves, others, and the future.

Second, behavior therapy for depression is based on the idea that depression is caused by a lack of **response-contingent reinforcement** (Lewinsohn, 1974). Specifically, people become depressed when they are unable to derive pleasure or satisfaction from their environments.

Image 13.3 Black Box Warning on Antidepressant Medication. Although very few children and adolescents experience dangerous side effects associated with SSRI use, this warning appears on antidepressant medication.

Suicidality in Children and Adolescents

Antidepressants increased the risk of suicidal thinking and behavior (suicidality) in short-term studies in children and adolescents with Major Depressive Disorder (MDD) and other psychiatric disorders. Anyone considering the use of [Insert established name] or any other antidepressant in a child or adolescent must balance this risk with the clinical need. Patients who are started on therapy should be observed closely for clinical worsening, suicidality, or unusual changes in behavior. Families and caregivers should be advised of the need for close observation and communication with the prescriber. [Insert established name] is not approved for use in pediatric patients. (See Warnings and Precautions: Pediatric Use) *[This sentence would be revised to reflect if a drug were approved for a pediatric indication(s). Such as, [Insert established name] is not approved for use in pediatric patients except for patients with [Insert approved pediatric indications(s)]. (See Warnings and Precautions: Pediatric Use)]*

Pooled analyses of short-term (4 to 16 weeks) placebo-controlled trials of 9 antidepressant drugs (SSRIs and others) in children and adolescents with major depressive disorder (MDD), obsessive compulsive disorder (OCD), or other psychiatric disorders (a total of 24 trials involving over 4400 patients) have revealed a greater risk of adverse events representing suicidal thinking or behavior (suicidality) during the first few months of treatment in those receiving antidepressants. The average risk of such events in patients receiving antidepressants was 4%—twice the placebo risk of 2%. No suicides occurred in these trials.

Source: Extracted from http://www.fda.gov.

For example, adolescents who lack adequate social or communication skills may frequently argue with parents and isolate themselves from peers. Consequently, they may spend much of their time alone, deriving little satisfaction from interpersonal relationships. Over time, they may become depressed and show even greater social isolation and mood problems. In behavior therapy, therapists try to improve adolescents' social and communication skills, increase their level of social activity, and teach them to reward themselves for their successes and accomplishments.

There are many cognitive-behavioral interventions designed for youths with depression. We will examine two of the best-studied treatments: Stark's cognitive-behavioral therapy (for school-age children) and the Coping With Depression program (for adolescents).

Stark's Cognitive-Behavioral Therapy for Children. One of the first CBT packages developed for depressed children was created by Kevin Stark and colleagues (Stark & Kendall, 1996; Stark, Hoke et al., 2005). The goal of treatment was to change children's problematic ways of thinking and to increase their satisfaction with themselves, others, and their surroundings. To accomplish this task, the therapist teaches children social, emotional, and behavioral skills so that they can effectively cope with negative feelings, solve problems, and interact with others. Treatment is conducted in small groups consisting of school-age children and a therapist. Sessions occur biweekly for 10 weeks.

In Stark's treatment (Stark et al., 2005), the therapist teaches four basic skills: (a) recognizing and understanding emotions, (b) solving social problems, (c) coping with negative feelings, and (d) cognitive restructuring. The first goal of therapy is to help children recognize and label emotions. Many children with depression have difficulty labeling their feelings. For example, some children can only differentiate "happy" and "sad." The therapist might use emotion flash cards, charades, or role play to teach children to differentiate within these mood states. For example, the facial expressions and physical sensations that accompany the feeling "embarrassed" are different from those that characterize feeling "angry" or "left out."

After children are able to recognize, differentiate, and label emotions, they learn basic problem-solving skills. That is, children must learn what to do when they feel embarrassed, angry, or left out. Many children with depression feel overwhelmed by their negative emotional states and withdraw from family and peers. Other depressed children express their negative emotions directly, through acting out and aggression. The goal of problem-solving training is to help children actively address social problems and the mood states they engender.

In problem-solving training, children are taught to systematically identify a social problem, brainstorm possible solutions, evaluate each solution, select and implement the best course of action, and evaluate outcomes (Crick & Dodge, 1996). In addition, problem-solving training for children with depression has two unique components. First, when children identify the problem, the therapist teaches them to "psych-up" (Stark et al., 2005, p. 249), or direct all of their attention and energy to solving it. Psyching-up helps children feel more empowered to confront and solve social problems and less hopeless. Second, after children evaluate the consequences of their actions, the therapist encourages them to reward their problem-solving efforts. Children are encouraged to praise themselves for their attempts at solving social problems, even if their solutions are not 100% effective.

Cognitive-behavioral therapists also teach coping skills. Many children with depression lack the ability to regulate their emotions. When they feel sad or helpless, they ruminate on their feelings rather than try to cope with them directly. The therapist might help children improve their coping skills in three ways. First, she might teach specific coping strategies, like relaxation. Second, she might ask children to interview their nondepressed peers and find out how these children cope with negative moods and everyday hassles. Third, she might ask children to actively plan pleasurable activities during the week so that they can experience positive emotions. For example, she might encourage children to go to a movie with friends or to a sporting event with family.

Finally, therapists use **cognitive restructuring**; that is, they attempt to challenge and alter the cognitive biases and distortions that maintain children's negative moods. Stark and colleagues (2005) discuss a number of games to help children look at themselves, others, and the future more objectively. In What's the Evidence, children must provide empirical support for their negative thinking. If a child is earning a low grade in reading class, she might conclude that she is not very smart. The therapist might challenge her conclusion by asking her for evidence to support her claim and by challenging her to provide evidence to the contrary (i.e., that she *is* smart). Although she may score poorly in reading, she may be extremely talented in art or math.

In another cognitive game, Alternative Interpretations, the therapist challenges children's automatic thoughts about ambiguous events by asking them to consider other ways of viewing the event. If a child is ignored by her classmates while walking down the hallway at school, she might conclude that her classmates are upset with her. The therapist might challenge this cognitive distortion and encourage her to consider other possibilities for their behavior: Perhaps her friends were late for class and in a hurry, or perhaps they did not see her.

A third strategy is to use the *what if* technique. Therapists use this technique to combat the high and (sometimes) unreasonable expectations children place on themselves and their tendency to engage in catastrophic thinking. For example, a boy who earns low grades might think, "Oh no. Now I'll never make the honor roll, and my parents are going to kill me!" The therapist might ask *what if* he does not make the honor roll; will his parents actually kill him? Will they disown him? Will they stop loving him?

Controlled studies of CBT for children with depression have shown it to be more effective than no treatment or placebo (Butler, Miezitis, Friedman, & Cole, 1980; Rossello & Bernal, 1999; Stark, Reynolds, & Kaslow, 1987; Weisz,

Thurber, Sweeney, Proffitt, & LeGagnoux, 1997). It has also been shown to be more effective than other forms of non-directive counseling (Brent et al., 1997; Stark, 1990; Stark, Rouse, & Livingston, 1991).

On the other hand, CBT is equally as effective at reducing depressive symptoms as supportive psychotherapy (Vostanis, Feehan, Grattan, & Bickerton,1996a, 1996b), social skills training (Butler et al., 1980), problem-solving training (Stark et al., 1987), and relaxation training (Kahn, Kehle, Jenson, & Clarke, 1990). In some studies, CBT was superior to alternative treatments like relaxation training and supportive therapy in the short term, but treatment groups showed comparable outcomes at long-term follow-up (Birmaher, Brent, & Benson, 2000; Wood, Harrington, & Moore, 1996). Overall, these results indicate that CBT is useful for reducing children's depressive symptoms. However, it is likely that certain components of the CBT package (i.e., problem-solving training, coping skills training) are sufficient to produce these benefits.

Cognitive-Behavioral Group Therapy for Adolescents. The adolescent coping with depression course (CWD-A; Clarke, Lewinsohn, & Hops, 1990; Lewinsohn, Clarke, Hops, & Andrews, 1990) is a group treatment for older adolescents (14–16 years) with MDD or Dysthymic Disorder. CWD-A was designed to be nonstigmatizing. It is conducted like a class, with the therapist playing the role of teacher. In class, adolescents learn and practice new skills to help them cope with depressive symptoms and daily stressors. Skills are taught using traditional instruction, role play and dialogue, workbook exercises, and quizzes. Adolescents complete homework to help generalize skills to use outside the therapy setting.

CWD-A is based heavily on the behavioral theory of depression developed by Lewinsohn and colleagues (Lewinsohn, Youngren, & Grosscup, 1979). According to this theory, adolescents become depressed because of a lack of positive reinforcement and an excess of punishment from their environments. When they succeed, these adolescents do not give themselves credit or enjoy their success. When they fail, they attribute their failure to internal and stable causes (i.e., personal faults) and assign self-blame. Over time, they experience only failure and frustration and perceive themselves as helpless and powerless. They also begin to show certain maladaptive thought patterns that contribute to their depressed mood, such as cognitive biases and distortions.

In CWD-A, adolescents learn new skills to cope with depressive symptoms, increase self-efficacy and pleasure, and change maladaptive thought patterns. Each week, the therapist-teacher introduces a new skill, which is practiced in the session and at home. In the first phase of treatment, the therapist teaches adolescents how to increase their energy levels and degree of positive emotions. First, adolescents learn to monitor their emotions and notice how changes in their behavior can improve their mood. For example, adolescents might notice how riding a bike, playing a sport, or calling a friend on the telephone usually results in greater energy. Later in treatment, the therapist uses social skills training to teach adolescents how to make friends and engage in social activities (Rohde, Lewinsohn, Clarke, Hops, & Seeley, 2005).

Finally, the therapist encourages adolescents to plan pleasurable activities in their daily lives. Specifically, the therapist encourages adolescents to identify activities that they formerly enjoyed and set realistic expectations for engaging in these activities. For example, a girl who formerly enjoyed going to school dances might plan on attending a dance over the weekend. An unrealistic expectation for the dance is that everyone would compliment her on her appearance and that she would be the center of attention. Such an expectation would set up the girl for disappointment. A more realistic expectation would be to attend the dance and spend some time with friends. The therapist encourages adolescents to deliberately schedule pleasurable events into their weekly routine. As adolescents engage in these pleasurable activities, they may derive greater reinforcement from their environment and improve their mood.

In the second phase of CWD-A, the therapist targets adolescents' negative moods. First, the therapist teaches relaxation techniques, like deep breathing and muscle relaxation, to help adolescents cope with anxiety and other negative moods. Later, the therapist teaches adolescents to recognize cognitive biases and distortions, using cartoons and role playing exercises. Adolescents are also taught to modify their thoughts with more realistic cognitions. In fact, the ability to replace negative automatic thoughts with more realistic cognitions may be one of the primary mechanisms by which CWD-A reduces depressive symptoms (Kaufman, Rohde, Seeley, Clarke, & Stice, 2005). Finally, adolescents are taught communication and conflict-resolution skills to help them negotiate interpersonal disputes. Typically, conflict-resolution training involves teaching adolescents how to listen to others with an open mind, avoid critical or accusatory comments, brainstorm possible solutions to interpersonal problems, and select a course of action that everyone can accept.

The efficacy of CWD-A has been examined in a number of randomized controlled studies. The first two studies involved a total of 155 adolescents with MDD or Dysthymic Disorder (Clarke, Rohde, Lewinsohn, Hops, & Seeley, 1999; Lewinsohn et al., 1990). Adolescents were randomly assigned to one of three treatment conditions. The first group participated in CWD-A. The second group participated in CWD-A, and their parents also participated in parallel parenting sessions. Adolescents in the third group served as waitlist controls. Adolescents' depressive symptoms were assessed before treatment, immediately after treatment, and 2 years after treatment. Results showed that adolescents who participated in CWD-A (e.g., the

first two groups) showed greater symptom reduction than adolescents on the waitlist. However, the adolescents in the two treatment conditions showed comparable outcomes, indicating that adding the parent group to CWD-A may be desirable, but not necessary.

In a more recent study, Clarke and colleagues (2002) compared the relative efficacy of CWD-A to treatment in the community. Specifically, 88 adolescents with MDD or Dysthymic Disorder were randomly assigned to traditional care alone or traditional care plus CWD-A. Adolescents in both treatment groups showed reductions in depressive symptoms. However, adolescents who also participated in CWD-A did not show better outcomes than adolescents who only participated in traditional care.

Interpersonal Psychotherapy for Adolescents

The underlying premise of interpersonal psychotherapy (IPT) is that depression is best understood as an adverse reaction to interpersonal problems (Mufson & Pollack Dorta, 2003; Mufson, Pollack Dorta, Moreau, & Weissman, 2005). Adolescents with depression have usually experienced disruptions in their interpersonal functioning or high levels of interpersonal stress (Puig-Antich et al., 1993; Stader & Hokanson, 1998). These interpersonal problems both contribute to and maintain their depressed mood (Hammen, 1999). IPT seeks to improve people's interpersonal functioning by helping them develop more satisfying and meaningful relationships, cope with the separation and loss of loved ones, and alleviate social distress and isolation.

Early in treatment, the adolescent and therapist select one or two problems to be the focus of therapy. These problems usually center on one of the following interpersonal themes: (a) grief and loss, (b) interpersonal role disputes, (c) role transitions, and (d) interpersonal deficits (Young, Mufson, & Davies, 2006).

Some adolescents become depressed following the loss of an important relationship. Adolescents can grieve the death of a family member, the separation from a parent, or the departure of a friend. When a relationship with a loved one is disrupted, adolescents can experience feelings of insecurity and helplessness. From the perspective of attachment theory, these adolescents have lost a secure base from which they derive comfort and interpersonal confidence. As a result, some adolescents become anxious, fearful, or unsure of themselves. Others become withdrawn and lethargic. Still others act out. The interpersonal therapist helps adolescents mourn the loss of the relationship and develop alternative sources of social support (McBride, Atkinson, Quilty, & Bagby, 2006).

Other adolescents become depressed due to interpersonal role disputes. Role disputes are usually between the adolescent and his parents; they typically reflect differences in values. Although parent-child disagreements are common during adolescence, they can become problematic if left unresolved. Adolescents who perceive their parents as unsympathetic or disinterested can feel low self-worth and helplessness. The interpersonal therapist teaches both parents and adolescents more effective communication skills and ways to resolve disagreements—ways that balance the authority of the parent with the autonomy of the adolescent.

Still other adolescents experience depression following a major role transition or psychosocial stressor. Adolescents experience considerable life transitions: entering junior and senior high school, beginning dating and serious romantic relationships, separating from family members, entering the workforce. At other times, life transitions are forced upon adolescents through the birth of a new sibling, an unexpected pregnancy, the deployment of a family member in the armed forces, or a chronic illness in the family. The interpersonal therapist helps the adolescent define, accept, and cope with his new social role. Coping may involve grieving the loss of the old role and learning new skills (or adjusting one's lifestyle) to suit new responsibilities.

Finally, adolescents can become depressed because of interpersonal deficits. Adolescents who lack appropriate social skills may have difficulty making friends, dating, and participating in extracurricular activities. Since adolescents' self-concepts are heavily influenced by peers, problems in peer functioning can cause a lack of self-esteem, self-confidence, and social isolation. The therapist teaches social skills, usually through role play exercises.

Although a number of randomized, controlled studies have supported the efficacy of interpersonal therapy for depression in adults, less research has focused on adolescents. In one study, 48 adolescents with depression were randomly assigned to one of two groups (Mufson, Weissman, Moreau, & Garfinkel, 1999). The first group participated in 12 weeks of IPT. The second group met with a counselor but did not receive any active form of treatment. Results showed that adolescents who participated in IPT were more likely to complete treatment (88%) than adolescents in the control group (46%). Furthermore, adolescents who received IPT showed greater improvement in mood, overall functioning, and social problem-solving skills than controls. A second study (Rossello & Bernal, 2005), using a slightly different version of IPT, showed similar results with Puerto Rican youths.

A more recent study compared the effectiveness of IPT and traditional counseling (Mufson, Pollack Dorta, Wickramaratne, Nomura, Olfson, & Weissman, 2004). Sixty-three adolescents with depression who were attending schools in low-income neighborhoods were randomly assigned to two treatment groups. The first group received 12 sessions of IPT at school. The second group received nondirective counseling at school; in most cases, counseling involved supportive psychotherapy. After treatment, adolescents in both groups showed improvement in depressive symptoms and overall functioning. Clinician ratings indicated that IPT was superior to traditional counseling in improving mood and functioning. Adolescents' self-reports indicated

that IPT was superior to traditional counseling in improving social functioning, but not in reducing depressive symptoms. Taken together, these results indicate that IPT is effective in treating adolescent depression, even when it is not administered as part of a university-based research trial. However, IPT may not always be superior to supportive psychotherapy in reducing adolescents' self-reported depressive symptoms.

Combining Medication and Psychotherapy

Many experts recommend combining medication and psychotherapy to treat child and adolescent depression (Birmaher et al., 1998; March & Wells, 2003). The rationale for combined treatment is threefold (Kratochvil et al., 2005). First, combining medication and psychotherapy might provide a greater "dose" of treatment, thereby, producing faster symptom reduction and greater treatment response. Second, medication plus psychotherapy might target different symptoms, thus, maximizing the range of symptoms that might be improved. For example, medication might target the physical symptoms of depression (e.g., fatigue, sleep, and appetite changes), whereas therapy might target cognitive symptoms (e.g., anhedonia, thoughts of death). Third, combined treatment might address a wider range of comorbid problems.

The **Treatment for Adolescents With Depression Study** (TADS, 2004) was designed to investigate the relative merits of medication and psychotherapy in treating adolescent depression. In TADS, researchers compared the efficacy of medication and CBT in adolescents aged 12 to 17 years. Four hundred and thirty-nine adolescents with MDD were randomly assigned to one of four treatment groups: (a) fluoxetine only, (b) CBT only, (c) combined fluoxetine and CBT, and (d) placebo (Figure 13.11). All treatments were administered for 12 weeks. Researchers measured adolescents' depressive symptoms before and after treatment. They also measured adolescents' self-harm during the course of treatment.

Children in all groups showed reductions in their depressive symptoms, although children in the combined treatment group showed the greatest symptom reduction at the fastest rate. At the end of treatment, the percentage of adolescents who showed significant improvement were 71% (combined treatment), 60.6% (medication only), 43.2% (CBT only), and 34.8% (placebo), respectively.

Follow-up tests revealed three important findings. First, the difference between adolescents who received combined treatment and adolescents who received medication alone was *not* statistically significant. In fact, another study published after TADS showed similar results: Combining psychotherapy with medication yielded no better outcomes than medication alone (Clarke et al., 2005). Second, adolescents who received combined treatment or medication alone showed significantly greater improvement than adolescents who received either CBT alone or placebo. Third, adolescents who received CBT alone and adolescents who received placebo *did not* statistically differ.

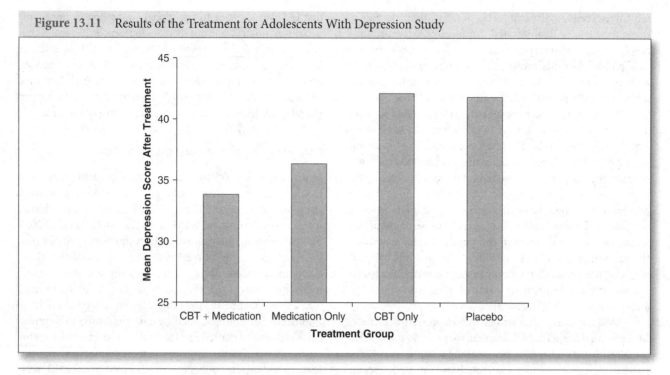

Source: Based on TADS (2004).

Note: Adolescents who received medication (either with or without CBT) showed lowest depression scores after treatment. Adding CBT to medication did not produce significantly greater effects than using medication alone. Youths who participated in CBT alone showed similar outcomes as youths who received placebo.

Some children do not respond to antidepressant medication. In the **Treatment of SSRI-Resistant Depression in Adolescents (TORDIA) study**, researchers examined the effects of adding CBT to medication in adolescents who did not respond to medication alone (Brent et al., 2008; Kennard et al., 2009). This study involved a large sample of 12- to 18-year-olds with severe depression. Adolescents were randomly assigned to one of four conditions: (a) SSRI alone, (b) non-SSRI antidepressant alone, (c) SSRI and CBT, or (d) Non-SSRI antidepressant and CBT. The cognitive-behavioral treatment included cognitive restructuring, problem-solving training, emotion regulation and social skills training, and parent-child sessions to improve family communication and problem-solving. After 12 weeks of treatment, the combination of any medication and CBT yielded greater reductions in depression than medication alone. Furthermore, problem-solving training seemed to be the most effective component of CBT. Unfortunately, 24 weeks after treatment the combination of medication and CBT was no longer superior to medication alone (Brent et al., 2009; Emslie et al., 2010).

The results of the TADS and TORDIA studies indicate that a combination of fluoxetine and CBT should be considered a first-line treatment for adolescent depression. However, the combination of CBT with medication may yield only modest benefits beyond medication alone (Ginsburg, Albano, Findling, Kratochvil, & Walkup, 2005).

CBT alone may be a useful alternative for adolescents and families unwilling to participate in pharmacotherapy, especially in light of recent FDA warnings against SSRIs (Jensen, 2005).

NON-SUICIDAL SELF-INJURY
What Is Non-Suicidal Self-Injury?

Non-Suicidal Self-Injury (NSSI) occurs when individuals repeatedly and intentionally damage the surface of their body in a manner that is likely to induce bleeding, bruising, or pain (Table 13.6, Proposed Diagnostic Criteria for Non-Suicidal Self-Injury). Individuals with NSSI do not have suicidal intent, that is, they do not want to die. Instead, they engage in self-injury with the expectation that they will cause only minor or moderate physical damage. The most common methods of self-injury among adolescents and young adults are cutting (70–90%), banging or hitting (20–40%), and burning (15–35%), although many youths who engage in self-injury use multiple methods (Rodham & Hawton, 2009).

Individuals with NSSI often report negative thoughts or feelings, such as depression, anxiety, or anger, which immediately precedes the self-injurious act. These individuals often feel intense urges to engage in self-injury. Immediately before or during the act, they may be preoccupied with the behavior and feel unable to resist engaging in it. Most

Table 13.6 Proposed Diagnostic Criteria for Non-Suicidal Self-Injury

A. In the last year, the individual has, on 5 or more days, engaged in intentional self-inflicted damage to the surface of his or her body of a sort likely to induce bleeding, bruising, or pain (e.g., cutting, burning, stabbing, hitting, excessive rubbing), with the expectation that the injury will lead to only minor or moderate physical harm (i.e., there is no suicidal intent).

Note: The absence of suicidal intent has either been stated by the individual or can be inferred by the individual's repeated engagement in behavior that the individual knows, or has learned, is not likely to result in death.

B. The individual engages in the self-injurious behavior with one or more of the following expectations:

　1. To obtain relief from a negative feeling or cognitive state.

　2. To resolve an interpersonal difficulty.

　3. To induce a positive feeling state.

Note: The desired relief or response is experienced during or shortly after the self-injury, and the individual may display patterns of behavior suggesting a dependence on repeatedly engaging in it.

C. The intentional self-injury is associated with at least one of the following:

　1. Interpersonal difficulties or negative feelings or thoughts, such as depression, anxiety, tension, anger, generalized distress, or self-criticism, occurring in the period immediately prior to the self-injurious act.

　2. Prior to engaging in the act, a period of preoccupation with the intended behavior that is difficult to control.

　3. Thinking about self-injury that occurs frequently, even when it is not acted upon.

D. The behavior is not socially sanctioned (e.g., body piercing, tattooing, part of a religious ritual) and is not restricted to picking a scab or nail biting.

E. The behavior or its consequences cause clinically significant distress or interference in interpersonal, academic, or other important areas of functioning.

F. The behavior is not better explained by another mental disorder (e.g., Intellectual Disability, Autism Spectrum Disorder, Trichotillomania, Excoriation Disorder). In individuals with a neurodevelopmental disorder, the behavior is not part of a pattern of repetitive stereotypies.

Source: Reprinted with permission from the *Diagnostic and Statistical Manual of Mental Disorders, Fifth Edition* (Copyright 2013). American Psychiatric Association.

Note: This disorder is classified as a "condition for further study" in *DSM-5*.

individuals with NSSI indicate that self-injury serves a specific function such as providing relief from negative feelings or inducing a positive mood state (Prinstein et al., 2009).

NSSI causes clinically significant distress or impairment in functioning (Image 13.4). It may interfere with work or school, family relationships, or interactions with peers. Self-injury that occurs because of a coexisting developmental disorder, another mental disorder, or intoxication is not an indicator of NSSI. For example, a boy with Intellectual Disability or Autism Spectrum Disorder who engages in stereotyped head banging would not be diagnosed with NSSI. Socially-sanctioned alteration of the body, such as body piercings or tattoos, are not indicators of NSSI (Favazza, 2012).

NSSI can be differentiated from suicide in three ways: intention, repetition, and lethality (Baetens, Claes, Muehlen-kamp, Grietens, & Onghena, 2011). First, adolescents who engage in NSSI do not indicate a desire to end their lives, whereas adolescents who attempt suicide may implicitly or explicitly express a desire to die. Second, most adolescents with NSSI typically engage in self-injurious acts repeatedly whereas adolescents who attempt suicide usually do so only once or twice (Nock, Joiner, Gordon, Lloyd-Richardson, & Prinstein, 2006). Third, NSSI involves only mild to moderate tissue damage; in contrast, suicide attempts usually result in more serious damage.

In *DSM-5*, NNSI is classified as a "disorder for future study." The developers of *DSM-5* did not believe there was sufficient research to classify NSSI as a mental disorder; however, they recognized the prevalence and seriousness of NSSI and wanted to encourage future research into its causes and treatment (American Psychiatric Association, 2013). In this section, we will examine what we know about NSSI and what we still need to learn.

Image 13.4 Self-Injury Awareness Day is an annual global event held on March 1st. On this day, organizations make special efforts to raise awareness about self-harm and self-injury.

Prevalence and Course

NSSI is surprisingly common among adolescents and young adults (Figure 13.12). In the community, between 13% and 29% of adolescents and 4% and 6% of adults engage in repeated acts of NSSI (Baetens et al., 2011; Klonsky, 2011; Muehlenkamp et al., 2012). As we might expect, the prevalence is higher among individuals participating in treatment. As many as 40% of adolescents and 21% of adults participating in inpatient treatment engage in NSSI (Jacobson, Muehlenkamp, Miller, & Turner, 2008).

Prepubescent children can also show NSSI. In one survey of college students with NSSI, 5% reported an age of onset beginning before age 10 years (Whitlock, Eckenrode, & Silverman, 2006). It is most common, however, for intentional self-injury to begin in middle adolescence (Nock, 2010). The prevalence of NSSI in early adolescence (e.g., 11–14 years) is 7% to 8%. In contrast, both prospective and longitudinal studies indicate that the prevalence increases to 18% to 23% between 15 and 18 years of age. Recent longitudinal data indicate that NSSI is moderately stable over time; approximately 50% of youths who begin self-injury in early adolescence continue the practice 2.5 years later (Hankin & Abela, 2011). Onset after early adulthood (e.g., age 24 years) is relatively uncommon (Shaffer & Jacobson, 2009).

In early adolescence, girls are approximately 4 times more likely than boys to show NSSI (Hawton, Rodham, Evans, & Weatherall, 2002). However, by late adolescence or early adulthood, the gender distribution becomes equal. These findings suggest that NSSI may emerge at an earlier age in females (Asarnow, Porta, et al. 2011; Bureau et al., 2010; Darke, Torok, Kaye, & Ross, 2010). Other studies suggest gender differences in the method adolescents use to harm themselves. Girls are more likely than boys to engage in cutting and scratching. In contrast, boys are more likely than girls to punch and hit themselves (Whitlock et al., 2006).

We do not know much about the natural course of NSSI. It appears that most people who engage in deliberate self-injury do so only occasionally. For example, in one large sample of college students who admitted to NSSI, 25% reported only one episode of self-injury and 33% reported two to five episodes (Whitlock et al., 2006). On the other hand, in the same study, 25% of the sample engaged in 10 or more instances of self-injury. Additional data suggest that when individuals repeatedly engage in NSSI, their behavior becomes sustained over time. In another study, 63% of young adults who repeatedly engaged in NSSI continued to do so over a one year period of time. The strongest predictors of repeated NSSI was the number of times individuals engaged in NSSI in the past, the severity of the previous self-injuries, and the person's degree of psychological distress (Klonsky et al., 2011).

Figure 13.12   The Prevalence of NSSI Over Time

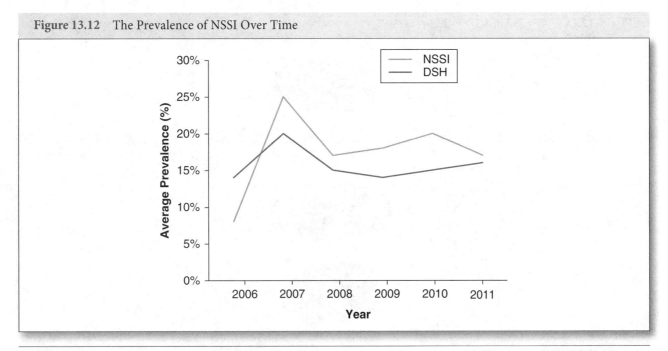

Source: Based on Muehlenkamp et al. (2012).

Note: NSSI and deliberate self-harm (DSH) in general have been relatively stable over the last few years. However, awareness of these problems has increased greatly among clinicians and members of the public.

Associated Problems

Psychiatric Disorders

NSSI is associated with a wide range of psychiatric conditions in adolescents. As we might expect, adolescents who engage in NSSI are up to 58% more likely than their peers without NSSI to experience depression, 38% more likely to have an anxiety disorder, and 24% more likely to have PTSD. It is likely that problems with emotion regulation help explain this association between NSSI and these internalizing problems (Klonsky et al., 2011).

Suicide

Identifying NSSI is important because it is a unique predictor of suicide. In three separate studies involving large samples of adolescents from the community, a history of NSSI increased adolescents' likelihood of attempting suicide by 18% to 40% (Brunner et al., 2007; Klonsky & Olino, 2008; Lloyd-Richardson, Perrine, Dierker, & Kelley, 2007). Furthermore, adolescents who engaged in NSSI more frequently and who used a greater variety of methods to injure themselves (e.g., cutting and burning) were at even greater risk for suicide. Interestingly, the relationship between NSSI and attempted suicide remained even after controlling for other indicators of psychological distress (Asarnow et al., 2011), such as depression (Gibb, Andover, & Beach, 2006) and family conflict (Wilkinson & Goodyer, 2011).

Hamza and colleagues (2012) have developed an integrated model to explain why NSSI might predict suicide attempts in adolescents (Figure 13.13). Specifically, the researchers identified three possible reasons for the association between NSSI and suicide:

- **Third variable theory:** According to this theory, NSSI and suicide often co-occur because both are elicited by a third variable. For example, severe depression can prompt individuals to seek relief from emotional pain through NSSI and, in extreme instances, attempt suicide. Other possible third variables might include chronic anxiety, ostracism, substance abuse, and personality attributes such as high neuroticism (e.g., proneness to negative emotions or emotional reactivity) or low inhibition.
- **Gateway theory:** According to this theory, NSSI and suicide exist along a continuum of self-harm ranging from mild (e.g., picking at a wound) to severe (e.g., deep cutting or stabbing). Adolescents typically begin by engaging in mild acts of self-injury which increase in severity in response to greater psychological distress. Support for this theory comes from research indicating that when adolescents both show NSSI and have a history of attempted suicide, NSSI almost always precedes the suicide attempt (Nock, Borges et al., 2008).
- **Acquired capacity for death theory:** A closely related theory is that NSSI habituates people to the fear of suicide. According to Joiner (Joiner, Brown, & Wingate, 2005; Joiner, 2009), individuals must acquire a "capacity for death" in order to attempt suicide. Increasingly

Figure 13.13   Why Might NSSI Lead to Suicide?

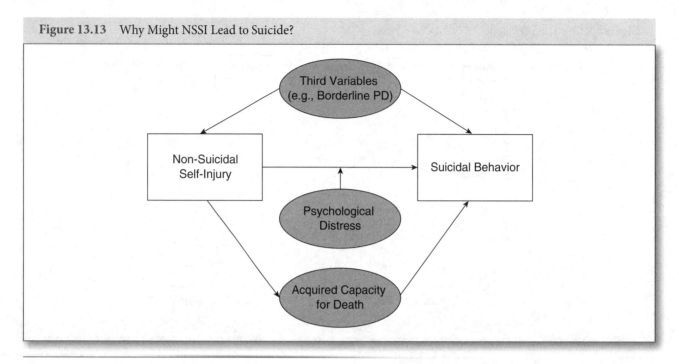

Note: According to Hamza and colleagues (2012), NSSI can directly lead to suicidal behavior because of increased psychological distress (gateway theory). In addition, a third variable, such as Borderline Personality Disorder, can elicit both NSSI and suicidal behavior (third variable theory). Finally, acquired capacity for death can mediate the relationship between NSSI and suicide (acquired capacity theory).

severe NSSI gradually builds this capacity and permits adolescents to engage in more serious acts of self-harm. Joiner posits that other acts of self-harm (e.g., alcohol abuse, exposure to violence) in addition to NSSI also build people's capacity for death and increase the likelihood of suicide. Support for Joiner's theory come from studies showing that adolescents who engage in more frequent NSSI, using a wider variety of methods (e.g., cutting *and* burning) are at greatest risk for suicide (Muehlenkamp & Gutierrez, 2004, 2007; Nock et al., 2006).

Hamza and colleagues (2012) integrate all three models to explain the relationship between NSSI and suicide. In some instances, people's level of psychological distress prompts them to engage in both NSSI and suicide. In other cases, NSSI serves as the gateway for more serious, suicidal self-harm. Finally, acquired capacity for death may mediate the relationship between NSSI and suicidal behavior. As individuals become habituated to the fear and pain of NSSI, they may be more likely to attempt suicide. Although the integrated model is based on previous research, future studies are necessary to test its predictive power.

Causes of Non-Suicidal Self-Injury (NSSI)

Learning Theory

Learning theory can be used to explain why adolescents engage in NSSI. Recall that learning theorists are interested in the function, or purpose, of behavior. NSSI must be maintained through some type of reinforcement or it would decrease over time. Table 13.7 shows Nock and Prinstein's (2004, 2005) **four-function model (FFM) of NSSI** (Table 13.7). According to this model, NSSI is maintained through either positive reinforcement (i.e., the presentation of a stimulus) or negative reinforcement (i.e., the removal or avoidance of a stimulus). Furthermore, reinforcement can be either automatic (i.e., within the person) or social (i.e., between people).

Most instances of NSSI are maintained through *automatic negative reinforcement*. Immediately after NSSI, many adolescents report a reduction in aversive thoughts and feelings. For example, they may feel calmer, experience less tension or anger, or think more clearly. The reduction or removal of these aversive mood and cognitive states can reinforce NSSI over time.

Some instances of NSSI are maintained through *automatic positive reinforcement*. Some adolescents report feeling lethargic, hopeless, numb, or altogether lacking in pleasure. These adolescents may engage in NSSI to feel something, even if the stimulus is moderately painful. Some physiological studies suggest that NSSI may elicit the release of endorphins. These endogenous opioids act as natural analgesics, which not only curtail pain associated with self-injury but also can produce feelings of pleasure, which may be positively reinforcing (Nock & Cha, 2009).

Sometimes, adolescents engage in NSSI for social reinforcement. NSSI is maintained through *social negative reinforcement* when acts of self-injury result in the removal

Table 13.7 Four-Function Model of NSSI

	Negative Reinforcement	Positive Reinforcement
Automatic	Automatic Negative Reinforcement *Reduction in emotional pain*	Automatic Positive Reinforcement *Increased feelings of pleasure*
Social	Social Negative Reinforcement *Avoidance of social demands*	Social Positive Reinforcement *Attention from parents, friends*

Source: Based on Nock & Cha (2009).

Note: Self-injury is maintained by either negative or positive reinforcement. This reinforcement can be automatic (i.e., within the individual) or social. Examples are provided in italics.

or withdrawal of a social demand. For example, some adolescents use NSSI to avoid age-appropriate responsibilities.

More commonly, NSSI is maintained through *social positive reinforcement*: Acts of self-injury are followed by attention or other desirable interactions from others. For example, one longitudinal study found that adolescents who engaged in NSSI experienced significant increases in the attention and the quality of interactions they received from their fathers immediately following self-injury. The researchers speculated that this increased attention might inadvertently reinforce acts of self-harm (Nock & Cha, 2009).

Modeling and Social Contagion

The four-factor model helps explain why NSSI is maintained over time. **Modeling** helps explain why adolescents engage in NSSI in the first place. In a recent survey, adolescents who engaged in NSSI reported that they first attempted deliberate self-injury because it was modeled or described by a peer (38%) or the media (13%; Deliberto & Nock, 2008). Modeling may also help explain a phenomenon called **social contagion**, that is, the tendency of NSSI to spread across adolescent peer groups (Prinstein et al., 2009). When one member of an adolescent peer group begins engaging in NSSI, the likelihood that his or her close friends will also engage in NSSI increases. Prinstein (2007) asked adolescents in the community to report the frequency and intensity of NSSI. Then, the researchers monitored NSSI acts in the adolescents' peer groups. The researchers noticed a significant increase in NSSI among the best friends of these adolescents over the following 2 years, supporting the notion of social contagion. In a second study, the researchers assessed NSSI in adolescents referred to counseling and their best friends over time. They found that adolescents' NSSI behavior at the beginning of the study

predicted an increase in their friends' NSSI behavior several months later.

The media can also contribute to the practice of NSSI among adolescents. Television, films, music, and Internet sites describe, demonstrate, and reinforce NSSI. Whitlock and colleagues (2009) found a marked increase in the number of popular songs, movies, and news stories that depicted, described, or included information about deliberate acts of self-harm. For example, between 1966 and 1990, the researchers identified only 253 stories about self-injury. Between 2000 and 2005, they identified 1,750 stories. Often, self-injury was portrayed as an effective means to regulate emotions and solve social problems.

More recently, Lewis and colleagues (2011) analyzed the 100 most popular YouTube videos depicting NSSI. These videos were viewed more than 2 million times and were usually accessible to a general audience. Approximately 90% of the videos showed explicit injuries (e.g., cuts, burns), and 28% demonstrated NSSI acts themselves. Most videos conveyed a hopeless or melancholic message. However, viewers generally rated these videos positively. The researchers concluded that these videos may normalize NSSI to adolescents who might otherwise avoid such practices.

Emotional Regulation Problems

Marsha Linehan (1993) has suggested that emotional dysregulation is a leading cause of self-harm in adolescents and adults. Linehan's **emotional dysregulation model** posits that individuals at risk for suicide and NSSI have difficulty modulating their emotions in adaptive ways. Specifically, these individuals have trouble identifying and tolerating negative emotions, generating and experiencing positive emotions, and controlling emotions in a manner that permits active coping with psychosocial stress. Instead, these individuals may use self-injury as a maladaptive way to regulate their emotions (Nock, 2009).

Considerable research supports the notion that NSSI is often used to cope with emotional pain. For example, adolescents and young adults who engage in NSSI often experience anxiety and depression. Compared to individuals who do not engage in NSSI, these adolescents and young adults react more negatively to stressful life experiences, cope with negative experiences in less adaptive ways, and spend more time and energy thinking about daily hassles. People who engage in NSSI also report great difficulty tolerating negative emotions; they express a desire to end distress more quickly than other individuals and may use self-injury as a means to convert emotional suffering into physical injury or pain (Klonsky et al., 2011).

It is likely that emotional dysregulation mediates the relationship between psychosocial stress and NSSI. Adrian and colleagues (2011) examined NSSI in a high-risk sample of adolescent girls participating in inpatient treatment. The researchers found that stress in the girls' family and peer relationships greatly reduced their capacity for emotional regulation. Problems with emotional regulation, in turn, often prompted NSSI.

Adolescents who engage in NSSI also report a rapid decrease in the intensity of negative emotions during and immediately following acts of self-injury. Many of these adolescents report calmness and relaxation. According to these reports, NSSI is especially effective at reducing anxiety, anger, and frustration (Klonsky et al., 2011).

Childhood Maltreatment

As many as 79% of adolescents and young adults who engage in NSSI report a history of child abuse or neglect (Yates, 2009). However, not all individuals who have NSSI report abuse histories, and most people who have experienced child maltreatment do not engage in NSSI. A recent meta-analysis indicated a moderate effect size for the relationship between abuse and NSSI ($r = .23$; Klonsky & Moyer, 2008). Therefore, child maltreatment is an important, but nonspecific risk factor for NSSI (Klonsky et al., 2011).

Sexual abuse is the most common type of childhood maltreatment associated with NSSI. Sexual abuse perpetrated by family members and abuse involving penetration is strongly associated with all acts of deliberate self-harm. For example, the percentage of incest survivors who later engage in NSSI may be as high as 58%. NSSI is also seen in adolescents and adults with histories of physical abuse, severe emotional abuse, and neglect (Yates, 2009). Specifically, adults who experienced sexual abuse in childhood reported using NSSI to regulate their emotions, to soothe, or to punish themselves. In contrast, adults who experienced physical abuse often admitted to using NSSI for social purposes, such as to obtain attention and sympathy or express anger and distress (Yates et al., 2008).

Yates (2009) has described three pathways by which childhood maltreatment might lead to later NSSI. According to the first pathway (i.e., the **reactive pathway**), child abuse or neglect disrupts the development of the child's biological stress response system. As a result, the child shows dysregulation in biochemical and neuroendocrine processes. For example, early maltreatment may directly affect the HPA axis which regulates arousal, the release of endogenous opioids, or the modulation of serotonin. As a result, the individual might engage in NSSI to gain control over these dysregulated systems.

According to the second pathway (i.e., the **regulatory pathway**), early maltreatment causes disruptions in children's cognitive and affective development. Specifically, childhood trauma is believed to disrupt the developmentally expected integration between thinking and feeling. As a result, children may not learn to cognitively recognize and label feelings, may not be able to tolerate negative emotions, and may not learn to cope with anxiety, depression, or anger. In adolescence or early adulthood, these adolescents may use NSSI to regulate their thoughts or emotions. Support for this pathway comes from recent studies showing that PTSD symptoms mediate the relationship between child abuse and later NSSI: Abuse predicts posttraumatic stress; stress, in turn, predicts later NSSI (Weierich & Nock, 2008).

The third pathway (i.e., the **representational pathway**) is based on attachment theory. Child abuse disrupts children's internal representation of themselves and their caregivers. Because of their early traumatic experiences, these children come to view others as insensitive or unresponsive to their needs. Furthermore, they come to view themselves as unworthy of receiving care from others and unable to take care of themselves. In young adulthood, these individuals use NSSI to punish themselves or to communicate with or manipulate others (Glassman, Weierich, Hooley, Deliberto, & Nock, 2007).

Diathesis-Stress

Recently, Nock and Cha (2009) offered a model of NSSI that includes many of the distal and proximal risk factors for the disorder. Their **diathesis-stress model of NSSI** (Figure 13.14) posits that individuals who experience certain cognitive, emotional, or social risks may develop NSSI. Distal risks include (a) cognitive variables that predispose them toward negative affect, such as cognitive biases and distortions or depressive attributions; (b) emotional variables, such as emotional dysregulation and depression; and (3) social variables, such as a history of maltreatment or current problems with parents or peers, that contribute to feelings of alienation, isolation, or loneliness.

NSSI is typically prompted by specific stressful events. These events involve autonomic overarousal, such as feelings of intense anxiety, depression, anger, or emotional pain. Sometimes, however, NSSI is brought about by autonomic underactivity, such as when someone who is experiencing depression or PTSD reports anhedonia or numbness. In these instances, NSSI may be used to regulate emotions either upward or downward. Stressful social events can also prompt episodes of NSSI. For example, criticism from parents, disputes with classmates or friends, or the disruption of interpersonal relationships can elicit NSSI. In these instances, NSSI may be used to obtain others' attention, to communicate emotional pain, or to avoid social responsibilities.

Of course, not everyone who experiences both distal risk factors and proximal stressors will develop NSSI. Indeed, most individuals will *not* show NSSI. According to the diathesis-stress model, NSSI-specific risk factors are also necessary. Chief among these risks is social exposure to NSSI. Peers and the media can model NSSI, encourage its use, and reduce inhibitions against using self-injury to regulate emotions and social interactions. The presence of self-criticism or self-hatred may also prompt individuals to direct negative feelings toward themselves.

Figure 13.14   Diathesis-Stress Model of NSSI

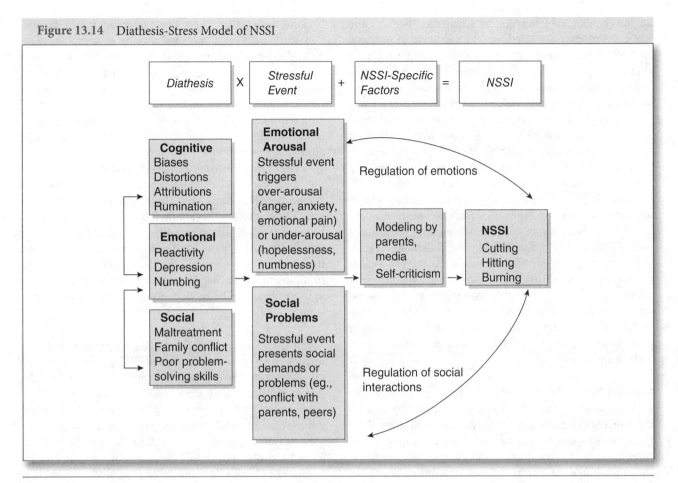

Source: Based on Nock and Cha (2009).

Finally, the diathesis-stress model posits that NSSI is either automatically reinforcing, through its effects on emotions, or socially reinforcing, through its effects on social interactions. Consequently, NSSI is likely to be repeated over time. The model predicts that interventions which reduce the distal and proximal risk factors for NSSI, or decrease their reinforcing properties, will be most efficacious.

Treatment for NSSI

Dialectical Behavior Therapy (DBT)

The Dialectic. DBT was developed by Marsha Linehan as a treatment for adults with Borderline Personality Disorder (BPD). BPD is characterized by long-standing difficulties with emotion regulation, unstable sense of identity, and tumultuous interpersonal relationships. Adults with BPD often, but not always, engage in NSSI to express psychological distress, to regulate emotions, or to gain attention from others. Because DBT has been shown to reduce self-injury in adults with BPD, many experts consider it the first-line treatment for adolescents with NSSI.

The goal of DBT is to help clients develop "a life that is worth living." To do so, the client and therapist use a dialectical approach to understanding the client and her relationship with others and the world. **Dialectic** is an approach to discovering truth used by classical philosophers, such as Socrates and Plato. It assumes that truth can be determined by following "the middle path" between two extremes. For example, philosophers might discern what "justice" is by offering two arguments. One philosopher might claim that justice is the will of the strongest person (i.e., a thesis). A second philosopher might offer a counterclaim that justice is the will of the majority (i.e., an antithesis). The dialectic assumes that neither position is entirely true; rather, truth likely falls somewhere in the middle of these extreme positions (i.e., the synthesis). For example, we might conclude that justice involves doing what is good, regardless of who wills it. This middle position can be further explored and subjected to inquiry.

Therapists who practice DBT help clients identify and modulate extreme beliefs. Often, individuals who engage in self-harm show black-and-white, **dichotomous thinking**. They may view themselves, others, and the world in extremes: either as *all* good or *all* bad. For example, an adolescent may view her English teacher as "perfect" and her math teacher as "worthless." She is likely to overlook all faults of the former teacher and focus exclusively on the shortcomings of the latter. More commonly, people who engage in dichotomous thinking oscillate between idealizing and demonizing the same person. For example, after arguing with her boyfriend, a girl might think, "He never cared about me; he only used me for sex." Later, however, the same girl might regret the argument, thinking, "Why did I lose my temper? I'm such a fool. I don't know why he puts up with me. I'll never find anyone as good as him."

Dichotomous thinking is a cognitive distortion. People are never "all good" or "all bad." Usually, people have qualities that are both admirable and disappointing. A primary goal of DBT is to help clients see the world in shades of gray, that is, to recognize and tolerate both good and bad aspects in themselves and others. DBT is also a behavioral therapy, which means that the therapist accomplishes goals by focusing on the client's current behavior: her thoughts, feelings, and actions. Although current behavior can be influenced by past experiences (e.g., abuse), most time in therapy is spent addressing current problems.

Linehan's Biosocial Model. DBT is based on the premise that people who engage in NSSI have underlying problems with emotion regulation. In response to psychosocial stress, these individuals experience negative emotions more quickly and more intensively than most other people. Furthermore, they take longer to return to baseline levels of emotional arousal. Linehan argues that this "emotional vulnerability" is inherited and likely manifests itself in the individual's neurophysiology.

Emotional vulnerability becomes problematic when individuals experience psychosocial stress. Linehan suggests that one particularly important stress is an **invalidating environment**, that is, interpersonal relationships during childhood or adolescence in which family and peers ignore, dismiss, or trivialize the extent of these individuals' emotional suffering. Invalidating environments are especially likely to emerge in abusive relationships, in which the physical, social, and emotional needs of children are minimized or ignored. Over time, children and adolescents are believed to internalize this invalidating environment, leading them to doubt or dismiss their own feelings, ignore their social-emotional needs, and abdicate their sense of self, autonomy, or identity. As a result, these individuals experience intense negative emotions in response to psychosocial stress, yet they lack the intrapersonal and interpersonal resources to cope in adaptive ways. Instead, they may use NSSI to regulate negative emotions and prompt others to acknowledge (rather than dismiss) the extent of their suffering.

Therapists use the dialectic as the primary strategy to help clients. During the course of therapy, they try to strike a balance between validating the clients' negative emotions and encouraging them to change. Validation is important,

because it shows the client that the therapist (unlike others) will accept good and bad aspects of her personality and behavior. Specifically, the therapist listens to and shows interest in the client's feelings and attempts to understand them in the context of her past experiences and current relationships. The therapist also tries to understand the client's self-harming behavior from the client's point-of-view; acknowledging ways that self-harm might serve certain emotional or social functions.

The therapist also encourages clients to consider changing their current behavior. Typically, the therapist can encourage behavioral change only after she has taken the time to accept the client's emotional distress. Acceptance, however, is not synonymous with approval. In the context of a validating therapeutic relationship (perhaps the first one the client has experienced), the therapist and client might find ways to tolerate negative emotions, view self and others in more flexible and forgiving ways, and increase the client's coping skills.

Multifamily Group DBT for Adolescents. Miller and colleagues (2009) describe a modified DBT program designed for adolescents who engage in deliberate self-injury. In addition to traditional individual therapy, adolescents and their parents participate in 16 weeks of twice-weekly multifamily group sessions. Families are exposed to other families who are experiencing similar problems, so they can support and learn from each other. Each session addresses one of the following five skills: (a) mindfulness, (b) distress tolerance, (c) emotional regulation, (d) interpersonal effectiveness, and (e) walking the middle path.

Mindfulness is based on Buddhist philosophy, although its application does not depend on a commitment to that religion. Mindfulness refers to the ability to see people and events as they are in the present moment. It depends on focusing one's attention and becoming aware of self, others, and one's surroundings in an accepting and nonjudgmental way. Mindful thinking is antithetical to the cognitive distortions shown by many people who engage in self-harm. Instead of avoiding negative feelings, being overwhelmed by emotions, and dichotomizing experience, mindfulness requires the individual to experience and accept thoughts and feelings—both positive and negative—as they occur.

A closely related skill is **distress tolerance**. Whereas many individuals attempt to avoid negative emotions, adolescents in DBT learn to recognize and validate unpleasant feelings. A premise of therapy is that adolescents can find meaning in suffering if they are able to accept and learn from it. For example, the death of a loved one or the loss of a romantic relationship can be extremely upsetting, but it can also be a source of growth and opportunity. During the course of therapy, clients learn strategies to cope with intense negative emotions, such as self-soothing and distraction. Clients also work to find ways to accept negative emotions and learn from them.

A critical component of therapy is **emotion regulation training**. Training begins by helping clients recognize and differentiate various negative emotions. For example, clients might be encouraged to identify and describe aspects of anger, such as "bitterness," "envy," or "wrath." Then, clients are asked to differentiate these feelings by identifying events or cognitions that often elicit them. For example, "bitterness" might arise from thoughts such as "He shouldn't have done that to me" whereas "wrath" might follow cognitions such as "I need to teach him a lesson." Clients also identify maladaptive ways of responding to these emotions, such as injuring oneself as a form of self-punishment (because of bitterness) or injuring oneself to make others feel guilty (because of wrath). Most important, clients work to change cognitions that often elicit maladaptive behavioral responses and find new, more adaptive means of coping with negative emotions.

The fourth component of group therapy is **interpersonal effectiveness training**. Recall that many people who engage in NSSI show deficits in social functioning. One aspect of interpersonal effectiveness training is to teach clients strategies for identifying problems, generating possible solutions, selecting and implementing the best solution, and evaluating outcomes. Because clients often react to interpersonal problems in an impulsive manner, therapists emphasize the need to consider the consequences of one's actions before implementing a solution to a problem. Although self-injury might result in immediate sympathy from family and peers, it may hurt the quality of relationships in the long run. Another aspect of interpersonal effectiveness training is improving capacity for effective communication. Recall that some people engage in NSSI to convey distress or obtain attention from others. In group therapy, clients learn how to ask for what they want more directly, to say no when appropriate, and to maintain their integrity and autonomy in their relationships.

The final component of therapy is "**walking the middle path**." Families learn dialectical thinking, that is, the need to view self and others in shades of gray rather than at extremes. Specifically, it is important for adolescents and parents to view each other more completely (i.e., as both/and) rather than dichotomously (i.e., as either/or). For example, an angry adolescent girl might feel both bitterness *and* sympathy for her mother, who has disappointed her many times in the past. Similarly, a frustrated mother might acknowledge that she can feel both love *and* resentment toward her daughter.

Efficacy of DBT. Several randomized controlled studies have shown that DBT causes a reduction in suicide attempts and deliberate self-injury among adult women with BPD. DBT is associated with improvements in adult's social-emotional and interpersonal functioning as well (Klonsky et al., 2011).

Unfortunately, we do not yet know if DBT is efficacious when used (a) to treat adolescents or (b) to treat individuals who engage in NSSI but who do not have BPD. No randomized controlled studies of DBT for adolescents have been conducted (Miller, Rathus, & Linehan, 2006). Quasi-experimental studies of DBT involving adolescents are extremely limited and have yielded mixed results (Washburn et al., 2012). For example, in one quasi-experimental study, adolescents who participated in 12 weeks of DBT had fewer hospitalizations, reported less suicidal ideation, and were more likely to complete treatment than adolescents who received traditional outpatient therapy. Unfortunately, DBT did not appear to have effects on suicidal behavior or NSSI (Rathus & Miller, 2002). In another small study, adolescents who participated in DBT showed improvements in mood and reduction in deliberate self-harm; however, gains were not superior to adolescents in the control group who received traditional treatment (Katz et al., 2004). Because of its success with adults, DBT remains a promising, but as yet unproven, treatment for adolescent NSSI.

Other Cognitive-Behavior Therapies

Although many consider DBT to be the treatment of choice for NSSI, other cognitive-behavioral interventions are available (Lynch & Cozza, 2009; Newman, 2009). Whereas a key component of DBT is to improve clients' capacity for emotion regulation, many other cognitive-behavioral treatments target clients' problem-solving skills and maladaptive ways of thinking.

Social problem-solving training is based on the premise that individuals who show suicidal and non-suicidal behaviors are often overwhelmed by interpersonal problems or attempt to solve these problems in impulsive, maladaptive ways. The two primary goals of therapy are to alter one's distressing reactions to problems so they do not become emotionally overwhelming and improve one's social problem-solving strategies to more effectively overcome these problems and achieve one's goals. Treatment involves (a) changing clients' problem orientation, (b) improving their problem-solving strategies, and (c) decreasing impulsive, destructive decision making.

Problem orientation can be either positive or negative. People with positive orientations view problems as challenges that can provide opportunities to learn and grow. These individuals also view themselves as having the self-efficacy to overcome problems. In contrast, people with negative orientations view problems as personally threatening. They tend to view themselves as lacking self-efficacy and may become inhibited or overwhelmed in problem situations. Problem orientation is largely determined by client's cognitions. Realistic, flexible thoughts lead people to adopt a positive orientation. Rigid, irrational thoughts tend to produce a negative orientation.

To change clients' problem orientation, a therapist might use the reverse advocacy role-play strategy. Specifically, the therapist would pretend to be a person (like the client) with a negative problem orientation. As the therapist states rigid,

ROLE REVERSAL IN THERAPY

Therapist: The problem I'm having with my boyfriend is really bad. No one else's boyfriend gives her such trouble.

Tonya: Really? None of your friends have problems with their boyfriends like you?

Therapist: No. All of their relationships are perfect.

Tonya: You know that can't be true. They're always coming to you with their relationship problems.

Therapist: OK, maybe they have problems with their boyfriends too. But this problem I'm having is worse. There's no way I can solve it.

Tonya: What have you tried so far? Have you tried talking to him about the problem?

Therapist: No. What's the point? I know it won't work. I know what he'll say already.

Tonya: How do you know if you haven't tried? It sounds like you're giving up before even starting.

---

distorted, and irrational beliefs about his problems, the client's job is to challenge these beliefs using more realistic, flexible thinking. Consider Tonya in the above Research to Practice, a client trying to change her therapist's attitude regarding her boyfriend.

The second component of therapy is systematic instruction in **rational problem solving**. Specifically, clients learn to follow several steps when confronted with social problems:

- *Recognize cues:* The client learns to recognize cues that indicate a social problem is occurring. These cues can be cognitive (e.g., a negative automatic thought, "I'm completely worthless"), emotional (e.g., shame), or physiological (e.g., flushed face). Clients are taught to identify problems instead of avoiding them.
- *Define the problem:* The client gathers as much information about the problem as possible, separates facts from assumptions, and states the problem in clear, direct language. A clear, concrete definition of the problem makes it more manageable. For example, the problem, "My boyfriend doesn't love me" is easily overwhelming, whereas the problem, "My boyfriend forgot my birthday" might be upsetting but more manageable. The client also identifies her goal, that is, what she hopes to accomplish. Goals might include communicating anger, getting revenge, or improving the relationship.
- *Generate solutions:* The client brainstorms as many solutions to the problem as possible. Solutions should be flexible and creative, rather than rigid and stereotyped. For example, possible solutions might include confronting her boyfriend directly, writing a letter to him without sending it, talking with a friend, going for a walk, or self-harm.
- *Decision making:* The client systematically considers the costs and benefits of each solution. For example, how

likely will each solution allow the client to reach her goal? Will the client be able to successfully implement each solution? What will be the effects of each solution on the client and others?

- *Solution implementation and verification:* The client selects and implements the best solution. The solution might be role-played during the session and then later implemented in real life. The client then evaluates how well the solution allowed her to reach her problem-solving goal. If the result was not satisfactory, the client and therapist recycle through the problem-solving steps to find a better solution in the future.

Systematic problem-solving is especially important to adolescents and young adults who engage in NSSI, because they tend to avoid interpersonal problems or react in impulsive ways. For example, researchers compared the social problem-solving skills of adolescents with and without histories of NSSI. Although both groups of adolescents were able to generate the same number of possible solutions to hypothetical interpersonal problems, adolescents with histories of NSSI tended to select solutions without considering their long-term consequences. Furthermore, their solutions were often prompted by negative emotions rather than clear, rational thoughts.

Unfortunately, studies examining the effectiveness of problem-solving training to treat NSSI have yielded mixed results (Washburn et al., 2012). Problem-solving therapy is efficacious in reducing anxiety, depression, and hopelessness in older adolescents and young adults; however, it does not consistently decrease self-injury. On the other hand, in another study, adolescents and young adults who engaged in deliberate self-harm were randomly assigned to a comprehensive CBT package or treatment in the community (Slee et al., 2008). The CBT package specifically targeted cognitions related to self-harm. Results were promising. Nine months after treatment, individuals who received CBT showed reductions in deliberate self-harm compared to controls. Furthermore, improvements in mood and social problem solving were associated with these reductions (Figure 13.15).

Taken together, these findings indicate that CBT may be helpful in reducing NSSI in adolescents. However, comprehensive CBT packages that target adolescents' depressive symptoms, maladaptive ways of thinking, and problem-solving skills may yield the best results. Clearly, more research on the application of CBT for adolescents with NSSI is needed (Washburn et al., 2012).

Figure 13.15   CBT May Be Efficacious for NSSI

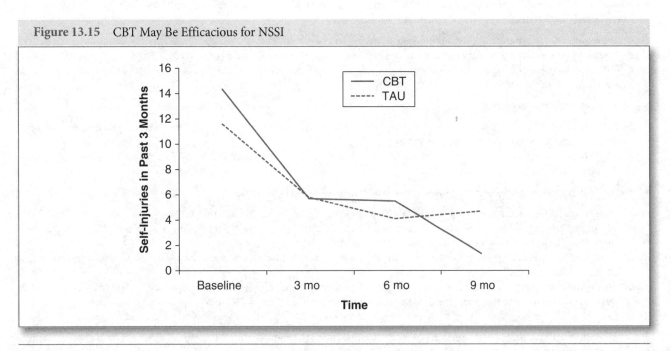

Source: Based on Slee et al. (2008).

Note: Adolescents and young adults randomly assigned to CBT showed significant reductions in NSSI, even compared to individuals assigned to treatment as usual (TAU). Improvements in depression and problem solving were associated with reductions in self-injury.

CHAPTER SUMMARY

Disruptive Mood Dysregulation Disorder (DMDD)

- DMDD is a mood disorder characterized by chronically irritable mood and recurrent, severe temper outbursts. Onset occurs in childhood, typically during the early school years.

  - DMDD is different from ADHD. Youths with DMDD tend to show angry and irritable moods not shown by youths with ADHD.
  - DMDD is different from ODD. The temper outbursts shown by youths with DMDD are severe, are directed toward many people in multiple settings, and typically involve aggressive and destructive acts directed toward people and objects.
  - DMDD is different from pediatric bipolar disorder. Youths with DMDD show chronic mood problems whereas youths with Bipolar Disorder show discrete episodes of mania and depression.

- In *DSM-5*, DMDD is classified as a mood disorder because (a) its most salient feature is irritable and angry mood and (b) youths with DMDD tend to develop anxiety and mood problems later in childhood and adolescence.
- Youths with DMDD tend to have problems recognizing and interpreting other people's emotional expressions and regulating their own emotional reactions to frustration. Over-activation of the amygdala and underactivation of the medial frontal gyrus and anterior cingulate may underlie these emotional processing and regulation problems.
- Traditional parent training and behavioral summer treatment programs have generally not been effective for youths with DMDD. Instead, comprehensive family treatment, which target's children's emotion-regulation skills, seems to work.
- Recent data suggest that improved sleep hygiene and chronotherapy may help some children with DMDD regulate their moods.

Major Depressive Disorder (MDD)

- In children and adolescents, MDD is characterized by a period of dysphoric or irritable mood that lasts at least 2 weeks and may be accompanied by anhedonia; changes in appetite, weight, and motor behavior; low energy, feelings of worthlessness or guilt, concentration problems, and thoughts of death.

  - In children and adolescents, Persistent Depressive Disorder is diagnosed when youths show depressive symptoms for more than one year. Typically, symptoms are not as severe as in MDD and do not involve suicidal ideation.
  - Anxiety disorders, disruptive behavior disorders, and substance use problems often occur alongside MDD. Whereas anxiety and conduct problems tend to emerge before MDD, substance use problems often emerge after MDD.

- Almost 3% of youths have made a serious suicide attempt. Many of these youths experienced depression, anxiety, or other forms of intense psychological distress prior to the attempt.

  - Professionals can assess the likelihood of suicide by asking youths directly.
  - Youths who express a desire to die, have a plan to kill themselves, and have a means to implement the plan are at greatest risk.
  - Psychosocial risks, such as child maltreatment, family conflict, social ostracism, and other mental health problems, can also increase the likelihood of suicide.

- MDD is relatively rare in prepubescent children; however, the prevalence is 3% to 7% in adolescents.

  - Girls are twice as likely to develop MDD as boys. Their increased risk may be due to increased empathy, compliance, and problems with emotion regulation that emerge after puberty.
  - MDD is fairly stable in childhood and adolescence. Approximately 20% of depressed youths show chronic mood problems, extending into late adolescence and adulthood.

- Research indicates genetic, biological, and environmental causes for MDD in children.

  - MDD is heritable; monozygotic concordance is 70% to 85% whereas dizygotic concordance is 19%.
  - The monoamine hypothesis implicates serotonin and norepinephrine in the development and maintenance of MDD. Most research supporting the hypothesis comes from research involving adults.
  - Some youths with MDD show dysregulation of the HPA axis. Dysregulation may underlie the high comorbidity of depression and anxiety in children.
  - Youths with MDD experience more stressful life events than nondepressed youths, and they cope with these events in less effective ways. Some data indicate that youths with MDD may also elicit negative events by their depressive behavior.
  - Cognitive theories suggest that youths' thoughts mediate the relationship between life events and depressed mood.

    - Beck's cognitive theory of depression posits that youths with MDD show cognitive biases and distortions that predispose them to depressed mood.
    - The learned helplessness hypothesis suggests that youths develop depression when they feel like environmental contingencies are beyond their control.
    - The reformulated learned helplessness model indicates that youths who attribute negative events to (a) internal, (b) stable, and (c) global causes are more likely to experience depression.

  - Several theories for MDD implicate family interactions as a cause for the disorder.

    - According to attachment theory, youths who develop internal working models of others based on inconsistent, insensitive care may experience relationship problems and depression in the future.
    - Maternal depression can compromise the quality of parent-child interactions during children's development and contribute to children's mood problems.
    - High family conflict, especially expressed emotion, can exacerbate depressed mood in children.

  - Peer interactions can contribute to depressed mood, especially in adolescents.

    - Several studies indicate that peer rejection in adolescence predicts the onset of MDD.
    - Youths who show biases in social information processing often experience both interpersonal problems and depressed mood.

- Several evidence-based treatments are available for youths with MDD.

  - The SSRI fluoxetine (Prozac) is superior to placebo in alleviating depressive symptoms in youths. Other medications yield benefits only slightly better than placebo. A very small number of children who take SSRIs show increased suicidal ideation.
  - Behavior therapy for MDD involves self-monitoring and response-contingent reinforcement. Children who behave in a nondepressed manner may experience improved mood.
  - Stark's CBT for depressed children and the adolescent coping with depression course are evidence-based psychosocial therapies that target both depressive behaviors and maladaptive ways of thinking and problem-solving.
  - Interpersonal therapy attributes depression to disruptions in interpersonal relationships. Therapy involves coping with interpersonal loss, managing role disruptions or transitions, or developing interpersonal skills to improve social functioning and mood.
  - Results of the TADS and TORDIA studies suggest that combining psychotherapy and medication may marginally improve the outcomes of youths with MDD compared to medication alone.

Non-Suicidal Self-Injury (NSSI)

- NSSI occurs when individuals repeatedly, intentionally damage the surface of their bodies in a manner that causes tissue damage. Unlike youths who attempt suicide, youths with NSSI do not indicate a willingness to die.
- NSSI is a "disorder for future study" in *DSM-5*, although it is a frequent problem among adolescents and young adults.
- Approximately 13% to 29% of adolescents in the community have engaged in self-injury. NSSI is 4 times more common among adolescent girls than boys. It tends to be fairly stable over time.
- NSSI is an important predictor of suicide. NSSI and suicide might be elicited by a third variable (e.g., depression); NSSI may serve as "gateway" behavior to more serious self-harm and suicide; or NSSI may gradually build up a person's pain tolerance and willingness to die.
- The four-functioning model suggests that NSSI is maintained by positive or negative reinforcement. Furthermore, reinforcement can either be social or automatic (i.e., within the individual).
- Social contagion theory asserts that youths develop NSSI chiefly through modeling or information from peers or the media.
- Linehan's emotion dysregulation model posits that NSSI is a maladaptive attempt to control mood states, either to displace emotional pain with physical pain or to reduce emotional numbness.
- Child abuse and neglect sometimes predisposes youths to NSSI. Child maltreatment can disrupt the development of (a) children's physiological stress response, (b) children's capacity for emotion regulation, or (c) children's internal representation of themselves and others.
- The diathesis-stress model asserts that early psychosocial risks combined with immediate psychosocial stressors and modeling can cause NSSI. Self-injury is then maintained through positive and/or negative reinforcement.
- Evidence-based treatments for NSSI are somewhat limited. Most treatments are extensions of therapies developed for adults.

  - Dialectical behavior therapy (DBT) challenges dichotomous thinking shown by many youths with NSSI. Therapists encourage youths to be mindful of their emotions and learn to tolerate and regulate negative feelings in more adaptive ways.
  - Multifamily group DBT is an extension of individual DBT for parents and adolescents. Family interpersonal skills are practiced in a group format.
  - Cognitive-behavior therapy for NSSI focuses chiefly on changing adolescent's problem orientation. Therapists encourage youths to view problems in realistic, flexile ways. Youths learn systematic ways to solve interpersonal problems.

KEY TERMS

acquired capacity for death theory   507

active coping   491

affect   468

anterior cingulate cortex (ACC)   476

attributions   493

avoidance coping   491

Bipolar Disorders   469

chronic depression   484

chronotherapy   479

cognitive biases   491

cognitive distortions   491

cognitive restructuring   501

cortisol   489

Depressive Disorders   469

depressogenic attributional style   493

dexamethasone suppression test (DST)   489

dialectic   511

diathesis-stress model of NSSI   510

dichotomous thinking   511

Disruptive Mood Dysregulation Disorder (DMDD)   469

distress tolerance   512

dysthymia   484

emotion regulation training   513

emotional dysregulation model   509

expressed emotion (EE)   495

four-function model (FFM) of NSSI   508

gateway theory   507

hypersomnia   480

hypothalamus-pituitary-adrenal (HPA) axis   489

insomnia   480

intergenerational interpersonal stress model   495

internal working models   494

interpersonal effectiveness training   513

invalidating environment   512

kindling hypothesis   487

Major Depressive Disorder (MDD)   480

Major Depressive Disorder, Recurrent   482

Major Depressive Disorder, Single Episode   482

medial frontal gyrus (MFG)   476

mindfulness   512

modeling   509

monoamine hypothesis   488

mood   468

negative automatic thoughts   491

CRITICAL THINKING EXERCISES

1. DMDD is very similar to (a) Oppositional Defiant Disorder and (b) Bipolar Disorder. How might a psychologist differentiate these two disorders in a 10-year-old child?

2. Why do you think traditional parent training programs and summer treatment programs are not as effective for youths with DMDD as they are for children with ADHD and ODD?

3. Imagine that you are a school psychologist. You want to help the teachers in your school recognize the symptoms of depression in middle school students. Create a list of symptoms (with examples) of what teachers should look for to identify students with depression.

4. Only trained professionals should evaluate someone's risk for suicide. However, it is often helpful for parents and paraprofessionals (e.g., teachers, coaches) to know suicide risk factors. What are some risk factors? If you suspected that an adolescent had suicidal thoughts, what would you do?

5. G. Stanley Hall, the first president of the American Psychological Association, described adolescence as a period of "storm and stress." He believed that adolescents typically show parental conflict and mood problems during the teenage years. Evaluate Hall's claim. Is it normal for adolescents to be depressed?

6. Alida is participating in cognitive therapy for depression. During therapy, Alida comments, "I messed up on my math test yesterday and got a D–. I just can't make myself study. I'm just no good at anything." If you were Alida's therapist, how might you use cognitive restructuring to change her ways of thinking?

7. Three treatment options for adolescent depression are (a) medication, (b) psychotherapy, and (c) a combination of medication and psychotherapy. If your adolescent was depressed, what course of treatment would you choose? Why?

8. Adolescents are sometimes introduced to NSSI through social media. How might you use social media to prevent NSSI?

EXTEND YOUR LEARNING

Videos, practice tests, flash cards, study guides, and links to online resources for this chapter are available to students online. Teachers also have access to lecture notes, PowerPoint presentations, suggestions for classroom activities, and possible exam questions. Visit: www .sagepub.com/weis2e.

CHAPTER 14

Bipolar Spectrum Disorders and Schizophrenia

BIPOLAR SPECTRUM DISORDERS

Bipolar Spectrum Disorders (BSDs) are serious mood disorders that are defined by the presence of manic symptoms. **Mania** refers to a discrete period of elevated, expansive, or irritable mood and increased level of energy and activity. All youths with BSDs have at least some manic symptoms. Many (but not all) youths with BSDs also show symptoms of depression. Consequently, these disorders are referred to as "bipolar" (i.e. manic-depressive) mood disorders, in contrast to "unipolar" depression.

DSM-5 recognizes four BSDs that are relevant to children and adolescents: Bipolar I Disorder, Bipolar II Disorder, Cyclothymic Disorder, and Other Specified Bipolar and Related Disorder. These disorders exist on a continuum, or "spectrum," of severity. Bipolar I Disorder (BP-I), defined by the presence of full-blown mania, is usually considered most severe. In contrast, Other Specified Bipolar and Related Disorder defined by subthreshold manic symptoms, is often considered least severe. Although symptom severity can vary, all of the BSDs are serious and can greatly disrupt the well-being of youths who experience them.

ENERGETIC EMILY

Sixteen-year-old Emily Gellar was referred to our clinic by her parents. Mrs. Gellar said that Emily had been more reclusive, sullen, and moody in recent weeks. Emily was often disrespectful, irritable, and upset. When her mother asked her to clean up after dinner, Emily replied, "Why don't you just do it—that's all you're good for around here anyway!" In the previous 4 weeks, Emily dropped out of two of her favorite activities at school. She also slept very little, ate even less, and was generally sluggish and mopey around the house.

Emily reluctantly agreed to a "trial run" of therapy with Brenda Turner, a social worker at an out clinic. Brenda diagnosed Emily with Major Depressive Disorder and began to use interpersonal therapy to improve Emily's mood. However, by the fourth session, Brenda noticed a dramatic change in Emily's affect and behavior. Emily arrived at the session in an unusually good mood. She spoke very fast: "I feel great today, Brenda, you know, like I can do anything. I think it's because I am in love." As Emily discussed her new boyfriend, Brenda noticed that her speech was extremely loud and her train of thought was difficult to follow. "Have you been drinking today?" Brenda asked. In a giddy tone of voice, Emily responded, "Not today, I don't feel like I need to."

During the session, Brenda noticed how distractible Emily was. Emily fidgeted in her chair, paced about the room, and kept complaining how "boring" it was to sit and talk. She reported a sudden increase in energy and mood. She added, "You know, I think I'm cured. Maybe we don't have to meet any more." Emily said she slept only about three or four hours in the previous 2 days but still did not feel tired. In fact, at 3 a.m. the night before, she decided to paint her room. "Thank God for Wal-Mart!" she said, "Do you know they're open 24 hours . . . and they sell paint?"

After the session, Brenda telephoned Mrs. Gellar to express her concern. Mrs. Gellar reported that Emily did, in fact, attempt to paint her bedroom in bright green but only managed to complete one and a half walls before moving on to another project. Emily also had been in trouble that week for skipping school, staying out all night, and going on a shopping spree with her mother's credit card. Mrs. Gellar stated, "She's been so distractible and flighty lately, I don't know what's gotten into her. Do you think she's just being a teenager?" Brenda answered, "No, I don't think so."

What Are Bipolar Spectrum Disorders?

Bipolar I Disorder

To be diagnosed with Bipolar I Disorder (BP-I), a person must have (or have had) at least one manic episode (Table 14.1, Diagnostic Criteria for Bipolar I Disorder). By definition, a manic episode is "a distinct period of abnormally, persistently elevated, expansive, or irritable mood and persistently increased activity and energy" (American Psychiatric Association, 2013, p. 127). By definition, manic episodes last at least one week and symptoms are present most of the day, nearly every day. In some instances, however, the duration criterion for mania (i.e., 7 days) is waived if the person requires hospitalization.

During manic episodes, adults with Bipolar I Disorder describe their mood as euphoric, cheerful, high, or elated. They seem to have boundless energy and may describe themselves as powerful or "on top of the world." Children and adolescents also typically report expansive mood, elation, and increased energy. Most experts view the presence of elated mood and increased energy as the cardinal symptom of BSDs. On average, 70% of youths with BSDs show uncharacteristically elated, expansive, or euphoric mood. Nearly 90% of these youths also show a dramatic increase in energy. These symptoms are highly specific to Bipolar Disorder; that is, they are common among youths with the disorder but relatively uncommon among youths with other psychiatric illnesses. Therefore, they are especially useful in identifying the disorder in children and adolescents (Youngstrom et al., 2008).

Children and adolescents also frequently display irritable mood during manic episodes. Their mood is often described as "touchy," angry, oppositional, or reactive. Young children with mania can be grouchy and easily set off. They may throw hour-long tantrums: yelling, crying, throwing objects, and acting physically aggressive toward others. Older children and adolescents sometimes display emotional outbursts or "affective storms." These tantrums often arise with little provocation (Kowatch, Fristad, Birmaher, Wagner, Findling, & Hellander, 2005).

Irritability is extremely common among youths with Bipolar Disorder, even those who also show expansiveness and increased energy. On average, 81% of youths with the disorder show a noticeable increase in irritability. However, irritability is not specific to Bipolar Disorder; it is a feature of pediatric depression, anxiety, and Oppositional Defiant Disorder as well. Therefore, many clinicians consider irritability to be a general indicator that "something's wrong" with the child, rather than a specific indicator of Bipolar Disorder. Irritability is analogous to a fever; it suggests that the child is sick but cannot specify which illness afflicts her (Youngstrom et al., 2008).

Table 14.1   Diagnostic Criteria for Bipolar I Disorder

A. Criteria have been met for at least one manic episode. A **manic episode** is defined by the following:

- A distinct period of abnormally and persistently elevated, expansive, or irritable mood and abnormally and persistently increased goal-directed activity or energy, lasting at least one week and present most of the day, nearly every day (or any duration if hospitalization is necessary).
- During the period of mood disturbance and increased energy or activity, three (or more) of the following symptoms (four if the mood is only irritable) are present to a significant degree and represent a noticeable change from usual behavior:

    1. Inflated self-esteem or grandiosity.

    2. Decreased need for sleep (e.g., feels rested after only 3 hours of sleep).

    3. More talkative than usual or pressure to keep talking.

    4. Flight of ideas or subjective experience that thoughts are racing.

    5. Distractibility (i.e., attention too easily drawn to unimportant or irrelevant external stimuli), as reported or observed.

    6. Increase in goal-directed activity (either socially, at work or school, or sexually) or psychomotor agitation (i.e., purposeless, non-goal-directed activity).

    7. Excessive involvement in activities that have a high potential for painful consequences (e.g., engaging in unrestrained buying sprees, sexual indiscretions, or foolish business investments).

- The mood disturbance is sufficiently severe to cause marked impairment in social or occupational functioning or to necessitate hospitalization to prevent harm to self or others, or there are psychotic features.
- The episode is not attributable to the physiological effects of a substance (e.g., a drug of abuse, a medication) or to another medical condition.

B. The occurrence of the manic episode is not better explained by Schizophrenia or another psychotic disorder.

Source: Reprinted with permission from the *Diagnostic and Statistical Manual of Mental Disorders, Fifth Edition* (Copyright 2013). American Psychiatric Association.

Note: Hypomanic and major depressive episodes are common in Bipolar I Disorder, but are not required for the diagnosis.

In addition to these changes in mood and energy, mania is characterized by at least three other symptoms (or four symptoms, if the person shows only irritable mood). On average, youths show five or six symptoms during a manic episode (Figure 14.1).

- Grandiosity or inflated self-esteem
- Racing thoughts or flight of ideas
- Activity level increase or psychomotor agitation
- Pressured speech or excessive talkativeness
- Excessive involvement in potentially harmful activities
- Sleep disturbance (i.e., decreased need for sleep)
- Distractibility

You can remember these symptoms using the acronym GRAPES+D (Diler & Birmaher, 2012).

Grandiosity or Inflated Self-Esteem. In adults, grandiosity is characterized by unusually high self-confidence, exaggerated self-esteem, and overrated self-importance. Some adults hold erroneous beliefs that they have special abilities, talents, or skills. Youths with mania are also capable of grandiosity and inflated self-esteem. Children may manifest grandiose thinking by claiming that they are special, have superhuman abilities, or hold magical powers. For example, a child with bipolar disorder may try to jump off the roof of his house because he thinks that he has unusual athletic abilities. Older children and adolescents might tell their coaches how to run the team, or their teachers how to instruct the class, because they believe that they have special talents or intelligence (Kowatch et al., 2005; Kowatch & Fristad, 2006).

Racing Thoughts or Flight of Ideas. Adults with mania often report that their thoughts are "racing" or occurring too fast to articulate to others. Some patients describe the sensation as watching two or three television programs at once. Racing thoughts are sometimes referred to as a **flight of ideas**. Children and adolescents also report racing thoughts. For example, they may say that their minds are going "100 miles an hour" or report that "there is an Energizer Bunny up there [in my head]" (Kowatch et al., 2005, p. 216).

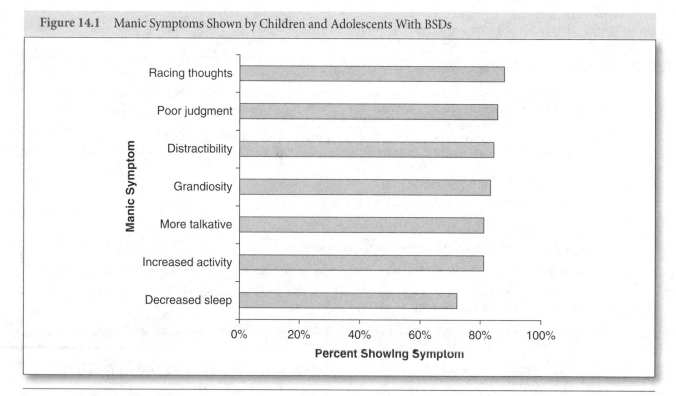

Source: Based on Findling and colleagues (2001).

Note: On average, youths display 5.5 of seven possible symptoms.

Increased Activity or Psychomotor Agitation. Adults with mania often show a marked increase in **goal-directed activity**; that is, they initiate a wide range of new activities and behaviors (see text box *DSM-IV → DSM-5* Changes: Increased Energy and Activity). For example, some adults with mania may decide to rebuild their car engine, write a novel, or start a new business with little preparation or training. Usually, these goal-directed activities are poorly planned and executed. Youths with mania can also show increased goal-directed activity. For example, children may draw, color, or build elaborate block towers. Older adolescents may begin a number of ambitious projects, like taking apart their computer. Youths with mania may also show **psychomotor agitation**; that is, they may appear hyperactive, restless, or impulsive. They often engage in short bursts of frenzied activity that do not have much purpose (Kowatch et al., 2005; Weller et al., 2004).

DSM-IV → DSM-5 CHANGES

INCREASED ENERGY AND ACTIVITY

In *DSM-5*, "increased activity or energy" is listed as a prominent symptom of a manic episode. *DSM-IV* also included increased "goal-directed activity" as a feature of mania and hypomania, but it was not emphasized. Instead, elevated or expansive mood was considered the defining feature of these conditions.

The *DSM-5* Mood Disorders Work Group decided to highlight "increased activity or energy" to help clinicians better identify manic and hypomanic episodes that patients might have experienced in the past. Many patients experience elevations in mood that they regard as "a part of themselves" rather than as an indicator of a psychiatric problem. When clinicians ask them, "Was there ever a time when you experienced a discrete period of elevated or expansive mood in the past?" they might answer "no."

In contrast, patients are more likely to remember discrete periods of increased energy and activity, especially when these bursts of energy seem out of the ordinary. When clinicians ask, "Was there ever a time when you experienced a discrete period of increased energy or a high amount of activity for days at a time?" they might be more likely to remember such an episode and answer "yes." Clinicians can then query their response to determine if other manic symptoms were present at the time, such as decreased need for sleep or increased high-risk activities.

Pressured Speech or More Talkative Than Usual. Many adults with mania talk rapidly in an attempt to keep up with racing thoughts. Their speech is typically fast, loud, and difficult to understand. Youths with mania may also speak rapidly. Their speech seems pressured; that is, they seem to keep talking in order to avoid periods of silence. Sometimes, they transition rapidly from one topic to the next. Some physicians call this phenomenon "knight's move thinking" because the person jumps from topic to topic like the knight on a chessboard jumps from one square to the next without moving in between.

Excessive Involvement in Activities With High Potential of Painful Consequences. Many adults with mania engage in pleasurable activities that are likely to have negative consequences. For example, some adults with mania go on shopping sprees, gambling trips, or risky sexual encounters. Youths with mania may also engage in pleasurable, but reckless, behaviors. Younger children may ride their bikes through dangerous intersections or perform stunts on their skateboards. Older children and adolescents may carelessly spend money, drive recklessly, steal items from a store, or indulge in alcohol and other drugs. Many youths with mania also show **hypersexuality**. Some show increased interest in pornography. Others engage in inappropriate, erotic behavior toward others. For example, some youths dance suggestively, attempt to touch others' private parts, or open-mouth kiss family members. Youths with mania may show these hypersexual behaviors even if they have never experienced sexual abuse.

Decreased Need for Sleep. Adults with mania show a marked decreased need for sleep. Some may feel rested after only 3 hours of sleep, while others go for days without feeling sleepy or fatigued. Youths with mania also show decreased need for sleep. Many youths with mania sleep only 4 or 5 hours at night and wake in the early morning feeling full of energy. Some wander the house, play video games, or watch TV into the early morning hours.

Distractibility. Adults with mania are easily distracted by irrelevant external stimuli or unimportant details. For example, an adult with mania may find it difficult to converse with another person because he is distracted by the pattern of the other person's tie or events occurring outside the room. Youths with mania almost always show distractibility. They may have problems concentrating on schoolwork or completing chores. Teachers and parents may describe them as disorganized or "flighty." These problems with distractibility reflect a marked change in the youth's typical behavior, not a general problem with inattention or hyperactivity-impulsivity (i.e., not due to ADHD).

Three manic symptoms are particularly useful in identifying Bipolar Disorder in children: grandiosity, decreased need for sleep, and involvement in high-risk sexual activity (Youngstrom et al., 2008). First, nearly 80% of youths with Bipolar Disorder show some form of grandiose thinking.

If grandiosity coincides with increased elation and energy, it is a good indicator of mania. Second, most (70%) youths with Bipolar Disorder show a decreased need for sleep. Typically, these youths feel rested after only a few hours of sleep. Decreased need for sleep is a good indicator of Bipolar Disorder because other disorders, such as anxiety and depression, are associated with problems of falling asleep or staying asleep. Third, high-risk sexual activity is a relatively specific symptom of Bipolar Disorder. A prepubescent child might begin acting or dressing in a sexually provocative manner at school, or an adolescent might engage in dangerous or exploitative sexual behavior with adults. A developmentally unexpected or marked change in sexual behavior is specific to only Bipolar Disorder and sexual abuse. Parents and clinicians who observe these changes in youths might suspect Bipolar Disorder, especially when the behavior is associated with increased elation and energy.

Bipolar II Disorder

To be diagnosed with Bipolar II Disorder (BP-II), a person must have (or have had) at least one major depressive episode and at least one hypomanic episode (Table 14.2, Diagnostic Criteria for Bipolar II Disorder). The prefix "hypo" means "below"; therefore, hypomania refers to less severe or prolonged manic symptoms. Like mania, hypomania is defined by a distinct period of elevated, expansive, or irritable mood and increased energy. Furthermore, the seven symptoms of hypomania are the same as the symptoms of mania. Hypomania differs from mania in three ways.

1. Hypomania lasts at least 4 days but less than one week
2. Hypomania *does not* cause significant impairment in social, occupational, or academic functioning
3. Hypomania *never* requires the person to be hospitalized

By definition, a person cannot be diagnosed with Bipolar II Disorder if she has ever had a manic episode. If the person has had a manic episode, she would be diagnosed with Bipolar I Disorder instead. Many individuals initially diagnosed with Bipolar II Disorder eventually experience a manic episode and are subsequently diagnosed with Bipolar I Disorder.

Hypomania is somewhat difficult to assess in children and adolescents. By definition, it does not lead to marked distress or impairment in functioning and does not require hospitalization. Consequently, many parents do not refer their children to treatment because of hypomania. It is also difficult to differentiate hypomania from developmentally normative behavior. For example, many adolescents are impulsive, have rapid changes in mood, or adopt irregular sleep habits, but they do not have hypomania (Youngstrom et al., 2010).

Youths with Bipolar I and II Disorders usually experience prolonged episodes of major depression. Episodes resemble Major Depressive Disorder. They are usually characterized by

Table 14.2 Diagnostic Criteria for Bipolar II Disorder

A. Criteria have been met for at least one hypomanic episode and at least one major depressive episode. A **hypomanic episode** is defined by the following:

- A distinct period of abnormally and persistently elevated, expansive, or irritable mood and abnormally and persistently increased activity or energy, lasting at least 4 days and present most of the day, nearly every day.
- During the period of mood disturbance and increased energy or activity, three (or more) of the following symptoms (four if the mood is only irritable) are present to a significant degree and represent a noticeable change from usual behavior:

  1. Inflated self-esteem or grandiosity.
  2. Decreased need for sleep (e.g., feels rested after only 3 hours of sleep).
  3. More talkative than usual or pressure to keep talking.
  4. Flight of ideas or subjective experience that thoughts are racing.
  5. Distractibility (i.e., attention too easily drawn to unimportant or irrelevant external stimuli), as reported or observed.
  6. Increase in goal-directed activity (either socially, at work or school, or sexually) or psychomotor agitation (i.e., purposeless, non-goal-directed activity).
  7. Excessive involvement in activities that have a high potential for painful consequences (e.g., engaging in unrestrained buying sprees, sexual indiscretions, or foolish business investments).

- The episode is associated with an unequivocal change in functioning that is uncharacteristic of the individual when not symptomatic.
- The disturbance in mood and the change in functioning are observable by others.
- The episode is not severe enough to cause marked impairment in social or occupational functioning or to necessitate hospitalization. If there are psychotic features, the episode is, by definition, manic.
- The episode is not attributable to the physiological effects of a substance (e.g., a drug of abuse, a medication) or to another medical condition.

B. There has never been a manic episode.

C. The occurrence of the hypomanic episode is not better explained by Schizophrenia or another psychotic disorder.

D. The symptoms of depression or the unpredictability caused by frequent alteration between periods of depression and hypomania causes clinically significant distress or impairment in social, occupational, or other important areas of functioning.

Source: Reprinted with permission from the *Diagnostic and Statistical Manual of Mental Disorders, Fifth Edition* (Copyright 2013). American Psychiatric Association.

Note: The symptoms of a major depressive episode are presented in Chapter 13.

depressed mood, low energy, and irritability. They may take several months to resolve. Some older adolescents experience a return to a normal mood state between manic and depressive episodes, but most children and younger adolescents simply experience prolonged episodes of manic and depressive symptoms (Carlson & Meyer, 2010).

On average, youths with BSDs spend more time in depressive episodes than manic or hypomanic episodes. However, it is important to note that a depressive episode is required only for Bipolar II Disorder. Although most youths with Bipolar I Disorder also experience periods of depression, these depressive episodes are not required for diagnosis of Bipolar I Disorder (Figure 14.2).

Cyclothymic Disorder

Cyclothymic Disorder is a BSD disorder that is rarely diagnosed in children and adolescents (see Table 14.3, Diagnostic Criteria for Cyclothymic Disorder). The disorder gets its name from the Greek words "kyklos" (cycle) and "thymos" (mood). It is defined by the presence of both periods of hypomanic symptoms (which do not meet full criteria for a manic episode) and periods of depressive symptoms (which do not meet full criteria for a depressive episode). Children and adolescents must experience these hypomanic and depressive symptoms for at least one year, and they must not be symptom free for more than 2 months.

Figure 14.2   Distinguishing Among the Bipolar Disorders

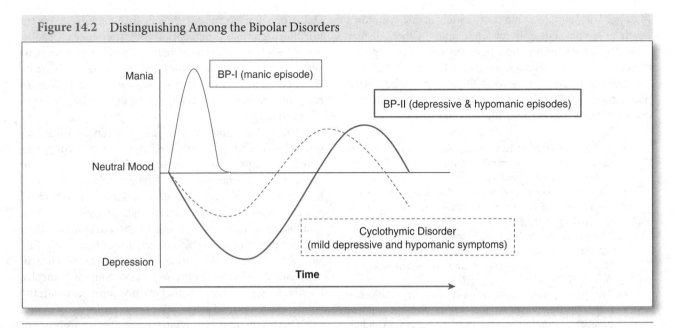

Note: BP-I is defined by at least one manic episode. BP-II is defined by at least one major depressive episode and at least one hypomanic episode (but no manic episodes). Cyclothymic Disorder is defined by recurrent depressive and hypomanic symptoms (but no major depressive or manic episodes).

Children and adolescents with Cyclothymic Disorder tend to describe their moods as a mixture of lethargy and low self-esteem, combined with racing thoughts and impulsivity (Van Meter, Youngstrom, & Findling, 2012). If Bipolar I and II Disorders are analogous to influenza, Cyclothymic Disorder would be analogous to the common cold—less severe but more long-lasting symptoms that cause distress or impairment. The most commonly reported problems are irritability and excessive activity, which rise and fall in an episodic fashion over the course of at least one year. Because irritability and excessive activity are symptoms shared by many psychiatric disorders, and because they are sometimes shown by healthy children, Cyclothymic Disorder is often misdiagnosed or overlooked by practitioners (Van Meter, Youngstrom, & Findling, 2012).

Other Specified Bipolar and Related Disorder

Other Specified Bipolar and Related Disorder is used to describe individuals with subthreshold bipolar symptoms. These people typically display symptoms of hypomania or depressed mood, but they fall short of the diagnostic criteria for any of the Bipolar Disorders. In some cases, the *number* of manic symptoms shown by these children fall just short of the three (or four) required by the definition of mania or hypomania. For example, many youths display a marked increase in irritability, motor activity, and distractibility, but they do not show enough criteria to be classified with mania. In other instances, children display a sufficient number of symptoms, but their mood episodes are not long enough to meet the *duration* criterion for mania (7 days) or hypomania

Table 14.3   Diagnostic Criteria for Cyclothymic Disorder

A. For at least 2 years (at least one year in children and adolescents) there have been numerous periods with hypomanic symptoms that do not meet criteria for a hypomanic episode and numerous periods with depressive symptoms that do not meet criteria for a major depressive episode.

B. During the above 2 year period (one year in children and adolescents), the hypomanic and depressive periods have been present for at least half the time and the individual has not been without the symptoms for more than 2 months at a time.

C. Criteria for a major depressive, manic, or hypomanic episode have never been met.

D. The symptoms of criterion A are not better explained by Schizophrenia or another Psychotic Disorder.

E. The symptoms are not attributable to the physiological effects of a substance (e.g., a drug of abuse, a medication) or another medical condition.

F. The symptoms cause clinically significant distress or impairment in social, occupational, or other important areas of functioning.

Source: Reprinted with permission from the *Diagnostic and Statistical Manual of Mental Disorders, Fifth Edition* (Copyright 2013). American Psychiatric Association.

(4 days). For example, some youths show manic symptoms nearly every day, but only for a few hours. Others display manic symptoms on multiple days but not on consecutive days (Fawcett, 2010; Fristad, Arnold, & Leffler, 2011).

DSM-5 specifies four ways individuals might be labeled with Other Specified Bipolar and Related Disorder (American Psychiatric Association, 2013):

- The person meets criteria for Bipolar II disorder, but the duration of their hypomanic symptoms is only 2–3 days, rather than the required 4 days.
- The person meets criteria for Bipolar II disorder except the number of hypomanic symptoms falls short of the required amount.
- The person meets full criteria for a hypomanic episode but has never experienced a major depressive episode. (Consequently, the person cannot be diagnosed with Bipolar II Disorder.)
- The person meets criteria for Cyclothymic Disorder, except the duration of symptoms is less than the required number of months (i.e., less than 12 months for children and adolescents).

Notice that Other Specified Bipolar and Related Disorder is only diagnosed when an individual shows a very specific symptom presentation. The diagnosis is meant to serve as a "red flag" that the person has significant bipolar symptoms and merits clinical attention and careful monitoring.

Indeed, youths with these subthreshold symptoms tend to show high rates of impairment and family distress, just like youths with Bipolar I Disorder (Birmaher, Axelson, Monk, Kalas, Goldstein et al., 2009). Furthermore, many youths initially diagnosed with subthreshold bipolar symptoms eventually meet full criteria for Bipolar I or II Disorder. In the largest longitudinal study yet conducted, researchers assessed 140 youths with subthreshold bipolar symptoms periodically for 5 years (Axelson et al., 2011). Nearly 45% of youths eventually met criteria for Bipolar I or II Disorder. On average, youths developed full-blown Bipolar I or II Disorder within 58 weeks of being first classified with subthreshold bipolar symptoms. Youths with a family history of Bipolar Disorder were especially likely to eventually develop a full-blown disorder themselves. This study highlights the importance of identifying and treating youths with subthreshold manic symptoms.

Specifying Symptoms

Bipolar I Disorder With Psychotic Features

Approximately 20% of youths with Bipolar I Disorder experience hallucinations or delusions during their manic episodes. **Hallucinations** are erroneous perceptions that do not correspond to reality. Although hallucinations can occur in any sensory modality, auditory hallucinations are most common. For example, children might hear voices telling them that they are special or possess unique talents.

Delusions are erroneous beliefs that usually involve a misinterpretation of perceptions or experiences. Usually, these beliefs are bizarre in nature or otherwise implausible. For example, an adolescent might believe that he is called to perform a special mission (i.e., delusions of reference) or has a special identity or power (i.e., delusion of grandiosity).

Youths' hallucinations and delusions can be either congruent or incongruent with their mood. Mood-congruent psychotic symptoms are consistent with the person's current mood state. For example, a child experiencing a manic episode might engage in dangerous or reckless actions because he believes he has superhuman strength or speed. Similarly, an adolescent experiencing mania might erroneously believe that her parents and friends are jealous of her, or plotting against her, because of her unusual beauty or intelligence. In contrast, mood-incongruent psychotic symptoms involve hallucinations or delusions that are not consistent with the youths' current mood state.

DSM-5 instructs clinicians to specify the presence of hallucinations and/or delusions when diagnosing Bipolar I Disorder. Furthermore, clinicians specify whether the symptoms are congruent or incongruent with mood. For example, a child might be diagnosed with Bipolar I Disorder with Mood-Congruent Psychotic Features (American Psychiatric Association, 2013). Specifying the presence of hallucinations and delusions is important because youths with Bipolar I Disorder who show psychotic symptoms tend to have poorer outcomes than their counterparts without these symptoms (Figure 14.3; Fristad et al., 2011).

Bipolar Disorder With Mixed Features

The diagnostic criteria for BSDs are the same for children, adolescents, and adults. However, the manifestation of these disorders depends on the person's age and level of development (Danielyan, Pathak, Kowatch, Arszman, & Johns, 2007; Masi, Perugi, Millepiedi et al., 2006). Most adults with bipolar disorders show classic, discrete episodes of mania and depression (i.e., Bipolar I Disorder). A typical adult patient has reasonably good functioning before his first mood episode. Then, usually between the age of 18 and 25 years, he experiences a clear manic episode marked by euphoria, inflated self-esteem and grandiosity, decreased need for sleep, racing thoughts and rapid speech, and risk-taking behavior. Following this clear-cut manic episode, which may last for a few weeks, he enters a period of major depression that can persist for weeks or months. Finally, his depression abates, and he shows a return to reasonably good functioning until his next mood episode.

Children and adolescents with bipolar disorders rarely show this classic presentation of mania and depression. Instead, youths often show mixed moods during a single

Figure 14.3 Bipolar I Disorder With and Without Psychotic Symptoms

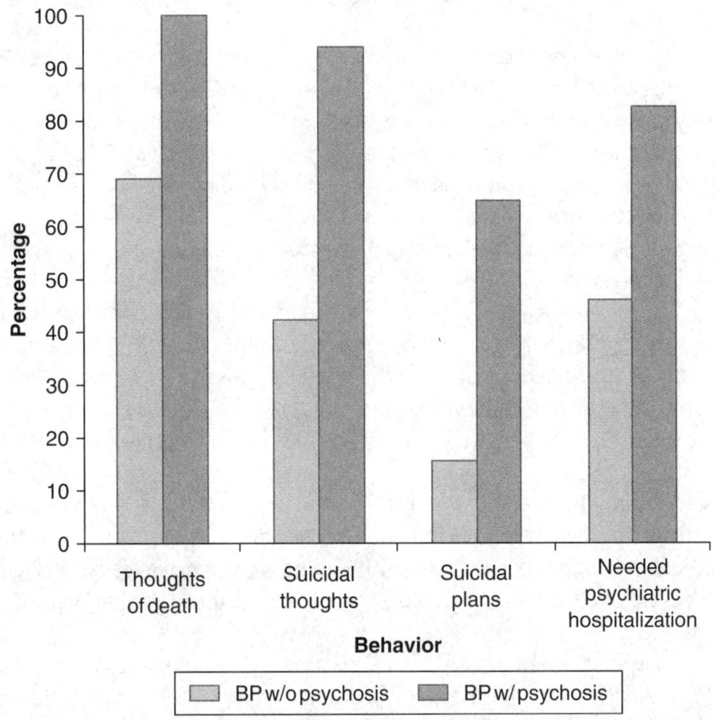

Source: Based on Caetano et al. (2006).

Note: Youths with Bipolar Disorders with Psychotic Symptoms show more severe impairment than youths with Bipolar Disorders alone.

mood episode. A **mixed mood** occurs when youths meet criteria for either a manic or hypomanic episode and simultaneously show subthreshold symptoms of depression. Alternatively, a mixed mood can occur when youths meet criteria for a major depressive episode and simultaneously show subthreshold hypomanic symptoms (American Psychiatric Association, 2013).

How might a child or adolescent show both mania or hypomania *and* depression? To understand mixed moods, experts have likened them to desserts (Youngstrom et al., 2008). Some mixed moods are analogous to "chocolate milk"; symptoms of mania and depression are dissolved together into a homogenous state that is different from either component. These children display a blend of crankiness, irritability, anger, high energy, and excitability. Other mixed moods are analogous to "fudge ripple"; chunks of manic and chunks of depressive symptoms remain identifiable in the child's symptoms. During the course of the day, the child's mood might cycle from brief periods of elation and energy superimposed on more predominant instances of irritability, tearfulness, and lethargy. Some youths experience these mood fluctuations multiple times each day. In *DSM-5*, clinicians indicate the presence of mixed mood symptoms by adding a "with mixed features" specifier to the Bipolar Disorder diagnosis (e.g., Bipolar

I Disorder with Mixed Features; American Psychiatric Association, 2013).

Mixed, fluctuating mood states are common among youths with BSDs (Findling, Gracious et al., 2001; Geller, Zimmerman et al., 2000). In one study, 81% of children with bipolar disorders displayed mood shifts from hypomania to normal mood to depression during a single 24-hour period. In another study, approximately one third of adolescents with bipolar disorders displayed these rapid changes in mood. In contrast, rapid changes in mood are relatively rare among adults with BSDs.

It is important to remember that these mood fluctuations occur within a single mood episode. Although some researchers have suggested these mood changes might reflect extremely rapid (i.e., "ultradian") mood episodes (B. Geller, Williams et al., 1998), most experts believe they are better seen as mixed mood states within a single manic or hypomanic episode. For example, longitudinal studies have shown that youths with BSDs experience discrete mood episodes lasting several days or weeks. These discrete mood episodes are similar to the episodes shown by adults with the disorder. Youths with Bipolar Disorder are more likely than adults to show mixed moods and rapid fluctuations in mood (Fawcett, 2010). However, this rapid cycling tends to occur within a specific mood episode (Youngstrom et al., 2008, 2009).

MIXED MOOD MAX

Max was a 9-year-old boy who was referred to our hospital after an apparent suicide attempt. One day, while traveling to school with his mother, Max began talking and laughing uncontrollably. Then, he unbuckled his seat belt and jumped out of their moving car, seriously injuring himself. After he was treated in the emergency department, Dr. Saunders, a pediatric psychologist at the hospital, interviewed Max and his mother.

Max was a "colicky" infant who was difficult to soothe. During his toddler years, however, Max's crying decreased, and he developed into an energetic, inquisitive child. Max was diagnosed with ADHD 3 years earlier, because of problems with hyperactivity and impulsiveness. He responded well to stimulant medication. Although he was considered "a handful" by his parents, Max was a likable, friendly boy.

Six months prior to the incident, however, Max's disposition began to change. His medication seemed to be increasingly less effective in managing his hyperactivity. He would frequently whine, complain, and talk back to family members. Max began having problems falling asleep at night and eventually refused to go to bed when asked. In the morning, Max was irritable and cranky. Max also became a "weepy" child; on one occasion, he cried for several hours because his sister ate the last piece of his favorite dessert. On several occasions, his mother overheard him sobbing in his room, "Nobody loves me."

Max's mood deteriorated rapidly the week before his hospitalization. He was highly active and boisterous, both at home and at school. He refused to sleep at night, claiming that he was not tired, but during the day, he seemed moody and easily set off. Instead of sleeping, Max snuck out of his room, watched television, played video games, and even began disassembling his bicycle "to see how it worked." His mother also caught him viewing adult-oriented material on the computer.

Two days earlier, Max was suspended from school after starting a fight in the lunchroom. When a classmate would not allow Max to sit next to him, Max threw his food at the child and hit him with his tray. Max was taken to the principal's office, where he continued to scream and tantrum until his mother arrived an hour later.

Dr. Saunders asked Max about his apparent suicide attempt. Max said he did not want to kill himself. He explained, "I told my mom that I didn't want to go to school and she wouldn't listen. So, I thought that if I just ran really fast, I could keep up with the car and hop out."

Dr. Saunders learned that Max's mother had a history of depression. Max's father was diagnosed with Bipolar I Disorder in his early 20s and managed his symptoms fairly well with medication. His mother added, "I just don't know what to do about Max. He used to be such a sweet, fun boy, but something's changed. I'm so scared what might happen next."

Epidemiology

Prevalence

There are very few epidemiological studies investigating the prevalence of BSDs in children and adolescents. Overall, the lifetime prevalence of Bipolar I Disorder ranges from 0% to 1.9% in youths, which is similar to the 1% lifetime prevalence seen in the adult population (Merikangas & Pato, 2009). However, the lifetime prevalence of all BSDs may be closer to 3% to 4% (Youngstrom et al., 2009). Most adults with BSDs report an age of onset either in childhood (15%–28%) or adolescence (50%–66%). Although prospective studies are rare, they also suggest that onset typically occurs between middle adolescence and young adulthood (Miklowitz, Mullen, & Chang, 2008).

The prevalence of BSDs is much higher among children and adolescents referred for treatment compared to youths in the community. In outpatient mental health clinics, approximately 6% to 7% of youths have Bipolar Disorder. Among youths receiving treatment in psychiatric hospitals, 26% to 34% were diagnosed with the disorder (Youngstrom et al., 2009).

Over the past two decades, there has been a marked increase in the number of children receiving the diagnosis of Bipolar Disorder. Between 1994 and 2003, there was a 40-fold increase in the number of psychiatric visits associated with a pediatric Bipolar Disorder diagnosis. However, the results of epidemiological studies, involving children in the community, indicate that the actual number of youths with Bipolar Disorder has remained relatively consistent over the years (Goldstein, 2010). For example, a meta-analysis involving 16,222 children and young adults (ages 7–21 years) in the community showed relative stability in the prevalence of Bipolar Disorder between 1985 and 2007 (i.e., 1.1–3.0%). Prevalence is similar in Ireland, Mexico, the Netherlands, New Zealand, United Kingdom, and the United States (Van Meter, Moreira, 2011).

Gender, Age, and Ethnicity

Data on gender differences in child and adolescent bipolar disorders are sparse. Adolescent and adult samples indicate that men and women are equally likely to develop Bipolar I Disorder. However, symptoms of bipolar disorders differ somewhat in men and women. Men tend to have earlier symptom onset and more frequent manic episodes than women. Women, on the other hand, tend to show higher frequency of mixed episodes and psychotic features than men. Bipolar II Disorder may be more common in females. One epidemiological study showed a slightly increased prevalence of Bipolar II in adolescent girls (3.3%) than boys (2.6%; Birmaher, Axelson, Goldstein et al., 2009). This gender disparity may be due to the fact that manic episodes are more common among males, whereas depressive episodes are more common among females (Duax, Youngstrom, Calabrese, & Findling, 2007).

Adolescent boys and girls with BSDs do show slightly different comorbid symptoms. Boys (91%) are somewhat more likely than girls (70%) to have comorbid ADHD. Girls (61%) are more likely than boys (46%) to have comorbid anxiety disorders (Biederman, Kwon et al., 2004).

Very few studies have investigated differences in pediatric BSDs as a function of ethnicity. Studies involving adults indicate that the prevalence of the disorder is similar regardless of income and education. The prevalence of bipolar disorders among African Americans is similar to the prevalence of the disorder among whites. However, some data indicate that the *presentation* of bipolar disorders may vary across ethnic groups. African American adolescents with bipolar disorders are more likely to show psychotic symptoms, especially auditory hallucinations, than white adolescents with the disorder. Researchers are uncertain what causes these ethnic differences in symptom presentation (Patel, DelBello, Keck, & Strakowski, 2006).

Course

Prodromal Phase and Onset. BSDs must be managed across the life span. Kowatch and Fristad (2006) liken bipolar disorders to diabetes. Both disorders are greatly influenced by the person's genes and biological functioning. However, the severity of these disorders and the extent to which they interfere with people's lives greatly depend on environmental experiences. Children with diabetes must monitor their blood sugar and regulate their diet to remain symptom-free and healthy. Children with BSDs must monitor their mood states and behavior, comply with physician's recommendations regarding medication, and improve the quality of their social-emotional environment in order to avoid mood episodes. There is currently no "cure" for either diabetes or BSDs. However, environmental experiences can determine whether these disorders are manageable or debilitating.

The onset of Bipolar Disorder is typically insidious (i.e., gradual and barely noticeable at first). Youths usually begin showing **prodromal**, subthreshold mood problems months or years before their first mood episode (Table 14.4). In one study, 52% of youths began experiencing minor mood problems one year before their first mood episode; only 4%

Table 14.4	Prodromal Symptoms in Childhood-Onset Bipolar Disorder

Symptom	Percentage Showing
Depressed mood	53
Increased energy	47
Tiredness or fatigue	38
Anger, quick temper	38
Irritability	33
Conduct problems	28
Decreased need for sleep	26
Crying	26
Oversensitivity	24

Source: Based on Egeland, Hosteller, Pauls, and Sussex (2000).

of youths experienced sudden symptom onset. The most commonly reported mood problems are dysphoria, difficulty thinking and concentrating, irritability, and agitation. These problems are sometimes experienced by healthy youths from time to time, so they often go unnoticed and untreated (Luby & Navsaria, 2010).

Manic symptoms are relatively common among youths referred for psychiatric treatment. In the Longitudinal Assessment of Manic Symptoms (LAMS) Study, researchers found that 43% of treatment-referred children showed some subthreshold manic symptoms as reported by parents. These children tended to show poorer overall functioning and more comorbid problems than clinic-referred children without subthreshold manic symptoms. However, only about 25% of these children eventually developed Bipolar Disorder (Findling, Youngstrom, et al., 2010). Predicting which children will develop the disorder is difficult.

Course and Outcomes: The COBY Study

Once youths experience a full-blown mood episode, symptoms usually persist for some time. The best data regarding the course of BSDs in children and adolescents come from the **Course and Outcome of Bipolar Youth (COBY) study**. In this study, researchers recruited 413 youths (ages 7–17 years) with Bipolar I, Bipolar II, or subthreshold symptoms. All youths were being treated for BSDs, typically with medication. The researchers assessed the youths' emotional functioning approximately every 9 months for 4 years in order to determine their outcomes (Birmaher, Axelson, Goldstein et al., 2009).

Approximately 2.5 years after their first mood episode, most (81.5%) youths fully recovered. Average time to recovery was 124 weeks. However, 1.5 years later, at the end of the study, most (62.5%) had experienced another mood episode, usually depression. On average, the time from recovery to recurrence was 71 weeks. Approximately one half of youths who experienced recurrence actually showed multiple mood episodes during the course of the 4-year study (Figure 14.4).

The researchers also asked families to comment on children's emotional functioning from week to week. Children tended to show discrete mood episodes, usually long episodes of depression. When not experiencing these episodes, however, youths still tended to show subthreshold symptoms of depression and irritability. Even after recovery, youths remained symptomatic 60% of the time. Youths also tended to show mixed mood symptoms, with frequent changes in mood from excitability to irritability to sadness. On average, youths' moods changed polarity 12 times during the course of one year.

Over the course of the study, 25% of youths with Bipolar II displayed sufficient manic symptoms to be diagnosed with Bipolar I Disorder. Furthermore, 38% of youths with subthreshold symptoms eventually showed sufficient manic or hypomanic symptoms to be diagnosed with either Bipolar I or II.

Altogether, results of the COBY study provided important information about the course of BSDs in youths:

- Youths with BSDs typically recover from their initial mood episode. However, relapse is likely and multiple mood episodes are fairly common.

- Youths with BSDs experience discrete mood episodes, usually long periods of depression. Between episodes, youths typically show subthreshold symptoms of depression.
- Youths with BSDs often show mixed mood symptoms, including excitability, agitation, irritability, and sadness.
- Many youths initially diagnosed with Bipolar II or subthreshold symptoms "convert" to Bipolar I Disorder. The BSDs exist on a spectrum of severity ranging from longer, severe mood problems (i.e., Bipolar I) to relatively shorter, subthreshold mood symptoms.

Another longitudinal study demonstrated persistence of Bipolar Disorder from childhood through adolescence (Wozniak et al., 2011). Researchers assessed a large group of children with Bipolar I Disorder in childhood (age 10 years) and 4 years later. Most youths continued to meet diagnostic criteria for Bipolar I Disorder as adolescents. Adolescents who did not meet criteria for Bipolar I Disorder either showed subthreshold bipolar symptoms or experienced problems with depression. Only 7% of youths completely recovered.

Individuals with childhood- and adolescent-onset bipolar disorders may have worse outcomes than individuals whose bipolar symptoms emerge during adulthood (Masi, Perugi, Toni et al., 2006). Carlson and colleagues (2000) compared individuals with early- and adult-onset bipolar disorders on a number of outcome variables. They found

Figure 14.4   Results of the COBY Study on Childhood Bipolar Disorder

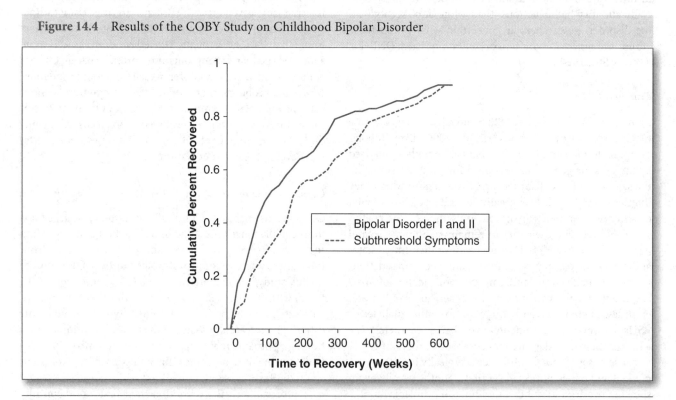

Source: Based on Birmaher, Axelson, Goldstein (2009).

Note: Most youths with BSDs recover from their first mood episode, although average time to recovery is 124 weeks. Recovery is faster for youths with Bipolar I or II Disorder than for youths with subthreshold symptoms. Unfortunately, 62.5% of youths who recover will relapse within 18 months.

that individuals whose symptom onset occurred during adolescence showed greater frequency of manic symptoms, less remission of symptoms and more relapse over time, and a greater number of psychiatric hospitalizations than individuals whose onset occurred during adulthood. Furthermore, individuals with early-onset Bipolar Disorder were more likely to have experienced educational, employment, and substance use problems than people whose symptoms emerged during adulthood.

BSDs can be debilitating if left untreated. Over time, individuals with bipolar disorders who do not participate in pharmacotherapy are at considerable risk for recurrent episodes of mania and depression, employment and relationship problems, legal problems, periodic hospitalizations, substance abuse, and suicide. These outcomes highlight the importance of identifying and managing bipolar disorders as early as possible (Findling et al., 2001; Lewinsohn, Seeley, & Klein, 2003).

Associated Problems

Approximately 70% of children and 31% of adolescents with BSDs also have ADHD (Birmaher, Axelson, Goldstein, 2009). Some of this apparent comorbidity may be due to symptoms common to both ADHD and mania, such as talkativeness, distractibility, and excessive motor activity. However, it is clear that many youths legitimately experience both disorders. Despite symptom overlap, the two disorders can be differentiated. A child with ADHD runs into the street because he forgot to look out for cars. A child with BSD runs out into the street because he believes he can outrun the cars (Fristad et al., 2011).

Although youths with BSDs are at risk for ADHD, the converse is not true: youths with ADHD are not at increased risk for developing BSDs. In one large study of children and adolescents with ADHD, only one child met diagnostic criteria for a BSD (Hassan, Agha, Langley, & Thapar, 2011).

Approximately 40% of youths with BSDs also have at least one anxiety disorder. Children with BSDs are especially at risk for Separation Anxiety Disorder (28%), whereas adolescents with Bipolar Disorder are at particular risk for Panic Disorder (8%).

Nearly 75% of youths with BSDs report sleep problems. This is not surprising, because sleep disturbance is a symptom of both mania and depression. During manic episodes, youths typically do not feel sleepy. They may stay awake for long periods of time and feel completely rested after sleeping only a few hours. In contrast, during depressive episodes, youths often have problems falling asleep and staying asleep for the duration of the night. They may wake early in the morning, feeling tired throughout the day. Alternatively, they may have difficulty getting out of bed (Fristad et al., 2011).

Disruptive behavior disorders are also comorbid conditions, although prevalence depends on age of onset

(Birmaher, Axelson, Goldstein, 2009). Youths with childhood-onset BSDs are most likely to develop Oppositional Defiant Disorder (43%), whereas youths with adolescent-onset BSDs are more likely to have Conduct Disorder (16%) or substance use problems (23%). Differentiating conduct problems and BSDs can be challenging. In general, youths with conduct problems are deliberately noncompliant, whereas youths with BSDs cannot comply because of their mood problems (Fristad et al., 2011).

Differential Diagnosis

The psychiatrist Emil Kraepelin was among the first diagnosticians to identify BSDs in children and adolescents. Indeed, Kraepelin documented episodes of mania, depression, and irritability in approximately one hundred youths. Kraepelin saw the essential features of BSDs in children and adolescents to be consistent with the features shown by adults with the disorder: severe mood episodes, which lasted several days or weeks, and marked impairment in functioning (Leibenluft et al., 2003).

Despite Kraepelin's early observations, BSDs came to be viewed as "adult" disorders—conditions rarely, if ever, shown by children. In the 1980s, however, Gabrielle Carlson described bipolar symptoms in prepubescent children, characterized by severe irritability and rapidly changing, mixed mood states. Carlson's description renewed interest among researchers and clinicians in pediatric BSDs. Two views gradually emerged.

The first view, consistent with Kraepelin, was that the essential features of BSDs were largely invariant across childhood, adolescence, and adulthood. All individuals with BSDs, regardless of age, showed discrete mood episodes, characterized by manic (and often depressive) symptoms associated with marked impairment in functioning (Leibenluft et al., 2003).

The second view was that the definition of BSDs should be expanded to include youths who showed *chronic* irritability and angry outbursts. According to this view, chronic mood problems, characterized by persistent irritability, anger, and violent or destructive tantrums, reflected an underlying mood disturbance consistent with BSDs (Biederman et al., 1995; Wozniak et al., 1995).

Expanding the definition of BSDs caused a marked increase in the number of youths diagnosed with BSDs. Increased diagnosis was also fueled by the publication of *The Bipolar Child* (Papolos & Papolos, 2000), a *Time Magazine* cover story about pediatric Bipolar Disorder (Kluger & Song, 2002), and a lead story in the *New York Times Magazine* (Egan, 2008). These popular publications led many parents and clinicians to suspect that chronically angry, irritable, and moody children, who often displayed fits, tantrums, or "rages" might have BSDs. Although the actual prevalence of BSDs never changed, the frequency of the diagnosis increased markedly in outpatient clinics and hospitals (Parens & Johnston, 2010).

Although experts still disagree regarding the best conceptualization of pediatric BSDs, research by Leibenluft and colleagues helped to resolve the issue (Leibenluft & Dickstein, 2008). Leibenluft and colleagues (2003) recognized that many children did show chronic problems with irritability and angry outbursts; however, they argued, these children do not have pediatric BSDs. Whereas bipolar disorder is an illness defined by mood *episodes*, these youths showed *chronic* problems with irritability, dysphoria, and anger. Prior to *DSM-5*, these children were "diagnostic orphans," that is, youths with serious emotional problems who desperately needed help. Many clinicians diagnosed them with BSDs because they did not fit any other diagnostic category, and they desperately needed treatment.

Rather than change *DSM* criteria to fit these children's symptoms, Leibenluft and colleagues (2003) created a new diagnostic classification, Severe Mood Dysregulation (SMD), defined by the presence of *chronic* irritability or anger, violent or destructive temper outbursts, and hyperactivity-impulsivity. Researchers identified a large group of children with SMD and studied the presentation, course, and causes of this condition. They found that young children with SMD often developed depression and anxiety disorders in adolescence and early adulthood; almost none developed BSDs. Furthermore, youths with SMD often had family members with depression or anxiety disorders, not BSDs. The researchers concluded that the chronic irritability and angry outbursts reflected depression, anxiety, and problems with emotion regulation and not BSDs.

Because of this research, a new diagnosis was included in *DSM-5*: Disruptive Mood Dysregulation Disorder (DMDD). DMDD is characterized by persistent problems with irritability and frequently angry outbursts. It is similar to the research definition of Severe Mood Dysregulation, but without symptoms of ADHD.

Children with DMDD and BSDs can show problems with both irritability and angry or aggressive outbursts. However, children with DMDD show these problems persistently, whereas youths with BSDs show a noticeable increase in these symptoms during mood episodes. DMDD is considered a depressive disorder, because it more closely resembles depression and anxiety than BSDs.

Etiology

Genetics

The single greatest risk factor for BSDs is having a biologically related family member with a bipolar disorder (Birmaher et al., 2010). The average concordance rate for monozygotic twins (40%) is much higher than the rate for dizygotic twins (5%; Merikangas & Pato, 2009). Although the lifetime prevalence of BSDs is appropriately 1%, the prevalence among the children of adults with BSDs ranges from

5% to 10%. Furthermore, the children of adults with BSDs are at increased risk for a wide range of psychiatric disorders. In the Pittsburgh Bipolar Offspring Study (BIOS), researchers compared a large sample of children whose parents had BSDs with a large sample of children from the community (Birmaher, Axelson, & Monk, 2009; Birmaher, Axelson, Monk, Kalas, et al., 2009; Birmaher, Axelson, Goldstein, Monk, 2010). After controlling for demographic variables, children (6–18 years old) of adults with the illness showed increased risk of developing BSDs, other mood disorders, and other anxiety disorders. They were also twice as likely to develop psychiatric disorders as the children of healthy parents. Even preschool-age children (2–5 years old) of adults with BSDs were at increased risk for psychiatric disorders, especially disruptive behavior problems (Figure 14.5).

Neuroimaging

Emotional Perception and Processing. Several neuroimaging studies have compared the brains of youths with and without BSDs. One of the most consistent neuroanatomical findings is that youths with BSDs often have smaller brains than unaffected youths. In several studies, adolescents with BSDs showed a 5% reduction in total cerebral volume compared to adolescents without bipolar disorders. These findings suggest that genetic factors may cause irregular neurological development, which results in smaller brain size (Frazier et al., 2005).

Since BSDs are mood disorders, researchers have focused on areas of the brain responsible for emotional processing and regulation. Researchers have known for some time that children and adults with BSDs often have problems correctly labeling others' facial expressions. When they are shown pictures of people displaying various emotions, they often misinterpret these expressions. Specifically, they tend to interpret benign facial expressions as sad, angry, or hostile. These problems with emotion recognition are seen even when youths are not experiencing mood episodes. As you might expect, problems interpreting the emotional expressions of others can interfere with their ability to interpret social situations and behave appropriately. If you often misinterpret others' benign expressions as hostile or threatening, you might be more likely to react negatively to others (Luby & Navsaria, 2010).

Youths with BSDs also show abnormalities in the several brain areas responsible for emotion regulation. First, youths with BSDs display hyperactivation of the **amygdala**, compared to healthy youths. Recall that the amygdala is part of the limbic system, a brain region that is critically important to the experience and expression of negative emotions, especially fear and rage. When youths with BSDs perceive negative facial expressions in others, they experience more negative emotions themselves and show over-activity in this brain region (Figure 14.6).

Figure 14.5 The Pittsburgh Bipolar Offspring Study

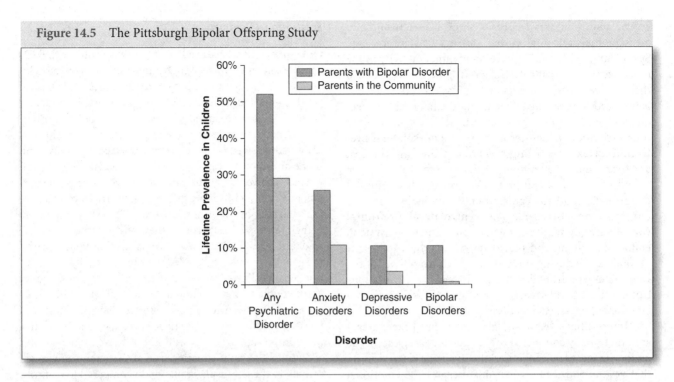

Source: Based on Birmaher, Axelson, Monk, Kalas, et al. (2009).

Note: The Pittsburgh Bipolar Offspring Study examined the children of adults with BSDs. These children showed increased risk for developing BSDs and other anxiety and mood disorders themselves.

Figure 14.6 Brain Abnormalities in Children With Bipolar Disorders

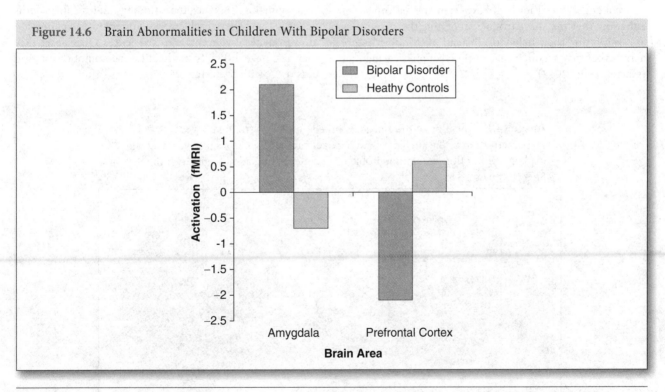

Source: Based on Garrett and colleagues (2012).

Note: Compared to healthy adolescents, youths with BSDs show over-activation of the amygdala and underactivation of the prefrontal cortices while completing a frustrating task. These abnormalities are associated with high emotional reactivity to stress and problems regulating their emotions.

Second, youths with BSDs show hypoactivation in areas of the prefrontal cortex, during facial processing. Specifically, fMRI studies have shown underactivity in the dorsolateral and ventrolateral prefrontal cortices. Recall that the prefrontal cortex is the brain's "executive" area; it is involved in planning, considering the long-term consequences of our actions, and inhibiting behavior that might interfere with our long-term goals. The **dorsolateral prefrontal cortex** plays an important role in directing, shifting, and sustaining our attention. When presented with negative stimuli, the dorsolateral prefrontal cortex helps to inhibit our behavior and to regulate our emotions by directing our attention elsewhere. The **ventrolateral prefrontal cortex** partially regulates our peripheral nervous system, endocrine system, and motor system—body regions that become active during times of stress. Underactivity of the ventrolateral prefrontal cortex would lead to difficulty controlling these bodily reactions and greater behavioral and emotional arousal (Luby & Navsaria, 2010).

Interestingly, the amygdala (and other limbic areas) are functionally connected to the prefrontal regions of the brain (Image 14.1). Together, the available data indicate that youths with BSDs often misinterpret the emotional expressions of others in a hostile or threatening way. They may have difficulty directing their attention away from these negative expressions in others and often experience greater or stronger negative emotions themselves as a consequence. Once they begin experiencing fear, anger, or agitation, they may have trouble regulating their emotions and inhibiting their behavior. Instead of thinking before acting, they may act out in an emotional or physical manner (Garrett et al., 2012).

Frustration Tolerance

Other researchers have tried to explain why youths with BSDs are so easily upset by seemingly minor stressors or setbacks. To answer this question, Rich and colleagues (2011) asked youths with and without BSDs to play a simple computer game. The game required youths to press one of two buttons, depending on which side of the screen a stimulus was displayed. Correct answers were rewarded by praise and monetary rewards (e.g., "Correct! Win 25 cents"). Although the task was very easy, the game was rigged to frustrate participants. On slightly more than half of the trials, youths were told that their answer was incorrect, or "too slow," regardless of their response. Furthermore, they were punished with false feedback (e.g., "Wrong! Lose 25 cents"). While youths played the game, researchers recorded their brain activity.

Results showed marked differences in the brain activity of youths with and without BSDs (Rich et al., 2011). As expected, youths with BSDs reported more sadness and negative emotion during the rigged task than healthy youths. More importantly, youths with BSDs showed much greater activity in the right superior frontal gyrus and much less activity in the left insula brain region compared to controls. The **superior frontal gyrus** is a large area of the frontal lobe responsible for many activities, including attention and working memory. The **insula** is a more centrally located brain area, close to the limbic area, that plays a role in emotion regulation. Together, these findings indicate that youths with BSDs may have problems with directing their attention away from negative events and experiences. Once upset, they may also have difficulty modulating their emotions to deal effectively with problems.

Image 14.1   Location of the amygdala in relation to the frontal cortex. Hyperactivation of the amygdala and hypoactivation of the frontal cortex may help explain the emotion-regulation problems of children and adolescents with Bipolar Spectrum Disorders.

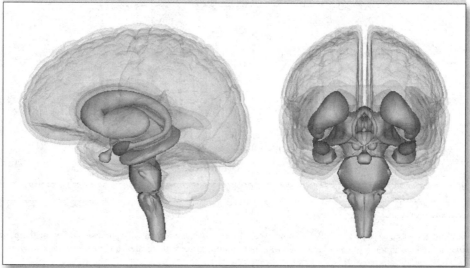

Of course, neuroimaging studies like these do not tell us whether these brain differences cause BSDs, whether the symptoms of BSDs cause deficits in emotion regulation, or whether a third variable, yet unidentified, might affect both brain and behavior. Longitudinal neuroimaging studies of youths with BSDs are sorely needed to address these questions about causality.

Cognition

Youths with BSDs often show cognitive deficits compared to healthy peers (Fristad et al., 2011). On average, their IQ scores are approximately 7 points lower than the scores of healthy youths. Approximately 22% earn IQ scores less than 80. The majority (79%) of children and adolescents with BSDs also have Specific Learning Disorder. In one study, 74% had problems with writing, 32% had problems with mathematics, and 28% had problems with reading (Mayes & Calhoun, 2006).

Youths with BSDs also frequently show more subtle, cognitive processing problems (Fristad et al., 2011). Most impairments are in the areas of executive functioning, that is, planning, organizing, and inhibiting behavior. Specifically, youths with BSDs show deficits in selective attention, sustained attention, behavioral inhibition, processing speed, and working memory. Some studies have also shown deficits in verbal learning and memory, social problem solving, and taking the perspective of others. Usually, these problems are only noticeable during formal neuropsychological testing. However, these cognitive processing problems likely interfere with youths' ability to regulate their actions and emotions.

At school, children with BSDs are more likely to show significant behavior problems and to earn low grades than children with ADHD and children without psychiatric diagnoses. Furthermore, children with BSDs show comparable rates of repeating a grade, being assigned to a remedial class, and being classified as having a learning disability as children with ADHD. In one large study, one third of adolescents with BSDs had failed at least one grade in school, and slightly more than one third were receiving special educational services for academic or behavioral problems (Biederman, Faraone et al., 2005).

Sleep-Wake Cycles

Although BSDs are highly heritable, their emergence is also dependent on environmental factors. We have known for some time that disruptions in the sleep-wake cycle of adults can contribute to the emergence of mania. Adults who report disruptions to their sleep-wake cycles are more likely to experience a recurrence of manic or depressive episodes compared to adults with the disorder who maintain regular sleep-wake cycles. Indeed, one psychosocial treatment for adults with BSDs is called **social rhythm therapy**. In this form of treatment, the therapist helps the client maintain regular sleep-wake cycles and avoid disruptions in day-to-day routines. For example, adults with bipolar disorders might be taught to avoid changes in work schedules, all-night studying for exams, late-night partying, or social stressors that can cause insomnia. Social rhythm therapy is associated with less frequent relapse among adults with the disorder (Rao, 2003).

Unfortunately, information about the sleep-wake cycles of children and adolescents with BSDs has been largely anecdotal. Clinical reports indicate that disruptions in daily routines and circadian rhythms can trigger manic symptoms in adolescents with BSDs, especially if they have a tendency toward rapid-cycling mood symptoms. Researchers do not yet know how sleep disturbance increases the likelihood of mania in youth. Sleep disruption may affect certain hormones (e.g., thyroid-stimulating hormone, cortisol) and neurotransmitters (e.g., serotonin) that are associated with mood regulation. Most psychosocial treatments for youths with bipolar disorders involve teaching these youths to maintain consistent sleep-wake schedules and avoid psychosocial stressors that could lead to sleep disturbance (Rao, 2003).

Stressful Life Events

Stressful events have also been shown to trigger manic and depressive episodes in adults with BSDs. The death of a loved one, the loss of a job, or a crisis at home can lead to relapse. Interestingly, stressful life events do not always have to be negative to trigger relapse. Any life experience that seriously disrupts day-to-day routines can contribute to a change in mood. For example, adults with bipolar disorders who get married, change jobs, or have a baby may be at increased risk (Johnson et al., 2000; Malkoff-Schwartz et al., 1998).

Only recently have stressful life events been studied among children and adolescents with BSDs. In the CODY study, youths with BSDs reported a very high number of stressful life events. Indeed, the number of stressful events reported by youths with BSDs was the same as the number reported by youths with depression. Furthermore, many of these negative events were a product of youths' own disruptive mood and behavior. For example, an adolescent might get suspended from school or break up with his long-term girlfriend, during a manic episode. The fact that youths might contribute to their own negative life events might help explain the chronicity of youths' mood problems (Romero et al., 2009).

Youths with BSDs also reported very few positive life events—even lower than the number reported by youths with depression. Furthermore, the scarcity of positive events in the lives of these youths seems to be dependent on their own mood and behavior problems. For example, an irritable or depressed adolescent will likely have problems developing close relationships with family and friends. Limited social support and cohesive family ties, in turn, can exacerbate youths' mood problems (Romero et al., 2009).

Family and Friends

Individuals with BSDs also frequently experience problems in their family relationships. Family tension typically arises in three ways. First, caring for a child or adolescents with a BSD can be extremely stressful to parents and older family members. Caregivers worry, "Will he forget to take his medication? Is she starting to show signs of mania again? What am I going to do if he's suspended from school?" Parenting stress creates tension in the home and interferes with parents' ability to provide sensitive, consistent care. Second, youths with BSDs frequently elicit negative thoughts, feelings, and actions from family members because of their disruptive mood and behavior. For example, parents might blame youths for their dysphoric mood, viewing their mood problems as a sign of disrespect, disobedience, or resentment. To the extent that parents attribute youths' disruptive mood and behavior to deliberate, willful acts of malice, parents may be more likely to become angry, hostile, and resentful toward their children. Third, many youths with BSDs often have parents with mood disorders themselves. Because of their own problems with depression or mania, parents may be less able to respond to their children's symptoms in effective ways (Hellander, Sisson, & Fristad, 2003; Kowatch & Fristad, 2006).

Expressed emotion (EE) reflects the degree to which caregivers display criticism, hostility, or emotional over-involvement (e.g., overprotectiveness, inordinate self-sacrifice) toward the family member with a psychiatric disorder. Typically, EE is assessed by counting the number of *critical, hostile,* or emotionally *over-involved* statements uttered by caregivers toward their children, during an interview or brief observation session. Here are some examples:

- *Criticism:* Why can't you be responsible like other kids your age and remember to do your homework?
- *Hostility:* I don't want to be around you when you act that way. You make me sick.
- *Over-involvement:* I lie awake at night, worrying about you. Are you safe? Who are you with?

EE is important because it predicts relapse in individuals with BSDs, Major Depressive Disorder, and Schizophrenia. After discharge from psychiatric treatment, individuals from high-EE families are 2 to 3 times more likely to relapse over the course of 2 years than individuals from low-EE families (Miklowitz, 2012).

In contrast, warm, supportive parent-child interactions may prevent the return of mood episodes in youths with BSDs (Figure 14.7). Two years after recovering from a mood

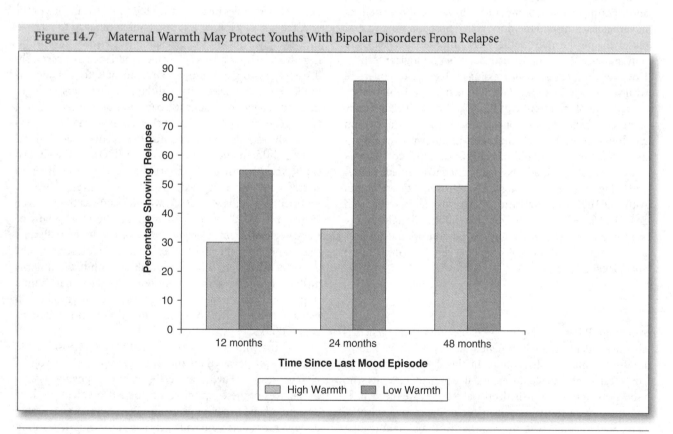

Figure 14.7   Maternal Warmth May Protect Youths With Bipolar Disorders From Relapse

Source: Based on Geller et al. (2004).

Note: Children whose mothers showed high levels of sensitive and responsive care were less likely to relapse over a 4-year time period. Helping parents provide sensitive and responsive care and avoid conflict is a key component of most psychosocial treatments for pediatric bipolar disorders.

episode, these youths were 4 times less likely to relapse in families characterized by high maternal warmth than low maternal warmth. Four years after recovery, children from high-warmth families (50.3%) were less likely to relapse than the children of low-warmth families (85.9%; Geller et al., 2004).

Children with BSDs often have considerable problems in their peer relationships. In one study, children with BSDs had fewer friends than children with ADHD. Although both children with ADHD and children with BSDs have difficulty making and keeping friends, children with ADHD usually know how they ought to behave toward others. In contrast, youths with BSDs often showed deficits in social skill and social problem solving. It is likely that peers find the mood problems of children with BSD to be off-putting, so they shy away from these children. Many psychosocial treatments for children with BSDs systematically teach children social skills and problem-solving strategies to help improve their interactions with family and friends (Geller, Zimmerman et al., 2000; Kowatch & Fristad, 2006).

Treatment

Medication

Pharmacotherapy is considered the primary form of treatment for BSDs (Pfeifer et al., 2010). The American Academy of Child and Adolescent Psychiatry recommends that a single medication should be tried initially to treat the youth's most recent mood episode. If the child responds only partially, additional medications can be administered until a desired response is achieved. Three classes of medications are used to treat pediatric BSDs: mood stabilizers (e.g., lithium), anticonvulsants (e.g., divalproex), and atypical antipsychotics (e.g., risperidone).

Mood Stabilizers and Anticonvulsants. The **mood stabilizing medication** lithium (Eskalith) was once considered the gold standard in treating pediatric BSDs. Several randomized controlled studies demonstrated its efficacy in reducing mania in adults with the disorder. The mechanism by which lithium decreases mania and stabilizes mood is unknown. Lithium seems to reduce the action of the neurotransmitters norepinephrine and serotonin, which play important roles in mood and emotional expression (Weller et al., 2004).

Unfortunately, no randomized, placebo-controlled studies investigating the efficacy of lithium on youths with BSDs have been published (Liu et al., 2011). Open trials (i.e., studies without control groups) have shown that, on average, only 38% of youths respond to lithium. In one study, researchers compared lithium with several other medications used to treat BSDs (Geller et al., 2012). The researchers found that only 35.6% of youths responded to lithium. Nearly as many youths, 32.2%, discontinued lithium and dropped out of the study before the end of the 8-week trial. Furthermore,

lithium was associated with side effects including nausea, headache, weight gain, thyroid dysfunction, diabetes, and tremor. For these reasons, lithium is usually not regarded as a first-line treatment for youths with BSDs.

Anticonvulsants, medications chiefly used to treat seizures, have also been used to treat mania in adults. These medications increase the inhibitory neurotransmitter GABA and/or decrease the excitatory neurotransmitter glutamate, causing a net decrease in neuronal activity, which may explain their effectiveness for both epilepsy and mania. The most widely studied anticonvulsant is divalproex (Depakote). Several studies suggest it may be effective in reducing mania in adolescents with BSDs; response rates vary from 24% to 53% (Geller et al., 2012; Pfeifer et al., 2010). The overall effect size, however, is not significantly higher than placebo (Liu et al., 2011). Common side effects include sedation, gastrointestinal problems, and weight gain. Rare, but severe side effects are inflammation of the pancreas, liver toxicity, and polycystic ovary syndrome, which can cause infertility. Other anticonvulsant medications, such as carbamazepine (Carbatrol), lamotrigine (Lamictal), and oxcarbazepine (Trileptal) have been chiefly studied in adults, rather than children, with the disorder.

Atypical Antipsychotics. **Atypical antipsychotics** are becoming the most frequently prescribed medications for youths with BSDs. These medications are called "atypical" because, unlike first-generation antipsychotics which bind to dopamine receptors, these antipsychotics affect dopamine and other neurotransmitters, such as serotonin and norepinephrine. They also seem to bind more weakly to dopamine receptors, causing fewer side effects (Pfeifer et al., 2010).

Both open-trial and randomized, controlled studies of atypical psychotics have shown them to be useful in reducing manic and mixed mood symptoms in children and adolescents (Singh et al., 2010). Response rates range from 73% for quetiapine (Seroquel) to 49% for olanzapine (Zyprexa) in randomized, controlled studies (Liu et al., 2011). Aripiprazole (Abilify), quetiapine (Seroquel), and risperidone (Risperdal) have been approved for children (10–17 years), whereas olanzapine (Zyprexa) has been approved for adolescents (13–17 years). Approximately half of youths who take these medications will show significant reduction in manic or mixed symptoms, compared to approximately one fourth of youths who respond to placebo (Figure 14.8).

Overall, response rates are significantly higher for youths taking atypical antipsychotics than traditional mood stabilizers or anticonvulsants (Liu et al., 2011). Researchers conducted a head-to-head comparison of these medications in the **Treatment of Early Age Mania (TEAM) study**. Specifically, 279 children and adolescents (6–15 years) with BSDs were randomly assigned to receive either the traditional mood stabilizer lithium (Eskalith), the anticonvulsant divalproex (Depakote), or the atypical

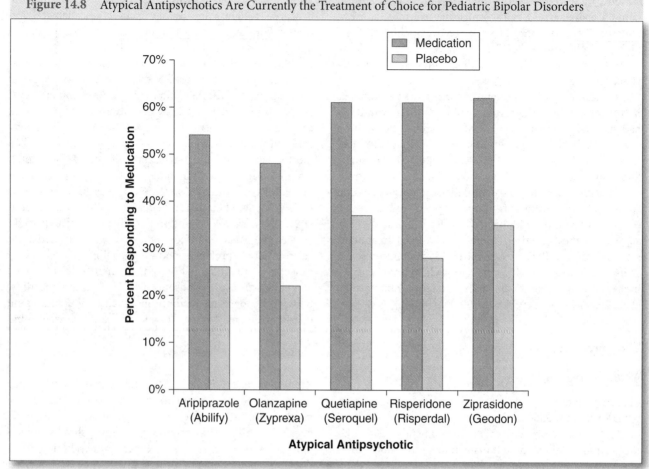

Source: Based on Singh and colleagues (2010).

Note: On average, 50% of youths with BSDs will show a reduction in manic symptoms after taking these medications compared to 25% who respond to placebo.

antipsychotic risperidone (Risperdal). All youths were experiencing a manic episode, but had not taken medication for BSDs previously. After 8 weeks of treatment, 41.9% of youths responded to their medication. More youths responded to risperidone (68.5%) than lithium (35.6%) or divalproex (24.0%). These findings supported the use of atypical antipsychotics in youths experiencing mania (Geller et al., 2012).

Treatment with atypical antipsychotics does have several limitations. First, only about half of youths respond to these medications. Often, multiple medications must be administered to reduce symptoms. Second, although *response* rates are relatively high, complete *recovery* rates are low. Most youths show improvement while taking these medications, but most also continue to show symptoms. Third, side effects are common. The most common side effect is significant weight gain, which occurs in 7% (ziprasidone) to 42% (olanzapine) of youths who take these medications. These medications may also cause diabetes and other metabolic difficulties (Singh et al., 2010).

Multiple Medications. Many youths with BSDs are prescribed multiple medications to treat their complex mood symptoms. However, very little evidence is available regarding the efficacy of combining medications to treat these youths. In a rare randomized, controlled trial, researchers compared adolescents taking divalproex (Depakote) and quetiapine (Seroquel) to adolescents taking divalproex (Depakote) and placebo. Significantly more adolescents showed a reduction in manic symptoms while taking the combination of medications (87%) than the single medication (53%). This finding provides initial evidence that multiple medications may be helpful to adolescents who do not respond to a single medication.

Although medication is efficacious in treating mania, we know very little about the usefulness of medication in treating depression in youths with BSDs (Pfeifer et al., 2010). Our lack of knowledge is important because, on average, youths with BSDs spend more time in a depressed mood state than a manic mood state. Often, physicians treat depressive episodes in adults with BSDs by augmenting mood stabilizing medication with antidepressants. However, the efficacy and safety of using this combination of medications in children and adolescents with the disorder is unknown. Selective serotonin reuptake inhibitors (SSRIs), which are useful in treating Major Depressive Disorder in adults, may exacerbate manic symptoms in children with BSDs. Approximately 10% of depressed adolescents with BSDs will actually "switch" from depression to mania following administration of an SSRI (Carlson & Meyer, 2010). Furthermore, SSRIs are associated with increased suicidal thoughts in some youths. Clearly, we need more information on effective treatments for depressive episodes in these children and adolescents.

Psychosocial Treatment

Psychosocial treatment for BSDs is typically used in combination with medication. The primary purpose of psychosocial treatment is twofold: (a) to increase the child's compliance with pharmacotherapy and (b) to prevent recurrence of another mood episode. The past decade has seen a marked increase in the number of evidence-based psychosocial interventions for youths with BSDs. These treatments have several components in common:

- *Psychoeducation:* Therapists teach clients about BSDs, their causes, course, and treatment.
- *Family involvement:* Therapy involves youths with BSDs, primary caregivers, and (sometimes) siblings.

- *Reducing blame:* Because family members often blame youths, or themselves, for their children's mood problems, therapists try to alleviate blame and feelings of guilt.
- *Skill building:* Therapists often teach skills that are deficient in children with BSDs and their parents. Skills might include recognizing and regulating one's emotions, solving social problems, communicating within the family, and maintaining a consistent lifestyle.

Although several evidence-based interventions are currently available for youths with BSDs, we will examine three which illustrate the use of psychosocial interventions across childhood and adolescence: Child- and family-focused cognitive-behavioral therapy (CFF-CBT), psychoeducational psychotherapy (PEP), and family-focused treatment for adolescents (FFT-A).

Child- and Family-Focused Cognitive-Behavioral Therapy

Mani Pavuluri (Pavuluri et al., 2004) developed **child- and family-focused cognitive-behavioral therapy (CFF-CBT)** for children aged 7–13 years with BSDs. Therapy consists of 12 sessions, some attended by children, some by parents, and some with children and parents together. Sessions provide information about BSDs and teach cognitive-behavioral strategies to improve children's behavior, mood, and social problem-solving skills (Table 14.5).

Table 14.5 Child- and Family-Focused Cognitive-Behavioral Therapy

R	Routine	To avoid mood problems, it is important for families to follow a routine. Waking, bedtime, meals, activities, and medication should be consistent. Transitions should be smooth and expected.
A	Affect Regulation	Parents and children should monitor children's moods each day. Families can decrease negative moods with coping strategies and parenting tactics to defuse situations.
I	I Can Do It!	Parents and children can solve disputes and arguments in positive ways. Parents can use a mixture of quiet confidence, calming tones, and a focus on empathy to help deescalate their children's negative moods.
N	No Negative Thoughts	Parents and children can identify and challenge cognitive distortions that contribute to negative moods. Negative thoughts (e.g., My child is terrible; nothing I do helps) can be reframed more realistically (e.g., My child's behavior is a problem that I can solve).
B	Be a Good Friend	Children are taught social skills to help them make and keep friends. Parents are encouraged to live a balanced lifestyle, to develop a social support network, and other ways to decrease stress.
O	Oh, How Can We Solve the Problem?	Parents and children can learn to use problem-solving strategies to deal with social problems. Breaking large problems into smaller steps, generating possible solutions, selecting and implementing the best solution, and evaluating outcomes can help.
W	Ways to Get Support	Children can identify family members, other adults, or friends who can help them when they have mood problems. Parents and therapists can advocate for their children at school to help them achieve.

Source: Based on West and Weinstein (2012).

Note: The acronym RAINBOW is used to remind families of the principles of treatment.

CFF-CBT is based on the assumption that children with BSDs have disturbances in their neural systems responsible for processing and regulating emotions (West & Weinstein, 2012). These children usually want to behave appropriately at home and school, but their mood regulation problems prevent them from doing so. Treatment involves teaching children and parents strategies to help regulate children's emotions and decrease the frequency and severity of mood episodes.

First, therapists teach children to recognize and regulate negative emotions. Strategies include recognizing and labeling feelings, identifying and avoiding triggers that might elicit dysphoria, and developing tactics to cope with expansive, irritable, or sad mood states. Therapists also teach parents how to monitor their children's moods and prompt their children to use emotion-regulation skills in times of stress. Parents are also encouraged to develop stress-reduction techniques of their own, to help manage the stress associated with caring for a child with a BSD.

Second, parents and children learn cognitive skills to improve the quality of parent-child interactions and children's social functioning. Some sessions focus on problem-solving skills training, to help family members navigate problems without anger and argument. Other sessions emphasize social skills training. Through role play and discussion, parents and children learn how to listen to each other and communicate their feelings in positive ways.

Third, therapists teach parents behavior management strategies to cope with children's angry, irritable mood states. In traditional parent-training for families with children who have ODD, therapists encourage parents to establish limits on children's behavior, to give clear commands, and to immediately respond to instances of noncompliance. However, children with BSDs may actually become more agitated by these tactics. Whereas children with ODD misbehave in a purposeful, manipulative manner, children with BSDs misbehave because of deficits in emotion-regulation skills. Rather than strict limit setting and punishment, children

with BSDs may respond to parenting strategies that defuse emotionally charged situations. Parents are encouraged to use a calming voice, to modulate their own affect, and to emphasize an empathic and collaborative problem-solving approach to stressful situations.

The feasibility of CFF-CBT therapy has been demonstrated in two open trials. In the first study, a small sample of youths with BSDs and their families participated in treatment. Participants reported a high degree of satisfaction with the program. Furthermore, children showed reductions in depression, mania, psychotic symptoms, and sleep problems and improvements in overall functioning over time (Pavuluri, Graczyk, et al., 2004). Families were able to maintain these gains 3 years later (West et al., 2007).

In the second study, researchers examined the feasibility of treatment when administered to groups of parents and children. A small sample of children with BSDs and their families participated in sessions together. After treatment, parents reported an increase in children's coping skills and a decrease in children's manic symptoms (West et al., 2009).

The chief limitation of these evaluation studies is that they did not include control groups. Although treatment seems effective, we cannot be certain that therapy caused these beneficial outcomes. Medication, other environmental factors, or the simple passage of time might be responsible for children's improvement.

Psychoeducational Psychotherapy (PEP)

Psychoeducational psychotherapy (PEP) was developed by Mary Fristad and colleagues (2011) to help children with BSDs and other mood disorders (Table 14.6). It is designed for children, ages 8 to 12 years and their caregivers, although it is often used for older and younger children. PEP can be administered to individual families (IF-PEP), like CFF-CBT. PEP can also be administered to multiple families together (MF-PEP) in

---

Table 14.6 Components of Psychoeducational Psychotherapy (PEP)

1. Parents and children discuss the group's purpose and symptoms of mood disorders.

2. Parents and children are taught about medications used to treat mood disorders, expected benefits, and possible side effects. Parents and children learn to use medication logs to monitor medication effects.

3. Parents learn about systems of care; that is, how professionals at the child's school and clinic can work together to provide comprehensive treatment. Children create a "tool kit" of skills designed to help them cope with negative events and emotions. Coping skills include four areas: creative coping (e.g., dance), physical coping (e.g., sports), social coping (e.g., playing with a friend), and rest/relaxation coping (e.g., mom giving a back rub).

4. Parents learn how children's mood symptoms can cause conflict in the family. They participate in the "Naming the Enemy" exercise, in which they differentiate the child from his/her symptoms. This exercise demonstrates that symptoms can cover up the positive aspects and strengths of the child. Children participate in the thinking-feeling-doing exercise to learn the connection between thoughts, feelings, and actions. Therapists demonstrate how thoughts mediate the relationship between events and behavioral responses.

5. Parents and children learn to break down social problems into multiple steps: (1) Stop, (2) Think, (3) Plan, (4) Do, (5) Check.

6. Therapists and parents discuss "helpful" and "hurtful" forms of communication with children. Children learn this distinction through role play.

7. Parents learn specific symptom management skills. Children continue to learn and practice communication skills.

8. Families review what they have learned and receive feedback regarding family/child strengths. They are also given resource material (i.e., books, support groups in the community).

Source: From Kowatch and Fristad (2006). Used with permission.

such a way that groups of children and groups of parents gain information, practice skills, and find support from one another.

As its name implies, PEP emphasizes **psychoeducation**. Considerable time is spent helping families understand mood disorders, their symptoms, course, causes, and treatments. Therapists conceptualize mood disorders as "no-fault brain disorders" that have biological underpinnings. Neither children nor parents are blamed for children's mood problems. The fundamental principle of PEP is reflected in the motto, "It's not your fault, but it's your challenge!" Although families do not cause BSDs, the way they respond to children's symptoms can either alleviate or exacerbate their problems.

A primary goal is to direct blame away from children by differentiating the child from his or her mood symptoms. Children participate in an activity called "Naming the Enemy" in which they are encouraged to see their mood problem as something external to themselves—something that needs to be targeted for treatment. Parents are also encouraged to differentiate their children from their children's symptoms and to pay attention to positive aspects of their children's behavior (see Research to Practice: Naming the Enemy). They learn to monitor and record their children's mood symptoms and create practical goals for therapy (i.e., a "Fit-it List").

RESEARCH TO PRACTICE

NAMING THE ENEMY

Annie

Annie's Symptoms

Annie	Annie's Symptoms
Excellent drawer, artist	**Mania**
Good to animals (especially cats)	Doesn't sleep much, refuses to sleep
Wonderful smile	Acts goofy, silly, wild
Athletic—swimming, soccer, basketball	Talks a lot; won't sit still
Always willing to help younger brother	Tantrums, throws, breaks things
Good at sharing	**Depression**
Very affectionate	Irritable, cranky, "mouthy"
Funny, practical joker	Cries, weepy
Likes to help dad outside	Doesn't want to play sports or be with others

Source: Based on Fristad and colleagues (2011).

Note: Parents learn to differentiate the child from his or her symptoms in the Naming the Enemy activity, a component of psychoeducational psychotherapy for children with BSDs and other mood disorders. The child's mood disorder (not the child) is to blame.

A second component of PEP is **emotion-regulation training**. Initially, children learn basic skills to gain control of their emotions. For example, therapists teach three breathing techniques (i.e., "the three Bs") to reduce anxiety and anger: belly breathing (e.g., deep breathing from the diaphragm), bubble breathing (i.e., slow and steady release), and balloon breathing (i.e., slow release with pursed lips). In later sessions, children build a "tool kit" of cognitive and behavioral skills that they can use to cope with negative emotions. Coping skills in their tool kit fall into four categories that children remember by the acronym CARS: creative (e.g., drawing), active (e.g., playing outside), rest and relaxation (e.g., breathing), and social (time with friends).

Therapists also help children understand the relationship between their thoughts, feelings, and actions. In one exercise called "Thinking, Feeling, and Doing," children learn that the way they think about or react to a problem influences the way they feel about it (Figure 14.9). If children change hurtful thoughts (e.g., She was mean to me on purpose) and actions (e.g., name calling, yelling) with helpful thoughts and actions (e.g., Maybe she didn't mean to hurt my feelings), they might feel better in stressful situations.

A third component of PEP is improving the family's **problem-solving skills**. Parents and children are encouraged to view children's mood disorders as a problem that needs to be addressed. Children learn simple problem-solving steps:

- *Stop:* take a moment to calm down
- *Think:* define the problem and generate possible solutions
- *Plan:* consider the best solution to use
- *Do:* carry out the solution
- *Check:* evaluate the outcome and decide what to do next

Parents practice responding to their children's mood symptoms without resorting to criticism, hostility, or blame. Although parents want to be empathetic and helpful, they often become frustrated when their efforts fail to regulate their children's emotions or behavior. Parents learn the "dos and don'ts" of responding to a moody child. They learn to recognize the early signs of anger, frustration, or guilt to avoid negative interactions with their children.

IF-PEP consists of 20 to 24 weekly family sessions, each lasting 45 to 50 minutes. Sessions typically alternate between parent-sessions and child-sessions. MF-PEP consists of 8

Figure 14.9 Thinking-Feeling-Doing Exercise

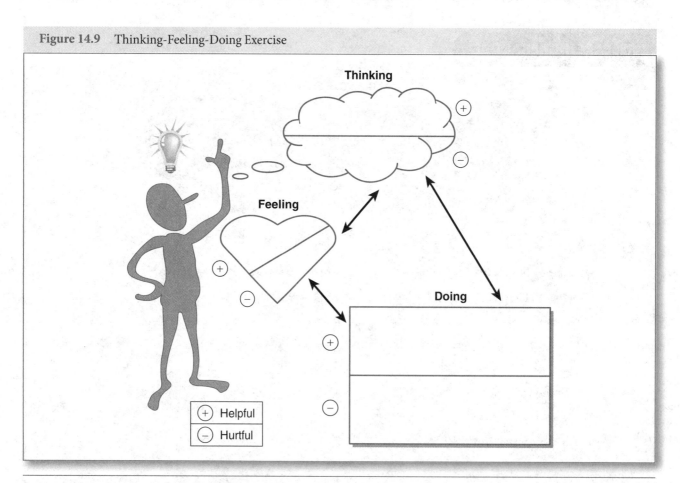

Source: From Goldberg-Arnold and Fristad (2003). Reprinted with permission.

Note: Children learn the connection between feelings (the heart), thoughts (the cloud), and actions (the box) in this game. Although it is unrealistic for children with mood problems to "wish" bad feelings away, they can change negative emotions by altering their behavior or ways of thinking.

weekly sessions, each lasting 90 minutes. Typically, six to eight families (parents and children) meet together at the beginning and end of each session. For most of each session, however, children and parents meet separately in groups that address a similar theme for the week. In this manner, children can observe and practice skills with their peers while parents gain support from other caregivers (Davidson & Fristad, 2008).

Support for PEP comes from a large, randomized controlled trial involving 165 children (8–12 years) with mood disorders and their parents (Fristad, Verducci, Walters, & Young, 2009). Approximately 70% of children had BSDs. Families were randomly assigned to receive eight sessions of MF-PEP immediately, or they were placed in a waitlist control group for 12 months. Families in both groups were also allowed to take medication for their mood disorder. One year later, children who participated in MF-PEP showed significantly fewer mood symptoms than children in the waitlist control group. When children assigned to waitlist were also allowed to participate in MF-PEP, they too showed a reduction in mood symptoms. Nearly 90% of families completed the program. These findings indicate that MF-PEP is helpful in augmenting standard treatment for pediatric mood disorders, especially BSDs.

MF-PEP may also be effective in preventing (or at least delaying) the onset of BSDs in young children at high risk for developing the disorder. In one study, researchers administered MF-PEP to a large sample of children with depression and transient symptoms of mania. Youths and their parents either received MF-PEP immediately or were placed on a waiting list. Within 12 months, 12% of youths who received MF-PEP developed Bipolar Disorder compared to 45% of youths placed on the waitlist. Overall, MF-PEP was associated with a fourfold reduction in developing the illness. The researchers suggested that MF-PEP might reduce conversion to Bipolar Disorder by helping families become better consumers of mental health care, by decreasing stress and increasing social support, and by improving family functioning (Nadkarni & Fristad, 2010).

Family-Focused Treatment for Adolescents (FFT-A)

Family-focused treatment (FFT) was developed by David Miklowitz (2012) and colleagues to treat adults with Bipolar Disorder. More recently, the therapy has been adapted to be used with adolescents and older children with the disorder (Table 14.7). Ideally, FFT-A involves all family members, including parents and siblings. FFT-A is typically administered in 21 sessions spread over 9 months (i.e., weekly for 3 months, biweekly for 3 months, monthly for 3 months).

FFT-A is based on a diathesis-stress model for BSDs. Both genetic risk (i.e., diathesis) and environmental stressors are necessary for someone to develop the disorder. Although one's genotype may place them at increased risk, "genetics is not destiny" (Miklowitz, Axelson, et al., 2008, p. 172). Adolescents and their parents can learn to identify and reduce psychosocial stressors that might exacerbate episodes of mania or depression. Possible stressors include child-family conflicts, sibling rivalries, peer or romantic relationship problems, school or neighborhood difficulties, or any disruption to family routines.

A primary goal of FFT-A is to reduce expressed emotion (EE) in the family (Figure 14.10). High-EE families often exacerbate their children's mood symptoms in three ways. First, families often attribute their children's disruptive behavior to internal, stable, and personal factors rather than to a medical illness. For example, they might blame their child for his disruptive actions, interpreting his misbehavior as a sign of disrespect or malice. Therefore, the first component of FFT-A is education. Families are taught about the

Table 14.7 Family-Focused Treatment for Adolescents With Bipolar Disorder

Sessions	Module	Description
1–9	Psychoeducation	Families learn about the causes, course, and treatment for Bipolar Disorder. Families learn that "genetics is not destiny"; adolescents can learn to avoid or reduce stressors that trigger mood episodes. Families develop a plan for relapse should it occur.
10–15	Communication Enhancement Training	Using role play, families practice four skills designed to improve communication at home: listening, expressing positive feelings, making positive requests for changes in others' behavior, and providing constructive negative feedback. Families identify and break negative communication cycles.
16–21	Problem-Solving Skills	Families learn steps to solve social problems and avoid arguments: break down problems into smaller steps, generate possible solutions, select and implement the best solution, and evaluate outcomes. Sessions may also focus on managing adolescents' disruptive behavior while respecting his or her emerging autonomy.
21+	Maintenance	Therapists periodically meet with families to trouble-shoot specific problems and review principles. Often, sessions involve the rehearsal of communication and problem-solving skills.

Source: Based on Miklowitz, Axelson, et al. (2008).

symptoms, course, and causes of BSDs. Therapists help parents view their children's disruptive behavior as a symptom of a medical illness rather than as an act of irresponsibility or disrespect.

Youths with BSDs often elicit negative thoughts, feelings, and actions from their parents. For example, when an adolescent skips school during a manic episode or yells at her parents during an episode of depression, parents might understandably react with feelings of anger or resentment. Often, families engage in a **negatively escalating cycle of communication**, in which criticism from one family member elicits countercriticism from another family member, until it is difficult to resolve amicably. Miklowitz (2008) calls this an "attack-counterattack" cycle of communication that usually follows a "three-volley sequence":

Parent: Why can't you pick up your things when you get home from school instead of just hiding in your room listening to music?

Adolescent: I wouldn't have to hide in my room if you didn't nag me so much and minded your own business.

Parent: Nag you? If I didn't nag, you wouldn't get anything done.

The second component of FFT is communication enhancement training. Through a series of role-playing exercises, parents learn to deescalate highly emotional, negative interactions with their children in order to avoid excessive displays of anger, hostility, or sadness. Families learn how to shift their attention away from immediate, negative feelings and instead to communicate their thoughts and feelings in constructive ways. Typically, communication enhancement training involves teaching families how to listen to each other, share positive feelings, make positive requests, and give feedback to each other in ways that do not result in criticism or condemnation.

Third, high-EE families often have difficulty solving social problems. When problems arise, families often resort to two, ineffective strategies. Some families engage in criticism and hostility, as described previously. Instead of solving the problem directly, they emotionally attack each other. In contrast, other families use avoidance coping when dealing with problems. For example, a mother might ignore her child's disruptive behavior until it becomes so excessive she lashes out in anger and resentment. Therefore, FFT-A seeks to teach families social problem-solving skills. First, families are taught to take large, abstract problems (e.g., "We don't respect each other") and break them down into objective, smaller steps (e.g., "We need to use a lower tone of voice when speaking to each other"). Then, families are taught to generate possible solutions to real-life family problems, to evaluate the pros and cons of each possible solution, and to select the best solution to implement.

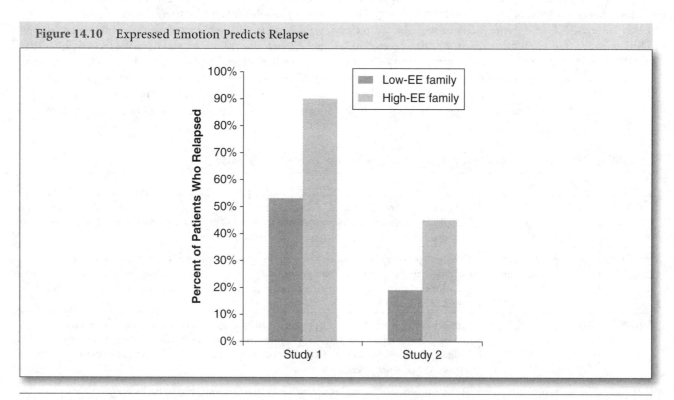

Figure 14.10   Expressed Emotion Predicts Relapse

Source: Based on Miklowitz (2008).

Note: In two studies, children from families with high expressed emotion were more likely to relapse than children from families with low expressed emotion. A primary goal of family therapy is to decrease expressed emotion to reduce relapse.

PROBLEM-SOLVING TRAINING FOR ADOLESCENTS WITH BIPOLAR SPECTRUM DISORDERS

Problem-solving training is an important component of therapy for adolescents with Bipolar Spectrum Disorders. The therapist and adolescent might practice social problem-solving strategies on hypothetical situations created by the therapist or generated by the family:

> This upcoming Saturday night is the big homecoming dance at our school. I am really excited because I am going to the dance with a person I really like. I don't know what to do because my date and all of my friends are allowed to stay out until 1:30 a.m. and my parents said that I have to be home by my normal curfew, which is midnight. My parents hate me—they want me to be unpopular! I am going to miss out on the big party after the dance because I have to go home! Everyone is going to think that I am so lame. I am thinking about just staying out and making up an excuse when I get home late. What do you think I should do? (Danielson et al., 2004)

By learning to engage in social problem solving in a methodical way, the families can weigh the strengths and weaknesses of each possible solution to the problem before acting. This can decrease the likelihood that he will act in an impulsive fashion, get into trouble, and experience a negative mood state.

Typically, problem-solving training is introduced during therapy sessions and practiced at home (see Research to Practice: Problem-Solving Training for Adolescents With Bipolar Spectrum Disorders).

FFT has been evaluated in several randomized, controlled trials of adults with BSDs (Miklowitz, 2012). Overall, adults who participate in FFT are less likely to relapse (36%–46%) than adults assigned to traditional supportive therapy (60%) or crisis management (83%).

Furthermore, a randomized, controlled study indicates that FFT-A may speed recovery of depression in adolescents with BSDs. Miklowitz and colleagues (Miklowitz, Axelson, et al., 2008) assigned adolescents to either FFT-A plus medication or "enhanced care" plus medication. FFT-A consisted of 21 sessions spread across 9 months, involving adolescents, parents, and (sometimes) siblings. Enhanced care involved 3 weekly sessions during which families were provided information about BSDs, medication management, and the importance of avoiding conflict in the home.

Two years after the beginning of the study, 91.4% of adolescents recovered from their initial mood episode. The recovery rates were similar for youths in both treatment conditions. However, youths who received FFT-A showed significantly faster reduction in depressive symptoms (10.2 weeks) than youths in the control condition (14.1 weeks). Youths who received FFT-A also showed faster recovery from mania (7.6 weeks) than youths in the control condition (13.8 weeks), although this difference only approached significance. The researchers suggested that FFT-A's focus on reducing family conflict, enhancing social support, and teaching interpersonal skills were responsible for its effectiveness in alleviating depression.

FFT-A may also be useful in preventing BSD in children at high risk for developing the disorder. In a pilot study, Miklowitz and colleagues (2011) administered a modified version of FFT-A to a small sample of older children and young adolescents who had a biological parent with a BSD. These youths were selected for the study because they were at increased genetic risk for the disorder themselves. Furthermore, children also had mood disorders themselves, most commonly depression. The modified FFT-A consisted of 12 family sessions which emphasized psychoeducation, communication enhancement, and problem-solving skills. One year later, youths showed significant improvement in depression, hypomania, and psychosocial functioning. Because this study did not include a control group, we cannot be certain that these benefits are attributable to FFT-A. However, these findings do suggest that FFT-A may be an effective avenue for treatment and prevention.

SCHIZOPHRENIA IN CHILDHOOD AND ADOLESCENCE

Schizophrenia is a serious mental disorder characterized by a disturbance in perception, thought, language, social interactions, and emotional expression. People with schizophrenia experience problems thinking clearly, differentiating idiosyncratic (and often bizarre) perceptions and thoughts from reality, and interacting with others. It is among the most debilitating illnesses and often leads to long-term impairment.

The term "schizophrenia" was coined by the famous psychiatrist Eugen Bleuler. Between 1908 and 1911, Bleuler

SPLIT MINDS, SPLIT BRAINS, AND MULTIPLE PERSONALITIES

Although schizophrenia means "split mind," it should not be confused with similar terms frequently used in psychology. For example, Schizophrenia should not be confused with Dissociative Identity Disorder (formerly Multiple Personality Disorder). People with Schizophrenia do not have multiple personalities that influence their behavior. People with Schizophrenia should also not be confused with the "split brain patients" who are usually described in introductory psychology textbooks. Split brain patients have undergone a surgical procedure to severe their corpus callosum, the bundle of nerves that connect the hemispheres of the brain. The surgery is usually conducted to alleviate severe epilepsy and results in a functional disconnect between certain left- and right-hemisphere brain processes. Their deficits are usually not observable, except under carefully controlled laboratory conditions. Split brain patients do not show symptoms of mental illness.

observed thought and perceptual disturbances in some of his young patients. He believed the patients' underlying problem was a separation of their intellectual and emotional faculties. Consequently, he used the term *schizophrenia*, meaning "split mind," to describe these patients (Fusar-Poli & Politi, 2008). He saw these individuals as lacking motivation and volition, avoiding interactions with others, displaying very little emotion, and having unusual thought processes (see text box Research to Practice: Split Minds, Split Brains, and Multiple Personalities). These symptoms remain part of our current conceptualization of the disorder today (Kuniyoshi & McClellan, 2010).

Although Schizophrenia is usually thought of as an "adult" disorder, it can also exist in children and adolescents (Palmen & van Engeland, 2012). Although rare, childhood- and adolescent onset Schizophrenia are conditions that greatly impact the lives of youths and families around the world.

Today, *DSM-5* classifies Schizophrenia as a Psychotic Disorder. The term *psychotic* derives from the Greek words "psyche" (mind) and "-osis" (an abnormal condition). **Psychotic Disorders** are thought disorders in which the person's cognitions, affect, and overt actions reflect a lack of contact or connection with their surroundings. Although there are many Psychotic Disorders, Schizophrenia is the most common.

CASE STUDY

MINA'S MACABRE VISIONS

Fourteen-year-old Mina was brought to the emergency department of our hospital by the police. According to the police report, Mina had attempted to strangulate her mother with a belt during a family argument. The on-call psychologist, Dr. Harrington, was asked to assess Mina's state of mind with respect to the incident and to recommend treatment.

Mina did not look up at Dr. Harrington when she entered the exam area. Although Mina's general appearance was disheveled, her behavior was calm, almost passive, and withdrawn. She responded to Dr. Harrington's questions with downcast eyes in a slow, monotone voice. Her affect was restricted; even while discussing the incident, her voice rarely fluctuated in tone, and her facial expression remained unchanged. Mina stared at the hospital blankets on her bed as she spoke as if they were the most interesting objects in the world.

"I didn't want to hurt her," Mina reported. "But I felt like I had to. It's really the only way to make things stop."

Dr. Harrington replied, "Tell me about those 'things."

After a long pause, Mina continued, "It's the voice I hear, especially when things get bad. It's the voice of a bad man—a really raspy, quick voice. It tells me to hurt or kill other people. I know it's not real, but it keeps going on and on in my head, telling me to do things I know I shouldn't."

During the interview, Dr. Harrington learned that Mina began experiencing auditory hallucinations at the age of 9. The hallucinations began as "whispers" which gradually became a male voice that told her to "hurt, kill, or choke" other people. At the age of 12, Mina also began to experience brief, but vivid, visual hallucinations. Usually, she saw bloody, dismembered, or mutilated bodies or a corpse that had been stabbed or cut into several pieces. Each scene usually lasted

5 to 10 seconds, but they often occurred multiple times each day. Understandably, the auditory and visual hallucinations caused Mina serious distress and interfered with her ability to do well at school and interact with family members and friends.

"Is there anything you can do to stop the voices or images?" Dr. Harrington asked.

Mina replied, "Sometimes, I don't know what to do. I just crawl into bed, under the covers, and try to hide from them. That usually doesn't work so well. I've thought about killing myself, but I'm too scared to do that. And I don't want to leave my mom all alone." Mina reluctantly added, "Other times, they are so bad, I need to do something, so I scratch on my arms to make them go away. It's like the pain on my arm clears my head." For the first time during the interview, Mina looked up at Dr. Harrington and sighed.

"Who else knows about the voice and the pictures you see?" Dr. Harrington asked.

"No one," Mina admitted, "I didn't want people to think I was crazy."

What Is Schizophrenia?

Core Features

Schizophrenia is a Psychotic Disorder in which the person's thoughts, feelings, and actions reflect a lack of contact with reality. It is defined by the presence of two or more of the following psychotic symptoms: hallucinations, delusions, disorganized speech, grossly abnormal behavior, and diminished emotional expression or lack of motor activity (Table 14.8, Diagnostic Criteria for Schizophrenia).

The most common feature of Schizophrenia in children and adolescents is hallucinations (Table 14.9). Hallucinations are "perception-like experiences that occur without an external stimulus" (American Psychiatric Associations, 2013, p. 87). Hallucinations are usually auditory, consisting of voices which may give commands, issue threats, or offer comments about

---

Table 14.8 Diagnostic Criteria for Schizophrenia

A. Two (or more) of the following, each present for a significant portion of time during a 1-month period (or less if successfully treated). At least one of these must be (1), (2), or (3):

1. Delusions.

2. Hallucinations.

3. Disorganized speech (e.g., frequent derailment or incoherence).

4. Grossly disorganized or catatonic behavior.

5. Negative symptoms (i.e., diminished emotional expression or avolition).

B. For a significant portion of the time since the onset of the disturbance, level of functioning in one or more major areas, such as work, interpersonal relations, or self-care, is markedly below the level achieved prior to the onset (or when the onset is in childhood or adolescence, there is failure to achieve the expected level of interpersonal, academic, or occupational functioning).

C. Continuous signs of the disturbance persist for at least 6 months. This 6-month period must include at least 1 month of symptoms (or less if successfully treated), that meet criterion A (i.e., active-phase symptoms) and may include periods of prodromal or residual symptoms. During these prodromal or residual periods, the signs of the disturbance may be manifested by only negative symptoms or by two or more symptoms in attenuated form (e.g., odd beliefs, unusual perceptual experiences).

D. Depressive and Bipolar Disorder with psychotic features have been ruled out because either (1) no major depressive or manic episodes have occurred concurrently with the active-phased symptoms, or (2) if mood episodes have occurred during active-phase symptoms, they have been present for a minority of the total duration of the active and residual periods of the illness.

E. The disturbance is not attributable to the physiological effects of a substance (e.g., a drug of abuse, a medication) or another medical condition.

F. If there is a history of Autism Spectrum Disorder or a Communication Disorder of childhood onset, the additional diagnosis of Schizophrenia is made only if predominant delusions or hallucinations, in addition to the other required symptoms, are also present for at least 1 month (or less if successfully treated).

Source: Reprinted with permission from the *Diagnostic and Statistical Manual of Mental Disorders, Fifth Edition* (Copyright 2013). American Psychiatric Association.

Table 14.9   Assessing Hallucinations in Children and Adolescents

1. Auditory Hallucinations:	Do you hear voices, sounds, or noises that other people do not hear? Where do the voices come from? Are they in your head or do you hear them on the outside through your ears? Do they sound as clear as someone speaking to you?
Commands	Do the voices tell you to do things? Have they ever told you to hurt or kill yourself or someone else?
Commentary	Do you hear voices that talk about what you're doing, feeling, or thinking?
Conversing	How many voices do you hear? Do they talk with each other?
Thoughts aloud	Do you ever hear your own thoughts spoken aloud?
Religious	Do you ever hear the voice of God (Jesus), angels, or demons?
Non-voices	Do you ever hear other sounds, music, or noises that others don't hear?
2. Visual Hallucinations:	Do you see things that other children don't see? Did you see something that looked real, or was it just like a shadow moving? How clear was it? Did you see it many times on different days?
3. Tactile Hallucinations:	Do you ever feel like someone or something is touching you, but when you look there is nothing there?
4. Olfactory Hallucinations:	Do you ever smell things that other people don't smell?
5. Illusions:	Have you ever looked around your room at night and seen things that you thought were something else? For example, did you ever look at a stuffed animal or shirt and think it was a monster? Have you ever looked at a belt or rope and thought it was a snake?
6. Cultural Acceptance:	Do other people in your family or church have the same experiences as you?

Source: Based on the Kiddie-Schedule for Affective Disorders and Schizophrenia, Psychosis Supplement, a semi-structured interview to diagnose Schizophrenia in youths (Endicott & Spitzer, 1978).

the youths' thoughts or actions (Figure 14.11). Sometimes, auditory hallucinations involve laughter, humming, whistling, or whispering. Visual hallucinations also occur frequently in children and adolescents with the disorder. Typically, youths do not see clear, fully formed images. Shadows, light, and brief

images are more common. When children do see clear images, they may be in the shape of animals (e.g., spiders), mythical figures (e.g., fairies), monsters, or cartoon characters. Olfactory (smell), gustatory (taste), and tactile/somatosensory (touch) hallucinations are rare in children and adolescents. If they do

Figure 14.11   Types of Hallucinations Experienced by Youths With Schizophrenia

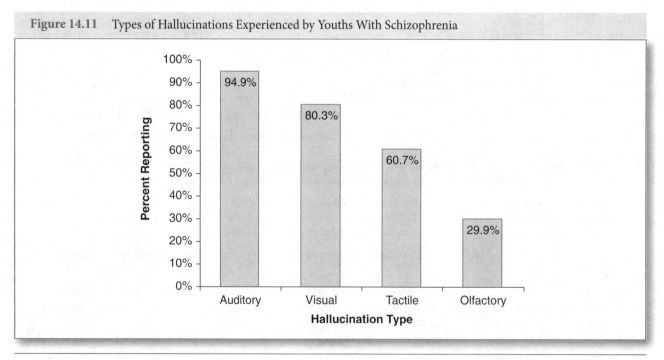

Source: Based on David and colleagues (2011).

Note: Auditory and visual hallucinations are most common. When other hallucinations occur, they usually accompany auditory and visual hallucinations.

occur, they usually present alongside auditory and visual hallucinations (David et al., 2011).

Youths with Schizophrenia also frequently experience delusions. Delusions are "fixed beliefs that are not amenable to change in light of conflicting evidence" (American Psychiatric Association, 2013). These beliefs usually reflect a misinterpretation of perceptions or experiences and may be bizarre in nature (Table 14.10). Adolescents may report delusions that others are controlling their actions or thoughts (i.e., delusions of control), that others are out to get them (i.e., delusions of persecution), or that other people are sending them special messages or signals (i.e., delusions of reference). Sometimes, youths believe that they are special or called to perform a certain task (i.e., delusions of grandiosity) or that their body is defective or distorted in some way (i.e., somatic delusions). Although delusions like these are clearly atypical, their content may reflect developmentally appropriate concerns, such as thoughts about autonomy, adolescent egocentrism, and preoccupation with appearance and the physical changes associated with puberty. Clearly developed and articulated delusions are relatively rare among children with Schizophrenia. They become more common in adolescents with the disorder, as youths acquire more sophisticated cognitive abilities (Hollis, 2010).

Children and adolescents with Schizophrenia also frequently display peculiar speech and language (Clark, 2011). Some youths speak very little (i.e., poverty of speech) whereas other are extremely talkative (i.e., logorrhea). Other children repeat words and phrases (i.e., perseverations), use highly rigid, stereotyped language, or seem usually preoccupied with certain topics. Some youths with Schizophrenia repeat words or phrases uttered by others (i.e., echolalia). Still other children insert made-up words into their language (i.e., neologisms).

Children's language can give clues regarding their cognitive functioning. Youths with Schizophrenia will often exhibit breaks in their train of thought (i.e., thought blockage), jump from one topic to another (i.e., knight's move thinking), discuss tangential or totally irrelevant topics, or use vague language. In rare cases, youths may complain that they can hear their own thoughts, as if they were spoken by someone else (i.e., thought echoing). Others report that people are inserting thoughts into their minds (i.e., thought insertion), that their thoughts are broadcast to others (i.e., thought broadcasting), or that someone has stolen their thoughts (i.e., thought withdrawal).

Table 14.10	Assessing Delusions in Children and Adolescents
1. Grandiosity:	Do you ever feel that you are a very important person or that you have special powers? Are you related to important people, like kings or the president? Do you have special powers like reading people's minds? Has God chosen you to do special tasks for him?
2. Guilt or Sin:	Did you ever feel like you did something terrible? Do you deserve punishment?
3. Delusions of Control:	Do you have feelings that you are being controlled by some force or power outside yourself? Do you feel like you are a puppet or robot and can't control what you do?
4. Somatic Delusions:	Do you think you have any serious diseases? Has something happened to your body or insides?
5. Nihilism:	Do you feel that something terrible will happen or has happened? Have you felt like the world was coming to an end?
6. Thought Broadcasting:	Do you ever feel like your thoughts are broadcast out loud so that other people know what you are thinking? Like on a radio, so that others could hear them? Have you actually heard your own thoughts spoken out loud?
7. Thought Insertion:	Do you feel that thoughts are put into your mind that are not your own?
8. Thought Withdrawal:	Have you had thoughts taken out of your mind by someone else or by a special force or power?
9. Message from Media:	Does the TV or radio ever talk to you or send you a message?
10. Persecution:	Has anyone been making things hard for you, purposely causing you trouble, trying to hurt you, or plotting against you?
11. Mind Reading:	Do people know what you are thinking? Is it because of the way you look, or is it because they can somehow read your mind?
12. Reference:	Do people seem to say things to you that have double meanings? Have things been especially arranged so that only you can understand their meaning?
13. Culture:	Do other people in your family or church have similar thoughts? Do your friends or other children at school believe what you believe?

Source: Based on the Kiddie-Schedule for Affective Disorders and Schizophrenia, Psychosis Supplement, a semi-structured interview to diagnose Schizophrenia in youths.

Many youths with Schizophrenia display disturbances in movement and coordination (Hollis, 2010). They may appear clumsy, engage in repetitive, purposeless movements of the hands, arms, or legs (e.g., stereotypies), or show other compulsive actions or rituals. They may seem dejected and walk slowly. In rare instances, they may assume bizarre postures or remain motionless and unresponsive for long periods of time (i.e., catatonia).

Nearly all youths with Schizophrenia show disturbances in affect. Youths with Schizophrenia often show "diminished emotional expression;" that is, they do not show typical feelings through smiling, laughing, making eye contact, looking surprised, or becoming tearful when discussing sad topics. Youths may also display **avolition**, that is, a lack of drive, energy, or meaningful goal-directed behavior. They may seem "mopey" and disinterested in friends, sports, or hobbies. They may speak in a monotonous voice and seem lethargic or apathetic. Sometimes, youths show inappropriate affect. Inappropriate affect refers to emotional expressions that are incongruent with the content of speech. For example, a child might giggle while discussing her expulsion from school or a recent suicide attempt (Clark, 2011).

Youths with Schizophrenia also frequently report mood problems. Some children describe their own mood as anxious, fearful, tense, or restless. Others experience listlessness and depression. Still others are touchy, angry, or irritable. Most experience considerable problems in interpersonal relationships and often avoid interactions with peers.

To be diagnosed with Schizophrenia, youths must show at least two of the five possible features of the illness: hallucinations, delusions, disorganized speech, abnormal behavior, and diminished emotional expression. Furthermore, at least one of these symptoms must include delusions, hallucinations, or disorganized speech—the most salient features of the disorder. Usually, children with Schizophrenia will show most, if not all symptoms.

DSM-5 also requires individuals with Schizophrenia to show signs of the illness for at least 6 months. For at least one month, the psychotic symptoms must be present (e.g., delusions, hallucinations, disorganized speech). For the other 5 months, the individual can continue to show these psychotic symptoms, display less severe (i.e., attenuated) symptoms, or display only problems with diminished emotional expression and avolition.

Schizophrenia should not be diagnosed if youths experience a mood disorder at the same time they show psychotic symptoms. For example, some youths with Major Depressive Disorder or BSDs experience auditory hallucinations. Clinicians only diagnose Schizophrenia after they have ruled out the possibility that youths' psychotic symptoms are not caused by depression or mania. Similarly, schizophrenia is not diagnosed when psychosis is caused by a medical illness, medication, or drug. As we shall see, many illnesses, medications, and drugs can mimic psychotic symptoms and can easily be mistaken for Schizophrenia.

Finally, young children with Schizophrenia often show several of the features of Autism Spectrum Disorder (ASD), such as marked deficits in social communication. However, children with ASD typically do not have delusions or hallucinations that last for extended periods of time. Schizophrenia can be diagnosed in children with ASD only when these other positive symptoms are present.

Positive and Negative Symptoms

Clinicians often divide the symptoms of Schizophrenia into two types: positive and negative (Crow, 1980). **Positive symptoms** reflect "behavioral over-expressions"; these symptoms are present in addition to or in excess of normal functioning. Examples of positive symptoms include hallucinations, delusions, disorganized behavior, excitement, grandiosity, suspiciousness, and hostility. **Negative symptoms** reflect behavioral "under-expressions"; they are absent or impoverished behavior with respect to normal functioning. Examples of negative symptoms include blunted or flat affect, avolition, social withdrawal, passivity or apathy, and a lack of spontaneity. Both positive and negative symptoms fluctuate over time (Kodish & McClellan, 2008).

Dividing symptoms into positive and negative types is useful to professionals for at least three reasons (Remschmidt & Theisen, 2012). First, positive and negative symptoms likely have different underlying neurobiological causes. For example, dopaminergic over-activity in central brain regions is associated with many positive symptoms, whereas underactivity in frontal brain regions is associated with many negative symptoms. Second, the prevalence and severity of positive and negative symptoms often change during the course of the illness. Typically, psychotic episodes begin with predominantly positive symptoms, which are gradually replaced by predominantly negative symptoms. Third, positive and negative symptoms respond differentially to treatment. Although antipsychotic medications are often helpful in reducing positive symptoms, they are usually less effective in treating negative symptoms (text box *DSM-IV → DSM-5* Changes: Where Have All the Subtypes Gone?).

DSM-IV → DSM-5 CHANGES

WHERE HAVE ALL THE SUBTYPES GONE?

For the past century, individuals with Schizophrenia were classified into one of several subtypes, based on their most salient symptoms. Subtypes included "paranoid" (i.e., delusions or auditory hallucinations involving persecution),

---

"disorganized" (i.e., disorganized speech and/or behavior and flat affect), "residual" (i.e., largely absent positive symptoms and predominantly negative symptoms), and "catatonic" (i.e., unusual muscular rigidity, repetitive purposeless movements, and/or echolalia). The subtypes were often used by clinicians to describe patients; however, their use was problematic in at least three ways (*DSM-5* Psychosis Working Group, 2012):

1. The subtypes had low inter-rater and test-retest reliability. Often, clinicians would classify the same patient with different subtypes. Furthermore, many patients would meet criteria for different subtypes over time as their signs and symptoms changed.

2. The subtypes were highly comorbid with each other. Many patients met criteria for two subtypes.

3. The subtypes were not very useful in planning treatment or predicting outcomes. Clinicians tended to use similar treatments (e.g., antipsychotic medication and psychotherapy) with all patients with similar rates of effectiveness.

Because of these problems, the subtypes of schizophrenia no longer appear in *DSM-5*. Instead, clinicians are encouraged to indicate the severity of each symptom. Nevertheless, some clinicians may continue to use the subtypes as a shorthand way to describe prominent features of their patients.

Epidemiology

Prevalence

Researchers differentiate Schizophrenia into three groups, based on symptom onset. Adult-onset Schizophrenia is most common; it is defined by the onset of symptoms after age 18. The lifetime prevalence of Schizophrenia among adults in the general population is approximately 1%. Schizophrenia typically emerges between the ages of 20 to 24 years in men and 25 to 29 years in women (Gur et al., 2005).

Adolescent-onset Schizophrenia (onset between 13–17 years) is much less common than adult-onset Schizophrenia. Only about 5% of people who develop Schizophrenia begin showing the disorder during adolescence. Although large

epidemiological studies have not yet been conducted, the best estimate is that only 0.23% of all youths will develop Schizophrenia during adolescence. **Childhood-onset Schizophrenia** (onset <12 years) is rarer still. Only about 1% of people who develop Schizophrenia begin manifesting the illness before puberty. Overall, the likelihood of a child developing Schizophrenia is approximately .0019%. Most clinicians will never see a child with Schizophrenia during their entire career (Remschmidt & Theisen, 2012).

Boys are approximately twice as likely as girls to develop Schizophrenia in childhood or adolescence (Kodish & McClellan, 2008). This is probably because, on average, males begin showing symptoms 5 to 7 years earlier than females (Figure 14.12). By middle adulthood, the prevalence of Schizophrenia across genders is similar (Nugent et al., 2012).

Figure 14.12 The Onset of Schizophrenia Depends on Gender

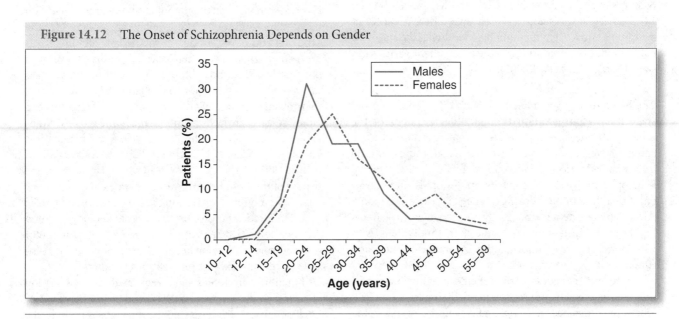

Source: Based on Gur and colleagues (2005).

Note: Males typically develop the disorder earlier than females.

CAROLINE'S CONVERSATIONS

Eight-year-old Caroline was referred to our clinic by her pediatrician who observed a marked decrease in her motor, language, and social skills over the past 6 months. Her pediatrician was unable to find a cause for these problems despite several physical exams and extensive testing. Recently, Caroline had shown a very dramatic decline in functioning: She was unable to dress herself, rarely made eye contact or spoke with others, and engaged in bizarre actions such as making unusual gestures and talking to herself.

During a diagnostic interview with Caroline's mother, Dr. Silverman learned that Caroline showed delays in her motor and language development. She did not learn to walk until age 18 months and continued to show problems with balance, coordination, and clumsiness as a preschooler. She did not utter her first meaningful words until age 26 months or speak clear sentences until age 4 years. By kindergarten, Caroline had made some progress, but she was still physically, linguistically, and cognitive behind her peers.

"About one year ago, I noticed a change in her behavior," Caroline's mother explained. "She started talking to herself a lot—you know, carrying on conversations. They were usually accompanied by hand motions and other gestures. I thought, 'most kids have vivid imaginations' so I didn't worry about it at first. Then, I started hearing her say strange things during these conversations, like, 'My friend died, somebody killed him with a knife' or 'We need to find a grave and bury him.' I also heard her say scary things to the cat, like 'Oh, Roscoe (the cat), why do you have bugs coming from your mouth?' This made me worried."

As Caroline's unusual behavior increased, her mood and social skills declined. She began having problems falling asleep at night and complained of nightmares and fears associated with going to bed alone. She was often tearful or irritable during the day and would sometimes tantrum violently. She showed a marked increase in hyperactivity and defiance and gradually refused to do most things for herself, like dress in the morning, brush her hair and teeth, and eat meals. She also lost interest in school and playing with neighborhood friends.

Dr. Silverman observed Caroline and her mother together in the clinic playroom. Caroline made very little eye contact. When Dr. Silverman attempted to play with her, she looked at him with an empty, meaningless expression and turned away. Caroline spent most of the session talking to herself quietly in the corner of the room.

Dr. Silverman questioned Caroline's mother about their family. Her mother replied, "Caroline lives with me and her younger brother. Her father really isn't in the picture anymore. He developed Schizophrenia shortly after we were married, and we separated a few months later. We haven't had contact with him for several years."

Course

People with schizophrenia typically progress through a series of stages over the course of several months or years (Figure 14.13). Each stage is characterized by a different cluster of symptoms and level of functioning. Identifying the stage of a patient's illness is important, because treatment varies from stage to stage (Gur et al., 2005).

The Premorbid Stage: Problems in Early Life. The premorbid stage lasts from gestation through the first signs of the illness. On the surface, children in the premorbid stage show no overt symptoms. However, several studies indicate that many adolescents and young adults who later develop Schizophrenia display deficits in motor skills and social-emotional functioning during infancy and early childhood. Although these deficits are usually not recognized by parents and teachers at the time, they indicate that individuals with Schizophrenia have abnormalities in brain structure and functioning very early in life.

One way to assess early deficits in individuals later diagnosed with Schizophrenia is to ask their parents to recall when they reached developmental milestones regarding basic motor skills and language. These retrospective studies reveal that infants and toddlers who later develop Schizophrenia are slower to crawl, walk, manipulate objects, and toilet train than their peers. Similarly, they show marked delays in expressive language and the ability to converse with other children and adults. These deficits are observed as early as the first year of life (Kodish & McClellan, 2008).

A chief problem with retrospective studies, however, is reporting bias. In hindsight, parents might magnify delays that were really quite minor to explain their children's current problems. To remedy this shortcoming of retrospective studies, researchers have examined the home movies of toddlers and preschoolers who later developed Schizophrenia as adults (E. Walker & J. Lewine, 1990; E. F. Walker & R. R. Lewine, 1993). Experts, who were not informed about the purpose of these studies, were asked to rate children's motor and social-emotional functioning based on the content of the films. Their ratings corroborated parents' reports; children who later developed Schizophrenia showed delays in motor skills and social behavior in their home movies. They also showed problems expressing emotions to others.

Longitudinal studies have replicated this association between early developmental delays and the later emergence of Schizophrenia. In these studies, researchers periodically assessed the development of large samples of children,

Figure 14.13 The Stages of Child- and Adolescent-Onset Schizophrenia

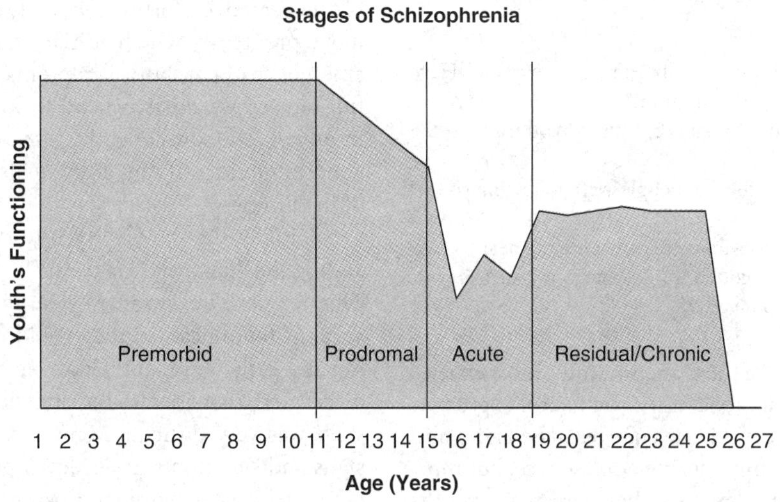

Stages of Schizophrenia

Youth's Functioning (y-axis)

Premorbid | Prodromal | Acute | Residual/Chronic

Age (Years): 1 2 3 4 5 6 7 8 9 10 11 12 13 14 15 16 17 18 19 20 21 22 23 24 25 26 27

Source: Based on Gur and colleagues (2005).

Note: Motor, language, and cognitive delays are often seen during the premorbid stage. The prodromal stage is characterized by changes in behavior and mood. Psychotic symptoms define the acute stage. The residual stage usually lasts a long time and most youths do not return to their premorbid level of functioning.

beginning in infancy and continuing through early adulthood. In all three studies, infants who later developed Schizophrenia in adulthood showed delays in sitting, standing, and walking. Their mothers reported delays in language acquisition. School personnel reported speech and language problems when these children began formal education. On average, 72% of youths later diagnosed with Schizophrenia showed marked delays in early language acquisition, speech, and motor development (Asarnow & Kernan, 2008). At the time, these delays did not greatly concern parents and school personnel; in hindsight, they provide the earliest warning signs for the disorder (Gur et al., 2005).

In elementary school, children who later develop Schizophrenia continue to show problems. Developmental tasks during elementary and middle school include the mastery of basic academic skills and the ability to make and keep friends. Unfortunately, children who later develop Schizophrenia often show marked problems with both tasks. On average, their cognitive functioning is one standard deviation below average. Their academic performance tends to be poor. These youths also experience considerable difficulty in interpersonal relationships. Family members frequently notice their preference for solitary play and their lack of confidence when interacting with peers. Teachers and classmates often describe them as more touchy, irritable, or moody during social interactions. Although these problems often concern parents and teachers, they are almost never seen as the early indicators of Schizophrenia. Indeed, academic and peer problems are so common

in childhood, they lack the specificity to predict such an uncommon disorder (Gur et al., 2005).

The Prodromal Stage: Noticeable Changes. The prodromal stage is characterized by a marked change in youths' academic, behavioral, and social-emotional functioning. Although children and adolescents in the prodromal stage may not show positive symptoms of Schizophrenia (e.g., hallucinations, delusions), family members usually notice a deterioration in their overall functioning. Many youths show significant problems with attention and concentration. They may seem restless and have difficulty completing their homework and studying for exams. Consequently, their grades in school decline. Parents usually describe their children as more "moody" or withdrawn. These youths may begin to avoid contact with family and friends, preferring to spend most of their time alone. They may quit clubs, sports, or other extracurricular activities. Sometimes, youths become more irritable and suspicious of others. Many youths begin to neglect their appearance and hygiene (Asarnow & Kernan, 2008)

Prodromal symptoms may emerge 2 to 6 years before the youth's first psychotic episode. Researchers have tried to better identify youths in the prodromal stage, with the hope of intervening early and avoiding (or at least delaying) the onset of Schizophrenia. For example, Poulton and colleagues (2000) conducted a longitudinal study of children in Dunedin, New Zealand. They followed children from age 11 to 26. They found that 11-year-olds who answered affirmatively to one of the five following questions were 16 times more likely to develop psychosis by the time they reached young adulthood than children who answered the questions negatively:

- Do you believe in mind reading or being psychic? Have other people ever read your mind?
- Have you ever had messages sent just to you through the television or radio?
- Have you ever thought that people were following you or spying on you?
- Have you heard voices that other people can't hear?
- Has somebody ever gotten inside your body, or has your body changed in some way?

Despite the findings of the Dunedin study, most experts have found it very difficult to identify youths in the prodromal stage. Many youths experience changes in behavior and social-emotional functioning during adolescence, but most have no mental health problems. Furthermore, many youths with anxiety, depression, peer problems, and substance use disorders display symptoms very similar to youths in the prodromal phase of Schizophrenia. Consequently, it is very difficult for clinicians to use prodromal symptoms to predict later psychosis (Gur et al., 2005).

The Acute Stage: Deterioration and Impairment. The acute phase begins with the onset of positive symptoms. Young children typically experience insidious (i.e., slow, barely noticeable) onset. In contrast, onset is typically more rapid among adolescents. The acute phase typically lasts one to 6 months, depending on how rapidly medication can be administered and how responsive youths are to medication (Kodish & McClellan, 2008).

The Residual Stage: Chronic Problems. After a psychotic episode, most youths enter a residual stage which may last for several months or years. Functioning in this stage is variable. Some youths experience a noticeable improvement in behavior and social-emotional skills; their functioning returns to levels similar to those before the prodromal phase. Sadly, however, most youths continue to show persistence of negative symptoms after a psychotic episode without a marked return to baseline functioning. These children remain withdrawn, moody, or irritable and experience long-term problems with relationships and school. Many of these youths will experience additional psychotic episodes later in adolescence or adulthood. With each subsequent episode, their functioning often deteriorates slightly. Thus, these youths experience problems which persist over time.

Predicting Schizophrenia: Attenuated Psychosis Syndrome

In recent years, researchers have become interested in identifying Schizophrenia in children, adolescents, and young adults as early as possible (*DSM-5* Psychosis Work Group, 2012). Early identification is critical, because long-term prognosis is related to the amount of time the disorder is left untreated. Unfortunately, early identification and treatment programs, which initiate treatment soon after the emergence of psychotic symptoms, do not seem to prevent full-blown psychosis or lead to long-term improvements in outcomes. Consequently, researchers have turned their attention to identifying individuals in the prodromal stage of the illness.

Initially, the *DSM-5* Psychosis Work Group considered adding the diagnosis "Psychosis Risk Syndrome" to *DSM-5*. This diagnosis was meant to identify youths in the prodromal stage of the illness, so they could receive careful monitoring and early treatment. However, the *DSM-5* Work Group discovered that identifying individuals in the prodromal stage was very difficult. Many individuals with prodromal signs and symptoms never developed psychosis, and many others who later developed psychosis did not show sufficient prodromal signs and symptoms. Furthermore, some experts worried that classifying youths with Psychosis Risk Syndrome might be stigmatizing.

Consequently, the *DSM-5* Work Group recommended that a different disorder, "Attenuated Psychosis Syndrome (APS)" be added to *DSM-5* as a "condition for future study." APS is a condition characterized by the very first signs and symptoms of psychosis, before the onset of full-blown psychosis. To be diagnosed, individuals must show at least one of the following:

- Delusions or delusional ideas
- Hallucinations or perceptual abnormalities
- Disorganized speech or communication

These features must be present at least once per week for the past month and they must have started or worsened in the past year. Furthermore, these signs and symptoms must have caused enough distress or impairment to individuals or their families to prompt them to seek professional help (American Psychiatric Association, 2013).

The research that is available regarding APS is promising. Early studies indicate that it can be diagnosed reliably. Furthermore, APS is associated with later psychosis: 18% of individuals who meet criteria for APS develop psychosis within 6 months, 22% within 12 months, 29% within 24 months, and 36% within 36 months. Most (73%) patients who later experience psychosis develop Schizophrenia; the remaining patients show mood disorders with psychotic features (e.g., Bipolar I Disorder).

Prognosis

The short-term prognosis of youths with Schizophrenia is poor. Psychotic symptoms usually persist for several months, even after they are recognized and treated. In one study, only 12% of individuals with Schizophrenia recovered completely by the time they were discharged from the hospital. If recovery does occur, it tends to be within 3 months after onset. Only about one fifth of patients have "good" outcomes, characterized by alleviation of positive symptoms, mild negative symptoms, and a general return to pre-psychotic levels of functioning. Even among these patients, long-term problems in social functioning, friendships, and romantic relationships are common (Hollis, 2010).

Researchers have identified several variables that predict the long-term outcomes of youths with Schizophrenia (Table 14.11). One of the strongest predictors is age of onset. Most studies suggest that people who manifest the disorder during childhood or adolescence have poorer long-term outcomes than people who develop the disorder in adulthood. For example, Lay and colleagues (2000) examined the outcomes of adolescents admitted to a psychiatric hospital because of Schizophrenia. As adults, 66% had serious deficits in social functioning and interpersonal relationships; 75% were dependent on their family. A more recent, retrospective study showed similarly poor outcomes (Reichert, Kreiker, Mehler-Wex, & Warnke, 2008). Twenty-two percent were currently experiencing acute psychosis, 31% reported serious depression, and 37% admitted suicidal thoughts or actions. Most adults with adolescent-onset Schizophrenia continued to live with their parents (48%) or in assisted living facilities (33%). Less than 19% completed high school.

A second important predictor is the duration of time between the onset of prodromal symptoms and the initiation of treatment. Youths who suffer through prodromal and early psychotic symptoms without medication and psychotherapy typically show more severe and persistent symptoms than youths whose symptoms are recognized and treated in a timely manner (Remschmidt & Theisen, 2012). Even with early intervention and optimal treatment, youths still frequently show residual symptoms of the illness years after their first psychotic episode (Rapoport, Gogtay, & Shaw, 2008).

Associated Problems

Comorbid Conditions

It is easy to overlook the comorbid problems of youths with Schizophrenia. The positive symptoms which characterize acute psychotic episodes, and the negative symptoms which often linger over time, demand most attention from parents and clinicians. However, as is the case with most mental disorders, comorbidity is the rule more than the exception. In one large study, only 27% of youths with Schizophrenia suffered from that disorder alone; 35% had one other psychiatric diagnosis, 30% had two other diagnoses, and 7% had three or more other conditions (Nugent et al., 2012).

Table 14.11   Prognosis for Youths With Schizophrenia

Better Outcomes	Worse Outcomes
No family history of psychosis	First-degree relative with psychosis
Meets developmental milestones	Developmental delays in infancy and early childhood
Good functioning before onset of illness	Low premorbid functioning
Onset in late adolescence or adulthood	Onset in childhood or early adolescence
Short duration of first psychotic episode	Long duration of first psychotic episode
Symptoms identified and treated rapidly	Symptoms not identified or treated
Mild to moderate symptoms	Severe symptoms requiring hospitalization

Source: Based on Remschmidt & Theisen (2012).

The most common coexisting disorders are Major Depressive Disorder (54%), Obsessive-Compulsive Disorder (21%), Generalized Anxiety Disorder (15%), and ADHD (15%). The treatment of ADHD is particularly challenging. Physicians are often reluctant to prescribe stimulant medications, which are effective in treating ADHD, because these medications may exacerbate the positive symptoms of Schizophrenia. Typically, psychotic symptoms are treated first; then, comorbid conditions can be addressed once children are stabilized (Rapoport et al., 2008).

Alcohol and other drug abuse is also comorbid with Schizophrenia. Approximately 20% to 40% of adults with Schizophrenia also have a Substance Use Disorder. Furthermore, the lifetime prevalence of substance use problems among adults with Schizophrenia is 40% to 60%. Available data suggest similarly high rates of comorbidity for adolescents with the disorder. The most frequently used drugs are alcohol and cannabis, although stimulants (e.g., cocaine) and hallucinogens are also used. Negative reinforcement is believed to maintain the substance use of many individuals with Schizophrenia. Depressants, such as alcohol, are frequently used to decrease unwanted positive symptoms. However, positive reinforcement may play a role in the abuse of stimulants; these medications may produce euphoria and increased energy among patients with predominantly negative symptoms (Milin, 2008).

Perhaps most concerning is the high prevalence of suicidal behaviors shown by youths with Schizophrenia. In one large epidemiological study, 31% of children and adolescents with Schizophrenia had attempted suicide at least once, compared to 16% of youths with other psychiatric conditions (Nugent et al., 2012). Retrospective studies indicate that youths contemplate suicide as a means to end psychological distress and stop persistent, positive symptoms.

Differential Diagnosis

The positive symptoms of Schizophrenia must be differentiated from the normal cognitive immaturity of young children and adolescents. Many youths have difficulty conveying their thoughts, jump from topic to topic, use incorrect vocabulary, and show lapses in logic. Clinicians must be able to differentiate hallucinations and delusions from normal childhood play. Many children engage in fantasy play, have imaginary friends, and engage in conversations with fictitious characters.

Psychotic delusions must also be differentiated from **culturally sanctioned beliefs**. For example, many adolescents and adults hold strong religious convictions or believe that they have communicated with God during prayer. These beliefs usually reflect culturally sanctioned religious beliefs rather than delusions. However, it is sometimes very challenging to differentiate delusions regarding religious persecution (e.g., *The devil is trying to kill me*) and extreme worthlessness or scrupulosity (e.g., *God is punishing me because I am evil*) from feelings of temptation and sinfulness experienced by followers of many faiths. Typically, delusions experienced by people with Schizophrenia are bizarre in nature, associated with risk or impairment, and uncommon even among members of the person's cultural or religious group.

Several medical illnesses can produce psychotic symptoms. Physicians sometimes refer to these symptoms as "organic psychosis," although the term is a bit misleading. Both Schizophrenia and psychotic symptoms caused by other medical problems have biological (i.e., "organic') underpinnings. Brain tumors and certain seizure disorders can produce hallucinations. Interestingly, the type of hallucinations reported often corresponds to the brain regions affected by the tumor. Olfactory and gustatory hallucinations, in particular, are sometimes reported in youths who experience seizures, although these types of hallucinations are infrequent among youths with Schizophrenia. Visual hallucinations caused by seizures are usually simple figures or shapes, not objects, animals, and people frequently perceived by youths with Schizophrenia. Seizures can also produce thought blockage, that is, temporary lapses in thinking and speaking that correspond to minor seizure activity. These lapses can mimic psychosis (Kodish & McClellan, 2008).

Delirium can also imitate many of the symptoms of Schizophrenia. **Delirium** is a temporary state of confusion or disorientation associated with a rapid change in functioning (e.g., from lethargy to excitement or agitation). Children are most likely to show delirium when they have an extremely high fever, experience an acute obstruction in breathing, or are exposed to alcohol and other drugs. Youths experiencing delirium may not know who they are, where they are, or what they are doing. They may experience transient hallucinations, short-term delusions, and fluctuating emotions (e.g., sadness, terror, euphoria). Youths with delirium often show marked problems with thinking and reasoning. Their train of thought may be difficult to follow. Delirium can be differentiated from Schizophrenia by the presence of other medical problems, especially fever and hypoxia (i.e., insufficient oxygen to the brain), and by its relatively brief duration.

Many children and adolescents with Autism Spectrum Disorder (ASD) display several of the negative symptoms of Schizophrenia. Most notably, youths with ASD display social avoidance and withdrawal, as well as other impairments in social communication. Many youths with ASD also engage in stereotypies and other motor disturbances seen in some youths with Schizophrenia (Palmen & van Engeland, 2012). Alternatively, young children in the prodromal stage of Schizophrenia often display social and linguistic deficits typically shown by youths with ASD. In one study, 39% of children with Schizophrenia also displayed significant delays in language, social skills, and motor behaviors; an additional 28% were formally diagnosed with ASD. Consequently, it is very challenging for clinicians to differentiate these two disorders (Rapoport, Chavez, & Greenstein, Addington, & Gogtay, 2009).

Despite their similarities, ASD and Schizophrenia can be differentiated based on their onset, course, and symptoms. First, ASD typically emerges in early life, often before age 5. In contrast, Schizophrenia does not arise before age 3 years and is exceptionally rare before age 5. Second, children with ASD usually show chronic problems with language, social, and motor functioning, beginning in infancy and continuing through childhood. In contrast, children with Schizophrenia usually show relatively normal functioning in early childhood, which is followed by a noticeable deterioration in language, social, and emotional functioning during the prodromal stage of the illness in late childhood or adolescence. Third, hallucinations and delusions are common among youths with Schizophrenia; they are seldom seen among children with ASD.

Several mood disorders can also mimic many of the features of Schizophrenia. Approximately 20% of youths with Major Depressive Disorder or Bipolar I Disorder experience transitory psychotic symptoms, such as hallucinations or delusions. By definition, they also show a marked deterioration in social-emotional functioning, such as depressed mood, lethargy, or irritability. The disorders are differentiated based on predominance and persistence of psychotic symptoms (Remschmidt & Theisen, 2012). If psychotic symptoms are present only during a major depressive or manic episode, the individual is more likely to have a Mood

Disorder. In contrast, if psychotic symptoms are independent of the individual's mood state, the diagnosis of Schizophrenia is probably more appropriate. Usually, a clinician must carefully assess a youth's social-emotional and family history and observe the adolescent over time before she can be confident in her diagnosis. Nevertheless, approximately one half of adolescents with Schizophrenia are initially misdiagnosed with a Bipolar Spectrum Disorder (Kodish & McClellan, 2008).

Several drugs and medications can induce or mimic psychotic states in adolescents and young adults. Most drugs that act as dopamine agonists or otherwise stimulate the central nervous system are candidates for eliciting psychosis: cocaine, amphetamines, hypnotics, and LSD. In rare instances, alcohol and anxiolytics can induce psychosis as well. Medications, especially when taken inappropriately, can elicit psychotic symptoms in some youths. They include antihistamines, corticosteroids, and psychostimulants. When a patient who has ingested these substances presents with psychotic symptoms, it is extremely difficult to determine whether these substances are a cause or consequence of the psychosis. Most clinicians can only diagnose Schizophrenia after learning about the patient's history and/or observing him after the immediate effects of the substance have passed (Kuniyoshi & McClellan, 2010).

Etiology
Genetics

Schizophrenia is a heritable disorder (Helenius, Munk-Jorgensen, & Steinhausen, 2012). Every major study published since 1980 has shown than the disorder runs in families (Figure 14.14). On average, individuals who have a first-degree family member with Schizophrenia are significantly more likely (5.9%) to develop the disorder than individuals without an affected first-degree relative (0.5%). Twin studies provide additional evidence for the influence of genetics. The average concordance rate for monozygotic twins is 55.8%; concordance drops to 13.5% among dizygotic twins. Even more compelling evidence comes from children born to parents with Schizophrenia but adopted by adults without the disorder. Epidemiological studies conducted in Denmark, Finland, and the United States each demonstrated that adopted children whose biological parents had Schizophrenia were more likely to develop the disorder themselves than adopted children whose biological parents did not have the disorder (Cardno & Gottesman, 2000).

Knowledge of genetic risk has practical importance to couples with a positive family history of Schizophrenia. For example, a woman without Schizophrenia may have a father or brother with the disorder. She can use these data

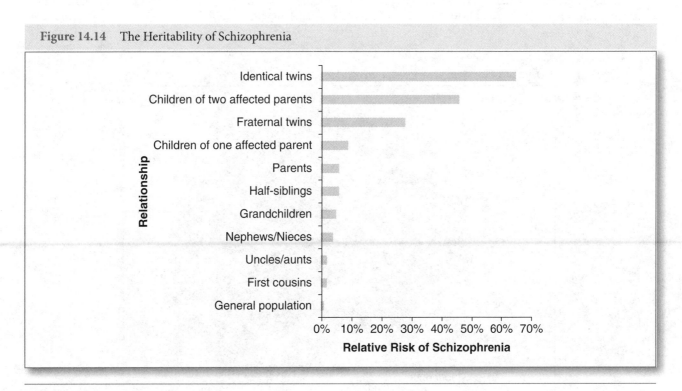

Figure 14.14 The Heritability of Schizophrenia

Source: Based on Walters, O'Donovan, and Owen (2011).

Note: The overall risk of developing schizophrenia is about 1%. The risk of schizophrenia increases if you have a biological relative with the disorder. However, even identical twins, who have 100% genetic similarity, are not 100% concordant for the disorder. Environmental factors are also important.

to determine the likelihood that she will have a child who will one day develop the disorder (i.e., a 2–3% likelihood assuming her husband does not have a family history of Schizophrenia). If the woman herself has Schizophrenia, her child's risk increases to 7%. If both she and her husband have the disorder, their child's risk jumps to 27% (Gur et al., 2005; Walters et al., 2011).

Researchers have identified several candidate genes that likely play specific roles in the development of schizophrenia. One of the most important genes in adolescent-onset Schizophrenia appears to be the **catechol-*O*-methyltransferase (COMT) gene**. The COMT gene produces an enzyme which regulates dopamine in several brain areas. It appears to produce excessive dopamine activity in brain regions responsible for positive symptoms and diminish dopamine activity in brain regions responsible for negative symptoms (Caspi et al., 2005).

Children with Schizophrenia have a higher rate of genetic abnormalities and mutations than their healthy peers. For example, young children with Schizophrenia sometimes show unusual deletions, duplications, or mutations of genetic material. Recently, researchers have discovered that several children with Schizophrenia have a specific abnormality known as **22q11 deletion syndrome**. Approximately 10% to 30% of youths who show this syndrome develop Schizophrenia or psychotic disorders (Kuniyoshi & McClellan, 2010).

Although a genetic propensity may be necessary for one to develop schizophrenia, it is unlikely that it is sufficient to explain the disorder. Even monozygotic twins, who have identical genetic similarity, are discordant for schizophrenia 44% of the time. Consequently, researchers have explored early environmental influences that, along with genes, might more fully explain the emergence of the disorder.

Brain Abnormalities

Three decades of research have documented differences in the brain structure of adults with and without Schizophrenia. Three abnormalities are most often replicated across studies. First, adults with Schizophrenia often show increased volumes of the **third and lateral ventricles**, the canals in the center of the brain that are filled with cerebrospinal fluid (Image 14.2). Typically, individuals with Schizophrenia show 40% greater ventricular enlargement than healthy adults. Second, adults with the disorder often show reductions in the total volume and thickness of the prefrontal, temporal, and parietal cortices. Overall, patients with Schizophrenia show 10% less cortical volume than healthy controls. These areas are important because they are responsible for sensory-motor processes, language, and higher order planning and reasoning. Third, adults with the disorder often display reductions in the size of the **hippocampus** and **thalamus**, two centrally located brain regions responsible for the integration of behavior. On average, the size of these brain regions is 4.5% to 10% smaller than in healthy adults (Hollis, 2010; Kuniyoshi & McClellan, 2010).

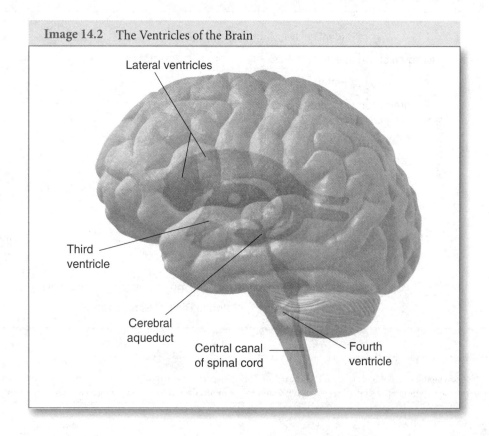

Image 14.2   The Ventricles of the Brain

Lateral ventricles

Third ventricle

Cerebral aqueduct

Central canal of spinal cord

Fourth ventricle

Until recently, however, researchers did not know if these brain abnormalities were a cause of Schizophrenia, a consequence of the disorder, or the result of a third variable such as antipsychotic medication. To answer these questions, researchers at the National Institute of Mental Health (NIMH) studied the brain structure and functioning of youths with childhood-onset schizophrenia from early childhood through young adulthood. MRIs of the brains of these youths were examined over time and compared to MRIs of the brains of a comparison sample of healthy youths. Because patients were young, did not have extensive experience taking medication, and could be followed over time, the researchers could begin to determine the relationship between brain structure and psychotic symptoms (Gogtay et al., 2004; Kodish & McClellan, 2008).

The NIMH studies yielded three important findings. First, older children and adolescents with Schizophrenia showed most of the same brain abnormalities as adults with the disorder. This finding was important because it suggested that youth-onset and adult-onset Schizophrenia reflect the same underlying disorder. Specifically, children and adolescents with Schizophrenia show ventricular enlargement, reductions in hippocampus and amygdala volumes, and a progressive decrease in the volume of the parietal (8.5% decrease), frontal (11% decrease), and temporal (8% decrease) lobes (Hollis, 2010).

Second, the abnormalities shown by young patients (e.g., reductions in hippocampal and thalamic volume, thinning of parietal, temporal, and frontal cortices) tended to occur early in the course of the disorder. This finding suggests that these brain abnormalities may cause many of the signs and symptoms of the illness that later emerge (Rapoport & Gogtay, 2011).

Third, and perhaps most importantly, young patients with Schizophrenia showed dramatic reductions in gray matter that correspond to the onset of psychosis (Kuniyoshi & McClellan, 2010). Healthy children experience a dramatic overproduction of synaptic connections in infancy and early childhood. Later, these children show reduction of 1% to 2% of gray matter per year across late childhood and adolescence. This loss of gray matter reflects normal synaptic "pruning." Much like a bush that needs to be pruned to allow it to grow in the appropriate way, the neural connections that are not needed atrophy during adolescence to allow the most important connections to work more efficiently. This atrophy or pruning progresses from lower order brain areas (central areas, parietal lobe) in childhood to higher order brain areas (e.g., frontal lobe, prefrontal cortex) in adolescence and young adulthood. The outcome of normal neural pruning is adolescents' ability to engage in more complex, graceful, and efficient cognitive and social-emotional tasks (Huttenlocher & Dabholkar, 1997; Kodish & McClellan, 2008).

Children with Schizophrenia, however, seem to show more rapid, excessive neural pruning (Image 14.3). Neuroimaging studies suggest a loss of 3% to 4% of gray matter per year on average. Furthermore, the loss of gray matter tends to occur shortly before and immediately after the onset of the child's first psychotic episode. Interestingly, neural loss

Image 14.3 Regions of greatest gray matter loss in children with Schizophrenia (*shaded areas*). Brain scans conducted on the same children with Schizophrenia between the ages of 12 and 16 years showed a progressive deterioration in gray matter not shown by healthy children. Notice how the gray matter loss moves from the parietal region to the frontal and temporal regions over time. This loss corresponds to the child's first psychotic episode.

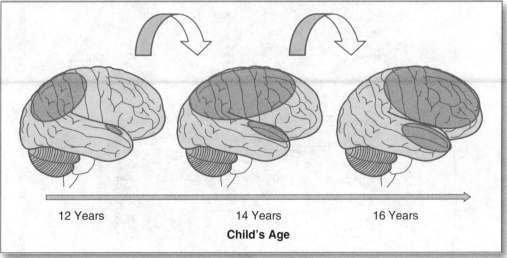

Source: Based on Rapoport and Gogtay (2011). Figure based on P. J. Lynch, Creative Commons.

progresses in the same parietal-to-frontal pattern as it does in healthy children. However, youths with Schizophrenia experience much more dramatic and rapid loss than would be developmentally expected. The result of this loss in gray matter appears to be the signs and symptoms of the disorder (Thompson et al., 2001; Vidal et al., 2006).

Perhaps because of this rapid and excessive pruning, many youths with Schizophrenia show deficits in intellectual functioning. Mean IQ scores are approximately two thirds of a standard deviation below average (i.e., IQ = 90). Approximately 10% to 20% of children and adolescents with Schizophrenia earn IQ scores in the borderline range or below (i.e., <80; Brown, Antonuccio, et al., 2008a). Youths with schizophrenia also earn below average scores on measures of academic achievement, especially math (Hooper et al., 2010). Longitudinal research indicates that youths' intellectual functioning is typically below average before the onset of psychosis and that it usually declines markedly during and immediately following the first psychotic episode. After recovery from the first psychotic episode, IQ typically stabilizes (Frangou et al., 2008).

Neural Pathways

There are two brain pathways implicated in Schizophrenia: the mesolimbic pathway and the mesocortical pathway. The **mesolimbic pathway** is a dopamine-rich neural pathway that many experts believe is involved in feelings of pleasure and the experience of rewards. It begins in the ventral tegmental area of the midbrain and connects to several structures in the limbic system: the amygdala, hippocampus, and nucleus accumbens. It also connects to the striatum, an area deep within the brain responsible for coordination and movement.

The **dopamine hypothesis** posits that Schizophrenia is caused by excessive stimulation of certain dopamine receptors (D2 receptors) along the mesolimbic pathway. Excessive dopaminergic activation is believed to produce many of the positive symptoms of Schizophrenia, such as hallucinations and delusions. Evidence supporting this hypothesis comes from the fact that antipsychotic drugs, which reduce these positive symptoms, are D2 receptor antagonists. They block D2 receptors and reduce many positive psychotic symptoms. Furthermore, certain stimulant drugs (e.g., cocaine, methamphetamine) act as D2 agonists; they augment dopaminergic activity along this pathway and can produce hallucinations and delusions among individuals susceptible to the disorder (Asarnow & Kernan, 2008)

The **mesocortical pathway** is another dopaminergic neural path. It also begins in the ventral tegmental area of the midbrain but connects to the dorsolateral prefrontal cortex (Image 14.4). The dorsolateral area is believed to be responsible for motivation and the expression of emotions. Emerging evidence suggests that many individuals with Schizophrenia show **hypofrontality**, that is, underactivity among certain dopamine receptors in the dorsolateral prefrontal region (D1 receptors). This underactivity is believed to be responsible for the negative symptoms of the disorder, including apathy and flat affect (Asarnow & Kernan, 2008).

The challenge in treating Schizophrenia is to find medications that block excessive dopamine activity along one

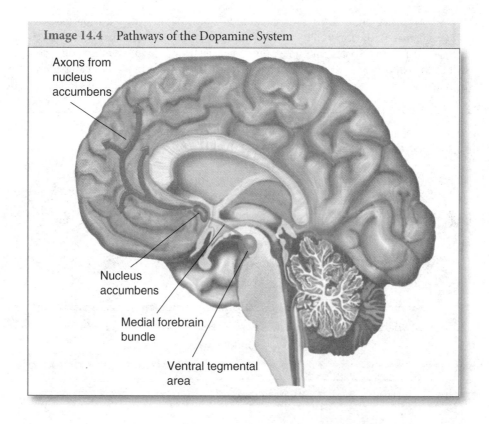

Image 14.4 Pathways of the Dopamine System

Axons from nucleus accumbens

Nucleus accumbens

Medial forebrain bundle

Ventral tegmental area

pathway, while simultaneously augmenting activity along the other pathway. To complicate matters, dopamine is involved in several other important activities of the central nervous system, such as the control of movement and the regulation of metabolism. Medications that affect dopamine receptors can adversely affect these other activities, producing side effects that make them intolerable to many patients.

Environmental Risks

Several early environmental risk factors are implicated in the development of Schizophrenia. These include in-utero maternal stress, exposure to disease, season of birth and pre- or perinatal complications (Palmen & van Engeland, 2012). Recent longitudinal studies have shown that major life events also predict the onset of Schizophrenia in individuals genetically predisposed to the illness. Interestingly, events that are perceived as "uncontrollable" are particularly salient predictors of psychosis. Furthermore, both positive and negative events place individuals at risk. For example, leaving home and transitioning to college, which many adolescents regard as a positive event, can elicit symptoms in youths predisposed to the disorder. Finally, the total number of daily hassles (i.e., minor stressful life events) is associated with both symptom onset and severity. Day-to-day troubles, such as oversleeping and arriving late for class, can influence the disorder (Kodish & McClellan, 2008).

Family Interactions

Years ago, several clinicians posited that Schizophrenia was caused by distant, harsh parenting or the maladaptive ways parents communicated with children. Today, we know that parenting behavior does not cause Schizophrenia; there is no such thing as a "Schizophrenogenic" parent. However, researchers have discovered that the quality of family interactions can influence the course of the disorder and the likelihood of relapse.

Specifically, researchers have studied expressed emotion (EE) in the families of adults with Schizophrenia. For example, some parents may blame their children with Schizophrenia for their illness, perceiving symptoms to be within their control. Parents may criticize them for not taking their medication, for failing to meet school or work responsibilities, or for disrupting the family. Other parents may be overly controlling and involved in their adolescents' lives, denying them the responsibility to manage their illness and make their own decision regarding treatment (Hooley & Campbell, 2002).

EE is important because it predicts relapse in adults. Butzlaff and Hooley (1998) examined the one-year outcomes of adult patients who returned to their families following a psychotic episode. Approximately 65% of patients who returned to homes with high EE relapsed within one year compared to 35% of patients who returned to families with low EE. More recent research has replicated these findings and has shown that EE predicts Schizophrenia relapse up to 7 years after hospitalization (Maron et al., 2005).

However, several studies suggest that EE may not be as relevant to adolescents with Schizophrenia compared to adults with the disorder. Asarnow and colleagues (1994) studied the verbal interactions between adolescents with psychosis and their families. Although EE was common among the families of adults with Schizophrenia (44%), EE was less common among the families of adolescents with the illness (23%). Another study examined EE in the families of adolescents and young adults experiencing their first psychotic episode (Nugter et al., 1997). Patients were randomly assigned to either individual therapy or individual therapy plus a family-based intervention. One year later, there were no differences in EE across treatment conditions. Furthermore, EE did not predict relapse.

The importance of EE may also depend on ethnicity. In African American families, high levels of critical and controlling parental behavior are associated with improved psychosocial outcomes over a 2-year period of time (Rosenfarb, Bellack, & Aziz, 2006). In Mexican American families, a combination of high warmth and moderate over-involvement are associated with the best outcomes (Lopez et al., 2004).

Cannabis Use

Considerable research has been directed at the relationship between marijuana and Schizophrenia in adolescents. Early studies showed a correlation between marijuana use in early adolescence and a greater likelihood of developing Schizophrenia in later adolescence and early adulthood. For example, researchers examined cannabis use in a large sample of Swedish adolescents and young adults (>97% of the county's male population). They found a direct relationship between early cannabis use and Schizophrenia 5 years later. Furthermore, there was a dose-dependent relationship between early cannabis use and later psychosis: the greater the use, the greater the likelihood of developing the disorder (Zammit et al., 2002). However, researchers could not tell whether marijuana caused later psychosis, whether prodromal symptoms led adolescents to use marijuana, or whether a third factor (such as impulsivity) might contribute to both marijuana use and Schizophrenia.

To answer this question, Arsenault and colleagues (2004) reviewed the research literature on the causal relationship between cannabis and Schizophrenia. They reached three conclusions. First, cannabis use in adolescence increased the likelihood of developing Schizophrenia in early adulthood two- or threefold. Second, the earlier and more frequent the cannabis use in adolescence, the greater the likelihood of later psychosis. Third, cannabis alone was not sufficient to cause Schizophrenia; it only led to Schizophrenia when adolescents were genetically at risk for the disorder (Milin, 2008).

Caspi and Moffitt (2006) conducted a prospective, longitudinal study to examine how adolescent cannabis use might interact with genes to place youths at risk for Schizophrenia. The researchers examined a large cohort of individuals from Dunedin, New Zealand, aged 11 to 26 years. They assessed participants' psychotic symptoms in late childhood, cannabis use in adolescence, and subsequent psychotic symptoms as young adults. They also collected DNA to study youths' genotype. The researchers discovered a significant gene-environment interaction that partially explains the relationship between cannabis use and psychosis.

The catechol-*O*-methyltransferase (COMT) gene has two variations (i.e., alleles): the COMT valine allele and the COMT methionine allele. Children can inherit two valine alleles, two methionine alleles, or one of each type. The researchers discovered that adolescents who avoided cannabis had lower risk of psychosis than adolescents who used cannabis, regardless of what alleles they inherited. However, adolescents who used cannabis and who inherited at least one COMT valine allele were significantly more likely to develop psychosis than adolescents who used cannabis but did not inherit a COMT valine allele. The COMT valine allele, which produces an enzyme which regulates dopaminergic activity, seems to place adolescents at risk for later Schizophrenia, but only if they are exposed to cannabis. In contrast, the COMT methionine allele seems to protect adolescents from psychosis, regardless of their cannabis exposure (Figure 14.15).

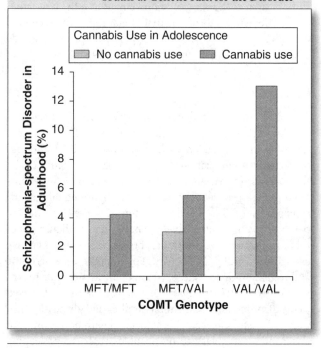

Figure 14.15 Cannabis in Adolescence Predicts Later Schizophrenia, but Only Among Youths at Genetic Risk for the Disorder

Source: Based on Caspi and Moffitt (2006).

Note: Youths who use cannabis and inherit the VAL allele of the COMT gene are at increased risk. Youths with a family history of Schizophrenia, therefore, should avoid cannabis.

Summary: The Neurodevelopmental Model of Schizophrenia

Today, most experts view childhood- and adolescent-onset Schizophrenia as a neurodevelopmental disorder (Brennan & Walker, 2010; Kodish & McClellan, 2008; Waddington & Buckley, 1996). The **neurodevelopmental model for Schizophrenia** is based on the notion that individuals who develop Schizophrenia have a diathesis (i.e., risk) for the disorder that is usually present at birth. Evidence for this claim comes from behavioral genetics research showing high heritability for the disorder and molecular genetics research suggesting specific genes that might place individuals at elevated risk. Genetic risk seems to be especially important for the development of schizophrenia; the likelihood of developing the disorder is <0.8% without a positive family history.

Genetic risk is not sufficient to explain the illness, however. The neurodevelopmental model posits that early environmental stressors, combined with biogenetic risk factors, lead to abnormalities in the organization and development of the central nervous system. Known environmental risk factors include maternal stress and illness during gestation, season of birth, obstetric complications, malnutrition and poverty, and stressors associated with immigration and acculturation. It is likely that other risks will be discovered. Abnormalities of the central nervous system initially manifest themselves as premorbid differences. Toddlers and preschoolers who later develop Schizophrenia often show deficits in language, social interaction, and motor skills.

Later, abnormalities in the organization and development of the brain become evident as prodromal signs and symptoms: marked changes in social behavior, mood, and cognitive functioning. These features, which often emerge years before the youth's first psychotic episode, correspond to the beginning of a documented pattern of excessive neural pruning that progresses from lower level to higher level brain regions. Indeed, the emergence of psychosis often coincides with dramatic reductions in gray matter in brain areas responsible for thinking, reasoning, and regulating emotions. The youth's first psychotic episode may be one step in a progression of events that began at (or before) birth (Rapoport & Gogtay, 2011).

Treatment

Prevention

Given the debilitating nature of Schizophrenia, the best form of intervention is prevention. Early identification and preventative treatment is essential. Youths' prognoses are related to the amount of time the illness is left unrecognized and untreated. Recent studies have indicated that outcomes correlate with the duration of the illness from the onset of prodromal symptoms to the time treatment begins. Consequently, most prevention strategies seek to identify and treat youths entering the prodromal stage or as soon thereafter (Gur et al., 2005).

Early identification and treatment programs for adolescents and young adults with prodromal or early psychotic symptoms have been developed in the United States and Europe. For example, in the United Kingdom, the Buckingham Integrated Mental Health Care Project was designed to identify individuals in the community showing the first indicators of the illness. Primary practice physicians were trained to routinely screen individuals for prodromal symptoms and to refer them to the early intervention program (Table 14.12). The intervention itself consisted of low doses of antipsychotic medication, education about psychosis, and psychotherapy to help patients manage stress. The incidence of Schizophrenia dropped from 7.4 per 100,000 people per year before the program to 0.75 per 100,000 per year after the program was initiated (Falloon, Kydd, Coverdale, & Laidlaw, 1996).

Early detection and prevention programs have also been developed at the Early Psychosis Prevention and Intervention Centre (EPPIC) in Australia. EPPIC works to identify youths at risk for developing Schizophrenia before the onset of psychotic symptoms. The program then provides medication, education, and psychotherapy services to youths and their families to ameliorate the effects of the illness. Staff members also offer support to help youths stay on track with regard to schooling and vocational planning. Youths who participate in EPPIC show better outcomes than individuals who do not receive these preventative and early intervention services. Specifically, youths show fewer positive symptoms, better adaptive functioning, fewer number of total psychotic episodes,

and better vocational outcomes. These findings speak to the importance of early identification and intervention (Amminger et al., 2011).

Other early identification and prevention programs include the Treatment and Intervention in Psychosis (TIPs) project in Norway and the Portland Identification and Early Referral Program (PIER) in the United States. Evaluations of these programs indicate that prodromal and early psychotic symptoms can be identified in adolescents and young adults. Furthermore, early intervention, consisting of medication and counseling, is effective at delaying the onset of a major psychotic episode. However, these programs have not been shown to prevent the onset of psychosis altogether (Gur et al., 2005).

Medication

Conventional Antipsychotics. The first-line treatment for the acute stage of Schizophrenia is antipsychotic medication. There are two broad classes of medications that are especially effective for the disorder: conventional antipsychotics and atypical antipsychotics.

Conventional antipsychotics have been used to treat adults with Schizophrenia for more than 50 years. **Conventional antipsychotics** act as dopamine antagonists by binding to D2 receptors, particularly in the mesolimbic pathway. Consequently, they are especially effective in reducing the positive symptoms of Schizophrenia, such as hallucinations and delusions. The most well-known conventional antipsychotics are haloperidol (Haldol), molindone (Moban), and perphenazine (Trilafon). Conventional antipsychotics are effective in reducing the positive symptoms of Schizophrenia in children and adolescents as well (Mattai et al., 2010). Overall, 54% to 93% of youths experience symptom reduction while taking these medications compared to 0% to 38% taking placebo (Rapoport et al., 2008).

Conventional antipsychotics have two main drawbacks. First, they are less effective at reducing the negative symptoms of Schizophrenia, such as apathy, restricted emotional expression, social withdrawal, and psychomotor problems. Second, and perhaps more importantly, they produce side effects in some patients that are distressing and occasionally life threatening.

Extrapyramidal side effects are most common. These effects are called "extrapyramidal" because they involve the extrapyramidal system, a neural network that regulates the body's control of movement. The extrapyramidal system includes regions that regulate movement, such as the substantial nigra, basal ganglia, and cerebellum. Unfortunately, these regions are rich in dopamine receptors and can be adversely affected by antipsychotics that block dopamine. Side effects include the inability to initiate movement (i.e., akinesia), intense feelings of restlessness and difficulty remaining motionless (i.e., akathisia), and tremors that

---

Table 14.12 Prodromal Signs Checklist

In the Buckingham early identification and intervention project, physicians routinely screened patients to detect prodromal signs of psychosis:

- Marked change in behavior, peculiar behavior
- Inappropriate emotions or loss of emotional expression
- Speech that is difficult to follow
- Marked lack of speech and thoughts
- Marked preoccupation with odd ideas
- Ideas of reference—belief that events and/or objects have special meanings
- Persistent feelings of unreality
- Changes in the way things appear, sound, or smell

Source: Based on Falloon et al. (1996).

resemble the symptoms of Parkinson's Disease. Other involuntary motor movements include spasms of the muscles of the face and mouth, writhing of the hands or wrists, and minor tongue protrusion or lip smacking. In adults, **tardive dyskinesia** can occur, characterized by involuntary, purposeless, and repetitive movements of the face, mouth, and jaw (Rapoport et al., 2008). A rare, but potentially life-threatening, side effect of these medications is **neuroleptic malignant syndrome** (NMS; Rapoport et al., 2008). NMS is most likely to develop shortly after the initiation of high doses of dopamine antagonists. Signs and symptoms include severe muscle rigidity, loss of motor control, elevated or highly fluctuating body temperature and blood pressure, and delirium.

Atypical Antipsychotics. In the past 20 years, psychiatrists have begun using a second class of medications, the atypical antipsychotics, to treat adults with Schizophrenia. Like conventional antipsychotics, **atypical antipsychotics** act as dopamine antagonists and are effective in reducing positive symptoms of the disorder. Unlike conventional antipsychotics, they bind more weakly to dopamine receptors, resulting in reduced likelihood of extrapyramidal side effects. Moreover, most atypical antipsychotics have higher affinity for serotonin receptors, making them more effective at regulating mood and reducing negative symptoms (Rapoport et al., 2008).

The most frequently used atypical antipsychotics are aripiprazaole (Abilify), olanzapine (Zyprexa), paliperidone (Invega), quetiapine (Seroquel), risperidone (Risperdal), and ziprasidone (Geodon).

Correll (2010) reviewed randomized controlled studies examining the effects of these medications on youths with the disorder. Overall, 38% to 72% of youths show symptom reduction while taking atypical antipsychotic medication compared to 26% to 35% of youths who show symptom reduction taking placebo.

Because antipsychotic medications are newer and associated with less severe side effects, most physicians use these medications as the first-line treatment of Schizophrenia (Correll, 2010). Recently, however, a large study called into question the superiority of atypical antipsychotics over conventional antipsychotics (Sikich et al., 2008). In the **Treatment of Early-Onset Schizophrenia Spectrum Disorders (TEOSS) Study**, 119 youths with Schizophrenia were randomly assigned to receive one of three medications: (a) molindone, a conventional antipsychotic; (b) olanzapine, an atypical antipsychotic; or (c) risperidone, another atypical antipsychotic. The researchers assessed outcome 8 weeks after treatment. Overall, treatment gains were modest, between 20% and 34% of youths showed significant reduction in positive and negative symptoms. Furthermore, there were no significant differences in the percentage of youths who responded to molindone (50%), olanzapine (34%), and resperidone

(46%). One year later, there were still no differences in the outcomes of youths in the three conditions (Findling, Johnson et al., 2010).

Atypical antipsychotics also have side effects (Correll, 2009). Approximately one half of children and adolescents prescribed olanzapine or risperidone still develop extrapyramidal side effects and approximately 5% to 10% develop akathisia. The most common non-motor side effects are weight gain and sedation. Significant weight gain is usually defined as an increase of 7% total body weight. According to this definition, 4% to 5% of adolescents show significant weight gain with aripiprazole, 15% to 16% with risperidone, and 45% to 46% with olanzapine. Weight gain is associated with other metabolic problems, such as risk for diabetes, obesity, and elevated trigylcerides and cholesterol. Weight gain can also lead to teasing or ostracism by peers. The prevalence of sedation varies considerably across medications; prevalence is lowest for aripiprazole (0%–33%) and highest for olanzapine (46%–90%). Sedation can interfere with children's academic and social functioning. Atypical antipsychotics are also associated with abnormalities in liver enzymes in 22% to 35% of youths. Consequently, children's metabolism must be carefully monitored by their pediatricians (Findling, et al., 2008; Kryzhanovskaya et al., 2009).

Clozapine (Clozaril) was the first atypical antipsychotic medication used to treat schizophrenia in the United States. Most, but not all, studies have shown it to be among the most effective antipsychotic medications for adults with the disorder (Rapoport et al., 2008). Furthermore, several studies have shown that clozapine is useful in treating youths who do not respond to other antipsychotic medications (Correll, 2009; Mattai et al., 2010). For example, Kumra and colleagues (2008) randomly assigned treatment-resistant youths with Schizophrenia to two treatment conditions: clozapine or a high dose of the atypical antipsychotic olanzapine. Significantly more youths responded to clozapine (66%) than olanzapine (33%).

Clozapine is not routinely given to children, however, because it is associated with severe side effects, including excessive salivation, seizure, and dangerous decreases in white blood cell count (i.e., agranulocytosis). Risk of side effects is significantly greater in children and adolescents compared to adults. Consequently, clozapine is used only in treatment-resistant cases. Furthermore, patients must be willing to undergo weekly blood tests to monitor the safety of the medication (Correll, 2010; Rapoport et al., 2008).

Antipsychotic medication should be used for 6 to 18 months after the onset of psychotic symptoms. However, because of their side effects, most youths are reluctant to take these medications for long periods of time. One large study found that 71% to 77% of youths prescribed atypical antipsychotics for early-onset Schizophrenia stopped taking these medications in the first 180 days after they were first prescribed (Olfson et al., 2011). This high rate of discontinuation is important because it predicts relapse. On average, patients who discontinue their medication have a 7 to 28 times greater likelihood of having another psychotic episode compared to patients who remain adherent to their medication (Subotnik et al., 2011). Consequently, clinicians usually augment medication with psychotherapy to improve the likelihood of adherence (Kodish & McClellan, 2008).

Psychotherapy

Description of Therapy Programs. Nearly all experts recommend that medication should be combined with psychosocial interventions to treat youths with Schizophrenia (Figure 14.16). Most psychosocial treatments have five components in common (Remschmidt & Theisen, 2012).

First, therapists provide information about the illness to youths and their families. Psychoeducation is critical to treatment success; family members often have many questions about the disorder and the best way to help youths cope with symptoms. Therapists can also be instrumental in dispelling myths about Schizophrenia and listening to families' concerns about caring for a youth with the disorder.

Second, therapists work with youths and their parents to encourage medication compliance. Because antipsychotic medications often have unpleasant side effects, such as weight gain, adolescents are often reluctant to take them for long periods of time. Nagging, pleading, and bribing on the part of parents are usually ineffective strategies to encourage compliance. Instead, therapists might use principles of motivational interviewing to help adolescents comply with pharmacotherapy. Instead of insisting that adolescents take their medication, therapists who use motivational interviewing acknowledge and try to understand adolescents' reluctance or apprehension. Therapists also encourage youths to weigh the costs and benefits of medication adherence. Of course, therapists hope adolescents will decide that the benefits of adherence outweigh those of noncompliance. The goal of therapy is to slowly move adolescents from medication refusal to greater acceptance of pharmacotherapy.

Third, adolescents with Schizophrenia may benefit from cognitive-behavioral interventions. Cognitive interventions might involve helping them to look at their symptoms more objectively and develop more effective coping strategies. For example, an adolescent with Schizophrenia might feel like she was treated unfairly by parents and

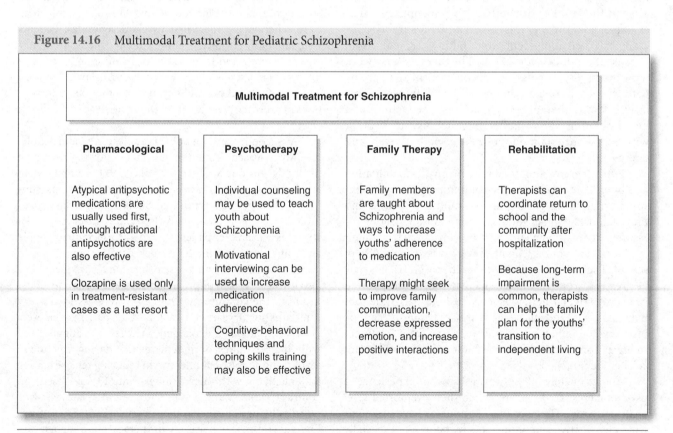

Figure 14.16 Multimodal Treatment for Pediatric Schizophrenia

Multimodal Treatment for Schizophrenia

Pharmacological	Psychotherapy	Family Therapy	Rehabilitation
Atypical antipsychotic medications are usually used first, although traditional antipsychotics are also effective Clozapine is used only in treatment-resistant cases as a last resort	Individual counseling may be used to teach youth about Schizophrenia Motivational interviewing can be used to increase medication adherence Cognitive-behavioral techniques and coping skills training may also be effective	Family members are taught about Schizophrenia and ways to increase youths' adherence to medication Therapy might seek to improve family communication, decrease expressed emotion, and increase positive interactions	Therapists can coordinate return to school and the community after hospitalization Because long-term impairment is common, therapists can help the family plan for the youths' transition to independent living

Source: Based on Clark (2011).

Note: Nearly all treatment programs involve (a) medication, (b) individual psychotherapy, (c) family therapy, and (d) planning for the child's return to school and family life.

teachers. A cognitive therapist might ask the adolescent for evidence of these beliefs and suggest alternative, more realistic ways to interpret adults' behavior toward the adolescent. Behavioral interventions might involve teaching specific communication skills to improve the quality of relationships with parents and teachers. For example, the therapist might teach and role-play ways the adolescent can express concerns to adults without starting an argument. Behavioral interventions might also involve introducing and practicing ways to cope with specific symptoms of Schizophrenia. For example, the adolescent might learn to distract herself when she begins to hear voices or respond to them in more rational ways (e.g., "Oh, there are those voices again. I need to find a way to keep them in the background of my life.")

Fourth, treatment may involve family-based interventions. Although the disorder is not caused by parenting, its severity and course may be influenced by the quality of interactions within the family system. Initially, family therapists try to establish a stable therapeutic alliance with family members. Typically, this involves listening empathically to the family's concerns, providing information, and offering emotional support to members. After forging an alliance with the family, therapists address areas of conflict or tension that often arise in the families of youths with Schizophrenia. For example, a family therapist might address parents' concerns that their adolescent avoids taking his medication, because it produces side effects. The therapist may work with the family to balance the concerns of the parents with the developing autonomy of the adolescent. Similarly, a family therapist might address the feelings of a healthy sibling who feels "left out" because her brother with Schizophrenia monopolizes her parents' time and energy.

Fifth, therapy almost always involves rehabilitation and integration back into the community. Psychotic episodes are both distressing and disruptive to youths and their families. Some youths require hospitalization or residential treatment and may be separated from their families. Many youths will miss several weeks or months of school. Their relationships with teachers and friends may be greatly disrupted. Youths who play sports, are involved in extracurricular activities, or who hold part-time jobs may also suspend these activities. Therapists can be instrumental in helping youths transition from treatment to life at home, school, and the community (Remschmidt & Theisen, 2012).

Approximately 40% of youths who experience a psychotic episode do not return to their premorbid level of functioning. These youths continue to have problems with the negative symptoms of Schizophrenia, especially dysphoria, apathy, and social withdrawal. For these youths, the goal of rehabilitation is not so much to return to their "old life" but to find new ways to cope with the illness and derive as much satisfaction from life as possible.

Effectiveness of Therapy. Are psychosocial interventions effective for Schizophrenia? Two reviews of cognitive-behavioral interventions involving adults with Schizophrenia have yielded disappointing results. In a qualitative review of the published research, Dickerson (2000) concluded that cognitive-behavior therapy was moderately effective in reducing positive symptoms of Schizophrenia, especially among patients with clearly defined psychotic symptoms. However, she found little evidence that cognitive-behavioral interventions were useful in alleviating negative symptoms or improving social functioning. Cormac and colleagues (2002) conducted a meta-analysis of the effectiveness of various psychosocial interventions for Schizophrenia. They found no differences in the effectiveness of CBT compared to supportive psychotherapy. Furthermore, when CBT was added to traditional pharmacotherapy, it did not reduce relapse or the rate of hospitalization more than medication alone.

Unfortunately, there are no randomized, controlled studies investigating the efficacy of psychosocial interventions for youths with Schizophrenia. However, three studies may be relevant. Lewis and colleagues (2002) studied the efficacy of treatment for adolescents *and* young adults who were experiencing their first psychotic episodes. Patients were randomly assigned to either CBT and medication, supportive therapy and medication, or medication alone. The intervention lasted only 5 weeks. Results showed modest benefits of CBT above and beyond the other two interventions in speeding recovery from the acute stage of the illness (Figure 14.17).

A second study involved adolescents and adults recently released from the hospital following an acute psychotic episode (Hogarty et al., 1997). Patients were randomly assigned to two psychosocial interventions: supportive therapy or skills training. Skills training consisted of progressively more complex skills to cope with psychosocial stress. For example, patients learned to recognize people and situations that might trigger negative emotions, to avoid these stimuli, and to use relaxation techniques. They also learned skills to improve social interactions and adjust to life in the community. Outcomes were assessed every 6 months for 3 years. Overall, 29% of patients relapsed. However, outcomes depended on whether patients lived with their families or independently during treatment. Skills training was very effective in reducing relapse among patients living with their families (only 13% relapsed). In contrast, skills training did not prevent relapse among patients living independently (44% relapsed). These findings suggest that the efficacy of therapy might depend on support from family and/or the stability of patients' lives outside the therapy setting.

Figure 14.17 Effects of CBT on Schizophrenia Symptoms in Children

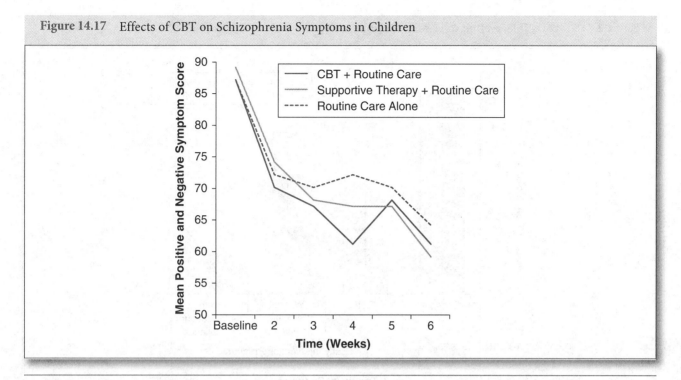

Source: Based on Lewis and colleagues (2002).

Note: Adding CBT to routine care (medication) modestly speeds recovery among adolescents with Schizophrenia. Youths who received supportive therapy and medication or medication alone improved about as well as youths in CBT.

Finally, McGorry and colleagues (2002) conducted a randomized, controlled study to examine the efficacy of a combination of cognitive-behavioral therapy and risperidone in preventing psychosis in adolescents and young adults at very high risk for developing Schizophrenia (Figure 14.18). Specifically, the researchers randomly assigned patients to either the early intervention program or to "needs-based intervention," that is, treatment for symptoms as they emerged. Immediately after treatment, patients who received early intervention were significantly less likely to develop psychotic symptoms than controls. At 12-month follow-up, differences between groups largely disappeared. However, outcomes were dependent on whether patients continued to consistently take antipsychotic medication. Patients who adhered to their medication continued to show low rates of psychosis. These findings speak to the importance of continued adherence to medication in the prevention of psychosis.

Family therapy is almost universally recommended for children and adolescents with Schizophrenia. Unfortunately, studies investigating the efficacy of family therapy for youths with Schizophrenia are limited. One relevant study involved 547 newly diagnosed patients who were experiencing their first psychotic episodes; many were older adolescents and young adults (Petersen et al., 2005). Researchers randomly assigned these youths to two treatment conditions: medication alone or medication plus family therapy and social skills training. Patients who received family therapy in addition to medication showed greater improvement in positive and negative symptoms than patients receiving medication alone. Patients who received family therapy were also less likely to use alcohol and other drugs, were more likely to adhere to medication, and were more satisfied with treatment.

There is also some evidence that family-based interventions can help younger patients with schizophrenia. In one study, youths with Schizophrenia were randomly assigned to either medication treatment or medication treatment plus family therapy (Rund, 1994). Family therapy consisted of sessions designed to teach family members about the disorder, improve family problem solving, and provide coordination of wide educational networks. Two years after treatment, overall functioning and relapse rates were better for youth who received medication plus family therapy. However, relapse was still quite high, supporting the notion that early-onset Schizophrenia is very resistant to treatment. Lenior and colleagues (2001) randomly assigned adolescents and young adults with Schizophrenia to either standard treatment or standard treatment plus family therapy. Patients who received family therapy spent an average of 10 months less in residential care at follow-up than patients who received only standard treatment. Family therapy is a promising intervention for youths with Schizophrenia. Clearly, more research is needed to determine its effectiveness.

Figure 14.18 Early Intervention to Prevent Schizophrenia in High-Risk Youths

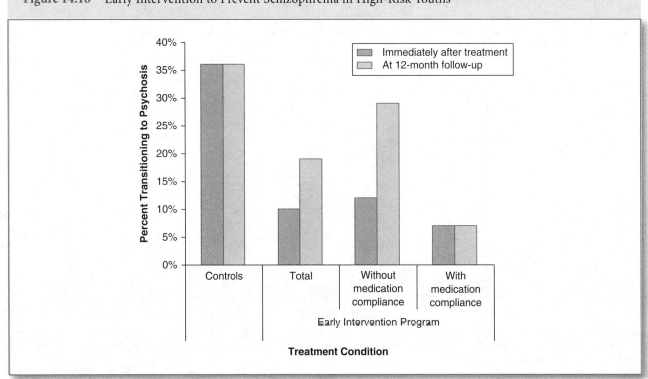

Source: Based on McGorry and colleagues (2002).

Note: Researchers examined the efficacy of early intervention to prevent Schizophrenia in high-risk youths. Immediately after treatment, youths who received early intervention were less likely to develop psychotic symptoms than controls. One year later, most youths who received early intervention continued to remain symptom free—but only if they remained on antipsychotic medication. These findings highlight the importance of early intervention and compliance with medication.

CHAPTER SUMMARY

Bipolar Spectrum Disorders (BSDs)

- BSDs are serious mood disorders characterized by the presence of manic symptoms and often (but not always) depressive symptoms.

  - Bipolar I Disorder is characterized by at least one manic episode.

    - Mania is defined by grandiosity, racing thoughts, increased activity, pressured speech, excessive risky activities, sleep disturbance, and distractibility (GRAPES+D).
    - Grandiosity, decreased sleep, and high-risk sexual activity are relatively specific indicators of mania in children and adolescents.

  - Bipolar II Disorder is characterized by hypomania and at least one depressive episode.
  - Bipolar Disorder, NEC is defined by bipolar symptoms that do not meet the duration or severity criterion for Bipolar I or II.
  - Cyclothymic Disorder is characterized by hypomania and depressive symptoms only, lasting at least one year in children and adolescents. The disorder is infrequently diagnosed in youths.
  - Children often show mixed moods, that is, mood episodes characterized by features of mania and depression.

- Approximately 3% of youths may develop BSDs. This prevalence is similar to that seen in adults.

  - Prevalence of Bipolar I is equal across genders, whereas Bipolar II is more common among females. Boys with BSDs often have comorbid ADHD. Girls with BSDs often have comorbid anxiety.
  - The course of BSD in youths consists of several phases.

    - The prodromal phase is marked by subthreshold mood problems, especially increased irritability.
    - Results of the COBY study indicate that most youths recover from mania, but most also experience subsequent depression. Recurrent mood problems are likely within four years of onset.

  - Most youths with BSDs have ADHD; however, youths with ADHD are not at increased risk for BSDs.
  - BSDs can be mistaken for Schizophrenia and DMDD. BSDs can be differentiated from these disorders by the presence of discrete mood episodes rather than chronic problems with psychotic symptoms or temper.

- Genetic, biological, and early experience have been implicated in the development of BSDs.

  - BSDs are heritable conditions. Concordance among monozygotic twins (40%) is much higher than among dizygotic twins (5%).
  - Neuroimaging studies indicate reduced cerebral volume in youths with BSDs. Furthermore, fMRI suggests dysfunction in the amygdala and prefrontal cortex, regions associated with emotional processing and regulation.
  - Youths with BSDs often show deficits in executive functioning and cognitive processing. IQ scores are lower than those of typically developing peers.
  - Stressful life events may elicit mood symptoms among youths predisposed to BSDs. Expressed emotion in families predict relapse, whereas supportive family interactions may protect youths from relapse.

- Atypical antipsychotic medication is usually considered the first-line treatment for children and adolescents with BSDs.

  - The TEAM study showed atypical antipsychotics to be superior to mood stabilizers and anticonvulsants in treating mania in children with BSDs.
  - Medication is less effective in managing depressive symptoms.

- Psychosocial treatment for pediatric BSDs usually involve family members.

  - Child- and family-focused CBT helps children identify and regulate their emotions and teaches parents behavior management and communication skills.
  - Psychoeducational psychotherapy can be administered to groups of children and parents. It consists of psychoeducation, emotion-regulation training, and instruction in problem-solving.
  - Family-focused treatment for adolescents is designed to improve parent-adolescent communication and problem solving and to reduce expressed emotion.

Schizophrenia

- Schizophrenia is a psychotic disorder characterized by hallucinations, delusions, and disturbances in speech, movement, and affect. Symptoms must exist for at least 6 months. Children tend to show the same symptoms as adults.

  - Positive symptoms include hallucinations and delusions. These are more sensitive to treatment.
  - Negative symptoms, such as flat affect, are less responsive to medication and often indicate poorer prognosis.

- The prevalence of Schizophrenia in adulthood is approximately 1%. Adolescent-onset (.23%) and childhood-onset (.0019%) are very rare.
- The course of pediatric Schizophrenia tends to progress through a series of phases.

  - In the premorbid phase, youths do not show psychotic symptoms. However, they often display delays in reaching motor, social, and emotional milestones. Cognitive problems are also common.
  - In the prodromal phase, youths show marked deterioration in functioning, often associated with irritability and social withdrawal.
  - In the acute stage, psychotic symptoms emerge.
  - In the residual stage, symptoms may last for months or years. Some youths return to baseline functioning, but most continue to show impairment in cognitive and social-emotional functioning.
  - Attenuated Psychosis Syndrome is a condition for future study. It may be used to classify youths at very high risk for Schizophrenia who show early signs and symptoms of psychosis.

- Schizophrenia must be differentiated from culturally sanctioned behaviors and beliefs as well as other conditions such as medical illness, delirium, and Autism Spectrum Disorder.
- The neurodevelopmental model for Schizophrenia suggests that genetic diathesis and psychosocial stress contribute to the emergence of the disorder in youths.

  - Monozygotic twin concordance (56%) is much higher than dizygotic twin concordance (14%). The COMT gene and 22q11 deletion syndrome may contribute to some cases of pediatric Schizophrenia.
  - Children and adults with Schizophrenia often show similar brain abnormalities, including enlarged ventricles, reduced cortical volume, and abnormalities in the hippocampus and thalamus.
  - Longitudinal studies also indicate rapid, excessive neural pruning in youths with Schizophrenia. Pruning often coincides with the onset of psychotic symptoms.
  - Abnormalities of the mesolimbic and mesocortical pathways implicate dopamine as a cause of Schizophrenia in adolescents and adults. Dopamine antagonists are often effective in treating psychotic symptoms.
  - High expressed emotion predicts relapse in adults with Schizophrenia; however, expressed emotion is not consistently associated with relapse in children and adolescents with the disorder.
  - Early cannabis use may elicit Schizophrenia later in life but only among youths genetically at risk for the disorder.

- Evidence-based treatment for Schizophrenia is based largely on studies involving adults.

  - Prevention programs can be useful in delaying Schizophrenia or lessening the severity of the disorder when it occurs. Programs consist of education about the disorder, antipsychotic medication, and stress management.
  - Conventional antipsychotics are effective in reducing positive symptoms, but they are associated with extrapyramidal side effects.

- Atypical antipsychotics are also effective in treating Schizophrenia. Side effects include weight gain and metabolic problems. Not all studies show them to be superior to conventional antipsychotics, however.
- Clozapine is sometimes effective in treatment-resistant cases of Schizophrenia. However, it can cause serious side effects in some individuals.
- Psychotherapy for Schizophrenia often consists of (a) education about the disorder, (b) strategies to increase medication adherence, (c) coping skills training, (d) family therapy to reduce expressed emotion, and (e) planning for the future.
- Randomized controlled trials of psychotherapy for older adolescents and young adults with Schizophrenia have yielded mixed results. Family involvement seems to be important to the success of treatment.

KEY TERMS

CRITICAL THINKING EXERCISES

1. Compare and contrast Disruptive Mood Dysregulation Disorder (DMDD) and Bipolar Spectrum Disorders. If you were a clinician, how might you determine whether a child has DMDD versus a Bipolar Spectrum Disorder?

2. BSDs are usually regarded as genetic disorders. What is the evidence that genes contribute to the development of child and adolescent BSDs? Do environmental factors play any role in the development of the disorder?

3. Brice is a 16-year-old adolescent with Bipolar I Disorder. Brice and his mother argue frequently because Brice often stays out too late with his friends. These arguments often exacerbate Brice's mood symptoms. If you were a family therapist, how might you use a behavioral contract to decrease arguments between Brice and his mother?

4. The treatment for youths with BSDs often involves families. How are families involved in the treatment of (1) young children and (2) adolescents with these disorders?

5. Most children who later develop Schizophrenia show premorbid delays in development and prodromal symptoms before their first psychotic episode. However, very few of these children are identified and treated early in life. Why?

6. Why is it important for a clinician to consider a family's religious beliefs and social-cultural background when assessing a child or adolescent for Schizophrenia?

7. The first-line treatment for Schizophrenia is antipsychotic medication. What role might psychotherapy play in the treatment for youths with the disorder? Is psychotherapy effective?

EXTEND YOUR LEARNING

Videos, practice tests, flash cards, study guides, and links to online resources for this chapter are available to students online. Teachers also have access to lecture notes, PowerPoint presentations, suggestions for classroom activities, and possible exam questions. Visit: www .sagepub.com/weis2e.

PART V

HEALTH-RELATED PROBLEMS

CHAPTER 15

Feeding and Eating Disorders

LEARNING OBJECTIVES

After reading this chapter, you should be able to answer these questions:

- What are feeding disorders? How do Pica, Rumination Disorder, and Avoidant/Restrictive Food Intake Disorder differ from each other?

- How can learning theory and the quality of parent-child relationships explain the development and maintenance of feeding problems? What evidence-based treatments are available to correct these problems?

- What are eating disorders? How might Anorexia Nervosa, Bulimia Nervosa, and Binge Eating Disorder present differently in children and adolescents compared to adults?

- In what way might genetic, biological, psychological, and familial factors explain the development of eating disorders in children and adolescents?

- How might social-cultural factors account for the development and maintenance of eating disorders in adolescents?

- What evidence-based treatments are available to youths with eating disorders? Why is family involvement often a critical component of effective treatment?

Feeding and eating disorders are grouped together into a single diagnostic category in *DSM-5*. These disorders involve disturbances in the natural and essential process of eating. Feeding disorders are usually seen in infants, toddlers, and young children, although they may also be seen in children and adults with developmental disabilities. These disorders are characterized by marked disturbances in the ingestion of food, cause considerable distress to caregivers, and place children at risk for malnutrition or physical illness. In contrast, eating disorders are almost exclusively seen in older children, adolescents, and adults. These disorders are characterized by disturbances in eating that result in very low body weight, binge eating, and/or dangerous compensatory behaviors to avoid weight gain. Eating disorders are among the most lethal of all mental disorders because of their effect on adolescents' physical development and their close relationship with depression, hopelessness, and self-harm.

In this chapter, we will first examine feeding disorders that typically present in infants and young children: Pica, Rumination Disorder, and Avoidant/Restrictive Food Intake Disorder. Then, we will consider the three most common eating disorders in older children and adolescents: Anorexia Nervosa, Bulimia Nervosa, and Binge Eating Disorder.

FEEDING DISORDERS IN INFANTS, TODDLERS, AND YOUNG CHILDREN

The transition from breast or bottle-feeding to the consumption of solid foods occurs gradually over the first two years of life. Although this transition might seem effortless, it is highly dependent on the child's physical, motoric, and social-emotional development. First, the child's gustatory and digestive systems must be able to accept and digest increasingly solid food, of different tastes, textures, and appearances. Second, the child must have the capacity to bite, chew, and swallow, as well as coordinate movements to place food in his mouth, use a spoon, and drink from a cup. Third, the child must be able to regulate his attention, emotions, and behavior long enough to focus on mealtime, to accept food, and to consume sufficient calories. Finally, children must learn to recognize signals of hunger and satiety and to negotiate with caregivers various feeding tasks (e.g., who will hold the spoon?). Feeding is a social activity between caregiver and child; self-feeding is an important milestone in an infant's emerging autonomy and sense of self.

At its best, mealtime for 10-month-olds can be messy; at its worse, it can be a source of anxiety and frustration. Approximately 25% to 50% of parents of infants and toddlers report at least moderate feeding problems. Furthermore, approximately 1% to 2% of children have feeding disorders, severe feeding problems characterized by food avoidance, limited diet, inappropriate diet, or recurrent regurgitation (Chatoor & Ammaniti, 2007). Feeding disorders can elicit great family distress and place children at risk for malnutrition, dehydration, growth suppression, and cognitive-behavioral problems (Chatoor, 2009).

What Is Pica and Rumination Disorder?

Two feeding disorders are most commonly seen among children with developmental disorders: Pica and Rumination Disorder. Pica refers to the persistent eating of nonnutritive, nonfood substances over the period of at least one month. The name "Pica" comes from the Latin word for magpie, a bird known for eating both edible and inedible objects. Table 15.1 lists some of the substances consumed by children with Pica. Some children with Pica eat nonfood substances indiscriminately, whereas others prefer specific items. Pica is not diagnosed when the mouthing or consumption of nonfoods might be considered developmentally appropriate; for example, an infant who eats small objects she finds on the floor of the house would not be diagnosed with Pica (Motta & Basile, 1998).

Pica is most commonly associated with severe or profound Intellectual Disability. Approximately 15% of

Table 15.1 Some Substances Consumed by Children With Pica
Burnt matches
Caulking, concrete, glass
Cigarette butts
Coins, nuts, bolts, screws
Crayons, chalk, glue, pencils
Dirt, sand, clay
Fibers, pillow and/or toy stuffing, carpet, cloth, sponge
Grass, leaves, acorns, pinecones
Hair
Insects
Laundry starch
Paint chips
Paper, toilet paper
Plastic toy parts
Rocks, gravel, pebbles
Wood, bark, twigs

Source: Adapted from Stiegler (2005).

individuals with intellectual disabilities have Pica. It is possible that Pica provides oral and gustatory stimulation to these individuals. Pica is also, sometimes, associated with iron or zinc deficiency. For example, children with medical disorders associated with these deficiencies (e.g., celiac disease, kidney and liver disease, sickle cell disease) sometimes show Pica. Pregnant women at risk for iron deficiency also sometimes engage in Pica. It is possible that these individuals eat substances to obtain necessary minerals. Pica is also associated with environmental stressors, such as major life events, impoverished home environments, or social neglect. Finally, some of the substances ingested by children with Pica are intrinsically reinforcing. For example, many youths with Pica ingest cigarette butts because of the nicotine they contain (Stiegler, 2005).

In typically developing children, Pica usually remits spontaneously. In youths with developmental disabilities, Pica tends to be persistent over time. In either case, Pica should be treated because of the risks associated with nonfood substances. Common risks include intestinal and bowel blockage from eating impassible substances (e.g., hair, pebbles), ingestion of harmful bacteria and parasites, perforation of the digestive system caused by sharp objects (e.g., glass, nails), and lead toxicity following repeated consumption of lead-based paint chips (Motta & Basile, 1998).

Rumination Disorder is also most often seen among children with developmental disabilities. Rumination involves the repeated regurgitation of stomach contents into the mouth. The regurgitated food may be re-chewed, re-swallowed, or spit out. Children are diagnosed with Rumination Disorder if this behavior is repeated over the course of at least one month. Youths with the disorder regurgitate out of habit; Rumination Disorder is not diagnosed if the child has a medical condition that might involve regurgitation, such as gastroesophageal reflux. Rumination Disorder is also not diagnosed if the person regurgitates food to avoid weight gain, as in the case of people with Anorexia or Bulimia Nervosa (Silverman & Tarbell, 2009).

Rumination Disorder typically develops in early childhood and is prevalent (92%) among children with severe or profound intellectual disabilities. It is 5 times more common among boys than girls. Operant conditioning, especially positive reinforcement, usually maintains regurgitation. Some children ruminate because they gain attention from caregivers or peers (i.e., social positive reinforcement). Other youths might ruminate to avoid an undesirable task (i.e., social negative reinforcement); for example, a child who does not want to participate in a group activity might regurgitate to avoid social contact. Sometimes, rumination is a form of self-stimulation (i.e., automatic reinforcement). Although regurgitation probably does not sound pleasant to most of us, it may be stimulating to severely disabled youths (Vollmer & Roane, 1998).

The repeated regurgitation of food can have physical and social consequences. The most common physical problems are weight loss and malnutrition, dental erosions (because of stomach acid), and electrolyte imbalance (because of fluid loss). Rumination Disorder often results in negative social interactions with caregivers and rejection by peers. Over time, these negative social experiences can hinder the development of children's social skills and relationships (Vollmer & Roane, 1998).

What Is Avoidant/Restrictive Food Intake Disorder?

Avoidant/Restrictive Food Intake Disorder (ARFID) is a feeding disorder seen in typically developing children, children with developmental disabilities, and children with chronic health problems (Table 15.2, Diagnostic Criteria for Avoidant/Restrictive Food Intake Disorder). Youths with ARFID show a lack of interest in eating, avoid certain foods based on their sensory characteristics (e.g., texture, color, smell), or are concerned about possible negative consequences of eating (e.g., nausea, choking, vomiting). By definition, all children with ARFID have persistent problems with meeting their nutritional or energy needs. For example, they may fail to gain weight or grow, develop nutritional deficiencies, or need a feeding tube to acquire sufficient nutrition. They are also disruptive during meals; they may talk, cry, tantrum, arch their backs, throw food, or leave their seat—anything to avoid eating.

Table 15.2   Diagnostic Criteria for Avoidant/Restrictive Food Intake Disorder

A. An eating or feeding disturbance (e.g., apparent lack of interest in eating or food; avoidance based on the sensory characteristics of food; concern about the aversive consequences of eating) as manifested by persistent failure to meet appropriate nutritional and/or energy needs associated with one (or more) of the following:

1. Significant weight loss (or failure to achieve expected weight gain or faltering growth in children).

2. Significant nutritional deficiency.

3. Dependence on enteral feeding or oral nutritional supplements.

4. Marked interference with psychosocial functioning.

B. The disturbance is not better explained by lack of available food or by an associated culturally sanctioned practice.

C. The eating disturbance does not occur exclusively during the course of Anorexia Nervosa or Bulimia Nervosa, and there is no evidence of a disturbance in the way in which one's body weight or shape is experienced.

D. The eating disturbance is not attributable to a current medical condition or not better explained by another mental disorder. When the eating disturbance occurs in the context of another condition or disorder, the severity of the eating disturbance exceeds that routinely associated with the condition or disorder and warrants additional clinical attention.

Source: Reprinted with permission from the *Diagnostic and Statistical Manual of Mental Disorders, Fifth Edition* (Copyright 2013). American Psychiatric Association.

There are three main subtypes of ARFID; each is associated with different causes and treatments:

1. Children who do not eat enough and show little interest in feeding (i.e., infantile anorexia)

2. Children who avoid certain foods because of their sensory characteristics, such as taste or texture (i.e., sensory food aversion)

3. Children who refuse foods because of a pervious aversive experience associated with eating (i.e., posttraumatic feeding disorder)

Children with all three conditions would be diagnosed with Avoidant/Restrictive Food Intake Disorder (American Psychiatric Association, 2013).

Infantile Anorexia

Some children with feeding disorders show little interest in eating and rarely report feeling hungry (Image 15.1). These children may accept a small bite of food or sip on milk and then report feeling full. They often turn away from food, attempt to leave the high chair or booster seat, or try to distract themselves or their parents from the meal. For example, they might play with food or utensils, talk, or tantrum. Because of their lack of interest in food and avoidance of meals, these children are often underweight and small for their age and gender.

Needless to say, most parents are concerned about their children's lack of interest in food, low body weight, and/or growth failure. Consequently, parents often attempt to use a variety of strategies to get their children to eat: coaxing, begging, distracting with toys, threatening with physical punishment, and force feeding. Mealtime eventually becomes a stressful and time-consuming process, during which children and parents struggle. Because these children show little interest in food and because they often struggle with parents to assert their autonomy, these children have been described as having infantile anorexia, literally "a lack of interest in food."

Infantile anorexia tends to develop during the transition from breast or bottle-feeding to the consumption of solid food (e.g., 6–36 months). At this time in development, children begin to develop autonomy independent of their parents: They can wander away, say no, defy requests, and assume more control over metabolic functions, such as toileting and sleeping. Eating is another domain in which older infants and toddlers develop autonomy. Specifically, they must learn to recognize signals of hunger and satiety, ask to be fed, and effectively work with parents to obtain and consume desirable foods.

Unfortunately, children with infantile anorexia do not seem to develop these autonomous behaviors during this sensitive period in development. Consequently, their disinterest in food persists over time. One longitudinal study followed infants with infantile anorexia into childhood. At

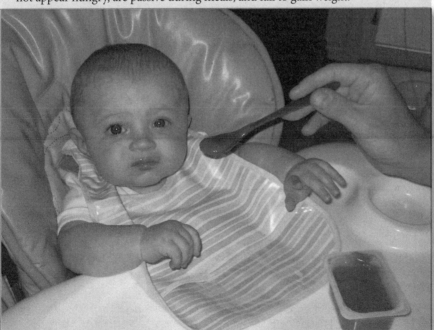

Image 15.1   Some children with Avoidant/Restrictive Food Intake Disorder show little interest in food. Parents often become upset when their children do not appear hungry, are passive during meals, and fail to gain weight.

4 to 6 years of age, 68% showed mild-moderate malnutrition and an additional 13% were severely malnourished. By age 7 to 8 years, only 21% showed weight within normal limits (Lucarelli, Cimino, Petrocchi, & Ammaniti, 2007). These children also showed increased rates of oppositional-defiant behavior, anxiety, school refusal, and somatic problems.

What causes infantile anorexia? Chatoor's (2009) **transactional model for feeding disorders**, posits that the disorder is caused by the interaction of child and caregiver characteristics over time. First, emerging data indicate that children with infantile anorexia often show high physiological arousal; they are active, need a great deal of cognitive stimulation, and are frequently "on the go." Consequently, they may be less sensitive to hunger signals (e.g., stomach contractions, empty feelings, fatigue). Second, these children often show temperaments that are described as "strong willed," making them more likely to engage in power struggles during mealtimes. Third, the parents of these children often report considerable anxiety about their children's eating and growth (Figure 15.1). Consequently, with the best of intentions, they may try to trick, coerce, or force their children to eat. The result is that the child's eating becomes entirely regulated by the parent; the child never

learns to recognize and respond to her own hunger signals. Treatment involves teaching the child to recognize hunger cues and rely on herself, rather than a parent, to feed and determine satiety (Owens & Burnham, 2009).

Sensory Food Aversion

Other children with ARFID report hunger and request food but accept only a limited diet. Most often, their diet consists of starches and grains, and it is often devoid of fruits, vegetables, and meats. They typically find certain foods aversive based on their taste, texture, temperature, or smell. In some cases, children will accept only certain brands of foods (e.g., only Tyson chicken nuggets), foods of a certain color (e.g., only "yellows" and "whites"), or foods in a certain package (e.g., McDonald's wrappers; Image 15.2).

"Picky" eating is a common problem among toddlers and preschool-aged children. As many as 50% of parents report that their children are selective eaters (Carruth, Ziegler, Gordon, & Barr, 2004). However, children are not diagnosed with ARFID unless their selectiveness affects their health or causes severe disruption in the family. Selective eating tends to persist across early childhood and taper off by late childhood or early adolescence.

Figure 15.1 Mothers' Worrying Moderates the Relationship Between Children's Weight and Interactions During Feeding

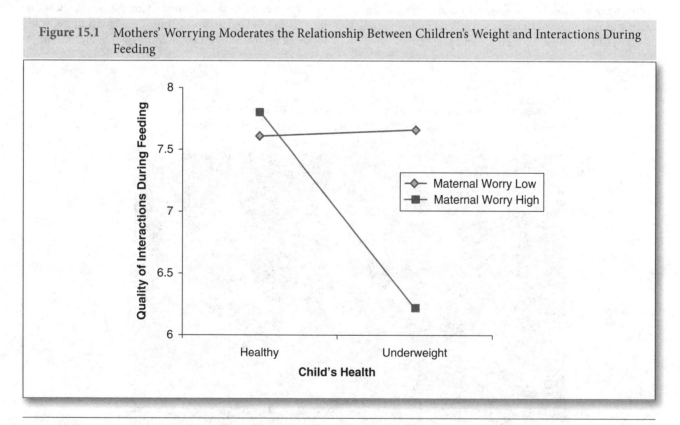

Source: Adapted from Gueron-Sela and colleagues (2011).

Note: The mothers of healthy infants provided structure and respected the autonomy of infants during meals. However, the feeding behavior of mothers of underweight children depended on the degree to which they worried about their children's weight. Parents who worried more about their children provided less structure and were more intrusive during mealtime.

Image 15.2 Many children with Avoidant/Restrictive Food Intake Disorder have aversions to certain foods. For example, they may refuse foods based on color, smell, or taste. Some children eat a very limited diet (e.g., chicken nuggets, plain spaghetti noodles) and trantrum when other, more nutritious foods are offered.

There are many causes for children's food aversions. Some children seem to be hypersensitive to texture. Indeed, approximately 17% of infants who later show sensory food aversion have difficulty switching from breast to bottle-feeding and trouble transitioning from Stage 1 (pureed) to Stages 2 and 3 (slightly textured) baby foods. Other children seem to be unusually sensitive to certain tastes, especially bitterness, spiciness, and fattiness. This hypersensitivity to certain tastes is heritable and is associated with an unusual concentration of fungiform papillae and taste buds on the child's tongue. Many of these children also show hypersensitivity to other tactile stimuli; they may avoid getting their hands dirty, their teeth brushed, or their hair washed (Chatoor, 2009).

Food aversions and restricted diets often develop through classical conditioning and are maintained through operant conditioning. A parent may present a food that elicits a negative reaction (e.g., disgust, nausea). The pairing of the food and the negative reaction results in aversion to that food. Often, children generalize this learned association to food with similar sensory properties (e.g., the same texture, smell, or color). Understandably, the child avoids these foods in the future by crying, tantrumming, or engaging in other inappropriate actions. These inappropriate behaviors are maintained through negative reinforcement; the child learns to avoid ingesting the aversive foods. Parents' acquiescence is also maintained through negative reinforcement; they learn that they can stop or avoid children's inappropriate displays by serving only their children's favorite foods. Negative reinforcement maintains a coercive cycle of parent-child interactions. Treatment, therefore, involves breaking this cycle—teaching children that cries and tantrums will not allow them to escape or avoid healthy foods.

Posttraumatic Feeding

Other children develop feeding disorders following one or more traumatic insults to the mouth, throat, or gastrointestinal tract. For example, some infants have gastroesophageal reflux disease (GERD), a condition in which stomach acid is involuntarily expelled into the esophagus. The acid produces irritation (similar to heartburn in adults), nausea, coughing, or vomiting. These symptoms usually follow feeding and are very distressing to infants. Through classical conditioning, children associate feeding with the consequences of GERD.

Posttraumatic feeding problems can also develop in the absence of medical illness. For example, some children aspirate, choke, or vomit on food as they transition from milk or formula to solids. In some cases, these negative events may become associated with feeding, causing children to refuse solids altogether.

Avoidance of feeding is maintained through negative reinforcement; children learn that they can avoid negative symptoms by abstaining from eating solids. Some children accept only milk, formula, or purees. Others, who are reluctant to eat even these substances, must be bottle-fed at night when they are relaxed and not aware that feeding is occurring. In severe cases, physicians may recommend nutrition through a gastric tube. Treatment for this feeding problem, similar to the treatment for Posttraumatic Stress Disorder (PTSD), requires extinction: the presentation of the feared stimulus (i.e., food) without refusal, escape, or avoidance.

Epidemiology

Approximately 1% to 2% of infants and young children have feeding disorders that merit treatment. Feeding disorders are much more common among children with medical illnesses (10%–49%), developmental disabilities (23%–43%), and physical disabilities (26%–90%). Approximately two thirds of infants and toddlers with feeding disorders are classified as **failure to thrive (FTT)**. Definitions of FTT vary; however, most professionals agree that it is characterized by nutritional deficiency and weight below the fifth percentile for age and gender on standardized growth charts (Owens & Burnham, 2009).

The various subtypes of ARFID are relatively distinct from one another. Most children with ARFID show only one subtype, probably because each subtype is associated with a specific cause. However, some children show symptoms of two or more subtypes. For example, 13% of children with feeding problems show both infantile anorexia and sensory food aversions. These children typically present with more serious feeding problems and are more resistant to treatment (Chatoor & Ammaniti, 2007).

Treatment

Pica and Rumination Disorder

The treatment of Pica and Rumination Disorder involves the use of reinforcement and/or punishment. Psychologists always try to use positive reinforcement first, because it is nonaversive and teaches appropriate behavior. One technique, **differential reinforcement of incompatible behavior (DRI)** is especially useful; children are positively reinforced for engaging in behavior that is incompatible with Pica or rumination. For example, a child might be allowed to chew his favorite gum, which is both intrinsically reinforcing and incompatible with Pica and rumination. Another strategy is **differential reinforcement of zero behavior (DRO)**; children are reinforced for not engaging in Pica or rumination. For example, a caregiver might give the child a bite of a snack

or a sip of a favorite beverage every minute he does not engage in the undesired behavior. A final technique to treat Pica is to identify the sensory properties of objects that are eaten and replace these objects with foods that have similar properties. For example, a caregiver might substitute licorice for plastic toys, Grape Nuts cereal for sand and pebbles, or beef jerky for bark and twigs (Stiegler, 2005).

If positive reinforcement is ineffective and the child's eating behavior places him at risk for serious injury, therapists might rely on punishment. Punishment is used only as a last resort and with the consent of parents. One method of positive punishment is **overcorrection**; the child is required to engage in a fairly long and mildly aversive series of actions, following Pica or rumination. For example, a child who ruminates might be required to immediately brush his teeth, rinse with mouthwash, and wash his face. Another method of positive punishment used to treat Pica is **facial screening**; a child who engages in Pica must wear a mask or bib over his mouth for 10 minutes. The screen is mildly uncomfortable and prohibits future pica (Stiegler, 2005; Vollmer & Roane, 1998).

Avoidant/Restrictive Food Intake Disorder

As we have seen, ARFID can be conceptualized in terms of learning theory. Some children have not learned to recognize hunger and lack the skills necessary to eat independently. Others have learned to avoid certain foods based on their sensory qualities. Still others avoid solid foods altogether. Treatment, therefore, involves three components: (a) increasing children's motivation to eat, (b) changing the antecedents of eating to increase the likelihood that children will accept food, and (c) altering the consequences of children's eating behavior to reinforce appropriate eating and extinguish inappropriate mealtime behavior.

Mild to moderate feeding disorders are typically treated on an outpatient basis; parents learn skills in a clinic and practice them at home with their children. Severe feeding disorders are best treated in a children's medical center. Hospitals allow medical professionals to monitor children's caloric intake and health and, if necessary, to provide supplemental fluid or nutrients. Hospitals also allow psychologists to carefully control the child's environment: when, how, and by whom food is presented. In this manner, psychologists have control over both the antecedents and consequences of meals (Martin & Dovey, 2011).

Appetite Manipulation

Treatment involves three main components: (a) appetite manipulation, (b) contingency management, and (c) parent training. Appetite manipulation is especially important for children who show little motivation to eat. In **appetite manipulation**, children are provided with fluids and essential electrolytes to maintain hydration but are prohibited from snacking. Children are offered food only during therapeutic meals, which are scheduled three to four times during the day, approximately 3 to 4 hours apart. Caloric restriction helps children recognize signs of hunger and increases their motivation to eat when food is presented. Children learn that food provides its own naturally reinforcing consequences (Silverman & Tarbell, 2009).

Contingency Management

Contingency management is practiced during each meal. Initially, trained therapists feed children with parents absent from the room. Therapists are in complete control of the presentation of food (antecedents) and consequences of children's food refusal.

As we have seen, most feeding problems are maintained through operant conditioning, especially negative reinforcement. We know that operant conditioning maintains feeding problems because researchers have studied the responses of parents to children's food refusal and disruptive mealtime behavior (Vaz & Piazza, 2011). Most parents react in one of three ways: (a) they withdraw their demand that children eat the food, (b) they reprimand the child or express displeasure, or (c) they try to distract the child or provide the child with a toy or desired object. The first strategy (withdrawing the demand) is most common and negatively reinforces children for food refusal. The other two strategies are often positively reinforcing to children; parents present children with attention or access to a desired object which increases their food refusal. Treatment, therefore, must involve the presentation of food, without the inadvertent use of positive or negative reinforcement (Piazza & Addison, 2007).

Escape extinction is critical to treatment. **Escape extinction** involves refusing to allow the child to escape or avoid eating through protests or tantrums. Escape extinction is typically practicing using (a) non-removal of the spoon and (b) physical guidance. After the child is seated in a high chair, the therapist might place a small amount of food on a spoon and place the spoon against the child's lips. The spoon is not removed until the child accepts the food. If the child does not accept the food in a few seconds, the therapist may apply gentle pressure to the child's lower manidibular joint to allow her to place the food in the child's mouth. In either case, the child must accept the food and is not allowed to escape from the situation because of cries and protests (Linscheid, 2006).

Most therapists supplement escape extinction with positive reinforcement. Potentially positively reinforcing behaviors might include verbally praising the child, providing the child with access to a desired object, or permitting the child to view a favorite video while feeding. These stimuli are contingent on the child's eating (Cornwell et al., 2010).

Some therapists also use mild punishment to reduce problem behavior. Time out is most commonly used. **Time out** is technically called "time out from positive reinforcement." It is a form of negative punishment in which all positively reinforcing stimuli are momentarily withdrawn contingent on the child's food refusal. For example, if the child tantrums, the therapist might turn the child's high chair away for a few seconds and ignore the child's bids for attention. When the child is quiet, the therapist then reintroduces the food and requires the child to accept it (Linscheid, 2006).

Meals are limited to 20 to 25 minutes, regardless of the number of calories consumed by the child. The child must wait until the next session to eat again.

Parent Training and Counseling

Nearly all professionals recognize the importance of including parents in treatment. Most important, parents must be taught how to implement the behavioral feeding intervention and to avoid inadvertently reinforcing inappropriate mealtime behaviors. After the child accepts a variety of foods from the therapist, the therapist models the contingency management procedure to parents. Often, with parents present, children show a reemergence of food refusal. In behavioral terms, parents act as discriminative stimuli for children; children have learned that food refusal will be reinforced by parents but not by the therapist. The therapist's job is to teach parents to implement the contingency management program and reinforce their child only for appropriate eating behavior. Therapists act as behavioral coaches, watching parents practice contingency management until they are successful.

Parents may also benefit from individual counseling, which addresses thoughts and feelings that might compromise their ability to follow through with their child's treatment. For example, parents of children with feeding disorders often show a lack of sensitivity and responsiveness to their child's hunger and satiety cues, have developmentally inappropriate or unrealistic expectations regarding their children's eating habits, or have difficulty establishing meal schedules. Sometimes, these parents are too preoccupied by anxiety, depression, family or job stress, or their own caregiving histories to successfully implement treatment. Some parents exhibit deficits in problem-solving or emotion-regulation skills and have difficulty responding to children's food refusal in a patient, objective manner. Parents of malnourished or chronically ill children may be so concerned about their children's health, they may have difficulty restricting feeding to develop hunger motivation in their children. All of these parents would likely benefit from counseling directed at their specific psychosocial needs (Bryant-Waugh et al., 2010; Gueron-Sela et al., 2011).

Efficacy

Most data supporting the behavioral treatment of feeding disorders come from single-subject research studies. Overall, these studies provide strong support for behavioral treatment, especially contingency management (Sharp et al., 2010). The overall effect size for treatment is very large ($d = 2.46$). Escape extinction seems to be essential to treatment; without it, few children show significant improvements. Gains are larger when escape extinction is paired with positive reinforcement and time out. Parent training also appears to be important for helping children generalize their feeding to the home environment (Mueller et al., 2003).

EATING DISORDERS IN OLDER CHILDREN AND ADOLESCENTS

What Is Anorexia Nervosa?

Individuals with Anorexia Nervosa (AN) show three essential features (Table 15.3, Diagnostic Criteria for Anorexia Nervosa). First, people with AN do not maintain normal body weight. Specifically, their weight is significantly below what is expected for their age, gender, and overall physical health (American Psychiatric Association, 2013).

Determining whether a person has "significantly low weight" requires both careful measurement and clinical judgment. *DSM-5* recommends that clinicians calculate an adult's body mass index (BMI): a ratio of weight to height squared (e.g., kg/m^2). Then, the adult's BMI can be compared to normative data gathered by the Centers for Disease Control and Prevention (CDC) to determine if the person is significantly underweight compared to other people of the same age and gender. According to *DSM-5*, BMI scores <17 indicate significantly low weight. For example, a BMI of 17 corresponds to a weight of approximately 96 pounds for an 18-year-old, 5 foot, 3 inch tall woman.

In the case of children and adolescents, *DSM-5* recommends that clinicians also calculate the youth's BMI and compare his or her score to the CDC normative data. A score falling in the lowest fifth percentile, compared to youths of the same age and gender, would likely constitute significantly low weight (American Psychiatric Association, 2013). For example, a weight of approximately 87 pounds or less would fall in the lowest 5th percentile for a 14-year-old, 5 foot,

---

Table 15.3 Diagnostic Criteria for Anorexia Nervosa

A. Restriction of energy intake relative to requirements, leading to a significantly low body weight in the context of age, sex, developmental trajectory, and physical health. *Significantly low weight* is defined as a weight that is less than minimally normal or, for children and adolescents, less than minimally expected.

B. Intense fear of gaining weight or of becoming fat, or persistent behavior that interferes with weight gain, even though at a significantly low weight.

C. Disturbance in the way in which one's body weight or shape is experienced, undue influence of body weight or shape on self-evaluation, or persistent lack of recognition of the seriousness of the current low body weight.

Specify current type:

Restricting type: During the past 3 months, the individual has not engaged in recurrent episodes of binge eating or purging behavior (i.e., self-induced vomiting or the misuse of laxatives, diuretics, or enemas). This subtype describes presentations in which weight loss is accomplished primarily through dieting, fasting, and/or excessive exercise.

Binge-eating/purging type: During the last 3 months, the individual has engaged in recurrent episodes of binge eating or purging behavior (i.e., self-induced vomiting or the misuse of laxatives, diuretics, or enemas).

Specify current severity:

The minimum level of severity is based, for adults, on current body mass index (BMI) or, for children and adolescents, on BMI percentile. The ranges below are derived from World Health Organization categories for thinness in adults; for children and adolescents, corresponding BMI percentiles should be used. The level of severity may be increased to reflect clinical symptoms, the degree of functional disability, and the need for supervision.

Mild: BMI ≥ 17 kg/m^2

Moderate: BMI 16–16.99 kg/m^2

Severe: BMI 15–15.99 kg/m^2

Extreme: BMI <15 kg/m^2

Source: Reprinted with permission from the *Diagnostic and Statistical Manual of Mental Disorders, Fifth Edition* (Copyright 2013). American Psychiatric Association.

JULIE: "PERFECTLY NORMAL"

Julie was a 15-year-old girl who was referred to the hospital because of malnourishment and dehydration. Although Julie was 5 foot, 5 inches tall, she weighed only 87 lbs. Her skin had a dry, yellow appearance and her clothes, which were stylish, hung from the frame of her body. Dr. Matyas escorted Julie and her mother to an examination room.

"We were brought to the hospital because Julie passed out after gym class at school," her mother explained. Julie interrupted her mother harshly, "It was nothing. I just felt lightheaded." Her mother interjected, almost in tears, "I'm very worried about her. She doesn't listen to me. She's irritable all the time." Dr. Matyas asked, "Julie, what did you eat for breakfast and lunch today?" Julie replied, "A hard-boiled egg for breakfast . . . and I think that I had some yogurt at lunch."

Dr. Matyas noticed Julie's emaciated body. Her ribs and pelvic bones were clearly visible, extruding from her skin. Her hair was dry and brittle. On her face and arms, Julie had soft, downy hair to protect her from the cold. Dr. Matyas listened to Julie's heart and asked, "Do you have regular periods?" Julie responded, "Yes . . . well I used to, but now I don't."

"Julie," said Dr. Matyas, "do you know that you're underweight?" Julie snapped, "If I was on television or in the movies, I'd be perfectly normal. It's just because I'm in high school that everybody thinks I'm too thin." Dr. Matyas handed Julie her pen. Pointing to the exam table, she said, "I want you to imagine that you're sitting up there. I want you to use my pen to mark the width of your thighs on the exam table." With a sigh, Julie grabbed the pen and made two marks on the butcher-block paper spread out on the examination table. The distance was almost 4 feet.

2 inch tall girl. BMI calculators for a person's exact age, gender, and weight can be found online and are also available at this book's website: www.sagepub.com/weis2e.

Clinicians must also be mindful of the person's developmental status and health history when determining if a person's low weight is attributable to AN. For example, a child or adolescent who falls slightly above the fifth percentile but who exhibits an unusual preoccupation with eating and thinness might still be diagnosed with the disorder. Alternatively, a child or adolescent with low weight who is recovering from a medical illness would not be diagnosed with AN. Clinicians must rely on professional judgment, in addition to actuarial data, in making the diagnosis of AN.

Second, individuals with AN show excessive concern over their body shape and weight. Almost all adolescents with AN report that they are afraid of becoming fat. However, it might be more precise to say that they have an intense fear of gaining any weight whatsoever. The self-esteem of these adolescents is closely connected to their abilities to control their weight, appear attractive, and gain the approval and acknowledgment of others. Failure to control weight is seen as a sign of personal weakness and a risk to self-esteem. An adolescent with AN who gains even one pound might see herself on the path to obesity, peer rejection, and worthlessness.

Third, individuals with AN usually deny the seriousness of their low body weight. AN tends to be **ego-syntonic**; that is, people with the disorder usually do not think that their eating is problematic (Stice, Wonderlich, & Wade, 2006). Instead, most adolescents with AN take pride in their ability to restrict their diet and avoid weight gain. They often derive a certain degree of pleasure from resisting the temptation to eat even though they are severely malnourished. Resisting the temptation to eat is seen as a sign of control; dieting is regarded as a personal accomplishment. Severe dieting is doubly reinforced when other people, like parents or friends, comment on their will power or slim figure. Since their self-esteem is dependent on their ability to avoid weight gain, they are usually resistant to treatment. Treatment, which would involve eating and gaining weight, would represent a loss of control and a reduction in self-worth.

DSM-5 requires clinicians to specify the severity of the individual's disorder, based on his or her BMI. Lower scores, indicative of severe or extreme weight loss, communicate an immediate need for intervention (American Psychiatric Association, 2013).

What Is Bulimia Nervosa?

The essential feature of Bulimia Nervosa (BN) is recurrent binge eating (Table 15.4, Diagnostic Criteria for Bulimia Nervosa). **Binge eating** occurs when a person (a) consumes an unusually large amount of food in a discrete period of time (e.g., within 2 hours), and (b) he or she feels out of control while eating. During binge episodes, some people with BN consume 1,000 to 2,000 calories, roughly one half to one full day's caloric requirements. Most individuals with BN prefer foods that are high in sugar and fat like breads, cakes, ice cream, and other desserts (Stice et al., 2006).

By definition, people with BN also engage in some form of **inappropriate compensatory behavior** to prevent weight gain. Most people with BN purge; that is, they induce vomiting or misuse laxatives, diuretics, or enemas

Table 15.4   Diagnostic Criteria for Bulimia Nervosa

A. Recurrent episodes of binge eating. An episode of binge eating is characterized by both of the following:

   1. Eating, in a discrete period of time (e.g., within any 2-hour period), an amount of food that is definitely larger than what most individuals would eat in a similar period of time under similar circumstances.

   2. A sense of lack of control over eating during the episode (e.g., a feeling that one cannot stop eating or control what or how much one is eating).

B. Recurrent inappropriate compensatory behaviors in order to prevent weight gain, such as self-induced vomiting; misuse of laxatives, diuretics, or other medications; fasting; or excessive exercise.

C. The binge eating and inappropriate compensatory behaviors both occur, on average, at least once a week for 3 months.

D. Self-evaluation is unduly influenced by body shape and weight.

E. The disturbance does not occur exclusively during episodes of Anorexia Nervosa.

Specify current severity:

The minimum level of severity is based on the frequency of inappropriate compensatory behaviors. The level of severity may be increased to reflect other symptoms and the degree of functional disability.

   Mild: An average of 1–3 episodes of inappropriate compensatory behaviors per week.

   Moderate: An average of 4–7 episodes of inappropriate compensatory behaviors per week.

   Severe: An average of 8–13 episodes of inappropriate compensatory behaviors per week.

   Extreme: An average of 14 or more episodes of inappropriate compensatory behaviors per week.

Source: Reprinted with permission from the *Diagnostic and Statistical Manual of Mental Disorders, Fifth Edition* (Copyright 2013). American Psychiatric Association.

to avoid caloric absorption. Some individuals with BN do not purge. Instead, they avoid weight gain primarily through excessive fasting or exercise. For example, an adolescent who consumes 1,200 calories during a midnight binge might decide to "make up for it" by fasting the next day or running an extra 4 miles. Individuals with BN binge and use compensatory means of weight control regularly, at least twice each week. In extreme cases, individuals binge and show compensatory behaviors multiple times each day.

Like individuals with AN, people with BN show unusual preoccupation with body shape and weight. Indeed, the self-esteem and mood of individuals with BN is closely connected to their subjective impressions of their appearance. In contrast to AN, BN is usually an **ego-dystonic** disorder (Stice et al., 2006). Individuals with Bulimia Nervosa usually regard their eating behavior as problematic. Indeed, people with BN often binge in private because bingeing produces guilt and shame. Adolescents will often go to great lengths to hide their bingeing and purging from family members, sometimes for months or years. Adolescents with Bulimia Nervosa usually seek treatment for their disorder only after they feel that they can no longer keep their eating habits a secret from loved ones or when they feel a complete lack of control over their behavior.

One problem in diagnosing BN is identifying what constitutes a "binge." A binge is usually defined as an amount of food that is definitely larger than most people would eat during a similar period of time and under similar circumstances. However, two people's conceptualizations of a "large" amount of food might differ. A related problem with this definition is that many people with BN do not consume an extremely large amount of food when they binge. In one study, approximately one third of patients with BN consumed fewer than 600 calories per binge, which is approximately one third of their daily dietary requirement. Most experts believe that the subjective experience of feeling out of control over one's eating is more important to the diagnosis and treatment of BN than exactly how much a person eats during each binge episode. Consequently, some experts use the term **subjective binge** to describe the feeling of being out of control while eating, even if the number of calories consumed is relatively small (Wilson, Becker, & Heffernan, 2003; see text box *DSM-IV → DSM-5* Changes: Eating Disorders Get a Makeover).

What Is Binge Eating Disorder?

Binge Eating Disorder (BED) is characterized by recurrent episodes of binge eating *without* inappropriate compensatory behaviors to avoid weight gain (Table 15.5, Diagnostic Criteria for Binge Eating Disorder). During binges, people with BED feel out of control of their eating behavior and find it very difficult to stop. For example, a boy with BED might consume a large bag of pretzels, an entire canister of potato chips, several handfuls of crackers, and a bowl of ice cream in a 30-minute period of time (American Psychiatric Association, 2013).

Often, people with BED are not subjectively hungry when they binge. For example, a girl with BED may eat dinner at 6:30 p.m., only to binge one hour later in her bedroom while

Table 15.5 Diagnostic Criteria for Binge Eating Disorder

A. Recurrent episodes of binge eating. An episode of binge eating is characterized by both of the following:

  1. Eating, in a discrete period of time (e.g., within any 2-hour period), an amount of food that is definitely larger than what most individuals would eat in a similar period of time under similar circumstances.

  2. A sense of lack of control over eating during the episode (e.g., a feeling that one cannot stop eating or control what or how much one is eating).

B. The binge-eating episodes are associated with three (or more) of the following:

  1. Eating much more rapidly than normal.

  2. Eating until feeling uncomfortably full.

  3. Eating alone because embarrassed by how much one is eating.

(Continued)

Table 15.5 (Continued)

4. Feeling disgusted with oneself, depressed, or very guilty afterward.

C. Marked distress regarding binge eating is present.

D. The binge eating occurs, on average, at least once a week for 3 months.

E. The binge eating is not associated with the recurrent use of compensatory behavior as in Bulimia Nervosa and does not occur exclusively during the course of Bulimia Nervosa or Anorexia Nervosa.

Specify current severity:

The minimum level of severity is based on the frequency of episodes of binge eating. The level of severity may be increased to reflect other symptoms and the degree of functional disability.

Mild: 1–3 binge-eating episodes per week.

Moderate: 4–7 binge-eating episodes per week.

Severe: 8–13 binge-eating episodes per week.

Extreme: 14 or more binge-eating episodes per week.

Source: Reprinted with permission from the *Diagnostic and Statistical Manual of Mental Disorders, Fifth Edition* (Copyright 2013). American Psychiatric Association.

completing her homework. Individuals with BED often eat until they are uncomfortably full. Then they may feel disgusted, ashamed, or guilty for consuming so many calories and for their lack of control. Most people with BED are embarrassed about their eating behavior; consequently, they typically binge alone. It is not uncommon for a child and adolescent with BED to hide the disorder from their parents for months before being detected (American Psychiatric Association, 2013).

Binges must occur at least once a week for 3 months for someone to be diagnosed with BED. This frequency and duration criterion is identical to BN. Unlike people with BN, however, individuals with BED do not engage in compensatory behaviors to avoid weight gain. Whereas people with BN might vomit, severely restrict their diet, or excessively exercise to avoid weight gain following a binge, individuals with BED do not. Because of their compensatory behaviors, most people with BN are average or slightly above average weight. In contrast, most people with BED are overweight or obese (American Psychiatric Association, 2013).

CASE STUDY

ANTS!

Mateo was an 11-year-old boy referred to our outpatient clinic by his mother because of his unusual eating habits. A short and overweight boy, Mateo refused to enter the psychologist's office at the time of his appointment, preferring instead to remain in the waiting room.

His mother explained, "I've always tried to keep a neat house and insist that Mateo keep his room clean. Then, I noticed ants in the house. We've never had problems before, so I thought this was strange. I followed the ants to Mateo's room where I found what was hidden under his bed: cookies, crackers, candy bars, cheese curls, and lots of wrappers, empty plastic bags, and crumbs. I even found wrappers from Halloween candy from several months ago! I asked him about it, but he blamed his little brother."

Eventually, the psychologist was able to coax Mateo into her office and interview him alone. She said, "So I guess you know why you're here." Mateo responded, "Yeah. It's about my stash. My mom gets upset about everything."

The psychologist replied, "She told me about the different kinds of foods you eat. Maybe you can tell me when you eat them." Mateo answered, "I eat mostly when I get home from school. I'm hungry, and I need some snacks to keep me going until dinner."

"That seems reasonable," the psychologist commented. "Do you eat at other times, too?" Mateo replied, "Then, I eat in my room after dinner, while I watch TV or play video games. Sometimes, I just feel bored so I eat. Sometimes, I need to take my mind off school and things. I just keep eating and eating and can't seem to stop. I even tell myself, 'OK that's enough' but I keep on going."

"How do you feel afterwards?" the psychologist asked. Mateo answered, "Terrible. Like I want to throw up." The psychologist replied, "Do you?" He answered, "No. That's gross. But I feel like a disgusting pig. I guess I just got into the habit of hiding stuff under my bed."

Differentiating Among Eating Disorders

Anorexia Versus Bulimia

Many people believe that AN is defined by excessive dieting while BN is defined by bingeing and purging. In fact, neither disorder is defined in this way. Individuals with AN are classified into two subtypes, based on their current symptom presentation. Individuals with **AN-Restricting Type** maintain their low body weight through caloric restriction, that is, through extreme dieting or fasting. In contrast, individuals with **AN-Binge Eating/Purging Type** maintain low body weight primarily through binge eating and purging (American Psychiatric Association, 2013).

Similarly, individuals with BN can exhibit either purging or nonpurging behaviors. Most people with BN purge; they regularly induce vomiting or misuse laxatives, diuretics, or enemas to avoid weight gain. However, some people with BN use other compensatory behaviors, such as excessive fasting or exercise, to avoid weight gain.

The difference between AN and BN is *not* based on whether the person fasts or purges. In fact, some people with AN binge and purge while some people with BN seldom purge at all.

AN and BN can be differentiated in two ways. First, all individuals with AN show unusually low body weight. In contrast, low body weight is not required for the diagnosis of BN. In fact, most individuals with BN have weight within the normal range, and some people with BN are overweight. Second, all individuals with BN show recurrent binge eating. In contrast, not all people with AN binge (American Psychiatric Association, 2013).

BED Versus AN/BN

AN is differentiated from BED by low body weight. By definition, individuals with AN have very low body weight; in contrast, people with BED are usually overweight or obese. BN is differentiated from BED in that people with BN engage in purging or other compensatory strategies to avoid weight gain. In contrast, people with BED do not purge, fast, or engage in excessive exercise after bingeing. People with BN also tend to spend a great deal of time thinking about food and dieting. In contrast, people with BED usually do not show obsessive interests in food and may even view food negatively (Wilson & Sysko, 2009; see text box *DSM-IV → DSM-5* Changes: A New Diagnosis for an Old Problem).

DSM-IV → DSM-5 CHANGES

A NEW DIAGNOSIS FOR AN OLD PROBLEM

Binge Eating Disorder (BED) first appeared in the appendix of *DSM-IV* as a diagnosis "for further study." It was first described in 1959 by Albert Stunkard as "night eating syndrome"—a condition characterized by nighttime binges. In 1994, when *DSM-IV* was published, clinicians could identify many people who binged but did not purge or engage in other compensatory strategies. However, researchers were uncertain whether BED was distinct from other eating disorders (especially Bulimia Nervosa) and whether BED was not merely a symptom of depression or anxiety (e.g., emotional overeating).

Since 1994, more than 1,000 peer-reviewed studies have been published on BED. Research has confirmed that BED is distinct from Anorexia and Bulimia Nervosa, that it is not merely a symptom of psychological distress, that it causes considerable distress to people who have it, and that it can adversely affect people's physical health, social-emotional functioning, and overall satisfaction with life (Wonderlich et al., 2009). Consequently, BED appears in *DSM-5* as an official psychiatric condition.

Unfortunately, most of what we know about BED comes from studies of adult women with the disorder. We know much less about men with BED and even less about children and adolescents with this condition. Hopefully, the inclusion of BED in *DSM-5* will encourage researchers to investigate the presentation, etiology, and treatment of this disorder in youths.

Although BED and BN are separate disorders, some individuals may transition from one disorder to the other over time (Fairburn & Gowers, 2010). It is most common for individuals with BED to begin purging or engaging in other compensatory behaviors. For example, Fichter and Quadflieg (2007) studied a sample of 60 people with BED for 2 years. Although none of the patients developed AN, many later met criteria for BN. Transitioning from BN to BED appears to be less common. Only 10% of women with BED report a history of BN (Striegel-Moore et al., 2001).

Associated Features and Problems

Psychiatric Disorders

Approximately 80% of adolescents with eating disorders meet diagnostic criteria for at least one other disorder. The most common comorbid problems are depression, anxiety, and substance use problems (Evans et al., 2005).

Depression and Suicide

The most common comorbid psychiatric condition among adolescents with eating disorders is Major Depressive Disorder (MDD; Lucka, 2006). The lifetime prevalence of MDD for individuals with eating disorders is approximately 50% to 60%. The prevalence of depression among adolescents with eating disorders is much higher than in the general adolescent population.

However, the prevalence of depression among adolescents with eating disorders is similar to rates of depression among other clinic-referred children without eating problems (B. McDermott, Forbes, Harris, McCormack, & Gibbon, 2006).

In the case of AN and BN, depression usually emerges after the onset of the eating disorder and often persists after treatment of the eating problem. In one study, nearly 70% of individuals who previously suffered from AN subsequently developed depression (Halmi, Eckert, Marchi, Sampagnaro, Apple, & Cohen, 1991). Depression, therefore, is often a consequence of AN and BN, not a primary cause of these conditions.

Adults with BED also typically experience depression and other emotional problems after the onset of their binge eating. However, children and adolescents with BED tend to show depression before the onset of their binges. Children with BED tend to be obese and are often alienated and teased by peers because of their weight or body shape. They are also more likely than children without BED to have parents with mental health problems and to develop low self-esteem and depression themselves. Many of these children use food to cope with feelings of loneliness and other negative moods (Marcus & Kalarchian, 2003).

Individuals with eating disorders, especially AN and BN, are also at risk for suicide. Overall, approximately 25% of individuals with eating disorders have attempted suicide. Attempts are most common among individuals who purge, as opposed to those people who use dietary restriction or exercise to control their weight (Figure 15.2).

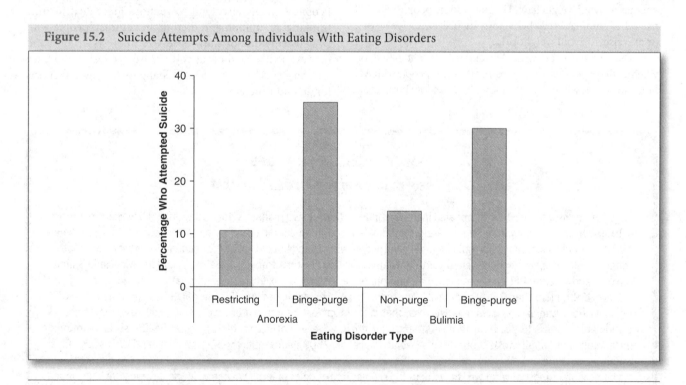

Figure 15.2 Suicide Attempts Among Individuals With Eating Disorders

Source: Based on Milos, Spindler, Hepp, and Schnyder (2004).

Note: Suicide attempts are more common among people who binge and purge, regardless of whether they have AN or BN. Impulsivity might underlie the tendency to binge-purge and attempt self-harm.

Rates of suicide completion are especially high among people with AN. Approximately 5% of individuals with AN commit suicide every decade that they live with the disorder. Indeed, malnourishment and suicide are the two leading causes of death associated with AN (Milos et al., 2004; Youssef et al., 2004).

Anxiety Disorders

Social Anxiety Disorder affects 30% to 50% of females with eating disorders (Wilson et al., 2003). Social Anxiety Disorder usually predates the emergence of AN and BN and persists after treatment. Many adolescent girls and women with eating disorders are extremely sensitive to criticism by others and have histories of avoiding situations in which they might be negatively evaluated by others. These individuals also frequently show a high need for approval by peers. Some may use dietary restriction and/or purging to assume physical appearances that meet the approval of others and enhance their social standing. Over time, these behaviors can lead to AN or BN (Atlas, 2004).

Approximately 30% to 40% of people with eating disorders show Obsessive-Compulsive Disorder (OCD). Most research indicates that perfectionism and OCD symptoms often precede the development of eating problems. Females with eating disorders often have long-standing problems with rigid, obsessive thinking. It is possible that rigid cognitive style places these individuals at risk for eating problems (Halmi et al., 2005).

Common genetic or environmental factors might partially account for the co-occurrence of eating disorders and anxiety disorders. Keel, Klump, Miller, McGue, and Iacono (2005) examined 14 monozygotic twins, aged 16 to 18 years, discordant for eating disorders; one of the twins had an eating disorder, while the other twin did not. Then, the researchers examined the prevalence of anxiety disorders among the twins who did not have an eating disorder. They found that these discordant twins were twice as likely to have an anxiety disorder as individuals in the general population. These findings suggest that common factors underlie both eating and anxiety disorders. However, we do not know whether these factors are predominantly genetic, environmental, or (most likely) a combination of the two.

Substance Use Disorders

Substance use problems frequently occur with eating disorders. The most frequently abused substances among individuals with AN or BN are nicotine, alcohol, marijuana, and cocaine. Overall, 20% to 25% of individuals with eating disorders show comorbid substance use disorders (Evans et al., 2005).

The prevalence of substance use disorders varies, depending on the subtype of eating disorder. Specifically, individuals who frequently engage in binge eating are 3 times more likely to show comorbid substance use problems than individuals with eating disorders who do not binge. Experts believe that underlying problems with impulsivity account for both the tendency to binge and the tendency to misuse alcohol and other drugs (Bulik et al., 2004). In most cases, substance use disorders emerge during or after the onset of the eating disorder. Consequently, many individuals with eating disorders seem to use alcohol and other drugs to reduce symptoms of anxiety (Bulik et al., 2004).

Personality

A central personality characteristic of AN is perfectionism. More than 30 years ago, Hilde Bruch (1973) described adolescents with AN as excessively compliant, eager to please, and lacking an autonomous sense of self. Subsequent research on adolescents with AN has generally confirmed Bruch's impressions. Even before they meet diagnostic criteria for AN, these adolescents are usually described as perfectionist, driven, and goal oriented. They are often overachievers, popular, and academically successful. They tend to be very conscientious about their appearance and the way they present themselves to others. They are often reluctant to take risks because they do not want to make mistakes or lose the approval of family or peers.

A second, related personality characteristic of adolescents with AN is rigidity and overcontrol (Tozzi et al., 2005). Adolescents with AN often show rigidity in their actions, feelings, and thoughts. With respect to actions, many of these individuals say that they need to have things "their way" in order to feel comfortable. They may become upset when they lack control over situations. Other people describe adolescents with AN as "obsessive" or excessively organized. With respect to their feelings, adolescents with AN are often guarded and emotionally reserved. They are especially reluctant to express sadness, frustration, and anger directly, preferring to keep these feelings hidden or to deny them altogether (Fairburn, Cooper, Doll, & Welch, 1999). Finally, adolescents with AN often show rigidity in their thoughts. Many show **black-and-white thinking**; that is, they view themselves and others as either "good" or "bad." This type of dichotomous thinking causes them to see the world in harsh, concrete, and simplistic ways. For example, if they gain one pound, they might regard themselves as "worthless" or "a complete failure."

Adolescents with BN show many of the same personality features as adolescents with AN (Tozzi et al., 2005). Perhaps the most salient characteristic of adolescents with BN is their low self-evaluation. In contrast to adolescents with AN, adolescents with BN tend to be more emotionally labile and impulsive. Adolescents with BN often show problems with temper and acting out. Some engage in self-harm or misuse alcohol and other drugs. Many youths with BN show chronic problems with emotion regulation.

Health Problems in Youths With AN/BN. Eating disorders can cause serious health problems. A frequent and serious medical complication associated with eating disorders is **electrolyte imbalance** (Evans et al., 2005). Electrolytes are minerals found in the body; they include calcium, sodium, and potassium. These minerals help maintain proper fluid levels throughout the body. They also regulate important metabolic functions, such as heart rate and brain activity. Activities that cause the body to lose excessive amounts of water (e.g., vomiting, excessive use of diuretics or laxatives) can lead to electrolyte imbalance.

Electrolyte imbalance can cause cardiac arrhythmias (i.e., irregular heart rate) and death. A serious condition called **hypokalemia**, caused by low potassium levels, can be fatal. People with AN are especially vulnerable to cardiac arrhythmias when they attempt to gain weight during treatment. In fact, physicians use the term **refeeding syndrome** to describe the cardiac and other health-related problems shown by patients with AN during the first 7 to 10 days of treatment. Because of the danger of arrhythmia, refeeding is conducted slowly and under close medical supervision.

Another serious medical complication associated with AN is **osteopenia**, that is, reduced bone mass. In healthy girls, bone density increases during childhood and early adolescence. Approximately 60% of a girl's bone density is acquired during her early adolescent years. However, AN interferes with this increase in bone density. The combination of poor nutrition, decreased estrogen levels caused by amenorrhea, and excessive exercise can lead to significantly lower bone density. Bone density loss is greatest in the spine and hips. Approximately 90% of adolescents and young adults with AN show osteopenia, placing them at risk for osteoporosis and hip fractures later in life. Bone loss may be irreversible.

Other medical complications associated with AN seem to be temporary. AN seems to disrupt hormone and endocrine functioning, which can lead to disturbances in appetite, physical growth, heart rate, and temperature regulation. Lack of body fat sometimes causes the development of fine downy hair (i.e., lanugo) on the trunk, limbs, and face. These soft hairs help conserve body temperature. Hair can become brittle, and skin may adopt a yellow color. Malnutrition associated with AN also seems to cause problems with concentration, memory, and problem solving.

Medical complications associated with BN are largely due to bingeing and purging. As mentioned above, hypokalemia is the most serious medical risk factor associated with BN. Frequent vomiting can cause enlargement of the salivary glands, erosion of dental enamel, and damage to the esophagus. Some individuals who use their fingers to induce vomiting show temporary scarring of the skin tissue up to the second or third knuckle (Image 15.3). Frequent laxative use can contribute to gastrointestinal problems, especially constipation.

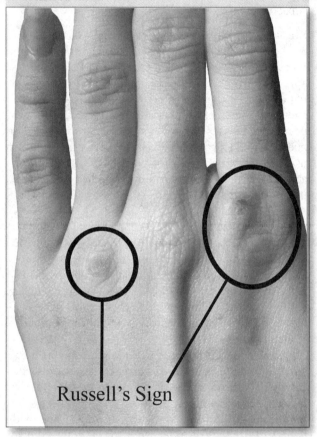

Image 15.3 Some people with AN or BN develop calluses on their knuckles due to repeated self-induced vomiting. The calluses arise when the knuckles repeatedly make contact with the incisor teeth. They are called "Russell's sign" after the British psychiatrist Gerald Russell who first described them.

Russell's Sign

Obesity in Youths with BED. Approximately 41.7% of individuals with BED are obese, compared to 15.8% of people without BED. Obesity is associated with a wide range of health-related problems. These problems include diabetes, high blood pressure, high cholesterol, heart disease, headaches, and other forms of chronic pain (Kessler et al., 2013).

BED also interferes with obesity treatment (Wonderlich et al., 2009). Individuals with BED who participate in weight loss programs lose less weight and are more likely to drop out than individuals without BED. Furthermore, adults who receive bariatric surgery to lose weight are more likely to regain their weight following surgery than their counterparts without BED. These difficulties with weight loss are due to their frequent binges (Blaine & Rodman, 2007).

Because most youths with BED are overweight or obese, they are at great risk for teasing and ostracism by peers. They frequently report avoidance of social situations, low self-esteem, and low confidence in social situations. Unfortunately, these negative feelings can contribute to depression and anxiety and elicit future binge episodes.

Indeed, children and adolescents with BED are at great risk for anxiety, depression, and other internalizing disorders (Fairburn & Gowers, 2010). Researchers examined the prevalence of BED in obese adolescents who sought weight loss treatment (Glasofer et al., 2007). Approximately 30% met criteria for BED. Furthermore, adolescents with BED showed more concerns about eating, body shape, and weight than obese adolescents without BED. Furthermore, adolescents with BED also showed significantly more problems with depression and anxiety (Figure 15.3).

Family Relationships. Research has consistently shown problems in the family functioning of girls with eating disorders. Adolescents with AN often come from highly rigid, overprotective homes. The parents of adolescents with AN typically adopt **authoritarian parenting** strategies: They place high demands on their children's behavior, but they show limited responsiveness to their children's needs. Parents usually assume considerable control over their children's lives and do not allow their adolescents to take much part in decision making.

Adolescents with BN also tend to come from homes that place a premium on obedience and achievement. However, their homes are usually chaotic and stress filled. These adolescents often report a high degree of family conflict and, sometimes, domestic violence. Adolescents with BN tend to have higher rates of insecure attachment compared to adolescents without eating problems.

Diet, weight, and body shape are given considerable attention in the families of girls with eating disorders (Smolak, 2006). Girls with AN often report that their parents frequently dieted in order to lose weight and made periodic comments about their weight and physical appearance. Indeed, some of these girls reported a history of eating disorders within the immediate family. In contrast, the family members of girls with BN are sometimes obese or overweight. These girls often report considerable tension during mealtime, parents who encourage them to lose weight, or family members who tease them about their weight, shape, or appearance.

Parents' comments about weight and body shape are associated with adolescents' body satisfaction, self-esteem, and eating habits (Field et al., 2001; Smolak, Levine, & Schermer, 1999). For example, the frequency of parents' comments about their daughters' body shape and weight is associated with body dissatisfaction in elementary school girls (Smolak, 2006). In one study, 23% of middle school girls said that at least one parent teased them about their appearance (Keery, Boutelle, van den Berg, & Thompson, 2005). Teasing by fathers was associated with body dissatisfaction, dietary restriction, and symptoms of BN. Teasing by mothers was associated with depression. Even mothers' comments about *their own* weight were associated with their daughters' body dissatisfaction (Tiggeman & Lynch, 2001). Although these associations do not necessarily mean that parental comments cause girls to feel poorly

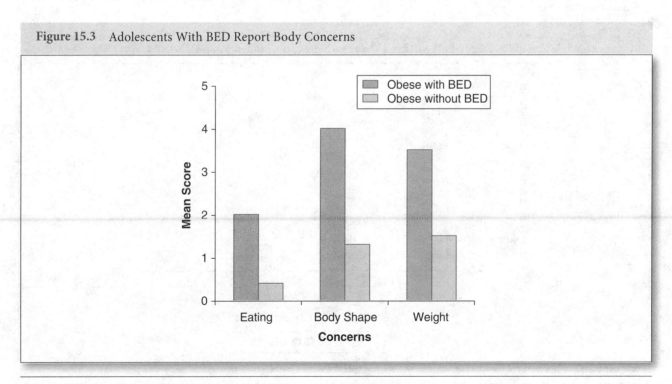

Figure 15.3 Adolescents With BED Report Body Concerns

Source: Based on Glasofer and colleagues (2007).

Note: Obese adolescents who seek treatment for weight loss report concerns about their eating behavior, shape, and weight. However, obese adolescents with BED report more concerns than obese adolescents without BED.

about their appearance, they suggest that parents' comments about shape and weight are connected with their daughters' feelings about their own bodies.

School and Sports. Adolescents with eating disorders are often overachievers and perfectionists when it comes to school and sports. These adolescents often derive self-esteem from their accomplishments, especially the praise and recognition of others. They tend to earn high grades, excel in sports, and assume leadership roles in extracurricular activities (Fairburn & Harrison, 2003).

On the other hand, adolescents with eating disorders are often unwilling to take risks because they fear that they will fail and lose the approval of others. Because their self-worth is so heavily dependent on their accomplishments, they do not tolerate failure. They often appear driven, perfectionistic, and obsessed about school work, sports, and other extracurricular activities. They may see setbacks in school and extracurricular activities as indicators of personal weakness and worthlessness.

Adolescents who experience severe malnourishment because of AN usually show some problems in academic and social functioning. Malnourishment leads to fatigue, irritability, and concentration problems that interfere with girls' abilities to perform academically and socially. Adolescents with advanced BN also tend to show academic problems. BN often leads to mood and substance use problems that affect adolescents' school performance (Stice et al., 2006).

Epidemiology

Prevalence

AN and BN. It has been difficult to estimate the prevalence of eating disorders among adolescents, for two reasons. First, most people with eating disorders, especially adolescents, are reluctant to admit their symptoms. Consequently, surveys, even those conducted anonymously, may underestimate prevalence. Second, eating disorders are relatively rare, especially among adolescents. Therefore, researchers need to gather data from large numbers of people in order to obtain a precise estimate of the prevalence of AN and BN (Evans et al., 2005).

Despite these limitations, researchers have been able to obtain rough estimates for the lifetime prevalence of eating disorders in the United States (Stice et al., 2006). The lifetime prevalence of AN is between 0.5% and 1% for females and less than 0.3% for males. The lifetime prevalence of BN is between 1.5% and 4% in females and less than 0.5% in males. The prevalence of AN and BN among adolescent girls is slightly lower than the prevalence for women (Wilson et al., 2003).

Available data probably underestimate the prevalence of eating problems among adolescents because most adolescents do not meet full diagnostic criteria for either AN or BN. Available data indicate that an additional 1% to 2% of adolescent girls show subthreshold levels of AN, while an additional 2% to 3% of adolescent girls show subthreshold symptoms of BN (Evans et al., 2005). Although full-blown eating disorders are relatively rare among adolescents, subthreshold eating problems are more common (Figure 15.4).

Figure 15.4   Maladaptive Weight Loss Methods Used by High School Students in the Last 30 Days

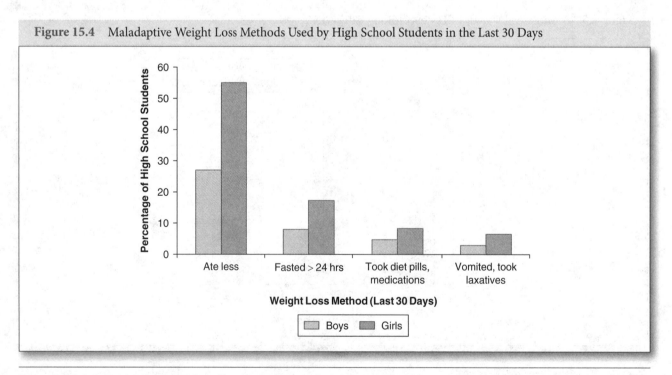

Source: Based on the Youth Risk Behavior Surveillance System (Centers for Disease Control, 2007).

Note: Data are based on a sample of approximately 14,000 adolescents in ninth through 12th grades. Although most youths do not have eating disorders, many (especially girls) use risky methods to lose weight.

BED. The lifetime prevalence of BED in adults in the United States is 2.6%. The prevalence is significantly greater than either AN or BN. At any point in time, approximately 1.2% of adults have BED (Kessler et al., 2013). The prevalence of BED among older children and adolescents is approximately 1% to 1.5%. However, many more children binge occasionally and feel out of control when they binge. In one large epidemiological study, almost 20% of high school students admitted to bingeing and feeling out of control at least once in the previous year (W. G. Johnson, Rohan, & Kirk, 2002; Kjelsas et al., 2004).

The prevalence of BED is very high among youths referred for treatment because of obesity. In one study, 36.5% of older children and adolescents referred to a residential treatment program for obesity binged at least once a week; 6% reported multiple binges weekly (Decaluwe et al., 2002).

Epidemiological studies consistently show BED to be 2.4 to 3.6 times more prevalent in women than in men. However, the gender distribution may be closer to equal in children and younger adolescents.

Eating Problems of Boys. The prevalence of eating disorders differs by gender. Adolescent girls are 10 to 15 times more likely than adolescent boys to develop AN or BN. The prevalence of AN among adolescent boys and young men is less than 0.16%. The prevalence of BN among boys and young men is less than 0.7%. Some researchers indicate that as many as 1% of adolescent boys and young men may have subthreshold eating problems.

Instead of AN and BN, some adolescent boys are at risk for eating problems caused by a desire to *gain* weight, body mass, and muscle. Many boys attempt to gain body mass and muscle in appropriate ways, such as by eating healthy foods and exercising. However, some boys rely on risky strategies such as overeating, excessive exercise, or use of dietary supplements. One fourth to one half of adolescent boys admit to using dietary supplements (e.g., protein shakes, creatine, ephedrine) to increase mass. Between 3% and 12% have used anabolic steroids to build muscle. Approximately 5% of adolescent boys exercise more than seven times each week, exercise despite pain and injury, and experience guilt or depression on days they are unable to exercise (McCabe & Ricciardelli, 2001).

Culture and Ethnicity

Eating Disorders Across Countries. For years, experts believed that eating disorders were found only in Western, industrialized countries, predominantly in high socioeconomic groups. Today, researchers have found eating disorders across all cultures and socioeconomic strata that have been studied (Polivy, Herman, Mills, & Wheeler, 2003).

AN and BN appear to be universal phenomena, existing across countries and cultures. For example, eating disorders have been identified in Asia, Africa, the Middle East, the Caribbean, the Pacific Islands, and Eastern Europe, in addition to Western Europe and the United States. However, eating disorders are more prevalent among Western societies and industrialized nations than non-Western and preindustrialized countries. For example, the prevalence of eating disorders in Eastern Europe, Japan, Singapore, South Africa, and Israel is generally equivalent to the prevalence of these disorders in the United States. In non-Western and preindustrialized countries like Nigeria and Belize, prevalence is lower (Anderson-Frye & Becker, 2004).

Considerable evidence indicates that globalization has spread eating disorders from industrialized countries to developing nations. For example, eating disorders were largely unknown in the island of Fiji in the South Pacific a generation ago. However, the prevalence of eating disorders rose dramatically after Western culture was introduced to the island by television and other media. Similarly, adolescents who immigrate to the United States from developing countries initially show low rates of eating disorders. However, after years of living in the United States, their likelihood of eating disorders increases dramatically (Anderson-Frye & Becker, 2004; Polivy et al., 2003).

Experts disagree as to how Western culture or industrialization might contribute to an increase in eating disorders. One popular explanation is that girls and women in non-Western and developing cultures compare themselves to the images of models and actresses portrayed in Western magazines and television. These comparisons cause girls in non-Western and developing countries to become dissatisfied with their bodies, to diet, and to engage in unsafe practices to lose weight (Thompson & Heinberg, 1993).

An alternative hypothesis is that girls and women notice a relationship between the physical attractiveness of Western models and other indicators of wealth, social status, and happiness. In order to enhance their social status, they attempt to emulate these models and actresses by losing weight. For example, shortly after the introduction of Western media in Fiji, many girls expressed a desire to lose weight. They reasoned that if they were more attractive, like the models and actresses on television, they might be able to lead more successful lives (Becker, Burwell, Gilman, Herzog, & Hamburg, 2002). In other developing countries, girls and women most at risk for eating disorders tend to come from upwardly mobile families. For example, in Curacao and Belize, girls and women who had aspirations of achieving wealth and social status, or who had economic ties to Western culture through tourism, showed rates of eating disorders similar to those of females in the United States. Upwardly mobile black females living in South Africa show greater prevalence of eating disorders than their white South African counterparts. For some girls and women, AN and BN may reflect a maladaptive attempt to emulate Western culture in order to share in its social and economic prosperity (Anderson-Frye & Becker, 2004).

THE EYE OF THE BEHOLDER

Grace was a 16-year-old girl who immigrated to the United States with her parents from the African nation of Rwanda following the 1994 genocide that occurred in that country. Although Grace's family was a member of the majority Hutus, her father aided and protected members of the minority Tutsis who were slaughtered by extremist Hutu militia. Fearing retribution, the family fled the country and eventually sought asylum in the United States.

In Africa, Grace was viewed as an intelligent and beautiful girl. In the United States, however, she had difficulty gaining acceptance from her peers because of her appearance. By Western standards, Grace was short and slightly overweight. She was unaccustomed to being teased by other girls at school and ostracized by classmates. Within 6 months of enrolling in high school, Grace developed symptoms of Bulimia Nervosa. She began to binge and purge multiple times each week.

Eating Disorders in the United States. Some experts have suggested that ethnic minorities in the United States are less likely to develop eating disorders than white adolescents. These experts argue that because ethnic minority adolescents come from subcultures that place less emphasis on slenderness, they may be less likely to diet and engage in problematic eating (Striegel-Moore, Silberstein, & Rodin, 1986). In fact, Latina and African American adolescent girls tend to be more tolerant than white adolescent girls of a heavier and more curvaceous body shape. Furthermore, Latina and African American girls are often less concerned about weight gain than their white counterparts (McKnight Risk Factor Study, 2003).

However, eating disorders exist across all ethnic groups in the United States, and the culturally specific preferences regarding weight and shape may not protect minority girls from developing eating disorders. Native American adolescents appear to have the highest rates of eating disorders among all ethnic groups in the United States (including whites), while Asian Americans appear to have the lowest rates. Most data indicate that the prevalence of eating disorders among Latina adolescents is comparable to the prevalence among whites.

Data regarding African American girls are mixed; prevalence for African American youths varies, depending on the type of eating disorder. Most studies show lower rates of AN among African American adolescents than white adolescents. However, most studies have found no differences in BN between African American and white adolescents (Anderson-Frye & Becker, 2004; Polivy et al., 2003).

Shaw and colleagues (2004) surveyed a large group of adolescent girls and young women to assess behaviors indicative of eating pathology and cognitions that might place them at risk for developing eating disorders. Behavioral indicators of eating problems included amenorrhea, low body mass, bingeing, purging, and fear of gaining weight. Risk factors for eating problems included a history of dieting, anxiety, depression, and a strong desire to be thin. The researchers were especially interested in whether participants' behaviors and risk factors varied as a function of ethnicity. The researchers found almost no differences across four ethnic groups: Asian Americans, African Americans, Latinos, and whites. They concluded that eating pathology is more similar across ethnic groups than previously thought.

Course

Anorexia Nervosa (AN) and Bulimia Nervosa (BN). AN and BN usually begin during adolescence. Early research indicated a bimodal age of onset for AN; some adolescents develop AN shortly after puberty, whereas other adolescents develop the disorder around age 18 years. More recent longitudinal research indicates that the peak age of onset for AN is between 16 and 19 years (Evans et al., 2005; Lewinsohn, Striegel-Moore, & Seeley, 2000). BN usually emerges at a somewhat later age than AN. The peak age of onset for BN is usually between 18 and 20 years. Although eating disorders can emerge at any age, they are extremely rare among prepubescent children, and they usually do not emerge after age 25 years.

The reasons for adolescents' maladaptive eating behaviors vary with age (Evans et al., 2005). Some young adolescents with eating disorders, especially AN, report a fear of physical maturation. Researchers have speculated that these young adolescents avoid weight gain in order to delay the onset of puberty and retain a childlike appearance and social status. In contrast, older adolescents and adults with eating disorders usually report fear of weight gain or becoming overweight.

The course of AN is variable. Approximately 50% of individuals with AN recover from the disorder, 30% improve but continue to meet diagnostic criteria for either AN or BN, and 10% to 20% have chronic symptoms of AN. Individuals with chronic symptoms are most at risk for death, either from malnourishment or suicide. Adolescents with AN who receive treatment shortly after symptom onset have the best chance of recovery (Evans et al., 2005; Wilson et al., 2003).

The prognosis of BN is somewhat better than for AN. In one large study of individuals previously diagnosed with BN, 15% continued to meet diagnostic criteria for the disorder 5 years later. Unfortunately, 36% of patients continued to show subthreshold eating problems while 41% met diagnostic criteria for MDD, instead. While the chance of recovery is greater for BN than AN, the majority of people diagnosed with either eating disorder continue to show psychiatric problems years later. The mortality rate for BN is approximately 0.5% (Fairburn, Cooper, Doll, Norman, & O'Connor, 2000).

A significant percentage of adolescents with eating problems change diagnostic classification over time, a phenomenon called **diagnostic migration**. For example, individuals might initially meet diagnostic criteria for AN and later be diagnosed with BN. In one large study, 36% of patients with AN later showed BN. Furthermore, 27% of patients with BN later developed AN (Tozzi et al., 2005). Diagnostic migration is especially common among adolescents with eating disorders, and it usually occurs within 5 years after the initial diagnosis.

BED: Childhood- Versus Adult-Onset. Recent research indicates that youths may manifest BED differently than adults (Fairburn & Gowers, 2010). Marcus and Kalarchian (2003) differentiate between early-onset and late-onset BED. **Early-onset BED** tends to emerge between 11 and 13 years of age. Youths with early-onset BED, like Mateo, usually have weight problems or obesity in childhood. They typically begin binge eating in late childhood (mean age = 12 years) and begin dieting a few years later (mean age = 14 years). They often have problems with depression and anxiety and tumultuous family relationships. They may also develop BN in adulthood.

In contrast, **late-onset BED** tends to emerge in early adulthood (e.g., >18 years). People with late-onset BED tend to have weight problems or obesity in early adulthood, rather than in childhood (mean age = 19 years). Furthermore, they often begin dieting (mean age = 20 years) *before* they engage in binge eating (mean age = 28 years). Late-onset BED is less closely associated with BN.

These findings suggest that BED in children and adolescents is closely associated with emotional problems, such as depression and anxiety. Food and eating may be a method of emotion-regulation for these youths. In contrast, BED in adults is more closely associated with dietary restriction. Adults with BED may binge to alleviate feelings of hunger, emptiness, and dysphoria while dieting (Marcus & Kalarchian, 2003).

People are more likely to recover from BED than other eating disorders. Fairburn and colleagues (2000) found that 85% of young women with BED no longer met criteria for the disorder 5 years after their initial diagnosis. A second longitudinal study also found high rates of recovery 2 years (65%) and 6 years (78%) after diagnosis (Fichter & Quadflieg, 2007).

Etiology of Anorexia/ Bulimia Nervosa

Genetics

Genes likely play a role in the development of eating disorders (Bulik, 2004). Behavioral geneticists have determined that eating disorders run in families. Females who have a first-degree relative with an eating disorder are 4 to 11 times more likely to develop an eating disorder themselves compared to females with no family history of eating problems (Strober, Freeman, Lampert, Diamond, & Kaye, 2000). This increased genetic risk for eating disorders is not specific to AN or BN. Instead, a family member with BN places other biological relatives at risk for *all* eating disorders, not BN per se. Genes probably predispose individuals to general eating pathology.

Behavioral geneticists have also tried to determine how much of the variance of eating disorders can be explained by genetic versus environmental factors. Twin studies indicate that the heritability of AN is between 48% and 74%, depending on the sample and the definition of AN that the researchers use (Bulik, 2004). Twin studies indicate that the heritability of BN is roughly the same: between 59% and 83%. The remaining variance is largely explained by nonshared environmental factors, that is, events and experiences unique to the adolescent and not her twin (e.g., different friends, teachers, sports, or hobbies). Shared environmental factors (e.g., same parents, house, socioeconomic status) seem to play relatively little role in explaining either AN or BN.

Molecular geneticists have tried to locate specific genes that might be responsible for placing individuals at risk for eating pathology (Bulik, 2004). Unfortunately, this line of research has produced inconsistent results. So far, researchers have been unable to identify a single gene or set of genes that are consistently associated with either AN or BN. Some evidence suggests that chromosome 1 may be involved in the development of AN-Restricting Type as well as in the tendency to obsess over thinness. Other data indicate that chromosome 10 may play a role in the development of purging behavior, especially vomiting. More research is needed.

Serotonin and Cholecystokinin

The neurotransmitter serotonin may be involved in the development of eating disorders, especially AN. In healthy individuals, serotonin is involved in general metabolism, mood, and personality. With respect to metabolism, serotonin plays a crucial role in appetite; it is partially responsible for feelings of satiety. With respect to mood, serotonin plays a major role in emotion regulation. Abnormalities in serotonergic functioning are likely involved in depression. With respect to personality, high levels of serotonin are associated with sensitivity to psychological stress, perfectionism, and a need for order and organization.

Some individuals with eating disorders show a disturbance in serotonin levels. For example, people with AN often show unusually high levels of serotonin, even after they have recovered from the disorder (Kaye, Weltzin, & Hsu, 1993). Similarly, individuals with BN show abnormalities in serotonin levels both during their illness and after recovery (Kaye et al., 1998). Kaye, Bastiani, and Moss (1995) suggest that elevated serotonin may make certain individuals prone to psychological distress, anxiety, and perfectionism. Restrictive dieting can temporarily decrease serotonin levels, causing a reduction in negative affect. Thus, dietary restriction is negatively reinforced and maintained over time.

Serotonin disturbance has also been suggested as a cause for bingeing and purging. In healthy individuals, serotonin plays a role in inhibiting eating. Individuals with BN, however, show low serotonin activity. These low levels of serotonin activity might explain their tendency to binge. Furthermore, individuals who recover from BN often show increased serotonin levels, indicating that recovery is partially dependent on changes in serotonergic activity (Ferguson & Pigott, 2000).

Some people with BN show low levels of a hormone called **cholecystokinin (CCK).** In healthy individuals, CCK is produced after eating a large meal. This hormone triggers satiety and regulates the amount of food consumed. However, people with BN produce much less CCK when they eat, perhaps allowing them to binge without experiencing satiety (Polivy et al., 2003).

Studies showing an association between serotonin, CCK, and eating disorders have relied on cross-sectional designs. These studies cannot tell us whether abnormalities in neurotransmitters or hormones are a cause or a consequence of eating disorders. For example, individuals with AN often have elevated levels of another neurotransmitter, norepinephrine. However, recent studies indicate that reductions in norepinephrine are the result of severe weight loss, not a cause of the disorder (Wilson et al., 2003). Although it is tempting to infer causal relationships from correlational data, such inferences can lead to an inaccurate understanding of adolescent eating disorders.

Sexual Development

Puberty. Experts have given considerable attention to the role of puberty in the emergence of eating disorders. Research has consistently shown that eating disorders usually develop sometime during or after puberty, and they rarely emerge before puberty or after age 25.

One explanation for the association between puberty and eating disorders is that the physical changes that characterize puberty are particularly stressful to adolescent girls. Before puberty, girls tend to have slender figures that are relatively low in body fat. Their body weight and shape are relatively close to the socially sanctioned ideal body promoted by Western society. With the onset of puberty, girls gain weight and body fat, making their bodies less compatible with this Western ideal. This increase in weight and change in shape can lead to body dissatisfaction in some girls, causing them to diet in order to regain their prepubescent shape (Smolak, 2006).

A related hypothesis is that the timing of puberty might be important in the development of eating disorders. Specifically, girls who mature earlier may be at particular risk for body dissatisfaction and eating pathology. These girls will not only violate socially sanctioned ideals regarding weight and shape, but they will do so when their peers are not developing in similar ways. Some early-maturing girls may be teased because of their precocious physical development.

Empirical studies have not consistently supported these hypotheses regarding the association between puberty, body dissatisfaction, and eating *problems*. Some studies have shown significant associations between pubertal development, pubertal timing, and body dissatisfaction; however, the strength of these associations has been relatively modest. Other studies have failed to support an association between pubertal development, pubertal timing, and body dissatisfaction altogether. Indeed, the only longitudinal study to test this hypothesis did not support the notion that puberty contributes to later body dissatisfaction (Stice, 2003).

Research investigating the association between pubertal development, pubertal timing, and eating *disorders* has also yielded mixed results. Pubertal development and timing is associated with dieting in some studies but not others. However, pubertal development and timing tends to be weakly correlated with the likelihood of eating disorders. Taken together, these findings indicate that puberty may be a developmental time frame, during which adolescents are vulnerable to the emergence of body dissatisfaction and eating pathology. However, there is relatively little evidence to suggest that puberty, by itself, *causes* eating problems or eating disorders.

Child Sexual Abuse

Some experts have speculated that a sexual victimization during childhood can lead to the development of eating pathology, especially BN (Kearney-Cooke & Striegel-Moore, 1994; Mannarino & Cohen, 1996). According to these theorists, the experience of sexual abuse makes girls feel helpless and shameful. Maltreated girls may be disgusted by their bodies or view their bodies as "tainted" by the abusive act. Some girls may express this shame and disgust by harming their bodies through starvation, bingeing, and purging. Other girls attempt to regain a sense of control over their bodies by dieting. In any case, girls place themselves at risk for developing eating disorders as a consequence of their abuse.

There is considerable evidence that child sexual abuse is associated with eating disorders, especially BN (Thompson & Wonderlich, 2004). Studies involving abused children, adolescents with eating disorders, and youths in the community have shown that girls who are sexually maltreated show increased likelihood of developing eating disorders later in life. Furthermore, adolescents and adults with eating disorders often report that their sexual victimization occurred before the onset of their eating disorders.

On the other hand, child sexual abuse seems to place children at risk for a host of psychiatric problems, not eating disorders per se. Fairburn and colleagues (1999) conducted a series of studies involving 102 women with BN, 102 women with other psychiatric disorders (usually depression), and 204 women with no mental health problems. Results showed that women with BN or another psychiatric disorder were more likely to have been sexually abused than women without a current mental illness. However, history of sexual abuse was equally as common among women with BN as it was among women with other psychiatric problems (Fairburn et al., 1999; Welch & Fairburn, 1996).

Child sexual abuse seems to lead to BN when individuals show other psychological problems, such as impulsivity, risk-taking behavior, and substance abuse. These findings indicate that child sexual abuse is a risk factor for many psychiatric illnesses, but it is probably not a unique predictor of eating pathology (Thompson & Wonderlich, 2004; Wonderlich et al., 2001).

Cognitive-Behavioral Theory

The cognitive-behavioral conceptualization of eating disorders is based on the notion that thoughts, feelings, and actions are closely connected. Each component of behavior affects the others. Cognitive-behavioral theorists believe eating disorders are caused by a disturbance among these three factors: an *affective* disturbance characterized by low self-esteem; a *cognitive* disturbance characterized by distorted perceptions of weight, shape, and body image; and a *behavioral* disturbance marked by dietary restriction (Pike, Devlin, & Loeb, 2004; Wilson, Fairburn, & Agras, 1997).

At the heart of the cognitive-behavioral model for eating disorders is low self-esteem. Adolescents at risk for AN and BN are believed to have underlying problems with dysphoria and generally low regard for themselves. Although the source of this low self-esteem is unknown, it likely stems from a combination of genetic and environmental factors. For example, individuals at risk for eating disorders tend to have personality dispositions that make them sensitive to psychological distress as well as highly critical of themselves and others. Furthermore, many youths with eating disorders come from disruptive or stressful family environments that can contribute to their feelings of low self-worth. To compensate for these negative emotions, adolescents may place considerable value on their physical appearance, especially their weight and body shape. They believe that by attaining a certain weight or shape, they can overcome feelings of low self-esteem and self-worth.

Most adolescents diet to attain ideal weight and shape. Severe dieting is negatively reinforced by the reduction of low self-esteem. Adolescents feel temporarily better about themselves and their appearance as they lose weight and receive compliments from others. Unfortunately, severe dieting usually exacerbates adolescents' dysphoria over time. First, adolescents usually hold such unrealistic ideals of weight and shape that no amount of dieting can allow them to reach these ideals. Second, dietary restriction causes feelings of hunger, irritability, and fatigue.

To compensate for feelings of frustration, hunger, and fatigue, many adolescents break their diets and binge. Binges are negatively reinforced by temporary reductions in negative affect. However, binges are quickly followed by more lasting feelings of guilt, disgust, and physical discomfort.

To alleviate guilt and avoid weight gain, some adolescents will engage in inappropriate compensatory behaviors. At first, these behaviors include fasting or extra exercise. Fasting is negatively reinforced by reductions in guilt and anxiety about weight gain. However, fasting also produces long-term feelings of dysphoria and hunger. Other adolescents purge in order to avoid weight gain. Purging is also negatively reinforced by temporary reductions of anxiety. However, purging usually exacerbates feelings of guilt and disgust over time. Furthermore, after purging, adolescents often feel the same sense of emptiness and dysphoria that existed before the binge.

In summary, low self-esteem and dysphoria form the basis for the cognitive-behavioral model of eating disorders. Dietary restriction causes a temporary reduction in dysphoria (negative reinforcement) but long-term feelings of frustration and hunger. Binge eating reduces feelings of hunger (negative reinforcement) but produces guilt and anxiety about weight gain. Fasting and purging can alleviate guilt and fears of weight gain (negative reinforcement) but exacerbate feelings of low self-worth. Eating disorders, therefore, are caused by underlying mood problems and maintained by problematic thoughts and a cycle of negative reinforcement.

Social-Cultural Theories

Dual Pathway Model. Other researchers are interested in how social and cultural factors might contribute to the emergence of eating disorders. Stice (2002) has offered one of the most influential social-cultural models to explain binge eating: the dual pathway model. According to the **dual pathway model**, eating disorders develop through two pathways: (a) dietary restriction and (b) negative affect.

At the center of the dual process model is the notion that society places great demands on adolescent girls to lose weight and appear attractive. Many girls internalize the socially sanctioned **thin ideal** because they are reinforced by others when they conform to this ideal and punished when their appearance violates this standard. For example, adolescent girls often praise peers who lose weight and ostracize peers who are overweight. Praise (positive reinforcement) and teasing or ostracism (punishment) can be powerful motivators.

Idealization of thinness contributes to body dissatisfaction, even in very young girls (Smolak, 2006). When girls are dissatisfied with their bodies, they may engage in dietary restriction to lose weight and achieve their ideal size and shape. Unfortunately, dieting is an ineffective means of long-term weight control. Instead, dieting usually produces feelings of hunger, irritability, and fatigue. Furthermore, failure to lose weight and achieve the thin ideal contributes to low self-esteem, frustration, and negative affect (Image 15.4).

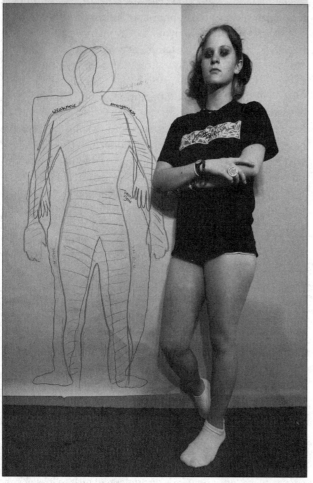

Image 15.4 Brittany stands next to her body tracing during a therapy session for girls with eating disorders. The body tracing exercise allows her to see the distortion between her actual body, traced by the therapist, and her perceived body image.

In some girls, dietary restriction and negative affect lead to binge eating. Bingeing causes a temporary reduction in both hunger and negative emotions. Indeed, binge foods tend to be high in fat and carbohydrates—foods we usually call "comfort foods." However, as described by the cognitive-behavioral model of eating disorders, bingeing also elicits increased guilt and the likelihood of purging or other compensatory behaviors.

Tripartite Influence Model. An alternative social-cultural model for the development of eating disorders is the tripartite influence model (Thompson, Coovert, & Stormer, 1999). According to this model, three social-cultural factors influence adolescent girls' eating behavior: peers, parents, and the media (Figure 15.5).

Peers can influence adolescent girls' eating when they place importance on weight and body shape, tease other girls about their weight or appearance, or diet themselves. Parents affect a girl's eating behavior when they make comments about their own weight, shape, or appearance, when they diet, or when they criticize their daughter's appearance or urge her to lose weight. The media can also affect girls' eating behavior. Models on television, in movies, and in magazines can convey the importance of physical attractiveness to girls' well-being. Similarly, television and magazines can provide girls with maladaptive ideas about dieting, exercise, and weight loss (Image 15.5).

According to the tripartite influence model, these three social-cultural factors (peers, parents, media) can lead to the development of eating problems in three ways. First, they can directly affect eating behavior by motivating a girl to diet. For example, a girl who sees her mother, her best friend, and her favorite television star dieting might regard dieting as a developmentally normative and socially expected means of losing weight. She might decide to diet in order to appear more like these significant people in her life. As we have seen before, however, dietary restriction is not an effective, long-term means of weight control. In fact, it often causes negative affect and can lead to binge eating.

Second, the relationship between these three social-cultural factors and girls' eating might be mediated by girls' internalization of the thin ideal. Messages from peers, parents, and the media about body shape, weight, or attractiveness might cause girls to internalize the often unrealistic standards for beauty conveyed in Western culture. For example, girls who read fashion magazines might internalize the often unrealistic standards for body shape and weight conveyed by the models in these magazines. Girls who internalize these standards, in turn, might experience dissatisfaction with their own shape and weight. Such body dissatisfaction can lead to dieting, negative emotions, and bulimic symptoms.

Third, the relationship between these three social-cultural factors and girls' eating might be mediated by girls' tendency to compare their appearance with the appearance

Figure 15.5 Tripartite Influence Model of Eating Disturbance

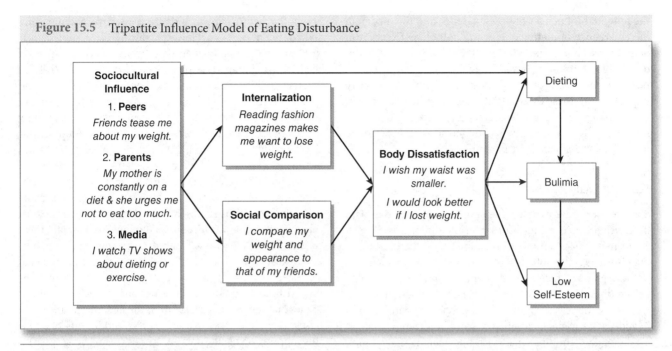

Source: From Shroff and Thompson (2006). Used with permission.

Note: Social-cultural factors lead to body dissatisfaction and BN in two ways: (a) by causing girls to internalize the thin ideal and (b) by causing girls to compare their appearance to others.

of others. For example, peers might make comments about classmates who are exceptionally thin and attractive or overweight and unattractive. Adolescent girls, in turn, might compare their own weight and body shape to these attractive and unattractive classmates. These social comparisons, in turn, might cause girls to feel dissatisfied with their bodies. Body dissatisfaction can contribute to dieting, emotional problems, and eating disorders.

Data from adolescents and adults indicate that the tripartite influence model might be a useful way of explaining

Image 15.5 According to the tripartite influence model, social-cultural factors (peers, parents, media) can lead to the development of eating problems in girls. Girls who internalize the "thin ideal" may be at particular risk.

the potential influences of peers, parents, and the media on the emergence of dieting and eating pathology (Keery, van den Berg, & Thompson, 2004; Shroff & Thompson, 2006; van den Berg, Thompson, Brandon, & Coovert, 2002). Future research will likely be directed at examining the relative importance of these three social-cultural influences in girls of various ages. For example, older adolescents may be greatly influenced by peers, whereas younger adolescents may be influenced more heavily by parents.

Feminist Theories

Some authors have adopted a feminist perspective to explain the development of eating disorders in adolescent girls (Smolak & Murnen, 2004). Central to the feminist understanding of eating disorders is the notion of gender roles. **Gender role** refers to the degree to which girls adopt masculine and/or feminine behaviors and internalize these gender-relevant attributes into their sense of selves. Traditionally masculine characteristics include assertiveness, dominance, and leadership abilities. Traditionally feminine characteristics include nurturance, empathy, and compassion for others. Some evidence indicates that girls who adopt masculine gender roles may be at lower risk for eating disorders, whereas girls who endorse feminine characteristics may be at slightly greater risk (Smolak, 2005).

Other theorists claim that feminine gender roles place some girls at risk for eating disorders. Carol Gilligan (1982) argues that before puberty, girls are as assertive, outgoing, and self-confident as boys. However, during early adolescence, girls suppress some of their assertiveness and self-reliance, while boys maintain these personality characteristics. Gilligan asserts that this difference in social behavior reflects boys' and girls' different values during early adolescence. The primary developmental task facing adolescent boys is establishing a personal identity and sense of self. Boys accomplish this developmental task by trying out a variety of social roles and achieving a sense of autonomy, independent of parents and family. In contrast, adolescent girls value interpersonal relationships more than boys. When girls' bids for autonomy come into conflict with their desire for intimacy in interpersonal relationships, girls sacrifice their autonomy to maintain these relationships. Boys gain self-esteem and recognition from others because of their accomplishments. In contrast, girls gain self-esteem and approval from others when they deny their own wishes and conform to the expectations of others. Gilligan argues that adolescent girls suppress their autonomy and sense of self in order to please parents, family, and friends. She calls this suppression of autonomy a "loss of voice" (Image 15.6).

Eating disorders reflect girls' loss of voice in two ways. First, girls gain social approval when they lose weight and conform to society's expectations with regard to weight and body shape. Second, girls with eating disorders assume control over the only area of their lives that they can control: their bodies.

Image 15.6   In Shakespeare's *Hamlet*, Ophelia drowns herself after Hamlet spurns her love. Feminist theorists have argued that stereotypical gender roles place girls at risk for a wide range of mental health problems including eating disorders. Mary Pipher's book, *Reviving Ophelia: Saving the Selves of Adolescent Girls,* argues that teenage girls are victimized, lost, and unsure of themselves, like Ophelia.

Source: Painting of Ophelia by John William Waterhouse (1889).

Other feminist theorists have argued that the objectification of women and girls contributes to eating disorders (Fredrickson & Roberts, 1997). Advocates of **objectification theory** assert that Western culture values women primarily for their appearance and sexual identities. Advertising, popular music, television, movies, and other media convey the notion that women are sexual objects whose primary value is to gratify the needs of men. At an early age, girls learn that appearing attractive brings reinforcement from society, whereas appearing unattractive leads to social rejection. Girls develop body dissatisfaction and eating pathology when they internalize society's standards of beauty and come to see themselves primarily as sexual objects to be viewed by others. Their self-esteem becomes dependent on their ability to please others rather than on internal indicators of self-worth.

Although feminist theories for the etiology of eating disorders are popular, they have not been adequately tested. A few studies have provided limited support for the notion that gender roles influence the likelihood of eating disorders (Murnen & Smolak, 1998). On the other hand, Gilligan's (1982) hypothesis that adolescent girls suppress autonomy in order to gain social approval has not been consistently supported by empirical data. Furthermore, Gilligan's concept of loss of voice has not been adequately studied with adolescents (Smolak & Murnen, 2004).

Objectification theory is relatively new, but emerging data provide initial support for some of its claims (Smolak, 2005). For example, girls who compare themselves to models in fashion magazines report greater body dissatisfaction and more concern about their weight and appearance than girls who do not make such comparisons (Smolak, 2005). In contrast, girls who actively reject the portrayal of women in the media show greater body satisfaction than girls who internalize these standards of attractiveness (Murnen, Smolak, Mills, & Good, 2003). Objectification theory holds considerable promise as a way of explaining some aspects of eating disorders in adolescents.

Etiology of Binge Eating Disorder (BED)

Individuals with BED almost certainly inherit a genetic diathesis for the disorder. Twin studies indicate heritability for binge eating to be .39. Furthermore, the approximately 50% of adults with BED have a family member with obesity or BED. Unfortunately, no genetic markers have been consistently implicated for the disorder, although most evidence suggests abnormalities in the serotonin and dopamine transporter genes (Wonderlich et al., 2009).

Neuroimaging studies have also yielded mixed results, regarding the biological underpinnings of BED. Most research suggests that people with BED may be unusually sensitive to certain properties of food (e.g., color, smell, texture, taste) that make it more likely they will binge. For

example, two studies have shown hyperactivation of the frontal and prefrontal lobes when presented with appealing foods (e.g., foods high in carbohydrates, fats, and salt; Wonderlich et al., 2009).

Children with BED are usually overweight or obese. Longitudinal data indicate these children often have weight problems in childhood, before they begin bingeing. Furthermore, these children often have parents with weight problems and family members who make negative comments about their shape, weight, or eating habits. Furthermore, parents of children with BED often have strict rules about eating. They insist that children "clean their plate" at mealtime or severely restrict children's access to snacks or sweets. Longitudinal studies indicate that parental preoccupation with their own weight, their children's weight or shape, or their children's diet predicts the development of eating disorder behavior in children. For example, children whose parents severely restrict their access to snacks in kindergarten tend to overeat in later childhood (Fisher & Birch, 2002).

BED in children and adolescents is closely associated with depression and anxiety. Unlike adults with BED, youths with the disorder typically begin bingeing several years *before* they begin dieting. Children with BED are often alienated and teased by peers because of their weight or body shape. They are also more likely than children without BED to have negative childhood experiences or have parents with mental health problems (Marcus & Kalarchian, 2003).

It is likely that bingeing is negatively reinforced by the alleviation of anxiety, depression, worry, or boredom. Johnson, Cohen, and colleagues (2002) prospectively studied children from late childhood through early adulthood. They found that depression at baseline predicted bingeing in adolescence and adulthood. Similarly, Stice and colleagues (1998) followed a large sample of adolescent girls over time. They found that negative affect predicted the onset of bingeing but not purging. These findings suggest that youths with BED may binge to alleviate depression and negative affect.

Treatment

Inpatient Treatment for Anorexia Nervosa

Behavioral Treatment. Inpatient treatment for AN initially focuses on changing the adolescent's eating behavior, rather than on providing relief for the adolescent's emotional distress. The primary goal of treatment is to monitor the adolescent's physical health and to help her gain weight. Since rapid weight gain is dangerous to severely malnourished patients, physicians monitor the refeeding process. Typically, adolescents with AN are required to consume 1,500 calories per day for the first few days of inpatient treatment. Then, their target caloric intake is increased by about 500 calories every other day until the target reaches 3,500 calories daily (almost twice the amount of daily calories needed for weight maintenance). Consumption of 3,500 calories per day usually results in a gain of 2 to 4 lbs. per week (Linscheid & Butz, 2003).

Most adolescents with AN are resistant to inpatient treatment because they fear any weight gain, no matter how small. Rigid, black-or-white thinking leads these adolescents to believe that if they gain even one pound, they have lost all control over their eating behavior and are on the road to obesity. Furthermore, adolescents with AN often derive self-worth from their ability to control their weight. To these adolescents, gaining weight means a loss of identity and self-esteem.

To help girls gain weight, the treatment team administers a behavioral protocol that reinforces caloric intake and participation in the treatment program. Usually, this behavioral protocol is based on the notion that girls with AN are afraid of weight gain. In order to overcome this fear, they are required to consume a wide variety of foods during regularly scheduled mealtimes and avoid behaviors designed to limit weight gain (e.g., purging, excessive exercise).

Meal completion is positively reinforced by hospital staff. Upon entering treatment, adolescents are denied most of the privileges they enjoyed at home: watching television and reading magazines, taking telephone calls and visits from friends, and access to makeup, favorite clothes, and accessories. Adolescents can earn these privileges by eating meals and participating in other aspects of the treatment program.

Some inpatient programs require patients to remain in their beds until they meet certain caloric intake goals. For example, hospital staff might explain that if the patient does not consume enough calories, she might be too weak to leave her bed or socialize with others. Under these circumstances, meal completion is negatively reinforced, by allowing patients to escape the confine of their rooms.

Patients are also prohibited from engaging in compensatory behaviors to avoid weight gain. Initially, nursing staff monitors patients to ensure that they do not purge or engage in covert exercise.

Group Therapy. In most inpatient treatment programs, adolescents participate in group therapy (Guarda & Heinberg, 2004). Groups consist of adolescents who are new to the inpatient program as well as adolescents nearing completion. **Supportive confrontation** between patients is encouraged by the group therapist. In supportive confrontation, senior group members are encouraged to challenge the cognitive distortions and food obsessions of newer members. For example, a new group member who complains that the food she is forced to consume will make her fat might be challenged by the other group members to avoid "fat talk" during the session. Attempts to lose weight or outsmart staff are discouraged by the group and lead to peer rejection. The therapist uses peer pressure during the session to promote healthy eating in the same way peer pressure likely contributed to the adolescent's eating problems outside of treatment.

Group therapy is structured along several tasks designed to teach adolescents about eating disorders,

manage emotions and cope with low self-esteem, develop social skills, maintain a healthy diet, and recognize and challenge beliefs that lead to problematic eating behavior (Table 15.6). Individuals with eating disorders often show two types of cognitive distortions. First, many erroneously believe that their self-worth is directly associated with their weight. They think, "If it is good to be thin, then you are the best if you are the thinnest" (Linscheid & Butz, 2003, p. 645). The second distortion involves dichotomous (i.e., black-or-white) thinking. Specifically, they believe that if they start eating, they will be unable to stop (Linscheid & Butz, 2003). Therapists try to teach patients to recognize and critically evaluate these faulty beliefs.

There is little evidence supporting the efficacy of inpatient group therapy for AN. In fact, no randomized controlled trials of group therapy for adolescents with AN have been published. Some researchers believe that individuals with AN are too malnourished to fully participate in group therapy. For example, problems with concentration and problem solving, caused by malnourishment, can interfere with adolescents' abilities to recognize and critically evaluate cognitive distortions (Linscheid & Butz, 2003). Other researchers have suggested that group therapy might even be dangerous, especially if adolescents compete with other members in the group to lose weight or share weight-loss techniques (Maher, 1980).

Partial Hospitalization. Inpatient treatment lasts about three to four weeks; however, some adolescents participate in inpatient treatment for much less time, while other programs routinely keep patients 6 weeks or longer. Because inpatient treatment is expensive, many hospitals have developed day treatment or **partial hospitalization programs** for patients with eating disorders. After discharge from the hospital, adolescents continue to receive services from hospital staff, but spend evenings with their families in their own homes. Day treatment is a less restrictive and intense form of treatment than inpatient hospitalization, although adolescents spend almost their entire day in the day treatment program. Day treatment can help adolescents transition from the hospital to their homes.

Inpatient treatment programs are efficacious in increasing the weight of patients with AN (Guarda & Heinberg, 2004). Programs that adopt behavioral strategies, like the kinds described above, tend to lead to weight gain of approximately two to four pounds per week. Partial hospitalization programs have also been shown to be effective in helping individuals with AN gain weight. Weight gain tends to be slower than in traditional inpatient treatment, with patients averaging only 0.5 to 1.0 lbs. per week. Unfortunately, 30% to 50% of patients with AN who successfully gain weight, during inpatient treatment or partial hospitalization, relapse within one year (Pike, 1998). Consequently, most clinicians recommend that girls with AN participate in outpatient therapy after they are discharged from a hospital or day treatment program.

Table 15.6 Group Therapy for Adolescent Eating Disorders

Topic	Description
Psychoeducation	Provides adolescents with information about eating disorders
Behavioral recovery	Teaches adolescents to recognize and challenge cognitive distortions that lead to eating problems; promotes weight gain and healthy eating using supportive confrontation between group members
Relaxation training	Teaches adolescents relaxation and emotion-regulation skills, such as deep breathing, imagery, yoga, and meditation
Nutrition	Teaches adolescents about basic nutrition, the risks associated with dieting, and alternative ways to manage weight and consume healthy foods
Meal planning	Helps adolescents select balanced meals and healthy portions; teaches social skills while eating
Body image	Teaches adolescents to correct maladaptive beliefs about their bodies, to critically evaluate images of women's bodies on TV and in magazines
Self-esteem	Provides adolescents with assertiveness training and communication skills training to improve self-confidence
Family issues	Helps adolescents understand how family relationships can lead to healthy or problematic eating; allows adolescents to develop more healthy patterns of interaction with family
Relapse prevention	Teaches adolescents to recognize and avoid environmental events or mood states that trigger problematic eating; helps adolescents plan for their return to family and school

Source: Based on Guarda and Heinberg (2004).

Note: Most inpatient treatment programs for adolescents with eating disorders require patients to participate in group therapy. Patients in the Johns Hopkins Eating Disorders Program participate in three group sessions daily. Each session covers one of the topics listed above.

Family Therapy for Anorexia Nervosa

Structural Family Therapy. After adolescents with AN gain sufficient weight, most professionals recommend family therapy as the first line of psychosocial treatment. Although many kinds of family therapy are available, the most well-known and widely used approach is structural family therapy, developed by Salvador Minuchin.

Structural family therapy focuses primarily on the quality and patterns of relationships between family members. Therapists place little emphasis on the adolescent's eating behavior, per se. In fact, the adolescent's AN symptoms are believed to serve a diversionary function. As long as family members concentrate their energy and efforts on the adolescent's problematic eating, they do not have to focus on the real source of the problem: family relationships and communication. Family therapists see their "client" as the entire family system, not just the adolescent with the eating disorder.

Minuchin believed that adolescents with AN belong to highly controlling, overprotective families. He used the term **enmeshment** to describe family relationships in which boundaries between parents and children were blurred or diffuse. In enmeshed families, parents control too many aspects of their adolescents' lives and do not

allow adolescents to express developmentally appropriate levels of autonomy. For example, parents might place excessive demands on adolescents' choice of after-school activities, show a lack of respect for the adolescents' privacy, and insist on strict obedience to rigid family rules. At the same time, parents of adolescents with AN are overly concerned with the appearance of the family to others. Family members avoid conflict with one another, preferring to ignore family problems rather than discuss them openly. Minuchin believed that adolescents from enmeshed families develop AN as a means to assert autonomy over the only aspect of their lives that they are able to control: their bodies.

Structural family therapists have two main goals. First, they try to open lines of communication among family members. Specifically, therapists help family members realize how their adolescent's eating problems might distract them from other relationship problems in the family, such as a mother's excessive alcohol use or a father's tendency toward anger. Improved communication between family members, especially between parents, will decrease overall tension in the family that can contribute to the adolescent's eating problems.

Second, the therapist helps the family recognize the adolescent's emerging needs for autonomy and finding developmentally appropriate ways for her to show self-direction. For example, parents might agree to knock on their adolescent's bedroom door before entering, to avoid snooping through her room when she is not home or resist listening to her telephone calls without her knowledge. They might also give their daughter more freedom to select classes and extracurricular activities. At the same time, the therapist might help the adolescent express concerns to her parents in direct and mature ways in order to reduce family conflict.

Data on the efficacy of family therapy are extremely limited. Minuchin's idea that adolescents with AN come from highly controlling, enmeshed families has not been adequately tested. Furthermore, structural family therapy has not been adequately evaluated using randomized controlled trials. Uncontrolled trials of structural family therapy indicate that 66% to 86% of adolescents with AN show improvements in weight gain and menstruation following family treatment (Minuchin, Rosman, & Baker, 1978; Stierlin & Weber, 1989). Despite its popularity, more research is needed to establish structural family therapy as an efficacious treatment.

The Maudsley Hospital Approach. Although structural family therapy is a popular form of outpatient treatment for AN, another variant of family therapy developed at Maudsley Hospital in London has received considerably more empirical support. Indeed, several randomized controlled trials have been conducted investigating the Maudsley approach to treatment, making it the best studied family approach to treating AN (Lock, 2004).

On the surface, the Maudsley approach to family therapy is quite different from traditional structural family therapy. Initially, clinicians using the Maudsley approach target the adolescent's eating disorder symptoms, rather than communication patterns in the family. During the first phase of treatment, the therapist encourages parents to take control of their adolescent's eating behavior and develop a plan for helping her gain weight. The therapist is usually not concerned with the tactics parents use to take control of their adolescent's eating, so long as both parents work together. At the same time, the therapist blames the adolescent's weight loss on the eating disorder itself, not on the parents or family-related problems. The goal of the initial phase of treatment is to help parents feel empowered over the adolescent's eating and to allow the adolescent to gain weight.

Under the surface, the initial phase of the Maudsley approach resembles that of structural family therapy. Both schools of therapy require parents to solidify their relationship and communicate with each other. Structural family therapists make this goal explicit, by focusing on communication patterns between parents. Practitioners of the Maudsley approach keep this goal implicit, by encouraging parents to find ways to "refeed" their adolescent. Accomplishing the refeeding task requires parents to

open lines of communication and work together to solve a common problem.

In the second phase of the Maudsley approach, parents are encouraged to gradually shift responsibility for refeeding to their adolescent. Again, it is more important that families work out for themselves how to transfer this responsibility than it is for the therapist to tell families the "right way" to do it. Accomplishing this task requires families to give their adolescent progressively greater freedom and autonomy over her eating behavior.

The third phase of treatment begins when the adolescent has achieved sufficient weight and menstruation has returned. In this phase, treatment focuses less on the adolescent's eating behavior and more on the developing autonomy of the adolescent. Parents and adolescents work together to help adolescents negotiate rights and responsibilities within the family that satisfy all family members.

The Maudsley approach to family therapy takes approximately one year. Randomized controlled trials indicate that the Maudsley approach is efficacious in treating adolescents who show relatively recent onset of AN. Furthermore, the Maudsley approach is associated with more rapid weight gain than individual psychotherapy (Robin et al., 1999).

Outpatient Treatment for Bulimia Nervosa

Cognitive-Behavioral Therapy. Cognitive-behavioral therapy is one of the most frequently used outpatient treatments for BN (Guarda & Heinberg, 2004). Recall that cognitive-behavioral therapists conceptualize BN as reflecting a disturbance in mood, cognition, and eating (Fairburn, Cooper, & Safran, 2002; Pike et al., 2004). All three aspects of functioning (mood, cognitions, and eating behaviors) are interrelated. Adolescents initially diet to achieve a highly idealized and unattainable weight or shape. By acquiring this ideal body, they believe that they will overcome feelings of low self-worth. Unfortunately, dieting often leads to binge eating, which causes adolescents to feel guilty and out of control. Many adolescents engage in further dietary restriction to alleviate these negative feelings, but continued dieting produces only more negative emotions. Other adolescents purge to reduce fears of weight gain, but purging exacerbates guilt and low self-esteem. The bulimic cycle is maintained through negative reinforcement. Binges are negatively reinforced by temporary reductions in hunger, irritability, and fatigue brought on by severe dieting. Purging is negatively reinforced by temporary reductions in guilt and dysphoria brought on by binges.

The goal of CBT is to break this cycle of negative reinforcement by exposing girls to normal amounts of food and prohibiting them from purging or engaging in other maladaptive means of avoiding weight. Clients initially experience considerable discomfort ingesting food and

IDENTIFYING TRIGGERS FOR BINGEING AND PURGING

Therapist: OK. Now I'd like you to complete the following form with me about the times when you binge and the times you make yourself throw up. Tell me about situations that almost always cause you to binge.

Sara: Well, you know, I binge a lot when I'm alone in the house. Like, before my brother gets home from school and my parents get home from work.

Therapist: What do you mean by "a lot"? Do you mean all of the time?

Sara: No, maybe about half of the time. Maybe three or four times each week.

Therapist: OK. Then let's say that being home alone triggers a binge about 50% of the time. What kinds of situations or feelings *almost always* cause you to binge?

Sara: Feelings?

Therapist: Yes. Sometimes you might find that certain emotions cause you to binge.

Sara: Like, whenever I get into an argument with my boyfriend or I feel like he doesn't care about me or is angry with me.

Therapist: That almost always causes you to binge?

Sara: All of the time. I feel terrible inside, you know, depressed. And then I eat.

Therapist: OK. And in what sorts of situations do you *never* binge?

Sara: Well, I never binge when other people are around, like with my friends or family. I also never binge when I'm having fun with the other kids.

Therapist: OK. So you never binge when you're with other people, especially when you're having fun with friends?

Sara: Yeah.

Therapist: OK. So you see that certain situations and feelings often cause you to binge, like when you're alone or feeling depressed about your boyfriend. When you're in other situations or in a good mood, you never binge. Do you see how situations and feelings can affect your likelihood of bingeing?

Sara: Yeah.

Therapist: Also, do you see your bingeing is not completely out of control? After all, in some situations you never binge, right?

Sara: Yes. I guess I never thought about it that way.

avoiding weight loss strategies; over time, however, anxiety is gradually reduced and compensatory behaviors are no longer negatively reinforced.

CBT for bulimia is typically conducted in 20 weekly sessions (Wilson & Pike, 2001) and is divided into three phases. In the first phase, the therapist introduces the cognitive-behavioral model for BN and shows how the client's emotions, thoughts, and eating behaviors are closely connected. Early in treatment, the therapist asks the adolescent to identify situations or events that do and do not trigger bingeing or purging. Consider the dialogue in the text box above, Research to Practice: Identifying Triggers for Bingeing and Purging.

Another early goal is to increase the adolescent's motivation to change her eating behavior. Although adolescents with BN usually recognize that they have an eating disorder, they may be unwilling to give up purging because they fear becoming fat. The therapist might ask the adolescent to complete a cost-benefit analysis (Figure 15.6). First, the therapist might ask the adolescent to consider the positive and negative consequences of maintaining her present eating habits. A perceived benefit might be to lose weight, while a perceived cost might be feeling that she is out of control. Second, the therapist asks the adolescent to consider the benefits and costs of

Figure 15.6 Cost-Benefit Analysis of Bingeing and Purging

Continue Bingeing and Purging

Benefits
- I'll lose weight.
- I'll get compliments from friends, boyfriend.

Costs
- I feel guilty and out of control for bingeing.
- I feel guilty (disgusting) after purging.
- I don't like lying to my family.

Change Eating Behavior

Benefits
- I won't feel guilty about bingeing and purging.
- I might feel better about myself—more in control.

Costs
- I will gain a lot of weight.
- People might criticize me (parents) or make fun of me (friends) if I get heavy.

changing her eating habits. A possible benefit might be to feel less guilty about bingeing and purging. A potential drawback might be that she gains weight and is rejected by her boyfriend.

After the adolescent completes the cost-benefit analysis, the therapist asks the adolescent to critically evaluate perceived benefits of maintaining her present eating habits and perceived costs associated with reducing her bingeing and purging.

RESEARCH TO PRACTICE

THE COSTS AND BENEFITS OF PURGING

Therapist:	So, you said that you'd like to stop purging, but purging helps you lose weight. Is that right?
Becca:	Yeah. If I stop throwing up or exercising and stuff, I'll probably gain 50 lbs. like that.
Therapist:	Well, let's look at that belief for a minute. Right now you're bingeing and purging pretty frequently . . . usually once or twice a day. How much weight have you lost over the last month?
Becca:	Well, none. But I haven't gained any either.
Therapist:	So purging hasn't caused you to lose weight?
Becca:	No.
Therapist:	Well, let's look at the alternative. If you stopped purging, would you really gain 50 lbs "just like that"?
Becca:	Maybe not 50. Maybe 25.
Therapist:	If you gained 25 lbs., do you think your friends would reject you?
Becca:	I don't know. I worry about that.
Therapist:	Well, if your best friend, Marcie, gained that much weight, would you stop being her friend or tease her or do something else mean like that?
Becca:	Of course not.
Therapist:	So you wouldn't do that to Marcie, but she might do that to you?
Becca:	I guess not. I guess my real friends wouldn't do that to me even if I gained the weight.

THE A-B-C'S OF EATING PROBLEMS

Therapist: So you said that you binged a lot this week and felt totally out of control?

Heather: Yeah. I was doing real well, you know, on my diet. I went two days eating very little. Just some low-fat yogurt and steamed vegetables and stuff like that. Then, I was so hungry and feeling sort of bored, and I started to eat some potato chips. They tasted real good at first, but then I felt so guilty for breaking my diet. But I just couldn't stop, so I ate the whole bag, and I kept on eating until I was stuffed. That was Wednesday, when my parents were out. Afterward, I felt terrible, like a pig. I felt, you know, real dirty and bloated. So I threw up. That made me feel even worse because I had been so good lately, and then, I was hungry again.

Therapist: OK. So let's look at the situation a little more closely. You were hungry and bored, so you started eating the potato chips? That was the event that started the binge?

Heather: Yeah. Then, I just kept right on eating.

Therapist: Actually, something occurred in between. What was going through your mind when you started eating the chips?

Heather: I don't know... nothing.

Therapist: You said you felt so guilty for breaking your diet?

Heather: Yeah. I guess I thought, "Oh well, what the hell, I might as well eat the whole bag and pig out since I broke my diet."

Therapist: That's what I mean. Eating one potato chip didn't cause you to eat the whole bag and all the rest of the food. Your *thought* caused you to binge. You thought, "Well, I'm terrible for breaking my diet, so I might as well pig out." That's what caused you to binge.

Heather: I guess so.

Therapist: Well, if you had another thought at the time, a different thought, might you have acted differently? For example, if you'd thought, "Well, I ate a few chips and broke my diet a little, but I was really hungry. Maybe I should eat something healthy now," maybe you wouldn't have binged.

Heather: Yeah. Probably not.

The cost-benefit analysis often increases adolescents' willingness to participate in therapy. Adolescents can view the cycle of bingeing and purging as the cause of their emotional problem, not the solution.

In the second phase of treatment, therapy focuses primarily on identifying and challenging dysfunctional thoughts that contribute to the adolescent's eating disorder. Adolescents are taught that situations and events do not directly affect behavior. Instead, beliefs mediate the relationship between antecedent events and behavioral consequences. Many therapists teach adolescents the A-B-C approach to analyzing the relationship between antecedent events, beliefs, and emotional and behavioral consequences. Consider the dialogue in the text box above, Research to Practice: The A-B-C's of Eating Problems.

The therapist spends the majority of the second phase of treatment teaching adolescents to recognize and challenge distorted thoughts that lead to bingeing and purging. In the example above, Heather displays a common cognitive distortion called dichotomous thinking. She sees herself in black-and-white terms, either all good or all bad. Therefore, she believes that if she violates her diet, she is a terrible person who is out of control over her eating.

In the final phase of treatment, the therapist and client prepare for termination and plan for the possibility of relapse. Since relapse is common among individuals with BN, the therapist openly talks about the possibility that some time in the future, the adolescent might binge and purge. The therapist encourages the adolescent to anticipate high-risk situations that might trigger relapse. Then, the therapist and client develop strategies to manage those high-risk situations.

Several randomized controlled trials have demonstrated the efficacy of CBT in treating Bulimia (Pike et al., 2004). CBT is associated with reductions in bingeing, purging, dietary restraint, and concern over shape and weight. Furthermore, CBT has been shown to cause clinically meaningful reductions in these symptoms; after treatment, many adolescents no longer meet diagnostic criteria for BN (Lundgren, Danoff-Burg, & Anderson, 2004). CBT appears to be most effective in reducing dietary restraint and purging, while it is somewhat less effective in reducing the frequency of bingeing and general concerns about weight and shape (Figure 15.7).

Although CBT is currently the treatment of choice for adolescents with Bulimia, it is not a panacea (Agras, Crow

Figure 15.7 Effectiveness of CBT for Bulimia Nervosa

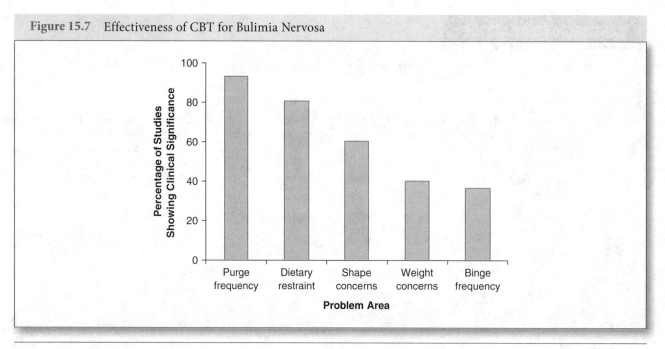

Source. Based on Lundgren et al. (2004).

Note: CBT is most effective in reducing purging and dietary restraint and least effective at reducing weight concerns and frequency of binges.

et al., 2000; Agras, Walsh, Fairburn, Wilson, & Kraemer, 2000). Approximately 20% to 30% of individuals who begin CBT withdraw before completion. Among those who complete CBT, 50% are not able to abstain from bingeing and purging after treatment. Finally, most studies have examined the efficacy of CBT with older adolescents and adults. More research is needed to confirm its utility with younger adolescents.

Interpersonal Therapy for BN. Although CBT is currently the treatment of choice for adolescents with BN, not all patients respond to CBT. An alternative treatment is interpersonal therapy (IPT). Interpersonal therapists focus on the number and quality of their client's relationships with others. While they do not necessarily believe that interpersonal problems *cause* eating disorders, therapists recognize that eating disorder symptoms are usually closely connected to adolescents' social functioning. Consequently, interpersonal therapists focus primarily on the adolescent's relationships with family members and friends, rather than on her eating disorder symptoms (Tantleff-Dunn, Cokee-LaRose, & Peterson, 2004).

IPT is based on the medical model of psychopathology; that is, clients are told that BN is a medical illness that is interfering with their physical, psychological, and social well-being. Adolescents are allowed to assume the sick role. They are not blamed for having an eating disorder, nor are their symptoms interpreted as indicators of personal weakness. Instead, symptoms are attributed to the medical illness.

The therapist initially teaches the adolescent about BN and demonstrates how interpersonal problems frequently coincide with (and sometimes elicit) maladaptive eating. Indeed, 75% of people with eating disorders experience a significant interpersonal stressor shortly before the onset of their eating problem (Schmidt, Tiller, Blanchard, Andrews, & Treasure, 1997). The therapist offers to help the adolescent improve the quality of her interpersonal relationships so that she might feel better about herself and correct her problematic eating habits.

Interpersonal therapists target one or two areas of interpersonal functioning that are associated with the adolescent's eating disorder. These problems can be loosely classified into four interpersonal problem areas: grief, role transitions, role disputes, and interpersonal deficits. First, some adolescents' symptoms are associated with grief, specifically, the death of a loved one or separation from a family member. For example, an adolescent might show severe depression and moderate symptoms of BN after her mother is sent overseas to serve in the army. In her mother's absence, she may have assumed many of the housekeeping and caregiving duties in the home and is generally not able to process the negative feelings associated with separation from her mother. An interpersonal therapist would help this adolescent grieve the loss (albeit temporary) of her mother's companionship.

Second, many eating disorder symptoms are associated with role transitions in the adolescent's life. Life-changing experiences, such as beginning a new school, moving to a new neighborhood, or coping with parental divorce, require adolescents to assume new roles. Often, these roles threaten the adolescent's self-esteem. For example, an adolescent who begins high school must abandon the old, comfortable roles that she played in junior high and create a new social niche. For some adolescents, this transition can be threatening. The interpersonal therapist helps the adolescent mourn the loss of her old social roles and embrace the challenges of her new surroundings. The therapist acts as a source of support as the adolescent begins to develop new areas of social competence.

Third, adolescent eating disorders are often associated with interpersonal role disputes. Role disputes usually occur when adolescents and their parents have mismatched expectations for each other's behaviors. For example, a 15-year-old adolescent might believe that she is old enough to start dating; however, her parents might believe that she should wait at least one more year and then only date boys with their approval. The adolescent might view herself as an emerging adult who deserves certain rights and responsibilities. Her parents, however, might still view the adolescent as a child who needs protection and guidance. Role disputes can lead to tension in the home, leaving the adolescent feeling misunderstood and unfairly treated. However, if role disputes are successfully resolved, they can lead to stronger parent-adolescent relationships. The interpersonal therapist's goal is to facilitate parent-adolescent communication so that both parties can achieve a greater understanding of each other's perspectives.

Fourth, eating disorders can be tied to adolescents' interpersonal deficits. Some adolescents lack adequate social skills to make and keep friends. Other adolescents are rejected by peers because they are socially withdrawn or disruptive. For example, an extremely shy adolescent might desperately want friends, but she might be unsure how to join peer groups. She might believe that if she were more attractive, she would gain social standing. Consequently, she might begin dieting and purging to lose weight. An interpersonal therapist might help her develop assertiveness skills so that she might feel more comfortable meeting peers and expanding her social network.

Preliminary evidence indicates that IPT is efficacious in reducing symptoms of BN, especially the frequency of bingeing and purging (Tantleff-Dunn et al., 2004). A large, randomized controlled study directly compared CBT and IPT (Agras, Walsh et al., 2000). In this study, 220 women and adolescent girls with BN received either CBT or IPT over the course of 20 weeks. Outcomes were assessed immediately after treatment and at one year follow-up. Immediately after treatment, clients who participated in CBT showed greater improvement than clients who participated in IPT. At follow-up, however, clients who participated in IPT continued to improve and showed comparable levels of functioning to clients who participated in CBT. These findings indicate that IPT may be a viable alternative for adolescents who do not respond to CBT (Figure 15.8).

Figure 15.8 Comparison of CBT and IPT in Treating Bulimia Nervosa

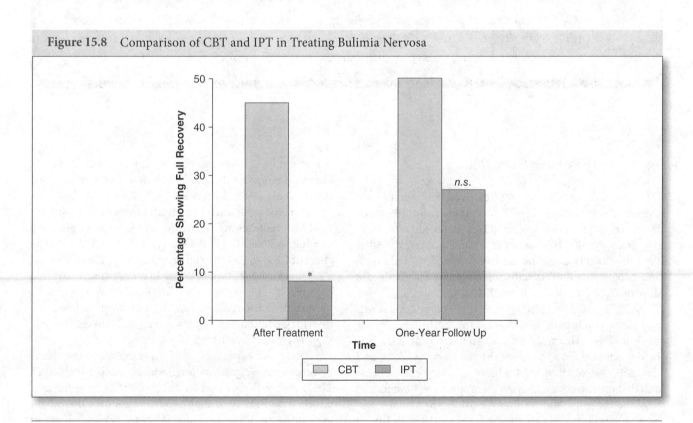

Source: Based on Wilson, Fairburn, Agras, Walsh, and Kraemer (2002).

Note: Immediately after treatment, more people improved after receiving CBT. One year later, people who received CBT and IPT showed similar outcomes.

*p < .05, n.s. = not significant.

IDENTIFYING ANTECEDENTS TO BED

Therapist:	So this week, for homework, you kept a record of the times you binged, where you were when you binged, and what you were doing and feeling. I'm really glad you followed through with this assignment.
Margo:	Yeah. I binged three times this week.
Therapist:	Did you see any patterns in your bingeing? Did you always binge at the same time every day?
Margo:	No, but I always binged in my room while I was using my computer. (Looks at notebook.) Once I was on Facebook. The other two times I was doing my homework.
Therapist:	And how were you feeling during those times?
Margo:	Depressed mostly. I was looking at an old friend's profile. We're not friends anymore because she was mean to me last year. I kind of missed her and was feeling pretty bad.
Therapist:	And the other times?
Margo:	I was feeling frustrated. You know I'm not very good at school, and I really didn't want to be working on homework. I just started eating and couldn't stop.
Therapist:	OK. So, this past week, you always binged in your room while on your computer or doing your homework. You also felt depressed or frustrated before you binged. How can you use that information to make a plan for *this* week?
Margo:	Well. I know I won't binge if I'm with someone else. I mean, I really can't binge if my mom or sister are around.
Therapist:	Can you bring your laptop to the kitchen table and work there?
Margo:	I guess so. It'll be a little distracting, but at least I won't binge. But there's not much I can do about my feelings.
Therapist:	Maybe you can make a promise to yourself: If you feel depressed or frustrated, you'll promise to leave your room and talk with someone about it. Do you have anyone to talk to?
Margo:	Yes. I've got two good friends. I guess I can try this plan for a week and see how it goes.

Psychotherapy for Binge Eating Disorder

Cognitive-Behavior Therapy for BED. Very few studies have examined the treatment of BED in children and adolescents. However, several evidence-based treatments for adult BED have been identified (Brownley et al., 2007). It is possible that these treatments might be modified for use with children and adolescents until specific interventions for youths are developed (Fairburn & Gowers, 2010).

CBT is the treatment of choice for older adolescents and young adults with BED (Vocks et al., 2010). Therapy for BED resembles treatment for BN. An initial goal of therapy is to teach clients to recognize the situations, feelings, and thoughts that often prompt a binge episode. Then, clients and therapists work on altering these antecedent events and negative thoughts and feelings. Consider the therapy session in the text box above, Research to Practice: Identifying Antecedents to BED.

Later sessions focus on identifying and challenging specific automatic thoughts about eating and body image that might elicit bingeing. Therapy can also include family sessions to improve the quality of parent-child interactions (Gorin et al., 2003; Grilo et al., 2005; Telch et al., 2001).

A recent meta-analysis indicates that cognitive-behavioral interventions are efficacious in reducing binge eating in adults with BED (Vocks et al., 2010; Figure 15.9). The effect of CBT on BED was large. On average, clients showed a 1.5 standard deviation decrease in binge eating compared to controls. Furthermore, medication (antidepressants in most studies) also reduced bingeing, but effects were smaller than for CBT. Combining CBT and medication yielded only slightly greater benefits than CBT alone.

Vocks and colleagues (2010) also examined the effects of behavioral weight loss programs on people with BED. These programs focus on weight loss, rather than the dysphoric mood states or maladaptive cognitions that might elicit bingeing. Overall, the effects of weight loss programs on BED were moderate and about one half the magnitude of the effects of CBT. This finding indicates that therapies for BED should address the psychosocial stressors, thoughts,

Figure 15.9 Cognitive-Behavior Therapy Can Reduce Binge Eating and Weight Concerns in People With BED

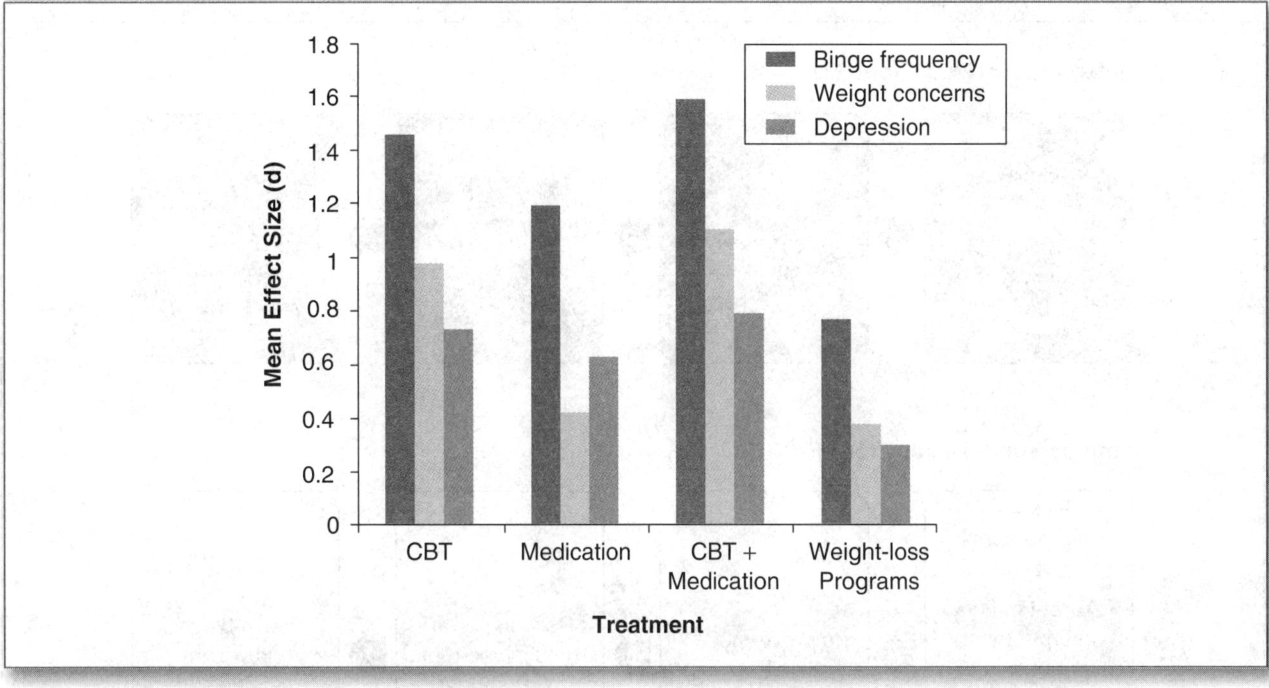

Source: Based on a meta-analysis by Vocks and colleagues (2010).

Note: Combining CBT with medication yields only slightly greater benefits than CBT alone. Weight-loss programs, those that do not target maladaptive thoughts and feelings, show lower effectiveness.

and feelings that precipitate bingeing, rather than focus on dietary habits alone (Wonderlich et al., 2009).

Interpersonal Therapy for BED. Because children's social-emotional functioning is so dependent on family members, interventions that target interpersonal relationships might be especially relevant to youths with BED. An alternative treatment for youths with BED is Interpersonal Therapy (IPT). Recall that IPT is based on the notion that interpersonal problems are often associated with people's depressive symptoms. IPT attempts to treat mood problems by identifying and alleviating the interpersonal problems that might underlie depression (Mufson et al., 2004; Young & Mufson, 2003).

Denise Wilfley and colleagues (1998) have adapted IPT to help children and adolescents with BED (Figure 15.10). IPT may be particularly useful for youths with BED because interpersonal problems, such as conflicts with parents or rejection by peers, are often closely related to their binge eating. These problems elicit depression and low self-esteem. In turn, youths may binge to temporarily alleviate these negative feelings. However, bingeing usually results in greater dysphoria over time and weight gain. If IPT can alleviate the interpersonal problems that contribute to dysphoria and low self-esteem, it may be helpful in reducing bingeing and weight gain.

At the core of IPT is the identification of the youth's interpersonal problems that might be associated with her low self-esteem and bingeing: (a) grief (e.g., loss or separation of a parent), (b) role disputes (e.g., arguments between parents and children), (c) role transitions (e.g., changing schools, parental divorce), and (d) interpersonal deficits (e.g., bullying, peer rejection). The therapist will help the child identify one interpersonal problem area for therapy. Then, therapist and client collaborate to solve the interpersonal problem and improve the client's mood and social functioning (Tanofsky-Kraff et al., 2007).

For example, a 12-year-old girl with BED might report frequent arguments with her mother. Specifically, her mother frequently nags her about her weight, poor school performance, and sloppy appearance. These arguments cause the girl to feel sad and tense at home. She uses food as a means to relax and gain a sense of satisfaction. An interpersonal therapist might conceptualize the girl's problem as a "role dispute" between herself and her mother. The goal of therapy might be to help the girl avoid arguments with her mother and, if arguments arise, to remain calm. Therapy might focus on improving the girl's communication skills. At first, the girl and therapist might role-play more effective ways to interact with her mother at home—ways to avoid yelling, screaming, and emotionally attacking each other. Later, the therapist

Figure 15.10 Interpersonal Therapy Identifies and Alleviates Interpersonal Problems That Contribute to Depression and Binge Eating

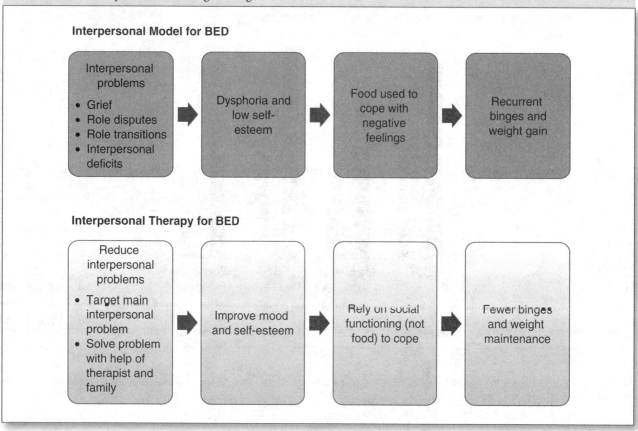

Source: Based on Tanofsky-Kraff and colleagues (2007).

Note: It may be especially useful for children and adolescents whose mood depends on relationships with family and friends.

might invite the girl's mother to join the sessions, to practice communication skills together.

Another child might be socially isolated from peers and teased because of his weight. He may have few friends and no hobbies or interests outside of school. His ostracism makes him feel lonely and depressed, and he often uses food to cope with these feelings. An interpersonal therapist might view the boy as having an "interpersonal deficit." The goal of therapy might be to help him overcome this deficit by learning how to make and keep friends. Initially, sessions might focus on basic social skills, such as how to introduce yourself to a peer group, how to join a game or activity that is already in progress, and how to respond to teasing. Later, with the help of parents, the child and therapist might identify ways the boy might be more involved in after-school activities, especially activities in which he might have relative strengths. For example, if he is a poor athlete but an excellent artist, he might take a drawing class rather than join the school basketball team.

IPT has been shown to be as effective as CBT in alleviating BED in adults. Furthermore, it is more effective than behavioral weight-loss programs at reducing bingeing. IPT seems to help clients by improving self-esteem and reducing dysphoria (Wilson et al., 2010). However, additional research is necessary to demonstrate its usefulness with children (Tanofsky-Kraff et al., 2007).

Medication

The first medications used to treat AN were conventional antipsychotics—medications that influenced the neurotransmitter dopamine. Clinicians reasoned that people with AN often had obsessions about their shape and weight that resembled the delusions of patients with psychotic disorders. Several randomized controlled trials of antipsychotic medications showed them to be ineffective. More recently, clinicians have used newer antipsychotic medications, which affect a wider range of neurotransmitters. Case studies indicate that these atypical antipsychotics may work for some patients, but there are not sufficient randomized controlled trials of these medications to support their widespread use (Flament, Furino, & Godart, 2005).

Antidepressant medications have been used to treat AN. Clinicians have speculated that antidepressant medications may be effective for three reasons. First, there is high comorbidity between eating disorders and depression; as many as 80% of individuals with eating disorders show significant mood problems (Lilenfeld et al., 1998). Second, many people believe low self-esteem and dysphoria underlie eating disorder symptoms. Decreasing dysphoria with medication might alleviate eating disorder symptoms. Third, serotonin is involved in both mood regulation and satiety. Antidepressant medications that affect serotonin might improve mood and eating.

Unfortunately, randomized controlled trials of tricyclic antidepressants and selective serotonin reuptake inhibitors (SSRIs) have shown them to be largely ineffective in treating anorexia. Both medications are generally equivalent to placebo in producing weight gain. One study indicates that the SSRI fluoxetine (Prozac) might be useful in preventing relapse after patients had already gained adequate weight (Kaye et al., 2001). However, another study suggests that patients treated with both SSRIs and psychotherapy showed poorer outcomes than patients treated with psychotherapy alone (Bergh, Eriksson, Lindberg, & Sodersten, 1996).

Consequently, medication is not regarded as a first-line treatment for AN (Flament et al., 2005).

Antidepressant medications have been shown to be effective in controlling BN (Flament et al., 2005). Two randomized controlled trials, involving more than 700 patients with BN, showed that fluoxetine (Prozac) was superior to placebo in reducing bingeing and purging (Fluoxetine Bulimia Nervosa Collaborative Study Group, 1992; Goldstein, Wilson, & Thompson, 1995). A second SSRI, fluvoxamine (Luvox), has been shown to prevent relapse in patients who have already recovered from BN (Fichter, Kruger, Rief, Holland, & Dohne, 1996). Unfortunately, the vast majority of patients treated with medication do not stop bingeing or purging. Approximately 75% to 80% of patients remain symptomatic even while taking the medication. Medication can reduce, but not eliminate, symptoms (Figure 15.11).

Furthermore, antidepressants should not replace psychotherapy for BN (Flament et al., 2005). Four randomized controlled studies that have compared CBT to antidepressant medication have found CBT to be superior to medication alone. Some recent data indicate that combining antidepressant medication with psychotherapy, especially CBT, may be slightly more efficacious than providing CBT alone (Bacaltchuk et al., 2000; Narash-Eisikovits, Dierberger, & Westen, 2002). Consequently, medication is probably used best as an adjunct to CBT or as a means to prevent relapse after treatment.

Figure 15.11 Effectiveness of Medication and Psychotherapy for Bulimia Nervosa

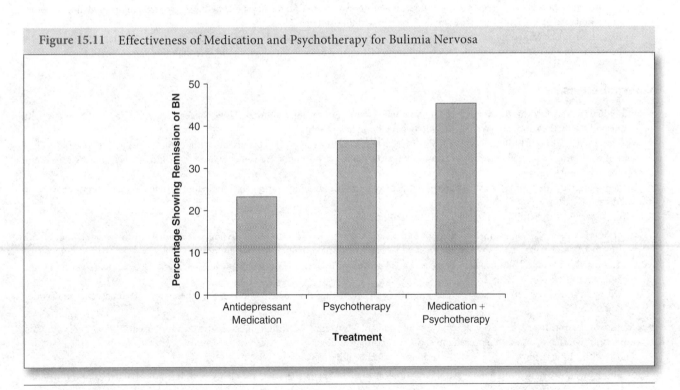

Source: Based on Bacaltchuk, Trefiglio, Oliveira, Hay, Lima, and Mari (2000).

Note: Combining SSRIs and psychotherapy (especially CBT) was slightly more effective in reducing BN than using therapy alone. Medication alone resulted in poorest outcomes.

Feeding Disorders

- Feeding disorders characterized by marked disturbances in the ingestion of food cause distress or adversely affect the child's health and development. They are usually seen in infants, toddlers, and young children as well as some youths with developmental disabilities.

  - Pica is the persistent ingestion of nonnutritive, nonfood substances (e.g., dirt, paper). It is often shown by youths with severe or profound Intellectual Disability.
  - Rumination Disorder involves the repeated regurgitation of stomach contents into the mouth. It occurs habitually and is not the result of a medical disorder.
  - Avoidant/Restrictive Food Intake Disorder (ARFID) is characterized by a lack of interest in eating, avoidance of certain foods, or concern about possible negative consequences of eating (e.g., choking, nausea).

    - Youths with infantile anorexia show little interest in eating. They are often inattentive at meals and resistant to parents' attempts to feed.
    - Youths with sensory food aversion refuse foods based on their physical properties (e.g., taste, temperature, texture).
    - Youths with posttraumatic feeding disorder avoid feeding because of a past stressful event associated with feeding.

- Approximately 1% to 2% of infants and toddlers have feeding disorders. Roughly two thirds of these infants and toddlers are classified as failure-to-thrive; that is, their weight is below the fifth percentile for age and gender.
- Treatment for Pica and Rumination Disorder usually involves operant conditioning.

  - Positive reinforcement is typically used as a first-line treatment. Differential reinforcement of incompatible behavior (DRI) and zero behavior (DRO) can increase appropriate eating behavior.
  - Punishment can be used, with the consent of parents, when positive reinforcement is ineffective. Techniques include overcorrection and facial screening.

- Treatment of ARFID also involves operant conditioning. In severe instances, treatment occurs in a pediatric hospital where children's health and nutrition can be monitored.

  - Appetite manipulation is used to increase children's desire to eat during therapeutic meals.
  - Contingency management is used to elicit appropriate eating behavior and decrease food refusal.
  - Escape extinction is critical to treatment. Children are not permitted to avoid or escape meals by engaging in tantrums or other undesired behaviors. Time out is used to decrease these undesired behaviors.
  - Parents are also trained to use contingency management, to generalize children's eating behavior to the home. Some parents also benefit from counseling to address social-emotional factors that affect their parent-child interactions (e.g., depression).

Eating Disorders

- Individuals with Anorexia Nervosa (AN) do not maintain normal body weight, show excessive concern over their body shape and weight, and usually deny the seriousness of their eating behavior and low weight.
- The essential feature of Bulimia Nervosa (BN) is recurrent binge eating and inappropriate compensatory behaviors to avoid weight gain. Binge eating occurs when a person consumes an unusually large amount of food in a discrete period of time, and she feels out of control while eating.
- Binge Eating Disorder (BED) is characterized by recurrent episodes of binge eating without inappropriate compensatory behaviors to avoid weight gain.
- Eating disorders can be differentiated by their symptoms.

  - Youths with AN show abnormally low weight. In contrast, youths with BN and BED do not have abnormally low weight. Youths with BN are often of average or above average weight. Youths with BED are often overweight or obese.
  - Youths with BN and BED engage in binge eating. However, youths with BN also engage in compensatory behaviors to avoid weight gain. Youths with BED do not.
  - Despite these distinctions, many youths migrate from one eating disorder to another over the course of adolescence and young adulthood.

- Youths with eating disorders are at risk for depression and anxiety. Depression often emerges after the onset of eating disorder symptoms. Anxiety and perfectionism often precede the onset of eating disorders.
- Youths with eating disorders are at risk for serious physical health problems.

  - Youths who restrict caloric intake are at risk for electrolyte imbalance, cardiac problems, and death. Prolonged caloric restriction can also lead to osteopenia.
  - Youths who binge and purge may also develop electrolyte imbalance and damage to their digestive track.
  - BED often causes obesity and associated health problems, such as diabetes.

- Children and adolescents with eating disorders often experience tense or tumultuous family relationships.

    - AN is associated with authoritarian parenting style and enmeshment in family interactions. Adolescents are usually given little autonomy in parent-child interactions.
    - BN is associated with poor family problem solving and high family conflict. Some families are disengaged.
    - BED is also associated with family conflict. Youths with BED often have a family history of weight problems or obesity.

- Between 0.5% and 1% of girls develop AN. Between 1.5% and 4% of girls develop BN. Prevalence of AN and BN is much lower in boys. As many as 2% of adolescent girls show subthreshold symptoms of AN, and 7% show subthreshold symptoms of BN. The prevalence of BED is approximately 2.5% in males and females.

- Eating disorders are seen across cultures. However, globalization seems to spread eating disorders to developing counties. In the United States, eating disorders are seen across all ethnicities and socioeconomic backgrounds.

- Onset of AN is typically in middle to late adolescence. Onset of BN is usually in late adolescence or early adulthood. BED can emerge in late childhood or adulthood. Childhood-onset BED is associated with much worse prognosis.

- Genetic, biological, and psychological factors are implicated as causes for eating disorders in adolescents.

    - Eating disorders are heritable. Heritability for AN is between 48% and 74%. Heritability for BN is between 59% and 83%.
    - Elevated serotonin may make certain individuals prone to psychological distress, anxiety, and perfectionism. Restrictive dieting can temporarily decrease serotonin levels, causing a reduction in negative affect. Some people with BN show low levels of a hormone called colycystikinen (CCK), which regulates appetite.
    - Women with BN are more likely to have been sexually abused than women without a current mental illness; however, history of sexual abuse is equally common among women with BN as it is among women with other psychiatric problems.
    - The cognitive-behavioral model for eating disorders posits that negative reinforcement maintains these problems. Binge eating reduces feelings of hunger (negative reinforcement) but produces guilt and anxiety about weight gain. Fasting and purging can alleviate guilt and fears of weight gain (negative reinforcement) but exacerbate feelings of low self-worth.

- Several social-cultural theories have been offered to explain eating disorders.

    - According to the dual pathway model, eating disorders develop through two pathways:

        - When girls are dissatisfied with their bodies, they may engage in dietary restriction to lose weight and achieve their ideal size and shape.
        - Dieting usually produces feelings of hunger, irritability, and fatigue.

    - According to the tripartite influence model, three social-cultural factors influence adolescent girls' eating behavior: peers, parents, and the media.

        - Peers can influence adolescent girls' eating when they place importance on weight and body shape, tease other girls about their weight or appearance, or diet themselves.
        - Parents affect a girl's eating behavior when they make comments about their own weight, shape, or appearance; when they diet; or when they criticize their daughter's appearance or urge her to lose weight.
        - The media can provide girls with maladaptive ideas about dieting, exercise, and weight loss.

    - Gilligan (1982) argues that before puberty, girls are as assertive, outgoing, and self-confident as boys; however, during early adolescence, girls suppress some of their assertiveness; lack of autonomy can contribute to eating problems.
    - Advocates of objectification theory assert that Western culture values women primarily for their appearance and sexual identities; girls develop body dissatisfaction and eating pathology when they internalize society's standards of beauty and come to see themselves primarily as sexual objects to be viewed by others.

- Inpatient treatment for AN initially focuses on changing the adolescent's eating behavior, rather than on providing relief for the adolescent's emotional distress.

    - The primary goal is to monitor the adolescent's physical health and to help her gain weight.
    - The treatment team administers a behavioral protocol that reinforces caloric intake and participation in the treatment program.
    - Adolescents participate in group therapy; supportive confrontation between patients may be encouraged by the group therapist.
    - Therapy often targets adolescents' cognitive distortions about eating.

- Structural family therapy focuses primarily on the quality and patterns of relationships between family members. Therapists have two main goals:

    - Open lines of communication among family members.
    - Help the family recognize the adolescent's emerging needs for autonomy and find developmentally appropriate ways for her to show self-direction.

- The Maudsley Hospital approach is an alternative treatment for AN.

    - During the first phase of treatment, the therapist encourages parents to take control of their adolescent's eating behavior and develop a plan for helping her gain weight.
    - In the second phase, parents gradually shift responsibility for refeeding to their adolescent; parents grant the adolescent greater freedom and autonomy.

- In the final phase of treatment, parents and adolescents work together to help adolescents negotiate rights and responsibilities within the family.

- A primary goal of CBT is to break the cycle of negative reinforcement that maintains BN.

  - Girls are exposed to normal amounts of food and prohibited from purging or engaging in other maladaptive means of avoiding weight.
  - Clients initially experience considerable discomfort ingesting food and avoiding weight loss strategies.
  - Over time, anxiety is gradually reduced and compensatory behaviors are no longer negatively reinforced.

- Another goal of CBT is to increase the adolescent's motivation to change her eating behavior; this is sometimes accomplished by conducting a cost-benefit analysis. CBT focuses primarily on identifying and challenging dysfunctional thoughts that contribute to the adolescent's eating disorder; adolescents learn to change their ways of thinking.

- Interpersonal therapists recognize that eating disorder symptoms are usually closely connected to adolescents' social functioning. Therapists help adolescents cope with four types of problems that might be associated with their symptoms:

  - Loss or separation of a loved one
  - Interpersonal role transitions
  - Interpersonal role disputes
  - Social skills deficits

- Antidepressant medications have been shown to be effective in reducing BN symptoms; however, 75% to 80% of patients remain symptomatic even while taking the medication. Antidepressants may also be helpful in reducing anxiety in depression as shown by many youths with BED.

KEY TERMS

AN-Binge Eating/Purging Type 587

AN-Restricting Type 587

appetite manipulation 580

authoritarian parenting 591

Avoidant/Restrictive Food Intake Disorder (ARFID) 576

binge eating 582

black-and-white thinking 589

cholecystokinin (CCK) 596

diagnostic migration 595

differential reinforcement of incompatible behavior (DRI) 580

differential reinforcement of zero behavior (DRO) 580

dual pathway model 597

early-onset BED 595

ego-dystonic 584

ego-syntonic 583

electrolyte imbalance 590

enmeshment 603

escape extinction 581

facial screening 580

failure to thrive (FTT) 580

gender role 600

hypokalemia 590

inappropriate compensatory behavior 583

late-onset BED 595

objectification theory 601

osteopenia 590

overcorrection 580

partial hospitalization programs 602

Pica (disorder) 575

refeeding syndrome 590

Rumination Disorder 576

structural family therapy 603

subjective binge 584

supportive confrontation 602

thin ideal 597

time out 581

transactional model for feeding disorders 578

CRITICAL THINKING EXERCISES

1. Behavior therapy is typically considered the treatment of choice to correct feeding disorders in infants and toddlers. Why might it also be important for a therapist to provide cognitive or supportive therapy to the *parents* of children with feeding disorders?

2. Is it possible for a 14-year-old girl who binges and purges to have AN? Is it possible for a 15-year-old girl to have BN but *never* purge?

3. How might the development of BED be different in children than in adults? What implications might this difference have on the way BED is treated in children?

4. Many people believe that girls develop eating disorders because of pressure placed on them by society and the media. What is the evidence that society and the media *cause* eating disorders in adolescent girls? Is there any evidence that genetic and biological factors also play some role in the development of eating disorders?

5. What role does (a) culture and (b) ethnicity play in the development of eating disorders among adolescent girls?

6. Ronnie is a 15-year-old girl with early signs of BN. In therapy, she explained to her counselor, "After I ate the pizza, ice cream, and soda, I felt disgusting—like I was an ugly slob with no self-control. I knew the other girls thought so too because they were watching me. So I went into the bathroom and threw it all up." If you were Ronnie's counselor, how might you challenge her ways of thinking?

EXTEND YOUR LEARNING

Videos, practice tests, flash cards, study guides, and links to online resources for this chapter are available to students online. Teachers also have access to lecture notes, PowerPoint presentations, suggestions for classroom activities, and possible exam questions. Visit: www .sagepub.com/weis2e.

CHAPTER 16

Health-Related Disorders and Pediatric Psychology

LEARNING OBJECTIVES

After reading this chapter, you should be able to answer these questions:

- What are elimination disorders? What are the most common causes of these disorders in children? How does their treatment involve physicians, therapists, and parents?

- What is Insomnia Disorder? How might the manifestation and causes of insomnia be different for (a) infants and toddlers, (b) school-aged children, and (c) adolescents?

- What evidence-based treatments are available for youths with Insomnia?

- What other sleep problems are commonly experienced by children and adolescents? How are these problems treated?

- What is pediatric psychology? What are some of the primary professional activities of pediatric psychologists who work in hospitals and clinics?

- How do pediatric psychologists work with medical professionals and families to help children experiencing chronic illnesses?

If you were to ask young parents to make a list of their main concerns regarding their toddlers or preschool-aged children, two items would likely be at the top: (a) toilet training and (b) sleeping. Although not glamorous, toilet training and "sleeping through the night" are two important developmental tasks that all young children must face and overcome. The way in which parents help their children reach these milestones, and children's ease in doing so, can greatly affect children's autonomy and self-efficacy and parents' competence and well-being.

Elimination (i.e., toileting) and sleep disorders have at least three features in common. First, they are both best conceptualized as disruptions in children's typical behavioral development. Over the first years of life, most children acquire bowel and bladder control and the ability to soothe themselves to sleep. However, elimination and sleep disorders reflect a fundamental delay or deviation from the typical developmental trajectory shown by most children. In some cases, children may have missed sensitive periods in their development to acquire these behavioral skills. For example, children who experience disruptions to family routines during the time that toilet training usually occurs may not acquire this skill in early childhood and may be resistant to learning later on. Treatment of these disorders, therefore, involves helping children acquire the skills possessed by typically developing peers and correct early developmental delays or deficits.

Second, children's ability to develop these skills depends on both their physiological and psychological functioning. Perhaps more than other childhood problems, elimination and sleep disorders illustrate the complex interrelationship between children's

618

physical and behavioral health. For example, many children with encopresis have chronic problems with constipation. However, treating constipation alone rarely solves their soiling problems. Instead, treatment typically involves both medication and techniques to teach children toileting skills (e.g., recognizing the "need to go") and overcome toileting problems (e.g., embarrassment, fear). Consequently, the assessment and treatment of these disorders almost always involves both medical and behavioral professionals.

Third, the development of children's elimination and sleeping skills occurs within the context of their relationships with caregivers. These disorders are probably best viewed as existing between parents and children rather than within children themselves. For example, many children have difficulty falling asleep. They may delay bedtime by asking for a drink of water, an additional story, or a trip to the bathroom. These sleep problems are often maintained by parents who intermittently reinforce their children for "stalling"—sometimes parents give in to their children's requests; at other times, they become upset and annoyed. These sleep problems, therefore, reflect a pattern of interaction between parents and children. Treatment, therefore, typically involves both members of the dyad (Owens & Burnham, 2009).

In this chapter, we will focus on the most common elimination and sleep disorders seen in infants, toddlers, and young children. Then, we will discuss the field of pediatric psychology, an area of clinical child psychology concerned with helping children cope with medical illness and injury. Throughout the chapter, pay attention to how children's problems reflect a deviation in typical development, the interaction between children's physical and psychological well-being, and the importance of parent-child interactions in treatment.

ELIMINATION DISORDERS
What Is Enuresis?

Typical and Atypical Development

On average, children attain daytime control of urination by age 2 and a half and nighttime continence by the end of age 3 (Houts, 2010). However, approximately 10 million children in the United States have difficulty with daytime or nighttime wetting and approximately 4% to 5% meet diagnostic criteria for enuresis (Shreeram, He, Kalaydjian, Brothers, & Merikangas, 2009). **Enuresis** is defined as the repeated voiding of urine into the bed or clothes in children aged 5 years or older (see Table 16.1, Elimination Disorders in Children). Voiding must occur at least twice a week for at least 3 consecutive months in order to meet diagnostic criteria. Furthermore, the voiding must not be caused by medications, such as diuretics or selective serotonin reuptake inhibitors (SSRIs), which are known to cause increased urination. Enuresis can be nocturnal (i.e., occurring only at night), diurnal (i.e., occurring only during the day), or both nocturnal and diurnal (Friman, 2008).

Although not part of the diagnostic criteria, most clinicians also specify whether enuresis is primary or secondary. *Primary enuresis* is seen in children who have never been able to stay dry during the night or day. *Secondary enuresis* is seen in children who had previously been toilet trained for at least 6 months and then began to show enuresis. Approximately 75% to 80% of children with enuresis show primary enuresis; the remainder show secondary enuresis (Friman, 2008).

The distinction between primary and secondary enuresis is important because it provides clinicians with clues regarding the cause and treatment of children's wetting. For example, whereas children with primary enuresis usually do

Table 16.1 Elimination Disorders in Children

Enuresis	Encopresis
Repeated voiding of urine into bed or clothes, whether involuntary or intentional	Repeated passage of feces into inappropriate places (e.g., clothing, floor), whether involuntary or intentional
Occurs either twice weekly for 3 months or causes distress/impairment	Occurs at least once per month for 3 months
Child is at least 5 years of age (of equivalent developmental level)	Child is at least 4 years of age (of equivalent developmental level)
Not attributable to a medication or medical condition	Not attributable to a medication (e.g., laxatives) or a medical condition except one causing constipation
Specify: Nocturnal only Diurnal only Nocturnal and diurnal	Specify: With constipation and overflow incontinence Without constipation and overflow incontinence

Source: Based on American Psychiatric Association (2013).

not have other behavior or emotional problems, children with secondary enuresis sometimes show ADHD and oppositional behavior (Butler, 2008). Furthermore, secondary enuresis sometimes follows a stressful event in children's lives, such as moving to a new home, the birth of a sibling, or parental separation. In one study, 81% of children experienced a stressful life event one month prior to the onset of secondary enuresis (Butler, 2008; Friman, 2008).

Experts have leveled three criticisms at the *DSM-5* conceptualization of enuresis (von Gontard, 2011). First, *DSM-5* makes no distinctions between the various types of enuresis (e.g., primary vs. secondary), despite etiology and treatment that sometimes differ across types. Second, some experts argue that the age requirement is arbitrary and that children younger than 5 should be treated for enuresis if it causes significant problems for families. Third, the frequency criterion (i.e., two times per week) ignores children who wet less frequently but who might respond to treatment. For example, a 4-year old boy who wets at preschool once per week poses problems for parents and teachers despite the fact that he meets neither the age nor frequency criteria for enuresis (Christophersen & Friman, 2010).

Epidemiology

About one in ten children experience occasional problems with daytime or nighttime wetting (Houts, 2010). In any given year, approximately 4.5% of children between the ages of 8 and 11 meet diagnostic criteria for enuresis. Enuresis is much more common among boys (6.2%) than girls (2.5%), perhaps because of delays in the maturation of the nervous and excretory systems of boys. As you might expect, the frequency of enuresis decreases with age. Whereas the prevalence of enuresis is 7.8% among 8-year olds, it drops to 3.8% among 9-year-olds and continues to decrease thereafter (Shreeram et al., 2009). Every year, approximately 15% of children will spontaneously recover from enuresis without any treatment, perhaps because of physical maturation. However, approximately 1% to 2% of adolescents and 1% of adults have enuresis, indicating that the disorder is persistent in some people (Brown et al., 2010; Butler, 2008; Mikkelsen, 2010).

Associated Problems

Early theories of enuresis were based on psychodynamic theory and suggested that enuresis reflected social-emotional disturbance. Recent, empirical research has not supported this hypothesis. Overall, children with and without enuresis do not differ in the number of social or emotional problems reported by parents and teachers (Erdogan et al., 2008). When children do show emotional problems, such as low self-esteem, it is typically a consequence rather than a cause of enuresis (Friman, 2008). For example, as children with enuresis grow older, their self-esteem and self-reported quality of life worsens (Ertan et al., 2009). Social-emotional problems are most likely to be present in girls, in youths with secondary enuresis, and in children who wet during the day (Mellon & Houts, 2007).

On the other hand, several studies indicate that enuresis is associated with ADHD (Ghanizadeh, 2010). Approximately 35% of children with enuresis also show significant ADHD symptoms, and children with ADHD are almost

3 times more likely to have enuresis than their unaffected peers. ADHD is most often seen in boys with daytime enuresis. New data indicate that problems with arousal underlie both disorders: Children with ADHD have difficulty with arousal and attention whereas children with enuresis often have difficulty recognizing and responding to indicators of a full bladder at night and during daytime activities (Butler, 2008; Elia et al., 2009; Shreeram et al., 2009).

Bed-wetting is stressful to all members of a family. Children often feel embarrassed or ashamed about their nighttime incontinence. Parents, too, may blame themselves or their children for their children's bed-wetting. Furthermore, bed-wetting can interfere with families' sleep cycles and lead to marital conflict. Enuresis places greater strain on families already experiencing psychosocial stress, such as single-parent families or families of low socioeconomic status (Houts, 2010).

Although parents do not cause enuresis, they can maintain or exacerbate children's bed-wetting in two ways. First, some parents attribute children's enuresis to laziness or defiance. Others believe that they have little control over their children's wetting and feel helpless as parents. Consequently, they may respond to their children's accidents in hostile and coercive ways, such as yelling, spanking, or inducing guilt (e.g., "Why do you make so much work for me, don't you care?"). Such attributions interfere with parents' abilities to effectively resolve children's enuresis. These thoughts also increase parent-child conflict and elicit stress and negative affect in the family (Friman, 2008; Mellon & Houts, 2007).

Sometimes, parents try to treat their children's enuresis in ways that are counterproductive (Butler, 2008; van Dommelen et al., 2009). For example, many parents allow younger children with nocturnal enuresis to wear diapers or Pull-Ups to bed. Because these underclothes absorb urine and keep children comfortable, these children usually do not learn to awaken when wet. Consequently, they never learn to detect feelings of a full bladder or inhibit bladder contractions to avoid wetting as typically developing children do. Other well-intentioned parents restrict children's fluids after dinner to decrease nighttime wetting. Although fluid restriction may reduce or delay wetting, it prohibits children from learning to recognize and respond to feelings of a full bladder. Finally, some parents engage in "lifting"; that is, when they discover a child has wet the bed, they lift or guide the child to the toilet and/or clean him or her without waking. Although lifting spares children embarrassment, it also prohibits them from learning to avoid nighttime wetting (Christophersen & Friman, 2010).

Causes of Nocturnal Enuresis

Approximately 85% of children with nocturnal enuresis show **monosymptomatic primary enuresis (MPE)**: They wet only at night, have never been able to stay dry *each* night for longer than 6 months, and have no known medical cause for their wetting (Houts, 2010). Children with MPE usually wet soon after falling asleep, void a normal amount of urine, and often do not wake up after urination. These children usually do not show other behavioral or emotional problems (Butler, 2008).

Most research points to four causes for MPE. First, MPE is highly heritable. Indeed, one of the best predictors of the age at which children will attain nighttime dryness is the age at which his or her parent accomplished the same feat as a child. If both parents have a history of enuresis, 77% of children will develop the disorder. In contrast, when one parent has a history of enuresis, the prevalence of enuresis in their children drops to 44%. Chromosomes 8, 12, 13, and 22 have been specifically implicated in placing children at risk for MPE (Friman, 2008; Mellon & Houts, 2007).

Second, approximately 20% of children with MPE show reduced secretion of **arginine vasopressin (AVP)**, a hormone that increases urine concentration and, thus, reduces its total volume. Low AVP secretion may cause nighttime urine production to exceed children's functional bladder capacity, leading children to wet the bed (Mellon & Houts, 2007).

Third, nearly all children with MPE have difficulty responding to signals of a full bladder during sleep. Although parents often describe these children as "deep sleepers," sleep studies indicate that MPE occurs at all stages of sleep, and children with MPE do not display atypical sleep patterns. However, most children with MPE do have problems with arousal from sleep. Arousal is important because it allows children to recognize their bladder is full so that they can (a) inhibit the flow of urine and/or (b) wake and use the toilet. However, children with MPE are often unaware that their bladder is full and may even remain asleep after wetting the bed (Houts, 2010).

Fourth, nearly all children with MPE have difficulty inhibiting urination during sleep. By age 4 and a half, most children learn to detect a full bladder and inhibit urination during sleep by contracting muscles of the pelvic floor. However, children with MPE typically do not actively inhibit nighttime urination and thus wet the bed. This lack of inhibition is probably caused by genetically influenced delays in physical maturation, increased urine production, a lack of awareness of a full bladder, and relatively few learning experiences that allow children to associate a full bladder with the contractions necessary to inhibit urination. The treatments for MPE involve helping children inhibit nighttime urination by recognizing sensations of a full bladder and associating these sensations with inhibition (Friman, 2008; Houts, 2010; Mellon & Houts, 2007).

Approximately 15% of children who wet at night have **polysymptomatic nocturnal enuresis (PSNE)**. In contrast to children with MPE, children with PSNE tend to wet throughout the night, void small amounts of urine, and wake after wetting. Children with PSNE also tend to wet during the day and often complain of frequent, sudden urges to wet.

PSNE is a complex disorder that can be caused by a wide range of biological and psychosocial factors. However, two factors are most common. First, approximately one third of children with PSNE have bladder instability; that is, they have uninhibited bladder contractions during the night, which prompt them to release urine. Second, some children with PSNE also have small functional bladder capacities; they are able to hold less urine before feeling the need for excretion. Consequently, children with PSNE often report "an urge to go" both during the day and at night (Brown, Antonuccio, et al., 2008b).

Causes of Daytime Wetting

The overall prevalence of daytime wetting (i.e., diurnal enuresis) is unknown. However, approximately 1% to 2% of children between the ages of 5 and 7 have frequent daytime accidents (Christophersen & Friman, 2010). Children engage in daytime wetting for different reasons. Most children who engage in daytime wetting have bladder instability (i.e., uninhibited bladder contractions) during the day and night. They experience a sudden, unexpected urge to urinate and typically show PSNE. Daytime wetting caused by bladder instability is more common in girls, is sometimes associated with medical problems, such as a urinary tract infection, and may be brought on by psychosocial stress.

Another reason for daytime wetting is **voiding postponement**. As most parents and teachers know, some children (mostly boys) have daytime accidents because they are engrossed in daily activities and are not aware that their bladder is full. Others are hyperactive and impulsive and may not take time to use the bathroom. Children who engage in voiding postponement are conspicuous; they urinate infrequently, engage in holding maneuvers (e.g., crossing their legs, fidgeting), and must be prompted by adults to use the toilet. Although many children have daytime accidents, children are classified as having daytime incontinence only when these accidents meet the frequency and duration criteria in *DSM-5* (Butler, 2008; Chrisophersen & Friman, 2010).

A very small number of children, mostly girls, engage in daytime wetting because they lack coordination of the muscles responsible for urination. These children contract (instead of relax) the external urethral sphincter muscles that permit urination. The result is that they strain to urinate, their flow of urination is often interrupted, and residual urine is often excreted after leaving the toilet (Butler, 2008).

Treatment

Treatment of Nocturnal Enuresis

Is enuresis a serious problem? Does it deserve treatment? Although most children with enuresis will eventually develop continence, recovery is often slow and stressful. Enuresis lowers children's self-esteem and quality of life, interferes with children's social activities (e.g., camps, sleepovers), and places great burden on parents. Furthermore, most children are able to significantly reduce daytime and/or nighttime wetting with

treatment, and treatment has been shown to lead to increases in children's self-esteem and social functioning. Still, many parents view enuresis as a condition that children will outgrow. Indeed, only 36% of children with enuresis in the United States receive treatment (Brown, Antonuccio, et al., 2008b; Shreeram et al., 2009).

The successful treatment of enuresis depends on collaboration between physicians, behavioral health professionals, and families (Mellon & Houts, 2007). Before treatment begins, children with enuresis should be assessed by their pediatrician to determine whether their wetting might be caused by a medical condition. For example, urinary tract infections, diabetes, and SSRIs are sometimes associated with enuresis in children. Constipation can also contribute to enuresis, as fecal matter may place pressure on the bladder. In very rare instances, children have anatomical abnormalities that contribute to their wetting. In 90% to 95% of cases, however, children's wetting is not attributable to medical causes and, consequently, a behavioral intervention is warranted (Campbell et al., 2009; Williams, Jackson, & Friman, 2007).

Behavioral interventions depend greatly on the resources and motivation of families. Therapists typically spend their first sessions with families assessing the nature of children's wetting as well as the family's ability and willingness to participate in behavioral treatment. Because behavioral treatments typically require time and energy on the part of parents and children (including lost sleep in the case of nocturnal enuresis), it is important for families to understand and commit to behavioral treatment. Often, therapists ask parents and children to sign a behavioral contract, that is, a written statement that describes what each family member is expected to do to participate in treatment (Stover, Dunlap, & Neff, 2008).

Behavioral Treatment. The treatment of choice for nocturnal enuresis is the use of a urine alarm (Brown, Antonuccio, et al., 2008b). A **urine alarm** is a small mechanical device worn in children's underpants in an area most likely to become wet during the night (Figure 16.1). The device is battery operated and connects to a small alarm that is clipped to the child's pajamas. When children wet, urine completes an electrical circuit in the mechanical device which triggers the alarm. The alarm typically wakes the child who becomes aware of his or her nighttime wetting (Friman, 2008; Shapira & Dahlen, 2010).

The urine alarm is believed to stop urination through classical conditioning. The alarm naturally startles the child, causing contraction of the muscles on the pelvic floor. This contraction inhibits urination. The classically conditioned response is maintained through negative reinforcement or avoidance learning. Over time, the child learns to avoid signaling the alarm by contracting the pelvic floor muscles when he or she senses a full bladder. Contraction during sleep delays urination until morning (Friman, 2008; Mellon & Houts, 2007).

Approximately 59% to 78% of children treated with a urine alarm stop bed-wetting in 8 to 14 weeks. Most children who do not improve do not wake to the alarm or eventually

Wireless Alarm Unit

Sensor

Note: The alarm wakes the child at the first detection of urine.

habituate to it (Houts, 2010). If a urine alarm alone is ineffective, clinicians may turn to full spectrum home training (FSHT; Mellon & Houts, 2007). FSHT has five components: (a) education and behavioral contracting, (b) urine alarm training, (c) cleanliness training, (d) retention control training, and (e) overlearning.

First, the therapist teaches families about the anatomy and physiology of nighttime urination. A behavior therapist will likely describe nocturnal enuresis as a problem in learning to associate a full bladder with the inhibition of urine flow during sleep. Treatment involves teaching the child to make this association by waking them using the alarm. Parents are told never to blame or scold their child for nighttime accidents but, rather, to acknowledge accidents in a matter-of-fact way: "Oh, you wet the bed. Let's get to work cleaning it up." Parents are also told to avoid restricting children's fluids or allowing them to use Pull-Ups at night—two strategies that can interfere with learning. Finally, the therapist asks family members to sign the Family Support Agreement, a behavioral contract that describes each family member's role in treatment.

Second, families begin using urine alarm training at home. Each night on a wall chart, families record whether the child remained dry, to monitor progress. The goal is for the child to stay dry for 14 consecutive nights. Each night the child remains dry, he is praised and receives a sticker or small reward. If the child wets and activates the alarm, the parents must make sure that the child immediately wakes and turns the alarm off. Once awake, the child is expected to go to the toilet and empty his bladder.

Third, after waking from the alarm, parents begin **cleanliness training** exercises. Depending on the child's age,

parents ask him to remove his bedding and pajamas and place them in the laundry area. Then, he is expected to put on fresh pajamas and bedding and reactivate the urine monitor before returning to bed. Responding to the alarm and engaging in cleanliness training may occur multiple times each night, depending on the frequency of the child's waking.

Fourth, children participate in **retention control training**. The purpose of retention control training is to increase the child's functional bladder capacity so that he can wait longer before urinating. During the day, parents ask the child to drink a large glass of water and refrain from using the toilet for 3 minutes. If he accomplishes this task, he is given a small reward. Each day, the duration for waiting is increased by 3 minutes until the child is able to delay urination for 45 minutes.

Fifth, after the child has remained dry for 24 consecutive nights, parents begin the overlearning procedure. **Overlearning** is designed to prevent relapse by giving children more practice associating full bladder sensations with the contractions needed to inhibit urination. Initially, parents ask the child to drink 4 ounces of water 15 minutes before bed and to refrain from wetting. If the child is able to accomplish this task, parents gradually increase the amount of water consumed prior to bedtime until the child is able to drink 8 to 10 ounces without night wetting.

Evaluations of multicomponent treatments, such as FSHT, for nocturnal enuresis indicate that they are slightly more effective at stopping nighttime wetting than using urine alarms alone (Table 16.2). However, multicomponent treatments are much better than urine alarm training alone at preventing relapse. Consequently, most therapists recommend including these components in treatment (Glazener et al., 2008; Houts, 2010).

Table 16.2	Urine Alarm Training Is the Most Effective Long-Term Treatment for Nocturnal Enuresis	
	Success Rate (Dry 14 Consecutive Nights)	
Treatment	Immediately After Treatment	One Year Later
Urine alarm only	59–78%	34–43%
Multicomponent treatment	64–86%	45–75%

Source: Based on Houts (2010).

Note: Supplementing it with cleanliness training, retention control training, and overlearning (e.g., multicomponent treatment) seems to reduce the likelihood of relapse.

Medication. Many physicians recommend medication for enuresis, either alone or in combination with behavioral interventions. However, medications are generally not regarded as long-term treatment options because they do not always reduce wetting and usually only work as long as children take them (Brown, Antonuccio, et al., 2008b).

Today, **desmopressin (DDAVP)** is the most commonly prescribed medication for nocturnal enuresis. It is a synthetic version of vasopressin, the hormone that reduces nighttime urine production. DDAVP is usually administered as a nasal spray or freeze-dried medication that melts in the mouth. Approximately 25% to 60% of children prescribed desmopressin stay dry shortly after taking the medication; however, only about 20% remain dry after discontinuing it. Desmopressin is also very expensive; consequently, it is typically used on a short-term basis (e.g., during a sleepover) or in treatment-resistant cases (Glazener & Evans, 2009; Mikkelsen, 2010).

Two other medications are less commonly used. Atomoxetine (Strattera), a selective norepinephrine inhibitor typically used to treat ADHD, has been prescribed for children with nocturnal enuresis. It is possible that atomoxetine increases arousal, allowing children to become more aware of full bladder sensations and thus inhibit nighttime urination. In a randomized controlled study, atomoxetine led to a small but significant reduction in nighttime wetting compared to placebo (Sumner, Schuh, Sutton, Lipetz, & Kelsey, 2006). Oxybutynin (Ditropan) is an antispasmic medication that is used to reduce the involuntary bladder contractions of children who engage in daytime wetting. Like DDAVP, however, oxybutynin is effective only when actively taken; relapse after discontinuation is 85% (Mellon & Houts, 2007).

Treatment for Daytime Wetting

Much less information is known about the etiology and treatment of daytime wetting. The underlying cause of most cases of diurnal enuresis is a lack of awareness of the sensations of an increasingly full bladder and the "urge to go" during daytime activities. Most children with diurnal enuresis are simply not cognizant of the fact that their bladder is full until it is too late. Even when parents and teachers prompt them to visit the bathroom because they are fidgeting, crossing their legs, or engaging in other "holding behaviors," they seem largely unaware that they need to urinate. Prolonged use of Pull-Ups seems to keep incontinence outside children's awareness and decrease their motivation to remain dry (Christophersen and Friman, 2010).

Treatment for daytime wetting, therefore, has three main components: (a) help children recognize feelings of a full bladder, (b) increase their control over pelvic floor muscles so that they can inhibit urination until they reach the toilet, and (c) increase their functional bladder capacity so that they can delay urination for longer periods of time.

To increase children's awareness of their need to urinate, most clinicians will recommend that children engage in scheduled bathroom breaks during the course of the day. Children who remain dry during a discrete time period (e.g., all morning) are reinforced for this accomplishment. If possible, scheduled toileting should occur at school. The child can also be given "bathroom passes" during the school day. To discourage their abuse, reinforcement may be awarded for unused passes at the end of the day. Some children may also wear a urine monitor during the day so that even small amounts of daytime urination cannot go unnoticed.

To strengthen the muscles of the pelvic floor, clinicians might teach children to practice **Kegel exercises,** that is, repeatedly stopping and starting the flow of urine during a toileting episode (Image 16.1). Kegel exercises, practiced at least three times a day, seem to increase children's ability to inhibit urination despite increased urges.

To increase functional bladder capacity, children may engage in retention control training. Retention control training may help children hold more urine before excretion, thereby, decreasing the frequency of urination. On weekends, some clinicians also suggest overlearning exercises, that is, asking children to drink progressively larger amounts of fluid during the day and avoid incontinence.

Empirical research supporting these interventions is limited (Christophersen & Friman, 2010). Daytime urine alarm training and Kegel exercises have been shown to decrease daytime wetting. Less is known about the other interventions.

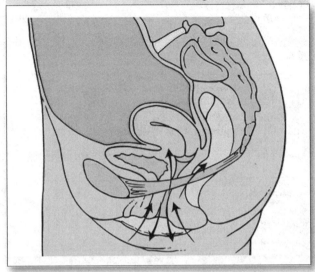

Image 16.1 Kegel exercises consist of repeatedly contracting and relaxing the muscles that form part of the pelvic floor, sometimes called the "Kegel muscles." Strengthening these muscles can help children reduce incontinence during the day.

What Is Encopresis?

Encopresis is the repeated passage of feces into inappropriate places, such as clothing or the floor. In most cases, the passage of feces is involuntary (e.g., children soil their clothes). However, some children's encopresis is intentional (e.g., defecating to upset parents). By definition, children must defecate inappropriately at least once a month for at least 3 months. Furthermore, they must be at least 4 years old. By definition, encopresis cannot be caused by a medication that typically causes incontinence, such as a laxative. Furthermore, it cannot be caused by a medical disorder, such as a bacterial or viral illness, that might result in accidents.

Although not part of the *DSM-5* diagnostic system, many clinicians differentiate primary encopresis from secondary encopresis. *Primary encopresis* is seen in children who have no history of controlling bowel movements. In contrast, *secondary encopresis* is characterized by the emergence of encopresis following a period of normal toilet use. It is important to determine the degree of volition and course of a child's encopresis, because this information can provide the clinician with clues regarding its cause and treatment. For example, a child with primary encopresis who has accidents during the day might benefit from systematic toilet training. In contrast, a child with secondary encopresis who deliberately defecates in his baby sister's crib might benefit from an intervention designed to address sibling rivalry or family stress.

Epidemiology

Approximately 3% of school-aged children in the United States meet diagnostic criteria for encopresis (Friman, 2008).

Approximately 1.4% of 7-year-old children soil once a week, whereas 6.8% soil only occasionally (von Gontard, 2011). Boys are 4 to 6 times more likely than girls to develop the disorder (Campbell et al., 2009).

Associated Problems

Studies investigating the psychosocial functioning of children with encopresis have yielded mixed results. Some research indicates that these children are more likely to have behavioral or social-emotional problems than their peers without encopresis (Friman et al., 2009). Children with primary encopresis sometimes report less satisfying social relationships, greater sadness, and more anxiety that is related to separation and social activities. Children with secondary encopresis and/or those who engage in deliberate defecation sometimes have problems with oppositional and defiant behavior and a recent history of psychosocial stressors. All children with encopresis are at risk for low self-esteem and social problems, given the negative reactions that their actions elicit from family and peers (Friman et al., 2009).

Approximately 30% of children with encopresis also show enuresis. Often, both disorders are caused by an enlarged colon, a result of prolonged constipation. The enlarged colon places pressure on the bladder which contributes to wetting (Campbell et al., 2009).

Etiology

In 80% to 95% of cases, encopresis is caused by constipation and overflow incontinence (Figure 16.2; Butler, 2008; Friman, 2008). Constipation usually develops because children do not defecate for a prolonged period of time. The reasons for delayed defecation are many: Children may be distracted by other activities (e.g., games, sports), children may not have easy access to a toilet (e.g., at school), children's diet may be restricted or irregular (e.g., too little fiber), or children may be experiencing periods of prolonged stress (e.g., moving). Oppositional and defiant children may simply refuse to use the toilet. Other children may feel embarrassed, ashamed, or unusually vulnerable when toileting. Still other children may experience discomfort or pain during a bowel movement and may subsequently avoid using the toilet (Friman, 2008).

Whatever the reason, fecal matter is retained in the anal canal, and the rectal wall is stretched to accommodate this mass (Figure 16.2). Retention has two consequences: (a) The rectum becomes enlarged, and (b) the nerves that line the rectum and allow the child to detect when it is full become less sensitive. Despite accumulating fecal matter in the canal, children gradually lose the normal sensation that they need to expel its contents.

Over time, water in the fecal mass is reabsorbed by the body. The mass becomes rock-like and difficult to pass. Through classical conditioning, the child quickly associates bowel movements with pain, increasing his avoidance of the toilet (Williams et al., 2007).

Figure 16.2 Encopresis Is Usually Caused by Constipation With Overflow

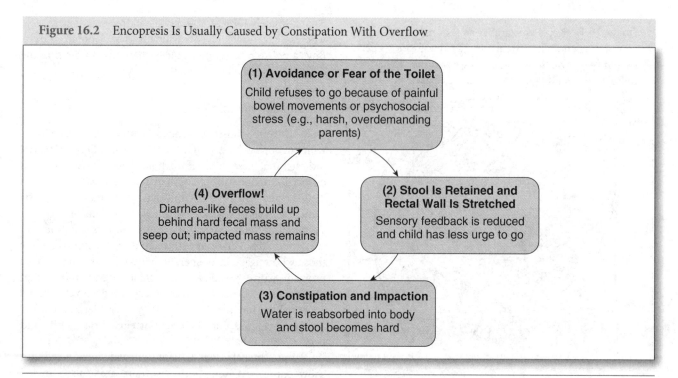

(1) Avoidance or Fear of the Toilet
Child refuses to go because of painful bowel movements or psychosocial stress (e.g., harsh, overdemanding parents)

(4) Overflow!
Diarrhea-like feces build up behind hard fecal mass and seep out; impacted mass remains

(2) Stool Is Retained and Rectal Wall Is Stretched
Sensory feedback is reduced and child has less urge to go

(3) Constipation and Impaction
Water is reabsorbed into body and stool becomes hard

Source: Based on Butler (2008).

Note: Treatment involves relieving constipation and teaching children to use the toilet regularly.

Image 16.2 The cause of encopresis is usually constipation. This image shows hardened fecal material in the large bowel and rectum. The material (seen as opaque white surrounded by black air) will make a regular bowel movement difficult. Eventually, seepage will occur around the mass resulting in soiling.

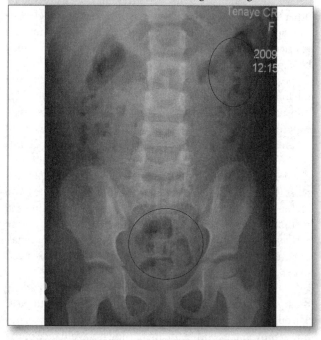

Source: Photo courtesy of James Heilman.

As new fecal matter continues to accumulate behind the fecal mass, it unexpectedly seeps around the mass, soiling the child's clothes. This new fecal matter usually resembles diarrhea. Consequently, many parents mistakenly administer anti-diarrhea medication which exacerbates the child's constipation (Friman et al., 2009).

As you can see, children who show constipation with overflow incontinence have little control over their encopresis. However, because they seldom complain of constipation, many parents misattribute this problem to stubbornness, laziness, or defiance. Punitive discipline almost always increases children's frustration and decreases the likelihood that children will cooperate with parents to resolve the problem (Butler, 2008).

Approximately 15% of children with encopresis do not have constipation. Most of these children have primary non-retentive encopresis; they have never achieved bowel control and often have accidents in their clothing. These children are often developmentally disabled or have neurological conditions that interfere with their ability to use the toilet. A few children, however, show secondary, non-retentive encopresis; they have bowel control but deliberately defecate in inappropriate places. These children are predominantly boys with histories of oppositional-defiant behavior. However, some children develop encopresis following major life events, such as parental separation, hospitalization, or sexual abuse. Although sexual abuse is a possible cause of encopresis, children are more likely to have encopresis for other reasons. Encopresis is not routinely an indicator of sexual victimization (Butler, 2008; Friman, 2008).

EXPLAINING ENCOPRESIS TO FAMILIES

Therapist:	So, over time, Brad's colon has become enlarged and distended—it's much bigger and more stretchy than it should be. Also, the nerves surrounding it don't work right—they don't tell the brain when it's full. The result is that Brad can't tell when he needs to go.
Mom:	So, it's not his fault when he goes in his underwear?
Therapist:	No. He probably doesn't even know until it happens. Right?
Brad:	(Nods)
Therapist:	So, rewarding Brad for staying clean all day or punishing him for having an accident won't do any good. Neither will making him feel bad about the accident. Instead, we need to get his colon back into shape. Right now, it's like an out-of-shape, soft, flabby athlete who can't perform very well. We need Brad to train his colon to get back into shape so it can perform at the top of its game. He can do that by doing some exercises every day. You (mom) can help him.

Treatment

Treating encopresis caused by constipation involves collaboration among physicians, therapists, and families. Before treatment begins, the child should be evaluated by his pediatrician to rule out the possibility that his encopresis is caused by one of several rare medical disorders. For example, Hirschsprung's disease is a rare condition in which the nerves that control the muscles that line the colon wall are absent, causing a lack of sensory input (Williams et al., 2007). The pediatrician can also determine whether the child is suffering from constipation and, if so, prescribe a laxative or enema to relieve this condition. After the child's colon is cleaned, the physician will likely recommend a mild laxative (e.g., Miralax) for daily use to soften stools, increase motility in his digestive system, and decrease the likelihood of constipation in the future (Campbell et al., 2009).

Behavior therapy usually begins with an explanation of the causes of encopresis, specifically, constipation with overflow. Then, the therapist provides the rationale for the interventions (see Research to Practice: Explaining Encopresis to Families).

To get the child's "colon into shape," the therapist will likely recommend dietary changes that include increased fiber (e.g., fruits, vegetables, whole grains), decreased dairy, and plenty of water.

Then, the child will be required to participate in scheduled toilet sitting. Approximately 15 to 20 minutes after breakfast and dinner, the child will be required to sit on the toilet for no more than 5 to 10 minutes with the intention to defecate. Parents should provide privacy and make the bathroom inviting to the child, perhaps by allowing him to read books or listen to music. It is also important for the toilet to be the correct size for the child and to have the child's feet supported to increase comfort.

To increase compliance with scheduled toileting, parents may provide small rewards for each successful time the child sits and larger rewards for successful defecation (Boles et al., 2010). To discourage soiling, parents may use cleanliness training and response cost. Cleanliness training requires the child to clean up after soiling (e.g., removing clothes and placing them in laundry area). Response cost involves withdrawing a reinforcer (e.g., reward, token) following an accident. Parents may also engage in positive practice following an accident, to emphasize appropriate toilet sitting. For example, parents might require children to practice running to the toilet and sitting down numerous times (Friman et al., 2009).

Several randomized controlled studies indicate that combining behavioral treatments, like scheduled toilet sitting and positive reinforcement with laxative therapy, is effective at reducing encopresis caused by constipation. Furthermore, behavioral interventions used in combination with laxatives often reduce encopresis more than laxative therapy alone (Brazzelli et al., 2011).

Treatment for non-retentive encopresis (i.e., not caused by constipation), depends on the cause of the disorder. Children with primary non-retentive encopresis will usually benefit from toilet training. Recall that many children who show this type of encopresis have developmental delays; consequently, the therapist must make sure that they have the cognitive ability to follow multiple-step commands necessary to successfully use the toilet (e.g., sit, wipe, wash). Children with secondary non-retentive encopresis should receive interventions that address possible causes of their soiling, before treating the encopresis itself. For example, oppositional-defiant children, fearful children, or sexually abused children should receive treatment specific to these problems (Friman, 2008).

SLEEP DISORDERS IN CHILDREN

Although sleep is a natural process, the ability to fall asleep independently, stay asleep during the course of the night, and gain enough sleep to feel rested are skills that children must develop over the first few years of life (Crabtree & Williams, 2009). The development of these skills depends greatly on the maturation of their nervous system, their temperament and behavior, and their parent's ability to foster healthy sleeping habits. Typically developing children show changes in their sleeping behavior and their **sleep architecture** (i.e., central nervous system activity) from birth through adolescence (Owens & Burnham, 2009). As children's sleep patterns and architecture develop, they may develop different types of sleep problems (Table 16.3).

Sleep disorders are identified using several methods. Usually, children's sleep problems are assessed through parental report. Psychologists may interview families about children's sleep habits, quality, and environment (Leu & Rosen, 2008). To screen for possible sleep disorders, some professionals use the mnemonic BEARS:

- Are there **bedtime difficulties** or problems going to sleep?
- Does the child seem **excessively sleepy** during the day?
- Does the child **awaken during the night** and can't go back to sleep?
- Does the child have a **regular sleep-wake schedule**?
- Does the child **snore** or have trouble breathing during sleep?

Parents may also complete a sleep log or diary to more accurately record children's sleeping and waking. To obtain

Table 16.3 Sleep Behavior, Architecture, and Possible Problems Across Development

Age	Behavior	Architecture	Possible Problems
Newborn	Sleeps in 3–4 hour segments spread evenly across a 34–hour period; sleeps 16–18 hours/day	Enters REM after falling asleep; most sleep is spent in REM; other stages are indistinct	Depends on parents to fall asleep and return to sleep, but this is considered normal
2–4 months	At 3 months, infants become entrained to a 24 hour sleep-wake cycle; they can sleep more during the night than day; they can self-soothe and return to sleep if awakened during the night	Infants begin entering non-REM after falling asleep; less time is spent in REM	Infants may have problems falling asleep without parent's help
6–12 months	By 9 months, most children sleep through the night (6–7 hours); total sleep is 14–15 hours with 2–3 daytime naps	By 6 months, infants have circadian rhythm that remains stable until puberty; non-REM stages are distinct (like adults)	Infants may have problems falling asleep or returning to sleep without parent's help; night wakings or problems "sleeping through the night"
1–2 years	Total sleep is 12–14 hours with one daytime nap	REM declines to 30% of child's total sleep time by age 3 years	Child shows separation anxiety; may refuse separations at bedtime
3–5 years	Total sleep is 11–12 hours; napping stops in 75% of children by age 5 years	Sleep cycle increases to 90 minutes (like adults)	Cognitive development makes nighttime fears common; children may refuse going to bed; arousal disorders may occur; some children show sleep apnea
6–12 years	Children require 10–11 hours of sleep but usually do not get enough; sleep latency (time till sleep) is about 20 minutes	By late childhood, most children show adult-like sleep cycle	Children may stall or refuse to go to bed; some children show insomnia due to anxiety
12–18 years	Adolescents need 9–11 hours of sleep but usually do not get enough; delay in circadian rhythm causes a desire to stay up late and rise later in the day	With puberty, adolescents show phase delay in melatonin which delays circadian rhythm	Adolescents may show anxiety-related insomnia; school and other activities encroach on sleep time causing daytime sleepiness

Source: Adapted from Owens and Burnham (2009) and Reite, Weissberg, and Ruddy (2009).

a more objective estimate of children's sleep duration and quality, children may wear an actometer. This small device attaches to the infant's leg or child's arm and provides a reliable and accurate measure of nighttime activity. The "gold standard" for assessing sleep is a **polysomnogram (PSG)** or "sleep study" (Crabtree & Williams, 2009). To perform a PSG, children must spend the night in the hospital while their sleep is monitored (Image 16.3). Brain activity (EEG), eye movements (EOG), muscle activation (EMG), and heart rhythm (ECG) are assessed. A PSG can assess sleep duration and quality, detect abnormalities in sleep architecture, and identify breathing-related sleep problems (Luginbuehl & Kohler, 2009; Wickwire, Roland, Elkin, & Schumacher, 2008).

Sleep disorders can cause distress and impairment in children (O'Brien, 2009). Adolescents with sleep disorders may exhibit the same signs and symptoms as adults (e.g., yawning, drowsiness). Most children, however, show paradoxical symptoms such as over-activity, impulsiveness, and irritability. Sleep problems are associated with attention, concentration, and higher order problem-solving problems. Not surprisingly, youths with sleep problems sometimes experience behavioral and academic difficulties in school (Paavonen et al., 2009; Sadeh, 2007).

Sleep disorders can be equally disruptive to parents. The caregivers of children with sleep disorders often report many of the same symptoms as their children: daytime drowsiness and fatigue, concentration problems, irritability, and dysphoria. Parenting a child with sleep problems can be extremely stressful, especially when parents are plagued by other psychosocial hardships (e.g., marital discord, single-parent status, irregular work schedules). The relationship between children's sleep problems and parental distress is also bidirectional: Children's problems cause, and are exacerbated by, parenting stress (Owens, 2007).

Approximately 25% of children experience some type of sleep problem at some point in their development (Owens, 2007). *DSM-5* recognizes 20 sleep-wake disorders. We will focus on five disorders most frequently seen in children: Insomnia Disorder, Circadian Rhythm Sleep Disorder, Sleep Arousal Disorders, Nightmare Disorder, and Obstructive Sleep Apnea Hypopnea (Figure 16.3).

What Is Insomnia Disorder?

Insomnia Disorder is, by far, the most common sleep problem experienced by youths. It is defined by dissatisfaction with the quantity or quality of sleep (Table 16.4, Diagnostic Criteria for Insomnia Disorder). It is noteworthy that dissatisfaction can be reported by either the child or his or her parents. Because infants and younger children typically do not report sleep problems, the diagnosis of insomnia depends on the degree to which children's sleep problems affect parents. Two children might show the same problems with bedtime refusal or nighttime waking; however, only one child (whose parent is upset by her child's sleep habits) might be diagnosed (Rabian & Bottjer, 2008).

Insomnia manifests itself differently, depending on the age and development of the child. Infants and toddlers typically have problems going to sleep and returning to sleep when they awaken during the night. Preschoolers and school-aged children may stall during bedtime or refuse to go to bed. Older children and adolescents may have difficulty with anxiety, which interferes with their ability to sleep (Reid, Huntley, & Lewin, 2009).

Sleep problems must occur at least 3 nights per week. Furthermore, the sleep problem should persist for at least 3 months to qualify for "persistent" Insomnia. Sleep problems of shorter duration are labeled as either "acute" (< 1 month) or "subacute" (1–3 months).

Adults with insomnia typically report daytime fatigue and sleepiness. They may yawn, mope, or complain of low energy. Insomnia in children typically has paradoxical effects: Children are often hyperactive, talkative, or impulsive. On the other hand, the parents of children with insomnia typically do report considerable daytime fatigue because of their children's sleep habits. Youths with insomnia also frequently show impairments in cognition (e.g., attention, concentration), academic achievement (e.g., schoolwork), and mood (e.g., dysphoria, irritability). Many of these effects of insomnia mimic psychiatric disorders, such as ADHD, conduct problems, and depression.

Epidemiology

Sleep problems are common among children. Approximately 25% to 50% of parents report at least occasional problems with their children's sleep habits. Approximately 30% of youths will

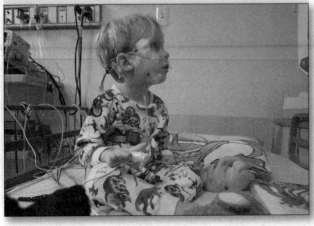

Image 16.3   This boy is preparing for a sleep study to determine the cause of his sleep problems. Polysomnography will measure his brain activity (EEG), eye movements (EOG), muscle activity or skeletal muscle activation (EMG), heart rhythm (ECG), and respiration during sleep.

Source: Photo courtesy of Robert Lawton.

Figure 16.3 Sleep Architecture in a Typically Developing Child

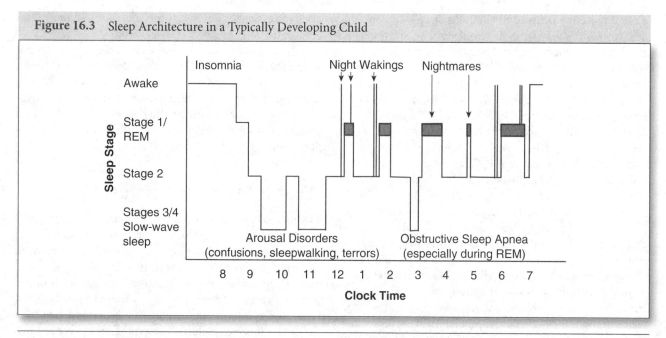

Source: Adapted from Leu & Rosen (2008).

Note: The sleep cycle (relaxed awake, non-REM, REM) repeats throughout the night with periodical night waking and returning to sleep. Possible sleep disorders by title describe where cyclic disruptions most frequently occur.

develop a sleep disorder at some point during childhood. Sleep disorders are generally more prevalent in early childhood and generally decline with a child's development. For example, approximately 25% of infants and toddlers have difficulty falling asleep independently or returning to sleep when awakened during the night. As many as 10% of preschoolers and

Table 16.4 Diagnostic Criteria for Insomnia Disorder

A. A predominant complaint of dissatisfaction with sleep quantity or quality, associated with one (or more) of the following symptoms:

1. Difficulty initiating sleep. (In children, this may manifest as difficulty initiating sleep without caregiver intervention.)

2. Difficulty maintaining sleep, characterized by frequent awakening or problems returning to sleep after awakenings. (In children, this may manifest as difficulty returning to sleep without caregiver intervention.)

3. Early-morning awakening with inability to return to sleep.

B. The sleep disturbance causes clinically significant distress or impairment in social, occupational, educational, academic, behavioral, or other important areas of functioning.

C. The sleep difficulty occurs at least 3 nights per week.

D. The sleep difficulty is present for at least 3 months.

E. The sleep difficulty occurs despite adequate opportunity for sleep.

F. The insomnia is not better explained by and does not occur exclusively during the course of another sleep-wake disorder.

G. The insomnia is not attributable to the physiological effects of a substance (e.g., a drug of abuse, a medication).

H. Coexisting mental disorders and medical conditions do not adequately explain the predominant complaint of insomnia.

school-aged children stall or resist bedtime. Approximately 5% to 10% of adolescents report anxiety that interferes with their ability to sleep. Certain children have chronic sleep problems that persist into adolescence and adulthood (Owens & Burnham, 2009). Sleep problems are especially common among youths with Intellectual Disability (30%–80%), Autism Spectrum Disorder (50%–70%), and chronic health problems (K. P. Johnson, Giannotti, & Cortesi, 2009; Sivertsen, Mysing, Elgen, Stormark, & Lundervold, 2009).

Etiology

Insomnia manifests itself in various ways, depending on children's age and development. Consequently, there is no single cause for insomnia. Nevertheless, several comprehensive models for childhood Insomnia have been developed (Rabian & Bottjer, 2008; Touchette, Petit, Tremblay, & Montplaisir, 2009).

These models assume that insomnias depend on characteristics of the child, characteristics of the parent, and the interactions between both members of the dyad (Figure 16.4). For example, certain children are at risk for sleep problems, such as infants who have trouble falling asleep because of difficult temperament, children who wake during the night because of medical problems, and adolescents with Generalized Anxiety Disorder who worry while lying in bed. Certain parents are also less likely to respond effectively to their children's sleep difficulties. For example, some parents might not recognize the importance of sleep to children's health and well-being. Other parents, experiencing psychosocial stress (e.g., single parents, parents working multiple jobs), might have trouble establishing regular bedtime routines. Indeed, children's sleep disorders are associated with parental risk factors, such as stress, fatigue, poor physical health, depression, and family disruption (Owens & Burnham, 2009; Reid et al., 2009).

Figure 16.4 Understanding Childhood Insomnia

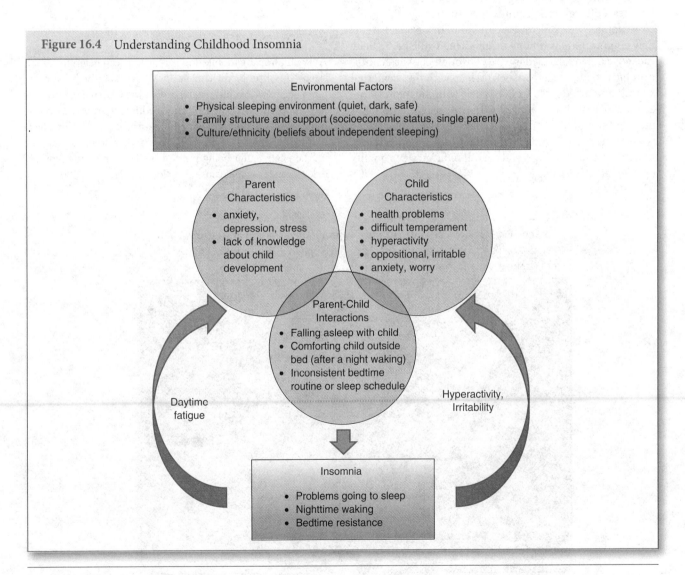

Source: Adapted from Owens & Burnham (2009) and Reite et al. (2009).

Note: Children's problems going to sleep and staying sleep depend on characteristics of the parent, child, and environment.

Parent and child risk factors can lead to interactions that cause or maintain children's sleep problems. These problems, in turn, depend on children's age and development.

Difficulty Falling Asleep Alone

The most common sleep problem shown by infants is difficulty falling asleep independently. Between birth and 6 months of age, most infants rely on parents to regulate their behavior and emotions sufficiently to fall asleep. Between 5 and 7 months of age, however, healthy infants begin to develop the capacity for self-soothing, sufficient to fall asleep on their own.

Problems occur when parents do not allow their children to acquire these skills. Approximately 12% to 30% of older infants and toddlers in the United States sleep in their parents' bed (Reid et al., 2009). Although the acceptability of co-sleeping varies considerably based on families' cultural backgrounds and childrearing histories, co-sleeping is a risk factor for childhood insomnia. Parents may condition their infants to fall asleep while being held, rocked, carried, cuddled, or fed. Through classical conditioning, infants learn to associate sleep with these external stimuli and are unable to fall asleep without them (Reite et al., 2009; Wickwire et al., 2008). Indeed, co-sleeping or putting the infant or toddler to bed after she falls asleep is associated with problems falling asleep independently, more nighttime wakings, and overall reduced sleep quality (Reid et al., 2009).

Night Waking

Conditioning infants to fall asleep only with the help of parents becomes especially problematic during the late night hours. As older infants and children transition from slow-wave (i.e., Stages 3 and 4) sleep through REM sleep, they typically experience a brief state of arousal. Infants and toddlers typically wake briefly four to six times each night as a result of their normal sleep cycles, that is, about every 90 to 120 minutes. Most older infants and children are able to rely on self-soothing techniques (e.g., sucking fingers, cuddling with blanket), during this period of arousal and return to sleep. However, children who have been conditioned to fall asleep only with parental help will have difficulty returning to sleep. Instead, they may wake parents several times during the night, expecting their assistance in returning to sleep. This behavior results in not only fragmented sleep on the part of the infant but also sleep loss on the part of the parent (Owens & Burnham, 2009).

Bedtime Resistance or Struggles

After children are mobile and verbal, they can begin to exhibit sleep refusal problems (Image 16.4). Typically, bedtime resistance begins when children make seemingly reasonable requests to parents shortly before or after bedtime: Can you read one more story? Can you talk with me just a little longer? Can I have a drink of water? It is not usual for children to make multiple "curtain calls" after being put to bed. These requests typically delay sleep onset and cause sleep loss (Moore et al., 2007).

Image 16.4 A story before bedtime can promote relaxation and parent-child relationships. However, sleep refusal can develop when parents give in to children's demands to stay up "just a little while longer."

Source: Image courtesy of Liron Dorfman.

Problems arise when parents occasionally give in to children's requests. When parents acquiesce, children are positively reinforced for their resistant behavior on an intermittent schedule (the most difficult type to extinguish). Furthermore, parents are negatively reinforced for giving in to their children's requests: They temporarily satisfy their children and keep them quiet! Inconsistent bedtime schedules and routines exacerbate bedtime refusal. Parents actively train their children to delay or refuse bedtime (Wickwire et al., 2008).

Even moderate delays in children's bedtimes, if they occur repeatedly, can adversely affect their daytime functioning. In an experimental study, researchers assessed the sleep habits and cognitive functioning of school-aged children for 2 days. On the third day of the study, families were randomly assigned to two treatment conditions. Some parents were told to keep their children up one hour later than usual; the parents of other children were told to put their children to bed one hour earlier than usual. After 3 days of either restricted or extended sleep, the researchers reassessed children's functioning. They found that the sleep restricted children had poorer sleep quality and more night wakings than children who went to bed early. Furthermore, sleep restricted children scored significantly lower on several measures of cognitive functioning, especially attention and concentration. Allowing children to stay up for "one more TV show" each night can take its toll over time (Sadeh, Gruber, & Raviv, 2003).

Anxiety and Impulsivity

Older children and adolescents often have difficulty falling asleep because of anxiety. Children with Separation Anxiety Disorder may fear harm befalling their parents. Alternatively, adolescents with Generalized Anxiety Disorder may worry about events scheduled for the following day. Even youths without anxiety disorders may adopt maladaptive ways of thinking that predispose them to anxiety and arousal. During the day, these youths can distract themselves from anxiety and worry with school, social activities, extracurricular involvement, and media. At night, when lying in bed, these anxiety-provoking cognitions may emerge (Alfano et al., 2009).

The most common cognitive error is **catastrophizing**, the tendency to expect the worst possible outcomes from a specific situation. For example, a child might worry about failing a test the following day and losing the respect of his parents and teacher. Another common error is **selective abstraction**, a cognitive bias in which events are taken out of context in a way that emphasizes their negative elements and downplays their positive elements. For example, an adolescent remembering a party that she attended that evening, might recall only an embarrassing interaction with a former boyfriend, rather than the good time she'd had more generally. A third cognitive error is **personalization**, in which the person attributes a negative event to

her own behavior when, in fact, there is no relationship. For example, an older adolescent might believe that her boyfriend did not call her that evening because he is mad at her when, in actuality, her boyfriend was simply working late (Gregory et al., 2009).

Adolescents often try to cope with bedtime anxieties by remaining in bed and forcing themselves to sleep. However, anxiety and sleep are antithetical processes: They cannot occur simultaneously. Sleep requires relaxation and inhibition; it necessarily makes us vulnerable to our surroundings. In contrast, anxiety makes us aroused, apprehensive, and vigilant. Adolescents who try to force themselves to sleep often experience increased frustration and anxiety. Other adolescents attempt to distract themselves by watching TV, playing video games, or talking with friends. Stimulating activities like these usually increase arousal, prolong sleep onset, and increase sleep loss (Dahl & Harvey, 2008).

Of course, children's sleep problems emerge in the context of the broader social and cultural surroundings (Rabian & Bottjer, 2008). These environmental factors include the physical sleeping environment (e.g., Does the child have a safe, quiet, and dark room in which to sleep?), family structure and resources (e.g., Does mom need to get up early the next morning for work?), and cultural or ethnic beliefs and values (e.g., Is it appropriate to allow children to sleep in their parents' bed?). Even within the United States, families of different ethnic and cultural backgrounds report different values and habits regarding children's sleep (Giannotti & Cortesi, 2009).

Insomnia is sometimes secondary to other childhood psychiatric disorders (Owens, Brown et al., 2009). Approximately, 30% of children with ADHD also have problems falling and staying asleep (Mayes et al., 2008). There are three possible explanations for this high comorbidity. First, problems with behavioral inhibition, which underlie ADHD symptoms, may also interfere with children's ability to soothe themselves to sleep. Indeed, most parents of children with ADHD report that their children have problems with repetitive movements and restlessness during sleep. However, sleep studies have usually not shown differences in the sleep architecture of youths with and without ADHD. Second, stimulant medication used to treat ADHD may cause insomnia. In this case, insomnia is caused by the treatment of ADHD, not ADHD per se. Third, the effects of medication used to treat ADHD typically lose their efficacy in the evening. It is possible that as the medication wears off, symptoms of hyperactivity-impulsivity emerge and interfere with sleep (Gruber, 2009; Reite et al., 2009).

Treatment

Behavioral Treatment. The treatment of pediatric Insomnia, and most sleep disorders, involves teaching parents and children about healthy **sleep hygiene**, that is, the behaviors and environmental conditions that promote restful sleep

(Table 16.5). Although the components of healthy sleep hygiene might seem obvious, it is surprising how many sleep problems can be attributed to poor sleep hygiene (Durand, 2008).

Infants must be taught to fall asleep independently and return to sleep when they awaken during the night. To help them learn this skill, parents should practice a consistent bedtime routine that helps infants relax (e.g., bathing, dressing, changing). Infants should be put to bed at the same time each night. Furthermore, parents should place the infant awake, but drowsy, in the crib and leave the room. Parents may also give the infant a transitional object, such as a small blanket or doll to help the child soothe himself to sleep (Owens & Burnham, 2009).

Mindell and colleagues (2009) demonstrated the efficacy of sleep hygiene in improving the sleep quality of infants and toddlers. A large sample of mothers of children (aged 7–18 months) were randomly assigned to two conditions. Half of the sample were instructed to put their children to bed at a consistent time each night, using a bedtime routine. The other half served as a no-treatment control group. After 3 weeks, infants and toddlers in the intervention group showed improved sleep habits: less time spent falling asleep, fewer and shorter night wakings, and better moods when rising in the morning. Furthermore, mothers of children in the intervention group experienced significant improvement in their mood and energy levels compared to mothers in the control group. The simple intervention benefited both members of the dyad!

Improved sleep hygiene alone will not correct all problems with insomnia. Other interventions should be used, depending on the child's age and specific problem. Extinction appears to be most effective in treating infants and toddlers who have problems falling asleep independently or returning to sleep after waking during the night. Recall that these problems arise through classical conditioning; infants associate falling asleep with the presence of a certain person (parent), object (bottle), or condition (being held) and cannot fall asleep alone. Extinction involves placing the child in the crib without the stimuli he associates with sleep. The goal is for the child to learn self-soothing techniques so that he can fall asleep independently (Durand, 2008).

Parents can practice extinction in several ways. The quickest treatment method is **planned ignoring**. Parents simply place their fed, dry, and drowsy infant in the crib and leave the room. The infant will likely cry because he is not provided with the conditions he has learned are necessary for sleep (e.g., mom, bottle). The parents ignore the infant's cries until sleep overcomes the infant. Needless to say, planned ignoring can be quite stressful on parents and infants. Indeed, many infants will show an extinction burst, that is, an initial increase in the intensity or duration of their cries after the implementation of the extinction procedure. The parent's job is to extinguish these cries by continuing to ignore the infant until he falls asleep independently. After several nights of training, infants are able to fall asleep (or return to sleep) alone (Moore et al., 2007).

Many parents find it difficult to ignore their infant's cries. In fact, some parents will initially allow their infants to cry, only later giving in to their protests and providing them with comfort or food. The practice of initially ignoring and then reinforcing children is problematic. In effect, parents are reinforcing children on an intermittent schedule, training them to cry longer and louder to receive the comfort they demand (Owens & Burnham, 2009).

An alternative, slightly less aversive technique, is **graduated ignoring** (Moore et al., 2007). In graduated ignoring, parents place their fed, dry, and drowsy child in the crib and leave the room. Then, they ignore the infant's cries for a specified period of time (e.g., 5 minutes). After that time, they may enter the room, check in on their infant, and briefly provide comfort (e.g., kiss, caress). Parents then leave the room again and ignore the child's cries for another specified period of time. The process repeats until the child falls asleep. It is important to note that the parent's decision to enter the room is based on time intervals; it is not contingent on the

Table 16.5   Sleep Hygiene for Families

Make sure the child's bedroom is safe, dark, and quiet

Establish a regular bedtime routine which may include bathing, putting on pajamas, and story time

No arousing stimuli before bed (e.g., television, video games, bright lights, sports)

Put the child to bed at the same time, 7 days/week (no late nights on weekends)

For infants, put the child to bed drowsy but awake so they learn to fall asleep independently

Put the child to bed without a bottle, music, or television

Maintain daytime naps through age 3 or 3 and a half to avoid sleep deprivation

For children and adolescents, avoid caffeine in the evening

Source: Adapted from Owens and Burnham (2009).

infant's crying. The infant is never reinforced for his protests. Some therapists recommend increasing the time intervals gradually over the course of a single night (e.g., 5 minutes until the first check in, 10 minutes until the next check in). Other therapists recommend increasing the intervals each night (e.g., 5 minute intervals on Monday, 10 minute intervals on Tuesday).

A third option is **bedtime fading**. This technique uses the infant's need for sleep to help her overcome her sleeping problems. Parents put their infant in the crib 30 minutes after her usual bedtime. If the infant does not fall asleep quickly, parents remove her from the crib for another 30 minutes and then put her back to bed. This process is repeated until the child falls asleep quickly when placed in the crib. The next night, the child is placed in the crib 30 minutes earlier than she fell asleep the night before. The child's bedtime is gradually "faded" to her regular bedtime on each subsequent night (Moore et al., 2007).

A fourth technique, **scheduled wakings**, is an option for children who wake during the night. In this technique, parents monitor children's sleep habits to determine when children are most likely to wake during the night. Then, parents wake and comfort the child for a short period of time before the child's regular night waking. These scheduled night wakings are faded over time until the child no longer awakens during the night (Durand, 2008).

Considerable research supports the use of all four behavioral treatments. Overall, 94% of children show clinically significant improvement in sleep after families implement these interventions (Moore et al., 2007). Furthermore, 80% of children maintain these improvements in sleep duration and quality over time (Mindell et al., 2006). Planned ignoring typically works more quickly than graduated ignoring and bedtime fading. The use of scheduled waking to treat nighttime wakings is considered probably efficacious, but it is difficult to use if children do not wake at a regular time (Rabian & Bottjer, 2008). Treatment for Insomnia is also associated with improvements in parents' sleep quality, sleep duration, daytime mood and behavior, and interactions with their children (Owens & Burnham, 2009).

Cognitive-Behavioral Therapy. Cognitive-behavioral interventions may be especially helpful in treating insomnia in older children and adolescents. Recall that anxiety often interferes with the ability of these adolescents to fall asleep or return to sleep when awakened. Consequently, treatment targets the behavior and thoughts that elicit anxiety (Dahl & Harvey, 2008).

Nearly all therapists would begin treatment by helping adolescents establish healthy sleep hygiene. It is especially important (and difficult) for adolescents to have predictable sleep-wake schedules, to avoid caffeine and other substances that might inhibit sleep, and to refrain from highly stimulating activities prior to bedtime (e.g., exercise, video games). In addition, cognitive-behavior therapists may also incorporate several other components into treatment (Meltzer & Mindell, 2008):

- *Relaxation training:* Adolescents might learn anxiety-reduction techniques, such as progressive muscle relaxation, focused breathing, or guided imagery. These techniques would be taught during therapy sessions, practiced at home, and used prior to bedtime.
- *Stimulus control:* If adolescents do not fall asleep within 20 to 30 minutes of going to bed, they are instructed to leave the bedroom and engage in another quiet activity (e.g., reading) until they feel sleepy. Stimulus control is designed to help adolescents associate the bedroom only with sleeping (e.g., not homework, eating, socializing) and to extinguish the association between the bedroom and feelings of anxiety or frustration.
- *Sleep restriction:* Sleep restriction involves limiting the total amount of time the adolescent is in bed. First, the adolescent monitors her usual sleep habits and determines the total number of hours she sleeps each night. Then, the adolescent is told to limit the number of hours she spends in bed to the average number of hours she sleeps. Sleep restriction and stimulus control, together, improve sleep efficiency, that is, the number of hours the adolescent is in bed *and* asleep.
- *Cognitive restructuring:* Adolescents learn to correct maladaptive thoughts that elicit anxiety and interfere with sleep. Cognitive restructuring involves three steps: (a) identifying distorted or irrational beliefs, (b) challenging the validity of these cognitions, and (c) replacing these incorrect thoughts with more rational, realistic beliefs.

RESEARCH TO PRACTICE

CHALLENGING IRRATIONAL BELIEFS ABOUT SLEEP

Lindsay: When I lie in bed at night I can hear the clock ticking in the hallway, and I know I've been in bed for hours. I just can't stop myself from thinking about the day and the things that I need to do tomorrow.

Therapist: The things you need to do tomorrow? Like what?

Lindsay: You know. I promised to call Jessie and talk with her about our service project that's scheduled for next week. I'm also supposed to help Savannah with a Spanish assignment she's having trouble with. Then, there's my own homework to worry about!

(Continued)

(Continued)

Therapist:	That's a lot of things to remember. But I wonder if what you said is true?
Lindsay:	What did I say?
Therapist:	You said you start thinking about all the things you need to do the next day. I'm wondering if that's true. Do you really need to do all those things?
Lindsay:	Of course, otherwise I'll let everyone down and look like a bad friend.
Therapist:	OK. Let's look at it more carefully—and clearly. Would you want Jessie or Savannah staying up all night worrying about all the things they promised to do for you?
Lindsay:	Of course not.
Therapist:	And, if Jessie or Savannah forgot to call or help you, and then apologized the next day for forgetting, would you be really angry? Would you think they were bad friends?
Lindsay:	No, of course not. I'd understand that they have a lot going on.
Therapist:	But you hold yourself up to a higher standard. You think that these are things you *have* to do, rather than things you *need* to do or *would like* to do.
Lindsay:	Yes, I'd like to do these things and be a good friend . . .
Therapist:	But you don't absolutely have to do them. You can still be a good friend if you forget sometimes or don't get around to it because of your schedule.
Lindsay:	I wouldn't like it, but I guess you're right.
Therapist:	So tonight, when you're thinking about all the things you need to do tomorrow, try changing the word "need" to "like"—all the things you'd like to do tomorrow. Let's practice right now.

Psychologists might also recommend interventions to combat worry or rumination (e.g., repetitively and passively thinking about negative events and feelings; Dahl & Harvey, 2008). For example, adolescents might be encouraged to keep a "to do" list for important tasks. If a task is on the list, they do not need to worry about it at bedtime. Similarly, adolescents may keep a "worry diary"—a journal in which they describe their worries. Adolescents set aside time each day to update the diary. If they find themselves worrying before bedtime, they remind themselves, "Now's not the time for that; I'll worry about that in my journal tomorrow." Still other psychologists teach adolescents guided imagery to help them direct their attention to positive, relaxing events before bedtime. For example, adolescents might imagine hiking in the mountains, relaxing on the beach, or swimming in a coral reef (Dahl & Harvey, 2008).

Cognitive-behavioral interventions like these are 70% to 80% effective at treating Insomnia in adults. However, relatively few randomized controlled studies have been conducted with adolescents (Buckhalt et al., 2009).

Medication. Medication is the most commonly used treatment for pediatric insomnia. In a recent, epidemiological study, physicians were much more likely to prescribe medication to treat pediatric sleep problems (81%) than recommend behavior or cognitive therapy (22%). Unfortunately, there are no medications approved by the U.S. Food and Drug Administration to treat insomnia in children and adolescents. Furthermore, there is very little research supporting the efficacy of these medications with children. Nevertheless, physicians often recommend these medications to help children sleep (Stojanovski et al., 2007).

The most frequently prescribed medications for pediatric Insomnia are **alpha-agonists**, such as clonidine (Catapres). These medications are typically used to treat hypertension in adults. They decrease blood pressure by lowering heart rate and relaxing blood vessels. They have sedating effects and, consequently, are helpful in promoting sleep. Alpha-agonists are most often used to treat children with ADHD and other neurodevelopmental disorders to fall asleep. Side effects include lightheadedness, dry mouth, and dizziness. Children can overdose from these medications, so their use must be carefully monitored by their physician and parents (Owens & Moturi, 2009).

The most frequently used over-the-counter medication for children's sleep problems are **antihistamines**. Histamines are neurotransmitters which regulate the body's immune system. They produce increased vascular permeability, causing fluid to escape from capillaries into bodily tissues. Consequently, they produce runny nose and watery eyes. Most antihistamines block histamine receptors, reducing these effects. Antihistamines, such as diphenhydramine (Benedryl) and hydroxyzine (Vistaril) also produce drowsiness and sedation, which make them conducive to sleep. These medications are generally not appropriate for the long-term treatment of insomnia because their effects are fairly long-lasting; many people experience drowsiness the day after taking them. Furthermore, they often impair sleep quality (Johnson & Ivanenko, 2010).

A third group of medications are the **benzodiazepine receptor agonists**. These medications act on receptors for GABA, the body's most important inhibitory neurotransmitter. Traditional benozodiazepines, such as temazepam (Restoril), estazolam (ProSom), and quazepam (Doral), bind to major GABA receptors and produce marked sedation. Unfortunately, they also seem to affect sleep quality, decreasing both slow-wave and REM sleep. Individuals can also develop tolerance for these medications and experience severe insomnia after discontinuing their use. Newer benzodiazepine receptor agonists bind only to specific GABA receptors. They produce sedation and anxiety reduction; consequently, they are referred to as "hypnotics." Examples of these newer medications are eszopiclone (Lunesta), zaleplon (Sonata), and zolpidem (Ambien).

Other Sleep Disorders

Circadian Rhythm Sleep-Wake Disorder

By early childhood, children become entrained to a sleep-wake cycle that causes them to rise and sleep at approximately the same time each day (Table 16.6 Common Sleep Disorders in Children). This circadian (i.e., "about a day") rhythm in sleeping and waking is regulated by environmental cues, such

as sunlight, and hormones that influence fatigue and arousal, such as cortisol and melatonin (Dahl & Harvey, 2008).

Many adolescents experience a delay in cortisol and melatonin secretion shortly after the onset of puberty. This delay can cause a corresponding phase delay in the circadian rhythm. We can see this phase delay in adolescents (including college students) who prefer to stay up until 2 or 3 a.m. and wake at 10 or 11 a.m. Problems arise when there is a mismatch between the adolescent's endogenous circadian rhythm and the sleep-wake cycle required by his social environment. High school students and younger college students know the difficulty of going to bed late and waking for an early morning class after only a few hours of sleep! **Circadian Rhythm Sleep-Wake Disorder** describes this persistent inability to fall asleep and wake at conventionally appropriate times (Dahl & Harvey, 2008).

Approximately 7% to 10% of adolescents meet diagnostic criteria for Circadian Rhythm Sleep-Wake Disorder. It can cause adolescents considerable distress and impairment. Some adolescents become upset when they cannot fall asleep at an appropriate hour because they know they need to rise early the next morning. Other adolescents, who wake up early for school, experience accumulated sleep loss, resulting in daytime fatigue, attention-concentration problems, and academic difficulties. Frustration over their sleep schedule and accumulated sleep loss can also contribute to dysphoria (Leu & Rosen, 2008; Wickwire et al., 2008).

The treatment of Circadian Rhythm Sleep-Wake Disorder involves matching the adolescent's endogenous sleep-wake cycle to the expectations of his social environment (e.g., school, work). Some psychologists refer to this adjustment in the adolescent's sleep-wake cycle as **chronotherapy**. Chronotherapy can be performed in two ways. One method

Table 16.6 Common Sleep Disorders in Children

Disorder	Description
Insomnia Disorder	Dissatisfaction with sleep quantity or quality associated with difficulty (1) initiating sleep, (2) maintaining sleep, or (3) early morning waking.
Circadian Rhythm Sleep-Wake Disorder	Persistent or recurrent sleep disruption caused by an alteration of the person's circadian rhythm or misalignment between the person's circadian rhythm and his or her daily schedule. Causes insomnia and/or daytime sleepiness.
Sleep Arousal Disorders	Recurrent episodes of incomplete awakening from non-REM sleep, accompanied by either (1) sleepwalking, or (2) sleep terrors. The person has no memory of the episode and recalls little or no dream imagery.
Nightmare Disorder	Repeated, extremely upsetting dreams that involve threats to personal integrity. Dreams occur during REM sleep. The person has memory of the dreams and becomes oriented and alert upon waking.
Obstructive Sleep Apnea Hypopnea	Recurrent, obstructed breathing during sleep (confirmed by a sleep study), usually associated with (1) nocturnal breathing disturbances (e.g., snoring, gasping), and (2) daytime sleepiness.

Source: Based on American Psychiatric Association (2013).

involves gradually advancing the adolescent's bedtime in 15-minute intervals over the course of several weeks. For example, an adolescent who feels the need to sleep at 2 a.m., might establish a bedtime of 1:45 a.m. for several nights until he falls asleep at that time. Then, he would move his bedtime forward another 15 minutes until eventually he is able to fall asleep at the desired hour (Wickwire et al., 2008).

A second method is to delay bedtime by several hours each night until the desired bedtime is achieved. For example, an adolescent who feels the need to sleep at 2 a.m., might delay bedtime until 7 a.m. On each successive night, he might delay bedtime an additional 4 hours (i.e., 11 a.m., 3 p.m., 7 p.m.) until he reaches his desired bedtime. Phase-delaying sleep onset in this manner is relatively quick, but it can be very disruptive to the adolescent's daytime activities (Wickwire et al., 2008).

Many therapists supplement chronotherapy with synthetic melatonin supplements and light stimulation. Melatonin, a dietary supplement sold at many health food stores, mimics the body's natural sleep hormone. At low doses, it may produce mild drowsiness and promote sleep. It is typically taken shortly before bedtime. Upon waking, adolescents are instructed to expose themselves to an array of high-intensity artificial light (or natural sunlight if available) to increase arousal (Buckhalt et al., 2009).

Limited data suggest that chronotherapy is effective in treating Circadian Rhythm Sleep-Wake Disorder in adolescents. Data regarding the effectiveness of melatonin and light therapy for this disorder are more mixed. Furthermore, the safety of melatonin for children and adolescents has not been established. Consequently, these components of treatment should be used only under professional supervision, cautiously, and in conjunction with chronotherapy (Johnson & Ivanenko, 2010).

Some communities try to prevent adolescent sleep problems by avoiding early school start times. When researchers compare adolescents who begin school early (e.g., before 7:15 a.m.) and later (e.g., after 8:40 a.m.), several findings emerge:

- Adolescents go to bed at approximately the same time, regardless of when they need to wake and be at school. Therefore, adolescents who awaken early get less sleep than adolescents who awaken later.
- Schools with earlier start times have greater absenteeism.
- Adolescents attending schools with early start times show more problems with attention, concentration, daytime sleepiness, and lower academic achievement than students with late start times.

Furthermore, delaying school start times is associated with improvements in adolescents' functioning (Buckhalt et al., 2009). Consequently, several researchers have advocated for later school start times and education to help children improve their sleep hygiene. For example, the Young Adolescent Sleep-Smart Pacesetter Program is a school-based prevention program designed for middle school students. Adolescents learn to keep consistent sleep-wake schedules, to develop a relaxing bedtime routine, to regulate sleep and arousal by reducing light exposure in the evening and maximizing it in the morning, and to avoid caffeine and other stimulating substances that might interfere with sleep. This program is effective in helping adolescents increase their total sleep time, develop more consistent sleep schedules, and improve confidence in their ability to get sufficient sleep (Vo, LeChasseur, Wolfson, & Marco, 2003).

Sleep Arousal Disorders

Sleep Arousal Disorders occur when children have recurrent episodes of "incompletely awakening" from non-REM sleep. There are two types of arousal disorders: (a) sleepwalking, and (b) sleep terrors. Both disorders have the following features in common (Mason & Pack, 2007; Wickwire et al., 2008):

- They usually occur early in the night, usually 60 to 90 minutes after sleep onset.
- They occur during slow-wave (i.e., non-REM, or "deep") sleep.
- Children are generally unresponsive during an arousal episode.
- Episodes are relatively brief in duration (10–30 minutes).
- Children usually fall back to sleep after the episode.
- Children usually have no memory of the episode the following morning.

How is it possible for children to be "incompletely awake"? To understand Sleep Arousal Disorders, it is important to realize that sleep is not a period of complete inactivity. During the various stages of sleep (e.g., relaxed alertness, non-REM, REM), some brain regions are highly active whereas others actively inhibit autonomic arousal and motor activity. Disorders of arousal usually occur when the child transitions from slow-wave sleep to the beginning of his or her first REM episode. The child presents in a mixed state of sleep: She appears unresponsive to her surroundings, disoriented, and has no memory of the event, like people in deep, slow-wave sleep, but she also shows a high degree of motor or autonomic activity, like people in REM sleep. Children with Sleep Arousal Disorders seem to be stuck between these two sleep states for a brief period of time until the episode passes (Kotagal, 2008).

Researchers are not completely sure what causes this mixed state. Sleep Arousal Disorders are highly heritable (Figure 16.5). Twin and family studies indicate high prevalence in first-degree relatives. It appears that children inherit the inability to transition smoothly from slow-wave sleep to REM. These children also have immature neural networks that are responsible for inhibiting autonomic arousal and motor activity. Consequently, they sometimes show both autonomic arousal and movement even though they are largely unresponsive to others. As their nervous systems mature, inhibition becomes complete and children outgrow the disorder. Finally, environmental stressors may precipitate the disorder. Sleep deprivation, changes to the child's sleep-wake cycle, and psychosocial stress often occur before an episode (Mason & Pack, 2007).

The exact prevalence of Sleep Arousal Disorders is unknown. A conservative estimate is that 15% of children experience sleepwalking or sleep terrors at some point during childhood. These problems are equally prevalent in boys and girls (Bloomfield & Shatkin, 2009).

As many as 17% of toddlers and preschoolers show **confusional arousals**. Children typically sit up in bed, with eyes open or closed, and appear disoriented and moderately distressed. They may wake parents with cries for help. However, they are usually unresponsive to parents, cannot describe the source of their distress, and appear confused. If parents attempt to hug or comfort them, some children become more distressed and agitated. Others may say "no" or "go away." Confusional arousals usually last 10 to 30 minutes, after which children return to restful sleep (Kotagal, 2009; Mason & Pack, 2007).

Sleepwalking is most common among children aged 4 to 8 years. Approximately 25% to 30% of children sleepwalk occasionally. Children typically leave the bed and wander about the house. Occasionally, they may engage in disruptive (e.g., urinating on the floor) or dangerous acts (e.g., leaving the house). Because sleepwalking occurs during non-REM sleep, sleepwalking children are not dreaming, nor are they acting out dreams. If parents discover their sleepwalking child, they can usually lead the child to bed and allow her to return to sleep. Most episodes of sleepwalking last approximately 10 to 20 minutes. Sleepwalkers typically have no memory of the event (Kotagal, 2009).

Sleep terrors are seen in 3% of prepubescent children. They are very upsetting to families. Children typically emit a blood-curdling scream early in the sleep cycle. They may sit up in bed, eyes open, with a look of terror, and cry inconsolably. They are usually unresponsive to parents' offers of comfort. Because sleep terrors occur during non-REM sleep, they do not occur during dreaming; consequently, children are usually unable to describe the source of their terror. Sleep terrors typically pass in 10 to 30 minutes, after which children return to restful sleep. Children usually have complete or partial amnesia for the event the next day (Kotagal, 2009).

Sleep Arousal Disorders are not associated with psychopathology. Parents of children with this disorder can be reassured that the disorder is not associated with neurological impairment, mood or anxiety disorders, or trauma. Children usually outgrow the disorder by late childhood or adolescence (Kotagal, 2009).

If children display confusional arousal or sleep terror, parents should attempt to reassure and comfort them to the degree possible. Sometimes, comfort simply involves being present and helping the child return to sleep after the episode. Parents of sleepwalkers should take precautions to avoid danger (Leu & Rosen, 2008). For example, parents might place a bell on their child's door to signal them if their child leaves the room. Some psychologists

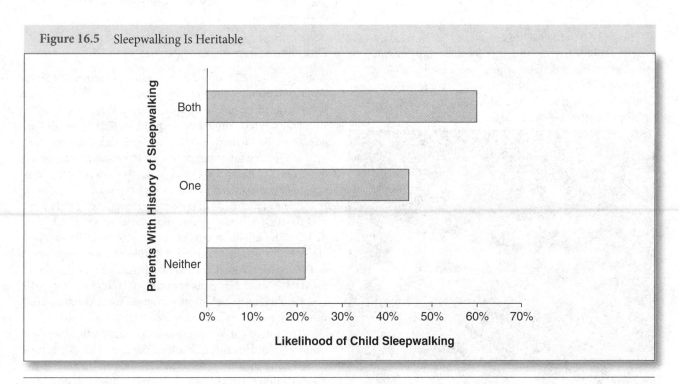

Figure 16.5 Sleepwalking Is Heritable

Source: Based on Reite et al. (2009).

Note: A child's likelihood of sleepwalking is correlated with his or her parent's history of sleepwalking as a child.

recommend that children sleep in a sleeping bag or a mattress on the floor. The sleeping bag makes it more difficult for the child to sleepwalk whereas the a mattress on the floor reduces the risk of injury if he manages to leave the bed. If children do leave the room, parents should gently encourage them to return to bed (Reite et al., 2009).

Nightmare Disorder

Nightmares are extremely common in children and adolescents. Approximately 2% to 11% of children report nightmares "always or often" whereas an additional 15% to 31% experience them "now and then." The content of nightmares often mirror the cognitive development of children. For example, preschoolers, who engage in preoperational thought, tend to dream about magical creatures or events (e.g., monsters, witches) whereas children, whose thought is largely restricted to concrete operations, may dream of actual physical dangers (e.g., wild animals, storms). The formal operations attained by adolescents allow them to incorporate more abstract content into their nightmares (e.g., social ostracism, abandonment, death, Kotagal, 2009).

Youths may be diagnosed with **Nightmare Disorder** if their nightmares are recurrent, they reflect actual dreams that involve threats to their survival or well-being, and they cause significant distress or impairment (e.g., sleep loss, daytime fatigue). As many as 50% of preschoolers have recurrent nightmares; the prevalence drops to 10% among adolescents. Relatively few of these children are formally treated for Nightmare Disorder (Image 16.5).

Image 16.5 *The Nightmare* (Henry Fuseli, 1781). The suffix "mare" is from the German word "maron" which refers to demons who are believed to sit on top of sleepers, paralyzing them. Certain rare sleep disorders, such as sleep paralysis and hypnagogic hallucinations, would produce this sensation.

Source: Wikimedia Commons.

Nightmares differ from sleep terrors in several ways. First, nightmares occur during REM sleep, whereas sleep terrors occur during non-REM sleep. Second, children who experience nightmares can be awakened during their dreams, either by themselves or their parents. Children who have sleep terrors are difficult to wake. Third, once awake, children can immediately recall the content of their nightmare. In contrast, children are usually unable to recall the content associated with a sleep terror. Fourth, after a nightmare, most children have difficulty returning to sleep. In contrast, children usually return to restful sleep after a sleep terror. Finally, recurrent nightmares are sometimes experienced by children exposed to considerable psychosocial stress or trauma. In contrast, anxiety, stress, and trauma are not associated with sleep terrors (Leu & Rosen, 2008).

Most youths with Nightmare Disorder are treated informally by parents. However, recurrent, severe nightmares that cause distress or disruption to the family merit professional attention. These nightmares occasionally (although certainly not always) reflect other sources of anxiety in children's lives. Professional treatment of Nightmare Disorder typically involves the assessment of possible psychosocial stressors that might elicit the nightmares, improving the child's sleep hygiene and teaching children relaxation and coping skills. One interesting technique, **nightmare imagery rehearsal therapy**, involves asking children to rewrite the nightmare in a manner that emphasizes mastery or resilience and then mentally rehearsing the dream daily. Younger children may be asked to draw pictures of their nightmare's content, changing it to produce a positive or benign outcome (Kotagal, 2009; Reite et al., 2009).

Obstructive Sleep Apnea Hypopnea

Approximately 1.2% of children may have **Obstructive Sleep Apnea Hypopnea**, a condition in which the child's airway is constricted or blocked during sleep (Bixler et al., 2009). Blockage is often caused by enlarged adenoids or tonsils (i.e., adenotonsillar hypertrophy), obesity, facial abnormalities, or thick tongue (as sometimes seen in children with Down Syndrome). The symptoms of apnea include snoring, disrupted or restless sleep, unusual sleeping positions (e.g., arching the head and neck to improve airflow), daytime fatigue, and daytime behavior problems, such as irritability, hyperactivity, and attention-concentration problems. Parents and children are usually not aware that children have sleep apnea, so the disorder is often unrecognized or may be misdiagnosed as ADHD. Snoring is fairly common in children (15%–20%) and should only be an indicator of apnea when children show other risk factors or symptoms (Wickwire et al., 2008).

Treatment for sleep apnea in children often involves removal of the tonsils. Adenotonsillectomy is 80% effective in reducing apnea. Older children may be treated using a **continuous positive air pressure (CPAP)** device. The child wears a mask connected by a tube to a small ventilator. The ventilator delivers continuous airflow to the child, opening his airway and reducing the likelihood of obstruction. Although CPAP is the treatment of choice for apnea in adults, it is less often used with children because some youths find the device uncomfortable or embarrassing (Dahl & Harvey, 2008).

Treatment for Obstructive Sleep Apnea Hypopnea is important because it can interfere with children's behavioral, cognitive, and social-emotional functioning. Treatment, either with surgery or CPAP, has been shown to cause improvements in children's sleep, daytime behavior, school performance, and overall quality of life (Reite et al., 2009).

PEDIATRIC PSYCHOLOGY

What Is Pediatric Psychology?

Pediatric psychology is an interdisciplinary field concerned with the application of psychology to the domain of children's health. Pediatric psychologists are scientists and practitioners who promote the physical and psychological health and development of youths (B. S. Aylward, Bender et al., 2009). Most pediatric psychologists (63%) work in medical facilities, such as academic hospitals, children's hospitals, or rehabilitation centers. They collaborate with medical staff to help children cope with physical illness. Some pediatric psychologists (22%) work in private practice settings, often helping children and families with a wide range of behavioral, social-emotional, and medical problems. Pediatric psychologists work in a variety of other settings including universities, outpatient clinics, and schools (Buckloh & Greco, 2009).

Most pediatric psychologists are clinical or counseling psychologists with specialized training in the intersection of children's mental and physical health and development. Pediatric psychologists are involved in wide range of professional activities; however, most of their activities can be classified into the following groups (Buckloh & Greco, 2009):

- *Inpatient consultation-liaison:* Pediatric psychologists work in hospitals to address the needs of children and adolescents with acute psychological problems. They also collaborate with medical staff to help patients participate in medical procedures, adhere to treatment, and cope with their illness.
- *Chronic conditions:* Pediatric psychologists work on interdisciplinary teams in hospitals and outpatient clinics to help children cope with long-term medical problems. For example, a pediatric psychologist might help children with severe asthma, cancer, or diabetes to comply with medical procedures related to their illness; address feelings of anxiety, depression, or anger associated with their medical problems; and improve their interactions with parents, siblings, and friends.
- *Specialized care:* Pediatric psychologists work in outpatient clinics to help children with behavior problems that require coordinated psychological and medical treatment. For example, children with feeding disorders,

elimination disorders, and sleep disorders typically require treatment by both psychologists and physicians.

Inpatient Consultation-Liaison

Many pediatric psychologists who work in children's hospitals engage in consultation and liaison (CL) with medical staff (Carter et al., 2009). **Consultation** occurs when a health care professional is treating a child with a behavioral, cognitive, or social-emotional problem that interferes with the child's treatment. The medical professional might ask the pediatric psychologist for her recommendations regarding how to address the child's psychological problems. For example, an adolescent might be brought to the emergency department because she swallowed a bottle of over-the-counter pain medicine. Her physicians might ask the psychologist to assess the adolescent and recommend a course of action after the girl is medically stable (e.g., should she go home or stay for observation).

Alternatively, a physician might request that the psychologist provide a service to help the child participate in treatment more effectively. For example, a child might be required to have a lumbar puncture to determine whether he has meningitis. This procedure involves inserting a needle into the lower spine to collect a small sample of cerebrospinal fluid. Because this procedure can be frightening and uncomfortable, the child might understandably refuse to participate. A psychologist might be asked to meet with the child and his family, discuss the procedure, and teach the child relaxation strategies so that he can undergo the procedure with less fear and pain (Abrams & Rauch, 2008).

Consultation is analogous to "firefighting." The psychologist's primary job is to address an immediate problem, to help solve the problem, or to recommend a course of action based on her knowledge of psychological science and child development.

In contrast, pediatric psychologists might also act as **liaisons** between medical and psychological staff for children with chronic illnesses. Rather than focus on specific problems, liaisons usually work as part of an interdisciplinary team of medical and behavioral professionals who serve youths with specific illnesses. Rather than fighting specific "fires," the liaison's job is to "fireproof" the medical procedures and hospital environment to avoid problems.

For example, a psychologist might work on the hospital's pediatric oncology team, helping medical staff find ways to facilitate the diagnosis, treatment, and recovery of children with cancer. When a child is newly diagnosed, the psychologist might provide support services to parents, to help them address emotions associated with their children's illness. The psychologist might also teach relaxation and coping strategies to children in the unit to help them participate in medical procedures. Before leaving the hospital, the psychologist might help the child return to school and interactions with peers.

Pediatric psychologists who practice consultation-liaison engage in a wide variety of activities; no 2 days are exactly alike. Carter and von Weiss (2005) classified these activities into five groups—the five Cs of consultation-liaison:

1. *Crisis:* Psychologists help children and families who are initially admitted to the hospital or newly diagnosed with an illness. They attempt to normalize the family's fears and help them take steps to address children's medical problems.

2. *Coping:* Psychologists help children and families cope with anxiety, fear, and discomfort associated with medical procedures in the hospital. They also work with families to help children adjust their lifestyles in response to the illness (e.g., a child with diabetes, limiting sugar intake).

3. *Compliance:* Psychologists help children follow medical recommendations, such as taking medication, monitoring health, altering behavior, or participating in checkups and medical procedures.

4. *Communication:* Psychologists act as liaisons between medical staff and families. They educate children and families about medical procedures and help them cope with stressors associated with medical care.

5. *Collaboration:* Psychologists function as part of an interdisciplinary team of professionals, which often include physicians; nurses; occupational, recreational, and physical therapists; social workers; dieticians; and family life experts. These professionals have a shared goal of promoting the health and well-being of children.

Adherence is a common reason for psychological consultation (LaGreca & Mackey, 2009). Adherence refers to the degree to which children and families follow the recommendations of medical staff. As you might imagine, many youths are unwilling to participate in medical procedures that might involve strange situations, separation from parents, or physical discomfort. Other children do not adhere to changes in diet or lifestyle that are necessary to manage their illness. Adherence varies, depending on the severity and duration of the child's disorder, the aversiveness of treatment, and the family's social-emotional resources. However, most studies indicate that only half of youths with chronic illnesses adhere to the recommendations of their physicians (Brown et al., 2007).

Children's cognitive and social-emotional development influences their likelihood of adherence. For example, younger children may resist parental separation or painful procedures whereas adolescents may avoid medication that limits their social activities or diet. Families can also influence children's adherence. For example, families with greater knowledge about their children's illness, coping and problem-solving skills, and tangible resources may be best able to address their children's needs and respond to their anxiety, frustration, and fears (Abrams & Rauch, 2008).

Children With Chronic Health Problems

Approximately 7% of children and adolescents have chronic medical conditions that necessitate ongoing care. Pediatric psychologists provide support for these children and their families during their stay in the hospital and after returning to their homes (Brown et al., 2007).

Children with chronic illnesses may be at risk for behavioral and social-emotional problems. However, studies investigating comorbid depression, anxiety, and disruptive behavior among youths with chronic illnesses have yielded mixed results. Most research points to two general conclusions. First, children's outcomes depend on the nature and severity of their illnesses. For example, certain disorders such as diabetes and sickle cell disease are known to place children at risk for anxiety and depression. Children with other disorders such as asthma and cancer have more mixed social-emotional outcomes.

Second, outcomes depend on how effectively children and families cope with the chronic illness. Some families seem to be more psychologically "hardy" than others. Psychologists have developed two models to explain the way families' coping might influence the effects of chronic illness on children's outcomes.

The **transactional stress and coping (TSC) model** views the child's illness as a stressor to which the family must respond (Thompson & Gustafson, 1996). The effectiveness of the response depends on (a) the family's cognitions, (b) the family's coping style, and (c) overall family functioning. First, the family's thoughts about the illness are important. Does the child and family understand the illness and the ways it can be treated? Do they view the illness as manageable and themselves in control, or do they view the situation as hopeless and themselves as helpless? Second, the family's coping style is important. Does the family actively try to respond to the illness or do family members react with anger or avoidance? Third, the quality of relationships in the family is important. Do parents agree regarding the best course of action or do they undermine each other's decisions? Do they give children responsibility for managing their illness or are they overcontrolling?

The TSC model emphasizes the family system in determining the social-emotional outcomes of children with chronic illnesses. Psychologists who adopt this model will try to help families by challenging biased or distorted perceptions regarding children's illnesses, teaching families more effective, active coping strategies and improving communication and the quality of relationships between family members (Brown et al., 2007).

Alternatively, the **disability stress coping (DSC) model** predicts that children's ability to cope with chronic illness depends on risk and resilience factors in the family. Recall that risk factors increase the likelihood that children will develop behavioral or social-emotional problems, whereas resilience factors buffer children from these deleterious effects. According to the model, risk factors include (a) aspects of the illness itself, including its severity, duration, and the age at which the child was first diagnosed; (b) behavioral or social-emotional problems experienced by the child before he was diagnosed; and (c) psychosocial stressors experienced by the family. Resilience factors include (a) characteristics of the child, such as easy temperament, well-developed problem-solving and social skills, or motivation; (b) the family's response to stress, such as their understanding of the illness, their sense of control, and their ability to cope; and (c) psychosocial resources, such as adequate access to health care, social support, and communication among family members.

According to the DSC model, risk and resilience factors moderate the relationship between children's illness and their social-emotional outcomes. Psychologists who adopt this model work with families to decrease risk and foster resilience to promote children's recovery (Brown et al., 2007).

Asthma

Asthma is a chronic condition caused by inflammation of the airways and intermittent periods of difficulty breathing. Approximately 6% of children have current asthma attacks that interfere with life activities (e.g., school, sports, family events). It is the most common chronic illness afflicting youths.

Children with asthma manage their symptoms by avoiding situations or activities that might trigger an asthma attack. Children also typically take medication and carry inhalers for asthmatic episodes. Some children resent limitations placed on their daily activities or are embarrassed to use medications or inhalers in front of peers. Other children develop anxiety problems because they fear future attacks (Image 16.6).

Pediatric psychologists might educate families about asthma and help modify the home environment to prevent attacks (e.g., installing a hypoallergenic filter, avoid smoking). Psychologists might help parents and children establish a behavioral contract, or written agreement, that designates the responsibilities of both parties in managing children's asthma. For example, parents agree to allow children to attend a scout camping trip if children agree to carry their inhaler at all times. For children with anxiety, psychologists might teach relaxation exercises, such as deep breathing or guided imagery, to help them cope with asthmatic episodes should they occur (McQuaid & Abramson, 2009).

Cancer

Cancer is the leading cause of death by disease for children in the United States. Although cancer is relatively rare in children, approximately 12,500 youths are diagnosed each year. Acute lymphoblastic leukemia (ALL) and malignant brain tumors are most common among children. Cancer, especially ALL, is usually curable in children; however, the medical procedures needed to diagnose and treat cancer often cause physical, cognitive, and social-emotional problems (Elkin & Stoppelbein, 2008).

Pediatric psychologists can be involved in all aspects of children's cancer treatment. Initially, they may help families cope with fears and worries associated with children's diagnoses. Later, children might become frustrated and irritable; psychologists might work with families to reduce conflict and increase cohesion among family members during treatment. Psychologists may also teach children ways to manage pain and nausea associated with treatment or to distract themselves to cope with medical procedures. Later, psychologists might help children plan for their return to school and cope with missed work and peers. Psychologists can also counsel children who experience specific problems, such as depression or possible sterility, following radiation therapy (Cohen, Maclaren, & Lim, 2008; Vannatta, Salley, & Gerhardt, 2009).

Image 16.6   Pediatric psychologists help children with asthma manage their symptoms. This girl uses an inhaler to breathe more easily.

Cystic Fibrosis

Cystic fibrosis is an inherited condition that causes thick mucus in the airways and lungs. Foreign particles in the air, such as dust, pollen, or other pollutants, can accumulate in this mucus causing chronic lung infections. Cystic fibrosis affects one in 3,500 children; most are diagnosed in infancy or early childhood. Besides respiratory and digestive problems, children with cystic fibrosis must participate in frequent exercises to clear their airways and lungs. These exercises can be time consuming, laborious, and distressing for children and their families.

Pediatric psychologists often help children and their families adhere to physicians' recommendations regarding the frequency of exercises. Young children may become oppositional and refuse to participate. In this case, psychologists might teach parents to use positive reinforcement and other behavioral techniques to increase compliance. Older children and adolescents, in contrast, may become depressed. They may believe that the exercises will not appreciably prolong their life span or improve their life satisfaction. Pediatric psychologists might challenge the maladaptive cognitions that rob these adolescents' of their motivation to manage their condition (Quittner, Barker, Marciel, & Grimley, 2009).

Diabetes Mellitus

Diabetes mellitus is a chronic disease caused by a deficiency in insulin, the hormone needed to regulate blood sugar. Type I diabetes, most often seen in children, is caused by the absence or destruction of cells in the pancreas responsible for manufacturing insulin. Type II diabetes, seen in 10% to 20% of youths with diabetes, occurs when the body develops a resistance to insulin and no longer uses it properly to control blood sugar. Approximately one in 600 children and adolescents has diabetes.

Diabetes can cause severe problems if children allow blood sugar levels to remain unregulated. Hypoglycemia (low blood sugar) occurs when children allow blood glucose levels to drop to dangerously low levels, usually resulting in fatigue, dizziness, and possible damage to internal organs. Hypoglycemia can occur when children skip meals or take too much insulin. In contrast, diabetic ketoacidosis occurs when blood glucose levels are unusually high. It usually occurs when children eat a large (or sugary) meal and do not take sufficient insulin to metabolize blood glucose. Over time, failure to regulate blood glucose can cause heart disease, stroke, and damage to the kidneys and eyes.

The chief problem with diabetes is adherence (Image 16.7). Younger children might avoid the frequent needle pricks necessary to monitor blood sugar. Older children and adolescents might be embarrassed about their condition or might resent having to monitor and restrict their diet to manage blood glucose. Pediatric psychologists try to increase compliance in ways that are developmentally appropriate. For example, they might teach younger children strategies to reduce pain associated with glucose testing or respond to teasing from peers. They might also teach children to monitor and record their glucose levels over time and encourage parents to reinforce children for accepting responsibility for this task. In contrast, psychologists might work with parents to find ways to avoid arguments about adolescents' diet and allow adolescents to take ownership of the management of their disorder (Elkin & Stoppelbein, 2008; Wysocki, Buckloh, & Greco, 2009).

Gastrointestinal Problems

Abdominal pain and gastrointestinal problems are fairly common among children and adolescents. Approximately 6% of older children and 14% of adolescents have symptoms of **Irritable Bowel Syndrome (IBS)**, a disorder characterized by abdominal discomfort and altered bowel functioning. Some youths with IBS show frequent diarrhea, others constipation, and still others both problems. IBS is painful, stressful, and potentially embarrassing. Youths will IBS often miss school and must forgo activities with family and peers because of these chronic symptoms.

The cause of IBS is unknown, although most evidence points to a hypersensitivity of the nerve endings surrounding the bowel. However, stress and behavior can greatly affect the timing and severity of symptoms. Consequently, treatment usually involves medical and psychological interventions. With respect to psychological treatment, pediatric

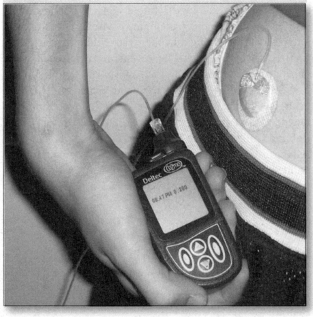

Image 16.7   Psychologists can help children with diabetes avoid high-risk foods and adhere to medication. This adolescent girl has an insulin pump which administers insulin to her after meals. Pumps like these are often more convenient than insulin injections.

psychologists may teach children relaxation skills, pain reduction techniques, and other ways to manage stress (Banez & Cunningham, 2009).

Inflammatory Bowel Disease (IBD) is a more serious disorder characterized by diarrhea, rectal bleeding, urgency, abdominal cramping, weight loss, fatigue, and fever. Chron Disease is probably the best known example of IBD; it is caused by severe inflammation of the digestive tract, especially the intestinal wall. The cause of IBD is unknown, although it is likely influenced by genetics, exposure to bacteria or viruses, and/or problems with the body's immune system.

Understandably, children with IBD are at risk for anxiety, depression, poor social relationships, and difficulty with school attendance. Their self-reported quality of life is often poor. Adherence is also usually a problem, because children must frequently take medication to manage their symptoms. Psychologists are often involved in helping children and families adhere to medication, overcome anxiety and mood problems, improve social competence and skills, and adjust to missed schooling (Banez & Cunningham, 2009).

Juvenile Rheumatoid Arthritis

Juvenile rheumatoid arthritis (JRA) is a leading cause of physical disability among children and adolescents. It is characterized by inflammation of the musculoskeletal system, blood vessels, and skin. In particular, children with JRA show synovitis, inflammation of the synovial membrane of a joint. The result is chronic pain, restricted range of motion, and possible growth problems. JRA is diagnosed based on whether it affects only certain joints, such as the ankles and knees (pauciarticular JRA); many joints including the hands, wrists, and neck (polyarticular JRA); or other body regions, such as the lymph nodes, spleen, liver, and heart (systemic-onset JRA; Rapoff, Lindsley, & Karlson, 2009).

The treatment of JRA typically involves long-term use of anti-inflammatory medication (e.g., ibuprofen), occasional use of corticosteroids in severe cases, and daily therapeutic exercises to maintain range and ease of motion. Pediatric psychologists are typically involved in the care of children or youths with JRA in three ways. First, psychologists may help patients manage chronic pain. Second, psychologists can develop ways to increase children's adherence to medication and their exercise-physical therapy program. Third, psychologists may work with parents and siblings to help reduce stress and conflict within the family, frequently caused by the child's chronic illness (Rapoff et al., 2009).

Sickle Cell Disease

Sickle cell disease is an inherited disorder characterized by abnormal, sickle-shaped red blood cells. The unusual shape of the cells can cause problems with blood flow. The disease also causes anemia, episodes of acute pain, and risk of infections and damage to vital organs. It occurs in one out of 500 African American children but is less common among youths of European-American ethnicity (Image 16.8).

Psychologists typically teach youths with sickle cell disease techniques to manage pain. Strategies such as deep breathing, guided imagery, and positive self-statements are often effective. Psychologists may also help children and families cope with other stressors associated with the disease, such as missed school, sleep problems, and restricted social activities (Elkin & Stoppelbein, 2008; Lemanek & Ranalli, 2009).

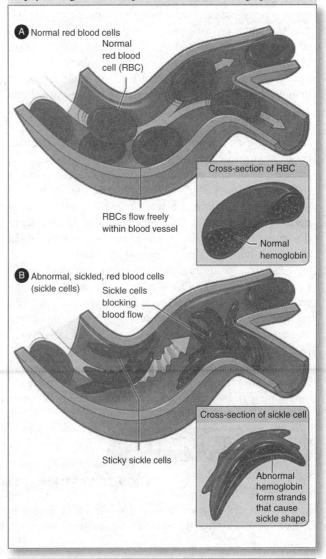

Image 16.8 Youths with sickle cell disease often experience acute pain and risk of infections. Pediatric psychologists can help these children manage pain.

Ⓐ Normal red blood cells
Normal red blood cell (RBC)
RBCs flow freely within blood vessel
Cross-section of RBC
Normal hemoglobin

Ⓑ Abnormal, sickled, red blood cells (sickle cells)
Sickle cells blocking blood flow
Sticky sickle cells
Cross-section of sickle cell
Abnormal hemoglobin form strands that cause sickle shape

Source: Courtesy of the National Institutes of Health.

Interventions for Youths with Chronic Health Problems

Behavior Therapy

Behavioral interventions used by pediatric psychologists are based on classical conditioning, operant conditioning, and observational learning. Systematic desensitization is a common intervention used to help children cope with painful (e.g., injections) or uncomfortable (e.g., MRI) medical procedures. Systematic desensitization is based on classical conditioning; it involves pairing relaxation with stimuli that elicit anxiety.

Systematic desensitization involves four steps. First, the psychologist teaches the child how to relax. Typically, relaxation is achieved through progressively tightening and relaxing muscle groups (e.g., arms, legs, middle) and concentrating on slow, deep breathing. Relaxation is introduced during a therapy session and practiced until it is achieved relatively quickly. Second, the child lists stimuli that elicit anxiety and orders them in a hierarchical fashion from least to most anxiety provoking. For example, viewing a picture of a hypodermic needle might elicit low anxiety, seeing an actual needle might elicit moderate anxiety, and seeing a needle while smelling the alcohol swab a nurse uses to clean the skin shortly before an injection might elicit high anxiety. Third, the child engages in imaginal exposure; after the child is relaxed, the psychologist asks him to imagine the stimulus that elicits the least anxiety. Imagined exposure continues until the child's anxiety is extinguished or, at least, is manageable. The child gradually progresses up the hierarchy, pairing relaxation with more anxiety-provoking stimuli. Fourth, the child engages in *in vivo* (real life) exposure; after the child is relaxed, the psychologist presents an actual stimulus that elicits the least amount of anxiety (e.g., a picture of a needle). Once the child can tolerate this stimulus, he gradually progresses up the hierarchy until he can successfully undergo the medical procedure.

Pediatric psychologists often rely on operant conditioning to increase children's adherence. Three frequently used procedures are positive reinforcement, negative reinforcement, and response cost. For example, when a child is diagnosed with Type I diabetes, physicians usually recommend that families keep a record of the child's diet, exercise, blood glucose, and insulin throughout the day. The record allows the physician and family to determine the best timing and amount of insulin for the child. However, the glucose tests are slightly painful and record-keeping can be bothersome.

Rather than nag children, parents might award the child one point each time he correctly records information and bonus points for doing so with minimal prompting or complaining. These points can be used to buy small toys or privileges. Awarding points to increase compliance is an example of positive reinforcement: the presentation of a stimulus resulting in an increase in behavior. As an additional incentive, if the child accurately records information throughout the entire day, he might be excused from a chore, such as taking out the garbage. Excusing a child from a chore to increase compliance is an example of negative reinforcement: the removal or avoidance of a stimulus resulting in an increase in behavior. Finally, if the child fails to record information, he might be penalized points. The removal of points is an example of response cost, a form of negative punishment in which a stimulus is withdrawn, resulting in a decrease in behavior.

Pediatric psychologists also rely on principles of observational learning. One particularly useful technique is participant modeling; the psychologist demonstrates the desired behavior, and a child is encouraged to imitate the action. For example, a child afraid of entering an MRI machine might be more likely to do so if he saw the psychologist (or parent) demonstrating the procedure.

Cognitive Therapy

Pediatric psychologists often use both cognitive and behavioral interventions to help older children with chronic illnesses. The underlying premise of cognitive-behavioral therapy is the notion that children's thoughts, feelings, and actions are connected; each affects and is affected by the other. Therefore, changing the way children think about their medical condition, a procedure, or their treatment can influence the way they think and act. Cognitive interventions typically work better with older children who have the ability to engage in metacognition, that is, to think about their own thinking. Consequently, these interventions are most often used for school-aged children and adolescents.

Perhaps the most common cognitive intervention is **cognitive restructuring**, a technique used to change biased or irrational thoughts to more realistic or rational thoughts. First, the psychologist helps the child become aware of thoughts, beliefs, assumptions, or self-statements that cause him or her to become sad, anxious, or angry.

RESEARCH TO PRACTICE

COGNITIVE RESTRUCTURING FOR KIDS WITH DIABETES

Psychologist: Your mom was pretty angry at you for going to the party and eating all of that pizza and soda. She worries about you because she sees you're not watching your blood sugar.

Lewis: Well, I don't like the fact that all the other kids can eat what they want and drink what they want and I can't. Nobody has this problem but me.

Psychologist:	Let's look at that statement for a second: "Nobody has this problem but me." Do you think that's really true?
Lewis:	Of course, I feel like I'm the only one who has to worry about blood sugar and diet and stuff like that.
Psychologist:	I'm sure that's how you *feel*—like you're the only one, like you're singled out. Now tell me what you *think*. Are you really the only kid with diabetes in the world?
Lewis:	Of course not.
Psychologist:	Are you the only kid with diabetes at your school?
Lewis:	No. I know other kids who have it.
Psychologist:	What about kids in your school who have other dietary restrictions? It's not exactly the same thing, but do any of your friends have allergies or food restrictions?
Lewis:	Sure. Will and James are lactose intolerant. Sam's allergic to peanuts. Another kid can't eat breads or anything with wheat.
Psychologist:	So there's no need to feel resentful or angry or singled out. There are other kids who have to watch their diet too.
Lewis:	I guess I never thought about it before.

The psychologist helps the child identify potentially problematic thoughts and test them empirically, to see if they are true. If they are not true, she encourages the child to adopt more accurate, rational beliefs in future situations. These more accurate, rational beliefs may reduce negative feelings and actions.

Cognitive therapists also use role-play and self-statements to help children adopt more accurate, rational thoughts. During a role play, the psychologist and the child act out a situation that often elicits negative thoughts, feelings, and actions. The child can practice replacing biased or distorted thoughts with more realistic cognitions. The psychologist might also teach the child to practice self-statements—short and simple phrases that the child can say when he experiences negative emotions.

Two other cognitive interventions are guided imagery and refocusing. In guided imagery, the child is taught to replace thoughts about a medical procedure or illness with thoughts about a pleasant, peaceful situation (e.g., lying on the beach, flying a kite). Guided imagery is often used in combination with other relaxation techniques. Refocusing involves redirecting the child's attention from the stressful or painful event to more relaxing or entertaining stimuli. For example, a child with chronic pain might be asked to think

RESEARCH TO PRACTICE

ROLE PLAYING TO PRACTICE NEW SKILLS

Psychologist:	So let's imagine that you're at a party and there's pizza and soda and other things. You've already had some, and you know you need to stop. I'll be Sam and I'm offering you another soda. What can you do?
Lewis:	Say "no."
Psychologist:	Right, but that might not always work because you really, really want to drink the soda. And when you want to drink the soda, and Sam wants you to drink the soda, and the soda desperately wants to be drunk, what do you think will happen?
Lewis:	I'll probably drink it.
Psychologist:	Yes. Almost certainly. So let me teach you three things you can say in this situation. First, say, "no thanks." Second, ask for something non-sugary to drink, "Do you have water?" Unless the party's in the Sahara, they'll probably have water. Third, when you're drinking the water say to yourself, "I can do this. I'm taking care of myself." Take three long drinks and say it to yourself each time as you drink. Can you do that?
Lewis:	I think so.
Psychologist:	OK. Let's practice it.

about his last birthday party, a favorite meal, or playing video games with his friends.

Family Therapy

Families with strong support, cohesion, and communication are best able to help children cope with medical illness. In contrast, families characterized by distress and conflict are less able to marshal their resources to meet children's needs. Consequently, many pediatric psychologists integrate family therapy into their practice. Family therapy is based on systems theory, the idea that an individual's ability to cope with his environment is dependent on the many relationships he has with other people in his life. Changing one of these relationships will necessarily affect all of the other relationships because they are interrelated. Family therapists view the entire family as their "client" rather than a single child. Their goal is to improve family functioning with the understanding that it will lead to a corresponding improvement in the child's behavior.

There are many schools of family therapy. Each school places different emphasis on certain relationships between family members or divisions between the family and the outside world. One of the best known approaches is structural family therapy, developed by Salvador Minuchin. **Structural family therapy** is chiefly concerned with special relationships, or *alliances,* between parents and children. Problems occur when parents show too much involvement (i.e., enmeshment) or too little involvement (i.e., disengagement) in the child's life. For example, enmeshed parents might take excessive control over their child's illness and deny the child any say in its management. The child, in turn, might resent parental overcontrol and assert her autonomy by sabotaging treatment. Alternatively, a father might feel left out of a relationship between a mother and a child with chronic illness. The father's disengagement might cause family strain and communication problems.

Structural family therapists are also concerned with boundaries between the family and the outside world. Ideally, *boundaries* should be flexible. They should clearly divide family activities from other important domains of life (e.g., school, friends, work) while also being open to involvement with these domains. Problems occur when boundaries become excessively rigid or diffuse. For example, families of chronically ill children need to work effectively with medical professionals, therapists, schools, and other people in children's lives (e.g., coaches, friends). Families who refuse to interact with these different groups or who become too preoccupied with extra-family responsibilities and activities, may experience a lack of coherence.

Structural therapists typically meet with parents and children together. They seek to understand relationships between family members and identify problematic relationships and boundaries. When problematic relationships are found, the therapist often tries to disrupt these relationships. For example, in an enmeshed family, the therapist might try to give the child greater autonomy and responsibility for managing her illness. Alternatively, in a family with rigid boundaries, the therapist might challenge the family's underlying mistrust for the outside world. Overall, structural family therapy is associated with improved coherence and communication among family members and reductions in children's behavior problems.

Behavior family systems therapy (BFST) combines cognitive-behavioral interventions with elements of structural family therapy. The primary goal of BFST is to reduce conflict and increase communication among families. Techniques are behavioral, cognitive, and structural in nature. First, therapists provide problem-solving and communication skills training to families. Specifically, families are taught to solve disputes in ways that respect each family member's autonomy, thoughts, and feelings. A primary goal is to avoid coercive parent-child interactions, such as yelling, threatening, or inducing guilt. Second, therapists try to identify and challenge biased or irrational beliefs held by family members that contribute to family conflict. For example, parents might misattribute an adolescent's frustration as "a lack of parental respect" whereas adolescents might misattribute parents' concern as "overcontrolling." A therapist might relabel these behaviors to help parents and children view interactions more accurately and avoid unnecessary conflict. Third, therapists attempt to identify and correct alliances or boundaries in the family in ways similar to structural family therapists. Although most often used for families of disruptive youths, BFST has been used effectively for adolescents with chronic illnesses, such as cystic fibrosis and diabetes.

Multisystemic family therapy (MFT) has also been used to improve family cohesion and communication. Recall that MFT is typically used to treat antisocial adolescents; however, recent studies have demonstrated its effectiveness for families of children with chronic illness, such as diabetes. MFT is similar to other family therapies in that the goal is to improve relationships between family members. Therapists seek to reduce conflict, miscommunication, and coercive parent-child interactions. In addition, MFT is concerned with the family's relationships with the outside world, especially schools, medical professionals, and peers. Therapists who practice MFT emphasize the "ecological validity" of their interactions, that is, they want to make sure that their treatments will generalize to "the real world." Consequently, MFT therapists will consult with children's teachers, physicians, dieticians, and leaders of extracurricular activities to help identify and resolve problems that interfere with the management of their illness.

Group and Peer-Assisted Therapy

Some therapists offer therapy to groups of children with similar pediatric disorders. Group therapy can be helpful

GROUP THERAPY: GETTING FEEDBACK FROM PEERS

Hannah: Maybe you don't have many friends, Kylie, because you're always in a bad mood?

Therapist: What do you think, Kylie? Is there any truth to that?

Kylie: No, that's dumb. (To Hannah) It's even stupid to say such a thing.

Therapist: Hannah, how do you feel right now, after what Kylie said?

Hannah: Not very good. Like I don't want to be around her.

Therapist: (To the group) Anyone else? How do you feel?

Molly: Me, too.

Therapist: So, if these girls don't want to be around you when you get mad, maybe others don't, too. These girls want to be your friend, but they're being scared away.

in at least three ways. First, children with medical illnesses often feel emotionally isolated, that their illness or problems are unique, and that no one else can understand the stressors they experience. Group therapy allows children to encounter youths with similar medical problems and reduce feelings of isolation. Second, some children with chronic illness have deficits in problem-solving and social skills. Group therapy gives these children a chance to practice skills with each other. Third, group therapy allows children to receive feedback from their peers, regarding their own behavior. For example, group members might notice that a particular child often appears angry and resentful, often blaming others for his troubles. The group might mention this to the child saying, "Maybe you don't have many friends because you're always in a bad mood?" Although interpersonal feedback like this might be initially off-putting, a skillful therapist might be able to use this feedback to help youths learn about themselves and change their behavior.

The brief transcript in the text box Research to Practice: Group Therapy: Getting Feedback From Peers illustrates two principles of group therapy. First, group therapists focus chiefly on the *process* of therapy (i.e., the pattern of interactions between group members) rather than the *content* of therapy (i.e., what is being said). Second, whenever possible, group therapists focus on participants' immediate thoughts, feelings, and actions, rather than events that happened in the past or outside the therapy session. Group therapists often focus on the "here-and-now" rather than on the "there-and-then." Focusing on immediate interactions between group members allows members to give and receive feedback regarding their own interpersonal behavior.

Plante, Lobato, & Engel (2001) conducted a meta-analysis of the effectiveness of group therapy for children with chronic illness. They found that group therapies which focus chiefly on managing children's symptoms and improving

social and problem-solving skills were associated with the largest improvements in children's functioning. Groups that focused chiefly on providing facts to families about specific illnesses were less effective.

Two new group interventions for children with chronic illness have emerged in recent years: summer treatment programs and peer group interventions. Summer treatment programs usually consist of groups of children with similar medical problems who participate in several days' worth of psychoeducational and skill-building activities in the context of a summer camp. For example, camps have been developed for children with asthma, cancer, diabetes, and gastrointestinal problems. Overall, these camps are associated with reductions in anxiety and depression, improvements in positive affect and self-efficacy, and more satisfying interactions with friends and family (Brown et al., 2007). Peer group interventions involve children with chronic illness and their best friends or classmates. Friends and classmates learn about children's illnesses and ways they can help them adhere to medical recommendations and support them through tough times. For example, a peer group intervention for children with diabetes might teach friends the importance of monitoring blood sugar and diet as well as ways to manage stress.

Efficacy of Pediatric Treatment

Several meta-analyses indicate that individual, family, and group interventions for children with chronic illness are efficacious. Overall, mean effect sizes from published studies range from .71 to .87, indicating moderate to large differences between children who participate in therapy and those who do not. Treatment efficacy does not seem to depend on the type of illness; children with a range of illnesses seem to benefit equally. However, some evidence indicates that therapies which focus primarily on symptom management, symptom reduction, and skills training yield greater benefits than therapies that provide only information and education.

Finally, some data indicate that the effects of treatment are fairly long lasting, with benefits seen 12 months after termination (Beale, 2006; Kibby et al., 1998; Wolf, Guevara, Grum, Clark, & Cates, 2002).

CHAPTER SUMMARY

Enuresis

- Enuresis is the repeated voiding of urine into the bed or clothes shown by children 5 years of age or older.

  - Approximately 4.5% of 8 to 11-year-olds have enuresis. Prevalence decreases with age.
  - ADHD is the most common comorbid problem. Other social-emotional problems are often a cause, rather than consequence of, enuresis.
  - Parents sometimes exacerbate children's enuresis by blaming children or using behavioral techniques that make it less likely that children will learn to detect a full bladder and stay dry.

- Approximately 85% of children with nocturnal enuresis have monosymptomatic primary enuresis (MPE). These children wet only at night and have never been able to stay dry.

  - MPE is highly heritable.
  - Children with MPE have problems detecting a full bladder at night.

- Approximately 15% of children with nocturnal enuresis have polysymptomatic nocturnal enuresis (PSNE). These children wet during the day and night. During the day, they often have frequent, sudden urges to wet.

  - Youths with PSNE often have smaller functional bladder capacities than other children.
  - Youths with PSNE also show bladder instability (i.e., uninhibited bladder contractions that cause them to wet).

- Most children who wet only during the day engage in voiding postponement. Some youths who wet during the day have bladder instability or they lack coordination of the muscles that control urination.
- The treatment of nocturnal enuresis (especially MPE) involves the use of a urine alarm. The alarm stops nighttime urination through classical conditioning. The alarm startles children, causing them to contract muscles of the pelvic floor, inhibiting urination.
- Some youths with MPE require full spectrum home training, a multi-component treatment that consists of (a) education, (b) urine alarm training, (c) cleanliness training, (d) retention control training, and (e) overlearning.

  - Cleanliness training is a form of overcorrection in which children must clean themselves and their bedding following a nighttime accident.
  - Retention control training involves drinking progressively more fluid while inhibiting urination during the day. It is designed to increase functional bladder capacity.
  - Overlearning involves drinking progressively more fluid before bedtime after the child is able to stay dry during the night.

- Desmopressin (DDAVP) is a synthetic version of vasopressin. It reduces nighttime urine production and helps children stay dry. Relapse is very high after the medication is discontinued. It is usually considered a short-term treatment.
- Treatment for daytime wetting involves (a) helping children recognize and respond to signs of a full bladder, (b) increase control over urine flow, and (c) increase functional bladder capacity.

Encopresis

- Encopresis is the repeated passage of feces into inappropriate places (e.g., clothing). Usually, defecation is involuntary, but it can be volitional (e.g., a sign of defiance or anger). It is diagnosed only in children 4-years-old or older.

  - Primary encopresis is seen in children who have no history of controlling bowel movements.
  - Secondary encopresis is seen in children who show encopresis after a period of regular toilet use.
  - Approximately 3% of school-aged children have encopresis. Boys are 4 to 6 times more likely than girls to develop the disorder.

- Encopresis is usually (85%) caused by constipation and overflow incontinence. Fecal matter hardens in the rectum, causing pain. Children avoid toilet use. Then, fluid fecal matter leaks out causing involuntary soiling.
- Sometimes (15%), children engage in encopresis deliberately. Deliberate defecation can be a sign of oppositional-defiant behavior, severe psychosocial stress (e.g., parental separation), or sexual abuse.
- The treatment of encopresis requires collaboration by parents, physician, and therapist.

  - A physician will rule out possible medical conditions that may cause encopresis. Then, she may prescribe a laxative or enema to relieve constipation.

- The therapist explains encopresis caused by constipation and overflow incontinence to parents. He may stress the importance that parents not blame or punish their child.
    - Behavior therapy involves scheduled toilet sitting. Children are reinforced for appropriate sitting and (eventually) defecation.
- Treatment for non-retentive, volitional encopresis depends on the nature of the child's underlying social-emotional problems.

Sleep Disorders

- Insomnia Disorder is characterized by a marked disturbance in the quantity or quality of sleep that causes distress or impairment. Children with insomnia have difficulty falling sleep, staying asleep, or attaining restful sleep.
- Insomnia can develop in children and adolescents for multiple reasons.

    - Some infants and toddlers often become conditioned to falling asleep while being held or fed by others. They may develop an inability to go to sleep alone.
    - Other infants and toddlers wake during the night and cannot soothe themselves back to sleep.
    - Children may resist or "stall" at bedtime. Parents may intermittently reinforce their bids to stay awake.
    - Older children and adolescents may experience anxiety that contributes to Insomnia. Cognitive distortions frequently underlie their anxiety.

- Infants and toddlers with Insomnia need to learn how to fall asleep and remain asleep independent of their parents. Sleep hygiene and planned ignoring can be used to prepare the infant for bedtime and extinguish cries and protests.
- Parents can also set firm limits on children's bedtimes and use planned ignoring to extinguish bedtime resistance.
- Cognitive-behavioral interventions are often useful to treat Insomnia in older children and adolescents. Techniques include (a) relaxation training, (b) stimulus control, (c) sleep restriction, and (d) cognitive restructuring to correct maladaptive thoughts.
- Some youths take medication to manage Insomnia. The most common medications are antihistamines (e.g., Benedryl) and hypnotics (e.g., Ambien). These medications can disrupt the quality of sleep and are sometimes associated with tolerance and dependence. Relapse is very high after medication is discontinued.
- Circadian Rhythm Sleep-Wake Disorder is characterized by a persistent inability to fall asleep and wake at conventionally appropriate times.

    - Adolescents sometimes show this disorder because of phase delays in hormone secretion associated with puberty.
    - Chronotherapy is often successful in advancing the circadian cycle, leading to earlier bedtime and waking.

- Sleep Arousal Disorders occur when children have recurrent problems awakening from non-REM sleep. Three arousal problems seen in children are (a) confusional arousals, (b) sleepwalking, and (c) sleep terrors.

    - Toddlers and preschoolers with confusional arousals have problems transitioning from non-REM sleep to wakefulness. They wake, display dysphoria, and show a lack of responsiveness to others.
    - Sleepwalking is typically seen in youths 4 to 8 years of age. It occurs during non-REM sleep. Youths usually have no memory of sleepwalking after the event.
    - Young children with sleep terrors experience extreme distress and disorientation during non-REM sleep. They wake and are difficult to soothe. They usually have no memory of the event the next morning.

- Nightmare Disorder is characterized by recurrent nightmares that cause distress or impairment. Unlike arousal disorders, nightmares occur during REM sleep, and youths can usually recall the content of their dreams. Most youths do not receive treatment for this disorder.
- Obstructive Sleep Apnea Hypopnea is caused by blocked or restricted oxygen flow during sleep. It causes the youth to become aroused during the night, thereby interfering with sleep duration and quality. Surgery or CPAP is typically used to treat children with this disorder.

Pediatric Psychology

- Pediatric psychology is an interdisciplinary field concerned with the application of psychology to the domain of children's health. Pediatric psychologists often work in children's hospitals and clinics.
- Inpatient consultation-liaison is a primary job of many pediatric psychologists who work in hospitals. Consultation involves providing recommendations to hospital staff regarding the behavioral treatment of a child with a medical illness. Psychologists also act as liaison between families and hospital staff to help coordinate services and facilitate the transition from hospital to home and school.
- Many pediatric psychologists work with families to help children adhere to their medical treatment (e.g., special diet, medications).
- Pediatric psychologists sometimes specialize in the behavioral treatment of children with specific medical problems. They provide behavior therapy and counseling to children and families to help youths cope with these illnesses.

    - Psychologists help children with asthma avoid situations in which they might experience an attack, cope with attacks when they occur, and adhere to their physician's treatment plan.
    - Psychologists help youths with cancer by providing information about the illness, helping them cope with the initial diagnosis and resulting psychosocial stress, and manage pain and nausea associated with treatment. Psychologists may also help youths with their return to school after treatment and provide long-term supportive therapy.

- ○ Psychologists help children with cystic fibrosis and their families adhere to treatment. They may also provide therapy to older children who experience mood problems because of the illness.
  - ○ Psychologists help youths with diabetes monitor their blood sugar and adhere to dietary restrictions. They may also provide support to families to improve parent-child communication about the disorder and symptom management.
  - ○ Psychologists help children with gastrointestinal problems manage stress that can exacerbate symptoms. They may also provide counseling for anxiety and depression often associated with the disorder.
  - ○ Psychologists help youths with arthritis and sickle cell disease by teaching relaxation and pain management techniques and adherence to medication.
- Systematic desensitization is often used to help youths cope with frightening or uncomfortable medical procedures.
- Positive reinforcement and response cost is helpful in helping children and families adhere to physician's recommendations regarding treatment.
- Cognitive restructuring is typically used to challenge older children's and adolescents' cognitive distortions regarding their illness. Therapists help children see their illness more objectively rather than catastrophically.
- Family therapy is used to improve communication between youths with medical illness and their families. Family therapists focus on parents' involvement in youths' lives and boundaries between the family and the outside world.
- Some children with medical problems benefit from group therapy. Groups can help children feel less isolated. Groups also provide feedback to youths about the way their behaviors affect others.
- Other children with medical problems benefit from peer-assisted therapy. In this treatment, friends or siblings learn how to support youths with chronic illnesses.

KEY TERMS

adherence   642

alpha-agonists   636

antihistamines   636

arginine vasopressin (AVP)   621

awaken during the night   628

bedtime difficulties   628

bedtime fading   635

behavior family systems therapy (BFST)   648

benzodiazepine receptor agonists   637

catastrophizing   633

chronotherapy   637

Circadian Rhythm Sleep-Wake Disorder   637

cleanliness training   623

cognitive restructuring   646

confusional arousals   639

consultation   641

continuous positive air pressure (CPAP)   640

desmopressin (DDAVP)   624

disability stress coping (DSC) model   642

encopresis   625

enuresis   619

excessively sleepy   628

graduated ignoring   634

Inflammatory Bowel Disease (IBD)   645

Insomnia Disorder   629

Irritable Bowel Syndrome (IBS)   644

Kegel exercises   624

liaisons   641

monosymptomatic primary enuresis (MPE)   621

multisystemic family therapy (MFT)   648

Nightmare Disorder   640

nightmare imagery rehearsal therapy   640

Obstructive Sleep Apnea Hypopnea   640

overlearning   623

pediatric psychology   641

personalization   633

planned ignoring   634

polysomnogram (PSG)   629

polysymptomatic nocturnal enuresis (PSNE)   621

regular sleep/wake schedule   628

retention control training   623

scheduled wakings   635

selective abstraction   633

sleep architecture   628

Sleep Arousal Disorders   638

sleep hygiene   634

sleep terrors   639

sleepwalking   639

snore   628

structural family therapy   648

systematic desensitization   646

transactional stress and coping (TSC) model   642

urine alarm   622

voiding postponement   622

1. Many parents try to treat their children's nocturnal enuresis by restricting fluids after dinner. Why is this usually not effective in resolving the problem?

2. A urine alarm is typically used to treat nocturnal enuresis. However, experts disagree on how the alarm decreases nighttime wetting. How might you use classical conditioning to explain its effectiveness in decreasing enuresis? Alternatively, how might you use negative reinforcement to explain its effectiveness?

3. Many parents blame children for encopresis. To what extent is encopresis volitional? How might blaming or punishing children exacerbate the problem?

4. The treatment of insomnia in infants and toddlers typically involves extinction through planned ignoring. Why might some parents have difficulty implementing this treatment? How might parents' social and cultural background influence their willingness to use planned ignoring?

5. What is the difference between nightmares and sleep terrors? What would you say to a parent who is concerned about her daughter's recurrent (a) nightmares or (b) sleep terrors?

6. One of the "Five Cs" of pediatric psychology is "collaboration." Why is it important that pediatric psychologists collaborate with parents, teachers, physicians, and other healthcare providers? Give two examples of how collaboration might be critical to the treatment of children with chronic illness.

EXTEND YOUR LEARNING

Videos, practice tests, flash cards, study guides, and links to online resources for this chapter are available to students online. Teachers also have access to lecture notes, PowerPoint presentations, suggestions for classroom activities, and possible exam questions. Visit: www.sagepub.com/weis2e.

References

Abbeduto, L., McDuffie, A., Brady, N., & Kover, S. T. (2012). Language development in Fragile X Syndrome. In J. A. Burack, R. M. Hodapp, G. Iarocci, & E. Zigler (Eds.), *The Oxford handbook of intellectual disability and development* (pp. 200–216). New York: Oxford University Press.

Abbott, P. J. (2007). Co-morbid alcohol/other drug abuse/dependence and psychiatric disorders in adolescent American Indian and Alaska natives. *Alcoholism Treatment Quarterly, 24*, 3–21.

Abela, J. R. Z., Hankin, B. L., Haigh, E. A. P., Adams, P., Vinokuroff, T., & Trayhern, L. (2005). Interpersonal vulnerability to depression in high-risk children: The role of insecure attachment and reassurance seeking. *Journal of Clinical Child and Adolescent Psychology, 34*, 182–192.

Aber, J. L., Gershoff, E. T., Ware, A., & Kotler, J. A. (2004). Estimating the effects of September 11th and other forms of violence on the mental health and social development of New York City's youth: A matter of context. *Applied Developmental Science, 8*, 111–129.

Abikoff, H., Hechtman, L., Klein, R. G., Gallagher, R., Fleiss, K., Etcovitch, J., et al. (2004a). Social functioning in children with ADHD treated with long-term methylphenidate and multimodal psychosocial treatment. *Journal of the American Academy of Child and Adolescent Psychiatry, 43*, 820–829.

Abikoff, H., Hechtman, L., Klein, R. G., Weiss, G., Fleiss, K., Etcovitch, J., et al. (2004b). Symptomatic improvement in children with ADHD treated with long-term methylphenidate and multimodal psychosocial treatment. *Journal of the American Academy of Child and Adolescent Psychiatry, 43*, 802–811.

Abikoff, H., Jensen, P., Arnold, L. E., Hoza, B., Hechtman, L., Pollack, S., et al. (2002). Observed classroom behavior of children with ADHD: Relationship to gender and comorbidity. *Journal of Abnormal Child Psychology, 30*, 349–359.

Abrams, A. N., & Rauch, P. K. (2008). Pediatric consultation. In M. Rutter (Ed.), *Rutter's child and adolescent psychiatry* (pp. 1143–1155). New York: Blackwell.

Abramson, L. Y., Seligman, M. E., & Teasdale, J. D. (1978). Learned helplessness in humans: Critique and reformulation. *Journal of Abnormal Psychology, 87*, 49–74.

Achenbach, T. M. (1982). Assessment and taxonomy of children's behavior disorders. In *Advances in clinical child psychology* (pp. 1–38). New York: Springer.

Achenbach, T. M., Howell, C. T., Quay, H. C., & Conners, C. K. (1991). National survey of problems and competencies among four- to sixteen-year-olds: Parents' reports for normative and clinical samples. *Monographs of the Society for Research in Child Development, 56*, 1–131.

Achenbach, T. M., McConaughy, S. H., & Howell, C. T. (1987). Child/adolescent behavioral and emotional problems: Implications of cross-informant correlations for situational specificity. *Psychological Bulletin, 101*, 213–232.

Ackerman, B. P., Brown, E., & Izard, C. E. (2003). Continuity and change in levels of externalizing behavior in school of children from economically disadvantaged families. *Child Development, 74*, 694–709.

Ackerman, P., Newton, J., McPherson, W. B., Jones, J., & Dykman, R. (1998). Prevalence of posttraumatic stress disorder and other psychiatric diagnoses in three groups of abused children (sexual, physical, and both). *Child Abuse and Neglect, 22*, 759–774.

Adams, G., & Carnine, D. (2003). Direct instruction. In H. L. Swanson, K. R. Harris, & S. Graham (Eds.), *Handbook of learning disabilities* (pp. 403–416). New York: Guilford Press.

Adrian, M., Zeman, J., Erdley, C., Lisa, L., & Sim, L. (2011). Emotional dysregulation and interpersonal difficulties as risk factors for non-suicidal self-injury in adolescent girls. *Journal of Abnormal Child Psychology, 39*, 389–400.

Agras, W. S., Crow, S. J., Halmi, K. A., Mitchell, J. E., Wilson, G. T., & Kraemer, H. C. (2000). Outcome predictors for the cognitive behavior treatment of bulimia nervosa: Data from a multisite study. *American Journal of Psychiatry, 757*, 1302–1308.

Agras, W. S., Walsh, B. T., Fairburn, C. G., Wilson, G. T., & Kraemer, C. H. (2000). A multi-center comparison of cognitive-behavioral therapy and interpersonal psychotherapy for bulimia nervosa. *Archives of General Psychiatry, 57*, 459–466.

Agrawal, A., Heath, A. C., & Lynskey, M. T. (2011). *DSM-IV* to *DSM-5*: The impact of proposed revisions on diagnosis of alcohol use disorders. *Addiction, 106*, 1935–1943.

Ahmann, P., Waltonen, S., Olson, K., Theye, F., Van Erem, A., & LaPlant, R. (1993). Placebo-controlled evaluation of Ritalin side effects. *Pediatrics, 91*, 1101–1106.

Ainsworth, M. D. S., Belhar, M. C., Waters, E., & Wall, S. (1978). *Patterns of attachment: A psychological study of the strange situation.* Hillsdale, NJ: Erlbaum.

Akinbami, L. J., Liu, X., Pastor, P. N., Reuben, C. A. (2011). *Attention deficit hyperactivity disorder among children aged 5–17 in the United States.* Washington, DC: US Department of Health and Human Services.

Al Otaiba, S., & Fuchs, S. (2002). Characteristics of children who are unresponsive to early literacy intervention. *Remedial and Special Education, 23*, 300–316.

Alanay, Y., Unal, F., Turanli, G., Alikasifoglu, M., Alehan, D., Akyol, U., et al. (2007). A multidisciplinary approach to the management of individuals with fragile X syndrome. *Journal of Intellectual Disability Research, 51*, 151–161.

Alarcon, R. D. (2009). Culture, cultural factors and psychiatric diagnosis: review and projections. *World Psychiatry, 8*(3), 131–139.

Albano, A. M., Chorpita, B. F., & Barlow, D. H. (1996). Childhood anxiety disorders. In E. J. Mash & R. A. Barkley (Eds.), *Child psychopathology* (pp. 196–242). New York: Guilford Press.

Albano, A. M., & Hayward, C. (2004). Social anxiety disorder. In T. H. Ollendick & J. S. March (Eds.), *Phobic and anxiety disorders in children and adolescents* (pp. 198–235). New York: Oxford University Press.

Alfano, C. A., & Gamble, A. L. (2009). The role of sleep in childhood psychiatric disorders. *Child and Youth Care Forum, 38*, 327–340.

Alfano, C. A., Zakem, A. H., Costa, N. M., Taylor, L. K., & Weems, C. F. (2009). Sleep problems and their relation to cognitive factors, anxiety, and depressive symptoms in children and adolescents. *Depression and Anxiety, 26*, 503–512.

Alger, J. R. (2012). The diffusion tensor imaging toolbox. *Journal of Neuroscience, 32*, 7418–7428.

Alloy, L. B., Abramson, L. Y., Raniere, D., & Dyller, I. M. (1999). Research methods in adult psychopathology. In P. C. Kendall, J. N. Butcher, & G. N. Holmbeck (Eds.), *Handbook of research methods in clinical psychology* (pp. 466–498). New York: Wiley.

Almeida, L. G., Ricardo-Garcell, J., Prado, H., Barajas, L., Frenandez-Bouzas, A., Avilia, D., & Martinez, R. B. (2010). Reduced right frontal cortical thickness in children, adolescents, and adults with ADHD and its correlation to clinical variables. *Journal of Psychiatric Research, 44,* 1214–1223.

Al-Yagon, M., & Margalit, M. (2012). Children with Down syndrome: Parents' perspectives. In J. A. Burack, R. M. Hodapp, G. Iarocci, & E. Zigler (Eds.), *The Oxford handbook of intellectual disability and development* (pp. 349–365). New York: Oxford University Press.

Aman, M. G., Collier-Crespin, A., & Lindsay, R. (2000). Pharmacotherapy of disorders in mental retardation. *European Child & Adolescent Psychiatry, 9,* 98–107.

Aman, M. G., De Smedt, G., Derivan, A., Lyons, B., Findling, R. L., & Risperidone Disruptive Behavior Study Group. (2002). Double-blind, placebo-controlled study of risperidone for the treatment of disruptive behaviors in children with subaverage intelligence. *American Journal of Psychiatry, 159,* 1337–1346.

American Academy of Child and Adolescent Psychiatry. (2001). Practice parameter for the assessment and treatment of children and adolescents with suicidal behavior. *Journal of the American Academy of Child and Adolescent Psychiatry, 40,* 24–51.

American Psychiatric Association. (1980). *Diagnostic and statistical manual of mental disorders* (3rd ed.). Washington, DC: Author.

American Psychiatric Association. (2000). *Diagnostic and statistical manual of mental disorders* (4th ed., Text Rev.). Washington, DC: Author.

American Psychiatric Association. (2013). *Diagnostic and statistical manual of mental disorders* (5th ed.) (*DSM-5*). Washington, DC: Author.

American Psychological Association (APA). (1947). Recommended graduate training program in clinical psychology. *American Psychologist, 2,* 539–558.

American Speech-Language-Hearing Association (ASHA). (2005). Roles and responsibilities of speech-language pathologists with respect to augmentative and alternative communication. Retrieved from asha.org/policy.

Amir, R. E., Van den Veyver, I. B., Wan, M., Tran, C. Q., Francke, U., & Zoghbi, H. Y. (1999). Rett syndrome is caused by mutations in X-linked MECP2, encoding methyl-CpG-binding protein 2. *Nature Genetics, 23,* 185–188.

Amminger, G. P., Henry, L. P., Harrigan, S. M., Harris, M. G., Alvarez-Jimenez, M., Herrman, H., et al. (2011). Outcome in early-onset schizophrenia revisited: Findings from the Early Psychosis Prevention and Intervention Centre long-term follow-up study. *Schizophrenia Research, 131,* 112–119.

Anastasi, A., & Urbina, S. (1997). *Psychological testing.* Upper Saddle River, NJ: Prentice Hall.

Anastopoulos, A. D., Shelton, T. L., & Barkley, R. A. (2005). Family-based psychosocial treatments for children and adolescents with attention-deficit/hyperactivity disorder. In E. D. Hibbs & P. S. Jensen (Eds.), *Psychosocial treatments for child and adolescent disorders: Empirically based strategies for clinical practice* (pp. 327–350). Washington, DC: American Psychological Association.

Anderson R. A., & Rees C. S. (2007). Group versus individual cognitive-behavioural treatment for obsessive-compulsive disorder: A controlled trial. *Behavior Research and Therapy, 45,* 123–137.

Anderson, K. G., Ramo, D. E., & Brown, S. A. (2006). Life stress, coping and comorbid youth: An examination of the stress-vulnerability model for substance relapse. *Journal of Psychoactive Drugs, 38,* 255–262.

Anderson, S. R., Avery, D. L., DiPietro, E. K., Edwards, G. L., & Christian, W. P. (1987). Intensive home-based intervention with autistic children. *Education and Treatment of Children, 10,* 352–366.

Anderson-Frye, E. P., & Becker, A. E. (2004). Sociocultural aspects of eating disorders. In J. K. Thompson (Ed.), *Handbook of eating disorders and obesity* (pp. 565–589). Hoboken, NJ: Wiley.

Andersson, U. (2010). Skill development in different components of arithmetic and basic cognitive functions: Findings from a 3-year longitudinal study of children with different types of learning difficulties. *Journal of Educational Psychology, 102,* 115.

Andrews, G., Hobbs, M. J., Borkovec, T. D., Beesdo, K., Craske, M. G., Heimberg, R. G., et al. (2010). Generalized worry disorder: A review of *DSM-IV* generalized anxiety disorder and options for *DSM-5. Depression and Anxiety, 27,* 134–147.

Andrews, G., Slade, T., & Peters, L. (2009). Classification in psychiatry: ICD-10 versus *DSM-IV. British Journal of Psychiatry, 174,* 3–5.

Andrews, J. A. (2005). Substance abuse in girls. In D. J. Bell, S. L. Foster, & E. J. Mash (Eds.), *Handbook of behavioral and emotional problems in girls* (pp. 181–209). New York: Kluwer/Plenum.

Angell, C. A. (2009). *Language development and disorders.* Boston, MA: Jones & Bartlett.

Angelman, H. (1965). "Puppet children": A report on three cases. *Developmental Medicine and Child Neurology, 7,* 681–688.

Angold, A., Costello, E. J., & Erkanli, A. (1999). Comorbidity. *Journal of Child Psychology and Psychiatry and Allied Disciplines, 40,* 57–87.

Antony, M. M. (2005). Five strategies for bridging the gap between research and clinical practice. *Behavior Therapist, 28,* 162–163.

Appel, A. E., & Holden, W. (1998). The co-occurrence of spouse and physical child abuse: A review and appraisal. *Journal of Family Psychology, 12,* 578–599.

Appleton, R., & Baldwin, T. (2006). *Management of brain injured children* (2nd ed.). New York: Oxford University Press.

Arbuthnot, J., & Gordon, D.A. (1986). Behavioral and cognitive effects of a moral reasoning development intervention for high-risk behavior-disordered adolescents. *Journal of Consulting and Clinical Psychology, 54,* 208–216.

Arnold, L. (1996). Sex differences in ADHD: Conference summary. *Journal of Abnormal Child Psychology, 24,* 555–569.

Arsenault, L., Cannon, M., Witton, J., & Murray, R. M. (2004). Causal association between cannabis and psychosis: Examination of the evidence. *British Journal of Psychiatry, 184,* 110–117.

Asarnow, J. R., Goldstein, M. J., Tompson, M., & Guthrie, D. (1993). One-year outcomes of depressive disorders in child psychiatric in-patients: Evaluation of the prognostic power of a brief measure of expressed emotion. *Journal of Child Psychology and Psychiatry, 34,* 129–137.

Asarnow, J. R., & Kernan, C. L. (2008). Childhood schizophrenia. In T. P. Beauchaine & S. P. Hinshaw (Eds.), *Child and adolescent psychopathology* (pp. 614–642). New York: Wiley.

Asarnow, J. R., Porta, G., Spirito, A., Emslie, G., Clarke, G., Wagner, K. D., et al. (2011). Suicide attempts and nonsuicidal self-injury in the treatment of resistant depression in adolescents: Findings from the TORDIA study. *Journal of the American Academy of Child and Adolescent Psychiatry, 50,* 772–781.

Asarnow, J. R., Tompson, M., Hamilton, E. B., Goldstein, M. J., & Guthrie, D. (1994). Family expressed-emotion, childhood-onset depression, and childhood-onset schizophrenia spectrum disorders: Is expressed emotion a nonspecific correlate of child psychopathology or a specific risk for depression? *Journal of Abnormal Child Psychology, 22,* 129–146.

Aschenbrand, S. G., Kendall, P. C., Webb, A., Safford, S. M., & Flannery-Schroeder, E. (2003). Is childhood separation anxiety disorder a predictor of adult panic disorder and agoraphobia? A seven-year longitudinal study. *Journal of the American Academy of Child & Adolescent Psychiatry, 42,* 1478–1485.

Asherson, P., & Gurling, H. (2011). Quantitative and molecular genetics of ADHD. In C. Stanford & R. Tannock (Eds.), *Behavioral neuroscience of attention deficit hyperactivity disorder and its treatment* (pp. 239–272). New York: Springer.

Atlas, J. G. (2004). Interpersonal sensitivity, eating disorder symptoms, and eating/thinness expectancies. *Current Psychology: Developmental, Learning, Personality, Social, 22,* 368–378.

Augustyniak, K., Murphy, J., & Phillips, D. K. (2006). Psychological perspectives in assessing mathematics learning needs. *Journal of Instructional Psychology, 32,* 277–286.

Autism and Developmental Disabilities Monitoring Network (ADDM Network). (2012). Prevalence of autism spectrum disorders. *Morbidity and Mortality Weekly Report, 61,* 1–19.

Autism Genome Project Consortium. (2007). Mapping autism risk loci using genetic linkage and chromosomal rearrangements. *Nature Genetics, 39,* 319–328.

Axelson, D. A., Birmaher, B., Strober, M. A., Goldstein, B. I., Ha, W., Gill, M. K., et al. (2011). Course of subthreshold bipolar disorder in youth: Diagnostic progression from bipolar disorder not otherwise specified. *Journal of the American Academy of Child and Adolescent Psychiatry, 50,* 1001–1016.

Axelson, D. A., Perel, J. M., Birmaher, B., Rudolph, G., Nuss, S., Yurasits, L., et al. (2005). Platelet serotonin reuptake inhibition and response to SSRIs in depressed adolescents. *American Journal of Psychiatry, 162,* 802–804.

Aylward, B. S., Bender, J. A., Graves, M. M., & Roberts, M. C. (2009). Historical developments and trends in pediatric psychology. In M. C. Roberts & R. G. Steele (Eds.), *Handbook of pediatric psychology* (pp. 3–18). New York: Guilford.

Aylward, E. H., Richards, T. L., Berninger, V. W., Nagy, W. E., Field, K. M., Grimme, A. C. et al. (2003). Instructional treatment associated with changes in brain activation in children with dyslexia. *Neurology, 61,* 212 219.

Azar, S. T., & Wolfe, D. A. (1998). Child physical abuse and neglect. In E. J. Mash & R. A. Barkley (Eds.), *Treatment of childhood disorders* (pp. 501–544). New York: Guilford.

Azrin, N. H., & Peterson, A. L. (1988). Habit reversal for the treatment of Tourette syndrome. *Behavior Research and Therapy, 26,* 347–351.

Bacaltchuk, J., Trefiglio, R. P., Oliveira, I. R., Hay, P., Lima, M. S., & Mari, J. J. (2000). Combination of antidepressants and psychological treatments for bulimia nervosa: A systematic review. *Acta Psychiatrica Scandinavica, 101,* 256–264.

Baddeley, A. D., & Hitch, G. (1974). Working memory. In G. A. Bower (Ed.), *The psychology of learning and motivation* (pp. 47–90). New York: Academic Press.

Baetens, I., Claes, L., Muehlenkamp, J., Grietens, H., & Onghena, P. (2011). Non-suicidal and suicidal self-injurious behavior among Flemish adolescents: A web-survey. *Archives of Suicide Research, 15,* 56–67.

Bagwell, C. L., Molina, B. S. G., Kashdan, T. B., Pelham, W. E., & Hoza, B. (2006). Anxiety and mood disorders in adolescents with childhood attention-deficit/hyperactivity disorder. *Journal of Emotional and Behavioral Disorders, 14,* 178–187.

Baker, D. B., & Benjamin, T. (2000). The affirmation of the scientist-practitioner: A look back at Boulder. *American Psychologist, 55,* 241–247.

Bakermans-Kranenburg, M. J., Dobrova-Krol, N., & van IJzendoorn, M. (2012). Impact of institutional care on attachment disorganization and insecurity of Ukrainian preschoolers: Protective effect of the long variant of the serotonin transporter gene (5HTT). *International Journal of Behavioral Development, 36,* 11–18.

Bakermans-Kranenburg, M. J., Steele, H., Zeanah, C. H., Muhamedrahimov, R. J., Vorria, P., Dobrova-Krol, N. A., et al. (2011). Attachment and emotional development in institutional care. *Monographs for the Society for Research in Child Development, 76,* 62–91.

Balthazar, C. H., & Scott, C. M. (2007). Syntax-morphology. In A. G. Kamhi, J. J. Masterson, & K. Apel (Eds.), *Clinical decision making in developmental language disorders.* (pp. 143–163). Baltimore, MD: Brookes.

Bandura, A. (1973). *Aggression: A social learning theory analysis.* New York: Prentice Hall.

Bandura, A., Ross, D., & Ross, S. A. (1961). Transmission of aggression through imitation of aggressive models. *Journal of Abnormal & Social Psychology, 63,* 575–582.

Banez, G. A., & Cunningham, C. L. (2009). Abdominal pain-related gastrointestinal disorders. In M.C. Roberts & R.G. Steele (Eds.), *Handbook of pediatric psychology* (pp. 403–419). New York: Guilford.

Barber, B. (2002). *Intrusive parenting: How psychological control affects children and adolescents.* Washington, DC: American Psychological Association.

Bardone, A. M., Moffitt, T. E., Caspi, A., Dickson, N., & Silva, P. A. (1996). Adult mental health and social outcomes of adolescent girls with depression and conduct disorder. *Development and Psychopathology, 8,* 811–829.

Bardone, M. S., Moffitt, T. E., Caspi, A., Dickson, N., Stanton, W. R., & Silva, P. A. (1998). Adult physical health outcomes of adolescent girls with conduct disorder, depression, and anxiety. *Journal of the American Academy of Child and Adolescent Psychiatry, 317,* 594–601.

Barkley, R. A. (1988). The effects of methylphenidate on the interactions of preschool ADHD children with their mothers. *Journal of the American Academy of Child and Adolescent Psychiatry, 27,* 336–341.

Barkley, R. A. (1997a). *ADHD and the nature of self-control.* New York: Guilford Press.

Barkley, R. A. (1997b). *Defiant children: A clinician's manual for assessment and parent training.* New York: Guilford Press.

Barkley, R. A. (1998). *Attention deficit hyperactivity disorder: A handbook for diagnosis and treatment* (2nd ed.). New York: Guilford Press.

Barkley, R. A. (2004). Adolescents with attention-deficit/hyperactivity disorder: An overview of empirically based treatments. *Journal of Psychiatric Practice, 10,* 39–56.

Barkley, R. A., DuPaul, G. J., & Connor, D. F. (1999). Stimulants. In J. S. Werry & M. G. Aman (Eds.), *Practitioner's guide to psychoactive drugs in children and adolescents* (pp. 213–247), New York: Plenum.

Barkley, R. A., Edwards, G., Laneri, M., Fletcher, K. E., & Metevia, L. (2001). The efficacy of problem-solving communication training alone, behavior management training alone, and their combination for parent-adolescent conflict in teenagers with ADHD and ODD. *Journal of Consulting and Clinical Psychology, 69,* 926–941.

Barkley, R. A., Fischer, M., Smallish, L., & Fletcher, K. R. (2002). Persistence of attention deficit hyperactivity disorder into young adulthood as a function of reporting source and definition of disorder. *Journal of Abnormal Psychology, 111,* 279–289.

Barkley, R. A., Shelton, T. L., Crosswait, C., Moorehouse, M., Fletcher, K., Barrett, S., et al. (2000). Multi-method, psycho-educational intervention for preschool children with disruptive behavior: Preliminary results at post-treatment. *Journal of Child Psychology and Psychiatry, 41,* 319–332.

Barlow, D. H. (2002). *Anxiety and its disorders: The nature and treatment of anxiety and panic* (2nd ed.). New York: Guilford Press.

Barnard, L., Stevens, T., To, Y. M., Lan, W. Y., & Mulsow, M. (2010). The importance of ADHD subtype classification for educational applications of DSM-5. *Journal of Attention Disorders, 13,* 573–583.

Barnes, G. M., Hoffman, J. H., Welte, J. W., Farrell, M. P., & Dintcheff, B. A. (2006). Effects of parental monitoring and peer deviance on substance use and delinquency. *Journal of Marriage and Family, 68,* 1084–1104.

Barnett, D., Ganiban, J., & Cicchetti, D. (1999). Maltreatment, negative expressivity, and the development of Type D attachments from 12 to 24 months of age. *Monographs of the Society for Research in Child Development, 64,* 97–118.

Barnow, S., Schultz, G., Lucht, M., Ulrich, I., Preuss, U., & Freyberger, H. (2004). Do alcohol expectancies and peer delinquency/substance use mediate the relationship between impulsivity and drinking behaviour in adolescence? *Alcohol and Alcoholism, 39,* 213–219.

Baron, R. M., & Kenny, D. A. (1986). The moderator-mediator variable distinction in social psychological research: Conceptual, strategic, and statistical considerations. *Journal of Personality and Social Psychology, 51,* 1173–1182.

Baron-Cohen, S. (1995). *Mindblindness: An essay on autism and theory of mind.* Boston: MIT Press/Bradford Books.

Baron-Cohen, S. (2005). Autism and the origins of social neuroscience. In A. Easton & N. Emery (Eds.), *The cognitive neuroscience of social behaviour* (pp. 239–255). New York: Psychology Press.

Baron-Cohen, S., Leslie, A. M., & Frith, U. (1985). Does the autistic child have a "theory of mind"? *Cognition, 21,* 37–46.

Baron-Cohen, S., Scahill, V. L., Izaguirre, J., Hornsey, H., & Robertson, M. M. (1999). The prevalence of Gilles de le Tourette syndrome in children and adolescents with autism: A large-scale study. *Psychological Medicine, 29*, 1151–1159.

Baron-Cohen, S., Scott, J. J., Allison, C., Williams, J., Bolton, P., Matthews, F. E., et al., (2009). Prevalence of autism-spectrum conditions. *British Journal of Psychiatry, 194*, 500–509.

Barrett, P. M., Dadds, M. R., & Rapee, R. M. (1996). Family treatment of childhood anxiety: A controlled trial. *Journal of Consulting and Clinical Psychology, 64*, 333–342.

Barrett, P. M., Duffy, A. L., Dadds, M. R., & Rapee, R. M. (2001). Cognitive-behavioral treatment of anxiety disorders in children: Long-term (6 year) follow-up. *Journal of Consulting and Clinical Psychology, 69*, 1–7.

Barrett, P. M., Rapee, R. M., Dadds, M. M., & Ryan, S. M. (1996). Family enhancement of cognitive style in anxious and aggressive children. *Journal of Abnormal Child Psychology, 24*, 187–203.

Barrios, A. A., & O'Dell, S. L. (1998). Fears and anxieties. In E. J. Mash & R. A. Barkley (Eds.), *Treatment of childhood disorders* (2nd ed., pp. 249–337). New York: Guilford Press.

Barrouillet, P., Fayol, M., & Lathuliere, E. (1997). Selecting between competitors in multiplication tasks: An explanation of the errors produced by adolescents with learning disabilities. *International Journal of Behavioral Development, 21*, 253–275.

Barry, C. T., Frick, P. J., Grooms, T., McCoy, M. G., Ellis, M. L., & Loney, B. R. (2000). The importance of callous-unemotional traits for extending the concept of psychopathy to children. *Journal of Abnormal Psychology, 109*, 335–340.

Bauermeister, J. J., Alegria, M., Bird, H., Rubio-Stipec, M. A., & Canino, G. (1992). Are attentional-hyperactivity deficits unidimensional and multidimensional syndromes? Empirical findings from a community survey. *Journal of the American Academy of Child and Adolescent Psychiatry, 31*, 423–431.

Baumeister, A. A., & Bacharach, V. R. (1996). A critical analysis of the Infant Health and Development Program. *Intelligence, 23*, 79–104.

Baumeister, A. A., & Bacharach, V. R. (2000). Early generic educational intervention has no enduring effect on intelligence and does not prevent mental retardation: The Infant Health and Development Program. *Intelligence, 28*, 161–192.

Baumrind, D. (1991). The influence of parenting style on adolescent competence and substance use. *Journal of Early Adolescence, 11*, 56–95.

Beale, I. L. (2006). Efficacy of psychological interventions for pediatric chronic illness. *Journal of Pediatric Psychology, 31*, 437–451.

Beardslee, W. R., Versage, E. M., & Gladstone, T. R. (1998). Children of affectively ill parents: A review of the past 10 years. *Journal of the American Academy of Child & Adolescent Psychiatry, 37*, 1134–1141.

Beauchaine, T. P., Webster-Stratton, C., & Reid, M. J. (2005). Mediators, moderators, and predictors of 1-year outcomes among children treated for early-onset conduct problems: A latent growth curve analysis. *Journal of Consulting and Clinical Psychology, 73*, 371–388.

Beck, A. T. (1967). *Depression: Clinical, experimental, and theoretical perspectives.* New York: Harper & Row.

Beck, A. T. (1976). *Cognitive therapy and the emotional disorders.* New York: International Universities Press.

Beck, A. T., & Emery, G. (1985). *Anxiety disorders and phobias: A cognitive perspective.* Philadelphia: Center for Cognitive Therapy.

Beck, A. T., & Weishaar, M. E. (2005). Cognitive therapy. In R. J. Corsini & D. Wedding (Eds.), *Current psychotherapies* (pp. 238–268). Belmont, CA: Brooks/Cole.

Beck, J. S., Liese, B. S., & Najavits, L. M. (2005). Cognitive therapy. In R. J. Frances, S. I. Miller, & A. H. Mack (Eds.), *Clinical textbook of addictive disorders* (3rd ed., pp. 474–501). New York: Guilford Press.

Beck, S. J. (1937). Introduction to the Rorschach method. *American Orthopsychiatric Association Monograph, 1*, 1–278.

Beck, S. J., Hanson, C.A., Puffenberger, S. S., Benninger, K. L., & Benninger, W. B. (2010). A controlled trial of working memory training for children and adolescents with ADHD. *Journal of Clinical Child and Adolescent Psychology, 39*, 825–836.

Becker, A. E., Burwell, R., Gilman, S. E., Herzog, D., & Hamburg, P. (2002). Eating behaviors and attitudes following prolonged exposure to television among ethnic Fijian adolescent girls. *British Journal of Psychiatry, 180*, 509–514.

Becker, A. E., Eddy, K. T., & Perloe, A. (2009). Clarifying criteria for cognitive signs and symptoms for eating disorders in *DSM-V. International Journal of Eating Disorders, 42*, 611–619.

Beesdo, K., Bittner, A., Pine, D. S., Stein, M. B., Hofler, M., Lieb, R., & Wittchen, H. (2007). Incidence of social anxiety disorder and the constituent risk for secondary depression in the first three decades of life. *Archives of general Psychiatry, 64*, 903–912.

Beesdo, K., Knappe, S., & Pine, D. S. (2009). Anxiety and anxiety disorders in children and adolescents. *Psychiatric Clinics of North America, 32*, 483–524.

Behrman, A., & Haskell, J. (2010). *Exercises for voice therapy.* San Diego, CA: Plural.

Beidel, D. C., Morris, T. L., & Turner, M. W. (2004). Social phobia. In T. L. Morris & J. S. March (Eds.), *Anxiety disorders in children and adolescents* (pp. 141–163). New York: Guilford Press.

Beidel, D. C., Turner, M. W., & Trager, K. N. (1994). Test anxiety and childhood anxiety disorders in African American and White school children. *Journal of Anxiety Disorders, 8*, 169–179.

Beidel, D. C., & Turner, S. M. (2007). Behavioral and cognitive-behavioral treatment of social anxiety disorder in children and adolescents. In D. C. Beidel & S. M. Turner (Eds.), *Shy children, phobic adults: Nature and treatment of social anxiety disorders* (pp. 261–313). Washington, DC: American Psychological Association.

Beidel, D. C., Turner, S. M., & Morris, T. L. (1999). Psychopathology of childhood social phobia. *Journal of the American Academy of Child and Adolescent Psychiatry, 38*, 643–650.

Bergevin, T. A., Bukowski, W. M., & Karavasilis, L. (2003). Childhood sexual abuse and pubertal timing: Implications for long-term psychosocial adjustment. In C. Hayward (Ed.), *Gender differences at puberty* (pp. 187–216). New York: Cambridge University Press.

Bergh, C., Eriksson, M., Lindberg, G., & Sodersten, P. (1996). Selective serotonin reuptake inhibitors in anorexia. *Lancet, 348*, 1459.

Berkeley, S., Bender, W. N., Peaster, L. G., & Saunders, L. (2009). Implementation of response to intervention: A snapshot of progress. *Journal of Learning Disabilities, 42*, 85–95.

Berkeley, S., Scruggs, T. E., & Mastropieri, M. A. (2010). Reading comprehension instruction for students with learning disabilities, 1995–2006: A meta-analysis. *Journal of Learning Disabilities, 31*, 423–436.

Berliner, L. (2000). What is sexual abuse? In H. Dubowitz & D. DePanfilis (Eds.), *Handbook for child protection* (pp. 18–22). Thousand Oaks, CA: Sage.

Berliner, L. (2005). The results of randomized clinical trials move the field forward. *Child Abuse & Neglect, 29*(2), 103–105.

Berliner, L., & Elliott, D. M. (2002). Sexual abuse of children. In J. E. B. Myers, L. Berliner, J. Briere, C. T. Hendrix, C. Jenny, & T. A. Reid (Eds.), *The APSAC handbook on child maltreatment* (2nd ed., pp. 55–78). Thousand Oaks, CA: Sage.

Bernard, K., Dozier, M., Bick, J., Lewis-Morrarty, E., Lindheim, O., & Carlson, E. (2012). Enhancing attachment organization among maltreated children. *Child Development, 83*, 623–636.

Bernstein, G. A., & Victor, A. M. (2010). Separation anxiety disorder and school refusal. In M. K. Dulcan (Eds.), *Child and adolescent psychiatry* (pp. 325–338). Washington, DC: American Psychiatric Publishing.

Bernthal, J. E., & Bankson, N. W. (2004). *Articulation and phonological disorders.* Boston, MA: Allyn & Bacon.

Bettelheim, B. (1967). *The empty fortress: Infantile autism and the birth of self.* New York: Free Press.

Beutler, L. E., Zetzer, H. A., & Williams, R. E. (1996). Research applications of prescriptive therapy. In W. Dryden (Ed.), *Research in counselling and psychotherapy: Practical applications* (pp. 25–48). Thousand Oaks, CA: Sage.

Biedel, D. C., Turner, M. W., & Trager, K. N. (1994). Test anxiety and childhood anxiety disorders in African American and White school children. *Journal of Anxiety Disorders, 8*, 169–179.

Biederman, J., & Faraone, S. V. (2004). The Massachusetts General Hospital studies of gender influences on attention-deficit/hyperactivity disorder in youths and relatives. *Psychiatric Clinics of North America, 27,* 225–232.

Biederman, J., Faraone, S. V., Wozniak, J., Mick, E., Kwon, A., & Aleardi, M. (2004). Further evidence of unique developmental phenotypic correlates of pediatric bipolar disorder. *Journal of Affective Disorders, 82S,* S45–58.

Biederman, J., Faraone, S. V., Wozniak, J., Mick, E., Kwon, A., Cayton, G. A., et al. (2005). Clinical correlates of bipolar disorder in a large, referred sample of children and adolescents. *Journal of Psychiatric Research, 39,* 611–622.

Biederman, J., Kwon, A., Wozniak, J., Mick, E., Markowitz, S., Fazio, V., et al. (2004). Absence of gender differences in pediatric bipolar disorder: Findings from a large sample of referred youth. *Journal of Affective Disorders, 83,* 207–214.

Biederman, J., Lopez, F. A., Boellner, S. W., & Chandler, M. C. (2002). A randomized, double-blind, placebo-controlled study of SLI381 (Adderall XR) in children with attention-deficit/hyperactivity disorder. *Pediatrics, 110,* 258–266.

Biederman, J., Mick, E., Faraone, S. V., Braaten, E., Doyle, A., Spencer, T., et al. (2002). Influence of gender on attention deficit hyperactivity disorder in children referred to a psychiatric clinic. *American Journal of Psychiatry, 159,* 36–42.

Biederman, J., Milberger, S., & Faraone, S. V. (1995). Family-environmental risk factors for attention-deficit hyperactivity disorder. *Archives of General Psychiatry, 52,* 464–470.

Biederman, J., Monuteaux, M. C., Doyle, A. E., Seidman, L. J., Wilens, T. E., Ferrero, F., et al. (2004). Impact of executive functioning deficits and attention-deficit/hyperactivity disorder (ADHD) on academic outcomes in children. *Journal of Consulting and Clinical Psychology, 72,* 757–766.

Biederman, J., Petty, C., Faraone, S. V., Henin, A., Hirshfeld-Becker, D., Pollack, M. H., et al. (2006). Effects of parental anxiety disorders in children at high risk for panic disorder: A controlled study. *Journal of Affective Disorders, 94,* 191–197.

Biederman, J., Petty, C. R., Clarke, A., Lomedico, A., & Faraone, S.V. (2011). Predictors of persistent ADHD. *Journal of Psychiatric Research, 45,* 150–155.

Biederman, J., Petty, C. R., Evans, M., Small, J., & Faraone, S.V. (2010). How persistent is ADHD? *Psychiatry Research, 177,* 299–304.

Biederman, J., Wilens, T., Mick, E., Spencer, T., & Faraone, S. V. (1999). Pharmacotherapy of attention deficit/hyperactivity disorder reduces risk for substance use disorder. *Pediatrics, 104,* 20.

Bifulco, A., Moran, P. M., Ball, C., Jacobs, C., Baines, R., Bunn, A., et al. (2002). Childhood adversity, parental vulnerability and disorder: Examining inter-generational transmission of risk. *Journal of Child Psychology and Psychiatry, 43,* 1075–1086.

Biklen, D. (1993). *Communication unbound.* New York: Teachers College Press.

Binet, A., & Simon, T. (1916). *The development of intelligence in children.* Baltimore, MD: Williams & Wilkins.

Birkeland, S., Murphy-Graham, E., & Weiss, C. (2005). Good reasons for ignoring good evaluation: The case of the drug abuse resistance education (D.A.R.E.) program. *Evaluation and Program Planning, 28,* 247–256.

Birmaher, B., Arbelaez, C., & Brent, D. (2002). Course and outcome of child and adolescent major depressive disorder. *Child and Adolescent Psychiatric Clinics of North America, 11,* 619–637.

Birmaher, B., Axelson, D., Goldstein, B., Monk, K., Kalas, C., Obreja, M., et al. (2010). Psychiatric disorders in preschool offspring of parents with bipolar disorder. *American Journal of Psychiatry, 167,* 321–330.

Birmaher, B., Axelson, D., Goldstein, B., Strober, M., Gill, M. K., Hunt, J., Houck, P., et al. (2009). Four-year longitudinal course of children and adolescents with bipolar spectrum disorder: The course and outcome of bipolar youth (COBY) study. *American Journal of Psychiatry, 166,* 795–804.

Birmaher, B., Axelson, D., & Monk, K. (2009). Lifetime psychiatric disorders in school-aged offspring of parents with Bipolar Disorder. *Archives of General Psychiatry, 66,* 287–296.

Birmaher, B., Axelson, D. A., Monk, K., Kalas, C., Clark, D. B., Ehmann, M., et al. (2003). Fluoxetine for the treatment of childhood anxiety disorders. *Journal of the American Academy of Child and Adolescent Psychiatry, 42,* 415–423.

Birmaher, B., Axelson, D., Monk, K., Kalas, C., Goldstein, B., Hickey, M. B., et al. (2009). Lifetime psychiatric disorders in school-aged offspring of parents with bipolar disorder: The Pittsburgh Bipolar Offspring study. *Archives of General Psychiatry, 66,* 287.

Birmaher, B., & Brent, D. A. (2010). Depression and dysthymia. In M. Dulcan (Ed.), Textbook of child and adolescent psychiatry (pp. 261–278). Washington, DC: American Psychiatric Press.

Birmaher, B., Brent, D. A., & Benson, R. S. (2000). Summary of the practice parameters for the assessment and treatment of children and adolescents with depressive disorders. *Journal of the American Academy of Child and Adolescent Psychiatry, 37,* 1234–1238.

Birmaher, B., & Ollendick, T. H. (2004). Childhood-onset panic disorder. In T. H. Ollendick & J. S. March (Eds.), *Phobic and anxiety disorders in children and adolescents* (pp. 306–333). New York: Oxford University Press.

Birmaher, B., Ryan, N., Williamson, D., Brent, D., Kaufman, J., Dahl, R., et al. (1996). Childhood and adolescent depression: A review of the past 10 years, Part 1. *Journal of the American Academy of Child and Adolescent Psychiatry, 35,* 1427–1439.

Birmaher, B., Waterman, G. S., Ryan, N. D., Perel, J., McNabb, J., Balach, L., et al. (1998). Randomized, controlled trial of amitriptyline versus placebo for adolescents with treatment-resistant major depression. *Journal of the American Academy of Child and Adolescent Psychiatry, 37,* 527–535.

Birmaher, B., Williamson, D. E., Dahl, R. E., Axelson, D. A., Kaufman, J., Dorn, L. D., et al. (2004). Clinical presentation and course of depression in youth: Does onset in childhood differ from onset in adolescence? *Journal of the American Academy of Child & Adolescent Psychiatry, 43,* 63–70.

Birnbrauer, J. S., & Leach, D. J. (1993). The Murdoch Early Intervention Program after two years. *Behaviour Change, 10,* 63–74.

Bishop, D. (2006). What causes specific language impairment in children? *Current Directions in Psychological Science, 15,* 217–221.

Bishop, D., & Rutter, M. (2010). Neurodevelopmental disorders: Conceptual issues. In M. Rutter (Ed.), Child and adolescent psychiatry (pp. 32–41). Malden, MA: Blackwell.

Bisson, J. I., & Lewis, C. (2009). *Systematic review of psychological first aid.* Cardiff, UK: World Health Organization.

Bisson, J. I., Ehlers, A., Matthews, R., Pilling, S., Richards, D., & Turner, S. (2007). Psychological treatments for chronic post-traumatic stress disorder: Systematic review and meta-analysis. *British Journal of Psychiatry, 190,* 97–104.

Bittner, A., Goodwin, R. D., Wittchen, H., Beesdo, K., Hifler, M., & Lieb, R. (2004). What characteristics of primary anxiety disorder predict subsequent major depressive disorder? *Journal of Clinical Psychiatry, 47,* 618–626.

Bixler, E. O., Vgontzas, A. N., Lin, H., Liao, D., Calhoun, S., Vela-Bueno, A., et al. (2009). Sleep disordered breathing in children in a general population sample. *Sleep, 32,* 731–736.

Black, J. E., Jones, T. A., Nelson, C. A., & Greenough, W. T. (1998). Neuronal plasticity and the developing brain. In N. E. Alessi, J. T. Coyle, S. I. Harrison, & S. Eth (Eds.), *Handbook of child and adolescent psychiatry* (pp. 31–53). New York: Wiley.

Blader, J. C., & Carlson, G. A. (2007). Increased rates of bipolar disorder diagnoses among US child, adolescent, and adult inpatients. *Biological Psychiatry, 62,* 107–114.

Blaine, B., & Rodman, J. (2007). Responses to weight loss treatment among obese individuals with and without BED. *Eating and Weight Disorders, 12,* 54–60.

Blair, C., & Wahlsten, D. (2002). Why early intervention works: A reply to Baumeister and Bacharach. *Intelligence, 30,* 129–140.

Blair, R. J., Mitchell, D., & Blair, K. (2005). *The psychopath: Emotion and the brain.* Malden, MA: Blackwell.

Bloch, M. H., Craiglow, B. G., & Landeros-Weisenberger, A. (2009). Predictors of early adult outcome in pediatric-onset obsessive-compulsive disorder. *Pediatrics, 124,* 1085–1093.

Blood, G., Ridenour, V., & Qualls, C. (2003). Co-occurring disorders in children who stutter. *Journal of Communication Disorders, 36,* 427–448.

Bloodstein, O. (1995). *Handbook of stuttering.* San Diego, CA: Singular.

Bloodstein, O. (1997). Stuttering as an anticipatory struggle reaction. In R. Curlee & W. Perkins (Eds.), *Nature and treatment of stuttering.* Needham Heights, MA: Allyn & Bacon.

Bloomfield, E. R., & Shatkin, J. P. (2009). Parasomnias and movement disorders in children and adolescents. *Child and Adolescent Psychiatric Clinics of North America, 18,* 947–965.

Boddaert, N., Chabane, N., Gervais, H., Good, C. D., Bourgeois, M., Plumet, M. H., et al. (2004). Superior temporal sulcus anatomical abnormalities in childhood autism: A voxel-based morphometry MRI study. *Neuroimage, 23,* 364–369.

Bogels, S. M., & van Melick, M. (2004). The relationship between child-report, parent self-report, and partner report of perceived parental rearing behaviors and anxiety in children and parents. *Personality and Individual Differences, 37,* 1583–1596.

Boggs, S. R., Eyberg, S. M., Edwards, D. L., Rayfield, A., Jacobs, J., Bagner, D., et al. (2004). Outcomes of parent-child interaction therapy: A comparison of treatment completers and study dropouts one to three years later. *Child & Family Behavior Therapy, 26,* 1–22.

Boles, R. E., Roberts, M. C., & Vernberg, E. M. (2010). Treating non-retentive encopresis with rewarded scheduled toilet visits. *Behavior Analysis in Practice, 1,* 68–72.

Bonati, M., & Clavenna, A. (2005). The epidemiology of psychotropic drug use in children and adolescents. *International Review of Psychiatry, 17,* 181–188.

Bond, L., Toumbourou, J. W., Thomas, L., Catalano, R., & Patton, G. C. (2005). Individual, family, school and community risk and protective factors for depressive symptoms in adolescents: A comparison of risk profiles for substance use and depressive symptoms. *Prevention Science, 6,* 73–88.

Bonner, B. L., Logue, M. B., & Kees, M. (2003). Child maltreatment. In M. C. Roberts (Ed.), *Handbook of pediatric psychology* (pp. 652–663). New York: Guilford Press.

Boone, D. R., McFarlane, S. C., Von Berg, S. L., & Zraick, R. I. (2010). *The voice and voice therapy.* Boston: Allyn & Bacon.

Borkovec, T. D., & Inz, J. (1990). The nature of worry in generalized anxiety disorder: A predominance of thought activity. *Behaviour Research and Therapy, 28,* 153–158.

Borkovec, T. D., Ray, W. J., & Stober, J. (1998). Worry: A cognitive phenomenon intimately linked to affective, physiological, and interpersonal behavioral processes. *Cognitive Therapy and Research, 22,* 561–576.

Bos, K., Zeanah, C. H., Fox, N. A., Drury, S. S., McLaughlin, K. A., & Nelson, C. A. (2011). Psychiatric outcomes in young children with a history of institutionalization. *Harvard Review of Psychiatry, 19,* 15–24.

Bos, K., Zeanah, C. H., Smyke, A. T., Fox, N. A., & Nelson, C. A. (2010). Stereotypies in children with a history of early institutional care. *Archives of Pediatric and Adolescent Medicine, 164,* 406–411.

Bouchard, S., Mendlowitz, S. L., Coles, M. E., & Franklin, M. (2004). Considerations in the use of exposure with children. *Cognitive and Behavioral Practice, 11,* 56–65.

Boudreau, D. (2007). Supporting the development of spoken narrative skills in children with language impairment. In A.G. Kamhi, J.J. Masterson, & K. Apel (Eds.), *Clinical decision making in developmental language disorders.* (pp. 203–222). Baltimore, MD: Brookes Publishing.

Bowlby, J. (1951). *Maternal Care and Mental Health.* New York: Schocken.

Bowlby, J. (1954). *Child care and the growth of love.* New York: Penguin.

Bowlby, J. (1969), *Attachment and loss, Vol. 1: Attachment.* New York: Basic Books.

Bowlby, J. (1973). *Attachment and loss, Vol. 2: Separation.* New York: Basic Books.

Bowlby, J. (1980). *Attachment and loss: Vol. 3. Loss: Sadness and depression.* New York: Basic Books.

Bowlby, J. (1988). *A secure base: Parent-child attachment and healthy human development.* New York: Basic Books.

Boyle, C. A., Boulet, S., Schieve, L. A., Cohen, R. A., Blumberg, S. J., Yeargin-Allsopp, M., et al. (2011). Trends in the prevalence of developmental disabilities in US children. *Pediatrics, 127,* 1023–1042.

Boyle, M. H., & Lipman, E. L. (2002). Do places matter? Socioeconomic disadvantage and behavioral problems of children in Canada. *Journal of Consulting & Clinical Psychology, 70,* 378–389.

Bradley, C. (1937). The behavior of children taking Benzedrine. *American Journal of Psychiatry, 94,* 577–585.

Bradley, C. (1950). Benzedrine and Dexedrine in the treatment of children's behavior problems. *Pediatrics, 5,* 24–36.

Bradley, J. D., & Golden, C. J. (2001). Biological contributions to the presentation and understanding of attention-deficit/hyperactivity disorder: A review. *Clinical Psychology Review, 21,* 907–929.

Brake, W. G., Sullivan, R. M., & Gratton, A. (2000). Perinatal distress leads to lateralized medial prefrontal cortical dopamine hypofunction in adult rats. *Journal of Neuroscience, 20,* 5538–5543.

Brazzelli, M., Griffiths, P. V., Cody, J. D., & Tappin, D. (2011). Behavioral and cognitive interventions with or without other treatments for the management of fecal incontinence in children. *Cochrane Reviews.*

Bregman, J. D. (2005). Definitions and characteristics of the spectrum. In D. Zager (Ed.), *Autism spectrum disorders: Identification, education, and treatment* (pp. 3–46). Mahwah, NJ: Erlbaum.

Brendgen, M., Wanner, B., Morin, A. J. S., & Vitaro, F. (2005). Relations with parents and with peers, temperament, and trajectories of depressed mood during early adolescence. *Journal of Abnormal Child Psychology, 33,* 579–594.

Brennan, P. A., & Walker, E. F. (2010). Vulnerability to schizophrenia in childhood and adolescence. In R. E. Ingram & J. M. Price (Eds.), *Vulnerability to psychopathology: Risk across the lifespan* (pp. 363–388). New York: Guilford.

Brent, D., & Weersing, V. R. (2010). Depressive disorders in childhood and adolescence. In M. Rutter (Ed.), *Rutter's child and adolescent psychiatry* (pp. 587–612). Malden, MA: Blackwell.

Brent, D., Emslie, G., Clarke, G., Asarnow, J., Spirito, A., Ritz, L., et al. (2009). Predictors of spontaneous and systematically assessed suicidal adverse events in the treatment of SSRI-resistant depression in adolescents (TORDIA) study. *American Journal of Psychiatry, 166,* 718–726.

Brent, D., Emslie, G., Clarke, G., Wagner, K. D., Asarnow, J. R., Keller, M., Vitiello, B., et al. (2008). Switching to another SSRI or to venlafaxine with or without cognitive behavioral therapy for adolescents with SSRI-resistant depression: The TORDIA randomized controlled trial. *JAMA, 299,* 901–913.

Brent, D., Holder, D., Kolko, D., Birmaher, B., Baugher, M., Roth, C., et al. (1997). A clinical psychotherapy trial for adolescent depression comparing cognitive, family, and supportive therapy. *Archives of General Psychiatry, 54,* 877–885.

Brereton, A. V., Tonge, B. J., & Einfeld, S. L. (2006). Psychopathology in children and adolescents with autism compared to young people with intellectual disability. *Journal of Autism and Developmental Disorders, 36,* 863–870.

Breslau, J., Lane, M., Sampson, N., & Kessler, R. C. (2008). Mental disorders and subsequent educational attainment in a US national sample. *Journal of Psychiatric Research, 42,* 708–716.

Brestan, E. V., & Eyberg, S. M. (1998). Effective psychosocial treatments of conduct-disordered children and adolescents: 29 years, 82 studies, 5,272 kids. *Journal of Clinical Child Psychology, 27,* 180–189.

Bretherton, I. (1992). The origins of attachment theory. *Developmental Psychology, 28,* 759–775.

Breton, J., Bergeron, L., Valla, J., Berthiaume, C., Gaudet, N., Lambert, J., et al. (1999). Quebec Child Mental Health Survey: Prevalence of DSM-III-R mental health disorders. *Journal of Child Psychology and Psychiatry, 40,* 375–384.

Brewin, C. R., Lanius, R. A., Novac, A., Schnyder, U., & Galea, S. (2009). Reformulating PTSD for *DSM-5*: Life after criterion A. *Journal of Traumatic Stress, 22,* 366–373.

Bridge, J., Iyengar, S., Salary, C. B., Barbe, R. P., Birmaher, B., Pincus, H., et al. (2007). Clinical response and risk of reported suicidal ideation and suicide attempts in pediatric antidepressant treatment. *JAMA: Journal of the American Medical Association, 297,* 1683–1696.

Briere, J., Berliner, L., Bulkley, J., Jenny, C. A., & Reid, T. A. (1996). *The APSAC handbook on child maltreatment.* Thousand Oaks, CA: Sage.

Brilleslijper-Kater, S. N., Friedrich, W. N., & Corwin, D. L. (2004). Sexual knowledge and emotional reaction as indicators of sexual abuse in young children: Theory and research challenges. *Child Abuse & Neglect, 28,* 1007–1017.

British Medical Association. (2006). *Child and adolescent mental health: A guide for healthcare professionals.* London: Author.

Brody, G. H., Ge, X., Conger, R., Gibbons, F. X., McBride Murry, V., Gerrard, M., et al. (2001). The influence of neighborhood disadvantage, collective socialization, and parenting on African American children's affiliation with deviant peers. *Child Development, 72,* 1231–1246.

Bronfenbrenner, U. (1979). *The ecology of human development: Experiments by design and nature.* Cambridge, MA: Harvard University Press.

Bronfenbrenner, U. (2000). Ecological system theory. In A. E. Kazdin (Ed.), *Encyclopedia of psychology* (Vol. 3, pp. 129–133). New York: Oxford University Press.

Bronfenbrenner, U., McClelland, P. D., Wethington, E., Moen, P., & Ceci, S. (1996). *The state of the Americas: This generation and the next.* New York: Free Press.

Bronfenbrenner, U., & Morris, P. A. (1998). The ecology of developmental process. In W. Damon (Ed.), *Handbook of child psychology: Vol. 1. Theory* (pp. 993–1028). New York: Wiley.

Brookes, K., Xu, X., Chen, W., Zhou, K., Neale, B., Lowe, N., et al. (2006). The analysis of 51 genes in *DSM-IV* combined type attention deficit hyperactivity disorder: Association signals in DRD4, DAT1 and 16 other genes. *Molecular Psychiatry, 11,* 935–953.

Brooks-Gunn, J., & Duncan, G. J. (1997). The effects of poverty on children. *The Future of Children, 7,* 55–71.

Brooks-Gunn, J., Duncan, G. J., Klebanov, P. K., & Sealand, N. (1993). Do neighborhoods influence child and adolescent development? *American Journal of Sociology, 99,* 353–395.

Brotman, M. A., Kassem, K., Reising, M. M., Guyer, A. E., Dickstein, D. P., Rich, B. A., et al. (2007). Parental diagnoses in youth with narrow phenotype bipolar disorder or severe mood dysregulation. *American Journal of Psychiatry, 164,* 1238–1241.

Brotman, M. A., Rich, B. A., Guyer, A. E., Lunsford, J. R., Horsey, S. E., Reising, M. M., et al. (2010). Amygdala activation during emotion processing of neutral faces in children with severe mood dysregulation versus ADHD or bipolar disorder. *American Journal of Psychiatry, 167,* 61.

Brotman, M. A., Schmajuk, M., Rich, B. A., Dickstein, D. P., Guyer, A. E., Costello, E. J., et al. (2006). Prevalence, clinical correlates, and longitudinal course of severe mood and behavioral dysregulation in children. *Biological Psychiatry, 60,* 991–997.

Brown, E. J., & Kolko, J. (1999). Child victims' attributions about being physically abused: An examination of factors associated with symptom severity. *Journal of Abnormal Child Psychology, 27,* 311–322.

Brown, M. L., Pope, A. W., & Brown, E. J. (2010). Treatment of primary nocturnal enuresis in children. *Child: Care, Health, and Development, 37,* 153–160.

Brown, R., Antonuccio, D., DuPaul, G., Fristad, M., King, C., Leslie, L., et al. (2008a). Schizophrenia spectrum disorders. In *Childhood mental health disorders: Evidence based and contextual factors for psychosocial, psychopharmacological, and combined interventions* (pp. 97–103). Washington, DC: American Psychological Association.

Brown, R. T., Antonuccio, D. O., DuPaul, G. J., Fristad, M. A., King, C. A., Leslie, L. K. et al. (2008b). *Childhood mental health disorders.* Washington, DC: American Psychological Association.

Brown, R. T., Daly, B. P., & Rickel, A. U. (2007). *Chronic illness in children and adolescents.* Cambridge, MA: Hogrefe.

Browne, A., & Finkelhor, D. (1986). Impact of child sexual abuse: A review of the research. *Psychological Bulletin, 99,* 66–77.

Brownley, K. A., Berkman, N. D., Sedway, J. A., Lohr, K. N., & Bulik, C. M. (2007). Binge eating disorder treatment. *International Journal of Eating Disorders, 40,* 337–348.

Brozina, K., & Abela, Z. (2006). Symptoms of depression and anxiety in children: Specificity of the hopelessness theory. *Journal of Clinical Child and Adolescent Psychology, 35,* 515–527.

Bruce, J., Tarullo, A. R., & Gunnar, M. R. (2009). Disinhibited social behavior among internationally adopted children. *Development and Psychopathology, 21,* 157–171.

Bruch, H. (1973). *Eating disorders: Obesity, anorexia nervosa, and the person within.* New York: Basic Books.

Brunner, R., Parzer, P., Haffner, J., Steen, R., Roos, J., Klett, M., & Resch, F. (2007). Prevalence and psychological correlates of occasional and repetitive deliberate self-harm in adolescents. *Archives of Pediatrics & Adolescent Medicine, 161,* 641.

Brutten, E. J., & Shoemaker, D. (1967). *The modification of stuttering.* Englewood Cliffs, NJ: Prentice-Hall.

Bryant-Waugh, R., Markham, L., Kreipe, R. E., & Walsh, B. T. (2010). Feeding disorders in childhood. *International Journal of Eating Disorders, 43,* 98–111.

Brymer, M., Jacobs, A., Layne, C., Pynoos, R., Ruzek, J., Steinberg, A., et al. (2006). Psychological first aid: Field operations guide. Durham, NC: National Child Traumatic Stress Network and National Center for PTSD.

Buckhalt, J. A., Wolfson, A. R., & El-Sheikh, M. (2009). Children's sleep and school psychology practice. *School Psychology Quarterly, 24,* 60–69.

Buckley, S. (1999). Promoting the cognitive development of children with Down Syndrome: The practical implications of recent psychological research. In J. A. Rondal, J. Perera, & L. Nadel (Eds.), *Down's syndrome: A review of current knowledge* (pp. 99–110). London: Whurr.

Buckley, S., Dodd, P., Burke, A., Guerin, S., McEvoy, J., & Hillery, J. (2006). Diagnosis and management of attention-deficit hyperactivity disorder in children and adults with and without learning disability. *Psychiatric Bulletin, 30,* 251–253.

Buckloh, L. M., & Greco, P. (2009). Professional development, roles, and practice patterns. In M. C. Roberts & R. G. Steele (Eds.), *Handbook of pediatric psychology* (pp. 35–51). New York: Guilford.

Bugental, D. B., Johnston, C., New, M., & Silvester, J. (1998). Measuring parental attributions: Conceptual and methodological issues. *Journal of Family Psychology, 12,* 459–480.

Bukstein, O. G. (2011). Attention deficit hyperactivity disorder and substance use disorders. In C. Stanford & R. Tannock (Eds.), *Behavioral neuroscience of attention deficit hyperactivity disorder and its treatment* (pp. 145–172). New York: Springer.

Bukstein, O. G., & Deas, D. (2010). Substance abuse and addictions. In M. K. Dulcan (Ed.), *Dulcan's textbook of child and adolescent psychiatry* (pp. 241–258). Washington, DC: American Psychiatric Publishing.

Bulik, C. M. (2004). Genetic and biological risk factors. In J. K. Thompson (Ed.), *Handbook of eating disorders and obesity* (p. 3–16). Hoboken, NJ: Wiley.

Bulik, C. M., Klump, K. L., Thornton, L., Kaplan, A. S., Devlin, B., Fichter, M. M., et al. (2004). Alcohol use disorder comorbidity in eating disorders: A multicenter study. *Journal of Clinical Psychiatry, 65,* 1000–1006.

Bureau, J. F., Martin, J., Freynet, N., Poirier, A. A., Lafontaine, M. F., & Cloutier, P. (2010). Perceived dimensions of parenting and non-suicidal self-injury in young adults. *Journal of Youth and Adolescence, 39,* 484–494.

Burke, J. D. (2012). An affective dimension within oppositional defiant disorder symptoms among boys. *Journal of Child Psychology and Psychiatry, 53,* 1176–1183.

Burke, J. D., Hipwell, A. E., & Loeber, R. (2010). Dimensions of oppositional defiant disorder as predictors of depression and conduct disorder in preadolescent girls. *Journal of the American Academy of Child and Adolescent Psychiatry, 49,* 484–492.

Burleson, J. A., & Kaminer, Y. (2005). Self-efficacy as a predictor of treatment outcome in adolescent substance use disorders. *Addictive Behaviors, 30,* 1751–1764.

Burlingham, D., & Freud, A. (1962). *Infants without families: The case for and against residential nurseries.* London: International Universities Press.

Burns, B. J., Costello, E. J., Angold, A., Tweed, D., Stangl, D., Farmer, E. M. Z., et al. (1995). Children's mental health service use across service sectors. *Health Affairs, 14,* 147–159.

Burt, K. B., Van Dulmen, M. H. M., Carlivati, J., Egeland, B., Sroufe, L. A., Forman, D. R., et al. (2005). Mediating links between maternal depression and offspring psychopathology: The importance of independent data. *Journal of Child Psychology and Psychiatry, 46,* 490–499.

Burt, S. A., McGue, M., DeMarte, J. A., Krueger, R. F., & Iacono, W. G. (2006). Timing of menarche and the origins of conduct disorder. *Archives of General Psychiatry, 63,* 890–896.

Burton, E., Stice, E., & Seeley, J. R. (2004). A prospective test of the stress-buffering model of depression in adolescent girls: No support once again. *Journal of Consulting and Clinical Psychology, 72,* 689–697.

Burwell, R. A., & Shirk, R. (2007). Subtypes of rumination in adolescence: Associations between brooding, reflection, depressive symptoms, and coping. *Journal of Clinical Child and Adolescent Psychology, 36,* 56–65.

Buschmann, A., Jooss B, & Rupp A., (2008). Children with developmental language delay at 24 months of age: Results of a diagnostic work-up. *Developmental Medicine and Child Neurology, 50,* 223–229.

Butcher, J. N., Williams, C. L., Graham, J. R., Archer, R. P., Tellegen, A., Ben-Porath, Y. S., et al. (1992). *MMPI-A: Manual for administration, scoring, and interpretation.* Minneapolis: University of Minnesota Press.

Butler, L., Miezitis, S., Friedman, R., & Cole, E. (1980). The effect of two school-based intervention programs on depressive symptoms in preadolescents. *American Educational Research Journal, 17,* 111–119.

Butler, R. J. (2008). Wetting and soiling. In M. Rutter (Ed.), *Rutter's child and adolescent psychiatry* (pp. 916–929). Malden, MA: Blackwell.

Butterworth, B. (1999). *The mathematical brain.* London: Macmillan.

Butterworth, B. (2005). Developmental dyscalculia. In J. I. D. Campbell (Ed.), *Handbook of mathematical cognition* (pp. 455–467). New York: Psychology Press.

Button, T. M. M., Hewitt, J. K., Rhee, S. H., Young, S. E., Corley, R. P., & Stalling, M. C. (2006). Examination of the causes of covariation between conduct disorder symptoms and vulnerability to drug dependence. *Twin Research and Human Genetics, 9,* 38–45.

Butzlaff, R. L., & Hooley, J. M. (1998). Expressed emotion and psychiatric relapse: A meta-analysis. *Archives of General Psychiatry, 55,* 547–552.

Byrne, B., Olson, R. K., Samuelsson, S., Wadsworth, S., Corley, R., DeFries, J. C., et al. (2006). Genetic and environmental influences on early literacy. *Journal of Research in Reading, 29,* 33–49.

Caetano, S. C., Olvera, R. L., Hunter, K., Hatch, J. P., Najt, P., Bowden, C., et al. (2006). Association of psychosis with suicidality in pediatric bipolar I, II and bipolar NOS patients. *Journal of Affective Disorders, 91,* 33–37.

Callaghan, R. C., Hathaway, A., Cunningham, J. A., Vettese, L. C., Wyatt, S., & Taylor, L. (2005). Does stage-of-change predict dropout in a culturally diverse sample of adolescents admitted to inpatient substance-abuse treatment? A test of the transtheoretical model. *Addictive Behaviors, 30,* 1834–1847.

Calzada, E. J., Eyberg, S. M., Rich, B., & Querido, J. G. (2004). Parenting disruptive preschoolers: Experiences of mothers and fathers. *Journal of Abnormal Child Psychology, 32,* 203–213.

Camarata, S. M., & Nelson, K. E. (2006). Conversational recast intervention with preschool and older children. In R. J. McCauley & M. E. Fey (Eds.), *Treatment of language disorders in children* (pp. 237–264). Baltimore, MD: Brookes Publishing.

Campbell, L. K., Cox, D. J., & Borowitz, S. M. (2009). Elimination disorders. In M.C. Roberts & R.G. Steele (Eds.), *Handbook of pediatric psychology* (pp. 481–490). New York: Guilford.

Cao, F., Bitan, T., Chou, T., Burman, D. D., & Booth, J. R. (2006). Deficient orthographic and phonological representations in children with dyslexia revealed by brain activation patterns. *Journal of Child Psychology and Psychiatry, 47,* 1041–1050.

Capaldi, D. M. (1992). Co-occurrence of conduct problems and depressive symptoms in early adolescent boys: II. A 2-year follow-up at grade 8. *Development and Psychopathology, 4,* 125–144.

Caputo, A. A., Frick, P. J., & Brodsky, S. L. (1999). Family violence and juvenile sex offending: Potential mediating roles of psychopathic traits and negative attitudes toward women. *Criminal Justice & Behavior, 26,* 338–356.

Carcani-Rathwell, I., Rabe-Hasketh, S., & Santosh, P. J. (2006). Repetitive and stereotyped behaviours in pervasive developmental disorders. *Journal of Child Psychology and Psychiatry, 47,* 573–581.

Cardno, A., & Gottesman, I. (2000). Twin studies of schizophrenia. *American Journal of Medical Genetics, 97,* 12–17.

Carlson, C. D., & Francis, D. J. (2002). Increasing the reading achievement of at-risk children through direct instruction: Evaluation of the Rodeo Institute for Teacher Excellence (RITE). *Journal of Education for Students Placed at Risk, 7,* 141–166.

Carlson, C. L., & Mann, M. (2002). Sluggish cognitive tempo predicts a different pattern of impairment in the attention deficit hyperactivity disorder predominantly inattentive type. *Journal of Clinical Child and Adolescent Psychology, 31,* 123–129.

Carlson, C. L., Shin, M., & Booth, J. (1999). The case for *DSM-IV* subtypes in ADHD. *Mental Retardation and Developmental Disabilities Research Reviews, 5,* 199–206.

Carlson, G. A., Bromet, E. J., & Sievers, S. (2000). Phenomenology and outcome of subjects with early and adult-onset psychotic mania. *American Journal of Psychiatry, 157,* 213–219.

Carlson, G. A., & Meyer, S. E. (2010). Bipolar disorder. In M. K. Dulcan (Ed.), *Dulcan's textbook of child and adolescent psychiatry* (pp. 279–298). Washington, DC: American Psychiatric Publishing.

Carpenter, M. (2006). Instrumental, social, and shared goals and interventions in imitation. In S. J. Rogers & J. H. G. Williams (Eds.), *Imitation and the social mind: Autism and typical development* (pp. 48–70). New York: Guilford Press.

Carr, E. G., & Durand, V. M. (1985). Reducing behavior problems through functional communication training. *Journal of Applied Behavior Analysis, 18,* 111–126.

Carr, E. G., Levin, L., McConnachie, G., Carlson, J. I., Kemp, D. C., & Smith, C. E. (1994). *Communication-based intervention for problem behavior: A user's guide for producing positive change.* Baltimore, MD: Paul H. Brooks.

Carrey, N., MacMaster, F. P., Sparkes, S. J., Khan, S. C., & Kusumakar, V. (2002). Glutamatergic changes with treatment in attention deficit hyperactivity disorder: A preliminary case series. *Journal of Child and Adolescent Psychopharmacology, 12,* 331–336.

Carrion, V. G., Weems, C. F., Ray, R. D., Glaser, B. H., Hassl, D., & Reiss, A. L. (2002). Diurnal salivary cortisol in pediatric posttraumatic stress disorder. *Biological Psychiatry, 51,* 575–582.

Carroll, J. B. (1997). Psychometrics, intelligence, and public perception. *Intelligence, 24,* 25–52.

Carruth, B. R., Ziegler, P. J., Gordon, A., & Barr, S. I. (2004). Prevalence of picky eaters among infants and toddlers and their caregivers' decisions about offering a new food. *Journal of the American Dietetic Association, 104*, 57–64.

Carter, A. S., Marakovitz, S. E., & Sparrow, S. A. (2006). Comprehensive psychological assessment: A developmental psychopathology approach for clinical and applied research. In D. Cicchetti & D. J. Cohen (Eds.), *Developmental psychopathology, Vol. 1: Theory and method* (2nd ed., pp. 181–210). Hoboken, NJ: Wiley.

Carter, B. D., Kronenberger, W. G., Scott, E., & Ernst, M. M. (2009). Inpatient consultation-liaison. In M. C. Roberts & R. G. Steele (Eds.), *Handbook of pediatric psychology* (pp. 114–129). New York: Guilford.

Carter, B. D., & von Weiss, R. (2005). Pediatric consultation-liaison: Applied child health psychology. In R. Steele & M. Roberts (Eds.), *Handbook of mental health services for children and adolescents* (pp. 63–77). New York: Kluwer.

Caseras, X., Gampietro, V., Lamas, A., Brammer, M., Vilarroya, O., Carmona, S., et al. (2010). The functional neuroanatomy of blood-injection-injury phobia: A comparison with spider phobics and healthy controls. *Psychological Medicine, 40*, 125–134.

Casey, R. J., & Berman, J. S. (1985). The outcome of psychotherapy with children. *Psychological Bulletin, 98*, 388–400.

Caspi, A. (2000). The child is the father of man: Personality continuities from childhood to adulthood. *Journal of Personality and Social Psychology, 78*, 158–172.

Caspi, A., Harrington, H., Moffitt, T. E., & Milne, B. J. (2002). Males on the life-course-persistent and adolescence-limited antisocial pathways: Follow-up at age 26 years. *Development and Psychopathology, 14*, 179–207.

Caspi, A., Lynam, D., Moffitt, T. E., & Silva, P. A. (1993). Unraveling girls' delinquency: Biological, dispositional, and contextual contributions to adolescent misbehavior. *Developmental Psychology, 29*, 19–30.

Caspi, A., & Moffitt, T. E. (2006). Gene–environment interactions in psychiatry: Joining forces with neuroscience. *Nature Reviews Neuroscience, 7*, 583–590.

Caspi, A., Moffitt, T. E., & Cannon, M. (2005). Moderation of the effect of adolescent-onset cannabis use an adult psychosis by a functional polymorphism in the catechol-O-methyltransferase gene: Longitudinal evidence of a gene X environment interaction. *Biological Psychiatry, 57*, 1117–1127.

Caspi, A., & Shiner, R. (2010). Temperament and personality. In M. Rutter (Ed.), *Rutter's child and adolescent psychiatry* (pp. 182–198). Malden, MA: Blackwell.

Caspi, A., Wright, B. R. E., Moffitt, T. E., & Silva, P. A. (1998). Early failure in the labor market: Childhood and adolescent predictors of unemployment in the transition to adulthood. *American Sociological Review, 63*, 424–451.

Cassidy, J., & Shaver, P. R. (1999). *Handbook of attachment.* New York: Guilford Press.

Cassoff, J., Wiebe, S. T., & Gruber, R. (2012). Sleep patterns and the risk of ADHD. *Nature and Science of Sleep, 4*, 74–80.

Castellanos, F. X. (2003). Anatomic brain abnormalities in monozygotic twins discordant for attention deficit hyperactivity disorder. *American Journal of Psychiatry, 160*, 1693–1695.

Castellanos, F. X., Giedd, J. N., Berquin, P. C., Walter, J. M., Sharp, W., Tran, T., et al. (2001). Quantitative brain magnetic resonance imaging in girls with attention-deficit/hyperactivity disorder. *Archives of General Psychiatry, 58*, 289–295.

Castellanos, F. X., Giedd, J. N., Eckburg, P., Marsh, W. L., Vaituzis, A. C., Kaysen, D., et al. (1994). Quantitative morphology of the caudate nucleus in attention deficit hyperactivity disorder. *American Journal of Psychiatry, 151*, 1791–1796.

Castellanos, F. X., Giedd, J. N., Marsh, W. L., Hamburger, S. D., Vaituzis, A. C., Dickstein, D. P., et al. (1996). Quantitative brain magnetic resonance imaging in attention deficit hyperactivity disorder. *Archives of General Psychiatry, 53*, 607–616.

Castellanos, F. X., Lee, P. P., Sharp, W., Jeffries, N. O., Greenstein, D. K., Clasen, L. S., et al. (2002). Developmental trajectories of brain volume abnormalities in children and adolescents with attention-deficit/hyperactivity disorder. *Journal of the American Medical Association, 288*, 1740–1748.

Castellanos, F. X., & Tannock, R. (2002). Neuroscience of attention-deficit/hyperactivity disorder. *Nature Review Neuroscience, 3*, 617–628.

Castelli, F., Happe, F., Frith, U., & Frith, C. (2000). Movement and mind: A functional imaging study of perception and interpretation of complex intentional movement patterns. *Neuroimage, 12*, 314–325.

Cavendish, W. (2013). Identification of learning disabilities. *Journal of Learning Disabilities, 46*, 52–57.

Centers for Disease Control. (2007). *Youth risk behavior surveillance system.* Retrieved June 19, 2007, from http://www.cfoc.org/Info/yrbss

Centers for Disease Control. (2012). *Developmental milestones.* Washington, DC: Author.

Centers for Disease Control and Prevention. (2004). Youth risk behavior surveillance. *Morbidity and Mortality Weekly Report, 53*, 1–96.

Chaffin, M., & Schmidt, S. (2006). An evidence-based perspective on interventions to stop or prevent child abuse. In J. R. Lutzker (Ed.), *Preventing violence: Research and evidence-based intervention strategies* (pp. 49–68). Washington, DC: American Psychological Association.

Chaffin, M., Silovsky, J. F., Funderburk, B., Valle, L. A., Brestan, E. V., Balachova, T., et al. (2004). Parent-child interaction therapy with physically abusive parents: Efficacy for reducing future abuse reports *Journal of Consulting and Clinical Psychology, 72*, 500–510.

Chaffin, M., Silovsky, J. F., & Vaughn, C. (2005). Temporal concordance of anxiety disorders and child sexual abuse: Implications for direct versus artifactual effects of sexual abuse. *Journal of Clinical Child and Adolescent Psychology, 34*, 210–222.

Chaffin, M., & Valle, L. (2003). Dynamic predictive validity of the child abuse potential inventory. *Child Abuse and Neglect, 27*, 463–482.

Chamberlain, P., Reid, J. B., Ray, J., Capaldi, D. M., & Fisher, P. (1997). Parent inadequate discipline (PID). In T. A. Widiger, A. J. Frances, H. A. Pincus, R. Ross, M. B. First, & W. Davis (Eds.), *DSM-IV sourcebook* (Vol. 3, pp. 569–629). Washington, DC: American Psychiatric Association.

Chapman, J. W., Tunmer, W. E., & Prochnow, J. E. (2001). Does success in the Reading Recovery program depend on developing proficiency in phonological processing skills? A longitudinal study in a whole language instruction context. *Scientific Studies of Reading, 5*, 141–176.

Chapman, R. S., & Bird, E. K. (2012). Language development in childhood, adolescence, and young adulthood in persons with Down Syndrome. In J.A. Burack, R.M. Hodapp, G. Iarocci, & E. Zigler (Eds.), *The Oxford handbook of intellectual disability and development* (pp. 167–183). New York: Oxford University Press.

Charach, A., Yeung, E., Climans, T., & Lillie, E. (2011). Childhood attention-deficit/hyperactivity disorder and future substance use disorders. *Journal of the American Academy of Child and Adolescent Psychiatry, 50*, 9–21.

Chard, D. J., Vaughn, S., & Tyler, B. (2003). A synthesis of research on effective interventions for building reading fluency with elementary students with learning disabilities. *Journal of Learning Disabilities, 35*, 386–406.

Charlop-Christy, M. H., & Jones, C. (2006). The Picture Exchange Communication System. In R. J. McCauley & M. E. Fey (Eds.), *Treatment of language disorders in children* (pp. 105–122). Baltimore, MD: Brookes.

Charman, T. (2003). Why is joint attention a pivotal skill in autism? In U. Frith & E. Hill (Eds.), *Autism: Mind and brain* (pp. 67–87). New York: Oxford University Press.

Charman, T., & Baird, G. (2002). Practitioner review: Diagnosis of autism spectrum disorder in 2- and 3-year-old children. *Journal of Child Psychology and Psychiatry, 43*, 289–305.

Charman, T., & Baron-Cohen, S. (2006). Screening for autism spectrum disorders in populations: Progress, challenges, and questions for future research and practice. In T. Charman & W. Stone (Eds.), *Social and communication development in autism spectrum disorders* (pp. 63–87). New York: Guilford Press.

Chase, C. D., Osinowo, T., & Pary, R. J. (2002). Medical issues in patients with Down syndrome. *Mental Health Aspects of Developmental Disabilities, 5*(2), 34–45.

Chase-Lansdale, P. L., & Gordon, R. A. (1996). Economic hardship and the development of five- and six-year-olds: Neighborhood and regional perspectives. *Child Development, 67,* 338–367.

Chassin, L., Pitts, S. C., & DeLucia, C. (1999). The relation of adolescent substance use to young adult autonomy, positive activity involvement, and perceived competence. *Development and Psychopathology, 11,* 915–932.

Chassin, L., Ritter, J., Trim, R. S., & King, K. M. (2003). Adolescent substance use disorders. In E. J. Mash & R. A. Barkley (Eds.), *Child psychopathology* (pp. 199–230). New York: Guilford Press.

Chatoor, I. (2009). *Diagnosis and treatment of feeding disorders in infants, toddlers, and young children.* Washington, DC: National Center for Infants, Toddlers, and Families.

Chatoor, I., & Ammaniti, M. (2007). Classifying feeding disorders of infancy and early childhood. In W. E. Narrow (Ed.), *Age and gender considerations in psychiatric diagnosis* (pp. 227–242). Arlington, VA: American Psychiatric Association.

Chavira, D. A., & Stein, M. B. (2005). Childhood social anxiety disorder: From understanding to treatment. *Child and Adolescent Psychiatric Clinics of North America, 14,* 797–818.

Chavira, D. A., Stein, M. B., Bailey, K., & Stein, M. T. (2004). Comorbidity of generalized social anxiety disorder and depression in a pediatric primary care sample. *Journal of Affective Disorders, 80,* 163–171.

Chemtob, C., Nakashima, J., & Carlson, J. (2002). Brief treatment for elementary school children with disaster-related posttraumatic stress disorder: A field study. *Journal of Clinical Psychology, 58,* 99–112.

Chen, K., & Kandel, D. B. (1995). The natural history of drug use from adolescence to the mid-thirties in a general population sample. *American Journal of Public Health, 85,* 41–47.

Chen, X., Hastings, P. D., Rubin, K. H., Chen, H., Cen, G., & Stewart, S. (1998). Child-rearing attitudes and behavioral inhibition in Chinese and Canadian toddlers: A cross-cultural study. *Developmental Psychology, 34,* 677–686.

Cheuk, D. K. L., Wong, V., Chen, W. X. (2011). Acupuncture for autism spectrum disorder. Cochrane Database of Systematic Reviews.

Chilcoat, H. D., & Breslau, N. (1998). Posttraumatic stress disorder and drug disorders: Testing causal pathways. *Archives of General Psychiatry, 55,* 913–917.

Christophersen, E. R., & Friman, P. C. (2010). *Elimination disorders in children and adolescents.* Cambridge, MA: Hogrefe.

Chronis, A. M., Fabiano, G. A., Gnagy, E. M., Onyango, A. N., Pelham, W. E., Lopez-Williams, A., et al. (2004). An evaluation of the summer treatment program for children with attention-deficit/hyperactivity disorder using a treatment withdrawal design. *Behavior Therapy, 35,* 561–585.

Chronis, A. M., Lahey, B. B., Pelham, W. E., Kipp, H. L., Baumann, B. L., & Lee, S. S. (2003). Psychopathology and substance abuse in parents of young children with attention-deficit/hyperactivity disorder. *Journal of the American Academy of Child and Adolescent Psychiatry, 42,* 1424–1432.

Chronis, A. M., Lahey, B. B., Pelham, W. E., Williams, S. H., Baumann, B. L., Kipp, H., et al. (2007). Maternal depression and early positive parenting predict future conduct problems in young children with attention-deficit/hyperactivity disorder. *Developmental Psychology, 43,* 70–82.

Chung, T., Martin, C. S., Armstrong, T. D., & Labouvie, E. W. (2002). Prevalence of *DSM-IV* alcohol diagnoses and symptoms in adolescent community and clinical samples. *Journal of the American Academy of Child & Adolescent Psychiatry, 41,* 546–554.

Cicchetti, D. (1990). A historical perspective on the discipline of developmental psychopathology. In J. Rolf, A. Masten, D. Cicchetti,

K. Nuechterlein, & S. Weintraub (Eds.), *Risk and protective factors in the development of psychopathology* (pp. 2–28). New York: Cambridge University Press.

Cicchetti, D. (2004). An odyssey of discovery: Lessons learned through three decades of research on child maltreatment. *American Psychologist, 59,* 731–741.

Cicchetti, D. (2006). Developmental psychopathology. In D. Cicchetti & D. J. Cohen (Eds.), *Developmental psychopathology, Vol. 1: Theory and method* (2nd ed., pp. 1–23). Hoboken, NJ: Wiley.

Cicchetti, D., & Aber, J. L. (1998). Contextualism and developmental psychopathology. *Development and Psychopathology, 10,* 137–426.

Cicchetti, D., & Barnett, D. (1991). Toward the development of a scientific nosology of child maltreatment. In D. Cicchetti & W. Grove (Eds.), *Thinking clearly about psychology: Essays in honor of Paul E. Meehl* (pp. 346–377). Minneapolis: University of Minnesota Press.

Cicchetti, D., & Curtis, W. J. (2006). The developing brain and neural plasticity: Implications for normality, psychopathology, and resilience. In D. Cicchetti & D. J. Cohen (Eds.), *Developmental psychopathology, Vol 2: Developmental neuroscience method* (2nd ed., pp. 1–64.). Hoboken, NJ: Wiley.

Cicchetti, D., & Toth, S. L. (1991). The making of a developmental psychopathologist. In J. Cantor, C. Spiker, & L. Lipsitt (Eds.), *Child behavior and development: Training for diversity* (pp. 34–72). Norwood, NJ: Ablex.

Cicchetti, D., & Toth, S. L. (1998). Perspectives on research and practice in developmental psychopathology. In W. Damon (Ed.), *Handbook of child psychology* (Vol. 4, pp. 479–583). New York: Wiley.

Cicchetti, D., Toth, S. L., & Maughan, A. (2000). An ecological-transactional model of child maltreatment. In A. J. Sameroff (Ed.), *Handbook of developmental psychopathology* (pp. 689–722). New York: Kluwer.

Clark, A. F. (2011). Schizophrenia and schizophrenia-like disorders. In C. Gillberg, R. Harrington, & H. Steinhausen (Eds.), *A clinician's handbook of child and adolescent psychiatry* (pp. 79–109). Cambridge, UK: Cambridge University Press.

Clark, D. B., De Bellis, M. D., Lynch, K. G., Cornelius, J. R., & Martin, C. (2003). Physical and sexual abuse, depression, and alcohol use disorders in adolescents: Onsets and outcomes. *Drug and Alcohol Dependence, 69,* 51–60.

Clark, D. B., Parker, A., & Lynch, K. (1999). Psychopathology and substance-related problems during early adolescence: A survival analysis. *Journal of Clinical Psychology, 28,* 333–341.

Clark, D. B., Vanyukov, M., & Cornelius, J. (2002). Childhood antisocial behavior and adolescent alcohol use disorders. *Alcohol Research and Health, 26,* 109–115.

Clark, D. B., Wood, D. S., & Cornelius, J. R. (2003). Clinical practices in the pharmacological treatment of comorbid psychopathology in adolescents with alcohol use disorders. *Journal of Substance Abuse Treatment, 25,* 293–295.

Clark, D. M., Salkovskis, P. M., & Chalkley, A. J. (1985). Respiratory control as a treatment for panic attacks. *Journal of Behavior Therapy and Experimental Psychiatry, 16,* 23–30.

Clarke, G. N., Hornbrook, M. C., Lynch, F. L., Polen, M. R., Gale, J., O'Connor, E., et al. (2002). Group cognitive behavioral treatment for depressed adolescent offspring of depressed parents in an HMO. *Journal of the American Academy of Child and Adolescent Psychiatry, 41,* 305–313.

Clarke, G. N., Lewinsohn, P. M., & Hops, H. (1990). *Instructor's manual for the adolescent coping with depression course.* Retrieved September 6, 2006, from http://www.kpchr.org/public/acwd/ acwd.html

Clarke, G. N., Rohde, P., Lewinsohn, P. M., Hops, H., & Seeley, J. R. (1999). Cognitive-behavioral treatment of adolescent depression: Efficacy of acute group treatment and booster sessions. *Journal of the American Academy of Child and Adolescent Psychiatry, 38,* 272–279.

Clarke, G., Debar, L., Lynch, F., Powell, J., Gale, J., O'Connor, E., et al. (2005). A randomized effectiveness trial of brief cognitive-behavioral therapy for depressed adolescents receiving antidepressant medication.

Journal of the American Academy of Child & Adolescent Psychiatry, 44, 888–898.

Claude, D., & Firestone, P. (1995). The development of ADHD in boys: A 12-year follow-up. *Canadian Journal of Behavioural Science, 27,* 226–249.

Claussen, A. H., & Crittenden, P. M. (1991). Physical and psychological maltreatment: Relations among types of maltreatment. *Child Abuse & Neglect, 15,* 5–18.

Clayton, R., Cattarello, A. M., & Johnstone, B. M. (1996). The effectiveness of drug abuse resistance education (project D.A.R.E.): 5-Year follow up results. *Preventative Medicine, 25,* 307–318.

Clayton-Smith, J. (2001). Angelman syndrome: Evolution of the phenotype in adolescents and adults. *Developmental Medicine & Child Neurology, 43,* 476–480.

Clifford, J. J., Tighe, O., Croke, D. T., Sibley, D. R., Drago, J., & Waddington, J. L. (1998). Topographical evaluation of the phenotype of spontaneous behaviour in mice with targeted gene deletion of the D1A dopamine receptor: Paradoxical elevation of grooming syntax. *Neuropharmacology, 37,* 1595–1602.

Clinton, D., & Norring, C. (2005). The comparative utility of statistically derived eating disorder clusters and *DSM-IV* diagnoses: Relationship to symptomatology and psychiatric comorbidity at intake and follow-up. *Eating Behaviors, 6,* 403–418.

Cobham, V. E., Dadds, M. R., & Spence, S. H. (1998). The role of parental anxiety in the treatment of childhood anxiety. *Journal of Consulting and Clinical Psychology, 66,* 893–905.

Coghill, D., & Seth, S. (2011). Do the diagnostic criteria for ADHD need to change? *European Child and Adolescent Psychiatry, 20,* 75–81.

Cohen, D., Gerardin, P., Mazet, P., Purper-Ouakil, D., & Flament, M. F. (2004). Pharmacological treatment of adolescent major depression. *Journal of Child and Adolescent Psychopharmacology, 14,* 19–31.

Cohen, J. (1988). *Statistical power analysis for the behavioral sciences* (2nd ed.). Hillsdale, NJ: Erlbaum.

Cohen, J. A. (2005). Treating traumatized children: Current status and future directions. *Journal of Trauma & Dissociation, 6,* 109–121.

Cohen, J. A., Deblinger, E., Mannarino, A. P., & Steer, R. A. (2004). A multisite, randomized controlled trial for children with sexual abuse-related PTSD symptoms. *Journal of the American Academy of Child & Adolescent Psychiatry, 43,* 393–402.

Cohen, J. A., & Mannarino, A. P. (1996). A treatment outcome study for sexually abused preschool children: Initial findings. *Journal of the American Academy of Child and Adolescent Psychiatry, 35,* 42–50.

Cohen, J. A., & Mannarino, A. P. (1997). A treatment study of sexually abused preschool children: Outcome during a one year follow-up. *Journal of the American Academy of Child and Adolescent Psychiatry, 36,* 1229–1235.

Cohen, J. A., & Mannarino, A. P. (2004). Posttraumatic stress disorder. In T. H. Ollendick & J. S. March (Eds.), *Phobic and anxiety disorders in children and adolescents* (pp. 405–432). New York: Oxford University Press.

Cohen, J. A., & Mannarino, A. P. (2010). Posttraumatic stress disorder. In M. K. Dulcan (Ed.), *Child and adolescent psychiatry* (pp. 339–348). Washington, DC: American Psychiatric Publishing.

Cohen, J. A., Mannarino, A. P., & Knudsen, K. (2005). Treating sexually abused children: 1 year follow-up of a randomized controlled trial. *Child Abuse & Neglect, 29,* 135–145.

Cohen, J. A., Mannarino, A. P., & Perel, J. M. (2007). A pilot randomized controlled trial of combined trauma-focused CBT and sertraline for childhood PTSD symptoms. *Journal of the American Academy of Child and Adolescent Psychiatry, 46,* 811–819.

Cohen, J. A., Perel, J. M., DeBellis, M. D., Friedman, M. J., & Putnam, F. W. (2002). Treating traumatized children: Clinical implications of the psychobiology of posttraumatic stress disorder. *Trauma, Violence, & Abuse, 3,* 91–108.

Cohen, J. B., Deblinger, E., Maedel, A. B., & Stauffer, L. B. (1999). Examining sex-related thoughts and feelings of sexually abused and nonabused children. *Journal of Interpersonal Violence, 14,* 701–712.

Cohen, L., Lehericy, S., Chochon, F., Lemer, C., Rivaud, S., & Dehaene, S. (2002). Language-specific tuning of visual cortex? Functional properties of the Visual Word Form Area. *Brain, 125,* 1054–1069.

Cohen, L. L., Maclaren, J. E., & Lim, C. S. (2008). Pain and pain management. In R. Steele, T. D. Elkin, & M. C. Roberts (Eds.), *Handbook of evidence-based therapies for children and adolescents* (pp. 283–295). New York: Springer.

Cohen, P., Cohen, J., Kasen, S., Velez, C., Hartmark, C., Johnson, J., et al. (1993). An epidemiological study of childhood disorders in late childhood and adolescence: I. Age and gender-specific prevalence. *Journal of Child Psychology, Psychiatry, and Allied Disciplines, 34,* 851–867.

Cohen, R. J., & Swerdlik, M. E. (2005). *Psychological testing and assessment: An introduction to tests and measurement.* New York: McGraw-Hill.

Coie, J. D., Dodge, K. A., & Kupersmidt, J. B. (1990). Peer group behavior and social status. In S. R. Asher & J. D. Coie (Eds.), *Peer rejection in childhood* (pp. 17–59). New York: Cambridge University Press.

Coie, J. D., Dodge, K. A., Terry, R., & Wright, V. (1991). The role of aggression in peer relations: An analysis of aggression episodes in boys' play groups. *Child Development, 62,* 812–826.

Cole, D. A., Peeke, L. G., Martin, J. M., Truglio, R., & Seroczynski, A. D. (1998). A longitudinal look at the relation between depression and anxiety in children and adolescents. *Journal of Consulting and Clinical Psychology, 66,* 451–460.

Cole, D. A., Tram, J. M., Martin, J. M., Hoffman, K. B., Ruiz, M. D., Jacquez, F. M., et al. (2002). Individual differences in the emergence of depressive symptoms in children and adolescents: A longitudinal investigation of parent and child reports. *Journal of Abnormal Psychology, 111,* 156–165.

Colman, I., Wadsworth, M. E. J., Croudace, T. J., & Jones, P. B. (2007). Forty-year psychiatric outcomes following assessment for internalizing disorders in adolescence. *American Journal of Psychiatry, 164,* 126–133.

Colton, R. H., Casper, J. K., & Leonard, R. (2011). *Understanding voice problems.* Philadelphia: Wolters Kluwer.

Comery, T. A., Harris, J. B., Willems, P. J., Oostra, B. A., & Greenough, W. T. (1997). Abnormal dendritic spines in fragile X knockout mice: Maturation and pruning deficits. *Proceedings of the National Academy of Sciences, 94,* 5401–5404.

Common Core State Standards (2013). *Common Core State Standards for English Language Arts.* Washington, DC: Council of Chief State School Officers.

Compas, B. E., Connor-Smith, J., & Jaser, S. S. (2004). Temperament, stress reactivity, and coping: Implications for depression in childhood and adolescence. *Journal of Clinical Child and Adolescent Psychology, 33,* 21–31.

Compton, D. L., Fuchs, L. S., Fuchs, D., Lambert, W., & Hamlett, C. (2012). The cognitive and academic profiles of reading and mathematics learning disabilities. *Journal of Learning Disabilities, 45,* 79–95.

Compton, S. N., Walkup, J. T., Albano, A. M., Piacentini, J. C., Birmaher, B., Sherrill, J. T., et al. (2010). Child/adolescent anxiety multimodal study (CAMS): Rationale, design, and methods. *Child and Adolescent Psychiatry and Mental Health, 4,* 1–15.

Conger, R. D., Ge, X. J., Elder, G. H., Lorenz, F. O., & Simons, R. L. (1994). Economic stress, coercive family process, and developmental problems of adolescents. *Child Development, 65,* 541–561.

Connolly, S. D., & Bernstein, A. (2007). Practice parameter for the assessment and treatment of children and adolescents with anxiety disorders. *Journal of the American Academy of Child & Adolescent Psychiatry, 46,* 267–283.

Connolly, S. D., & Suarez, L. M. (2010). Generalized anxiety disorder, specific phobia, panic disorder, social phobia, and selective mutism. In M. K. Dulcan (Eds.), *Child and adolescent psychiatry* (pp. 299–323). Washington, DC: American Psychiatric Publishing.

Connor, D. F., Steingard, R. J., Cunningham, J. A., Anderson, J. J., & Melloni, R. H. (2004). Proactive and reactive aggression in referred children and adolescents. *American Journal of Orthopsychiatry, 74,* 129–136.

Connor-Smith, J. K., Compas, B. E., Wadsworth, M. E., Thomsen, A. H., & Saltzman, H. (2000). Responses to stress in adolescence: Measurement of coping and involuntary stress responses. *Journal of Consulting and Clinical Psychology, 68,* 976–992.

Constantino, J. N., Chackes, L. M., Wartner, U. G., Gross, M., Brophy, S. L., Vitale, J., et al. (2006). Mental representations of attachment in identical female twins with and without conduct problems. *Child Psychiatry & Human Development, 37,* 65–72.

Coolidge, F. L., Thede, L. L., & Young, S. E. (2000). Heritability of the comorbidity of attention deficit hyperactivity disorder with behavioral disorders and executive function deficits: A preliminary investigation. *Developmental Neuropsychology, 17,* 273–287.

Copeland, W. E., Keeler, G., Angold, A., & Costello, E. J. (2007). Traumatic events and posttraumatic stress in childhood. *Archives of General Psychiatry, 64,* 577–584.

Coppus, A., Evenhuis, H., Verberne, G., Visser, F., van Gool, P., Eikelenboom, P., et al. (2006). Dementia and mortality in persons with Down's syndrome. *Journal of Intellectual Disability Research, 50,* 768–777.

Cormac, I., Jones, C., Campbell, C. (2002). Cognitive behavior therapy for Schizophrenia. *Cochrane Database Systematic Review, 2004,* CD000524.

Cornish, K. M., Bertone, A., Kogan, C.S., & Scerif, G. (2012). Linking genes to cognition: The case of Fragile X Syndrome. In J.A. Burack, R.M. Hodapp, G. Iarocci, & E. Zigler (Eds.), *The Oxford handbook of intellectual disability and development* (pp. 42–59). New York: Oxford University Press.

Cornish, K. M., Munir, F., & Cross, G. (1998). The nature of spatial deficit in young females with fragile-X syndrome: A neuropsychological and molecular perspective. *Neuropsychologia, 36,* 1239–1246.

Cornwell, S. L., Kelly, K., & Austin, L. (2010). Pediatric feeding disorders: Effectiveness of multidisciplinary inpatient treatment of gastronomy-tube dependent children. *Children's Health Care, 39,* 214–231.

Correll, C. U. (2009). Managing the health outcomes of schizophrenia treatment in children and adolescents. In J. M. Meyer & H. A. Nasrallah (Eds.), *Medical illness and schizophrenia* (pp. 343–373). Washington, DC: American Psychiatric Publishing.

Correll, C. U. (2010). Antipsychotic medications. In M. K. Dulcan (Eds.), *Dulcan's textbook of child and adolescent psychiatry* (pp. 743–775). Washington, DC: American Psychiatric Association.

Corsini, R. J. (2005). Introduction to current psychotherapies. In R. J. Corsini & D. Wedding (Eds.), *Current psychotherapies* (7th ed., pp. 1–14). Belmont, CA: Brooks/Cole.

Costantino, G., Malgady, R. G., & Cardalda, E. (2005). TEMAS narrative treatment: An evidence-based culturally competent therapy modality. In E. D. Hibbs & P. S. Jensen (Eds.), *Psychosocial treatments for child and adolescent disorders: Empirically based strategies for clinical practice* (pp. 717–742). Washington, DC: American Psychological Association.

Costello, E. J. (2005). The developmental epidemiology of anxiety disorders: Phenomenology, prevalence, and comorbidity. *Child and Adolescent Psychiatric Clinics of North America, 14,* 631–648.

Costello, E. J., Angold, A., Burns, B., Stangl, D. K., Tweed, D. L., Erkanli, A., et al. (1996). The Great Smoky Mountains Study of Youth: Goals, design, methods, and the prevalence of DSM-III-K disorders. *Archives of General Psychiatry, 53,* 1129–1136.

Costello, E. J., Egger, H. L., & Angold, A. (2004). Developmental epidemiology of anxiety disorders. In T. H. Ollendick & J. S. March (Eds.), *Phobic and anxiety disorders in children and adolescents* (pp. 61–91). New York: Oxford University Press.

Costello, E. J., Erkanli, A., & Angold, A. (2006). Is there an epidemic of child or adolescent depression? *Journal of Child Psychology and Psychiatry, 47,* 1263–1271.

Costello, E. J., Erkanli, A., Federman, E., & Angold, A. (1999). Development of psychiatric comorbidity with substance abuse in adolescents: Effects of timing and sex. *Journal of Clinical Child Psychology, 28,* 298–311.

Costello, E. J., Pine, D. S., Hammen, C. M., John, S., Plotsky, P. M., & Weissman, M. (2002). Development and natural history of mood disorders. *Biological Psychiatry, 52,* 529–542.

Cowan, P. A., & Cowan, C. P. (2006). Developmental psychopathology from family systems and family risk factors perspectives. In D. Cicchetti & D. J. Cohen (Eds.), *Developmental psychopathology, Vol 1: Theory and method* (2nd ed., pp. 530–587). Hoboken, NJ: Wiley.

Coyne, J. C., & Whiffen, V. E. (1995). Issues in personality as diathesis for depression: The case of sociotropy-dependency and autonomy-self-criticism. *Psychological Bulletin, 118,* 358–378.

Coyne, P., Pisha, B., Dalton, B., Zeph, L. A., & Smith, N. C. (2012). Literacy by design. *Remedial and Special Education, 33,* 162–172.

Crabtree, V. M., & Williams, N. A. (2009). Normal sleep in children and adolescents. *Child and Adolescent Psychiatric Clinics of North America, 18,* 799–811.

Craig, A., Handcock, K., Tran, Y., Craig, M., & Peters, K. (2002). Epidemiology of stuttering in the community acress of the entire life span. *Journal of Speech, Language, and Hearing Research, 45,* 1097–1105.

Craske, M. G., Kircanski, K., Epstein, A., Wittchen, H., Pine, D. S., Lewis-Fernandez, R., et al. (2010). Panic disorder: A review of *DSM-IV* panic disorder and proposals for *DSM-5. Depression and Anxiety, 27,* 93–112.

Creswell, C., Schniering, C. A., & Rapee, R. M. (2005). Threat interpretation in anxious children and their mothers: Comparison with non-clinical children and the effects of treatment. *Behaviour Research and Therapy, 43,* 1375–1381.

Crick, N. R. (1995). Relational aggression: The role of intent attributions, feelings of distress, and provocation type. *Development and Psychopathology, 7,* 313–322.

Crick, N. R. (1997). Engagement in gender normative versus non-normative forms of aggression: Links to social-psychological adjustment. *Developmental Psychology, 33,* 610–617.

Crick, N. R., & Bigbee, M. A. (1998). Relational and overt forms of peer victimization: A multi-informant approach. *Journal of Consulting and Clinical Psychology, 66,* 337–347.

Crick, N. R., & Dodge, K. A. (1994). A review and reformulation of social information-processing mechanisms in children's social adjustment. *Psychological Bulletin, 115,* 74–101.

Crick, N. R., & Dodge, K. A. (1996). Social information-processing mechanisms in reactive and proactive aggression. *Child Development, 67,* 993–1002.

Crick, N. R., & Grotpeter, J. K. (1995). Relational aggression, gender, and social-psychological adjustment. *Child Development, 66,* 710–722.

Critchley, H. D., Daly, E. M., Bullmore, E. T., Williams, S. C., Van Amelsvoort, T., Robertson, D. M., et al. (2000). The functional neuroanatomy of social behaviour: Changes in cerebral blood flow when people with autistic disorder process facial expressions. *Brain, 123,* 2203–2212.

Crittenden, P. (1992). Children's strategies for coping with adverse home environments: An interpretation using attachment theory. *Child Abuse & Neglect, 16,* 329–343.

Crittenden, P. M., Claussen, A. H., & Sugarman, D. B. (1994). Physical and psychological maltreatment in middle childhood and adolescence. *Development & Psychopathology, 6,* 145–164.

Crnic, K., & Low, C. (2002). Everyday stresses and parenting. In M. H. Bornstein (Ed.), *Handbook of parenting* (pp. 243–268). Mahwah, NJ: Lawrence Erlbaum.

Crockett, J. L., Fleming, R. K., Doepke, K. J., & Stevens, J. S. (2007). Parent training: Acquisition and generalization of discrete trials teaching skills with parents of children with autism. *Research in Developmental Disabilities, 28,* 23–36.

Crome, I., & Bloor, R. (2005). Substance misuse and psychiatric comorbidity in adolescents. *Current Opinion in Psychiatry, 18,* 435–439.

Crow, T. J. (1980). Molecular pathology of schizophrenia: More than one disease process? *British Medical Journal, 280,* 66.

Cuckle, H. S., Wald, N. J., & Thompson, S. G. (1987). Estimating a woman's risk of having a pregnancy associated with Down's syndrome using her age and serum alpha-fetoprotein level. *British Journal of Obstetrics and Gynecology, 94,* 387–402.

Cunningham, C. E., & Boyle, H. (2002). Preschoolers at risk for attention-deficit hyperactivity disorder and oppositional defiant disorder: Family, parenting, and behavioral correlates. *Journal of Abnormal Child Psychology, 30,* 555–569.

Cunningham, M., Rapee, R., & Lyneham, H. (2007). Overview of the *Cool Teens* CD-ROM for anxiety disorders in adolescents. *The Behavior Therapist, 30,* 15–19.

Cupples, B. (2011). Language disorders in children. In R. B. Hoodin (Ed.), *Intervention in child language disorders* (pp. 33–44). Boston, MA: Jones & Bartlett.

Curry, J. F., March, J. S., & Hervey, A. S. (2004). Comorbidity of childhood and adolescent anxiety disorders. In T. H. Ollendick & J. S. March (Eds.), *Phobic and anxiety disorders in children and adolescents* (pp. 116–140). New York: Oxford University Press.

Curry, J., Silva, S., Rohde, P., Ginsburg, G., Kennard, B., Kratochvil, C., et al. (2012). Onset of alcohol or substance use disorders following treatment for adolescent depression. *Journal of Consulting and Clinical Psychology, 80,* 299–312.

Cyr, M., McDuff, P., Wright, J., Theriault, C., & Cinq-Mars, C. (2005). Clinical correlates and repetition of self-harming behaviors among female adolescent victims of sexual abuse. *Journal of Child Sexual Abuse, 14,* 49–68.

D'Agostino, J. V., & Murphy, J. A. (2004). A meta-analysis of Reading Recovery in the United States schools. *Educational Evaluation and Policy Analysis, 26,* 23–38.

Dahl, R. E., & Harvey, A. G. (2008). Sleep in children and adolescents with behavioral and emotional disorders. *Sleep Medicine Clinics, 2,* 501–511.

Dadds, M. R., Barrett, P. M., Rapee, R. M., & Ryan, A. (1996). Family process and child anxiety and aggression: An observational analysis. *Journal of Abnormal Child Psychology, 24,* 715–734.

Dadds, M. R., Fraser, J., Frost, A., & Hawes, D. J. (2005). Disentangling the underlying dimensions of psychopathy and conduct problems in childhood: A community study. *Journal of Consulting and Clinical Psychology, 73,* 400–410.

Dadds, M. R., & McHugh, A. (1992). Social support and treatment outcome in behavioral family therapy for child conduct problems. *Journal of Consulting and Clinical Psychology, 60,* 252–259.

Dadds, M. R., & Salmon, K. (2003). Learning and temperament as alternate pathways to punishment insensitivity in antisocial children. *Clinical Child and Family Psychology Review, 6,* 69–86.

Dahl, R. E., & Harvey, A. G. (2008). Sleep disorders. In M. Rutter (Ed.), *Rutter's child and adolescent psychiatry* (pp. 894–905). New York: Blackwell.

Danielson, C. K., de Arellano, M. A., Kilpatrick, D. G., Saunders, B. E., & Resnick, H. S. (2005). Child maltreatment in depressed adolescents: Differences in symptomatology based on history of abuse. *Child Maltreatment, 10,* 37–48.

Danielson, C. K., Feeny, N. C., Findling, R. L., & Youngstrom, E. A. (2004). Psychosocial treatment of bipolar disorders in adolescents: A proposed cognitive-behavioral intervention. *Cognitive and Behavioral Practice, 11,* 283–297.

Danielyan, A., Pathak, S., Kowatch, R. A., Arszman, S. P., & Johns, E. S. (2007). Clinical characteristics of bipolar disorder in very young children. *Journal of Affective Disorders, 97,* 51–59.

Darke, S., Ross, J., & Lynskey, M. (2003). The relationship of conduct disorder to attempted suicide and drug use history among methadone maintenance patients. *Drug and Alcohol Review, 22,* 21–25.

Darke, S., Torok, M., Kaye, S., & Ross, J. (2010). Attempted suicide, self-harm, and violent victimization among regular illicit drug users. *Suicide and Life-Threatening Behavior, 40,* 587–596.

David, C. N., Greenstein, D., Clasen, L., Gochman, P., Miller, R., Tossell, J. W. (2011). Childhood onset schizophrenia: High rate of visual hallucinations. *Journal of the American Academy of Child and Adolescent Psychiatry, 50,* 681–686.

Davidovitch, M., Click, L., Holtzman, G., Tirosh, E., & Safir, M. P. (2000). Developmental regression in autism: Maternal perception. *Journal of Autism and Developmental Disorders, 30,* 113–119.

Davidson, K. H., & Fristad, M. A. (2008). Psychoeducational psychotherapy. In B. Geller & M. P. DelBello (Eds.), *Treatment of bipolar disorder in children and adolescents* (pp. 184–201).New York: Guilford.

Davila, J., Steinberg, S. J., Kachadourian, L., Cobb, R., & Fincham, F. (2004). Romantic involvement and depressive symptoms in early and late adolescence: The role of a preoccupied relational style. *Personal Relationships, 11,* 161–178.

Dawson, G. (2008). Early behavioral intervention, brain plasticity, and the prevention of autism spectrum disorder. *Development and Psychopathology, 20,* 775–803.

Dawson, D. A., Goldstein, R. B., & Grant, B. F. (2013). Differences in the profiles of *DSM-IV* and *DSM-5* alcohol use disorders. *Alcoholism, 37,* 305–313.

de Haan, E., Hoogduin, K. A., Buitelaar, J. K., & Keijsers, G. P. (1998). Behavior therapy versus chlomipramine for the treatment of obsessive-compulsive disorder in children and adolescents. *Journal of the American Academy of Child and Adolescent Psychiatry, 37,* 1022–1029.

De La Paz, S., Swanson, P., & Graham, S. (1998). The contribution of executive control to the revising of students with writing and learning difficulties. *Journal of Educational Psychology, 90,* 448–460.

Dean, A. J., McDermott, B. M., & Marshall, R. T. (2006). Psychotropic medication utilization in a child and adolescent mental health service. *Journal of Child and Adolescent Psychopharmacology, 16,* 273–285.

Deas, D., Roberts, J. S., & Grindlinger, D. (2005). The utility of *DSM-IV* criteria in diagnosing substance abuse/dependence in adolescents. *Journal of Substance Use, 10,* 10–21.

Deas, D., & Thomas, S. E. (2001). An overview of controlled studies of adolescent substance abuse treatment. *American Journal of Addictions, 10,* 178–189.

Deater-Deckard, K., Dodge, K. A., Bates, J. E., & Pettit, G. S. (1996). Physical discipline among African American and European American mothers: Links to children's externalizing behaviors. *Developmental Psychology, 32,* 1065–1072.

DeBellis, M. D. (2001). Developmental traumatology. *Development and Psychopathology, 13,* 539–564.

DeBellis, M. D., Chrousos, G. P., Dorn, L. D., Burke, L., Helmers, K., Kling, M. A., et al. (1994). Hypothalamic-pituitary-adrenal axis dysregulation in sexually abused girls. *Journal of Clinical Endocrinology and Metabolism, 78,* 249–255.

Deblinger, E., & Heflin, A. H. (1996). *Cognitive behavioral interventions for treating sexually abused children.* Thousand Oaks, CA: Sage.

Deblinger, E., Lippmann, J., & Steer, R. (1996). Sexually abused children suffering posttraumatic stress symptoms: Initial treatment outcome findings. *Child Maltreatment, 1,* 310–321.

Deblinger, E., Steer, R. A., & Lippmann, J. (1999a). Maternal factors associated with sexually abused children's psychosocial adjustment. *Child Maltreatment, 4,* 13–20.

Deblinger, E., Steer, R. A., & Lippmann, J. (1999b). Two-year follow-up study of cognitive-behavioral therapy for sexually abused children suffering from post-traumatic stress symptoms. *Child Abuse & Neglect, 23,* 1371–1378.

Decaluwe, V., Braet, C., & Fairburn, C. G. (2002). Binge eating in obese children and adolescents. *International Journal of Eating Disorders, 33,* 78–84.

Dehaene, S., Piazza, M., Pinel, P., & Cohen, L. (2003). Three parietal circuits for number processing. *Cognitive Neuropsychology, 20,* 487–506.

Dehon, C., Weems, C. F., Stickle, T. R., Costa, N. M., & Berman, S. L. (2005). A cross-sectional evaluation of the factorial invariance of anxiety sensitivity in adolescents and young adults. *Behaviour Research and Therapy, 43,* 799–810.

Dejong, P. J., & Merckelbach, H. (1998). Blood-injection-injury phobia and fear of spiders: Domain-specific individual differences in disgust sensitivity. *Personality & Individual Differences, 24,* 153–158.

Dekkers, J., van der Leeuw, P., & van der Weijer, J. (2000). *Optimality theory: Phonology, syntax, and acquisition.* Oxford, UK: Oxford University Press.

Delaney-Black, V., Chiodo, L. M., Hannigan, J. H., Greenwald, M. K., Janisse, J., Patterson, G., & Sokol, R. J. (2010). Just say "I don't": Lack of concordance between teen report and biological measures of drug use. *Pediatrics, 126*(5), 887–893.

Delate, T., Gelenberg, A. J., Simmons, V. A., & Motheral, B. R. (2004). Trends in the use of antidepressants in a national sample of commercially insured pediatric patients, 1998 to 2002. *Psychiatric Services, 55,* 387–391.

Deliberto, T. L., & Nock, M. K. (2008). An exploratory study of correlates, onset, and offset of non-suicidal self-injury. *Archives of Suicide Research, 12,* 219–231.

Denckla, M.B., & Rudel, R.G. (1976). Rapid automatized naming (RAN): Dyslexia differentiated from other learning disorders. *Neuropsychologia, 14,* 471–479.

De Nil, L., Kroll, R., Kapur, S., & Houle, S. (2000). A positron emission tomography study of silent oral single word reading in stuttering and nonstuttering adults. *Journal of Speech, Language, and Hearing Research, 43,* 1038–1053.

De Nil, L., Kroll, R., Lafaille, S., & Houle, S. (2003). A positron emission tomography study of short- and long-term treatment effects on functional brain activation in adults who stutter. *Journal of Fluency Disorders, 28,* 357–380.

Dennis, M., Godley, S. H., Diamond, G., Tims, F. M., Babor, T., Donaldson, J., et al. (2004). The Cannabis Youth Treatment (CYT) Study: Main findings from two randomized trials. *Journal of Substance Abuse Treatment, 27,* 197–213.

Dennis, M. L., Titus, J. C., Diamond, G., Donaldson, J., Godley, S. H., Tims, P., et al. (2002). The Cannabis Youth Treatment (CYT) experiment: Rationale, study design and analysis plans. *Addiction, 97,* 16–34.

de Roos, C., Greenwald, R., den Hollander-Gijsman, M., Noorthoorn, E., van Buuren, S., & de Jongh, A. (2011). A randomised comparison of cognitive behavioural therapy (CBT) and eye movement desensitisation and reprocessing (EMDR) in disaster exposed children. *European Journal of Psychotraumatology, 2,* 5694.

DeShazo Barry, T., Lyman, R. D., & Grofer Klinger, L. (2002). Academic underachievement and attention-deficit/hyperactivity disorder: The negative impact of symptom severity on school performance. *Journal of School Psychology, 40,* 259–283.

DeYoung, A. C., Kenardy, J. A., & Cobham, V. E. (2011). Diagnosis of post-traumatic stress disorder in preschool children. *Journal of Clinical Child and Adolescent Psychology, 40,* 375–384.

Dhalla, S., Zumbo, B. D., & Poole, G. (2011). A review of the psychometric properties of the CRAFFT instrument: 1999-2010. *Current Drug Abuse Review, 4,* 57–64.

Diamond, G., Godley, S. H., Liddle, H. A., Sampl, S., Webb, C., Tims, F. M., et al. (2002). Five outpatient treatment models for adolescent marijuana use: A description of the Cannabis Youth Treatment Interventions. *Addiction, 97,* 70–83.

Dick, D., Li, T., Edenberg, H., Hesselbrock, V., Kramer, J., Kuperman, S., et al. (2004). A genome-wide screen for genes influencing conduct disorder. *Molecular Psychiatry, 9,* 81–86.

Dick, D. M., & Todd, R. D. (2006). Genetic contributions. In D. Cicchetti & D. J. Cohen (Eds.), *Developmental psychopathology, Vol. 2: Developmental neuroscience* (pp. 16–28). Hoboken, NJ: Wiley.

Dick, D. M., Viken, R. J., Kaprio, J., Pulkkinen, L., & Rose, R. J. (2005). Understanding the covariation among childhood externalizing symptoms: Genetic and environmental influences on Conduct Disorder, Attention Deficit Hyperactivity Disorder, and Oppositional Defiant Disorder symptoms. *Journal of Abnormal Child Psychology, 33,* 219–229.

Dickerson, F. B. (2000). Cognitive behavioral therapy for schizophrenia: A review of recent empirical studies. *Schizophrenia Research, 43,* 71–90.

Dickstein, D. P., Towbin, K. E., Can Der Veen, J. W., Rich, B. A., Brotman, M. A., Knopf, L., et al. (2009). Randomized, double-blind, placebo-controlled trial of lithium in youths with severe mood dysregulation. *Journal of Child and Adolescent Psychopharmacology, 19,* 61–73.

Didden, R., Sturmey, P., Sigafoos, J., Lang, R., O'Reilly, M. F., & Lancioni, G. E. (2012). Nature, prevalence, and characteristics of challenging behavior. In J. L. Matson (Ed.), *Functional assessment for challenging behavior* (pp. 25–44). New York: Springer.

Diler, R. S., & Birmaher, B. (2012). Bipolar disorder in children and adolescents. In J. M. Rey (Ed.), *IACAPAP e-textbook of child and adolescent mental health.* Geneva: International Association for Child and Adolescent Psychiatry and Allied Professions.

Dilworth-Bart, J. E., & Moore, F. (2006). Mercy mercy me: Social injustice and the prevention of environmental pollutant exposures among ethnic minority and poor children. *Child Development, 77,* 247–265.

Dimitropoulos, A., Feurer, I. D., Butler, M. G., & Thompson, T. (2001). Emergence of compulsive behavior and tantrums in children with Prader-Willi syndrome. *American Journal on Mental Retardation, 106,* 39–51.

Dirks, E., Spyer, G., van Lieshout, E. C., & de Sonneville, L. (2008). Prevalence of combined reading and arithmetic disabilities. *Journal of Learning Disabilities, 41,* 460–473.

Dishion, T. J., Andrews, D. W., & Crosby, L. (1995). Antisocial boys and their friends in early adolescence: Relationship characteristics, quality and interactional process. *Child Development, 66,* 139–151.

Dishion, T. J., Capaldi, D., Spracklen, K. M., & Li, F. (1995). Peer ecology of male adolescent drug use. *Development and Psychopathology, 7,* 803–824.

Dishion, T. J., Eddy, J. M., Haas, E., Li, F., & Spracklen, K. M. (1997). Friendships and violent behavior during adolescence. *Social Development, 6,* 207–223.

Dishion, T. J., McCord, J., & Poulin, F. (1999). When interventions harm: Peer groups and problem behavior. *American Psychologist, 54,* 755–764.

Dishion, T. J., Spracklen, K. M., Andrews, D. W., & Patterson, G. R. (1996). Deviancy training in male adolescent friendships. *Behavior Therapy, 27,* 373–390.

Dix, T. (1993). Attributing dispositions to children: An interactional analysis of attribution in socialization. *Personality and Social Psychology Bulletin, 19,* 633–643.

Dix, T., & Lochman, J. (1990). Social cognition and negative reactions to children: A comparison of mothers of aggressive and nonaggressive boys. *Journal of Social and Clinical Psychology, 9,* 418–438.

Dodge, K. A. (1993). Social-cognitive mechanisms in the development of conduct disorder and depression. *Annual Review of Psychology, 44,* 559–584.

Dodge, K. A. (2003). Do social information-processing patterns mediate aggressive behavior? In B. B. Lahey, T. E. Moffitt, & A. Caspi (Eds.), *Causes of conduct disorder and juvenile delinquency* (pp. 254–274). New York: Guilford Press.

Dodge, K. A. (2006). Translational science in action: Hostile attributional style and the development of aggressive behavior problems. *Development and Psychopathology, 18,* 791–814.

Dodge, K. A., & Coie, J. D. (1987). Social-information processing factors in reactive and proactive aggression in children's peer groups. *Journal of Personality and Social Psychology, 53,* 1146–1158.

Dodge, K. A., Lansford, J. E., Burks, V. S., Bates, J. E., Pettit, G. S., Fontaine, R., et al. (2003). Peer rejection and social information-processing factors in the development of aggressive behavior problems in children. *Child Development, 74,* 374–393.

Dodge, K. A., & Pettit, G. S. (1990). Mechanisms in the cycle of violence. *Science, 250,* 1678–1683.

Dodge, K. A., & Pettit, G. S. (2003). A biopsychosocial model of the development of chronic conduct problems in adolescence. *Developmental Psychology, 39,* 349–371.

Dodge, K. A., Pettit, G. S., & Bates, J. E. (1997). How the experience of early physical abuse leads children to become chronically aggressive. *Developmental perspectives on trauma: Theory, research and intervention* (pp. 263–288). Rochester, NY: University of Rochester Press.

Dodge, K. A., Pettit, G. S., Bates, J. E., & Valente, E. (1995). Social information-processing patterns partially mediate the effect of early physical abuse on later conduct problems. *Journal of Abnormal Psychology, 104,* 632–643.

Doyle, A. E., Faraone, S. V., DuPre, E. P., & Biederman, J. (2001). Separating attention deficit hyperactivity disorder and learning disabilities in girls: A familial risk analysis. *American Journal of Psychiatry, 158,* 1666–1672.

Dozier, M., Dozier, D., & Manni, M. (2002). Attachment and biobehavioral catch-up. *Zero to Three, 11,* 7–13.

Drabick, D. A. G., & Gadow, K. D. (2012). Deconstructing oppositional defiant disorder: Clinic-based evidence for an anger/irritability phenotype. *Journal of the American Academy of Child and Adolescent Psychiatry, 51,* 384–393.

Drabick, D. A. G., & Goldfried, R. (2000). Training the scientist-practitioner for the 21st century: Putting the bloom back on the rose. *Journal of Clinical Psychology, 56,* 327–340.

DSM-5 Childhood and Adolescent Disorders Working Group. (2010a). *Issues pertinent to a developmental approach to bipolar disorder in DSM-5.* Washington, DC: American Psychiatric Association.

DSM-5 Childhood and Adolescent Disorders Working Group. (2010b). *Justification for temper dysregulation disorder with dysphoria.* Washington, DC: American Psychiatric Association.

DSM-5 Psychosis Working Group. (2012). Rationale for including Attenuated Psychosis Syndrome (APS) in Section 3 of *DSM-5.* Retrieved from www.dsmorg.

Duax, J. M., Youngstrom, E. A., Calabrese, J. R., & Findling, R. L. (2007). Sex differences in pediatric bipolar disorder. *Journal of Clinical Psychiatry, 68,* 1565–1573.

Dubowitz, H., & Black, M. (2002). Neglect of children's health. In J. E. B. Meyers, L. Berliner, J. Briere, C. T. Hendrix, C. Jenny, & T. A. Reid (Eds.), *The APSAC handbook on child maltreatment* (2nd ed., pp. 269–292). Thousand Oaks, CA: Sage.

Dubowitz, H., Newton, R. R., Litrownik, A. J., Lewis, T., Briggs, E. C., Thompson, R., et al. (2005). Examination of a conceptual model of child neglect. *Child Maltreatment, 10,* 173–189.

Dukes, R. L., Stein, J. A., & Ullman, J. B. (1997). Long-term impact of drug abuse resistance education (D.A.R.E.): Results of a 6-year follow-up. *Evaluation Review, 21,* 483–500.

Duncan, G. J., & Brooks-Gunn, J. (2000). Family poverty, welfare reform, and child development. *Child Development, 71,* 188–196.

DuPaul, G. J., & Eckert, T. L. (1997). The effects of school-based interventions for attention deficit hyperactivity disorder: A meta-analysis. *School Psychology Digest, 26,* 5–27.

DuPaul, G. J., & Stoner, G. (2003). *ADHD in the schools: Assessment and intervention strategies.* New York: Guilford.

Durand, V. M. (2005). Past, present, and emerging directions in education. In D. Zager (Ed.), *Autism spectrum disorders: Identification, education, and treatment* (pp. 89–109). Mahwah, NJ: Erlbaum.

Durand, V. M. (2008). *When children don't sleep well: Interventions for pediatric sleep disorders.* New York: Oxford University Press.

Durand, V. M., & Christodulu, K. V. (2006). Mental retardation. In M. Hersen (Ed.), *Clinician's handbook of child behavioral assessment* (pp. 459–475). San Diego, CA: Elsevier.

Durkin, M. S., Maenner, M. J., Meaney, F. J., Levy, S. E., DiGuiseppi, C., Nicholas, J. S., et al. (2010). Socioeconomic inequality in the prevalence of autism spectrum disorder. *PLOS ONE, 5*(7), e11551.

Dwight, D. M. (2006). *Here's how to do therapy: Hands-on core skills in speech-language pathology.* San Diego, CA: Plural.

Dykens, E. (2001). Introduction to the special issue on behavioral phenotypes. *American Journal on Mental Retardation, 106,* 1–3.

Dykens, E. M. (1995). Measuring behavioral phenotypes: Provocations from the "new genetics." *American Journal on Mental Retardation, 99,* 522–532.

Dykens, E. M. (2000). Contaminated and unusual food combinations: What do people with Prader-Willi syndrome choose? *Mental Retardation, 38,* 163–171.

Dykens, E. M. (2003). Anxiety, fears, and phobias in persons with Williams syndrome. *Developmental Neuropsychology, 23,* 291–316.

Dykens, E. M., & Cassidy, S. B. (1999). Prader-Willi syndrome. In S. Goldstein & C. R. Reynolds (Eds.), *Handbook of neurodevelopmental and genetic disorders in children* (pp. 525–554). New York: Guilford Press.

Dykens, E. M., Cassidy, S. B., & King, B. H. (1999). Maladaptive behavior differences in Prader-Willi syndrome due to paternal deletion versus maternal uniparental disomy. *American Journal on Mental Retardation, 104,* 66–77.

Dykens E. M., & Hodapp, R. M. (2001). Research in mental retardation: Toward an etiologic approach. *Journal of Child Psychology and Psychiatry, 42,* 49–71.

Dykens, E. M., Hodapp, R. M., & Evans, D. W. (2006). Profiles and development of adaptive behavior in children with Down syndrome. *Down Syndrome: Research & Practice, 9,* 45–50.

Dykens, E., Hodapp, R. M., & Finucane, B. M. (2000). *Genetics and mental retardation.* Baltimore: Brookes.

Dykens, E. M., & Kasari, C. (1997). Maladaptive behavior in children with Prader-Willi syndrome, Down syndrome, and nonspecific mental retardation. *American Journal on Mental Retardation, 102,* 228–237.

Dykens, E. M., & Shah, B. (2003). Psychiatric disorders in Prader-Willi syndrome. *CNS Drugs, 17,* 167–178.

Edwards, G., & Gross, M. (1976). Alcohol dependence: Provisional description of a clinical syndrome. *British Medical Journal, 1,* 1058–1061.

Egan, J. (2008, September 14). The bipolar puzzle. *New York Times Magazine.*

Egeland, J. A., Hostetter, A. M., Pauls, D. L., & Sussex, J. N. (2000). Prodromal symptoms before onset of manic-depressive disorder suggested by first hospital admission histories. *Journal of the American Academy of Child & Adolescent Psychiatry, 39,* 1245–1252.

Egger, H. L., Costello, E. J., & Angold, A. (2003). School refusal and psychiatric disorders. *Journal of the American Academy of Child and Adolescent Psychiatry, 42,* 797–807.

Ehren, T. C., & Ehren, B. J. (2007). Legal mandates. In A.G. Kamhi, J.J. Masterson, & K. Apel (Eds.), *Clinical decision making in developmental language disorders* (pp. 337–359). Baltimore, MD: Brooks.

Ehrensaft, M. K. (2005). Interpersonal relationships and sex differences in the development of conduct problems. *Clinical Child and Family Psychology Review, 8,* 39–63.

Eigsti, I., & Cicchetti, D. (2004). The impact of child maltreatment on expressive syntax at 60 months. *Developmental Science, 7,* 88–102.

Einfeld, S. L. (2005). Behaviour problems in children with genetic disorders causing intellectual disability. *Educational Psychology, 25,* 341–346.

Einfeld, S. L., Piccinin, A. M., Mackinnon, A., Hofer, S. M., Taffe, J., Gray, K. M., et al. (2006). Psychopathology in young people with intellectual disability. *Journal of the American Medical Association, 296,* 1981–1989.

Eisenberg, N., Cumberland, A., & Spinrad, T. L. (1998). Parental socialization of emotion. *Psychological Inquiry, 9,* 241–273.

Eisenberg, N., Cumberland, A., Spinrad, T. L., Fabes, R. A., Shepard, S. A., Reiser, M., et al. (2001). The relations of regulation and emotionality to children's externalizing and internalizing problem behavior. *Child Development, 72,* 1112–1134.

Eisenberg, N., Fabes, R. A., Guthrie, I. K., & Reiser, M. (2000). Dispositional emotionality and regulation: Their role in predicting quality of social functioning. *Journal of Personality and Social Psychology, 78,* 136–157.

Eisenstadt, T. H., Eyberg, S., McNeil, C. B., Newcomb, K., & Funderburk, B. (1993). Parent-child interaction therapy with behavior problem children: Relative effectiveness of two stages and overall treatment outcome. *Journal of Clinical Child Psychology, 22,* 42–51.

Elbaum, B., Vaughn, S., Hughes, M. T., & Moody, S. W. (2000). How effective are one-to-one tutoring programs in reading for elementary students at risk for reading failure? A meta-analysis of the intervention research. *Journal of Educational Psychology, 92,* 605–619.

Eley, T. C., Sugden, K., Corsico, A., Gregory, A. M., Sham, P., McGuffin, P., et al. (2004). Gene-environment interaction analysis of serotonin system markers with adolescent depression. *Molecular Psychiatry, 9,* 908–915.

Elhai, J. D., Kashdan, T. D., & Freuh, B. C. (2005). What is a traumatic event? *British Journal of Psychiatry, 187,* 189–190.

Elia, J., Takeda, T., Deberardinis, R., Burke, J., Accardo, J., Ambrosini, P. J., Blum, N. J., et al. (2009). *Journal of Pediatrics, 155,* 239–244.

Elkin, T. D., & Stoppelbein, L. (2008). Evidence-based treatments for children with chronic illnesses. In R. Steele, T. D. Elkin, & M. C. Roberts (Eds.), *Handbook of evidence-based therapies for children and adolescents* (pp. 297–309). New York: Springer.

Elkind, D., & Bowen, R. (1979). Imaginary audience behavior in children and adolescence. *Developmental Psychology, 15,* 38–44.

Elkins, I. J., King, S. M., McGue, M., & Iacono, W. G. (2006). Personality traits and the development of nicotine, alcohol, and illicit drug disorders: Prospective links from adolescence to young adulthood. *Journal of Abnormal Psychology, 115,* 26–39.

Elkins, I. J., McGue, M., & Iacono, W. G. (2007). Prospective effects of attention-deficit/hyperactivity disorder, conduct disorder, and sex on adolescent substance use and abuse. *Archives of general psychiatry, 64,* 1145.

Elliott, L., Orr, L., Watson, L., & Jackson, A. (2005). Secondary prevention interventions for young drug users: A systematic review of the evidence. *Adolescence, 40,* 1–22.

Ellis, A. (2005). *The myth of self-esteem: How rational emotive behavior therapy can change your life forever.* Amherst, NY: Prometheus Books.

Ellis, A. (2011). Rational emotive behavior therapy. In R. J. Corsini & D. Wedding (Eds.), *Current psychotherapies* (pp. 196–234). Belmont, CA: Brooks/Cole.

Ellis, A., & Harper, R. A. (1961). *A guide to rational living.* Hollywood, CA: Wilshire Books.

Elsabbagh, M., & Karmiloff-Smith, A. (2012). The contribution of developmental models toward understanding gene-to-behavior mapping. In J.A. Burack, R.M. Hodapp, G. Iarocci, & E. Zigler (Eds.), *The Oxford handbook of intellectual disability and development* (20–41). New York: Oxford University Press.

Emslie, G. J., Heiligenstein, J. H., Wagner, K. D., Hoog, S. L., Ernest, D. E., Brown-Nilson, M., et al. (2002). Fluoxetine for acute treatment of depression in children and adolescents: A placebo-controlled, randomized clinical trial. *Journal of the American Academy of Child & Adolescent Psychiatry, 41,* 1205–1215.

Emslie, G. J., Mayes, T., Porta, G., Vitiello, B., Clarke, H., Wagner, K. D., et al. (2010). Treatment of resistant depression in adolescents (TORDIA): Week 24 outcomes. *American Journal of Psychiatry, 167,* 782–791.

Emslie, G. J., Rush, J., Weinberg, W. A., Kovatch, R. A., Hughes, C. W., Carmody, T., et al. (1997). A double-blind, randomized, placebo-controlled trial of fluoxetine in children and adolescents with depression. *Archives of General Psychiatry, 54,* 1031–1037, 1997.

Endicott, J., & Spitzer, R. L. (1978, July). A diagnostic interview: The schedule for affective disorders and Schizophrenia. *Archives of General Psychiatry, 35*(7), 873–843.

Engelhardt, P. E., Nigg, J. T., Carr, L. A., Ferreira, F. (2008). Cognitive inhibition and working memory in attention-deficit/hyperactivity disorder. *Journal of Abnormal Psychology, 117,* 591–605.

Engelmann, S., & Carnine, D. (1975). *DISTAR arithmetic.* Columbus, OH: Science Research Associates.

Ennett, S. T., Tobler, N. S., Ringwalt, C. L., & Flewelling, R. L. (1994). Resistance education? A meta-analysis of Project D.A.R.E. outcome evaluations. *American Journal of Public Health, 84,* 1394–1401.

Erdogan, A., Akkurt, H., Boettjer, N. K., Yurtseven, E., Can, G., & Kiran, S. (2008). Prevalence and behavioral correlates of enuresis in young children. *Journal of Pediatrics and Child Health, 44,* 297–301.

Erhardt, D., & Hinshaw, S. P. (1994). Initial sociometric impressions of attention-deficit/hyperactivity disorder and comparison boys: Predictions from social behaviors and from nonbehavioral variables. *Journal of Consulting and Clinical Psychology, 62,* 833–842.

Erickson, M. F., & Egeland, B. (2002). Child neglect. In J. E. B. Meyers, L. Berliner, J. Briere, C. T. Hendrix, C. Jenny, & T. A. Reid (Eds.), *The APSAC handbook on child maltreatment* (pp. 3–20). Thousand Oaks, CA: Sage.

Erikson, E. H. (1963). *Childhood and society.* New York: Norton.

Ertan, P., Yilmaz, O., Caglayan, M., Sogut, A., Aslan, S., & Yuksel, H. (2009). Relationship of sleep quality and quality of life in children with monosymptomatic enuresis. *Child: Care, Health, and Development, 35,* 469–474.

Essau, C. A. (2003). *Conduct and oppositional defiant disorders: Epidemiology, risk factors, and treatment.* New York: Erlbaum.

Essau, C. A. (2004). The association between family factors and depressive disorders in adolescents. *Journal of Youth and Adolescence, 33,* 365–372.

Essau, C. A., Conradt, J., & Petermann, F. (1999). Frequency of panic attacks and panic disorder in adolescents. *Depression and Anxiety, 9,* 19–26.

Essau, C. A., Conradt, J., & Petermann, F. (2000). Frequency, comorbidity, and psychosocial impairment of anxiety disorders in German adolescents. *Journal of Anxiety Disorders, 14,* 263–279.

Essau, C. A., & Merikangas, K. R. (1999). Familial and genetic factors. In C. A. Essau & F. Petermann (Eds.), *Depressive disorders in children and adolescents: Epidemiology, risk factors, and treatment* (pp. 261–285). Lanham, MD: Aronson.

Essau, C. A., Sasagawa, S., & Frick, P. J. (2006). Callous-unemotional traits in a community sample of adolescents. *Assessment, 13,* 454–469.

Essex, M. J., Klein, M. H., Cho, E., & Kalin, N. H. (2002). Maternal stress beginning in infancy may sensitize children to later stress exposure: Effects on cortisol and behavior. *Biological Psychiatry, 52,* 776–784.

Estes, A., Shaw, D. W. W., Sparks, B. F., Friedman, S., Giedd, J. N., Dawson, G., et al. (2011). Basal ganglia morphology and repetitive behavior in young children with autism spectrum disorder. *Autism Research, 4,* 212–220.

Evans, D. L., Beardslee, W., Biederman, J., Brent, D., Charney, D., Coyle, J., et al. (2005). Depression and bipolar disorder. In D. L. Evans, E. B. Foa, R. E. Gur, H. Hendin, C. P. O'Brien, M. E. P. Seligman, & B. T. Walsh (Eds.), *Treating and preventing adolescent mental health disorders* (pp. 3–74). New York: Oxford University Press.

Ewing, J. A. (1984). Detecting alcoholism: The CAGE questionnaire. *Journal of the American Medical Association, 252,* 1905–1907.

Exner, J. E. (2003). *The Rorschach: A comprehensive system.* New York: Wiley.

Eyberg, S. M. (2006). Oppositional defiant disorder. In J. E. Fisher & W. T. O'Donohue (Eds.), *Practitioner's guide to evidence-based psychotherapy* (pp. 461–468). New York: Springer.

Eyberg, S. M., Funderburk, B. W., Hembree-Kigin, T. L., McNeil, C. B., Querido, J. G., & Hood, K. K. (2001). Parent-child interaction therapy with behavior problem children: One and two year maintenance of treatment effects in the family. *Child & Family Behavior Therapy, 23,* 1–20.

Eyler, L. T., Pierce, K., & Courchesne, E. (2012). A failure of left temporal cortex to specialize for language is an early emerging and fundamental property of autism. *Brain, 135,* 949–960.

Eysenck, H. J. (1959). *Behaviour therapy and the neuroses: Readings in modern methods of treatment derived from learning theory.* Oxford, UK: Pergamon Press.

Eysenck, M. W., Derakshan, N., Santos, R., & Calvo, M. G. (2007). Anxiety and cognitive performance: Attentional control theory. *Emotion, 7,* 336.

Ezpeleta, L., Domenech, J. M., & Angold, A. (2006). A comparison of pure and comorbid CD/ODD and depression. *Journal of Child Psychology and Psychiatry, 47,* 704–712.

Ezrati-Vinacour, R., Platzky, R., & Yairi, E. (2001). The young child's awareness of stuttering-like disfluency. *Journal of Speech, Language, and Hearing Research, 44,* 368–380.

Fabiano, G. A., Pelham, W. E., Coles, E. K., Gnagy, E. M., Chronis-Tuscano, A., & O'Connor, B. C. (2009). A meta-analysis of behavioral treatments for attention-deficit/hyperactivity disorder. *Clinical Psychology Review, 29*, 129–140.

Fabiano, G. A., Pelham, W. E., Cunningham, C. E., Yu, J., Gangloff, B., Buck, M., et al. (2012). A waitlist-controlled trial of behavioral parent training for fathers of children with ADHD. *Journal of Clinical Child and Adolescent Psychology, 41*, 337–345.

Fagan, P. J., Wise, T. N., Schmidt, C. W., & Berlin, F. S. (2002). Pedophilia. *Journal of the American Medical Association, 288*, 2458–2465.

Fairburn, C. G., Cooper, Z., & Safran, R. (2002). Cognitive behavior therapy for eating disorders: A "transdiagnostic" theory and treatment. *Behavior Research and Therapy, 41*, 509–528.

Fairburn, C. G., Cooper, Z., Doll, H. A., Norman, P., & O'Connor, M. (2000). The natural course of bulimia nervosa and binge eating disorder in young women. *Archives of General Psychiatry, 57*, 659–665.

Fairburn, C. G., Cooper, Z., Doll, H. A., & Welch, S. L. (1999). Risk factors for anorexia nervosa: Three integrated case-control comparisons. *Archives of General Psychiatry, 56*, 468–476.

Fairburn, C. G., & Gowers, S. G. (2010). Eating disorders. In M. Rutter (Ed.), *Rutter's child and adolescent psychiatry* (pp. 670–685.). Malden, MA: Blackwell.

Fairburn, C. G., & Harrison, P. J. (2003). Eating disorders. *Lancet, 361*, 407–416.

Falck-Yttr, T., Fernell, E., Hedvall, A.L., von Vofsten, C., & Gillberg, C. (2012). Gaze performance in children with autism spectrum disorder when observing communicative actions. *Journal of Autism and Developmental Disorders, 42*, 2236–2245.

Falloon, I. R., Kydd, R. R., Coverdale, J. H., & Laidlaw, T. M. (1996). Early detection and intervention for initial episodes of Schizophrenia. *Schizophrenia Bulletin, 22*, 271–282.

Famularo, R., Fenton, T., Augustyn, M., & Zuckerman, B. (1996). Persistence of pediatric post traumatic stress disorder after 2 years. *Child Abuse & Neglect, 20*, 1245–1248.

Famularo, R., Fenton, T., Kinscherff, R., Ayoub, C., & Barnum, R. (1994). Maternal and child posttraumatic stress disorder in cases of child maltreatment. *Child Abuse & Neglect, 18*, 27–36.

Faraone, S. V., & Biederman, J. (1998). Neurobiology of attention-deficit hyperactivity disorder. *Biological Psychiatry, 44*, 951–958.

Faraone, S. V., Biederman, J., Weber, W., & Russell, R. L. (1998). Psychiatric, neuropsychological, and psychosocial features of *DSM-IV* subtypes of attention-deficit/hyperactivity disorder: Results from a clinically referred sample. *Journal of the American Academy of Child and Adolescent Psychiatry, 37*, 185–193.

Faraone, S. V., & Buitelaar, J. (2010). Comparing the efficacy of stimulants for ADHD in children and adolescents using meta-analysis. *European Child and Adolescent Psychiatry, 19*, 353–364.

Farmer, C., & Aman, M. (2011). Aggressive behavior in a sample of children with autism spectrum disorders. *Reearch in Autism Spectrum Disorders, 5*, 317–323.

Farran, D. C. (2000). Another decade of intervention for children who are low income or disabled: What do we know now? In J. P. Shonkoff & S. J. Meisels (Eds.), *Handbook of early childhood intervention* (pp. 510–548). New York: Cambridge University Press.

Farrington, D. P. (1998). Predictors, causes, and correlates of male youth violence. In M. Tonry & M. Moore (Eds.), *Youth violence* (pp. 317–371). Chicago: University of Chicago Press.

Favazza, A. R. (2012). Nonsuicidal self-injury: How categorization guides treatment. *Current Psychiatry, 11*, 21–25.

Fawcett, J. (2010). *DSM-5* perspectives on classification of bipolar disorder. In L. N. Yatham & M. Maj (Eds.), *Bipolar disorder* (pp. 44–51). New York: Wiley.

Feeley, K. M., & Jones, A. (2006). Addressing challenging behaviour in children with Down syndrome: The use of applied behaviour analysis for assessment and intervention. *Down Syndrome: Research & Practice, 11*, 64–77.

Feinberg, D. T. (2006). The cost of over-the-counter substance abuse. *Journal of Child and Adolescent Psychopharmacology, 16*, 801–802.

Feindler, E. L., & Engel, E. C. (2011). Assessment and intervention for adolescents with anger and aggression difficulties in school settings. *Psychology in the Schools, 48*, 243–253.

Feinstein, A. (2010). *A history of autism: Conversations with the pioneers.* New York: Wiley-Blackwell.

Feiring, C., & Taska, S. (2005). The persistence of shame following sexual abuse: A longitudinal look at risk and recovery. *Child Maltreatment, 10*, 337–349.

Fenske, E. C., Zalenski, S., Krantz, P. J., & McClannahan, L. E. (1985). Age at intervention and treatment outcome for autistic children in a comprehensive intervention program. *Analysis and Intervention in Developmental Disabilities, 5*, 49–58.

Ferguson, C. P., & Pigott, T. A. (2000). Anorexia and bulimia nervosa: Neurobiology and pharmacotherapy. *Behavior Therapy, 31*, 237–263.

Fergusson, D. M., & Horwood, L. J. (1995). Early disruptive behavior, IQ, and later school achievement and delinquent behavior. *Journal of Abnormal Child Psychology, 23*, 183–199.

Fergusson, D. M., Horwood, L. J., & Nagin, D. S. (2000). Offending trajectories in a New Zealand birth cohort. *Criminology, 38*, 525–552.

Fergusson, D. M., Horwood, L. J., & Ridder, E. M. (2005). Show me the child at seven: The consequences of conduct problems in childhood for psychosocial functioning in adulthood. *Journal of Child Psychology and Psychiatry, 46*, 837–849.

Fergusson, D. M., & Lynskey, M. T. (1998). Conduct problems in childhood and psychosocial outcomes in young adulthood: A prospective study. *Journal of Emotional and Behavioral Disorders, 6*, 2–18.

Fergusson, D. M., Lynskey, M. T., & Horwood, L. J. (1997). Attentional difficulties in middle childhood and psychosocial outcomes in young adulthood. *Journal of Child Psychology and Psychiatry, 38*, 633–644.

Fichter, M. M., Kruger, R., Rief, W., Holland, R., & Dohne, J. (1996). Fluvoxamine in prevention of relapse in bulimia nervosa: Effects on eating-specific psychopathology. *Journal of Clinical Psychopharmacology, 16*, 9–18.

Fichter, M. M., & Quadflieg, N. (2007). Long-term stability of eating disorder diagnoses. *International Journal of Eating Disorders, 40*, 61–66.

Field, A., Camargo, C., Taylor, C., Berkey, C., Robert, S., & Colditz, G. (2001). Peer, parent, and media influences on the development of weight concerns and frequent dieting among preadolescent girls and boys. *Pediatrics, 107*, 54–60.

Filipek, P. A., Semrud-Clikeman, M., Steingrad, R., Kennedy, D., & Biederman, J. (1997). Volumetric MRI analysis: Comparing subjects having attention-deficit hyperactivity disorder with normal controls. *Neurology, 48*, 589–601.

Finch, A. J., Nelson, W. M., & Hart, K. J. (2006). Conduct disorder: Description, prevalence, and etiology. In W. M. Nelson, A. J. Finch, & K. J. Hart (Eds.), *Conduct disorders: A practitioner's guide to comparative treatments* (pp. 1–13). New York: Springer.

Findling, R. L. (2005). Update on the treatment of bipolar disorder in children and adolescents. *European Psychiatry, 20*, 87–91.

Findling, R. L., Aman, M. G., Eerdekens, M., Derivan, A., Lyons, B., & Risperidone Behavior Study Group. (2004). Long-term, open-label study of risperidone in children with severe disruptive behaviors and below-average IQ. *American Journal of Psychiatry, 161*, 677–684.

Findling, R. L., Gracious, B. L., McNamara, N. K., Youngstrom, E. A., Demeter, C. A., Branicky, L. A., et al. (2001). Rapid, continuous cycling and psychiatric co-morbidity in pediatric bipolar I disorder. *Bipolar Disorders, 3*, 202–210.

Findling, R. L., Johnson, J. L., McClellan, J., Frazier, J. A., Vitiello, B., Hamer, R. M., et al. (2010). Double-blind maintenance safety and effectiveness findings from the treatment of early-onset schizophrenia spectrum (TEOSS) study. *Journal of the American Academy of Child and Adolescent Psychiatry, 49*, 583–594.

Findling, R. L., Robb, A., Nyilas, M., Forbes, R. A., Jin, N., Ivanova, S., et al. (2008). A multiple-center, randomized, double-blind, placebo controlled study of oral aripiprazole for treatment of adolescents with schizophrenia. *American Journal of Psychiatry, 165*, 1432–1441.

Findling, R. L., Youngstrom, E. A., Fristad, M. A., Birmaher, B., Kowatch, R. A., Arnold, L. E., et al. (2010). Characteristics of children with elevated symptoms of mania. *Journal of Clinical Psychiatry, 71,* 1664–1672.

Finkelhor, D., & Browne, A. (1985). The traumatic impact of child sexual abuse: A conceptualization. *American Journal of Orthopsychiatry, 55,* 530–541.

Finkelhor, D., Cross, T. P., & Cantor, E. N. (2005). The justice system for juvenile victims: A comprehensive model of case flow. *Trauma, Violence, & Abuse, 6,* 83–102.

Finkelhor, D., Hotaling, G. T., Lewis, I. A., & Smith, C. (1989). Sexual abuse and its relationship to later sexual satisfaction, marital status, religion, and attitudes. *Journal of Interpersonal Violence, 4,* 379–399.

Fiorello, C. A., Hale, J. B., Decker, S. L., & Coleman, S. (2009). Neuropsychology in school psychology. In E. Garcia-Vazquez, T.D. Crespi, & C.A. Riccio (Eds.), *Handbook of education, training, and supervision of school psychologists in school and community* (pp. 213–232). New York: Taylor & Francis.

First, M. B., & Wakefield, J. C. (2010). Defining mental disorder in *DSM-5*. *Psychological Medicine, 40,* 1779–1782.

Fischer, D. J., Himle, J. A., & Thyer, B. A. (1999). Separation anxiety disorder. In R. T. Ammerman, M. Hersen, & C. G. Last (Eds.), *Handbook of prescriptive treatments for children and adolescents* (pp. 141–154). Boston: Allyn & Bacon.

Fischer, M., Barkley, R. A., Smallish, L., & Fletcher, K. (2002). Young adult follow-up of hyperactive children: Self-reported psychiatric disorders, comorbidity, and the role of childhood conduct problems. *Journal of Abnormal Child Psychology, 30,* 463–475.

Fisher, J. O., & Birch, L. L. (2002). Eating in the absence of overweight girls from 5 to 7 years of age. *American Journal of Clinical Nutrition, 76,* 226–231.

Fisher, P. A., & Stoolmiller, M. (2008). Intervention effects on foster parent stress: Associations with child cortisol levels. *Development and Psychopathology, 20,* 1003–1021.

Flament, M. F., Furino, C., & Godart, N. (2005). Evidence-based pharmacotherapy of eating disorders. In D. J. Stein, B. Lerer, & S. Stahl (Eds.), *Evidence-based psychopharmacology* (pp. 204–254). New York: Cambridge University Press.

Flanagan, D. P., Alfonso, V. C., & Mascolo, J. T. (2011). A CHC-based operational definition of SLD. In D. P. Flanagan & V. C. Alfonso (Eds.), *Essentials of specific learning disability identification* (pp. 233–298). Hoboken, NJ: Wiley.

Flanagan, D. P., Fiorello, & Ortiz, S. O. (2010). Enhancing practice through application of Cattell-Horn-Carroll theory and research. *Psychology in the Schools, 47,* 739–760.

Flannery-Schroeder, E. C. (2004). Generalized anxiety disorder. In T. L. Morris & J. S. March (Eds.), *Anxiety disorders in children and adolescents* (pp. 125–140). New York: Guilford Press.

Flannery-Schroeder, E., Choudhury, M. S., & Kendall, P. C. (2005). Group and individual cognitive-behavioral treatments for youth with anxiety disorders: One-year follow-up. *Cognitive Therapy and Research, 29,* 253–259.

Flannery-Schroeder, E. C., & Kendall, P. C. (2000). Group and individual cognitive-behavioral treatments for youth with anxiety disorders: A randomized clinical trial. *Cognitive Therapy and Research, 24,* 251–278.

Fleischner, J. E., & Manheimer, M. A. (1997). Math interventions for students with learning disabilities: Myths and realities. *School Psychology Review, 26,* 397–413.

Fleming, J., & Offord, D. (1990). Epidemiology of childhood depressive disorders: A critical review. *Journal of the American Academy of Child and Adolescent Psychiatry, 29,* 571–580.

Fletcher, J. M., Lyon, G. R., Barnes, M., Stuebing, K. K., Francis, D. J., Olson, R. K., et al. (2002). Classification of learning disabilities: An evidenced-based evaluation. In R. Bradley, L. Danielson, & D. P. Hallahan (Eds.), *Identification of learning disabilities: Research to policy* (pp. 185–250). Mahwah, NJ: Erlbaum.

Flett, G. L., Hewitt, P. L., Oliver, J. M., & Macdonald, S. (2002). Perfectionism in children and their parents: A developmental analysis. In G. L. Flett & P. L. Hewitt (Eds.), *Perfectionism: Theory, research, and treatment* (pp. 89–132). Washington, DC: American Psychological Association.

Flore, L.A., Milunsky, J.M. (2012). Updates in the genetic evaluation of the child with global developmental delay or intellectual disability. *Seminars in Pediatric Neurology, 19,* 173–180.

Fluoxetine Bulimia Nervosa Collaborative Study Group. (1992). Fluoxetine in the treatment of bulimia nervosa: A multicenter, placebo-controlled, double-blind trial. *Archives of General Psychiatry, 49,* 139–147.

Fogle, P.T. (2008). *Foundations of communication sciences and disorders.* Clifton Park, NY: Delmar.

Fombonne, E. (2005). Epidemiological studies of pervasive developmental disorders. In F. R. Volkmar, R. Paul, A. Klin, & D. Cohen (Eds.), *Handbook of autism and pervasive developmental disorders, Vol. 1: Diagnosis, development, neurobiology, and behavior* (pp. 42–69). Hoboken, NJ: Wiley.

Fombonne, E., Wostear, G., Cooper, V., Harrington, R., & Rutter, M. (2001). The Maudsley long-term follow-up of child and adolescent depression: 1. Psychiatric outcomes in adulthood. *British Journal of Psychiatry, 179,* 210–217.

Forbes, D., Fletcher, S., Lockwood, E., O'Donnell, M., Creamer, M., Bryant, R. A., et al. (2011). Requiring both avoidance and emotional numbing in *DSM-5* PTSD: Will it help? *Journal of Affective Disorder, 130,* 483–486.

Fox, N. A., Almas, A. N., Degnan, K. A., Nelson, C. A., & Zeanah, C. H. (2011). The effects of severe psychosocial deprivation and foster care intervention on cognitive development at 8 years of age: Findings from the Bucharest Early Intervention Project. *Journal of Child Psychology and Psychiatry, 52,* 919–928.

Frackowiak, R., Friston, K., Frith, C., Dolan, R., Price, C., Zeki, S., et al. (2004): *Human brain function.* San Diego: Academic Press, Elsevier Science.

Frances, A. (2009). Whither *DSM-5*? *British Journal of Psychiatry, 195,* 391–392.

Frangou, S., Madjulis, M., & Vourdas, A. (2008). The Maudsley early onset schizophrenia study: Cognitive function over a 4-year follow-up period. *Schizophrenia Bulletin, 34,* 52–59.

Frank, J. D. (1973). *Persuasion and healing.* Baltimore, MD: Johns Hopkins University Press.

Frank, J. D., & Frank, J. (2004). Therapeutic components shared by all psychotherapies. In A. Freeman, M. J. Mahoney, P. DeVito, & D. Martin (Eds.), *Cognition and psychotherapy* (pp. 45–78). New York: Springer.

Franklin, M. E., Kozak, M. J., Cashman, L. A., Coles, M. E., Rheingold, A. A., & Foa, E. B. (1998). Cognitive-behavioral treatment of pediatric obsessive-compulsive disorder: An open clinical trial. *Journal of the Academy of Child and Adolescent Psychiatry, 37,* 412–419.

Franklin, M. E., Rynn, M. A., Foa, E. B., & March, J. S. (2004). Pediatric obsessive-compulsive disorder. In T. H. Ollendick & J. S. March (Eds.), *Phobic and anxiety disorders in children and adolescents* (pp. 381–404). New York: Oxford University Press.

Franklin, M. E., Sapyta, J., Freeman, J. B., Khanna, M., Compton, S., & Almirall, D., et al. (2011). Cognitive Behavior Therapy Augmentation of Pharmacotherapy in Pediatric Obsessive-Compulsive Disorder: *JAMA: Journal of the American Medical Association, 306,* 1224–1232.

Franklin, M., March, J. S., & Gracia, A. (2007). Treating obsessive-compulsive disorder in children and adolescents. In M. M. Antony, C. Purdon, & L. J. Summerfeldt (Eds.), *Psychological treatment of obsessive compulsive disorders: Fundamentals and beyond* (pp. 253–266). Washington, DC: American Psychological Association.

Frazier, J. A., Chiu, S., Breeze, J. L., Makris, N., Lange, N., Kennedy, D. N., et al. (2005). Structural brain magnetic resonance imaging of limbic and thalamic volumes in pediatric bipolar disorder. *American Journal of Psychiatry, 162,* 1256–1265.

Frazier, T. W., Youngstrom, E. A., Speer, L., Embacher, R., Law, P., Costantino, J., et al. (2012). Validation of proposed *DSM-5* criteria for autism spectrum disorder. *Journal of the American Academy of Child and Adolescent Psychiatry, 51,* 28–40.

Fredrickson, B., & Roberts, T. (1997). Objectification theory: Toward understanding women's lived experiences and mental health risks. *Psychology of Women Quarterly, 21,* 173–206.

Freitag, C. M. (2007). The genetics of autistic disorders and its clinical relevance: A review of the literature. *Molecular Psychiatry, 12,* 2–22.

Fremont, W. P. (2004). Childhood reactions to terrorism-induced trauma: A review of the past 10 years. *Journal of the American Academy of Child & Adolescent Psychiatry, 43,* 381–392.

Freud, A. (1936). *The ego and the mechanisms of defense.* New York: International Universities Press.

Freud, A. (1956). *Research at the Hampstead Child-Therapy Clinic.* New York: International University Press.

Freud, A., & Burlingham, D. (1943). *Children in war.* New York: Medical War Books.

Freud, S. (1961). The ego and the id. In J. Strachey (Ed. & Trans.), *The standard edition of the complete psychological works of Sigmund Freud* (Vol. 19). London: Hogarth Press. (Original work published 1923)

Frick, P. J. (2004). Developmental pathways to conduct disorder: Implications for serving youth who show severe aggressive and antisocial behavior. *Psychology in the Schools, 41,* 823–834.

Frick, P. J., Bodin, S. D., & Barry, C. T. (2000). Psychopathic traits and conduct problems in community and clinic-referred samples of children: Further development of the psychopathy screening device. *Psychological Assessment, 12, 382 393.*

Frick, P. J., Cornell, A. H., Barry, C. T., Bodin, S. D., & Dane, H. A. (2003). Callous-unemotional traits and conduct problems in the prediction of conduct problem severity, aggression, and self-report of delinquency. *Journal of Abnormal Child Psychology, 31,* 457–470.

Frick, P. J., Cornell, A. H., Bodin, S. D., Dane, H. A., Barry, C. T., & Loney, B. R. (2003). Callous-unemotional traits and developmental pathways to severe conduct problems. *Developmental Psychology, 39,* 246–260.

Frick, P. J., Lahey, B. B., Applegate, B., Kerdyck, L., Ollendick, T., Hynd, G., et al. (1994). *DSM-IV* field trials for the disruptive behavior disorders: Symptom utility estimates. *Journal of the American Academy of Child and Adolescent Psychiatry, 33,* 529–539.

Frick, P. J., Lahey, B. B., Loeber, R., Stouthamer-Loeber, M., Christ, M. A., & Hanson, K. (1992). Familial risk factors to oppositional defiant disorder and conduct disorder: Parental psychopathology and maternal parenting. *Journal of Consulting and Clinical Psychology, 60,* 49–55.

Frick, P. J., Lahey, B. B., Loeber, R., Tannenbaum, L. E., Van Horn, Y., Christ, M. A. G., et al. (1993). Oppositional defiant disorder and conduct disorder: A meta-analytic review of factor analyses and cross-validation in a clinic sample. *Clinical Psychology Review, 13,* 319–340.

Frick, P. J., & Loney, B. R. (2002). Understanding the association between parent and child antisocial behavior. In R. J. McMahon & R. De V. Peters (Eds.), *The effects of parental dysfunction on children* (pp. 105–126). New York: Kluwer Academic/Plenum.

Frick, P. J., & Moffitt, T. E. (2010). *A proposal to the DSM-5 childhood disorders and the ADHD and disruptive behavior disorders work groups to include a specifier to the diagnosis of conduct disorder based on the presence of callous-unemotional traits.* Washington, DC: American Psychiatric Association.

Frick, P. J., & Morris, A. S. (2004). Temperament and developmental pathways to conduct problems. *Journal of Clinical Child and Adolescent Psychology, 33,* 54–68.

Frick, P. J., & Munoz, L. (2006). Oppositional defiant disorder and conduct disorder. In C. A. Essau (Ed.), *Child and adolescent psychopathology: Theoretical and clinical implications* (pp. 26–51). New York: Routledge.

Frick, P. J., Stickle, T. R., Dandreaux, D. M., Farrell, J. M., & Kimonis, E. R. (2005). Callous-unemotional traits in predicting the severity and stability of conduct problems and delinquency. *Journal of Abnormal Child Psychology, 33,* 471–487.

Friedrich, W. N. (1997). *Child sexual behavior inventory.* Odessa, FL: Psychological Assessment Resources.

Friedrich, W. N. (2002). An integrated model of psychotherapy for abused children. In J. E. B. Meyers, L. Berliner, J. Briere, C. T. Hendrix, C. Jenny, & T. A. Reid (Eds.), *The APSAC handbook on child maltreatment* (pp. 141–158). Thousand Oaks, CA: Sage.

Friedrich, W. N., Fisher, J. L., Dittner, C. A., Acton, R., Berliner, L., Butler, J., et al. (2001). Child sexual behavior inventory: Normative, psychiatric, and sexual abuse comparisons. *Child Maltreatment, 6,* 37–49.

Frijters, J. C., Lovett, M. W., Steinbach, K. A., Wolf, M., Sevcik, R. A, & Morris, R. D. (2011). Neurocognitive predictors of reading outcomes for children with reading disabilities. *Journal of Learning Disabilities, 44,* 150–166.

Friman, P. C. (2008). Encopresis and enuresis. In D. Reitman (Ed.), *Handbook of psychological assessment, case conceptualization, and treatment* (pp. 589–621). New York: Wiley.

Friman, P. C., Resetar, J., & DeRuyk, K. (2009). Encopresis: Biobehavioral treatment. In W. O'Donohue & J. E. Fisher (Eds.), *General principles and empirically supported techniques of cognitive behavior therapy* (pp. 285–294). New York: Wiley.

Fristad, M. A., Arnold, J. S. G., Leffler, J. M. (2011). *Psychotherapy for children with bipolar and depressive disorders.* New York: Guilford.

Fristad, M. A., Verducci, J. S., Walters, K., & Young, M. E. (2009). Impact of multifamily psychoeducational psychotherapy in treating children aged 8 to 12 years with mood disorders. *Archives of General Psychiatry, 66,* 1013–1021.

Frith, C. D., & Frith, U. (1999). Interacting minds: a biological basis. *Science, 286,* 1692–1695.

Frost, L., & Bondy, A. (2002). *The picture exchange communication system training manual.* Newark, DE: Pyramid Educational Products.

Fuchs, L. S., Fuchs, D., & Compton, D. L. (2012). The early prevention of mathematics difficulty. *Journal of Learning Disabilities, 45,* 257–269.

Fulford, K. W. M. (1994). Closet logics: Hidden conceptual elements in the DSM and ICD classification of mental disorders. In J. Z. Sadler, O. P. Wiggins, & M. A. Schwartz (Eds.), *Philosophical perspectives on psychiatric diagnostic classification* (pp. 211–232). Baltimore, MD: Johns Hopkins University Press.

Funderburk, B. W., Eyberg, S. M., Newcomb, K., McNeil, C. B., Hembree-Kigin, T., & Capage, L. (1998). Parent-child interaction therapy with behavior problem children: Maintenance of treatment effects in the school setting. *Child & Family Behavior Therapy, 20,* 17–38.

Fusar-Poli, P., & Politi, P. (2008). Paul Eugen Bleuler and the birth of schizophrenia. *American Journal of Psychiatry, 165,* 1407.

Galambos, N. L., Barker, E. T., & Almeida, D. M. (2003). Parents do matter: Trajectories of change in externalizing and internalizing problems in early adolescence. *Child Development, 74,* 578–594.

Garb, H. N., & Boyle, P. A. (2004). Understanding why some clinicians use pseudoscientific methods. In S. O. Lilienfeld, S. J. Lynn, & J. M. Lohr (Eds.), *Science and pseudoscience in clinical psychology* (pp. 17–38). New York: Guilford Press.

Garber, J., & Flynn, C. (2001). Vulnerability to depression in childhood and adolescence. In R. Ingram & J. Price (Eds.), *Vulnerability to psychopathology: Risk across the lifespan* (pp. 175–225). New York: Guilford Press.

Garber, J., Keiley, M. K., & Martin, N. C. (2002). Developmental trajectories of adolescents' depressive symptoms: Predictors of change. *Journal of Consulting and Clinical Psychology, 70,* 79–95.

Garland, J. (2004). Facing the evidence: Antidepressant treatment in children and adolescents. *Canadian Medical Association Journal, 170,* 489–491.

Garner, A.A., Mrug, S., Hodgens, B., & Patterson, C. (2012). Do symptoms of sluggish cognitive tempo in children with ADHD symptoms represent comorbid internalizing difficulties? *Journal of Attention Disorders.*

Garrett, A. S., Reiss, A. L., Howe, M. E., Kelley, R. G., Singh, M. K., Adleman, N. E., et al. (2012). Abnormal amygdala and prefrontal cortex activation to facial expressions in pediatric bipolar disorder. *Journal of the American Academy of Child and Adolescent Psychiatry, 51,* 821–831.

Gau, S. S. F., Chong, M., Yang, P., Yen, C., Liang, K., & Cheng, A. T. A. (2007). Psychiatric and psychosocial predictors of substance use disorders among adolescents. Longitudinal study. *British Journal of Psychiatry, 190,* 42–48.

Gaub, M., & Carlson, C. L. (1997). Behavioral characteristics of *DSM-IV* ADHD subtypes in a school-based population. *Journal of Abnormal Child Psychology, 25,* 103–111.

Gaynor, S. T., Baird, S. C., & Nelson-Gray, R. O. (1999). Application of time-series (single-subject) designs in clinical psychology. In P. C. Kendall, J. N. Butcher, & G. N. Holmbeck (Eds.), *Handbook of research methods in clinical psychology* (pp. 297–329). Hoboken, NJ: Wiley.

Gazelle, H. (2006). Class climate moderates peer relations and emotional adjustment in children with an early history of anxious solitude. *Developmental Psychology, 42,* 1179–1192.

Ge, X., Coger, R. D., & Elder, G. H. (2001). Pubertal transition, stressful life events, and the emergence of gender differences in adolescent depressive symptoms. *Developmental Psychology, 37,* 404–417.

Geary, D. C. (2010). Mathematical disabilities: Reflections on cognitive, neuropsychological, and genetic components. *Learning and Individual Differences, 20,* 130–133.

Geary, D. C. (2011). Consequences, characteristics, and causes of mathematical learning disabilities and persistent low achievement in mathematics. *Journal of Developmental and Behavioral Pediatrics, 32,* 250–263.

Geary, D. C., Bailey, D. H., & Hoard, M. K. (2009). Predicting mathematical achievement and mathematical learning disability with a simple screening tool. *Journal of Psychoeducational Assessment, 27,* 265–279.

Geary, D. C., & Hoard, M. K. (2005). Learning disabilities in arithmetic and mathematics: Theoretical and empirical perspectives. In J. I. D. Campbell (Ed.), *Handbook of mathematical cognition* (pp. 253–267). New York: Psychology Press.

Geary, D. C., Hoard, M. K., & Bailey, D. H. (2011). How SLD manifests in mathematics. In D. P. Flanagan & V. C. Alfonso (Eds.), *Essentials of specific learning disability identification* (pp. 43–64). Hoboken, NJ: Wiley.

Geary, D. C., Hoard, M. K., Byrd-Craven, J., Nugent, L., & Numtee, C. (2007). Cognitive mechanisms underlying achievement deficits in children with mathematical learning disability. *Child development, 78,* 1343–1359.

Geary, D. C., Hoard, M. K., Nugent, L., & Bailey, D.H. (2012). Mathematical cognition deficits in children with learning disabilities and persistent low achievement. *Journal of Educational Psychology, 104,* 206–223.

Gelhorn, H., Hartmen, C., Sakai, J., Stallings, M., Young, S., Rhee, S. H., et al. (2008). Toward *DSM-5*: An item response theory analysis of the diagnostic process for alcohol abuse and dependence. *Journal of the American Academy of Child and Adolescent Psychiatry, 47,* 1329–1339.

Gelhorn, H. L., Stallings, M. C., Young, S. E., Corley, R. P., Rhee, S. H., & Hewitt, J. K. (2005). Genetic and environmental influences on conduct disorder: Symptom, domain and full-scale analyses. *Journal of Child Psychology and Psychiatry, 46,* 580–591.

Geller, B., Cooper, T. B., & Sun, K. (1998). Double-blind and placebo-controlled study of lithium for adolescent bipolar disorders with secondary substance dependency. *Journal of the American Academy of Child and Adolescent Psychiatry, 37,* 171–178.

Geller, B., Cooper, T. B., Sun, K., Zimmerman, B., Frazier, J., Williams, M., et al. (1998). Double-blind and placebo-controlled study of lithium for adolescent bipolar disorders with secondary substance dependency. *Journal of the American Academy of Child and Adolescent Psychiatry, 37,* 171–178.

Geller, B., Luby, J. L., & Joshi, P. (2012). A randomized controlled trial of risperidone, lithium, or divalproex for initial treatment of bipolar I disorder, manic or mixed phase, in children and adolescents. *Archives of General Psychiatry, 69,* 515–528.

Geller, B., Tillman, R., Craney, J. L., & Bolhofner, K. (2004). Four-year prospective outcome and natural history of mania in children with a prepubertal and early adolescent bipolar disorder phenotype. *Archives of General Psychiatry, 61,* 459–467.

Geller, B., Williams, M., Zimmerman, B., Frazier, J., Beringer, L., & Warner, K. L. (1998). Prepubertal and early adolescent bipolarity differentiate from ADHD by manic symptoms, grandiose delusions, ultra-rapid or ultradian cycling. *Journal of Affective Disorders, 51,* 81–91.

Geller, B., Zimmerman, B., Williams, M., Bolhofher, K., Craney, J. L., Delbello, M. P., et al. (2000). Diagnostic characteristics of 93 cases of a prepubertal and early adolescent bipolar disorder phenotype by gender, puberty and comorbid attention deficit hyperactivity disorder. *Journal of Child and Adolescent Psychopharmacology, 10,* 157–164.

Geller, D. A. (2010). Obsessive-compulsive disorder. In M. K. Dulcan (Eds.), *Child and adolescent psychiatry* (pp. 349–363). Washington, DC: American Psychiatric Publishing.

Gelman, R., & Gallistel, C. R. (1978). *The child's understanding of number.* Cambridge, MA: Harvard University Press.

Gentile, D. (2009). Pathological Video-Game Use Among Youth Ages 8 to 18: A National Study. *Psychological Science, 20*(5), 594–602.

Gentile, D. A., Choo, H., Liau, A., Sim, T., Li, D., Fung, D., & Khoo, A. (2011). Pathological video game use among youths: A two-year longitudinal study. *Pediatrics, 127, e319–e329.*

Georgiades, S., Szatmari, P., Zwaigenbaum, L., Duku, E., Bryson, S., Roberts, W., et al. (2007). Structure of the autism symptom phenotype: A proposed multidimensional model. *Journal of the American Academy of Child & Adolescent Psychiatry, 46,* 188–196.

Gersten, R., Chard, D. J., Jayanthi, M., Baker, S. K., Morphy, P., & Flojo, J. (2009). Mathematics instruction for students with learning disabilities: A meta-analysis of instructional components. *Review of Educational Research, 79,* 1202–1242.

Ghanizadeh, A. (2010). Comorbidity of enuresis in children with Attention-Deficit/Hyperactivity Disorder. *Journal of Attention Disorders, 13,* 464–467.

Ghera, M. M., Marshall, P. J., Fox, N. A., Zeanah, C. H., Nelson, C. A., Smyke, A. T., et al. (2009). The effects of foster care intervention on socially deprived institutionalized children's attention and positive affect. *Journal of Child Psychology and Psychiatry, 50,* 246–253.

Giaconia, R. M., Reinherz, H. Z., Silverman, A. B., Pakiz, B., Frost, A. K., & Cohen, E. (1995). Traumas and posttraumatic stress disorder in a community population of older adolescents. *Journal of the American Academy of Child and Adolescent Psychiatry, 34,* 1369–1380.

Giannotti, F., & Cortesi, F. (2009). Family and cultural influences on sleep development. *Child and Adolescent Psychiatric Clinics of North America, 18,* 849–861.

Gibb, B. E., Abramson, L. Y., & Alloy, L. B. (2004). Emotional maltreatment from parents, verbal peer victimization, and cognitive vulnerability to depression. *Cognitive Therapy and Research, 28,* 1–21.

Gibb, B. E., Andover, M. S., & Beach, S. R. (2006). Suicidal ideation and attitudes toward suicide. *Suicide and Life-Threatening Behavior, 36,* 12–18.

Gibbs, J. C. (2010). *Moral development and reality: Beyond the theories of Kohlberg and Hoffman* (2nd ed.). Boston: Pearson.

Giedd, J. M., Shaw, P., Wallace, G., Gogtay, N., & Lenroot, R. K. (2006). Anatomic brain imaging studies of normal and abnormal brain development in children and adolescents. In D. Cicchetti & D. J. Cohen (Eds.), *Developmental psychopathology, Vol 2: Developmental neuroscience* (pp. 127–196). Hoboken, NJ: Wiley.

Giedd, J. N., Blumenthal, J., Molloy, E., & Castellanos, F. X. (2001). Brain imaging of attention-deficit/hyperactivity disorder. *Annals of the New York Academy of Sciences, 931,* 33–34.

Gil, A. G., Vega, W. A., & Turner, R. J. (2002). Early and mid-adolescence risk factors for later substance abuse by African-Americans and European Americans. *Public Health Reports, 177,* 15–29.

Gilligan, C. (1982). *In a different voice: Psychological theory and women's development*. Cambridge, MA: Harvard University Press.

Gillon, G. T., Moran, C. A., & Page, F. (2007). Semantic intervention. In A.G. Kamhi, J.J. Masterson, & K. Apel (Eds.), *Clinical decision making in developmental language disorders*. (pp. 165–183). Baltimore, MD: Brookes Publishing.

Gil-Rivas, V., Holman, E. A., & Silver, R. C. (2004). Adolescent vulnerability following the September 11th terrorist attacks: A study of parents and their children. *Applied Developmental Science, 8*, 130–142.

Ginsburg, G. S., Albano, A. M., Findling, R. L., Kratochvil, C., & Walkup, J. (2005). Integrating cognitive behavioral therapy and pharmacotherapy in the treatment of adolescent depression. *Cognitive and Behavioral Practice, 12*, 252–262.

Ginsburg, G. S., Lambert, S. F., & Drake, K. L. (2004). Attributions of control, anxiety sensitivity, and panic symptoms among adolescents. *Cognitive Therapy and Research, 28*, 745–763.

Ginsburg, G. S., & Schlossberg, M. C. (2002). Family-based treatment of childhood anxiety disorders. *International Journal of Psychiatry, 14*, 142–153.

Ginsburg, G. S., Siqueland, L., Masia-Warner, C., & Hedtke, K. A. (2004). Anxiety disorders in children: Family matters. *Cognitive and Behavioral Practice, 11*, 28–43.

Ginsburg, G. S., & Walkup, J. T. (2004). Specific phobia. In T. H. Ollendick & J. S. March (Eds.), *Phobic and anxiety disorders in children and adolescents* (pp. 175–197). New York: Oxford University Press.

Gladstone, T. G., & Kaslow, N. J. (1995). Depression and attributions in children and adolescents: A meta-analytic review. *Journal of Abnormal Child Psychology, 23*, 597–606.

Glasofer, D. R., Tanofsky-Kraff, M., Eddy, K. T., Yanovsky, S. Z., Theim, K. R., Mirch, M. C., et al. (2007). Binge eating in overweight treatment-seeking adolescents. *Journal of Pediatric Psychology, 32*, 95–105.

Glassman, L. H., Weierich, M. R., Hooley, J. M., Deliberto, T. L., & Nock, M. K. (2007). Child maltreatment, non-suicidal self-injury, and the mediating role of self-criticism. *Behavior Research and Therapy, 45*, 2483–2490.

Glazener, C. M. A., & Evans, J. H. C. (2009). Desmopressin for nocturnal enuresis in children. *Cochrane Reviews.*

Glazener, C. M. A., Evans, J. H. C., & Peto, R. E. (2008). Complex behavioral and educational interventions for nocturnal enuresis in children. *Cochrane Reviews.*

Gleason, M. M., Fox, N. A., Drury, S., Smyke, A. T., Egger, H. L., Nelson, C. A., Gregas, M. G., & Zeanah, C. H. (2011). Validity of evidence-derived criteria for reactive attachment disorder: Indiscriminately social/disinhibited and emotionally withdrawn/inhibited types. *Journal of the American Academy of Child and Adolescent Psychiatry, 50*, 216–231.

Glick, B. (2006). ART: A comprehensive intervention for aggressive youth. In B. Glick (Ed.), *Cognitive behavioral interventions for at-risk youth* (pp. 11.1–11.27). Kingston, NJ: Civic Research Institute.

Glick, B., & Gibbs, J.C. (2011). *Aggression replacement training (3rd ed).* Champaign, IL: Research Press.

Glidden, L. M. (2012). Family well-being and children with developmental disability. In J.A. Burack, R.M. Hodapp, G. Iarocci, & E. Zigler (Eds.), *The Oxford handbook of intellectual disability and development* (pp. 303–317). New York: Oxford University Press.

Glowinski, A. L. (2011). Reactive attachment disorder: An evolving entity. *Journal of the American Academy of Child and Adolescent Psychiatry, 50*, 210–212.

Goenjian, A. K., Karayan, I., Pynoos, R. S., Minassian, D., Najarian, L. M., Steinberg, A. M., et al. (1997). Outcome of psychotherapy among early adolescents after trauma. *American Journal of Psychiatry, 154*, 536–542.

Gogtay, N., Giedd, J. N., Lusk, L., Hayashi, K. M., Greenstein, D., Vaituzis, A. C., et al. (2004). Dynamic mapping of human cortical development during childhood through early adulthood. *Proceedings of the National Academy of Sciences, 101*, 8174–8179.

Gold, C., Wigram, T., & Elefant, C. (2010). Music therapy for autistic spectrum disorder. Cochrane Database of Systematic Reviews.

Gold, S. R., Sinclair, B. B., & Balge, K. A. (1999). Risk of sexual revictimization: A theoretical model. *Aggression and Violent Behavior, 4*, 457–470.

Goldberg, D. P., Krueger, R. F., Andrews, G., & Hobbs, M. J. (2009). Emotional disorders: Cluster 4 of the proposal meta-structure for DSM-5 and ICD-11. *Psychological Medicine, 39*, 2043–2059.

Goldberg-Arnold, J. S., & Fristad, M. A. (2003). Psychotherapy for children with bipolar disorder. In B. Geller & M. DelBello (Eds.), *Bipolar disorder in childhood and early adolescence* (pp. 272–294). New York: Guilford Press.

Goldman, S. R. (1989). Strategy instruction in mathematics. *Learning Disability Quarterly, 12*, 43–55.

Goldman, S., Wang, C., Salgado, M., Greene, P., Kim, M., & Rapin, I. (2009). Motor stereotypies in children with autism and other developmental disorders. *Developmental Medicine and Child Neurology, 51*, 30–38.

Goldsmith, S. (2012). *Universal design.* Oxford, Architectural Press.

Goldstein, A. P. (1997). *Skillstreaming the adolescent.* Champaign, IL: Research Press.

Goldstein, A. P. (2002). *The psychology of group aggression.* New York: Wiley.

Goldstein, A. P., & Martens, B. K. (2000). *Lasting change: Methods for enhancing generalization of gain.* Champaign, IL: Research Press.

Goldstein, B. I. (2010). Pediatric bipolar disorder: More than a temper problem. *Pediatrics, 125*, 1283–1285.

Goldstein, D. J., Wilson, M. G., & Thompson, V. L. (1995). Long-term fluoxetine treatment of bulimia nervosa. *British Journal of Psychiatry, 166*, 660–667.

Gomez, S., & Nygren, M. A. (2012). *DSM-5 draft diagnostic criteria for Intellectual Developmental Disorder.* Washington, DC: AAIDD.

Goodman, E., & Capitman, J. (2000). Depressive symptoms and cigarette smoking among teens. *Pediatrics, 706*, 748–755.

Goodman, K. S. (1992). Why whole language is today's agenda in education. *Language Arts, 69*, 354–363.

Goodman, S., & Gotlib, I. (1999). Risk for psychopathology in the children of depressed mothers: A developmental model for understanding mechanisms of transmission. *Psychological Review, 106*, 458–490.

Goodman, Y. M. (1989). Roots of the whole-language movement. *Elementary School Journal, 90*, 113–127.

Goods, K.S., Ishijima, E., Chang, Y., Kasari, C. (2013). Preschool based JASPER intervention in minimally verbal children with autism. *Journal of Autism and Developmental Disorders.*

Goodwin, J. (1988). Posttraumatic stress symptoms in abused children. *Journal of Traumatic Stress, 1*, 475–488.

Goodwin, R. D., Fergusson, D. M., & Horwood, L. J. (2004). Association between anxiety disorders and substance use disorders among young persons: Results of a 21-year longitudinal study. *Journal of Psychiatric Research, 38*, 295–304.

Goodwin, R. D., Lieb, R., Hoefler, M., Pfister, H., Bittner, A., Beesdo, K., et al. (2004). Panic attack as a risk factor for severe psychopathology. *American Journal of Psychiatry, 161*, 2207–2214.

Goodyer, I. M., Herbert, J., & Tamplin, A. (2000). First episode major depression in adolescents: Affective, cognitive and endocrine characteristics of risk status and predictors of onset. *British Journal of Psychiatry, 176*, 142–149.

Goodyer, I. M., Herbert, J., Tamplin, A., & Altham, P. M. (2000). Recent life events, cortisol, dehydroepiandrosterone and the onset of major depression in high-risk adolescents. *British Journal of Psychiatry, 177*, 499–504.

Goodyer, I. M., Park, R. J., & Herbert, J. (2001). Psychosocial and endocrine features of chronic first-episode major depression in 8-16 year olds. *Biological Psychiatry, 50*, 351–357.

Gorin, A. A., Le Grange, D., & Stone, A. A. (2003). Effectiveness of spouse involvement in cognitive behavioral therapy for binge eating disorder. *International Journal of Eating Disorders, 33*, 421–433.

Gorman-Smith, D., Tolan, P. H., & Henry, D. B. (2000). A developmental-ecological model of the relation of family functioning to patterns of delinquency. *Journal of Quantitative Criminology, 16*, 169–198.

Gosselin, P., Langlois, F., Freeston, M. H., Ladouceur, R., Laberge, M., & Lemay, D. (2007). Cognitive variables related to worry among adolescents. *Behavior Research and Therapy, 45,* 225–233.

Gotlib, I. H., & Sommerfeld, B. K. (1999). Cognitive functioning in depressed children and adolescents: A developmental perspective. In C. A. Essau & F. Petermann (Eds.), *Depressive disorders in children and adolescents: Epidemiology, risk factors, and treatment* (pp. 195–236). Lanham, MD: Aronson.

Gottesman, I. I. (1963). Genetic aspects of intelligent behavior. In N. R. Ellis (Ed.), *Handbook of mental deficiency: Psychological theory and research* (pp. 253–296). New York: McGraw-Hill.

Gottlieb, G., & Willoughby, M. T. (2006). Probabilistic epigenesis of psychopathology. In D. Cicchetti & D. J. Cohen (Eds.), *Developmental psychopathology, Vol 1: Theory and method* (pp. 673–700). Hoboken, NJ: Wiley.

Gould, M. S., Marrocco, F. A., & Kleinman, M. (2005). Evaluating iatrogenic risk of youth suicide screening programs. *JAMA: Journal of the American Medical Association, 293,* 1635–1643.

Grabill, K., Storch, E. A., & Geffken, G. R. (2007). Intensive cognitive-behavioral therapy of pediatric obsessive-compulsive disorder. *Behavior Therapist, 30,* 19–21.

Graham, C. A., & Easterbrooks, M. A. (2000). School-aged children's vulnerability to depressive symptomatology: The role of attachment security, maternal depressive symptomatology, and economic risk. *Development and Psychopathology, 12,* 201–213.

Graham, S. (2006). Strategy instruction and the teaching of writing: A meta-analysis. In C. A. MacArthur, S. Graham, & J. Fitzgerald (Eds.), *Handbook of writing research* (pp. 187–207). New York: Guilford Press.

Graham, S., & Harris, K. R. (2000). The role of self-regulation and transcription skills in writing and writing development. *Educational Psychologist, 35,* 3–12.

Graham, S., & Harris, K. R. (2003). Students with learning disabilities and the process of writing: A meta-analysis of SRSD studies. In H. L. Swanson, K. R. Harris, & S. Graham (Eds.), *Handbook of learning disabilities* (pp. 323–344). New York: Guilford Press.

Graham, S., Harris, K. R., & Fink, B. (2000). Is handwriting causally related to learning to write? Treatment of handwriting problems in beginning writers. *Journal of Educational Psychology, 92,* 620–633.

Graham, S., Harris, K. R., & Fink, B. (2002). Contributions of spelling instruction to the spelling, writing, and reading of poor spellers. *Journal of Educational Psychology, 94,* 669–686.

Graham, S., Harris, K. R., & MacArthur, C. (2004). Writing instruction. In B. Y. L. Wong, (Ed.), *Learning about learning disabilities* (pp. 281–313). San Diego: Elsevier Academic Press.

Graham, S., Harris, K. R., MacArthur, C., & Schwartz, S. (1991). Writing and writing instruction with students with learning disabilities: A review of a program of research. *Learning Disability Quarterly, 14,* 89–114.

Graham, S., & Juvonen, J. (2001). An attributional approach to peer victimization. In J. Juvonen & S. Graham (Eds.), *Peer harassment in school* (pp. 49–72). New York: Guilford Press.

Graham-Bermann, S. A. (2002). Child abuse in the context of domestic violence. In J. E. B. Meyers, L. Berliner, J. Briere, C. T. Hendrix, C. Jenny, & T. A. Reid (Eds.), *The APSAC handbook on child maltreatment* (pp. 119–130). Thousand Oaks, CA: Sage.

Grant, B. F., Goldstein, R. B., Chou, S. P., Huang, B., Stinson, F. S., Dawson, D. A., et al. (2009). Sociodemographic and psychopathologic predictors of first incidence of *DSM-IV* substance abuse, mood, and anxiety disorders. *Molecular Psychiatry, 14,* 1051–1066.

Grant, J. E., Odlaug, B. L., Chamberlain, S. R., Keuthen, N. J., Lochner, C., & Stein, D. J. (2012). Skin picking disorder. *American Journal of Psychiatry, 169.*

Gray, J. A. (1982). *The neuropsychology of anxiety: An inquiry into the functions of the septo-hippocampal system.* New York: Oxford University Press.

Gray, J. A. (1987). *The psychology of fear and stress.* Cambridge: Cambridge University Press.

Gray, J. A. (1994). Three fundamental emotion systems. In P. Ekman & R. J. Davidson (Eds.), *The nature of emotion: Fundamental questions* (pp. 243–247). New York: Oxford University Press.

Greenberg, M. T., Lengua, L. J., Coie, J. D., & Pinderhughes, E. E. (1999). Predicting developmental outcomes at school entry using a multiple-risk model: Four American communities. *Developmental Psychology, 35,* 403–417.

Greenhill, L. L. (2005). The science of stimulant abuse. *Psychiatric Annals, 35,* 210–214.

Greenhill, L. L., & Ford, R. E. (2002). Childhood attention-deficit hyperactivity disorder: Pharmacological treatments. In P. E. Nathan, & J. M. Gorman (Eds.), *A guide to treatments that work* (pp. 25–55). New York: Oxford University Press.

Greenhill, L. L., Pliszka, S. R., & Dulcan, M. K. (2002). Practice parameter for the use of stimulant medication in the treatment of children, adolescents and adults. *Journal of the American Academy of Child and Adolescent Psychiatry, 41,* 26S–29S.

Gregory, A. M., Cox, J., Crawford, M. R., Holland, J., Haravey, A. G., & The STEPS Team. (2009). Dysfunctional beliefs and attitudes about sleep in children. *Journal of Sleep Research, 18,* 422–426.

Grella, C. E., Hser, Y. I., Joshi, V., & Rounds-Bryant, J. (2001). Drug treatment outcomes for adolescents with comorbid mental and substance use disorders. *Journal of Nervous and Mental Disease, 189,* 384–392.

Grenard, J. L., Ames, S. L., Wiers, R. W., Thush, C., Stacy, A. W., & Sussman, S. (2007). Brief intervention for substance use among at-risk adolescents: A pilot study. *Journal of Adolescent Health, 40,* 188–191.

Grigorenko, E. L. (2001). Developmental dyslexia: An update on genes, brains, and environments. *Journal of Child Psychology and Psychiatry, 42,* 91–125.

Grilo, C. M., Masheb, R. M., & Wilson, G. T. (2005). Efficacy of cognitive behavioral therapy and fluoxetine for the treatment of binge eating disorder. *Biological Psychiatry, 57,* 301–309.

Groth-Marnat, G. (2003). *Handbook of psychological assessment.* New York: Wiley.

Gruber, R. (2009). Sleep characteristics of children with Attention-Deficit/Hyperactivity Disorder. *Child and Adolescent Psychiatric Clinics of North America, 18,* 863–876.

Gruber, R., Cassoff, J., Frenette, S., Wiebe, S., & Carrier, J. (2012). Impact of sleep extension and restriction on children's emotional lability and impulsivity. *Pediatrics, 130,* 1155–1161.

Gruber, R., Michaelsen, S., Bergmame, L., Frenette, S., Bruni, P., Fontil, L., & Carrier, J. (2012). Short sleep duration is associated with teacher-reported inattention and cognitive problems in healthy school-age children. *Nature and Science of Sleep, 4,* 33–40.

Guarda, A. S., & Heinberg, L. J. (2004). Inpatient and partial hospital approaches to the treatment of eating disorders. In J. K. Thompson (Ed.), *Handbook of eating disorders and obesity* (pp. 297–320). Hoboken, NJ: Wiley.

Gueron-Sela, N., Atzaba-Poria, N., Meiri, G., & Yerushalmi, B. (2011). Maternal worries about child underweight mediate and moderate the relationship between child feeding disorders and mother-child feeding. *Journal of Pediatric Psychology, 36,* 827–836.

Guitar, B. (2006). *Stuttering: An integrated approach to its nature and treatment.* Baltimore, MD: Lippincott.

Gunnar, M. R. (2010). Reversing the effects of early deprivation after infancy. *Frontiers of Neuroscience, 4,* 1–2.

Gunnar, M. R., & Fisher, P. A. (2006). Bringing basic research on early experience and stress neurobiology to bear on preventative interventions for neglected and maltreated children. *Development and Psychopathology, 18,* 651–677.

Gur, R. E., Andreasen, N., Asarnow, R., Gur, R., Jones, P., Kendler, K., et al. (2005). Schizophrenia. In *Treating and preventing adolescent mental health disorders* (pp. 77–156). Oxford: Oxford University Press.

Guttmann-Steinmetz, S., & Crowell, A. (2006). Attachment and externalizing disorders: A developmental psychopathology perspective. *Journal of the American Academy of Child & Adolescent Psychiatry, 45*(4), 440–451.

Guyer, A. E., McClure, E. B., Adler, A. D., Brotman, M. A., Rich, B. A., Kimes, A. S., et al. (2007). Specificity of facial expression labeling deficits in childhood psychopathology. *Journal of Child Psychology and Psychiatry, 48*, 863–871.

Halberda, J., & Feigenson, L. (2008). Developmental change in the acuity of the number sense. *Developmental Psychology, 44*, 1457–1465.

Hale, J., Alfonso, V., Berninger, V., Bracken, B., Christo, C., Clark, E., et al. (2010). Critical issues in response-to-intervention, comprehensive evaluation, and specific learning disabilities identification and intervention: An expert white paper consensus. *Learning Disabilities Quarterly, 33*, 223–235.

Hale, L. R., & Calamari, J. E. (2007). Panic symptoms and disorder in youth: What role does anxiety sensitivity play? In C. M. Velotis (Ed.), *New developments in anxiety disorders research* (pp. 131–162). Hauppauge, NY: Nova Biomedical.

Hale, W. W., Engels, R., & Meeus, W. (2006). Adolescent's perceptions of parenting behaviours and its relationship to adolescent Generalized Anxiety Disorder symptoms. *Journal of Adolescence, 29*, 407–417.

Hallahan, D. P., & Mock, D. R. (2003). A brief history of the field of learning disabilities. In H. L. Swanson, K. R. Harris, & S. Graham (Eds.), *Handbook of learning disabilities* (pp. 16–29). New York: Guilford Press.

Halligan, S. L., Herbert, J., Goodyer, I. M., & Murray, L. (2004). Exposure to postnatal depression predicts elevated cortisol in adolescent offspring. *Biological Psychiatry, 55*, 376–381.

Halmi, K. A., Eckert, E., Marchi, P., Sampagnaro, V., Apple, R., & Cohen, J. (1991). Comorbidity of psychiatric diagnoses in anorexia nervosa. *Archives of General Psychiatry, 48*, 712–718.

Halmi, K. A., Tozzi, F., Thornton, L. M., Crow, S., Fichter, M. M., Kaplan, A. S., et al. (2005). The relation among perfectionism, obsessive compulsive personality disorder and obsessive compulsive disorder in individuals with eating disorders. *International Journal of Eating Disorders, 38*, 371–374.

Hammen, C. (1992). Cognitive, life stress, and interpersonal approaches to a developmental psychopathology model of depression. *Development and Psychopathology, 4*, 189–206.

Hammen, C. (1999). The emergence of an interpersonal approach to depression. In T. Joiner & J. Coyne (Eds.), *The interactional nature of depression: Advances in interpersonal approaches* (pp. 22–36). Washington, DC: American Psychological Association.

Hammen, C. (2002). The context of stress in families of children with depressed parents. In S. Goodman & I. Gotlib (Eds.), *Children of depressed parents: Mechanisms of risk and implications for treatment* (pp. 175–199). Washington, DC: American Psychological Association.

Hammen, C. L. (1991). *Depression runs in families: The social context of risk and resilience in children of depressed mothers.* New York: Springer-Verlag.

Hammen, C., Shih, J. H., & Brennan, P. A. (2004). Intergenerational transmission of depression: Test of an interpersonal stress model in a community sample. *Journal of Consulting and Clinical Psychology, 72*, 511–522.

Hamza, C. A., Stewart, S. L., & Willoughby, T. (2012, August). Examining the link between nonsuicidal self-injury and suicidal behavior. *Clinical Psychology Review, 32*, 482–496.

Han, C., McGue, M. K., & Iacono, W. G. (1999). Lifetime tobacco, alcohol and other substance use in adolescent Minnesota twins: Univariate and multivariate behavioral genetic analyses. *Addiction, 94*, 981–993.

Hancock, T.B., & Kaiser, A.P. (2006). Enhanced milieu teaching. In R.J. McCauley & M.E. Fey (Eds.), *Treatment of language disorders in children* (pp. 203–236). Baltimore, MD: Brookes.

Handen, B.L., & Gilchrist, R. (2006). Practitioner review: Psychopharmacology in children and adolescents with mental retardation. *Journal of Child Psychology and Psychiatry, 47*, 871–882.

Handleman, J. S., Harris, S. L., & Martins, M. P. (2005). Helping children with autism enter the mainstream. In F. R. Volkmar, R. Paul, A. Klin, & D. Cohen (Eds.), *Handbook of autism and pervasive developmental disorders, Vol. 2: Assessment, interventions, and policy* (pp. 1029–1042). New York: Wiley.

Handler, S. M., Fierson, W. M., and the American Academy of Ophthalmology. (2011). Learning disabilities, dyslexia, and vision. *Pediatrics, 127*, 818–856.

Hankin, B. L., & Abela, J. R. Z. (2005). *Development of psychopathology: A vulnerability-stress perspective.* Thousand Oaks, CA: Sage.

Hankin, B. L., & Abela, J. R. Z. (2011). Nonsuicidal self-injury in adolescence: Prospective rates and risk factors in a 2 ½ year longitudinal study. *Psychiatry Research, 186*, 65–70.

Hankin, B. L., Abramson, L. Y., Moffitt, T. E., Silva, P. A., McGee, R., & Angell, K. E. (1998). Development of depression from preadolescence to young adulthood: Emerging gender differences in a 10-year longitudinal study. *Journal of Abnormal Psychology, 107*, 128–140.

Hanley, G. P., Iwata, B. A., & McCord, B. E. (2003). Functional analysis of problem behavior: A review. *Journal of Applied Behavior Analysis, 36*, 147–185.

Hanna, G. L. (2000). Clinical and family-genetic studies of childhood obsessive-compulsive disorder. In W. K. Goodman, M. V. Rudorfer, & J. D. Maser (Eds.), *Obsessive-compulsive disorder.* New York: Erlbaum.

Hanna, S. E., Rosenbaum, P. L., Bartlett, D. J., Palisano, R. J., Walter, S. D., Avery, L., et al. (2009). Stability and decline in gross motor function among children and youth with cerebral palsy aged 2 to 21 years. *Developmental Medicine and Child Neurology, 51*, 295–302.

Hanson, R. K., Saunders, B. E., Kilpatrick, D. G., Resnick, H., Crouch, J. A., & Duncan, R. (2001). Impact of childhood rape and aggravated assault on adult mental health. *American Journal of Orthopsychiatry, 71*, 108–119.

Harford, T. C., Grant, B. F., Yi, H., Chen, C. M. (2005). Patterns of *DSM-IV* alcohol abuse and dependence criteria among adolescents and adults. *Alcoholism, 20*, 810–828.

Harford, T. C., Yi, H., Faden, V. B., & Chen, C. M. (2009). The dimensionality of *DSM-IV* alcohol use disorders among adolescent and adult drinkers and symptom patterns by age, gender, and race/ethnicity. *Alcoholism, 33*, 868–877.

Harkness, K. L., Bruce, A. E., & Lumley, M. N. (2006). The role of childhood abuse and neglect in the sensitization to stressful life events in adolescent depression. *Journal of Abnormal Psychology, 115*, 730–741.

Harrington, K. M., & Waldman, I. D. (2010). Evaluating the utility of sluggish cognitive tempo in discriminating among *DSM-IV* ADHD subtypes. *Journal of Abnormal Child Psychology, 38*, 173–184.

Harrington, R., Fudge, H., Rutter, M., Pickles, A., & Hill, J. (1990). Adult outcomes of childhood and adolescent depression: I. Psychiatric status. *Archives of General Psychiatry, 47*, 465–473.

Harris, S., Handleman, J., Gordon, R., Kristoff, B., & Fuentes, F. (1991). Changes in cognitive and language functioning of preschool children with autism. *Journal of Autism and Developmental Disabilities, 21*, 281–290.

Hart, E. L., Lahey, B. B., Loeber, R., Applegate, B., Green, S. M., & Frick, P. J. (1995). Developmental changes in attention-deficit hyperactivity disorder in boys: A four-year longitudinal study. *Journal of Abnormal Child Psychology, 23*, 729–750.

Hart, K. J., Nelson, W. M., & Finch, A. J. (2006). Comparative treatments of conduct disorder: Summary and conclusions. In W. M. Nelson, A. J. Finch, & K. J. Hart (Eds.), *Conduct disorders: A practitioner's guide to comparative treatments* (pp. 321–343). New York: Springer.

Hart, S. N., Brassard, M. R., Binggeli, N. J., & Davidson, H. A. (2002). Psychological maltreatment. In J. E. B. Meyers, L. Berliner, J. Briere, C. T. Hendrix, C. Jenny, & T. A. Reid (Eds.), *The APSAC handbook on child maltreatment* (pp. 79–104). Thousand Oaks, CA: Sage.

Harter, S. (1997). The development of self-representations. In W. Damon (Series Ed.) & N. Eisenberg (Vol. Ed.), *Handbook of child psychology* (5th ed., Vol. III). New York: Wiley.

Harter, S. (1999). *The construction of self: A developmental perspective.* New York: Guilford Press.

Hartley, S. L., & Sikora, D. M. (2009). Sex differences in autism spectrum disorder. *Journal of Autism and Developmental Disorders, 39*, 1715–1722.

Hartmen, C. A., Gelhorn, H., Crowley, T. J., Sakai, J. T., Stallings, M., Young, S. E., et al. (2008). Item response theory of *DSM-IV* cannabis abuse and dependence criteria in adolescents. *Journal of the American Academy of Child and Adolescent Psychiatry, 47,* 165–173.

Harwood, M. D., & Eyberg, M. (2006). Child-directed interaction: Prediction of change in impaired mother-child functioning. *Journal of Abnormal Child Psychology, 34,* 335–347.

Haselager, G. J. T., Cillessen, A. H. N., Van Lieshout, C. F. M., Riksen-Walraven, J. M. A., & Hartup, W. W. (2002). Heterogeneity among peer-rejected boys across middle childhood: Developmental pathways of social behavior. *Developmental Psychology, 38,* 446–456.

Hasin, D., & Paykin, A. (1999). Dependence symptoms but no diagnosis. *Drug and Alcohol Dependence, 53,* 215–222.

Hassan, A., Agha, S. S., Langley, K., & Thapar, A. (2011). Prevalence of bipolar disorder in children and adolescents with attention-deficit hyperactivity disorder. *British Journal of Psychiatry, 198,* 195–198.

Hawes, D. J., & Dadds, M. R. (2005). The treatment of conduct problems in children with callous-unemotional traits. *Journal of Consulting and Clinical Psychology, 73,* 737–741.

Hawke, J. L., Wadsworth, S. J., & Defries, J. C. (2006). Genetic influences on reading difficulties in boys and girls: The Colorado twin study. *Dyslexia: An International Journal of Research and Practice, 12,* 21–29.

Hawton, K., Rodham, K., Evans, E., & Weatherall, R. (2002). Deliberate self-harm in adolescents: Self-report survey in schools in England. *British Medical Journal, 325,* 1207.

Hayes, J., & Flower, L. (1980). Identifying the organization of writing processes. In L. Gregg & E. Steinberg (Eds.), *Cognitive processes in writing* (pp. 3–30). Hillsdale, NJ: Erlbaum.

Hayward, C., Killen, J. D., Kraemer, H. C., & Barr Taylor, C. (2000). Predictors of panic attacks in adolescents. *Journal of the American Academy of Child and Adolescent Psychiatry, 39,* 207–214.

Hazell, P., O'Connell, D., Heathcote, D., & Henry, D. (2002). Tricyclic drugs for depression in children and adolescents. *Cochrane Systematic Reviews, 2,* 2317.

Headley, L. M., Hoffart, A. (2001). Agoraphobia without history of Panic Disorder. *Clinical Psychology and Psychotherapy, 8,* 436–443.

Heal, D. J., Smith, S. L., & Findling, R. L. (2011). ADHD: Current and future therapies. In C. Stanford & R. Tannock (Eds.), *Behavioral neuroscience of attention deficit hyperactivity disorder and its treatment* (pp. 361–390). New York: Springer.

Heath, A. C., Lynskey, M. T., & Waldron, M. (2010). Substance use and substance use disorder. In M. Rutter (Ed.), *Rutter's child and adolescent psychiatry* (pp. 565–586). Malden, NJ: Blackwell.

Hebb, D. O. (1949). *The organization of behavior.* New York: Wiley.

Hechtman, L., Abikoff, H., & Jensen, P. S. (2005). Multimodal therapy and stimulants in the treatment of children with attention-deficit/ hyperactivity disorder. In E. D. Hibbs & P. S. Jensen (Eds.), *Psychosocial treatments for child and adolescent disorders: Empirically based strategies for clinical practice* (pp. 411–437). Washington, DC: American Psychological Association.

Hechtman, L., Abikoff, H., Klein, G., Greenfield, B., Etcovitch, J., Cousins, L., et al. (2004a). Children with ADHD treated with long-term methylphenidate and multimodal psychosocial treatment: Impact on parental practices. *Journal of the American Academy of Child and Adolescent Psychiatry, 43,* 830–838.

Hechtman, L., Abikoff, H., Klein, R. G., Weiss, G., Respitz, C., Kouri, J., et al. (2004b). Academic achievement and emotional status of children with ADHD treated with long-term methylphenidate and multimodal psychosocial treatment. *Journal of the American Academy of Child and Adolescent Psychiatry, 43,* 812–819.

Hedge, M. N. (2008). *Hedge's pocket guide to communication disorders in children.* Clifton Park, NY: Delmar.

Heflin, A. H., & Deblinger, E. (2003). Treatment of a sexually abused adolescent with posttraumatic stress disorder. In M. A. Reinecke, F. M. Dattilio, & A. Freeman (Eds.), *Cognitive therapy with children and adolescents: A casebook for clinical practice* (pp. 214–246). New York: Guilford Press.

Hegde, M. N., & Maul, C. A. (2006). *Language disorders in children.* Boston: Pearson.

Heikkila, R., Narhi, V., Aro, M., & Ahonen, T. (2009). Rapid automatized naming and learning disabilities. *Child Neuropsychology, 15,* 343–358.

Heiler, S., Legenbauer, T., Bogen, T., Jensch, T., & Holtmann, M. (2011). Severe mood dysregulation: In the "light" of circadian functioning. *Medical Hypotheses, 77,* 692–695.

Heiman, J. R., & Heard-Davison, A. R. (2004). Child sexual abuse and adult sexual relationships: Review and perspective. In L. J. Koenig, L. S. Doll, A. O'Leary, & W. Pequegnat (Eds.), *From child sexual abuse to adult sexual risk: Trauma, revictimization, and intervention* (pp. 13–47). New York: American Psychological Association.

Helenius, D., Munk-Jorgensen, P., & Steinhausen, H. (2012). Family load estimates of schizophrenia and associated risk factors in a nationwide population study of former child and adolescent patients up to forty years of age. *Schizophrenia Research, 139,* 193–188.

Hellander, M., Sisson, D. P., & Fristad, M. A. (2003). Internet support for parents of children with early-onset bipolar disorder. In B. Geller & M. P. DelBello (Eds.), *Bipolar disorder in childhood and early adolescence* (pp. 314–329). New York: Guilford Press.

Helzer, J. E. (2011). A proposal for incorporating clinically relevant dimensions into *DSM-5.* In D. A. Reiger (Ed.), *The conceptual evolution of DSM-5* (pp. 81–96). Washington, DC: American Psychiatric Publishing.

Henggeler, S. W., & Lee, T. (2003). Multisystemic treatment of serious clinical problems. In A. E. Kazdin & J. R. Weisz (Eds.), *Evidence-based psychotherapies for children and adolescents* (pp. 301–322). New York: Guildford Press.

Henggeler, S. W., Pickrel, S. G., Brondino, M. J., & Crouch, J. L. (1996). Eliminating (almost) treatment dropout of substance abusing or dependent delinquents through home-based multisystemic therapy. *American Journal of Psychiatry, 153,* 427–428.

Henry, B., Feehan, M., McGee, R., Stanton, W., Moffitt, T. W., & Silva, P. (1993). The importance of conduct problems and depressive symptoms in predicting adolescent substance use. *Journal of Abnormal Child Psychology, 21,* 469–480.

Herschell, A. D., & McNeil, C. B. (2005). Parent-child interaction therapy for children experiencing externalizing behavior problems. In L. A. Reddy, T. M. Files-Hall & C. E. Schaefer (Eds.), *Empirically based play interventions for children* (pp. 169–190). Washington, DC: American Psychological Association.

Hettema, J. M., Neale, M. C., & Kendler, K. S. (2001). A review and meta-analysis of the genetic epidemiology of anxiety disorders. *American Journal of Psychiatry, 158,* 1568–1578.

Heyman, R. E., Slep, A. M. S., Beach, S. R., Wamboldt, M. Z., Kaslow, N. J., & Reiss, D. (2009). Relationship problems and the DSM: needed improvements and suggested solutions. *World Psychiatry, 8,* 7–14.

Hill, D. E., Yeo, R. A., Campbell, R. A., Hart, B., Vigil, J., & Brooks, W. (2003). Magnetic resonance imaging correlates of attention-deficit/ hyperactivity disorder in children. *Neuropsychology, 17,* 498–506.

Hill, J. L. Brooks-Gunn, J., & Waldfogel, J. (2003). Sustained effects of high participation in an early intervention for low-birth-weight premature infants. *Developmental Psychology, 39,* 730–744.

Hinshaw, S. P. (2005). Stigma of mental disorders in children and parents: Developmental issues, family concerns, and research needs. *Journal of Child Psychology and Psychiatry, 36,* 714–734.

Hinshaw, S. P. (2006). Stigma and mental illness: Developmental issues and future prospects. In D. Cicchetti & D. J. Cohen (Eds.), *Developmental psychopathology, Vol. 3: Risk, disorder, and adaptation* (pp. 841–881). New York: Wiley.

Hinshaw, S. P., Klein, R. G., & Abikoff, H. B. (2002). Childhood attention-deficit hyperactivity disorder: Nonpharmacological treatments and their combination with medication. In P. E. Nathan & J. M. Gorman (Eds.), *A guide to treatments that work* (pp. 3–23). New York: Oxford University Press.

Hippler, K., & Klicpera, C. (2003). A retrospective analysis of the clinical case records of "autistic psychopaths" diagnosed by Hans Asperger and his team at the University Children's Hospital, Vienna. In U. Frith & E. Hill (Eds.), *Autism: Mind and brain* (pp. 21–42). New York: Oxford University Press.

Hiroto, D. S., & Seligman, E. (1975). Generality of learned helplessness in man. *Journal of Personality and Social Psychology, 31,* 311–327.

Hirshfeld, D. R., Biederman, J., Brody, L., Faraone, S. V., & Rosenbaum, J. F. (1997). Expressed emotion toward children with and without behavioral inhibition: Associations with maternal anxiety disorders. *Journal of the American Academy of Child and Adolescent Psychiatry, 36,* 910–917.

Hirshfeld-Becker, D. R., Biederman, J., & Rosenbaum, J. F. (2004). Behavioral inhibition. In T. L. Morris & J. S. March (Eds.), *Anxiety disorders in children and adolescents* (pp. 27–58). New York: Guilford Press.

Hock, E., Hart, M., Kang, M. J., & Lutz, W. J. (2004). Predicting children's reactions to terrorist attacks: The importance of self-reports and preexisting characteristics. *American Journal of Orthopsychiatry, 74,* 253–262.

Hocutt, A. M. (1996). Effectiveness of special education: Is placement the critical factor? In D. Terman (Ed.), *The future of children: Special education* (pp. 77–102). Los Altos, CA: David and Lucille Packard Foundation.

Hodapp, R. M., & DesJardin, J. L. (2002). Genetic etiologies of mental retardation: Issues for interventions and interventionists. *Journal of Developmental and Physical Disabilities, 14,* 323–338.

Hodapp, R. M., & Dykens, E. M. (2006). Mental retardation. In K. A. Renninger, I. E. Sigel, W. Damon, & R. M. Lerner (Eds.), *Handbook of child psychology: Vol. 4, Child psychology in practice* (6th ed., pp. 453–496). Hoboken, NJ: Wiley.

Hodapp, R. M., Zakemi, E., Rosner, B. A., & Dykens, E. M. (2006). Mental retardation. In D. A. Wolfe & E. J. Marsh (Eds.), *Behavioral and emotional disorders in adolescents* (pp. 383–409). New York: Guilford Press.

Hodges, J., & Tizard, B. (1989). Social and family relationships of ex-institutional adolescents. *Journal of Child Psychology and Psychiatry, 30,* 77–97.

Hofer, M. A. (2006). Psychobiological roots of early attachment. *Current Directions in Psychological Science, 15,* 84–88.

Hogarty, G. E., Kornblith, S. J., Greenwald, D., DiBarry, A. L., Cooley, S., Ulrich, R. F., et al. (1997). Three-year trials of personal therapy among schizophrenic patients living with or independent of family. *American Journal of Psychiatry, 154,* 1504–1513.

Hogue, A., Dauber, S., Samuolis, J., & Liddle, H. A. (2006). Treatment techniques and outcomes in multidimensional family therapy for adolescent behavior problems. *Journal of Family Psychology, 20,* 535–543.

Hogue, A., Liddle, H. A., Dauber, S., & Samuolis, J. (2004). Linking session focus to treatment outcome in evidence-based treatments for adolescent substance abuse. *Psychotherapy: Theory, Research, Practice, Training, 41,* 83–96.

Holburn, S. (2005). Severe aggressive and self-destructive behavior: Mentalistic attribution. In J. W. Jacobson, R. M. Foxx, & J. A. Mulick (Eds.), *Controversial therapies for developmental disabilities: Fad, fashion and science in professional practice* (pp. 279–293). Mahwah, NJ: Erlbaum.

Holden, B., & Gitlesen, P. (2006). A total population study of challenging behaviour in the county of Hedmark, Norway: Prevalence and risk markers. *Research in Developmental Disabilities, 27,* 456–465.

Hollin, C. R. (2004). ART: The cognitive-behavioral context. In A.P. Goldstein, R. Nensen, B. Daleflod, & M. Kalt (Eds.), *New perspectives on Aggression Replacement Training* (pp. 3–19). New York: Wiley.

Hollin, C. R., & Bloxsom, C. A. J. (2007). Treatments for angry aggression. In T. A. Gannon, T. Ward, A. R. Beech, & D. Fisher (Eds.), *Aggressive offenders' cognition* (pp. 215–229). New York: Wiley.

Hollis, C. (2010). Schizophrenia and allied disorders. In M. Rutter (Ed.), *Rutter's child and adolescent psychiatry* (pp. 737–758). Malden, MA: Blackwell.

Holmbeck, G. H., Zebracki, K., & McGoron, K. (2009). Research design and statistical applications. In M.C Roberts & R.G. Steele (Eds.), *Handbook of pediatric psychology* (pp. 52–70). New York: Guilford.

Hood, K. K., & Eyberg, S. M. (2003). Outcomes of parent-child interaction therapy: Mothers' reports of maintenance three to six years after treatment. *Journal of Clinical Child and Adolescent Psychology, 32,* 419–429.

Hoodin, R. B. (2011). *Intervention in child language disorders.* Boston, MA: Jones & Bartlett.

Hooley, J. M., & Gotlib, I. H. (2000). A diathesis-stress conceptualization of expressed emotion and clinical outcome. *Applied and Preventive Psychology, 9,* 135–151.

Hooley, J. M., & Campbell, C. (2002). Control and controllability: Beliefs and behavior in high and low expressed emotion relatives. *Psychological Medicine, 32,* 1091–1099.

Hooper, S. R., Giuliano, A. J., Youngstrom, E. A., Breiger, D., Sikich, L., Frazier, J. A., et al. (2010). Neurocognition in early-onset schizophrenia and schizoaffective disorders. *Journal of the American Academy of Child and Adolescent Psychiatry, 49,* 52–60.

Hornstein, N. L. (1996). Complexities of psychiatric differential diagnosis in children with dissociative symptoms and disorders. In J. Silberg (Ed.), *The dissociative child* (pp. 27–46). Lutherville, MD: Sidran Press.

Horwitz, S. M., Kelleher, K., Boyce, T., Jensen, P., Murphy, M., Perrin, E., et al. (2002). Barriers to health care research for children and youth with psychosocial problems. *Journal of the American Medical Association, 288,* 1508–1512.

Hoskyn, M., & Swanson, L. (2000). Cognitive processing of low achievers and children with reading disabilities: A selective meta-analytic review of the published literature. *School Psychology Review, 29,* 102–119.

Houts, A. C. (2010). Behavioral treatment for enuresis. In J. R. Weisz & A. E. Kazdin (Eds.), *Evidence-based psychotherapies for children and adolescents* (pp. 359–374). New York: Guilford.

Hoven, C. W., Mandell, D. J., & Duarte, C. S. (2003). Mental health of New York City public school children after 9/11: An epidemiologic investigation. In S. W. Coates, J. L. Rosenthal, & D. S. Schechter (Eds.), *September 11: Trauma and human bonds* (pp. 51–74). Hillsdale, NJ: Analytic Press.

Howard, K. I., Kopta, S. M., Krause, M. S., & Orlinsky, D. E. (1986). The dose-effect relationship in psychotherapy. *American Psychologist, 41,* 159–164.

Howes, P. W., Cicchetti, D., Toth, S. L., & Rogosch, F. A. (2000). Affective, organizational, and relational characteristics of maltreating families: A systems perspective. *Journal of Family Psychology, 14,* 95–110.

Howlin, P. (2006). Augmentative and alternative communication systems for children with autism. In T. Charman & W. Stone (Eds.), *Social and communication development in autism spectrum disorders* (pp. 236–266). New York: Guilford Press.

Hoyson, M., Jamieson, B., & Strain, P. S. (1984). Individualized group instruction of normally developing and autistic-like children: A description and evaluation of the LEAP curriculum model. *Journal of the Division of Early Childhood, 8,* 157–181.

Hoza, B., Mrug, S., Gerdes, A. C., Hinshaw, S. P., Bukowski, W. M., Gold, J. A., et al. (2005). What aspects of peer relationships are impaired in children with attention-deficit/hyperactivity disorder? *Journal of Consulting and Clinical Psychology, 73,* 411–423.

Hoza, B., Mrug, S., Pelham, W. E., Greiner, A. R., & Gnagy, E. M. (2003). A friendship intervention for children with attention-deficit/hyperactivity disorder: Preliminary findings. *Journal of Attention Disorders, 6,* 87–98.

Hser, Y. I., Grella, C. E., & Hubbard, R. L. (2001). An evaluation of drug treatments for adolescents in four US cities. *Archives of General Psychiatry, 58,* 689–695.

Hsieh, S., & Hollister, D. (2004). Examining gender differences in adolescent substance abuse behavior: Comparisons and implications for treatment. *Journal of Child & Adolescent Substance Abuse, 13,* 53–70.

Hudson, J. L., & Rapee, R. M. (2002). Parent-child interactions in clinically anxious children and their siblings. *Journal of Clinical Child and Adolescent Psychology, 31,* 548–555.

Hudson, J., & Rapee, R. (2004). From anxious temperament to disorder: An etiological model of generalized anxiety disorder. In R. G. Heimberg, C. L. Turk, & D. S. Mennin (Eds.), *Generalized anxiety disorder: Advances in research and practice* (pp. 51–76). New York: Guilford Press.

Hudziak, J. J., Heath, A. C., Madden, P. F., Reich, W., Bucholz, K. K., Slutske, W., et al. (1998). Latent class and factor analysis of *DSM-IV* ADHD: A twin study of female adolescents. *Journal of the American Academy of Child and Adolescent Psychiatry, 36,* 848–857.

Hudziak, J., van Beijstervveldt, C. E., & Althoff, R. R. (2004). Genetic and environmental contributions to the Child Behavior Checklist Obsessive-Compulsive Scale. *Archives of General Psychiatry, 61,* 608–616.

Huerta, M., Bishop, S. L., Duncan, A., Hus, V., & Lord, C. (2012). Application of *DSM-5* criteria for autism spectrum disorder to three samples of children with *DSM-IV* diagnoses of pervasive developmental disorders. *American Journal of Psychiatry, 169,* 1056–1064.

Huey, S. J., Henggeler, S. W., Brondino, M. J., & Pickrel, S. G. (2000). Mechanisms of change in multisystemic therapy: Reducing delinquent behavior through therapist adherence and improved family and peer functioning. *Journal of Consulting and Clinical Psychology, 68,* 451–467.

Humeniuk, R., Henry-Edwards, S., Ali, R., Poznyak, V., & Monteiro, M. G. (2010). *The Alcohol, Smoking and Substance involvement Screening Test (ASSIST).* Geneva, Switzerland: World Health Organization.

Hurwitz, S., & Minshawi, N. F. (2012). Methods of defining and observing behaviors. In J. L. Matson (Ed.), *Functional assessment for challenging behavior* (pp. 91–103). New York: Springer.

Huttenlocher, P. R., & Dabholkar, A. S. (1997). Regional differences in synaptogenesis in the human cerebral cortex. *Journal of Comparative Neurology, 387,* 167–178.

Hyman, S.E. (2011). Repairing a plane while it is flying—reflections on Rutter (2011). *Journal of Child Psychology and Psychiatry, 52,* 661–662.

Iacono, W. G., Carlson, S. R., Taylor, J., Elkins, I. J., & McGue, M. (1999). Behavioral disinhibition and the development of substance-use disorders: Findings from the Minnesota Twin Family Study. *Development and Psychopathology, 11,* 869–900.

Iarocci, G., & Petrill, S.A. (2012). Behavioral genetics, genomics, intelligence, and mental retardation. In J.A. Burack, R.M. Hodapp, G. Iarocci, & E. Zigler (Eds.), *The Oxford handbook of intellectual disability and development* (pp. 13–29). New York: Oxford University Press.

Ingersoll, B. (2010a). Pilot randomized controlled trial of reciprocal imitation training or teaching elicited and spontaneous imitation to children with autism. *Journal of Autism and Developmental Disorders, 40,* 1154–1160.

Ingersoll, B. (2010b). Teaching social communication: A comparison of naturalistic behavioral and developmental social pragmatic approaches for children with autism spectrum disorders. *Journal of Positive Behavioral Interventions, 12,* 33–43.

Ingersoll, B. (2011). Recent advances in early identification and treatment of autism. *Current Directions in Psychological Science, 20,* 335–339.

Ingersoll, B. (2012). Effect of a focused imitation intervention on social functioning in children with autism. *Journal of Autism and Developmental Disorders, 42,* 1768–1773.

Ingersoll, B., & Dvortcsak, A. (2010). *Teaching social communication to children with autism.* New York: Guilford.

Ingoldsby, E. M., & Shaw, D. S. (2002). Neighborhood contextual factors and early-starting antisocial pathways. *Clinical Child & Family Psychology Review, 5,* 21–55.

Iwata, B. A., Dorsey, M. F., Slifer, K. J., Bauman, K. E., & Richman, G. S. (1994). Toward a functional analysis of self-injury. *Journal of Applied Behavior Analysis, 27,* 197–209.

Jackson, D. M., & Westlind-Danielsson, A. (1994). Dopamine receptors: Molecular biology, biochemistry and behavioural aspects. *Pharmacological Therapy, 64,* 291–370.

Jacobson, C. M., Muehlenkamp, J. J., Miller, A. L., & Turner, J. B. (2008). Psychiatric impairment among adolescents engaging in different types of deliberate self-harm. *Journal of Clinical Child and Adolescent Psychology, 37,* 363–375.

Jacobson, J. W., & Mulick, J. A. (1996). *Manual of diagnosis and professional practice in mental retardation.* Washington, DC: American Psychological Association.

Jairam, R., Prabhuswamy, M., & Dullur, P. (2012). Do we really know how to treat a child with Bipolar Disorder or one with Severe Mood Dysregulation? *Depression Research and Treatment, 2012,* 1–9.

Jenkins, E. J., & Bell, C. C. (1994). Violence among inner city high school students and post-traumatic stress disorder. In S. Friedman (Ed.), *Anxiety disorders in African Americans* (pp. 76–88). New York: Springer.

Jenkins, R. (1998). Mental health and primary care—implications for policy. *International Review of Psychiatry, 10,* 158–160.

Jensen, P. S. (2005). NIMH's TADS: More than just a tad of progress? *Cognitive and Behavioral Practice, 12,* 156–158.

Jensen, P. S., Hoagwood, K., & Zitner, L. (2006). What's in a name? Problems versus prospects in current diagnostic approaches. In D. Cicchetti & D. J. Cohen (Eds.), *Developmental psychopathology, Vol 1: Theory and method* (pp. 24–40). New York: Wiley.

Johnson, C. F. (2002). Physical abuse: Accidental versus intentional trauma in children. In J. E. B. Meyers, L. Berliner, J. Briere, C. T. Hendrix, C. Jenny, & T. A. Reid (Eds.), *The APSAC handbook on child maltreatment* (pp. 249–268). Thousand Oaks, CA: Sage.

Johnson, C. P., Myers, S. M., & American Academy of Pediatrics. (2007). Identification and evaluation of children with autism spectrum disorders. *Pediatrics, 120,* 1183–1215.

Johnson, D. E., & Gunnar, M. R. (2011). Growth failure in institutionalized children. *Monographs for the Society for Research in Child Development, 76,* 92–126.

Johnson, E. S., Humphrey, M., Mellard, D. F., Woods, K., & Swanson, H. L. (2010). Cognitive processing deficits and students with specific learning disabilities: A selective meta-analysis of the literature. *Learning Disability Quarterly, 33,* 3–18.

Johnson, J. G., Cohen, P., Kasen, S., Smailes, E., & Brook, J. S. (2001). Association of maladaptive parental behavior with psychiatric disorder among parents and their offspring. *Archives of General Psychiatry, 58,* 453–460.

Johnson, J. G., Cohen, P., Kotler, L., Kasen, S., & Brook, J. S. (2002). Psychiatric disorders associated with risk for the development of eating disorders during adolescence and early adulthood. *Journal of Consulting and Clinical Psychology, 70,* 1119–1128.

Johnson, K. P., Giannotti, F., & Cortesi, F. (2009). Sleep patterns in autism spectrum disorders. *Child and Adolescent Psychiatric Clinics of North America, 18,* 917–928.

Johnson K. P., & Ivanenko, A. (2010). Medications used for sleep. In M. K. Dulcan (Ed.), *Dulcan's textbook of child and adolescent psychiatry* (pp. 787–794). Washington, DC: American Psychiatric Publishing.

Johnson, M. H., & de Haan, M. (2006). Typical and atypical human functional brain development. In D. Cicchetti & D. J. Cohen (Eds.), *Developmental psychopathology, Vol 2: Developmental neuroscience* (pp. 197–215). Hoboken, NJ: Wiley.

Johnson, S. L., Sandrow, D., Meyer, B., Winters, R., Miller, I., Solomon, D., et al. (2000). Increases in manic symptoms after life events involving goal attainment. *Journal of Abnormal Psychology, 109,* 721–727.

Johnson, T. C., & Friend, C. (1995). Assessing young children's sexual behaviors in the context of child sexual abuse evaluations. In T. Ney (Ed.), *True and false allegation of child sexual abuse: Assessment and case management* (pp. 49–72). New York: Brunner Mazel.

Johnson, W. G., Rohan, K. J., & Kirk, A. A. (2002). Prevalence and correlates of binge eating in white and African American adolescents. *Eating Behaviors, 3,* 179–189.

Johnston, C. (2005). The importance of parental attributions in families of children with attention-deficit/hyperactivity and disruptive behavior disorders. *Clinical Child and Family Psychology Review, 8,* 167–182.

Johnston, C., & Freeman, W. (1997). Attributions for child behavior in parents of children without behavior disorders and children with attention deficit-hyperactivity disorder. *Journal of Consulting and Clinical Psychology, 65,* 636–645.

Johnston, L. D., O'Malley, P. M., Bachman, J. G., & Schulenberg, J. E. (2005). *Monitoring the future national survey results on drug use, 1975–2004. Volume I: Secondary school students* (NIH Publication No. 05-5727). Bethesda, MD: National Institute on Drug Abuse.

Johnston, L. D., O'Malley, P. M., Bachman, J. G., & Schulenberg, J. E. (2006). *Monitoring the future national results on adolescent drug use: Overview of key findings, 2005.* (NIH Publication No. 06–5882). Bethesda, MD: National Institute on Drug Abuse.

Joiner, T. (2009). *Why people die by suicide.* Boston, MA: Harvard University Press.

Joiner, T. E., Jr., Brown, J. S., & Wingate, L. R. (2005). The psychology and neurobiology of suicidal behavior. *Annual Review of Psychology., 56,* 287–314.

Joiner, T. E., Metalsky, G. I., Katz, J., & Beach, S. R. H. (1999). Depression and excessive reassurance-seeking. *Psychological Inquiry, 10,* 269–278.

Joiner, T. E., & Wagner, K. D. (1995). Attribution style and depression in children and adolescents: A meta-analytic review. *Clinical Psychology Review, 15,* 777–798.

Jonas, R., Nguyen, S., Hu, B., Asarnow, R. F., LoPresti, C., Curtiss, S., et al. (2004). Cerebral hemispherectomy: Hospital course, seizure, developmental, language, and motor outcomes. *Neurology, 62,* 1712–1721.

Jones, M. C. (1924). A laboratory study of fear: The case of Peter. *Pedagogical Seminary, 31,* 308–315.

Jones, M., Onslow, M., Harrison, E., & Packman, A. (2000). Treating stuttering in young children. *Journal of Speech, Language, and Hearing Research, 43,* 1440–1450.

Jones, W., Carr, K., & Klin, A. (2008). Absence of preferential looking to the eyes of approaching adults predicts level of social disability in 2-year-old toddlers with autism spectrum disorder. *Archives of General Psychiatry, 65,* 946–954.

Jordan, N. C., Hanich, L. B., & Kaplan, D. (2003). A longitudinal study of mathematical competencies in children with specific mathematics difficulties versus children with co-morbid mathematics and reading difficulties. *Child Development, 74,* 834–850.

Joshi, S. V. (2004). Psychostimulants, atomoxetine, and alpha-agonists. In H. Steiner (Ed.), *Handbook of mental health interventions in children and adolescents* (pp. 258–287). San Francisco: Jossey-Bass.

Juffer, F., Palacios, J., LeMare, L., Sonuga-Barke, E., Tieman, W., Bakermans-Kraneburg, M. J., et al. (2011). Development of adopted children with histories of adversity. *Monographs for the Society for Research in Child Development, 76,* 31–61.

Kaderavek, J. N. (2011). *Language disorders in children: Fundamental concepts of assessment and intervention.* Boston: Pearson.

Kagan, J., Reznick, J. S., & Snidman, N. (1988). Biological bases of childhood shyness. *Science, 240,* 167–171.

Kahn, J. S., Kehle, T. J., Jenson, W. R., & Clarke, E. (1990). Comparison of cognitive-behavioral, relaxation, and self-modeling interventions for depression among middle-school students. *School Psychology Review, 19,* 196–208.

Kahn, R. E., Frick, P. J., Youngstrom, E., Findling, R. L., & Youngstrom, J. K. (2012). The effects of including a callous-unemotional specifier for the diagnosis of conduct disorder. *Journal of Child Psychology and Psychiatry, 53,* 271–282.

Kahng, S., Iwata, B. A., & Lewin, A. B. (2002). Behavioral treatment of self-injury, 1964 to 2000. *American Journal on Mental Retardation, 107,* 212–221.

Kamhi, A. G., Masterson, J. J., Apel, K. (2007). *Clinical decision making in developmental language disorders.* Baltimore, MD: Brookes.

Kaminer, Y., Blitz, C., Burleson, J. A., Sussman, J., & Rounsaville, B. J. (1998). Psychotherapies for adolescent substance abusers: treatment outcome. *Journal of Nervous and Mental Disease, 186,* 684–690.

Kaminer, Y., & Bukstein, O. G. (2005). Treating adolescent substance abuse. In R. J. Frances, S. I. Miller, & A. H. Mack (Eds.), *Clinical textbook of addictive disorders* (pp. 559–587). New York: Guilford Press.

Kaminer, Y., Burleson, J. A., & Goldberger, R. (2002). Cognitive-behavioral coping skills and psychoeducation therapies for adolescent substance abuse. *Journal of Nervous and Mental Disease, 190,* 737–745.

Kaminski, R. A., & Cummings, K. D. (2008). *Linking assessment to instruction: Using Dynamic Indicators of Basic Early Literacy Skills in an outcomes-driven model.* Eugene, OR: Dynamic Measurement Group.

Kamphaus, R. W., & Frick, P. J. (2002). *Clinical assessment of child and adolescent personality and behavior.* Boston: Allyn & Bacon.

Kamphaus, R. W., Reynolds, C. R., & Imperato-McCammon, C. (1999). Roles of diagnosis and classification in school psychology. In C. R. Reynolds & T. B. Gutkin (Eds.), *Handbook of school psychology* (pp. 292–306). New York: Wiley.

Kandel, D. B., Yamaguchi, K., & Chen, K. (1992). Stages of progression in drug involvement from adolescence to adulthood: Further evidence for the gateway theory. *Journal of Studies on Alcohol, 53,* 447–457.

Kanne, S., & Mazurek, M. (2011). Aggression in children and adolescents with ASD. *Journal of Autism and Developmental Disorders, 41,* 926–937.

Kanner, L. (1943). Autistic disturbances of affective contact. *Nervous Child, 2,* 217–250.

Karrass, J., Walden, T. A., Conture, E. G., Graham, C. G., Arnold, H. S., Hartfield, K. N., & Schwenk, K. A. (2006). Relation of emotional reactivity and regulation to childhood stuttering. *Journal of Communication Disorders, 39,* 402–423.

Kasari, C., Freeman, S., & Paparella, T. (2006). Joint attention and symbolic play in young children with autism. *Journal of Child Psychology and Psychiatry, 47,* 611–620.

Kasari, C., Gulsrud, A. C., Freeman, S., Paparella, T., & Hellemann, G. (2012). Longitudinal follow-up of children with autism receiving targeted interventions on joint attention and play. *Journal of the American Academy of Child and Adolescent Psychiatry, 51,* 487–495.

Kasari, C., Gulsrud, A. C., Wong, C., Kwon, S., & Locke, J. (2010). Randomized controlled caregiver mediated joint engagement intervention for toddlers with autism. *Journal of Autism and Developmental Disorders, 40,* 1045–1056.

Kashani, J. H., & Orvaschel, H. (1990). A community study of anxiety in children and adolescents. *American Journal of Psychiatry, 147,* 313–318.

Kaslow, N. J., Deering, G. G., & Racusin, G. R. (1994). Depressed children and their families. *Clinical Psychology Review, 14,* 39–59.

Kaslow, N. J., & Thompson, M. P. (1998). Applying the criteria for empirically supported treatments to studies of psychosocial interventions for child and adolescent depression. *Journal of Clinical Child Psychology, 27,* 146–155.

Kates, W. R., Frederikse, M., Mostofsky, S. H., Folley, B. S., Cooper, K., Mazur-Hopkins, P., et al. (2002). MRI parcellation of the frontal lobe in boys with attention deficit hyperactivity disorder or Tourette syndrome. *Psychiatry Research, 116,* 63–81.

Katz, L. Y., Cox, B. J., Gunasekara, S., & Miller, A. L. (2004). Feasibility of dialectical behavior therapy for suicidal adolescent inpatients. *Journal of the American Academy of Child and Adolescent Psychiatry, 43,* 276–282.

Kaufman, N. K., Rohde, P., Seeley, J. R., Clarke, G. N., & Stice, E. (2005). Potential mediators of cognitive-behavioral therapy for adolescents with comorbid major depression and conduct disorder. *Journal of Consulting and Clinical Psychology, 73,* 38–46.

Kavale, K. A., Kaufmann, J. M., Bachmeier, R. J., & LeFever, G. B. (2008). Response to intervention: Sparing the rhetoric of self-congratulation from the reality of specific learning disability identification. *Learning Disability Quarterly, 31,* 135–150.

Kaye, W. H., Bastiani, A. M., & Moss, H. (1995). Cognitive style of patients with anorexia nervosa and bulimia nervosa. *International Journal of Eating Disorders, 18,* 287–290.

Kaye, W. H., Greeno, C. G., Moss, H., Fernstrom, J., Fernstrom, M., Lilenfeld, L. R., et al. (1998). Alterations in serotonin activity and psychiatric symptoms after recovery from bulimia nervosa. *Archives of General Psychiatry, 55,* 927–935.

Kaye, W. H., Nagata, T., Weltzin, T. E., Hsu, L. K., Sokol, M. S., McConaha, C., et al. (2001). Double-blind placebo-controlled administration of fluoxetine in restricting and restricting-purging type anorexia nervosa. *Biological Psychiatry, 49,* 644–652.

Kaye, W. H., Weltzin, T., & Hsu, L. G. (1993). Relationship between anorexia nervosa and obsessive and compulsive behaviors. *Psychiatric Annals, 23,* 365–373.

Kazdin, A. E. (1999). Overview of research design issues in clinical psychology. In P. C. Kendall, J. N. Butcher, & G. N. Holmbeck (Eds.), *Handbook of research methods in clinical psychology* (pp. 3–30). New York: Wiley.

Kazdin, A. E. (2003). *Research design in clinical psychology.* Boston: Allyn & Bacon.

Kazdin, A. E. (2005a). Child, parent, and family-based treatment of aggressive and antisocial child behavior. In E. D. Hibbs & P. S. Jensen (Eds.), *Psychosocial treatments for child and adolescent disorders: Empirically based strategies for clinical practice* (pp. 445–476). Washington, DC: American Psychological Association.

Kazdin, A. E. (2005b). *Parent management training: Treatment for oppositional, aggressive, and antisocial behavior in children and adolescents.* New York: Oxford University Press.

Kazdin, A. E., & Marciano, P. L. (1998). Childhood and adolescent depression. In E. J. Mash & R. A. Barkley (Eds.), *Treatment of childhood disorders* (pp. 211–248). New York: Guilford Press.

Kazdin, A. E., & Whitley, K. (2006). Comorbidity, case complexity, and effects of evidence-based treatment for children referred for disruptive behavior. *Journal of Consulting and Clinical Psychology, 74,* 455–467.

Kazdin, A. E., Bass, D., Ayers, W. A., & Rodgers, A. (1990). Empirical and clinical focus of child and adolescent psychotherapy research. *Journal of Consulting and Clinical Psychology, 58,* 729–740.

Kazdin, A. F., & Weisz, J. (2003). *Evidence-based psychotherapies for children and adolescents.* New York: Guilford Press.

Kearney, C. A., & Albano, A. M. (2000). *When children refuse school: A cognitive-behavioral therapy approach.* San Antonio, TX: Psychological Corporation.

Kearney-Cooke, A., & Striegel-Moore, H. (1994). Treatment of childhood sexual abuse in anorexia nervosa and bulimia nervosa: A feminist psychodynamic approach. *International Journal of Eating Disorders, 15,* 305–319.

Keel, P. K., Klump, K. L., Miller, K. B., McGue, M., & Iacono, W. G. (2005). Shared transmission of eating disorders and anxiety disorders. *International Journal of Eating Disorders, 38,* 99–105.

Keenan, K., Gunthorpe, D., & Young, D. (2002). Patterns of cortisol reactivity in African American neonates from low-income environments. *Developmental Psychobiology, 41,* 1–13.

Keenan, K., & Hipwell, A. E. (2005). Preadolescent clues to understanding depression in girls. *Clinical Child and Family Psychology Review, 8,* 89–105.

Keenan, K., Hipwell, A., Duax, J., Stouthamer-Loeber, M., & Loeber, R. (2004). Phenomenology of depression in young girls. *Journal of the American Academy of Child & Adolescent Psychiatry, 43,* 1098–1106.

Keenan, K., Loeber, R., & Green, S. (1999). Conduct disorder in girls: A review of the literature. *Clinical Child & Family Psychology Review, 2,* 3–19.

Keenan, K., & Shaw, D. S. (2003). Starting at the beginning: Exploring the etiology of antisocial behavior in the first years of life. In B. B. Lahey, T. E. Moffitt, & A. Caspi (Eds.), *Causes of conduct disorder and juvenile delinquency* (pp. 153–181). New York: Guilford Press.

Keenan, K., & Wakschlag, S. (2004). Are oppositional defiant and conduct disorder symptoms normative behaviors in preschoolers? A comparison of referred and nonreferred children. *American Journal of Psychiatry, 161,* 356–358.

Keery, H., Boutelle, K., van den Berg, P., & Thompson, J. K. (2005). The impact of appearance-related teasing by family members. *Journal of Adolescent Health, 37,* 120–127.

Keery, H., van den Berg, P., & Thompson, J. K. (2004). An evaluation of the tripartite influence model of body dissatisfaction and eating disturbance with adolescent girls. *Body Image, 1,* 237–251.

Keller, M. B., Lavori, P. W., Wunder, J., Beardslee, W. R., Schwartz, C. E., & Roth, J. (1992). Chronic course of anxiety disorders in children and adolescents. *Journal of the American Academy of Child and Adolescent Psychiatry, 31,* 595–599.

Keller, M. B., Ryan, N. D., Strober, M., Klein, R. G., Kutcher, S., Birmaher, B., et al. (2001). Efficacy of paroxetine in the treatment of adolescent major depression: A randomized, controlled trial. *Journal of the American Academy of Child and Adolescent Psychiatry, 40,* 762–772.

Kempes, M., Matthys, W., de Vries, H., & van Engeland, H. (2005). Reactive and proactive aggression in children: A review of theory, findings and the relevance for child and adolescent psychiatry. *European Child & Adolescent Psychiatry, 14,* 11–19.

Kempler, D. (2005). *Neurocognitive disorders in aging.* Thousand Oaks, CA: Sage.

Kendall, P. C. (1992). *Coping cat workbook.* Ardmore, PA: Workbook Publishing.

Kendall, P. C. (1994). Treating anxiety disorders in children: Results of a randomized clinical trial. *Journal of Consulting and Clinical Psychology, 62,* 100–110.

Kendall, P. C., Flannery-Schroeder, E. C., & Ford, J. D. (1999). Therapy outcome research methods. In P. C. Kendall, J. N. Butcher, & G. N. Holmbeck (Eds.), *Handbook of research methods in clinical psychology* (pp. 330–363). New York: Wiley.

Kendall, P. C., Flannery-Schroeder, E. C., Panichelli-Mindel, S., Southam-Gerow, M., Henin, A., & Warman, M. (1997). Therapy for youth with anxiety disorders: A second randomized clinical trial. *Journal of Consulting and Clinical Psychology, 65,* 366–380.

Kendall, P. C., Hudson, J. L., Choudhury, M., Webb, A., Pimentel, S. (2005). Cognitive-behavioral treatment for childhood anxiety disorders. In E. D. Hibbs & P. S. Jensen (Eds.), *Psychosocial treatments for child and adolescent disorders: Empirically based strategies for clinical practice* (2nd ed., pp. 47–73). Washington, DC: American Psychological Association.

Kendall, P. C., Krain, A., & Treadwell, K. (1999). Generalized anxiety disorders. In R. T. Ammerman, M. Hersen, & C. G. Last (Eds.), *Handbook of prescriptive treatments for children and adolescents* (pp. 155–171). Needham Heights, MA: Allyn & Bacon.

Kendall, P. C., Marrs-Garcia, A., Nath, S. R., & Sheldrick, R. C. (1999). Normative comparisons for the evaluation of clinical significance. *Journal of Consulting and Clinical Psychology, 67,* 285–299.

Kendall, P. C., Pimentel, S., Rynn, M. A., Angelosante, A., & Webb, A. (2004). Generalized anxiety disorder. In T. H. Ollendick & J. S. March (Eds.), *Phobic and anxiety disorders in children and adolescents* (pp. 334–380). New York: Oxford University Press.

Kendall, P. C., Safford, S., Flannery-Schroeder, E., & Webb, A. (2004). Child anxiety treatment: Outcomes in adolescence and impact on substance use and depression at 7.4-year follow-up. *Journal of Consulting and Clinical Psychology, 72,* 276–287.

Kendall, P. C., & Southam-Gerow, M. (1996). Long-term follow-up of treatment for anxiety-disordered youth. *Journal of Consulting and Clinical Psychology, 65,* 883–888.

Kendall-Tackett, K. A., Williams, L. M., & Finkelhor, D. (1993). Impact of sexual abuse on children: A review and synthesis of recent empirical studies. *Psychological Bulletin, 113,* 164–180.

Kennard, B. D., Clarke, G. N., Weersing, V. R., Asarnow, J. R., Shamseddeen, W., Porta, G., et al. (2009). Effective components of TORDIA cognitive-behavioral therapy for adolescent depression. *Journal of Consulting and Clinical Psychology, 77*, 1033–1041.

Kennard, B. D., Ginsburg, G. S., Feeny, N. C., Sweeney, M., & Zagurski, R. (2005). Implementation challenges to TADS cognitive-behavioral therapy. *Cognitive and Behavioral Practice, 12*, 230–239.

Kenney-Benson, G. A., & Pomerantz, M. (2005). The role of mothers' use of control in children's perfectionism: Implications for the development of children's depressive symptoms. *Journal of Personality, 73*, 23–46.

Keogh, B. K., Bernheimer, L. P., & Guthrie, D. (1997). Stability and change over time in cognitive level of children with delays. *American Journal on Mental Retardation, 101*, 365–373.

Kerins, M. (2006). The effects of systematic reading instruction on three classifications of readers. *Reading Research and Instruction, 45*, 243–260.

Kerr, M., & Stattin, H. (2000). What parents know, how they know it, and several forms of adolescent adjustment: Further support for a reinterpretation of monitoring. *Developmental Psychology, 36*, 366–380.

Kerstjens, J. M., DeWinter, A. F., Bocca-Tjeertes, I., Bos, A. F., & Reijnveld, S.A. (2013). Risk of developmental delay increases exponentially as gestational age of preterm infants decreases. *Developmental Medicine and Child Neurology.*

Kessler, R. C., Berglund, P. A., Chiu, W. T., Deitz, A. C., Hudson, J. I., Shahly, V., et al. (2013). The prevalence and correlates of binge eating disorder in the World Health Organization world mental health surveys *Biological Psychiatry.*

Kessler, R., Berglund, P., Dernier, O., Jin, R., & Walters, E. (2005). Lifetime prevalence and age-of-onset distributions of *DSM-IV* disorders in the National Co-morbidity Survey replication. *Archives of General Psychiatry, 62*, 593–602.

Key, A. P. F., & Thornton-Wells, T. A. (2012). Brain-based methods in the study of developmental disabilities. In J.A. Burack, R.M. Hodapp, G. Iarocci, & E. Zigler (Eds.), *The Oxford handbook of intellectual disability and development* (pp. 149–166). New York: Oxford University Press.

Khanna, M., Aschenbrand, S. G., & Kendall, P. C. (2007). New frontiers: Computer technology in the treatment of anxious youth. *The Behavior Therapist, 30*, 22–25.

Khantzian, E. J. (1995). Self-regulation vulnerabilities in substance abusers: Treatment implications. In S. Dowling (Ed.), *The psychology and treatment of addictive behavior* (pp. 17–41). Madison, CT: International Universities Press.

Kibby, M. Y., Tye, V. L., & Mulhern, P. K. (1998). Effectiveness of psychological intervention for children and adolescents with chronic medical illness: A meta-analysis. *Clinical Psychology Review, 18*, 103–117.

Kilpatrick, D. G., Ruggiero, K. J., Acierno, R., Saunders, B. E., Resnick, H. S., & Best, C. (2003). Violence, risk of PTSD, major depression, substance abuse/dependence, and comorbidity: Results from the National Survey of Adolescents. *Journal of Consulting and Clinical Psychology, 71*, 692–700.

Kim, J. A., Szatmari, P., Bryson, S. E., Streiner, D. L., & Wilson, F. J. (2000). The prevalence of anxiety and mood problems among children with autism and Asperger syndrome. *Autism, 4*, 117–132.

Kim, J. E., Hetherington, E. M., & Reiss, D. (1999). Associations among family relationships, antisocial peers, and adolescents' externalizing behaviors: Gender and family type differences. *Child Development, 70*, 1209–1230.

Kim-Cohen, J., Arseneault, L., Caspi, A., Tomas, M. P., Taylor, A., & Moffitt, T. E. (2005). Validity of *DSM-IV* conduct disorder in 4½–5-year-old children: A longitudinal epidemiological study. *American Journal of Psychiatry, 162*, 1108–1117.

Kim-Cohen, J., Arseneault, L., Newcombe, P., Adams, F., Bolton, H., Cant, L., et al. (2009). Five-year predictive validity of *DSM-IV* conduct disorder research diagnosis in 4 1/2–and 5-year-old children. *European Child and Adolescent Psychiatry, 18*, 284–291.

King, J. M. (2011). Augmentative and alternative communication (AAC) systems and individuals with complex communication needs. In

J. N. Kaderavek (Ed.), *Language disorders in children* (pp. 356–382). Boston: Pearson.

King, K. M., & Chassin, L. (2004). Mediating and moderated effects of adolescent behavioral undercontrol and parenting in the prediction of drug use disorders in emerging adulthood. *Psychology of Addictive Behaviors, 18*, 239–249.

King, N. J., & Bernstein, G. A. (2001). School refusal in children and adolescents. *Journal of the American Academy of Child and Adolescent Psychiatry, 40*, 197–205.

King, N. J., Gullone, E., Tonge, B. J., & Ollendick, T. H. (1993). Self-reports of panic attacks and manifest anxiety in adolescents. *Behavior Therapy and Research, 31*, 111–116.

King, N. J., Muris, P., & Ollendick, T. H. (2004). Specific phobia. In T. L. Morris & J. S. March (Eds.), *Anxiety disorders in children and adolescents* (pp. 263–279). New York: Guilford Press.

King, S., Waschbusch, D. A., Frankland, B. W., Andrade, B. F., Thurston, C. M., McNutt, L., et al. (2005). Taxonomic examination of ADHD and conduct problem comorbidity in elementary school children using cluster analyses. *Journal of Psychopathology and Behavioral Assessment, 27*, 77–88.

King, S. M., Iacono, W. G., & McGue, M. (2004). Childhood externalizing and internalizing psychopathology in the prediction of early substance use. *Addiction, 99*, 1548–1559.

Kingston, M. Huber, A., Onslow, M., Jones, M., & Packman, A. (2003). Predicting treatment time with the Lidcombe program. *International Journal of Language and Communication Disorders, 38*, 165–177.

Kirisci, L., Tarter, R. E., Vanyukov, M., Reynolds, M., & Habeych, M. (2004). Relation between cognitive distortions and neurobehavior disinhibition on the development of substance use during adolescence and substance use disorder by young adulthood: A prospective study. *Drug and Alcohol Dependence, 76*, 125–133.

Kirisci, L., Vanyukov, M., & Tarter, R. (2005). Detection of youth at high risk for substance use disorders: A longitudinal study. *Psychology of Addictive Behaviors, 19*, 243–252.

Kirk, S. A. (1962). *Educating exceptional children*. Oxford, UK: Houghton Mifflin.

Kjelsas, E., Bjornstrom, C., & Gotestam, K. G. (2004). Prevalence of eating disorders in female and male adolescents. *Eating Behaviors, 5*, 13–25.

Klein, R. G., Abikoff, H., Hechtman, L., & Weiss, G. (2004). Design and rationale of controlled study of long-term methylphenidate and multimodal psychosocial treatment in children with ADHD. *Journal of the American Academy of Child and Adolescent Psychiatry, 43*, 792–801.

Klein, R. G., Abikoff, H., Klass, E., Ganeles, D., Seese, L. M., & Pollack, S. (1997). Clinical efficacy of methylphenidate in conduct disorder with and without attention deficit hyperactivity disorder. *Archives of General Psychiatry, 54*, 1073–1080.

Klerman, G. L., & Weissman, M. M. (1993). Interpersonal psychotherapy for depression: Background and concepts. In G. L. Klerman & M. M. Weissman (Eds.), *New applications of interpersonal psychotherapy* (pp. 3–26). Washington, DC: American Psychiatric Press.

Klimes-Dougan, B., & Kopp, C. B. (1999). Children's conflict tactics with mothers: A longitudinal investigation of the toddler and preschool years. *Merrill-Palmer Quarterly, 45*, 226–241.

Klin, A. (2000). Attributing social meaning to ambiguous visual stimuli in higher functioning autism and Asperger syndrome: The social attribution task. *Journal of Child Psychology, Psychiatry and Allied Disciplines, 33*, 763–769.

Klin, A., Jones, W., Schultz, R. T., & Volkmar, F. R. (2003). The enactive mind: From actions to cognition: Lessons from autism. *Philosophical Transactions of the Royal Society, Biological Sciences, 358*, 345–360.

Klin, A., McPartland, J., & Volkmar, F. R. (2005). Asperger syndrome. In F. R. Volkmar, R. Paul, A. Klin, & D. Cohen (Eds.), *Handbook of autism and pervasive developmental disorders, Vol. 1: Diagnosis, development, neurobiology, and behavior* (pp. 88–125). Hoboken, NJ: Wiley.

Klinger, L. G., Dawson, G., & Renner, P. (2003). Autistic disorder. In E. J. Mash & R. A. Barkley (Eds.), *Child psychopathology* (pp. 409–454). New York: Guilford Press.

Klomek, A. B., Marrocco, F., Kleinman, M., Schonfeld, I. S., & Gould, M. S. (2007). Bullying, depression, and suicidality in adolescents. *Journal of the American Academy of Child & Adolescent Psychiatry, 46*, 40–49.

Klonsky, E. D. (2011). Non-suicidal self-injury in United States adults: Prevalence, sociodemographics, topography and functions. *Psychological Medicine, 41*, 1981–1986.

Klonsky, E. D., & Moyer, A. (2008). Childhood sexual abuse and non-suicidal self-injury: Meta-analysis. *The British Journal of Psychiatry, 192*, 166–170.

Klonsky, E. D., Muehlenkamp, J. J., Lewis, S. P., & Walsh, B. (2011). *Nonsuicidal self-injury.* Cambridge, MA: Hogrefe.

Klonsky, E. D., & Olino, T. M. (2008). Identifying clinically distinct subgroups of self-injurers among young adults: A latent class analysis. *Journal of Consulting and Clinical Psychology, 76*, 22.

Kluger, J., & Song, S. (2002). Young and bipolar. *Time, 160*, 38.

Knappe, S., Beesdo-Baum, K., Fehm, L., Stein, M. B., Lieb, R., & Wittchen, H. (2011). Social fear and Social Anxiety Disorder types among community youth: Differential clinical features and vulnerability factors. *Journal of Psychiatric Research, 45*, 111–120.

Knell, S. M., & Ruma, C. D. (2003). Play therapy with a sexually abused child. In M. A. Reinecke, F. M. Dattilio, & A. Freeman (Eds.), *Cognitive therapy with children and adolescents: A casebook for clinical practice* (pp. 338–368). New York: Guilford Press.

Knight, J. R., Shrier, L. A., Bravender, T. D., Farrell, M., Vander Bilt, J., & Shaffer, H. J. (1999). A new brief screen for adolescent substance abuse. *Archives of Pediatrics and Adolescent Medicine, 153*, 591.

Knutson, J. F., DeGarmo, D., Koeppl, G., & Reid, J. B. (2005). Care neglect, supervisory neglect, and harsh parenting in the development of children's aggression: A replication and extension. *Child Maltreatment, 10*, 92–107.

Kochanska, G., & Aksan, N. (2006). Children's conscience and self-regulation. *Journal of Personality, 74*, 1587–1617.

Kodish, I., & McClellan, J. (2008). Early-onset schizophrenia. In D. Reitman (Ed.), *Handbook of psychological assessment, case conceptualization, and treatment* (pp. 405–443). New York: Wiley.

Koegel, L. K. (1995). Communication and language intervention. In R. L. Koegel & L. K. Koegel (Eds.), *Teaching children with autism: Strategies for initiating positive interaction and improving learning opportunities* (pp. 17–32). Baltimore: Brookes.

Koegel, L. K. (2000). Interventions to facilitate communication in autism. *Journal of Autism and Developmental Disorders, 30*, 383–391.

Koegel, L. K., Carter, C. M., & Koegel, R. L. (2003). Teaching children with autism self-initiations as a pivotal response. *Topics in Language Disorders, 23*, 134–145.

Koegel, L. K., Koegel, R. L., & Brookman, L. I. (2005). Child-initiated interactions that are pivotal in intervention for children with autism. In E. D. Hibbs & P. S. Jensen (Eds.), *Psychosocial treatments for child and adolescent disorders: Empirically based strategies for clinical practice* (pp. 633–657). Washington, DC: American Psychological Association.

Koegel, L. K., Koegel, R. L., Shoshan, Y., & McNerney, E. (1999). Pivotal response intervention II: Preliminary long-term outcome data. *Journal of the Association for Persons With Severe Handicaps, 24*, 186–198.

Koenig, A. L., Cicchetti, D., & Rogosch, F. A. (2004). Moral development: The association between maltreatment and young children's prosocial behaviors and moral transgressions. *Social Development, 13*, 97–106.

Koenig, K., & Tsatsanis, K. D. (2005). Pervasive developmental disorders in girls. In D. J. Bell, S. L. Foster, & E. J. Mash (Eds.), *Handbook of behavioral and emotional problems in girls* (pp. 211–237). New York: Kluwer Academic/Plenum Publishers.

Koenig, L. J., & Clark, J. (2004). Sexual abuse of girls and HIV infection among women: Are they related? In L. J. Koenig, L. S. Doll, A. O'Leary, & W. Pequegnat (Eds.), *From child sexual abuse to adult sexual risk: Trauma, revictimization, and intervention* (pp. 69–92). Washington, DC: American Psychological Association.

Kogan, M. D., Blumberg, S. J., Schieve, L. A., Boyle, C. A., Perrin, J. M., & Ghandour, R. M. (2009). Prevalence of parent-reported diagnosis of autism spectrum disorder among children in the US. *Pediatrics, 124*, 1395–1403.

Kolko, D. J. (1996). Individual cognitive behavioral treatment and family therapy for physically abused children and their offending parents: A comparison of clinical outcomes. *Child Maltreatment, 1*, 322–342.

Kolko, D. J. (2002). Child physical abuse. In J. E. B. Meyers, L. Berliner, J. Briere, C. T. Hendrix, C. Jenny, & T. A. Reid (Eds.), *The APSAC handbook on child maltreatment* (pp. 21–54). Thousand Oaks, CA: Sage.

Kolko, D. J., Selelyo, J., & Brown, E. J. (1999). The treatment histories and service involvement of physically and sexually abusive families: Description, correspondence, and clinical correlates. *Child Abuse & Neglect, 23*, 459–476.

Kolko, D. J., & Swenson, C. C. (2002). *Assessing and treating physically abused children and their families: A cognitive-behavioral approach.* Thousand Oaks, CA: Sage.

Konidaris, J. B. (2005). A sibling's perspective on autism. In F. R. Volkmar, R. Paul, A. Klin, & D. Cohen (Eds.), *Handbook of autism and pervasive developmental disorders, Vol. 2: Assessment, interventions, and policy* (pp. 1265–1275). New York: Wiley.

Koob, G. F., & LeMoal, M. (2006). *Neurobiology of addiction.* Amsterdam: Elsevier.

Koocher, G. P., & LaGreca, A. M. (2010). *The parents' guide to psychological first aid.* Oxford, UK: Oxford University Press.

Kopta, S. M. (2003). The dose-effect relationship in psychotherapy: A defining achievement for Dr. Kenneth Howard. *Journal of Clinical Psychology, 59*, 727–733.

Koskentausta, T., Iivanainen, M., & Almqvist, F. (2007). Risk factors for psychiatric disturbance in children with intellectual disability. *Journal of Intellectual Disability Research, 51*, 43–53.

Kosten, T. R., George, T. P., & Kleber, H. D. (2005). The neurobiology of substance dependence. In R. J. Frances, S. I. Miller, & A. H. Mack (Eds.), *Clinical textbook of addictive disorders* (pp. 3–15). New York: Guilford Press.

Kotagal, S. (2008). Parasomnias in childhood. *Sleep Medicine Reviews, 13*, 157–168.

Kovacs, M. (1997). Depressive disorders in childhood: An impressionistic landscape. *Journal of Child Psychology and Psychiatry, 38*, 287–298.

Kovacs, M., & Devlin, B. (1998). Internalizing disorders in childhood. *Journal of Child Psychology & Psychiatry & Allied Disciplines, 39*, 47–63.

Kovelman, I., Norton, E. S., Christodoulou, J. A., Gaab, N., Lieberman, D. A., Triantafyllou, C., et al. (2012). Brain basis of phonological awareness for spoken language in children and its disruption in dyslexia. *Cerebral Cortex, 22*, 754–764.

Kowatch, R. A., & Fristad, M. A. (2006). Bipolar disorders. In R. T. Ammerman (Ed.), *Comprehensive handbook of personality and psychopathology* (pp. 217–232). Hoboken, NJ: Wiley.

Kowatch, R. A., Fristad, M., Birmaher, B., Wagner, K. D., Findling, R. L., & Hellander, M. (2005). Treatment guidelines for children and adolescents with bipolar disorder. *Journal of the American Academy of Child & Adolescent Psychiatry, 44*, 213–235.

Kratochvil, C. J., Simons, A., Vitiello, B., Walkup, J., Emslie, G., Rosenberg, D., et al. (2005). A multisite psychotherapy and medication trial for depressed adolescents: Background and benefits. *Cognitive and Behavioral Practice, 12*, 159–165.

Krieger, F. V., Pheula, G. F., Coelho, R., Zeni, T., Tramontina, S., Zeni, C. P., et al. (2011). An open-label trial of risperidone in children and adolescents with severe mood dysregulation. *Journal of Child and Adolescent Psychopharmacology, 21*, 237–243.

Kroesbergen, E. H., & VanLuit, H. (2003). Mathematics interventions for children with special educational needs: A meta-analysis. *Remedial and Special Education, 24*, 97–114.

Kroneman, L., Loeber, R., & Hipwell, A. E. (2004). Is neighborhood context differently related to externalizing problems and delinquency for girls compared with boys? *Clinical Child and Family Psychology Review, 7*, 109–122.

Krueger, R. F. (1999). The structure of common mental disorders. *Archives of General Psychiatry, 56*, 921.

Krueger, R. F., & Bezdjian, S. (2009). Enhancing research and treatment of mental disorders with dimensional concepts. *World Psychiatry, 8*, 5–6.

Kruh, I. P., Frick, P. J., & Clements, C. B. (2005). Historical and personality correlates to the violence patterns of juveniles tried as adults. *Criminal Justice and Behavior, 92*, 69–96.

Kryzhanovskaya, L., Schulz, S. C., McDougle, C., Frazier, J., Dittmann, R., Robertson-Plouch, C., et al. (2009). Olanzapine versus placebo in adolescents with schizophrenia. *Journal of the American Academy of Child and Adolescent Psychiatry, 48*, 60–70.

Kuehn, B. M. (2006). Shift seen in patterns of drug use among teens. *Journal of the American Medical Association, 295*, 612–613.

Kuhn, M. R., & Stahl, S. A. (2003). Fluency: A review of developmental and remedial practices. *Journal of Educational Psychology, 95*, 3–21.

Kumin, L. (1994). Intelligibility of speech in children with Down syndrome in natural settings: Parents' perspective. *Perceptual and Motor Skills, 78*, 307–313.

Kumra, S., Kranzler, H., Gerbino-Rosen, G., Kester, H. M., DeThomas, C., Kafantaris, V., et al. (2008). Clozapine and "high dose" olanzapine in refractory early-onset schizophrenia. *Biological Psychiatry, 63*, 524–529.

Kumsta, R., Kreppner, J., Rutter, M., Beckett, C., Castle, J., Stevens, S., & Sonuga-Barke, E. J. (2011). III. Deprivation-specific psychological patterns. *Monographs of the Society for Research in Child Development, 75*, 48–78.

Kuniyoshi, J. S., & McClellan, J. M. (2010). Early-onset schizophrenia. In M. K. Dulcan (Eds.), *Dulcan's textbook of child and adolescent psychiatry* (pp. 367–379). Washington, DC: American Psychiatric Association.

Kupersmidt, J. B., Griesler, P. C., DeRosier, M. E., Patterson, C. J., & Davis, P. W. (1995). Childhood aggression and peer relations in the context of family and neighborhood factors. *Child Development, 66*, 360–375.

Lackaye, T., Margalit, M., Ziv, O., & Ziman, T. (2006). Comparisons of self-efficacy, mood, effort, and hope between students with learning disabilities and their non-LD-matched peers. *Learning Disabilities Research & Practice, 21*, 111–121.

Lacourse, E., Nagin, D. S., Vitaro, F., Cote, S., Arseneault, L., & Tremblay, R. E. (2006). Prediction of early-onset deviant peer group affiliation: A 12-year longitudinal study. *Archives of General Psychiatry, 63*, 562–568.

LaGreca, A. M., & Harrison, M. (2005). Adolescent peer relations, friendships, and romantic relationships: Do they predict social anxiety and depression? *Journal of Clinical Child and Adolescent Psychology, 34*, 49–61.

LaGreca, A. M., & Mackey, E. R. (2009). Type 1 diabetes mellitus. In *Behavioral approaches to chronic disease in adolescence* (pp. 85–100). New York: Springer.

LaGreca, A. M., & Silverman, W. K. (2006). Treating children and adolescents affected by disasters and terrorism. In P. C. Kendall (Ed.), *Child and adolescent therapy: Cognitive-behavioral procedures* (3rd ed., pp. 356–382). New York: Guilford Press.

LaGreca, A. M., Silverman, W. K., & Wasserstein, S. B. (1998). Children's pre-disaster functioning as a predictor of posttraumatic stress following Hurricane Andrew. *Journal of Consulting and Clinical Psychology, 66*, 883–892.

LaGreca, A. M., Silverman, W. K., Vernberg, E. M., & Roberts, M. C. (2002). Introduction. In A. M. La Greca, W. K. Silverman, E. M. Vernberg, & M. C. Roberts (Eds.), *Helping children cope with disasters and terrorism* (pp. 3–8). Washington, DC: American Psychological Association.

Lahey, B. B., Carlson, C. L., & Frick, P. J. (1997). Attention-deficit disorder without hyperactivity. In T. A. Widiger, A. J. Frances, H. A. Pincus, R. Ross, M. B. First, & W. Davis (Eds.), *DSM-IV sourcebook* (Vol. 3; pp. 163–188). Washington, DC: American Psychiatric Association.

Lahey, B. B., & Loeber, R. (1994). Framework for a developmental model of oppositional defiant disorder and conduct disorder. In D. K. Routh (Ed.), *Disruptive behavior disorders in childhood* (pp. 139–180). New York: Plenum.

Lahey, B. B., Loeber, R., Burke, J. D., & Applegate, B. (2005). Predicting future antisocial personality disorder in males from a clinical assessment in childhood. *Journal of Consulting and Clinical Psychology, 73*, 389–399.

Lahey, B. B., Loeber, R., Quay, H. C., Frick, P. J., & Grimm, J. (1992). Oppositional defiant and conduct disorders: Issues to be resolved for *DSM-IV. Journal of the American Academy of Child & Adolescent Psychiatry, 31*, 539–546.

Lahey, B. B., McBurnett, K., & Loeber, R. (2000). Are attention-deficit/hyperactivity disorder and oppositional defiant disorder developmental precursors to conduct disorder? In A. J. Sameroff, M. Lewis, & S. M. Miller (Eds.), *Handbook of developmental psychopathology* (pp. 431–446). New York: Kluwer Academic/Plenum.

Lahey, B. B., Pelham, W. E., Loney, J., Kipp, H., Ehrhardt, A., Lee, S. S., et al. (2004). Three-year predictive validity of *DSM-IV* attention deficit hyperactivity disorder in children diagnosed at 4–6 years of age. *American Journal of Psychiatry, 161*, 2014–2020.

Lahey, B. B., Pelham, W. E., Stein, M. A., Loney, J., Trapani, C., Nugent, K., et al. (1998). Validity of *DSM-IV* attention-deficit/hyperactivity disorder for younger children. *Journal of the American Academy of Child and Adolescent Psychiatry, 37*, 695–702.

Lahey, B. B., & Waldman, I. D. (2003). A developmental propensity model of the origins of conduct problems during childhood and adolescence. In B. B. Lahey, T. E. Moffitt, & A. Caspi (Eds.), *Causes of conduct disorder and juvenile delinquency* (pp. 76–117). New York: Guilford Press.

Lahey, B. B., Waldman, I. D., & McBurnett, K. (1999). The development of antisocial behavior: An integrative causal model. *Journal of Child Psychology and Psychiatry, 40*, 669–682.

Lahey, B. B., & Willcutt, E.G. (2010). Predictive validity of a continuous alternative to nominal subtypes of attention-deficit hyperactivity disorder for *DSM-5. Journal of Clinical Child and Adolescent Psychology, 39*, 761–775.

Laird, R. D., Pettit, G. S., Dodge, K. A., & Bates, J. E. (2003). Change in parents' monitoring knowledge: Links with parenting, relationship quality, adolescent beliefs, and antisocial behavior. *Social Development, 12*, 401–419.

Lambert, M. J., & Ogles, B. M. (2004). The efficacy and effectiveness of psychotherapy. In M. J. Lambert (Ed.), *Bergin and Garfield's handbook of psychotherapy and behavior change* (pp. 139–193). New York: Wiley.

Lancioni, G. E., Singh, N. N., O'Reilly, M. F., Sigafoos, J., & Didden, R. (2012). Function of challenging behaviors. In J. L. Matson (Ed.), *Functional assessment for challenging behavior* (pp. 45–64). New York: Springer.

Landau, B. (2012). The organization and development of spatial representation: Insights from Williams Syndrome. In J. A. Burack, R. M. Hodapp, G. Iarocci, & E. Zigler (Eds.), *The Oxford handbook of intellectual disability and development* (pp. 61–88). New York: Oxford University Press.

Landerl, K., & Moll, K. (2010). Comorbidity of learning disorders. *Journal of Child Psychology and Psychiatry, 51*, 287–294.

Langberg, J. M., Becker, S. P., & Dvorsky, M. R. (2013). The associations between sluggish cognitive tempo and academic functioning in youth with attention-deficit/hyperactivity disorder (ADHD). *Journal of Abnormal Child Psychology.*

Langleben, D. D., Austin, G., Krikorian, G., Ridlehuber, H. W., Goris, M. L., & Strauss, H. W. (2001). Interhemispheric asymmetry of regional cerebral blood flow in prepubescent boys with attention deficit hyperactivity disorder. *Nuclear Medicine, 22*, 1333–1340.

Lansford, J. E., Deater-Deckard, K., Dodge, K. A., Bates, J. E., & Pettit, G. S. (2004). Ethnic differences in the link between physical discipline and later adolescent externalizing behaviors. *Journal of Child Psychology and Psychiatry, 45*, 801–812.

Larsson, H. J., Eaton, W. W., Madsen, K. M., Vestergaard, M., Olesen, A., Averbo, E., et al. (2005). Risk factors for autism. *American Journal of Epidemiology, 161,* 916–925.

Larsson, J., Larsson, H., & Lichtenstein, P. (2004). Genetic and environmental contributions to stability and change of ADHD symptoms between 8 and 13 years of age: A longitudinal twin study. *Journal of the American Academy of Child and Adolescent Psychiatry, 43,* 1267–1275.

Last, C. G., Perrin, S., Hersen, M., & Kazdin, A. E. (1992). DSM-III-R anxiety disorders in children: Sociodemographic and clinical characteristics. *Journal of the American Academy of Child and Adolescent Psychiatry, 31,* 1070–1076.

Last, C. G., Perrin, S., Hersen, M., & Kazdin, A. E. (1996). A prospective study of childhood anxiety disorders. *Journal of the American Academy of Child and Adolescent Psychiatry, 35,* 1502–1510.

Latimer, W. W., Ernst, J., Hennessey, J., Stinchfield, R. D., & Winters, K. C. (2004). Relapse among adolescent drug abusers following treatment: The role of probable ADHD status. *Journal of Child & Adolescent Substance Abuse, 13,* 1–16.

Latimer, W. W., Newcomb, M., Winters, K. C., & Stinchfield, R. D. (2000). Adolescent substance abuse treatment outcome: The role of substance abuse problem severity, psychosocial, and treatment factors. *Journal of Consulting and Clinical Psychology, 68,* 684–696.

Laumann, E. O., Paik, A., & Rosen, R. C. (1999). Sexual dysfunction in the United States: Prevalence and predictors. *Journal of the American Medical Association, 281,* 537–544.

Lawrence, C. J., Lott, I., & Haier, R. J. (2005). Neurobiology of autism, mental retardation, and Down syndrome. In C. Stough (Ed.), *Neurobiology of exceptionality* (pp. 125–142). New York: Kluwer Academic/Plenum.

Lawton, K., & Kasari, C. (2012). Teacher-implemented joint attention intervention. *Journal of Consulting and Clinical Psychology, 80,* 687–693.

Lay, B., Blanz, B., Hartmann, M., & Schmidt, M. (2000). The psychosocial outcome of adolescent schizophrenia: A 12-year follow-up. *Schizophrenia Bulletin, 26,* 801–816.

Layne, A. E., Bernat, D. H., Vitor, A. M., & Bernstein, G. A. (2009). Generalized anxiety disorder in a nonclinical sample of children. *Journal of Anxiety Disorders, 23,* 283–289.

Leach, J. M., Scarborough, H. S., & Rescorla, L. (2003). Late-emerging reading disabilities. *Journal of Educational Psychology, 95,* 211–224.

LeBeau, R. T., Glenn, D., Liao, B., Wittchen, H., Beesdo-Baum, K., Ollendick, T., & Craske, M. G. (2010). Specific phobia: A review of *DSM-IV* specific phobia and preliminary recommendations for *DSM-5. Depression and Anxiety, 27,* 148–167.

Leckman, J. F., & Bloch, M. H. (2010). Tic disorders. In M. Rutter (Ed.), *Rutter's child and adolescent psychiatry* (pp. 719–736). Malden, MA: Blackwell.

Leckman, J. F., Denys, D., Simpson, H. B., Mataix-Cols, D., Hollander, E., Saxena, S., et al. (2010). Obsessive-compulsive disorder: A review of the diagnostic criteria and possible subtypes and dimensional specifiers for *DSM-5. Depression and Anxiety, 27,* 507–527.

Lee, J. S., Kim, B. N., Kang, E., Lee, D. S., Kim, Y. K., Chung, J., et al. (2004). Regional cerebral blood flow in children with attention deficit hyperactivity disorder: Comparison before and after methylphenidate treatment. *Human Brain Mapping, 24,* 157–164.

Lee, S. S., Humphreys, K. L., Flory, K., Liu, R., Glass, K. (2011). Prospective association of childhood attention-deficit/hyperactivity disorder (ADHD) and substance use and abuse/dependence. *Clinical Psychology Review, 31,* 328–341.

Legenbauer, T., Heiler, S., Holtmann, M., Fricke-Oerkermann, L., & Lehmkuhl, G. (2012). The affective storms of school children during night time. *Journal of Neural Transmission, 119,* 989–998.

Leibenluft, E. (2011). Severe mood dysregulation, irritability, and the diagnostic boundaries of bipolar disorder. *American Journal of Psychiatry, 168,* 129–142.

Leibenluft, E., Charney, D. S., Towbin, K. E., Bhangoo, R. K., & Pine, D. S. (2003). Defining clinical phenotypes of juvenile mania. *American Journal of Psychiatry, 160,* 430–437.

Leibenluft, E., & Dickstein, D. P. (2008). Bipolar disorder in children and adolescents. In M. Rutter (Ed.), *Rutter's child and adolescent psychiatry* (pp. 613–627). Malden, MA: Blackwell.

Leibenluft, E., Uher, R., & Rutter, M. (2012). Disruptive mood dysregulation with dysphoria disorder. A proposal for ICD-11. *World Psychiatry, 11S,* 77–81.

Lekhwani, M., Nair, C., Nikhinson, I., & Ambrosini, P. J. (2004). Psychotropic prescription practices in child psychiatric inpatients 9 years old and younger. *Journal of Child and Adolescent Psychopharmacology, 14,* 95–103.

Lemanek, K. L., & Ranalli, M. (2009). Sickle cell disease. In M. C. Roberts & R. G. Steele (Eds.), *Handbook of pediatric psychology* (pp. 303–318). New York: Guilford.

Lengua, L. J., Long, A. C., Smith, K. I., & Meltzoff, A. N. (2005). Preattack symptomatology and temperament as predictors of children's responses to the September 11 terrorist attacks. *Journal of Child Psychology and Psychiatry, 46,* 631–645.

Lenior, M., Dingemans, P., Linszen, D., de Haan, L., & Schene, A. (2001). Social functioning and the course of early-onset schizophrenia: Five-year follow-up of a psychosocial intervention. *British Journal of Psychiatry, 179,* 53–58.

Leu, R. M., Rosen, C. L. (2008). Sleep and pediatrics. In H. R. Smith, C. L. Comella, & B. Hogl (Eds.), *Sleep medicine* (pp. 208–223). Cambridge: Cambridge University Press.

Leventhal, B. L. (2012). Lumpers and splitters: Who knows? Who cares? *Journal of the American Academy of Child and Adolescent Psychiatry, 51,* 6–7.

Leventhal, T., & Brooks-Gunn, J. (2000). The neighborhoods they live in: The effects of neighborhood residence on child and adolescent outcomes. *Psychological Bulletin, 126,* 309–337.

Levy, F., Hay, D. A., Bennett, K. S., & McStephen, M. (2005). Gender differences in ADHD subtype comorbidity. *Journal of the American Academy of Child and Adolescent Psychiatry, 44,* 368–376.

Levy, S. E., Giarelli, E., Lee, L., Schieve, L. A., Kirby, R. S., Cunniff, C., et al. (2010). Autism spectrum disorder and co-occurring developmental, psychiatric, and medical conditions among children in multiple populations in the United States. *Journal of Developmental Behavioral Pediatrics, 31,* 267–275.

Lewinsohn, P. M. (1974). A behavioral approach to depression. In R. J. Friedman, & M. M. Katz (Eds.), *The psychology of depression: Contemporary theory and research* (pp. 157–184). Washington, DC: Winston-Wiley.

Lewinsohn, P. M., Allen, N. B., Gotlib, I. H., & Seeley, J. R. (1999). First onset versus recurrence of depression: Differential processes of psychosocial risk. *Journal of Abnormal Psychology, 108,* 483–498.

Lewinsohn, P. M., Clarke, G. N., Hops, H., & Andrews, J. (1990). Cognitive-behavioral group treatment of depression in adolescents. *Behavior Therapy, 21,* 385–401.

Lewinsohn, P. M., Hops, H., Roberts, R. E., Seeley, J. R., & Andrews, J. A. (1993). Adolescent psychopathology: I. Prevalence and incidence of depression and other DSM-III-R disorders in high school students. *Journal of Abnormal Psychology, 102,* 133–144.

Lewinsohn, P. M., Roberts, R. E., Seeley, J. R., Rohde, P., Gotlib, I. H., & Hops, H. (1994). Adolescent psychopathology: II. Psychosocial risk factors for depression. *Journal of Abnormal Psychology, 103,* 302–315.

Lewinsohn, P. M., Rohde, P., & Seeley, J. R. (1998). Major depressive disorder in older adolescents: Prevalence, risk factors, and clinical implications. *Clinical Psychology Review, 18,* 765–794.

Lewinsohn, P. M., Seeley, J. R., & Klein, D. N. (2003). Epidemiology and suicidal behavior. In B. Geller & M. P. DelBello (Eds.), *Bipolar disorder in childhood and early adolescence* (pp. 7–24). New York: Guilford Press.

Lewinsohn, P. M., Striegel-Moore, R. H., & Seeley, J. R. (2000). Epidemiology and natural course of eating disorders in young women from adolescence to young adulthood. *Journal of the American Academy of Child and Adolescent Psychiatry, 39,* 1284–1292.

Lewinsohn, P. M., Youngren, M. A., & Grosscup, S. J. (1979). Reinforcement and depression. In R. A. Dupue (Ed.), *The psychobiology of depressive disorders: Implications for the effects of stress* (pp. 291–316). New York: Academic Press.

Lewis, S. P., Heath, N. L., St. Denis, J. M., & Noble, R. (2011). The scope of nonsuicidal self-injury on YouTube. *Pediatrics, 127,* 1–6.

Lewis, S., Tarrier, N., Haddock, G., Bentrall, R., Kinderman, P., Kingdon, D., et al. (2002). Randomized controlled trial of cognitive-behavioral therapy in early schizophrenia: Acute-phase outcomes. *British Journal of Psychiatry, 181,* s91–s97.

Li, C. E., DiGiuseppe, R., & Froh, J. (2006). The roles of sex, gender, and coping in adolescent depression. *Adolescence, 41,* 409–415.

Libby, A. M., Orton, H. D., Novins, D. K., Spicer, P., Buchwald, D., Beals, J., et al. (2004). Childhood physical and sexual abuse and subsequent alcohol and drug use disorders in two American-Indian tribes. *Journal of Studies on Alcohol, 65,* 74–83.

Libby, A. M., Orton, H. D., Stover, S. K., & Riggs, P. D. (2005). What came first, major depression or substance use disorder? Clinical characteristics and substance use comparing teens in a treatment cohort. *Addictive Behaviors, 30,* 1649–1662.

Libby, S., Reynolds, S., Derisley, J., & Clark, S. (2004). Cognitive appraisals in young people with obsessive-compulsive disorder. *Journal of Child Psychology and Psychiatry, 45,* 1076–1084.

Liddle, H. A. (2004). Family-based therapies for adolescent alcohol and drug use: Research contributions and future research needs. *Addiction, 99,* 76–92.

Liddle, H. A., Dakof, G. A., Diamond, G. S., Parker, G. S., Barrett, K., & Tejeda, M. (2001). Multidimensional family therapy for adolescent substance abuse: Results of a randomized clinical trial. *American Journal of Drug and Alcohol Abuse, 27,* 651–687.

Liddle, H. A., & Hogue, A. (2001). Multidimensional family therapy for adolescent substance abuse. In E. F. Wagner & H. B. Waldron (Eds.), *Innovations in adolescent substance abuse interventions* (pp. 229–261). Amsterdam: Pergamon/Elsevier Science.

Liddle, H. A., & Rowe, C. L. (2006). *Adolescent substance abuse: Research and clinical advances.* New York: Cambridge University Press.

Liddle, H. A., Rowe, C. L., Dakof, G. A., Ungaro, R. A., & Henderson, C. E. (2004). Early intervention for adolescent substance abuse: Pretreatment to posttreatment outcomes of a randomized clinical trial comparing multidimensional family therapy and peer group treatment. *Journal of Psychoactive Drugs, 36,* 49–63.

Lilenfeld, L. R., Kaye, W. H., Greeno, C. G., Merikangas, K. R., Plotnicov, K., Pollice, C., et al. (1998). A controlled family study of anorexia nervosa and bulimia nervosa: Psychiatric disorders in first-degree relatives and effects of proband comorbidity. *Archives of General Psychiatry, 55,* 603–610.

Lin, H., Katsovich, L., Ghebremichael, M., Findley, D. B., Grantz, H., Lombroso, P. J., et al. (2007). Psychosocial stress predicts future symptom severities in children and adolescents with Tourette syndrome and/or obsessive-compulsive disorder. *Journal of Child Psychology and Psychiatry, 48,* 157–166.

Linan-Thompson, S., & Miciak, J. (2012). Reading interventions for students in early primary grades. In B. Wong & D. Butler (Eds.), *Learning about learning disabilities* (pp. 175–190).New York: Elsevier.

Linehan, M. M. (1993). *Cognitive-behavioral treatment of personality disorder.* New York: Guilford.

Linnet, K. M., Dalsgaard, S., Obel, C., Wisborg, K., Henriksen, T. B., Rodriguez, A., et al. (2003). Maternal lifestyle factors in pregnancy risk of attention deficit hyperactivity disorder and associated behaviors: Review of the current evidence. *American Journal of Psychiatry, 160,* 1028–1040.

Linscheid, T. R. (2006). Behavioral treatments for pediatric feeding disorders. *Behavior Modification, 30,* 6–23.

Linscheid, T. R., & Butz, C. (2003). Anorexia nervosa and bulimia nervosa. In M. C. Roberts (Ed.), *Handbook of pediatric psychology* (636–651). New York: Guilford Press.

Lipka, O., & Siegel, L. S. (2006). Learning disabilities. *Behavioral and emotional disorders in adolescents* (pp. 410–443). New York: Guilford.

Lipton, J. S., & Spelke, S. (2003). Origins of number sense: Large-number discrimination in human infants. *Psychological Science, 14,* 396–401.

Little, S. A., & Garber, J. (2005). The role of social stressors and interpersonal orientation in explaining the longitudinal relation between externalizing and depressive symptoms. *Journal of Abnormal Psychology, 114,* 432–443.

Liu, H. Y., Potter, M. P., Woodworth, K. Y., Yorks, D. M., Petty, C. R., Wozniak, J. R., et al. (2011). Pharmacologic treatments for pediatric bipolar disorder. *Journal of the American Academy of Child and Adolescent Psychiatry, 50,* 749–762.

Lloyd-Richardson, E. E., Perrine, N., Dierker, L., & Kelley, M. L. (2007). Characteristics and functions of non-suicidal self-injury in a community sample of adolescents. *Psychological Medicine, 37,* 1183.

Lock, J. (2004). Family approaches to anorexia nervosa and bulimia nervosa. In J. K. Thompson (Ed.), *Handbook of eating disorders and obesity* (pp. 218–231). Hoboken, NJ: Wiley.

Loeber, R., & Farrington, D. P. (2000). Young children who commit crime: Epidemiology, developmental origins, risk factors, early interventions, and policy implications. *Development & Psychopathology, 12,* 737–762.

Loeber, R., Green, S. M., & Lahey, B. B. (1990). Mental health professionals' perception of the utility of children, mothers, and teachers as informants on childhood psychopathology *Journal of Clinical Child Psychology, 19,* 136–143.

Loeber, R., & Hay, D. (1997). Key issues in the development of aggression and violence from childhood to early adulthood. *Annual Review of Psychology, 48,* 371–410.

Loeber, R., & Stouthamer-Loeber, M. (1986). Family factors as correlates & predictors of juvenile conduct problems and delinquency. In M. Tonry & N. Morris (Eds.), *Crime and justice: An annual review of research* (pp. 29–149). Chicago: University of Chicago Press.

Loeber, R., & Stouthamer-Loeber, M. (1998). Development of juvenile aggression and violence: Some common misconceptions and controversies. *American Psychologist, 53,* 242–259.

Loesch, D. Z., Bui, Q. M., Grigsby, J., Butler, E., Epstein, J., Huggins, R. M., et al. (2003). Effect of the fragile X status categories and the fragile X mental retardation protein levels on executive functioning in males and females with fragile X. *Neuropsychology, 17,* 646–657.

Loney, B. R., Frick, P. J., Clements, C. B., Ellis, M. L., & Kerlin, K. (2003). Callous-unemotional traits, impulsivity, and emotional processing in antisocial adolescents. *Journal of Clinical Child and Adolescent Psychology, 32,* 139–152.

Lonigan, C. J., Elbert, J. C., & Johnson, S. B. (1998). Empirically supported psychosocial interventions for children: An overview. *Journal of Clinical Child Psychology, 27,* 138–145.

Loomis, J. W. (2006). Learning disabilities. In R. T. Ammerman, (Ed.) *Comprehensive handbook of personality and psychopathology* (pp. 272–284). Hoboken, NJ: Wiley.

Lopez, S. R., Hipke, K. N., & Polo, A. J. (2004). Ethnicity, expressed emotion, attributions, and course of schizophrenia: Family warmth matters. *Journal of Abnormal Psychology, 113,* 428–439.

Lord, C., & McGee, J. P. (2001). *Educating children with autism: Committee on Educational Interventions for Children With Autism.* Washington, DC: National Academy Press.

Lord, C., & Richler, J. (2006). Early diagnosis of children with autism spectrum disorders. In T. Charman & W. Stone (Eds.), *Social and communication development in autism spectrum disorders* (pp. 35–59). New York: Guilford Press.

Lovaas, O. I. (1987). Behavioral treatment and normal educational and intellectual functioning in young autistic children. *Journal of Consulting and Clinical Psychology, 55,* 3–9.

Lovaas, O. I., Cross, S., & Revlin, S. (2006). Autistic disorder. In J. E. Fisher & W. T. O'Donohue (Eds.). *Practitioner's guide to evidence-based psychotherapies* (pp. 101–114). New York: Springer.

Lovaas, O. I., Koegel, R. L., Simmons, J. Q., & Long, J. S. (1973). Some generalization and follow-up measures on autistic children in behavior therapy. *Journal of Applied Behavior Analysis, 6,* 131–166.

Lovaas, O. I., & Smith, T. (2003). Early and intensive behavioral intervention in autism. In A. E. Kazdin & J. R. Weisz (Eds.), *Evidence-based psychotherapies for children and adolescents* (pp. 325–340). New York: Guilford Press.

Lovejoy, M. C., Graczyk, P. A., O'Hare, E., & Neuman, G. (2000). Maternal depression and parenting behavior: A meta-analytic review. *Clinical Psychology Review, 20,* 561–592.

Lovejoy, M. C., Weis, R., O'Hare, E., & Rubin, E. C. (1999). Development and initial validation of the Parent Behavior Inventory. *Psychological Assessment, 11,* 534–545.

Luby, J. L., Belden, A. C., & Spitznagel, E. (2006). Risk factors for preschool depression: The mediating role of early stressful life events. *Journal of Child Psychology and Psychiatry, 47,* 1292–1298.

Luby, J. L., & Navsaria, N. (2010). Pediatric bipolar disorder: Evidence for prodromal states and early markers. *Journal of Child Psychology and Psychiatry, 51,* 459–471.

Lucarelli, L., Cimino, S., Petrocchi, M., & Ammaniti, M. (2007). Infantile anorexia: A longitudinal study on maternal and child psychopathology. *Scientific Program and Abstracts,* 25–27.

Lucka, I. (2006). Depressive disorders in patients suffering from anorexia nervosa. *Archives of Psychiatry and Psychotherapy, 8*(2), 55–61.

Luckasson, R., Borthwick-Duffy, S., Buntinx, W. H. E., Coulter, D. L., Craig, E. M., Reeve, A., et al. (2002). *Mental retardation: Definition, classification, and systems of support.* Washington, DC: American Association on Mental Retardation.

Luginbuehl, M., & Kohler, W.C. (2009). Screeing and evaluations for sleep disorders in children and adolescents. *Child and Adolescent Psychiatric Clinics of North America, 18,* 825–838.

Luman, M., van Meel, C. S., Oosterlaan, J., & Geurts, H. M. (2012). Reward and punishment sensitivity in children with ADHD. *Journal of Abnormal Child Psychology, 40,* 145–157.

Lundahl, B., Risser, H. J., & Lovejoy, M.C. (2006). A meta-analysis of parent training: Moderators and follow-up effects. *Clinical Psychology Review, 26,* 86–104.

Lundgren, J. D., Danoff-Burg, S., & Anderson, D. A. (2004). Cognitive-behavioral therapy for bulimia nervosa: An empirical analysis of clinical significance. *International Journal of Eating Disorders, 35,* 262–274.

Luntz, B., & Widom, C. S. (1994). Antisocial personality disorder in abused and neglected children grown up. *American Journal of Psychiatry, 151,* 670–674.

Luthar, S. S. (2006). Resilience in development: A synthesis of research across five decades. In D. Cicchetti & D. J. Cohen (Eds.), *Developmental psychopathology, Vol. 3: Risk, disorder, and adaptation* (pp. 739–795). Hoboken, NJ: Wiley.

Luthar, S. S., & Latendresse, J. (2005). Children of the affluent: Challenges to well-being. *Current Directions in Psychological Science, 14,* 49–53.

Lynch, T. R., & Cozza, C. (2009). Behavior therapy for nonsuicidal self-injury. In M. K. Nock (Ed.), *Understanding nonsuicidal self-injury* (pp. 221–249). Washington, DC: American Psychological Association.

Lyon, G. R., Fletcher, J. M., & Barnes, M. C. (2003). Learning disabilities. In E. J. Mash & R. A. Barkley (Eds.), *Child psychopathology* (2nd ed., pp. 520–588). New York: Guilford Press.

Maag, J. W., & Irvin, M. (2005). Alcohol use and depression among African-American and caucasian adolescents. *Adolescence, 40,* 87–101.

MacArthur, C., Graham, S., & Schwartz, S. (1991). Knowledge of revision and revising behavior among students with learning disabilities. *Learning Disability Quarterly, 14,* 61–74.

MacArthur, C. A., Philippakos, Z., Graham, S., & Harris, K. (2012). Writing instruction. In B. Wong & D. Butler (Eds.), *Learning about learning disabilities* (pp. 247–270). New York: Elsevier.

Maccoby, E. E., & Martin, J. A. (1983). Socialization in the context of the family: Parent–child interaction. In P. H. Mussen (Ed.) &

E. M. Hetherington (Vol. Ed.), *Handbook of child psychology: Vol. 4. Socialization, personality, and social development* (pp. 1–101). New York: Wiley.

MacMaster, F. P., & Kusumakar, V. (2004). MRI study of the pituitary gland in adolescent depression. *Journal of Psychiatric Research, 38,* 231–236.

MacPhee, A. R., & Andrews, W. (2006). Risk factors for depression in early adolescence. *Adolescence, 41,* 435–466.

Maehler, C., & Schuchardt, K. (2009). Working memory functioning in children with learning disabilities: Does intelligence make a difference? *Journal of Intellectual Disability Research, 53,* 3–10.

Maglione, M., Gans, D., Das, L., Timbie, J., & Kasari, C. (2012). Nonmedical interventions for children with ASD. *Pediatrics, 130,* s169–s178.

Maher, M. S. (1980). Group psychotherapy for anorexia nervosa. In P. S. Powers & R. C. Fernandez (Eds.), *Current treatment for anorexia nervosa and bulimia* (pp. 265–276). Basel, Switzerland: Karger.

Main, M., Kaplan, K., & Cassidy, J. (1985). Security in infancy, childhood and adulthood: A move to the level of representation. In I. Bretherton & E. Waters (Eds.), *Growing points of attachment theory and research, Monographs of the Society for Research in Child Development, 50*(1–2, Serial No. 209), 66–104.

Mak-Fan, K. M., Taylor, M. J., Roberts, W., & Lerch, J. P. (2012). Measures of cortical grey matter structure and development in children with autism spectrum disorder. *Journal of Autism and Developmental Disorders, 42,* 419–427.

Malkoff-Schwartz, S., Frank, E., Anderson, B., Sherrill, J. T., Siegel, L., Patterson, D., et al. (1998). Stressful life events and social rhythm disruption in the onset of manic and depressive bipolar episodes: A preliminary investigation. *Archives of General Psychiatry, 55,* 702–707.

Manassis, K. (2001). Child-parent relations: Attachment and anxiety disorders. In W. K. Silverman & P. D. A. Treffers (Eds.), *Anxiety disorders in children and adolescents* (pp. 255–272). New York: Cambridge University Press.

Manassis, K., Bradley, S., Goldberg, S., Hood, J., & Swinson, R. P. (1994). Attachment in mothers with anxiety disorders and their children. *Journal of the American Academy of Child & Adolescent Psychiatry, 33,* 1106–1113.

Mandlawitz, M. R. (2004). Educating children with autism: Current legal issues. In F. R. Volkmar, R. Paul, A. Klin, & D. Cohen (Eds.), *Handbook of autism and pervasive developmental disorders, Vol. 2: Assessment, interventions, and policy* (pp. 1161–1173). New York: Wiley.

Mandy, W. P. L., Charman, T., & Skuse, D. H. (2012). Testing the construct validity of proposed criteria for *DSM-5* autism spectrum disorder. *Journal of the American Academy of Child and Adolescent Psychiatry, 51,* 41–50.

Mannarino, A., & Cohen, J. (1996). Abuse-related attributions and perceptions, general attributions, and locus of control in sexually abused girls. *Journal of Interpersonal Violence, 11,* 162–180.

Manning, S. E., Davin, C. A., Barfield, W. D., Kotelchuck, M., Clements, K., Diopo, H., et al. (2011). Early diagnosis of autism spectrum disorders in Massachusetts birth cohorts. *Pediatrics, 127,* 1043–1051.

March, J. (1998). Cognitive behavioral psychotherapy for pediatric OCD. In M. Jenike, L. Baer, & W. E. Minichiello (Eds.), *Obsessive-compulsive disorders* (pp. 400–420). Philadelphia: Mosby.

March, J., & Wells, K. (2003). Combining medication and psychotherapy. In A. Martin, L. Scahill, D. S. Charney, & J. F. Leckman (Eds.), *Pediatric psychopharmacology: Principles and practice* (pp. 326–346). London: Oxford University Press.

March, J. S., Franklin, M. E., Leonard, H. L., & Foa, E. (2004). Obsessive-compulsive disorder. In T. L. Morris & J. S. March (Eds.), *Anxiety disorders in children and adolescents* (pp. 212–240). New York: Guilford Press.

March, J. S., Franklin, M., & Foa, E. (2005). Cognitive-behavioral psychotherapy for pediatric obsessive-compulsive disorder. In E. D. Hibbs & P. S. Jensen (Eds.), *Psychosocial treatments for child and adolescent disorders: Empirically based strategies for clinical practice* (pp. 121–142). Washington, DC: American Psychological Association.

March, J. S., Mulle, K., & Herbel, B. (1994). Behavioral psychotherapy for children and adolescents with obsessive-compulsive disorder: An open trial of a new protocol-driven treatment package. *Journal of the American Academy of Child and Adolescent Psychiatry, 33,* 333–341.

Marcus, M. D., & Kalarchian, M. A. (2003). Binge eating in children and adolescents. *International Journal of Eating Disorders, 34,* 47–57.

Margulies, D. M., Weintraub, S., Basile, J., Grover, P. J., & Carlson, G. A. (2012). Will disruptive mood dysregulation disorder reduce false diagnosis of bipolar disorder in children? *Bipolar Disorders, 14,* 488–496.

Markie-Dadds, C., & Sanders, R. (2006). Self-directed Triple P (positive parenting program) for mothers with children at risk of developing conduct problems. *Behavioural and Cognitive Psychotherapy, 34,* 259–275.

Marlatt, G. A., & Gordon, J. R. (1985). *Relapse prevention: Maintenance strategies in the treatment of addictive behaviors.* New York: Guilford Press.

Marmorstein, N. R., & Iacono, G. (2004). Major depression and conduct disorder in youth: Associations with parental psychopathology and parent-child conflict. *Journal of Child Psychology and Psychiatry, 45,* 377–386.

Maron, S., Munitz, H., Jones, P. B., Weizman, A., & Hermesh, H. (2005). Expressed emotion: Relevance to rehospitalization in schizophrenia over seven years. *Schizophrenia Bulletin, 31,* 751–758.

Marsh, P. J., & Williams, L. M. (2004). An investigation of individual typologies of attention deficit hyperactivity disorder using cluster analysis of *DSM-IV* criteria. *Personality and Individual Differences, 36,* 1187–1195.

Marshal, M. P., Molina, B. S. G., & Pelham, W. E. (2003). Childhood ADHD and adolescent substance use: An examination of deviant peer group affiliation as a risk factor. *Psychology of Addictive Behaviors, 17,* 293–302.

Martin, A., Scahill, L., Klin, A., & Volkmar, F. R. (1999). Higher-functioning pervasive developmental disorders: Rates and pattern of psychotropic drug use. *Journal of the American Academy of Child & Adolescent Psychiatry, 38,* 923–931.

Martin, C., & Dovey, T. M. (2011). Intensive intervention for childhood feeding disorders. In A. Southall & C. Martin (Eds.), *Feeding problems in children* (pp. 277–293). Oxon, UK: Radcliffe.

Martin, C. S., Chung, T., Kirisci, L., & Langenbucher, J. W. (2006). Item response theory analysis of diagnostic criteria for alcohol and cannabis use disorders in adolescents: Implications for DSM-V. *Journal of Abnormal Psychology, 115,* 807–814.

Martin, G., Bergen, H. A., Richardson, A. S., Roeger, L., & Allison, S. (2004). Sexual abuse and suicidality: Gender differences in a large community sample of adolescents. *Child Abuse & Neglect, 28,* 491–503.

Martin, R. R., Kuhl, P., & Haroldson, S. (1972). An experimental treatment with two preschool stuttering children. *Journal of Speech and Hearing Research, 15,* 743–752.

Martinussen, R., Hayden, J., Hogg-Johnson, S., & Tannock, R. (2005). A meta-analysis of working memory impairments in children with Attention-Deficit/Hyperactivity Disorder. *Journal of the American Academy of Child and Adolescent Psychiatry, 44,* 344–3854.

Maser, J. D., Norman, S. B., Zisook, S., Everall, I. P., Stein, M. B., Schettler, P. J., et al. (2009). Psychiatric nosology is ready for a paradigm shift in *DSM-5. Clinical Psychology: Science and Practice, 16,* 24–40.

Mash, E. J., & Johnston, C. (1990). Determinants of parenting stress: Illustrations from families of hyperactive children and families of physically abused children. *Journal of Clinical Psychology, 19,* 313–328.

Masi, G., Favilla, L., Mucci, M., & Millepiedi, S. (2000). Depressive comorbidity in children and adolescents with generalized anxiety disorder. *Child Psychiatry and Human Development, 30,* 205–215.

Masi, G., Millepiedi, S., Mucci, M., Poli, P., Bertini, N., & Milantoni, L. (2004). Generalized anxiety disorder in referred children and adolescents. *Journal of the American Academy of Child & Adolescent Psychiatry, 43,* 752–760.

Masi, G., Perugi, G., Millepiedi, S., Mucci, M., Toni, C., Bertini, N., et al. (2006). Developmental differences according to age at onset in juvenile bipolar disorder. *Journal of Child & Adolescent Psychopharmacology, 16,* 679–685.

Masi, G., Perugi, G., Toni, C., Millepiedi, S., Mucci, M., Bertini, N., & Akiskal, H. S. (2006). The clinical phenotypes of juvenile bipolar disorder. *Biological psychiatry, 59,* 603–610.

Mason, L. H., & Hagaman, J. L. (2012). Highlights in reading comprehension intervention research for students with learning disabilities. In B. Wong & D. Butler (Eds.), *Learning about learning disabilities* (pp. 191–215). New York: Elsevier.

Mason, T. B. A., & Pack, A. I. (2007). Pediatric parasomnias. *Sleep, 30,* 141–151.

Masten, A. S., Burt, K. B., & Coatsworth, J. D. (2006). Competence and psychopathology in development. In D. Cicchetti & D. J. Cohen (Eds.), *Developmental psychopathology, Vol 3: Risk, disorder, and adaptation* (pp. 696–738). Hoboken, NJ: Wiley.

Mather, N., & Wendling, B. J. (2011). *Essentials of dyslexia assessment and intervention.* New York: Wiley.

Matson, J. L., Sipes, M., Horovitz, M., Worley, S., Shoemaker, M., & Kozlowski, A.M. (2011). Behaviors and corresponding functions addressed via functional assessment. *Research in Developmental Disabilities, 32,* 625,629.

Mattai, A. K., Hill, J. L., & Lenroot, R. K. (2010). Treatment of early-onset schizophrenia. *Current Opinions in Psychiatry, 23,* 304–310.

Maughan, B., Rowe, R., Messer, J., Goodman, R., & Meltzer, H. (2004). Conduct disorder and oppositional defiant disorder in a national sample: Developmental epidemiology. *Journal of Child Psychology and Psychiatry, 45,* 609–621.

Maughan, B., & Rutter, M. (2010). Development and psychopathology: A life course perspective. In M. Rutter (Ed.), *Rutter's child and adolescent psychiatry* (pp. 160–182). Malden, NJ: Blackwell.

Maxfield, M. G., & Widom, C. S. (1996). The cycle of violence: Revisited six years later. *Archives of Pediatrics and Adolescent Medicine, 150,* 390–395.

Mayes, S. D., Black, A., & Tierney, C. D. (2013). *DSM-5* under-identifies PDDNOS. *Research in Autism Spectrum Disorders, 7,* 298–306.

Mayes, S. D., & Calhoun, L. (2006). Frequency of reading, math, and writing disabilities in children with clinical disorders. *Learning and Individual Differences, 16,* 145–157.

Mayes, S. D., Calhoun, S. L., Bixler, E. O., Vgontgas, A. N., Mahr, F., Hillwig-Garcia, J., et al. (2008). ADHD subtypes and comorbid anxiety, depression, and oppositional-defiant disorder. *Journal of Pediatric Psychology, 34,* 328–337.

Mazzocco, M. M., & McCloskey, M. (2005). Math performance in girls with Turner or fragile X syndrome. In J. I. D. Campbell (Ed.), *Handbook of mathematical cognition* (pp. 269–297). New York: Psychology Press.

Mazzocco, M. M., Pennington, B. F., & Hagerman, R. J. (1993). The neurocognitive phenotype of female carriers of fragile X: Further evidence for specificity. *Journal of Developmental and Behavioural Pediatrics, 14,* 328–335.

McBride, C., Atkinson, L., Quilty, L. C., & Bagby, R. M. (2006). Attachment as moderator of treatment outcome in major depression: A randomized control trial of interpersonal psychotherapy versus cognitive behavior therapy. *Journal of Consulting and Clinical Psychology, 74,* 1041–1054.

McBurnett, K. (1997). Attention-deficit/hyperactivity disorder: A review of diagnostic issues. In T. A. Widiger, A. J., Frances, H. A. Pincus, R. Ross, M. B. First, & W. Davis (Eds.), *DSM-IV sourcebook* (Vol. 3; pp. 111–143). Washington, DC: American Psychiatric Association.

McBurnett, K., Lahey, B. B., Rathouz, P. J., & Loeber, R. (2000). Low salivary cortisol and persistent aggression in boys referred for disruptive behavior. *Archives of General Psychiatry, 57,* 38–43.

McBurnett, K., Pfiffner, L. J., & Frick, P. J. (2001). Symptom properties as a function of ADHD type: An argument for continued study of the sluggish cognitive tempo. *Journal of Abnormal Child Psychology, 29,* 207–213.

McBurnett, K., Raine, A., Stouthamer-Loeber, M., Loeber, R., Kumar, A. M., Kumar, M., et al. (2005). Mood and hormone responses to psychological challenge in adolescent males with conduct problems. *Biological Psychiatry, 57,* 1109–1116.

McCabe, M. P., & Ricciardelli, A. (2001). Body image and body change techniques among young adolescent boys. *European Eating Disorders Review, 9,* 335–347.

McCall, R., & St. Petersburg-USA Orphanage Research Team (2008). The effects of early social-emotional and relationship experience on the development of young orphanage children. *Monographs of the Society for Research in Child Development, 73,* 1–297.

McCambridge, J., & Strang, J. (2004). The efficacy of single-session motivational interviewing in reducing drug consumption and perceptions of drug-related risk and harm among young people: Results from a multi-site cluster randomized trial. *Addiction, 99,* 39–52.

McCandliss, B., Cohen, L., & Dehaene, S. (2003). The visual word form area: Expertise in reading in the fusiform gyrus. *Trends in Cognitive Science, 7,* 293–299.

McCauley, E., Myers, K., Mitchell, J., Calderon, R., Schloredt, K., & Treder, R. (1993). Depression in young people: Initial presentation and clinical course. *Journal of the American Academy of Child and Adolescent Psychiatry, 32,* 714–722.

McClead, R. E., Menke, J. A., & Coury, D. L. (1996). Major technological breakthroughs in the diagnosis of mental retardation. In J. W. Jacobson & J. A. Mulick (Eds.), *Manual of diagnosis and professional practice in mental retardation* (pp. 179–190). Washington, DC: American Psychological Association.

McDermott, B., Forbes, D., Harris, C., McCormack, J., & Gibbon, P. (2006). Non-eating disorders psychopathology in children and adolescents with eating disorders: Implications for malnutrition and symptom severity. *Journal of Psychosomatic Research, 60,* 257–261.

McEachin, J. J., Smith, T., & Lovaas, O. I. (1993). Long-term outcome for children with autism who received early intensive behavioral treatment. *American Journal on Mental Retardation, 97,* 359–372.

McFall, R. M. (1991). Manifesto for a science of clinical psychology. *The Clinical Psychologist, 44,* 75–88.

McGoey, K. E., DuPaul, G. J., Eckert, T. L., Volpe, R. J., & van Brakle, J. (2005). Outcomes of a multi-component intervention for preschool children at-risk for attention-deficit/hyperactivity disorder. *Child and Family Behavior Therapy, 27,* 33–56.

McGorry, P. D., Yung, A. R., Phillips, L. J., Yuen, H. P., Francey, S., Cospgrave, E. M. et al. (2002). Randomized controlled trial of interventions designed to reduce the risk of progression to first-episode psychosis in a clinical sample with subthreshold symptoms. *Archives of General Psychiatry, 59,* 921–928.

McGough, J. J., Biederman, J., Wigal, S. B., Lopez, F. A., McCracken, J. T., Spencer, T., et al. (2005). Long-term tolerability and effectiveness of once-daily mixed amphetamine salts (Adderall XR) in children with ADHD. *Journal of the American Academy of Child and Adolescent Psychiatry, 44,* 530–538.

McGue, M., Iacono, W. G., Legrand, L. N., & Elkins, I. (2001). Origins and consequences of age at first drink II. Familial risk and heritability. *Alcoholism: Clinical and Experimental Research, 25,* 1166–1173.

McGue, M., Iacono, W. G., Legrand, L., Malone, S., & Elkins, I. (2001). Origins and consequences of age at first drink I. Associations with substance-use disorders, disinhibitory behavior and psychopathology, and P3 amplitude. *Alcoholism: Clinical and Experimental Research, 25,* 1156–1165.

McGue, M., Pickens, R. W., & Svikis, D. S. (1992). Sex and age effects on the inheritance of alcohol problems: A twin study. *Journal of Abnormal Psychology, 101,* 3–17.

McKee, T. E., Harvey, E., Danforth, J. S., Ulaszek, W. R., & Friedman, J. L. (2004). The relation between parental coping styles and parent-child interactions before and after treatment for children with ADHD and oppositional behavior. *Journal of Clinical Child and Adolescent Psychology, 33,* 158–168.

McKenzie, R. G. (2009). Obscuring vital distinctions: The oversimplification of learning disabilities within RTI. *Learning Disability Quarterly, 32,* 203–215.

McKnight, C. D., Compton, S. N., & March, J. S. (2004). Posttraumatic stress disorder. In T. L. Morris & J. S. March (Eds.), *Anxiety disorders in children and adolescents* (pp. 241–262). New York: Guilford Press.

McKnight Risk Factor Study. (2003). Risk factors for the onset of eating disorders in adolescent girls: Results of the McKnight Longitudinal Risk Factor Study. *American Journal of Psychiatry, 160,* 248–254.

McLaren, J., & Bryson, E. (1987). Review of recent epidemiological studies of mental retardation: Prevalence, associated disorders, and etiology. *American Journal on Mental Retardation, 92,* 243–254.

McLaughlin, K. A., Fox, N. A., Zeanah, C. H., Sheridan, M. A., Marshall, P., & Nelson, C. A. (2011). Delayed maturation in brain electrical activity partially explains the association between early environmental deprivation and symptoms of attention-deficit/hyperactivity disorder. *Biological Psychiatry, 68,* 329–336.

McLaughlin, K. A., Zeanah. C. H., Fox, N. A., & Nelson, C. A. (2012). Attachment security as a mechanism linking foster care placement to improved mental health outcomes in previously institutionalized children. *Journal of Child Psychology & Psychiatry, 53,* 46–55.

McLeer, S. V., Deblinger, E., Henry, D., & Orvaschel, H. (1992). Sexually abused children at high risk for post-traumatic stress disorder. *Journal of the American Academy of Adolescent and Child Psychiatry, 31,* 875–879.

McLoyd, V. C. (1998). Socioeconomic disadvantage and child development. *American Psychologist, 53,* 185–204.

McLoyd, V. C., Hill, N. E., & Dodge, K. A. (2005). *African American family life: Ecological and cultural diversity.* New York: Guilford Press.

McMahon, R. J., & Frick, J. (2005). Evidence-based assessment of conduct problems in children and adolescents. *Journal of Clinical Child and Adolescent Psychology, 34,* 477–505.

McNally, R. J. (2003). Progress and controversy in the study of posttraumatic stress disorder. *Annual Review of Psychology, 54,* 229–252.

McNally, R. J. (2009). Can we fix PTSD in DSM-5? *Depression and Anxiety, 26,* 597–600.

McPartland, J. C., Reichow, B., & Volkmar, F. R. (2012). Sensitivity and specificity of proposed *DSM-5* diagnostic criteria for autism spectrum disorder. *Journal of the American Academy of Child and Adolescent Psychiatry, 51,* 368–383.

McPheeters, M. L., Warren, Z., Sathe, N., Bruzek, J. L., Krishnaswami, S., Jerome, R. N., et al. (2011). A systematic review of medical treatments for children with autism spectrum disorders. *Pediatrics, 127,* 1312–1321.

McQuaid, E. L., & Abramson, N. W. (2009). Pediatric asthma. In M. C. Roberts & R. G. Steele (Eds.), *Handbook of pediatric psychology* (pp. 254–270). New York: Guilford.

Meiser-Stedman, R., Yule, W., Smith, P., Glucksman, E., & Dalgeish, T. (2005). Acute stress disorder and posttraumatic stress disorder in children and adolescents involved in assaults or motor vehicle accidents. *American Journal of Psychiatry, 162,* 1381–1383.

Melik, E., Babar-Melik, E., Ozgunen, T., & Binokay, S. (2000). Median raphe nucleus mediates forming long-term but not short-term contextual fear conditioning in rats. *Behavioural Brain Research, 112,* 145–150.

Mellon, M. W., & Houts, A. C. (2007). Home-based treatment for primary enuresis. In J. M. Briesmeister & C. E. Schaefer (Eds.), *Handbook of parent training* (pp. 429–466). New York: Wiley.

Meltzer, H., Gatward, R., Goodman, R., & Ford, T. (2003). Mental health of children and adolescents in Great Britain. *International Review of Psychiatry, 15,* 185–187.

Meltzer, L. J., & Mindell, J. A. (2008). Behavioral sleep disorders in children and adolescents. *Sleep Medicine Clinics, 3,* 269–279.

Mendenhall, A. N., Fristad, M. A., & Early, T. J. (2009). Factors influencing service utilization and mood symptom severity in children with mood disorders: Effects of Multifamily Psychoeducation Groups (MFPGs). *Journal of Consulting and Clinical Psychology, 77,* 463–473.

Merikangas, K. R. (2005). Vulnerability factors for anxiety disorders in children and adolescents. *Child and Adolescent Psychiatric Clinics of North America, 14,* 649–679.

Merikangas, K. R., & Pato, M. (2009). Recent developments in the epidemiology of bipolar disorder in adults and children. *Clinical Psychology: Science and Practice, 16,* 121–133.

Mervis, C. B. (2012). Language development in Williams Syndrome. In J. A. Burack, R. M. Hodapp, G. Iarocci, & E. Zigler (Eds.), *The Oxford handbook of intellectual disability and development* (pp. 217–237). New York: Oxford University Press.

Mesibov, G. (1997). Formal and informal measures on the effectiveness of the TEACCH program. *Autism, 1,* 25–35.

Mesibov, G. B., & Shea, V. (1996). Full inclusion and students with autism. *Journal of Autism and Developmental Disorders, 26,* 337–346.

Mesibov, G. B., Shea, V., & Schopler, E. (2005). *The TEACCH approach to autism spectrum disorders.* New York: Springer.

Metz, B., Mulick, J. A., & Butter, E. M. (2005). Autism: A late 20th-century fad magnet. In J. W. Jacobson, R. M. Foxx, & J. A. Mulick (Eds.), *Controversial therapies for developmental disabilities: Fad, fashion and science in professional practice* (pp. 237–263). Mahwah, NJ: Erlbaum.

Meyer, J. S., & Quenzer, L. F. (2005). *Psychopharmacology: Drugs, the brain, and behavior.* Sunderland, MA: Sinauer Associates.

Meyer, J., Rutter, M., Silberg, J., Maes, H., Simonoff, E., Shillady, L., et al. (2000). Familial aggregation for conduct disorder symptomatology: The role of genes, marital discord and family adaptability. *Psychological Medicine, 30,* 759–774.

Mezulis, A. H., Hyde, J. S., & Abramson, L. Y. (2006). The developmental origins of cognitive vulnerability to depression: Temperament, parenting, and negative life events in childhood as contributors to negative cognitive style. *Developmental Psychology, 42,* 1012–1025.

Mick, E., Biederman, J., Faraone, S. V., Sayer, J., & Kleinman, S. (2002). Case-control study of attention-deficit hyperactivity disorder and maternal smoking, alcohol use, and drug use during pregnancy. *Journal of the American Academy of Child and Adolescent Psychiatry, 41,* 378–385.

Mick, E., Spencer, T., Wozniak, J., & Biederman, J. (2005). Heterogeneity of irritability in attention-deficit/hyperactivity disorder subjects with and without mood disorders. *Biological Psychiatry, 58,* 576–582.

Mikkelsen, E. J. (2010). Elimination disorders. In M. K. Dulcan (Ed.), *Dulcan's textbook of child and adolescent psychiatry* (pp. 435–447). Washington, DC: American Psychiatric Publishing.

Miklowitz, D. J. (2008). *Bipolar disorder: A family-focused treatment approach.* New York: Guilford.

Miklowitz, D. J. (2012). Family-focused treatment for children and adolescents with bipolar disorder. *International Journal of Psychiatry and Related Sciences, 49,* 95–103.

Miklowitz, D. J., Axelson, D. A., Birmaher, B., George, E. L., Taylor, D. O., Schneck, C. D., et al. (2008). Family-focused treatment for adolescents with bipolar disorder. *Archives of General Psychiatry, 65,* 1053–1061.

Miklowitz, D. J., Chang, K. D., Taylor, D. O., George, E. L., Singh, M. K., Schneck, C. D., et al. (2011). Early psychosocial intervention for youth at risk for bipolar I or II disorder. *Bipolar Disorders, 13,* 67–75.

Miklowitz, D. J., Mullen, K. L., & Chang, K. D. (2008). Family-focused treatment for bipolar disorder in adolescence. In B. Geller & M. P. DelBello (Eds.), *Treatment of bipolar disorder in children and adolescents* (pp. 166–183). New York: Guilford.

Milin, R. (2008). Comorbidity of schizophrenia and substance use disorders in adolescents and young adults. In Y. Kaminer & O. G. Bukstein (Eds.), *Adolescent substance abuse* (pp. 355–378). New York: Routledge.

Milin, R., Walker, S., & Chow, J. (2003). Major depressive disorder in adolescence: A brief review of the recent treatment literature. *Canadian Journal of Psychiatry, 48,* 600–606.

Miller, A. L., Muehlenkamp, J. J., & Jacobson, C. M. (2009). Special issues in treating adolescent nonsuicidal self-injury. In M. K. Nock (Ed.), *Understanding nonsuicidal self-injury* (pp. 251–270). Washington, DC: American Psychological Association.

Miller, A. L., Rathus, J. H., & Linehan, M. M. (2006). *Dialectical behavior therapy with suicidal adolescents.* New York: Guilford.

Miller, B. A., & Mancuso, F. (2004). Connecting childhood victimization to later alcohol/drug problems: Implications for prevention. *Journal of Primary Prevention, 25,* 149–169.

Miller, E. T., Turner, A. P., & Marlatt, G. A. (2001). The harm reduction approach to the secondary prevention of alcohol problems in adolescents and young adults. In P. Monti, S. M. Colby, & T. A. O'Leary (Eds.), *Adolescents, alcohol, and substance abuse: Reaching teens through brief interventions* (pp. 58–79). New York: Guilford Press.

Miller, R., & Prosek, E. A. (2013). Trends and implications of proposed Changes to the *DSM-5* for vulnerable populations. Journal of Counseling & Development, 91, 359-366.

Miller, W. R., & Rollnick, S. (2002). *Motivational interviewing: Preparing people for change.* New York: Guilford Press.

Millichap, J. G. (2010). *Attention deficit hyperactivity disorder handbook.* New York: Springer.

Millward, C., Ferriter, M., Calver, S. J., & Connell-Jones, G. G. (2009). Gluten- and casein-free diets for autistic spectrum disorder. Cochrane Database of Systematic Reviews. Retrieved from http://www.ncbi.nlm.nih.gov/pubmed/18425890

Milos, G., Spindler, A., Hepp, U., & Schnyder, U. (2004). Suicide attempts and suicidal ideation: Links with psychiatric comorbidity in eating disorder subjects. *General Hospital Psychiatry, 26,* 129–135.

Mindell, J. A., Kuhn, B., Lewin, D. S., Meltzer, L. J., Sadeh, A., & American Academy of Sleep Medicine. (2006). Behavioral treatment of bedtime problems and night wakings in infants and young children. *Sleep, 29,* 1263–1276.

Mindell, J. A., Telpfski, L. S., Wiegand, B., & Kurtz, E. S. (2009). A nightly bedtime routine: Impact on sleep in young children. *Sleep, 32,* 599–606.

Minuchin, S. (1974). *Families and family therapy.* Cambridge, MA: Harvard University Press.

Minuchin, S., Rosman, B., & Baker, I. (1978). *Psychosomatic families: Anorexia nervosa in context.* Cambridge, MA: Harvard University Press.

Misener, V. L., Luca, P., Azeke, O., Crosbie, J., Waldman, I., Tannock, R., et al. (2004). Linkage of the dopamine receptor D1 gene to attention-deficit/hyperactivity disorder. *Molecular Psychiatry, 9,* 500–509.

Missale, C., Nash, S. R., Robinson, S. W., Jaber, M., & Caron, M. G. (1998). Dopamine receptors: From structure to function. *Physiological Review, 78,* 189–225.

Moffitt, T. E. (1993). Adolescence-limited and life-course persistent antisocial behavior: A developmental taxonomy. *Psychological Review, 100,* 674–701.

Moffitt, T. E. (2003). Life-course persistent and adolescence-limited antisocial behavior: A 10-year research review and research agenda. In B. B. Lahey, T. E. Moffitt, & A. Caspi (Eds.), *Causes of conduct disorder and juvenile delinquency* (pp. 49–75). New York: Guilford Press.

Moffitt, T. E., & Caspi, A. (2001). Childhood predictors differentiate life-course persistent and adolescence-limited antisocial pathways in males and females. *Development & Psychopathology, 13,* 355–376.

Moffitt, T. E., Caspi, A., & Harrington, H. (2007). Generalized anxiety disorder and depression: Childhood risk factors in a birth cohort followed to age 32. *Psychological Medicine, 37,* 441–452.

Moffitt, T. E., Caspi, A., Harrington, H., & Milne, B. (2002). Males on the life-course persistent and adolescence-limited antisocial pathways: Follow-up at age 26. *Development and Psychopathology, 14,* 179–206.

Moffitt, T. E., Caspi, A., Rutter, M., & Silva, P. A. (2001). *Sex differences in antisocial behaviour: Conduct disorder, delinquency, and violence in the Dunedin Longitudinal Study.* Cambridge, UK: Cambridge University Press.

Monroe, B. W., & Troia, A. (2006). Teaching writing strategies to middle school students with disabilities. *Journal of Educational Research, 100,* 21–33.

Monroe, S. M., Rhode, P., Seeley, J. R., & Lewinsohn, P. M. (1999). Life events and depression in adolescence: Relationship loss as a prospective risk factor for the first onset major depressive disorder. *Journal of Abnormal Psychology, 108,* 606–614.

Montgomery, C. S. (2006). The treatment of stuttering: From the hub to the spoke. In N.B. Ratner & J. Tetnowski (Eds.), *Current issues in stuttering research and practice* (pp. 159–204). Mahwah, NJ: Erlbaum.

Monti, P. M., Barnett, N. P., O'Leary, T. A., & Colby, S. M. (2001). Motivational enhancement for alcohol-involved adolescents. In P. M. Monti, S. M. Colby, & T. A. O'Leary (Eds.), *Adolescents, alcohol, and substance abuse: Reaching teens through brief interventions* (pp. 145–182). New York: Guilford Press.

Monti, P. M., Colby, S. M., Barnett, N. P., Spirito, A., Rohsenow, D. J., Myers, M., et al. (1999). Brief intervention for harm reduction with alcohol-positive older adolescents in a hospital emergency department. *Journal of Consulting and Clinical Psychology, 67,* 989–994.

Monuteaux, M. C., Fitzmaurice, G., Blacker, D., Buka, S. L., & Biederman, J. (2004). Specificity in the familial aggregation of overt and covert conduct disorder symptoms in a referred attention-deficit hyperactivity disorder sample. *Psychological Medicine, 34,* 1113–1127.

Moore, M., Meltzer, L. J., & Mindell, J. A. (2007). Bedtime problems and night wakings in children. *Sleep Medicine Clinics, 2,* 377–385.

Moore, P. S., Whaley, S. E., & Sigman, M. (2004). Interactions between mothers and children: Impacts of maternal and child anxiety. *Journal of Abnormal Psychology, 113,* 471–476.

Moran, M. (2013). Trauma disorder criteria reflect variability of response to events. *Psychiatric News, 48,* 6–7.

Moran, P., Rowe, R., Flach, C., Briskman, J., Ford, T., Maughan, B., et al. (2009). Predictive value of callous-unemotional traits in a large community sample. *Journal of the American Academy of Child and Adolescent Psychiatry, 48,* 1079–1084.

Moreno, C., Laje, G., Blanco, C., Jiang, H., Schmidt, A. B., & Olfson, M. (2007). National trends in the outpatient diagnosis and treatment of bipolar disorder in youth. *Archives of general psychiatry, 64,* 1032.

Morris, R. D., Lovett, M. W., Wolf, M., Sevcik, R. A., Steinbach, K. A., Frijters, J. C., & Shapiro, M. B. (2012). Multiple-component remediation for developmental reading disabilities. *Journal of Learning Disabilities, 45,* 99–127.

Morris, T. L. (2004). Social development. In T. L. Morris & J. S. March (Eds.), *Anxiety disorders in children and adolescents* (pp. 59–70). New York: Guilford Press.

Mostofsky, S., Cooper, K., Kates, W., Denckla, M., & Kaufmann, W. (2002). Smaller prefrontal and premotor volumes in boys with attention-deficit/hyperactivity disorder. *Biological Psychiatry, 52,* 785–794.

Motta, R. W., & Basile, D. M. (1998). Pica. In L. Phelps (Ed.), *Health-related disorders in children and adolescents* (pp. 524–527). Washington, DC: American Psychological Association.

Mowrer, O. (1960). *Learning theory and behavior.* New York: Wiley.

MTA Cooperative Group. (1999). A 14-month randomized clinical trial of treatment strategies for attention-deficit/hyperactivity disorder. (Multimodal Treatment Study of Children with ADHD; MTA Study). *Archives of General Psychiatry, 56,* 1073–1086.

Muehlenkamp, J. J., Claes, L., Havertape, L., & Plener, P. L. (2012). International prevalence of adolescent non-suicidal self-injury and deliberate self-harm. *Child and Adolescent Psychiatry and Mental Health, 6,* 1–9.

Muehlenkamp, J. J., & Gutierrez, M. (2004). An investigation of differences between self-injurious behavior and suicide attempts in a sample of adolescents. *Suicide and Life-Threatening Behavior, 34,* 12–23.

Muehlenkamp, J. J., & Gutierrez, P. M. (2007). Risk for suicide attempts among adolescents who engage in non-suicidal self-injury. *Archives of Suicide Research, 11,* 69–82.

Mueller, M. M., Piazza, C. C., Moore, J. W., Kelley, M. E., Bethke, S. A., Pruett, A. E., et al. (2003). Training parents to implement pediatric feeding protocols. *Journal of Applied Behavior Analysis, 36,* 545–562.

Mufson, L., & Pollack Dorta, K. (2003). Interpersonal psychotherapy for depressed adolescents. In A. E. Kazdin & J. R. Weisz (Eds.), *Evidence-based psychotherapies for children and adolescents* (pp. 148–164). New York: Guilford Press.

Mufson, L., Pollack Dorta, K., Moreau, D., & Weissman, M. M. (2005). Efficacy to effectiveness: Adaptations of interpersonal psychotherapy for adolescent depression. In E. D. Hibbs & P. S. Jensen (Eds.), *Psychosocial treatments for child and adolescent disorders: Empirically based strategies for clinical practice* (pp. 165–186). Washington, DC: American Psychological Association.

Mufson, L., Pollack Dorta, K., Wickramaratne, P., Nomura, Y., Olfson, M., & Weissman, M. M. (2004). A randomized effectiveness trial of interpersonal psychotherapy for depressed adolescents. *Archives of General Psychiatry, 61,* 577–584.

Mufson, L., Weissman, M. M., Moreau, D., & Garfinkel, R. (1999). Efficacy of interpersonal psychotherapy for depressed adolescents. *Archives of General Psychiatry, 56,* 573–579.

Mullen, P. E., Martin, J. L., Anderson, J. C., Romans, S. E., & Herbison, G. P. (1994). The effect of child sexual abuse on social, interpersonal and sexual function in adult life. *British Journal of Psychiatry, 165,* 35–47.

Mundy, P., & Burnette, C. (2005). Joint attention and neurodevelopmental models of autism. In F. R. Volkmar, R. Paul, A. Klin, & D. Cohen (Eds.), *Handbook of autism and pervasive developmental disorders, Vol. 1: Diagnosis, development, neurobiology, and behavior* (pp. 650–681). Hoboken, NJ: Wiley.

Murberg, T. A., & Bru, E. (2005). The role of coping styles as predictors of depressive symptoms among adolescents: A prospective study. *Scandinavian Journal of Psychology, 46,* 385–393.

Muris, P., Mayer, P., & Meesters, C. (2000). Self-reported attachment style, anxiety, and depression in children. *Social Behavior and Personality, 28,* 157–162.

Muris, P., Merckelbach, H., Gadet, B., & Moulaert, V. (2000). Fears, worries, and scary dreams in 4- to 12-year-old children: Their content, developmental pattern, and origins. *Journal of Clinical Child Psychology, 29,* 43–52.

Muris, P., Merckelbach, H., Mayer, B., & Meesters, C. (1998). Common fears and their relationship to anxiety disorders symptomatology in normal children. *Personality and Individual Differences, 24,* 575–578.

Murnen, S. K., Smolak, L., Mills, I. A., & Good, L. (2003). Thin, sexy women and strong, muscular men: Grade-school children's responses to objectified images of women and men. *Sex Roles, 49,* 427–437.

Murnen, S., & Smolak, L. (1998). Femininity, masculinity, and disordered eating: A meta-analytic approach. *International Journal of Eating Disorders, 22,* 231–242.

Murphy, T. K., Kurlan, R., & Leckman, J. (2010).The immunobiology of Tourette's disorder, pediatric autoimmune neuropsychiatric disorders associated with Streptococcus, and related disorders: A way forward. *Journal of Child and Adolescent Psychopharmacology, 20,* 317–331.

Nace, E. P. (2005). Alcohol. In R. J. Frances, S. I. Miller, & A. H. Mack (Eds.), *Clinical textbook of addictive disorders* (pp. 75–104). New York: Guilford Press.

Nadder, T. S., Rutter, M., Silberg, J. L., Maes, H. H., & Eaves, L. J. (2002). Genetic effects on the variation and covariation of attention deficit-hyperactivity disorder (ADHD) and oppositional-defiant disorder/conduct disorder (ODD/CD) symptomalogies across informant and occasion of measurement. *Psychological Medicine, 32,* 39–53.

Nadel, J., & Aouka, N. (2006). Imitation: Some cues for intervention approaches in autism spectrum disorders. In T. Charman & W. Stone (Eds.), *Social and communication development in autism spectrum disorders* (pp. 219–235). New York: Guilford Press.

Nadkarni, R. B., & Fristad, M. A. (2010). Clinical course of children with a depressive spectrum disorder and transient manic symptoms. *Bipolar Disorders, 12,* 494–503.

Najjar, F., Welch, C., Grapentine, W. L., Sachs, H., Siniscalchi, J., & Price, L. H. (2004). Trends in psychotropic drug use in a child psychiatric hospital from 1991-1998. *Journal of Child and Adolescent Psychopharmacology, 14,* 87–93.

Narash-Eisikovits, O., Dierberger, A., & Westen, D. (2002). A multidimensional meta-analysis of pharmacotherapy for bulimia nervosa: Summarizing the range of outcomes in controlled clinical trials. *Harvard Review of Psychiatry, 10,* 193–211.

Nathan, P. E., & Gorman, J. M. (2002). *A guide to treatments that work.* New York: Oxford University Press.

Nation, K., & Penny, S. (2008). Sensitivity to eye gaze in autism. *Development and Psychopathology, 20,* 79

National Center for Educational Statistics. (2003). *National assessment of educational progress: The nation's report card.* Washington, DC: U.S. Department of Education.

National Institute for Health and Clinical Excellence (2005). *Post Traumatic Stress Disorder, National Clinical Practice Guideline Number 26.* London: Author.

National Institute on Child Health and Human Development (NICHD). (2010). *Speech and language developmental milestones.* Bethesda, MD: Author

National Institute on Drug Abuse. (2013). *ASSIST.* Bethesda, MD: Author.

National Reading Panel. (2000). *Teaching children to read: An evidence-based assessment of the scientific research literature on reading and its implications for reading instruction.* Washington, DC: National Institute of Child Health and Human Development.

Nelson, C. A., Bos, K., Gunnar, M. R., & Sonuga-Barke, E. J. (2011). V. The neurobiological toll of early human deprivation. *Monographs of the Society for Research in Child Development, 76,* 127–146.

Nelson, C. A., Furtado, E. A., Fox, N. A., & Zeanah, C. H. (2009). The deprived human brain. *American Scientist, 97,* 222–229.

Nelson, C. A., Zeanah, C. H., Fox, N. A., Marshall, P. J., Smyke, A. T., & Guthrie, D. (2007). Cognitive recovery in socially deprived young children. *Science, 318,* 1937–1940.

Nelson, J. M., Harwood, H. (2011). Learning disabilities and anxiety: A meta-analysis. *Journal of Learning Disabilities, 44,* 3–17.

Nelson, J. R., Benner, G. J., & Gonzalez, J. (2003). Learner characteristics that influence the treatment effectiveness of early literacy interventions: A meta-analytic review. *Learning Disabilities Research and Practice, 18,* 255–267.

Nemeroff, R., Gipson, P., & Jensen, P. (2004). From efficacy to effectiveness research: What we have learned over the last 10 years. In T. H. Ollendick & J. S. March (Eds.), *Phobic and anxiety disorders in children and adolescents: A clinician's guide to effective psychosocial and pharmacological interventions* (pp. 476–505). New York: Oxford University Press.

Newberger, D. S. (2000). Down syndrome: Prenatal risk assessment and diagnosis. *American Family Physician, 62,* 825–832.

Newbury, D. F., Bishop, D. V., & Monaco, A. P. (2005). Genetic influences on language impairment and phonological short-term memory. *Trends in cognitive sciences, 9,* 528–534.

Newcorn, J. H., Halperin, J. M., Jensen, P. S., Abikoff, H. B., Arnold, L. E. Cantwell, D. P., et al. (2001). Symptom profiles in children with ADHD: Effects of comorbidity and gender. *Journal of the American Academy of Child and Adolescent Psychiatry, 40,* 137–146.

Newman, C. F. (2009). Cognitive therapy for nonsuicidal self-injury. In M. K. Nock (Ed.), *Understanding nonsuicidal self-injury* (pp. 201–219). Washington, DC: American Psychological Association.

Newsom, C., & Hovanitz, C. A. (2005). The nature and value of empirically validated interventions. In J. W. Jacobson, R. M. Foxx, & J. A. Mulick (Eds.), *Controversial therapies for developmental disabilities: Fad, fashion and science in professional practice* (pp. 31–44). Mahwah, NJ: Erlbaum.

Nigg, J. T. (2001). Is ADHD a disinhibitory disorder? *Psychological Bulletin,127,* 571.

Nigg, J. T. (2006). Temperament and developmental psychopathology. *Journal of Child Psychology and Psychiatry, 47,* 395–422.

Nigg, J. T., Hinshaw, S. P., & Huang-Pollock, C. (2006). Disorders of attention and impulse regulation. In D. Cicchetti & D. J. Cohen (Eds.), *Developmental psychopathology, Vol. 3: Risk, disorder, and adaptation* (pp. 358–403). Hoboken, NJ: Wiley.

Nikolas, M. A., & Burt, S. A. (2010). Genetic and environmental influences of ADHD symptom dimensions of inattention and hyperactivity. *Journal of Abnormal Psychology, 119,* 1–17.

Niles, A. N., Lebeau, R. T., Liao, B., Glenn, D. E., & Craske, M. G. (2012). Dimensional indicators of generalized anxiety disorder severity for *DSM-5. Journal of Anxiety Disorders, 26,* 279–286.

Nixon, R. D. V. (2002). Treatment of behavior problems in preschoolers: A review. *Clinical Psychology Review, 22,* 525–546.

Nixon, R. D. V., Sweeney, L., Erickson, D. B., & Touyz, S. W. (2003). Parent-child interaction therapy: A comparison of standard and abbreviated treatments for oppositional defiant preschoolers. *Journal of Consulting and Clinical Psychology, 71,* 251–260.

Nixon, R. D. V., Sweeney, L., Erickson, D. B., & Touyz, S. W. (2004). Parent-child interaction therapy: One- and two-year follow-up of standard and abbreviated treatments for oppositional preschoolers. *Journal of Abnormal Child Psychology, 32,* 263–271.

Nock, M. K. (2009). Why do people hurt themselves? New insights into the nature and functions of self-injury. *Current Directions in Psychological Science, 18,* 78–83.

Nock, M. K. (2010). Self-injury. *Annual Review of Clinical Psychology, 6,* 339–363.

Nock, M. K., Borges, G., Bromet, E. J., Cha, C. B., Kessler, R. C., & Lee, S. (2008). Suicide and suicidal behavior. *Epidemiologic Reviews, 30,* 133–154.

Nock, M. K., & Cha, C. B. (2009). Psychological models of nonsuicidal self injury. In M. K. Nock (Ed.), *Understanding nonsuicidal self injury* (pp. 65–77). Washington, DC: American Psychological Association.

Nock, M. K., Joiner Jr., T. E., Gordon, K. H., Lloyd-Richardson, E., & Prinstein, M. J. (2006). Non-suicidal self-injury among adolescents: Diagnostic correlates and relation to suicide attempts. *Psychiatry Research, 144,* 65–72.

Nock, M. K., & Prinstein, M. J. (2004). A functional approach to the assessment of self-mutilative behavior. *Journal of Consulting and Clinical Psychology, 72,* 885.

Nock, M. K., & Prinstein, M. J. (2005). Contextual features and behavioral functions of self-mutilation among adolescents. *Journal of Abnormal Psychology, 114,* 140.

Nolen-Hoeksema, S. (2000). The role of rumination in depressive disorders and mixed anxiety/depressive symptoms. *Journal of Abnormal Psychology, 109,* 504–511.

Nolen-Hoeksema, S., Girgus, J. S., & Seligman, M. E. (1992). Predictors and consequences of childhood depressive symptoms: A 5-year longitudinal study. *Journal of Abnormal Psychology, 101,* 405–422.

Norris, F. H. (2007). Impact of mass shootings on survivors, families, and communities. *PTSD Research Quarterly, 18,* 1–8.

Norton, E. S., & Wolf, M. (2012). Rapid Automatized Naming (RAN) and reading fluency. *Annual Review of Psychology, 63,* 427–452.

Novaco, R. W. (1975). *Anger control: The development and evaluation of an experimental treatment.* Lexington, MA: Heath.

Nowicki, E. A. (2003). A meta-analysis of the social competence of children with learning disabilities compared to classmates of low and average to high achievement. *Learning Disability Quarterly,* 171–188.

Nugent, K. L., Daniels, A. M., & Azur, M. J. (2012). Correlates of schizophrenia spectrum disorders in children and adolescents cared for in community settings. *Child and Adolescent Mental Health, 17,* 101–108.

Nugter, M. A., Dingemans, P. M., Linszen, D. H., van der Does, A. J., Gersons, B. P. (1997). Parental communication deviance: Its stability and the effect of family treatment in recent-onset schizophrenia. *Acta Psychiatrica Scandanavica, 95,* 199–204.

Nye, C., & Brice, A. (2009). Combined vitamin B6-magnesium treatment in autism spectrum disorder. *Cochrane Database of Systematic Reviews.*

O'Brien, B. A., Wolf, M., & Lovett, M. W. (2012). A toxometric investigation of developmental dyslexia subtypes. *Dyslexia, 18,* 16–39.

O'Brien, C. (2011). Addiction and dependence in *DSM-5. Addiction, 106,* 866–867.

O'Brien, C. P., Anthony, J. C., Carroll, K., Childress, A. R., Dackis, C., Diamond, G., et al. (2005). Substance use disorders. In D. L. Evans, E. B. Foa, R. E. Gur, et al. (Eds.), *Treating and preventing adolescent mental health disorders: What we know and what we don't know: A research agenda for improving the mental health of our youth* (pp. 335–426). New York: Oxford University Press.

O'Brien, L. M. (2009). The neurocognitive effects of sleep disruption in children and adolescents. *Child and Adolescent Psychiatric Clinics of North America, 18,* 813–823.

O'Brien, M. P., Gordon, J. L., Bearden, C. E., Lopez, S. R., Kopelowicz, A., & Cannon, T. D. (2006). Positive family environment predicts improvement in symptoms and social functioning among adolescents at imminent risk for onset of psychosis. *Schizophrenia Research, 81,* 269–275.

O'Connor, T. G. (2003). Early experiences and psychological development: Conceptual questions, empirical illustrations, and implications for intervention. *Development and Psychopathology, 15,* 671–690.

Odlaug, B. L., Lust, K., Schreiber, L. R. N., Christenson, G., Derbyshire, K., & Grant, J. E. (2013). Skin picking disorder in university students: Health correlates and gender differences. *General Hospital Psychiatry, 35,* 168–173.

Offord, D. R., Boyle, M. H., Szatmari, P., Rae-Grant, N. I., Links, P. S., Cadman, D. T., et al. (1987). Ontario child health study: II. Six-month prevalence of disorder and rates of service utilization. *Archives of General Psychiatry, 44,* 832–836.

Olfson, M., Gameroff, M. J., Marcus, S. C., & Jensen, P. S. (2003). National trends in the treatment of attention deficit hyperactivity disorder. *American Journal of Psychiatry, 160,* 1071–1077.

Olfson, M., Gerhard, T., Huang, C., Lieberman, J. A., Bobo, W. V., & Crystal, S. (2011). Comparative effectiveness of second-generation antipsychotic medications in early-onset schizophrenia. *Schizophrenia Bulletin*, Advance Access.

Olfson, M., Marcus, S. C., Weissman, M. M., & Jensen, P. S. (2002). National trends in the use of psychotropic medications by children. *Journal of the American Academy of Child & Adolescent Psychiatry, 41,* 514–521.

Ollendick, T. H., Birmaher, B., & Mattis, S. G. (2004). Panic Disorder. In T. L. Morris & J. S. March (Eds.), *Anxiety disorders in children and adolescents* (pp. 189–211). New York: Guilford Press.

Ollendick, T. H., & King, N. J. (1998). Empirically supported treatments for children with phobic and anxiety disorders. *Journal of Clinical Child Psychology, 27,* 156–167.

Ollendick, T. H., Mattis, S. G., & King, N. J. (1994). Panic in children and adolescents: A review. *Journal of Child Psychology and Psychiatry, 35,* 113–134.

Osterling, J., & Dawson, G. (1994). Early recognition of children with autism: A study of first birthday home videotapes. *Journal of Autism and Developmental Disorders, 24,* 247–257.

Owens, J. A. (2007). Classification and epidemiology of childhood sleep disorders. *Sleep Medicine Clinics, 2,* 353–361.

Owens, J. A., Brown, T. E., Modestino, E. J. (2009). ADHD with sleep/arousal disturbances. In T. E. Brown (Ed.), *ADHD comorbidities* (pp. 279–291). Arlington, VA: American Psychiatric Publishing.

Owens, J. A., & Burnham, M. M. (2009). Sleep disorders. In C. H. Zeanah (Ed.), *Handbook of infant mental health* (pp. 362–391). New York: Guilford.

Owens, J., & Hoza, B. (2003). Diagnostic utility of *DSM-IV*-TR symptoms in the prediction of *DSM-IV*-TR ADHD subtypes and ODD. *Journal of Attention Disorders, 7,* 11–27.

Owens, J. A., & Moturi, S. (2009). Phramacologic treatment of pediatric insomnia. *Child and Adolescent Psychiatric Clinics of North America, 18,* 1001–1016.

Ozechowski, T. J., & Liddle, A. (2000). Family-based therapy for adolescent drug abuse: Knowns and unknowns. *Clinical Child and Family Psychology Review, 3,* 269–298.

Ozonoff, S. (2012). *DSM-5* and autism spectrum disorders. *Journal of Child Psychology and Psychiatry, 53,* 4–6.

Ozonoff, S., & Cathcart, K. (1998). Effectiveness of a home program intervention for young children with autism. *Journal of Autism and Developmental Disorders, 28,* 25–32.

Ozonoff, S., Cook, I., Coon, H., Dawson, G., Joseph, R. M., Klin, A., et al. (2004). Performance on Cambridge Neuropsychological Test automated battery subtests sensitive to frontal lobe function in people with autistic disorder: Evidence from the Collaborative Programs of Excellence in Autism Network. *Journal of Autism and Developmental Disorders, 34,* 139–150.

Ozonoff, S., Young, G.S., Carter, A., Messinger, D., Yirmiya, N., Zwaigenbaum, L., et al. (2011). Recurrence risk for autism spectrum disorders: A baby siblings research consortium study. *Pediatrics, 128,* 488–495.

Paavonen, E. J., Porkka-Heiskanen, T., & Lahikainen, A. R. (2009). Sleep quality, duration, and behavioral symptoms among 5–6-year-old children. *European Child and Adolescent Psychiatry, 18,* 747–754.

Palacios, E. D., & Semrud-Clikeman, M. (2005). Delinquency, hyperactivity, and phonological awareness: A comparison of adolescents with ODD and ADHD. *Applied Neuropsychology, 12,* 94–105.

Palmen, S., & van Engeland, H. (2012). The relationship between Autism and Schizophrenia. In M. E. Garralda & J. Raynaud (Eds.), *Brain, mind, and developmental psychopathology in childhood* (pp. 123–143). Lanham, MD: Aronson.

Palmer, E. J. (2007). Moral cognition and aggression. In T. A. Gannon, T. Ward, A. R. Beech, & D. Fisher (Eds.), *Aggressive offenders' cognition* (pp. 199–214). New York: Wiley.

Papolos, D., & Papolos, J. (2000). *The bipolar child.* New York: Broadway.

Pardini, D. A., & Fite, P. J. (2010). Symptoms of conduct disorder, oppositional defiant disorder, attention-deficit/hyperactivity disorder, and callous-unemotional traits as unique predictors of psychosocial maladjustment in boys. *Journal of the American Academy of Child and Adolescent Psychiatry, 49,* 1134–1144.

Pardini, D. A., Lochman, J. E., & Frick, P. J. (2003). Callous/unemotional traits and social cognitive processes in adjudicated youth. *Journal of the American Academic of Child and Adolescent Psychiatry, 42,* 364–371.

Parens, E., & Johnston, J. (2010). Controversies concerning the diagnosis and treatment of bipolar disorder in children. *Child and Adolescent Psychiatry and Mental Health, 4,* 1–14.

Parker, J. G., Rubin, K. H., Erath, S. A., Wojslawosicz, J. C., & Buskirk, A. A. (2006). In D. Cicchetti & D. J. Cohen (Eds.), *Developmental psychopathology, Vol. 1: Theory and method* (2nd ed., pp. 419–493). Hoboken, NJ: Wiley.

Parker, J. S., & Benson, J. (2005). Parent-adolescent relations and adolescent functioning: Self-esteem, substance abuse, and delinquency. *Family Therapy, 32,* 131–142.

Parloff, M. B. (1984). Psychotherapy research and its incredible credibility crisis. *Clinical Psychology Review, 4,* 95–109.

Patel, N. C., DelBello, M. P., Keck, P. E., & Strakowski, S. M. (2006). Phenomenology associated with age at onset in patients with bipolar disorder at their first psychiatric hospitalization. *Bipolar Disorders, 8,* 91–94.

Patterson, G. R., & Capaldi, D. M. (1991). Antisocial parents: Unskilled and vulnerable. In P. A. Cowan & E. M. Hetherington (Eds.), *Family transitions* (pp. 195–218). Hillsdale, NJ: Erlbaum.

Patterson, G. R., DeGarmo, D. S., & Knutson, N. (2000). Hyperactive and antisocial behaviors: Comorbid or two points in the same process? *Development and Psychopathology, 12,* 91–107.

Patterson, G. R., Reid, J. B., & Dishion, T. J. (1992). *Antisocial boys.* Eugene, OR: Castalia.

Patterson, G. R., & Yoerger, K. (2002). A developmental model for early- and late-onset delinquency. In J. B. Reid, G. R. Patterson & J. Snyder (Eds.), *Antisocial behavior in children and adolescents: A developmental analysis and model for intervention* (pp. 147–172). Washington, DC: American Psychological Association.

Patterson, H. O., & O'Connell, D. F. (2003). Recovery maintenance and relapse prevention with chemically dependent adolescents. In

M. A. Reinecke, F. M. Dattilio, & A. Freeman (Eds.), *Cognitive therapy with children and adolescents* (pp. 70–94). New York: Guilford Press.

Patterson, T., & Kaslow, F. W. (Eds.). (2004). *Comprehensive handbook of psychotherapy: Cognitive-behavioral approaches.* New York: Wiley.

Patton, G. C., Coffey, C., Carlin, J. B., Degenhardt, L., Lynskey, M. T., & Hall, W. D. (2002). Cannabis use and mental health in young people: Cohort study. *British Medical Journal, 525,* 1195–1198.

Pauly, H., Linkersdorfer, J., Lindberg, S., Woerner, W., Hasselhorn, M., & Lonnemann, J. (2011). Domain-specific rapid automatized naming deficits in children at risk for learning disabilities. *Journal of Neurolinguistics, 24,* 602–610.

Pavuluri, M. N., Graczyk, P. A., Henry, D. B., Carbray, J. A., Heidenreich, J., & Miklowitz, D. J. (2004). Child- and family-focused cognitive-behavioral therapy for pediatric bipolar disorder. *Journal of the American Academy of Child and Adolescent Psychiatry, 43,* 528–537.

Pears, K. C., Bruce, J., Fisher, P. A., & Kim, H. K. (2010). Indiscriminate friendliness in maltreated foster children. *Child Maltreatment, 15,* 64–75

Pearson, M., Sweeting, H., West, P., Young, R., Gordon, J., & Turner, K. (2006). Adolescent substance use in different social and peer contexts: A social network analysis. *Drugs: Education, Prevention & Policy, 13,* 519–536.

Pediatric OCD Treatment Study Team (POTS). (2004). Cognitive-behavior therapy, sertraline, and their combination for children and adolescents with obsessive-compulsive disorder. *Journal of the American Medical Association, 292,* 1969–1976.

Pelham, W. E., & Bender, M. E. (1982). Peer relationships in hyperactive children: Description and treatment. In K. Gadow & I. Bailer (Eds.), *Advances in learning and behavioral disabilities* (Vol. 1, pp. 365–436). Greenwich, CT: JAI Press.

Pelham, W. E., Carlson, C., Sams, S. E., Dixon, M. J., & Hoza, B. (1993). Separate and combined effects of methylphenidate and behavior modification on boys with attention-deficit hyperactivity disorder in the classroom. *Journal of Consulting and Clinical Psychology, 61,* 506–515.

Pelham, W. E., Fabiano, G. A., Gnagy, E. M., Greiner, A. R., & Hoza, B. (2005). The role of summer treatment programs in the context of comprehensive treatment for attention-deficit/hyperactivity disorder. In E. D. Hibbs & P. S. Jensen (Eds.), *Psychosocial treatments for child and adolescent disorders: Empirically based strategies for clinical practice* (pp. 377–409). Washington, DC: American Psychological Association.

Pelham, W. E., Gnagy, E. M., Greiner, A. R., Hoza, B. Hinshaw, S. P., Swanson, J. M., et al. (2000). Behavioral vs. behavioral and pharmacological treatment in ADHD children attending a summer treatment program. *Journal of Abnormal Child Psychology, 28,* 507, 526.

Pelham, W. E., & Hinshaw, S. P. (1992). Behavioral intervention for attention-deficit hyperactivity disorder. In S. M. Turner, K. S. Calhoun, & H. E. Adams (Eds.), *Handbook of clinical behavior therapy* (pp. 259–283). New York: Wiley.

Pelham, W. E., & Hoza, B. (1996). Intensive treatment: A summer treatment program for children with ADHD. In E. D. Hibbs & P. S. Jensen (Eds.), *Psychosocial treatments for child and adolescent disorders: Empirically based strategies for clinical practice* (pp. 311–340). Washington, DC: American Psychological Association.

Pelham, W. E., & Waschbusch, D. A. (1999). Behavioral intervention in attention-deficit/hyperactivity disorder. In H. C. Quay & A. E. Hogan (Eds.), *Handbook of disruptive behavior disorders* (pp. 255–278). Dordrecht, Netherlands: Kluwer.

Pelham, W. E., Wheeler, T., & Chronis, A. (1998). Empirically supported psychosocial treatments for attention deficit hyperactivity disorder. *Journal of Clinical Child Psychology, 27,* 190–205.

Pena-Brooks, A., & Hedge, M. N. (2007). *Assessment and treatment of articulation and phonological disorders in children.* Austin, TX: Pro-Ed.

Pennington, B. F., & Ozonoff, S. (1996). Executive functions and developmental psychopathology. *Journal of Child Psychology and Psychiatry, 37,* 51–87.

Perham, N., Moore, S. C., Shepherd, J., & Cusens, B. (2007). Identifying drunkenness in the night-time economy. *Addiction, 102,* 377–380.

Perwien, A. R., & Bernstein, G. A. (2004). Separation anxiety disorder. In T. H. Ollendick & J. S. March (Eds.), *Phobic and anxiety disorders in children and adolescents* (pp. 272–305). New York: Oxford University Press.

Petersen, L., Jeppesen, P., & Thorup, A. (2005). A randomized, multicenter trial of integrated versus standard treatment for patients with a first episode of psychotic illness. *British Medical Journal, 331,* 602.

Peterson, A. L., & Azrin, N. H. (1992). Behavioral and pharmacological treatments for Tourette syndrome: A review. *Applied and Preventive Psychology, 2,* 231–242.

Petras, H., Schaeffer, C. M., Ialongo, N., Hubbard, S., Muthen, B., Lambert, S. F., et al. (2004). When the course of aggressive behavior in childhood does not predict antisocial outcomes in adolescence and young adulthood: An examination of potential explanatory variables. *Development and Psychopathology, 16,* 919–941.

Pfeifer, J. C., Kowatch, R. A., & DelBello, M. P. (2010). Pharmacotherapy of bipolar disorder in children and adolescents. *CNS Drugs, 24,* 575–593.

Pfiffner, L. J., & O'Leary, S. G. (1993). School-based psychological treatments. In J. L. Matson (Ed.), *Handbook of hyperactivity in children* (pp. 234–255). Boston: Allyn & Bacon.

Phelps, L. (2005). Health-related issues among ethnic minority and low-income children: Psychoeducational outcomes and prevention models. In C. L. Frisby & C. R. Reynolds (Eds.), *Comprehensive handbook of multicultural school psychology* (pp. 928–944). Hoboken, NJ: Wiley.

Phillips, D., Prince, S., & Schiebelhut, L. (2004). Elementary school children's responses 3 months after the September 11 terrorist attacks: A study in Washington, DC. *American Journal of Orthopsychiatry, 74,* 509–528.

Phillips, K. A., Stein, D. J., Rauch, S. L., Hollander, E., Fallon, B. A., Barsky, A., et al. (2010). Should obsessive-compulsive spectrum grouping of disorders be included in *DSM-5? Depression and Anxiety, 27,* 528–555.

Piazza, C. C., & Addison, L. R. (2007). Function-based assessment and treatment of pediatric feeding disorders. In P. Sturmey (Ed.), *Functional analysis in clinical treatment* (pp. 129–149). Burlington, MA: Elsevier.

Piazza, M., Giacomini, E., Le Bihan, D., & Dehaene, S. (2003). Single-trial classification of parallel pre-attentive and serial attentive processes using functional magnetic resonance imaging. *Proceedings of the Royal Society, 270,* 1237–1245.

Pickles, A., & Hill, J. (2006). Developmental pathways. In D. Cicchetti & D. J. Cohen (Eds.), *Developmental psychopathology, Vol. 1: Theory and method* (pp. 211–243). Hoboken, NJ: Wiley.

Pierce, K., Muller, R. A., Ambrose, J., Allen, G., & Courchesne, E. (2001). Face processing occurs outside the fusiform "face area" in autism: evidence from functional MRI. *Brain, 124,* 2059–2073.

Pieretti, M., Zhang, F., Fu, Y. H., Warren, S. T., Oostra, B. A., Caskey, C. T., et al. (1991). Absence of expression of the FMR1 gene in the fragile X syndrome. *Cell, 66,* 817–822.

Pike, K. M. (1998). Long-term course of anorexia nervosa: Response, relapse, remission, and recovery. *Clinical Psychology Review, 18,* 447–475.

Pike, K. M., Devlin, M. J., & Loeb, K. L. (2004). Cognitive-behavioral therapy in the treatment of anorexia nervosa, bulimia nervosa, and binge eating disorder. In J. K. Thompson (Ed.), *Handbook of eating disorders and obesity* (pp. 130–162). Hoboken, NJ: Wiley.

Pina-Camacho, L., Villero, S., Fraguas, D., Boada, L., Janssen, J., Navas-Sanchez, F. J., et al. (2012). Autism spectrum disorder: Does neuroimaging support the *DSM-5* proposal for a symptom dyad? *Journal of Autism and Developmental Disorders, 42,* 1326–1341.

Pine, D. S. (2006). A primer on brain imaging in developmental psychopathology: What is it good for? *Journal of Child Psychology and Psychiatry, 47*(10), 983–986.

Pine, D. S., Cohen, P., Gurley, D., Brook, J., & Ma, Y. (1998). The risk for early-adulthood anxiety and depressive disorders in adolescents with anxiety and depressive disorders. *Archives of General Psychiatry, 55,* 56–64.

Pine, D. S., Costello, E. J., Dahl, R., James, R., Leckman, J. F., Leibenluft, E., et al. (2011). Increasing the developmental focus in *DSM-5.* In D. A. Reiger (Ed.), *The conceptual evolution of DSM-5* (pp. 305–321). Washington, DC: American Psychiatric Publishing.

Pine, D. S., & Grun, J. S. (1999). Childhood anxiety: Integrating developmental psychopathology and affective neuroscience. *Journal of Child and Adolescent Psychopharmacology, 9,* 1–12.

Pine, D. S., & Klein, R. G. (2010). Anxiety disorders. In M. Rutter (Ed.), *Rutter's child and adolescent psychiatry* (pp. 628–647). Malden, MA: Blackwell.

Piquero, A. R., & Brezina, T. (2001). Testing Moffitt's account of adolescence-limited delinquency. *Criminology, 39,* 353–370.

Plante, W. A., Lobato, D., & Engel, R. (2001). Review of group interventions for pediatric chronic conditions. *Journal of Pediatric Psychology, 26,* 435–453.

Pliszka, S. R. (2003). *Neuroscience for the mental health clinician.* New York: Guilford Press.

Pliszka, S. R., Lancaster, J., Liotti, M., & Semrud-Clikeman, M. (2006). Volumetric MRI differences in treatment-naive vs. chronically treated children with ADHD. *Neurology, 67*(6), 1023–1027.

Plybon, L. E., & Kliewer, W. (2001). Neighborhood types and externalizing behavior in urban school-age children: Tests of direct, mediated, and moderated effects. *Journal of Child & Family Studies, 10,* 419–437.

Polanczyk, G., Caspi, A., Houts, R., Kollins, S. H., Rohde, L. A., & Moffitt, T. E. (2010). Implication of extending the ADHD age-of-onset criterion to age 12. *Journal of the American Academy of Child and Adolescent Psychiatry, 49,* 210–216.

Polivy, J., Herman, P. C., Mills, J. S., & Wheeler, H. B. (2003). Eating disorders in adolescence. In G. R. Adams & M. D. Berzonsky (Eds.), *Blackwell handbook of adolescence* (pp. 523–549). Malden, MA: Blackwell.

Pollack, S. D., Nelson, C. A., Schlaak, M. F., Roeber, B. J., Wewerka, S. S., Wiik, K. L., et al. (2010). Neurodevelopmental effects of early deprivation in postinstitutionalized children. *Child Development, 81,* 224–236.

Pomerantz, J. M. (2005). After the black box warning: Treating children and adolescents who have depression. *Drug Benefit Trends, 17,* 183–184.

Pontifex, M. B., Saliba, B. J., Raine, L. B., Picchietti, D. L., & Hillman, C. H. (2012). Exercise improves behavioral, neurocognitive, and scholastic performance in children with attention-deficit/hyperactivity disorder. *Journal of Pediatrics.*

Pope, H. G., & Yurgelun-Todd, D. (2004). Residual cognitive effects of long-term cannabis use. In D. Castle & R. Murray (Eds.), *Marijuana and madness: Psychiatry and neurobiology* (pp. 198–210). New York: Cambridge University Press.

Post, R., Weiss, S., Leverich, G., George, M., Frye, M., & Ketter, T. (1996). Developmental psychobiology of cyclic affective illness: Implications for early therapeutic intervention. *Development and Psychopathology, 8,* 273–305.

Postma, A., & Kolk, H. (1992). Error monitoring in people who stutter. *Journal of Speech and Hearing Research, 35,* 1024–1032.

Potter, D., Chevy, C., Amaya-Jackson, L., O'Donnell, K., & Murphy R. A. (2009). *Reactive attachment disorder (RAD): Appropriate and inappropriate application of the reactive attachment disorder diagnosis on an age continuum from birth though age 18.* Washington, DC: American Academy of Child and Adolescent Psychiatry.

Poulton, R., Caspi, A., Moffit, T. E., Cannon, M., Murray, R. M., & Harrington, H. L. (2000). Children's self-reported psychotic symptoms and adult schizophreniform disorder: A 15-year longitudinal study. *Archives of General Psychiatry, 57,* 1053–1058.

Power, T. J., Costigan, T. E., Eiraldi, R. B., & Leff, S. S. (2004). Variations in anxiety and depression as a function of ADHD subtypes defined by *DSM-IV*: Do subtype differences exist or not? *Journal of Abnormal Child Psychology, 32,* 27–37.

President's New Freedom Commission on Mental Health. (2003). *Achieving the promise: Transforming mental health care in America. Final report.* Rockville, MD: U.S. Department of Health and Human Services.

Price, J. M., & Dodge, K. A. (1989a). Peers' contributions to children's social maladjustment: Description and intervention. In T. J. Berndt & G. W. Ladd (Eds.), *Peer relationships and social development* (pp. 341–370). New York: Wiley.

Price, J. M., & Dodge, K. A. (1989b). Reactive and proactive aggression in childhood: Relations to peer status and social context dimensions. *Journal of Abnormal Child Psychology, 17,* 455–471.

Price, J. M., & Glad, K. (2003). Hostile attributional tendencies in maltreated children. *Journal of Abnormal Child Psychology, 31,* 329–343.

Pringsheim, T., & Steeves, T. (2012). Pharmacological treatment for attention deficit hyperactivity disorder (ADHD) in children with comorbid tic disorders. *Evidence-based Child Health, 4,* 1196–1230.

Prinstein, M. J. (2007). Moderators of peer contagion: A longitudinal examination of depression socialization between adolescents and their best friends. *Journal of Clinical Child and Adolescent Psychology, 36,* 159–170.

Prinstein, M. J., & Aikins, W. (2004). Cognitive moderators of the longitudinal association between peer rejection and adolescent depressive symptoms. *Journal of Abnormal Child Psychology, 32,* 147–158.

Prinstein, M. J., Boergers, J., & Vernberg, E. M. (2001). Overt and relational aggression in adolescents: Social-psychological adjustment of aggressors and victims. *Journal of Clinical Child Psychology, 30,* 479–491.

Prinstein, M. J., Cheah, C. S. L., & Guyer, A. E. (2005). Peer victimization, cue interpretation, and internalizing symptoms: Preliminary concurrent and longitudinal findings for children and adolescents. *Journal of Clinical Child and Adolescent Psychology, 34,* 11–24.

Prinstein, M. J., Guerry, J. D., Browne, C. B., & Rancourt, D. (2009). Interpersonal models of nonsuicidal self-injury. In M. K. Nock (Ed.), *Understanding nonsuicidal self-injury* (pp. 79–98). Washington, DC: American Psychological Association.

Prochaska, J. O., DiClemente, C. C., & Norcross, J. C. (1992). In search of how people change: Applications to addictive behaviors. *American Psychologist, 47,* 1102–1114.

Prochaska, J. O., & Norcross, J. C. (2003). *Systems of psychotherapy: A transtheoretical analysis* (5th ed.). Belmont, CA: Brooks/Cole.

Puig-Antich, J., Kaufman, J., Ryan, N. D., Williamson, D. E., Dahl, R. E., Lukens, E., et al. (1993). The psychosocial functioning and family environment of depressed adolescents. *Journal of the American Academy of Child and Adolescent Psychiatry, 32,* 244–253.

Pulsifer, M. B., Brandt, J., Salorio, C. F., Vining, E. P. G., Carson, B. S., & Freeman, J. M. (2004). The cognitive outcome of hemispherectomy in 71 children. *Epilepsia, 45,* 243–254.

Pumariega, A. J., Rodriguez, L., & Kilgus, M. D. (2004). Substance abuse among adolescents: Current perspectives. *Addictive Disorders & Their Treatment, 3,* 145–155.

Purcel, D. W., Malow, R. M., Dolezal, C., & Carballo-Dieguez, A. (2004). Sexual abuse of boys: Short- and long-term associations and implications for HIV prevention. In L. J. Koenig, L. S. Doll, A. O'Leary, & W. Pequegnat (Eds.), *From child sexual abuse to adult sexual risk: Trauma, revictimization, and intervention* (pp. 93–114). New York: American Psychological Association.

Putwain, D. W. (2007). Test anxiety in UK schoolchildren. *British Journal of Educational Psychology, 77,* 579–593.

Querido, J., & Eyberg, S. M. (2005). Parent-child interaction therapy: Maintaining treatment gains of preschoolers with disruptive behavior disorders. In E. D. Hibbs & P. S. Jensen (Eds.), *Psychosocial treatments for child and adolescent disorders: Empirically based strategies for clinical practice* (pp. 575–597). Washington, DC: American Psychological Association.

Querido, J., Eyberg, S. M., & Boggs, S. (2001). Revisiting the accuracy hypothesis in families of young children with conduct problems. *Journal of Clinical Child Psychology, 30,* 253–261.

Quiggle, N. L., Garber, J., Panak, W. E., & Dodge, K. A. (1992). Social information processing in aggressive and depressed children. *Child Development, 63,* 1305–1320.

Quinton, D., & Rutter, M. (1998). *Parenting and breakdown: The making and breaking of intergenerational links.* Aldershot, UK: Avebury.

Quittner, A. L., Barker, D. H., Marciel, K. K., & Grimley, M. E. (2009). Cystic fibrosis: A model for drug discovery and patient care. In M. C. Roberts & R. G. Steele (Eds.), *Handbook of pediatric psychology* (pp. 271–286). New York: Guilford.

Rabian, B., & Bottjer, S. J. (2008). Sleep problems. In A. R. Eisen (Ed.), *Treating childhood behavioral and emotional problems* (pp. 365–410). New York: Guilford.

Raghavan, R., & Small, N. (2004). Cultural diversity and intellectual disability. *Current Opinion in Psychiatry, 17,* 371–375.

Raine, A. (2002). Biosocial studies of antisocial and violent behavior in children and adults: A review. *Journal of Abnormal Child Psychology, 50,* 311–326.

Ramirez, S. Z., Feeney-Kettler, K. A., Flores-Torres, L., Kratochwill, T. R., & Morris, R. J. (2006). Fears and anxiety disorders. In G. G. Bear & K. M. Minke (Eds.), *Children's needs III: Development, prevention, and intervention* (pp. 267–279). Washington, DC: National Association of School Psychologists.

Ramo, D. E., Anderson, K. G., Tate, S. R., & Brown, S. A. (2005). Characteristics of relapse to substance use in comorbid adolescents. *Addictive Behaviors, 30,* 1811–1823.

Ramsay, M. C., Reynolds, C. R., & Kamphaus, R. W. (2002). *Essentials of behavioral assessment.* New York: Wiley.

Ransby, M. J., & Swanson, H. L. (2003). Reading comprehension skills of young adults with childhood diagnosis of dyslexia. *Journal of Learning Disabilities, 36,* 538–555.

Rao, U. (2003). Sleep and other biological rhythms. In B. Geller & M. DelBello (Eds.), *Bipolar disorder in childhood and early adolescence* (pp. 215–246). New York: Guilford Press.

Rao, U., Daley, S. E., & Hammen, C. (2000). Relationship between depression and substance use disorders in adolescent women during the transition to adulthood. *Journal of the American Academy of Child and Adolescent Psychiatry, 39,* 215–222.

Rapee, R. M. (1997). The potential role of childrearing practices in the development of anxiety and depression. *Clinical Psychology Review, 17,* 47–67.

Rapee, R. M., Abbott, M. J., & Lyneham, H. J. (2006). Bibliotherapy for children with anxiety disorders using written materials for parents: A randomized controlled trial. *Journal of Consulting and Clinical Psychology, 74,* 436–444.

Rapoff, M. A., Lindsley, C. B., & Karlson, C. (2009). Medical and psychosocial aspects of juvenile rheumatoid arthritis. In M. C. Roberts & R. G. Steele (Eds.), *Handbook of pediatric psychology* (pp. 366–380). New York: Guilford.

Rapoport, J. L., Chavez, A., Greenstein, D., Addington, A., & Gogtay, N. (2009). Autism spectrum disorders and childhood-onset schizophrenia: Clinical and biological contributions to a relation revisited. *Journal of the American Academy of Child and Adolescent Psychiatry, 48,* 10–18.

Rapoport, J. L., & Gogtay, N. (2011). Childhood onset schizophrenia: Support for a progressive neurodevelopmental disorder. *International Journal of Developmental Neuroscience, 29,* 251–258.

Rapoport, J. L., Gogtay, N., & Shaw, P. (2008). Schizophrenia and psychotic illness. In R. L. Findling (Ed.), *Clinical manual of child and adolescent psychopharmacology* (pp. 337–373). Washington, DC: American Psychiatric Association.

Rapoport, J. L., & Shaw, P. (2010). Obsessive-compulsive disorder. In M. Rutter (Ed.), *Rutter's child and adolescent psychiatry* (pp. 696–718). Malden, MA: Blackwell.

Rapport, M. D., Scanlan, S. W., & Denney, C. B. (1999). Attention-deficit/hyperactivity disorder and scholastic achievement: A model of dual developmental pathways. *Journal of Child Psychology and Psychiatry, 40,* 1169–1183.

Rathus, J. H., & Miller, A. L. (2002). Dialectical behavior therapy adapted for suicidal adolescents. *Suicide and life-threatening behavior, 32*(2), 146–157.

Ratner, N. B., & Guitar, B. (2006). Treatment of very early stuttering and parent-administered therapy. In N.B. Ratner & J. Tetnowski (Eds.), *Current issues in stuttering research and practice* (pp. 99–124). Mahwah, NJ: Erlbaum.

Ratner, N. B., & Tetnowski, J. (2006). *Current issues in stuttering research and practice.* Mahwah, NJ: Erlbaum.

Ray, R., & Dhawan, A. (2011). Diagnostic orphans. *Addiction, 106,* 867–868.

Rayner, K., Foorman, B. R., Perfetti, C. A., Pesetsky, D., & Seidenberg, M. S. (2001). How psychological science informs the teaching of reading. *Psychological Science in the Public Interest, 2,* 31–74.

Raz, M. H. (1995). *Help me talk right: How to teach a child to say the "L" sound in 15 easy lessons.* Scottsdale, AZ: Gerstenweitz.

Reddy, L. A., & Goldstein, A. P. (2001). ART: A multimodal intervention for aggressive adolescents. *Residential Treatment for Children and Youth, 18,* 47–62.

Redmond, S. M., & Rice, M. L. (1998). The socioemotional behaviors of children with SLI: Social adaptation or social deviance? *Journal of Speech, Language and Hearing Research, 41,* 688–700.

Redmond, S. M., & Timler, G. R. (2007). Addressing the social concomitants of developmental language impairments. In A. G. Kamhi, J. J. Masterson, & K. Apel (Eds.), *Clinical decision making in developmental language disorders* (pp. 185–202). Baltimore, MD: Brookes.

Reichert, A., Kreiker, S., Mehler-Wex, C., Warnke, A. (2008). The psychopathological and psychosocial outcome of early-onset schizophrenia: Preliminary data of a 13-year follow-up. *Child and Adolescent Psychiatry and Mental Health, 6,* 1–9.

Reid, G., Hong, R. Y., Wade, T. J. (2009). The relation between common sleep problems and emotional and behavioral problems among 2- and 3-year-olds in the context of known risk factors for psychopathology. *Journal of Sleep Research, 18,* 49–59.

Reid, G., Huntley, E. D., & Lewin, D. S. (2009). Insomnias of childhood and adolescence. *Child and Adolescent Psychiatric Clinics of North America, 18,* 979–1000.

Reid, R. R., Harris, K. R., Graham, S., & Rock, M. (2012). Self-regulation among students with LD and ADHD. In B. Wong & D. Butler (Eds.), *Learning about learning disabilities* (pp. 141–173). New York: Elsevier.

Reilly, J., Klima, E. S., & Bellugi, U. (1990). Once more with feeling: Affect and language in atypical populations. *Development and Psychopathology, 2,* 367–391.

Reinecke, M. A. (2006). Cognitive-developmental treatment of conduct disorder. In W. M. Nelson, A. J. Finch, & K. J. Hart (Eds.), *Conduct disorders: A practitioner's guide to comparative treatments* (pp. 99–135). New York: Springer.

Reinecke, M. A., & Simons, A. (2005). Vulnerability to depression among adolescents: Implications for cognitive-behavioral treatment. *Cognitive and Behavioral Practice, 12,* 166–176.

Reiss, S. (1990). Prevalence of dual diagnosis in community-based day programs in the Chicago metropolitan area. *American Journal on Mental Retardation, 94,* 578–585.

Reite, M., Weissberg, M., & Ruddy, J. (2009). *Clinical manual for evaluation and treatment of sleep disorders.* Arlington, VA: American Psychiatric Publishing.

Remschmidt, H., & Theisen, F. (2012). Early-onset schizophrenia. In M. E. Garralda & J. Raynaud (Eds.), *Brain, mind, and developmental psychopathology in childhood* (pp. 145–172). Lanham, MD: Aronson.

Rende, R., & Waldman, I. (2006). Behavioral and molecular genetics and developmental psychopathology. In D. Cicchetti & D. J. Cohen (Eds.), *Developmental psychopathology, Vol. 2: Developmental neuroscience* (pp. 427–464). Hoboken, NJ: Wiley.

Renz, K., Lorch, E. P., Milich, R., Lemberger, C., Bodner, A., Welsh, R. (2003). On-line story representation in boys with attention deficit hyperactivity disorder. *Journal of Abnormal Child Psychology, 31,* 93–104.

Reschly, D. J. (2006). Legal influences on the identification and treatment of educational disabilities. In I. B. Weiner & A. K. Hess (Eds.), *The handbook of forensic psychology* (pp. 167–189). Hoboken, NJ: Wiley.

Reschly, D. J., & Bergstrom, M. K. (2009). Response to intervention. In T. B. Gutkin & C. R. Reynolds (Eds.), *Handbook of school psychology* (pp. 434–460). Hoboken, NJ: Wiley.

Reschly, D. J., Tilly, W. D., & Grimes, J. P. (1999). *Special education in transition: Functional assessment and noncategorical programming.* Longmont, CO: Sopris West.

Rescorla, L., Ross, G. S., & McClure, S. (2007). Language delay and behavioral/emotional problems in toddlers. *Journal of Speech, Language, and Hearing Research, 50,* 1063–1078.

Resick, P. A., & Miller, M. W. (2009). Posttraumatic stress disorder: Anxiety or traumatic stress disorder. *Journal of Traumatic Stress, 22,* 384–390.

Reuther, E. T., Davis, T. E., Rudy, B. M., Jenkins, W. S., Whiting, S. E., & May, A. C. (2013). Intolerance of uncertainty as a mediator of the relationship between perfectionism and obsessive-compulsive symptom severity. *Depression and Anxiety, 30,* 773–777.

Reynolds, C. R., & Kamphaus, R. W. (2004). *Behavior assessment system for children* (2nd ed.). Circle Pines, MN: AGS.

Reynolds, C.R., & Shaywitz, S.E. (2009). Response to intervention: Ready or not? *School Psychology Quarterly, 24,* 1–19.

Rhee, S. H., & Waldman, D. (2002). Genetic and environmental influences on antisocial behavior: A meta-analysis of twin and adoption studies. *Psychological Bulletin, 128,* 490–529.

Riccio, C. A., Homack, S., Jarratt, K. P., & Wolfe, M. E. (2006). Differences in academic and executive function domains among children with ADHD predominantly inattentive and combined types. *Archives of Clinical Neuropsychology, 21,* 657–667.

Rice, K. G., Leever, B. A., Noggle, C. A., & Lapsley, D. K. (2007). Perfectionism and depressive symptoms in early adolescence. *Psychology in the Schools, 44,* 139–156.

Rich, B. A., Carver, F. W., Holroyd, T., Rosen, H. R., Mendoza, J. K., Cornwell, B. R., et al. (2011). Different neural pathways to negative affect in youth with pediatric bipolar disorder and severe mood dysregulation. *Journal of Psychiatric Research, 45,* 1283–1294.

Rich, C. L., Combs-Lane, A. M., Resnick, H. S., & Kilpatrick, D. G. (2004). Child sexual abuse and adult sexual revictimization. In L. J. Koenig, L. S. Doll, A. O'Leary, & W. Pequegnat (Eds.), *From child sexual abuse to adult sexual risk: Trauma, revictimization, and intervention* (pp. 49–68). Washington, DC: American Psychological Association.

Richter, M. A., Summerfeldt, L. J., Antony, M. M., & Swinson, R. P. (2003). Obsessive-compulsive spectrum conditions in obsessive-compulsive disorder and other anxiety disorders. *Depression and Anxiety, 18,* 118–127.

Richters, J. E., & Cicchetti, D. (1993). Mark Twain meets DSM–III–R: Conduct disorder, development, and the concept of harmful dysfunction. *Development and Psychopathology, 5,* 5–29.

Rieder, C., & Cicchetti, D. (1989). Organizational perspective on cognitive control functioning and cognitive-affective balance in maltreated children. *Developmental Psychology, 25,* 382–393.

Riggs, P. D., Hall, S., & Mikulich-Gilbertson, S. K. (2004). A randomized controlled trial of pemoline for attention-deficit/hyperactivity disorder in substance-abusing adolescents. *Journal of the American Academy of Child and Adolescent Psychiatry, 43,* 420–429.

Riggs, P. D., Mikulich-Gilbertson, S. K., & Davies, R. D. (2007). A randomized controlled trial of fluoxetine and cognitive behavioral therapy in adolescents with major depression, behavior problems, and substance use disorders. *Archives of Pediatric and Adolescent Medicine, 161,* 1026–1034.

Rimland, B. (1964). *Infantile autism: The syndrome and its implications for a neural theory of behavior.* New York: Appleton-Century-Crofts.

Ringel, J. S., & Sturm, R. (2001). National estimates of mental health utilization and expenditures for children in 1998. *Journal of Behavioral Health and Research, 28,* 319–333.

Riou, E. M., Ghosh, S., Francoeur, E., & Shevell, M. I. (2009). Global developmental delay and its relationship to cognitive skills. *Developmental Medicine and Child Neurology, 51,* 600–606.

Rissanen, A., Niemimaa, M., Suonpää, M., Ryynänen, M., & Heinonen, S. (2007). First trimester Downs Syndrome screening shows high detection rate for trisomy 21, but poor performance in structural abnormalities. *Fetal Diagnosis and Therapy, 22,* 45–50.

Robert, R., Blakeney, P. E., & Villarreal, C. (1999). Imipramine treatment in pediatric burn patients with symptoms of acute stress disorder. *Journal of the American Academy of Child and Adolescent Psychiatry, 38,* 873–882.

Robin, A., Siegal, P., Moye, A., Gilroy, M., Dennis, A., & Sikand, A. (1999). A controlled comparison of family versus individual therapy for adolescents with anorexia nervosa. *Journal of the American Academy of Child and Adolescent Psychiatry, 38,* 1482–1489.

Robins, E. & Guze, S. B. (1970). Establishment of diagnostic validity in psychiatric illness: Its application to schizophrenia. *American Journal of Psychiatry, 126,* 983–987.

Rodham, K., & Hawton, K. (2009). Epidemiology and phenomenology of nonsuicidal self-injury. In M. K. Nock (Ed.), *Understanding nonsuicidal self-injury* (pp. 37–62). Washington, DC: American Psychological Association.

Roemer, L., & Borkovec, T. D. (1993). Worry: Unwanted cognitive activity that controls unwanted somatic experience. In D. M. Wegner & J. W. Pennebaker (Eds.), *Handbook of mental control* (pp. 220–238). Englewood Cliffs, NJ: Prentice Hall.

Rogers, C. R. (1957). The necessary and sufficient conditions of therapeutic personality change. *Journal of Consulting Psychology, 21,* 95–103.

Rogers, S. J. (1998). Empirically supported comprehensive treatments for young children with autism. *Journal of Clinical Child Psychology, 27,* 168–179.

Rogers, S. J., & Williams, J. H. G. (2006). Imitation in autism: Findings and controversies. In S. J. Rogers & J. H. G. Williams (Eds.), *Imitation and the social mind: Autism and typical development* (pp. 277–309). New York: Guilford Press.

Rogosch, F., Cicchetti, D., & Abre, J. L. (1995). The role of child maltreatment in early deviations in cognitive and affective processing abilities and later peer relationship problems. *Development & Psychopathology, 7,* 591–609.

Rohrbach, L. A., Sussman, S., Dent, C. W., & Sun, P. (2005). Tobacco, alcohol, and other drug use among high-risk young people: A five-year longitudinal study from adolescence to emerging adulthood. *Journal of Drug Issues, 35,* 333–356.

Rohde, P., Lewinsohn, P. M., Clarke, G. N., Hops, H., & Seeley, J. R. (2005). The adolescent coping with depression course: A cognitive-behavioral approach to the treatment of adolescent depression. In E. D. Hibbs & P. S. Jensen (Eds.), *Psychosocial treatments for child and adolescent disorders: Empirically based strategies for clinical practice* (pp. 219–237). Washington, DC: American Psychological Association.

Rohde, P., Lewinsohn, P. M., & Seeley, J. R. (1991). Comorbidity of unipolar depression: II. Comorbidity with other mental disorders in adolescents and adults. *Journal of Abnormal Psychology, 100,* 214–222.

Romero, S., Birmaher, B., Axelson, D. A., Iosif, A., Williamson, D. E., Gill, M. K., et al. (2009). Negative life events in children and adolescents with bipolar disorder. *Journal of Clinical Psychiatry, 70,* 1452–1460.

Romski, M., Sevicik, R.A., Cheslock, M., & Barton, A. (2006). The System for Augmenting Language. In R.J. McCauley & M.E. Fey (Eds.), *Treatment of language disorders in children* (pp. 123–148). Baltimore, MD: Brookes.

Roodman, A. A., & Clum, G. A. (2001). Revictimization rates and method variance: A meta-analysis. *Clinical Psychology Review, 21,* 183–204.

Root, R. W., Resnick, R. J. (2003). An update on the diagnosis and treatment of attention-deficit/hyperactivity disorder in children. *Professional Psychology: Research and Practice, 34,* 34–41.

Rose, A. J. (2002). Co-rumination in the friendship of girls and boys. *Child Development, 73,* 1830–1843.

Rose, S., Bisson, J., Churchill, R., & Wessely, S. (2002). Psychological debriefing for preventing posttraumatic stress disorder (PTSD). *Cochrane Database Reviews, 2,* CD000560.

Rosenbaum, D. P., Gordon, S., & Hanson, S. (1998). Assessing the effects of school-based drug education: A six-year multilevel analysis of project D.A.R.E. *Journal of Research in Crime and Delinquency, 35,* 381–412.

Rosenberg, D. R., & Keshavan, M. S. (1998). A. E. Bennett Research Award: Toward a neurodevelopmental model of obsessive-compulsive disorder. *Biological Psychiatry, 43,* 623–640.

Rosenberg, R. E., Daniels, A. M., Law, J. K., Law, P. A., & Kaufmann, W. E. (2009). Trends in autism spectrum disorder diagnoses. *Journal of Autism and Developmental Disorders, 39,* 1099–1111.

Rosenfarb, I. S., Bellack, A. S., & Aziz, N. (2006). Family interactions and the course of schizophrenia in African American and White patients. *Journal of Abnormal Psychology, 115,* 112–120.

Rosenshine, B., Meister, C., & Chapman, S. (1996). Teaching students to generate questions: A review of the intervention studies. *Review of Educational Research, 66,* 181–221.

Rosenzweig, S. (1936). Some implicit common factors in diverse methods of psychotherapy. *American Journal of Orthopsychiatry, 6,* 412–415.

Rosner, B. A., Hodapp, R. M., Fidler, D. J., Sagun, J. N., & Dykens, E. M. (2004). Social competence in persons with Prader-Willi, Williams and Down's Syndromes. *Journal of Applied Research in Intellectual Disabilities, 17,* 209–217.

Rossello, J., & Bernal, G. (1999). The efficacy of cognitive-behavioral and interpersonal treatments for depression in Puerto Rican adolescents. *Journal of Consulting and Clinical Psychology, 67,* 734–745.

Rossello, J., & Bernal, G. (2005). New developments in cognitive-behavioral and interpersonal treatments for depressed Puerto Rican adolescents. In E. D. Hibbs & P. S. Jensen (Eds.), *Psychosocial treatments for child and adolescent disorders: Empirically based strategies for clinical practice* (pp. 187–217). Washington, DC: American Psychological Association.

Rosso, I. M., Cintron, C. M., Steingard, R. J., Renshaw, P. F., Young, A. D., & Yurgelun-Todd, D. A. (2005). Amygdala and hippocampus volumes in pediatric major depression. *Biological Psychiatry, 57,* 21–26.

Rothbart, M. K., & Bates, J. E. (1998). Temperament. In W. Damon (Ed.), *Handbook of child psychology: Vol. 3. Social, emotional, and personality development* (pp. 105–176). New York: Wiley.

Rowe, C. L., Liddle, H. A., Greenbaum, P. E., & Henderson, C. E. (2004). Impact of psychiatric comorbidity on treatment of adolescent drug abusers. *Journal of Substance Abuse Treatment, 26,* 129–140.

Rowe, R., Maughan, B., Pickles, A., Costello, E. J., & Angold, A. (2002). The relationship between *DSM-IV* oppositional defiant disorder and conduct disorder: Findings from the Great Smoky Mountains Study. *Journal of Child Psychology and Psychiatry, 43,* 365–373.

Rubin, K. H., Bukowski, W., & Parker, J. G. (1998). Peer interactions, relationships, and groups. In W. Damon & N. Eisenberg (Eds.), *Handbook of child psychology: Social, emotional, and personality development* (pp. 619–700). New York: Wiley.

Rubin, K. H., & Rose-Krasnor, L. (1992). Interpersonal problem solving and social competence in children. In V. B. Van Hassett & M. Hersen (Eds.), *Handbook of social development: A life-span perspective* (pp. 283–323). New York: Plenum.

Ruchkin, V. V., Schwab-Stone, M., Koposov, R. A., Vermeiren, R., & King, R. A. (2003). Suicidal ideations and attempts in juvenile delinquents. *Journal of Child Psychology and Psychiatry, 44,* 1058–1066.

Rueda, M. R., Rothbart, M. K., McCandliss, B. D., Saccomanno, L., & Posner, M. I. (2005). Training, maturation, and genetic influences on the development of executive attention. *Proceedings of the National Academy of Sciences, 41,* 14931–14936.

Rumpf, H. J., Wohlert, T., Freyer-Adam, J., Grothues, J., & Bischof, G. (2012). Screening questionnaires for problem drinking in adolescents: Performance of AUDIT, AUDIT-C, CRAFFT and POSIT. *European Addiction Research, 19*(3), 121–127.

Rund, B. R. (1994). The relationship between psychosocial and cognitive functioning in schizophrenic patients and expressed emotion and communication deviance in their parents. *Acta Psychiatrica Scandinavica, 90,* 133–140.

Runyon, M. K., Deblinger, E., Ryan, E. E., & Thakkar-Kolar, R. (2004). An overview of child physical abuse: Developing an integrated parent-child cognitive-behavioral treatment approach. *Trauma, Violence, & Abuse, 5,* 65–85.

Runyon, M. K., & Kenny, M. C. (2002). Relationship of attributional style, depression, and posttrauma distress among children who suffered physical or sexual abuse. *Child Maltreatment, 7,* 254–264.

Runyon, M. K., Kenny, M. C., Berry, E. J., Deblinger, E., & Brown, E. J. (2006). Etiology and surveillance in child maltreatment. In J. R. Lutzker (Ed.), *Preventing violence: Research and evidence-based intervention strategies* (pp. 23–47). Washington, DC: American Psychological Association.

Rutter, M. (2005). Genetic influences and autism. In F. R. Volkmar, R. Paul, A. Klin, & D. Cohen (Eds.), *Handbook of autism and pervasive developmental disorders, Vol. 1: Diagnosis, development, neurobiology, and behavior* (pp. 425–452). Hoboken, NJ: Wiley.

Rutter, M. (2011). Research review: Child psychiatric diagnosis and classification. *Journal of Child Psychology and Psychiatry, 32,* 647–660.

Rutter, M., Sonuga-Barke, E. J., Beckett, C., Castle, J., Kreppner, J., Kumsta, R., et al. (2011). Deprivation-specific psychological patterns: Effects of institutional deprivation. *Monographs of the Society for Research in Child Development, 75*(1), 1–252.

Rutter, M., Sonuga-Barke, E. J., & Castle, J. (2011). Investigating the impact of early institutional deprivation on development: Background and research strategy of the English and Romanian adoptees (ERA) study. *Monographs of the Society for Research in Child Development, 75,* 1–20.

Rutter, M., & Sroufe, A. (2000). Developmental psychopathology: Concepts and challenges. *Development and Psychopathology, 12,* 265–296.

Ruzek, J. I., Brymer, M. J., Jacobs, A. K., Layne, C. M., Vernberg, E. M., & Watson, P. J. (2007). Psychological first aid. *Journal of Mental Health Counseling, 29,* 17–49.

Sadeh, A. (2007). Consequences of sleep loss or sleep disruption in children. *Sleep Medicine Clinics, 2,* 513–520.

Sadeh, A., Gruber, R., & Raviv, A. (2003). The effects of sleep restriction and extension on school-age children: What a difference an hour makes. *Child Development, 74,* 444–455.

Sadock, B. J., & Sadock, V. A. (2003). *Kaplan and Sadock's synopsis of psychiatry: Behavioral sciences/clinical psychiatry.* Philadelphia, PA: Lippincott Williams & Wilkins.

Saenz, L. M., & Fuchs, L. S. (2002). Examining the reading difficulty of secondary students with learning disabilities. *Remedial and Special Education, 23,* 31–41.

Saldana, L., & Henggeler, S. W. (2006). Multisystemic therapy in the treatment of adolescent conduct disorder. In W. M. Nelson, A. J. Finch, & K. J. Hart (Eds.), *Conduct disorders: A practitioner's guide to comparative treatments* (pp. 217–258). New York: Springer.

Salkovskis, P., Forrester, E., & Richards, C. (1998). Cognitive behavioural approach to understanding obsessional thinking. *British Journal of Psychiatry, 173,* 53–63.

Salvy, S. J., Mulick, J. A., Butter, E., Bartlett, K. K., & Linscheid, T. R. (2004). Contingent electric shock (SIBIS) and a conditioned punisher eliminate severe head banging in a preschool child. *Behavioral Interventions, 19,* 59–72.

Sambrano, S., Springer, J. F., Sale, E., Kasim, R., & Hermann, J. (2005). Understanding prevention effectiveness in real-world settings: The national cross-site evaluation of high risk youth programs. *American Journal of Drug and Alcohol Abuse, 31,* 491–513.

Sameroff, A. J. (2000). Developmental systems and psychopathology. *Development and Psychopathology, 12,* 297–312.

Sameroff, A. J., Peck, S. C., & Eccles, J. S. (2004). Changing ecological determinants of conduct problems from early adolescence to early adulthood. *Development and Psychopathology, 16,* 873–896.

Samms-Vaughn, M. (2006). Learning disorders. In C. A. Essau (Ed.), *Child and adolescent psychopathology: Theoretical and clinical implications* (pp. 271–289). New York: Routledge.

Sandberg, S., McGuinness, D., Hillary, C., & Rutter, M. (1998). Independence of childhood life events and chronic adversities. *Journal of the American Academy of Child & Adolescent Psychiatry, 37*, 728–735.

Sandman, C. A., Hetrick, W. P., & Taylor, D. V. (1997). Dissociation of POMC peptides after self-injury predicts responses to centrally acting opiate blockers. *American Journal of Mental Retardation, 102,* 182–199.

Sandman, C. A., Spence, M. A., & Smith, M. (1999). Proopiomelanocortin (POMC) disregulation and response to opiate blockers. *Mental Retardation and Developmental Disabilities Research Reviews, 5,* 314–321.

Sattler, J. M. (2001). *Assessment of children: Cognitive applications.* San Diego, CA: Jerome M. Sattler.

Sattler, J. M. (2002). *Assessment of children: Behavioral and clinical applications.* San Diego, CA: Jerome M. Sattler.

Sattler, J. M., & Dumont, R. (2004). *Assessment of children: WISC-IV and WPPSI-III supplement.* San Diego, CA; Jerome M. Sattler.

Scahill, L., Hallett, V., Aman, M. G., McDougle, C. J., Arnold, L. E., McCracken, J. T. (2013). Social disability in autism spectrum disorder: Results from Research Units on Pediatric Psychopharmacology (RUPP) Autism Network trials. *Journal of Autism and Developmental Disorders, 43*(3), 739–746.

Scanlon, D. (2013). Specific learning disability and its newest definition. *Journal of Learning Disabilities, 46*, 26–33.

Scarr, S., & McCartney, K. (1983). How people make their own environments: Environment effects. *Child Development, 54, 424*–435.

Schab, D. W., & Trinh, N. H. T. (2004). Do artificial food colors promote hyperactivity in children with hyperactive syndromes? A meta-analysis of double-blind placebo-controlled trials. *Journal of Developmental & Behavioral Pediatrics, 25,* 423–434.

Schaeffer, C. M., & Borduin, M. (2005). Long-term follow-up to a randomized clinical trial of multisystemic therapy with serious and violent juvenile offenders. *Journal of Consulting and Clinical Psychology, 73,* 445–453.

Schalock, R. L., Borthwick-Duffy, S. A., Bradley, V. J., Buntinx, W. H. E., Coulter, D. L., Craig, E. M., et al. (2010). *Intellectual Disability: Definition, classification, and systems of supports* (11th ed.). Washington, DC: AAIDD.

Schalock, R. L., Thompson, J. R., & Tasse, M. J. (2008). *Relating Supports Intensity Scale information to individual service plans.* Washington, DC: AAIDD.

Schechter, D. S. (2012). Editorial: The developmental neuroscience of emotional neglect, its consequences, and the psychological interventions that can reverse them. *American Journal of Psychiatry, 169,* 452–454.

Scheeringa, M. S., Zeanah, C. H., & Cohen, J. A. (2011). PTSD in children and adolescents. *Depression and Anxiety, 28,* 770–782.

Schlenger, W. E., Caddell, J. M., Ebert, L., Jordan, B. K., Rourke, K. M., Wilson, D., et al. (2002). Psychological reactions to terrorist attacks: Findings from the National Study of Americans' Reactions to September 11th. *Journal of the American Medical Association, 288,* 581–588.

Schmidt, U., Tiller, J., Blanchard, M., Andrews, D., & Treasure, J. (1997). Is there a specific trauma precipitating anorexia nervosa? *Psychological Medicine, 27,* 523–530.

Schniering, C. A., & Rapee, M. (2004a). The relationship between automatic thoughts and negative emotions in children and adolescents: A test of the cognitive content-specificity hypothesis. *Journal of Abnormal Psychology, 113,* 464–470.

Schniering, C. A., & Rapee, M. (2004b). The structure of negative self-statements in children and adolescents: A confirmatory factor-analytic approach. *Journal of Abnormal Child Psychology, 32,* 95–109.

Schopler, E., Mesibov, G., & Baker, A. (1982). Evaluation of treatment for autistic children and their parents. *Journal of the American Academy of Child Psychiatry, 21,* 262–267.

Schopler, E., Mesibov, G., DeVellis, R., & Short, A. (1981). Treatment outcome for autistic children and their families. In P. Mittler (Ed.), *Frontiers of knowledge in mental retardation* (pp. 293–301). Baltimore, MD: University Park Press.

Schreibman, L., & Koegel, R. L. (2005). Training for parents of children with autism: Pivotal responses, generalization, and individuation of interventions. In E. D. Hibbs & P. S. Jensen (Eds.), *Psychosocial treatments for child and adolescent disorders: Empirically based strategies for clinical practice* (pp. 605–631). Washington, DC: American Psychological Association.

Schroeder, S. R., Oster-Granite, M. L., Berkson, G., Bodfish, J. W., Breese, G. R., Cataldo, M. F., et al. (2001). Self-injurious behavior: Gene-brain-behavior relationships. *Mental Retardation and Developmental Disabilities Research Reviews, 7,* 3–12.

Schuengel, C., Oosterman, M., & Sterkenburg, P. S. (2009). Children with disrupted attachment histories. *Child and Adolescent Psychiatry and Mental Health, 3,* 1–10.

Schuhmann, E. M., Foote, R. C., Eyberg, S. M., Boggs, S. R., & Algina, J. (1998). Efficacy of parent-child interaction therapy: Interim report of a randomized trial with short-term maintenance. *Journal of Clinical Child Psychology, 27,* 34–45.

Schultz, J. R. (2006). Behavioral treatment for youth with conduct disorder. In W. M. Nelson, A. J. Finch, & K. J. Hart (Eds.), *Conduct disorders: A practitioner's guide to comparative treatments* (pp. 137–175). New York: Springer.

Schultz, R. T., Grelotti, D. J., Klin, A., Kleinman, J., Van der Gaag, C, Marois, R., et al. (2003). Autism and movement disturbance. In U. Frith & E. Hill (Eds.), *Autism: Mind and brain* (pp. 267–293). New York: Oxford University Press.

Schultz, R. T., & Robins, D. L. (2005). Functional neuroimaging studies of autism spectrum disorders. In F. R. Volkmar, R. Paul, A. Klin, & D. Cohen (Eds.), *Handbook of autism and pervasive developmental disorders, Vol. 1: Diagnosis, development, neurobiology, and behavior* (pp. 515–533). Hoboken, NJ: Wiley.

Schumann, C. M., & Amaral, G. (2006). Stereological analysis of amygdala neuron number in autism. *Journal of Neuroscience, 26,* 7674–7679.

Schuster, M., Stein, B., Jaycox, L., Collins, R., Marshall, G., Elliot, M., et al. (2001). A national survey of stress reactions after the September 11, 2001 terrorist attacks. *New England Journal of Medicine, 345,* 1507–1512.

Schwartz, D., Dodge, K. A., Coie, J. D., Hubbard, J. A., Cillessen, A. H., Lemerise, E. A., et al. (1998). Social-cognitive and behavioral correlates of aggression and victimization in boys' playgroups. *Journal of Abnormal Child Psychology, 26,* 431–440.

Scott, J., & Baldwin, W. L. (2005). The challenge of early intensive intervention. In D. Zager (Ed.), *Autism spectrum disorders: Identification, education, and treatment* (pp. 173–228). Mahwah, NJ: Erlbaum.

Sedlak, A. J., & Broadhurst, D. D. (1996). *Executive summary of the Third National Incidence Study of Child Abuse and Neglect.* Washington, DC: U.S. Department of Health and Human Services.

Seeman, P., & Madras, B. K. (1998). Anti-hyperactivity medication: Methylphenidate and amphetamine. *Molecular Psychiatry, 3,* 386–396.

Seidler, G., & Wagner, F. (2006). Comparing the efficacy of EMDR and trauma-focused cognitive-behavioral therapy in the treatment of PTSD: A meta-analytic study. *Psychological Medicine, 36,* 1515–1522.

Seidman, L. J., Biederman, J., Faraone, S. V., Weber, W., & Ouellette, C. (1997). Toward defining a neuropsychology of attention-deficit/hyperactivity disorder: Performance of children and adolescents from a large clinically referred sample. *Journal of Consulting and Clinical Psychology, 65,* 150–160.

Seidman, L. J., Biederman, J., Monuteaux, M., Weber, W., & Faraone, S. V. (2000). Neuropsychological functioning in nonreferred siblings of children with attention-deficit/hyperactivity disorder. *Journal of Abnormal Psychology, 109,* 252–265.

Seidman, L. J., Biederman, J., Weber, W., Hatch, M., & Faraone, S. V. (1998). Neuropsychological functioning in adults with attention-deficit hyperactivity disorder. *Biological Psychiatry, 44,* 260–268.

Seidman, L. J., Valera, E. M., Makris, N. (2005). Structural brain imaging of attention-deficit/hyperactivity disorder. *Biological Psychiatry, 57,* 1263–1272.

Seligman, M. E. P. (1975). *Helplessness: On depression, development, and death.* San Francisco: Freeman.

Senel, H. G. (2010). Parents' views and experiences about complementary and alternative medicine treatments for their children with autistic spectrum disorder. *Journal of Autism and Developmental Disorders, 40,* 494–503.

Shaffer, D., Fisher, P., Dulcan, M. K., Davies, M., Piacentini, J., Schwab-Stone, M. E., et al. (1996). The NIMH diagnostic interview schedule for children version 2.3 (DISC): Description, acceptability, prevalence rates, and performance in the MECA study. *Journal of the American Academy of Child and Adolescent Psychiatry, 35,* 865–877.

Shaffer, D., Fisher, P., Lucas, C. P., Dulcan, M. K., & Schwab-Stone, M. E. (2000). The NIMH diagnostic interview schedule for children version IV (DISC-IV). *Journal of the American Academy of Child and Adolescent Psychiatry, 39,* 28–38.

Shaffer, D., & Jacobson, C. (2009). *Proposal to the DSM-V childhood disorder and mood disorder work groups to include non-suicidal self-injury (NSSI) as a DSM-5 disorder.* Washington, DC: American Psychiatric Association.

Shafritz, K. M., Marchione, K. E., Gore, J. C., Shaywitz, S. E., & Shaywitz, B. A. (2004). The effects of methylphenidate on neural systems of attention in attention deficit hyperactivity disorder. *American Journal of Psychiatry, 161,* 1990–1997.

Shahar, G., Blatt, S. J., Zuroff, D. C., Kuperminc, G. P., & Leadbeater, B. J. (2004). Reciprocal relations between depressive symptoms and self-criticism (but not dependency) among early adolescent girls (but not boys). *Cognitive Therapy and Research, 28,* 85–103.

Shain, B. N. (2007). Suicide and suicide attempts in adolescence. *Pediatrics, 120,* 669–676.

Shapira, B. E., & Dahlen, P. (2010). Therapeutic treatment protocol for enuresis using an enuresis alarm. *Journal of Counseling and Development, 88,* 246–252.

Shapiro, D. A., & Shapiro, D. (1982). Meta-analysis of comparative therapy outcome studies: A replication and refinement. *Psychological Bulletin, 92,* 581–604.

Shapiro, F. (2001). *EMDR: Eye Movement Desensitization of Reprocessing: Basic principles, protocols and procedures* (2nd ed.). New York: Guilford Press.

Sharp, W. H., Jaquess, D. L., Morton, J. F., & Herzinger, C. V. (2010). Pediatric feeding disorders: A quantitative synthesis of treatment outcomes. *Child and Family Psychology Review, 13,* 348–365.

Shaw, D. S., Gilliom, M., Ingoldsby, E. M., & Nagin, D. (2003). Trajectories leading to school-age conduct problems. *Developmental Psychology, 39,* 189–200.

Shaw, D. S., Lacourse, E., & Nagin, D. S. (2005). Developmental trajectories of conduct problems and hyperactivity from ages 2 to 10. *Journal of Child Psychology and Psychiatry, 46,* 931–942.

Shaw, H., Ramirez, L., Trost, A., Randall, P., & Stice, E. (2004). Body image and eating disturbances across ethnic groups: More similarities than differences. *Psychology of Addictive Behaviors, 18,* 12–18.

Shaw, J., Applegate, B., & Schorr, C. (1996). Twenty-one month follow-up study of school-age children exposed to Hurricane Andrew. *American Journal of Child and Adolescent Psychiatry, 35,* 359–364.

Shaywitz, B. A., Holford, T. R., Holahan, J. M., & Fletcher, J. M. (1995). A Matthew effect for IQ but not for reading: Results from a longitudinal study. *Reading Research Quarterly, 30,* 894–906.

Shaywitz, B. A., Shaywitz, S. E., Blachman, B. A., Pugh, K. R., Fulbright, R. K., Skudlarski, P., et al. (2004). Development of left occipitotemporal systems for skilled reading in children after a phonologically-based intervention. *Biological Psychiatry, 55,* 926–933.

Shaywitz, B. A., Shaywitz, S. E., Pugh, K. R., Mencl, W. E., Fulbright, R. K., Skudlarski, P., et al. (2002). Disruption of posterior brain systems for reading in children with developmental dyslexia. *Biological Psychiatry, 52,* 101–110.

Shaywitz, S. E., & Shaywitz, B. A. (2005). Dyslexia (specific reading disability). *Biological Psychiatry, 57,* 1301–1309.

Shea, A., Walsh, C., MacMillan, H., & Steiner, M. (2005). Child maltreatment and HPA axis dysregulation: Relationship to major depressive disorder and posttraumatic stress disorder in females. *Psychoneuroendocrinology, 30,* 162–178.

Sheehan, J. (1970). *Stuttering: Research and therapy.* New York: Harper & Row.

Sheeringa, M. S., Zeanah, C. H., & Cohen, J. A. (2011). PTSD in children and adolescents: Toward an empirically based algorithm. *Depression & Anxiety, 28,* 770–782.

Sher, K. J. (1991). *Children of alcoholics: A critical appraisal of theory and research.* Chicago: University of Chicago Press.

Sherman, D. K., Iacono, W. G., & McGue, M. K. (1997). Attention-deficit hyperactivity disorder dimensions: A twin study of inattention and impulsivity-hyperactivity. *Journal of the American Academy of Child and Adolescent Psychiatry, 36,* 745–753.

Shevell, M. I. (2008). Global developmental delay and mental retardation or intellectual disability. *Pediatric Clinics of North America, 55,* 1071–1084.

Shevell, M. I. (2010). Present conceptualization of early childhood neurodevelopmental disabilities. *Journal of Child Neurology, 25,* 120–126.

Shevell, M. I., Ashwal, S., Donley, D., Flint, J., Gingold, M., Hirtz, D. et al. (2003). Practice parameter: Evaluation of the child with global developmental delay. *Neurology, 60,* 367–380.

Shifrer, D., Muller, C., Callahan, R. (2011). Disproportionality and learning disabilities. *Journal of Learning Disabilities, 44,* 246–257.

Shirk, S. R., Gudmundsen, G. R., & Burwell, R. A. (2005). Links among attachment-related cognitions and adolescent depressive symptoms. *Journal of Clinical Child and Adolescent Psychology, 34,* 172–181.

Shoal, G. D., Castaneda, J. O., & Giancola, P. R. (2005). Worry moderates the relation between negative affectivity and affect-related substance use in adolescent males: A prospective study of maladaptive emotional self-regulation. *Personality and Individual Differences, 38,* 475–485.

Shreeram, S., He, J., Kalaydjian, A., Brothers, S., & Merikangas, K. R. (2009). Prevalence of enuresis and its association with Attention-Deficit/Hyperactivity Disorder among US children. *Journal of the American Academy of Child and Adolescent Psychiatry, 48,* 35–41.

Shroff, H., & Thompson, K. (2006). The tripartite influence model of body image and eating disturbance: A replication with adolescent girls. *Body Image, 3,* 17–23.

Sibley, M. H., Waxmonsky, J. G., Robb, J. A., & Pelham, W. E. (2013). Implications of changes for the field: ADHD. *Journal of Learning Disabilities, 46,* 34–42.

Siegel, B., & Ficcaglia, M. (2006). Pervasive developmental disorders. In R. T. Ammerman (Ed.), *Comprehensive handbook of personality and psychopathology* (pp. 254–271). Hoboken, NJ: Wiley.

Sikich, L., Frazier, J. A., McClellan, J., Findling, R. L., Vitiello, B., Ritz, L., et al. (2008). Double-blind comparison of first- and second-generation antipsychotics in early-onset schizophrenia and schizoaffective disorder. *American Journal of Psychiatry, 165,* 1420–1431.

Siklos, S., & Kerns, A. (2007). Assessing the diagnostic experiences of a small sample of parents of children with autism spectrum disorders. *Research in Developmental Disabilities, 28,* 9–22.

Silver, A. A., & Hagin, R. A. (2002). *Disorders of learning in childhood.* New York: Wiley.

Silverman, A. H., & Tarbell, S. (2009). Feeding and vomiting problems in pediatric populations. In M. C. Roberts & R. G. Steele (Eds.), *Handbook of pediatric psychology* (pp. 429–445). New York: Guilford.

Silverman, W. K., & Carmichael, W. K. (1999). Phobic disorders. In R. T. Ammerman, M. Hersen, & C. L. Last (Eds.), *Handbook of prescriptive treatments for children and adolescents* (pp. 172–192). Boston: Allyn & Bacon.

Silverman, W. K., & Dick-Niederhauser, A. (2004). Separation anxiety disorder. In T. L. Morris & J. S. March (Eds.), *Anxiety disorders in children and adolescents* (pp. 164–188). New York: Guilford Press.

Silverman, W. K., Kurtines, W., Ginsburg, G. S., Weems, C. F., Lumpkin, P. W., & Carmichael, D. H. (1999). Treating anxiety disorders in children with group cognitive-behavioral therapy: A randomized clinical trial. *Journal of Consulting and Clinical Psychology, 67,* 995–1003.

Silverthorn, P., Frick, P. J., & Reynolds, R. (2001). Timing of onset and correlates of severe conduct problems in adjudicated girls and boys. *Journal of Psychopathology and Behavioral Assessment, 23,* 171–181.

Simeon, J. C., Dinicola, V. F., Ferguson, B. H., & Copping, W. (1990). Adolescent depression: A placebo-controlled fluoxetine study and follow-up. *Progress in Neuro-Psychopharmacology & Biological Psychiatry, 14,* 791–795.

Simonoff, E., Pickles, A., Meyer, J. M., Silberg, J. L., Maes, H. H., Loeber, R., et al. (1997). The Virginia Twin Study of Adolescent Behavioral Development: Influence of age, sex, and impairment on rates of disorder. *Archives of General Psychiatry, 54,* 801–808.

Simons, A. D., Rohde, P., Kennard, B. D., & Robins, M. (2005). Relapse and recurrence prevention in the treatment for adolescents with depression study. *Cognitive and Behavioral Practice, 12,* 240–251.

Simos, P. G., Fletcher, J. M., Bergman, E., Breier, J. I., Foorman, B. R., Castillo, E. M., et al. (2002). Dyslexia-specific brain activation profile becomes normal following successful remedial training. *Neurology, 58,* 1203–1213.

Simos, P. G., Fletcher, J. M., Sarkari, S., Billingsley, R. L., Francis, D. J., Castillo, E. M., et al. (2005). Early development of neurophysiological processes involved in normal reading and reading disability: A magnetic source imaging study. *Neuropsychology, 19,* 787–798.

Simpson, R. L., de Boer-Ott, S. R., Griswold, D. E., Myles, B. S., Byrd, S. E. Ganz, J. B., et al. (2005). *Autism spectrum disorders.* Thousand Oaks, CA: Corwin Press.

Sinclair, B. B., & Gold, S. R. (1997). The psychological impact of withholding disclosure of child sexual abuse. *Violence and Victims, 12,* 137–145.

Singer, H. S., Gilbert, D. L., Wolf, D. S., Mink, J. W., & Kurlan, R. (2011). Moving from PANDAS to CANS. *Journal of Pediatrics, 160,* 725–731.

Singh, A. N., Matson, J. L., Cooper, C. L., Dixon, D., & Sturmey, P. (2005). The use of risperidone among individuals with mental retardation: Clinically supported or not? *Research in Developmental Disabilities, 26,* 203–218.

Singh, M. K., DelBello, M. P., Kowatch, R. A., & Strakowski, S. M. (2006). Co-occurrence of bipolar and attention-deficit hyperactivity disorders in children. *Bipolar Disorders, 8,* 710–720.

Singh, M. K., Ketter, T. A., & Chang, K. D. (2010). Atypical antipsychotics for acute manic and mixed episodes in children and adolescents with bipolar disorder. *Drugs, 70,* 433–442.

Singh, N. N., Ellis, C. R., & Wechsler, H. (1997). Psychopharmacoepidemiology of mental retardation: 1966 to 1995. *Journal of Child and Adolescent Psychopharmacology, 7,* 255–266.

Singh, N. N., Osborne, J. G., & Huguenin, N. H. (1996). Applied behavioral interventions. In J. W. Jacobson & J. A. Mulick (Eds.), *Manual of diagnosis and professional practice in mental retardation* (pp. 341–353). Washington, DC: American Psychological Association.

Sinha, Y., Silove, N., Hayen, A., & Williams, K. (2011). Auditory integration training and other sound therapies for autistic spectrum disorders. Cochrane Database of Systematic Reviews.

Sivertsen, B., Mysing, M., Elgen, I., Stormark, K. M., & Lundervold, A. J. (2009). Chronicity of sleep problems in children with chronic illness. *Child and Adolescent Psychiatry and Mental Health, 3,* 22–29.

Skiba, R. J., Simmons, A. B., Ritter, S., Gibb, A. C., Rausch, M. K., Cuadrado, J., & Chung, C. G. (2008). Achieving equity in special education: History, status, and current challenges. *Exceptional Children, 74,* 264–288.

Skiba, T., Landi, N., Wagner, R., & Grigorenko, E. L. (2011). In search of the perfect phenotype: An analysis of linkage and association studies of reading and reading-related processes. *Behavior genetics, 41,* 6–30.

Skinner, B. F. (1974). *About behaviorism.* New York: Knopf.

Slade, T. I. M., & Watson, D. (2006). The structure of common *DSM-IV* and ICD-10 mental disorders in the Australian general population. *Psychological Medicine, 36,* 1593–1600.

Slee, N., Garnefski, N., van der Leeden, R., Arensman, E., & Spinhoven, P. (2008). Cognitive-behavioral intervention for self-harm: Randomized controlled trial. *British Journal of Psychiatry, 192,* 202–211.

Smith, M. L., & Glass, G. V. (1977). Meta-analysis of psychotherapy outcome studies. *American Psychologist, 32,* 752–760.

Smith, P., Yule, W., Perrin, S., Tranah, T. Dalgeish, T., & Clark, D. M. (2007). A randomized controlled trial of cognitive behavior therapy for PTSD in children and adolescents. *Journal of the American Academy of Child and Adolescent Psychiatry, 46,* 1–51–1061.

Smith, T., Groen, A. D., & Wynn, J. W. (2000). Randomized trial of intensive early intervention for children with pervasive developmental disorder. *American Journal on Mental Retardation, 105,* 269–285.

Smolak, L. (2005). Eating disorders in girls. In D. J. Bell, S. L. Foster, & E. J. Mash (Eds.), *Handbook of behavioral and emotional problems in girls* (pp. 463–487). New York: Kluwer Academic/Plenum.

Smolak, L. (2006). Body image. In J. Worell & C. D. Goodheart (Eds.), *Handbook of girls' and women's psychological health: Gender and well-being across the lifespan* (pp. 69–76). New York: Oxford University Press.

Smolak, L., Levine, M. P., & Schermer, F. (1999). Parental input and weight concerns among elementary school children. *International Journal of Eating Disorders, 25,* 263–271.

Smolak, L., & Murnen, S. K. (2004). A feminist approach to eating disorders. In J. K. Thompson (Ed.), *Handbook of eating disorders and obesity* (pp. 590–605). Hoboken, NJ: Wiley.

Smoller, J. W., Yamaki, L. H., Fagerness, J. A., Biederman, J., Racette, S., Laird, N. M., et al. (2005). The corticotropin-releasing hormone gene and behavioral inhibition in children at risk for panic disorder. *Biological Psychiatry, 57,* 1485–1492.

Smyke, A. T., Dumitrescu, A., & Zeanah, C. H. (2002). Attachment disturbances in young children. *Journal of the American Academy of Child and Adolescent Psychiatry, 41,* 972–982.

Smyke, A. T., Zeanah, C. H., Fox, N. A., Nelson, C. A., & Guthrie, D. (2010). Placement in foster care enhances quality of attachment among young institutionalized children. *Child Development, 81,* 212–223.

Snorrason, I., Belleau, E. L., & Woods, D. W. (2012). How related are hair pulling disorder (trichotillomania) and skin picking disorder? A review of evidence for comorbidity, similarities and shared etiology. *Clinical Psychology Review, 32,* 618–629.

Snowling, M. J., Bishop, D. V. M., Stothard, S. E., Chipchase, B., & Kaplan, C. (2006). Psychosocial outcomes at 15 years of children with a preschool history of speech-language impairment. *Journal of Child Psychology and Psychiatry, 47,* 759–765.

Snyder, H. (2001). Epidemiology of official offending. In R. Loeber & D. P. Farrington (Eds.), *Child delinquents: Development, intervention and service needs* (pp. 25–46). Thousand Oaks, CA: Sage.

Snyder, J., Cramer, A., Afrank, J., & Patterson, G. R. (2005). The contributions of ineffective discipline and parental hostile attributions of child misbehavior to the development of conduct problems at home and school. *Developmental Psychology, 41,* 30–41.

Snyder, J., Reid, J., & Patterson, G. (2003). A social learning model of child and adolescent antisocial behavior. In B. B. Lahey, T. E. Moffitt, & A. Caspi (Eds.), *Causes of conduct disorder and juvenile delinquency* (pp. 27–48). New York: Guilford Press.

Snyder, R., Turgay, A., Aman, M., Binder, C., Fisman, S., & Carroll, A. (2002). Effects of risperidone on conduct and disruptive behavior disorders in children with subaverage IQs. *Journal of the American Academy of Child & Adolescent Psychiatry, 41,* 1026–1036.

Snyderman, M., & Rothman, S. (1987). Survey of expert opinion on intelligence and aptitude testing. *American Psychologist, 42,* 137–144.

Solanto, M. V. (1998). Neuropsychopharmacological mechanisms of stimulant drug action in attention-deficit hyperactivity disorder: A review and integration. *Behavioral Brain Research, 94,* 127–152.

Solanto, M. V., Wasserstein, J., Marks, D. J., & Mitchell, K. J. (2013). Diagnosis of ADHD in adults: What is the appropriate *DSM-5* symptom threshold for hyperactivity-impulsivity? *Journal of Attention Disorders, 16,* 631–634.

Sotelo-Dynega, M., Flanagan, D. P., & Alfonso, V. C. (2011). Overview of specific learning disabilities. In D.P. Flanagan & V.C. Alfonso (Eds.), *Essentials of specific learning disability identification* (pp. 1–20). Hoboken, NJ: Wiley.

Sowell, E. R., Thompson, P. M., Welcome, S. E., Henkenius, A. L., Toga, A. W., & Peterson, B. S. (2003). Cortical abnormalities in children and adolescents with attention-deficit hyperactivity disorder. *Lancet, 362*, 1699–1707.

Spence, S. H., Donovan, C., & Brechman-Toussaint, M. (2000). The treatment of childhood social phobia: The effectiveness of a social skills training-based, cognitive-behavioural intervention, with and without parental involvement. *Journal of Child Psychology and Psychiatry, 41*, 713–726.

Spence, S., & Reinecke, M. (2003). Cognitive approaches to understanding, preventing, and treating child and adolescent depression. In M. Reinecke & D. Clark (Eds.), *Cognitive therapy across the lifespan* (pp. 358–395). Cambridge, UK: Cambridge University Press.

Spencer, T., Biederman, J., Harding, M. Faraone, S., & Wilens, T. (1996). Growth deficits in ADHD children revisited: Evidence for disorder related growth delays. *Journal of the American Academy of Child and Adolescent Psychiatry, 35*, 1460–1467.

Spencer, T. J., Biederman, J., & Wilens, T. E. (2010). Medications used for attention-deficit/hyperactivity disorder. In M. K. Dulcan (Ed.), *Dulcan's textbook of child and adolescent psychiatry* (pp. 681–671). Washington, DC: American Psychiatric Publishing.

Spencer, T., Heiligenstein, J. H., Biederman, J., Faries, D. E., Kratochvil, C. J., Conners, C. K., & Potter, W. Z. (2002). Results from 2 proof-of-concept, placebo-controlled studies of atomoxetine in children with attention-deficit/hyperactivity disorder. *Journal of Clinical Psychiatry, 63*, 1140.

Spessot, A. L., & Peterson, B. S. (2006). Tourette's syndrome: A multifactorial, developmental psychopathology. In D. Cicchetti & D. J. Cohen (Eds.), *Developmental psychopathology, Vol. 3: Risk, disorder, and adaptation* (2nd ed., pp. 436–469). Hoboken, NJ: Wiley.

Spitz, R. A. (1965). *The first year of life: A psychoanalytic study of normal and deviant development of object relations*. Oxford: International Universities Press.

Spitz, R. A., & Wolf, K. M. (1946). Anaclitic depression. *Psychoanalytic Study of the Child, 2*, 313–342.

Sroufe, L. A. (1989a). Pathways to adaptation and maladaptation: Psychopathology as developmental deviation. In D. Cicchetti (Ed.), *Rochester symposium on developmental psychopathology: The emergence of a discipline* (pp. 13–40). Hillsdale. NJ: Erlbaum.

Sroufe, L. A. (1989b). Relationships, self and individual adaptation. In A. J. Sameroff & R. N. Emde (Eds.), *Relationship disturbances in early childhood* (pp. 70–94). New York: Basic Books.

Sroufe, L. A. (1997). Psychopathology as an outcome of development. *Development and Psychopathology, 9*, 251–268.

Sroufe, L. A., & Rutter, M. (1984). The domain of developmental psycho pathology. *Child Development, 55*, 17–29.

Sroufe, L. A., & Waters, B. (1977). Attachment as an organizational construct. *Child Development, 49*, 1184–1199.

St Clair, M. C., Pickles, A., Durkin, K., & Conti-Ramsden, G. (2011). A longitudinal study of behavioral, emotional and social difficulties in individuals with a history of specific language impairment (SLI). *Journal of Communication Disorders, 44*, 186–199.

Stader, S., & Hokanson, J. (1998). Psychological antecedents of depressive symptoms: An evaluation using daily experiences methodology. *Journal of Abnormal Psychology, 107*, 17–26.

Stahl, S. A., McKenna, M. C., & Pagnucco, J. R. (1994). The effects of whole-language instruction: An update and a reappraisal. *Educational Psychologist, 29*, 175–185.

Stallard, P., & Smith, E. (2007). Appraisals and cognitive coping styles associated with chronic post-traumatic symptoms in child road traffic accident survivors. *Journal of Child Psychology and Psychiatry, 48*, 194–201.

Stanovich, K. E. (1986). Matthew effects in reading: Some consequences of individual differences in the acquisition of literacy. *Reading Research Quarterly, 21*, 360–407.

Stark, K. D. (1990). *The treatment of depression during childhood: A school-based program*. New York: Guilford Press.

Stark, K. D., Hoke, J., Ballatore, M., Valdez, C., Scammaca, N., & Griffin, J. (2005). Treatment of child and adolescent depressive disorders. In E. D. Hibbs & P. S. Jensen (Eds.), *Psychosocial treatments for child and adolescent disorders: Empirically based strategies for clinical practice* (pp. 239–265). Washington, DC: American Psychological Association.

Stark, K. D., & Kendall, P. C. (1996). *Treating depressed children*. Ardmore, PA: Workbook.

Stark, K. D., Reynolds, W. M., & Kaslow, N. J. (1987). A comparison of the relative efficacy of self-control therapy and a behavioral problem-solving therapy for depression in children. *Journal of Abnormal Child Psychology, 15*, 91–113.

Stark, K. D., Rouse, L., & Livingston, R. (1991). Treatment of depression during childhood and adolescence: Cognitive behavioral procedures for the individual and family. In P. C. Kendall (Ed.), *Child and adolescent therapy: Cognitive-behavioral procedures* (pp. 165–208). New York: Guilford Press.

Starkey, P., & Cooper, R. G. (1980). Perception of number by human infants. *Science, 210*, 1033–1035.

Stein, D. J., Craske, M. G., Friedman, M. J., & Phillips, K. A. (2011). Meta-structure issues for the *DSM-5*. *Current Psychiatry Reports, 13*, 248–250.

Stein, D. J., Fineberg, N. A., Bienvenu, O. J., Denys, D., Lochner, C., Nestadt, D., et al. (2010). Should OCD be classified as an anxiety disorder? *Depression and Anxiety, 27*, 495–506.

Stein, D. J., Grant, J. E., Franklin, M. E., Keuthen, N., Lochner, C., Singer, H. S., & Woods, D. W. (2010). Trichotillomania (hair pulling disorder), skin picking disorder, and stereotypic movement disorder: Toward *DSM-5*. *Depression and Anxiety, 27*, 611–626.

Stein, D. J., Keating, J., Zar, H. J., & Hollander, E. (1994). A survey of the phenomenology and pharmacotherapy of compulsive and impulsive-aggressive symptoms in Prader-Willi syndrome. *Journal of Neuropsychiatry and Clinical Neurosciences, 6*, 23–29.

Stein, D. J., Phillips, K. A., Bolton, D., Fulford, K. W. M., Sadler, J. Z., & Kendler, K. S. (2010). What is a mental/psychiatric disorder? From *DSM-IV* to *DSM-5*. *Psychological Medicine, 40*, 1759–1765.

Stein, M. A., Waldman, I. D., Sarampote, C. S., Seymour, K. E., Robb, A. S., Conlon, C., et al. (2005). Dopamine transporter genotype and methylphenidate dose response in children with ADHD. *Neuropsychopharmacology, 30*, 1374–1382.

Stein, M. B., & Seedat, S. A. (2004). Pharmacotherapy. In T. L. Morris & J. S. March (Eds.), *Anxiety disorders in children and adolescents* (pp. 329–354). New York: Guilford Press.

Steiner, H., & Remsing, L. (2007). Practice parameter for the assessment and treatment of children and adolescents with oppositional defiant disorder. *Journal of the American Academy of Child & Adolescent Psychiatry, 46*, 126–141.

Steinhausen, H. C., & Metzke, C. W. (2000). Adolescent self-rated depressive symptoms in a Swiss epidemiological study. *Journal of Youth & Adolescence, 29*, 421–439.

Stemple, J. C., & Fry, L. T. (2010). *Voice therapy*. San Diego, CA: Plural.

Stevens, E. A., & Prinstein, J. (2005). Peer contagion of depressogenic attributional styles among adolescents: A longitudinal study. *Journal of Abnormal Child Psychology, 33*, 25–37.

Stevens, J., Harman, J. S., & Kelleher, K. J. (2005). Race/ethnicity and insurance status as factors associated with ADHD treatment patterns. *Journal of Child & Adolescent Psychopharmacology, 15*, 88–96.

Stevens, L. C. (2011). Augmentative/alternative communication. In R. B. Hoodin (Ed.), *Intervention in child language disorders* (pp. 109–124). Boston, MA: Jones & Bartlett.

Stevens, L. J., Kuczek, T., Burgess, J. R., Hurt, E., & Arnold, L. E. (2011). Dietary sensitivities and ADHD symptoms. *Clinical Pediatrics, 50,* 279–293.

Stevens, S. E., Kumsta, R., Kreppner, J. M., Brookes, K. J., Rutter, M., & Sonuga-Barke, E. J. (2009). Dopamine transporter gene polymorphism moderates the effects of severe deprivation on ADHD symptoms: Developmental continuities in gene–environment interplay. *American Journal of Medical Genetics Part B: Neuropsychiatric Genetics, 150,* 753–761.

Stevens, T. N., Ruggiero, K. J., Kilpatrick, D. G., Resnick, H. S., & Saunders, B. E. (2005). Variables differentiating singly and multiply victimized youth: Results from the National Survey of Adolescents and implications for secondary prevention. *Child Maltreatment, 10,* 211–223.

Stevenson, R. E., Schwartz, C. E., & Rogers, R. C. (2012). *Atlas of X-linked intellectual disability syndromes.* New York: Oxford University Press.

Stewart, S. E., Geller, D. A., Jenike, M., Pauls, D., Shaw, D., Mullin, B., & Faraone, S. V. (2004). Long-term outcome of pediatric obsessive-compulsive disorder: A meta-analysis and qualitative review of the literature. *Acta Psychiatrica Scandinavica, 110,* 4–13.

Stewart, S. M., Kennard, B. D., Lee, P. W. H., Hughes, C. W., Mayes, T. L., Emslie, G. J., et al. (2004). A cross-cultural investigation of cognitions and depressive symptoms in adolescents. *Journal of Abnormal Psychology, 113,* 248–257.

Stice, E. (2002). Risk and maintenance factors for eating pathology: A meta-analytic review. *Psychological Bulletin, 128,* 825–848.

Stice, E. (2003). Puberty and body image. In C. Hayward (Ed.), *Gender differences at puberty* (pp. 61–76). New York: Cambridge University Press.

Stice, E., Killen, J. D., Hayward, C., & Taylor, C. B. (1998). Age on onset for binge eating and purging during late adolescence. *Journal of Abnormal Psychology, 107,* 671–675.

Stice, E., Kirz, J., & Borbely, C. (2002). Disentangling adolescent substance use and problem use within a clinical sample. *Journal of Adolescent Research, 17,* 122–142.

Stice, E., Wonderlich, S., & Wade, E. (2006). Eating disorders. In R. T. Ammerman (Ed.), *Comprehensive handbook of personality and psychopathology* (pp. 330–347). Hoboken, NJ: Wiley.

Stiegler, L. N. (2005). Understanding pica behavior. *Focus of Autism and Other Developmental Disabilities, 20,* 27–38.

Stierlin, H., & Weber, G. (1989). *Unlocking the family door: A systemic approach to the understanding and treatment of anorexia nervosa.* New York: Brunner/Mazel.

Stojanovski, S. D., Rasu, R. S., Balkrishnan, R., & Nahata, M. C. (2007). Trends in medication prescribing for pediatric sleep difficulties in US outpatient settings. *Sleep, 30,* 1013–1017.

Stoolmiller, M. (2001). Synergistic interaction of child manageability problems and parent-discipline tactics in predicting future growth in externalizing behavior for boys. *Developmental Psychology, 37,* 814–825.

Stover, A. C., Dunlap, G., & Neff, B. (2008). The effects of a contingency contracting program on the nocturnal enuresis of three children. *Research on Social Work Practice, 18,* 421–428.

Striegel-Moore, R. H., Cachelin, F. M., Dohm, F. A., Pike, K. M., Wilfley, D. E., & Fairburn, C. G. (2001). Comparison of binge eating disorder and bulimia nervosa in a community sample. *International Journal of Eating Disorders, 29,* 157–165.

Striegel-Moore, R. H., Silberstein, L. R., & Rodin, J. (1986). Toward an understanding of risk factors for bulimia. *American Psychologist, 41,* 246–263.

Stringaris, A. (2011). Irritability in children and adolescents: A challenge for *DSM-5. European Child and Adolescent Psychiatry, 20,* 61–66.

Stringaris, A., Baroni, A., Haimm, C., Brotman, M., Lowe, C. H., Myers, F., et al. (2010). Pediatric bipolar disorder versus severe mood dysregulation: Risk for manic episodes on follow-up. *Journal of the American Academy of Child and Adolescent Psychiatry, 49,* 397–405.

Stringaris, A., Cohen, P., Pine, D. S., & Leibenluft, E. (2009). Adult outcomes of adolescent irritability: A 20-year community follow-up. *American Journal of Psychiatry, 166,* 1048–1054.

Stringaris, A., & Goodman, R. (2009). Three dimensions of oppositionality in youth. *Journal of Child Psychology and Psychiatry, 50,* 216–223.

Strober, M., Freeman, R., Lampert, C., Diamond, J., & Kaye, W. (2000). Controlled family study of anorexia nervosa and bulimia nervosa: Evidence of shared liability and transmission of partial syndromes. *American Journal of Psychiatry, 157,* 393–401.

Stromme, P., & Hagberg, G. (2000). Etiology in severe and mild mental retardation: A population-based study of Norwegian children. *Developmental Medicine & Child Neurology, 42,* 76–86.

Stromme, P., & Magnus, P. (2000). Correlations between socioeconomic status, IQ and aetiology in mental retardation: A population-based study of Norwegian children. *Social Psychiatry and Psychiatric Epidemiology, 35,* 12–18.

Stuber, J., Galea, S., Pfefferbaum, B., Vandivere, S., Moore, K., & Fairbrother, G. (2005). Behavior problems in New York City's children after the September 11, 2001, terrorist attacks. *American Journal of Orthopsychiatry, 75,* 190–200.

Stuebing, K. K., Fletcher, J. M., LeDoux, J. M., Lyon, G. R., Shaywitz, S. E., & Shaywitz, B. A. (2002). Validity of IQ-discrepancy classifications of reading disabilities: A meta-analysis. *American Educational Research Journal, 39,* 469–518.

Suarez, L., & Bell-Dolan, D. (2001). The relationship of child worry to cognitive biases: Threat interpretation and likelihood of event occurrence. *Behavior Therapy, 32,* 425–442.

Suarez, L., Bennett, S., Goldstein, C. R., & Barlow, D. (2008). Understanding anxiety disorders from a "triple vulnerability" framework. In M. M. Anthony & M. B. Stein (Eds.), *Oxford handbook of anxiety and related disorders* (pp. 153–172). Oxford, UK: Oxford University Press.

Subotnik, K. L., Nuechterlein, K. H., Ventura, J., Gitlin, M. J., Marder, S., Mintz, J., et al. (2011). Risperidone nonadherence and return of positive symptoms in the early course of schizophrenia. *American Journal of Psychiatry, 168,* 286–292.

Sullivan, H. S. (1953). *The interpersonal theory of psychiatry.* New York: Norton.

Sullivan, K., Hooper, S., & Hatton, D. (2007). Behavioural equivalents of anxiety in children with fragile X syndrome: Parent and teacher report. *Journal of Intellectual Disability Research, 51,* 54–65.

Sullivan, M., Finelli, J., Marvin, A., Garrett-Mayer, E., Bauman, M., & Landa, R. (2007). Response to joint attention in toddlers at risk for autism spectrum disorder. *Journal of Autism and Developmental Disabilities, 37,* 37.

Sumner, C. R., Schuh, K. J., Sutton, V. K., Lipetz, R., & Kelsey, D. K. (2006). Placebo-controlled study of the effects of atomoxetine on bladder control in children with nocturnal enuresis. *Journal of Child and Adolescent Psychopharmacology, 16,* 699–711.

Suveg, C., Zeman, J., Flannery-Schroeder, E., & Cassano, M. (2005). Emotion socialization in families of children with an anxiety disorder. *Journal of Abnormal Child Psychology, 33,* 145–155.

Swanson, H. L., & Stomel, D. (2012). Learning disabilities and memory. In B. Wong & D. Butler (Eds.), *Learning about learning disabilities* (pp. 27–57). New York: Elsevier.

Swanson, J. M., Kraemer, H. C., Hinshaw, S. P., Arnold, L. E., Conners, C. K., Abikoff, H. B., et al. (2001). Clinical relevance of the primary findings of the MTA: Success rates based on severity of ADHD and ODD symptoms at the end of treatment. *Journal of the American Academy of Child and Adolescent Psychiatry, 40,* 168–179.

Sweeney, M., & Pine, D. (2004). Etiology of fear and anxiety. In T. H. Ollendick & J. S. March (Eds.), *Phobic and anxiety disorders in children and adolescents* (pp. 34–60). New York: Oxford University Press.

Sweeney, P. D., Anderson, K., & Bailey, S. (1986). Attributional style in depression: A meta-analytic review. *Journal of Personality and Social Psychology, 50,* 974–991.

Swenson, C. C., & Brown, E. J. (1999). Cognitive-behavioral group treatment for physically abused children. *Cognitive & Behavioral Practice, 6,* 212–220.

Szabo, M., & Lovibond, F. (2004). The cognitive content of thought-listed worry episodes in clinic-referred anxious and nonreferred children. *Journal of Clinical Child and Adolescent Psychology, 33,* 613–622.

Szatmari, P., Offord, D. R., & Boyle, M. H. (1989). Ontario child health study: Prevalence of attention deficit disorder with hyperactivity. *Journal of Child Psychology and Psychiatry, 30,* 219–230.

Szymanski, L. S., & Kaplan, L. C. (2006). Mental retardation. In M. K. Dulcan & J. M. Weiner (Eds.), *Essentials of child and adolescent psychiatry* (pp. 121–152). Washington, DC: American Psychiatric Publishing.

Tackett, J. L., Krueger, R. F., Iacono, W. G., & McGue, M. (2005). Symptom-based subfactors of DSM-defined conduct disorder: Evidence for etiologic distinctions. *Journal of Abnormal Psychology, 114,* 483–487.

Tackett, J. L., Krueger, R. F., Sawyer, M. G., & Graetz, B. W. (2003). Subfactors of *DSM-IV* conduct disorder: Evidence and connections with syndromes from the child behavior checklist. *Journal of Abnormal Child Psychology, 31,* 647–654.

Tager-Flusberg, H., Boshart, J., & Baron-Cohen, S. (1998). Reading the windows to the soul: Evidence of domain-specific sparing in Williams syndrome. *Journal of Cognitive Neuroscience, 10,* 631–639.

Tager-Flusberg, H., & Joseph, R. M. (2003). Identifying neurocognitive phenotypes in autism. In U. Frith & E. Hill (Eds.), *Autism: Mind and brain* (pp. 43–66). New York: Oxford University Press.

Tager-Flusberg, H., Paul, R., & Lord, C. (2005). Language and communication in autism. In F. R. Volkmar, R. Paul, A. Klin, & D. Cohen (Eds.), *Handbook of autism and pervasive developmental disorders, Vol. 1: Diagnosis, development, neurobiology, and behavior* (pp. 335–364). Hoboken, NJ: Wiley.

Tallal, P. (1999). Children with language impairment can be accurately identified using temporal processing measures: A response to Zhang and Tomblin. *Brain and Language, 69,* 222–229.

Tamm, L., Menon, V., & Reiss, A. L. (2006). Parietal attentional system aberrations during target detection in adolescents with attention deficit hyperactivity disorder: Event-related fMRI evidence. *American Journal of Psychiatry, 163,* 1033–1043.

Tanaka, H., Black, J. M., Hulme, C., Stanley, L. M., Kesler, S. R., Whitfield-Gabrieli, S., et al. (2011). The brain basis of the phonological deficit in dyslexia is independent of IQ. *Psychological Science, 22,* 1442–1451.

Tannock, R. (2000). Attention-deficit/hyperactivity disorder with anxiety disorders. In T. E. Brown (Ed.), *Attention deficit disorders and comorbidities in children, adolescents, and adults* (pp. 125–170). Washington, DC: American Psychiatric Press.

Tannock, R. (2013). Rethinking ADHD ad LD in *DSM-5*. *Journal of Learning Disabilities, 46,* 5–25.

Tanofsky-Kraff, M., Wilfley, D. E., Young, J. F., Mufson, L., Yanovski, S. Z., Glasofer, D. R., et al. (2007). Preventing excessive weight gain in adolescents. *Obesity, 14,* 1345–1355.

Tantleff-Dunn, S., Cokee-LaRose, J., & Peterson, R. D. (2004). Interpersonal psychotherapy for the treatment of anorexia nervosa, bulimia nervosa, and binge eating disorder. In J. K. Thompson (Ed.), *Handbook of eating disorders and obesity* (pp. 163–185). Hoboken, NJ: Wiley.

Tarter, R. E., Kirisci, L., Mezzich, A., Cornelius, J., Pajer, K., Vanyukov, M., et al. (2003). Neurobehavior disinhibition in childhood predicts early age onset of substance disorder. *American Journal of Psychiatry, 160,* 1078–1085.

Tarter, R., Kirisci, L., Habeych, M., Reynolds, M., & Vanyukov, M. (2004). Neurobehavior disinhibition in childhood predisposes to substance use disorder by young adulthood: Direct and mediated etiologic pathway. *Drug and Alcohol Dependence, 73,* 121–132.

Tassé, M. J., Schalock, R. L., Balboni, G., Bersani, H., Borthwick-Duffy, S. A., Spreat, S. et al. (2012). The construct of adaptive behavior: Its conceptualization, measurement, and use in the field of Intellectual Disability. *American Journal on Intellectual and Developmental Disabilities, 117,* 291–303.

Tassé, M. J., Schalock, R. L., Balboni, G., Bersani, H., Borthwick-Duffy, S. A., Spreat, S., et al. (2011, June). *Development of the Diagnostic Adaptive Behavior Scale.* Paper presented at the 135th American Associationon Intellectual and Developmental Disabilities Annual Meeting, Saint Paul, MN.

Tassone, F., Hagerman, R. J., Ikle, D., Dyer, P. N., Lampe, M., & Willemsen, R. (1999). FMRP expressions as a potential prognostic indicator in fragile X syndrome. *American Journal of Medical Genetics, 84,* 250–261.

Taylor, E., & Sonuga-Barke, E. (2010). Disorders of attention and activity. In M. Rutter (Ed.), *Rutter's child and adolescent psychiatry* (pp. 521–542). Malden, MA: Blackwell.

Telch, C. F., Agras, W. S., & Linehan, M. M. (2001). Dialectical behavior therapy for binge eating disorder. *Journal of Consulting and Clinical Psychology, 69,* 1061–1065.

Temple, C. M., & Sherwood, S. (2002). Representation and retrieval of arithmetical facts: Developmental difficulties. *Quarterly Journal of Experimental Psychology, 55,* 733–752.

Tems, C. L., Stewart, S. M., Skinner, J. R., Hughes, C. W., & Emslie, G. (1993). Cognitive distortions in depressed children and adolescents: Are they state dependent or traitlike? *Journal of Clinical Child Psychology, 22,* 316–326.

Terr, L. C. (1991). Childhood traumas: An outline and overview. *American Journal of Psychiatry, 148,* 10–20.

Tervo, R.C. (2012). Developmental and behavior problems predict parenting stress in young children with global delay. *Journal of Child Neurology, 27,* 291–296.

Tevyaw, T., & Monti, M. (2004). Motivational enhancement and other brief interventions for adolescent substance abuse: Foundations, applications and evaluations. *Addiction, 99,* 63–75.

Thapar, A., & Rutter, M. (2010). Genetics. In M. Rutter (Ed.), *Rutter's child and adolescent psychiatry* (pp. 339–358). Malden, MA: Blackwell.

Therrien, W. J., Wickstrom, K., & Jones, K. (2006). Effect of a combined repeated reading and question generation intervention on reading achievement. *Learning Disabilities Research & Practice, 21,* 89–97.

Thomas, C. P., Conrad, P., Casler, R., & Goodman, E. (2006). Trends in the use of psychotropic medications among adolescents, 1994 to 2001. *Psychiatric Services, 57,* 63–69.

Thomas, P., Zahorodny, W., Peng, B., Kim, S., Jani, N., Halperin, W., et al. (2012). The association of autism diagnosis with socioeconomic status. *Autism, 16,* 201–213.

Thompson, J. K., Coovert, M. D., & Stormer, S. M. (1999). Body image, social comparison, and eating disturbance: A covariance structure modeling investigation. *International Journal of Eating Disorders, 26,* 43–51.

Thompson, J. K., & Heinberg, L. J. (1993). Preliminary test of two hypotheses of body image disturbance. *International Journal of Eating Disorders, 14,* 59–63.

Thompson, K. M., & Wonderlich, S. A. (2004). Child sexual abuse and eating disorders. In J. K. Thompson (Ed.), *Handbook of eating disorders and obesity* (pp. 679–694). Hoboken, NJ: Wiley.

Thompson, P. M., Vidal, C., Giedd, J. N., Gochman, P., Blumenthal, J., Nicolson, R., et al. (2001). Mapping adolescent brain change reveals dynamic wave of accelerated gray matter loss in very early-onset schizophrenia. *Proceedings of the National Academy of Sciences, 98,* 11650–11655.

Thompson, R. J., Jr., & Gustafson, K. E. (1996). *Adaptation to chronic childhood illness.* Washington, DC: American Psychological Association.

Thompson, T., & Caruso, M. (2002). Self-injury: Knowing what we're looking for. In S. R. Schroeder, M. L. Oster-Granite, & T. Thompson (Eds.), *Self-injurious behavior: Gene-brain-behavior relationships* (pp. 1–21). Washington, DC: American Psychological Association.

Tiet, Q. Q., Wasserman, G. A., Loeber, R., McReynolds, L. S., & Miller, L. S. (2001). Developmental and sex differences in types of conduct problems. *Journal of Child and Family Studies, 10,* 181–197.

Tiggeman, M., & Lynch, J. (2001). Body image across the life span in adult women: The role of self-objectification. *Developmental Psychology, 37*, 243–253.

Tirosch, E., Jaffe, M. (2011). Global developmental delay and mental retardation: A pediatric perspective. *Developmental Disabilities Research Reviews, 17*, 85–92.

Tizard, B., & Hodges, J. (1978). The effect of early institutional rearing on the development of eight year old children. *Journal of Child Psychology and Psychiatry, 19*, 99–118.

Tizard, B., & Rees, J. (1974). A comparison of the effects of adoption, restoration to the natural mother, and continued institutionalization on the cognitive development of four-year-old children. *Child Development, 45*, 92–99.

Tizard, B., & Rees, J. (1976). The effect of early institutional rearing on the behavior problems and affectional relationships of four-year-old children. *Journal of Child Psychology and Psychiatry, 16*, 61–73.

Tolan, P. H., & Dodge, A. (2005). Children's mental health as a primary care and concern: A system for comprehensive support and service. *American Psychologist, 60*, 601–614.

Toll, S. W. M., van der Ven, S. H. G., Kroesbergen, E. H., & van Luit, J. E. H. (2011). Executive functions as predictors of math learning disabilities. *Journal of Learning Disabilities, 44*, 521–532.

Tomlinson, K. L., Brown, S. A., & Abrantes, A. (2004). Psychiatric comorbidity and substance use treatment outcomes of adolescents. *Psychological Addictive Behavior, 18*, 160–169.

Toolan, J. M. (1962). Suicide and suicidal attempts in children and adolescents. *American Journal of Psychiatry, 118*, 719–724.

Torgesen, J. (2009). The response to intervention instructional model: Some outcomes from a large-scale implementation in reading first schools. *Child Development Perspectives, 3*, 38–40.

Toth, S. L., & Cicchetti, D. (1999). Developmental psychopathology and child psychotherapy. In S. Russ & T. Ollendick (Eds.), *Handbook of psychotherapies with children and families* (pp. 15–44). New York: Plenum Press.

Toth, S. L., Cicchetti, D., Macfie, J., Maughan, A., & Vanmeenen, K. (2000). Narrative representations of caregivers and self in maltreated preschoolers. *Attachment and Human Development, 2*, 271–305.

Touchette, E., Petit, D., Tremblay, R. E., & Montplaisir, J. Y. (2009). *Sleep Medicine Reviews, 13*, 355–361.

Towbin, K. E. (2010). Tic disorders. In M. K. Dulcan (Eds.), *Child and adolescent psychiatry* (pp. 417–433). Washington, DC: American Psychiatric Publishing.

Tozzi, F., Thornton, L. M., Klump, K. L., Fichter, M. M., Halmi, K. A., Kaplan, A. S., et al. (2005). Symptom fluctuation in eating disorders: Correlates of diagnostic crossover. *American Journal of Psychiatry, 162*, 732–740.

Tran, L., Sanchez, T., Arellano, B., & Swanson, H. L. (2011). A meta-analysis of the RTI literature for children at risk for reading disabilities. *Journal of Learning Disabilities, 44*, 283–295.

Treadwell, K. H., & Kendall, P. C. (1996). Self-talk in anxiety-disordered youth: States-of-mind, content specificity, and treatment outcome. *Journal of Consulting and Clinical Psychology, 64*, 941–950.

Treatment for Adolescents With Depression Study Team (TADS). (2004). Fluoxetine, cognitive-behavioral therapy, and their combination for adolescents with depression: Treatment for Adolescents With Depression Study (TADS) randomized controlled trial. *Journal of the American Medical Association, 292*, 807–820.

Treatment for Adolescents With Depression Study Team. (2005). Treatment for adolescents with depression study (TADS): Demographic and clinical characteristics. *Journal of American Academy of Child and Adolescent Psychiatry, 44*, 28–40.

Tremblay, R. E. (2003). Why socialization fails: The case of chronic physical aggression. In B. B. Lahey, T. E. Moffitt & A. Caspi (Eds.), *Causes of conduct disorder and juvenile delinquency* (pp. 182–224). New York: Guilford Press.

Tsai, L. Y. (2004a). Autistic disorder. In J. M. Wiener & M. K. Dulcan (Eds.), *The American psychiatric publishing textbook of child and adolescent psychiatry* (pp. 261–315). Washington, DC: American Psychiatric Publishing.

Tsai, L. Y. (2004b). Other pervasive developmental disorders. In J. M. Wiener & M. K. Dulcan (Eds.), *The American psychiatric publishing textbook of child and adolescent psychiatry* (pp. 317–349). Washington, DC: American Psychiatric Publishing.

Tsai, L. Y. (2005). Medical treatment in autism. In D. Zager (Ed.), *Autism spectrum disorders: Identification, education, and treatment* (pp. 395–492). Mahwah, NJ: Erlbaum.

Tsatsanis, K. D. (2005). Neuropsychological characteristics in autism and related conditions. In F. R. Volkmar, R. Paul, A. Klin, & D. Cohen (Eds.), *Handbook of autism and pervasive developmental disorders, Vol. 1: Diagnosis, development, neurobiology, and behavior* (pp. 365–381). Hoboken, NJ: Wiley.

Tucker, J. S., Ellickson, P. L., Orlando, M., Martino, S. C., & Klein, D. J. (2005). Substance use trajectories from early adolescence to emerging adulthood: A comparison of smoking, binge drinking, and marijuana use. *Journal of Drug Issues, 35*, 307–332.

Turkheimer, E., Haley, A., Waldron, M., D'Onofrio, B., & Gottesman, I. I. (2003). Socioeconomic status modifies heritability of IQ in young children. *Psychological Science, 14*, 623–628.

Turner, H., & Bryant-Waugh, R. (2004). Eating disorder not otherwise specified (EDNOS): Profiles of patients presenting at a community eating disorder service. *European Eating Disorders Review, 12*, 18–26.

United Nations Children's Fund (UNICEF). (2012), *Orphans*. Retrieved from http://www.unicef.org/media/media_45279.html

Upadhyaya, H. P., Desaiah, D., Schuh, K. J., Bymaster, F. P., Kallman, M. J., Clarke, D. O., et al. (2013). A review of the abuse potential assessment of atomoxetine. *Psychopharmacology, 226*, 189–200.

Urberg, K. A., Luo, Q., Pilgrim, C., & Degirmencioglu, S. M. (2003). A two-stage model of peer influence in adolescent substance use: Individual and relationship-specific differences in susceptibility to influence. *Addictive Behaviors, 28*, 1243–1256.

U.S. Census Bureau. (2006). *Population estimates*. Retrieved November 1, 2006, from http://www.census.gov/popest/estimates.

U.S. Department of Education. (1977). Assistance to states for education of handicapped children: Procedures for evaluating specific LD. *Federal Register, 42*, 65082–65085.

U.S. Department of Education. (2006). Additional procedures for identifying children with specific learning disabilities. *Federal Register, 71*, 46786–46788.

U.S. Department of Education, National Center for Education Statistics (2012). *Digest of Education Statistics, 2011* (NCES 2012–001). Washington, DC: National Center for Education Statistics.

U.S. Department of Health and Human Services. (2002). *Child maltreatment, 2000: Reports from the states for the national child abuse and neglect data systems*. Washington, DC: Government Printing Office.

Vaidya, C. J. (2011). Neurodevelopmental abnormalities in ADHD. In C. Stanford & R. Tannock (Eds.), *Behavioral neuroscience of attention deficit hyperactivity disorder and its treatment* (pp. 49–66). New York: Springer.

Vaidya, C. J., Austin, G., Kirkorian, G., Ridlehuber, H. W., Desmond, J. E., Glover, G. H., et al. (1998). Selective effects of methylphenidate in attention deficit hyperactivity disorder: A functional magnetic resonance study. *Proceedings of the National Academy of Sciences, 95*, 14494–14499.

Van Acker, R., Loncola, J. A., & Van Acker, E. Y. (2005). Rett syndrome: A pervasive developmental disorder. In F. R. Volkmar, R. Paul, A. Klin, & D. Cohen (Eds.), *Handbook of autism and pervasive developmental disorders, Vol. 1: Diagnosis, development, neurobiology, and behavior* (pp. 126–164). Hoboken, NJ: Wiley.

van den Berg, P., Thompson, J. K., Brandon, K. O., & Coovert, M. (2002). The tripartite influence model of body image and eating disturbance: A covariance structural modeling investigation testing the mediational role of comparison. *Journal of Psychosomatic Research, 53*, 1007–1020.

Van Dommelen, P., Kamphuis, M., van Leerdam, F., deWilde, J. A., Rijpstra, A., Campagne, A. E., et al. (2009). The short- and long-term effects of simple behavioral interventions for nocturnal enuresis in young children. *Journal of Pediatrics, 154,* 662–666.

Van Empelen, R., Jennekens-Schinkel, A., Buskens, E., Helders, P. J. M., & Van Nieuwenhuizen, O. (2004). Functional consequences of hemispherectomy. *Brain, 127,* 2071–2079.

van Goozen, S. H. M., Cohen-Kettenis, P. T., Snoek, H., Matthys, W., Swaab-Barneveld, H., & van Engeland, H. (2004). Executive functioning in children: A comparison of hospitalised ODD and ODD/ ADHD children and normal controls. *Journal of Child Psychology and Psychiatry, 45,* 284–292.

van Goozen, S. H. M., & Fairchild, G. (2006). Neuroendocrine and neurotransmitter correlates in children with antisocial behavior. *Hormones and Behavior, 50,* 647–654.

van Goozen, S. H., Fairchild, G., Snoek, H., & Harold, G. T. (2007). The evidence for a neurobiological model of childhood antisocial behavior. *Psychological Bulletin, 133,* 149–182.

van IJzendoorn, M., Palacios, P., Sonuga-Barke, E., Gunnar, M. R., Vorria, P., McCall, R. B., et al., (2011). Children in institutional care: Delayed development and resilience. *Monographs for the Society for Research in Child Development, 76,* 8–30.

van Kammen, W. B., Loeber, R., & Stouthamer-Loeber, M. (1991). Substance use and its relationship to conduct problems and delinquency in young boys. *Journal of Youth and Adolescence, 20,* 399–413.

van Lang, N. D. J., Ferdinand, R. F., & Verhulst, F. C. (2007). Predictors of future depression in early and late adolescence. *Journal of Affective Disorders, 97,* 137–144.

Van Meter, A. R., Moreira, A. L., & Youngstrom, E. A. (2011). Meta-analysis of epidemiological studies of pediatric bipolar disorder. *Journal of Clinical Psychiatry, 72,* 1250–1256.

Van Meter, A. R., Youngstrom, E. A., Demeter, C., & Findling, R. L. (2012). Examining the validity of cyclothymic disorder in a youth sample. *Journal of Abnormal Child Psychology,* Springer online.

Van Meter, A. R., Youngstrom, E. A., & Findling, R. L. (2012). Cyclothymic disorder: A critical review. *Clinical Psychology Review, 32,* 229–243.

van Oppen, P., de Haan, E., van Balkom, A. J., Spinhoven, P., Hoogduin, K., & van Dyck, R. (1995). Cognitive therapy and exposure in vivo in the treatment of obsessive-compulsive disorder. *Behavior Research and Therapy, 33,* 379–390.

Van Voorst, W., & Quirk, S. (2003). Are relations between parental history of alcohol problems and changes in drinking moderated by positive expectancies? *Alcoholism: Clinical and Experimental Research, 26,* 25–30.

Vander Stoep, A., McCauley, E., Flynn, C., & Stone, A. (2009). Thoughts of death and suicide in early adolescence. *Suicide and Life Threatening Behavior, 39,* 599.

Vannatta, K., Salley, C. G., & Gerhardt, C. A. (2009). Pediatric oncology: Progress and future challenges. In M. C. Roberts & R. G. Steele (Eds.), *Handbook of pediatric psychology* (pp. 319–333). New York: Guilford.

Vanyukov, M. M., & Tarter, R. E. (2000). Genetic studies of substance abuse. *Drug and Alcohol Dependence, 59,* 101–123.

Vasey, M. W., Crnic, K. A., & Carter, W. G. (1994). Worry in childhood: A developmental perspective. *Cognitive Therapy & Research, 18,* 529–549.

Vaz, P. C. M., & Piazza, C. C. (2011). Behavioral approaches to the management of pediatric feeding problems. In A. Southall & C. Martin (Eds.), *Feeding problems in children* (pp. 53–73). Oxon, UK: Radcliffe.

Vega, W. A., Gil, A. G., & Wagner, E. (1998). Cultural adjustment and Hispanic adolescent drug use. In H. B. Kaplan, A. E. Gottfried, & A. W. Gottfried (Series Eds.), W. A. Vega, & A. G. Gil (Vol. Eds.), *Longitudinal research in the social and behavioral sciences: Vol. 2. Drug use and ethnicity in early adolescence* (pp. 125–148). New York: Plenum Press.

Vellutino, F. R., Scanlon, D. M., & Lyon, G. R. (2000). Differentiating between difficult to remediate and readily remediated poor readers: More evidence against the IQ Achievement discrepancy definition of reading disability. *Journal of Learning Disabilities, 33,* 223–238.

Veness, C., Prior, M., Bavin, E., Eadie, P., Cini, E., & Reilly, S. (2012). Early indicators of autism spectrum disorders at 12 and 24 months of age. *Autism, 16,* 163–177.

Verges, A., Steinley, D., Trull, T. J., & Sher, K. (2010). It's the algorithm! *Journal of Abnormal Psychology, 119,* 650–661.

Verhoeven, L., & Vermeer, A. (2006). Literacy achievement of children with intellectual disabilities and differing linguistic backgrounds. *Journal of Intellectual Disability Research, 50,* 725–738.

Vickers, K. S., Patten, C. A., Lane, K., Clark, M. M., Crogan, I. T., Schroeder, D. R., et al. (2003). Depressed versus nondepressed young adult tobacco users: Differences in coping style, weight concerns and exercise level. *Health Psychology, 22,* 498–503.

Vidal, C. N., Rapoport, J. L., Hayashi, K. M., Geaga, J. A., Sui, Y., McLemore, L. E., et al. (2006). Dynaically spreading frontal and cingulate deficits in adolescents with schizophrenia. *Archives of General Psychiatry, 63,* 25–34.

Viding, E., Blair, J. R., Moffitt, T. E., & Plomin, R. (2004). Psychopathic syndrome indexes strong genetic risk for antisocial behavior in 7-year-olds. *Journal of Child Psychology and Psychiatry, 46,* 592–597.

Vismara, L. A., & Rogers, S. J. (2010). Behavioral treatments in autism spectrum disorder: What do we know? *Annual Review of Clinical Psychology, 6,* 447–468.

Vo O. T., LeChasseur, K., Wolfson, A., & Marco, C. (2003). Sleepy preteens: Second pilot of Sleep-Smart Program in 7th graders. *Sleep, 26,* A411.

Vocks, S., Tuschen-Caffier, B., Pietrowsky, R., Rustenbach, S. J., Kersting, A., & Herpertz, S. (2010). Meta-analysis of the effectiveness of psychological and pharmacological treatments for binge eating disorder. *International Journal of Eating Disorders, 43,* 205–217.

Volkmar, F. R., Cohen, D. J., & Paul, R. (1986). An evaluation of *DSM-III* criteria for infantile autism. *Journal of the American Academy of Child and Adolescent Psychiatry, 25,* 190–197.

Volkow, N. D., Wang, G., Fowler, J. S., Logan, J., Gerasimov, M., Maynard, L. et al. (2001). Therapeutic doses of oral methylphenidate significantly increase extracellular dopamine in the human brain. *Journal of Neuroscience, 21,* 121.

Vollebergh, W. A., Iedema, J., Bijl, R. V., de Graaf, R., Smit, F., & Ormel, J. (2001). The structure and stability of common mental disorders: The NEMESIS study. *Archives of General Psychiatry, 58,* 597.

Vollmer, T. R., & Roane, H. S. (1998). Rumination. In L. Phelps (Ed.), *Health-related disorders in children and adolescents* (pp. 564–570). Washington, DC: American Psychological Association.

Volpe, J. J. (2008). Brain injury in premature infants. *Lancet Neurology, 8,* 110–124.

Von Gontard, A. (2011). Elimination disorders: A critical comment on *DSM-5* proposals. *European Child and Adolescent Psychiatry, 20,* 83–88.

Vostanis, P., Feehan, C., Grattan, E., & Bickerton, W. (1996a). A randomized, controlled, out-patient trial of cognitive-behavioural treatment for children and adolescents with depression: 9-month follow-up. *Journal of Affective Disorders, 40,* 105–116.

Vostanis, P., Feehan, C., Grattan, E., & Bickerton, W. (1996b). Treatment for children and adolescents with depression: Lessons from a controlled trial. *Clinical Child Psychology and Psychiatry, 1,* 199–212.

Vygotsky, L. S. (1962). *Thought and language.* Cambridge, MA: Wiley.

Vygotsky, L. S. (1978). *Mind in society: The development of higher psychological processes.* Cambridge, MA: Harvard University Press.

Waaktaar, T., Borge, A. I. H., Fundingsrud, H. P., Christie, H. J., & Torgersen, S. (2004). The role of stressful life events in the development of depressive symptoms in adolescence: A longitudinal community study. *Journal of Adolescence, 27,* 153–163.

Waddington, J., & Buckley, P. (1996). *The neurodevelopmental basis of schizophrenia.* Austin, TX: Landes.

Wade, T. J., & Cairney, J. (2006). Sociological contributions. In R. T. Ammerman (Ed.), *Comprehensive handbook of personality and psychopathology* (Vol. 3, pp. 44–63). Hoboken, NJ: Wiley.

Wagner, E. F., & Austin, A. M. (2006). Substance use disorders. In R. T. Ammerman (Ed.), *Comprehensive handbook of personality and psychopathology* (Vol. 3, pp. 348–366). Hoboken, NJ: Wiley.

Wagner, K. D. (2005). Pharmacotherapy for major depression in children and adolescents. *Progress in Neuro-Psychopharmacology & Biological Psychiatry, 29,* 819–826.

Wagner, K. D., Ambrosini, P., Rynn, M., Wohlberg, C., Yang, R., Greenbaum, M. S., et al. (2003). Efficacy of sertraline in the treatment of children and adolescents with major depressive disorder: Two randomized controlled trials. *Journal of the American Medical Association, 290,* 1033–1041.

Wagner, K. D., Berard, R., Stein, M. B., Wetherhold, E., Carpenter, D. J., Perera, P., et al. (2004). A multicenter, randomized, double-blind, placebo-controlled trial of paroxetine in children and adolescents with social anxiety disorder. *Archives of General Psychiatry, 61,* 1153–1162.

Wagner, K. D., Robb, A. S., Findling, R. L., Jin, J., Gutierrez, M., & Heydorn, W. E. (2004). A randomized, placebo-controlled trial of citalopram for the treatment of major depression in children and adolescents. *American Journal of Psychiatry, 161,* 1079–1083.

Wakefield, A. J., Murch, S. H., Anthony, A., Linnell, J., Casson, D. M., Malik, M., et al. (1998). Ileal lymphoid-nodular hyperplasia, non-specific colitis, and pervasive developmental disorder in children. *Lancet, 351,* 637–641.

Wakefield, J. C. (1992). Disorder as harmful dysfunction: A conceptual critique of DSM-III-R's definition of mental disorder. *Psychological Review, 99,* 232–247.

Wakefield, J. C. (1997). When is development disordered? Developmental psychopathology and the harmful dysfunction analysis of mental disorder. *Development and Psychopathology, 9,* 269–290.

Wakschlag, L. S., Choi, S. W., Carter, A. S., Hullsiek, H., Burns, J., McCarthy, K., et al. (2012). Defining the developmental parameters of temper loss in early childhood. *Journal of Child Psychology and Psychiatry, 53,* 1099–1108.

Waldron, H. B., & Kaminer, Y. (2004). On the learning curve: The emerging evidence supporting cognitive-behavioral therapies for adolescent substance abuse. *Addiction, 99,* 93–105.

Waldron, H. B., Slesnick, N., Brody, J. L., Charles W. T., & Thomas R. P. (2001). Treatment outcomes for adolescent substance abuse at 4- and 7-month assessments. *Journal of Consulting and Clinical Psychology, 69,* 802–813.

Walker, D. D., Roffman, R. A., Stephens, R. S., Wakana, K., & Berghuis, J. (2006). Motivational enhancement therapy for adolescent marijuana users: A preliminary randomized controlled trial. *Journal of Consulting and Clinical Psychology, 74,* 628–632.

Walker, E., & Lewine, J. (1990). Prediction of adult-onset Schizophrenia. *American Journal of Psychiatry, 1,* 47.]

Walker, E. F., & Lewine, R. R. (1993). Sampling biases in studies of gender and schizophrenia. *Schizophrenia Bulletin, 19,* 1.

Walkup, J. T., Albano, A. M., Piacentini, J., Birmaher, B., Compton, S. N., Sherrill, J. T., et al. (2008). Cognitive behavioral therapy, sertraline, or a combination in childhood anxiety. *New England Journal of Medicine, 359,* 2753–2766.

Wallander, J. L., Dekker, M. C., & Koot, H. M. (2006). Risk factors for psychopathology in children with intellectual disability: A prospective longitudinal population-based study. *Journal of Intellectual Disability Research, 50,* 259–268.

Walters, J. T. R., O'Donovan, M., & Owen, M. J. (2011). The genetics of schizophrenia. In W. Gaebel (Ed.), *Schizophrenia: Current science and clinical practice* (pp. 109–140). New York: Wiley.

Warner, L. A., Pottick, K. J., & Mukherjee, A. (2004). Use of psychotropic medications by youths with psychiatric diagnoses in the U.S. mental health system. *Psychiatric Services, 55,* 309–311.

Warren, S. L., Emde, R. N., & Sroufe, L. A. (2000). Internal representations: Predicting anxiety from children's play narratives. *Journal of the American Academy of Child and Adolescent Development, 39,* 100–107.

Warren, S. L., Huston, L., Egeland, B., & Sroufe, L. A. (1997). Child and adolescent anxiety disorders and early attachment. *Journal of the American Academy of Child and Adolescent Psychiatry, 36,* 637–644.

Warren, S. L., & Simmens, J. (2005). Predicting toddler anxiety/depressive symptoms: Effects of caregiver sensitivity of temperamentally vulnerable children. *Infant Mental Health Journal, 26,* 40–55.

Warren, S. L., & Sroufe, L. A. (2004). Developmental issues. In T. H. Ollendick & J. S. March (Eds.), *Phobic and anxiety disorders in children and adolescents* (pp. 92–115). New York: Oxford University Press.

Waschbusch, D. A. (2002). A meta-analytic examination of comorbid hyperactive-impulsive-attention problems and conduct problems. *Psychological Bulletin, 128,* 118–150.

Waschbusch, D. A., Willoughby, M. T., & Pelham, W. E. (1998). Criterion validity and the utility of reactive and proactive aggression: Comparisons to attention deficit hyperactivity disorder, oppositional defiant disorder, conduct disorder, and other measures of functioning. *Journal of Clinical Child Psychology, 27,* 396–405.

Washburn, J. J., Richardt, S. L., Styer, D. M., Gebhardt, M., Juzwin, K. R., Yourek, A., & Aldridge, D. (2012). Psychotherapeutic approaches to non-suicidal self-injury in adolescents. *Child and Adolescent Psychiatry and Mental Health, 6,* 1–21.

Wasserman, G. A., & Seracini, A. M. (2001). Family risk factors and interventions. *Child delinquents: Development, intervention, and service needs* (pp. 165–189). Thousand Oaks, CA: Sage.

Watson, H. J., & Rees, C. S. (2008). Meta-analysis of randomized, controlled treatment for pediatric obsessive-compulsive disorder. *Journal of Child Psychology and Psychiatry, 49,* 489–498.

Watson, J. B., & Rayner, R. (1920). Conditioned emotional reactions. *Journal of Experimental Psychology, 3,* 1–14.

Watson, P. J., Brymer, M. J., & Bonanno, G. A. (2011). Postdisaster psychological intervention since 9/11. *American Psychologist, 66,* 482–494.

Waxmonsky, J. G., Wymbs, F. A., Pariseau, M. E., Belin, P. J., Waschbusch, D. A., Baboscai, L., et al. (2012). A novel group therapy for children with ADHD and severe mood dysregulation. *Journal of Attention Disorders, 17,* 527–541.

Waxmonsky, J., Pelham, W., Cummings, M., O'Connor, B., Majumdar, A., Verley, J., et al. (2008). The impact of manic-like symptoms on the multimodal treatment of pediatric attention deficit hyperactivity disorder. *Journal of Child and Adolescent Psychopharmacology, 18,* 573–588.

Webster-Stratton, C. (1990). Long-term follow-up of families with young conduct problem children: From preschool to grade school. *Journal of Clinical Child Psychology, 19,* 144–149.

Webster-Stratton, C. (2005). The incredible years: A training series for the prevention and treatment of conduct problems in young children. In E. D. Hibbs & P. S. Jensen (Eds.), *Psychosocial treatments for child and adolescent disorders: Empirically based strategies for clinical practice* (pp. 507–555). Washington, DC: American Psychological Association.

Webster-Stratton, C., & Hammond, M. (1990). Predictors of treatment outcome in parent training for families with conduct problem children. *Behavior Therapy, 21,* 319–337.

Webster-Stratton, C., & Hammond, M. (1999). Marital conflict management skills, parenting style, and early-onset conduct problems: Processes and pathways. *Journal of Child Psychology and Psychiatry, 40,* 917–927.

Webster-Stratton, C., & Reid, M. J. (2007). Incredible years parents and teachers training series: A Head Start partnership to promote social competence and prevent conduct problems. In P. Tolan, J. Szapocznik, & S. Sambrano (Eds.), *Preventing youth substance abuse: Science-based programs for children and adolescents* (pp. 67–88). Washington, DC: American Psychological Association.

Webster-Stratton, C., Reid, M. J., & Hammond, M. (2001). Preventing conduct problems, promoting social competence: A parent and teacher training partnership in Head Start. *Journal of Clinical Child Psychology, 30,* 283–302.

Webster-Stratton, C., Reid, M. J., & Hammond, M. (2004). Treating children with early-onset conduct problems: Intervention outcomes for parent, child, and teacher training. *Journal of Clinical Child and Adolescent Psychology, 33,* 105–124.

Wechsler, D. (1958). *The measurement and appraisal of adult intelligence.* Baltimore, MD: Williams & Wilkins.

Wechsler, D. (2003). *Wechsler intelligence scale for Children: Administration and scoring manual* (4th ed.). San Antonio, TX: The Psychological Corporation.

Weems, C. F., Berman, S. L., Silverman, W. K., & Saavedra, L. M. (2001). Cognitive errors in youth with anxiety disorders: The linkages between negative cognitive errors and anxious symptoms. *Cognitive Therapy and Research, 25,* 559–575.

Weems, C. F., Pina, A. A., Costa, N. M., Watts, S. E., Taylor, L. K., & Cannon, M. F. (2007). Predisaster trait anxiety and negative affect predict posttraumatic stress in youths after hurricane Katrina. *Journal of Consulting and Clinical Psychology, 75,* 154–159.

Weems, C. F., Silverman, W. K., & La Greca, A. M. (2000). What do youth referred for anxiety problems worry about? Worry and its relation to anxiety and anxiety disorders in children and adolescents. *Journal of Abnormal Child Psychology, 28,* 63–72.

Weems, C. F., & Watts, S. E. (2005). Cognitive models of childhood anxiety. In C. M. Velotis (Ed.), *Anxiety disorder research* (pp. 205–232). Hauppauge, NY: Nova Science.

Weierich, M. R., & Nock, M. K. (2008). Posttraumatic stress symptoms mediate the relation between childhood sexual abuse and nonsuicidal self-injury. *Journal of Consulting and Clinical Psychology, 76,* 39.

Weinfield, N. S., Sroufe, L. A., & Egeland, B. (2000). Attachment from infancy to early adulthood in a high-risk sample: Continuity, discontinuity, and their correlates. *Child Development, 71,* 695–702.

Weis, R., & Pucke, E. R. (2013). Aggression replacement training for disruptive adolescents: Efficacy, effectiveness, and new directions involving families. In E. Trejos-Castillo (Ed.), *Youth: Practices, perspectives and challenges* (pp. 179–206). Hauppauge NY: Nova.

Weismer, S. E. (2008). Speech perception in specific language impairment. In D. B. Pisoni, R. E. Remez, & S. E. Weismer (Eds.), *The handbook of speech perception* (pp. 567–588). Malden, MA: Blackwell.

Weiss, L. H., & Schwarz, J. C. (1996). The relationship between parenting types and older adolescents' personality, academic achievement, adjustment, and substance use. *Child Development, 67*(5), 2101–2114.

Weisz, J. R. (1990). Cultural-familial mental retardation: A developmental perspective on cognitive performance and "helpless" behavior. In R. M. Hodapp, J. A. Burack, & E. Zigler (Eds.), *Issues in the developmental approach to mental retardation* (pp. 137–168). New York: Cambridge University Press.

Weisz, J. R., Doss, A. J., & Hawley, K. M. (2005). Youth psychotherapy outcome research: A review and critique of the evidence base. *Annual Review of Psychology, 56,* 337–363.

Weisz, J. R., & Jensen, A. L. (2001). Child and adolescent psychotherapy in research and practice contexts: Review of the evidence and suggestions for improving the field. *European Child & Adolescent Psychiatry, 10,* S12–S18.

Weisz, J. R., Jensen, A. L., & McLeod, B. D. (2005). Development and dissemination of child and adolescent psychotherapies: Milestones, methods, and a new deployment-focused model. In E. D. Hibbs & P. S. Jensen (Eds.), *Psychosocial treatments for child and adolescent disorders: Empirically based strategies for clinical practice* (pp. 9–39). Washington, DC: American Psychological Association.

Weisz, J. R., Thurber, C. A., Sweeney, L., Proffitt, V. D., & LeGagnoux, G. L. (1997). Brief treatment of mild-to-moderate child depression using primary and secondary control enhancement training. *Journal of Consulting and Clinical Psychology, 65,* 703–707.

Weisz, J. R., Weiss, B., Alicke, M. D., & Klotz, M. L. (1987). Effectiveness of psychotherapy with children and adolescents: A meta-analysis for clinicians. *Journal of Consulting and Clinical Psychology, 55,* 542–549.

Weisz, J. R., Weiss, B., Han, S. S., Granger, D. A., & Morton, T. (1995). Effects of psychotherapy with children and adolescents revisited: A meta-analysis of treatment outcome studies. *Psychological Bulletin, 117,* 450–468.

Welch, S. L., & Fairburn, C. G. (1996). Childhood sexual and physical abuse as risk factors for the development of bulimia nervosa: A community-based case control study. *Child Abuse and Neglect, 20,* 633–642.

Weller, E. B., Weller, R. A., & Danielyan, A. K. (2004). Mood disorders in prepubertal children and adolescents. In J. M. Wiener & M. K. Dulcan (Eds.), *The American Psychiatric Publishing textbook of child and adolescent psychiatry* (pp. 411–481). Washington, DC: American Psychiatric Publishing.

Wellington, T. M., Semrud-Clikeman, M., Gregory, A. L., Murphy, J. M., & Lancaster, J. L. (2006). Magnetic resonance imaging volumetric analysis of the putamen in children with ADHD: Combined type versus control. *Journal of Attention Disorders, 10,* 171–180.

Wells, K. C., Pelham, W. E., Kotkin, R. A., Hoza, B., Abikoff, H. B., Abramowitz, A., et al. (2000). Psychosocial treatment strategies in the MTA study: Rationale, methods, and critical issues in design and implementation. *Journal of Abnormal Child Psychology, 28,* 483–505.

Wendling, P. (2009). PTSD can present months after a shooting. *Clinical Psychiatry News, 21,* 20–21.

Werba, B. E., Eyberg, S. M., Boggs, S. R., & Algina, J. (2006). Predicting outcome in parent-child interaction therapy: Success and attrition. *Behavior Modification, 30,* 618–646.

West, A. E., Henry, D. B., & Pavuluri, M. N. (2007). Maintenance model of integrated psychosocial treatment in pediatric bipolar disorder: A pilot feasibility study. *Journal of the American Academy of Child & Adolescent Psychiatry, 46,* 205–212.

West, A. E., Jacobs, R. H., Westerholm, R., Lee, A., Carbray, J., Heidenreich, J., et al. (2009). Child- and family-focused cognitive-behavioral therapy for pediatric bipolar disorder: Pilot study of group treatment format. *Journal of the Canadian Academy of Child and Adolescent Psychiatry, 18,* 239–246.

West, A. E., & Weinstein, S. M. (2012). A family-based psychosocial treatment model. *International Journal of Psychiatry and Related Sciences, 49,* 86–94.

Westen, D., Novotny, C. M., & Thompson-Brenner, H. (2004). The empirical status of empirically supported psychotherapies: Assumptions, findings, and reporting in controlled clinical trials. *Psychological Bulletin, 130,* 631–663.

Wetherby, A. M., Watt, N., Morgan, L., & Shumway, S. (2007). Social communication profiles of children with autism spectrum disorders late in the second year of life. *Journal of Autism and Developmental Disorders, 37,* 960–975.

Whalen, C. K., Henker, B., King, P. S., Jamner, L. D., & Levine, L. (2004). Adolescents react to the events of September 11, 2001: Focused versus ambient impact. *Journal of Abnormal Child Psychology, 32,* 1–11.

White, H. R., Labouvie, E. W., & Papadaratsakis, V. (2005). Changes in substance use during the transition to adulthood: A comparison of college students and their noncollege age peers. *Journal of Drug Issues, 35,* 281–306.

White, H. R., McMorris, B. J., Catalano, R. F., Fleming, C. B., Haggerty, K. P., & Abbott, R. D. (2006). Increases in alcohol and marijuana use during the transition out of high school into emerging adulthood: The effects of leaving home, going to college, and high school protective factors. *Journal of Studies on Alcohol, 67,* 810–822.

Whiteman, M., Fanshel, D., & Grundy, J. F. (1987). Cognitive-behavioral interventions aimed at anger of parents at risk of child abuse. *Social Work, 32,* 469–474.

Whitlock, J., Eckenrode, J., & Silverman, D. (2006). Self-injurious behaviors in a college population. *Pediatrics, 117,* 1939–1948.

Whitlock, J., Purington, A., & Gershkovich, M. (2009). Media, the internet, and nonsuicidal self-injury. In M. K. Nock (Ed.), *Understanding nonsuicidal self-injury* (pp. 139–155). Washington, DC: American Psychological Association.

Whittinger, N. S., Langley, K., Fowler, T. A., Thomas, H. V., & Thapar, A. (2007). Clinical precursors of adolescent conduct disorder in children with attention-deficit/hyperactivity disorder. *Journal of the American Academy of Child & Adolescent Psychiatry, 46,* 179–187.

Whittington, C. J., Kendall, T., & Fonagy, P. (2004). Selective serotonin reuptake inhibitors in childhood depression: Systematic review of published versus unpublished data. *Lancet, 363,* 1341–1345.

Wickwire, E. M., Roland, M. M. S., Elkin, T. D., & Schumacher, J. A. (2008). Sleep disorders. In D. Reitman (Ed.), *Handbook of psychological assessment, case conceptualization, and treatment* (pp. 622–651). New York: Wiley.

Widom, C. S., & Kuhns, J. B. (1996). Childhood victimization and subsequent risk for promiscuity, prostitution, and teenage pregnancy: A prospective study. *American Journal of Public Health, 86,* 1607–1612.

Wight, R. G., Sepulveda, J. E., & Aneshensel, C. S. (2004). Depressive symptoms: How do adolescents compare with adults? *Journal of Adolescent Health, 34,* 314–323.

Wild, L. G., Flisher, A. J., & Lombard, C. (2004). Suicidal ideation and attempts in adolescents: Associations with depression and six domains of self-esteem. *Journal of Adolescence, 27,* 611–624.

Wilens, T. E., Biederman, J., Kwon, A., Ditterline, J., Forkner, P., Moore, H., et al. (2004). Risk of substance use disorders in adolescents with bipolar disorder. *Journal of the American Academy of Child & Adolescent Psychiatry, 43,* 1380–1386.

Wilens, T. E., & Spencer, T. J. (2000). The stimulants revisited. *Child and Adolescent Psychiatric Clinics of North America, 9,* 573–603.

Wilens, T. E., Spencer, T., & Biederman, J. (1996). Attention deficit disorder with substance abuse. In T. E. Brown (Ed.), *Subtypes of attention deficit disorder in children, adolescents, and adults* (pp. 319–339). Washington, DC: American Psychiatric Press.

Wilfley, D., Frank, M., Welch, R., Spurrell, E., & Rounsaville, B. (1998). Adapting interpersonal psychotherapy to a group format (IPT-G) for Binge Eating Disorder: Toward a model for adapting empirically supported treatments. *Psychotherapy Research, 8,* 379–391.

Wilkinson, P., & Goodyer, I. (2011). Non-suicidal self-injury. *European Child & Adolescent Psychiatry, 20,* 103–108.

Wilkinson, P. O., & Goodyer, M. (2006). Attention difficulties and mood-related ruminative response style in adolescents with unipolar depression. *Journal of Child Psychology and Psychiatry, 47,* 1284–1291.

Willcutt, E. G., Pennington, B. F., Olson, R. K., Chhabildas, N., & Hulslander, J. (2005). Neuropsychological analyses of comorbidity between reading disability and attention deficit hyperactivity disorder: In search of the common deficit. *Developmental Neuropsychology, 27,* 35–78.

Willcutt, E. G., Nigg, J. T., Pennington, B. F., Solanto, M. V., Rohde, L. A., Tannock, R., et al. (2012). Validity of *DSM-IV* attention-deficit/hyperactivity disorder symptom dimensions and subtypes. *Journal of Abnormal Psychology.*

Williams, C. A. (2005). Neurological aspects of the Angelman syndrome. *Brain & Development, 27,* 88–94.

Williams, R. J., Chang, S. Y., & Addiction Center Adolescent Research Group. (2000). A comprehensive and comparative review of adolescent substance abuse treatment outcome. *Clinical Psychology: Science and Practice, 7,* 138–166.

Williams, W. L., Jackson, M., & Friman, P. C. (2007). Encopresis and enuresis. In P. Sturmey (Ed.), *Functional analysis in clinical treatment* (pp. 171–190). Burlington, MA: Academic Press.

Williamson, D. E., Birmaher, B., Frank, E., Anderson, B. P., Matty, M. K., & Kupfer, D. J. (1998). Nature of life events and difficulties in depressed adolescents. *Journal of the American Academy of Child & Adolescent Psychiatry, 37,* 1047–1057.

Williamson, P., McLeskey, J., Hoppey, D., & Rentz, T. (2006). Educating students with mental retardation in general education classrooms. *Exceptional Children, 72,* 347–361.

Willoughby, M. T. (2003). Developmental course of ADHD symptomatology during the transition from childhood to adolescence: A review with recommendations. *Journal of Child Psychology and Psychiatry, 4,* 88–106.

Wilson, C., Hall, M., Abramowitz, J. S., Whiteside, S., Kalsy, S. A., Tolin, D. F., et al. (2012). Thought control strategies in adolescents: Links with OCD symptoms and meta-cognitive beliefs. *Behavioral and Cognitive Psychotherapy, 40,* 438.

Wilson, G. T., Becker, C. B., & Heffernan, K. (2003). Eating disorders. In E. J. Mash & R. A. Barkley (Eds.), *Child psychopathology* (pp. 687–715). New York: Guilford Press.

Wilson, G. T., Fairburn, C. G., & Agras, W. S. (1997). Cognitive-behavioral therapy for bulimia nervosa. In D. M. Garner & P. Garfinkel (Eds.), *Handbook of treatment for eating disorders* (pp. 67–93). New York: Guilford Press.

Wilson, G. T., Fairburn, C. C., Agras, W. S., Walsh, B. T., & Kraemer, H. (2002). Cognitive-behavioral therapy for bulimia nervosa: Time course and mechanisms of change. *Journal of Consulting and Clinical Psychology, 70,* 267–274.

Wilson, G. T., & Pike, K. M. (2001). Eating disorders. In D. H. Barlow (Ed.), *Clinical handbook of psychological disorders: A step-by-step treatment manual* (pp. 332–375). New York: Guilford Press.

Wilson, G. T., & Sysko, R. (2009). Frequency of binge eating episodes in bulimia nervosa and binge eating disorder. *International Journal of Eating Disorders, 42,* 603–610.

Wilson, G. T., Wilfley, D. E., Agras, W. S., & Bryson, S. W. (2010). Psychological treatments of binge eating disorder. *Archives of General Psychiatry, 67,* 94–101.

Wilson, J. J., & Levin, R. (2005). Attention-deficit/hyperactivity disorder and early-onset substance use disorders. *Journal of Child and Adolescent Psychopharmacology, 15,* 751–763.

Wilson, J. K., & Rapee, R. M. (2005). The interpretation of negative social events in social phobia: Changes during treatment and relationship to outcome. *Behaviour Research and Therapy, 43,* 373–389.

Windle, M., & Davies, P. T. (1999). Depression and heavy alcohol use among adolescents: Concurrent and prospective relations. *Development and Psychopathology, 11,* 823–844.

Wing, L. (1981). Asperger's syndrome: A clinical account. *Psychological Medicine, 11,* 115–129.

Wing, L. (2000). Past and future of research on Asperger syndrome. In A. Klin, F. R. Volkmar, & S. S. Sparrow (Eds.), *Asperger syndrome* (pp. 418–432). New York: Guilford Press.

Winters, K. C., Martin, C. S., & Chung, T. (2011). Commentary on O'Brien: Substance use disorders in *DSM-5* when applied to adolescents. *Addiction, 106,* 882–897.

Winters, K. C., Stinchfield, R. D., Opland, E., Weller, C., & Latimer, W. W. (2000). The effectiveness of the Minnesota model approach in the treatment of adolescent drug abusers. *Addiction, 95,* 601–612.

Wise, B. K., Cuffe, S. P., & Fischer, T. (2001). Dual diagnosis and successful participation of adolescents in substance abuse treatment. *Journal of Substance Abuse Treatment, 21,* 161–165.

Wittchen, H., Gloster, A. T., Beesdo-Baum, K., Fava, G. A., & Craske, M. G. (2010). Agoraphobia: A review of the diagnostic classification position and criteria. *Depression and Anxiety, 27,* 113–133.

Wittchen, H., Kessler, R. C., Pfister, H., Hofler, M., & Lieb, R. (2000). Why do people with anxiety disorders become depressed? *Acta Psychiatrica Scandinavica, 102,* 14–23.

Wittchen, H., Reed, V., & Kessler, R. C. (1998). The relationship of agoraphobia and panic in a community sample of adolescents and young adults. *Archives of General Psychiatry, 55,* 1017–1024.

Witwer, A. N., & Lecavalier, L. (2008). Examining the validity of autism spectrum disorder subtypes. *Journal of Autism and Developmental Disorders, 38,* 1611–1624.

Wohlfarth, T., Lekkerkerker, F., & van Zwieten, B. (2004). Use of selective serotonin reuptake inhibitors in childhood depression. *Lancet, 364,* 659–660.

Wolf, F. M., Guevara, J. P., Grum, C. M., Clark, N. M., & Cates, C. J. (2002). Educational interventions for asthma in children. *Cochrane Database Sys Reviews, 4.*

Wolf, M., Barzillai, M., Gottwald, S., Miller, L., Spencer, K., Norton, E., et al. (2009). The RAVE-O intervention. *Mind, Brain, and Education, 3,* 84–91.

Wolf, M., & Bowers, P. G. (1999). The double-deficit hypothesis for the developmental dyslexias. *Journal of Educational Psychology, 91,* 415.

Wolf, M., Gottwald, S., & Orkin, M. (2009). Serious word play: How multiple linguistic emphasis in RAVE-O instruction improve multiple reading skills. *Mind, Brain, and Education, 3,* 21–24.

Wolf, M., Miller, L., & Donnelly, K. (2000). Retrieval, Automaticity, Vocabulary, Elaboration, Orthography (RAVE-O). *Journal of Learning Disabilities, 33,* 375–386.

Wolfberg, P. J., & Schuler, A. L. (2006). Promoting social reciprocity and symbolic representation in children with autism spectrum disorders. In T. Charman & W. Stone (Eds.), *Social and communication development in autism spectrum disorders* (pp. 180–218). New York: Guilford Press.

Wolpe, J. (1958). *Psychotherapy by reciprocal inhibition.* Stanford, CA: Stanford University Press.

Wonderlich, S. A., Gordon, K. H., Mitchell, J. E., Crosby, R. D., & Engel, S. G. (2009). The validity and clinical utility of binge eating disorder. *International Journal of Eating Disorders, 42,* 687–705.

Wonderlich, S., Crosby, R., Mitchell, J., Thompson, K., Redlin, J., Demuth, G., et al. (2001). Pathways mediating sexual abuse and eating disturbance in children. *International Journal of Eating Disorders, 29,* 270–279.

Wong, B. (1997). Research on genre-specific strategies in enhancing writing in adolescents with learning disabilities. *Learning Disability Quarterly, 20,* 140–159.

Wood, A., Harrington, R., & Moore, A. (1996). Controlled trial of a brief cognitive-behavioural intervention in adolescent patients with depressive disorders. *Journal of Child Psychology and Psychiatry, 37,* 737–746.

Wood, L. A., & Hart, P. (2007). Facilitating language skills in individuals who use augmentative and alternative communication. In A. G. Kamhi, J. J. Masterson, & K. Apel (Eds.), *Clinical decision making in developmental language disorders.* (pp. 323–336). Baltimore, MD: Brookes.

Woodcock, R. W., McGrew, K. S., & Mather, N. (2001). *The Woodcock-Johnson III.* Itasca, IL: Riverside.

Woodward, L. J., & Fergusson, D. M. (1999). Early conduct problems and later risk of teenage pregnancy in girls. *Development and Psychopathology, 11,* 127–141.

Woodward, L. J., & Fergusson, D. M. (2001). Life course outcomes of young people with anxiety disorders in adolescence. *Journal of the American Academy of Child and Adolescent Psychiatry, 40,* 1086–1094.

World Health Organization. (2001). *Mental health: New understanding, new hope.* Geneva, Switzerland: Author.

Wozniak, J., Biederman, J., Kiely, K., Ablon, J. S., Faraone, S. V., Mundy, E., et al. (1995). Mania-like symptoms suggestive of childhood-onset bipolar disorder in clinically referred children. *Journal of the American Academy of Child and Adolescent Psychiatry, 34,* 867–876.

Wozniak, J., Petty, C. R., Schreck, M., Moses, A., Faraone, S. V., & Biederman, J. (2011). High level of persistence of pediatric bipolar-I disorder from childhood into adolescent years. *Journal of Psychiatric Research, 45,* 1273–1282.

Wu, K. K., Anderson, V., & Castiello, U. (2006). Attention-deficit/hyperactivity disorder and working memory: A task switching paradigm. *Journal of Clinical and Experimental Neuropsychology, 28*(8), 1288–1306.

Wu, P., Hoven, C. W., Liu, X., Cohen, P., Fuller, C. J., & Shaffer, D. (2005). Substance use, suicidal ideation and attempts in children and adolescents. *Suicide and Life-Threatening Behavior, 34,* 408–420.

Wynn, K. (1992). Addition and subtraction by human infants. *Nature, 358,* 749–750.

Wysocki, T., Buckloh, L. M., & Greco, P. (2009). The psychological context of diabetes mellitus in youths. In M. C. Roberts & R. G. Steele (Eds.), *Handbook of pediatric psychology* (pp. 287–302). New York: Guilford.

Xu, F., & Spelke, E.S. (2000). Large number discrimination in 6-month-old infants. *Cognition, 74,* 1–11.

Yairi, E., & Ambrose, N. (2005). *Early childhood stuttering.* Austin, TX: Pro-Ed.

Yairi, E., & Seery, C.H. (2011). *Stuttering: Foundations and clinical applications.* Boston: Pearson.

Yates, T. M. (2009). Developmental pathways from child maltreatment to nonsuicidal self-injury. In M. K. Nock (Ed.), *Understanding nonsuicidal self-injury* (pp. 117–137). Washington, DC: American Psychological Association.

Yates, T. M., Tracy, A. J., & Luthar, S. S. (2008). Nonsuicidal self-injury among "privileged" youths: Longitudinal and cross-sectional approaches to developmental process. *Journal of Consulting and Clinical Psychology, 76,* 52.

Yeargin-Allsop, M., Boyle, C., & van Naarden, K. (2008). The epidemiology of developmental disabilities. In P. J. Accardo (Ed.), *Neurodevelopmental disabilities in infancy and childhood* (pp. 61–100). Baltimore, MD: Brookes.

Yoder, P. J., & McDuffie, A. S. (2006). Treatment responding to and initiating joint attention. In T. Charman & W. Stone (Eds.), *Social and communication development in autism spectrum disorders* (pp. 117–142). New York: Guilford Press.

Young, J. F., & Mufson, L. (2003). *Manual for interpersonal psychotherapy-adolescent skills training (IPT-AST).* New York: Columbia University.

Young, J. F., Mufson, L., & Davies, M. (2006). Efficacy of interpersonal psychotherapy-adolescent skills training: An indicated preventive intervention for depression. *Journal of Child Psychology and Psychiatry, 47,* 1254–1262.

Young, S., Amarasinghe, M. (2010). Non-pharmacological treatments for ADHD: A lifespan approach. *Journal of Child Psychology and Psychiatry, 51,* 116–133.

Young, S., Stallings, M., Corley, R., Krauter, K., & Hewitt, J. (2000). Genetic and environmental influences on behavioral disinhibition. *American Journal of Medical Genetics, 96,* 684–695.

Youngstrom, E. A., Birmaher, B., & Findling, R. L. (2008). Pediatric bipolar disorder: Validity, phenomenology, and recommendations for diagnosis. *Bipolar Disorders, 10,* 194–214.

Youngstrom, E. A., Freeman, A. J., & Jenkins, M. M. (2009). The assessment of children and adolescents with bipolar disorder. *Child and Adolescent Psychiatric Clinics of North America, 18,* 353–390.

Youngstrom, E. A., van Meter, A., Algorta, G. P. (2010). The bipolar spectrum: Myth or reality? *Current Psychiatry Reports, 12,* 479–489.

Youssef, G., Plancherel, B., Laget, J., Corcos, M., Flament, M. F., & Halfon, O. (2004). Personality trait risk factors for attempted suicide among young women with eating disorders. *European Psychiatry, 19,* 131–139.

Yssledyke, J., Burns, M., Scholin, S., & Parker, D. (2010). Instructionally valid assessment within response to intervention. *Teaching Exceptional Children, 42,* 54–61.

Ystgaard, M., Hestetun, I., Loeb, M., & Mehlum, L. (2004). Is there a specific relationship between childhood sexual and physical abuse and repeated suicidal behavior? *Child Abuse & Neglect, 28,* 863–875.

Yule, W., & Smith, P. (2010). Post-traumatic stress disorder. In M. Rutter (Ed.), *Rutter's child and adolescent psychiatry* (pp. 686–697). Malden, MA: Blackwell.

Zahn-Waxler, C. (2000). The development of empathy, guilt, and internalization of distress. In R. J. Davidson (Ed.), *Anxiety, depression, and emotion* (pp. 222–265). New York: Oxford University Press.

Zahn-Waxler, C., Cole, P. M., & Barrett, K. C. (1991). Guilt and empathy: Sex differences and implications for the development of depression. In J. Garber & K. A. Dodge (Eds.), *The development of emotion regulation and dysregulation* (pp. 243–272). Cambridge: Cambridge University Press.

Zahr, N. M., & Sullivan, E. V. (2008). Translational studies of alcoholism bridging the gap. *Alcohol Research & Health, 31,* 215.

Zammit, S., Allebeck, P., Andreasson, S., Lundberg, I., & Lewis, G. (2002). Self reported cannabis use as a risk factor for schizophrenia in

Swedish conscripts of 1969: Historical cohort study. *British Medical Journal, 325,* 1–5.

Zane, T. (2005). Fads in special education: An overview. In J. W. Jacobson, R. M. Foxx, & J. A. Mulick (Eds.), *Controversial therapies for developmental disabilities: Fad, fashion, and science in professional practice* (pp. 175–191). Mahwah, NJ: Erlbaum.

Zeanah, C. H., Berlin, L. J., & Boris, N. W. (2011). Practitioner review: Clinical applications of attachment theory and research for infants and young children. *Journal of Clinical Child Psychology and Psychiatry, 52,* 819–833.

Zeanah, C. H., Egger, H. L., Smyke, A. T., Nelson, C. A., Foz, N. A., Marshall, P. J., et al. (2009). Institutional rearing and psychiatric disorders in Romanian preschool children. *American Journal of Psychiatry, 166,* 777–785.

Zeanah, C. H., Fox, N. A., & Nelson, C. A. (2012). The Bucharest Early Intervention Project: Case study in the ethics of mental health research. *Journal of Nervous and Mental Disease, 200,* 243–247.

Zeanah, C. H., & Gleason, M. M. (2010). *Reactive attachment disorder: A review for DSM-5.* Washington, DC: American Psychiatric Association.

Zeanah, C. H., & Smyke, A. T. (2008). Attachment disorders in family and social context. *Infant Mental Health Journal, 29, 219-233.*

Zeanah, C. H., Smyke, A. T., Koga, S. F., & Carlson, E. (2005). Attachment in institutionalized and community children in Romania. *Child Development, 76,* 1015–1028.

Zigler, E. (1969). Developmental versus difference theories of mental retardation and the problem of motivation. *American Journal of Mental Deficiency, 73,* 536–556.

Zigler, E., Balla, D., & Hodapp, R. M. (1986). On the definition and classification of mental retardation. *American Journal of Mental Deficiency, 89,* 215–230.

Zigler, E., Hodapp, R. M., & Edison, M. R. (1990). From theory to practice in the care and education of mentally retarded individuals. *American Journal on Mental Retardation, 95,* 1–12.

Zirkel, P. A., & Thomas, L. B. (2010). State laws and guidelines for implementing RTI. *Teaching Exceptional Children, 43,* 60–73.

Zuckerman, M. (2007). Sensation seeking and substance use and abuse: Smoking, drinking, and drugs. In M. Zuckerman (Ed.), *Sensation seeking and risky behavior* (pp. 107–143). Washington, DC: American Psychological Association.

Zwaigenbaum, L., Bryson, S., Lord, C., Rogers, S., Carter, A., Carver, L., et al. (2009). Clinical assessment and management of toddlers with suspected autism spectrum disorder. *Pediatrics, 123,* 1383–1392.

Index

child/adolescent presentation, 396–398
diagnosing, 370, 394–396, 589
etiology, 398–399
Excoriation Disorder, 401–402
summary, 413–414
tic disorders, 399–401, 408–409
treatment, 408–409
Trichotillomania, 401
Panic Disorder, 381–383, 385–386,
    406–407, 411, 413
prevalence, 367–369
school refusal, 380–381
Separation Anxiety Disorder, 370–373,
    387, 403–406, 412
Social Anxiety Disorder, 376–379,
    403–406, 412–413
Specific Phobia, 373–376, 402–403, 411, 412
summary, 412–414
test anxiety, 380
treatment
    behavior therapy, 402–403
    cognitive-behavior therapy, 403–408
    exposure therapy, 402
    habit reversal training, 408–409
    pharmacotherapy, 409–411
    self-monitoring treatment, 408
    summary, 414
vulnerability to, 368–369
Anxiety sensitivity, 386
Anxiolytics, 325
APD (Antisocial Personality Disorder),
    259, 301–302, 455
Aphonia, 143
Apoptosis, 43
Appetite manipulation, 580–581
Applied behavior analysis (ABA),
    21 (image), 117–121
Approach-avoidance theory of stuttering, 154
APSAC (American Professional Society on the
    Abuse of Children), 451
APS (Attenuated Psychosis Syndrome), 554
Arginine vasopressin (AVP), 621
Aripiprazole (Abilify), 197
Arithmetic computation, 241–242, 242 (figure)
Arnold, J. S. G., 540
Arsenault, L., 561
Asarnow, J. R., 495, 561
Asperger, Hans, 168
Asperger's Disorder, 174–175
    See also Autism Spectrum Disorder
Assessment of child behavior
    behavioral observations, 59–60
    clinical interviews, 57–59, 58–59 (table)
    components, 56–57
    evaluating tests, 69–72
    norm-referenced testing, 60–69
    purposes, 55–56
    subjectivity in, 7
    summary, 83–84
    See also Diagnosis; Psychotherapy;
        specific disorders
ASSIST (Alcohol, Smoking, and Substance
    Involvement Screening Test),
    331, 332 (table)
Assistive technology, 117
Association studies, 41
Asthma, 643, 643 (image)

Atomoxetine (Strattera), 272
Attachment
    depressive disorders and, 494
    quality of, 456
    theory of, 437–438
    See also Parent-child interaction; Reactive
        Attachment Disorder (RAD)
Attachment and biobehavioral catch-up (ABC),
    446–447, 446 (image)
Attention-Deficit/Hyperactivity Disorder
    (ADHD)
    associated disorders
        Antisocial Personality Disorder, 259
        Autism Spectrum Disorder, 174
        Bipolar Disorder, 260
        conduct problems, 259, 298
        Disruptive Mood Dysregulation Disorder,
            471–472
        elimination disorders, 620–621
        Oppositional Defiant Disorder, 259
        Schizophrenia, 555, 556
        sleep disorders, 633
        Substance Use Disorder, 339, 350
        summary, 283–284
        trauma-related disorders, 443–444
    associated problems, 260–262, 283–284
    case studies, 256, 258
    diagnosing, 252–258, 253–254 (table), 283
    epidemiology, 262–265, 284
    etiology
        Barkley's neurodevelopment model,
            269–270, 269 (figure)
        brain structure/functioning, 266–269
        early environment, 265–266
        genetic factors, 265
        summary, 284
    summary, 283–285
    symptoms
        adults, 258–259
        children, 256–258
        hyperactive/impulsive presentation, 257
        inattentive presentation, 257–258
    treatment
        comparisons of, 279–281,
            281–282 (figure)
        diet, 281, 282 (figure)
        evidence-based, 271
        medication, 271–275, 272 (figure),
            273 (image), 274 (figure)
        psychosocial, 275–279, 278 (figure)
        sleep and exercise, 282–283, 283 (image)
        summary, 284–285
Attention-placebo control group, 33
Attention problems. See Attention-Deficit/
    Hyperactivity Disorder
Attenuated Psychosis Syndrome (APS), 554
Attributions for misbehavior, 308
Attrition in research studies, 35
Atypical antipsychotics, 537–538,
    538 (figure), 564–565
Auditory feedback, 144–145
Auditory integration training, 198
Auditory perception problems, 134–135
Auditory processing deficit model, 155
Augmentative/alternative communication
    (AAC), 140–142
Authoritarian parents, 50

Authoritative parents, 50
Autism and Developmental Disabilities
    Monitoring (ADDM) Network,
    175, 176–177
Autism Genome Project, 179
Autism Spectrum Disorder (ASD)
    associated disorders
        Attention-Deficit/Hyperactivity
            Disorder, 174
        communication disorders,
            161, 166–167, 173–174
        Fragile X, 107
        Intellectual Disability, 166–167,
            170, 172–173
        Rett syndrome, 171
        Schizophrenia, 550, 556
        seizures, 174
        trauma-related, 437
    case studies, 167, 171
    definitions, 168–169 (table), 168–171,
        200–201
    developmental model, 188 (figure)
    empirical data, 20
    epidemiology, 175–178, 201
    etiology
        brain structure/function,
            177, 179–183, 189
        genes and early environment, 179
        language problems,
            189–190, 189 (image)
        social cognition deficits, 183–189
        summary, 201
    specifiers, 171–172
    treatment
        best practices, 200
        early identification, 190–191, 200
        home-based, 191–194
        infant/toddler interventions, 195–197
        medication, 197–198
        options with limited empirical support,
            198–200, 199 (table)
        school-based, 194–195
        summary, 201–202
Autonomous children, 309–310, 310 (figure)
Aversion therapy, 350
Avoidance, 134, 376, 491
Avoidant/Restrictive Food Intake Disorder
    (ARFID), 576–580, 576 (table),
    577 (image), 579 (image)
AVP (arginine vasopressin), 621
Axelson, D. A., 544

Babar-Melik, E., 375
Baboscai, L., 478
Baker, S. K., 244
Bandura, A., 46, 393
Barkley's neurodevelopmental model,
    269–270, 269 (figure)
Barlow, D., 368
Barnard, L., 273
Baron-Cohen, S., 180, 183, 187
Barriers to children's services, 6
Bartlett, K. K., 120
Basal ganglia, 44, 44 (image), 189
BASC-2, 70 (figure), 74–75
Bauman, K. E., 120
Baumrind, D., 49–50

Bayley Scales of Infant and Toddler Development Third Edition (BSID-III), 95, 96
BEARS mnemonic, 628–629, 628 (table)
Beck, A., 77, 491–492
Beck, S. J., 278
BED. *See* Binge Eating Disorder
Bedtime fading strategy, 635
Bedtime resistance, 632–633
   See also Sleep disorders
Bedwetting. *See* Elimination disorders
Behavioral contract, 402
Behavioral genetics, 39–40, 265
Behavioral inhibition system (BIS), 268, 378–379, 379 (figure)
Behavioral learning, 46–48
Behavioral observation, 59–60
Behavioral phenotypes, 103–104
Behavioral rigidity, 7
Behavior family systems therapy (BFST), 648
Behavior functioning, tests of, 69
Behavior therapies, 76–77, 81, 646
   See also specific disorders
BEIP (Bucharest Early Intervention Project), 440–442, 441 (table), 443, 448
Belhar, M. C., 48
Belin, P. J., 478
Benefits and costs of alcohol use, 352–353, 352 (figure)
Benninger, K. L., 278
Benninger, W. B., 278
Bentrall, R., 566
Benzodiazepine receptor agonists, 637
Bereavement, 490
Berghuis, J., 35
Berliner, L., 450
Bernard, K., 445
Betrayal, 457–458
Bettelheim, Bruno, 20, 178–179
BFST (behavior family systems therapy), 648
Bibliotherapy, 34, 34 (figure)
Bick, J., 445
Biederman, J., 264, 273
Biklen, D., 20
Binet, A., 62
Binge drinking, 333–334, 341, 342 (figure)
Binge Eating Disorder (BED)
   course, 595
   diagnosing, 585–587, 585 (table)
   etiology, 601
   psychotherapy, 610–611, 611 (figure)
   See also Bulimia Nervosa
Binggeli, N. J., 456
Binokay, S., 375
Bioecological systems theory, 51–52
Biology and behavior, 9–10, 41–46
   See also Brain structure/function; Genetic factors; Neurological development and biology
Biopsychosocial model of substance abuse, 344–347
Biosocial model of NSSI, 512
Bipolar I Disorder, 520–523, 541 (table)
Bipolar II Disorder, 523–524, 524 (table)
Bipolar Spectrum Disorders (BSDs)
   associated disorders/features, 260, 473–474, 525–526, 531–532, 535
   Bipolar I Disorder, 520–523, 541 (table)

Bipolar II Disorder, 523–524, 524 (table)
   case studies, 520, 528
   Cyclothymic Disorder, 524–525, 525 (table)
   diagnosing, 469
   epidemiology, 528–531
   etiology, 532–537
   specifying symptoms, 526–527
   summary, 568–569
   treatment
      cognitive-behavioral therapy, 539–540
      family-focused treatment, 543–545
      medication, 537–539
      psychoeducational psychotherapy, 540–543
      social rhythm therapy, 535
      types, 519, 525 (figure)
Birkeland, S., 348
Birmaher, B., 544
BIS (behavioral inhibition system), 268, 378–379, 379 (figure)
Bishop, S. L., 175
Black-and-white (dichotomous) thinking, 589
Blanz, B., 555
Bleuler, E., 545–546
Blocking effects of medication, 350
Blood-injection-injury phobias, 375
BMI scores, 582–583
Boellner, S. W., 273
Bondy, A., 140
Borderline Personality Disorder (BPD), 302, 511
Bowley, J., 48, 78, 436–439
Bradley, C., 271
Brain structure/function
   alcohol effects, 334–336
   anxiety disorders and, 375, 398–399, 398 (image)
   Attention-Deficit/Hyperactivity Disorder and, 266–269, 266 (figure), 267 (image)
   Autism Spectrum Disorder and, 177, 179–183, 180 (figure), 181 (image), 189, 189 (image)
   depressive disorders and, 475–476
   development of, 43–45
   language disorder and, 134
   learning disabilities and, 210
   Schizophrenia and, 558–560
   stuttering and, 153
   trauma-related disorders and, 427–428, 442–443
   word reading problems and, 223–225, 223 (image), 224 (image)
   See also Genetic factors; Neurological development and biology
Brassard, M. R., 456
Brennan, P. A., 495
Broca's area, 153
Bronfenbrenner, U., 51
Brotman, M. A., 473, 475
Browne, A., 457
Bruce, J., 441
BSDs. *See* Bipolar Spectrum Disorders
BSID-III (Bayley Scales of Infant and Toddler Development Third Edition), 95, 96
Bucharest Early Intervention Project (BEIP), 440–442, 441 (table), 443, 448

Buckley, S., 104
Bukowski, W. M., 260–261
Bulimia Nervosa (BN)
   course, 594–595
   diagnosing, 583–585, 584 (table)
   etiology, 595–601
   medication, 613, 613 (figure)
   treatment, 604–609
Burton, E., 496
Buschmann, A., 131
Butter, E., 120
Butter, E. M., 198
Butterworth, B., 240
Butzlaff, R. L., 561
Byrd-Craven, J., 239

CAGE questionnaire, 331
Callahan, R., 216
Callous-unemotional traits, 295–296, 296 (figure)
Campbell, C., 566
CAMS (Child-Adolescent Anxiety Multimodal Study), 409–410, 409 (figure)
Canalization, 45
Cancer, 643
Cannabis. *See* Marijuana
Cannabis Youth Treatment Study, 357–358, 358 (figure)
Cannon, M., 553–554, 561
Cantor, E. N., 453
Cardiac arrhythmias, 590
Carlson, E., 445
Carlson, G., 531
Carlson, J. I., 100
Carr, E. G., 100
Carrier, J., 282
Carroll, J., 62
Carter, B. D., 641–642
Carver, F. W., 475
Case studies. *See specific disorders*
Casoff, J., 282
Caspi, A., 553–554, 562
Casson, D. M., 20
Castelli, F., 182
Catastrophic thinking, 386–387, 393, 407, 633
Catechol-*O*-methyltransferase (COMT), 442, 558
Causes of disorders
   behavioral influences, 46–48
   biological influences, 9–10, 41–46
   correlations and, 20, 29–30, 29–31, 30 (figure)
   single-subject research and, 38
   social-cultural influences, 51–52
   summary, 52–53
   See also Brain structure/function; Environment; Families; Genetic factors; Research studies; *specific disorders*
CCK (cholecystokinin), 596
Cerebral palsy, 97
Cerebellum, 45
Cha, C. B., 510
Chandler, M. C., 273
Chang, K. D., 545
Chantoor, I., 578
Chard, D. J., 244

Child Abuse Prevention and Treatment Act, 448–449

Child-Adolescent Anxiety Multimodal study (CAMS), 409–410, 409 (figure)

Childhood deprivation. *See* Trauma-related disorders

Childhood-onset fluency disorder. *See* Stuttering

Child maltreatment
  case studies, 450–451, 452, 453
  confidentiality issues, 24
  defined, 448–453
  depressive disorders, 510–511
  diagnosing, 448–453, 449 (table)
  effects, 454–457, 454–458
  prevalence, 453–454
  summary, 465–466
  types, 451–452 (table)

Child-parent interaction. *See* Parent-child interaction

Children in the Community Study, 474

Cholecystokinin (CCK), 596

Chorionic villus sampling (CVS), 115

Choudhury, M., 403

Chromosomal abnormalities
  about, 38–39
  Angelman's Syndrome, 108–109, 108 (image)
  Down Syndrome, 104–106, 104 (figure), 105 (image)
  Fragile X Syndrome, 106–107, 106 (image)
  organic *vs.* cultural familial, 102 (table)
  Prader-Willi Syndrome, 107–108, 107 (image)
  Williams Syndrome, 109–110, 109 (image)

Chromosomal microarray (CMA), 97–98, 98 (image)

Chronic health problems
  conditions, 642–645
  efficacy of treatment, 649–650
  interventions, 646–649

Chronis, A., 247, 277

Chronis-Tuscano, A., 280–281

Chronotherapy, 480, 637–638

Circadian Rhythm Sleep-Wake Disorder, 637–638

Clark, D. M., 433

Clarke, A., 264

Clarke, G. N., 502

Classical conditioning
  about, 46
  elimination disorders and, 622–623, 624 (table)
  sleep disorders and, 632
  Social Anxiety Disorder and, 378
  Specific Phobia and, 375
  Substance Use Disorders and, 351

Classroom universal design, 116–117, 118 (figure)

Cleanliness training, 623

Clinical behavior therapy, 275–276
  See also Behavior therapies

Clinicians and research, 21–22

Clozapine (Clozaril), 564

CMA (chromosomal microarray), 97–98, 98 (image)

COACHES intervention program, 275

COBY (Course and Outcome of Bipolar Children) study, 529–530, 535

Coercive parent-child cycle, 306–307, 306 (figure)

Cognition, 59, 443, 491, 535

Cognitive appraisal of trauma, 429–430

Cognitive avoidance theory, 392–393

Cognitive-behavioral therapies (CBT)
  for anxiety disorders, 34, 34 (figure), 403–408
  behavior family systems therapy, 648
  for child abuse/neglect, 460–461
  child- and family-focused (CFF-CBT), 539–540, 539 (table)
  for depressive disorders, 478–479, 478 (table), 499–502, 513–515, 515 (figure)
  for eating disorders, 597, 604–608, 606 (figure), 608 (figure), 609 (figure)
  for sleep disorders, 635–636
  for substance use disorders, 351–353, 351 (figure)

Cognitive biases, 491

Cognitive delays from trauma, 456–457

Cognitive distortion, 393, 463–464, 491, 492 (table)

Cognitive numbing, 420

Cognitive processing problems, 134–135, 214, 225, 229–230, 535

Cognitive restructuring techniques, 406–407, 462–464, 501, 646–647

Cognitive Strategy Instruction, 235–237

Cognitive therapy, 77, 80, 158, 158 (table), 646–648

Cohen, J. A., 462

Coles, E. K., 280–281

Cologne Sleep Study, 479

Columbine High School killings, 7, 8

Combined presentation of ADHD, 256

Communication disorders
  Autism Spectrum Disorder associated with, 161, 166–167, 173–174
  definitions, 128
  late language emergence, 128–131
  prevalence, 127
  social (pragmatic) disorder, 159–163
  specific language impairment, 131–134
  See also Language Disorders; Speech disorders

Communication enhancement training, 544

Comorbid mental health problems, 72, 75, 101
  See also specific disorders

Competence boundaries of professionals, 23–24

Complex sentences, 137–138

Composition. *See* Written expression

Comprehension problems. *See* Reading fluency/comprehension problems

Comprehensive assessment of learning disabilities, 212–214, 215 (figure)

Comprehensive (Exner) System, 68–69

Compulsions, 395

Computed tomography (CT), 41

Computer-based therapy, 405–406

COMT (catechol-*O*-methyltransferase), 442, 558

Conceptual skills, 91, 92 (table)

Concurrent validity, 72

Conduct problems
  associated disorders/features, 101, 259, 298–300, 455, 484–485, 531
  case studies, 291, 293, 297
  childhood-onset *vs.* adolescent-onset, 294–295
  Conduct Disorder (CD), 291–297, 294 (table), 321, 455, 531
  diagnosing, 287, 289, 292 (table), 295, 297
  epidemiology, 300–302, 322
  etiology
    adolescent-limited conduct problems, 312
    genetic factors, 302–303, 303 (figure)
    neighborhoods, 311–312
    neurological development, 304–305
    parent-child interactions, 306–310
    peer relationships, 310–311
    social information processing, 310
    summary, 322
    temperament, 303, 305
  Oppositional Defiant Disorder (ODD), 288–289 (table), 288–290, 321
  summary, 321–322
  treatment
    children with limited prosocial emotions, 296
    older children/adolescents, 317–318
    summary, 322
    younger children, 312–317

Confidentiality, 24–25

Conflict theory of stuttering, 154

Confusional arousals, 639

Constipation, 625–627

Consultation and liaison in pediatric psychology, 641–642

Contingency management, 402–403, 581

Continuous positive air pressure (CPAP) device, 640–641

Control groups, 36 (figure)

Controlling behavior, 378–379

Convergent validity, 71

Conversational recast training, 138–139

Conversational repair, 161, 162

Conversation initiations, 161–162

Conversation maintenance, 162

Cook, I., 182

Cool Teens, 405

Coon, H., 182

Cooper, R. G., 239

Cooper, Z., 595

Coping skills
  for chronic health problems, 642–643
  for depressive disorders, 501–502
  for mood problems, 489–491
  for trauma-related, 429–430, 432

Cormac, I., 566

Cornwell, B. R., 475

Corpus callosum, 44, 45

Correlations, 20, 29–31, 30 (figure)

Correll, C. U., 564

Corsico, A., 489

Corsini, R., 75–76

Cortez, 43

Cortico-striatal-thalamic circuit, 398–399, 398 (image)

Cortisol levels, 427–428, 489

Co-sleeping approach, 632

INTRODUCTION TO ABNORMAL CHILD AND ADOLESCENT PSYCHOLOGY

Substance Use Disorder, 345
testing for chromosomal microarray, 97–98, 98 (image)
trauma-related disorders, 442
See also Chromosomal abnormalities
Genotypes, 39
George, E. L., 544, 545
George, M., 487
Gerdes, A. C., 260–261
GERD (gastroesophageal reflux disease), 579
Gershkovich, M., 509
Gersten, R., 244
Gilligan, C., 600, 601
Global Developmental Delay (GDD), 94–97, 95 (table), 123
See also Intellectual Disability
Glucksman, E., 426
Glutamate functioning, 334
Gnagy, E. M., 277, 280–281
Gold, J. A., 260–261
Goldfried, R., 19
Goldstein, M. J., 495, 561
Gottesman, I. I., 46
Graduated ignoring strategy, 634–635
Graham, S., 238
Grammar, 133, 235
Grandiosity, 521, 522 (table)
Grand mal seizures, 174
Granger, D. A., 81
GRAPES+D, 521–523, 522 (figure)
Graphemes, 221
Gray, J. A., 268, 298
Great Smokey Mountains Study, 380, 474, 475
Greenbaum, M. S., 497
Gregory, A. M., 489
Greiner, A. R., 280
Grief, 608
Grimm, J., 301
Group therapy, 602, 603 (table), 648–349
Growth dysregulation hypothesis, 180
Guided imagery, 647
Gunnar, M. R., 441
Guthrie, D., 495, 561
Gutierrez, M., 497
Guyer, A. E., 473, 475

Haddock, G., 566
Hair loss. *See* Trichotillomania
Hair pulling, 401
Hallucinations, 547–549, 548 (figure), 548 (table), 556
Hallucinogens, 325
Hamilton, E. B., 561
Hammen, C., 495
Hamza, C. A., 507–508
Han, S. S., 81
Hand-over-hand assistance, 194
Handwriting instruction, 237–238
Hanley, G. P., 100, 121
Hanson, C. A., 278
Happe, F., 182
Harmful dysfunction perspective, 7–8
Harm reduction approach to treatment, 354–355
Harrington, H. L., 553–554
Harris, Eric, 7, 8
Harris, K. R., 238

Hart, S. N., 456
Hartmann, M., 555
Hawes, D. J., 296
Hazardous situations and substance use, 330
Head circumference, 442–443, 445
Heath, N. L., 509
Hebb, D. O., 46
Helplessness, 493–494
Henderson, C. E., 357
Herpertz, S., 610
Heuristics, 245–246
Heydorn, W. E., 497
High comorbidity, 72–73
Hillman, C. H., 282
Hinshaw, S. P., 260–261, 280
Hippocampus, 428, 558–559
Hipwell, A. E., 486–487
Hispanic culture and eating disorders, 594
HIV (human immunodeficiency virus), 111
Hoard, M. K., 239
Hodapp, R. M., 110
Holroyd, T., 475
Homotypic continuity, 3
Hooley, J. M., 561
Hornbrook, M. C., 502
Hornsey, H., 180
Horovitz, M., 101
Horwood, L. J., 301
Hostile parenting behavior, 306–307, 308, 379
Hoza, B., 260–261, 277, 280
HPA dysregulation, 443
Hudson, J. L., 403
Huerta, M., 175
Human immunodeficiency virus (HIV), 111
Hus, V., 175
Hyperactivity, 252–256
See also Attention-Deficit/Hyperactivity Disorder (ADHD)
Hypernasality, 143
Hyperphagia, 107
Hypersensitivity to dopamine, 100
Hypnotics, 325
Hypomania, 523
Hyponasality, 143
Hypopigmentation, 109
Hypothalamus-pituitary-adrenal (HPA) axis, 304, 489
Hypotheses, 28–29, 56

Iacono, W. G., 589
IBD (Inflammatory Bowel Disease), 645
IDEA (Individuals with Disabilities Education Act), 74, 116
IDEA 2004 (Individuals with Disabilities Education Improvement Act), 208–209, 213
Identification in speech therapy, 157
IEP (Individualized Education Program), 116
IFSP (Individualized Family Services Plan), 116
Immature speech production, 147
Impaired control, 326–327
Impulsiveness, 257
See also Attention-Deficit/Hyperactivity Disorder (ADHD); Conduct problems
Inappropriate compensatory behavior, 583–584, 597

Inattentive presentation, 257–258
See also Attention-Deficit/Hyperactivity Disorder (ADHD)
Incidental teaching, 139
Inclusion, 116, 195
Incontinence. *See* Enuresis
Incredible Years Programs, 316–317
Independent silent reading, 230–231
Individual differences, focus on, 16–17
Individualized Education Program (IEP), 116
Individualized Family Services Plan (IFSP), 116
Individuals with Disabilities Education Act (IDEA), 74, 116
Individuals with Disabilities Education Improvement Act (IDEA 2004), 208–209, 213
Indulgent parents, 50
Infant deprivation. *See* Trauma-related disorders
Infant Health and Development Program (IHDP), 115
Infantile anorexia, 577–578
Infant/preschool prevention of Intellectual Disability, 115
Infant/toddler intervention in ASD, 195–197
Inflammatory Bowel Disease (IBD), 645
Influences on development. *See* Causes of disorders
Informants, 57
Informational transmission of anxiety, 376
Informed consent, 26
Inhalants, 325
Inhibition, lack of. *See* Disinhibited Social Engagement Disorder (DSED)
Inpatient treatment for substance use, 350–351
Insecure attachment, 48, 49, 456, 458
Insight of children, 59
Insomnia
associated disorders, 633
diagnosing, 629, 630 (table)
epidemiology, 629–631
etiology, 631–632, 631 (figure)
specific difficulties, 632–633
treatment, 633–637
Insula brain region, 534
Intellectual Disability
associated disorders
Autism Spectrum Disorder, 166–167, 170, 172–173, 178
Pica, 575
Specific Learning Disorder, 207
case studies, 89, 96, 112
causes
Angelman's Syndrome, 108 (image)
behavioral phenotypes, 103–104
childhood illness/injury, 113
chromosomal abnormalities, 103–110, 219
cultural-familial disability, 102–103, 102 (table), 113–114
Down Syndrome, 104 (figure), 105 (image)
embryonic teratogen exposure, 111–112
Fragile X Syndrome, 106 (image)
metabolic disorders, 110–111
Prader-Willi Syndrome, 107 (image)

Multiple relationships, 25–26
Multisystemic Family Therapy (MFT), 648
Multisystemic Therapy (MST), 6, 318–319, 320 (figure)
Murch, S. H., 20
Murphy-Graham, E., 348
Murray, R. M., 553–554, 561
Music therapy, 198
Myelination, 43
MZ (monozygotic), 488

Nadder, T. S., 298
Naltrexone, 122, 350
"Naming the Enemy" activity, 541
Narrative skills, 160–163
Narrative text comprehension, 232
National Health Interview Survey, 215
National Institutes for Mental Health (NIMH), 473, 474, 559
National Reading Panel (NRP), 225, 230
National Survey of Children's Health (NSCH), 175, 176–177
Naturalistic observation, 60
Naturally fluent speech, 156
Natural opioids, 335
Needed supports for Intellectual Disability, 94
Negative affect pathways, 345–346
Negative automatic thoughts, 491–492, 493 (table)
Negatively escalating cycle of communication, 544
Negative punishment, 47, 121
Negative reinforcement, 47, 376, 378, 392–393, 399, 430, 579–580
Negative self-statements, 404, 462–464
Negative symptoms of Schizophrenia, 550
Neglect of children, 452–457
    See also Child maltreatment
Neighborhood influence on conduct disorders, 311–312
Neural plasticity, 45–46
Neural pruning, 559–560, 559 (image)
Neural tubes, 43
Neurobehavioral disinhibition, 346–347
Neuroleptic malignant syndrome (NMS), 564
Neurological development and biology
    advances in neuroimaging, 41–43, 42 (image), 98
    Bipolar Spectrum Disorders and, 532–535
    conduct disorders and, 302–305
    depressive disorders and, 488–489, 495
    Schizophrenia and, 550, 560–562
    stuttering and, 153–154
Nightmare Disorder, 640, 640 (image)
Night waking, 632
NIMH (National Institutes for Mental Health), 473, 474, 559
NMS (neuroleptic malignant syndrome), 564
Noble, R., 509
Nock, M. K., 508, 510
Nocturnal enuresis, 622
Non-retentive encopresis, 626, 627–628
Nonshared environmental factors, 40
Non-Suicidal Self-Injury (NSSI)
    associated problems, 507–508
    causes, 508–511
    diagnosing, 504–505, 505 (table)

prevalence and course, 506, 507 (figure)
    summary, 517
    treatment, 511–515
Non-Western cultures and eating disorders, 593
Norepinephrine, 334
Norepinephrine inhibitor, 624
Normalization for ADHD, 276
Norman, P., 595
Norm-referenced testing, 60–69, 61, 91
NOS (Not Otherwise Specified) category, 73
No-treatment control group, 33
NRP (National Reading Panel), 225
NSCH (National Survey of Children's Health), 175, 176–177
NSSI. See Non-Suicidal Self-Injury
Nucleotides, 38
Nucleus accumbens, 335 (image)
Nugent, L., 239
Number Line Test, 239, 240 (figure)
Number sense, 239–241, 240 (figure)
Number Sets Test, 239, 240 (figure)
Numtee, C., 239

Obesity, 590, 591 (figure)
Objectification theory, 601
Observation, 118–119
Observational learning, 376
Obsessive-Compulsive Disorder (OCD)
    associated disorders, 589
    child/adolescent presentations, 396–398
    diagnosing, 370, 394–396
    etiology, 398–399
    Excoriation Disorder, 401–402
    summary, 413–414
    tic disorders, 399–401, 408–409
    treatment, 408–409
    Trichotillomania, 401
Obstructive Sleep Apnea Hypopnea, 640–641
Occipital lobe, 43, 44 (image)
OCD. See Obsessive-Compulsive Disorder
O'Connor, B. C., 280–281
O'Connor, E., 502
O'Connor, M., 595
Omen formation, 422
Onyango, A. N., 277
Operant conditioning, 46–48, 47 (figure), 156–157, 351, 376, 581
Ophelia, 600 (image)
Opioids, 325
Oppositional Defiant Disorder (ODD)
    associated disorders
        Bipolar Spectrum Disorders, 531
        Disruptive Mood Dysregulation Disorder, 472–473
        trauma-related disorders and, 455
    diagnosing, 74, 288–289 (table), 288–291, 293
Orbitofrontal cortex, 267
Organic vs. cultural-familial Intellectual Disability, 102–103, 102 (table), 113–114
Ortiz, S. O., 214
Orton, Samuel, 233
Osteopenia, 590
Osterling, J., 31
Overcorrection, 121
Overgeneralizations, 393

Overlearning procedure, 623
Overprotective parents, 372–373, 379
Overt vs. covert conduct problems, 294
Ozgunen, T., 375
Ozonoff, S., 182

Pagnucco, J. R., 226
PANDA (Pediatric Autoimmune Neuropsychiatric Disorder Associated with Streptococcus), 399
Panic Disorder
    associated disorders, 385–386, 411
    diagnosing, 369, 381–383, 381 (table)
    etiology, 386–387
    summary, 413
    treatment, 406–407
    types, 383 (figure)
Parent-child interaction
    about, 49–51, 50 (table)
    anxiety disorders and, 368–369, 378–379, 380–381
    Attention-Deficit/Hyperactivity Disorder and, 260, 275–276
    Autism Spectrum Disorder and, 195, 200
    child abuse/neglect and, 460
    communication disorders and, 135
    conduct problems and, 304, 306–310, 315–316, 316 (table)
    depressive disorders and, 494–495
    dimensions of, 49–50
    eating disorders and, 591–592, 603, 611
    in family therapy, 356–357
    feeding disorders and, 578 (figure), 581
    Intellectual Disability and, 122–123
    in Multisystemic Therapy, 6, 318–319, 320 (figure)
    parent-infant attachment, 48–49, 49 (table)
    Reactive Attachment Disorder and, 437–438
    Separation Anxiety Disorder and, 372–373
    Substance Use Disorder and, 347–348
    trauma-related disorders and, 430–431
Parent-Child Interaction Therapy (PCIT), 315–316, 315 (image), 316 (table), 460, 461 (figure)
Parent management training (PMT), 312–315, 313 (image), 314 (table)
Parents
    absence of. See Trauma-related disorders
    cognition of, 308
    feeding concerns of, 578 (figure)
    hostility/coercion of, 50–51
    mental health of, 309
    under stress, 122–123
    See also Parent-child interaction
Parietal lobe, 43, 44 (image)
Pariseau, M. E., 478
Partial hospitalization programs, 602
Partial seizures, 174
Participant modeling, 403
Partnership for a Drug Free America (PDFA), 348
Passive gene-environment correlation, 41
Pathway model of substance abuse, 344–347
Pathways of development, 13–14 (table), 13–15
Patterson, G. R., 306–307, 309
Pavlov's experiments, 46
Pavuluri, M., 539

PDFA (Partnership for a Drug Free
America), 348
Peabody Picture Vocabulary Test, 128
PECS (Picture Exchange Communication
System), 140, 141 (figure)
Pediatric Autoimmune Neuropsychiatric
Disorder Associated with Streptococcus
(PANDA), 399
Pediatric OCD Treatment Studies (POTS),
410–411, 410 (figure), 411 (figure)
Pediatric psychology
chronic health problems and, 642–645
consultation and liaison, 641–642
defined, 641
efficacy of treatment, 649–650
interventions, 646–649
summary, 651–652
Peer groups, 649
Peer interactions
Attention-Deficit/Hyperactivity Disorder
and, 260–261, 261 (figure)
Bipolar Spectrum Disorders and, 537
conduct disorders and, 310–311
depressive disorders and, 495–496
deviancy and, 319
disinhibition affecting, 347
eating disorders and, 612
learning disabilities and, 218–219
peer-assisted therapy, 648–649
rejection in, 304
substance abuse and, 347
teasing, 158
Pelham, W. E., 247, 277, 280–281
PEP (psychoeducational psychotherapy),
540–543
Permissive parents, 307
Perrin, S., 433
Persistent Depressive Disorder,
482–484, 483 (table)
Personality characteristics for eating
disorders, 589
Personalization of negative events,
386, 393, 633
Petit mal seizures, 174
Petty, C. R., 264
PFA (psychological first aid),
431–432, 432 (image)
Pharmacodynamic tolerance, 335–336, 337
Pharmacology criteria for substance use
disorders, 327
Pharmacotherapy
for anxiety disorders, 409–411
for Attention-Deficit/Hyperactivity
Disorder, 274–275
increases in, 4–6, 5 (figure), 5 (table)
Phenotypes, 41
Phenylketonuria (PKU), 110–111, 114
Phillips, L. J., 567
Phonemes
acquisition, 147
awareness, 132, 221, 221 (table), 225,
226 (figure), 229
mediation, 222
practice, 149
See also Word reading problems
Phonics, 221–222, 222 (image), 225
Phonological processing skills, 225

Phonological short-term memory, 135
Phonology, 132, 145–146
Physical abuse, 449–450, 454–457
Physical aggression, 101
Physical neglect of children, 452–453
See also Child maltreatment
Pica, 575, 580
Picchietti, D. L., 282
Picky eaters, 578–579
Picture Exchange Communication System
(PECS), 140, 141 (figure)
Pietrowsky, R., 610
Pimentel, S., 403
Pisha, B., 117
Pitch of voice, 142–143
Pivotal response training, 193–194
PKU (Phenylketonuria), 110–111, 114
Placebo effect, 33
Planned ignoring strategy, 634
Planning process for writing, 234
Plante, W. A., 649
Plasticity, neural, 45–47
PMT (parent management training),
312–315, 313 (image), 314 (table)
Polen, M. R., 502
Polysomnogram (PSG), 629, 629 (image)
Polysymptomatic nocturnal enuresis (PSNE),
621–622
Pomerantz, M., 31–32
Pontifex, M. B., 282
Popular children, 261, 261 (figure)
Positive expectations and pleasurable
effects, 345
Positive practice, 121
Positive punishment, 47, 120–121, 307
Positive reinforcement, 47, 120, 581
Positive symptoms of Schizophrenia, 550
Post, R., 487
Posttraumatic feeding problems, 579–580
Posttraumatic Stress Disorder (PTSD)
associated disorders, 458
defined for older children and adolescents,
417–422, 418–419 (table)
defined for preschoolers and young
children, 422–424, 423–424 (table)
epidemiology, 425–426
etiology, 426–431
summary, 464–465
treatment, 431–434
POTS (Pediatric OCD Treatment Studies),
410–411, 410 (figure), 411 (figure)
Poulton, R., 553–554
Powerlessness, 458
POWER strategy for written expression, 236
Practical skills, 91, 92 (table)
Practice and science, 19–21
Prader-Willi Syndrome, 107–108, 107 (image)
Precocious sexual knowledge, 457
Predictive validity, 72
Predominantly hyperactive/impulsive
presentation, 257
Predominantly inattentive presentation,
257–258
Prefrontal cortex
Attention-Deficit/Hyperactivity Disorder
and, 266–267, 267 (image)
Autism Spectrum Disorder and, 182–183

Bipolar Spectrum Disorders and,
533 (figure), 534, 534 (image)
Pregnancy/delivery complications, 112–113,
113 (figure)
Prenatal environment, 177, 179
Prenatal screening, 114–115
Pretend play. See Symbolic play
Preterm birth, 112–113, 113 (figure)
Prevalence of disorders, 3–4, 3 (table), 4 (table)
See also specific disorders
Primary encopresis, 625
Primary enuresis, 619–620, 621
Primary prevention programs, 348–349
Prinstein, M. J., 496, 508
Proactive aggression, 294
Probabilistic epigenesis, 11–13
Problem-focused coping, 429
Problem orientation strategy, 513–514
Problem-solving skills, 500–501, 542
Processing speed, 229
Prodromal symptoms, 529, 529 (table)
Profound intellectual disability, 93
Prognosis, 16–17
Progress monitoring, 56, 200
Projective measures of personality, 67–69
Prosocial emotions, 305, 305 (figure)
Prospective longitudinal studies, 31
Protective factors, 17–19, 17 (table)
Proximal development in math instruction, 247
Proximal risk factors, 51
See also Brain structure/function; Families;
Genotypes
Proximity to trauma, 426–427, 427 (figure)
PSG (polysomnogram), 629, 629 (image)
PSST (Problem-Solving Skills Training),
317–318, 318 (table)
Psychobiological causes of disorders, 9–10
Psychodynamic therapy, 78–79
Psychoeducational psychotherapy (PEP),
540–543
Psycholinguistics, 154–155, 155
Psychological abuse, 451–452, 451–452 (table)
Psychological debriefing, 431
Psychological distress, 7
Psychological first aid (PFA), 431–432,
432 (image)
Psychological problems vs. disorders, 4
Psychology students, 22–23
Psychosocial history, 58 (table)
Psychosocial treatments vs. medication,
279–281
Psychostimulants, 271–275
Psychotherapy
child vs. adult, 79–80
common factors, 76
defined, 75–76
efficacy of, 80–83
summary, 84–85
systems of, 76–79
See also specific disorders
Psychotic disorders, 339
See also Schizophrenia
Psychotropic medication, 5, 5 (figure), 5 (table)
See also Pharmacology
Puberty and eating disorders, 596
Puffenberger, S. S., 278
Punishment, 46–48, 47, 120–121

Purging behavior, 583–584, 597
Purington, A., 509

Quality of voice, 142–143
Quasi-experiments, 34–35
Quay, H. C., 301
Questions (in language therapy), 137

Racial differences in learning disabilities,
    216–217
Racing thoughts, 521, 522 (table)
RAD. *See* Reactive Attachment Disorder
Raine, L. B., 282
Ramirez, L., 594
Randall, P., 594
Random assignment, 35
Randomized controlled trials,
    22, 33–34, 34 (figure)
RAN (rapid automatized naming), 230
Rapee, R. M., 34
Rapid automatized naming (RAN), 230
Rapid temporal processing, 135
Rational emotive therapy, 158, 158 (table)
Rational problem solving, 514
RAVE-O (retrieval, automaticity, vocabulary,
    elaboration, and orthography), 231–232
Rayner, R., 375
Reaction range, 46
Reactive aggression, 294
Reactive Attachment Disorder (RAD)
    causes, 439–445
    comparison to Disinhibited Social
        Engagement Disorder, 440 (table)
    diagnosing, 435–436 (table), 435–438,
        435–440, 440 (table)
    early studies, 436–437
    parent-child attachment and, 437–438
    treatment, 445–447
Reactive pathway, 510
Reactive *vs.* proactive aggression, 294
Reading fluency/comprehension problems
    skill deficits, 228–230
    summary, 248
    treatment, 230–234, 231 (figure),
        233 (image)
    See also Word reading problems
Reading Recovery, 227
Receptive language, 128
Reciprocal imitation training (RIT),
    196, 196 (figure)
Reciprocal vulnerability, 492–493
Rees, J., 439
Refeeding syndrome, 590
Refocusing activities, 648
Regular Education Initiative, 116
Regulatory pathway, 510
Reichow, B., 175
Reid, J. B., 306–307
Reinforcement, 46–48, 47, 307
Reinforcement pathways, 345
Reising, M. M., 473
Reiss, A. L., 42–43
Relapse prevention, 358–360, 408
Relational aggression, 302
Relaxation, 432, 501–502, 635
Relaxation response, 403
Reliability of tests, 69–70, 71 (image)

Repeated testing threat, 35
Repetitive behaviors, 170–171, 188–189
Representational pathway, 510
Requests, teaching, 136
Research studies
    clinicians and, 21–22
    evidence-based treatment, 22
    experiments, 32–34
    quasi-experiments, 34–35
    single-subject, 35–38, 37 (figure)
    summary of methods, 52
    variables' relationships, 31–32, 32 (figure)
    See also Causes of disorders; Scientific study
        of behavior
Research Unit on Pediatric
    Psychopharmacology (RUPP) Anxiety
    Study, 409
Research Unit on Pediatric
    Psychopharmacology (RUPP) Autism
    Network, 197
Reverse advocacy role-play strategy, 513–514
Resilience of youths, 18–19, 18 (image)
Resonance, 143
Response-contingent reinforcement, 499–500
Response costs, 121
Response to intervention (RTI), 210–212
Retention control training, 623
Reticular formation, 334–335, 334 (image),
    335 (image)
Retrieval, automaticity, vocabulary, elaboration,
    and orthography (RAVE-O), 231–232
Retrospective longitudinal study, 31
Rett syndrome, 171
Reversal design. *See* ABAB design method
Reviews of written work, 235
Reward sensitivity, 268–269
Rich, B. A., 473, 475
Richman, G. S., 120
Ridder, E. M., 301
Right fusiform gyrus, 181, 182 (image)
Rigidity of thoughts/actions, 589
Rimland, B., 179
Risk and substance use disorders, 327
Risk factors, 17, 17 (table)
Risky behavior, 522 (table), 523
Risperidone Disruptive Behavior Study
    Group, 121
Risperidone (Risperdal), 121, 197,
    197 (image), 538
Risser, H. J., 51
RIT (reciprocal imitation training),
    196, 196 (figure)
Ritualistic behaviors, 170
Robb, A. S., 497
Robertson, M. M., 180
Roffman, R. A., 35
Rogers, C., 76
Role-play activity, 320, 647
Role reversal, 514
Role transitions, 608–609
Romanian orphanages, 448
Romantic relationships, 496
Rorschach test, 67–69, 69 (image)
Rosa's Law, 90
Rosen, H. R., 475
Ross, D., 46
Ross, S. A., 46

Rounsaville, B., 611
Routines, 170
Rowe, C. L., 357
RTI (response to intervention), 210–212
Rumination Disorder, 576, 580
Rupp A., 131
RUPP (Research Unit on Pediatric
    Psychopharmacology), 197, 409
Russell's sign, 590 (image)
Rustenbach, S. J., 610
Rutter, M., 298, 444–445
Rynn, M., 497

SAD. *See* Separation Anxiety Disorder
Safety plan, 461
Saliba, B. J., 282
SAL (System for Augmenting Language),
    141–142
Salvy, S. J., 120
Sameroff, A., 11
Sandy Hook Elementary shooting,
    416–417, 417 (image)
Santana High School shooting, 426
Scaffolding technique, 194, 247
Scahill, V. L., 180
Scarr, S., 35
Scheduled waking strategy, 635
Schene, A., 567
Schizophrenia
    associated problems, 555–557
    background, 545–546
    case studies, 546–547, 552
    diagnosing, 547–548 (table), 547–551
    epidemiology, 551–555
    summary, 569–570
    treatment
        efficacy of early intervention, 568 (figure)
        medication, 563–565
        prevention, 562–563
        psychotherapy, 565–567
Schmidt, M., 555
Schneck, C. D., 544, 545
School failure hypothesis, 218
Schools
    conduct problems and, 319
    D.A.R.E program, 348–349, 349 (image)
    educational interventions, 115–117
    start times of, 638
Scientific study of behavior
    correlations, 29–32, 30 (figure)
    empirical data, 20, 29
    evidence-based treatment, 22
    hypotheses, 28–29
    integrating with clinical practice, 19–22
    scientific inquiry features, 28–29
    students of, 22–23
    See also Research studies
Scientist-practitioner approach, 19–23
Scripts, 163
Secondary encopresis, 625, 626
Secondary enuresis, 619–620
Secondary prevention programs for substance
    use, 349
Secondary reaction theory, 218
Secure attachment relationships, 48–49
Sedatives, 325
Seeley, J. R., 496

Seizures, 109, 174, 556
Selection biases, 35
Selective affiliation, 311
Selective norepinephrine reuptake inhibitor
    (SNRI), 272, 273
Selective serotonin reuptake inhibitors
    (SRRIs), 409, 410, 497–499, 499 (figure),
    500 (image), 613
Self-actualization, 456
Self-concept, 218
Self-Directed Strategy Instruction (SRSD), 246
Self-efficacy, 393
Self-esteem, 597, 608, 611–612
Self-harm, 458, 459 (figure)
Self-injurious behaviors (SIBs),
    99–101, 120–121, 122
Self-instruction, 244–245
Self-monitoring treatment, 408
Self-regulated strategy development (SRSD),
    235–237, 237 (figure)
Self-report ratings, 67, 69
Self-statements, 647
Seligman, M. E., 493
Semantic facilitation, 231–232
Semantics, 133–134
Sensory deficits, 98–99
Sensory food aversion, 578–579
Sensory integration training, 198
Sentence complexity, 235
Sentences (teaching), 137–138
Separation Anxiety Disorder (SAD),
    74, 368 (image), 369, 370–373,
    370 (table), 387, 403–406, 412
September 11 terrorist attack, 426–427, 429
Sequential processing, 107
Serotonin, 399, 442, 595–596
Serum screening, 114
Severe Mood Dysregulation (SMD), 532
Severity of intellectual impairments,
    92–93, 92 (table)
Sexual abuse
    associated disorders, 510, 596–597
    case studies, 450–451
    defined, 450
    effects of, 457–458
    treatment, 462–464
Sexual development, 596
Sexualized behavior, 457
Shaken baby syndrome, 454
Shakow, D., 19–20
Sham, P., 489
Shapiro, F., 433
Shared environmental factors, 40
Shaw, D. S., 304
Shaw, H., 594
Sher, K. J., 344–347
Shifrer, D., 216
Shih, J. H., 495
Shoemaker, M., 101
Short-term memory, 135
Sickle cell disease, 645, 645 (image)
Silberg, J. L., 298
Silent reading, 230–231
Sim, L., 509–510
Similar sequence hypothesis, 103
Similar structure hypothesis, 103
Simmens, J., 372

Simon, T., 62
Simultaneous processing, 107
Singh, M. K., 545
Single-subject studies, 35–38, 37 (figure), 38
Sipes, M., 101
Skillstreaming activity, 320
Skinner, B. F., 76, 117
Sleep disorders
    associated disorders
        Attention-Deficit/Hyperactivity
            Disorder, 262, 281, 282,
            283 (image)
        Bipolar Spectrum Disorders,
            522 (table), 523, 531, 535
        elimination disorders, 621
    Circadian Rhythm Sleep-Wake Disorder,
        637–638
    developmental concerns, 618–619
    Insomnia Disorder
        associated disorders, 633
        diagnosing, 629, 630 (table)
        epidemiology, 629–631
        etiology, 631–632, 631 (figure)
        specific difficulties, 632–633
        treatment, 633–637
    Nightmare Disorder, 640, 640 (image)
    Obstructive Sleep Apnea Hypopnea,
        640–641
    sleep architecture, 628–629, 628 (table),
        630 (table)
    sleep arousal disorders, 638–640
    summary, 651
    types of, 637 (table)
Sleep enhancement, 479–480
Sleep hygiene, 634, 634 (table), 635
Sleep refusal, 632–633, 633 (image)
Sleep terrors, 638–639
Sleepwalking, 638–640, 639 (figure)
Slifer, K. J., 120
Sluggish cognitive tempo,
    257–258, 257 (table)
Small, J., 264
Smith, C. E., 100
Smith, N. C., 117
Smith, P., 426, 433
Smoking risks, 259
Smyke, A. T., 448
SNRI (selective norepinephrine reuptake
    inhibitor), 272, 273
Social Anxiety Disorder
    associated disorders, 589
    diagnosing, 369, 376–377 (table),
        376–379, 378 (table)
    school refusal and, 380
    summary, 412–413
    treatment, 403–406
Social cognition deficits, 183–189
Social communication problems. See Autism
    Spectrum Disorder (ASD); Social
    (Pragmatic) Communication Disorder
Social contagion, 509
Social-cultural context in diagnoses,
    7–8, 9 (image)
Social-cultural influences on development,
    51–52
Social-cultural theories of eating disorders,
    597–598

Social-emotional deprivation. See Disinhibited
    Social Engagement Disorder (DSED);
    Reactive Attachment Disorder (RAD)
Social-emotional functioning, 67, 69
Social engagement, 178
Social impairment in substance use
    disorders, 327
Social information processing,
    310, 317–318, 455, 496–497, 496 (figure)
Social inhibition, 441
Social learning, 48, 351
Social orientation, 184–185, 185 (image),
    186 (figure)
Social Phobia, 378 (table)
Social (Pragmatic) Communication Disorder
    definition, 159–161, 159 (table), 160 (table)
    summary, 164
    treatment, 161–163
Social problem-solving training, 513
Social rhythm therapy, 535
Social skills, 91, 92 (table), 277, 609
Socioeconomic status, 4, 114, 177,
    216, 217 (figure)
Special education, 213
Specific Language Impairment (SLI), 131–134
Specific Learning Disorder
    features, 205–207, 206 (table),
        207–208 (table)
    specifiers, 207–208
Specific Phobia, 369, 373–376, 402–403,
    411, 412
Speech disorders
    case studies, 142
    Speech Sound Disorder (SSD), 145–150
    stuttering
        case study, 150–151
        definition, 150–152, 150 (table),
            151 (table)
        epidemiology and course,
            152, 152 (figure), 153 (figure)
        etiology, 153–155
        treatment, 156–158, 156–158 (table)
    summary, 163–164
    voice problems, 142–145
    See also Language Disorders; Social
        (Pragmatic) Communication Disorder
Speech modification programs, 156
Speech therapy, 146, 147–149
Spelling instruction, 237–238, 238
Spelling problems, 234–235
Spitz, R., 436
Spurrell, E., 611
Sroufe, L. A., 372
SRRIs (selective serotonin reuptake inhibitors),
    409, 410, 497–499, 499 (figure),
    500 (image), 613
SRSD (self-regulated strategy development),
    235–237, 237 (figure), 246
St. Denis, J. M., 509
St. Petersburg-USA Orphanages Research
    Project, 448
Stages of Schizophrenia, 552–554, 553 (figure)
Stahl, S. A., 226
Standardization/standard scores, 60–61, 60–62
Standard-treatment control group, 33–34
Stanovich, K., 230
Stark, K., 500–501

Starkey, P., 239
Statistical deviancy perspective, 6–7
Stephens, R. S., 35
Stereotyped behaviors, 188–189
Stereotypies, 99, 122, 443
Stevens, T., 273
Stewart, S. L., 507–508
Stice, E., 496, 594, 597
Stigma, 6, 75, 458
Stimulants, 271–275, 325
Stimulus control, 635
Story content problems, 235
Strange situation tests, 48–49, 49 (table)
Strep throat, 399
Stress
    anxiety disorders and, 443
    Bipolar Spectrum Disorders and, 535
    mood disorders and, 443, 489–491
    of parents, 122–123
    Schizophrenia and, 561
    sleep disorders and, 640
Stress response, 45
Striatum, 267–268, 267 (image)
Structured diagnostic interviews, 59
Structured family therapy, 77–78, 603–604, 648
Structured teaching, 194
Students as scientists/practitioners, 22–23
Stunkard, A., 587
Stuttering
    case study, 150–151
    definition, 150–152, 150 (table), 151 (table)
    epidemiology and course, 152, 152 (figure), 153 (figure)
    etiology, 153–155
    treatment, 156–158, 156–158 (table)
Subjective assessment of distress, 7
Subjectivity of diagnoses, 75
Substance-Induced Mental Disorder, 332–333, 333 (table)
Substance Use Disorders
    alcohol use/abuse, 325, 333–336
    associated disorders/features
        anxiety, 339
        Attention-Deficit Hyperactivity Disorder, 259
        comorbidity rates, 338
        conduct problems, 299, 300 (figure), 339
        depressive disorders, 339, 485
        eating disorders, 589
        psychotic disorders, 339, 555
    case studies, 327–328, 355–356
    definitions, 360–361
    diagnosing, 325–333, 326 (table)
    epidemiology, 339–344
    etiology, 344–348
    list of substances, 325
    marijuana use/abuse, 336–337
    parental experiences, 260
    pregnancy concerns, 111–113
    protective factors, 347–348
    summary, 360–361
    treatment
        medication, 350
        primary prevention programs, 348–349
        psychosocial programs, 350–355
        relapse prevention, 358–360
        secondary prevention programs, 349

Substitution therapy, 350
Sugden, K., 489
Suicide
    depression and, 485–486
    eating disorders and, 588–589, 588 (figure)
    NSSI as predictor of, 507–508
    risk factors for, 486 (figure)
    Schizophrenia and, 555–556
Sullivan, H. S., 78, 495
Summer treatment programs, 276–277, 649
Superior frontal gyrus, 534
Supportive confrontation, 602
Supportive therapy, 458–460
Support levels for Intellectual Disability, 94
Susceptibility hypothesis, 218
Swanson, J. M., 280
Symbolic play, 185–187, 186 (image)
Symbols in AAC systems, 140
Synaptic density/neural connections, 179–180
Synaptogenesis, 46
Syntactical errors, 133 (table)
Syntactic-semantic language problems, 189–190
System for Augmenting Language (SAL), 141–142
Systemic problem-solving, 514

Tacts (comments/descriptions), 136–137
TADS (Treatment for Adolescents with Depression Study), 503–504
Talkativeness, 522 (table), 523
Tamm, L., 42–43
Tarrier, N., 566
Tarullo, A. R., 441
Tasks of childhood, 13–14 (table)
TAU (treatment as usual) group, 34
Taylor, D. O., 544, 545
TEACCH program, 194–195, 200
TEAM (Treatment of Early Age Mania) study, 537–538
Teasdale, J. D., 493
Teasing, 158
Telpfski, L. S., 634
Temperament
    conduct disorder and, 303, 305
    depressive disorders and, 489
Temper tantrums, 471, 471 (figure)
    See also Bipolar Spectrum Disorders (BSDs); Disruptive Mood Dysregulation Disorder (DMDD)
Temporal lobe, 43, 44 (image)
TEOSS (Treatment of Early-Onset Schizophrenia Spectrum Disorders Study), 564
Teratogens, 111
Test-retest reliability, 70
Text enhancements, 232–233
TF-CBT (Trauma-Focused CBT), 432–433, 462, 463 (figure)
Thalamus, 558–559
THC (delta-9-tetrahydroccannabinol), 336
Theories. See Causes of disorders
Theory of mind, 187
Therapy. See Psychotherapy
Thin ideal, 596–601
"Thinking, Feeling, Doing" exercise, 542, 542 (figure)

Third variable theory, 507
Thought-action fusion, 399
Thought content, 59
Tic disorders, 399–401, 408–409
Time outs, 121, 581
Time-series studies. See Single-subject studies
Tizard, B., 439
To, Y. M., 273
Tobacco, 259, 325
Toileting skills. See Elimination disorders
Toilet sitting, 627
Tolan, P. H., 6
Tolerance in substance abuse, 330, 337
Tompson, M., 495, 561
Topographic theory of mind, 78
Tourette's Disorder, 400, 400 (image)
Tranah, T., 433
Transactional model for feeding disorders, 578
Transactional stress and coping (TSC) model, 642
Transference, 78–79
Translation of thoughts onto paper, 234, 237–238
Trauma-Focused CBT (TF-CBT), 432–433, 462, 463 (figure)
Trauma-related disorders
    Acute Stress Disorder, 424, 426
    case studies, 436, 450–451, 452, 453
    child maltreatment
        case studies, 450–451, 452, 453
        diagnosing, 448–453, 449 (table)
        effects, 454–457, 454–458
        prevalence, 453–454
        summary, 465–466
    Disinhibited Social Engagement Disorder
        causes, 440–445
        comparison to RAD, 440 (table)
        diagnosing, 438–440, 439 (table)
        treatment, 447–448
    Reactive Attachment Disorder
        causes, 439–445
        comparison to DSED, 440 (table)
        diagnosing, 435–436 (table), 435–438
        early studies of, 436–437
        parent-child attachment and, 437–438
        treatment, 445–447
    sexual abuse
        case studies, 450–451
        definition, 450
        effects of, 457–458
        treatment, 462–464
    See also Posttraumatic Stress Disorder (PTSD)
Traumatic sexualization, 457
Treadwell, K., 391
Treatment, 74, 83
    See also under specific disorders
Treatment and Education of Autistic and Related Communication-Handicapped Children (TEACCH), 194–195, 200
Treatment as usual (TAU) group, 34
Treatment for Adolescents with Depression Study (TADS), 503–504
Treatment of Early Age Mania (TEAM) study, 537–538
Treatment of Early-Onset Schizophrenia Spectrum Disorders Study (TEOSS), 564

⊛SAGE researchmethods

The essential online tool for researchers from the world's leading methods publisher

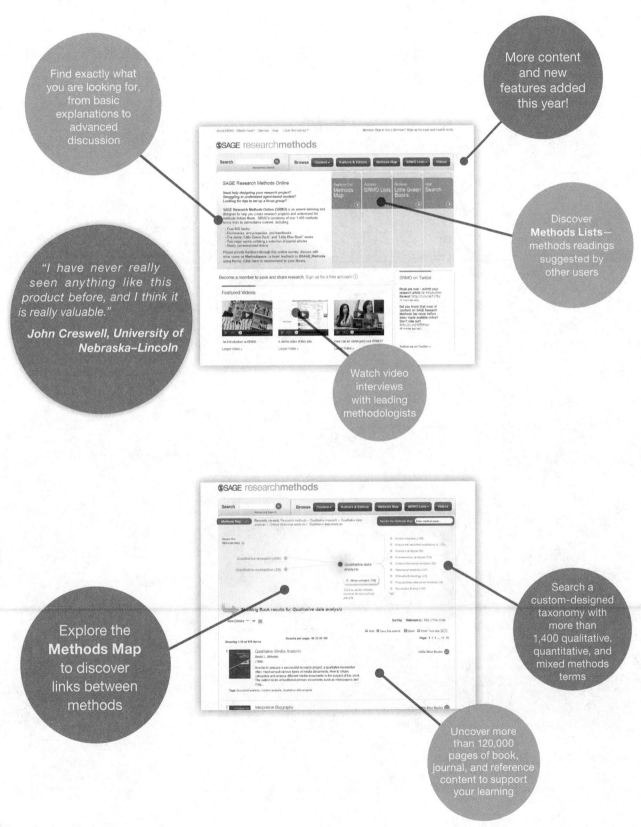

Find exactly what you are looking for, from basic explanations to advanced discussion

More content and new features added this year!

Discover **Methods Lists**— methods readings suggested by other users

"*I have never really seen anything like this product before, and I think it is really valuable.*"

John Creswell, University of Nebraska–Lincoln

Watch video interviews with leading methodologists

Explore the **Methods Map** to discover links between methods

Search a custom-designed taxonomy with more than 1,400 qualitative, quantitative, and mixed methods terms

Uncover more than 120,000 pages of book, journal, and reference content to support your learning

Find out more at
www.sageresearchmethods.com